Anthropological Theory

AN INTRODUCTORY HISTORY

Eighth Edition

R. JON McGEE
Texas State University

RICHARD L. WARMS
Texas State University

ROWMAN &
LITTLEFIELD

Lanham • Boulder • New York • London

Acquisitions Editor: Alyssa Palazzo
Assistant Acquisitions Editor: Hannah Eveland
Sales and Marketing Inquiries: textbooks@rowman.com

Credits and acknowledgments for material borrowed from other sources, and
reproduced with permission, appear on the appropriate pages within the text.

Published by Rowman & Littlefield
An imprint of The Rowman & Littlefield Publishing Group, Inc.
4501 Forbes Boulevard, Suite 200, Lanham, Maryland 20706
www.rowman.com

86-90 Paul Street, London EC2A 4NE

British Library Cataloguing in Publication Information Available

Library of Congress Cataloging-in-Publication Data

Names: McGee, R. Jon, 1955– author. | Warms, Richard L., 1955– author.
Title: Anthropological theory : an introductory history / R. Jon McGee, Richard L.
   Warms.
Description: Eighth edition. | Lanham, Maryland : Rowman & Littlefield, 2024. |
   Includes bibliographical references and index.
Identifiers: LCCN 2024026909 (print) | LCCN 2024026910 (ebook) | ISBN
   9781538183915 (paperback) | ISBN 9781538183922 (epub)
Subjects: LCSH: Anthropology—Philosophy—History—Sources. | Anthropology—
   Methodology—History—Sources.
Classification: LCC GN33 .M33 2024 (print) | LCC GN33 (ebook) | DDC 301.01—
   dc23/eng/20240617
LC record available at https://lccn.loc.gov/2024026909
LC ebook record available at https://lccn.loc.gov/2024026910

Contents

Preface

THEORY IS THE CORE of anthropology. Students often do not realize that the ethnographic materials they read in their textbooks and discuss in class are interpretations of data collected by anthropologists whose theoretical training determines the types of questions they ask and the sorts of information they collect. Without a solid understanding of theory, anthropology is reduced to a collection of exotic ethnographic vignettes. With a knowledge of theory, these vignettes become attempts to answer important philosophical and practical problems. Thus, it is crucial for anthropologists to understand theory and its historical context.

Students face two choices if they wish to understand the theoretical perspectives that ultimately drive ethnographic fieldwork: they can read original articles, or they can read someone's interpretations of those articles. For readers who are not well versed in anthropological theory, neither choice is ideal. We created this volume to provide an accessible means of introducing readers to the past century and a half of theory in anthropology.

We believe that it is essential for students to read complete original essays by influential scholars whose work has determined the paths in which anthropology has developed. Reading complete original works promotes depth of understanding and opens possibilities of analysis that even the best books providing short excerpts of original work or describing theory can never provide. What better introduction to nineteenth-century evolutionary thinking than reading Herbert Spencer and E. B. Tylor? To develop an in-depth understanding of Marxist analysis in anthropology, what could be more effective than reading Karl Marx, Eleanor Leacock, or Philippe Bourgois? If you are interested in knowing about practice theory or thinking about globalization in anthropology, shouldn't you read the men and women who developed those fields such as Pierre Bourdieu, Michel Foucault, Arjun Appadurai, and Sherry Ortner?

One of the most important features of this book is that it presents complete essays. In the few cases in which we abridge essays, we carefully indicate how many words we've removed and provide a summary of the subjects covered in the passages removed. This is critical since when editors present brief extracts from essays, they inevitably choose them according to their own interests or what they consider the most important passages. However, there is no telling what passages the essay authors considered most important, and the passages an editor considers most important today may seem irrelevant tomorrow. Over the decades that we've worked on this book, our ideas about what is critical in each essay have changed repeatedly. Having whole essays enables students and professionals to engage with thinkers of the past and present in far deeper and more knowledgeable ways than having only brief extracts would.

Many students find reading original essays extremely demanding. Sometimes we do too. The language is often difficult, and the intellectual disputes, references to other thinkers, and historical contexts may be obscure. We have attempted to make the task less onerous by providing detailed commentary, in close proximity to difficult passages in the original essays, to illuminate obscure references, arcane language, and unfamiliar contexts.

You are now reading the eighth edition of *Anthropological Theory*. We have struggled to refine the book's approach for more than a quarter century (the first edition came out in 1996). As we have repeatedly revised this text, our goals for the book have grown. *Anthropological Theory* is primarily a textbook designed for students in advanced undergraduate and beginning graduate classes. However, we have increasingly tried to write a reference work that both students and professionals will want to keep within easy reach. We have done this by writing extensive footnotes on an enormous variety of individuals and topics and by providing an extensive two-level index with well over one thousand entries. You will find basic information on everyone from Leo Frobenius to Daisy Bates, from Ibn Khaldun to Dina Dreyfus. Of course, no book can possibly include information on everyone and everything, but we believe that there is no other single book in anthropology that has as much basic information about as many different theories and people as this volume. In addition to the notes, we have also added a timeline to help readers place authors and significant works in the context of what was going on in the world at the time the piece was published.

APPROACH

We have assembled a diverse collection of essays by authors who are important thinkers in anthropology. We deliberately favor essays that are ethnographic examples of theoretical positions over those that are simply declarations of theory. We have selected essays that are well written, concise, and accessible. The collection begins in the mid-nineteenth century and ends in 2017. It is divided into sections encompassing well-known theoretical positions that are represented by authors generally considered to be the outstanding spokespersons for their points of view, or essays that are especially vivid illustrations of a perspective. In each section, our selections fit together either because they illustrate different aspects of a theoretical perspective or because they are good ethnographic examples of a theory.

PEDAGOGY

We have provided extensive support material to help students understand the forty-one essays that make up this volume. Each of the sixteen sections begins with an introduction to acquaint readers with some of the most important advocates of a school of thought, the problems they set out to solve, the methods they used, and the dilemmas they faced. Extensive editorial footnotes that provide additional information to help the reader understand and interpret the reading accompany each essay. In addition to providing definitions, translations of foreign phrases, and historical information, the notes help students trace the intellectual connections among thinkers both inside and outside of anthropology. The notes are meant to inform, raise interesting questions, and foster further creative and original thinking. They make essential but sometimes difficult information accessible to students and provide some interesting little-known background details. Anthropological theory, even that of a century ago, is alive and vital. We hope our commentary helps readers see it that way.

In this edition, the placement of our notes has been standardized. All our notes appear at the end of paragraphs. When our notes define words that appear in the essays, those words appear in bold in the essay and in the notes. Original notes by the essay's author appear as endnotes.

No book of theory and commentary can ever be entirely without bias, but we have tried to come as close to this ideal as we can. In our introductions and commentary, we point to both the strengths and weaknesses of each theoretical position. Although astute readers can probably figure out which perspectives we like and which we dislike, we do not intend to promote one theory at the expense of another. In fact, we come from quite different theoretical perspectives, and our ideas have evolved through the years as we have taught our theory classes and prepared new editions of this text. Every introductory section and note in this volume was written and rewritten by both of us, and we have been willing to accept substantial criticism and revision of ideas we hold dear. For us, editing this volume continues to be an exciting process of discovery and interpretation. Research, careful reading, discussion, and argumentation, as well as the comments of numerous reviewers and readers of earlier editions, have greatly deepened our understanding of the works of the great thinkers in anthropology. Writing this book has forced us to rethink what we believed we knew, and in the process we have become better scholars of theory. Selecting these essays and writing the introductions and commentary for them has been profoundly rewarding for us. We hope that reading the original material and our comments will be as productive for students and colleagues.

NEW TO THIS EDITION

Our eighth edition is a substantial revision of the seventh, and we owe a great deal to our editor, Alyssa Palazzo, for her guidance and vision for the book. The edition contains five new essays as well as a new section: "Decolonization and Whiteness." We have incorporated new information and brought an expanded selection of authors and opinions to the volume. Some of the notable changes in this edition include the following new sections and essays:

- In structural anthropology we've brought back "Is Female to Male as Nature Is to Culture?" by Sherry Ortner. This essay appeared in some earlier editions of the book, and we find that its importance has increased over time. It remains a frequently quoted and referenced work. We've rewritten and updated our notes.
- In postmodernism, we now present Michel-Rolph Trouillot's "Anthropology and the Savage Slot: The Poetics and Politics of Otherness." We've written extensive footnotes to help contextualize this essay and identify and explain the many historical references he employs.
- We've replaced our "Anthropology of the Good" section with "Phenomenological Anthropology and the Anthropology of the Good." It now has a greater emphasis on phenomenology and existential anthropology and includes Jason Throop's essay "Ambivalent Happiness and Virtuous Suffering." Throop gives us an experiential account of the Yapese way of understanding happiness and suffering that is both heartfelt and challenging to American notions of the idea of a good life.
- We've added a new section that addresses recent developments in anthropology. In "Decolonization and Whiteness," we feature the work of Audra Simpson based on her work among her own people, the Kahnawa'kehró:non, a Mohawk group whose land is southwest of Montreal. In "The Ruse of Consent and the Anatomy of 'Refusal': Cases from Indigenous North America and Australia," Simpson examines

the way that Indigenous people refuse participation in settler society, a tactic she employs herself in declining to tell the readers certain things about the Kahnawa'kehró:non. Our second essay in this section, Orisanmi Burton's "To Protect and Serve Whiteness," examines the nature of policing in the United States and its relation to the maintenance of white supremacy. We've written a new introduction for this section of the book, putting the anthropology of resistance in historical context, exploring the history of the anthropology of decolonization and whiteness, and presenting some recent controversies in anthropology.

In addition to our new introduction for "Decolonization and Whiteness," we updated each introduction in the book. The introductions include annotated lists of suggested readings chosen from important works in each subject area.

Unhappily, each new edition means saying good-bye to some essays as well. This is particularly true of this edition. For the first time since we began writing this book, the current edition includes essays on neither ethnoscience/cognitive anthropology nor sociobiology and behavioral ecology. We always face space limitations as we prepare revisions of the book, and that is the primary reason why these fields are no longer covered. However, we also find that we are no longer able to keep up with developments in biological approaches to culture, which have become more and more specialized and different from other culture theory. Readers will still find ethnoscience described in the introduction to the section on structural anthropology, and we continue to believe that it played an important role in the development of culture theory. However, reviewers tell us, and we agree, that readers will find Ortner's essay on female, male, nature, and culture more interesting and central to their work than an example of ethnoscience.

Of course, it is impossible to reprint essays from all of the scholars who have made significant contributions to anthropology, but we discuss many of these in the introductions and in our notes. Thus, you will find information about the contributions of people such as Jeremy Bentham, A. C. Haddon, James Frazer, Antonio Gramsci, Monica Wilson, Andrew Vayda, Michelle Rosaldo, Edith Turner, Frantz Fanon, and hundreds of others whose work has played a major role in anthropological theory. We have also included information on women who have been influential in anthropology but are often left out of general textbooks. For example, among the scores of scholars included you will find information on Elsie Clews Parsons, Dina Dreyfus, Gene Weltfish, Hilda Kuper, Hortense Powdermaker, Rhoda Métraux, Winifred Hoernle, Monica Wilson, Hildred Geertz, Emily Martin, Sarah Franklin, Edith Turner, and many others.

We have been particularly gratified by the reactions of readers of the first seven editions. We have received many letters and emails from the United States, Canada, and Europe. Both professors and students have asked questions, sent thoughtful commentary, and offered recommendations. We have been able to incorporate some of these into this edition. We deeply regret that editorial constraints and issues of timing and space have prevented us from including more of these suggestions, but we appreciate your feedback and hope you will continue to advise us.

ACKNOWLEDGMENTS

Writing this book has involved the labor and forbearance of many people. First and foremost, we would like to thank our families—Stacie, Jake, and Hannah McGee and Karen, Benjamin, Veronikah, and Nathan Warms. Without their support, this project would have been impossible. We continue to be grateful for the advice, help, and guidance of Alyssa Palazzo, our editor at Rowman & Littlefield, as well as R&L staff members, including Hannah Eveland and Alden Perkins.

One result of writing this kind of book is that we have had the privilege of having contact with several of the scholars whose work appears in this volume. We are indebted to the many people who made suggestions, reviewed, and commented on the text in various stages of preparation. Our work has benefited greatly from their comments, and our ideas were altered by their insights. We deeply appreciate their advice, even though we were not always able to follow it. Since the publication of the first edition of this book, we have benefited from the insights and advice of numerous individuals, including Tom Boellstorff, Roy D'Andrade, Regna Darnell, Jonathan Friedman, Allan Hanson, Marvin Harris, Joe Heyman, Robert Launay, Herbert Lewis, George Marcus, Naomi Quinn, Roy Rappaport, Sally Slocum, Ann Stoler, Claudia Strauss, David Valentine, and numerous others. Finally, the current edition would not have been possible without the careful analysis and useful suggestions from our reviewers, and we thank them for the time and energy they put into this volume:

Jessica Bradford, *University of California, Riverside*
Julia Cassaniti, *Washington State University*
Jay Fancher, *Washington State University*
Jessie Fly, *Eckerd College*
Nicole Kellett, *University of Maine, Farmington*
Endre Nyerges, *Centre College*
Matthew Pawlowicz, *Virginia Commonwealth University*
Kartikeya Saboo, *Wichita State University*
Matt Sumera, *Hamline University*
Lauren Wynne, *Ursinus College*

Timeline

Anthropology

Lamarck publishes his ideas on evolution in Recherches sur l'organisation des corps vivants **1802**	
The Phenomenology of Spirit (Hegel) **1807**	
Charles Darwin born **1809**	
J. J. Bachofen born **1815**	
L. H. Morgan born **1818**	
Karl Marx born **1818**	
Herbert Spencer born **1820**	
Friedrich Engels born **1820**	
Rudolf Virchow born **1821**	
Alfred R. Wallace born **1823**	
Adolf Bastian born **1826**	
Principles of Geology (Lyell) **1830**	
Darwin's voyage on HMS Beagle **1831–1836**	
E. B. Tylor born **1832**	
Wilhelm Wundt born **1832**	
Jeremy Bentham dies **1832**	
Guide to Northern Antiquity (Thomsen) **1836**	
Alice C. Fletcher born **1838**	
Fredric W. Putnam born **1839**	
American Ethnological Society founded **1842**	
Ethnology Society of London founded **1843**	
Friedrich Ratzel born **1844**	
The German Ideology (Marx and Engels) **1846**	
William H. Holmes born **1846**	
Communist Manifesto (Marx and Engels) **1848**	
League of the Iroquois (L. H. Morgan) **1851**	
Social Statics (Spencer) **1851**	
William J. McGee born **1853**	
James G. Frazer born 1854	
A. C. Haddon born **1855**	
Ferdinand de Saussure born **1857**	
Auguste Comte dies **1857**	
Émile Durkheim born **1858**	
Franz Boas born **1858**	
On the Origin of Species (Darwin) **1859**	
Man in History (Bastian) **1860**	
Ancient Law (Maine) **1861**	
Mother Right (Bachofen) **1861**	
Max Weber born **1864**	
Principles of Biology (Spencer) **1864**	
C. J. Thomsen dies **1865**	
Researches into the Early History of Mankind (Tylor) **1865**	
Prehistoric Times (Lubbock) **1865**	
Primitive Marriage (McLennan) **1865**	
Capital, Vol. 1 (Marx) **1867**	
Berlin Anthropology Society founded **1869**	

Timeline markers

1800

1810

1820

1830

1840

1850

1860

Wider World

Napoleonic Wars **1803–1815**
First steam locomotive **1804**
Battle of Trafalgar **1805**
Lewis and Clark expedition **1804–1806**
Joseph Nicephore Niepce attempts first photographic image **1814**
Napoleon defeated at Waterloo **1815**
First steamship crossing of the Atlantic **1819**
Countries in Mexico, Central America, and South America declare independence **1820–1828**
Babbage's calculating machine **1822**
Megalosaurus skeleton discovered in England **1824**
Treaty of London establishes an independent Greek state **1827**
French conquer Algeria **1830**
US Congress passes the Indian Removal Act **1830**
Slavery abolished in the British Empire **1833**
Victoria becomes Queen of England **1837**
Morse files for a telegraph patent **1837**
Oliver Twist (Dickens) **1837**
British seize Hong Kong starting First Opium War **1839**
Great Famine of Ireland **1845**
Mexican-American War **1845–1848**
First use of anesthesia **1846**
Principles of Political Economy (J. S. Mill) **1848**
Worker uprisings in Western and Central Europe **1848**
"Declaration of Sentiments" affirming the rights of women signed at Seneca Falls, NY **1848**
Great Exposition (Crystal Palace, London) **1851**
Louis-Napoleon stages "self-coup" in France **1851**
Crimean War **1853–1856**
First Neanderthal skeleton discovered in Germany **1856**
Indians rebel against British East India Company **1857**
First transatlantic telegraph cable **1858**
Edmund Husserl born **1859**
Lincoln elected president **1860**
Italian states unified by King Victor Emmanuel II **1861**
American Civil War **1861–1865**
First machine gun patented **1862**
Emancipation Proclamation **1863**
French invade Mexico installing Maximillian I as emperor **1864**
Gregor Mendel publishes his laws of inheritance **1866**
Alfred Nobel invents dynamite **1866**
Mexicans defeat the French and execute Maximillian I **1867**
Unification of Austria and Hungary forms the Austro-Hungarian Empire **1867**
Meiji Restoration (Japan) **1868**
Suez Canal opened **1869**
First US transcontinental railway completed **1869**

Anthropology

Systems of Consanguinity and Affinity (Morgan) **1870**	
Descent of Man (Darwin) **1871**	
Primitive Culture (Tylor) **1870**	
Heinrich Schliemann begins excavation of Troy **1871**	
Marcel Mauss born **1872**	
Charles Seligman born **1873**	
Arnold Van Gennep born **1873**	
Ethnological Museum of Berlin founded **1873**	
American Museum of Natural History establishes Anthropology Dept. **1873**	
Elsie Clews Parsons born **1875**	
A. L. Kroeber born **1876**	
Ancient Society (Morgan) **1877**	
Bureau of American Ethnology founded **1879**	
Anthropological Society of Washington founded **1879**	

L. H. Morgan dies **1881**
A. R. Radcliffe-Brown born **1881**
Charles Darwin dies **1882**
Franz Boas on Baffin Island **1883**
Karl Marx dies **1883**
Robert Lowie born **1883**
Paul Radin born **1883**
Edward Sapir born **1884**
Bronislaw Malinowski born **1884**
The Origin of the Family, Private Property and the State (Engels) **1884**
Women's Anthropological Society of America founded **1885**
Karl Polanyi born **1886**
J. J. Bachofen dies **1887**
Ruth Benedict born **1887**
Henry Maine dies **1888**
American Anthropologist founded **1888**

The Golden Bough (Frazer) **1890**
Dept. of Archaeology and Ethnology founded at Harvard University **1890**
Antonio Gramsci born **1891**
The Division of Labor in Society (Durkheim) **1893**
Friedrich Engels dies **1895**
The Rules of Sociological Method (Durkheim) **1895**
Columbia University hires Franz Boas **1896**
Benjamin L. Whorf born **1897**
George P. Murdock born **1897**
Suicide (Durkheim) **1897**
Bureau of American Ethnology established **1897**
Ruth Bunzel born **1898**
Torres Straits Expedition **1898**
L'Année Sociologique founded **1898**
American Anthropologist (new series) begins **1899**
Franz Boas appointed Professor at Columbia University **1899**
Audrey Richards born **1899**

Leslie White born **1900**
Dept. of Anthropology at UC Berkeley founded **1901**
Margaret Mead born **1901**
Dept. of Anthropology founded at Columbia by Franz Boas **1902**
E. E. Evans-Pritchard born **1902**
Julian Steward born **1902**
American Anthropological Association founded **1902**
Rudolf Virchow dies **1902**
Herbert Spencer dies **1903**
Cora Du Bois born **1903**
Reo Fortune born **1903**
Gregory Bateson born **1904**
Friedrich Ratzel dies **1904**

Wider World

1870

Franco-Prussian War **1870–1871**
Chicago Fire **1871**
Unification of Germany **1871**
Stanley and Livingstone meet in Africa **1871**
Paris Commune **1871**

Alexander G. Bell patents telephone **1876**
Custer defeated at Little Big Horn **1876**

1880

First Boer War begins **1880**
Edison patents light bulb **1880**
Congress passes the Chinese Exclusion Act **1882**
The Origin of the Family, Private Property, and the State (Engels) **1884**
Berlin Conference to regulate European colonization of Africa begins **1884**
European partition of Africa **1884**
Coca-Cola invented **1886**
Statue of Liberty dedicated **1886**
Michelson-Morely experiment performed **1887**

Karl Benz starts production of gasoline-powered automobiles **1889**
The French start construction on the Panama Canal **1889**

1890

Wounded Knee massacre **1890**

World's Columbian Exposition (Chicago) **1893**

Plessy v. Ferguson decision legalizes racial segregation **1896**

US annexes Hawaii **1898**
Spanish-American War **1898**

Second Boer War begins **1899**
The Interpretation of Dreams (Freud) **1899**

1900

Queen Victoria dies 1901
First transatlantic radio transmission **1901**

Wright Brothers' first flight **1903**

Russo-Japanese War **1904–1905**
Louisiana Purchase Exposition (St. Louis) **1904**

Anthropology

Adolf Bastian dies **1905**
The Protestant Ethic and the Spirit of Capitalism
  (Weber) **1905**
Clyde Kluckhohn born **1905**
Isaac Shapera born **1905**
Meyer Fortes born **1906**
Claude Lévi-Strauss born **1908**
Monica Wilson born **1908**
Rites of Passage (Van Gennep) **1909**

Edmund Leach born **1910**
Dina Dreyfus born **1911**
Max Gluckman born **1911**
The Mind of Primitive Man (Boas) **1911**
The Elementary Forms of the Religious Life
  (Durkheim) **1912**
William J. McGee dies **1912**
Alfred R. Wallace dies **1913**
Ferdinand de Saussure dies **1913**
Fredric W. Putnam dies **1915**
E. B. Tylor dies **1917**
Émile Durkheim dies **1917**
David Schneider born **1918**
Louis Althusser born **1918**
Franz Boas censured by the American
  Anthropological Association **1919**

Wilhelm Wundt dies **1920**
Victor Turner born **1920**
Primitive Society (Lowie) **1920**
Mary Douglas born **1921**
Sindney Mintz born **1922**
W. H. R. Rivers dies **1922**
Eleanor B. Leacock born **1922**
Argonauts of the Western Pacific (Malinowski) **1922**
The Andaman Islanders (Radcliffe-Brown) **1922**
Morton Fried born **1923**
Eric Wolf born **1923**
Alice C. Fletcher dies **1923**
Raymond Dart discovers *Australopithecus africanus* **1924**
Frantz Fanon born **1925**
The Gift (Mauss) **1925**
Harold C. Conklin born **1926**
Clifford Geertz born **1926**
Michel Foucault born **1926**
*Crashing Thunder: The Autobiography
  of an American Indian* (Radin) **1926**
Roy Rappaport born **1926**
Marvin Harris born **1927**
June Nash born **1927**
Primitive Art (Boas) **1927**
Sex and Repression in Savage Society (Malinowski) **1927**
Coming of Age in Samoa (Mead) **1928**
E. O. Wilson born **1929**

Pierre Bourdieu born **1930**
Marshall Sahlins born **1930**
*The Protestant Ethic and the
  Spirit of Capitalism* (Weber) **1930**
William H. Holmes dies **1933**

Wider World

Einstein formulates theory of special relativity **1905**
Niagara Falls Conference **1905**

San Francisco earthquake **1906**

Robert Peary reaches the North Pole. **1909**
NAACP founded **1909**

1910

Last Chinese emperor overthrown **1912**

Panama Canal opens **1914**
US Postal Service rules that children may not
  be shipped by parcel post **1914**

Margaret Sanger opens first birth control clinics **1916**
Communist Revolution in Russia **1917**

Influenza epidemic **1918–1820**, more than
  21 million deaths worldwide
Women over age 30 gain the vote in Britain **1918**

1920
Women's suffrage in US **1920**
Prohibition begins **1920** (US)
League of Nations founded **1920**
First commercial radio broadcast **1920**
Irish Uprising **1920–1921**
Insulin discovered **1921**
USSR formed **1922**
Benito Mussolini seizes power in Italy **1922**

Congress enacts the Asian Exclusion Act **1924**
Vladimir Lenin dies **1924**
End of Ottoman Empire. Republic of
  Turkey formed. **1924**
J. Edgar Hoover appointed FBI director **1924**
Mein Kampf (Hitler) **1925**
Scopes Trial (*State of Tennessee v. John Scopes*) **1925**
Ford announces first 40-hour workweek **1926**
Prison Notebooks (Gramsci) **1926**

Lindbergh, first solo transatlantic flight **1927**

Stock market crash in US **1929**

1930

Empire State Building completed **1931**
Hitler becomes chancellor of Germany **1933**
US Prohibition ends **1933**

Anthropology

Patterns of Culture (Benedict) **1934**
Sex and Temperament in Three Primitive Societies (Mead) **1935**
Coral Gardens and Their Magic (Malinowski) **1935**
Mules and Men (Hurston) **1935**
The Crow Indians (Lowie) **1935**
Their Eyes Were Watching God (Hurston) **1937**
Antonio Gramsci dies **1937**
Murdock establishes Cross-Cultural Survey **1937**
Edward Sapir dies **1939**
Sally Slocum born **1939**
Naomi Quinn born **1939**
Cultural and Natural Areas of Native North America (Kroeber) **1939**

Charles Seligman dies **1940**
HRAF founded at Yale University **1940**
Alexander Goldenweiser dies **1940**
A. C. Haddon dies **1940**
The Nuer (Evans-Pritchard) **1940**
Louise Lamphere born **1940**
Benjamin L. Whorf dies **1941**
James G. Frazer dies **1941**
Elsie Clews Parsons dies **1941**
Sherry Ortner born **1941**
Renato Rosaldo born **1941**
Franz Boas dies **1942**
Bronislaw Malinowski dies **1942**
Energy and the Evolution of Culture (White) **1943**
Paul Rabinow born **1944**
Michelle Rosaldo born **1944**
Nancy Scheper Hughes born **1944**
Veena Das born **1945**
Jonathan Friedman born **1946**
The Chrysanthemum and the Sword (Benedict) **1946**
Ruth Benedict dies **1948**
Anthropology: Race, Language, Culture, Psychology, Pre-history (Kroeber) **1948**
Arjun Appadurai born **1949**
The Elementary Structures of Kinship (Lévi-Strauss) **1949**
The Science of Culture (White) **1949**
Human Relations Area Files (HRAF) founded at Yale **1949**
Michel-Rolph Trouillot born **1949**

Marcel Mauss dies **1950**

Cheryl Mattingly born **1951**

Lila Abu-Lughod born **1952**
Structure and Function in Primitive Society (Radcliffe-Brown) **1952**

The Political Systems of Highland Burma (Leach) **1954**

A. R. Radcliffe-Brown dies **1955**
(R. Jon McGee and R. L. Warms born) **1955**
Theory of Culture Change (Steward) **1955**
Tristes Tropiques (Lévi-Strauss) **1955**

Wider World

Alan Turing describes a computing machine **1936**
Spanish Civil War **1936–1939**

Hindenburg disaster **1937**
Edmund Husserl dies **1938**
Kristallnacht pogrom in Germany 1938

World War II begins **1939**
First commercial transatlantic flight **1939**

Winston Churchill becomes prime minister of Britain **1940**
Lascaux cave paintings found **1940**

Pearl Harbor bombed **1941**

Manhattan project begins **1942**
US creates internment camps for Japanese Americans **1942**
First electronic computer **1943**

Atomic bombs dropped on Hiroshima and Nagasaki **1945**
World War II ends **1945**
United Nations formed **1945**

Transistor invented **1947**
Independence of India **1948**
Assassination of Mahatma Gandhi **1948**

People's Republic of China proclaimed **1949**

Korean War begins **1950**
King Solomon's Ring (Lorenz) **1952**
The Second Sex (de Beauvoir) **1952**
Mau Mau Uprising (Kenya) **1953**
Joseph Stalin dies **1953**
Structure of DNA published **1953**
French-Algerian War begins **1954**
Korean War ends **1953**
Senator Joseph McCarthy accuses public figures of being communists **1954**
Brown v. Board of Education ends legal racial segregation **1954**
Vietnamese defeat French forces at Diên Biên Phu **1954**
US military advisors sent to Vietnam **1955**
US Supreme Court orders integration of all public schools **1955**

1940

1950

Anthropology

Philippe Bourgois born **1956**
Nuer Religion (Evans Pritchard) **1956**
Language, Thought and Reality (Whorf) **1956**
Robert Lowie dies **1957**
Paul Radin dies **1959**
Mary Leakey discovers hominid fossils and tools at
    Olduvai Gorge **1959**
Structural Anthropology (Lévi-Strauss) **1959**
Paul Farmer born **1959**

Zora Neale Hurston dies **1960**
A. L. Kroeber dies **1960**
Evolution and Culture (Sahlins and Service) **1960**
Frantz Fanon dies **1961**
The Wretched of the Earth (Fanon) **1961**
Franz Fanon dies **1961**
Structural Anthropology (Lévi-Strauss) **1963**

Karl Polanyi dies **1964**

On Aggression (Lorenz) **1966**
David Valentine born **1966**
Cultural Ecology of India's Sacred Cattle (Harris) **1966**
Homo Hierarchicus (Dumont) **1966**
Purity and Danger (Douglas) **1966**
Pigs for the Ancestors (Rappaport) **1967**
The Forest of Symbols (Turner) **1967**
The Evolution of Political Society (Fried) **1967**
Rise of Anthropological Theory (Harris) **1968**
American Kinship (Schneider) **1968**
Archaeology of Knowledge (Foucault) **1969**
Ethnic Groups and Boundaries (Barth) **1969**
*Basic Color Terms: Their Universality and
    Evolution* (Berlin and Kay) **1969**
Tom Boellstorff born **1969**
Audra Simpson born **1969**

Association of Black Anthropologists established **1970**

Julian Steward dies **1972**
Stone Age Economics (Sahlins) **1972**

Anthropology and the Colonial Encounter (Asad) **1973**
The Interpretation of Cultures (Geertz) **1973**
E. E. Evans-Pritchard dies **1973**

Tim White and Donald Johanson discover "Lucy"
    Australopithecus afarensis **1974**
The Modern World System (Wallerstein) **1974**
Women, Culture, and Society (Lamphere) **1974**

Toward an Anthropology of Women (Reiter) **1975**
Max Gluckman dies **1975**
Leslie White dies **1975**
Discipline and Punish (Foucault) **1975**
Sociobiology: The New Synthesis (Wilson) **1975**

Outline of a Theory of Practice (Bourdieu) **1977**
Reflections on Fieldwork in Morocco (Rabinow) **1977**
Orientalism (Said) **1978**
History of Sexuality (Foucault) **1978**
Margaret Mead dies **1978**
Reo Fortune dies **1979**

1960

1970

Wider World

Sputnik orbits earth **1957**
First computer chip **1958**
Many African nations become independent
    1958–1966
European Common Market established **1957**
Sputnik orbits earth **1957**
First computer chip **1958**

"Second Wave Feminism" movement **1960–1980**
The Wretched of the Earth (Fanon) **1961**
Cuban missile crisis **1961**
Berlin Wall built **1961**
Bays of Pigs invasion **1961**
John Glenn orbits earth **1962**
The Feminine Mystique (Friedan) **1963**
Martin Luther King delivers his "I Have a Dream"
    speech in Washington, D.C. **1963**
Bombing of 16th Street Baptist Church in
    Birmingham **1963**
JFK Assassination **1963**
Civil Rights Act signed **1964**
Gulf of Tonkin resolution authorizes use of force in
    Vietnam **1964**
National Organization for Women (NOW) founded in
    the US **1966**
The Development of Underdevelopment
    (Gunder-Frank) **1966**
Martin Luther King assassinated **1968**
Robert F. Kennedy assassinated **1968**
Student strikes in France **1968**
Tet offensive in Vietnam **1968**
General System Theory (von Bertalanfy) **1968**
First moon landing **1969**
Stonewall Riots in New York mark beginning of the
    Gay Liberation/LGBTQ movement **1969**

Kent State shootings in US **1970**
Our Bodies, Ourselves published **1970**
Ray Tomlinson sends first email **1971**
Nixon visits China **1972**
Ms. magazine founded as a forum for feminist
    issues **1972**
Shirley Chisholm becomes the first major-party Black
    candidate and first woman to run for president
    of the United States **1972**
Title IX Women's Educational Equity Act passes,
    prohibiting sex discrimination in educational
    institutions and activities **1972**
President Salvador Allende assassinated
    in coup d'etat **1973**
US Supreme Court decides *Roe v. Wade*,
    legalizing abortion **1973**
Richard Nixon resigns as president of the US **1974**
Last US troops leave Vietnam **1975**
First UN World Conference on Women **1975**
Death of Mao Zedong **1976**
Apple II introduced **1977**
Combahee River Collective publishes a manifesto on
    Black feminism **1977**
Equal Rights Amendment fails to receive the
    necessary 38 state approvals for ratification **1977**
Iranian revolution **1979**

Anthropology

Gregory Bateson dies **1980**
The Logic of Practice (Bourdieu) **1980**
Knowledge and Passion (M. Rosaldo) 1980
Michelle Rosaldo dies **1981**
Europe and the People Without History (Wolf) **1982**
James P. Spradley dies **1982**
Monica Wilson dies **1982**
Victor Turner dies **1983**
Meyer Fortes dies **1983**
Audrey Richards dies **1984**
Michel Foucault dies **1984**
Theory in Anthropology since the Sixties (Ortner) **1984**
The Postmodern Condition (Lyotard) **1984**
A Critique of the Study of Kinship (Schneider) **1984**
*Weapons of the Weak (*Scott) **1985**
George Murdock dies **1985**
Sweetness and Power (Mintz) **1985**
Morton Fried dies **1986**
Writing Culture (Clifford and Marcus) **1986**
Eleanor B. Leacock dies **1987**
The Gender of the Gift (Strathern) **1988**
Culture and Truth (R. Rosaldo) **1989**
The Condition of Postmodernity (Harvey) **1989**
Edmund Leach dies **1989**
Culture and Truth (Rosaldo) **1989**

Native American Graves Protection and Repatriation Act
 (NAGPRA) becomes US law **1990**
Gender Trouble (Butler) **1990**
Louis Althusser dies **1990**
Ruth Bunzel dies **1990**
Of Revelation and Revolution Vol. 1.
 (Comaroff and Comaroff) **1991**
*Decolonizing Anthropology: Moving Further toward
 an Anthropology of Liberation* (Harrison) **1991**
We Have Never Been Modern (Latour) **1991**
Cora Du Bois dies **1991**
*Gender at the Crossroads of Knowledge:
 Feminist Anthropology in the
 Postmodern Era* (Di Leonardo) **1991**
Death Without Weeping (Scheper-Hughes) **1992**
*Beyond Culture – Space, Identity, and the politics of
 Difference* (Gupta and Ferguson) **1992**
Gender Trouble (Butler) **1992**
Mimesis and Alterity (Taussig) **1993**
Balinese Worlds (Barth) **1993**
Writing Women's Worlds (Abu-Lughod) **1993**
Luther Cressmasn dies **1994**
Colin Turnbull dies **1994**
David Schneider dies **1995**
*In Search of Respect: Selling Crack in
 El Barrio* (Bourgois) **1995**
Women Writing Culture (Behar) **1995**
Sol Tax dies **1995**

1980

1990

Wider World

Civil war in El Salvador **1980–1992**
Second UN World Conference on Women **1980**

First PC introduced **1981**
First official reporting of what will become known as
 the AIDS epidemic **1981**

Imagined Communities (Anderson) **1983**

Third UN World Conference on Women **1985**

Space shuttle *Challenger* explodes **1986**

Berlin Wall falls **1989**
Tim Berners-Lee invents the World Wide Web, and
 creates first web server and browser **1989–1990**

Han Dynasty vault with throusands of terra cotta
 figures discovered in China **1990**
Nelson Mandela freed **1990**
East and West Germany reunited **1990**
American with Disabilities Act passed **1990**

Breakup of the Soviet Union **1991**
Ötzi "The Iceman" discovered in the Alps **1991**

Bosnian genocide begins **1992**
Rebecca Walker coins the term "Third Wave
 Feminism" in *Ms.* magazine **1992**

European Union founded **1993**

End of apartheid in South Africa **1994**
Rwandan genocide **1994**
Amazon.com founded **1994**

Oklahoma City bombings **1995**
Fourth UN World Conference on Women **1995**

Anthropology

Anthropological Theory: An Introductory History (1st ed.)
   (McGee and Warms) **1996**
Modernity at Large (Appadurai) **1996**
Mary Leakey dies **1996**
Elman Service dies **1996**
Roy Rappaport dies **1997**
Louis Dumont dies **1998**
Dina Dreyfus dies **1999**
Eric Wolf dies **1999**
Flexible Citizenship (Ong) **1999**

On the Postcolony (Mbembe) **2001**
Marvin Harris dies **2001**
Derek Freeman dies **2001**
*Lines in the Water: Nature and Culture
   at Lake Titicaca* (Orlove) **2002**
Pierre Bourdieu dies **2002**
"Do Muslim Women Really Need Saving?"
   (Abu-Lughod) **2002**
Raymond Firth dies **2002**
Pathologies of Power (Farmer) **2003**
Isaac Schapera dies **2003**
Edward Said dies **2003**
Jacques Derrida dies **2004**
Friction: An Ethnography of Global Connection (Tsing) **2005**
*The Gay Archipelago: Sexuality and Nation
   in Indonesia* (Boellstorff) **2005**
Censure of Boas rescinded by the
   American Anthropological Association **2005**
Clifford Geertz dies **2006**
Anthropology and Social Theory (Ortner) **2006**
Life and Words (Das) **2006**
Mary Douglas dies **2007**
Claude Lévi-Strauss dies **2009**

"The Emergence of Multispecies Ethnography"
   (Kirksey and Helmrich) **2010**

Debt: The First 5,000 Years (Graeber) **2011**
Michel-Rolph Trouillot dies **2012**
"Toward an Ecology of Materials" (Ingold) **2012**

*"Beyond the Suffering Subject: Toward an
   Anthropology of the Good"* (Robbins) **2013**

*Mohawk Interruptus: Political Life across the
   Borders of Settler States* (Simpson) **2014**

Sidney Mintz dies **2015**

Wider World

Dolly the sheep (first cloned mammal) born **1996**
First Harry Potter book released **1997**

Google founded **1998**
Construction begins on
   International Space Station **1998**

Columbine High School killings **1999**
Protests against the World Trade Organization
   meetings in Seattle, WA, lead to
   antiglobalization movement **1999**

Terrorist attacks of 9/11 **2001**
US invades Afghanistan **2001**
The Netherlands is first country to
   legalize same-sex marriage **2001**

First *Homo floriensis* remains found **2003**

US war in Iraq starts **2003**
First successful Mars Rover landing **2003**
Human genome mapped **2003**
Facebook founded **2004**
YouTube founded **2005**
Hurricane Katrina **2005**

Twitter created **2006**
Pluto reclassified as dwarf planet **2006**
First iPhone **2007**
International financial crisis **2008**
Barack Obama elected as first
   Black president of the United States **2008**
Astrophysicists estimate the age of the
   Universe at 13.7 billion years **2009**
WHO declares H1N1 (swine flu) a pandemic **2009**

Beginning of "Arab Spring" **2010**
Affordable Care Act (Obamacare)
   signed by President Obama **2010**
National Oceanic and AtmosphericAdministration
   (NOAA) announces **2010** is hottest year on record
Fukushima nuclear disaster **2011**
Occupy Wall Street movement **2011**
Global population reaches seven billion people **2011**
Black Lives Matter movement **2013**
Boston Marathon bombing **2013**
Michael Brown killed by Ferguson Police **2014**
Eric Garner killed by New York City Police **2014**
More than 50% of US population
   has a smartphone **2014**
Flint, Michigan, water crisis **2014**
NOAA announces **2014** is the hottest year on record
Same-sex marriage legalized in the US **2015**
CRISPR gene editing method developed **2015**

2000

2010

Anthropology

The Seductions of Quantification: Measuring Human Rights, Gender Violence, and Sex Trafficking (Merry) **2016**
Fredrick Barth dies **2016**
Harold Conklin dies **2016**
Down and Out in the New Economy (Gershon) **2017**

Naomi Quinn dies **2019**
Napoleon Chagnon dies **2019**
June Nash dies **2019**

Marchall Sahlins dies **2021**
Mary Catherine Bateson dies **2021**
Paul Rabinow dies **2021**

Paul Farmer dies **2022**
Hildred Geertz dies **2022**
Bruno Latour dies **2022**

Wider World

US signs Paris Climate Agreement **2016**
Donald Trump elected US president **2016**
TikTok founded **2016**
NOAA announces **2016** is the hottest year on record
Women's March on Washington **2017**
US withdraws from Paris Climate Agreement **2017**
Unite the Right white supremacist rally in
    Charlottesville, Virginia, **2017**
#MeToo movement **2017**
SpaceX launches Falcon Heavy Rocket **2018**
Marjory Stoneman Douglas High School
    mass shooting, Parkland, Florida **2018**
US government shut down for 35 days **2018–2019**
Initial COVID outbreak in Wuhan, China,
    December **2019**

2020

CDC identifies first case of COVID in the US,
    December 20, **2020**
WHO declares COVID-19 a global pandemic,
    March 11, **2020**
Brexit: Britain withdraws from
    the European Union **2020**
Black Lives Matter protest begin nationwide
    following the police killings of George Floyd
    and Breonna Taylor **2020**
NASA announces **2020** has tied with 2016 as the
    hottest year on record
Worldwide number of recorded COVID-19 cases
    surpasses 100 million **2021**
US reenters Paris Climate Agreement **2021**
Afghanistan falls to the Taliban **2021**
Half the world's population owns a smartphone **2021**
Russia invades Ukraine **2022**
The number of recorded deaths in the US due to
    COVID-19 reaches one million; worldwide deaths
    are 15 million, May **2022**
Robb Elementary School mass shooting,
    Uvalde, Texas **2022**
Roe v. Wade reversed by US Supreme Court **2022**
ChatGPT launched **2022**
Hamas attacks Israel; war in Gaza begins **2023**
NOAA announces that **2023** is the hottest
    year on record

Introduction

ANTHROPOLOGY IS CONCERNED with understanding people. Typically, anthropologists study the behavior, beliefs, and lifestyles of communities. Some examine current cultures; others study the remains of past societies to re-create the lives of people who disappeared long ago; still others study primates to see what our closest relatives can tell us about being human. What unites this diverse work is a common ground in some fundamental theoretical ideas concerning biological evolution and social behavior.

We teach both undergraduate and graduate courses in anthropological theory at Texas State University. Each fall as the semester begins, we face the same issues: Some students want to know why, if they are studying X (fill in the blank), the theory course is required, and others worry about reading original works by authors and delving into a subject that seems esoteric. Because these matters are important, we begin this book by telling you why we think theory is essential in anthropology and why it is valuable to read complete original works rather than predigested theoretical summaries or brief extracts.

WHY STUDY THEORY?

Whether stated explicitly or assumed, theories are the tools anthropologists use to decide what are and what are not data. Theories enable anthropologists to observe and analyze human behavior. Examine the same topic from different theoretical perspectives and you will likely observe different things, collect different data, and come to different conclusions. Anthropologists' understandings of the events they witness and record are derived from their theoretical perspective. It is only through the application of a theoretical perspective that one can interpret designs carved into a rock ten thousand years ago, a cache of silver coins buried with a victim of the plague in fourteenth-century London, or the meaning of a wink as distinguished from the twitch of an eyelid. Theories are the tools anthropologists use to sort what they believe is significant from the trivial.

One's choice of theory determines the data to be collected in the first place. A structuralist interested in the unconscious meaning of mythology probably will not spend too much time studying subsistence patterns. Conversely, an economic anthropologist might ignore mythology and folklore focusing instead on precisely the subsistence patterns that the structuralist declares irrelevant. Without theory, one cannot do anthropology of any sort.

Although this is a book about theory in sociocultural anthropology, the different branches of anthropology have always freely borrowed ideas from each other and from other sciences. For example, in the nineteenth century, Herbert Spencer, a sociologist, and Charles Darwin, a naturalist, greatly influenced each other's work while Karl Marx and Friedrich Engels were inspired by the work of Lewis Henry Morgan. Interpretive anthropologists and postmodernists rely on tools developed in the study of literature, and many current anthropologists base their work on philosophers such as Edmund Husserl, Stanley Cavell, and Ludwig Wittgenstein. In the course of their research, anthropologists today delve into biology, geology, psychology, history, literature, physics, chemistry, medicine, and other subjects.

Modern anthropology is built on the work of earlier generations of researchers. Indeed, anthropologists today ask many of the same questions that occupied scholars in the nineteenth and early twentieth centuries.

Another reason to become familiar with anthropology's early history is that nineteenth-century ideas continue to resonate in popular culture. Have you ever heard the phrase "survival of the fittest," for example? It was first used by Herbert Spencer in his 1864 book *Principles of Biology*. Do you think that technology is a measure of a society's development? Then you will be comfortable reading Lewis Henry Morgan's *Ancient Society*, first published in 1877. To fully comprehend anthropological writing, you must appreciate the history of the ideas that inform it. These are, ultimately, the principles upon which current work is based.

Anthropological theory, and indeed anthropology in general is also important because it helps us think about who and what we are as human beings. It does this by asking us to consider how we view and understand each other. Historically, anthropology developed in Europe and the United States. As Europeans and their descendants in the United States confronted others who looked different from them and had different languages and customs (what anthropologists have come to call different *cultures*), they wondered if such people were inferior to them, superior to them, or just different. Were their cultures unchanging, following their own paths, or bound to those of Europeans in a grand evolutionary scheme? How should such people be treated? Although anthropology developed in Europe and the United States and in a context that was both colonial and racist, the questions it raises are universal in a world in which different people and cultures are in constant contact with each other. No matter who you are, the experience of confronting the other, and the questions and problems it raises is now universal and perhaps always was.

Studying other cultures leads anthropologists to think deeply and critically about their own cultures. The process of understanding and asking questions about others leads to questions about understanding ourselves. For well over a century, anthropologists have offered insights and critiques into their own cultures. In the past half-century, they have particularly focused on thinking about the histories, meanings, and pathways of power in Europe and the United States. They have challenged mainstream understandings of history, race, gender, and ethnicity.

At a second level, anthropology forces us to consider if we, as human beings, are fundamentally part of the natural world. If so, perhaps we can be studied by the scientific methods and principles used by biologists, physicists, and other scholars in the traditional physical sciences. Alternatively, are human beings sufficiently different from the rest of the world that studying them with these methods will produce only trivial and confusing results? If that is true, the skills needed might be creative insight, imaginative interpretation, and empathy—analytic tools traditionally associated with the arts and humanities.

A final level of discourse deals with the otherness of culture itself. By directing us to the comparison of cultures, anthropology ultimately points toward the study of human nature. If we could strip away the cultural clothing of all peoples, would we be left with some set of basic principles or underlying essence? Would this be equivalent to finding human nature before us in the buff? If so, how are we to understand human culture? Is it that which permits the full and satisfying expression of human nature, that which creates the prejudices, bigotries, and hierarchies that prevent the full achievement of human potential, that which prevents human nature from destroying human society, or that which throws humans together in violent confrontation? Can it be all of these things? At some level, all theory in anthropology, whether written in the eighteenth, nineteenth, twentieth, or twenty-first centuries, addresses these essential questions about culture. Sometimes individual theorists take extreme postures and for a time quiet the voices of those who hold alternative positions. However, no definitive conclusion has ever been reached on any of these issues. Perhaps these questions are ultimately unanswerable. But the fact that no authoritative conclusion has been reached does not lessen the importance of the debate, for how we answer these questions has practical applications in our world. The answers determine our understanding of ourselves and our behavior toward others. In a world of instantaneous communication and virtually unlimited capacity for violence, ethnic strife, war, and terrorism, surely these are among the most important questions that face us.

WHY READ ORIGINAL WORKS?

We believe it is important to read complete original works for several reasons. First, commentary on a theory cannot replace the original work because commentators unavoidably (and frequently intentionally) place their own interpretations on the material. For instance, Robert Lowie's 1937 *History of Ethnological Theory* and Marvin Harris's 1968 *The Rise of Anthropological Theory* are both comprehensive summaries of the anthropological theory of their eras, but they provide strikingly different perspectives on the field. Each is an ideological document supporting a particular interpretation of the history and proper goals of anthropology.

Second, part of the importance of classic works in theory is their subtlety and complexity. The current work of anthropology is part of an ongoing dialogue with earlier thinkers. As our understandings change, we return to these older works. Sometimes we find insights that advance our thinking or perceive errors against which we react. Through this process, new theory is generated. When works are summarized, when we read only brief extracts of works, or only an analysis, the theoretical dialogue is flattened, simplified, and ultimately impoverished.

In this volume, we provide what we believe is useful commentary on the essays we present, but reading these analyses cannot replace your careful reading of the original texts. As new insights are made, many of our notes will become outdated. The essays themselves have a much longer shelf life.

Finally, a firsthand reading of the original sources helps one avoid what one early commenter on this book referred to as "received untruths." In preparing this text, we have run across numerous cases in which the popularly accepted information was incorrect. Some of the folk wisdom of anthropology consists of half-truths or worse. The tendency to set up then critique simplified, straw-man versions of earlier anthropological thinkers has not diminished in the years we have been writing the now eight editions of this book. We bring this up not to point fingers or assign blame but to suggest that reading original sources can serve as a partial corrective for this problem.

USING THIS TEXTBOOK

This book is designed to help readers understand critical concepts in cultural anthropology through the work of ethnographers and social scientists over the last 150 years and to help you formulate your theoretical position in the field today. It is a historical overview of some of the principal developments in culture theory since the 1850s.

Theory texts are problematic because their contents tend to become accepted doctrine. Readers and critics suppose that the authors of such a text have chosen to present those pieces universally considered the most important works in the field. Should you entertain this notion, let us disabuse you of it. No group of professional anthropologists, however small, will agree on a single set of critical works. We have selected what we feel are representative articles by individuals associated with particular theories and works that seem to us to be good examples of theories in practice. An enormous corpus of work in anthropology now exists. We believe that the best way to study anthropological theory is to read as widely as possible. No collection of diverse writings, however artfully chosen, will be able to substitute for years of reading in the field, and that is what is ultimately required for a solid background in theory. We believe that all serious students of anthropology should have a solid knowledge of the history of their discipline and should read the works of earlier anthropologists. However, we reject the idea that there is a canon of authors and works that constitute the field's history that should be read by all. This volume is not an attempt to create or reinforce such a canon. It is an *Introductory History* that is, a reasonable place to begin what we hope will be your long engagement with the ideas, personalities, and histories of anthropology.

The book is different from others because it includes our introductions and paragraph-by-paragraph comments to inform your reading, raise interesting points, and ask questions about the essays. You will find that our commentary on the texts varies from extremely straightforward definitions and explanations to fairly elaborate speculation on the motives of authors and influences upon them. Although it is almost impossible to entirely eliminate mistakes in a book this long, we have checked our work carefully; when we point to a fact, you may be reasonably certain that it is correct. However, please remember that our interpretations are just that. They are meant to guide your reading, stimulate discussion, call your attention to certain ideas, and get you to think about different issues. If you read through this book and find nothing with which to disagree, you are not reading carefully enough or critically enough.

Although our likes and dislikes may become apparent to the careful reader, we do not intend to promote any particular viewpoint. In fact, we were trained in very different theoretical perspectives (McGee in interpretive-symbolic and Warms in positivist-materialist). While we have tried to present the key strengths and weaknesses of each position, we sometimes differ in our interpretations of theory and amuse our students by arguing about them. In short, while we hope that readers will agree with most of what we have written, we have tried to write at least something bound to rile your theoretical sensibilities, no matter who you are. You are invited to disagree with the text and debate with us if you wish, or at the very least contact us if you have a question. You can send us e-mail at r.warms@txstate.edu for Warms or rm08@txstate.edu for McGee.

THE ARRANGEMENT OF ESSAYS AND THE NOTATIONAL SYSTEM

The arrangement of essays presents a surprising number of problems. Should the texts be arranged strictly chronologically or by intellectual association or descent? If the text is to be divided into sections, what about those authors who do not quite fit? What about works that represent more than one area? We have taught our theory course both chronologically and thematically and concluded that a chronological presentation works best. Thus, we have chosen to arrange the theories in a rough chronological order to show readers the progression of ideas and to demonstrate the relationship between concepts. We have divided our chronology into named sections. Each begins with an introduction describing the theorists represented in the section, the principal ideas presented in their work, and suggested readings for those who wish to pursue a topic further. However, our scheme is not entirely consistent. Different schools of thought often overlap both intellectually and chronologically. Exploiting these inconsistencies and thinking about other possible arrangements of the text may prove an intellectually useful experience. New arrangements may provide new insights.

Space limitations and, occasionally, copyright regulations have forced us to make difficult decisions about the original material we have reprinted. Works included in earlier drafts of the book have been removed from the final, and we have added or subtracted articles as our own knowledge base has grown. You will see that we have occasionally eliminated fairly large passages of some essays or chosen to remove particularly lengthy sets of original footnotes or endnotes. These are not decisions we took lightly, nor do they indicate that we believe the notes and passages removed were of no significance. It was simply a question of space. We have often had to choose between removing notes and passages or cutting entire essays. Although there are good intellectual reasons for selecting either of these options, we believe that most readers are better served by the first. In doing this editing, we have tried to preserve a sense of the original by including notes telling the reader exactly how much text was removed and briefly summarizing the content of the lost passage. We also note where footnotes have been removed and how many how many there were. This gives readers a feel for the number and pacing of the notes.

Each essay in the volume is accompanied by our notes, which appear as footnotes and are numbered with Arabic numerals. The numbers for our notes are always placed at the end of the paragraph to which they refer. We frequently provide definitions for terms that the average reader might not be familiar with. When we define a word, the word is in bold in the text and the definition appears in the note for the paragraph in which the word appears, directly below any other commentary. Footnotes or endnotes created by the original authors are indicated by lowercase letters and appear as endnotes to the essays. In most cases, authors have provided references in their work, and these appear at the end of their essays. Our own references along with an index appear at the end of the volume.

PART I

Historical Foundations of Anthropological Theory

Nineteenth-Century Evolutionism

In the English-speaking world, the word *anthropologist* first appeared in print in 1805 (Kuklick 1991: 6). It was another seventy-nine years before the first university position in anthropology was created. The emerging discipline of anthropology combined three long-existing streams of thought. The first was the study of what we have come to call cultural differences among societies. The second dealt with the struggle to explain the antiquity of humans and the artifacts left from these ancient lives. The final line of thought, closely related to the second, was the investigation of the biological origins of humans and other species. All of these areas have been the subject of investigation and speculation for much of the past millennium. Though it is far beyond the scope of this text to analyze all the antecedents of anthropology, we will briefly review some of the principal developments that led to its origin before exploring evolutionary and anthropological thinking in the nineteenth century.

It is probably fair to say that wherever literate civilizations came into contact with members of different societies, something like ethnographic writing occurred. For example, ancient authors such as Herodotus, a Greek historian of the fifth century BCE, offered readers fanciful descriptions of other societies. In the fourteenth century, Ibn Khaldun, a Tunisian politician and historian, wrote the *Muqaddimah, or Introduction to History*, in which he proposed that the study of human civilization and social organization was an entirely original science (Ibn Khaldun 1989: 38–39).

In Europe, there was a long tradition of interest in the exotic. Writings such as *The Wonders of the East*, written in the eleventh century, and *The Travels of Marco Polo*, written around 1300, fascinated Europeans. Until the fifteenth century, however, Europe remained relatively provincial. Then developments in sailing technology and advances in weaponry allowed Europeans to expand their influence across the globe. For the first time, they were in frequent contact with people from societies radically different from their own. This exposure raised a host of ethical and philosophical problems. Were these other people human in the same way that Europeans were? Did their societies function according to brute natural law, or were they moral beings possessed of free will? How were social differences to be explained?

From the Renaissance until the eighteenth century, the concept of degenerationism provided Europeans with a biblically based explanation of cultural diversity. In this view, prior to the destruction of the Tower of Babel, all people belonged to a single civilization. When God destroyed the tower, creating differences in language and dispersing the people, some degenerated, losing their civilization and eventually becoming savages. Much of the European experience seemed to confirm degenerationism. For example, the recovery of texts and artifacts from ancient Greek and Roman civilizations seemed to show that these were far more advanced than those of later times.

Progressivism was an alternative view of social life. Progressivists believed that, rather than deteriorating from a previously civilized condition, societies had started out primitive but were progressing toward a more advanced state. For example, in "An Essay Concerning Human Understanding," published in 1690, the British philosopher John Locke (1632–1704) proposed that the human mind was a blank slate and that knowledge and reason were derived from experience. Thus different sorts of experiences would provide different sorts of ideas. Individuals growing up in different societies would have varied experiences. This, rather than degeneration, explained the differences among human societies.

The idea that people had progressed rather than degenerated became popular as scientific investigation and empirical observation increasingly yielded both academic and commercial results. By the late 1700s, few Europeans doubted that humankind was making progress and that they were the most advanced of all people.

With the general idea of progress firmly entrenched, philosophers devised various schemes to explain the nature and course of social evolution. Their goal was to construct a universal history of humankind that moved from a primitive past to the development of European nations. One of the most influential of these works was *The Decline and Fall of the Roman Empire* (1776–1788) by Edward Gibbon (1737–1794), but there were others as well. Italian philosopher Giambattista Vico (1668–1744), in his 1744 work *The New Science*, attempted to write a universal history of humanity. Vico believed that human nature was shaped by history and hence changed over time. Thus he thought that history was a better guide to understanding humanity than the natural sciences. French statesman Anne-Robert-Jacques Turgot (1727–1781) published "Plan for Two Discourses on Universal History" in 1750. He argued that, after the biblical flood, humans had passed through stages of savagery and barbarism to agriculture and urban-based civilization. Finally, there is *Sketch for a Historical Picture of the Progress of the Human Mind*, written by Marie-Jean-Antoine-Nicolas de Caritat, Marquis de Condorcet (1743–1794). Condorcet proposed a ten-stage scheme describing human progress from early tribal society through the founding of the French Republic and beyond, to a future in which human society would be perfected.

Condorcet was a philosophe, a friend of Turgot and of Voltaire, Benjamin Franklin, and Thomas Paine as well. He was a widely respected mathematician who became the secretary of the Legislative Assembly after the French Revolution. Condorcet supported liberal and rationalist causes but fell out of favor as the radical Montagnards rose to power. His opposition to the execution of the king and to the constitution proposed by the Montagnards led the increasingly powerful radicals to consider him a traitor and call for his arrest. In 1793 Condorcet went into hiding at a friend's home in Paris. *Sketch for a Historical Picture of the Progress of the Human Mind* was written in the months that followed. In 1794, fearing his hiding place was no longer safe, he attempted to flee Paris but was arrested and imprisoned. He was found dead in his cell two days later. Controversy remains over whether he committed suicide or was murdered.

The rise of the violent and radical Montagnards and the death of Condorcet signaled an important moment in British, American, and French social thought. The late eighteenth century had been characterized by optimism, progressivism, rationalism, and secularism. The violent overthrow of the social order in France and the increasing disorder and poverty of urban life in England, including the destruction of factories by Luddites, led to a retreat from these values. The result was a revival of religion and deep questioning of the notion of progress. There had been clear advances in technology, and for many, the standard of living had improved. However, the French Revolution and turbulence among the British lower classes suggested that optimism for humanity's future might not be justified. Clearly, if progress was being made, its course was not smooth. How were intellectuals to reconcile ideas of progress and rationalism with an increasingly disordered society?

The European expansion that began in the fifteenth century had a profound effect on the natural sciences as well as philosophy. Explorers' accounts of the flora and fauna of new lands challenged Europeans' biblical view of life, particularly the stories of creation and the flood. Long before Darwin, naturalists were confronted with distributions and variations in plants and animals that could not be explained in biblical terms. Scholars also struggled to explain evidence of human antiquity that did not correspond to biblical chronologies. This evidence became more widely available in the early nineteenth century as large-scale, nationwide engineering projects, such as the construction of canal and railroad systems, exposed geological strata, fossils, and human artifacts to the study of naturalists and geologists. Scientists were confronted with questions such as why objects of human manufacture were found in association with extinct mammals.

The foundation of biological-evolutionary speculation was laid down in the descriptive writings of seventeenth-century naturalists such as John Ray (1627–1705) and Gilbert White (1720–1793), who attempted to classify and describe the diversity of life-forms they observed. Ray influenced Carl Linné (Latinized as Carolus Linnaeus; 1707–1778), best known for the taxonomic categorization of life-forms he presented in *Systema Naturae* in 1735. Previously, there had been no single naming system for plants and animals, and identical species were called by different names in different places. Linnaeus's taxonomic system provided the systematic, organized, and, for Europeans, universal framework for the classification of life-forms that was necessary for the scientific investigation of biological evolution to take place.

The immutability of species was one aspect of thinking in the natural philosophy of Linnaeus's era. Almost all scholars believed that life-forms were created separately by God in their present form and could not change. The task of biology was to name and classify them. However, challenges to this position were developed by several scholars. For example, in *Telliamed* [. . .] *or Discourses between an Indian Philosopher and a French Missionary on the Diminution of the Sea, the Formation of the Earth, the Origin of Men and Animals* [. . .], a book widely read in the mid-eighteenth century, Benoit de Maillet (1656–1738) outlined a scheme for biological evolution. He speculated that the age of the earth was much greater than popularly believed, he recognized that fossils were the remains of life-forms, and he suggested that some of these fossils represented extinct species. De Maillet did not dare to speak of his theories in his own voice, choosing instead to frame his work as a conversation between "Telliamed," a fictitious Indian philosopher, and a Christian missionary and placing the radical observations in the mouth of the Indian. Alert readers will realize that "Telliamed" is de Maillet spelled backward.

Another naturalist, second in importance only to Linnaeus, was Georges Louis Leclerc, Comte de Buffon (1707–1788). The forty-four volumes of Buffon's *Natural History* (1752–1799) outlined an evolutionary theory that he called "degeneration" but which contained many of the elements that Darwin used in his theory of natural selection more than one hundred years later. Some of Buffon's key observations were that physical variation occurred within species; that different animals had underlying structural similarities; that life multiplied faster than its food supply, promoting a struggle for existence; and that some life-forms had become extinct.

Jean Lamarck (1744–1829) and Charles Darwin's grandfather Erasmus Darwin (1731–1802) were two great evolutionists of the late eighteenth century whose work exerted a profound influence on the development of later evolutionary theory. Although they held similar views, Lamarck's theories were more systematically presented, and his work is better known today. Lamarck believed that changes in geographic areas and climatic zones placed pressures on plant and animal life. In his view, changes in environmental conditions led to changes in animal species. Species did not go extinct but rather changed their forms as their environments changed. Lamarck argued that changed conditions would place stresses on particular body parts, requiring them to be used more often or in new ways. Body parts thus used would grow in size and strength. Changes acquired through the use and disuse of body parts during the life of individuals would be passed on to their offspring. Lamarck's most famous example was the giraffe. Lamarck argued that as the climate changed, the acacia leaves on which giraffes fed grew higher and higher. As a result, giraffes were forced to stretch to reach them. Thus giraffes lengthened their necks and forelimbs during their lifetimes. These changes were then passed down to their offspring. The result of this process was that the height of the entire species increased over time. This aspect of Lamarck's work is referred to as the inheritance of acquired characteristics.

Although the idea of the inheritance of acquired characteristics was deeply influential in the biology of the nineteenth and early twentieth centuries (e.g., agricultural policies of the Soviet Union through much of the twentieth century were based upon it), it is a fallacy. Heritable biological changes must be based on changes in DNA, and these cannot be acquired through use and disuse. However, the same is not true of cultural changes: people can be taught new cultural characteristics and pass these acquired traits on to anyone willing to watch or listen. For example, when McGee and Warms started at Texas State University in the 1980s, class registration was done by hand in the basketball arena. Students walked from department table to department table to select their classes. Then the World Wide Web was created by Tim Berners-Lee in 1989, and students were soon able to register for classes online from their desktop computers. Less than twenty years later, the first iPhone was introduced (2007), and by the mid-2010s, it became commonplace for students to register and pay for classes using their mobile phones. None of these cultural changes is dependent on biological inheritance.

By the end of the eighteenth century, the philosophical and biological frameworks for anthropology were in place. Nineteenth-century thinkers, driven by an abundance of new data, from fossil finds in England to explorers' accounts of Africa, built on this framework. They produced new theories of biological and social evolution that were key to the development of anthropology. The insights of Charles Darwin (1809–1882) and Herbert Spencer (1820–1903) were particularly important.

Between 1831 and 1836, Darwin traveled on the HMS *Beagle* on a mission to survey the southern coast of South America, one of the most famous voyages in the history of science. Darwin sailed over forty thousand miles and collected more than five thousand specimens. When he returned, he published a journal of his voyages (1839) as well as a major multivolume work on coral reefs (1846) and several works on barnacles (1851–1854). In 1837 he also began to write secret notebooks in which he organized his thoughts about evolution. He studied the materials he had collected and gave considerable attention to commercial plant and animal breeders in whose work he saw a practical application of his concepts. He collected data, organized his notes, and, in 1844, composed a draft of his ideas that he showed to his close friend, the eminent botanist Joseph Dalton Hooker (1817–1911). However, aware of the controversy his ideas would arouse, he refrained from publishing his work.

Darwin had been refining his ideas for twenty years when he received a letter in June 1858 from Alfred Russel Wallace (1823–1913), a young naturalist with whom he had been corresponding. From his observations in Malaysia, Wallace had independently formulated the theory that Darwin had been working so diligently to substantiate. Darwin was greatly disheartened by Wallace's letter, but his colleagues Charles Lyell (1797–1875) and Hooker arranged the joint presentation of the two men's ideas in July 1858, and Darwin was granted the opportunity to publish first. He published *On the Origin of Species by Means of Natural Selection* in November 1859.

Darwin held that change within species must follow natural laws like those found in the physical sciences. In *On the Origin of Species*, he named and outlined his theory of natural selection and proposed that it was the fundamental principle of biological change. Darwin began with the idea that more organisms were born than survived to adulthood. This was a widely accepted concept derived in part from "An Essay on the Principle of Population," published in 1798 by Thomas Malthus (1766–1834). He then speculated about the factors that determined which individuals survived while others did not. Darwin observed that no two individuals of any species were precisely alike; small variations occur in the appearance or behavioral characteristics of members of any population. Darwin hypothesized that some variations were better than others in that they led those who possessed them to more successfully compete for food, shelter, and mates. These individuals would subsequently produce more offspring who themselves would survive and reproduce. Darwin called the characteristics that led to increased numbers of surviving and reproducing offspring "adaptive." Though he did not have any understanding of the mechanisms of heredity, he observed that parents were capable of passing traits to their offspring and that those possessing the adaptive traits were "naturally selected" over those who lacked them. Consequently, over a long period, and through the slow, incremental accumulation of adaptive traits, the appearance of a species could be altered or a new species could develop.

Darwin's theory was extraordinarily important for several reasons. First, it was a scientifically convincing explanation of how life-forms could change over time and new species emerge. Natural selection also explained fossils and extinction. As such, the theory forms the basis of much of modern biology. Additionally, Darwin's theory was a powerful social metaphor. Darwin's theory explained how it was possible to have both progress and social disruption. It showed how progress, rather than being a smooth upward climb, was achieved through struggle and conflict.

Darwin's work was controversial in religious circles and met with ridicule from the popular press. It was disparaged by French intellectuals (who presented Darwin's theory in a seriously flawed translation when it first appeared) and generally rejected in Germany until the turn of the twentieth century. However, in Britain and America, scholars had been moving toward a theory of evolution for half a century, and Darwin's work was widely (if not universally) accepted.

Darwin had become extremely well respected in scientific circles for his publications on his voyages, geology, coral reefs, and barnacles. His support made the ideas of evolution and trans-mutation of species much more popular in both scientific and popular circles. However, many scientists of Darwin's era rejected natural selection. Some, such as William Thompson, Lord Kelvin, argued that even though the earth was ancient, it was not ancient enough to provide the time necessary for natural selection to occur. Others, such as Fleeming Jenkin, believed that any favorable mutations that did occur would be swamped by the size of existing populations. George Douglas Campbell, Duke of Argyle, proposed that natural selection could not account for the beauty of the world. Darwin used his theory of sexual selection to answer the Duke of Argyle's objections, but the problems raised by Lord Kelvin and Fleeming Jenkin were not solved until the late nineteenth and early twentieth centuries when radioactivity and genetics were better understood.

Herbert Spencer had been working on a theory of human social evolution years before Darwin published *Origin of Species*, and Darwin had applied some of Spencer's concepts in his work, but Spencer's work gained increased credibility because of Darwin.

Though Spencer was the son of a schoolmaster, he was largely self-educated. He worked as a civil engineer for the Birmingham and London Railway and then as a subeditor for *The Economist*, a magazine that promoted free-market capitalism. In 1853, having received a small inheritance, Spencer was able to leave *The Economist* to devote himself full time to writing.

Spencer was interested in evolution as a general phenomenon, and he applied his evolutionary approach to many fields of study. His concept of the law of equal freedom and related ideas on social evolution had an enormous impact in Britain and the United States, not only on science but on literature, politics, and popular culture. Spencer considered a person's right to make his or her own choices (and to benefit or suffer the consequences of those choices) to be the foundation of cultural evolution. He believed that the evolutionary process was a natural law expressed in four ways. According to Spencer, evolution was progressive, and over time evolution made small units larger, simple things became more complex, and entities composed of independent parts evolved into more complex units with interdependent components. Among people, however, Spencer believed that evolution was driven by a struggle for survival in which only those with superior skills and traits succeeded.

Spencer was the first to use the phrase "survival of the fittest" in his book *Principles of Biology* (1864). Darwin adopted Spencer's phrase in later editions of *On the Origin of Species*, which tended to obscure the important differences between the two. Spencer and Darwin understood the mechanisms of evolution in very different ways. For Spencer, survival of the fittest meant that evolution favored the physically strong, intellectually clever, and, among humans, financially most prosperous. For Darwin, fitness was a matter of reproduction. The most fit were those most successful at producing fertile offspring. Although Spencer viewed Darwin's work as supporting his own, there is little evidence Spencer understood what Darwin meant by natural selection. Spencer's view of biological evolution was based on Lamarck.

The organic analogy, a critical part of Spencer's thinking, is illustrated in "The Social Organism" (1860), which is the first essay of this book. Spencer compared human societies to biological organisms. He used this analogy to link biological and social evolution, implying both followed the same processes and direction. This suggested that societies could be studied in the same fashion as biological organisms.

In making the analogy between societies and biological organisms, Spencer was also proposing that there was an analogy between the organs within an organism and the various parts of society.

This implied a research agenda: these social organs should be accurately identified and their role and function in maintaining society described. This idea, in various forms, set the agenda for much of anthropology in the century following the publication of "The Social Organism."

All humans are ethnocentric to one degree or another, and nineteenth-century Europeans and Americans were no exception. Looking with pride at their industrial advances and burgeoning economic and military power, members of Western societies believed they were at the pinnacle of social evolution. One consequence of Spencer's work was the popularization of a point of view called social Darwinism. Social Darwinists interpreted theories of evolution to mean that progress could only be achieved through the strong dominating the weak. They equated strength with military and financial power. Thus they believed that it was not only the right but the obligation of the rich to dominate the poor and of Western powers to dominate those who were less technologically advanced. It was only in this manner that humanity as a whole could progress. This was a convenient philosophy for the rapidly expanding European powers and was used to justify their imperialism, colonialism, and racism. In the United States, social Darwinism was invoked as a justification for free enterprise capitalism, the doctrine of "manifest destiny," and imperialist projects such as the Spanish-American War of 1898.

It should be remembered, however, that although Spencer and the other evolutionary thinkers represented here thought Western society more highly evolved than any other, they were also highly critical of it. The evolutionists believed that societies moved continually toward perfection. Western society might be more advanced than any other, but it was far from perfect. It is true that Spencer argued, on one hand, that state-funded welfare, education, and public health programs were contrary to the laws of nature and should be avoided because the taxes that paid for them were an unjust use of a citizen's earnings, and they slowed the evolutionary process that was weeding out the unfit members of society. On the other hand, he also argued against the military, the Church of England, and the perquisites of the landowning class because these institutions were contrary to his notions of human freedom. Despite the use of theories like his to justify colonial conquest, Spencer himself was an adamant opponent of British imperialism. In his autobiography, he wrote that as early as 1879 he had spoken to friends concerning the possibility of doing something toward checking the aggressive tendencies displayed by us [the British] all over the world—sending as pioneers, missionaries of "the religion of love," and then picking quarrels with the native races and taking possession of their lands (1904: 443).

The English scholar Sir Edward Burnett Tylor (1832–1917) and the American Lewis Henry Morgan (1818–1881) were also interested in the evolution of culture as a general human phenomenon. Both men believed there were universal evolutionary stages of cultural development that characterized the transition from primitive to complex societies. Because of this belief, Morgan and Tylor are known as unilineal evolutionists.

E. B. Tylor was probably the leading English anthropologist of the nineteenth century. As one of the heirs of a family fortune based in brass manufacturing and coal mining, he was able to devote much of his life to anthropology. In his principal work, *Primitive Culture* (1871), an excerpt of which appears in essay 2, Tylor argued that all human minds followed the same course of development, an idea generally known as psychic unity. In formulating this idea, he drew heavily on the work of Adolf Bastian (1826–1905), who, in his 1860 book *Der Mensch in der Geschichte* (Man in History), describes *Elementargedanken* or "elementary ideas," which he believed appeared in almost all cultures and religions of the world. Tylor frequently cited *Der Mensch* and other works by Bastian in *Primitive Culture*.

Tylor believed that the fact that similar material artifacts were found in different areas of the world showed that human society developed along a single evolutionary pathway. He proposed that environments and social formations presented specific problems to human groups. Because human minds all worked along the same lines, faced with similar problems, humans would always come up with similar solutions. This resulted in a single path of social-evolutionary development. Throughout the process, human rationality increased; people thought their way to progress.

Tylor proposed that one could reconstruct earlier stages of cultural evolution by studying the customs of indigenous peoples and examining "survivals." These were elements from earlier societies that were still present in contemporary societies. Using existing "primitive" societies and the idea of "survivals," Tylor hoped to show examples of all stages of social evolution.

In *Primitive Culture*, Tylor also attempted to reconstruct the evolutionary stages of religion. He postulated that the most basic concept underlying the invention of religion was animism, the belief that all objects and aspects of the world are imbued with spirit. He outlined a developmental sequence for religion that began with animism, evolved into polytheism, and finally progressed into what he viewed as the highest form of religious belief, enlightened monotheism.

At the same time that Tylor was introducing evolutionary anthropology to an English audience, Lewis Henry Morgan was formulating a similar theory in the United States. Morgan was the son of a wealthy landowner in western New York State who made his own fortune as a lawyer, politician, and investor. As a young man, he became interested in Native American culture, especially the Iroquois of upstate New York. This led to his first book, *The League of the Iroquois*, in 1851. Morgan was particularly interested in patterns of marriage and descent, which he believed were related to social evolution. His success in business gave him the time and money to travel, and he visited a variety of Native American groups. Morgan used the data he collected on these trips to write his 1871 book, *Systems of Consanguinity and Affinity*, the first comparative study of kinship.

Morgan is most remembered for his book *Ancient Society*, published in 1877; essay 3 of this volume is the section "Ethnical Periods" from that work. In *Ancient Society*, Morgan attempted to trace the evolution of human society from primeval times to the Victorian era (which he considered the high point of human civilization). Following Turgot and other eighteenth-century writers, Morgan divided human cultural development into three grand stages—savagery, barbarism, and civilization—with the first two stages further subdivided into lower, middle, and upper phases.

Morgan accepted Spencer's idea that evolution proceeded from simple to complex and, in *Ancient Society*, outlined this progress by correlating states of social evolution with specific developments in family structure, subsistence, and technology. For example, in Morgan's scheme, middle savagery begins with the acquisition of fish subsistence, whereas upper savagery is marked by the invention of the bow and arrow.

Unlike Spencer, Morgan believed that evolutionary progress was not achieved through competition but was propelled by the "flowering" of "germs of thought." The increasingly complex technologies and family structures produced after such events were markers of evolutionary progress. Like Tylor, Morgan believed in psychic unity and the uniform nature of the human mind. All humans had the same germs of thought. However, these had not germinated equally in all societies. For Morgan, this explained both why human societies must move along a single evolutionary pathway and why not all had progressed equally.

The unilineal-evolutionary perspective of the late nineteenth century revolved around several related themes. First, it was generally supposed that all societies evolved through the same stages and were progressing toward civilization. Victorian society represented civilization in its highest currently extant form but would be surpassed by future societies.

Second, the whole perspective was rooted in the comparative method. In the nineteenth century, the term *comparative method* referred to the belief that contemporary "primitive" cultures were like "living fossils," similar to the early stages of current advanced cultures. As such, they were clues to cultural evolutionary development. One could study the evolutionary history of Western society by examining contemporary primitive societies.

The validity of the comparative method rested on an acceptance of the concept of psychic unity. Simple and complex societies were comparable because human minds were believed to develop along the same lines. If the human mind worked the same way in all cultures, then it was assumed that unrelated societies would develop in a parallel fashion. Beliefs in the comparative method, psychic unity, parallel evolution, and progress were woven together to support the unilineal view of social evolution.

Karl Marx (1818–1883) and his frequent coauthor Friedrich Engels (1820–1895) are far better known for their contributions to other disciplines—in particular, economic and political theory—than for their studies in anthropology. Despite this, their ideas are critical to anthropology and have been the subject of much debate among anthropologists.

Marx derived his theory of social evolution from a variety of sources including the theory of dialectical change advanced by the philosopher Georg Wilhelm Friedrich Hegel (1770–1831), the materialism of British philosophers like Adam Smith (1723–1790), and the romantic utopianism of French thinkers such as Pierre-Joseph Proudhon (1809–1865) and Henri de Saint-Simon (1760–1825). Whereas scholars such as Locke and Tylor believed that cultural institutions were the product of rational thought, Marx argued that all thought was a product of cultural institutions rather than their cause. Marx, a materialist philosopher, gave primacy to the analysis of the conditions of production within society.

Much of the work of Marx and Engels examined the conflict generated by the increasing wealth of the capitalist class, whom they called the "bourgeoisie," at the expense of the working class, referred to as the "proletariat," who only sank deeper into poverty. Marx and Engels viewed social change as an evolutionary process marked by revolutions in which new levels of social, political, and economic development were achieved through class struggle. They viewed history as a sequence of evolutionary stages, each marked by a unique mode of production. Just as unilineal-evolutionary theorists traced the social evolution of humans from savagery to civilization, Marx and Engels saw the history of Europe in terms of the transition from feudalism to capitalism and on to communism—which they believed was the next inevitable step in this process.

In their later work, Marx and Engels were deeply influenced by Morgan's work. In *Ancient Society*, Morgan correlated evolutionary stages of human culture with material achievements and technology. Marx and Engels viewed Morgan as a materialist and believed that his work validated their evolutionary theory. Additionally, although Marx despised Spencer (whom he viewed as an apologist for capitalism), both Marx and Spencer focused on the notion of conflict as the mechanism for social evolution.

Marx's work drew little attention in early twentieth-century anthropology. Although some scholars, such as Durkheim, were political socialists, until the late 1920s, Marx had relatively little effect on ethnographic analysis outside of the Soviet Union. However, in the 1920s, Australian archaeologist V. Gordon Childe (1892–1957) became one of the first Western advocates of Marxist analysis, and since that time, anthropologists have come to depend increasingly on his ideas. Many theories in both cultural anthropology and archaeology have come to rely on Marxist insights. Today, a background in Marxist thought is basic to reading culture theory. Essay 4 of this volume presents "Feuerbach," from *The German Ideology*.

SUGGESTED READINGS

Carneiro, Robert L. 1981. "Herbert Spencer as an Anthropologist." *Journal of Libertarian Studies* 5(2): 153–210.
A detailed account of Spencer's contribution to anthropology, especially to the work of Leslie White and other twentieth-century evolutionists.

Moses, Daniel Noah. 2009. *The Promise of Progress: The Life and Work of Lewis Henry Morgan*. Columbia: University of Missouri Press.
A comprehensive biography of Morgan that considers his life as an anthropologist and as a public figure.

Ratnapalan, Laavanyan. 2008. "E. B. Tylor and the Problem of Primitive Culture." *History and Anthropology* 19(2): 131–142.
An analysis of Tylor's theory of survivals and the contradictions that emerged as primitive beliefs were considered in light of Victorian ideas.

Roseberry, William. 1997. "Marx and Anthropology." *Annual Review of Anthropology* 26:25–46.
A study of the continuing influence of Marx that focuses on the analysis of *The German Ideology* (from which the essay in this book is taken), volume 1 of *Capital*, and *The Eighteenth Brumaire of Louis Bonaparte*.

Service, Elman R. 1981. "The Mind of Lewis H. Morgan." *Current Anthropology* 22(1): 25–43.

An analysis of Morgan's thought with particular regard to the question of whether or not he was a materialist thinker.

Singer, Peter. 1980. *Marx: A Very Short Introduction*. Oxford: Oxford University Press.

A concise introduction to Marx from an important current-day philosopher. Singer focuses on Marx as a social theorist rather than an economist.

Stocking, George. 1963. "Matthew Arnold, E. B. Tylor, and the Uses of Invention." *American Anthropologist* 65(4): 783–799.

———. 1971. "Animism in Theory and Practice: E. B. Tylor's Unpublished Notes on Spiritualism." *Man* 6(1): 88–104.

———. 1987. *Victorian Anthropology*. New York: Free Press.

George Stocking has written several important books and essays about E. B. Tylor and the emergence of anthropology in England.

Taylor, Michael W. 2007. *The Philosophy of Herbert Spencer*. New York: Continuum.

A recent review and analysis of all of Spencer's work. Taylor presents Spencer as a philosopher in search of universal societal laws.

Tooker, Elisabeth. 1992. "Lewis H. Morgan and His Contemporaries." *American Anthropologist* 94(2): 357–375.

An analysis of Morgan's research and his relations with his contemporaries based on his archives.

1. The Social Organism

Herbert Spencer (1820–1903)

SIR JAMES MACINTOSH got great credit for the saying, that "constitutions are not made, but grow." In our day the most significant thing about this saying is, that it was ever thought so significant. As from the surprise displayed by a man at some familiar fact you may judge of his general culture: so from the admiration which an age accords a new thought, its average degree of enlightenment may be safely inferred. That this **apothegm** of Macintosh should have been quoted and requoted as it has, shows how profound has been the ignorance of social science—how a small ray of truth has seemed brilliant, as a distant rush light looks like a star in the surrounding darkness. Such a conception could not indeed fail to be startling when let fall in the midst of a system of thought to which it was utterly alien. Universally in Macintosh's day, as by an immense majority in our own day, all things were explained on the hypothesis of manufacture, rather than that of growth. It was held that the planets were severally projected round the sun from the Creator's hand, with exactly the velocity required to balance the sun's attraction. The formation of the earth, the separation of the sea from land, the production of animals, were mechanical works from which God rested as a laborer rests. Man was supposed to be molded after a manner somewhat akin to that in which a modeler makes a clay figure. And of course, in harmony with such ideas, societies were tacitly assumed to be arranged thus or thus by direct interposition of Providence; or by the regulations of lawmakers; or by both.[1]

Yet that societies are not artificially put together, is a truth so manifest, that it seems wonderful men should have ever overlooked it. Perhaps nothing more clearly shows the small value of historical studies as they have been commonly pursued. You need but to look at the changes going on around, or observe social organization in its leading peculiarities, to see that these are neither supernatural, nor are determined by the wills of individual men, as by

From *Westminster Review* (1860)

1. Spencer begins with a quote from the Scottish philosopher and politician James Macintosh (1765–1832). Spencer argues that Macintosh's idea that constitutions grow is virtually a self-evident truth. The fact that others consider it a significant insight reflects their ignorance. Macintosh's work was influenced by the French Revolution and this context is interesting and important for Spencer. The French Revolution set the stage for many of the nineteenth-century debates in social science. Edmund Burke (1729–1797), a conservative critic of the revolution, wrote *Reflections on the Revolution in France* (1790). Macintosh, an early supporter of the revolutionaries, wrote *Vindiciae Gallicae* (1791) attacking Burke's position. Spencer's quote from Macintosh is a paraphrase of a passage in Macintosh's 1799 *Discourse on the Study of the Law of Nature and Nations*. Macintosh says a constitution must "arise out of the character and situation of a people . . . [and] grow with its progress" (1828 [1799]: 66). Thus, government cannot be imposed following abstract logical principles that have little to do with the lives and history of the people to be governed. Although Macintosh penned the line about growth, the idea became identified with Burke, who argued that government must be grounded in the mysticism and traditions of the past. Attempts to create new social forms were doomed to failure. For Spencer, society is neither grounded in organic, mystical traditions nor a result of rational human design. Rather, society reflects natural laws. It is the ever-changing result of conflict and struggle. Spencer sees society as growing from the past, but for him, this growth is a challenge to tradition, not its defense.

"**Apothegm**": a short saying or aphorism.

implication historians commonly teach; but are consequent on general natural causes. The one case of the division of labor suffices to show this. It has not been by the command of any ruler that some men have become manufacturers, while others have remained cultivators of the soil. In Lancashire millions have devoted themselves to the making of cotton fabrics; in Yorkshire, perhaps another million live by producing woollens; and the pottery of Staffordshire, the cutlery of Sheffield, the hardware of Birmingham, severally occupy their hundreds of thousands. These are large facts in the structure of English society; but we can ascribe them neither to miracle, nor to legislation. It is not by "the hero as king," any more than by "collective wisdom," that men have been segregated into producers, wholesale distributors, and retail distributors. The whole of our industrial organization, from its most conspicuous features down to its minutest details, has become what it is, not only without legislative guidance, but, to a considerable extent, in spite of legislative hindrances. It has arisen under the pressure of human wants and activities. While each citizen has been pursuing his individual welfare, and none taking thought about division of labor, or indeed conscious of the need for it, division of labor has yet been ever becoming more complete. It has been doing this slowly and silently; scarcely any having observed it until quite modern times. By steps so small, that year after year the industrial arrangements have seemed to men just what they were before—by changes as insensible as those through which a seed passes into a tree; society has become the complex body of mutually dependent workers which we now see. And

this economic organization, mark, is the all-essential organization. Through the combination thus spontaneously evolved it is, that every citizen is supplied with daily necessaries, at the same time that he yields some product or aid to others. That we are severally alive today, we owe to the regular working of this combination during the past week; and could it be suddenly abolished, a great proportion of us would be dead before another week was ended. If these most conspicuous and vital arrangements of our social structure have arisen without the devising of any one, but through the individual efforts of citizens severally to satisfy their own wants, we may be tolerably certain that all the other less important social arrangements have similarly arisen.[2]

"But surely," it will be said, "the social changes directly produced by law cannot be classed as spontaneous growths. When parliaments or kings dictate this or that thing to be done, and appoint officials to do it, the process is clearly artificial; and society to this extent becomes a manufacture rather than a growth." No, not even these changes are exceptions, if they be real and permanent changes. The true sources of such changes lie deeper than the acts of legislators. To take first the simplest instance. We all know that the enactments of representative governments ultimately depend on the national will: they may for a time be out of harmony with it, but eventually they have to conform to it. And to say that the national will is that which finally determines them, is to say that they result from the average of individual desires; or in other words—from the average of individual natures. A law so initiated, therefore, really grows out of the popular

---

2. Here Spencer claims that societies were not supernaturally manufactured but evolved through a natural process of growth, which he illustrates with examples from the social changes in English society caused by industrialization. Spencer's thinking reflected both evolutionism and the work of economist Adam Smith (1723–1790). In *The Wealth of Nations* (1776) Smith argued that individual actions guided by self-interest would benefit society. Spencer presents a similar idea here. There is also an evolutionary undercurrent. Like Charles Darwin (1809–1882), Spencer conceived of evolution as operating through the accumulation of minute changes over long periods of time. Spencer contrasts this idea with the notion that society is the work of individuals. His use of the phrase "the hero as king" is a reference to Thomas Carlyle (1795–1881). In *Lectures on Heroes, Hero-Worship, and the Heroic in History* (1841), Carlyle argued that history was driven by great men. "The Hero as King" is the title of one of the chapters of Carlyle's book. Carlyle was a frequent target of American anthropologists in the first half of the twentieth century. Both A. L. Kroeber (1876–1960) and Leslie White (1900–1975) argued against the importance of the individual in society.

character. In the case of a Government representing but a limited class, the same thing still holds, though not so manifestly. For the very existence of a supreme class monopolizing all power, is itself due to certain sentiments in the commonalty. But for the feeling of loyalty on system could not exist. We see in the protest of the Highlanders against the abolition of heritable jurisdictions, that they preferred that kind of local rule. And if thus to the popular nature must be ascribed the growth of an irresponsible ruling class; then to the popular nature must be ascribed the social arrangements which that class creates in the pursuit of its own ends. Even where the Government is despotic, the doctrine still holds. It is not simply that the existence of such a form of government is consequent on the character of the people, and that, as we have abundant proof, other forms suddenly created will not act, but rapidly retrograde to the old form; but it is that such regulations as a despot makes, if really operative, are so because of their fitness to the social state. Not only are his acts very much swayed by general opinion—by precedent, by

the feeling of his nobles, his priesthood, his army—and are so in part results of the national character; but when they are out of harmony with the national character, they are soon practically abrogated. The utter failure of Cromwell permanently to establish a new social condition, and the rapid revival of suppressed institutions and practices after his death, show how powerless is a monarch to change the type of the society he governs. He may disturb, he may retard, or he may aid the natural process of organization; but the general course of this process is beyond his control.[3]

Thus that which is so obviously true of the industrial structure of society, is true of its whole structure. The fact that constitutions are not made, but grow, is simply a fragment of the much larger fact, that under all its aspects and through all its ramifications, society is a growth and not a manufacture.

A dim perception that there exists some analogy between the body politic and a living individual body, was early reached, and from time to time re-appeared in literature. But this perception was necessarily vague and more or less fan-

---

3. Spencer here suggests that there is some palpable force in a society that conditions its members to act in certain ways. Even actions that appear to be extremely personal are ultimately the result of this social force. This suggestion provides a portion of the foundation for Émile Durkheim's (1858–1917) idea of collective consciousness (see essay 5) and Kroeber's of the superorganic (see essay 9). Notice that he says that actions by rulers or other individuals may disturb evolution's workings, but that the general process is natural and beyond human control.

Note also the strong conservatism of Spencer's work. By his argument, all governments, no matter how oppressive, arise out of the general will. If social change fails it does so because it violates this will (rather than, for example, because it was opposed by wealth and power). To prove his point, Spencer offers the example of Oliver Cromwell's rule of England. Cromwell (1599–1658) rose to power during the English Civil Wars of the mid-seventeenth century. He ruled as Lord Protector of England from 1653 to 1658 and signed the death warrant for the execution of King Charles I. However, in 1660, two years after Cromwell's death, Charles's son Charles II (1630–1685) returned to England and was crowned king. Spencer seems to suggest that the Civil War and Cromwell's rule changed nothing in Britain. This, however, is a particularly myopic view. Events during the Interregnum (the period of Parliamentary rule between the execution of Charles I in 1649 and his son, Charles II's resumption of the throne in 1660) changed Britain. For example, the power of Parliament and the end of the absolute power of the monarchy were confirmed, as was the dominance of the Anglican Church over Catholicism.

Although Spencer wrote about the English Civil War, he may have had the more recent French revolutions of the 1780s and 1840s in mind. These revolutions and the violence that accompanied them shocked and frightened the English upper classes, who interpreted the mass riots as evidence of the bestiality of the working class. The restoration of the monarchy in France was a comforting reassurance that the upper class was indeed superior and that the social-evolutionary scheme of things had balanced out. As Spencer writes, "other forms suddenly created will not act, but rapidly retrograde to the old form."

Early in the passage, Spencer mentions the protest of the Highlanders. He is referring to the Heritable Jurisdiction Act of 1746 in which the traditional rights of Scottish clan chiefs were abolished.

ciful. In the absence of physiological science, and especially of those comprehensive generalizations which it has but recently reached, it was impossible to discern the real parallelisms.

[*It is a law of nature, in Spencer's view, that societies change from simple to complex. The purposes of his article are to outline this process of change and to demonstrate that social processes are analogous to those in biological organisms. In a 950-word passage eliminated from this edition, Spencer discusses similar analogies made by Plato and Thomas Hobbes. Plato, in The Republic, compares society to the human psyche. Hobbes, in Leviathan, compares it to the human body. Spencer finds that both of these analogies result in inconsistencies, and faults both scholars for suggesting that society was created by man. Plato, Hobbes, and others saw only faint shadows of the truth because they lacked the insights of modern biology. Spencer proposes to show us accurate analogies disclosed by modern science.*]

Let us set out by succinctly stating the points of similarity and the points of difference. Societies agree with individual organisms in three conspicuous peculiarities:—

1. That commencing as small aggregations they insensibly augment in mass; some of them reaching eventually perhaps a hundred thousand times what they originally were.
2. That while at first so simple in structure as to be almost considered structureless, they assume, in the course of their growth, a continually increasing complexity of structure.
3. That though in their early undeveloped state there exists in them scarcely any mutual dependence of parts, these parts

gradually acquire a mutual dependence, which becomes at last so great, that the activity and life of each part is made possible only by the activity and life of the rest.[4]

These three parallelisms will appear the more significant the more we contemplate them. Observe that, while they are points in which societies agree with individual organisms, they are points in which all individual organisms agree with each other, and disagree with everything else. In the course of its existence, every plant and animal increases in mass, which, with the exception of crystals, can be said of no inorganic objects. The orderly progress from simplicity to complexity displayed by societies in common with every living body whatever, is a characteristic which substantially distinguishes living bodies from the inanimate bodies amid which they move. And that functional dependence of parts, which is scarcely more manifest in animals or plants than in societies, has no counterpart elsewhere. Moreover, it should be remarked, not only that societies and organisms are alike in these peculiarities, in which they are unlike all other things; but, further, that the highest societies, like the highest organisms, exhibit them in the greatest degree. Looking at the facts in their ensemble, we may observe that the lowest types of animals do not increase to anything like the size of the higher ones; and similarly we see that aboriginal societies are comparatively limited in their growth. In complexity, our large civilized nations as much exceed the primitive savage ones, as a vertebrate animal does a zoophyte. And while in simple communities, as in simple creatures, the mutual dependence of parts is so slight, that subdivision or mutilation causes but little inconvenience; in complex communities as in complex creatures, you cannot remove or

---

4. This paragraph contains the fundamental ideas upon which Spencer builds his evolutionary theory. He writes that societies are like organisms in three ways: (1) they grow from small groups to large aggregations; (2) they grow from simple to complex structures; and (3) they grow from a collection of independent units to an organism composed of interdependent parts. The second and third points are particularly important to his theory and were incorporated into most of the evolutionary and structural functionalist theories of the nineteenth and twentieth centuries. Durkheim, for example, used the idea of directional movement from simplicity to complexity and relational movement from independence to interdependence in his formulation of the differences between mechanical and organic solidarity, and these ideas were fundamental in how A. R. Radcliffe-Brown (1881–1955) perceived the relationships between cultural institutions (see essay 15).

injure any considerable organ without producing great disturbance or death of the rest.[5]

On the other hand, the leading differences between societies and individual organisms are these:

1. That they have no specific external forms. This, however, is a point of contrast which loses much of its importance, when we remember that throughout the entire vegetal kingdom, as well as in some lower divisions of the animal kingdom, the forms are very indefinite, and are manifestly in part determined by surrounding physical circumstances, as the forms of societies are. If, too, it should eventually be shown, as we believe it will, that the form of every species of organism has resulted from the average play of the external forces to which it has been subject during its evolution as a species; then, that the external forms of societies should depend, as they do, on surrounding conditions, will be a further point of community.

2. That whereas the living tissue whereof an individual organism consists, forms one continuous mass, the living elements which make up a society, do not form a continuous mass, but are more or less widely dispersed over some portion of the earth's surface. This, which at first sight appears to be a fundamental distinction, is one which yet to a great extent disappears when we contemplate all the facts.

[*In a four-hundred-word passage, Spencer argues that human society is in this respect similar to several primitive life-forms. He further suggests, though not in these terms, that the environment in which people live must be considered part of the social organism and that, if this is taken into account, societies do form a continuous mass.*]

3. That while the ultimate living elements of an individual organism are mostly fixed in their relative positions, those of the social organism are capable of moving from place to place, seems a marked point of disagreement. But here, too, the disagreement is much less than would be supposed. For while citizens are locomotive in their private capacities, they are fixed in their public capacities. As farmers, manufacturers, or traders, men carry on their businesses at the same spots, often throughout their whole lives; and if they go away for a time, they leave behind others to discharge their functions in their absence. Not only does each great center of production, each manufacturing town or district, continue always in the same place; but many of

---

5. Note that Spencer's analogy proceeds on two levels. He argues that individual bodies grow in size, complexity, and interdependence and that species also evolve in these same directions. He will similarly argue that both individual groups within society and society itself evolve in this fashion. According to Spencer, evolution is progressive, and societies that are large, complex, and integrated are more evolved than those that are not. Industrialized Europe was, in Spencer's view, the best society that evolution had thus far created.

For Spencer, social evolution was driven by competition among people, through which the best suited to survive were selected. Following this line of thought, he coined the phrase "survival of the fittest." Though this process may have meant misery for some, Spencer believed that it would lead to the perfection of society. His ideas, popularized largely by others as social Darwinism, were often used to justify the American and English class systems and colonial political systems. However, it is important to note that Spencer himself was deeply critical of both imperialism and the landed aristocracy (for example, see *Facts and Comments* [1902] in which Spencer argues that imperialism makes all men slaves of the state). In America, however, Spencer's work was seen as supporting both the wealthy and imperial expansion. William Graham Sumner (1840–1910) was one of Spencer's most prominent followers and among the best-known promoters of social Darwinism. In an essay defending the concentration of wealth, he wrote, "No man can acquire a million without helping a million men to increase their little fortunes. . . . The millionaires are a product of natural selection. . . . They may fairly be regarded as the naturally selected agents of society for certain work" (1963a [1914]: 156–57).

the firms in such town or district are for generations carried on either by the descendants or successors of those who founded them. Just as in a living body, the individual cells that make up some important organ, severally perform their functions for a time and then disappear, leaving others to supply their vacant places; so in each part of a society, while the organ remains, the persons who compose it change. Thus, in social life, as in the life of an animal, the units as well as the larger agencies composed of them, are in the main stationary as respects the places where they discharge their duties and obtain their sustenance. So that the power of individual locomotion does not practically affect the analogy.[6]

4. That while in the body of an animal only a special tissue is endowed with feeling, in a society all the members are endowed with feeling, is the last and perhaps the most important distinction. Even this distinction, however, is by no means a complete one. For in some lower divisions of the animal kingdom, characterized by the absence of a nervous system, such sensitiveness as exists is possessed by all parts. It is only in the more organized forms that feeling is monopolized by one particular class of vital elements. Moreover, we must not forget that societies, too, are not without a certain differentiation of this kind. Though the units of a community are all sensitive, yet they are so in unequal degrees. The classes

engaged in agriculture and laborious occupations in general, are far less susceptible, intellectually and emotionally, than the rest; and especially less so than the classes of highest mental culture. Still we have here a tolerably decided contrast between bodies politic and individual bodies. And it is one which we should keep constantly in view. For it reminds us that while in individual bodies the welfare of all other parts is rightly subservient to the welfare of the nervous system, whose pleasurable or painful activities make up the good or evil of life; in bodies politic the same thing does not hold good, or holds good to but a very slight extent. It is well that the lives of all parts of an animal should be merged in the life of the whole, because the whole has a corporate consciousness capable of happiness or misery. But it is not so with a society; since its living units do not and cannot lose individual consciousness; and since the community as a whole has no general or corporate consciousness distinct from those of its components. And this is an everlasting reason why the welfare of its citizens cannot rightly be sacrificed to some supposed benefit of the State; but why, on the other hand, the State must be regarded as existing solely for the benefit of citizens. The corporate life must here be subservient to the life of the parts, instead of the life of the parts being subservient to the corporate life.[7]

---

6. Spencer's ideas in this passage are somewhat surprising. Although he lived in an era of international trade and rapid social change, he seems to imagine a romantic English village where each business has been located in the same place for generations. However, the paragraph also includes an important insight: Entities such as businesses can exist independently of the individuals who compose them. The idea that institutions have an independent existence apart from the people who make them is an important insight for both anthropology and sociology in the twentieth century, variously echoed in Durkheim's notion of the collective conscious, Kroeber's work on the superorganic, Radcliffe-Brown's on social structure, and work by Max Weber (1864–1920) on bureaucracy.

7. In this paragraph, Spencer clearly expresses his conviction that some groups of people (particularly those of the "highest mental culture," that is, the educated elites) are better than others. In this case, he argues that the intellectual classes are capable of greater feeling than the laboring classes. Statements such

Such, then, are the points of analogy and the points of difference. May we not say that the points of difference serve but to bring into clearer light the points of analogy? While comparison makes definite the obvious contrast between organisms commonly so called, and the social organism, it shows that even these contrasts are not nearly so decided as was to be expected. The indefiniteness of form, the discontinuity of the parts, the mobility of the parts, and the universal sensitiveness, are not only peculiarities of the social organism which have to be stated with considerable qualifications; but they are peculiarities to which the inferior classes of animals present approximations. Thus we find but little to conflict with the all important analogies. That societies slowly augment in mass; that they progress in complexity of structure; that at the same time their parts become more mutually dependent; and further, that the extent to which they display these peculiarities is proportionate to their vital activity; are traits that societies have in common with all organic bodies. And these traits in which they agree with all organic bodies and disagree with all other things—these traits which in truth constitute the very essence of organization, entirely subordinate the minor distinctions: such distinctions being scarcely greater than those which separate one half of the organic kingdom from the other. The principles of organization are the same; and the differences are simply differences of application.

Thus a general survey of the facts seems quite to justify the comparison of a society to a living body. We shall find that the parallelism becomes the more marked the more closely it is traced. Let us proceed to consider it in detail.[8]

The lowest forms of animal and vegetable life—Protozoa and Protophyta—are chiefly inhabitants of the water. They are minute bodies, most of which are made individually visible only by the microscope. All of them are extremely simple in structure; and some of them, as the Amoeba and Actinophris, almost structureless. Multiplying, as they do, by the spontaneous division of their bodies, they produce halves, which may either become quite separate and move away in different direc-

---

as these have led most scholars since the early twentieth century to be highly critical of Spencer, considering him an apologist for ethnocentrism and racism.

The second half of this paragraph is a statement of Spencer's political views. Since the state has no consciousness capable of happiness or misery, citizens should never sacrifice for the benefit of the state. Spencer tells us that the state exists solely for the benefit of its citizens. He understands this as being the promotion of the most complete possible individual freedom of action, a radical form of laissez-faire that rejects almost all forms of collective action. For example, in *The Man versus the State* (1884) Spencer opposes government taxation to support "free libraries, public museums, washhouses, recreation grounds, etc." as well as many other things. He argues that increasing taxation restricts individual freedom since the justification for every additional request is "Hitherto you have been free to spend this portion of your earnings in any way which pleased you; hereafter you shall not be free so to spend it, but we will spend it for the general benefit" (Spencer 1884: 1.20).

Spencer's emphasis on the individual at the expense of the state has made his work popular among some groups on the American political right; examples include the Liberty Fund and the Cato Institute.

8. Spencer concludes the outline of his organic analogy at this point. In the paragraphs below, he makes a highly detailed argument in support of the analogy between the evolution of biological organisms and that of society. The ideas of simple and complex societies, social structures, and social functions explored here imply a research program. That is, the goal of anthropology (or sociology) should be to identify social "organs" and describe their functioning.

Contemporaneously with this essay, Spencer issued a prospectus for a future work, *Principles of Sociology*, in which he planned to develop empirical generalizations about social evolution from the comparative study of society. This project was never fully realized, but Spencer's research agenda was central to the development of social anthropology in the first decades of the twentieth century and influenced such thinkers as Durkheim, Radcliffe-Brown, Julian Steward (1902–1972), and George Murdock (1897–1985). The work of Franz Boas (1858–1942) and his students also engages Spencer's work, but largely by rejecting it.

tions, or may continue attached. And by the repetition of this process of fission, aggregations of various sizes and kinds are formed. Thus among the Protophyta we have some classes, as the Diatomacea and the yeast-plant, in which the individuals may be either separate, or attached in groups of two, three, four or more; other classes in which a considerable number of individual cells are united into a thread (Conferva, Monilia); others in which they form a network (Hydrodictyon); others in which they form plates (Ulva); and others in which they form masses (Laminaria, Agaricus): all which vegetal forms, having no distinction of root, stem or leaf, are called Thallogens. Among the Protozoa we find parallel facts. Immense numbers of Amoeba-like creatures massed together in a framework of horny fibers, are found in the extensive family of the sponges. In the Foraminifera we see smaller groups of such creatures arranged into more definite shapes. Not only do these almost structureless Protozoa unite into regular or irregular aggregations of various sizes; but among some of the more organized ones, as the Vorticellae, there are also produced clusters of individuals, proceeding from a common stock. But these little societies of monads, or cells, or whatever else we may call them, are societies in the lowest sense: there is no subordination of parts among them—no organization. Each of the component units lives by and for itself, neither giving nor receiving aid; there is no mutual dependence, save that consequent upon mere mechanical union.

Now do we not here clearly discern analogies to the first stages of human societies? Among the lowest races, as the Bushmen, we find but incipient aggregations: sometimes single families, sometimes two or three families wandering about together. The number of associated units is small and variable, and their union inconstant. No division of labor exists except between the sexes; and the only kind of mutual aid is that of joint attack or defence. We have nothing beyond an undifferentiated group of individuals forming the germ of a society; just as in the groups of similar cells above described, we have only the initial stage of animal and vegetal organization.[9]

[*In a 1,475-word passage removed from this edition, Spencer elaborates on his analogy. He argues that just as more advanced plants and animals show some specialization of function, more advanced societies show evidence of social structure. Beyond sexual division of labor, government is the first structure to emerge. However, as in lower plants, specialization remains imprecise. Cells can change function and a society's leaders may also do other jobs. The next phase is the spread of similar biological or social units across the landscape. Physical barriers may cause such social units to coalesce into nations. Spencer argues that just as some individuals among a large aggregate of hydra will develop special functions, some communities within a large society will develop specific functions, thus a division of labor develops.*]

The general doctrine of the progressive division of labor, to which we are here introduced, is more or less familiar to all readers. And further, the analogy between the economical division of labor and the "physiological division of labor" is so striking, as long since to have drawn the attention of scientific naturalists: so striking, indeed, that the expression "physiological division of labor," has been suggested by it. It is not needful, therefore, that

---

9. Notice that Spencer here describes the relationship between these *Protozoa* (single-celled organisms with animal-like behavior, such as amoebas) and *Protophyta* (single-celled organisms with plant-like behavior, such as algae and fungi) as being "mere mechanical union." He says that "each of the component units lives by and for itself, and envisions the first human societies to have been similar, just families wandering together." Durkheim will describe such societies in much the same way and uses the term "mechanical solidarity" to describe social relations in them. The similarity is probably not accidental. Although Durkheim disagreed with Spencer on many things, he was a close reader of Spencer and developed his own theories both in agreement and in contrast to Spencer's work. Durkheim developed his ideas about mechanical and organic solidarity in *The Division of Labor in Society* (1893). The index to that work cites Spencer almost fifty times (Corning 1982: 359).

we should treat this part of our subject in great detail. We shall content ourselves with noting a few general and significant facts not manifest on a first inspection.

Throughout the whole animal kingdom, from the **Coelenterata** upwards, the first stage of evolution is the same. Equally in the germ of a polype and in the human ovum, the aggregated mass of cells out of which the creature is to arise, gives origin to a peripheral layer of cells, slightly differing from the rest which they include; and this layer subsequently divides into two—the inner one lying in contact with the included yolk being commonly called the mucous layer, and the outer exposed to surrounding agencies being called the serous layer: or in the terms used by Professor Huxley, in describing the development of the Hydrozoa—the endoderm and the ectoderm. This primary division marks out the fundamental contrast of parts in the future organism. Out of the mucous layer or endoderm is developed the apparatus of nutrition; while out of the serous layer, or ectoderm, is developed the apparatus of external action. From the one arise the organs by which food is prepared and absorbed, oxygen imbibed, and blood purified; while out of the other arise the nervous, muscular, and **osseous** systems, by whose combined actions the movements of the body as a whole are effected. Though this is not a rigorously correct distinction, seeing that some organs involve both of these primitive membranes, yet the highest authorities agree in stating it as a broad general one. Well, in the evolution of a society we see a primary differentiation of analogous kind, which similarly underlies the whole future structure. As already pointed out, the only contrast of parts which is visible in primitive societies, is that between the government and the governed. In the least organized tribes, the council of chiefs may be a body of men distinguished simply by greater courage or experience. In more organized tribes, the chief-class is definitely separated from the lower class, and often regarded as different in nature—sometimes as god-descended. And later we find these two becoming respectively freemen and slaves, or nobles and serfs. A glance at their respective functions makes it obvious that the great divisions thus early formed, stand to each other in a relation similar to that in which the primary divisions of the embryo stand to each other. For from its first appearance, the class of chiefs is that by which the external actions of the society are controlled: alike in war, in negotiation, and in migration. As we advance, we see that while the upper class grows distinct from the lower, and at the same time becomes more and more exclusively regulative and defensive in its functions, alike as kings and subordinate rulers, as priests, and as military leaders; the inferior class becomes more and more exclusively occupied in providing the necessaries of life for the community at large. From the soil, with which it comes in most direct contact, the mass of the people takes up and prepares for use the food and such rude articles of manufacture as are known; while the overlying mass of superior men, supplied with the necessaries of life by those below them, deals with circumstances external to the community—circumstances with which, by position, it is more immediately concerned. Ceasing by-and-by to have any knowledge of, or power over, the concerns of the society as a whole, the serf class becomes devoted to the processes of alimentation; while the noble class, ceasing to take any part in the process of alimentation, becomes devoted to the co-ordination and movements of the entire body politic.[10]

---

10. Congratulations, you've made it through one of the many arcane passages of this text. Note that the vocabulary Spencer uses when describing biology in the first part of the passage is quite technical, especially considering that this essay appeared in a general intellectual journal rather than one specifically devoted to biology. The vocabulary he uses when referring to social formations, on the other hand, is quite simple. The effect of combining the technical language of biology with the rather simple vocabulary of society is to make Spencer's comments on society seem much more scientifically compelling than they actually are. Of course, in a modern sense, Spencer is simply presenting an argument by analogy which is not scientific at all. It is neither an attempt to explore and describe the range of human social organization nor a set of conclusions based on controlled experimentation.

Equally remarkable is a further analogy of like kind. After there has taken place in the embryo the separation of the mucous and serous layers, there presently arises between the two, a third, known to physiologists as the vascular layer—a layer out of which is developed the system of blood-vessels. The mucous layer absorbs nutriment from the mass of yolk it encloses; this nutriment has to be transferred to the overlying serous layer, out of which the nervo-muscular system is being developed; and between the two arises the system of vessels by which the transfer is effected—a system of vessels which continues ever after to be the transferrer of nutriment from the places where it is absorbed and prepared, to the places where it is needed for growth and repair. Well, may we not clearly trace a parallel step in social progress? Between the governing and the governed there at first exists no intermediate class; and even in some societies that have reached a considerable size, there are scarcely any but the nobles and their kindred on the one hand, and the serfs on the other: the social structure being such, that the transfer of commodities takes place directly from slaves to their masters. But in societies of a higher type, there grows up between these two primitive classes, another—the trading or middle class. Equally at first as now, we may see that, speaking generally, this middle class is the analogue of the middle layer in the embryo. For all traders are essentially distributors. Whether they be wholesale dealers, who collect into large masses the commodities of various producers; or whether they be retailers, who divide out to those who want them the masses of commodities thus collected together; all mercantile men are agents of transfer from the places where things are produced to the places where they are consumed. Thus the distributing apparatus of a society answers to the distributing apparatus in a living body, not only in its functions, but in its intermediate origin and subsequent position, and in the time of its appearance.

Without enumerating the minor differentiations which these three great classes afterwards undergo, we will merely note that throughout, they follow the same general law with the differentiations of an individual organism. In a society, as in a rudimentary animal, we have seen that the most general and broadly contrasted divisions are the first to make their appearance; and of the subdivisions it continues true in both cases, that they arise in the order of their generality.[11]

Note also that logical problems in Spencer's analogy begin to be evident almost immediately. For example, in an animal, the intestines don't suddenly decide they want to be the brain. However, in society, not only do individuals change positions but classes might rise and fall. On the one hand, Spencer's political philosophy is based on extreme meritocracy which implies social movement. On the other, the vision of society he presents here is very static.

In the first part of the passage, Spencer mentions Thomas Henry Huxley (1825–1895), a prominent biologist who became famous for his defense of Darwin and the theory of natural selection in a series of public debates with Samuel Wilberforce, the Bishop of Oxford. Because of this spirited defense, Huxley earned the nickname "Darwin's bulldog." Huxley and Spencer knew each other well. They were members of the X Club, a dining club composed of leading scientists, devoted, in the words of one of its members, to "science, pure and free, untrammelled by religious dogmas" (in Gardner and Wilson 1993: 832). Huxley and Spencer later split over Spencer's radical political views; Huxley, writing to Sir Joseph Hooker (a leading botanist and close friend of Darwin), described Spencer as a "long winded vanitous pedant" with "as much tact as a hippopotamus" (in Desmond 2001: 3).

"Coelenterata": an obsolete term for animals with a simple tissue organization consisting of two layers.

"Osseous": bony; "osseous system": skeleton.

11. In this passage, Spencer will compare the development of human embryos with different animal species and then with the development of society as a whole. Embryology was one of the leading fields of study of Spencer's day, and he was strongly influenced by it, particularly by the work of the pioneering German-Russian embryologist Karl Ernst von Baer (1792–1876). Von Baer argued that structures that form early in embryological development are more widely distributed among groups of organisms than structures that arise later in development, an idea now called von Baer's law. Spencer believed von Baer's

[*In an 875-word passage, Spencer argues that both societies and organisms develop in the direction of increased specialization of function. He compares the development of states to that of segmented worms. Among these, he says, lower forms are composed of many identical segments, while higher forms have organs that transcend segments. Similarly, early states are composed of many similar independent fiefdoms, but larger states have structures that completely transcend them. He then turns to a consideration of the reasons there are analogies between organisms and societies.*]

If, after contemplating these analogies of structure, we inquire whether there are any such analogies between causes and processes of organic growth, the answer is—yes. The causes which lead to the increase of bulk in any part of the body politic, are strictly analogous to those which lead to increase of bulk in any part of an individual body. In both cases the antecedent is greater functional activity consequent on greater demand. Each limb, viscus, gland, or other member of an animal, is developed by exercise—by actively discharging the duties which the body at large requires of it; and similarly, any class of laborers or artisans, any manufacturing center, or any official agency, begins to enlarge when the community devolves upon it an increase of work. Moreover, in each case growth has its conditions and its limits. That any organ in a living being may grow by exercise, there needs a due supply of blood: all action implies waste; blood brings the materials for repair; and before there can

be growth, the quantity of blood supplied must be more than that requisite for repair only. So is it in a society. If to some district which elaborates for the community particular commodities—say the woollens of Yorkshire—there comes an augmented demand; and if in fulfillment of this demand a certain expenditure and wear of the manufacturing organization are incurred; and if in payment for the extra supply of woollens sent away, there comes back only such quantity of commodities as replaces the expenditure and makes good the waste of life and machinery; there can clearly be no growth. That there may be growth, the commodities obtained in return must be somewhat more than is required for these ends; and just in proportion as the excess is great will the growth be rapid. Whence it is manifest that what in commercial affairs we call profit, answers to the excess of nutrition over waste in a living body. To which let us add, that in both cases, where the functional activity is great and the nutrition defective, there results not growth but decay. If in an animal any organ is worked so hard that the channels which bring blood cannot furnish enough for repair, the organ dwindles; and if in the body-politic some part has been stimulated into great productivity, and cannot afterwards get paid for all its produce, certain of its members become bankrupt and it decreases in size.

One more parallelism to be here noted is, that the different parts of the social organism, like the different parts of an individual organism, compete for nutriment; and obtain more or less of it according as they are discharging

---

work demonstrated that movement from homogeneity to heterogeneity was a law of organic progress and proposed that it was a general law of all progress (1857: 446 [Progress, its law and causes]). Spencer, and others, particularly the German biologist Ernst Heinrich Haeckel (1834–1919), also believed that von Baer's work suggested that the embryological development of an organism illustrated all the stages of its evolution. In 1866 (six years after this essay) Haeckel famously (and incorrectly) proclaimed that "ontogeny recapitulates phylogeny," that is, the embryological growth of an individual repeats the evolutionary history of its phylum. When applied to the evolution of society, this meant that the growth of individuals within advanced societies mirrored the stages through which human social evolution had passed. Someone believing this would conclude that adults in primitive societies were similar to children in advanced societies. Spencer and numerous other thinkers (particularly Sigmund Freud [1856–1939]) had frequent recourse to "the child/savage equation" (Stocking 1987: 22).

Here and below Spencer reiterates a basic principle of evolution as he understood it: Things appear "in order of their generality." In other words, they move from the simple (most generalized) to the complex (least generalized). This understanding was shared by most nineteenth-century thinkers and many more recent scholars. Today it is largely rejected.

more or less duty. If a man's brain be suddenly very much excited, it will abstract blood from his viscera and stop digestion; or, digestion actively going on will so affect the circulation through the brain as to cause drowsiness; or great muscular exertion will determine such a quantity of blood to the limbs as to arrest digestion or cerebral action, as the case may be. And in like manner in a society, it frequently happens that great activity in some one direction causes partial arrests of activity elsewhere, by abstracting capital, that is, commodities: as instance the way in which the sudden development of our railway system hampered commercial operations; or the way in which the raising of a large military force temporarily stops the growth of leading industries.[12]

The last few paragraphs naturally introduce the next division of our subject. Almost unawares we have come upon the analogy which exists between the blood of a living body and the circulating mass of commodities in the body-politic. We have now to trace out this analogy from its simplest to its most complex manifestations.

[*In a 2,350-word passage, Spencer compares certain aspects of society to the blood and circulatory system of organisms. Lower animals like sponges have no blood or circulatory system; every cell fends for itself. Similarly, he claims that in primitive tribes there is no system of exchange, and every family supports itself. Somewhat more complex organisms have extremely simple digestive tracts; likewise, somewhat more complex societies have some trade in agricultural commodities along simple paths. As specialization proceeds in an organism, blood and a circulatory system are required to nourish the now specialized organs. As societies become more complex, the demands for circulation of products between laboring groups similarly increase. Spencer notes that the circulatory material (either blood for organisms or products for societies) increases*

not only in quantity but in complexity as well. As animals evolve, they develop what Spencer calls "blood discs" (corpuscles) to facilitate nutrition. Spencer argues that in societies money plays a similar role, which he elaborates on in a series of analogies. Like blood cells, money itself is not consumed. Blood cells are found in greatest abundance in large organs, and money in greatest abundance in large cities. Blood in lower animals has no corpuscles, and lower societies have no money. Just as lower animals have minimally organized circulatory systems, countries where civilization is beginning have only rudimentary paths for the exchange of goods. More advanced animals have blood vessels, and more advanced societies have fenced and gravelled roads. In the highest organisms and societies, there are major blood vessels and capillaries or large main roads and small minor ones. The development of railroads that have a track for each direction is analogous to veins and arteries in a body. The analogy between society and organisms includes not only the circulatory system but also the pattern of motion of nutrients through it. In low creatures, the movement is a slow reciprocating motion. Similarly in lower societies there is movement now toward this fair or market, now toward that. In more advanced societies and animals there are "constant currents in definite directions." Moreover, as organisms evolve, they develop hearts that pump blood through the circulatory system, and societies develop large commercial centers. Blood flows more rapidly the closer it is to the heart, and trains move more rapidly and frequently the closer they are to commercial centers. Thus, Spencer concludes, the analogy between biological and social distribution systems is "wonderfully close."]

We come at length to the nervous system. Having noticed the primary differentiation of societies into the governing and governed classes, and observed its analogy to the differentiation of the two primary tissues which

---

12. Note that the description of the evolution of both organisms and society presented here is Lamarckian rather than Darwinian. Spencer argues that those organs that are used more grow more (and since this is an evolutionary argument, implies that these changes are passed to future generations).

Note also that in this passage, Spencer naturalizes capitalism. Profit and bankruptcy have their precedents in the animal kingdom. The movement of blood to or away from organs is the addition or subtraction of capital. Capitalism is thus (by the organic analogy) part of natural law and an inevitable part of human societies.

respectively develop into the organs of alimentation and those of external action; having noticed some of the leading analogies between the development of industrial organization and that of the alimentary apparatus; and having above more fully traced the analogies between the distributing systems, social and individual; we have now to compare the appliances by which a society, as a whole, is regulated, with those by which the movements of an organism are regulated. We shall find here parallelisms equally striking with those already detailed.[13]

The class out of which governmental organization originates is, as we have said, analogous, by origin and position, to the ectoderm of the lowest animals and of embryonic forms. And as this primitive membrane, out of which the nervo-muscular system is evolved, must, even in the first stage of its differentiation, be slightly distinguished from the rest by that greater **impressibility** and **contractility** characterizing the organ to which it gives rise; so, in that superior class which is eventually transformed into the nervo-muscular system of a society (its legislative and defense appliances), does there exist in the beginning a larger endowment of the capacities required for these higher social functions. Always, in rude assemblages of men, there is a tendency for the strongest, most courageous, and most sagacious to become rulers and leaders; and

in a tribe of some standing, this results in the establishment of a ruling class characterized on the average by those mental and bodily qualities which fit them for deliberation and vigorous combined action. Very significant, too, is the fact that those units of a society, who from the beginning discharge the directive and executive functions, are those in whom the directive and executive organs predominate: in other words, that what by analogy we call the nervo-muscular apparatus of a society begins to grow out of those units whose nervo-muscular systems are most developed. For the chiefs who, as individuals, or as a class, first separate themselves from the mass of a tribe, and begin to exercise control over their respective dependents and over the society as a whole, are men who have the greatest bodily vigor, the greatest bravery, or the greatest cunning—more powerful limbs, or more powerful brains, or both; while those to whom the industrious processes are chiefly left—in the smallest tribes the women, and in larger ones the least masculine men—are of less nervo-muscular power. Thus that greater impressibility and contractility which in the rudest animal forms characterize the units of the ectoderm, characterize also the units of the primitive social ectoderm; since impressibility and contractility are the respective roots of intelligence and strength.[14]

---

13. By this point, you may be tired of Spencer's examples. To modern readers, Spencer's writing style may seem repetitive. However, he was writing for an audience that was largely unfamiliar with the ideas he was presenting. Further, his readers had time to read and an aesthetic taste for copious examples. Gould (1994) has pointed out that, while modern American museums concentrate on the display of one or a few specimens, Victorian museums attempted to overwhelm the senses through the display of the enormous variety of nature. Here Spencer, a model Victorian, does the same thing with words; he overwhelms with detail and examples. We have removed about 40 percent of Spencer's original 14,250-word essay, but we have tried to leave enough of what, by modern standards, is excess verbiage for you to get a feel for this sort of writing.

14. In this passage, Spencer focuses on the relationship between fitness, power, and leadership. He declares that those who lead society are the most fit, distinguished by physical strength, bravery, and intelligence. Spencer claims that within a society, leadership, wealth, and power are determined by competition. The social arrangements that result are determined by natural law and the power of elites is justified by evolution. Note that Spencer's reasoning here is both completely without evidence and tautological. He simply declares that the leaders are the most fit. How do you know they are the most fit? Because they're the leaders. Note also that women are counted among the unfit.

Born to relative poverty, in his early career Spencer opposed the power of the landed aristocracy and supported rights for women. In his book *Social Statics* (1851), Spencer argued in favor of a concept he called the "law of equal freedom." He wrote, "If, then, the assumption that land can be held as property, involves that the whole globe may become the private domain of a part of its inhabitants; and if, by

[*In a 450-word passage, Spencer notes that as animals and societies move to higher levels of organization, they are increasingly specialized. Chiefs play roles in society analogous to those played by simple nervous centers in organisms. In simple societies, the chief both commands and coerces. But, as societies become more organized, the chief directs and leaves others to enforce his will. As this happens, cunning replaces strength as the key characteristic of leadership. In larger more complex communities, kings require advisors who inform them and carry out their orders. This is analogous to animals that have a chief ganglion with minor ganglia under its control.*]

The analogies between the evolution of governmental structure in a society, and the evolution of governmental structures in living bodies, are, however, more strikingly displayed during the formation of nations by the coalescence of small communities—a process already shown to be in several respects parallel to the development of those creatures that primarily consist of many like segments. Among the other points of community between the successive rings which make up the body in the **lower Articulata**, is the possession of similar pairs of ganglia. These pairs of ganglia, though united together by nerves, are very incompletely dependent on any general controlling power. Hence it results, that when the body is cut in two, the hinder part continues to move forward under the propulsion of its numerous legs; and that when the chain of ganglia has been divided without severing the body, the hinder limbs may be seen trying to propel the body in one direction, while the fore limbs are trying to propel it in another. Among the **higher Articulata**, however, a number of the anterior pairs of ganglia, besides growing severally much larger, unite into one mass; and this great cephalic ganglion, becoming the coordinator of all the creature's movements, there no longer exists much local independence. Now may we not in the growth of a consolidated kingdom out of petty sovereignties or baronies, observe analogous changes. Like the chiefs and primitive rulers above described, feudal lords, exercising supreme power over their respective groups of retainers, discharge functions analogous to those rudimentary nervous centers; and we know that at first they, like their prototypes, were distinguished by superiority of directive and executive organization. Among these local governing centers, we see in early feudal times very little subordination. They are in frequent antagonism; they are individually restrained chiefly by the influence of large parties in their own class; and are but imperfectly and irregularly subject to that most powerful member

---

consequence, the rest of its inhabitants can then exercise their faculties—can then exist even—only by consent of the landowners; it is manifest, that an exclusive possession of the soil necessitates an infringement of the law of equal freedom" (1851: 115). In the same work, he devotes an entire chapter to women's rights, writing, "The rights of women must stand or fall with those of men" (1851: 156). Both of these positions are consistent with Spencer's extreme laissez-faire philosophy. The landed rich are to be opposed since they achieved their wealth through inheritance rather than merit. If someone is meritorious, it should not matter if the person is male or female. Later in his career, as Spencer became more conventionally conservative and more beholden to wealthy patrons, he reversed both of these positions. He joined the Liberty and Property Defense League and wrote in support of the wealthy and powerful regardless of how their wealth was obtained. Similarly, Spencer later argued that the needs of reproduction arrested the mental evolution of females at an early age (Stocking 1987: 205).

Spencer's relationship with women was problematic. He never married and, by modern standards, was likely asexual. He had a decades-long intellectual friendship with the English novelist Mary Ann Evans (1819–1880), better known by her pen name George Eliot. Eliot loved Spencer but he did not return her feelings. Some of the tenor of their relationship can be seen in a letter she wrote to him in 1852. There was a heat wave in London and she's gone to the seashore. Spencer writes saying that she's taken the cooler weather with her. She replies: "Dear Friend, No credit to me for my virtues as a refrigerant. I owe them all to a few lumps of ice which I carried away with me from that tremendous glacier of yours," a clever way of calling Spencer cold and unfeeling. They remained friends but she found other romantic interests (Hardy 2006: 114).

"Impressibility" and **"contractility"**: in Spencer's usage, the ability of the ectoderm, or outer cell layer, in a very simple animal or embryo to remember (or learn) and to move, respectively.

of their order who has gained the position of head suzerain or king. Gradually, however, as the growth and organization of the society progresses, we find these local directive centers falling more and more under the control of a chief directive center. Closer commercial and distributive union between the several segments, is accompanied by closer governmental union; and these minor rulers end in being little more than agents who superintend the execution of the commands of the supreme ruler; just as the local ganglia, above described, eventually become agents which enforce in their respective segments the orders of the cephalic ganglion. Note now a further step in which the parallelism equally holds. We remarked above, when speaking of the rise of aboriginal kings, that in proportion as their territories and duties became greater, they were obliged not only to perform their executive functions by deputy, but also to gather round themselves advisers to aid them in their directive functions; and that thus, in place of a solitary governing unit, there grew up a group of governing units, comparable to a ganglion consisting of many cells. Let us here further remark, that the advisers and chief officers who thus form the rudiment of a ministry, tend from the beginning to exercise a certain control over the ruler. By the information they give and the opinions they express, they sway his judgment and affect his commands. To this extent he therefore becomes a channel through which are communicated the directions originating with them; and in course of time, when the advice of ministers becomes the acknowledged source of a king's actions, we see that he assumes very much the character of an automatic center reflecting the impressions made upon him from without.[15]

Beyond this complication in the governmental structure, many societies do not progress; but in some a much further development takes place. Our own case best illustrates this further development, and its further analogies. To kings and their ministries have been added in course of time other great directive centers, exercising a control which, at first small, has been gradually becoming predominant; as with the great governing ganglia that especially distinguish the highest class of living beings. Strange as the assertion will be thought, our Houses of Parliament discharge in the social economy, functions that are in sundry respects comparable to those discharged by the great cerebral masses in a vertebrate animal. As it is in the nature of a single ganglion to be affected only by special stimuli from particular parts of the body; so it is in the nature of a single ruler to be swayed in his acts by exclusive personal or class interests. As it is in the nature of an aggregation of ganglia, closely connected with the primary one, to convey to it a greater variety of influences from more numerous organs, and thus to make its acts conform to more numerous requirements; so it is in the nature of a king surrounded by subsidiary controlling powers to adapt his rule to a greater number of public exigencies. And as it is in the nature of those great and latest developed ganglia which distinguish the highest creatures, to interpret and combine the more numerous and more complex impressions conveyed to them from all parts of the system, and to regulate the actions in such a way as duly to regard them all; so it is in the nature of those great and latest developed legislative bodies which distinguished the most advanced societies, to interpret and combine the wishes and complaints of all classes and localities, and to regulate public affairs as much as possible in harmony with the general wants. It is the function of the cerebrum to coordinate the countless heterogeneous considerations which affect the present and future welfare of the individual as a whole; and it is the function of the House of Commons to coordinate the countless heterogeneous considerations which affect the immediate and remote welfare of the entire community. We may describe the office of the

---

15. If you're wading carefully through the verbiage, you'll have noted that in this paragraph Spencer compares feudal societies to earthworms and centralized kingdoms to spiders! Feudal lords are like more-or-less independent ganglia. As society progresses, these fall under the control of the king and are more like spiders or centipedes.

   "Lower Articulata" is an archaic term from biology. Spencer uses it to refer to earthworms, leeches, and other similarly segmented animals. **"Higher Articulata"** include centipedes and spiders.

brain as that of averaging the interests of life, physical, intellectual, moral, social; and a good brain is one in which the desires answering to these respective interests are so balanced, that the conduct they jointly dictate, sacrifices none of them. Similarly, we may describe the office of a Parliament as that of averaging the interests of the various classes in a community; and a good parliament is one in which the parties answering to these respective interests are so balanced, that their united legislation concedes to each class as much as consists with the good of the rest. Besides being comparable in their duties, these great directive centers, social and individual, are also comparable in the processes by which their duties are discharged. It is now a well-understood fact in Psychology, that the cerebrum is not occupied with direct impressions from without, but with the ideas of such impressions: instead of the actual sensations produced in the body, and directly appreciated by the sensory ganglia or primitive nervous centers, the cerebrum receives only the representations of these sensations; and its consciousness is called representative consciousness, to distinguish it from the original or presentative consciousness. Is it not significant that we have hit upon the same word to distinguish the function of our House of Commons? We call it a representative body, because the interests with which it deals—the pains and pleasures about which it consults—are not directly presented to it, but represented to it by its various members; and a debate is a conflict of representations of the evils or benefits likely to follow from a proposed course—a description which applies with equal truth to a debate in the individual consciousness. Further it should be remarked, that in both cases, these great governing masses take no part in the executive functions. As, after a conflict of motives in the cerebrum, those which finally predominate act on the subjacent ganglia, and through their instrumentality determine the bodily actions; so the parties who, after a parliamentary struggle, finally gain the victory, do not themselves carry out their desires, but get them carried out by the executive divisions of the Government. The fulfillment of all legislative decisions continues still to devolve upon the original directive centers—the impulse passing from the Parliament to the Ministers, and from the Ministers to the King, in whose name everything is done; just as those smaller first developed ganglia, which in the lowest vertebrata are the chief controlling agents, are still in a man's brain, the agents through which the dictates of the cerebrum are worked out. And yet once more, observe that in both cases these original centers become more and more automatic. In the individual they have now little function beyond that of executing the determinations of the larger centers. In the State we see that the monarch has long been lapsing into a mere passive agent of Parliament; and that now ministries are rapidly falling into the same position. Nay, between the two cases there is a parallelism, even in respect of the exceptions to this automatic action. For in the individual it happens that under circumstances of sudden alarm, as from a loud sound close at hand, an unexpected object starting up in front, or a slip from insecure footing, the danger is guarded against by some quick involuntary jump, or adjustment of the limbs, that takes place before there is time to consider the impending evil, and take deliberate measures to avoid it: the rationale of which is, that these violent impressions produced on the senses are reflected from the sensory ganglia to the spinal cord and muscles, without, as in ordinary cases, first passing through the cerebrum. In like manner on national emergencies calling for prompt action, the king and ministry, not having time to lay the matter before the great deliberative bodies, themselves issue commands for the requisite movements or precautions: the primitive, and now almost automatic directive centers resume for a moment their original uncontrolled power. And then, strangest of all, observe that in either case there is an after-process of approval or condemnation. The individual, on recovering from his automatic start, at once contemplates the cause of his fright; and, according to the case, concludes that it was well he moved as he did, or condemns himself for his groundless alarm. In like manner the deliberative powers in the State, discuss, as soon as may be, the unauthorized acts of the executive powers; and, deciding that the reasons were or were not sufficient, grant or withhold a bill of indemnity.[16]

Thus far in comparing the governmental organization of the body-politic with that of an individual body, we have considered only the respective co-ordinating centers. We have yet to consider the channels through which these co-ordinating centers receive information and convey commands. In the simplest societies, as in the simplest organisms, there is no "internuncial apparatus," as Hunter styled the nervous system. Consequently, impressions can be but slowly propagated from unit to unit throughout the whole mass. The same progress, however, which in animal organization shows itself in the establishment of ganglia or directive centers, shows itself also in the establishment of nerve-threads, through which the ganglia receive and convey impressions, and so control remote organs. And in societies the like eventually takes place. After a long period during which the directive centers communicate with the various parts of the society through other means, there at length comes into existence an "internuncial apparatus" analogous to that found in individual bodies. The comparison of telegraph wires to

nerves is familiar to all. It applies, however, to an extent not commonly supposed. We do not refer to the near alliance between the subtle forces employed in the two cases; though it is now held that the nerve-force, if not literally electric, is still a special form of electric action, related to the ordinary form much as magnetism is. But we refer to the structural arrangements of our telegraph system. Note first the fact that throughout the vertebrate sub-kingdom, we find the great nerve-bundles diverging from the vertebrate axis, side by side with the great arteries; and similarly we see that our groups of telegraph-wires are carried along the sides of our railways. But the most striking parallelism is this,—that into each great bundle of nerves as it leaves the axis of the body along with an artery, there enters a branch of the sympathetic nerve, which branch, accompanying the artery throughout its ramifications, has the function of regulating its diameter and otherwise controlling the flow of blood through it according to the local requirements. In like manner we find that in the group of telegraph wires running alongside each railway, there is one for the purpose of regulating the traffic— for retarding or expediting the flow of passen-

---

16. In this very long paragraph, Spencer fits the British Parliamentary system into his analogy. Spencer positions this system as the highest form of society. Until now he has been making comparisons with single-celled animals, earthworms, and centipedes. In this paragraph, he compares his leadership in his own society to the human brain.

Throughout this passage Spencer naturalizes British parliamentary democracy, arguing that, since it arises following the organic analogy in fine detail, its emergence is the result natural of natural law and hence inevitable. This defense of government must be read in the context of its time. The *Communist Manifesto* had been published in 1848, a year in which a series of unsuccessful revolutions had swept through Europe. Spencer argues by implication that revolutionary demands for radical change in government and ownership must fail since the form of the government is dictated by evolutionary law.

Spencer's understanding of the role of government was strongly influenced by John Locke (1632–1704) as well as Jeremy Bentham (1748–1832) and John Stuart Mill (1806–1873). Mill and Spencer were well known to each other. In fact, Mill had offered to cover the entire cost of publication of Spencer's work in the early 1860s (Derry 1902: 3). Though not a member, Mill was also associated with the X Club (Barton 1998: 439).

Bentham and Mill are closely associated with *utilitarianism*, the philosophical principle that societies should attempt to achieve the greatest good for the greatest number. This passage presents a utilitarian view of representative government: It acts by balancing the interests of all to achieve the best possible outcome for all. It is important to remember that contrary to Spencer's vision, governments, including the British government of Spencer's era tended to benefit particular groups and classes much more than others.

Early in the passage, Spencer presents the ideas of representative and presentative consciousness as if they were well established in philosophic discourse. They probably come from the work of Henry Mansel, a philosopher Spencer acknowledged as one source of his ideas (Taylor 2007: 136). Spencer expands on these ideas in *Principles of Psychology* (1855). However, they were controversial and were widely discussed and critiqued in his own lifetime (see Cairnes 1875; Mercier 1883).

gers and commodities as the local conditions demand. Probably when our now rudimentary telegraph system is fully developed, other analogies will be traceable.[17]

Such, then, is a general outline of the evidence which justifies in detail the comparison of a society to a living organism. The general peculiarities that societies gradually increase in mass, that they become little by little more complex, and that at the same time their parts grow more mutually dependent—these broad peculiarities which societies display in common with all living bodies, and in which they and living bodies differ from everything else; we find to involve minor analogies far closer than might have been expected. To these we would gladly have added others. We had hoped to say something respecting the different types of social organization, and something also on social metamorphoses; but we have reached our assigned limits.

---

17. For the modern reader, one of the most striking things about Spencer is the extraordinary degree of analogical detail he claims. Today, some of his suggestions can sound comic. In *The Principles of Sociology, Volume 1* (1898 [1874]: 479–82) he compares the transition from household to factory-based production to processes within the human liver. As Spencer notes, analogies between nerves and telegraph wires were common in the nineteenth century, for example, an anonymously written child's book from 1850 makes such a comparison. However, the specificity of Spencer's analogy is surprising. He suggests not only a general analogy between nerves and telegraph wires but one between specific nerves and particular arrangements of wires within the system. Note that for Spencer, the organic analogy is predictive. He says that as the telegraph develops, more analogies will be discovered. Thus, the development of the telegraph must parallel that of the nervous system. What would Spencer have made of the fact that modern communication uses wholly different technologies? The beauty of argument by analogy is flexibility. You can almost always say that one thing is like another in some conceivable way. Spencer would no doubt argue that today's smartphones were analogous to some aspect of physiology.

2. The Science of Culture

Sir Edward Burnett Tylor (1832–1917)

CULTURE OR CIVILIZATION, taken in its wide ethnographic sense, is that complex whole which includes knowledge, belief, art, morals, law, custom, and any other capabilities and habits acquired by man as a member of society. The condition of culture among the various societies of mankind, in so far as it is capable of being investigated on general principles, is a subject apt for the study of laws of human thought and action. On the one hand, the uniformity which so largely pervades civilization may be ascribed, in great measure, to the uniform action of uniform causes; while on the other hand its various grades may be regarded as stages of development or evolution each the outcome of previous history, and about to do its proper part in shaping the history of the future. To the investigation of these two great principles in several departments of ethnography, with especial consideration of the civilization of the lower tribes as related to the civilization of the higher nations, the present volumes are devoted.[1]

Our modern investigators in the sciences of inorganic nature are foremost to recognize, both within and without their special fields of work, unity of nature, the fixity of its laws, the definite sequence of cause and effect through which every fact depends on what has gone before it, and acts upon what is to come after it. They grasp firmly the Pythagorean doctrine of pervading order in the universal Kosmos. They affirm, with Aristotle, that nature is not full of incoherent episodes, like a bad tragedy. They agree with Leibnitz in what he calls "my axiom, that nature never acts by leaps (**La nature n'agit jamais par saut**)," as well as in his "great principle, commonly little employed, that nothing happens without its sufficient reason." Nor, again, in studying the structure and habits of plants and animals, or in investigating the lower functions even of man, are these leading ideas unacknowledged. But when we come to talk of the higher processes of human feeling and action, of thought and language, knowledge and art, a change appears in the prevalent tone of opinion. The world at large is scarcely prepared to accept the general study of human life as a branch of natural science, and to carry out, in a large sense, the poet's injunction to "Account for moral as for natural things." To many educated minds there seems something presumptuous and repulsive in the view that the history of mankind is part and parcel of the history of nature, that our thoughts, wills, and actions accord with laws

---

From *Primitive Culture* (1871)

1. Throughout this essay, Tylor reaffirms his faith in the possibility of a science of human society analogous to the physical sciences. In this, he is very much like the other thinkers of his era, particularly Herbert Spencer. The opening sentence of this essay is one of the most frequently quoted definitions of culture in anthropology. Despite this, Tylor's understanding of the meaning of culture is different from that of most modern anthropologists. Whereas most anthropologists today believe that there are a great many different cultures, Tylor believed that "Culture" was, ultimately, a single body of information of which different human groups had greater or lesser amounts. This understanding was based on his belief in the psychic unity of humankind, here referred to as "the uniform action of uniform causes." The volumes Tylor refers to are the two volumes of *Primitive Culture* (1871), generally considered Tylor's masterpiece. The first volume has chapters about the way that culture developed, Tylor's doctrine of survivals (discussed below), language, counting, mythology, and animism. The second volume is largely given to a discussion of animism.

as definite as those which govern the motion of waves, the combination of acids and bases, and the growth of plants and animals.[2]

The main reasons of this state of the popular judgment are not far to seek. There are many who would willingly accept a science of history if placed before them with substantial definiteness of principle and evidence, but who not unreasonably reject the systems offered to them, as falling too far short of a scientific standard. Through resistance such as this, real knowledge always sooner or later makes its way, while the habit of opposition to novelty does such excellent service against the invasions of speculative dogmatism, that we may sometimes even wish it were stronger than it is. But other obstacles to the investigation of laws of human nature arise from considerations of metaphysics and theology. The popular notion of free human will involves not only freedom to act in accordance with motive, but also a power of breaking loose from continuity and acting without cause,—a combination which may be roughly illustrated by the simile of a balance sometimes acting in the usual way, but also possessed of the faculty of turning by itself without or against its weights. This view of an anomalous action of the will, which it need hardly be said is incompatible with scientific argument, subsists as an opinion patent or latent in men's minds, and strongly affecting their theoretic views of history, though it is not, as a rule, brought prominently forward in

systematic reasoning. Indeed the definition of human will, as strictly according with motive, is the only possible scientific basis in such enquiries. Happily, it is not needful to add here yet another to the list of dissertations on supernatural intervention and natural causation, on liberty, predestination, and accountability. We may hasten to escape from the regions of transcendental philosophy and theology, to start on a more hopeful journey over more practicable ground. None will deny that, as each man knows by the evidence of his own consciousness, definite and natural cause does, to a great extent, determine human action. Then, keeping aside from considerations of extra-natural interference and causeless spontaneity, let us take this admitted existence of natural cause and effect as our standing ground, and travel on it so far as it will bear us. It is on this same basis that physical science pursues, with ever-increasing success, its quest of laws of nature. Nor need this restriction hamper the scientific study of human life, in which the real difficulties are the practical ones of enormous complexity of evidence, and imperfection of methods of observation.[3]

Now it appears that this view of human will and conduct, as subject to definite law, is indeed recognized and acted upon by the very people who oppose it when stated in the abstract as a general principle, and who then complain that it annihilates man's free will, destroys his sense of personal responsibility,

---

2. In this paragraph, Tylor refers to the principle of sufficient reason—the idea that if a thing exists or an event occurs, there is a sufficient explanation for it—proffered by philosopher Gottfried Wilhelm Leibniz (1646–1716). Tylor gives us a poetic interpretation of this idea from the words of the English poet Alexander Pope (1688–1744). In *An Essay on Man,* Pope wrote, "From pride, from pride, our very reas'ning springs;/ Account for moral as for natural things:/Why charge we Heav'n in those, in these acquit?/In both, to reason right is to submit." In this same poem, we also find the line "The proper study of Mankind is Man."

"La nature n'agit jamais par saut": French, "nature never acts by leaps."

3. In this passage, Tylor rejects both religious explanations of social phenomena and objections to social science based on the supposition of human free will. He does not deny free will but rather sidesteps the question, suggesting that we begin to investigate human behavior scientifically and leave questions of free will for later debate. Tylor was stridently anticlerical. He saw human history as proceeding toward increasing rationality. His religious background is significant in this context. Tylor was from a Quaker family and was highly influenced by Quaker theology. Quakers (members of the Society of Friends) believe that God speaks through each individual. One implication of this is that Quakers have no formal clergy and very little ritual. Quakers also insist on the unity of humanity and, in the nineteenth century, emphasized tolerance and humanitarianism. Tylor's Quaker background is reflected in his tendency to dismiss all religious ritual as irrational superstition and in his idea that all humans are on a single path of social evolution.

and degrades him to a soul-less machine. He who will say these things will nevertheless pass much of his own life in studying the motives which lead to human action, seeking to attain his wishes through them, framing in his mind theories of personal character, reckoning what are likely to be the effects of new combinations, and giving to his reasoning the crowning character of true scientific enquiry, by taking it for granted that in so far as his calculation turns out wrong, either his evidence must have been false or incomplete, or his judgment upon it unsound. Such a one will sum up the experience of years spent in complex relations with society, by declaring his persuasion that there is a reason for everything in life, and that where events look unaccountable, the rule is to wait and watch in hope that the key to the problem may some day be found. This man's observation may have been as narrow as his inferences are crude and prejudiced, but nevertheless he has been an inductive philosopher "more than forty years without knowing it." He has practically acknowledged definite laws of human thought and action, and has simply thrown out of account in his own studies of life the whole fabric of motiveless will and uncaused spontaneity. It is assumed here that they should be just so thrown out of account in wider studies, and that the true philosophy of history lies in extending and improving the methods of the plain people who form their judgments upon facts, and check them upon new facts. Whether the doctrine be wholly or but partly true, it accepts the very condition under which we search for new knowledge in the lessons of experience, and in a word the whole course of our rational life is based upon it.[4]

"One event is always the son of another, and we must never forget the parentage," was a remark made by a Bechuana chief to Casalis the African missionary. Thus at all times historians, so far as they have aimed at being more than mere chroniclers, have done their best to show not merely succession, but connection, among the events upon their record. Moreover, they have striven to elicit general principles of human action, and by these to explain particular events, stating expressly or taking tacitly for granted the existence of a philosophy of history. Should any one deny the possibility of thus establishing historical laws the answer is ready with which Boswell in such a case turned on Johnson: "Then, sir, you would reduce all history to no better than almanack." That nevertheless the labors of so many eminent thinkers should have as yet brought history only to the threshold of science need cause no wonder to those who consider the bewildering complexity of the problems which come before the general historian. The evidence from which he is to draw his conclusions is at once so multifarious and so doubtful that a full and distinct view of its bearing on a particular question is hardly to be attained, and thus the temptation becomes all but irresistible to garble it in support of some rough and ready theory of the course of events. The philosophy of history at large, explaining the past and predicting the future phenomena of man's life in the world by reference to general laws, is in fact a subject with which, in the present state of knowledge, even genius aided by wide research seems but hardly able to cope. Yet there are departments of it which, though difficult enough, seem comparatively accessible. If the field of inquiry be nar-

---

4. In this passage, Tylor continues his attack on those he considers the enemies of the application of the scientific method to social science. He argues that simply thinking about the way that people judge the actions of others shows widespread understanding that human actions have causes. He quotes the play *The Bourgeois Gentleman* by Molière (Jean-Baptiste Poquelin [1622–1673]). In the play, "the philosophy master" informs "Mr. Jourdain" that speech is a form of prose, and Jourdain replies, "By my faith! For more than forty years I have been speaking prose without knowing anything about it, and I am much obliged to you for having taught me that." Molière's play is comedic, but Tylor really does want to teach us that human action is determined, at least substantially, by cause and effect, whether we realize it or not.

Note also that Tylor here refers to his work as creating a philosophy of history. Tylor's anthropology was based in part on his reconstruction of the history of humankind's evolution to civilization. Many later anthropologists rejected such historical reconstruction as unscientific or impossible.

rowed from History as a whole to that branch of it which is here called Culture, the history, not of tribes or nations, but of the condition of knowledge, religion, art, custom, and the like among them, the task of investigation proves to lie within far more moderate compass. We suffer still from the same kind of difficulties which beset the wider argument, but they are much diminished. The evidence is no longer so wildly heterogeneous, but may be more simply classified and compared, while the power of getting rid of extraneous matter, and treating each issue on its own proper set of facts, makes close reasoning on the whole more available than in general history. This may appear from a brief preliminary examination of the problem, how the phenomena of Culture may be classified and arranged, stage by stage, in a probable order of evolution.[5]

Surveyed in a broad view, the character and habit of mankind at once display that similarity and consistency of phenomena which led the Italian proverb-maker to declare that "all the world is one country" "tutto il mondo e paese." To general likeness in human nature on the one hand, and to general likeness in the circumstances of life on the other, this similarity and consistency may no doubt be traced, and they may be studied with especial fitness in comparing races near the same grade of civilization. Little respect need be had in such comparisons for date in history or for place on the map; the ancient Swiss lake-dweller may be set beside the medieval Aztec, and the Ojibwa of North America beside the Zulu of South Africa. As Dr. Johnson contemptuously said when he had read about Patagonians and South Sea Islanders in Hawkesworth's Voyages, "one set of savages is like another." How true a general-

ization this really is, any Ethnological Museum may show. Examine for instance the edged and pointed instruments in such a collection; the inventory includes hatchet, adze, chisel, knife, saw, scraper, awl, needle, spear and arrowhead, and of these most or all belong with only differences of detail to races the most various. So it is with savage occupations; the wood-chopping, fishing with net and line, shooting and spearing game, fire-making, cooking, twisting cord and plaiting baskets, repeat themselves with wonderful uniformity in the museum shelves which illustrate the life of the lower races from Kamchatka to Tierra del Fuego, and from Dahome to Hawaii. Even when it comes to comparing barbarous hordes with civilized nations, the consideration thrusts itself upon our minds, how far item after item of the life of the lower races passes into analogous proceedings of the higher, in forms not too far changed to be recognized, and sometimes hardly changed at all. Look at the modern European peasant using his hatchet and his hoe, see his food boiling or roasting over the log-fire, observe the exact place which beer holds in his calculation of happiness, hear his tale of the ghost in the nearest haunted house, and of the farmer's niece who was bewitched with knots in her inside till she fell into fits and died. If we choose out in this way things which have altered little in a long course of centuries, we may draw a picture where there shall be scarce a hand's breadth difference between an English ploughman and a negro of Central Africa. These pages will be so crowded with evidence of such correspondence among mankind, that there is no need to dwell upon its details here, but it may be used at once to override a problem which would complicate the

---

5. In this passage, Tylor argues that the success of a philosophy of history depends on restricting the subject matter: By focusing on culture, the historian may ignore specific events in favor of general developmental trends. Because Tylor understood culture as a unitary phenomenon that characterized all people and societies to one degree or another, the project was practical. For Tylor, describing culture as an evolutionary phenomenon implied tracing the history of its development. Simple societies could be understood as living history or living fossils.

Tylor mentions Dr. Samuel Johnson (1709–1784) several times in this essay. Johnson is considered by many to be the greatest English author of the eighteenth century. James Boswell (1740–1795) was his biographer and frequent companion. Tylor quotes Boswell's reply to Johnson to point out that if there are no possible laws of history, then history is simply a list of events.

argument, namely, the question of race. For the present purpose it appears both possible and desirable to eliminate considerations of hereditary varieties or races of man, and to treat mankind as homogeneous in nature, though placed in different grades of civilization. The details of the enquiry will, I think, prove that stages of culture may be compared without taking into account how far tribes who use the same implement, follow the same custom, or believe the same myth may differ in their bodily configuration and the color of their skin and hair.[6]

A first step in the study of civilization is to dissect it into details, and to classify these in their proper groups. Thus, in examining weapons, they are to be classed under spear, club, sling, bow and arrow, and so forth; among textile arts are to be ranged matting, netting, and several grades of making and weaving threads; myths are divided under such headings as myths of sunrise and sunset, eclipse-myths, earthquake-myths, local myths which account for the names of places by some fanciful tale, **eponymic** myths which account for the par-

entage of a tribe by turning its name into the name of an imaginary ancestor; under rites and ceremonies occur such practices as the various kinds of sacrifice to the ghosts of the dead and to other spiritual beings, the turning to the east to worship, the purification of ceremonial or moral uncleanness by means of water or fire. Such are a few miscellaneous examples from a list of hundreds, and the ethnographer's business is to classify such details with a view to making out their distribution in geography and history, and the relations which exist among them. What this task is like may be almost perfectly illustrated by comparing these details of culture with the species of plants and animals as studied by the naturalist. To the ethnographer, the bow and arrow is a species, the habit of flattening children's skulls is a species, the practice of reckoning numbers by tens is a species. The geographical distribution of these things, and their transmission from region to region, have to be studied as the naturalist studies the geography of his botanical and zoological species. Just as certain plants and

---

6. When Tylor speaks here about "comparing races near the same grade of civilization" and placing ethnographic materials next to each other on display, he is probably thinking about actual museum displays. In 1816, Christian Jürgensen Thomsen (1788–1865) became curator of the Museum of Northern Antiquities in Copenhagen (later the National Museum of Denmark). Because he had no means to date artifacts in the museum's collection, he attempted to arrange the museum's collections chronologically based on the material and style of their construction. In so doing, he established the sequence of stone to bronze to iron. Thomsen's "Three Age System" became extremely influential in European and American archaeology and museum-collection displays worldwide. One example was the Great Exhibition of 1851, also known as the Crystal Palace Exhibition. Held in London in the summer of 1851, the Great Exhibition brought together some fourteen thousand international exhibitors. It showed the latest technology as well as archaeological and current-day artifacts from around the world. Ancient and modern artifacts were displayed together in order of their presumed technical sophistication. This method of display showed similarities between ancient European artifacts and material from current-day indigenous societies. It seemed to demonstrate that societies could be placed in evolutionary sequence with, as Tylor says above, "little respect . . . for date in history or place on the map." This idea became a cornerstone of the comparative method.

More than six million people attended the exhibition, and it had a profound influence on both the general public and scholars of the era. Tylor had several connections to the exhibition. His family's firm, a brass factory, exhibited its wares there, and Tylor's friend and mentor, the Quaker ethnologist and archaeologist Henry Christy, was a juror for the exposition.

Note also that, at the end of the paragraph, Tylor appears to reject explanations of cultural differences based on race. Tylor's Quaker theology committed him to the notion of *monogenesis*—the belief that all human races belonged to the same species and shared the same evolutionary origins. He wrote, "The facts collected seem to favor the view that the wide differences in the civilization and mental state of the various races of mankind are rather differences of development than of origin, rather of degree than kind" (quoted in Stocking 1987: 159). This notion was contested by the Americans Samuel G. Morton (1799–1851) and Louis Agassiz (1807–1873), key promoters of *polygenesis*, a theory that argued human races represented different and unequal species and was used as a "scientific" justification for slavery. Although to modern readers some of Tylor's writing has a decidedly racist cast, he was liberal by the standards of his day.

animals are peculiar to certain districts, so it is with such instruments as the Australian boomerang, the Polynesian stick-and-groove for fire making, the tiny bow and arrow used as a lancet or **phleme** by tribes about the Isthmus of Panama, and in like manner with many an art, myth, or custom found isolated in a particular field. Just as the catalogue of all the species of plants and animals of a district represents its Flora and Fauna, so the list of all the items of the general life of a people represents that whole which we call its culture. And just as distant regions so often produce vegetables and animals which are analogous, though by no means identical, so it is with the details of the civilization of their inhabitants. How good a working analogy there really is between the diffusion of plants and animals and the diffusion of civilization comes well into view when we notice how far the same causes have produced both at once. In district after district, the same causes which have introduced the cultivated plants and domesticated animals of civilization, have brought in with them a corresponding art and knowledge. The course of events which carried horses and wheat to America carried with them the use of the gun and the iron hatchet, while in return the old world received not only maize, potatoes, and turkeys, but the habit of smoking and the sailor's hammock.[7]

It is a matter worthy of consideration that the accounts of similar phenomena of culture, recurring in different parts of the world, actually supply incidental proof of their own authenticity. Some years since, a question which brings out this point was put to me by a great historian, "How can a statement as to customs, myths, beliefs, &c., of a savage tribe be treated as evidence where it depends on the testimony of some traveler or missionary, who may be a superficial observer, more or less ignorant of the native language, a careless retailer of unsifted talk, a man prejudiced or even wilfully deceitful?" This question is, indeed, one which every ethnographer ought to keep clearly and constantly before his mind. Of course he is bound to use his best judgment as to the trustworthiness of all authors he quotes, and if possible to obtain several accounts to certify each point in each locality. But it is over and above these measures of precaution that the test of recurrence comes in. If two independent visitors to different countries, say a medieval Mohammedan in Tartary and a modern Englishman in Dahome, or a Jesuit missionary in Brazil and a Wesleyan in the Fiji Islands, agree in describing some analogous art or rite or myth among the people they have visited, it becomes difficult or impossible to set down such correspondence to accident or willful fraud. A story by a bushranger in Australia may, perhaps, be objected to as a mistake or an invention, but did a Methodist minister in Guinea conspire with him to cheat the public by telling the same story there? The possibility of intentional or unintentional mystification is often barred by such a state of things as that a similar statement is made in two remote lands, by two witnesses, of whom A lived a century before B, and B appears never to have heard of A. How distant are the countries, how wide

---

7. Tylor, like Spencer, draws an analogy between cultural and biological evolution. In Tylor's view, the ethnographer's primary job is the classification of cultural traits. Following the analogy with biology, Tylor here proposes that to study civilization one must catalog all the practices of humankind and then arrange them into evolutionary and hierarchical order, producing something analogous to the Linnaean classification of plants and animals.

Unlike modern anthropologists, who tend to see field research as inseparable from the practice of anthropology, Tylor did not believe that anthropologists needed to be involved in data collection. Their primary job was to compile, organize, and classify data. Despite this, Tylor did have some field experience. During a year he spent in North America in 1856, he traveled for four months by horseback in Mexico with his friend Christy. He published an account of this trip (*Anahuac: Or Mexico and the Mexicans, Ancient and Modern*) in 1861.

"**Eponymic**": a word or name derived from a proper noun. For example, the guillotine is named for Dr. Joseph-Ignace Guillotin (1738–1814), who proposed the use of a machine as a humane method of capital punishment.

"**Phleme**" (or fleam): a medical device used for bloodletting, whose blade was at right angles to the handle.

apart the dates, how different the creeds and characters of the observers, in the catalogue of facts of civilization, needs no farther showing to any one who will even glance at the foot-notes of the present work. And the more odd the statement, the less likely that several people in several places should have made it wrongly. This being so, it seems reasonable to judge that the statements are in the main truly given, and that their close and regular coincidence is due to the cropping up of similar facts in various districts of culture. Now the most important facts of ethnography are vouched for in this way. Experience leads the student after a while to expect and find that the phenomena of culture, as resulting from widely-acting similar causes, should recur again and again in the world. He even mistrusts isolated statements to which he knows of no parallel elsewhere, and waits for their genuineness to be shown by corresponding accounts from the other side of the earth, or the other end of history. So strong, indeed, is this means of authentication that the ethnographer in his library may sometimes presume to decide, not only whether a particular explorer is a shrewd and honest observer, but also whether what he reports is conformable to the general rules of civilization. "**Non quis, sed quid**."[8]

To turn from the distribution of culture in different countries, to its diffusion within these countries. The quality of mankind which tends most to make the systematic study of civilization possible is that remarkable tacit consensus or agreement which so far induces whole populations to unite in the use of the same language, to follow the same religion and customary law, to settle down to the same general level of art and knowledge. It is this state of things which makes it so far possible to ignore exceptional facts and to describe nations by a sort of general average. It is this state of things which makes it so far possible to represent immense masses of details by a few typical facts, while, these once settled, new cases recorded by new observers simply fall into their places to prove the soundness of the classification. There is found to be such regularity in the composition of societies of men that we can drop individual differences out of sight, and thus can generalize on the arts and opinions of whole nations, just as, when looking down upon an army from a hill, we forget the individual soldier, whom, in fact, we can scarce distinguish in the mass, while we see each regiment as an organized body, spreading or concentrating, moving in advance or in retreat. In some branches of the study of social laws it is now possible to call in the aid of statistics, and to set apart special actions of large mixed communities of men by means of tax-gatherers' schedules, or the tables of the insurance office. Among modern arguments on the laws of human action, none have had a deeper effect than generalizations such as those of M. Quetelet, on the regularity, not only of such matters as average stature and the annual rates of birth and death, but the recurrence, year after year, of such obscure and seemingly incalculable products of national life as the numbers of murders and suicides, and the proportion of the very weapons of crime. Other striking cases are the annual regularity of persons killed accidentally in the London streets, and of undirected letters dropped into post-

---

8. In this paragraph, Tylor anticipates criticism of his data collection. How can we rely on reports from untrained observers? He responds that we know these reports are accurate since people in disparate times and places report similar things. He claims that this fact is a powerful argument for psychic unity and the idea that all groups pass through identical stages of development. However, he also claims that his evidence is so powerful that it allows him to determine whether the data is accurate or not. Tylor says that his principle is so well established that if traits are reported that do not fit in the sequence, the reports must be false. Thus, Tylor eliminates data that do not correspond to this theory, and he assumes what he is trying to prove. Tylor also states that similar traits found in widely different places and times are evidence of psychic unity and that the same concept can be used to verify or refute ethnographic data without leaving one's library. Pointing out the faults in this kind of logic was one of the main ways that Franz Boas (1858–1942) and his followers discredited the work of Tylor and other evolutionists.

"***Non quis, sed quid***": Latin, "not who, but what." It is not who made the report that is important, but rather what they reported.

office letterboxes. But in examining the culture of the lower races, far from having at command the measured arithmetical facts of modern statistics, we may have to judge of the condition of tribes from the imperfect accounts supplied by travelers or missionaries, or even to reason upon relics of prehistoric races of whose very names and languages we are hopelessly ignorant. Now these may seem at the first glance sadly indefinite and unpromising materials for a scientific enquiry. But in fact they are neither indefinite nor unpromising, but give evidence that is good and definite, so far as it goes. They are data which, for the distinct way in which they severally denote the condition of the tribe they belong to, will actually bear comparison with the statistician's returns. The fact is that a stone arrow-head, a carved club, an idol, a grave-mound where slaves and property have been buried for the use of the dead, an account of a sorcerer's rites in making rain, a table of numerals, the conjugation of a verb, are things which each express the state of a people as to one particular point of culture, as truly as the tabulated numbers of deaths by poison, and of chests of tea imported, express in a different way other partial results of the general life of a whole community.[9]

That a whole nation should have a special dress, special tools and weapons, special laws of marriage and property, special moral and religious doctrines is a remarkable fact, which we notice so little because we have lived all our lives in the midst of it. It is with such general qualities of organized bodies of men that ethnography has especially to deal. Yet, while generalizing on the culture of a tribe or nation, and

setting aside the peculiarities of the individuals composing it as unimportant to the main result, we must be careful not to forget what makes up this main result. There are people so intent on the separate life of individuals that they cannot grasp a notion of the action of a community as a whole—such an observer, incapable of a wide view of society, is aptly described in the saying that he "cannot see the forest for the trees." But, on the other hand, the philosopher may be so intent upon his general laws of society as to neglect the individual actors of whom that society is made up, and of him it may be said that he cannot see the trees for the forest. We know how arts, customs, and ideas are shaped among ourselves by the combined actions of many individuals, of which actions both motive and effect often come quite distinctly within our view. The history of an invention, an opinion, a ceremony, is a history of suggestion and modification, encouragement and opposition, personal gain and party prejudice, and the individuals concerned act each according to his own motives, as determined by his character and circumstances. Thus sometimes we watch individuals acting for their own ends with little thought of their effect on society at large, and sometimes we have to study movements of national life as a whole, where the individuals co-operating in them are utterly beyond our observation. But seeing that collective social action is the mere resultant of many individual actions, it is clear that these two methods of enquiry, if rightly followed, must be absolutely consistent.

In studying both the recurrence of special habits or ideas in several districts and their

---

9. Adolphe Quetelet (1796–1874) was a Belgian astronomer and mathematician whose examination of French crime records in the 1830s showed that behavior in large groups of people could be predicted through the use of statistics. Quetelet called his theory "social physics," implying that he had created a science of society similar to physics (Durkheim also makes use of Quetelet's work. See essay 5, note 8). In Tylor's time, statistics was a relatively recent and influential discovery. By providing a way to match numbers with social phenomena, statistics seemed to be a method by which natural laws determining human behavior could be ascertained. Here Tylor argues that ethnographic and archaeological data are comparable to demographic data collected in tax records and by insurance companies and can be considered equally valid. This proposition, if accepted, would provide further evidence that a valid science of culture was possible. In doing this, he enters a key area of controversy: To what degree may anthropologists ignore individual and group differences in favor of an average description of culture? Tylor asserts that cultures can be best represented by their averages. But can you average men and women, Protestants and Catholics, masters and slaves? This issue continues to be debated in anthropology today.

prevalence within each district, there come before us ever reiterated proofs of regular causation producing the phenomena of human life, and of laws of maintenance and diffusion according to which these phenomena settle into permanent standard conditions of society, at definite stages of culture. But, while giving full importance to the evidence bearing on these standard conditions of society, let us be careful to avoid a pitfall which may entrap the unwary student. Of course the opinions and habits belonging in common to masses of mankind are to a great extent the results of sound judgment and practical wisdom. But to a great extent it is not so. That many numerous societies of men should have believed in the influence of the evil eye and the existence of a firmament, should have sacrificed slaves and goods to the ghosts of the departed, should have handed down traditions of giants slaying monsters and men turning into beasts—all this is ground for holding that such ideas were indeed produced in men's minds by efficient causes, but it is not ground for holding that the rites in question are profitable, the beliefs sound, and the history authentic. This may seem at the first glance a truism, but, in fact, it is the denial of a fallacy which deeply affects the minds of all but a small critical minority of mankind. Popularly, what everybody says must be true, what everybody does must be right—"**Quod ubique, quod semper, quod ab omnibus creditum est, hoc est vere proprieque Catholicum**"—and so forth. There are various topics, especially in history,

law, philosophy, and theology, where even the educated people we live among can hardly be brought to see that the cause why men do hold an opinion, or practice a custom, is by no means necessarily a reason why they ought to do so. Now collections of ethnographic evidence, bringing so prominently into view the agreement of immense multitudes of men as to certain traditions, beliefs, and usages, are peculiarly liable to be thus improperly used in direct defence of these institutions themselves, even old barbaric nations being polled to maintain their opinions against what are called modern ideas. As it has more than once happened to myself to find my collections of traditions and beliefs thus set up to prove their own objective truth, without proper examination of the grounds on which they were actually received, I take this occasion of remarking that the same line of argument will serve equally well to demonstrate, by the strong and wide consent of nations, that the earth is flat, and nightmare the visit of a demon.[10]

It being shown that the details of Culture are capable of being classified in a great number of ethnographic groups of arts, beliefs, customs, and the rest, the consideration comes next how far the facts arranged in these groups are produced by evolution from one another. It need hardly be pointed out that the groups in question, though held together each by a common character, are by no means accurately defined. To take up again the natural history illustration, it may be said that they are species which tend to run widely into varieties. And when it

---

10. Tylor's goal in *Primitive Culture* was to scientifically examine the development of religion and expose laws underlying its evolution. He aimed to show that the history of religion is characterized by increasing rationality. The path of his argument led him to explain the rationality of many "primitive" practices. Here he distinguishes between explaining such practices and defending them; it was important to him that his work was perceived as an explanation of religion rather than a defense of particular beliefs. There is an implicit criticism of Tylor's own society in this passage as well. The reader might ask if all the beliefs of his or her society will withstand Tylor's scrutiny. Tylor believed that over time, society would grow increasingly rational. He held that his own society was the most rational yet developed. However, this did not mean that it was perfected. In the famous concluding passage of the second volume of *Primitive Culture* Tylor writes: "It is a harsher, and at times even painful, office of ethnography to expose the remains of crude old culture which have passed into harmful superstition, and to mark these out for destruction. Yet this work, if less genial, is not less urgently needful for the good of mankind. Thus, active at once in aiding progress and removing hindrance, the science of culture is essentially a reformer's science" (1871: 410). One of the societies Tylor wishes to reform is his own.

"*Quod Ubique . . .*": Tylor quotes a definition of orthodoxy that was offered by Saint Vincent of Lérins (d. circa 445), "That which is believed everywhere, always, and by everyone, this is truly and properly Catholic."

comes to the question what relations some of these groups bear to others, it is plain that the student of the habits of mankind has a great advantage over the student of the species of plants and animals. Among naturalists it is an open question whether a theory of development from species to species is a record of transitions which actually took place or a mere ideal scheme serviceable in the classification of species whose origin was really independent. But among ethnographers there is no such question as to the possibility of species of implements or habits or beliefs being developed one out of another, for development in culture is recognized by our most familiar knowledge. Mechanical invention supplies apt examples of the kind of development which affects civilization at large. In the history of fire-arms, the clumsy wheel-lock, in which a notched steel wheel was turned by a handle against the flint till a spark caught the priming, led to the invention of the more serviceable flint-lock, of which a few still hang in the kitchens of our farmhouses, for the boys to shoot small birds with at Christmas; the flint-lock in time passed by an obvious modification into the percussion-lock, which is just now changing its old-fashioned arrangement to be adapted from muzzle-loading to breech-loading. The medieval astrolabe passed into the quadrant, now discarded in its turn by the seaman, who uses the more delicate sextant, and so it is through the history of one art and instrument after another. Such examples of progression are known to us as direct history, but so thoroughly is this notion of development at home in our minds, that by means of it we reconstruct lost history without scruple, trusting to general knowledge of the principles of human thought and action as a guide in putting the facts in their proper order. Whether chronicle speaks or is silent on the point, no one comparing a longbow and a cross-bow would doubt that the cross-bow was a development arising from the simpler instrument. So among the fire-drills for igniting by friction, it seems clear on the face of the matter that the drill worked by a cord or bow is a later improvement on the clumsier primitive instrument twirled between the hands. That instructive class of specimens which antiquaries sometimes discover, bronze celts modelled on the heavy type of the stone hatchet, are scarcely explicable except as first steps in the transition from the Stone Age to the Bronze Age, to be followed soon by the next stage of progress, in which it is discovered that the new material is suited to a handier and less wasteful pattern. And thus, in the other branches of our history, there will come again and again into view series of facts which may be consistently arranged as having followed one another in a particular order of development, but which will hardly bear being turned round and made to follow in reversed order. Such for instance are the facts I have here brought forward in a chapter on the Art of Counting, which tend to prove that as to this point of culture at least, savage tribes reached their position by learning and not unlearning, by elevation from a lower rather than by degradation from a higher state.[11]

Among evidence aiding us to trace the courses which the civilization of the world has

---

11. Tylor believed in evolution and progress. He refers in the opening of this passage to the debate between biological evolutionists and creationists, still raging in 1871 when this piece was first published. For Tylor, the proposition that societies evolved from the most simple to the most complex was self-evident. He wrote, "The educated world of Europe and America practically settles a standard by simply placing its own nations at one end of the social series and savage tribes at the other, arranging the rest of mankind between these limits according as they correspond more closely to savage or cultured life" (quoted in Stocking 1987: 162). For Tylor, the force driving this evolution was the natural development of increasingly rational thinking. Although Tylor's thinking is evolutionary, he downplayed the importance of Darwinian evolution. In Darwinian thinking competition for food, shelter, and mates drives the evolutionary selection process, but there is little evidence for the role of competition in *Primitive Culture* (in fact, the word "competition" does not appear in the book). In his preface to the 1873 edition of *Primitive Culture*, Tylor explained the absence of references to Darwin and Spencer in the work by claiming that his work came "scarcely into contact of detail with the previous works of these eminent philosophers." However, Darwin references Tylor extensively in *The Descent of Man* (1871).

Note also that Tylor once again relies on his ideas of psychic unity, as well as Spencer's notion that evolution leads to increases in complexity, heterogeneity, and interdependence, in order to make claims without

actually followed, is that great class of facts to denote which I have found it convenient to introduce the term "survivals." These are processes, customs, opinions, and so forth, which have been carried on by force of habit into a new state of society different from that in which they had their original home, and they thus remain as proofs and examples of an older condition of culture out of which a newer has been evolved. Thus, I know an old Somersetshire woman whose handloom dates from the time before the introduction of the "flying shuttle," which new-fangled appliance she has never even learnt to use, and I have seen her throw her shuttle from hand to hand in true classic fashion; this old woman is not a century behind her times, but she is a case of survival. Such examples often lead us back to the habits of hundreds and even thousands of years ago. The ordeal of the Key and Bible, still in use, is a survival; the Midsummer bonfire is a survival; the Breton peasants' All Souls' supper for the spirits of the dead is a survival. The simple keeping up of ancient habits is only one part of the transition from old into new and changing times. The serious business of ancient society may be seen to sink into the sport of later generations, and its serious belief to linger on in nursery folk-lore, while superseded habits of old-world life may be modified into new-world forms still powerful for good and evil. Sometimes old thoughts and practices will burst out afresh, to the amazement of a world that thought them long since dead or dying; here survival passes into revival, as has lately happened in so remarkable a way in the history of modern spiritualism, a subject full of instruction from the ethnographer's point of view. The study of the principles of survival has, indeed, no small practical importance, for most of what we call superstition is included within survival, and in this way lies open to the attack of its deadliest enemy, a reasonable explanation. Insignificant, moreover, as multitudes of the facts of survival are in themselves, their study is so effective for tracing the course of the historical development through which alone it is possible to understand their meaning, that it becomes a vital point of ethnographic research to gain the clearest possible insight into their nature. This importance must justify the detail here devoted to an examination of survival, on the evidence of such games, popular sayings, customs, superstitions, and the like, as may serve well to bring into view the manner of its operation.[12]

Progress, degradation, survival, revival, modification are all modes of the connexion that binds together the complex network of civilization. It needs but a glance into the trivial details of our own daily life to set us thinking

---

data. In this paragraph, he declares that implements, habits, and beliefs develop along a single path and in predictable ways. An anthropologist should be able to place any collection of implements, habits, or beliefs in the correct chronological order. Tylor ignores the possibility that different processes may have led to similar outcomes or that things might change in unexpected ways. It might be relatively easy to place European firearms in the correct chronological order. To do the same thing with beliefs, art, stories, or aspects of social order is another thing entirely.

12. Although other thinkers such as Henry Sumner Maine (see note 20) also used the idea of survivals; it is considered one of Tylor's key contributions to anthropology. To him, almost any practice that seemed illogical or smacked of superstition was an example of the survival of the traits and beliefs of an earlier social form. Studying survivals was crucial, since through them—and with the theory of psychic unity—a researcher could trace the course of cultural evolution.

Notice Tylor's frequent references to the customs of the English peasantry in this passage. For Tylor and other evolutionists, European peasantry represented a crucial intermediate step between civilization and savagery. Notice also Tylor's mention of spiritualism. Tylor wrote in an era when the occult was becoming a popular middle-class pastime. He had seen and written on psychic phenomena. Although he did not believe in psychic phenomena, he did admit to being very impressed by the demonstrations he witnessed and unable to offer rational explanations for them (Stocking 1987: 191).

And, for true connoisseurs of historical trivia, Tylor mentions the ordeal of the Key and Bible. Tylor describes this later in *Primitive Culture* and again in an 1876 essay in *Popular Science Monthly*. The Key and Bible is a magical process to identify a thief. The key is placed or tied to the Bible at a verse of Psalm 50 that men-how far we are really its originators, and how far but the transmitters and modifiers of the results of long past ages. Looking round the rooms we live in, we may try here how far he who only knows his own time can be capable of rightly comprehending even that. Here is the "honeysuckle" of Assyria, there the fleur-de-lis of Anjou, a cornice with a Greek border runs round the ceiling, the style of Louis XIV and its parent the Renaissance share the looking-glass between them. Transformed, shifted, or mutilated, such elements of art still carry their history plainly stamped upon them; and if the history yet farther behind is less easy to read, we are not to say that because we cannot clearly discern it there is therefore no history there. It is thus even with the fashion of the clothes men wear. The ridiculous little tails of the German **postilion**'s coat show themselves how they came to dwindle to such absurd rudiments; but the **English clergyman's bands** no longer so convey their history to the eye, and look unaccountable enough till one has seen the intermediate stages through which they came down from the more serviceable wide collars, such as Milton wears in his portrait, and which gave their name to the "bandbox" they used to be kept in. In fact, the books of costume, showing how one garment grew or shrank by gradual stages and passed into another, illustrate with much force and clearness the nature of the change and growth, revival and decay, which go on from year to year in more important matters of life. In books, again, we see each writer not for and by himself, but occupying his proper place in history; we look through each philosopher, mathematician, chemist, poet, into the background of his education—through Leibnitz into Descartes, through Dalton into Priestley, through Milton into Homer. The study of language has, perhaps, done more than any other in removing from our view of human thought and action the ideas of chance and arbitrary invention, and in substituting for them a theory of devel-

opment by the cooperation of individual men, through processes ever reasonable and intelligible where the facts are fully known. Rudimentary as the science of culture still is, the symptoms are becoming very strong that even what seem its most spontaneous and motiveless phenomena will, nevertheless, be shown to come within the range of distinct cause and effect as certainly as the facts of mechanics. What would be popularly thought more indefinite and uncontrolled than the products of the imagination in myths and fables? Yet any systematic investigation of mythology, on the basis of a wide collection of evidence, will show plainly enough in such efforts of fancy at once a development from stage to stage, and a production of uniformity of result from uniformity of cause. Here, as elsewhere, causeless spontaneity is seen to recede farther and farther into shelter within the dark precincts of ignorance; like chance, that still holds its place among the vulgar as a real cause of events otherwise unaccountable, while to educated men it has long consciously meant nothing but this ignorance itself. It is only when men fail to see the line of connexion in events that they are prone to fall upon the notions of arbitrary impulses, causeless freaks, chance and nonsense, and indefinite unaccountability. If childish games, purposeless customs, absurd superstitions are set down as spontaneous because no one can say exactly how they came to be, the assertion may remind us of the like effect that the eccentric habits of the wild rice-plant had on the philosophy of a Red Indian tribe, otherwise disposed to see in the harmony of nature the effects of one controlling personal will. The Great Spirit, said these Sioux theologians, made all things except the wild rice; but the wild rice came by chance.[13]

"Man," said Wilhelm von Humboldt, "ever connects on from what lies at hand (der Mensch Knüpft immer an Vorhandenes an)." The notion of the continuity of civilization contained in this maxim is no barren philosophic principle, but

---

tions thieves. The Bible is then passed among the suspects until the key falls out or if suspended on a string, swings toward an individual. Thus, the thief is identified.

13. Here Tylor gives numerous examples of survivals. Tylor's great strength is his ability as a cultural historian; he was a master of the many details of cultural life. This passage also affirms his faith that laws of

is at once made practical by the consideration that they who wish to understand their own lives ought to know the stages through which their opinions and habits have become what they are. Auguste Comte scarcely overstated the necessity of this study of development, when he declared at the beginning of his "Positive Philosophy" that "no conception can be understood except through its history" and his phrase will bear extension to culture at large. To expect to look modern life in the face and comprehend it by mere inspection is a philosophy whose weakness can easily be tested. Imagine any one explaining the trivial saying, "a little bird told me" without knowing of the old belief in the language of birds and beasts, to which Dr. Dasent, in the introduction to the Norse Tales, so reasonably traces its origin. To ingenious attempts at explaining by the light of reason things which want the light of history to show their meaning, much of the learned nonsense of the world has indeed been due. Sir H. S. Maine, in his "Ancient Law," gives a perfect instance. In all the literature which enshrines the pretended philosophy of law, he remarks, there is nothing more curious than the pages of elaborate sophistry in which

Blackstone attempts to explain and justify that extraordinary rule of English law, only recently repealed, which prohibited sons of the same father by different mothers from succeeding to one another's land. To Sir H. S. Maine, knowing the facts of the case, it was easy to explain its real origin from the "Customs of Normandy" where according to the system of agnation, or kinship on the male side, brothers by the same mother but by different fathers were of course no relations at all to one another. But when this rule "was transplanted to England, the English judges, who had no clue to its principle, interpreted it as a general prohibition against the succession of the half-blood, and extended it to consanguineous brothers, that is to sons of the same father by different wives." Then, ages after, Blackstone sought in this blunder the perfection of reason, and found it in the argument that kinship through both parents ought to prevail over even a nearer degree of kinship through but one parent.[a] Such are the risks that philosophers run in detaching any phenomenon of civilization from its hold on past events, and treating it as an isolated fact, to be simply disposed of by a guess at some plausible explanation.[14]

---

culture, similar to the cause-and-effect principles of Newtonian physics, could be found. Virtually every paragraph of this essay stresses the ability of rational men to divine cause-and-effect relationships.

Tylor had an early interest in linguistics and was particularly influenced by Friedrich Max Müller (1823–1900). Linguistic scholarship in Tylor's day was almost entirely historical, and Müller used the study of Sanskrit writings to reconstruct the histories of Indo-European languages. Similarly, Tylor's attempt to reconstruct the history of human culture was modeled on Müller's work in linguistics.

Note also the strong superorganic element in this paragraph. Changes in elements of culture such as fashion or philosophy follow a pattern separate from the individuals who create them. Leibniz and Descartes are important not for their individual ideas but as markers in a predetermined pattern of human social development. In essay 9 of this volume, A. L. Kroeber (1876–1960) uses some of these same ideas (but without arguing for evolution).

"Postilion": a person who rides the horse on the left of the leading pair when four or more horses are used to draw a carriage, or simply the horse on the left when only one pair is used.

"English clergyman's bands": two white cloth strips hanging from the front of the collar, worn by some Protestant clergy.

14. Tylor mentions numerous important scholars in this passage. Wilhelm von Humboldt (1767–1835) was a German diplomat, a humanist, and the founder of the University of Berlin. Humboldt's enduring legacy was his work in language. His appreciation of linguistic differences foreshadowed the work of Edward Sapir (1884–1939) and Benjamin L. Whorf (1897–1941) in the twentieth century. In 1820 he wrote, "The differences between languages are not those of sounds and signs but those of differing world view" (1963: 246). He was also the brother of explorer and naturalist Alexander von Humboldt (1769–1859).

Auguste Comte (1798–1857) was one of the architects of the philosophical school of *positivism*. Comte and other positivists denied the possibility of metaphysical knowledge, asserting that social phenomena were subject to general laws that could be discovered using the scientific method. He proposed a science of soci-

In carrying on the great task of rational ethnography, the investigation of the causes which have produced the phenomena of culture, and the laws to which they are subordinate, it is desirable to work out as systematically as possible a scheme of evolution of this culture along its many lines. In the following chapter [of Primitive Culture], on the Development of Culture, an attempt is made to sketch a theoretical course of civilization among mankind, such as appears on the whole most accordant with the evidence. By comparing the various stages of civilization among races known to history, with the aid of archaeological inference from the remains of prehistoric tribes, it seems possible to judge in a rough way of an early general condition of man, which from our point of view is to be regarded as a primitive condition, whatever yet earlier state may in reality have lain behind it. This hypothetical primitive condition corresponds in a considerable degree to that of modern savage tribes, who, in spite of their difference and distance, have in common certain elements of civilization, which seem remains of an early state of the human race at large. If this hypothesis be true, then, notwithstanding the continual interference of degeneration, the main tendency of culture from primeval up to modern times has been from savagery towards civilization. On the problem of this relation of savage to civilized life, almost every one of the thousands of facts discussed in the succeeding chapters has its direct bearing. Survival in Culture, placing all along the course of advancing civilization way-marks full

of meaning to those who can decipher their signs, even now sets up in our midst primeval monuments of barbaric thought and life. Its investigation tells strongly in favor of the view that the European may find among the Greenlanders or Maoris many a trait for reconstructing the picture of his own primitive ancestors. Next comes the problem of the Origin of Language. Obscure as many parts of this problem still remain, its clearer positions lie open to the investigation whether speech took its origin among mankind in the savage state, and the result of the enquiry is that, consistently with all known evidence, this may have been the case. From examination of the Art of Counting a far more definite consequence is shown. It may be confidently asserted that not only is this important art found in a rudimentary state among savage tribes, but that satisfactory evidence proves numeration to have been developed by a rational invention from this low stage up to that in which we ourselves possess it. The examination of Mythology contained in the first volume is for the most part made from a special point of view, on evidence collected for a special purpose, that of tracing the relation between the myths of savage tribes and their analogues among more civilized nations. The issue of such enquiry goes far to prove that the earliest myth-maker arose and flourished among savage hordes, setting on foot an art which his more cultured successors would carry on, till its results came to be fossilized in superstition, mistaken for history, shaped and draped in poetry, or cast aside as lying folly.[15]

---

ety and is often considered a founder of sociology. Comte had a profound influence on the social scientists of Tylor's generation and was a particularly powerful influence on Émile Durkheim (1858–1917) and his followers in the early years of the twentieth century.

G. W. Dasent (1817–1896) was a translator of Scandinavian folktales, a lawyer, and a professor of English Literature and Modern History at King's College London. In his discussion of Norse tales, Dasent argues that the saying to which Tylor refers comes from the belief that some people can understand the language of animals which is evidenced in folktales.

Sir Henry Sumner Maine (1822–1888) was a legal historian and cultural evolupionist whose *Ancient Law* (1861) informed many of the anthropological discussions of Tylor's day. This passage shows an example of Maine's use of survivals.

William Blackstone (1723–1780) was an English jurist best known for writing *Commentaries on the Laws of England*.

15. This and the following passages introduce the rest of *Primitive Culture*. In subsequent chapters, Tylor, using the comparative method and focusing on the presence of survivals will trace out his version of the origin and development of language, counting, mythology, and especially religion.

Nowhere, perhaps, are broad views of historical development more needed than in the study of religion. Notwithstanding all that has been written to make the world acquainted with the lower theologies, the popular ideas of their place in history and their relation to the faiths of higher nations are still of the mediaeval type. It is wonderful to contrast some missionary journals with Max Muller's Essays, and to set the unappreciating hatred and ridicule that is lavished by narrow hostile zeal on Brahmanism, Buddhism, Zoroastrism, beside the catholic sympathy with which deep and wide knowledge can survey those ancient and noble phases of man's religious consciousness; nor, because the religions of savage tribes may be rude and primitive compared with the great Asiatic systems, do they lie too low for interest and even for respect. The question really lies between understanding and misunderstanding them. Few who will give their minds to master the general principles of savage religion will ever again think it ridiculous, or the knowledge of it superfluous to the rest of mankind. Far from its beliefs and practices being a rubbish heap of miscellaneous folly, they are consistent and logical in so high a degree as to begin, as soon as even roughly classified, to display the principles of their formation and development; and these principles prove to be essentially rational, though working in a mental condition of intense and inveterate ignorance. It is with a sense of attempting an investigation which bears very closely on the current theology of our own day, that I have set myself to examine systematically, among the lower races, the development of Animism; that is to say, the doctrine of souls and other spiritual beings in general. More than half of the present work is occupied with a mass of evidence from all regions of the world, displaying the nature and meaning of this great element of the Philosophy of Religion, and tracing its transmission, expansion, restriction, modification, along the course of history into the midst of our own modern thought. Nor are the questions of small practical moment which have to be raised in a similar attempt to trace the development of certain prominent Rites and Ceremonies—customs so full of instruction as to the inmost powers of religion, whose outward expression and practical result they are.[16]

In these investigations, however, made rather from an ethnographic than a theological point of view, there has seemed little need of entering into direct controversial argument, which indeed I have taken pains to avoid as far as possible. The connexion which runs through religion, from its rudest forms up to the status of an enlightened Christianity, may be conveniently treated of with little recourse to dogmatic theology. The rites of sacrifice and purification may be studied in their stages of development without entering into questions of their authority and value, nor does an examination of the successive phases of the world's belief in a future life demand a discussion of the arguments adduced for or against the doctrine itself. The ethnographic results may then be left as materials for professed theologians, and it will not perhaps be long before evidence so fraught with meaning shall take its legitimate place. To fall back once again on the analogy of natural history, the time may soon come when it will be thought as unreasonable for a scientific student of theology not to have a competent acquaintance with the principles of the religions of the lower races, as for a

---

16. Note Tylor's treatment of religion in this paragraph. He begins by condemning those who dismiss or condemn the religion of others and argues for a careful appraisal and appreciation of the religions of other societies, even those he and his contemporaries thought of as primitive. This critique is aimed not only at the Christian missionaries that Tylor mentions but also at other scholars. Many of Tylor's contemporaries suggested that since "primitive" religion was illogical and irrational, it did not lend itself to scientific study. These included Lewis Henry Morgan (1818–1881), who, though he wrote on Iroquois beliefs, considered all "primitive" religions to be "grotesque and to some extent unintelligible" (see essay 3). Tylor, on the other hand, asserted that, properly understood, "primitive" religious beliefs had rational bases. He further insisted that the development of religion, like most everything else, followed progressive, evolutionary laws. In much of the text that follows this assertion, Tylor traced what he believed was the evolution of religion from animism (a term he coined) to "enlightened Christianity."

physiologist to look with the contempt of fifty years ago on evidence derived from the lower forms of life, deeming the structure of mere invertebrate creatures matter unworthy of his philosophic study.[17]

Not merely as a matter of curious research, but as an important practical guide to the understanding of the present and the shaping of the future, the investigation into the origin and early development of civilization must be pushed on zealously. Every possible avenue of knowledge must be explored, every door tried to see if it is open. No kind of evidence need be left untouched on the score of remoteness or complexity, of minuteness or triviality. The tendency of modern enquiry is more and more toward the conclusion that if law is anywhere, it is everywhere. To despair of what a conscientious collection and study of facts may lead to, and to declare any problem insoluble because difficult and far off, is distinctly to be on the wrong side in science; and he who will choose a hopeless task may set himself to discover the limits of discovery. One remembers Comte starting in his account of astronomy with a remark on the necessary limitation of our knowledge of the stars: we conceive, he tells us, the possibility of determining their form, distance, size, and movement, whilst we should never by any method be able to study their chemical composition, their mineralogical structure, &c. Had the philosopher lived to see the application of spectrum analysis to this very problem his proclamation of the dispiriting doctrine of necessary ignorance would perhaps have been recanted in favor of a more hopeful view. And it seems to be with the philosophy of remote human life somewhat as with the study of the nature of the celestial bodies. The processes to be made out in the early stages of our mental evolution lie distant from us in time as the stars lie distant from us in space, but the laws of the universe are not limited with the direct observation of our senses. There is vast material to be used in our enquiry; many workers are now busied in bringing this material into shape, though little may have yet been done in proportion to what remains to do; and already it seems not too much to say that the vague outlines of a philosophy of primaeval history are beginning to come within our view.[18]

AUTHOR'S NOTE

a. Blackstone, "Commentaries," "As every man's own blood is compounded of the bloods of his respective ancestors, he only is properly of the whole or entire blood with another, who hath (so far as the distance of degrees will permit), all the same ingredients in the composition of his blood that the other hath," etc.

---

17. Tylor is careful to distinguish his ethnographic work from a theological defense of or attack on particular beliefs. However, notice the passage here about his evidence taking its legitimate place. Tylor believed that rational, scientific knowledge was displacing religious belief. Although Tylor was certainly no atheist, he implies that many of the religious practices of his day are survivals of early humans' misunderstanding of the world. Note the anticlerical undercurrents in these passages. Tylor obliquely implies that Christianity itself was a survival that would not endure rational examination.

18. In this final paragraph, Tylor positions himself in the early years of an anthropology which he believes will have the same scientific rigor as astronomy. *Primitive Culture* and Tylor's other work, particularly his editing of and contributions to the fieldworker's guide *Notes and Queries* had an important influence on future generations of anthropologists. Some of his ideas about animism continued to be used in the anthropology of religion. However, though he held a museum position at Oxford University from 1884 until his death and received a knighthood in 1912, he was unable to establish anthropology as a university discipline. His hopes for a scientific anthropology based on the evolutionary comparison of society were also frustrated. In Britain, later anthropologists would turn to the detailed investigation of individual societies and largely ignore questions of social evolution. In the United States, anthropologists in the early twentieth century would vigorously reject Tylor's style of evolutionary thinking.

By the 1930s, evolutionary anthropology was being reconsidered by some American scholars, particularly Leslie White (1900–1975) and Julian Steward (1902–1972) (see essays 16 and 17). But this new evolutionism rejected key elements of Tylor's theory.

3. Ethnical Periods

Lewis Henry Morgan (1818–1881)

THE LATEST investigations respecting the early condition of the human race are tending to the conclusion that mankind commenced their career at the bottom of the scale and worked their way up from savagery to civilization through the slow accumulations of experimental knowledge.[1]

As it is undeniable that portions of the human family have existed in a state of savagery, other portions in a state of barbarism, and still other portions in a state of civilization, it seems equally so that these three distinct conditions are connected with each other in a natural as well as necessary sequence of progress. Moreover, that this sequence has been historically true of the entire human family, up to the status attained by each branch respectively, is rendered probable by the conditions under which all progress occurs, and by the known advancement of several branches of the family through two or more of these conditions.

An attempt will be made in the following pages to bring forward additional evidence of the rudeness of the early condition of mankind, of the gradual evolution of their mental and moral powers through experience, and of their protracted struggle with opposing obstacles while winning their way to civilization. It will be drawn, in part, from the great sequence of inventions and discoveries which stretches along the entire pathway of human progress; but chiefly from domestic institutions, which express the growth of certain ideas and passions.[2]

As we re-ascend along the several lines of progress toward the primitive ages of mankind, and eliminate one after the other, in the order in which they appeared, inventions and discoveries on the one hand, and institutions on the other, we are enabled to perceive that the former stand to each other in progressive, and the latter in unfolding relations. While the former class have had a connection, more or less direct,

---

From *Ancient Society* (1877)

1. In this first paragraph, Morgan shows that he, like other nineteenth-century anthropologists, viewed cultural evolution as progressive. His statement that humans worked their way up "to civilization through the slow accumulations of experimental knowledge" sounds Darwinian, but the relationship between Morgan's and Darwin's work is difficult to judge. Morgan had corresponded with Charles Darwin (1809–1882) and visited him at Down House in 1871. However, Morgan's ideas are closer to those of Jean-Baptiste Lamarck (1744–1829) than to Darwin's. Further, his understanding of the progressive nature of human evolution was rooted in the Presbyterian theology of his close friend Joshua McIlvaine (1815–1897). McIlvaine was a philologist who lectured at Princeton and the University of Pennsylvania. He opposed degenerationism and supported the idea that humanity had risen from low origins to a high estate. However, McIlvaine (and probably Morgan) as well rejected any possibility of a biological connection between humans and nonhuman animals. McIlvaine wrote, "Man has come up from a low state and there is a splendid future before him. But he never came from the beast" (quoted in Service 1981: 28).

2. Like many others of his day, Morgan held that progress was a moral force. Humanity had not only developed increasingly complex and sophisticated institutions and technologies but modern people were also morally superior to "savages" whom he described as "held down by [their] low animal appetites and passions" (1910: 41). Notice that Morgan speaks of "winning" civilization. The influence of the concept of evolution as a battle for survival is evident in Morgan's characterization of cultural evolution as a "protracted struggle." Both competition and struggle play a greater role in Morgan's work than in that of E. B. Tylor (1832–1917).

the latter have been developed from a few primary germs of thought. Modern institutions plant their roots in the period of barbarism, into which their germs were transmitted from the previous period of savagery. They have had a lineal descent through the ages, with the streams of the blood, as well as a logical development.[3]

Two independent lines of investigations thus invite our attention. The one leads through inventions and discoveries, and the other through primary institutions. With the knowledge gained therefrom, we may hope to indicate the principal stages of human development. The proofs to be adduced will be drawn chiefly from domestic institutions; the references to achievements more strictly intellectual being general as well as subordinate.[4]

The facts indicate the gradual formation and subsequent development of certain ideas, passions, and aspirations. Those which hold the most prominent positions may be generalized as growths of the particular ideas with which they severally stand connected. Apart from inventions and discoveries they are the following:

I.	Subsistence,	V.	Religion,
II.	Government,	VI.	House Life and
III.	Language,		Architecture,
IV.	The Family,	VII.	Property.

First. Subsistence has been increased and perfected by a series of successive arts, introduced at long intervals of time, and connected more or less directly with inventions and discoveries.[5]

Second. The germ of government must be sought in the organization into **gentes** in the

---

3. Several aspects of Morgan's thought are evident in this paragraph. Note that Morgan discusses two different types of evolution: first, the growth of intelligence, illustrated by inventions and discoveries, and second, the evolution of institutions. Part 1 of *Ancient Society* deals with the first of these. The remaining three parts deal with the growth of institutions that Morgan deemed central: government, the family, and property.

4. Morgan was interested in the evolution of culture as a pan-human event but divides the evidence used in his analysis. He proposed to trace the development of "inventions and discoveries" but considered them subordinate to the development of the primary institutions of government, family, and property. Morgan believed that inventions and discoveries were correlated with stages of cultural evolution but developed by different processes. Inventions evolve by logically building from one to the next. Primary institutions have "unfolding relations." They were seeded as germs of thought in the period of Savagery, germinated in the period of Barbarism, and flowered in Civilization.

5. The importance Morgan places on the role of subsistence has given rise to a long debate on the role of materialism in his work. Karl Marx (1818–1883) and Friedrich Engels (1820–1895) believed that Morgan's work was materialist and supported their own. In 1884, in the preface to *The Origin of the Family, Private Property, and the State,* Engels wrote, "Morgan, in his own way . . . discovered afresh in America the materialistic conception of history discovered by Marx." Marxist anthropologists such as Eleanor Leacock (1922–1987) have also seen Morgan as a materialist. However, there are also clear differences between Morgan and Marx. To be truly materialist, Morgan must believe that social evolution is driven by the physical conditions of society. However, in many places, it is obvious that he believes that social evolution has biological roots and is associated with the "gradual enlargement of the brain itself, particularly of the cerebral portion" (1910: 36). For example, in *Ancient Society*, Morgan writes, "We have the same brain . . . which worked in the skulls of barbarians. . . . It is the same brain grown older and larger with the experience of the ages. . . . Out of a few germs of thought have been evolved all the principal institutions of mankind. . . . The evolution of these germs of thought has been guided by a natural logic which formed an essential attribute of the brain itself" (1910: 59–60). In another section of *Ancient Society* Morgan speaks of the inferior brain size of Native Americans and the "pre-eminent endowment" of the Aryan and Semitic families. Morgan's understanding of the brain sizes of different groups was based on the work of Samuel G. Morton (1799–1851). Thomas Trautmann and Karl Sanford Kabelac's 1994 study of Morgan's library shows he had taken notes on Morton's work. In Morton's most famous works, *Crania Americana* (1839) and *Crania Aegyptica* (1844), Morton claimed that whites had bigger brains than any other group and concluded that they were intellectually and morally superior to those other groups. Morton's data (although not his conclusions) were largely accepted until 1981 when Harvard biologist Stephen Jay Gould

Status of savagery; and followed down, through the advancing forms of this institution, to the establishment of political society.[6]

Third. Human speech seems to have been developed from the rudest and simplest forms of expression. Gesture or sign language, as intimated by Lucretius,[a] must have preceded articulate language, as thought preceded speech. The monosyllabical preceded the syllabical, as the latter did that of concrete words. Human intelligence, unconscious of design, evolved articulate language by utilizing the vocal sounds. This great subject, a department of knowledge by itself, does not fall within the scope of the present investigation.[7]

Fourth. With respect to the family, the stages of its growth are embodied in systems of consanguinity and affinity, and in usages relating to marriage, by means of which, collectively, the family can be definitely traced through several successive forms.[8]

Fifth. The growth of religious ideas is environed with such intrinsic difficulties that it may never receive a perfectly satisfactory exposition. Religion deals so largely with the imaginative and emotional nature, and consequently with such uncertain elements of knowledge, that all primitive religions are grotesque and to some extent unintelligible. This subject also falls without the plan of this work excepting as it may prompt incidental suggestions.[9]

---

published an analysis showing Morton had committed gross errors in sampling and had incorrectly analyzed his data. When Gould corrected these errors and reanalyzed Morton's skulls, he found no significant differences between the skull volumes of different ethnic groups in Morton's collection. Perhaps unsurprisingly, Gould's work has also been challenged. Lewis et al. (2011), also re-examined both Morton and Gould. They reject Morton's racism and note that cranial capacity is not correlated with race or intelligence, and "largely a function of climate." However, they argue that given the materials Morton had and the techniques he used, his report was accurate despite his clear biases. They charge that it was Gould whose biases affected his analysis. But this work has been challenged as well. Weisberg and Paul (2016) argue that Lewis et al.'s analysis does not address Morton's key claims and that Gould's account of the effect of Morton's bias on his research and analysis remains intact.

6. **"Gentes"**: Latin, "a patrilineal clan."

7. Morgan here refers to the Roman philosopher and poet Lucretius (96?–55 BCE), author of *De rerum natura,* a lengthy poem that explicates his understanding of Epicurean philosophy. Morgan gives the Latin original in endnote a. The translation by William Ellery Leonard (Lucretius 1916) is "And urged for children and the womankind/Mercy, of fathers, whilst with cries and gestures/They stammered hints how meet it was that all/Should have compassion on the weak."

Book 5 of *De rerum natura* was an important text for many nineteenth-century scholars. In it, Lucretius describes the origin and evolution of animals and plants, the origins of humanity, and its rise from savagery to civilization. Although Lucretius's version of evolution is fanciful, it clearly shows movement from the simple to the complex. In his 2011 book *The Swerve: How the World Became Modern*, Stephen Greenblatt argues that the recovery of Lucretius's work in the fifteenth century was a key moment in the making of the modern world.

8. The evolution of the family had long been a major focus of Morgan's work. He had published *Systems of Kinship and Affinity of the Human Family*, one of the founding documents of kinship studies, in 1871. In *Systems,* Morgan divides all kinship systems into descriptive and classificatory systems and identifies the kinships now known as Omaha, Crow, Iroquois, and Malayan. Morgan understood the family as evolving from primitive promiscuity to civilized monogamy. An important influence on Morgan was Johann Jakob Bachofen (1815–1887). In his 1861 book *Das Mutterrecht (Mother Right)*, Bachofen argued that motherhood was the prehistoric source of human society and that matriarchal societies were an earlier stage of social evolution. Bachofen's work was influential in the thinking of Morgan and Engels.

9. The idea that religion was not fit for scientific study because it was "imaginative and emotional" was common among nineteenth-century anthropologists. However, it was specifically rejected by E. B. Tylor, who attempted to trace the evolutionary history of religion in *Primitive Culture* (see essay 2).

Sixth. House architecture, which connects itself with the form of the family and the plan of domestic life, affords a tolerably complete illustration of progress from savagery to civilization. Its growth can be traced from the hut of the savage, through the communal houses of the barbarians, to the house of the single family of civilized nations, with all the successive links by which one extreme is connected with the other. This subject will be noticed incidentally.

Lastly. The idea of property was slowly formed in the human mind, remaining nascent and feeble through immense periods of time. Springing into life in savagery, it required all the experience of this period of barbarism to develop the germ, and to prepare the human brain for the acceptance of its controlling influence. Its dominance as a passion over all other passions marks the commencement of civilization. It not only led mankind to overcome the obstacles which delayed civilization, but to establish political society on the basis of territory and of property. A critical knowledge of the evolution of the idea of property would embody, in some respects, the most remarkable portion of the mental history of mankind.[10]

It will be my object to present some evidence of human progress along these several lines, and through successive ethnical periods, as it is revealed by inventions and discoveries, and by the growth of the ideas of government, of the family, and of property.

It may be here premised that all forms of government are reducible to two general plans, using the word plan in its scientific sense. In their bases the two are fundamentally distinct. The first, in the order of time, is founded upon persons, and upon relations purely personal, and may be distinguished as a society (societas). The **gens** is the unit of this organization; giving as the successive stages of integration, in the archaic period, the gens, the **phratry**, the tribe, and the confederacy of tribes, which constituted a people or nation (populus). At a later period a coalescence of tribes in the same area into a nation took the place of a confederacy of tribes occupying independent areas. Such, through prolonged ages, after the gens appeared, was the substantially universal organization of ancient society; and it remained among the Greeks and Romans after civilization supervened. The second is founded upon territory and upon property, and may be distinguished as a state (civitas). The township or ward, circumscribed by **metes** and **bounds**, with the property it contains, is the basis or unit of the latter, and political society is the result. Political society is organized upon territorial areas, and deals with property as well as with persons through territorial relations. The successive stages of integration are the township or ward, which is the unit of organization; the county or province, which is an aggregation of townships or wards; and the national domain or territory, which is an aggregation of counties or provinces; the people of each of which are organized into a body politic. It taxed the Greeks and Romans to the extent of their capacities, after they had gained civilization, to invent the deme or township and the city ward; and thus inaugurate the second great plan of government, which remains among civilized nations to the present hour. In ancient society this territorial plan was unknown. When it came in it fixed the boundary line between

---

10. Morgan's assertion that the concept of property led to the beginning of civilization as well as the establishment of political organizations may have had its origin in the work of John Locke (1632–1704), but it dovetails nicely with Marxist concerns. One can see why Marx and Engels were so interested in Morgan's work. Marx read and extensively annotated *Ancient Society* but died before he was able to publish anything about it. Thus it was Engels who had the task of integrating Morgan into Marxist theory. In 1884, Engels, working from Marx's annotations, published *The Origin of the Family, Private Property and the State*, which he subtitled *In the Light of the Researches of Lewis Henry Morgan*. There, he claimed Morgan had proven Marx's theory by demonstrating that private property and the state were only passing phases in the continuing evolution of human society. Although Engels believed *Ancient Society* confirmed the truth of Marxist analysis, Morgan was not a Marxist. His ideas of psychic unity and unilineal evolution are very different from Marx's notions that human nature is contingent and created through labor (see essay 4, note 11).

ancient and modern society, as the distinction will be recognized in these pages.[11]

It may be further observed that the domestic institutions of the barbarous, and even of the savage ancestors of mankind, are still exemplified in portions of the human family with such completeness that, with the exception of the strictly primitive period, the several stages of this progress are tolerably well preserved. They are seen in the organization of society upon the basis of sex, then upon the basis of kin, and finally upon the basis of territory; through the successive forms of marriage and of the family, with the systems of consanguinity thereby created; through house life and architecture; and through progress in usages with respect to the ownership and inheritance of property.[12]

The theory of human degradation to explain the existence of savages and of barbarians is no longer tenable. It came in as a corollary from the Mosaic cosmogony, and was acquiesced in from a supposed necessity which no longer exists. As a theory, it is not only incapable of explaining the existence of savages, but it is without support in the facts of human experience.[13]

The remote ancestors of the Aryan nations presumptively passed through an experience similar to that of existing barbarous and savage tribes. Though the experience of these nations embodies all the information necessary to illustrate the periods of civilization, both ancient and modern, together with a part of that in the Later period of barbarism, their anterior experience must be deduced, in the main, from the traceable connection between the elements of their existing institutions and inventions, and similar elements still preserved in those of savage and barbarous tribes.[14]

---

11. Morgan postulated that there were two basic forms of government: one based on kinship and one based on property. He believed that ancient society was founded on kinship whereas the modern state was founded upon notions of territory and property.

"***Gens*** and ***gentes***" are synonymous terms for patrilineal clan.

A "**phratry**" is a unilineal descent group composed of related clans.

"**Metes** and **bounds**" are terms used for describing parcels of land. "Metes" refers to a boundary defined by the measurement of a straight run between two terminal points while "bounds" refers to a general boundary description based on landmarks.

12. This passage clearly illustrates Morgan's ideas of unilineal evolution and "primitive" societies as "living fossils." If all human societies are evolving along a single path, and if Europeans have the most advanced society, then it follows that non-European societies are earlier stages of European society. We can understand earlier stages in the evolution of European civilization by studying these primitive societies.

13. The "theory of degradation," or *degenerationism*, was based on the story of Adam and Eve's fall from Grace in Genesis (Morgan's "Mosaic cosmogony"). A leading degenerationist, W. Cooke Taylor (1800–1849), outlined this view in his 1840 book *Natural History of Society in the Barbarous and Civilized State*. Taylor described a sequence of fall from grace, flood, Tower of Babel, and diaspora after which some groups degenerated into savagery, while others, aided by God, progressed toward civilization (Taylor 1840: 311–28). The "supposed necessity" Morgan mentions here refers to the view that there had been a relatively brief period of time since creation. If humans had only been in existence for five thousand years, then there was time for them to degenerate from a perfect state but, scholars of the nineteenth century believed, insufficient time for them to advance from a primitive state. Morgan thought that advances in geology, particularly the work of Charles Lyell (1797–1875), had shown that the earth had great antiquity. He begins the preface of *Ancient Society* by declaring that "The great antiquity of mankind upon the earth has been conclusively established" (1910: v). Thus, there was adequate time for societies to evolve.

14. Morgan, like Tylor (see essay 2, note 19), follows the German linguist Max Müller (1823–1900) in his use of the term "Aryan." For Müller, a scholar of Hindu and Sanskrit, Aryan referred to the Indo-Iranian peoples of the Vedic period about 1500 BCE. However, in the late nineteenth century, Europeans adopted the term as a racial classification referring to light-skinned, fair-haired Europeans. That is not how Morgan is using the word here. Morgan had purchased a book of Müller's lectures in 1862 and was much impressed with his use of linguistic techniques to discover the relationships among people. He was particularly attracted by Müller's argu-

It may be remarked finally that the experience of mankind has run in nearly uniform channels; that human necessities in similar conditions have been substantially the same; and that the operations of the mental principle have been uniform in virtue of the specific identity of the brain of all the races of mankind. This, however, is but a part of the explanation of uniformity in results. The germs of the principal institutions and arts of life were developed while man was still a savage. To a very great extent the experience of the subsequent periods of barbarism and of civilization have been expended in the further development of these original conceptions. Wherever a connection can be traced on different continents between a present institution and a common germ, the derivation of the people themselves from a common original stock is implied.[15]

The discussion of these several classes of facts will be facilitated by the establishment of a certain number of Ethnical Periods; each representing a distinct condition of society, and distinguishable by a mode of life peculiar to itself. The terms "Age of Stone," "of Bronze," and "of Iron," introduced by Danish archaeologists, have been extremely useful for certain purposes, and will remain so for the classification of objects of ancient art; but the progress of knowledge has rendered other and different subdivisions necessary. Stone implements were not entirely laid aside with the introduction of tools of iron, nor of those of bronze. The invention of the process of smelting iron ore created an ethnical epoch, yet we could scarcely date another from the production of bronze. Moreover, since the period of stone implements overlaps those of bronze and of iron, and since that of bronze also overlaps that of iron, they are not capable of a circumscription that would leave each independent and distinct.[16]

It is probable that the successive arts of subsistence which arose at long intervals will ultimately, from the great influence they must have exercised upon the condition of mankind, afford the most satisfactory bases for these divisions. But investigation has not been carried far enough in this direction to yield the necessary information. With our present knowledge the main result can be attained by selecting such other inventions or discoveries as will afford sufficient tests of progress to character-

---

ment that the root of the word "Aryan" was derived from a word that meant "those who plow" (Tooker 1992: 365). Morgan adopted the word Aryan and argued that Aryans represented the highest degree of civilization.

Although he does not make it explicit, Morgan is referring in this paragraph to E. B. Tylor's concept of survivals. For more on survivals, see essay 2, note 16.

15. This paragraph contains a brief powerful expression of several of Morgan's key ideas. He argues that all human societies have followed (and will follow) similar paths because all humans have similar brains and similar mental processes (this is the result of the common origin of all humanity). However, this message of uniformity is modified by the second half of the paragraph. There he argues that although the origins of the principal institutions of human society date to the period of savagery, these institutions have developed through later periods. In the last sentence, he implies that this development is, at root, biological. The presence of similar, more advanced institutions in different places implies a common biological origin of the people whose society exhibits these institutions.

Morgan believed that his work showed that all humans had descended from a single creation and that all societies had the potential to evolve. Thus, he believed that all humans had the potential to be equal. But do not mistake this for a belief in actual, current-day equality. Morgan, like most scientists of his day, believed people of Northern European descent were superior to all others. You will note that he consistently identifies the Greek, Roman, and Aryan peoples as evolving first and fastest, consigning Asian, African, and Mesoamerican civilizations to earlier stages in his evolutionary scheme.

16. The terms Stone Age, Bronze Age, and Iron Age were introduced by the first curator of the Danish National Museum, Christian J. Thomsen (1788–1865), to chronologically rank European artifacts in an 1807 exhibit. This "three-age system," as it came to be known, was soon widely used throughout Europe (Fagan 1989: 34). Morgan critiques Thomsen's system as unable to create historically consistent non-overlapping classes of society. Ironically, this was a criticism later leveled against Morgan's work.

ize the commencement of successive ethnical periods. Even though accepted as provisional, these periods will be found convenient and useful. Each of those about to be proposed will be found to cover a distinct culture, and to represent a particular mode of life.[17]

The period of savagery, of the early part of which very little is known, may be divided, provisionally, into three subperiods. These may be named respectively the Older, the Middle, and the Later period of savagery; and the condition of society in each, respectively, may be distinguished as the Lower, the Middle, and the Upper Status of savagery.[18]

In like manner, the period of barbarism divides naturally into three subperiods, which will be called, respectively, the Older, the Middle, and the Later period of barbarism; and the condition of society in each, respectively, will be distinguished as the Lower, the Middle, and the Upper Status of barbarism.

It is difficult, if not impossible, to find such tests of progress to mark the commencement of these several periods as will be found absolute in their application, and without exceptions upon all the continents. Neither is it necessary, for the purpose in hand, that exceptions should not exist. It will be sufficient if the principal tribes of mankind can be classified, according to the degree of their relative progress, into conditions which can be recognized as distinct.

I.   Lower Status of Savagery[19]
This period commenced with the infancy of the human race, and may be said to have ended with the acquisition of a fish subsistence and of a knowledge of the use of fire. Mankind were then living in their original restricted habitat, and subsisting upon fruits and nuts. The commencement of articulate speech belongs to this period. No exemplification of tribes of mankind in this condition remained to the historical period.

II. Middle Status of Savagery
It commenced with the acquisition of a fish subsistence and a knowledge of the use of fire, and ended with the invention of the bow and arrow. Mankind, while in this condition, spread from their original habitat over the greater portion of the earth's surface. Among tribes still existing it will leave in the Middle Status of savagery, for example, the Australians and the greater part of the Polynesians when discovered. It will be sufficient to give one or more exemplifications of each status.

III. Upper Status of Savagery
It commenced with the invention of the bow and arrow, and ended with the invention of the art of pottery. It leaves in the Upper Status of Savagery the Athapascan tribes of the Hudson's Bay Territory, the tribes of the valley of the Columbia, and certain coast tribes of North and South America; but with relation to the time of their discovery. This closes the period of Savagery.

---

17. Morgan's goal was to outline the stages of cultural evolution. He proposed that ultimately, these would be marked by changes in subsistence patterns. However, arguing that not enough is known about these, he chooses to mark the beginnings and ends of stages by the acquisition of specific technological innovations and kin patterns. Half a century later, the links Morgan made between subsistence, technology, and cultural evolution would be essential in the work of the neoevolutionists Leslie White (1900–1975) and Julian Steward (1902–1972) (see essays 16 and 17). White in particular would see Morgan's work as an inspiration for his own. In the next several paragraphs Morgan outlines his design for separating one stage of cultural evolution from another.

18. Note that Morgan tells us that the oldest periods of savagery are very little known. This is because he believed that all societies had already passed through these periods and thus, no current-day ethnographic example of them could be found to study. They remained conjectural.

19. Here Morgan begins to outline the factors upon which he distinguishes the stages of cultural evolution. Morgan noted above that such markers need not be absolutely reliable. However, later critics charged that Morgan's markers were so unreliable as to be useless, lumping together societies that we now consider to have vastly different levels of social organization.

IV. Lower Status of Barbarism

The invention or practice of the art of pottery, all things considered, is probably the most effective and conclusive test that can be selected to fix a boundary line, necessarily arbitrary, between savagery and barbarism. The distinctness of the two conditions has long been recognized, but no criterion of progress out of the former into the latter has hitherto been brought forward. All such tribes, then, as never attained to the art of pottery will be classed as savages, and those possessing this art but who never attained a phonetic alphabet and the use of writing will be classed as barbarians.

The first sub-period of barbarism commenced with the manufacture of pottery, whether by original invention or adoption. In finding its termination, and the commencement of the Middle Status, a difficulty is encountered in the unequal endowments of the two hemispheres, which began to be influential upon human affairs after the period of savagery had passed. It may be met, however, by the adoption of equivalents. In the Eastern hemisphere, the domestication of animals, and the Western, the cultivation of maize and plants by irrigation, together with the use of adobe-brick and stone in house building have been selected as sufficient evidence of progress to work a transition out of the Lower and into the Middle Status of barbarism. It leaves, for example, in the Lower Status, the Indian tribes of the United States east of the Missouri River, and such tribes of Europe and Asia as practiced the art of pottery, but were without domestic animals.

V. Middle Status of Barbarism

It commenced with the domestication of animals in the Eastern hemisphere, and in the Western with cultivation by irrigation and with the use of abode-brick and stone in architecture, as shown. Its termination may be fixed with the invention of the process of smelting iron ore. This places in the Middle Status, for example, the Village Indians of New Mexico, Mexico, Central America and Peru, and such tribes in the Eastern hemisphere as possessed domestic animals but were without a knowledge of iron. The ancient Britons, although familiar with the use of iron, fairly belong in this connection. The vicinity of more advanced continental tribes had advanced the arts of life among them far beyond the state of development of their domestic institutions.[20]

VI. Upper Status of Barbarism

It commenced with the manufacture of iron, and ended with the invention of a phonetic alphabet, and the use of writing in literary composition. Here civilization begins. This leaves in the Upper Status, for example, the Grecian tribes of the Homeric age, the Italian tribes shortly before the founding of Rome, and the Germanic tribes of the time of Caesar.

VII. Status of Civilization

It commenced, as stated, with the use of a phonetic alphabet and the production of literary records, and divides into Ancient and Modern. As an equivalent, hieroglyphical writing upon stone may be admitted.

Each of these periods has a distinct culture and exhibits a mode of life more or less special

---

20. A society's evolutionary stage was gauged by its technology, subsistence pattern, and kin and family structure together. Consequently, although groups such as the ancient Britons had acquired technological achievements of more advanced societies, such as the use of iron (diagnostic of Upper Barbarism), Morgan believes that the development of their domestic institutions places them squarely in the stage of Middle Barbarism.

and peculiar to itself. This specialization of ethnical periods renders it possible to treat a particular society according to its condition of relative advancement, and to make it a subject of independent study and discussion. It does not affect the main result that different tribes and nations on the same continent, and even of the same linguistic family, are in different conditions at the same time, since for our purpose the condition of each is the material fact, the time being immaterial.

Since the use of pottery is less significant than that of domestic animals, of iron, or of a phonetic alphabet, employed to mark the commencement of subsequent ethnical periods, the reasons for its adoption should be stated. The manufacture of pottery presupposes village life, and considerable progress in the simple arts.[b] Flint and stone implements are older than pottery, remains of the former having been found in ancient repositories in numerous instances unaccompanied by the latter. A succession of inventions of greater need and adapted to a lower condition must have occurred before the want of pottery would be felt. The commencement of village life, with some degree of control over subsistence, wooden vessels and utensils, finger weaving with filaments of bark, basket making, and the bow and arrow make their appearance before the art of pottery. The Village Indians who were in the Middle Status of barbarism, such as the Zuñians, the Aztecs and the Cholulans, manufactured pottery in large quantities and in many forms of considerable excellence; the partially Village Indians of the United States, who were in the Lower Status of barbarism, such as the Iroquois, the Choctas, and the Cherokees, made it in smaller quantities and in a limited number of forms; but the non-horticultural Indians, who were in the Status of savagery, such as the Athapascans, the tribes of California and of the valley of the Columbia, were ignorant of its use.[c] In Lubbock's Pre-Historic Times, in Tylor's Early History of Mankind, and in Peschel's Races of Man, the particulars respecting this art, and the extent of its distribution, have been collected with remarkable breadth of research. It was unknown in Polynesia (with the exception of the Islands of the Tongans and Fijians), in Australia, in California, and in the Hudson's Bay Territory. Mr. Tylor remarks that "the art of weaving was unknown in most of the Islands away from Asia," and that "in most of the South Sea Islands there was no knowledge of pottery."[d] The Rev. Lorimer Fison, an English missionary residing in Australia, informed the author in answer to inquiries, that "the Australians had no woven fabrics, no pottery, and were ignorant of the bow and arrow." This last fact was also true in general of the Polynesians. The introduction of the ceramic art produced a new epoch in human progress in the direction of an improved living and increased domestic conveniences. While flint and stone implements—which came in earlier and required long periods of time to develop all their uses—gave the canoe, wooden vessels and utensils, and ultimately timber and plank in house architecture,[e] pottery gave a durable vessel for boiling food, which before that had been rudely accomplished in baskets coated with clay, and in ground cavities lined with skin, the boiling being effected with heated stones.[f, 21]

---

21. In this paragraph, Morgan defends his choice of pottery as a marker of evolutionary stages. However, the passage is noted chiefly for Morgan's citations of key scholars of his age. Morgan begins by citing Tylor, Lubbock, and Fison, whose works were influential to his thinking.

John Lubbock (1834–1913), also known as Lord Avebury for his purchase of the prehistoric Avebury Circle, was an amateur ethnologist and natural historian. A prosperous banker and liberal member of Parliament, Lubbock served as president of the Royal Anthropological Institute and Ethnological Society of London. His boyhood home was near that of Darwin, with whom he became a close friend. Later, he became a staunch defender of Darwin's *On the Origin of Species*. Lubbock developed an evolutionary theory of human society based on his study of European and North American archaeology. He proposed a natural progression of social evolution from the primitive to the civilized, inventing the terms *paleolithic* and *neolithic*. He published his ideas in *Prehistoric Times* (1865) and *The Origin of Civilization* (1870). Morgan had met Lubbock on his European tour in 1870 and purchased his books on his return to the United States (Tooker 1992: 369).

Lorimer Fison (1832–1907) was a missionary, journalist, and anthropologist. Morgan's studies of kinship were based on extensive questionnaires sent to European travelers and missionaries. While in Fiji in 1869,

Recapitulation

Periods.	Conditions.
I. Older Period of Savagery,	I. Lower Status of Savagery,
II. Middle Period of Savagery,	II. Middle Status of Savagery,
III. Later Period of Savagery,	III. Upper Status of Savagery,
IV. Older Period of Barbarism,	IV. Lower Status of Barbarism,
V. Middle Period of Barbarism,	V. Middle Status of Barbarism,
VI. Later Period of Barbarism,	VI. Upper Status of Barbarism,
	VII. Status of Civilization.
I. Lower Status of Savagery,	From the Infancy of the Human Race to the commencement of the next Period.
II. Middle Status of Savagery,	From the acquisition of a fish subsistence and the knowledge of the use of fire, to etc.
III. Upper Status of Savagery,	From the Invention of the Bow and Arrow, to etc.
IV. Lower Status of Barbarism,	From the Invention of the Art of Pottery, to etc.
V. Middle Status of Barbarism,	From the Domestication of animals on the Eastern Hemisphere, and on the Western, from the cultivation of maize and plants by Irrigation, with the use of adobe-brick and stone, to etc.
VI. Upper Status of Barbarism,	From the Invention of the process of smelting Iron Ore, with the use of Iron tools, to etc.
VII. Status of Civilization,	From the Invention of a Phonetic Alphabet, with the use of writing, to the present time.

Whether the pottery of the aborigines was hardened by fire or cured by the simple process of drying, has been made a question. Prof E. T. Cox, of Indianapolis, has shown by comparing the analyses of ancient pottery and hydraulic cements, "that so far as chemical constituents are concerned it (the pottery) agrees very well with the composition of hydraulic stones." He

---

Fison received one of these. It drew his interest to anthropology, and he became an ardent follower of Morgan, with whom he corresponded extensively. Fison's research into Australian aboriginal kinship systems, based on interviews with European settlers, provided important data for Tylor, J. G. Frazer (1854–1941), and Émile Durkheim (1858–1917), as well as Morgan.

Morgan also cites the German geographer Oscar Peschel (1826–1875), whose most famous work *The Races of Man and Their Geographical Distribution* (1876) classified humans into seven races—Australians and Tasmanians, Papuans, Mongoloids, Dravidians, Hottentots, and Bushmen, Negroes, and Mediterraneans—and is a compilation of the ethnography and archaeology of his day. Among many topics, it discusses human evolution, language, technology, religion, marriage, and family. In an 1876 review, Alfred Russel Wallace wrote that the book "impresses one painfully with the still chaotic state of the infant science of anthropology." Wallace anticipated some of the later critiques of nineteenth-century evolutionary anthropology when he complained that Peschel focused on easily obtainable facts rather than on information that could only be obtained by systematic, long-term observation.

Also note that in this paragraph Morgan places Polynesians in Middle Savagery together with Australian Aborigines. Morgan's later critics saw this as an example of an illogical grouping created by his theory. Aboriginal society was organized by family-based foraging bands. Polynesian society, though without pottery or the technological innovations Morgan mentions here, was composed of highly stratified chiefdoms and was far more complex.

By the way, it's interesting to note the typographical errors in Morgan's footnote b. Morgan substitutes Edwin for Edward and Minkind for Mankind. These errors date to the original 1877 edition of the work (in the British edition the Minkind/Mankind error is corrected but the Edwin/Edward error is not) and are reproduced in many subsequent editions.

remarks further, that "all the pottery belonging to the mound-builders' age, which I have seen, is composed of alluvial clay and sand, or a mixture of the former with pulverized freshwater shells. A paste made of such a mixture possesses in a high degree the properties of hydraulic Puzzuolani and Portland cement, so that vessels formed of it hardened without being burned, as is customary with modern pottery. The fragments of shells served the purpose of gravel or fragments of stone as at present used in connection with hydraulic lime for the manufacture of artificial stone."[g] The composition of Indian pottery in analogy with that of hydraulic cement suggests the difficulties in the way of inventing the art, and tends also to explain the lateness of its introduction in the course of human experience. Notwithstanding the ingenious suggestion of Prof. Cox, it is probable that pottery was hardened by artificial heat. In some cases the fact is directly attested. Thus Adair, speaking of the Gulf Tribes, remarks that "they make earthen pots of very different sizes, so as to contain from two to ten gallons, large pitchers to carry water, bowls, dishes, platters, basins, and a prodigious number of other vessels of such antiquated forms as would be tedious to describe, and impossible to name. Their method of glazing them is, they place them over a large fire of smoky pitchpine, which makes them smooth, black and firm."[h, 22]

Another advantage of fixing definite ethnical periods is the direction of special investigation to those tribes and nations which afford the best exemplification of each status, with the view of making each both standard and illustrative. Some tribes and families have been left in geographical isolation to work out the problems of progress by original mental effort; and have, consequently, retained their arts and institutions pure and homogeneous; while those of other tribes and nations have been adulterated through external influence. Thus, while Africa was and is an ethnical chaos of savagery and barbarism, Australia and Polynesia were in savagery, pure and simple, with the arts and institutions belonging to that condition. In like manner, the Indian family of America, unlike any other existing family, exemplified the condition of mankind in three successive ethnical periods. In the undisturbed possession of a great continent, of common descent, and with homogeneous institutions, they illustrated, when discovered, each of these conditions, and especially those of the Lower and of the Middle Status of barbarism, more elaborately and completely than any other portion of mankind. The far northern Indians and some of the coast tribes of North and South America were in the Upper Status of savagery, the partially Village Indians east of the Mississippi were in the Lower Status of barbarism, and the Village Indians of North and South America were in the Middle Status. Such an opportunity to recover full and minute information of the course of human experience and progress in developing their arts and institutions through these successive conditions has not been offered within the historical period. It must be added that it has been indifferently improved. Our greatest deficiencies relate to the last period named.[23]

---

22. Edward Travers Cox (1821–1907) was the state geologist for Indiana.

23. For Morgan, all humans shared a single origin but different groups represented different branches on a human cultural evolutionary tree. In this passage, he proposes that ideal types for each status can be found, particularly in Australia, Polynesia, and America. Africans, however, pose particular problems, and Africa is described as being in "ethnical chaos." Morgan's understanding of Africa and of Africans in the United States is, by modern standards, disturbing. In *Systems of Consanguinity* (1871: 462), Morgan wrote, "The people of pure negro stock are known to be limited in numbers on the African continent. . . . Unimportant in numbers, feeble in intellect, and inferior in rank to every other portion of the human family, they yet center in themselves, in their unknown past and mysterious present, one of the greatest problems in the science of the families of mankind. They seem to challenge and to traverse all the evidences of the unity of origin of the human family by their excessive deviation from such a standard of the species as would probably be adopted on the assumption of unity of origin." Of Morgan's understanding of the African presence in the United States, Yael Ben-Zvi (2007: 209) writes, "By leaping from an imagined Native American past to the post–Civil War United States, Morgan imagines that slavery never existed, and portrays the colonization of Native American lands as a natural event. The existence

Differences in the culture of the same period in the Eastern and Western hemispheres undoubtedly existed in consequence of the unequal endowments of the continents; but the condition of society in the corresponding status must have been, in the main, substantially similar.

The ancestors of the Grecian, Roman, and German tribes passed through the stages we have indicated, in the midst of the last of which the light of history fell upon them. Their differentiation from the undistinguishable mass of barbarians did not occur, probably, earlier than the commencement of the Middle Period of barbarism. The experience of these tribes has been lost, with the exception of so much as is represented by the institutions, inventions and discoveries which they had brought with them, and possessed when they first came under historical observation. The Grecian and Latin tribes of the **Homeric and Romulian periods** afford the highest exemplification of the Upper Status of barbarism. Their institutions were likewise pure and homogeneous, and their experience stands directly connected with the final achievement of civilization.[24]

Commencing, then, with the Australians and Polynesians, following with the American Indian tribes, and concluding with the Roman and Grecian who afford the highest exemplifications respectively of the six great stages of human progress, the sum of their united experiences may be supposed fairly to represent that of the human family from the Middle Status of savagery to the end of ancient civilization.

Consequently, the Aryan nations will find the type of the condition of their remote ancestors, when in savagery, in that of the Australians and Polynesians; when in the Lower Status of barbarism in that of the partially Village Indians of America; and when in the Middle Status in that of the Village Indians, with which their own experience in the Upper Status directly connects. So essentially identical are the arts, institutions and mode of life in the same status upon all the continents, that the archaic form of the principal domestic institutions of the Greeks and Romans must even now be sought in the corresponding institution of the American aborigines, as will be shown in the course of this volume. This fact forms a part of the accumulating evidence tending to show that the principal institutions of mankind have been developed from a few primary germs of thought; and that the course and manner of their development was predetermined, as well as restricted within narrow limits of divergence, by the natural logic of the human mind and the necessary limitations of its powers. Progress has been found to be substantially the same in kind in tribes and nations inhabiting different and even disconnected continents, while in the same status, with deviations from uniformity in particular instances produced by special causes. The argument when extended tends to establish the unity of origin of mankind.

In studying the condition of tribes and nations in these several ethnical periods we are dealing, substantially, with the ancient history and condition of our own remote ancestors.[25]

---

of Africans is perceived as an aberration in national, scientific, and human terms." Brad Hume (2008: 146) notes that Morgan argued in favor of interbreeding Europeans and Native Americans and believed that it would benefit both groups. The same was not true of interbreeding with Africans. Morgan hoped the biological and cultural mixing of Europeans and Native Americans would "establish a new national and scientific order that would absorb red into white and make black disappear" (Ben-Zvi 2007: 209).

24. The **Homeric and Romulian periods** refer to the times of Homer, the Greek poet of the eighth century BCE, and Romulus, the mythological founder of Rome in 753 BCE.

25. In these concluding paragraphs Morgan outlines key aspects of his theory. Societies evolve through specific stages from savagery to civilization. Because all human minds operate by the same "natural logic" (an idea often called *psychic unity*), the course of this evolution is virtually identical everywhere. Thus, currently existing non-European societies are "living fossils" and are comparable to earlier states of today's most advanced societies. By comparing societies in the states of savagery and barbarism to each other and to earlier states of civilized society, a complete picture of the evolution of human society can be developed. This idea is usually called the comparative method. (Note that in this context the comparative method is

AUTHOR'S NOTES

a. Et pueros commendarunt mulierbreque saeclum Vocibus, et gestu, cum balbe significarent, Imbecillorum esse aequm miserier omnium.
—De Rerum Natura, lib. v, 1020.

b. Mr. Edwin B. Tylor observes that Goquet "first propounded, in the last century, the notion that the way in which pottery came to be made, was that people daubed such combustible vessels as these with clay to protect them from fire, till they found that clay alone would answer the purpose, and thus the art of pottery came into the world."—*Early History of Minkind*, p. 237. Goquet relates of Capt. Gonneville who visited the southeast coast of South America in 1503, that he found "their household utensils of wood, even their boiling pots, but plastered with a kind of clay, a good finger thick, which prevented the fire from burning them."—Ib. 273.

c. Pottery has been found in aboriginal mounds in Oregon within a few years past.—Foster's *Pre-Historic Races of the United States*, I, 152. The first vessels of pottery among the Aborigines of the United States seem to have been made in baskets of rushes or willows used as moulds which were burned off after the vessel hardened.—Jones's *Antiquities of Southern Indians*, p. 461. Prof. Rau's article on Pottery. *Smithsonian Report*, 1866, p. 352.

d. *Early History of Mankind*, p. 181; *Pre-Historic Times*, pp. 437, 441, 462, 477, 533, 542.

e. Lewis and Clarke (1805) found plank in use in houses among the tribes of the Columbia River.—*Travels*, Longman's Ed., 1814, p. 503. Mr. John Keast Lord found "cedar plank chipped from the solid tree with chisels and hatchets made of stone," in Indian houses on Vancouver's Island.—*Naturalist in British Columbia*, I, 169.

Moisture at 212 F., 1.00	
Silica,	36.00
Carbonate of Lime,	25.50
Carbonate of Magnesia,	3.02
Alumina,	5.00
Peroxide of Iron,	5.50
Sulphuric Acid,	.20
Organic Matter (alkalies and loess),	23.60
	100.00

f. Tylor's *Early History of Mankind*, p. 265, et seq.

g. *Geological Survey of Indiana*, 1873, p. 119. He gives the following analysis: Ancient Pottery, "Bone Bank," Posey Co., Indiana.

h. *History of the American Indians*, London. ed., 1775, p. 424. The Iroquois affirm that in ancient times their forefathers cured their pottery before a fire.

---

not simply the comparison of different societies. It implies using this comparison to place societies on an evolutionary scale.) The doctrine of psychic unity justified the belief that cultures evolved following a single pathway and that this pathway could be discerned using the comparative method. However, note the circular logic used in this argument: Why are we justified in using the comparative method? Because cultures evolved following a single pathway. Why did cultures evolve following a single pathway? Because of the psychic unity of mankind. How do we know that the psychic unity of humans exists? Because cultures evolve along a single pathway.

4. Feuerbach: Opposition of the Materialist and Idealist Outlook

Karl Marx (1818–1883) and Friedrich Engels (1820–1895)

THE ILLUSIONS OF GERMAN IDEOLOGY

AS WE HEAR FROM German ideologists, Germany has in the last few years gone through an unparalleled revolution. The decomposition of the Hegelian philosophy, which began with Strauss, has developed into a universal ferment into which all the "powers of the past" are swept. In the general chaos mighty empires have arisen only to meet with immediate doom, heroes have emerged momentarily only to be hurled back into obscurity by bolder and stronger rivals. It was a revolution beside which the French Revolution was child's play, a world struggle beside which the struggles of the **Diadochi** appear insignificant. Principles ousted one another, heroes of the mind overthrew each other with unheard-of rapidity, and in the three years 1842–45 more of the past was swept away in Germany than at other times in three centuries.[1]

All this is supposed to have taken place in the realm of pure thought.

Certainly it is an interesting event we are dealing with: the putrescence of the absolute spirit. When the last spark of its life had failed, the various components of this **caput mortuum** began to decompose, entered into new combinations and formed new substances. The industrialists of philosophy, who till then had lived on the exploitation of the absolute spirit, now seized upon the new combinations. Each with all possible zeal set about retailing his apportioned share. This naturally gave rise to competition, which, to start with, was carried on in moderately staid bourgeois fashion. Later when the German market was glutted, and the commodity in spite of all efforts found no response in the world market, the business was spoiled in the usual German manner by fabricated and fictitious production, deterioration in quality, adulteration of the raw materials, falsification of labels, fictitious purchases,

---

1. Marx and Engels, living in exile in Belgium, collaborated on *The German Ideology* in 1845 and 1846. They sent the manuscript to Germany for publication, but political crises prevented it from appearing. Marx later remarked that it had been abandoned to "the gnawing criticism of the mice" (1970 [1846]: 1). At the time *The German Ideology* was written, Marx and Engels were developing a thoroughly materialist worldview, which separated them from other German philosophers. *The German Ideology* is the first relatively complete statement of this worldview, although the materialist position it presents is foreshadowed in works like "On the Jewish Question" (1963 [1844]) and *The Holy Family* (1975 [1845]). The complete version of *The German Ideology* was not available until the 1930s. Thus, while theorists of the early twentieth century were profoundly affected by Marx, they did not have this particular work.

Ludwig Andreas Feuerbach (pronounced to rhyme with "lawyer-lock") (1804–1872) was a radical Hegelian philosopher whose critical work *The Essence of Christianity* had appeared in 1841. Feuerbach argues that religion in general and Christianity in particular are projections of human nature. Attributes such as love and charity are not divine because God possesses them but, rather, God possesses them because humans think they are divine. Thus, he proposed that religion had a material basis in human thought (and no "real" God existed). Marx was deeply impressed by Feuerbach's work. Shortly before writing *The German Ideology* he penned "Theses on Feuerbach," which consists of eleven brief responses to Feuerbach's work. "Theses on Feuerbach" was first published decades later as an appendix to Engels's 1888 work *Ludwig Feuerbach and the End of Classical German Philosophy*.

"Diadochi": the successors of Alexander the Great who fought among each other for control of the empire he left.

bill jobbing and a credit system devoid of any real basis. The competition turned into a bitter struggle, which is now being extolled and interpreted to us as a revolution of world significance, the begetter of the most prodigious results and achievements.[2]

If we wish to rate at its true value this philosophic charlatanry, which awakens even in the breast of the honest German citizen a glow of national pride, if we wish to bring out clearly the pettiness, the parochial narrowness of this whole Young-Hegelian movement and in particular the tragicomic contrast between the illusions of these heroes about their achievements and the actual achievements themselves, we must look at the whole spectacle from a standpoint beyond the frontiers of Germany.[3]

German criticism has, right up to its latest efforts, never quitted the realm of philosophy. Far from examining its general philosophic premises, the whole body of its inquiries has actually sprung from the soil of a definite philosophical system, that of Hegel. Not only in their answers but in their very questions there was a mystification. This dependence on Hegel is the reason why not one of these modern critics has even attempted a comprehensive criticism of the Hegelian system, however much each professes to have advanced beyond Hegel. Their polemics against Hegel and against one another are confined to this—each extracts one side of the Hegelian system and turns this against the whole system as well as against the sides extracted by the others. To begin with they extracted pure unfalsified Hegelian categories such as "substance" and "self-consciousness," later they desecrated these categories with more secular names such as "species," "the Unique," "Man," etc.

The entire body of German philosophical criticism from Strauss to Stirner is confined to criticism of religious conceptions. The critics started from real religion and actual theology. What religious consciousness and a religious conception really meant was determined variously as they went along. Their advance consisted in subsuming the allegedly dominant metaphysical, political, juridical, moral and other conceptions under the class of religious or theological conceptions; and similarly in pronouncing political, juridical, moral consciousness as religious or theological, and the political, juridical, moral man—"man" in the last resort—as religious. The dominance of religion was taken for granted. Gradually every dominant relationship was pronounced

---

2. Marx, like all German philosophers of the nineteenth century, was profoundly influenced by the work of Georg Wilhelm Friedrich Hegel (1770–1831). Hegel's philosophy described history as the complex relationship between human beings and absolute spirit, or God. Hegel related the history of this relationship to human freedom under different political conditions. Hegel was both deeply religious and conservative.

In this and subsequent paragraphs, Marx and Engels provide a satirical history of philosophy in Germany following the death of Hegel. After Hegel's death, his supporters split into two camps: the Right Hegelians and the Young Hegelians. The Right Hegelians stayed close to Hegel's teaching, concerning themselves with a spiritual and essentially conservative understanding of philosophy. The Young Hegelians, with whom Marx associated as a young man, held on to Hegel's ideas of historical progress toward freedom but rejected the notion that freedom was possible under existing forms of the state. They supported political programs varying from liberal democracy to anarchism. In this paragraph, Marx makes fun of these philosophical camps and claims that their contributions are worthless.

"Caput mortuum": Latin, "death's head"; in chemistry and alchemy, the worthless residue of a chemical operation.

3. Although he opposed the Right Hegelians, Marx's target here is the Young Hegelians, the group with whom he had formerly been associated. Additionally, Marx writes from a position outside of Germany. In 1842, Marx had become editor of a liberal newspaper called *Rheinische Zeitung*. In this position, he published increasingly radical critiques of the Prussian government and calls for democratization. This resulted in government censorship. In March 1843, the Prussian government closed the paper, and Marx fled to Paris. He lived in Paris from 1843 to 1845 when the French government, acting on a request from the Prussian government, expelled him. He moved on to Brussels, where he remained until 1848. *The German Ideology* was begun during Marx's stay in Paris but completed in Belgium.

a religious relationship and transformed into a cult, a cult of law, a cult of the State, etc. On all sides it was only a question of dogmas and belief in dogmas. The world sanctified to an ever-increasing extent till at last our venerable Saint Max was able to canonize it en bloc and thus dispose of it once for all.[4]

The Old Hegelians had comprehended everything as soon as it was reduced to an Hegelian category. The Young Hegelians criticized everything by attributing to it religious conceptions or by pronouncing it a theological matter. The Young Hegelians are in agreement with the Old Hegelians in their belief in the rule of religion, of concepts, of a universal principle in the existing world. Only, the one party attacks this dominion as usurpation, while the other extols it as legitimate.[5]

Since the Young Hegelians consider conceptions, thoughts, ideas, in fact all the products of consciousness, to which they attribute an independent existence, as the real chains of men (just as the Old Hegelians declared them the true bonds of human society) it is evident that the Young Hegelians have to fight only against these illusions of consciousness. Since, according to their fantasy, the relationships of men, all their doings, their chains and their limitations are products of their consciousness, the Young Hegelians logically put to men the moral postulate of exchanging their present consciousness for human, critical or egoistic consciousness, and thus of removing their limitations. This demand to change consciousness amounts to a demand to interpret reality in another way, i.e. to recognize it by means of another interpretation. The Young-Hegelian ideologists, in spite of their allegedly "world-shattering" statements, are the staunchest conservatives. The most recent of them have found the correct expression for their activity when they declare they are only fighting against "phrases." They forget, however, that to these phrases they themselves are only opposing other phrases, and that they are in no way combating the real existing world when they are merely combating the phrases of this world. The only results which this philosophic criticism could achieve were a few (and at that thoroughly one-sided) elucidations of Christianity from the point of view of religious history;—all the rest of their assertions are only further embellishments of their claim to have furnished, in these unimportant elucidations, discoveries of universal importance.

It has not occurred to any one of these philosophers to inquire into the connection of

---

4. Much of *The German Ideology* is a critique of the Young Hegelians, a group of which David Friedrich Strauss (1808–1874) and Max Stirner (born Kaspar Schmidt, 1806–1856) were prominent members. Strauss and Stirner were both radical and influential. In *The Life of Jesus* (1835) Strauss argued that the gospels were not literally true, and that Jesus was not divine but simply a historic human figure. The gospels were poetic evidence of man's desire to transcend history and reach for the absolute spirit described by Hegel.

Stirner, an anarchist ridiculed here as Saint Max, bears the brunt of Marx and Engels's attack. Stirner's influential book *The Ego and Its Own* was published in 1844. In it, he attacked Feuerbach, pointing out inconsistencies in his analysis of Christianity and calling for radical atheism. For Stirner, oppression and alienation are created through ideas that people accept as holy or sacred (hence Marx and Engels's epithets "holy" and "Saint"); freedom, on the other hand, originates through the ego's creation of its own ideas. The implication of this was individualist anarchy: People should be concerned only with their own welfare and accept no constraints on their actions. Identification with groups such as social classes was a form of oppression. For Marx and Engels, who saw individuals as existing primarily within social groups such as classes, this notion was radically wrong.

5. Both the Right Hegelians (here the Old Hegelians) and the Young Hegelians were much concerned with religion. However, religion was largely a surrogate for discussing politics and the state, taboo subjects for debate within Germany. Hegel had been quite conservative. He saw the relationship of individuals to the state as a historical and spiritual process fueled by dialectical contradiction and culminating in absolute freedom. He believed this freedom was possible under the Prussian monarchy (which, incidentally, employed him). In supporting the truths of religion, the Right Hegelians were closely following Hegel and supporting the Prussian state. In arguing that religion could not be understood as truth, the Young Hegelians were arguing against the state.

German philosophy with German reality, the relation of their criticism to their own material surroundings.[6]

FIRST PREMISES OF MATERIALIST METHOD

The premises from which we begin are not arbitrary ones, not dogmas, but real premises from which abstraction can only be made in the imagination. They are the real individuals, their activity and the material conditions under which they live, both those which they find already existing and those produced by their activity. These premises can thus be verified in a purely empirical way.[7]

The first premise of all human history is, of course, the existence of living human individuals. Thus the first fact to be established is the physical organization of these individuals and their consequent relation to the rest of nature. Of course, we cannot here go either into the actual physical nature of man, or into the natural conditions in which man finds himself— geological, **oreohydrographical**, climatic

and so on. The writing of history must always set out from these natural bases and their modification in the course of history through the action of men.

Men can be distinguished from animals by consciousness, by religion or anything else you like. They themselves begin to distinguish themselves from animals as soon as they begin to produce their means of subsistence, a step which is conditioned by their physical organization. By producing their means of subsistence men are indirectly producing their actual material life.[8]

The way in which men produce their means of subsistence depends first of all on the nature of the actual means of subsistence they find in existence and have to reproduce. This mode of production must not be considered simply as being the production of the physical existence of the individuals. Rather it is a definite form of activity of these individuals, a definite form of expressing their life, a definite mode of life on their part. As individuals express their life, so they are. What they are, therefore, coincides with their production, both with what they produce and with how they produce. The nature of

---

6. Marx and Engels accuse the Hegelians of believing that changing the way that people think will lead to changes in the world. For example, the Marxist scholars Howard Selsem and Harry Martel write that for Stirner, "All one had to do to get rid of the state, of religion, of poverty, etc., was to recognize that they were merely spooks, and to assert in the loudest possible tones that the only thing that counts is one's own ego" (1963: 280). Marx argues that the work of Hegel's followers, Right and Left, had only minimal effect since they have ignored the relationship between ways of thinking and the material conditions of life. Note also the strong implication that the goal of philosophy is social change. In the eleventh thesis on Feuerbach, Marx wrote, "The philosophers have only interpreted the world, in various ways; the point is to change it."

7. For Hegel and his followers, the world was conditioned by ideas, and history was about the progress of the human spirit. For Marx, human society was based on specific material conditions, and history was driven by conflicts at the core of society. This is the root of Marx and Engels's disagreements with Hegelians. Here and in the following paragraphs they lay out a preliminary materialist understanding of the world. Note the emphasis on empirical verification. Marx and Engels and their followers claimed that their philosophy was scientific and, because of this, believed that Marx's predictions, such as a worldwide communist revolution and the fall of capitalism, were as inevitable as gravity.

8. This paragraph contains a critical Marxist insight. For Hegel, humans are separated from animals by self-consciousness, but this self-consciousness entails alienation from God. For Marx and Engels, humans are distinguished from all other creatures by conscious control of the processes of production. Animals simply eat. Humans, on the other hand, must produce their food. Thus, human consciousness derives from the fact that labor is necessary for human existence and society.

"Oreohydrography": the study of drainage phenomena in mountains.

individuals thus depends on the material conditions determining their production.[9]

This production only makes its appearance with the increase of population. In its turn this presupposes the intercourse of individuals with one another. The form of this intercourse is again determined by production.

The relations of different nations among themselves depend upon the extent to which each has developed its productive forces, the division of labour and internal intercourse. This statement is generally recognized. But not only the relation of one nation to others, but also the whole internal structure of the nation itself depends on the stage of development reached by its production and its internal and external intercourse. How far the productive forces of a nation are developed is shown most manifestly by the degree to which the division of labour has been carried. Each new productive force, insofar as it is not merely a quantitative extension of productive forces already known (for instance the bringing into cultivation of fresh land), causes a further development of the division of labour.[10]

The division of labour inside a nation leads at first to the separation of industrial and commercial from agricultural labour, and hence to the separation of town and country and to the conflict of their interests. Its further development leads to the separation of commercial from industrial labour. At the same time through the division of labour inside these various branches there develop various divisions among the individuals co-operating in definite kinds of labour. The relative position of these individual groups is determined by the methods employed in agriculture, industry and commerce (patriarchalism, slavery, estates, classes). These same conditions are to be seen (given a more developed intercourse) in the relations of different nations to one another.[11]

The various stages of development in the division of labour are just so many different forms of ownership, i.e. the existing stage in the division of labour determines also the relations of individuals to one another with reference to the material, instrument, and product of labour.[12]

The first form of ownership is tribal ownership. It corresponds to the undeveloped stage of production, at which a people lives by hunting and fishing, by the rearing of beasts or, in the highest stage, agriculture. In the latter case it presupposes a great mass of uncultivated stretches of land. The division of labour is at

---

9. Here Marx and Engels pursue the importance of labor further: Production is more than simply feeding oneself; through labor people create their society. Since human nature is determined by the social conditions under which people live, humans, through labor, create their own nature.

10. Note that Marx believes that history is characterized by evolutionary progress through a series of stages. Different nations are at different stages of this process. Like the Hegelians, Marx and Engels believed that history had a beginning and an end. For Marx, its beginning was awareness of production, and its end was the emergence of a worldwide communist society. Between these two, society passed through a series of scientifically knowable stages, each characterized by a particular mode of production and its associated forms of property. Changes in human consciousness are part of this historical progression. There can be no experience of transcendental human nature before the end of history and the emergence of a universal communist society.

11. The developments Marx and Engels outline here are reminiscent of work by Adam Smith (1723–1790) on the division of labor. Marx had read Smith's *The Wealth of Nations* in 1843 (Levine 1987: 435) and was deeply influenced by his work. However, while Smith saw the division of labor as leading to the achievement of the greatest good for the greatest number, Marx and Engels focused on the alienation and oppression it generates. For them, these conflicts were critical to social development.

12. The interplay between technology and the social relationships through which technology is put to work is central to Marx and Engels's theory. The idea of ownership is key to this. Note Marx's emphasis on ownership as a particular kind of social relationship rather than simply a natural aspect of the world.

this stage still very elementary and is confined to a further extension of the natural division of labour existing in the family. The social structure is, therefore, limited to an extension of the family; patriarchal family chieftains, below them the members of the tribe, finally slaves. The slavery latent in the family only develops gradually with the increase of population, the growth of wants, and with the extension of external relations, both of war and of barter.[13]

The second form is the ancient communal and State ownership which proceeds especially from the union of several tribes into a city by agreement or by conquest, and which is still accompanied by slavery. Beside communal ownership we already find movable, and later also immovable, private property developing, but as an abnormal form subordinate to communal ownership. The citizens hold power over their labouring slaves only in their community, and on this account alone, therefore, they are bound to the form of communal ownership. It is the communal private property which compels the active citizens to remain in this spontaneously derived form of association over against their slaves. For this reason the whole structure of society based on this communal ownership, and with it the power of the people, decays in the same measure as, in particular, immovable private property evolves. The division of labour is already more developed. We already find the antagonism of town and country; later the antagonism between those states which represent town interests and those which represent country interests, and inside the towns themselves the antagonism between industry and maritime commerce. The class relation between citizens and slaves is now completely developed.[14]

With the development of private property, we find here for the first time the same conditions which we shall find again, only on a more exten-

---

13. Marx and Engels have stated that humans produce their own nature through labor. However, in this passage, they ground their analysis in a claim about the "natural division of labour existing in the family." These assertions seem to contradict each other. Note that Marx and Engels envision the "natural" family as consisting of a patriarch who controls the members of his tribe. Although a powerful male head of the household was a feature of European society of their time, it is hardly a universal aspect of primitive societies. Additionally, Marx and Engels cite no evidence to support their understanding of the family. They were aware of this problem, but almost thirty years would pass before the 1877 publication of *Ancient Society* by Lewis Henry Morgan, which they believed provided the evidence that proved their point.

Both Marx and Engels had interesting family lives. Shortly before he wrote *The German Ideology* Marx had married his childhood sweetheart, Jenny von Westphalen (1814–1881). They remained married until her death. They had seven children together but only three survived to adulthood. Marx was deeply critical of bourgeois society, but at the same time wanted Victorian respectability. However, his claims to respectability were challenged by his poverty and the birth of Henry Frederick Demuth (1851–1929), the child of Marx's housekeeper Helen Demuth (1820–1890). Demuth left the father's name off Henry Frederick's birth certificate. Though questions remain about his paternity (Carver 2005), most current scholars believe he was Marx's child and further, that to retain Marx's respectability Engels took credit for Henry Frederick. Engels could easily do this because he supported Marx financially as well as intellectually and did not believe in marriage at all. Engels had long-term relationships with two proletarian Irish sisters, Mary and Lizzy Burns (Beatty 2021). Mary (1821–1863) was Engels's partner from the 1840s until her sudden death in 1863. After Mary's death, Engels lived with her sister Lizzy (1827–1878) until her death in 1878. In her final days, Lizzie became worried about religion and the afterlife. To help quiet her fears, Engels married Lizzie hours before her death. Engel's relationship with the Burns sisters had a deep effect on his understanding of the proletariat, nationalism, and feminism (Hunt 2009).

14. Marx and Engels's description of the evolution of society is fanciful but note that the emphasis in this paragraph is on groups of individuals that stand in particular relationships to each other (town and country, citizen and slave, industry and commerce). Further, citizens are compelled to group together and hold certain forms of property because of their relationship to slaves. Thus, a relation of production (slavery) compels a social relation. Marx and Engels see the actions of individuals as largely subordinate to the key social classes of which they are members. Note as well that the relationships among these groups are characterized by conflict. Marx and Engels believed that progress was driven by conflict between groups.

sive scale, with modern private property. On the one hand, the concentration of private property, which began very early in Rome (as the **Licinian agrarian law** proves) and proceeded very rapidly from the time of the civil wars and especially under the Emperors; on the other hand, coupled with this, the transformation of the plebeian small peasantry into a proletariat, which, however, owing to its intermediate position between propertied citizens and slaves, never achieved an independent development.[15]

The third form of ownership is feudal or estate property. If antiquity started out from the town and its little territory, the Middle Ages started out from the country. This different starting-point was determined by the sparseness of the population at that time, which was scattered over a large area and which received no large increase from the conquerors. In contrast to Greece and Rome, feudal development at the outset, therefore, extends over a much wider territory, prepared by the Roman conquests and the spread of agriculture at first associated with it. The last centuries of the declining Roman Empire and its conquest by the barbarians destroyed a number of productive forces; agriculture had declined, industry had decayed for want of a market, trade had died out or been violently suspended, the rural and urban population had decreased. From these conditions and the mode of organization of the conquest determined by them, feudal property developed under the influence of the Germanic military constitution. Like tribal and communal ownership, it is based again on a community; but the directly producing class standing over against it is not, as in the case of the ancient community, the slaves, but the enserfed small peasantry. As soon as feudalism is fully developed, there also arises antagonism to the towns. The hierarchical structure of landownership, and the armed bodies of retainers associated with it, gave the nobility power over the serfs. This feudal organization was, just as much as the ancient communal ownership, an association against a subjected producing class; but the form of association and the relation to the direct producers were different because of the different conditions of production.[16]

This feudal system of landownership had its counterpart in the towns in the shape of corporative property, the feudal organization of trades. Here property consisted chiefly in the labour of each individual person. The necessity for association against the organized robber nobility, the need for communal covered markets in an age when the industrialist was at the same time a merchant, the growing competition of the escaped serfs swarming into the rising towns, the feudal structure of the whole coun-

---

15. Classical Greece and Rome provided key texts for authors of the nineteenth century. Most scholars of this era had an intimate knowledge of Greek and Roman history and philosophy (Marx himself had written his doctoral thesis on an issue in classical Greek philosophy). Additionally, because human life on earth was generally assumed to have had a fairly brief history, scholars assumed that the practices of early Greeks and Romans were fairly close to those of the most primitive people.

Notice here that Marx identifies three social classes in the late Roman Republic and early empire (so starting around 90 BCE): the landowners, the proletariat (those who sold their labor to the landowners for wages), and slaves.

"The Licinian law": (367 BCE) limited the amount of common land a Roman citizen could hold to about three hundred acres.

16. In Marx and Engels's view, feudal ownership derived from the material conditions of the end of the Roman Empire, in particular the collapse of the Roman economy. Both feudalism and the ancient society that preceded it involved the oppression of those who produced. The differences between these societies resulted from depopulation, disruption of distribution networks, and a change in the workforce from slaves to serfs. Once again social form is vitally influenced by production.

Marx's understanding of the conditions of Roman landownership and European feudalism as well as the importance these played in understanding society was deeply influenced by the members of the German historical school, particularly Georg Niebuhr (1776–1831). Niebuhr had argued that there were five forms of property ownership: oriental, tribal, classical, feudal, and modern (Levine 1987: 446). Marx built on this idea in this and other works.

try: these combined to bring about the guilds. The gradually accumulated small capital of individual craftsmen and their stable numbers, as against the growing population, evolved the relation of journeyman and apprentice, which brought into being in the towns a hierarchy similar to that in the country.[17]

Thus the chief form of property during the feudal epoch consisted on the one hand of landed property with serf labour chained to it, and on the other of the labour of the individual with small capital commanding the labour of journeymen. The organization of both was determined by the restricted conditions of production—the small-scale and primitive cultivation of the land, and the craft type of industry. There was little division of labour in the heyday of feudalism. Each country bore in itself the antithesis of town and country; the division into estates was certainly strongly marked; but apart from the differentiation of princes, nobility, clergy and peasants in the country, and masters, journeymen, apprentices and soon also the rabble of casual labourers in the towns, no division of importance took place. In agriculture it was rendered difficult by the **strip-system**, beside which the cottage industry of the peasants themselves emerged. In industry there was no division of labour at all in the individual trades themselves, and very little between them. The separation of industry and commerce was found already in existence in older towns; in the newer it only developed later, when the towns entered into mutual relations.[18]

The grouping of larger territories into feudal kingdoms was a necessity for the landed nobility as for the towns. The organization of the ruling class, the nobility, had, therefore, everywhere a monarch at its head.

The fact is, therefore, that definite individuals who are productively active in a definite way enter into these definite social and political relations. Empirical observation must in each separate instance bring out empirically, and without any mystification and speculation, the connection of the social and political structure with production. The social structure and the State are continually evolving out of the life-process of definite individuals, but of individuals, not as they may appear in their own or other people's imagination, but as they really are; i.e. as they operate, produce materially, and hence as they work under definite material limits, presuppositions and conditions independent of their will.[19]

The production of ideas, of conceptions, of consciousness, is at first directly interwoven with the material activity and the material intercourse of men, the language of real life. Conceiving, thinking, the mental intercourse of men, appear at this stage as the direct **efflux** of their material behaviour. The same applies to mental production as expressed in the language of politics, laws, morality, religion, metaphysics, etc. of a people. Men are the producers of their conceptions, ideas, etc.—real, active men, as they are conditioned by a definite development of their productive forces and of the intercourse corresponding to these, up to its furthest forms.

---

17. Guilds are created as a result of purely material processes. The urban organization master (or small capitalist), journeyman, and apprentice recapitulates the rural social organization of lord, military retainer, and enserfed peasant. Notice that Marx and Engels understood property as including both material goods and labor. The idea of labor as a commodity that can be bought and sold is crucial to their later analysis of capitalism.

18. **"Strip system"**: in medieval farming, peasant families had rights to a small strip of land (or several strips) within a large open field. Since only one crop was planted in a field, the strip system meant that many farming decisions had to be made by the community rather than the individual farmer.

19. Here Marx and Engels repeatedly stress that the processes they are talking about concern particular physical individuals and their specific physical actions. They mean to distinguish their materialist approach from the idealism of many Hegelians. However, also note that Marx and Engels talk of individuals "as they really are." They have no interest in characteristics like individual personality, imagination, soul, or destiny. For them, individuals "really are" the actions they take as they engage in production and the context in which these actions occur.

Consciousness can never be anything else than conscious existence, and the existence of men is their actual life-process. If in all ideology men and their circumstances appear upside-down as in a **camera obscura**, this phenomenon arises just as much from their historical life-process as the inversion of objects on the retina does from their physical life-process.[20]

In direct contrast to German philosophy which descends from heaven to earth, here we ascend from earth to heaven. That is to say, we do not set out from what men say, imagine, conceive, nor from men as narrated, thought of, imagined, conceived, in order to arrive at men in the flesh. We set out from real, active men, and on the basis of their real life-process we demonstrate the development of the ideological reflexes and echoes of this life-process. The phantoms formed in the human brain are also, necessarily, sublimates of their material life-process, which is empirically verifiable and bound to material premises. Morality, religion, metaphysics, all the rest of ideology and their corresponding forms of consciousness, thus no longer retain the semblance of independence. They have no history, no development; but men, developing their material production and their material intercourse, alter, along with this their real existence, their thinking and the products of their thinking. Life is not determined by consciousness, but consciousness by life. In the first method of approach the starting-point is consciousness taken as the living individual; in the second method, which conforms to real life, it is the real living individuals themselves, and consciousness is considered solely as their consciousness.[21]

This method of approach is not devoid of premises. It starts out from the real premises and does not abandon them for a moment. Its premises are men, not in any fantastic isolation and rigidity, but in their actual, empirically perceptible process of development under definite conditions. As soon as this active life-process is described, history ceases to be a collection of dead facts as it is with the empiricists (themselves still abstract), or an imagined activity of imagined subjects, as with the idealists.[22]

Where speculation ends—in real life—there real, positive science begins: the representation of the practical activity, of the practical process of development of men. Empty talk about consciousness ceases, and real knowledge has to take its place. When reality is depicted, philos-

---

20. Marx is arguing that society is created by the lives and actions of people as they exist in particular historical contexts. In 1852, in *The Eighteenth Brumaire of Louis Bonaparte*, Marx famously wrote, "Men make their own history, but they do not make it just as they please; they do not make it under circumstances chosen by themselves, but under circumstances directly encountered, given and transmitted from the past." Marx further argues that sometimes history can appear to be driven by ideas. However, he claims, this is an illusion created by natural law (in the same way an image appears upside down in a pinhole camera).

"**Efflux**": flowing outward.

"*Camera obscura*": what we might call a pinhole camera.

21. In this famous passage, Marx and Engels declare that consciousness does not create the material conditions of life but rather arises from them. Engels later said that with Hegel, the dialectic "is standing on its head. It must be turned right side up again, if you would discover the rational kernel within the mystical shell" (Engels, "On Dialectics"). Jonathan Friedman (1974) stresses the importance of understanding this passage. He points out that Marx and Engels are not promoting simple materialist determinism (which, following Marx, he calls vulgar materialism) but dialectical materialism, a process of change driven by opposition and contradiction.

22. In this paragraph, Marx is contrasting two philosophical perspectives, empiricism and idealism. Empiricism is the view that all knowledge is based on sensory experience. Idealism in general is the notion that reality is a mental construction.

In philosophy, a premise is a statement presumed to be true as the basis of a logical argument. Such premises are frequently unverifiable statements about the world, such as Hegel's presumption that absolute spirit exists. Marx, on the other hand, claims that his presumption is the existence of physical, empirical men living in verifiable historical conditions.

ophy as an independent branch of knowledge loses its medium of existence. At the best its place can only be taken by a summing-up of the most general results, abstractions which arise from the observation of the historical development of men. Viewed apart from real history, these abstractions have in themselves no value whatsoever. They can only serve to facilitate the arrangement of historical material, to indicate the sequence of its separate strata. But they by no means afford a recipe or schema, as does philosophy, for neatly trimming the epochs of history. On the contrary, our difficulties begin only when we set about the observation and the arrangement—the real depiction—of our historical material, whether of a past epoch or of the present. The removal of these difficulties is governed by premises which it is quite impossible to state here, but which only the study of the actual life-process and the activity of the individuals of each epoch will make evident. We shall select here some of these abstractions, which we use in contradistinction to the ideologists, and shall illustrate them by historical example.[23]

HISTORY: FUNDAMENTAL CONDITIONS

Since we are dealing with the Germans, who are devoid of premises, we must begin by stating the first premise of all human existence and, therefore, of all history, the premise, namely, that men must be in a position to live in order to be able to "make history." But life involves before everything else eating and drinking, a habitation, clothing and many other things. The first historical act is thus the production of the means to satisfy these needs, the production of material life itself. And indeed this is an historical act, a fundamental condition of all history, which today, as thousands of years ago, must daily and hourly be fulfilled merely in order to sustain human life. Even when the sensuous world is reduced to a minimum, to a stick as with Saint Bruno, it presupposes the action of producing the stick. Therefore in any interpretation of history one has first of all to observe this fundamental fact in all its significance and all its implications and to accord it its due importance. It is well known that the Germans have never done this, and they have never, therefore, had an earthly basis for history and consequently never an historian. The French and the English, even if they have conceived the relation of this fact with so-called history only in an extremely one-sided fashion, particularly as long as they remained in the toils of political ideology, have nevertheless made the first attempts to give the writing of history a materialistic basis by being the first to write histories of civil society, of commerce and industry.[24]

The second point is that the satisfaction of the first need (the action of satisfying, and the instrument of satisfaction which has been acquired) leads to new needs; and this produc-

---

23. This paragraph continues the contrast between Hegel's idealism and Marx and Engels's empiricism. Marx and Engels argue that Hegel is speculation, or "empty talk" about consciousness. They say that philosophical abstractions have little value except "to facilitate the arrangement of historical material." Marx and Engels's claim that human societies (and human beings themselves) can only be understood in an historical perspective and that there are fundamental laws that drive the process of history. They propose to sketch a brief outline of these laws in the following section.

24. Marx and Engels open this section with yet another satirical attack on the Young Hegelians, particularly Bruno Bauer (1809–1842) (their "Saint Bruno"). Bruno Bauer was the author of the 1841 *Critique of the Evangelical Gospels*, which traced the Greco-Roman roots of Christianity. Originally a conservative, Bauer had moved steadily to the left and by 1840 was associated with the Young Hegelians.

Marx and Engels's assertion that Germans have never had historians may strike the reader as odd, given Marx's reliance on German historians in the preceding paragraphs. However, by "history," Marx and Engels mean a materialist theory of history rather than either a listing of events or ideas.

The French and English referred to here are most likely the British economists Adam Smith and David Ricardo (1772–1823) and the French anarchist thinker Pierre-Joseph Proudhon (1809–1865). Although Marx and Engels disagreed with these thinkers, they were profoundly influenced by them.

tion of new needs is the first historical act. Here we recognize immediately the spiritual ancestry of the great historical wisdom of the Germans who, when they run out of positive material and when they can serve up neither theological nor political nor literary rubbish, assert that this is not history at all, but the "prehistoric era." They do not, however, enlighten us as to how we proceed from this nonsensical "prehistory" to history proper; although, on the other hand, in their historical speculation they seize upon this "prehistory" with especial eagerness because they imagine themselves safe there from inter-ference on the part of "crude facts," and, at the same time, because there they can give full rein to their speculative impulse and set up and knock down hypotheses by the thousand.[25]

The third circumstance which, from the very outset, enters into historical development, is that men, who daily remake their own life, begin to make other men, to propagate their kind: the relation between man and woman, parents and children, the family. The family, which to begin with is the only social rela-tionship, becomes later, when increased needs create new social relations and the increased population new needs, a subordinate one (excepting Germany), and must then be treated and analyzed according to the existing empiri-cal data, not according to "the concept of the family," as is the custom in Germany.[a]

These three aspects of social activity are not of course to be taken as three different stages, but just as three aspects or, to make it clear to the Germans, three "moments," which have existed simultaneously since the dawn of his-tory and the first men, and which still assert themselves in history today.[26]

The production of life, both of one's own in labour and of fresh life in procreation, now appears as a double relationship: on the one hand as a natural, on the other as a social relationship. By social we understand the co-operation of several individuals, no matter under what conditions, in what manner and to what end. It follows from this that a certain mode of production, or industrial stage, is always com-bined with a certain mode of co-operation, or social stage, and this mode of co-operation is itself a "productive force." Further, that the multitude of productive forces accessible to men determines the nature of society, hence, that the "history of humanity" must always be studied and treated in relation to the history of industry and exchange. But it is also clear how in Germany it is impossible to write this sort of history, because the Germans lack not only the necessary power of comprehension and the material but also the "evidence of their senses," for across the Rhine you cannot have any expe-rience of these things since history has stopped happening. Thus it is quite obvious from the start that there exists a materialistic connection of men with one another, which is determined by their needs and their mode of production, and which is as old as men themselves. This

---

25. In this paragraph, Marx and Engels provide a critical insight: The satisfaction of basic needs creates new needs. However, most of the paragraph is filled with invective against German intellectuals. This mixture of name-calling, satirical intellectual humor, polemic, and hyperbole set the tone for much of later writing by Marxists, although their indulgence in these tactics marginalized Marxists within academic discourse. This hyperbole may have been useful for political propaganda, but it made their work easier for others to dismiss.

26. Here Marx and Engels turn from production to the reproduction of society. They understood repro-duction as including both the biological process of human reproduction and the reproduction of social forms through time. Just as people must produce to live, societies must reproduce themselves to survive. The "three moments" comment is a reference to Hegel's *The Phenomenology of Spirit* (1807) in which he sorts his philo-sophical system into three parts: logic, philosophy of nature, and philosophy of spirit. Hegel divides the last part into three sections on subjective, objective, and absolute spirit. Marx and Engels satirically reproduce these three points as three moments manifested in the material world (people must produce to live, such pro-duction creates new needs, and people must reproduce). However, the critical point is that these "moments" are not a sequence but rather three continuous aspects of society.

This paragraph also contains Marx's footnote (printed at the end of this essay). Take a moment to read it. It includes an critical political idea. Marx believed that the Industrial Revolution was a necessary prerequisite for communism. This note explains his position.

connection is ever taking on new forms, and thus presents a "history" independently of the existence of any political or religious nonsense which in addition may hold men together.[27]

Only now, after having considered four moments, four aspects of the primary historical relationships, do we find that man also possesses "consciousness," but, even so, not inherent, not "pure" consciousness. From the start the "spirit" is afflicted with the curse of being "burdened" with matter, which here makes its appearance in the form of agitated layers of air, sounds, in short, of language. Language is as old as consciousness, language is practical consciousness that exists also for other men, and for that reason alone it really exists for me personally as well; language, like consciousness, only arises from the need, the necessity, of intercourse with other men. Where there exists a relationship, it exists for me: the animal does not enter into "relations" with anything, it does not enter into any relation at all. For the animal, its relation to others does not exist as a relation. Consciousness is, therefore, from the very beginning a social product, and remains so as long as men exist at all. Consciousness is at first, of course, merely consciousness concerning the immediate sensuous environment and consciousness of the limited connection with other persons and things outside the individual who is growing self-conscious. At the same time it is consciousness of nature, which first appears to men as a completely alien, all-powerful and unassailable force, with which men's relations are purely animal and by which they are overawed like beasts; it is thus a purely animal consciousness of nature (natural religion) just because nature is as yet hardly modified historically. (We see here immediately: this natural religion or this particular relation of men to nature is deter-

mined by the form of society and vice versa. Here, as everywhere, the identity of nature and man appears in such a way that the restricted relation of men to nature determines their restricted relation to one another, and their restricted relation to one another determines men's restricted relation to nature.) On the other hand, man's consciousness of the necessity of associating with the individuals around him is the beginning of the consciousness that he is living in society at all. This beginning is as animal as social life itself at this stage. It is mere herd-consciousness, and at this point man is only distinguished from sheep by the fact that with him consciousness takes the place of instinct or that his instinct is a conscious one. This sheep-like or tribal consciousness receives its further development and extension through increased productivity, the increase of needs, and, what is fundamental to both of these, the increase of population. With these there develops the division of labour, which was originally nothing but the division of labour in the sexual act, then that division of labour which develops spontaneously or "naturally" by virtue of natural predisposition (e.g. physical strength), needs, accidents, etc. Division of labour only becomes truly such from the moment when a division of material and mental labour appears. (The first form of ideologists, priests, is concurrent.) From this moment onwards consciousness can really flatter itself that it is something other than consciousness of existing practice, that it really represents something without representing something real; from now on consciousness is in a position to emancipate itself from the world and to proceed to the formation of "pure" theory, theology, philosophy, ethics, etc. But even if this theory, theology, philosophy, ethics, etc. comes into contradiction with the existing relations, this can only occur because existing

---

27. In this paragraph, Marx and Engels have described one of their most fundamental concepts, the "mode of production." A mode of production involves the combination of specific technologies and resources with a particular type of social relationship. Marx and Engels view history as a series of such relationships and say that the study of history must be focused on issues of resources, technology, and associated social relationships. They continue their satirical attack on German philosophers, claiming that in Germany, history has ended. The Right Hegelians asserted that Germans could attain freedom under the Prussian monarchy. Marx and Engels (as well as the Young Hegelians in Germany) thought this assertion absurd. Note also that Marx and Engels assert that real history is the history of people's needs and modes of production. Matters of religion and daily politics are simply the surface manifestation of these underlying forces.

social relations have come into contradiction with existing forces of production; this, moreover, can also occur in a particular national sphere of relations through the appearance of the contradiction, not within the national orbit, but between this national consciousness and the practice of other nations, i.e. between the national and the general consciousness of a nation (as we see it now in Germany).[28]

Moreover, it is quite immaterial what consciousness starts to do on its own: out of all such muck we get only the one inference that these three moments, the forces of production, the state of society, and consciousness, can and must come into contradiction with one another, because the division of labour implies the possibility, nay the fact that intellectual and material activity—enjoyment and labour, production and consumption—devolve on different individuals, and that the only possibility of their not coming into contradiction lies in the negation in its turn of the division of labour. It is self-evident, moreover, that "specters," "bonds," "the higher being," "concept," "scruple," are merely the idealistic, spiritual expression, the conception apparently of the isolated individual, the image of very empirical fetters and limitations, within which the mode of production of life and the form of intercourse coupled with it move.[29]

PRIVATE PROPERTY AND COMMUNISM

With the division of labour, in which all these contradictions are implicit, and which in its turn is based on the natural division of labour in the family and the separation of society into individual families opposed to one another, is given simultaneously the distribution, and indeed the unequal distribution, both quantitative and qualitative, of labour and its products, hence property: the nucleus, the first form, of which lies in the family, where wife and children are the slaves of the husband. This latent slavery in the family, though still very crude, is the first property, but even at this early stage it corresponds perfectly to the definition of modern economists who call it the power of disposing of the labour-power of others. Division of labour and private property are, moreover, identical expressions: in the one the same thing is affirmed with reference to activity as is affirmed in the other with reference to the product of the activity.[30]

---

28. In this long paragraph, Marx and Engels make one of their key assertions: It is production and social life that creates consciousness, not consciousness that creates social life. They describe human language linked to consciousness and resulting from problems posed by the processes of production and material life (Holborow 2007). They further argue that particular forms of consciousness arise from specific modes of production. The earliest of these is simply the consciousness of being part of a society and different from the natural world. Under such conditions, consciousness is very limited. Marx and Engels describe it as "herd-consciousness." The development of consciousness that is distinctly human is dependent on increased population and division of labor. As the division of labor becomes more complex, consciousness appears to seem independent of the world, but this is an illusion.

29. Marx and Engels conclude this section by focusing on conflict. They argue that the division of labor leads to different sorts of consciousnesses and gives different people different interests and positions within society. This necessarily leads to conflict, and such conflict drives history. Like all Hegelians, Marx and Engels believed that history was propelled by dialectical conflict. Each state of society (and for Marx and Engels, this meant each mode of production) could be considered a thesis. Each was characterized by internal contradiction which, in time, manifested as an antithesis. This led to a revolutionary clash between thesis and antithesis which resulted in a synthesis that, at the same time, was a new thesis.

30. Marx and Engels argue that the division of labor entails both inequality and the origin of private property. The division of labor implies control over both a portion of the labor process and the products of that process. Notice the concern with gender and the subjugation of women and children present in this paragraph. Because it was a good tool for analyzing relations of inequality, Marxism proved appealing to many feminist scholars. See essay 23, by Eleanor Leacock (1922–1987), for an example of Marxist-feminist

Further, the division of labour implies the contradiction between the interest of the separate individual or the individual family and the communal interest of all individuals who have intercourse with one another. And indeed, this communal interest does not exist merely in the imagination, as the "general interest," but first of all in reality, as the mutual interdependence of the individuals among whom the labour is divided. And finally, the division of labour offers us the first example of how, as long as man remains in natural society, that is, as long as a cleavage exists between the particular and the common interest, as long, therefore, as activity is not voluntarily, but naturally, divided, man's own deed becomes an alien power opposed to him, which enslaves him instead of being controlled by him. For as soon as the distribution of labour comes into being, each man has a particular, exclusive sphere of activity, which is forced upon him and from which he cannot escape. He is a hunter, a fisherman, a shepherd, or a critical critic, and must remain so if he does not want to lose his means of livelihood; while in communist society, where nobody has one exclusive sphere of activity but each can become accomplished in any branch he wishes, society regulates the general production and thus makes it possible for me to do one thing today and another tomorrow, to hunt in the morning, fish in the afternoon, rear cattle in the evening, criticize after dinner, just as I have a mind, without ever becoming hunter, fisherman, shepherd or critic. This fixation of social activity, this consolidation of what we ourselves produce into an objective power above us, growing out of our control, thwarting our expectations, bringing to naught our calculations, is one of the chief factors in historical development up till now.[31]

(And out of this very contradiction between the interest of the individual and that of the community the latter takes an independent form as the State, divorced from the real interests of individual and community, and at the same time as an illusory communal life, always based, however, on the real ties existing in every family and tribal conglomeration—such as flesh and blood, language, division of labour on a larger scale, and other interests—and especially, as we shall enlarge upon later, on the classes, already determined by the division of labour, which in every such mass of men separate out, and of which one dominates all the others. It follows from this that all struggles within the State, the struggle between democracy, aristocracy, and monarchy, the struggle for the franchise, etc. etc. are merely the illusory forms in which the real struggles of the different classes are fought out among one another. Of this the German theoreticians have not the faintest inkling, although they have received a sufficient introduction to the subject in the *Deutsch-Französische Jahrbücher* and *Die Heilige Familie*. Further, it follows that every class which is struggling for mastery, even when its domination, as is the case with the proletariat, postulates the abolition of the old form of society in its entirety and of domina-

scholarship. Marx and Engels, however, wrote little about women's issues, generally considering these part of the general topic of oppression of workers. In an 1885 letter to the German women's rights activist Gertrude Guillaume-Shack, Engels wrote, "It is my conviction that real equality of women and men can come true only when the exploitation of either by capital has been abolished and private housework has been transformed into a public industry."

31. Division of labor makes society possible, but it also destroys freedom and creates alienation. Alienation or estrangement, a key Marxist concept, refers to the separation of the individual from either the preconditions or the products of labor, or, in this case, from life's necessities. Here they argue that specializing in one activity creates alienation. A person becomes a hunter, fisherman, shepherd, or critical critic. In doing so, people lose the rest of their potential and hence lose their freedom. Here Marx and Engels argue that in a communist society people would be continuously free to choose what they do and hence this alienation would end. Almost all of Marx and Engels's work is devoted to describing and analyzing history and the rise of capitalism. They devote little space to describing how a communist society might actually be structured. Here they suggest that people in such a society might occupy any job they feel like at any time they feel like it. But can one be an engineer one day and a doctor the next?

tion itself, must first conquer for itself political power in order to represent its interest in turn as the general interest, which immediately it is forced to do. Just because individuals seek only their particular interest, which for them does not coincide with their communal interest, the latter will be imposed on them as an interest "alien" to them, and "independent" of them, as in its turn a particular, peculiar "general" interest; or they themselves must remain within this discord, as in democracy. On the other hand, too, the practical struggle of these particular interests, which constantly really run counter to the communal and illusory communal interests, makes practical intervention and control necessary through the illusory "general" interest in the form of the State.)[32]

The social power, i.e. the multiplied productive force, which arises through the co-operation of different individuals as it is determined by the division of labour, appears to these individuals, since their cooperation is not voluntary but has come about naturally, not as their own united power, but as an alien force existing outside them, of the origin and goal of which they are ignorant, which they thus cannot control, which on the contrary passes through a peculiar series of phases and stages independent of the will and the action of man, nay even being the prime governor of these.[33]

How otherwise could for instance property have had a history at all, have taken on different forms, and landed property, for example, according to the different premises given, have proceeded in France from parcellation to centralization in the hands of a few, in England from centralization in the hands of a few to parcellation, as is actually the case today? Or how does it happen that trade, which after all is nothing more than the exchange of products of various individuals and countries, rules the whole world through the relation of supply and demand—a relation which, as an English economist says, hovers over the earth like the fate of the ancients, and with invisible hand allots fortune and misfortune to men, sets up empires and overthrows empires, causes nations to rise and to disappear—while with the abolition of the basis of private property, with the communistic regulation of production (and, implicit in this, the destruction of the alien relation between men and what they themselves produce), the power of the relation of supply and demand is dissolved into nothing, and men get exchange, production, the mode of their mutual relation, under their own control again?[34]

---

32. This entire paragraph appeared as a marginal note to the paragraph above it in the original manuscript. Several important Marxist principles are laid out in it. First, as Marx and Engels were to write in *The Communist Manifesto* of 1848, "The history of all hitherto existing society is the history of class struggles." Second, these struggles between the different classes are the underlying dynamic driving political and economic history. Third, the state is an instrument of control and oppression, and seizing control of the state is a necessary step in changing society.

Marx and Engels mention the *Deutsch-Französische Jahrbücher* (*The German-French Annals*, 1844) and *Die Heilige Familie* (*The Holy Family*, 1845). The first of these was a radical periodical edited in France by Marx and Arnold Ruge (1802–1880). Only one issue appeared. The second was Marx and Engels's first collaboration; a mocking attack on Bruno Bauer and other Young Hegelians.

33. In this and the next paragraph, Marx and Engels argue that although people create society, it appears to them as something external with a life of its own. Similarly, Hegel had argued that that the spirit is part of humanity but appears to be separated from humanity. Hegel viewed history as the process of dissolving the alienation between humanity and spirit. Marx and Engels view history as the process of dissolving the alienation between human beings and society.

34. Marx refers here to Adam Smith's idea of the invisible hand. In discussing domestic and foreign investment, Smith had written that individuals, intending their own gain, are frequently "led by an invisible hand" to promote the interests of society. He continues with the caution that those who claim to make their economic decisions to promote the public good rarely do much good. Thus, Smith sees the invisible hand as a generally positive force. Marx and Engels, however, see it as a force of alienation, causing nations to rise and fall in arbitrary ways. They suggest that the laws of supply and demand are not natural laws but the products of a

In history up to the present it is certainly an empirical fact that separate individuals have, with the broadening of their activity into world historical activity, become more and more enslaved under a power alien to them (a pressure which they have conceived of as a dirty trick on the part of the so-called universal spirit, etc.), a power which has become more and more enormous and, in the last instance, turns out to be the world market. But it is just as empirically established that, by the overthrow of the existing state of society by the communist revolution (of which more below) and the abolition of private property which is identical with it, this power, which so baffles the German theoreticians, will be dissolved; and that then the liberation of each single individual will be accomplished in the measure in which history becomes transformed into world history. From the above it is clear that the real intellectual wealth of the individual depends entirely on the wealth of his real connections. Only then will the separate individuals be liberated from the various national and local barriers, be brought into practical connection with the material and intellectual production of the whole world and be put in a position to acquire the capacity to enjoy this all-sided production of the whole earth (the creations of man). All-round dependence, this natural form of the world-historical cooperation of individuals, will be transformed by this communist revolution into the control and conscious mastery of these powers, which, born of the action of men on one another, have till now overawed and governed men as powers completely alien to them. Now this view can be expressed again in speculative-idealistic, i.e. fantastic, terms as "self-generation of the species" ("society as the subject"), and thereby the consecutive series of interrelated individuals connected with each other can be conceived as a single individual, which accomplishes the mystery of generating itself. It is clear here that individuals certainly make one another, physically and mentally, but do not make themselves.[35]

This "alienation" (to use a term which will be comprehensible to the philosophers) can, of course, only be abolished given two practical premises. For it to become an "intolerable" power, i.e. a power against which men make a revolution, it must necessarily have rendered the great mass of humanity "propertyless," and produced, at the same time, the contradiction of an existing world of wealth and culture, both of which conditions presuppose a great increase in productive power, a high degree of its development. And, on the other hand, this development of productive forces (which itself implies the actual empirical existence of men in their world-historical, instead of local, being) is an absolutely necessary practical premise because without it want is merely made general, and with destitution the struggle for necessities and all the old filthy business would necessarily be reproduced; and furthermore, because only with this universal development of productive forces is a universal intercourse between men established, which produces in all nations simultaneously the phenomenon of the "propertyless" mass (universal competition), makes each nation dependent on the revolutions of the others, and finally has put world-historical, empirically universal individuals in place of local ones. Without this, (1) communism could only exist as a local event; (2) the forces of intercourse themselves could not have developed as universal, hence intoler-

---

particular form of society. This society seems alien and imposed but is created by people and can be ended by them. Marx and Engels propose that in a communist society, such laws would cease to exist.

35. Marx and Engels believed that history would eventually produce communist society. They envisioned such a society as being completely without contradictions. Since they also believed that contradictions created the historical process, the arrival of communism would end the historical process. Time, of course, would continue; but history (events driven by dialectical conflict) would end. They believed that the movement toward communism must be a world-historical movement. A communist revolution in one place must lead to communist revolution in all places. Such a revolution would enable individuals to transcend the alienation between humans and society. At the end of the paragraph, Marx and Engels once again make fun of the "idealistic, i.e. fantastic" ideas of German idealist philosophers.

able powers: they would have remained home-bred conditions surrounded by superstition; and (3) each extension of intercourse would abolish local communism. Empirically, communism is only possible as the act of the dominant peoples "all at once" and simultaneously, which presupposes the universal development of productive forces and the world intercourse bound up with communism. Moreover, the mass of propertyless workers—the utterly precarious position of labour-power on a mass scale cut off from capital or from even a limited satisfaction and, therefore, no longer merely temporarily deprived of work itself as a secure source of life—presupposes the world market through competition. The proletariat can thus only exist world-historically, just as communism, its activity, can only have a "world-historical" existence. World historical existence of individuals means, existence of individuals which is directly linked up with world history.

Communism is for us not a state of affairs which is to be established, an ideal to which reality [will] have to adjust itself. We call communism the real movement which abolishes the present state of things. The conditions of this movement result from the premises now in existence.[36]

AUTHOR'S NOTE

a. The building of houses. With savages each family has as a matter of course its own cave or hut like the separate family tent of the nomads. This separate domestic economy is made only the more necessary by the further development of private property. With the agricultural peoples a communal domestic economy is just as impossible as a communal cultivation of the soil. A great advance was the building of towns. In all previous periods, however, the abolition of individual economy, which is inseparable from the abolition of private property, was impossible for the simple reason that the material conditions governing it were not present. The setting-up of a communal domestic economy presupposes the development of machinery, of the use of natural forces and of many other productive forces—e.g., of water-supplies, of gas-lighting, steam-heating, etc., the removal [of the antagonism] of town and country. Without these conditions a communal economy would not in itself form a new productive force; lacking any material basis and resting on a purely theoretical foundation, it would be a mere freak and would end in nothing more than a monastic economy—What was possible can be seen in the towns brought about by condensation and the erection of communal buildings for various definite purposes (prisons, barracks, etc.). That the abolition of individual economy is inseparable from the abolition of the family is self-evident.

---

36. Marx and Engels understand history as having created ever more oppressive conditions and people as ever more enslaved. At the same time, they saw that the prosperity of certain sectors of society was increasing. They argue here that the contradiction between the poverty and propertyless condition of the masses and the wealth produced by industrialization would lead to revolution. This revolution would logically begin where both industrial wealth and poverty were most developed. From there it would quickly spread to become a general world revolution. In 1845, as they wrote *The German Ideology*, Marx and Engels believed that the conditions for such a revolution were rapidly being met. In 1848, when revolution did break out in Germany, they believed it to be the beginning of world communist revolution. Marx and Engels hurriedly returned to Germany, where Marx began to publish another radical newspaper, the *Neue Rheinische Zeitung* (recall that the paper he originally edited was called the *Rheinische Zeitung*). However, the 1848 revolutions were quickly and violently suppressed. In the spring of 1849, the government closed the newspaper and Marx was forced to flee to England, where he spent the remainder of his life.

The Foundations of Sociological Thought

Like anthropology, sociology is based on the work of philosophers and scientists of the nineteenth century, and the two disciplines share many ideas in common. Indeed, at the end of the nineteenth century, there was no clear distinction between anthropology and sociology; all the scholars discussed here adopted a cross-cultural approach in their work. The theories of these early sociological thinkers are worth exploring because they exerted a profound influence on anthropology that continues today.

Émile Durkheim (1858–1917) is a central figure in both sociology and anthropology. He is responsible for formulating some of the basic concepts of these disciplines and training the first generation of French sociologists. As a university student, Durkheim studied the works of the positivist philosopher Auguste Comte (1798–1857) as well as Herbert Spencer. Like Comte and Spencer, Durkheim believed that human society followed laws like those in the natural sciences and that these laws could be discovered by empirical observation and testing. In 1885 and 1886, Durkheim took a leave of absence from high school teaching to conduct research in Germany with the social psychologist Wilhelm Wundt (1832–1920). His experiences with Wundt convinced him that a scientific study of society was possible. On his return to France, Durkheim accepted a position at the University of Bordeaux, where over the next fifteen years he produced some of his best-known work. In 1902 he moved to the Sorbonne in Paris and held positions of increasing responsibility there until his death in 1917.

Durkheim believed that society was much more than simply a collection of individuals, and in his first book, *The Division of Labor in Society* (1893), he sought to discover the laws by which society operated. He began by questioning the nature of social cohesion (the term he used was *social solidarity*): What was it exactly that held societies together? He concluded that social solidarity was primarily the result of a force arising from participation in a shared system of beliefs and values that shaped and controlled individual behavior. Durkheim called this force *l'âme collective*, a phrase usually translated into English as "the collective conscience." However, the French word âme can also be translated as "soul," "spirit," "sentiment," or "sensibility," and Durkheim intended all of these meanings. In this book, we will continue Durkheim's use of *l'âme collective*, but we write it with the English article *the*.

Durkheim believed that the collective conscience originated in the communal interactions and experiences of members of a society. Because people were born and raised within this shared context of the collective conscience, it shaped their values, beliefs, and behaviors. Ultimately, Durkheim believed that the *l'âme collective* made life possible and meaningful. For the most part, social cohesion was maintained because everyone in a society participated in the *l'âme collective*. As you can see, Durkheim's notion of the collective conscience foreshadowed the modern concept of culture, although he did not use this term in his work.

Durkheim argued that the collective conscience was a psychological entity that, although carried by members of a society, superseded individual existence and could not be explained in terms of individual behavior. Once formed (through a process Durkheim called *social condensation*), it had an existence of its own and operated by its own rules. In other words, the collective conscience was not contained within any individual organism; the existence of the *l'âme collective* was superorganic.

Given that it was not a material thing, how could the *l'âme collective* be scientifically studied? Durkheim proposed that the appropriate units of analysis were social facts. These were the social and behavioral rules and principles that exist in a society before an individual is born and which that person learns and follows as a member of society. Social facts can be recognized by their pervasiveness within a society (they are collectively recognized, not individual rules) and because they are coercive. People feel obligated to observe their constraints. Durkheim believed that such social facts could be observed in people's actions and studied independently through the use of statistics. His 1897 book *Suicide* is a classic example of this form of analysis. Suicide seems the ultimate act of individual decision-making. However, Durkheim's analysis showed that there were patterns in the act of suicide which meant that people were following unspoken cultural rules, or social facts, in Durkheim's terms.

The influence of nineteenth-century evolutionary thought can be clearly seen in Durkheim's study of primitive societies. Like the other theorists of his day, Durkheim supposed technologically primitive peoples to be examples of earlier stages of cultural evolution. Though he did no fieldwork, Durkheim studied reports of primitive societies, in particular the Australian Aborigines, attempting to determine the form and nature of the *l'âme collective* in these societies.

Durkheim believed that societies evolved from mechanical to organic solidarity, concepts he had developed in his earlier work, *The Division of Labor in Society*. This notion parallels Herbert Spencer's views on evolution outlined in his work "The Social Organism," which is the first essay in the volume. Following the evolutionary sequence first proposed by Spencer in 1860, in which evolution moves from simple to complex, Durkheim stated that societies organized by mechanical solidarity were simple and undifferentiated but that those organized by organic solidarity were more complex and specialized.

Cohesion in societies organized by mechanical solidarity was created through face-to-face interaction. They were mechanical in that every person occupied the same functional role as every other person. Durkheim believed that in such societies, there were no individuals in the modern sense. Rather, "collective conscience completely envelopes [individual] conscience and coincides with it at every point" (1933 [1893]: 43). Because societies characterized by mechanical solidarity were undifferentiated, segments could break away without disrupting the functioning of the entire society. In these societies, kinship formed the primary bond between people.

Durkheim proposed that since mechanical solidarity was based primarily on face-to-face interaction, as population increased, it became a less effective mechanism of cohesion. In more complex societies, mechanical solidarity was replaced by organic solidarity. Leaning heavily on Spencer's organic analogy, Durkheim argued that in more complex societies, individuals formed interdependent groups (as more complex organisms have specialized organs). The primary ties between individuals thus came from economic and occupational cooperation rather than from kinship. In such societies, the *l'âme collective* was at least partially differentiated from individual conscience.

Unlike Spencer, Darwin, and Marx, who wrote in terms of the human struggle for survival, Durkheim focused on the solidarity within a society. Societies progressed from mechanical to organic solidarity not through competition and strife but rather through attempts to achieve greater solidarity at higher levels of population and complexity. Although he certainly did not view societies as free from conflict, Durkheim believed that social differentiation and specialization led to increased social cohesion and broadened the possibilities for individuals to achieve their full potential as human beings. Strife in modern society resulted from the incomplete elaboration of organic solidarity. Durkheim and many of his followers had a profound faith in the ability of science and rationality to help people create a better, more peaceful society in the future. This faith was sorely tested when Europe descended into the carnage of World War I.

Following his work on social facts, Durkheim proposed that all people understood the world through socially created systems of classification. He developed these ideas in his book *Primitive Classification* (Durkheim and Mauss 1963, orig. 1903) and *The Elementary Forms of the Religious Life* (1965, orig. 1912). Both works focused on Australian Aboriginal societies. He was interested in these societies because he believed that, since they were relatively simple, social processes in them could be more easily seen and analyzed.

In these works, Durkheim argued that systems of classification were not derived from simple observation of nature. Rather, their source was partly in the biology of the brain and partly in the collective conscience. They were social facts. Thus systems of classification did not reflect the natural world but rather imposed structure upon it. Durkheim developed this thought in his book *The Elementary Forms of the Religious Life*, in which he proposed that human societies developed systems of classification that projected their social organization on the material world. In the realm of religion, these systems became sacred. Thus, when societies engaged in religious worship, what they were actually venerating was their own social order. In Durkheim's view, this act of devotion invested society itself with a sacred character and was a critical element in creating and maintaining social solidarity.

Durkheim proposed that some social facts were universal. For example, he claimed that all human thought was binary. In all human societies, people tend to classify things in pairs with their opposites (good/bad, day/night, right/left, and so on). In *The Elementary Forms of the Religious Life*, Durkheim suggested that the most fundamental of these divisions was into the categories of sacred and profane. Durkheim's emphasis on systems of classification and binary opposition would have an enormous effect on later theories, in particular, French structuralism, ethnoscience, and cognitive anthropology.

Durkheim adopted what anthropologists in later decades termed a *functionalist* approach to the analysis of society. His analysis of social institutions and beliefs was often couched in terms of their contribution to promoting and maintaining social solidarity. This aspect of his work forms the basis of the British functionalist and structural-functionalist schools of anthropological thought exemplified by Bronislaw Malinowski and A. R. Radcliffe-Brown (see essays 14 and 15).

Around 1900, Durkheim's work attracted a very influential group of scholars, including his son, André, and his nephew Marcel Mauss. Together, between 1898 and 1912, they published a journal called *L'Année Sociologique* that presented and critiqued new findings in sociology. The scholars that gathered around Durkheim and their direct intellectual descendants are collectively known as the L'Année Sociologique school.

Unhappily, World War I exacted a profound toll on Durkheim and his students. Fearing German nationalism and anti-Semitism, Durkheim supported the war. He was on numerous war-related committees and wrote several propaganda pamphlets against German expansionism, particularly criticizing the work of Heinrich von Treitschke (1834–1896), a profoundly nationalist and anti-Semitic German politician and author. Unfortunately, a great many of Durkheim's students were killed in the war. These included Durkheim's only son, André, a promising young linguist who died in 1915 during the French army's retreat from Serbia. André was initially listed as missing, so Durkheim did not definitively know about his death for most of a year. Bereft of his son, Durkheim withdrew into silence. LaCapra writes: "Iron self-discipline remained the dominant force in Durkheim's life, and it finally broke him. In 1917, he died of what has been called a 'broken heart'" (1972: 78).

Durkheim's nephew Marcel Mauss (1872–1950) was one of the few members of L'Année Sociologique to survive the war and was considered one of the school's leading thinkers. In 1890, Mauss had moved to Bordeaux to study with Durkheim but, by 1895, had begun to have an independent scholarly career focusing on the analysis of Sanskrit texts and Indian religion. He worked in both Holland and England (his fluency in English led to his wartime employment as a translator, and probably his survival as well). After the war and Durkheim's death, Mauss became the central figure of French anthropology. He helped to found the Institut d'Ethnologie, and he was elected to the College de France, a prestigious research institution.

In 1925, Mauss published "Essai sur le don" ("The Gift"), his best-known work, a portion of which is reprinted here. In this essay, Mauss explored gift giving as a social fact. He showed that in primitive societies, *prestation*, as he called it, was typically a part of political and social obligations, reflecting or expressing the society's underlying social structure. He also proposed a special class of social facts called total social phenomena and illustrated this concept in his discussion of the potlatch.

Mauss produced a substantial body of work, but it is scattered across many different kinds of writing. He wrote book reviews and obituaries and published debates and articles. His students published his lecture notes (e.g., his 1947 *Manuel d'Ethnographie* prepared by his student Denise Paulme). Mauss's work ranged over many subjects, including history, religion, systems of classification, and philosophy. Beside "The Gift," Mauss's most influential essay is probably his 1934 lecture "Techniques of the Body," which explores cultural differences in physical activities from sleeping to sex. In a well-known passage that proved basic to Pierre Bourdieu's idea of *habitus* (see essay 27), Mauss described the different gaits of the French and English and the difficulties they had marching together as a result (Mauss 2009: 79).

Mauss and Durkheim believed that social evolution would be characterized by a progression of ever better social forms, but their personal lives were tragic. Mauss's mentor Durkheim died in 1917. Few of the members of L'Année Sociologique, many of whom were Mauss's close friends, survived World War I. In 1925, as he wrote "The Gift," Mauss also wrote an opening essay for the new series of *L'Annee Sociologique* in memory of his mentor Durkheim, and the other members of L'Annee Sociologique who had died in the war or shortly after. These were Henri Beauchat (1878–1914) (who died on an arctic expedition), Maxime David, Antoine Bianconi (d. 1915), Robert Hertz (1881–1915), Jean Reynier, R. Gelly (d. 1918), A. Vacher, J.-P. Laffitte, R. Chaillie, Paul Huvelin (1873–1924), and André Durkheim (1892–1915). It is hard to imagine the impact of losing so many friends and associates. You can get some sense of Mauss's feeling (and his fatalism) in his brief statement about Gelly: "For a long time we thought that at least Gelly would be left to us. Right to the end he underwent a great many dangers. One day in 1918, like the rest, he was taken from us. He had just turned 31" (1925: 25, our translation).

Mauss was successful between the wars, leading the Institut d'Ethnologie and gaining a chair in sociology at the College de France. He continued to edit and publish the work of his lost friends and colleagues, and he wrote a small number of influential publications, including "The Gift" and "Techniques of the Body."

However, after the Nazi invasion of France in 1940, Mauss was forced from his academic positions and from his Paris apartment (he was both a socialist and of Jewish ancestry). Beginning in 1942, he was forced to wear a yellow star on his coat. Possibly because his work was admired in Germany, and possibly because he continued to have some friends in high places, Mauss again survived. However, many of his friends, students, and colleagues did not. His students Deborah Lifszyc and Bernard Maupoil died at Auschwitz and Dachau, respectively. Friends and colleagues Henri Maspero and Maurice Halbwachs died at Buchenwald. Marc Bloch, an important social historian, was executed for his participation in the resistance. After the war, Mauss's position and apartment were returned to him, but his health and his spirit were broken. Increasingly, Mauss "withdrew into silence" (Fournier 2006: 345–49).

Though Mauss undoubtedly inspired many others, he did not attract a united group of followers (Allen 2013: 536). This may be because he did not produce a well-organized body of theory. It may also be because the last decade of his life, between the Nazi invasion of France in 1940 and his death in 1950, was so deeply troubled.

The last contributor to this section is the German sociologist Max Weber (1864–1920). Although best known for his work in sociology, Weber was trained in law and history and held academic posts in economics. Weber was relatively poorly versed in the ethnography of "primitive" societies, but he was extremely interested in Asia and wrote extensively on religion in China and India.

Much of Weber's work was influenced by Marx, and he attempted to develop Marx's thoughts on social class. Like Marx, he believed that social class was related to property ownership and control of the means of production. Unlike Marx, he believed that classes, in and of themselves, could not act and that status (or honor) and party could also cut across class lines. In his essay "Class, Status, Party," Weber develops this theory of class stratification and parties (groups that exist to pursue power) and their relationship to the role of the individual in society.

Contrary to Marx (but not Durkheim), Weber emphasized ideology. *The Protestant Ethic and the Spirit of Capitalism*, originally published in 1930, is perhaps Weber's best-known explanation of the role of ideology. Like Marx, Weber analyzed the rise of capitalism, and like Marx, he saw the roots of capitalism in fundamental changes in relations of production, such as the displacement of peasants. However, unlike Marx, he found these material causes insufficient to explain the emergence and success of capitalism. Instead, he proposed that it was material factors, coupled with a new Calvinist ethic emphasizing moral accountability and self-discipline, that explained capitalism's rise. It is critical to Weber's point that Calvinism did not emerge from capitalism. It was aimed at assuring personal salvation, not profits. However, coinciding with changes in relations of production, it greatly favored the emergence of a powerful capitalist bourgeoisie.

Another critical feature that differentiates Weber's work from both Marx's and Durkheim's is the prominent place he gave to individual action. Weber believed that the ultimate base of social action is individual behavior and that behavior is best judged by whether the action is rational. Both Marx and Weber saw individuals as ultimately grounded in systems of production, but in Weber's work, individuals take on the capacity for action that is much less evident in Marx and Durkheim.

Weber believed that individuals could profoundly affect their societies. Prophets could emerge who could change the way people thought. He called the ability of an individual to influence others *charisma*, which he defined in *The Sociology of Religion* (1993, orig. 1920) as an "extraordinary power," a sort of spiritual force possessed by an individual. Weber did not explain the source of charisma, asserting that it simply exists naturally in some people; in others, it is a germ that must be awakened. The power of charisma enables certain individuals to lead their societies and change the thinking of those around them.

Weber's influence on later anthropological work is subtle but significant. His emphasis on individual, rational, social action was incorporated by Bronislaw Malinowski into his theory of psychological functionalism. His work on forms of authority influenced many anthropological thinkers, as did his analysis of the Protestant ethic and capitalism (see Julian Steward, essay 17, and Clifford Geertz, essay 26). Weber's work on religion influenced Roy Rappaport (Rappaport 1994: 167) as well as Anthony F. C. Wallace, Peter Worsley, and Jean and John Comaroff (Erickson and Murphy 1998: 112). Especially important to contemporary anthropologists is his notion of *verstehen*, usually translated as "understanding." Weber used the term to mean the empathetic identification with those you are observing in order to better understand their motives and the meaning of their behavior. This is one of the fundamental concepts of the school of interpretive anthropology. In particular, Clifford Geertz (essay 26) and Renato Rosaldo (essay 29) illustrate how this principle has been used by anthropologists.

SUGGESTED READINGS

Allen, N. J. 2000. *Categories and Classifications: Maussian Reflections on the Social.* Oxford: Berghahn.
 A series of essays interpreting and analyzing Mauss's work across a wide variety of topics.
Bendix, Reinhard. 1977. *Max Weber: An Intellectual Portrait.* Berkeley: University of California Press.
 A good, if long, introduction to Weber's work.
Besnard, Philippe, ed. 1983. *The Sociological Domain: The Durkheimians and the Founding of French Sociology.* Cambridge: Cambridge University Press.
 A series of essays by different authors providing useful insight on Durkheim and many of his students.
Fournier, Marcel. 2006. *Marcel Mauss: A Biography.* Princeton, NJ: Princeton University Press.
 The most comprehensive biography of Mauss.
Jones, Robert Alun. 1986. *Emile Durkheim: An Introduction to Four Major Works.* Beverly Hills, CA: Sage.
 Jones, who was a professor of religion, history, and sociology, provides thoughtful introductions to Durkheim's works *The Division of Labor in Society*, *The Rules of Sociological Method*, *Suicide*, and *The Elementary Forms of the Religious Life*.
Keyes, Charles F. 2002. "Weber and Anthropology." *Annual Review of Anthropology* 31:233–255.
 A review of Weber's work focusing on connections between Weber and issues of interpretation and power, particularly as they relate to interpretive anthropology and the anthropology of religion.
Pickering, W. S. F., and H. Martings. 1994. *Debating Durkheim.* New York: Routledge.
 A collection of essays covering Durkheim's analysis of social facts, classification, method, and nationalism.

5. What Is a Social Fact?

Émile Durkheim (1858–1917)

BEFORE INQUIRING Into the method suited to the study of social facts, it is important to know which facts are commonly called "social." This information is all the more necessary since the designation "social" is used with little precision. It is currently employed for practically all phenomena generally diffused within society, however small their social interest. But on that basis, there are, as it were, no human events that may not be called social. Each individual drinks, sleeps, eats, reasons; and it is to society's interest that these functions be exercised in an orderly manner. If, then, all these facts are counted as "social" facts, sociology would have no subject matter exclusively its own, and its domain would be confused with that of biology and psychology.[1]

But in reality there is in every society a certain group of phenomena which may be differentiated from those studied by the other natural sciences. When I fulfill my obligations as brother, husband, or citizen, when I execute my contracts, I perform duties which are defined, externally to myself and my acts, in law and in custom. Even if they conform to my own sentiments and I feel their reality subjectively, such reality is still objective, for I did not create them; I merely inherited them through my education. How many times it happens, moreover, that we are ignorant of the details of the obligations incumbent upon us, and that in order to acquaint ourselves with them we must consult the law and its authorized interpreters! Similarly, the church-member finds the beliefs and practices of his religious life ready-made at birth; their existence prior to his own implies their existence outside of himself. The system of signs I use to express my thought, the system of currency I employ to pay my debts, the instruments of credit I utilize in my commercial relations, the practices followed in my profession, etc., function independently of my own use of them. And these statements can be repeated for each member of society. Here, then, are ways of acting, thinking, and feeling that present the noteworthy property of existing outside the individual consciousness.

These types of conduct or thought are not only external to the individual but are, moreover, endowed with coercive power, by virtue of which they impose themselves upon him, independent of his individual will. Of course, when I fully consent and conform to them, this constraint is felt only slightly, if at all, and is therefore unnecessary. But it is, nonetheless, an intrinsic characteristic of these facts, the proof thereof being that it asserts itself as soon as I attempt to resist it. If I attempt to violate the law, it reacts against me so as to prevent my act before its accomplishment, or to nullify my vio-

---

From *The Rules of the Sociological Method* (1895)

1. Durkheim's goal in writing this essay was to show that sociology could be a field of study distinct from other sciences. He wrote at a time when the divisions between anthropology, sociology, and psychology, as we know them today, did not exist. Durkheim was concerned to establish what he considered a new and independent science, which required having something in particular to study, a subject matter that could distinguish it from other sciences. That subject matter, Durkheim proposed, was social facts. As a follower of the French positivist Auguste Comte (1798–1857), Durkheim was vitally concerned with establishing the reality of social facts. Comte insisted that philosophy (and social science) be based on precise, observable facts subject to general laws. If the existence of such facts could not be demonstrated, the study of society had no place in science.

lation by restoring the damage, if it is accomplished and reparable, or to make me expiate it if it cannot be compensated for otherwise.[2]

In the case of purely moral maxims; the public conscience exercises a check on every act which offends it by means of the surveillance it exercises over the conduct of citizens, and the appropriate penalties at its disposal. In many cases the constraint is less violent, but nevertheless it always exists. If I do not submit to the conventions of society, if in my dress I do not conform to the customs observed in my country and in my class, the ridicule I provoke, the social isolation in which I am kept, produce, although in an attenuated form, the same effects as a punishment in the strict sense of the word. The constraint is nonetheless efficacious for being indirect. I am not obliged to speak French with my fellowcountrymen nor to use the legal currency, but I cannot possibly do otherwise. If I tried to escape this necessity, my attempt would fail miserably. As an industrialist, I am free to apply the technical methods of former centuries; but by doing so, I should invite certain ruin. Even when I free myself from these rules and violate them successfully, I am always compelled to struggle with them. When finally overcome, they make their constraining power sufficiently felt by the resistance they offer. The enterprises of all innovators, including successful ones, come up against resistance of this kind.[3]

Here, then, is a category of facts with very distinctive characteristics: it consists of ways of acting, thinking, and feeling, external to the individual, and endowed with a power of coercion, by reason of which they control him. These ways of thinking could not be confused with biological phenomena, since they consist of representations and of actions; nor with psychological phenomena, which exist only in the individual consciousness and through it. They constitute, thus, a new variety of phenomena; and it is to them exclusively that the term "social" ought to be applied. And this term fits them quite well, for it is clear that, since their source is not in the individual, their substratum can be no other than society, either the political society as a whole or some one of the partial groups it includes, such as religious denominations, political, literary, and occupational associations, etc. On the other hand, this term "social" applies to them exclusively, for it has a distinct meaning only if it designates exclusively the phenomena which are not included in any of the categories of facts that have already been established and classified. These ways of thinking and acting therefore constitute the proper domain of sociology. It is true that, when we define them with this word "constraint," we risk shocking the zealous partisans of absolute individualism. For those who profess the complete autonomy of the individual, man's dignity is diminished whenever he is made to feel that he is not completely selfdeterminant. It is generally accepted today, however, that most of our ideas and our tendencies are not developed by ourselves but come to us from without. How can they become a part of us except by imposing themselves upon us?

---

2. A critical aspect of Durkheim's argument is that individuals do not create their society but rather are born into preexisting duties, obligations, rights, ways of speaking, and ways of believing. This insight was to have a profound effect on some American scholars, particularly A. L. Kroeber (1876–1960) and Leslie White (1900–1975).

3. Durkheim argues that social facts are real because their effects can be felt. People may be unaware of these facts until they violate them. But, when they are violated, people face penalties that range from legal restrictions (if, for example, a person steals), to incomprehension (if, for example, a person addresses others in an unexpected language), to ridicule (think of the power of peer pressure in high school).

Note that this paragraph and the one previous begin to identify a theory of society. Durkheim was concerned with the forces that held society together, which created what he termed "social solidarity." Here he identifies some of these.

In the last sentence of this paragraph, Durkheim discusses resistance to new ideas. A famous modern example occurred when a Hewlett-Packard engineer named Steve Wozniak (b. 1950) built a prototype of a personal computer. He showed it to his supervisors, who rejected the idea because they couldn't imagine why anyone would want one. Wozniak went on to partner with Steve Jobs (1955–2011) and found the company Apple.

This is the whole meaning of our definition. And it is generally accepted, moreover, that social constraint is not necessarily incompatible with the individual personality.[a, 4]

Since the examples that we have just cited (legal and moral regulations, religious faiths, financial systems, etc.) all consist of established beliefs and practices, one might be led to believe that social facts exist only where there is some social organization. But there are other facts without such crystallized form which have the same objectivity and the same ascendancy over the individual. These are called "social currents." Thus the great movements of enthusiasm, indignation, and pity in a crowd do not originate in any one of the particular individual consciousnesses. They come to each one of us from without and can carry us away in spite of ourselves. Of course, it may happen that, in abandoning myself to them unreservedly, I do not feel the pressure they exert upon me. But it is revealed as soon as I try to resist them. Let an individual attempt to oppose one of these collective manifestations and the emotions that he denies will turn against him. Now, if this power of external coercion asserts itself so clearly in cases of resistance, it must exist also in the first-mentioned cases, although we are unconscious of it. We are then victims of the illusion of having ourselves created that which actually forced itself from without. If the complacency with which we permit ourselves to be carried along conceals the pressure undergone, nevertheless it does not abolish it. Thus, air is no less heavy because we do not detect its weight. So, even if we ourselves have spontaneously contributed to the production of the common emotion, the impression we have received differs markedly from that which we would have experienced if we had been alone. Also, once the crowd has dispersed, that is, once these social influences have ceased to act upon us and we are alone again, the emotions which have passed through the mind appear strange to us, and we no longer recognize them as ours. We realize that these feelings have been impressed upon us to a much greater extent than they were created by us. It may even happen that they horrify us, so much were they contrary to our nature. Thus, a group of individuals, most of whom are perfectly inoffensive, may, when gathered in a crowd, be drawn into acts of atrocity. And what we say of these transitory outbursts applies similarly to those more permanent currents of opinion on religious, political, literary, or artistic matters which are constantly being formed around us, whether in society as a whole or in more limited circles.[5]

---

4. Durkheim will present a formal definition of social fact at the end of this essay, but he has provided the background for it in this paragraph. Notice that he has created a new species: social facts, he insists, are real, exist outside the individual, and come from society. This is extremely useful, but also problematic in at least two ways: First, Durkheim wants to construct a science of sociology that is analogous to sciences like physics. However, do social facts exist in the same sense that atoms or gamma rays exist? Second, Durkheim insists that social facts cannot be reduced to individual psychology or physiology, but what exactly is the relation between the individual and social fact? Exactly what part of a person is individual and what part is simply a collection of social facts?

Some more recent theorists, such as Bruno Latour (1947–2022) have been deeply critical of Durkheim's idea of both social facts and society. For Durkheim and those he influenced, society had a real existence analogous to the existence of physical objects. Human actions were to be explained in terms of the interaction of social facts. Latour calls the people who maintain this position "sociologists of the social." He argues that there is no special reality that lies behind social phenomena and that "social is not a place, a thing, a domain, or a kind of stuff but a provisional movement of new associations" (2005: 238).

5. Durkheim differentiates social facts, which are enduring, from transitory social currents. He is far more interested in social facts but uses social currents, such as the momentary emotions sweeping a crowd, to give his readers a taste of the power of phenomena that he believes are both compelling and originate outside of the self. As members of a crowd, we are capable of emotions (and actions) beyond our individual capabilities or desires.

Issues of crowd behavior were very much on the minds of writers of this era. The unsuccessful European revolutions of 1848 and the Paris Commune of 1871 had included striking displays of mob and government

To confirm this definition of the social fact by a characteristic illustration from common experience, one need only observe the manner in which children are brought up. Considering the facts as they are and as they have always been, it becomes immediately evident that all education is a continuous effort to impose on the child ways of seeing, feeling, and acting which he could not have arrived at spontaneously. From the very first hours of his life, we compel him to eat, drink, and sleep at regular hours; we constrain him to cleanliness, calmness, and obedience; later we exert pressure upon him in order that he may learn proper consideration for others, respect for customs and conventions, the need for work, etc. If, in time, this constraint ceases to be felt, it is because it gradually gives rise to habits and to internal tendencies that render constraint unnecessary; but nevertheless it is not abolished, for it is still the source from which these habits were derived. It is true that, according to Spencer, a rational education ought to reject such methods, allowing the child to act in complete liberty; but as this pedagogic theory has never been applied by any known people, it must be accepted only as an expression of personal opinion, not as a fact which can contradict the aforementioned observations. What makes these facts particularly instructive is that the aim of education is, precisely, the socialization of the human being; the process of education, therefore, gives us in a nutshell the historical fashion in which the social being is constituted. This unremitting pressure to which the child is subjected is the very pressure of the social milieu which tends to fashion him in its own image, and of which parents and teachers are merely the representatives and intermediaries.[6]

It follows that sociological phenomena cannot be defined by their universality. A thought which we find in every individual consciousness, a movement repeated by all individual manifestations, is not thereby a social fact. If sociologists have been satisfied with defining them by this characteristic, it is because they confused them with what one might call their reincarnation in the individual. It is, however, the collective aspects of the beliefs, tendencies, and practices of a group that characterize truly social phenomena. As for the forms that the collective states assume when refracted in the individual, these are things of another sort. This duality is clearly demonstrated by the fact that these two orders of phenomena are frequently found dissociated from one another. Indeed, certain of these social manners of acting and thinking acquire, by reason of their repetition, a certain rigidity which on its own

---

violence. In 1894, a year before the publication of this essay, Alfred Dreyfus (1859–1935), the only Jewish officer in the French army's General Staff, was wrongly convicted of spying for the Germans. The affair inflamed mob passion against Jews, socialists, and other minorities. The proto-fascist politician and author Maurice Barrès (1862–1923) called for a leader who would be an embodiment of the collective will of the masses. Durkheim, as a secular, Jewish socialist, must have been deeply concerned.

6. Durkheim's ideas about the importance of early childhood and education (as well as those of Sigmund Freud) had an important effect on later generations. American anthropologists of the mid-twentieth century such as Margaret Mead (1901–1978), Ruth Benedict (1887–1948), and Cora Du Bois (1903–1991) conducted studies on the relationship between culture and personality. They referred to early childhood experience as *enculturation* and tried to demonstrate the effect of child-rearing practices on adult personality. Pierre Bourdieu (1930–2002), as well as many others in the late twentieth century, studied the ways in which early experiences and education created class distinctions and reproduced the social order.

Durkheim cites Herbert Spencer, who published a series of essays on education in the mid-nineteenth century. These were collected in the book *Education: Intellectual, Moral, and Physical* in 1861. In many ways, Spencer follows Jean-Jacques Rousseau, who had written on education a century earlier, in his 1762 *Emile*. Like Rousseau, Spencer argued for experimental education and an emphasis on natural consequences. Unlike Rousseau, he emphasized the practical value of scientific education. It is interesting that Durkheim cites Spencer rather than Rousseau, who wrote in French and spent much of his life in France. He probably does so because he considered Spencer a scientist and Rousseau a philosopher, and Durkheim wished to emphasize the scientific nature of his work.

account crystallizes them, so to speak, and isolates them from the particular events which reflect them. They thus acquire a body, a tangible form, and constitute a reality in their own right, quite distinct from the individual facts which produce it. Collective habits are inherent not only in the successive acts which they determine but, by a privilege of which we find no example in the biological realm, they are given permanent expression in a formula which is repeated from mouth to mouth, transmitted by education, and fixed even in writing. Such is the origin and nature of legal and moral rules, popular aphorisms and proverbs, articles of faith wherein religious or political groups condense their beliefs, standards of taste established by literary schools, etc. None of these can be found entirely reproduced in the applications made of them by individuals, since they can exist even without being actually applied.[7] No doubt, this dissociation does not always manifest itself with equal distinctness, but its obvious existence in the important and numerous cases just cited is sufficient to prove that the social fact is a thing distinct from its individual manifestations. Moreover, even when this dissociation is not immediately apparent, it may often be disclosed by certain devices of method. Such dissociation is indispensable if one wishes to separate social facts from their alloys in order to observe them in a state of purity. Currents of opinion, with an intensity varying according to the time and place, impel certain groups either to more marriages, for example, or to more suicides, or to a higher or lower birthrate, etc. These currents are plainly social facts. At first sight they seem inseparable from the forms they take in individual cases. But statistics furnish us with the means of isolating them. They are, in fact, represented with considerable exactness by the rates of births, dividing the average annual total of marriages, births, suicides, by the number of persons whose ages lie within the range in which marriages, births, and suicides occur.[b] Since each of these figures contains all the individual cases indiscriminately, the individual circumstances which may have had a share in the production of the phenomenon are neutralized and, consequently, do not contribute to its determination. The average, then, expresses a certain state of the group mind.[8]

Such are social phenomena, when disentangled from all foreign matter. As for their individual manifestations, these are indeed, to a certain extent, social, since they partly reproduce a social model. Each of them also depends, and to a large extent, on the organo-psychological constitution of the individual and on the particular circumstances in which he is placed. Thus they are not sociological phenomena in the strict sense of the word.

---

7. Since they are beyond the individual, social facts must have an existence apart from their individual manifestations. Indeed, individual behavior can only approximate the rules of social behavior. Durkheim was familiar with Platonic philosophy, and his argument parallels that perspective. Plato, in *The Republic*, proposed that objects on earth are imperfect representations of ideal forms existing beyond human consciousness; Durkheim suggests that actual behavior is the imperfect representation of crystallized social facts existing beyond individual awareness. A problem with this view is that a social fact must somehow be teased out of a myriad of individual manifestations, none of which accurately reflects it. Will all observers find the same social facts?

8. The use of statistics to predict behavior was of relatively recent origin when Durkheim wrote this article. The astronomer-turned-statistician Adolphe J. Quetelet (1796–1874) published two volumes, *On Man and the Development of His Faculties* (1835) and *Of the Social System and the Laws Which Rule It* (1848), in which probability theory was first applied to population characteristics. (Tylor also refers to Quetelet in essay 2.) Because the behavioral characteristics of a population are predictable through statistical analysis, Durkheim saw statistics as a scientific method for identifying social facts. In this paragraph, he mentions their use in analyzing suicide rates. *Suicide: A Study in Sociology* (1897), which appeared two years after this essay, was one of Durkheim's most influential works and makes extensive use of statistics.

At the end of this paragraph, there is a phrase translated as "group mind" that refers to the statistically identifiable behavior of a group. The French phrase Durkheim used was *l'âme collective*. This term is typically translated as "collective conscious" and refers to what today we would call *culture*.

They belong to two realms at once; one could call them sociopsychological. They interest the sociologist without constituting the immediate subject matter of sociology. There exist in the interior of organisms similar phenomena, compound in their nature, which form in their turn the subject matter of the "hybrid sciences," such as physiological chemistry, for example.

The objection may be raised that a phenomenon is collective only if it is common to all members of society, or at least to most of them in other words, if it is truly general. This may be true; but it is general because it is collective (that is, more or less obligatory), and certainly not collective because general. It is a group condition repeated in the individual because imposed on him. It is to be found in each part because it exists in the whole, rather than in the whole because it exists in the parts. This becomes conspicuously evident in those beliefs and practices which are transmitted to us ready-made by previous generations; we receive and adopt them because, being both collective and ancient, they are invested with a particular authority that education has taught us to recognize and respect. It is, of course, true that a vast portion of our social culture is transmitted to us in this way; but even when the social fact is due in part to our direct collaboration, its nature is not different. A collective emotion which bursts forth suddenly and violently in a crowd does not express merely what all the individual sentiments had in common; it is something entirely different, as we have shown. It results from their being together, a product of the actions and reactions which take place between individual consciousnesses; and if each individual consciousness echoes the collective sentiment, it is by virtue of the special energy resident in its collective origin. If all hearts beat in unison, this is not the result of a spontaneous and preestablished harmony but rather because an identical force propels them in the same direction. Each is carried along by all.[9]

We thus arrive at the point where we can formulate and delimit in a precise way the domain of sociology. It comprises only a limited group of phenomena. A social fact is to be recognized by the power of external coercion which it exercises or is capable of exercising over individuals, and the presence of this power may be recognized in its turn either by the existence of some specific sanction or by the resistance offered against every individual effort that tends to violate it. One can, however, define it also by its diffusion within the group, provided that, in conformity with our previous remarks, one takes care to add as a second and essential characteristic that its own existence is independent of the individual forms it assumes in its diffusion. This last criterion is perhaps, in certain cases, easier to apply than the preceding one. In fact, the constraint is easy to ascertain when it expresses itself externally by some direct reaction of society, as is the case in law, morals, beliefs, customs, and even fashions. But when it is only indirect, like the constraint which an economic organization exercises, it cannot always be so easily detected. Generality combined with externality may, then, be easier to establish. Moreover, this second definition is but another form of the first; for if a mode of behavior whose existence is external to individual consciousnesses becomes general,

---

9. Although the wording may be confusing, Durkheim makes an important point at the outset of this paragraph. He argues that people share beliefs or behaviors because they are collective. They are not collective because everyone shares them. This both separates the social fact from psychology and finesses an important problem. If social facts are collective because everyone shares them, it is difficult to explain the occurrence of individuals who don't share them. If on the other hand, they are external to individuals and people share them because they are collective, this problem is less important. However, Durkheim is proposing the existence of entities that can only be inferred indirectly by studying people's actions. A social fact cannot be directly observed.

Durkheim also returns to the problem of the crowd. He suggests that mob psychology is not simply the sum total of the individual feelings, it is rather a manifestation of a social fact created by their shared existence. Here Durkheim talks about something occurring "between individual consciousnesses." Durkheim hypothesized that this is where social facts and collective representations resided.

this can only be brought about by its being imposed upon them.[c, 10]

But these several phenomena present the same characteristic by which we defined the others. These "ways of existing" are imposed on the individual precisely in the same fashion as the "ways of acting" of which we have spoken. Indeed, when we wish to know how a society is divided politically, of what these divisions themselves are composed, and how complete is the fusion existing between them, we shall not achieve our purpose by physical inspection and by geographical observations; for these phenomena are social, even when they have some basis in physical nature. It is only by a study of public law that a comprehension of this organization is possible, for it is this law that determines the organization, as it equally determines our domestic and civil relations. This political organization is, then, no less obligatory than the social facts mentioned above. If the population crowds into our cities instead of scattering into the country, this is due to a trend of public opinion, a collective drive that imposes this concentration upon the individuals. We can no more choose the style of our houses than of our clothing—at least, both are equally obligatory. The channels of communication prescribe the direction of internal migrations and commerce, etc., and even their extent. Consequently, at the very most, it should be necessary to add to the list of phenomena which we have enumerated as presenting the distinctive criterion of a social fact only one additional category, "ways of existing"; and as this enumeration was not meant to be rigorously exhaustive, the addition would not be absolutely necessary.[11]

Such an addition is perhaps not necessary, for these "ways of existing" are only crystallized "ways of acting." The political structure of a society is merely the way in which its component segments have become accustomed to live with one another. If their relations are traditionally intimate, the segments tend to fuse with one another, or, in the contrary case, to retain their identity. The type of habitation imposed upon us is merely the way in which our contemporaries and our ancestors have been accustomed to construct their houses. The methods of communication are merely the channels which the regular currents of commerce and migrations have dug, by flowing in the same direction. To be sure, if the phenomena of a structural character alone presented this permanence, one might believe that they constituted a distinct species. A legal

---

10. In this paragraph, Durkheim summarizes the characteristics of social facts: They are external to individuals and coercive. Sometimes social facts are enshrined in law or can be recognized by the negative reaction of others when a principle is violated. Frequently they can be determined by the statistical analysis of a population's behavior. Notice that Durkheim says that constraints may be caused by economic organization. Some much more recent analysts understand this constraint in terms of "structural violence." The idea that social institutions constrain and disadvantage people relies on the idea that such institutions are social facts.

Note also the similarity between Durkheim's reference to "laws, morals . . ." and Tylor's 1871 definition of culture (see essay 2).

Durkheim's footnote comments on the work of the French criminologist Gabriel Tarde (1843–1904). In opposition to Durkheim, Tarde thought of society as simply a grouping of individuals and believed that individuals engaged one another through invention, imitation, and opposition. In the early 2000s, Bruno Latour (2002) returned to the dispute between Durkheim and Tarde and argued that Tarde's understanding was ultimately more useful. In general, Latour argued that what Durkheim thought of as social fact and collective conscience is the result of rather than the cause of the behaviors and actions of individuals, institutions, and technologies.

11. In these paragraphs, Durkheim considers the degree to which physical environmental factors can be considered social facts. Although he adds some caveats, in general, he dismisses this idea, believing that our ways of acting, feeling, and thinking are (mostly) independent of our environment. Though he distanced himself from socialist political movements, he was very sympathetic to socialist ideas and probably considered himself a socialist. However, he rejected Marx's analysis of society. He wrote, "Socialism is not a science, a sociology in miniature: it is a cry of pain." For Durkheim, socialism would be neither revolutionary nor class-based but instead a "carefully considered, progressive transformation of society" (Cotterrell 1999: 187).

regulation is an arrangement no less permanent than a type of architecture, and yet the regulation is a "physiological" fact. A simple moral maxim is assuredly somewhat more malleable, but it is much more rigid than a simple professional custom or a fashion. There is thus a whole series of degrees without a break in continuity between the facts of the most articulated structure and those free currents of social life which are not yet definitely molded. The differences between them are, therefore, only differences in the degree of consolidation they present. Both are simply life, more or less crystallized. No doubt, it may be of some advantage to reserve the term "morphological" for those social facts which concern the social substratum, but only on condition of not overlooking the fact that they are of the same nature as the others. Our definition will then include the whole relevant range of facts if we say: A social fact is every way of acting, fixed or not, capable of exercising on the individual an external constraint; or again, every way of acting which is general throughout a given society, while at the same time existing in its own right independent of its individual manifestations.[d, 12]

AUTHOR'S NOTES

a. We do not intend to imply, however, that all constraint is normal. We shall return to this point later.

b. Suicides do not occur at every age, and they take place with varying intensity at the different ages in which they occur.

c. It will be seen how this definition of the social fact diverges from that which forms the basis of the ingenious system of M. Tarde. First of all, we wish to state that our researches have nowhere led us to observe that preponderant influence in the genesis of collective facts which M. Tarde attributes to imitation. Moreover, from the preceding definition, which is not a theory but simply a résumé of the immediate data of observation, it seems indeed to follow, not only that imitation does not always express the essential and characteristic features of the social fact, but even that it never expresses them. No doubt, every social fact is imitated; it has, as we have just shown, a tendency to become general, but that is because it is social, that is, obligatory. Its power of expansion is not the cause but the consequence of its sociological character. If, further, only social facts produced this consequence, imitation could perhaps serve, if not to explain them, at least to define them. But an individual condition which produces a whole series of effects remains individual nevertheless. Moreover, one may ask whether the word "imitation" is indeed fitted to designate an effect due to a coercive influence. Thus, by this single expression, very different phenomena, which ought to be distinguished, are confused.

d. This close connection between life and structure, organ and function, may be easily proved in sociology because between these two extreme terms there exists a whole series of immediately observable intermediate stages which show the bond between them. Biology is not in the same favorable position. But we may well believe that the inductions on this subject made by sociology are applicable to biology and that, in organisms as well as in societies, only differences in degree exist between these two orders of facts.

---

12. In this paragraph, Durkheim continues to argue that physical facts of environment are no different from sociological facts, such as law, and that physical facts cannot be considered a separate species of social fact. He also suggests that social facts exist in a broad range of gradations, from the most fixed (the type of dwellings we live in) to the most flexible (fashion). In his footnote to this passage, he suggests that the gradations in social fact are analogous to those that exist between structure, organ, and function in biology and says that arguing from sociology to biology is sound reasoning. Many of Durkheim's followers saw strong connections between society and the body. Robert Hertz, for example, argued that people are right-handed because of the social values associated with right and left. Marcel Mauss (1872–1950) wrote on "body techniques," and much later, Bourdieu understood *habitus* to include aspects of the body. Durkheim concludes this essay with a famous concise definition of social fact.

6. Excerpts from *The Gift*

Marcel Mauss (1872–1950)

[*Our reprint of Mauss's work opens with section 3 of chapter 2. In sections 1 and 2 of that chapter, comprising about five thousand words, Mauss describes the rules of generosity on the Andaman Islands and the kula trade in Melanesia, as well as other associated exchange practices. These exchanges, he believes, are the material expressions of what Durkheim called social facts. They are used to forge and maintain alliances, and they replicate the divisions between the people involved in them. The interdependence of the exchange network increases social solidarity. He continues here with a discussion of potlatch among Native Americans.*]

HONOUR AND CREDIT (NORTH-WEST AMERICA)

From these observations on Melanesian and Polynesian peoples our picture of gift economy is already beginning to take shape. Material and moral life, as exemplified in gift exchange, functions there in a manner at once interested and obligatory. Furthermore, the obligation is expressed in myth and imagery, symbolically and collectively; it takes the form of interest in the objects exchanged; the objects are never completely separated from the men who exchange them; the communion and alliance they establish are well-nigh indissoluble. The lasting influence of the objects exchanged is a direct expression of the manner in which sub-groups within **segmentary societies** of an archaic type are constantly embroiled with and feel themselves in debt to each other.

Indian societies of the American North-West have the same institutions, but in a more radical and accentuated form. Barter is unknown there. Even now after long contact with Europeans it does not appear that any of the considerable and continual transfers of wealth take place otherwise than through the formality of the potlatch.* We now describe this institution as we see it.[1]

First, however, we give a short account of these societies. The tribes in question inhabit the North-West American coast—the Tlingit and Haida of Alaska,* and the Tsimshian and Kwakiutl of British Columbia.* They live on the sea or on the rivers and depend more on fishing than on hunting for their livelihood; but in contrast to the Melanesians and Polynesians they do not practice agriculture. Yet they are very wealthy, and even at the present day their fishing, hunting and trapping activities yield surpluses which are considerable even when reckoned on the European scale. They have the most substantial houses of all the American tribes, and a highly evolved cedar industry. Their canoes are good; and although they seldom venture out on to the open sea they are skillful in navigating around their islands and in coastal waters. They have a high standard of material culture. In particular, even back in the eighteenth century, they collected, smelted,

From *L'Année Sociologique* (1925)

1. Mauss implies here that the purpose of these practices cannot be explained simply by economics. If their root purposes were economic, they would have disappeared with European contact.

"*" Mauss's original includes 120 notes. Space limitations prevent us from reproducing them here, but asterisks have been included to show where they were placed.

molded and beat local copper from Tsimshian and Tlingit country. Some of the copper in the form of decorated shields they used as a kind of currency. Almost certainly another form of currency was the beautifully embellished Chilkat blanket-work still used ornamentally, some of it being of considerable value.* The peoples are excellent carvers and craftsmen. Their pipes, clubs and sticks are the pride of our ethnological collections. Within broad limits this civilization is remarkably uniform. It is clear that the societies have been in contact with each other from very early days, although their languages suggest that they belong to at least three families of peoples.*²

Their winter life, even with the southern tribes, is very different from their summer life. The tribes have a two-fold structure: at the end of spring they disperse and go hunting, collect berries from the hillsides and fish the rivers for salmon; while in winter they concentrate in what are known as towns. During this period of concentration they are in a perpetual state of effervescence. The social life becomes intense in the extreme, even more so than in the concentrations of tribes that manage to form in the summer. This life consists of continual movement. There are constant visits of whole tribes to others, of clans to clans and families to families. There is feast upon feast, some of long duration. On the occasion of a marriage, on various ritual occasions, and on social advancement, there

is reckless consumption of everything which has been amassed with great industry from some of the richest coasts of the world during the course of summer and autumn. Even private life passes in this manner; clansmen are invited when a seal is killed or a box of roots or berries opened; you invite everyone when a whale runs aground.³

Social organization, too, is fairly constant throughout the area though it ranges from the matrilineal phratry (Tlingit and Haida) to the modified matrilineal clan of the Kwakiutl; but the general characters of the social organization and particularly of totemism are repeated in all the tribes. They have associations like those of the Banks Islanders of Melanesia, wrongly called "secret societies," which are often intertribal; and men's and women's societies among the Kwakiutl cut across tribal organization. A part of the gifts and counterprestations which we shall discuss goes, as in Melanesia,* to pay one's way into the successive steps* of the associations. Clan and association ritual follows the marriage of chiefs, the sale of coppers, initiations, shamanistic seances and funeral ceremonies, the latter being more particularly pronounced among the Tlingit and Haida. These are all accomplished in the course of an indefinitely prolonged series of potlatches. Potlatches are given in all directions, corresponding to other potlatches to which they are the response. As in Melanesia the process is one of constant give-and-take.⁴

---

2. This and the next several paragraphs provide a broad ethnographic description of the potlatch customs of several Northwest Native American groups, much of which is drawn from the work of Franz Boas (1858–1942). Mauss's description is a catalog of material culture, but his real interests lie in examining patterns of social interaction.

3. For Émile Durkheim and his followers, members of *l'Année Sociologique* school, the idea of periods of "effervescence" was critical in the binary separation of sacred and profane. For example, discussing Australian Aborigines in *The Elementary Forms of the Religious Life*, Durkheim wrote that sacred times, when people assemble, were marked by "a sort of electricity . . . which transports them to exaltation. Every sentiment expressed finds a place without resistance in all the minds . . . each re-echoes the others, and is re-echoed by the others. . . . How could such experiences as these . . . fail to leave [an individual convinced] that there really exist two heterogeneous and mutually incomparable worlds?" (1965: 245–250). Mauss's use of the word "effervescence" here, and his division of the year into winter and summer seasons, mirrors the Durkheimian division of sacred (the winter) and profane (the summer).

4. Mauss's work deals with a class of phenomena he calls "prestations," which are a type of gift exchange between groups. Prestations appear "disinterested and spontaneous" but are neither. Rather, in prestation,

The potlatch, so unique as a phenomenon, yet so typical of these tribes, is really nothing other than gift-exchange. The only differences are in the violence, rivalry and antagonism aroused, in a lack of **jural** concepts, and in a simpler structure. It is less refined than in Melanesia, especially as regards the northern tribes, the Tlingit and the Haida,* but the collective nature of the contract is more pronounced than in Melanesia and Polynesia.* Despite appearances, the institutions here are nearer to what we call simple total prestations. Thus the legal and economic concepts attached to them have less clarity and conscious precision. Nevertheless, in action the principles emerge formally and clearly.[5]

There are two traits more in evidence here than in the Melanesian potlatch or in the more evolved and discrete institutions of Polynesia: the themes of credit and honour.*

As we have seen, when gifts circulate in Melanesia and Polynesia the return is assured by the virtue of the things passed on, which are their own guarantees. In any society it is in the nature of the gift in the end to being its own reward. By definition, a common meal, a distribution of **kava**, or a charm worn, cannot be repaid at once. Time has to pass before a counterprestation can be made. Thus the notion of time is logically implied when one pays a visit, contracts a marriage or an alliance, makes a treaty, goes to organized games, fights or feasts of others, renders ritual and honorific service and "shows respect," to use the Tlingit term.* All these are things exchanged side by side with

other material objects, and they are the more numerous as the society is wealthier. [6]

On this point, legal and economic theory is greatly at fault. Imbued with modern ideas, current theory tends towards a priori notions of evolution,* and claims to follow a so-called necessary logic; in fact, however, it remains based on old traditions. Nothing could be more dangerous than what Simiand called this "**unconscious sociology**." For instance, Cuq could still say in 1910: "In primitive societies barter alone is found; in those more advanced, direct sale is practiced. Sale on credit characterizes a higher stage of civilization; it appears first in an indirect manner, a combination of sale and loan."* In fact the origin of credit is different. It is to be found in a range of customs neglected by lawyers and economists as uninteresting: namely the gift, which is a complex phenomenon especially in its ancient form of total prestation which we are studying here. Now a gift necessarily implies the notion of credit. Economic evolution has not gone from barter to sale and from cash to credit. Barter arose from the system of gifts given and received on credit, simplified by drawing together the moments of time which had previously been distinct. Likewise purchase and sale—both direct sale and credit sale—and the loan, derive from the same source. There is nothing to suggest that any economic system which has passed through the phase we are describing was ignorant of the idea of credit, of which all archaic societies around us are aware. This is a simple and realistic manner

---

both gift and return gift are obligatory and enacted under a highly specific system of reciprocity. Note again the intersection of Durkheim's and Mauss's work. In *The Elementary Forms of the Religious Life,* Durkheim analyzes and connects effervescence, clans, and other divisions of Australian aboriginal society and totemism.

5. Mauss follows Durkheim's idea of social evolution from mechanical to organic solidarity. Mauss believes that the Northwest Pacific societies he is describing are simpler than those of Melanesia and that they are characterized by what Durkheim called "mechanical solidarity." In mechanical societies, solidarity is maintained by face-to-face contact and social institutions are not separated from each, as in complex societies. Instead, a few phenomena—called "total social phenomena"—simultaneously express a great many institutions. Potlatch exchange, as Mauss details below, is such a phenomenon.

"Jural": legal.

6. **"Kava"**: a Polynesian ritual beverage consumed to produce a euphoric state. Made from the roots of the kava plant, *Piper methysticum.*

of dealing with the problem, which Davy has already studied, of the "two moments of time" which the contract unites.*7

No less important is the role which honour plays in the transactions of the Indians. Nowhere else is the prestige of an individual as closely bound up with expenditure, and with the duty of returning with interest gifts received in such a way that the creditor becomes the debtor. Consumption and destruction are virtually unlimited. In some potlatch systems one is constrained to expend everything one possesses and to keep nothing.* The rich man who shows his wealth by spending recklessly is the man who wins prestige. The principles of rivalry and antagonism are basic. Political and individual status in associations and clans, and rank of every kind, are determined by the war of property, as well as by armed hostilities, by chance, inheritance, alliance or marriage.* But everything is conceived as if it were a war of wealth.* Marriage of one's children and one's position at gatherings are determined solely in the course of the potlatch given and returned. Position is also lost as in war, gambling,* hunting and wrestling.* Sometimes there is no question of receiving return; one destroys simply in order to give the appearance that one has no desire to receive anything back.* Whole cases of candlefish or whale oil,* houses, and blankets by the thousand are burnt; the most valuable coppers are broken and thrown into the sea to level and crush a rival. Progress up the social ladder is made in this way not only for oneself but also for one's family. Thus in a system of this kind much wealth is continually being consumed and transferred. Such transfers may if desired be called exchange or even commerce or sale;* but it is an aristocratic type of commerce characterized by etiquette and generosity; moreover, when it is carried out in a different spirit, for immediate gain, it is viewed with the greatest disdain.*8

---

7. Here Mauss takes aim at simple linear evolutionary schemes that see the practices of European societies as the most evolved.

"Unconscious sociology": François Simiand (1873–1935) was a student of Durkheim and a core member of the L'Annee Sociologique group. By "unconscious sociology" Simiand meant the tendency of amateur and professional social analysts to attempt, frequently incorrectly, to extrapolate practices of other societies and other times, from the practices of their own. In this example, it is the idea that since modern society depends on credit, earlier or simpler societies must have used something simpler. Barter is simpler than credit, ergo, less advanced societies must use barter. Mauss argues on the contrary that credit is an ancient practice and is fundamental to simpler societies.

Economics plays a critical role in Durkheim's and Mauss's thinking about evolution. Credit is important because it is a force of social solidarity. Individuals are held together in society by their mutual debt. This implies an economic model propelled by cooperation as well as competition. Durkheim and Mauss were hostile to Darwinian models of social evolution, which stressed conflict and competition. In Durkheim's model, social evolution is driven by the need to achieve social solidarity at greater levels of population density and complexity.

Mauss refers positively to the work of François Simiand and Georges Davy (1883–1955) and negatively to the work of Edouard Cuq (1850–1934). Simiand was a French economic historian, a student of Durkheim, member of L'Année Sociologique, and a socialist. He was critical of scholars of his day and suggested that history could not be studied apart from social and economic structures. Davy, another member of L'Année Sociologique, was a specialist in the sociology of law. He made extensive use of Mauss's analysis of the potlatch in describing the transition from statute to contractual law. Cuq was an historian and specialist in ancient law with no personal connection to Durkheim.

8. This paragraph discusses Mauss's understanding of the potlatch as a competition for prestige. For Mauss, neither psychology nor economics could explain the vast destruction of property caused by the potlatch or the seemingly illogical behavior of its participants. Instead, he believed that potlatch was about the status of groups, their maintenance of internal cohesion, and their relations with each other. The degree to which the potlatch involved the destruction of property and Mauss's emphasis on destruction in this paragraph have both been highly controversial. Authors such as Gail Ringel (1979) and Sergei Kan (1986) have seen

We see, then, that the notion of honour, strong in Polynesia, and present in Melanesia, is exceptionally marked here. On this point the classical writings made a poor estimate of the motives which animate men and of all that we owe to societies that preceded our own. Even as informed a scholar as Huvelin felt obliged to deduce the notion of honour—which is reputedly without efficacy—from the notion of magical efficacy.* The truth is more complex. The notion of honor is no more foreign to these civilizations than the notion of magic.* Polynesian mana itself symbolizes not only the magical power of the person but also his honour, and one of the best translations of the word is "authority" or "wealth."* The Tlingit or Haida potlatch consists in considering mutual services as honours.* Even in really primitive societies like the Australian, the "point of honor" is as ticklish as it is in ours; and it may be satisfied by prestations, offerings of food, by precedence or ritual, as well as by gifts.* Men could pledge their honor long before they could sign their names.[9]

The North-West American potlatch has been studied enough as to the form of the contract. But we must find a place for the researches of Davy and Adam in the wider framework of our subject. For the potlatch is more than a legal phenomenon; it is one of those phenomena we propose to call "total." It is religious, mythological and shamanistic because the chiefs taking part are incarnations of gods and ancestors, whose names they bear, whose dances they dance and whose spirits possess them.* It is economic; and one has to assess the value, importance, causes and effects of transactions which are enormous even when reckoned by European standards. The potlatch is also a phenomenon of social morphology; the reunion of tribes, clans, families and nations produces great excitement. People fraternize but at the same time remain strangers; community of interest and opposition are revealed constantly in a great whirl of business.* Finally, from the jural point of view, we have already noted the contractual forms and what we might call the human element of the contract, and the legal status of the contracting parties—as clans or families or with reference to rank or marital condition; and to this we now add that the material objects of the contracts have a virtue of their own which causes them to be given and compels the making of counter-gifts.[10]

---

the destruction of goods in the potlatch as a product of interactions between native and European economic systems and specific to the late nineteenth century Additionally, Jacques Derrida (1930–2004), who argues that a genuine gift exists only outside the kind of calculative reasoning Mauss implies, suggests that in this passage, Mauss is guilty of "a certain excess of the gift" and that his sociological narrative has gone "a little mad" (1992: 46). Derrida contends that Mauss's work is about the word "gift" rather than the gift itself.

9. In this paragraph, Mauss talks about the importance of honor and the different ways it is manifested in different societies. Here, and in other passages, Mauss attacks simplistic understandings of primitive people as morally inferior to Europeans. Although optimistic about the future of civilization, he was highly critical of his own society and, to some degree, romanticized the primitive. In the conclusion to *The Gift*, he wrote, "Hence, we should return to the old and elemental. Once again we shall discover . . . the joy of giving in public, the delight in generous artistic expenditure, the pleasure of hospitality in the public or private feast. . . . We can visualize a society in which these principles obtain. . . . For honour, disinterestedness and corporate solidarity are not vain words, nor do they deny the necessity for work" (1967: 67).

Paul Huvelin (1873–1924) was a specialist in Roman law and a member of the law faculty at the University of Lyon. He was a friend of Mauss and an important member of the *L'Année Sociologique* group. Huvelin theorized that the origins of law were magical. Note how gently Mauss critiques him.

10. In this passage, Mauss first identifies the potlatch as a total social phenomenon. It is total because it implicates so many different aspects of society: religion, economy, kinship structures, and the law.

Georges Davy's contribution is described in note 7. Leonhard Adam (1891–1960) was a German-born anthropologist, lawyer, and art historian who, after fleeing the Nazis in 1933, spent his career primarily in

It would have been useful, if space had been available, to distinguish four forms of American potlatch: first, potlatch where the phratries and chiefs' families alone take part (Tlingit); second, potlatches in which phratries, clans, families and chiefs take more or less similar roles (Haida); third, potlatch with chiefs and their clans confronting each other (Tsimshian); and fourth, potlatch of chiefs and fraternities (Kwakiutl). But this would prolong our argument, and in any case three of the four forms (with the exception of the Tsimshian) have already been comparatively described by Davy.* But as far as our study is concerned all the forms are more or less identical as regards the elements of the gift, the obligation to receive and the obligation to make a return.

THE THREE OBLIGATIONS: GIVING, RECEIVING, REPAYING

The Obligation to Give

This is the essence of potlatch. A chief must give a potlatch for himself, his son, his son-in-law or daughter* and for the dead.* He can keep his authority in his tribe, village and family, and maintain his position with the chiefs inside and outside his nation,* only if he can prove that he is favorably regarded by the spirits, that he possesses fortune* and that he is possessed by it.* The only way to demonstrate his fortune is by expending it to the humiliation of others, by putting them "in the shadow of his name."* Kwakiutl and Haida noblemen have the same notion of "face" as the Chinese mandarin or officer.* It is said of one of the great mythical chiefs who gave no feast that he had a "rotten face."* The expression is more apt than it is even in China; for to lose one's face is to lose one's spirit, which is truly the "face," the dancing mask, the right to incarnate a spirit and wear an emblem or totem. It is the veritable persona which is at stake, and it can

be lost in the potlatch* just as it can be lost in the game of gift-giving,* in war,* or through some error in ritual.* In all these societies one is anxious to give; there is no occasion of importance (even outside the solemn winter gatherings) when one is not obliged to invite friends to share the produce of the chase or the forest which the gods or totems have sent;* to redistribute everything received at a potlatch; or to recognize services* from chiefs, vassals or relatives* by means of gifts. Failing these obligations—at least for the nobles—etiquette is violated and rank is lost.*

The obligation to invite is particularly evident between clans or between tribes. It makes sense only if the invitation is given to people other than members of the family, clan or phratry.* Everyone who can, will or does attend the potlatch must be invited.* Neglect has fateful results.* An important Tsimshian myth* shows the state of mind in which the central theme of much European folklore originated: the myth of the bad fairy neglected at a baptism or marriage. Here the institutional fabric in which it is sewn appears clearly, and we realize the kind of civilization in which it functioned. A princess of one of the Tsimshian villages conceives in the "Country of the Otters" and gives birth miraculously to "Little Otter." She returns with her child to the village of her father, the chief. Little Otter catches halibut with which her father feeds all the tribal chiefs. He introduces Little Otter to everyone and requests them not to kill him if they find him fishing in his animal form: "Here is my grandson who has brought for you this food with which I serve you, my guests." Thus the grandfather grows rich with all manner of wealth brought to him by the chiefs when they come in the winter hunger to eat whale and seal and the fresh fish caught by Little Otter. But one chief is not invited. And one day when the crew of a canoe of the neglected tribe meets Little Otter at sea the bowman kills him and takes the seal. The grandfather and all the tribes search high and low for Little Otter until they hear about the

---

Australia. Adam studied the potlatch (among other things), and his work was cited by Franz Boas in his 1940 book *Race, Language, and Culture.*

neglected tribe. The latter offers its excuses; it has never heard of Little Otter. The princess dies of grief; the involuntarily guilty chief brings the grandfather all sorts of gifts in expiation. The myth ends: "That is why the people have great feasts when a chief's son is born and gets a name; for none may be ignorant of him."* The potlatch—the distribution of goods—is the fundamental act of public recognition in all spheres, military, legal, economic and religious. The chief or his son is recognized and acknowledged by the people.[11]

Sometimes the ritual in the feasts of the Kwakiutl and other tribes in the same group expresses this obligation to invite.* Part of the ceremonial opens with the "ceremony of the dogs." These are represented by masked men who come out of one house and force their way into another. They commemorate the occasion on which the people of the three other tribes of Kwakiutl proper neglected to invite the clan which ranked highest among them, the Guetela who, having no desire to remain outsiders, entered the dancing house and destroyed everything.*

The Obligation to Receive

This is no less constraining. One does not have the right to refuse a gift or a potlatch.* To do so would show fear of having to reply, and of being abased in default. One would "lose the weight" of one's name by admitting defeat in advance.* In certain circumstances, however, a refusal can be an assertion of victory and invincibility.* It appears at least with the Kwakiutl that a recognized position in the hierarchy, or a victory through previous potlatches, allows one to refuse an invitation or even a gift without war ensuing. If this is so, then a potlatch must be carried out by the man who refuses to accept the invitation. More particularly, he has to contribute to the "fat festival" in which a ritual of refusal may be observed.* The chief who considers himself superior refuses the spoonful of fat offered him: he fetches his copper and returns with it to "extinguish the fire" (of the fat). A series of formalities follow which mark the challenge and oblige the chief who has refused to give another potlatch or fat festival.* In principle, however, gifts are always accepted and praised.* You must speak your appreciation of food prepared for you.* But you accept a challenge at the same time.* You receive a gift "on the back." You accept the food and you do so because you mean to take up the challenge and prove that you are not unworthy.* When chiefs confront each other in this manner they may find themselves in odd situations and probably they experience them as such. In like manner in ancient Gaul and Germany, as well as nowadays in gatherings of French farmers and students, one is pledged to swallow quantities of liquid to "do honor" in grotesque fashion to the host. The obligation stands even although one is only heir to the man who bears the challenge.* Failure to give or receive,* like failure to make return gifts, means a loss of dignity.*[12]

The Obligation to Repay

Outside pure destruction the obligation to repay is the essence of potlatch.* Destruction is very often sacrificial, directed towards the spirits, and apparently does not require a return unconditionally, especially when it is the work of a superior clan chief or of the chief

---

11. The comparison of the Tsimshian myth to European folklore in this paragraph presupposes an evolutionary framework. Mauss, like many other social thinkers of the time, saw primitive cultures as living fossils. Given this premise, it followed that current Tsimshian myths were equivalent to ancient European folktales. Note also the emphasis on social being. Little Otter is a social being for the chiefs to whom he has been introduced. He is killed by a group to whom he was not introduced, for whom he had no social existence.

12. Notice that, though Mauss has said that prestations do sometimes serve an economic role, his discussion of potlatch is not economic. Instead, he sees the potlatch as symbolic of social relations between groups, which is why he can say that the obligation to receive is "no less constraining" than the obligation to give.

Note also that at the end of this paragraph, Mauss is talking humorously about drinking alcohol at parties. The current equivalent is doing shots or playing drinking games. Does one lose dignity if one doesn't drink (or maybe if one drinks too much)?

of a clan already recognized as superior.* But normally the potlatch must be returned with interest like all other gifts. The interest is generally between 30 and 100 per cent a year. If a subject receives a blanket from his chief for a service rendered he will return two on the occasion of a marriage in the chief's family or on the initiation of the chief's son. But then the chief in his turn redistributes to him whatever he gets from the next potlatch at which rival clans repay the chief's generosity.

The obligation of worthy return is imperative.* Face is lost for ever if it is not made or if equivalent value is not destroyed.*

The sanction for the obligation to repay is enslavement for debt. This is so at least for the Kwakiutl, Haida and Tsimshian. It is an institution comparable in nature and function to the Roman **nexum**. The person who cannot return a loan or potlatch loses his rank and even his status of a free man. If among the Kwakiutl a man of poor credit has to borrow he is said to "sell a slave." We need not stress the similarity of this expression with the Roman one.* The Haida say, as if they had invented the Latin phrase independently, that a girl's mother who gives a betrothal payment to the mother of a young chief "puts a thread on him." [13]

Just as the Trobriand kula is an extreme case of gift exchange, so the potlatch in North-West America is the monster child of the gift system. In societies of phratries, amongst the Tlingit and Haida, we find important traces of a former total prestation (which is characteristic of the Athabascans, a related group). Presents are exchanged on any pretext for any service, and everything is returned sooner or later for redistribution.* The Tsimshian have almost the same rules.* Among the Kwakiutl these rules, in many cases, function outside the potlatch.* We shall not press this obvious point; old authors described the potlatch in such a way as to make it doubtful whether it was or was not a distinct institution.* We may recall that with the Chinook, one of the least known tribes but one which would repay study, the word "potlatch" means "gift."*[14]

THE POWER IN OBJECTS OF EXCHANGE

Our analysis can be carried farther to show that in the things exchanged at a potlatch there is a certain power which forces them to circulate, to be given away and repaid.

To begin with, the Kwakiutl and Tsimshian, and perhaps others, make the same distinction between the various types of property as do the Romans, Trobrianders and Samoans. They have the ordinary articles of consumption and distribution and perhaps also of sale (I have found no trace of barter). They have also the valuable family property—talismans, decorated coppers, skin blankets and embroidered fabrics.* This class of articles is transmitted with that solemnity with which women are given in marriage, privileges are endowed on sons-in-law, and names and status are given to children and daughters' husbands.* It is wrong to speak here of alienation, for these things are loaned rather than sold and ceded. Basically they are **sacra** which the family parts with, if at all, only with reluctance.[15]

---

13. **"Nexum"**: a system of contracting a loan in ancient Rome in which the loan was made in the presence of five witnesses. Debtors could be held in bondage for failure to repay.

14. Note Mauss's widely quoted description of the potlatch as "the monster child of the gift system." The phrase actually belongs to the translator, Ian Cunnison (1923–2013). The original French reads that the potlatch is the *produit monstrueux du systeme des présents*. It would be fair to translate this, as W. D. Halls does, as the "monstrous product of the system of presents." However, that is much less quotable. Cunnison was a protégé of E. E. Evans-Pritchard, who did extensive fieldwork in Sudan and was the first professor of anthropology at the University of Khartoum in Sudan (Clark 2013).

15. Mauss's comment on alienation illustrates his insistence that the transactions he describes are not economic—that is, they are not driven by the desire to maximize material profit or minimize loss. Objects cannot really be alienated since they take their meaning not from their exchange value but rather from their

Closer observation reveals similar distinctions among the Haida. This tribe has in fact sacralized, in the manner of Antiquity, the notions of property and wealth. By a religious and mythological effort of a type rare enough in the Americas they have managed to reify an abstraction: the "Property Woman," of whom we possess myths and a description.* She is nothing less than the mother, the founding goddess of the dominant phratry, the Eagles. But oddly enough—a fact which recalls the Asiatic world and Antiquity—she appears identical with the "queen," the principal piece in the game of tipcat, the piece that wins everything and whose name the Property Woman bears. This goddess is found in Tlingit* country and her myth, if not her cult, among the Tsimshian* and Kwakiutl.*[16]

Together these precious family articles constitute what one might call the magical legacy of the people; they are conceived as such by their owner, by the initiate he gives them to, by the ancestor who endowed the clan with them, and by the founding hero of the clan to whom the spirits gave them.* In any case in all these clans they are spiritual in origin and nature.* Further, they are kept in a large ornate box which itself is endowed with a powerful personality, which speaks, is in communion with the owner, contains his soul, and so on.*

Each of these precious objects and tokens of wealth has, as amongst the Trobrianders, its name,* quality and power.* The large abalone shells,* the shields covered with them, the decorated blankets with faces, eyes, and animal and human figures embroidered and woven into them, are all personalities.* The houses and decorated beams are themselves beings.* Everything speaks—roof, fire, carvings and paintings; for the magical house is built not only by the chief and his people and those of the opposing phratry but also by the gods and ancestors; spirits and young initiates are welcomed and cast out by the house in person.*

Each of these precious things has, moreover, a productive capacity within it.* Each, as well as being a sign and surety of life, is also a sign and surety of wealth, a magico-religious guarantee of rank and prosperity.* Ceremonial dishes and spoons decorated and carved with the clan totem or sign of rank, are animate things.* They are replicas of the never ending supply of tools, the creators of food, which the spirits gave to the ancestors. They are supposedly miraculous. Objects are confounded with the spirits who made them, and eating utensils with food. Thus Kwakiutl dishes and Haida spoons are essential goods with a strict circulation and are carefully shared out between the families and clans of the chiefs.[17]

---

identification with particular individuals and social groups. Severing the connection between the object and these would render the transaction meaningless. In current day society, when we buy an object, a basic part of the transaction is that the object is alienated from its former owner who now has no claims on it.

"**Sacra**": Latin, "objects of devotion."

16. To reify an abstraction: that is, to turn an abstract idea, the sacredness of certain kinds of property and wealth, into a thing; in this case, "property woman." The game referred to in this passage is obscure. Tip-cat was a British field game that was a forerunner of baseball and cricket. However, in Mauss's original, he says "jeu de bâtonnets" which is a French tabletop game (but current versions do not have a queen). Halls (2000: 56) translates the passage as "'the game of sticks' ('tip-it')," but it is not clear what this is either.

17. Notice the fluidity with which Mauss moves among different cultures. In this section, he has mentioned Kwakiutl (current day Kwakwaka'wakw), Tsimshian, Romans, Trobrianders, Samoans, and Haida. The Kwakiutl, Tsimshian, and Haida peoples live in fairly close proximity to one another, but Trobrianders, Samoans, and Romans are separated from them by vast distances of space and, in the case of the Romans, time. Mauss believed that all of these cultures presented examples of the same class of gift giving. American anthropologists writing in the same era held that cultural practices must be described within their social and historical context. Therefore, the kind of analysis that Mauss presents here was inappropriate since it did violence to the data by taking cultural practices out of their context.

MONEY OF RENOWN (**RENOMMIERGELD**) * 18

Decorated coppers* are the most important articles in the potlatch, and beliefs and a cult are attached to them. With all these tribes copper, a living being, is the object of cult and myth.* Copper, with the Haida and Kwakiutl at least, is identified with salmon, itself an object of cult.* But in addition to this mythical element each copper is by itself an object of individual belief.* Each principal copper of the families of clan chiefs has its name and individuality;* it has also its own value,* in the full magical and economic sense of the word which is regulated by the vicissitudes of the potlatches through which it passes and even by its partial or complete destruction.*

Coppers have also a virtue which attracts other coppers to them, as wealth attracts wealth and as dignity attracts honours, spirit-possession and good alliances.* In this way they live their own lives and attract other coppers.* One of the Kwakiutl coppers is called "Bringer of Coppers" and the formula describes how the coppers gather around it, while the name of its owner is "Copper-Flowing-Towards-Me."* With the Haida and Tlingit, coppers are a "fortress" for the princess who owns them; elsewhere a chief who owns them is rendered invincible.* They are the "flat divine objects" of the house.* Often the myth identifies together the spirits who gave the coppers, the owners and the coppers themselves.* It is impossible to discern what makes the power of the one out of the spirit and the wealth of the other; a copper talks and grunts, demanding to be given away or destroyed;* it is covered with blankets to keep it warm just as a chief is smothered in the blankets he is to distribute.*

From another angle we see the transmission of wealth and good fortune.* The spirits and minor spirits of an initiate allow him to own coppers and talismans which then enable him to acquire other coppers, greater wealth, higher rank and more spirits (all of these being equivalents). If we consider the coppers with other forms of wealth which are the object of hoarding and potlatch—masks, talismans and so on—we find they are all confounded in their uses and effects.* Through them rank is obtained; because a man obtains wealth he obtains a spirit which in turn possesses him, enabling him to overcome obstacles heroically. Then later the hero is paid for his shamanistic services, ritual dances and trances. Everything is tied together; things have personality, and personalities are in some manner the permanent possession of the clan. Titles, talismans, coppers and spirits of chiefs are homonyms and synonyms, having the same nature and function.* The circulation of goods follows that of men, women and children, of festival ritual, ceremonies and dances, jokes and injuries. Basically they are the same. If things are given and returned it is precisely because one gives and returns "respects" and "courtesies." But in addition, in giving them, a man gives himself, and he does so because he owes himself—himself and his possessions—to others.[19]

Primary Conclusion

From our study of four important groups of people we find the following: first, in two or three of the groups, we find the potlatch, its leading motive and its typical form. In all groups we see the archaic form of exchange—the gift and the return gift. Moreover, in these societies we note the circulation of objects side by side with the circulation of persons and rights. We

---

18. "**Renommiergeld**" is translated here as "money of reknown." "Bragging money," the translation given by Johan Huizinga (1872–1945) in his book *Homo Ludens* (1949: 62), might be more apt. The concept refers to owning an object that brings one status.

19. In this paragraph, Mauss claims that the goods given in potlatch are, in essence, indistinguishable from the people giving them. The goods have personalities and are members of households. Giving them is then spiritually the same as the movement of people from household to household. Twenty-five years later, in his first major work, *Les Structures Élémentaires de la Parenté* (*The Elementary Structures of Kinship*, 1949), Lévi-Strauss expanded this line of argument by analyzing the exchange of women between groups as a fundamental social phenomenon.

might stop at this point. The amount, distribution and importance of our data authorize us to conceive of a regime embracing a large part of humanity over a long transitional phase, and persisting to this day among peoples other than those described. We may then consider that the spirit of gift exchange is characteristic of societies which have passed the phase of "total prestation" (between clan and clan, family and family) but have not yet reached the stage of pure individual contract, the money market, sale proper, fixed price, and weighed and coined money.[20]

[*The Gift, in its entirety, is a reasonably short essay (only about eighty pages plus extensive notes in the Norton Library edition). The passage you have just read is the conclusion of chapter 2. Chapter 3, titled "Survivals in Early Literature," discusses written evidence for Mauss' theory of gift-giving from ancient Roman law, ancient Hindu legal documents, early Germanic society, and, very briefly, Chinese law. Chapter 4 is titled "Conclusions." The first two sections, which we have excluded here, are moral conclusions and political and economic conclusions. They consist of about 4,750 words and 23 footnotes. We rejoin the text with the sociological and ethical conclusions with which Mauss ends his essay.*]

SOCIOLOGICAL AND ETHICAL CONCLUSIONS

We may be permitted another note about the method we have used. We do not set this work up as a model; it simply proffers one or two suggestions. It is incomplete: the analysis could be pushed farther.* We are really posing questions for historians and anthropologists and offering possible lines of research for them rather than resolving a problem and laying down definite answers. It is enough for us to be sure for the moment that we have given sufficient data for such an end.

This being the case, we would point out that there is a heuristic element in our manner of treatment. The facts we have studied are all "total" social phenomena. The word "general" may be preferred although we like it less. Some of the facts presented concern the whole of society and its institutions (as with potlatch, opposing clans, tribes on visit, etc.); others, in which exchanges and contracts are the concern of individuals embrace a large number of institutions.[21]

These phenomena are at once legal, economic, religious, aesthetic, morphological and so on. They are legal in that they concern individual and collective rights, organized and diffuse morality; they may be entirely obligatory, or subject simply to praise or disapproval. They are at once political and domestic, being of interest both to classes and to clans and families. They are religious; they concern true religion, animism, magic and diffuse religious mentality. They are economic, for the notions of value, utility, interest, luxury, wealth, acquisition, accumulation, consumption and liberal and sumptuous expenditure are all present, although not perhaps in their modern senses. Moreover, these institutions have an important aesthetic side which we have left unstudied; but the dances performed, the songs and shows, the dramatic representations given between camps or partners, the objects made,

---

20. This conclusion points once again to the evolutionary nature of Mauss's thinking. He saw exchange as evolving from encompassing every aspect of society to a specialized area of society. This follows Durkheim's understanding of social evolution as proceeding from mechanical to organic solidarity. However, the distinction between mechanical and organic solidarity is not as absolute as Durkheim supposed. Are there not elements of American society, such as sports teams, that create mechanical solidarity within a larger society with organic solidarity? Similarly, does not gift giving in our society share many of the characteristics that Mauss identifies in this essay?

21. In this paragraph and below, Mauss provides a comprehensive definition of total social phenomena, and suggests that the investigation of such phenomena provides an outstanding pathway for developing an understanding of society in general. Mauss claims that total social phenomena are morphological. That is, they reveal the underlying structure of the groups practicing them.

used, decorated, polished, amassed and transmitted with affection, received with joy, given away in triumph, the feasts in which everyone participates—all these, the food, objects and services, are the source of aesthetic emotions as well as emotions aroused by interest.* This is true not only of Melanesia but also, and particularly, of the potlatch of North-West America and still more true of the market-festival of the Indo-European world. Lastly, our phenomena are clearly morphological. Everything that happens in the course of gatherings, fairs and markets or in the feasts that replace them, presupposes groups whose duration exceeds the season of social concentration, like the winter potlatch of the Kwakiutl or the few weeks of the Melanesian maritime expeditions. Moreover, in order that these meetings may be carried out in peace, there must be roads or water for transport and tribal, inter-tribal or international alliances—**commercium and connubium**.*[22]

We are dealing then with something more than a set of themes, more than institutional elements, more than institutions, more even than systems of institutions divisible into legal, economic, religious and other parts. We are concerned with "wholes," with systems in their entirety. We have not described them as if they were fixed, in a static or skeletal condition, and still less have we dissected them into the rules and myths and values and so on of which they are composed. It is only by considering them as wholes that we have been able to see their essence, their operation and their living aspect, and to catch the fleeting moment when the society and its members take emotional stock of themselves and their situation as regards others. Only by making such concrete observation of social life is it possible to come upon facts such as those which our study is beginning to reveal. Nothing in our opinion is more urgent or promising than research into "total" social phenomena.[23]

The advantage is twofold. Firstly there is an advantage in generality, for facts of widespread occurrence are more likely to be universal than local institutions or themes, which are invariably tinged with local color. But particularly the advantage is in realism. We see social facts in the round, as they really are. In society there are not merely ideas and rules, but also men and groups and their behaviours. We see them in motion as an engineer sees masses and systems, or as we observe octopuses and anemones in the sea. We see groups of men, and active forces, submerged in their environments and sentiments.[24]

Historians believe and justly resent the fact that sociologists make too many abstractions and separate unduly the various elements of society. We should follow their precepts and observe what is given. The tangible fact is Rome or Athens or the average Frenchman or

---

22. **"*Commercium and connubium*"**: Latin, "commerce and lawful marriage"; these also referred to contract law and family law. To have commercium and connubium was to have full legal citizenship rights.

23. Here Mauss seems to emphasize direct observation through fieldwork and viewing cultures as integrated wholes. However, this is somewhat deceptive. Mauss did no fieldwork himself, relying instead on the work of Boas, Bronislaw Malinowski (1884–1942), and many others. Additionally, though Mauss has examined how gift giving implicates many different aspects of culture, he has also decontextualized gift giving, comparing specific practices of many different cultures. This makes his work quite different from the fieldwork-based holistic anthropology promoted by Boas and his students in the United States. However, Mauss's essay has been extremely important to the development of anthropology.

24. Mauss relies on Durkheim's idea of a social fact. For Durkheim, sociology was the analysis of social facts. He defines these as "every way of acting, fixed or not, capable of exercising on the individual an external constraint; or again, every way of acting which is general throughout a given society, while at the same time existing in its own right independent of its individual manifestations" (see essay 5). Durkheim and his followers believed in the possibility of a science of sociology. Note here that Mauss compares work in sociology to engineering (physics) and biology. The notion of sociology as science was persistent in the twentieth century. In the 1970s, a senior sociology professor at Texas State University gave lectures wearing a white lab coat to emphasize this fact.

the Melanesian of some island, and not prayer or law as such. Whereas formerly sociologists were obliged to analyze and abstract rather too much, they should now force themselves to reconstitute the whole. This is the way to reach incontestable facts. They will also find a way of satisfying psychologists who have a pronounced viewpoint, and particularly psycho-pathologists, since there is no doubt that the object of their study is concrete. They all observe, or at least ought to, minds as wholes and not minds divided into faculties. We should follow suit. The study of the concrete, which is the study of the whole, is made more readily, is more interesting and furnishes more explanations in the sphere of sociology than the study of the abstract. For we observe complete and complex beings. We too describe them in their organisms and **psychai** as well as in their behavior as groups, with the attendant psychoses: sentiments, ideas and desires of the crowd, of organized societies and their sub-groups. We see bodies and their reactions, and their ideas and sentiments as interpretations or as motive forces. The aim and principle of sociology is to observe and understand the whole group in its total behavior.[25]

It is not possible here—it would have meant extending a restricted study unduly—to seek the morphological implications of our facts. It may be worth while, however, to indicate the method one might follow in such a piece of research.

All the societies we have described above with the exception of our European societies are segmentary. Even the Indo-Europeans, the Romans before **the Twelve Tables**, the Germanic societies up to the **Edda**, and Irish society to the time of its chief literature, were still societies based on the clan or on great families more or less undivided internally and isolated from each other externally. All these were far removed from the degree of unification with which historians have credited them or which is ours today. Within these groups the individuals, even the most influential, were less serious, avaricious and selfish than we are; externally at least they were and are generous and more ready to give. In tribal feasts, in ceremonies of rival clans, allied families or those that assist at each other's initiation, groups visit each other; and with the development of the law of hospitality in more advanced societies, the rules of friendship and the contract are present—along with the gods—to ensure the peace of markets and villages; at these times men meet in a curious frame of mind with exaggerated fear and an equally exaggerated generosity which appear stupid in no one's eyes but our own. In these primitive and archaic societies there is no middle path. There is either complete trust or mistrust. One lays down one's arms, renounces magic and gives everything away, from casual hospitality to one's daughter or one's property. It is in such conditions that men, despite themselves, learnt to renounce what was theirs and made contracts to give and repay. [26]

But then they had no choice in the matter. When two groups of men meet they may move away or in case of mistrust or defiance they may resort to arms; or else they can come to terms. Business has always been done with foreigners, although these might have been allies. The people of Kiriwina said to Malinowski:

---

25. At the turn of the century, academic disciplines were not divided the same way they are today. One of Durkheim's concerns, here echoed by Mauss, was to show that sociology is a discipline with its own area of study and was distinct from history or psychology. Here he is concerned with positioning sociology as a science similar to but separate from psychology and psychiatry. He does this by emphasizing the concrete aspects of the subject matter of sociology.

"*Psychai*": daughters of the Greek goddess Psyche. Here probably simply used as a synonym for psyche or psychology.

26. "**Segmentary societies**": those whose organization is segmented by kin groups, such as a lineage, clan, and moiety.

"**The Twelve Tables**": the earliest Roman law, circa 540 BCE.

"**The *Edda***": a poetry and prose collection of Norse mythology written in Iceland in the thirteenth century.

"The Dobu man is not good as we are. He is fierce, he is a man-eater. When we come to Dobu, we fear him, he might kill us! But see! I spit the charmed ginger root and their mind turns. They lay down their spears, they receive us well."* Nothing better expresses how close together lie festival and warfare.[27]

Thurnwald describes with reference to another Melanesian tribe, with genealogical material, an actual event which shows just as clearly how these people pass in a group quite suddenly from a feast to a battle.* Buleau, a chief, had invited Bobal, another chief, and his people to a feast which was probably to be the first of a long series. Dances were performed all night long. By morning everyone was excited by the sleepless night of song and dance. On a remark made by Buleau one of Bobal's men killed him; and the troop of men massacred and pillaged and ran off with the women of the village. "Buleau and Bobal were more friends than rivals," they said to Thurnwald. We all have experience of events like this.[28]

It is by opposing reason to emotion and setting up the will for peace against rash follies of this kind that peoples succeed in substituting alliance, gift and commerce for war, isolation and stagnation.[29]

The research proposed would have some conclusion of this kind. Societies have progressed in the measure in which they, their sub-groups and their members, have been able to stabilize their contracts and to give, receive and repay. In order to trade, man must first lay down his spear. When that is done he can succeed in exchanging goods and persons not only between clan and clan but between tribe and tribe and nation and nation, and above all between individuals. It is only then that people can create, can satisfy their interests mutually and define them without recourse to arms. It is in this way that the clan, the tribe and nation have learnt—just as in the future the classes and nations and individuals will learn—how to oppose one another without slaughter and to give without sacrificing themselves to others. That is one of the secrets of their wisdom and solidarity.

There is no other course feasible. The Chronicles of Arthur* relate how King Arthur, with the help of a Cornish carpenter, invented the marvel of his court, the miraculous Round Table at which his knights would never come to blows. Formerly because of jealousy, skirmishes, duels and murders had set blood flowing in the most sumptuous of feasts. The carpenter says to Arthur: "I will make thee a fine table, where sixteen hundred may sit at once, and from which none need be excluded . . . And no knight will be able to raise combat, for there the highly placed will be on the same level as the lowly." There was no "head of the table" and hence no more quarrels. Wherever Arthur took his table, contented and invincible remained his noble company. And this today is the way of the nations that are strong, rich, good and happy. Peoples, classes, families and individuals may become rich, but they will not achieve happiness until they can sit down like the knights around their common riches. There is no need to seek far for goodness and happiness. It is to be found in the imposed peace, in the rhythm of communal and private labor, in wealth amassed and redistributed, in the mutual respect and reciprocal generosity that education can impart.

---

27. Malinowski, best known for his work in the Trobriand Islands, is a key source for Mauss's discussion of the kula exchange network. We present an extract from Malinowski's *Argonauts of the Western Pacific* (1922) in essay 14.

28. Richard Thurnwald (1869–1954) led research expeditions to the South Pacific in the early twentieth century. He was the founder of the journal *Sociologus* and a key voice in midcentury German anthropology.

29. Note that in the paragraphs you have just read, Mauss is both perceptive and romantic. He is perceptive in that he understands that gift giving and conflict are closely related. Gift exchange may be a continuation of war by other means (Pyyhtinen 2014: 64). He is romantic in understanding people in very positive terms and in connecting gift giving and the will for peace.

Thus we see how it is possible under certain circumstances to study total human behavior; and how that concrete study leads not only to a science of manners, a partial social science, but even to ethical conclusions—"civility," or "civics" as we say today. Through studies of this sort we can find, measure and assess the various determinants, aesthetic, moral, religious and economic, and the material and demographic factors, whose sum is the basis of society and constitutes the common life, and whose conscious direction is the supreme art— politics in the Socratic sense of the word.[30]

---

30. According to Durkheim's ideas about evolution, primitive mechanical solidarity gives way to modern organic solidarity. In this scheme, there is constant progress toward interdependence, and society reaches ever higher levels of integration. Rather than segments of society being opposed to each other in class warfare as Marxist analysts claim, or engaged in a Malthusian struggle for survival, as Spencerians believed, every part of society should be seen as working for the peace and benefit of the whole. In this condition, each individual should be able to fully achieve his or her potential.

Mauss's philosophy was optimistic but when *The Gift* was published in 1925, conditions in Europe were far from stable. The value of the franc had collapsed in 1924 and the French government, led by Edouard Herriot (1872–1957), was unstable and unable to solve the financial problems (it lasted only from June 1924 to April 1925). The essay's concluding paragraphs must be read in this context. They are, at the same time, an affirmation of Mauss's belief in progress and a plea for peace and harmony in the aftermath of war. Of course, it was not to be. The prosperity of the early postwar years soon turned to economic depression and political turmoil. The Nazi Party arose in Germany, and the world was on the path to an even greater war.

7. Class, Status, Party[a]

Max Weber (1864–1920)

ECONOMICALLY DETERMINED POWER AND THE SOCIAL ORDER

LAW EXISTS when there is a probability that an order will be upheld by a specific staff of men who will use physical or psychical compulsion with the intention of obtaining conformity with the order, or of inflicting sanctions for infringement of it. The structure of every legal order directly influences the distribution of power, economic or otherwise, within its respective community. This is true of all legal orders and not only that of the state. In general, we understand by "power" the chance of a man or of a number of men to realize their own will in a communal action even against the resistance of others who are participating in the action.[1]

"Economically conditioned" power is not, of course, identical with "power" as such. On the contrary, the emergence of economic power may be the consequence of power existing on other grounds. Man does not strive for power only in order to enrich himself economically. Power, including economic power, may be valued "for its own sake." Very frequently the striving for power is also conditioned by the social "honor" which it entails. Not all power, however, entails social honor: The typical American Boss, as well as the typical big speculator, deliberately relinquishes social honor. Quite generally, "mere economic" power, and especially "naked" money power, is by no means a recognized basis of social "honor." Nor is power the only basis of social "honor." Indeed, social honor, or prestige, may even be the basis of political or economic power, and very frequently has been. Power, as well as honor, may be guaranteed by the legal order, but, at least normally, it is not their primary source. The legal order is rather an additional factor that enhances the chance to hold power or honor; but it cannot always secure them.[2]

From *Economy and Society* (1922)

1. This essay was part of Weber's massive posthumously published work, *Wirtschaft und Gesellschaft (Economy and Society)*. Probably written between 1915 and 1920, it was first published in 1922. *Wirtschaft und Gesellschaft* was one volume of an extensive series of studies in the social sciences that Weber organized for the German publishing house Siebeck. Much of Weber's work was written in response to Karl Marx, and the relationship between the two is complex. The first section of the essay sets Weber's argument. In contrast to Marx, Weber insists that individual identity is not subsumed by class identity. Status and party may, and frequently do, cut across class membership. In this essay, he presents and discusses each of these forms of identity. Note the importance of compulsion in Weber's definition of power. Power is not the same as influence or authority. Power implies the possibility of coercion to a far greater extent than influence and authority.

G and M in the author's endnote a refer to the translators Hans Heinrich Gerth (1908–1978) and C. Wright Mills (1916–1962). Gerth and Mills were eminent sociologists and frequent coauthors.

2. Social thinkers and political activists (and Weber was both) in the Germany of Weber's time were extreme conservatives (generally members of the landowning upper class) or radicals who often espoused Marxist ideals (generally those identified with industrial workers). Weber—from a family whose wealth was based in textile manufacturing—identified with neither the conservative landowners nor the radical workers but was a political liberal trying to sit midway between the two.

The way in which social "honor" is distributed in a community between typical groups participating in this distribution, we may call the "social order." The social order and the economic order are, of course, similarly related to the "legal order." However, the social and the economic order are not identical. The economic order is for us merely the way in which economic goods and services are distributed and used. But, of course, the social order is conditioned by the economic order to a high degree, and in its turn reacts upon it.[3]

Now: "classes," "status groups," and "parties" are phenomena of the distribution of power within a community.

DETERMINATION OF CLASS-SITUATION BY MARKET-SITUATION

In our terminology, "classes" are not communities; they merely represent possible, and frequent, bases for communal action. We may speak of a "class" when (1) a number of people have in common a specific causal component of their life chances, in so far as (2) this component is represented exclusively by economic interests in the possession of goods and opportunities for income, and (3) is represented under the conditions of the commodity or labor markets. These points refer to "class situation," which we may express more briefly as the typical chance for a supply of goods, an "external" life fate, and an internal life fate, in so far as this chance is determined by the amount and kind of power, or lack of such, to dispose of goods or services in a market situation. The term "class" refers to any group of people that is found in the same class situation.[4]

It is the most elemental economic fact that the way in which disposition over material *property* is distributed among a plurality of people, meeting competitively in the market for the purpose of exchange, in itself creates specific life chances. According to the law of marginal utility this mode of distribution excludes the non-owners from competing for highly valued

---

Weber makes a distinction between mere wealth and wealth with social honor. Both in the United States and (particularly) the European nations of Weber's era, there were struggles between old wealth (in Europe, the aristocracy, in the United States those who made fortunes in the eighteenth and early nineteenth centuries) and rising industrial wealth. Weber viewed new wealth as money without social honor (as in the "American Boss"). Is this distinction relevant in our own era?

3. Weber felt that Marx's methods of analysis produced valuable insights. However, he believed that they leaned too heavily on economics and dialectical conflict between forces of production and relations of production as the motor driving social evolution. Weber incorporated much Marxist thought into his theories, yet he was not a Marxist and did not believe in a communist utopia. In the days of the Cold War, this might have been a factor in his appeal to American sociologists and anthropologists. In this paragraph, Weber links social order to both the distribution of wealth and the distribution of honor. He understands these as overlapping but far from identical.

4. Weber's definition of class overlapped Marx's, yet differed from it. For Marx, class signified a specific relationship to the means of production. In a class society, one class has ownership or control of the means of production, and another is employed producing surplus for that owner class. Further, classes are born in the struggle for control of the means of production. For Marx, understanding the role of class was key to the analysis of society; all other identifications were secondary. Although focused on ownership of property as the constitutive element of class, Weber downplayed other elements of Marx's analysis. In particular, Weber suggested that class does not necessarily have analytic primacy—other elements of identity may be of equal or greater importance. Moreover, Weber gave conflict less of a role in generating and maintaining class relationships than Marx did. For Weber, other forces are of much greater importance in social change. For example, Weber saw social evolution as a generalized process toward increased rationalization and bureaucratization that necessarily entailed the restriction of individual liberties. He believed that charisma acted in opposition to this process. Through strength of personality, the charismatic individual was able to break the bonds of routine and radically redirect society.

A later version of this essay by the same translators glosses external and internal life fates as external living conditions and personal life experiences.

goods; it favors the owners and, in fact, gives to them a monopoly to acquire such goods. Other things being equal, this mode of distribution monopolizes the opportunities for profitable deals for all those who, provided with goods, do not necessarily have to exchange them. It increases, at least generally, their power in price wars with those who, being property-less, have nothing to offer but their services in native form or goods in a form constituted through their own labor and who above all are compelled to get rid of these products in order barely to subsist. This mode of distribution gives to the propertied a monopoly on the possibility of transferring property from the sphere of use as a "fortune," to the sphere of "capital goods"; that is, it gives them the entrepreneurial function and all chances to share directly or indirectly in returns on capital. All this holds true within that sphere in which pure market conditions prevail. "Property" and "lack of property" are, therefore, the basic categories of all class situations. It does not matter whether these two categories become effective in price wars or in competitive struggles.[5]

However, within these categories, class situations are further differentiated, on the one hand, according to the kind of property that is usable for returns; and, on the other hand, according to the kind of services that can be offered in the market. Ownership of domestic buildings; productive establishments; warehouses; stores; agriculturally usable land, large and small holdings—quantitative differences with possibly qualitative consequences—; ownership of mines; cattle; men (slaves); disposition over mobile instruments of production, or capital goods of all sorts, especially money or objects that can be exchanged for money easily and at any time; disposition over products of one's own labor or of other's labor differ-

ing according to their various distances from consumability; disposition over transferable monopolies of any kind—all these distinctions differentiate the class situations of the propertied just as does the "meaning" which they can and do give to the utilization of property, especially to property which has money equivalence. Accordingly, the propertied, for instance, may belong to the class of rentiers or to the class of entrepreneurs.[6]

Those who have no property but who offer services are just as much differentiated according to their kinds of services and according to the way in which they make use of these services in a continuous or discontinuous relation to a recipient. But always this is the generic connotation of the concept of class: that the kind of chance in the *market* is the decisive moment which presents a common condition for the individual's fate. "Class situation" is, in this sense, ultimately "market situation." The effect of naked possession *per se*, which among cattle breeders gives the non-owning slave or serf into the power of the cattle owner, is only a forerunner of real "class" formation. However, in the cattle loan and in the naked severity of the law of debts in such communities for the first time mere "possession" as such emerges as decisive for the fate of the individual. This is very much in contrast to the agricultural communities based on labor. The creditor-debtor relation becomes the basis of "class situations" only in those cities where a "credit market," however primitive, with rates of interest increasing according to the extent of dearth and a factual monopolization of credits, is developed by a plutocracy. Therewith "class struggles" begin.[7]

A number of men whose fate is not determined by the chance of using goods or services for themselves on the market, e.g., slaves, are

---

5. Thus, Weber sees society as divided into those with and without property. Enormous advantages accrue to those with property and powerful disadvantages to those without. Those without property are forced into the market at disadvantageous terms. Those with property have more freedom to buy and sell as they please.

6. Property owners are further differentiated according to the type of property they own and its meaning within their society. Thus, like Marx, Weber sees types of ownership and types of production as critical to the shape of society. However, he gives a stronger role to meaning.

7. Notice the evolutionism implicit in this paragraph. In *The Gift* (essay 6), Marcel Mauss argued that credit was implicit in primitive societies. Here, Weber argues that class is incipient in herding societies but emerges with the credit markets in agricultural societies with strong, wealthy, property-owning classes.

not, however, a "class" in the technical sense of the term. They are, rather, a "status group."[8]

COMMUNAL ACTION FLOWING FROM CLASS INTEREST

According to our terminology, the factor which creates the "class" is unambiguously economic interest, and indeed, only those interests involved in the existence of the "market." Nevertheless, the concept of "class-*interest*" is an ambiguous one: even as an empirical concept it is ambiguous as soon as one understands by it something other than the factual direction of interests following with a certain probability from the class situation for a certain "average" of those people subjected to the class situation. The class situation and other circumstances remaining the same, the direction in which the individual worker, for instance, is likely to pursue his interests may vary widely according to whether he is constitutionally qualified for the task at hand to a high, to an average, or to a low degree. In the same way, the direction of interests may vary according to whether or not a *communal* action of a larger or smaller portion of those commonly affected by the "class situation," or even an association among them, e.g., a "trade union," has grown out of the class situation from which the individual may or may not expect promising results. Communal action refers to that action which is oriented to the feeling of the actors that they belong together. Societal action, on the other hand, is oriented to a rationally motivated adjustment of interests. The rise of societal or even of communal action from a common class situation is by no means a universal phenomenon.[9]

The class situation may be restricted in its effects to the generation of essentially *similar* reactions, that is to say, within our terminology, of "mass actions." However, it may not even have this result. Furthermore, often merely an amorphous communal action emerges. For example, the "murmuring" of the workers known in ancient oriental ethics: the moral disapproval of the work-master's conduct, which in its practical significance probably was equivalent to an increasingly typical phenomenon of precisely the latest industrial development, namely, the "slow down" (the deliberate limiting of work effort) of laborers by virtue of tacit agreement. The degree in which "communal action" and possibly "societal action," emerges from the "mass actions" of the members of a class is linked to general cultural conditions, especially to those of an intellectual sort, and to the extent of the already evolved contrasts; it is especially linked to the *transparency* of the connections between the causes and the consequences of the "class situation." However strongly life chances may be differentiated, this fact in itself, according to all experience, by no means gives birth to "class action" (communal action by the members of a class). The fact of being conditioned and the results of the class situation must be distinctly recognizable. For only then the contrast of life chances cannot be felt to be

---

8. Since Weber sees class as emerging from participation in the market. Slaves, because they do not participate in the market (or so Weber argues) are not a class. In Marx, class is a particular relationship not to the market but to the means of production, and slaves are certainly a class.

9. Underlying Weber's analysis is a concern for the issues of action and abstraction. For Weber, a class is an abstraction and therefore, in and of itself, could not act. Thus the actions that flow from class interest are problematic. To act, a group must be organized. In this passage, Weber shows that the actions of classes must be performed by individuals. However, individual variation within a class may be so great that it prevents the emergence of any generalized class consciousness or class struggle. Parties and status groups, discussed below, play key roles in organizing classes.

Note again the strong difference between Marx and Weber. For Marx, class determined the workers' interests. Marxists generally interpreted this to mean that all members of a class had identical interests. If individuals in the class failed to realize this, they were defective, had false consciousness, and were, in some instances, class traitors. Weber, on the other hand, is far more concerned with the individual. He points to the different ways that individuals are positioned within their class, and he understands class consciousness as variable: Many people in a class might think a certain way and express certain interests, but not all.

an absolutely given fact to be accepted, but can be felt to be a resultant from either (1) the given distribution of property, or (2) the structure of the concrete economic order. It is only then that people may react against the class structure, not only through acts of an intermittent and irrational protest but in the form of rational associations. There have been "class situations" of the first category (1), of such a specifically naked and transparent sort in the urban centers of antiquity and during the Middle Ages; especially then, when great fortunes were accumulated by factually monopolized trading in industrial products of these localities or in food stuffs. Furthermore, under certain circumstances, in the rural economy of the most diverse periods when agriculture was increasingly exploited in a profit-making manner. The most important historical example of the second category (2) is the class situation of the modern "proletariat."[10]

TYPES OF CLASS STRUGGLE

Thus every class may be the carrier of any one of the possibly innumerable forms of "class action," but this is not necessarily so. In any case, a class does not in itself constitute a community. To treat "class" conceptually as having the same value as "community" leads to distortion. That men in the same class situation regularly react in mass actions to such palpable situations as economic ones in the direction of those interests which are most adequate to their average number is an important and after all simple fact for the understanding of historical events. Above all, this fact must not lead to that kind of pseudo-scientific operation with the concepts of "class" and "class interests" so frequently found these days and which has found its most classic expression in the statement of a talented author,[b] that the individual may be in error concerning his interests but that the "class" is "infallible" about its interests. But if classes as such are not communities, nevertheless class situations emerge only on the basis of communalization. But the communal action which brings forth class situations is not basically action between members of the identical class; it is an action between members of different classes. Communal actions which directly determine the class situation of the worker and the entrepreneur are: the labor market, the commodities market, and the capitalistic enterprise. But, in its turn, the existence of a capitalistic enterprise presupposes a very specific communal action to exist which is specifically structured so as to protect the possession of goods *per se*, and especially the power of individuals to dispose, in principle freely, over means of production. The existence of a capitalistic enterprise is preconditioned by a specific kind of "legal order." Each kind of class situation, and above all when it rests upon the power of property *per se*, will come to efficacy in the clearest way when all other determinants of reciprocal relations are, as far as possible, eliminated in their significance. It is in this way that the utilization of the power of property in the market obtains its most sovereign importance.[11]

Now "status groups" hinder the strict carrying through of the sheer market principle.

---

10. Like the Marxists, Weber saw ideology as frequently masking the true nature of relations among people. Society could be understood by debunking the myths and ideological assertions that often cover economically or politically motivated action. Here he suggests that for class action to take place, class consciousness must already exist. However, various ideological structures may prevent classes from becoming aware of the true nature of their oppression and hence prevent the formation of class consciousness. Although Weber wrote about India and China, by far his primary interest was European history and society, and most of his analysis was driven by his understanding of these. His original scholarly interest was in history, and he wrote his doctoral thesis on trading companies during the Middle Ages. He later wrote essays on the social structure of ancient society. He refers frequently to the European Middle Ages and ancient Greece and Rome throughout his writing.

11. The translators, Gerth and Mills, identify the "talented author" as the Hungarian Marxist György Lukács (1885–1971); however, Weber was probably referring to Marx himself. Lukács had been a friend of Weber as well as numerous other key intellectuals of the era. He became the preeminent philosopher of Marxism as well

In the present context they are of interest to us only from this one point of view. Before we briefly consider them, note that not much of a general nature can be said about the more specific kinds of antagonism between "classes" (in our meaning of the term). The great shift, which has been going on continuously in the past, and up to our times, may be summarized, although at the cost of some precision: the struggle in which class situations are effective has progressively shifted from consumption credit toward, first, competitive struggles in the commodity market and, then, toward price wars on the labor market. The "class struggles" of antiquity—to the extent that they were genuine class struggles and not struggles between status groups—were initially carried on by indebted peasants, and perhaps also by artisans threatened by debt bondage struggling against urban creditors. For debt bondage is the normal result of the differentiation of wealth in commercial cities, especially in seaport cities. This situation has been similar among cattle breeders. Debt relationships as such produced class action up to the time of **Cataline**. Along with this, and with an increase in provision of grain

for the city by transporting it from the outside, the struggle over the means of sustenance emerged. It centered in the first place around the provision of bread and the determination of the price of bread. It lasted throughout antiquity and the entire Middle Ages. The propertyless as such flocked together against those who actually and supposedly were interested in the dearth of bread. This fight spread to involve all commodities essential to the way of life and to handicraft production. There were only incipient discussions of wage disputes in antiquity and in the Middle Ages. And slowly they have been increasing up into modern times. In the earlier periods they were completely secondary to slave rebellions as well as to fights in the commodity market.[12]

The propertyless of antiquity and of the Middle Ages protested against monopolies, preemption, forestalling, and the withholding of goods from the market for the purpose of raising prices. Today the central issue is the determination of the price of labor.

The transition is represented by the fight for access to the market and for the determination of the price of products. These fights

---

as Leninism and Stalinism in the middle third of the twentieth century. However, his move to Marxism probably came after Weber had written this essay.

The point Weber makes here highlights his disagreement with the Marxists. Marxism is a theory of class and group action in which the individual plays little role. For Weber, on the other hand, individuals and their relationships to social groups were of great importance. For Marxists, conflict between social groups is the key force that drives history. Weber suggests that such conflict can only exist when classes and groups are organized under quite specific conditions. A class, in the example here, cannot be infallible about its interests because a class is an abstraction and cannot have interests outside the interests of specific individuals in specific contexts. Weber here notes that the individuals who compose a class have interests outside of that class identification. It is only in particular contexts that their class interests outweigh other interests. In this passage, he illustrates some of the conditions under which class interests and struggle are likely to exist or historically did exist.

12. In this passage, Weber responds to Marx's dictum from the opening lines of *The Communist Manifesto* (1848): "the history of all hitherto existing society is the history of class struggles." Weber says that, on the contrary, history has sometimes involved class struggles and sometimes not. Here he presents particular cases in which class struggles were important and others in which they were not. Weber viewed sociology as the background information necessary to do history. The goal of his sociology was to propose general principles, but he believed that the actual unfolding of history was predicated on individual action and thus beyond any law. He wrote that "The reduction of empirical reality . . . to 'laws' is meaningless" and that "A systematic science of culture . . . would be senseless in itself" (Weber 1949: 81). Franz Boas (1858–1942) was probably quite familiar with Weber's work and had a similar understanding of the role of the individual. He, too, was "deeply concerned about individuals and individuality" (Lewis 2015: 19).

"**Cataline**": Lucius Sergius Catilina (108–62 BCE), a soldier and politician in the Roman Republic and the leader of an unsuccessful revolt.

went on between merchants and workers in the putting-out system of domestic handicraft during the transition to modern times. Since it is quite a general phenomenon we must mention here that the class antagonisms which are conditioned through the market situation are usually most bitter between those who actually and directly participate as opponents in price wars. It is not the rentier, the share-holder, and the banker who suffer the ill will of the worker, but almost exclusively the manufacturer and business executive who are direct opponents of workers in price wars. This is so in spite of the fact that it is precisely the cash boxes of the rentier, the share-holder, and the banker into which the more or less "unearned" gains flow, rather than into the pockets of the manufacturers or of the business executives. This simple state of affairs has very frequently been decisive for the role which the class situation has played in the formation of political parties. For example, it has made possible the varieties of patriarchal socialism and the frequent attempts—formerly, at least—of threatened status groups to form alliances with the proletariat against the "bourgeoisie."[13]

STATUS HONOR

In contrast to classes, *status groups* are normally communities. They are, however, often of an amorphous kind. In contrast to the purely economically determined "class situation" we wish to designate as "status situation" every typical component of the life fate of men which is determined by a specific, positive or negative, social estimation of *"honor."* This honor may be connected with any quality shared by a plurality.

Also, this honor can be knit to a class situation: class distinctions are linked in the most varied ways with status distinctions. Property as such is not always recognized as a status qualification, but in the long run it is, and with extraordinary regularity. In the subsistence economy of the organized neighborhood, very often the richest man is simply chieftain. However, this often means only honorific preference. For example, in the so-called pure modern "democracy," *i.e.*, one devoid of any expressly ordered status privileges for individuals, it happens that only the families coming under approximately the same tax class dance with one another. This example is reported of certain smaller Swiss cities. But status honor need not *necessarily* be linked with a "class situation." On the contrary, it normally stands in sharp opposition to the pretensions of sheer property.[14]

Both propertied and propertyless people can belong to the same status group, and frequently they do with very palpable consequences. This "equality" of social esteem may, however, in the long run become quite precarious. The "equality" of status among the American "gentlemen," for instance, is expressed in that outside the subordination determined by the different functions of "business" it would be considered strictly repugnant—wherever the old tradition still prevails—if even the richest "chief," while playing billiards or cards in his club in the evening, would not treat his "clerk" as in every sense fully his equal in birthright. It would be repugnant if the American "chief" would bestow upon his "clerk" the condescending "benevolence" which marks a distinction of "position," which the German chief can never **dissever** from his attitude. This is one of the most important reasons why in America the German "clubby-ness" has never

---

13. Here, Weber points out that class struggles are often misdirected. If class struggles were truly between classes, owners such as rentiers, shareholders, and bankers should suffer the wrath of the working class as much as manufacturers and business executives. Weber claims, however, that they do not because they are less likely to be in direct contact with the workers.

14. Above, Weber has described the operation of class within society. Here and below, he adds what he considers two other forces that cut across class identification and compete with it for prominence in social action: status and party. For Weber, class, status, and party are overlapping identifications. None of them has universal analytic priority, but rather identification with one or the other is dependent on circumstances. This idea of overlapping identities anticipates much of current anthropology including Kimberlé Crenshaw's idea of intersectionality (Crenshaw 1989).

been able to attain the attraction which the American clubs have.[15]

GUARANTEES OF STATUS STRATIFICATION

In content, status honor is normally expressed by the fact that above all else a specific *style of life* can be firmly expected from all those who wish to belong to the circle. Linked with this expectation are restrictions on "social" intercourse (*i.e.*, intercourse which is not subservient to economic or any other of business's "functional" purpose). These restrictions may confine normal intermarriages to the status circle and may lead to complete endogamous closure. As soon as there is, not a mere individual and socially irrelevant imitation of another style of life but, an agreed-upon communal action of this closing character, the "status" development is under way. In its characteristic way, stratification by "status groups" on the basis of conventional *styles of life* evolves at the present time in the United States out of the traditional democracy. For example, only the resident of a certain street ("the street") is considered as belonging to "society," is qualified for social intercourse, and is visited and invited. Above all, this differentiation evolves in such a way as to make for strict submission to the fashion that is dominant at a given time in

society. This submission to fashion also exists among men in America to a degree unknown in Germany. Such submission is considered to be an indication of the fact that a given man *pretends* to qualify as a gentleman. This submission decides, at least **prima facie**, that he will be treated as such. And this recognition becomes just as important for his employment chances in "swank" establishments, and above all, for social intercourse and marriage with "esteemed" families, as the qualification for "dueling" among Germans in the Kaiser's day. As for the rest: certain families resident for a long time (and, of course, correspondingly wealthy), families [*sic*] (*e.g.*, "F.F.V.," i.e., **First Families of Virginia**") or the actual or alleged descendants of the "Indian Princess" Pocahontas, of the Pilgrim fathers, or of the **Knickerbockers**, the members of almost inaccessible sects and all sorts of circles setting themselves apart by means of any other characteristics and badges . . . all these elements usurp "status" honor. The development of status is essentially a question of stratification resting upon usurpation. Such usurpation is the normal origin of almost all status honor. But the road from this purely conventional situation to legal privilege, positive or negative, is everywhere easily traveled as soon as a certain stratification of the social order has in fact been "lived in" and has achieved stability by virtue of the stabilization in the distribution of economic power.[16]

---

15. Weber's 1904 visit to America made a profound and lasting impression on him. Though greatly disturbed by the position of African Americans and immigrants, in many respects he viewed America as, for better and worse, the model of a new society. He felt that in America, rationalization and bureaucratization had proceeded to the greatest extent. The example of boss and worker treating each other as equals may appear fanciful to the modern reader, but for Weber, it illustrated the compartmentalization and bureaucratization of American life. It may also have reflected the intense formality of German life in Weber's era.

Note also the extensive use of scare quotes (quotes around particular words such as "clerk" and "position") in this and other passages in this essay. These appear in Weber's German original as well.

One of Weber's key contributions to sociology is the idea of *Entzauberung*, usually translated as "disenchantment." Weber believed that the magical and mystical elements of the world would be replaced by increasingly logical, secular, and rational thinking. Weber thought that this process of disenchantment was inevitable but not wholly desirable. The scare quotes around many words in this essay imply that these words are enchanted, not in the sense of being magical but in the sense of covering and explaining away a series of logical, rational propositions that sociology can uncover. Sociologists sometimes speak of the goal of sociology as demystifying society. In 2023, Warms performed a JSTOR search for "demystifying" and "sociology" that resulted in more than 2,500 hits.

"Dissever": divide or sever.

16. Although Weber recognized a link between economic position and status, he also believed that there were many other ways to acquire status. The examples he uses here are drawn from American society but reflect the extremely status-conscious German society. Weber came from a family of factory owners. He had

ETHNIC SEGREGATION AND CASTE

Where the consequences have been realized to their full extent the status group evolves into a closed "caste." This means that the status distinctions are guaranteed not merely by conventions and laws, but also by *rituals*. This occurs in such a way that every physical contact with a member of any caste which is considered to be "lower" by the members of a "higher" caste is evaluated as making for a ritualistic impurity and to be a stigma which must be expiated by a religious act. Individual castes develop in part quite disparate cults and gods.[17]

In general, however, the status structure reaches such extreme consequences only where differences which are defined as "ethnic" lie at its bottom. The "caste" is, indeed, the normal form in which ethnic communities usually live side by side in a "societalized" manner. These ethnic communities believe in blood relationship and exclude exogamous marriage and social intercourse. Such a caste situation exists with the phenomenon of "pariah" peoples which is found all over the world. These people form communities which have acquired specific occupational traditions of handicrafts or of other arts and which cultivate the belief in their ethnic community. Such people then live in a "diaspora" strictly segregated from all personal intercourse except that of an unavoidable sort; and their situation is legally precarious. But by virtue of their economic indispensability, pariah people are tolerated, indeed, frequently privileged, and they live in interspersed political communities. The Jews are the most impressive example in history.[18]

The "status" segregation grown into the "caste" and the mere "ethnic" segregation

---

trained in law at Heidelberg and was a member of his father's prestigious dueling fraternity. He had scars from the dueling he refers to in this passage (Franz Boas, six years older than Weber, also had dueling scars [Zumwalt 2013]). . After his studies and a year of military training, he was commissioned as an officer in the German army.

Much of Weber's writing in this essay feels very Victorian. It may be hard for people today to relate to his concern over who may dance with whom or billiards playing bosses. However, his ideas about the ways that status and honor are achieved, demonstrated, and retained remain relevant.

"*Prima facie*": Latin, "at first sight."

"**First Families of Virginia**": wealthy families that claimed descent from seventeenth-century European settlers. Many also claimed descent from Pocahontas.

"**Knickerbockers**": descendants of the Dutch settlers of New York.

17. Weber developed his notions of caste more fully in his work on the Indian caste system, but he clearly believed the term *caste* applied to a wide variety of social systems. He spends a good deal of time discussing caste here because he sees it as an extreme manifestation of status differences. One of Weber's contributions to sociology is the idea of the ideal type, a "one-sided accentuation of one or more points of view" (Weber 1949: 90). Weber uses "ideal" in the sense of the most extreme logical possibility rather than in the sense of best. He looked for, or logically constructed, extreme examples to gain insight into more typical social forms. Although the use of ideal types provides clear examples amenable to analysis, it may also obscure the complexity of social life.

18. Weber's position on Jews as "pariah people" has been deeply controversial. Weber wrote extensively on Judaism (for example, *Ancient Judaism*, in 1921). According to Abraham (1992), Weber's ideas about Jews are strongly influenced by his belief in the desirability of a unitary German culture. Weber believed that Jews could not be completely emancipated until they were fully assimilated into German culture and gave up all elements of cultural distinctiveness. The Nazi era proved that Weber was entirely wrong. Assimilation did not protect German Jews from genocide.

Weber was also embroiled in an intellectual dispute with Werner Sombart (1863–1941), a leading German economist and sociologist. Sombart argued that the origins of capitalism lay in the Jewish response to exclusion from the European economic system. Weber argued that the origins of capitalism lay in the Protestant Reformation. Sombart was deeply anti-Semitic and argued that Jews were responsible for the worst evils of capitalism (Funnell 2001), which he viewed largely in negative terms. Weber's anti-Semitism was less conscious and more subtle.

differ in their respective structures: the caste structure transforms the horizontal and unconnected coexistences of the ethnically segregated groups into a vertical social system of super- and sub-ordination. Correctly formulated: a comprehensive societalization integrates the ethnically divided communities into specific political and communal action. In their consequences they differ precisely in this way: whereas the ethnic coexistences condition the reciprocal repulsion and disdain but allow each ethnic community to consider its own honor as the highest one; the caste structure brings about a social subordination and an acknowledgment of "more honor" in favor of the privileged caste and status groups. This is due to the fact that in the caste structure ethnic distinctions as such have become "functional" distinctions within the political societalization (warriors, priests, artisans that are politically important for war and for buildings, and so on). But even the pariah people who are most despised are usually apt to continue cultivating in some manner that which is equally peculiar to ethnic and the status communities: the belief in their own specific "honor." This is the case with the Jews.[19]

Only with the negatively privileged "status groups" does the "sense of dignity" take a specific deviation. A sense of dignity is the precipitation in individuals of social honor and of conventional demands which the positively privileged "status group" raises for the deportment of its members. The sense of dignity which characterizes positively privileged status groups is naturally related to their "being" which does not transcend itself, that is, to their "beauty and excellence" (The Good and the Beautiful). Their kingdom is "of this world." They live for the present and by exploiting their great past. The sense of dignity of the negatively privileged strata can naturally refer to a future lying beyond the present, be it of this life or of another. In other words, it must be nurtured by the belief in a providential "mission" and by a belief in a specific honor before God as the "chosen people," that is, by beliefs either that in the beyond "the last will be the first" or that in this life a messiah will appear to bring forth into the light of the world which has cast them out the hidden honor of the pariah people. This simple state of affairs, and not the "resentment" which is so strongly emphasized in Nietzsche's much admired construction in the *Genealogy of Morals,* is the source of the religiosity cultivated by pariah status groups. In passing, we note that this trait, resentment, may be accurately applied only to a limited extent; for one of Nietzsche's main examples, Buddhism, it is not at all applicable.[20]

---

19. Notice Weber's use of the words "society" and "societalization." He theorized that there were three basic types of social structure: the community, the association, and the society (Gerth and Mills 1946: 57). To some degree, he understood history as a progression from community to society, with society marked by increased rationalization and bureaucratization. In Weber's usage, society is what modern anthropologists might refer to as *state-level society*. For Weber, when a group became societalized, it also became bureaucratized.

20. The work of Friedrich Wilhelm Nietzsche (1844–1900) was extremely influential for German social thinkers of the late nineteenth century. The reference here is to Nietzsche's *On the Genealogy of Morals* (1956 [1887]). In this work, Nietzsche proposed that there were two types of morality: master and slave. Master morality is the morality of the strong-willed; slave morality is based on resentment, and is created in opposition to what master morality considers good. Because they cannot bear the psychological burden of low position, oppressed people turn the characteristics of their subjugation, such as humility, charity, and pity into sources of honor. Thus, Nietzsche believed that ascetic Christian morality reflected the resentment of early Christians who were often slaves (Gerth and Mills 1946: 62). Nietzsche was deeply critical of both Buddhism and Christianity, describing them as world-weary and nihilistic (Nietzsche 1967: 18–23). However, he also argued that, since it had done away with the concept of God and posed problems "objectively and cooly," Buddhism was "a hundred times more realistic than Christianity" (Nietzsche 1968: 586). Although Weber is concerned with individual psychology, he understands the self-attribution of elevated moral status to oppressed peoples as a group function—one that maintains the status differentials of the caste system—rather than as an individual psychological coping mechanism. Weber probably considered resentment theory inapplicable to Buddhism because that religion's founder, the Indian prince Siddhartha Gautama (563?–483? BCE), was a man of high status.

Incidentally, the development of status groups from ethnic segregations is by no means the normal phenomenon. On the contrary, since objective "racial differences" are in no way basic to every subjective sentiment of "ethnic" community, the ultimately racial foundation of status structure is rightly and absolutely a question of the concrete individual case. Very frequently the "status group" is instrumental in the production of a thoroughbred anthropological type. Certainly the "status group" is to a high degree effective in producing extreme types and consists in a selection of personally qualified individuals (e.g., the Knighthood selects those who are fit for warfare, physically and psychically). But the selection of persons is far removed from being the only, or the predominant, way in which status groups are formed: Political membership or class situation has at least as frequently, in all times, been decisive. Today the class situation is by far the predominant factor. For the possibility of a style of life expected for members of "status groups" is, of course, usually conditioned economically.[21]

STATUS PRIVILEGES

For all practical purposes, stratification by status everywhere goes hand in hand with a monopolization of ideal and material goods or chances in the manner which we have come to know as typical. Besides the specific status honor, which always rests upon distance and exclusiveness, we find all sorts of material monopolies. Such honorific preferences may consist of the privilege to wear special costumes, to eat special dishes denied others by taboo, the privilege to carry arms which is most palpable in its consequences, the right to pursue certain non-professional dilettante artistic practices, e.g., to play certain musical instruments. Of course, material monopolies do provide the most effective motives for the exclusiveness of the status group, although, in themselves, they are rarely sufficient. But almost always they come into play to some extent. Within a status circle there is the question of intermarriage: the interest of the families in the monopolization of potential bridegrooms is at least of equal importance and is parallel to the interest in the monopolization of daughters. The daughters of the circle must be provided for. With an increased enclosure of the status group, the conventional preferential opportunities for special employment grow into a legal monopoly of special offices for the members of these delimited groups. Certain goods become objects for monopolization by status groups. In typical fashion these everywhere include "entailed estates"; frequently they also include the possessions of serfs or bondsmen and, finally, special trades. This monopolization occurs positively or negatively:

Positively: when the status group is exclusively entitled to own and to manage them;

Negatively: when, in order to maintain its specific way of life, the status group must *not* own and manage them. For the decisive role of the "style of life" in status "honor" means that the "status groups" are the specific bearers of all "conventions." In whatever way it may be manifest, all "stylization" of life either originates in status groups or at least is conserved by them. Even if the principles of status conventions differ greatly, they reveal certain typical traits, especially among those strata which are most privileged. Quite generally, among privileged status groups there is a status disqualification that operates against the performance of common physical labor. This disqualification is now "setting in" in America against the old tradition of esteem for labor. Very frequently every rational economic pursuit, and especially "entrepreneurial activity," is looked upon as a disqualification of status. Artistic and literary activity is also considered to be degrading work as soon as it is exploited for income, or at least

---

The "beauty and excellence" quote in this passage and following Greek is a reference to Plato's "Philebus," one of the Socratic dialogues. The "of this world" quote refers to the Christian Bible. In John 18:36 Jesus says, "My kingdom is not of this world."

21. Note that Weber argues that caste groups may be separated by perceived racial distinctions but are not created by these. Rather, differential status may, in time, create distinctions that are then perceived as racial.

when it is connected with hard physical exertion. An example is the sculptor working like a mason in his dusty smock as over against the painter in his salon-like "studio" and those forms of musical practice that are acceptable to the status group.[22]

ECONOMIC CONDITIONS AND EFFECTS OF STATUS STRATIFICATION

The frequent disqualification of the gainfully employed as such is a direct result of the principle of status stratification peculiar to the social order, and of course, of this principle's opposition to a distribution of power which is regulated exclusively through the market. These two factors operate along with various individual ones, which will be touched upon below.

We have seen above that the market and its processes "knows no personal distinctions": "functional" interests dominate it. It knows nothing of "honor." The status order means precisely the reverse, *viz.*: stratification in terms of "honor" and of style of life peculiar to status groups as such. If mere economic acquisition and naked economic power still bearing the stigma of its extra status origin could bestow upon anyone who has won it the same honor as those who are interested in status by virtue of style of life claim for themselves, the status order would be threatened at its very root. This is the more so as, given equality of status honor, everywhere property *per se* represents an addition even if it is not overtly acknowledged to be such. But if such economic acquisition and power gave the agent any honor at all, his wealth would result in his attaining more "honor" than those who successfully claim honor by virtue of style of life. Therefore all groups having interests in the status order react with special sharpness precisely against the pretensions of purely economic acquisition. In most cases they react the more vigorously the more they feel themselves threatened. Calderon's respectful treatment of the peasant, for instance, as opposed to Shakespeare's simultaneous and ostensible disdain of the "**canaille**" illustrates the different way in which a firmly structured status order reacts as compared with a status order which has become economically precarious. This is an expression of a state of affairs that recurs everywhere. Precisely because of the rigorous reactions against the claims of property *per se,* the "**parvenu**" is never personally and without reservation accepted by the privileged status groups, no matter how completely his style of life has been adjusted to theirs. They will only accept his descendants who have been educated in the conventions of their status group and who have never besmirched the honor of the status group by their own economic labor. Hence, as to the general *effect* of the status order, only one consequence can be stated, but it is very important. It is that the hindrance of the free development of the market occurs first for those goods which status groups directly withheld from free exchange by monopolization. This monopolization may be effected either legally or conventionally. For example, in many Hellenic cities during the epoch of status groups and also originally in Rome the inherited estate (as is shown by the old formula for **indiction against spendthrifts**) was monopolized just as were the estates of knights, peasants, priests,

---

22. In this paragraph, Weber described the material benefits of status, in addition to honor. He argues that material monopolies reinforce the exclusiveness of a status group such as the entailing of property. An entailed estate is a property that cannot be sold but must be passed to a predetermined heir. In Jane Austen's novel *Pride and Prejudice*, for example, Mrs. Bennet is very concerned for the future of her daughters because their home and land are entailed to a male relative. She and Mr. Bennet have no sons, thus when Mr. Bennet dies, their estate will be inherited by a distant and rather unpleasant cousin, Mr. Collins. In his emphasis on consumption as a marker of status, Weber's ideas are similar to those of his contemporary, the economic and social theorist Thorstein Veblen (1857–1929). Veblen's *The Theory of the Leisure Class* (1912 [1899]) suggested that there was a conflict between making goods and making money: Monied classes increasingly freed themselves from any involvement in labor. Veblen also introduces his concept of conspicuous consumption in this work. Weber expands upon this topic in the section below.

and especially the clientele of the craft and merchant guilds. The market is restricted and the power of naked property *per se* which gives its stamp to "class formation" is pushed into the background. The results of this process can be most diverse. Of course, by no means do they necessarily take the direction of weakening the contrasts in the economic situation. Frequently the reverse holds. In any case, where stratification by status permeates a community as strongly as was the case in all political communities of antiquity and of the Middle Ages, one can never speak of a genuinely free market competition as we understand it today. There are wider effects than this direct exclusion of special goods from the market. There is a circumstance which follows from the abovementioned contrariety between the status order and purely economic order. It is that in most instances the notion of honor peculiar to status absolutely abhors that which is essential to the market: **higgling**. This notion of honor abhors higgling among peers and occasionally it taboos higgling for the members of a status group in general. Therefore, everywhere there are status groups, and usually the most influential, who consider almost any kind of overt participation in economic acquisition as absolutely stigmatizing.[23]

Thus, with some over-simplification, one might say that "classes" are stratified according to their relations to the production and acquisition of goods; whereas "status groups" are stratified according to the principles of their *consumption* of goods as represented by special "styles of life." An "occupational group" is also a "status group." For normally, it successfully claims social honor only by virtue of the special "style of life" which may be determined by occupation. However, the difference between classes and status groups frequently overlap. It is precisely those status communities most strictly segregated in terms of "honor," *viz.*, the Indian castes, who today show, although within very rigid limits, a relatively high degree of indifference with regard to pecuniary income. However, the Brahmins seek such income in quite heterogeneous ways.

As to the general economic conditions making for the predominance of stratification by "status" only very little can be said. When the bases of the acquisition and distribution of goods are relatively stable, stratification by status is favored. Every techno-economic repercussion and transformation threatens stratification by status and pushes the "class situation" into the foreground. Epochs and countries in which the naked class situation is of predominant significance are regularly the periods of techno-economic transformations. And every slowing down of the shifting of economic stratifications in due course lead to the growth of "status" structures and makes for a resuscitation of the important role of social "honor."[24]

---

23. To a modern American reader, this passage may sound terribly anachronistic. For most of us, enormous wealth is likely to confer status almost instantly. Our culture heroes tend to conform (or want to appear to conform) to the Horatio Alger myth, the notion of the individual who becomes successful based largely on their own energy, hard work, and talent. Part of their status derives from the fact that they do not come from (or claim not to come from) an elite background. In Weber's nineteenth-century world, quick wealth was often considered tainted, and the old rich had little respect for those who acquired their money more recently. To Weber—member of a dueling society, officer, and nationalist—honor and the acquisition of status played a role that is, for most of us today, quite alien. In fact, his vocabulary (parvenu) and literary references (Calderón de la Barca, Nietzsche) are markers of Weber's status.

Spanish playwright Pedro Calderón de la Barca (1600–1681).

"*Canaille*": French, "mob."

"Parvenu": a newly rich person, an upstart, or social climber.

"Indiction against spendthrifts": Table 5 of the Roman Twelve Tables (the earliest Roman law, circa 540 BCE) forbids a spendthrift from administering his own goods).

"Higgling": bargaining.

24. Compare the conception of change here with Marx's understanding of change caused by conflict between classes. In both cases, conflict between ideological superstructure and technological base plays a crucial role.

PARTIES

Whereas the genuine locus of "classes" is within the "economic order," the locus of "status groups" is within the "social order," *i.e.*, within the sphere of the distribution of "honor." From within these spheres, classes and status groups influence one another and they influence the legal order and are in turn influenced by it. But "parties" live in a house of "power."

Their action is oriented toward the acquisition of social "power," that is to say, toward influencing a communal action no matter what its content. In principle, parties may exist in a social "club" as well as in a "state." As over against the actions of "classes" and "status groups," for which this is not necessarily the case, the communal actions of "parties" always mean a societalization. For party actions are always directed toward a goal which is striven for in planned manner. This goal may be a "cause" (the party may aim at realizing a program for ideal or material purposes), or the goal may be "personal" (sinecures, power, and from these, honor for the leader and the followers of the parties). But usually the party action aims at all these simultaneously. Parties are, therefore, only possible within communities which are somehow societalized, that is to say, which have some rational order and a staff of persons available who are ready to enforce it. For parties aim precisely at influencing this staff, and if possible, to recruit it from party followers.[25]

In any individual case, parties may represent interests determined through "class situation" or "status situation," and they may recruit their following respectively from one or the other. But they need be neither purely "class" nor purely "status" parties. In most cases they are partly class parties and partly status parties, and frequently they are neither. They may represent ephemeral or enduring structures. Their means of attaining power may be quite varied, ranging from naked violence of any sort to canvassing for votes with coarse or subtle means: money, social influence, the force of speech, suggestion, clumsy hoax, and so on to the rougher or more artful tactics of obstruction in parliamentary bodies.[26]

The sociological structure of parties differs in a necessarily basic way according to the kind of communal action which they struggle to influence. Also, parties differ according to whether or not the community is stratified by status or by classes. Before all else, they vary to the structure of "domination" within the community. For their leaders normally deal with the conquest of a community. They are, in the general concept which is maintained here, not only products of specially modern forms of domination. We shall also designate as parties the ancient and medieval "parties," despite the fact that their structure differs basically from the structure of modern parties. By virtue of these structural differences of domination it is impossible to say anything about the structure

---

25. Weber understood a party, broadly, as a group committed to using power to achieve a certain goal. Thus, his understanding of party was not limited to official state political parties. For Weber, two things separated parties from classes and status groups: They existed to pursue power, and they strove to achieve a specific goal or cause. These gave them much more definite shape than Weber perceives in either class or status groups.

Recall from above that Weber uses the term "societalization" to refer to complex, state-level societies.

26. This brief paragraph brings us close to the critical point of the essay. Individual identifications are not singular, fixed, and enduring. Depending on circumstances and the issues involved, class, status, and party identification may be the same or different for any individual. None of these identities is always primary. Individuals often have multiple and contradictory identities. This makes sociological analysis complex and also means that people cannot be relied on to act in the interest of their class when this may conflict with the interest of their status group or party.

of parties without discussing the structural forms of social domination *per se*. Parties which are always themselves structures struggling for domination are very frequently organized in a very strict "authoritarian" fashion.[27]

Concerning "classes," "status groups," and "parties," it must be said in general that they necessarily presuppose a comprehensive societalization, and especially a political framework of communal action, within which they operate. This does not mean that parties would be confined by the frontiers of any individual political community. On the contrary, at all times it has been the order of the day that the societalization (even when it aims at the use of military force in common) reaches beyond the frontiers of politics. This has been the case in the solidarity of interests among the Oligarchs and among the democrats in Hellas, among the Guelfs and among Ghibelines in the Middle Ages, and within the Calvinist party during the period of religious struggles. It has been the case up to the solidarity of the landlords (international congress of agrarian landlords), and has continued among princes (holy alliance, Karlsbad decrees), socialist workers, conservatives (the longing of Prussian conservatives for Russian intervention in 1850). But their aim is not necessarily the establishment of new international political, *i.e., territorial*, dominion. In the main they aim to influence the existing dominion.[28]

AUTHOR'S NOTES

a. From *Wirtschaft und Gesellschaft* (Tübingen 1922), pp. 631–40. The definitions of the following terms do not occur in the original German passage; we have taken them from other contexts of *W. und G.* and inserted them as parts of this text: "law," "societal action," "communal action." We have also inserted definitions of "class situations" and "class." One cross reference, to a passage in *W. und G.*, p. 277, has been omitted and one footnote has been placed in the text. Otherwise, the translation is as literal as grammar and clarity seemed to permit. G. & M.

b. Probably Georg Lukacs. (Translators)

---

27. Note that Weber does not confine his notion of party to Western political parties. A party is any group in a stratified society that is struggling to gain power.

28. Weber makes numerous historical references in this paragraph. Hellas refers to classical Greece. The Guelfs and the Ghibellines were the major political factions of twelfth- and thirteenth-century Italy. The Calvinist party in the wars of religion refers to a series of religious wars in Europe between the mid-sixteenth and mid-seventeenth centuries, including the French wars of religion, the Thirty Years War, and the Eighty Years War. "International congress of agrarian landlords" is obscure. The Holy Alliance of 1815 joined Russia, Austria, and Prussia against a possible resurgence of French republicanism. The Karlsbad decrees of 1819 united the German states in outlawing both liberal and nationalist organizations. In each of these cases, elites across different states and cultures joined to pursue a common goal of power.

PART II

Culture Theory in the Early Twentieth Century

The Boasians

A great deal of ethnographic writing took place in late-nineteenth-century America. We have already discussed Lewis Henry Morgan (1818–1881), who published his major works between 1851 and 1881 (see essay 3). In addition to Morgan, ethnologists such as Alice Cunningham Fletcher (1838–1923) actively pursued ethnographic investigations and were given an institutional base by Frederic Ward Putnam (1839–1914) at Harvard's Peabody Museum.

In 1897 the Smithsonian Institution established the Bureau of American Ethnology (BAE) to organize anthropological research in America. Its first director was John Wesley Powell (1834–1902), better known as the explorer of the Grand Canyon. The BAE sponsored the work of many scholars, including Matilda Coxe Stevenson (1849–1915), Otis Mason (1838–1908), James Mooney (1861–1921), and Frank Cushing (1857–1900).

Despite this variety of anthropological activity, anthropology was largely a self-taught occupation, and it was not until 1890, when Harvard founded its Department of Archaeology and Ethnology, that anthropology began to coalesce as an academic discipline in America. When it did, the ideas of a single individual, Franz Boas (1858–1942), had an enormous impact on the development of anthropology as an academic discipline. The method of research Boas pioneered is widely considered the first American-born school of anthropological thought, and he is considered one of the founders of American anthropology.

Boas was born to a secular and intellectual German Jewish family. His father, a merchant, held liberal political views, and his mother was a radical freethinker who founded a kindergarten devoted to the "consciousness of mutual interdependence" in children (Frank 1997: 733). Boas described his home as a place in which "the ideals of the revolution of 1848 were a living force" (1974a [1938]: 41). His upbringing emphasized the freedom, dignity, and fundamental equality of all peoples, and Boas remained deeply devoted to these ideas throughout his life.

Boas's education emphasized the physical sciences. After graduating from *Gymnasium* (secondary school) in 1877, he went first to the University of Heidelberg, then to Bonn, and finally to Kiel, where he received his PhD. His examination subjects were geography, physics, and philosophy, and his dissertation, "Contribution to the Understanding of the Color of Water," was about the relationship between physical stimuli and the perceptions they evoke, what we would call *psychophysics*. Although his training emphasized quantitative data, he later wrote that these studies caused him to realize that "there are domains of our experience in which the concepts of quantity . . . are not applicable" (1974a [1938]: 42). While Boas believed in a science of anthropology, he also recognized that there was a distinction between the social and natural sciences.

As a Jewish liberal, Boas had few opportunities for academic employment in late-nineteenth-century Germany, and by 1882, he had begun contemplating immigration to the United States. In 1883, he seized an opportunity to do research on migration patterns and seawater among the Eskimo on Baffin Island. Boas spent fifteen months in "the sublime loneliness of the arctic" (quoted in Stocking 1974: 22), and the experience changed him from a geographer to an ethnographer. Living among the Eskimo convinced him that the liberal and humanistic values of his childhood could be applied to the study of human society.

Not long before Boas left for Baffin Island, he had become engaged to Marie Krackowizer. During his fieldwork, he kept a diary in the form of a single long letter to her. In an oft-quoted passage written on December 23, 1883, he wrote,

> I believe, if this trip has for me (as a thinking person) a valuable influence, it lies in the strengthening of the viewpoint of the relativity of all cultivation [*bildung*] and that the evil as well as the

129

value of a person lies in the cultivation of the heart, which I find or do not find here just as much as amongst us, and that all service, therefore, which a man can perform for humanity must serve to promote truth. (quoted in Cole 1983: 33)

A month later, on January 22, 1884, he wrote,

I do not want a German professorship because I know I would be restricted to my science and to teaching, for which I have little inclination. I should much prefer to live in America in order to be able to further those ideas for which I live. . . . What I want to live and die for, is equal rights for all, equal possibilities to learn and work for poor and rich alike! Don't you believe that to have done even the smallest bit for this, is more than all science taken together? (quoted in Cole 1983: 37)

After spending the winter of 1884–1885 in New York, Boas returned to Germany in 1885 to take a position at the Berlin Ethnological Museum (the Museum fur Volkenkunde), where he worked with Rudolf Virchow (1821–1902) and Adolf Bastian (1826–1905). However, he soon left Germany once more, this time to visit the Kwakiutl (now usually called the Kwakwaka'wakw) and other tribes on Northern Vancouver Island in Canada, groups he was to study for the rest of his life. In 1886, after a brief return to Germany, he decided to immigrate to the United States.

Boas had the good fortune to be mentored in his early career by the Harvard anthropologist Frederic Ward Putnam. Putnam was a member of a prominent New England family who came to Massachusetts in 1640. Although he is not well known today, he was one of the leading archaeologists of the nineteenth century. In 1873, Putnam was elected secretary of the American Association for the Advancement of Science (AAAS) and was hired as an editor of the journal *Science*. In 1875 he became curator of the Peabody Museum, and in 1879 he cofounded the Archaeological Institute of America. In 1887 Putnam was appointed Peabody Professor of American Archaeology and Ethnology at Harvard. In 1890, the Department of Archaeology and Ethnology was founded, and consequently Putnam became one of the first American anthropologists to train PhD students.

Putnam used his positions as secretary of the AAAS and curator at the American Museum of Natural History to provide funding and research projects for his students. He also mentored the young Franz Boas, whom he first met at a meeting of the AAAS in 1886 and to whom he was related by marriage (Boas's uncle Abraham Jacobi married Putnam's cousin Mary Corinna Putnam in 1871). As George Stocking (1974: 284) points out, Boas followed in Putnam's footsteps in the 1890s. Putnam helped Boas get his first job as the geographic editor of *Science* in 1887, and in 1891, when Boas resigned from Clark University, Putnam offered him a position as his assistant in charge of Physical Anthropology at the Chicago World's Fair. When the fair ended in 1893, Putnam put Boas in charge of curating the anthropology materials exhibited at the fair for what was to become the Field Museum of Natural History. And when Boas was forced out of that position in 1894, Putnam hired Boas as his assistant in charge of Ethnology and Physical Anthropology at the American Museum of Natural History. Finally, in 1896, Putnam helped arrange a teaching position for Boas at Columbia University. From that point, their relationship became more equal as they exchanged students (Boas sent Putnam students for archaeology instruction, and Putnam sent Boas students for training in ethnology and linguistics), collaborated in research, and were among the founders of the American Anthropological Association (AAA). When Putnam retired in 1909 at the age of seventy, Boas organized a collection of writings in Putnam's honor (called a *Festschrift*). In his speech at the reception for Putnam, Boas identified Putnam, along with John Wesley Powell and Daniel Garrison Brinton (1837–1899), a biological anthropologist based at the University of Pennsylvania, as the three most prominent anthropologists of their generation (Tozzer 1909: 286).

Boas began his career at a time when anthropology was not recognized as a science or even as a field of university study, and he was personally determined to make anthropology a university-based discipline. Once established at Columbia, Boas spent as much time planning the disciplinary orga-nization of anthropology as he did conducting his own research. Boas helped create the indepen-dent Department of Anthropology at Columbia, expanded its faculty, helped to found the American Anthropological Association and its main journal, *American Anthropologist*, and trained students who went on to establish Boasian-style anthropology in universities across the country.

Boas's emphasis on the careful collection of ethnographic data and his rejection of nine-teenth-century evolutionary theories in favor of ethnographic field experience were, in part, a reaction to the uncritical use of the comparative method by the unilineal evolutionists of his day. Boas maintained that the sweeping generalizations of the unilineal social evolutionists were not scientifically valid. He based much of his attack on the distinction between convergent and parallel evolution.

Evolutionists assumed that similar cultural traits were the result of parallel development driven by universal evolutionary law. Boas showed that the same characteristics could come about through different processes. In "The Limitations of the Comparative Method in Anthropology" (1896), he demonstrated that cultures may have similar traits for a variety of reasons, including diffusion and independent invention. Such traits may be produced by corresponding environments or historical accidents independent of any universal evolutionary process. Thus the existence of such traits could not be used as evidence for universal stages of cultural evolution.

Boas believed that to explain cultural customs, one must examine them from three perspectives: the environmental conditions under which they developed, individual psychological factors, and the historical development of the culture in which they occurred. Of these, the third was the most important. He felt that societies were created by their historical circumstances. Thus the best explanations of cultural phenomena were to be acquired by studying the historical development of the societies in which they were found. The fact that Boas focused on the specific histories of individual societies led his approach to anthropology to often be called *historical particularism*, a phrase coined by Marvin Harris (1927–2001) in the 1960s.

Boas advocated a four-field perspective that included studying prehistory, linguistics, and phys-ical anthropology in addition to the observation of culture. This idea shaped the anthropology department Boas created at Columbia and the departments his students founded at other univer-sities. The hallmark of Boasian-style anthropology became the intensive study of specific cultures through long periods of fieldwork. Boas argued that it was only through living with a people and learning their language that one could develop an accurate understanding of a culture.

Boas and his students were driven by the belief that "primitive" societies were rapidly dis-appearing. In particular, the situation of Native Americans, forced onto reservations and their populations decimated, gave Boas and his students a sense of urgency. They believed that if these cultures were not recorded immediately, knowledge of them would be lost entirely. The sense that anthropology was an urgent salvage operation conditioned much of the theory and method in American anthropology and caused it to develop in a different direction than anthropology in Britain and France.

Boas also pioneered the concept that has become known as *cultural relativism*. He never used the term, which became popular in the 1950s, but it accurately describes his position. As we have noted, cultural evolutionists had argued that all societies were following the same path of develop-ment from savagery to civilization. If this was so, then it was perfectly reasonable to say that some societies were more or less advanced, more or less "primitive," than others. Boas rejected unilineal evolution and argued that societies were the result of their own unique histories. If this was the case, then there could be no universal yardstick by which to judge them. A society's traits were the result of its historical and environmental circumstances and could only be understood within that context. Consequently, terms such as *primitive*, *inferior*, and *superior* could not apply.

Because Boas discredited the unilineal-evolutionary schemes popular in his day and insisted that societies were the result of their particular histories and could not be compared, contemporary critics often dismissed him as antitheoretical. His students argued that this was not the case and pointed out that Boas believed that the foundations of cultural analysis were history and psychology and that he discussed the possibility of finding laws governing the growth of culture (Darnell 2001: 43). However, by 1906, Boas wrote,

> As we have penetrated more deeply into these problems we have observed that the general laws for which we have been searching prove elusive, that the forms of primitive culture are infinitely more complex than had been supposed. (1906: 642)

Today it is generally understood that the central tenet of Boas's notion that cultures are primarily the result of their unique histories is inimical to any general theory of culture.

Boas had a profound effect on the development of American anthropology. In his long career at Columbia (he retired in 1936), Boas almost single-handedly trained the first generation of American anthropologists and directed their initial field studies. Ruth Fulton Benedict (1887–1948), Ruth Bunzel (1898–1990), Melville Herskovits (1895–1963), Zora Neale Hurston (1891–1960), Alfred Louis Kroeber (1876–1960), Robert Lowie (1883–1957), Margaret Mead (1901–1978), Ashley Montagu (1905–1999), Paul Radin (1883–1959), Edward Sapir (1884–1939), Clark Wissler (1870–1947), and many others were his students.

In addition to training students, Boas lived his life as a citizen scientist, true to the ideals he had expressed in his Baffin Island letter-diary. He was an indefatigable campaigner for justice, equality, and the rights of individuals. He spoke out against World War I and the xenophobia and jingoism the war had triggered in America. A staunch champion of the rights of immigrants and African Americans, he fought against racial discrimination, the intimidation of teachers in colleges and high schools, and the rise of Nazism in Europe.

Boas was what we today would call a human rights activist. He was one of the very few educators of his day to welcome women, Native Americans, and African Americans as students. He had strong ties to leading black scholars, such as W. E. B. Du Bois and E. Franklin Frazier, and was deeply involved in the early years of the NAACP. He contributed the lead article for the second issue of that organization's journal, *The Crisis*, and spoke out on the subject of race and racism repeatedly throughout his life. Boas died in 1942 at a luncheon in honor of Paul Rivet, a leading French anthropologist and founder of the Musée de l'Homme, whose escape from Nazi-occupied France Boas had championed. Rivet reported that Boas's last words were "One must never tire of repeating that racism is a monstrous error or an impudent lie" (in Lewis 2001: 456).

Boas was deeply disturbed by the race-based anthropology practiced by physical anthropologists in the late nineteenth and early twentieth centuries. At the Berlin Ethnological Museum, Boas had learned anthropometrics, or techniques of human measurement, from Rudolf Virchow, which he later put to use in his studies debunking the notion that race was a factor in cultural development or that cultural differences were due to heredity. In one of his most famous studies, Boas set out to investigate the plasticity of different human groups, using as his sample immigrants and their children. The study was conducted for the US Immigration Commission and involved conducting anthropometric measurements on a sample of more than seventeen thousand people. Boas found that the average cranial size of immigrants was significantly different from those of their children born in the United States. Moreover, he discovered that the average cranial size of children born within ten years of their mother's arrival was significantly different from the average cranial size of children born more than ten years after their mothers' arrival. He concluded that the environment influenced these features (Boas 1912).

Boas and his students dominated American anthropology from about 1911 until after World War II (Stocking 1992: 117), but he was not unopposed. In the late nineteenth century, anthropology in America was dominated by museum-based scholars principally from Harvard and the Peabody Museum, the University of Pennsylvania and its affiliated museum, and the Smithsonian, drawn largely from old WASP families. Scholars from these institutions subscribed to theories of evolutionary anthropology. Many supported the American eugenics movement and were devoted to race-science attempts to prove the superiority of Northern Europeans. Several members of these institutions objected to Boas and his students, many of whom were either immigrants themselves or the sons or daughters of immigrants, and many of whom were Jewish. They opposed Boas's notions of cultural relativism and racial equality and objected to his support of female students, whom they believed were not suited to do anthropology. Boas's most virulent enemies were members of the anthropology division of the National Research Council (an organization founded to promote American aims in World War I) and the Galton Society, which promoted racial science and eugenics. Key members of both organizations included Charles B. Davenport (1866–1944), Madison Grant (1865–1937), and Ales Hrdlicka (1869–1943) (Stocking 1968: 289).

Boas's conflicts with other anthropologists over cultural relativism, racism, eugenics, and hostility to immigrants were intensified by his pacifism and opposition to World War I. In 1919, Boas wrote a letter to *The Nation* castigating unnamed anthropologists for working as spies for the American government. He wrote that such actions undermined belief in the "truthfulness of science" and "raised a new barrier" against international scientific cooperation (quoted in Stocking 1968: 274). Additionally, he called President Woodrow Wilson a hypocrite. The letter brought a series of old grievances and resentments against Boas to the surface at the American Anthropological Association meeting ten days after its publication. The Harvard and Smithsonian anthropologists moved successfully to have Boas censured by the AAA and stripped of membership in its governing council; he was also pressured to resign from the National Research Council (Stocking 1968: 273). Despite these setbacks, Boas and his students already controlled key positions in anthropology departments around the country and were the most important group of scholars shaping the direction of American anthropology. Although the place of Boas and his students in American anthropology was assured by the 1920s, the AAA censure of Boas stood for ninety-six years. In 2005, by a vote of 1,245 to 73, the organization finally rescinded and repudiated its 1919 motion of censure.

Next to Boas, the most influential figures in American anthropology during the first half of the twentieth century were his students, and we include the work of several of them (A. L. Kroeber, Edward Sapir, Ruth Benedict, Margaret Mead, and Zora Neale Hurston) in this volume. Kroeber was the first of Boas's students at Columbia to receive a doctorate in anthropology, which he earned in 1901. In that same year, Kroeber was hired by the University of California, Berkeley. At the age of twenty-five, he became the first instructor in the newly created anthropology program and the curator of the university's museum of anthropology. Kroeber stayed at Berkeley for the rest of his career, retiring in 1946. He stayed active in research and writing until his death in 1960.

Throughout his life, Kroeber maintained a Boasian perspective. Both Kroeber and Boas were antievolutionists, believed in integrating the four subfields of anthropology, and taught that a historical perspective was necessary to understand other cultures. However, Kroeber also had several disagreements with Boas. The most significant of these concerned the role of the individual in culture. Boas believed that individuals played a significant role in a culture's development and change. Kroeber, however, argued that although culture came from and is carried by human beings, humans played little if any active role in shaping the cultures in which they lived. He maintained that culture was a pattern that transcended and controlled individuals and played a powerful determining role in individual human behavior. This idea is similar to the concept of *l'âme collective* (collective conscience) expressed by French sociologist Émile Durkheim (1858–1917; see essay 5).

In Kroeber's view, individual accomplishment resulted from historical trends within society. Although Kroeber recognized that some individuals have special abilities, he argued that it is social and historical circumstances that determine what those individuals achieved. Kroeber developed these ideas at length in his 1917 essay "The Superorganic" (a term borrowed from Herbert Spencer [1820–1903]), where he wrote,

A hundred Aristotles among our cave-dwelling ancestors would have been Aristotles in their birthright no less; but they would have contributed far less to the advance of science than a dozen plodding mediocrities in the twentieth century. . . . Bach born in the Congo instead of Saxony could have composed not even a fragment of choral or sonata, though we can be equally confident that he would have outshone his compatriots in some manner of music. (1917: 195)

To illustrate his theory of the relationship between individuals and culture, Kroeber studied how patterns of art, technology, and fashion changed through time, independent of individual artists, inventors, and designers. In essay 9 of this volume, Kroeber illustrates his point using high-fashion women's clothing. He argues that basic features of women's gowns appear and then go out of fashion with predictable regularity and that the pattern is independent of any individual designer.

Kroeber published this article in 1919, and it is worth noting that this approach is similar to the culture history approach in American archaeology that was practiced at that time. Much as archaeologists carefully traced the changes in material culture at their sites, such as documenting shifting pottery styles through time, so too Kroeber performed a similar kind of analysis by documenting changing elements of women's clothing over time.

It was part of the Boasian program to study culture from a historical perspective, incorporating linguistics and both geographical and archaeological data when possible. Kroeber focused especially on the geographic distribution of cultural traits and on studying cultures in relation to their environment. Much of his research consisted of surveys of culture traits among Native Americans in California and on the Great Plains. Unlike Boas, who advocated the intensive study of individual societies, Kroeber was more interested in mapping the distribution of cultural traits into larger geographic patterns (Jacknis 2002: 525). As early as 1903, he had already conceived of the ethnological survey that would become his 1925 volume *Handbook of the Indians of California*. In *Cultural and Natural Areas of Native North America* (1939), he mapped geographic, climatological, and vegetation distribution in relation to Native American cultures. This work was influential among his students, particularly Julian Steward (1902–1972), who went on to develop the cultural ecological approach to the analysis of culture.

Ruth Benedict, Margaret Mead, and Edward Sapir were among Franz Boas's closest associates. Benedict taught at Columbia with Boas and, in turn, was one of Mead's professors. Sapir, one of Boas's most gifted students, was a close friend of Benedict and mentor to Benjamin L. Whorf (1897–1941). Benedict, Mead, and Sapir were also central figures in an anthropological movement known as the culture and personality school. Other culture and personality theorists of their era include Abram Kardiner (1891–1981), Cora Du Bois (1903–1991), Ralph Linton (1893–1953), and Clyde Kluckhohn (1905–1960). Sapir and Whorf are particularly remembered for their work on language.

Benedict came to anthropology from literature. She had taught secondary-school English and published numerous poems of her own before starting her career in anthropology. She first took classes in anthropology with Elsie Clews Parsons (1875–1941) at the New School for Social Research. Parsons was a pioneering feminist who earned her PhD in sociology but who had become an intellectual and political ally of Franz Boas. Parsons, the daughter of a banker and wife of a congressman, was also a very wealthy woman. She took no salary for her work, and she helped fund Columbia's anthropology department (Rosenberg 2004: 147).

Benedict was introduced to Boas by another of her professors at the New School for Social Research, Alexander Goldenweiser (1880–1940). Goldenweiser earned his PhD at Columbia under Boas's direction in 1910, and he encouraged Benedict to study with Boas. In 1921 Benedict moved to Columbia to work with Boas. She received her PhD in 1923 but remained with Boas at Columbia, serving as his teaching and administrative assistant. Boas relied on Benedict for his correspondence, and she remained extremely close to him throughout his life. Benedict's position at Boas's side gave her knowledge of and access to research being done by other Boasians.

Benedict started teaching students almost as soon as she arrived at Columbia but was not appointed assistant professor until 1931. After Boas retired in 1936, Benedict was named the acting executive director of Columbia's anthropology department. In 1937, to Boas's dismay, rather than confirming Benedict as department head, the university appointed Ralph Linton, a former Boas student who had quarreled with his mentor. However, Benedict was promoted to associate professor with tenure. She was the first woman to hold such a position at Columbia (Rosenberg 2004: 177). Benedict's slow advance at Columbia was due to the fact that she was a woman and that anthropology was unpopular with the university administration. She was not promoted to full professor until a few months before her death in 1948.

A theme in much of Benedict's work was the relationship between culture and personality. The most comprehensive expression of Benedict's ideas was her book *Patterns of Culture* (1934). There Benedict proposed that each culture had a unique pattern, called a *cultural configuration*, that determined the fundamental personality characteristics of its members. To illustrate this concept, Benedict selected three societies: Zuni, Dobu, and Kwakiutl. Relying on her own and Elsie Clews Parsons's observations among the Zuni, the work of Reo Fortune (1903–1979) with the people of Dobu, and Boas's writings on the Kwakiutl, she described the configuration for each society based on the dominant personality characteristics observed in those cultures. Famously, she argued that culture was "personality writ large."

During World War II, Benedict was a special advisor for the Office of War Information. In that position, she argued that understanding national character was key to both winning the war and establishing a lasting peace. Basing her work on interviews with first- and second-generation immigrants, statistics, and her reading of relevant literature, Benedict attempted to write analyses that illuminated "the loyalties, habits, fears, hopes, likes and dislikes of the target peoples" (Benedict in Van Ginkel 1992: 52). Benedict wrote several pieces on the Dutch, but her best-known effort of this nature was *The Chrysanthemum and the Sword* (1946), a study of the Japanese.

Trying to analyze a mass society such as Japan at a distance proved difficult, and *The Chrysanthemum and the Sword* included many errors. It was strongly critiqued by both American and Japanese scholars (e.g., Bennett and Nagai 1953; Lummis 1982). However, it also proved highly influential. The book played an important role in determining the nature of the American occupation of Japan (1945–1952) and has been much discussed and debated since, particularly in Japan. In 1999 Nanako Fukui reported that more than 2.3 million copies of the book had been sold in Japan, and its pocket-size Japanese edition, first published in 1967, has gone through more than one hundred printings (Ryang 2004).

Mention must also be made of Benedict's campaign against racism. As we noted, Boas took a strong stand against racism. Benedict followed him and extended his work. In 1940, Benedict published *Race: Science and Politics*. She followed this with many essays in both the professional and popular press. In these, she argued against any connection between the biology of race and culture, and she developed a historical account of race as a form of oppression (Anderson 2014: 395). The pamphlet *The Races of Mankind* (1943), coauthored with Gene Weltfish, is perhaps Benedict's best-known work on race. It was released as an illustrated children's book, an animated film, a series of posters, and a traveling exhibition (Burkholder 2006: 25). You can see the ten-and-a-half-minute film on YouTube: search for "Benedict the brotherhood of man."

Finally, Benedict was also an ardent cultural relativist. The essay we have chosen for this volume, "The Science of Custom," was published in 1929. In it, Benedict argues for anthropology's role in helping people become more culture conscious and that this can help people to intelligently direct culture change.

Margaret Mead and later culture and personality theorists largely accepted Benedict's notion of cultural configuration and focused on discovering its sources. Their investigations centered on the interplay of biological and cultural factors, particularly during childhood, and their effect on adult personality. They were influenced by the work of Sigmund Freud (1856–1939) and by the neo-Freudian analysts Harry Stack Sullivan (1892–1949), Karen Horney (1885–1952), and Erich Fromm (1900–1980). Margaret Mead's work clearly illustrates this theme. In a series of studies, starting with *Coming of Age in Samoa* (1928) and continuing with *Growing Up in New Guinea* (1930) and one of her more controversial books, *Sex and Temperament in Three Primitive Societies* (1935), Mead attempted to separate the biological and cultural factors that control human behavior and personality development. She anticipated the distinction between sex and gender found in much more recent work. Together with Benedict's *Patterns of Culture* (1934b), Mead's trilogy established the cultural configuration and national character approaches in American anthropology.

Mead was also one of the most colorful figures in American anthropology. She was born in Philadelphia, the daughter of a professor at the Wharton School of the University of Pennsylvania. Like her mentor, Benedict, she had an early interest in literature. During her undergraduate career at Barnard College in New York City, she was a member of a literary group called the Ash Can Cats (Lutkehaus 1995: 189).

In 1923, Mead began her graduate career at Columbia University, working with both Ruth Benedict and Franz Boas. Mead's relationship with her mentor Benedict was particularly intense. Mead's correspondence, published in 2006 as *To Cherish the Life of the World*, shows the passion and intensity of the relationship (see 2006: 53–54 for an example).

In 1925, Mead, only twenty-three years old, did her first fieldwork in Samoa. Her Samoan experience was the only fieldwork she was to undertake alone, and it became the basis of her first book, *Coming of Age in Samoa* (1928). This book was an immediate hit and launched Mead on a long career as one of anthropology's most prolific authors. She published thirty-nine books (fifteen of them collaborations) and almost fourteen hundred other pieces of various kinds. Many of these were brief essays designed for popular consumption. She wrote regularly for *The Nation* and the *New York Times*. For seventeen years, with her partner, Rhoda Métraux (1914–2003), she wrote a monthly column for the women's magazine *Redbook*.

In addition to her writing, Mead made films and appeared frequently on radio and television. By the late 1950s, her regular appearances on television talk shows made her one of the best-known academics in American life, and certainly the best-known anthropologist, a fame that continued well beyond her death. Publication in the popular press placed Mead squarely in the tradition of Franz Boas, who frequently wrote for a general, rather than professional, audience.

Mead's personal life was particularly tumultuous. In addition to her relationship with Benedict, she was married three times. Her first marriage to her childhood sweetheart, Luther Cressman, began in 1923. Cressman was ordained an Episcopal priest that same year but also studied sociology and anthropology at Columbia, receiving a PhD in sociology in 1928. In 1925, Cressman left New York to continue his studies in theology in Europe, and Mead began her fieldwork in Samoa. On the way back from Samoa, she met and fell in love with the Australian anthropologist and psychologist Reo Fortune. She divorced Cressman and married Fortune in 1928. Cressman went on to found the anthropology department at the University of Oregon and conducted some of the first research in the history and prehistory of the Northwest.

In the late 1920s and early 1930s, Fortune and Mead continued to do fieldwork together in New Guinea. In 1932, while working on the Sepik River in New Guinea, they met British anthropologist and psychologist Gregory Bateson. From 1932 to 1935, Mead, Fortune, and Bateson worked together and occasionally lived together. During this time, Mead fell in love with Bateson. In 2014, Mead's experiences in New Guinea and her relationship with Bateson and Fortune were the basis of a best-selling novel *Euphoria* by Lily King. When the three returned from the field in 1935, Mead divorced Fortune and, in 1936, married Bateson. Soon after, they left to conduct research together in Bali. Mead's only child, Mary Catherine Bateson, was born to the couple in 1939. While Mead and Bateson divorced in 1950, their daughter went on to become an accomplished anthropologist and linguist specializing in Middle Eastern culture. She died in January 2021.

In 1942 Mead began a professional collaboration with Métraux as her research assistant. In 1955, after Métraux's divorce, Mead and Métraux began to share the same residence. This relationship continued for twenty-three years, until Mead's death in 1978. In addition to their columns for *Redbook*, Mead and Métraux collaborated on several books.

We are often asked why we choose to present Mead's personal life in these pages. There are several reasons. First, all serious students of anthropology will surely hear something of Mead's private life, and because of this, it is important that the outline of her life and context of her many relationships be presented clearly. Second, there is a complex relationship between Mead's sexual and family life and her work, which focused extensively on family and sexual roles in different societies. Clearly, readers of Mead should ask to what extent her personal life colored her research, and vice versa. For example, the research Mead did for *Sex and Temperament in Three Primitive Societies* was done while she, Fortune, and Bateson lived together in New Guinea. Mead's daughter later wrote,

> It is not accidental that when Margaret was on the Sepik, struggling with the question of diversity in herself and in her ways of loving, she was formulating the contrasts between three New Guinea peoples who dealt very differently with maleness and femaleness, with assertion and creativity. (Bateson 1984: 160)

In addition, Mead seems almost larger than life, and her relationships show this. There are numerous other authors in this book who had spouses, lovers, or children who made contributions to their work or were independent scholars in their own right. You will notice that we do mention these (some good examples are Edith Turner and Michelle Rosaldo [1944–1981]). However, no one comes close to Mead. Of the five relationships we have mentioned here, Benedict, a major theorist, appears in this volume; Cressman and Fortune made important contributions to archaeology and anthropology; Bateson made contributions to many different fields, including anthropology, linguistics, psychology, and cybernetics, and became a critical cultural figure of the 1960s; and Métraux collaborated with Mead for more than two decades. It is hard to think of any major scholar in the social sciences who had as many deep relationships with other important thinkers as Mead.

Like Benedict's "The Science of Custom," the introduction to *Coming of Age in Samoa* (essay 11) clearly shows Mead's interest in culture as a primary factor determining the experience of adolescence and the social and behavioral characteristics of adolescents. The book, written for a popular rather than a professional audience, aimed to promote the Boasian notion of cultural relativity, criticized biological theories of causality, and increased readers' appreciation for cultural diversity.

Mead was always a controversial scholar, both within anthropology and outside of it. Books such as *Coming of Age in Samoa* were intended as a critique of American culture and were read as such. Mead was involved in politics for much of her life and consistently stood for liberal causes. Wilton Dillon wrote that "perhaps no citizen in modern times has testified on so many different topics before more different professional committees as Mead" (1980: 327). Although Mead posthumously received the Presidential Medal of Freedom in 1979, she also made many enemies in the course of her life, particularly among conservative thinkers. *Coming of Age in Samoa* figures prominently on several lists put together by conservative organizations featuring the "worst" books of the twentieth century. In fact, in 2014, the archconservative Intercollegiate Studies Institute named it the number-one worst book of that century (https://isi.org/intercollegiate-review/the-50-worst-books-of-the-20th-century).

Within academia, Mead's work, as well as Benedict's, also faced criticism. Benedict was critiqued for ignoring aspects of culture that did not fit her cultural configuration model, such as the incidence of alcoholism among the Pueblo Indians and the calculating self-control practiced by the Kwakiutl. In 1983, five years after Mead's death, Australian anthropologist Derek Freeman (1916–2001) ignited controversy with the publication of *Margaret Mead and Samoa: The Making and Unmaking of an Anthropological Myth*, in which he claimed that Mead's *Coming of Age in Samoa* was factually incorrect. Freeman charged that Mead's informants, embarrassed by her questions about intimate matters, deceived her with wild tales of sexual abandon. The debate over Freeman's assertions was a major issue in anthropology in the 1980s and early 1990s and remains unresolved.

A recent addition to this section is a chapter from Zora Neale Hurston's *Mules and Men* (1935), a collection of African American folklore collected in Florida in the late 1920s. Hurston began her university education at Howard University, receiving an associate's degree there in 1924. In 1927 she moved to Barnard College, graduating with a bachelor's degree in 1928. She continued on to graduate school at Columbia University but never earned a graduate degree (though, in 1939, she received an honorary doctorate from Morgan State College).

Boas and his students were often willing to accept black students, but racism and expense made it extraordinarily difficult for African American students to earn doctoral degrees. The first African American PhD should have been Boas's student Louis Eugene King (1898–1962), who completed his doctoral dissertation in 1932 but lacked the funds to print the twenty-seven copies of it that Columbia required. King eventually received his degree in 1951 but was never able to get an academic job (Bernstein 2002: 559). The first African American to receive a cultural anthropology PhD was Edward Sapir's student Mark Hanna Watkins (1903–1976), who graduated from the University of Chicago in 1933. It would be almost a decade before there was a second black PhD cultural anthropologist: W. Allison Davis (1902–1983) in 1942 (Drake 1980: 18). Davis was also one of the first African Americans to teach at a major predominantly white university (the University of Chicago) and, in 1947, the first to be hired to a tenured position (Slater 1998–1999: 98). Other prominent African Americans with training in anthropology included Roosevelt University and Stanford professor St. Clair Drake (1911–1990), choreographer and dancer Katherine Dunham (1909–2006), Morgan State University professor Irene Diggs (1906–1998), school principal and activist Arthur Huff Fauset (1899–1993), and biological anthropologists William Montague Cobb (1904–1990) and Caroline Bond Day (1889–1948). However, St. Clair Drake reports that when World War II ended, fewer than a half dozen African Americans were teaching in predominantly white universities in all disciplines combined (1980: 86). In these circumstances, it is unsurprising that Hurston never found a career in either a museum or a university.

Although Hurston was not as well known to the anthropologists of her era as others we have mentioned in this section, her work has had a profound influence on contemporary anthropology and literature. Hurston began working with Boas in the mid-1920s while a student at Barnard College. Boas was an outspoken advocate for equal rights and actively sought students from different ethnic and racial backgrounds. However, he also believed that such students could be perfect "insider" cultural observers (Salamone 2014: 218). Boas and many of his students understood themselves to be documenting disappearing cultures, what today is termed *salvage ethnography*. Consequently, in Boas's view, a student like Hurston could work in African American communities and record the last remnants of a disappearing African culture. Hurston shared this view and was deeply committed to recording African American folklore. In her article "High John De Conqueror," Hurston wrote:

> Maybe, now, we used-to-be black African folks can be of some help to our brothers and sisters who have always been white. You will take another look at us and say that we are still black and, ethnologically speaking, you will be right. But nationally and culturally, we are as white as the next one. (1943: 450)

In 1926, Hurston began her work on African American folklore in Harlem, where she became friends with black writers such as Langston Hughes (1902–1967), Alain Locke (1885–1954), and

Wallace Thurman (1902–1934). In 1927, Hurston moved to Florida to begin collecting the African American folklore that would form the basis for much of her later writing. This work was followed by time collecting folktales in New Orleans. Hurston also studied healing rituals in Jamaica and Haiti. Her first novel, *Jonah's Gourd Vine*, was a fictionalized account of her childhood published in 1934. This was soon followed by her collection of Florida folktales, *Mules and Men*, published one year later. In 1937 she published her best-known novel, *Their Eyes Were Watching God*. Widely criticized when first published, *Their Eyes* is now considered Hurston's best novel, and contemporary authors, such as Alice Walker (b. 1944) and Toni Morrison (1931–2019), were deeply influenced by it. *Their Eyes Were Watching God* was followed in 1938 by *Tell My Horse: Voodoo and Life in Haiti and Jamaica*, which was based on her research there. She ended this decade by publishing a third novel, *Moses, Man of the Mountain*, in 1939.

For the research on which *Mules and Men* was based, Hurston relied on funding from wealthy white patrons, in particular, Charlotte Osgood Mason, whose support was based on the condition that Hurston could not publish her research (Salamone 2014: 221). Consequently, Hurston published much of her fieldwork experiences in her novels rather than in academic journals. As you read the selection from *Mules and Men*, you can see how representative it is of Boasian-style anthropology. Hurston writes the folktales as she heard them, trying to preserve the voices and language of her collaborators. Unlike most authors of her time, she also documents her own role in the settings where she collected the stories, aiming for ethnographic accuracy that predates the autoethnographies of the 1980s and 1990s by fifty years. Reading *Mules and Men*, we also feel Hurston's pride in the culture of the black communities in which she studied. Compare Hurston's writing to that of Radcliffe-Brown in "On Joking Relationships," written just a couple of years after *Mules and Men*. You can feel the affection Hurston had for the people she studied and how deeply personal the work is compared to Radcliffe-Brown's.

Hurston led a dramatic and tumultuous life. She was a central figure in the Harlem Renaissance of the 1920s and 1930s, with close ties to its key figures, and her books were well received. However, she never earned much money from them. Additionally, she was politically conservative, opposing both Roosevelt's New Deal and the Supreme Court's *Brown v. Board of Education* decision. These positions alienated her from many in the African American community. Linguist John McWhorter, in an essay that goes on to praise Hurston, says she was "a thoroughly black *wav-man* who would gladly have peddled her wares on Fox News today" (2011). Hurston's conservatism was not a denial of racism but rather a belief in individuals and in working within the existing system. Hurston put many of her political ideas in the final chapter of her autobiographical book *Dust Tracks on the Road*. However, the chapter was removed from the first edition of the book in 1942 because it was deemed insufficiently patriotic (Bordelon 1997: 20). It was restored as an appendix in later editions. There she said:

> Race pride is a luxury I cannot afford. . . . I *do* glory when a Negro does something fine, I gloat because he or she has done a fine thing, but not because he was a negro. That is incidental and accidental. . . . I know that I cannot accept responsibility for thirteen million people. Every tub must sit on its own bottom regardless. . . . Races have never done anything. What seems race achievement is the work of individuals. The white race did not go into a laboratory and invent incandescent light. That was Edison. The Jews did not work out Relativity. That was Einstein. The Negroes did not find out the inner secrets of peanuts and sweet potatoes, nor the secret of the development of the egg. That was Carver and Just. If you are under the impression that every white man is an Edison, just look around a bit. (1984: 249)

In 1948 Hurston was accused of sexually molesting a ten-year-old boy. Although she proved she was in Honduras at the time of the crime and was acquitted when the boy admitted he had fabricated his story, the charges were widely published in the tabloids of the day, and Hurston was personally devastated. During the last years of her life, Hurston returned to Florida and worked as a freelance writer, but she struggled to support herself. She took work where she could find it, such as substitute teaching and working as a maid. In 1956 Hurston lost her home, and in 1958 she suffered a stroke and was forced to enter the St. Lucie Country Welfare Home. Hurston died in January 1960 and was buried in Fort Pierce, Florida, in an unmarked grave. A week after her death, most of her possessions were burned. Luckily, Patrick Duval, St. Lucie County deputy sheriff, rescued her manuscripts and personal papers from the fire (Abbott 1991: 177). In 1973 the author Alice Walker erected a marker in Hurston's memory near her burial site. In recent years, Hurston has been awarded numerous posthumous honors, including induction into the National Women's Hall of Fame in 1994, the American Library Association's Zora Neale Hurston Award established in 2008, and, in 2010, induction into the New York Writers Hall of Fame.

Language was a key area of interest for Boas. Among Boas's students, Sapir was the most involved in language study. Sapir and Whorf, his student, developed methods of linguistic analysis that were consistent with Boasian views of culture. Their key ideas of linguistic relativity and linguistic determinism have come to be known as the *Sapir-Whorf hypothesis*, though this term was coined by Sapir's student Harry Hoijer (1904–1976) in 1954, long after the deaths of both Sapir and Whorf.

Whorf earned a degree in chemical engineering at the Massachusetts Institute of Technology in 1918, then worked for the Hartford Fire Insurance Company in Connecticut. He pursued his interests in language primarily as a hobby. Although Whorf received several offers of professorships, he refused them, claiming that his work with the insurance company provided him with greater freedom and more money than an academic position could (Lavery 2001). In 1931, Whorf began to study linguistics at Yale University with Edward Sapir (1884–1939), one of the leading linguists of the period.

Whorf's main area of interest was Mayan and Aztec iconography. However, he is most remembered for his work on the Hopi language and for his ideas about the relationship of language to culture and thought. The Sapir-Whorf hypothesis contains two basic elements: *linguistic determinism* and *linguistic relativity*. The first deals with the manner in which the structure of a language affects cognition. Linguistic determinists propose that the grammatical and lexical categories of the language a person speaks organize the way the person thinks and shapes the person's behavior. The second, linguistic relativity, refers to the idea that just as cultures are the result of their history, so too are languages. This has two implications: First, no language can be judged better or worse than any other, and second, since the grammatical and lexical categories of a language are unique to that language, speakers of different languages inhabit separate conceptual worlds. You can see how the notion of linguistic relativity reflects the Boasian view of culture.

The work of Sapir and Whorf inspired research on the relationship between language and culture that continues to the current day. Anthropologists, linguists, and psychologists sought to test the notion of linguistic determinism. The concept of linguistic relativity was instrumental in the development of the ethnoscience and cognitive anthropology schools. In particular, the influence of Sapir and Whorf is evident in the studies of subjects such as ethnobotany and ethnomedicine and in the work of scholars like James P. Spradley (1933–1982), Ward Goodenough (1919–2013), William Sturtevant (1926–2007), and Charles O. Frake (1930–2021).

Whorf's "The Relation of Habitual Thought and Behavior to Language" (essay 13) is one of his best-known statements of his understanding of language. It includes many examples derived from his investigative work for the Hartford Insurance Company and his study of the Hopi language.

In most European universities, archaeology and linguistics are separate departments from social anthropology, and biological anthropology is typically a part of biology. The four-field focus of anthropology departments in American universities today is a reflection of Boas and his students' view of anthropology. Though anthropologists today rarely identify themselves as Boasians, it is almost impossible to overestimate the influence of Boas and his students on mainstream American anthropology. The effects of Boas's critical insights are seen most clearly in the work of his students in the first half of this century, but clear echoes of Boasian thought are present in ethnoscience and cognitive anthropology as well as in the symbolic and postmodern approaches to the study of culture.

SUGGESTED READINGS

Benedict, Ruth. 1934. *Patterns of Culture*. New York: Houghton Mifflin.
    Benedict's famous description of Puebloan, Dobuan, and Kwakiutl cultural personalities.
Boas, Franz. 1911. *The Mind of Primitive Man*. New York: Macmillan.
    Eloquent and readable statement of Boas's argument against cultural evolutionism and for universal human equality.
Caffrey, Margaret. 1989. *Ruth Benedict: Stranger in This Land*. Austin: University of Texas.
    Comprehensive biography of Benedict with analysis of her work and her relationships with other anthropologists.
Darnell, Regna. 2001. *Invisible Genealogies: A History of Americanist Anthropology*. Lincoln: University of Nebraska Press.
    Traces the connections among many of the students of Boas and their relevance to current-day anthropology.
Harrison, Ira E., and Faye V. Harrison. 1998. *African American Pioneers in Anthropology*. Urbana: University of Illinois Press.
    A collection of thirteen essays about the lives and struggles of African American anthropologists in the twentieth century.
Hurston, Zora Neale. 1990 (1935). *Mules and Men*. New York: Harper & Row.
    Hurston's groundbreaking collection of African American folklore collected in Florida in the 1920s.
King, Charles. 2019. *Gods of the Upper Air: How a Circle of Renegade Anthropologists Reinvented Race, Sex, and Gender in the Twentieth Century*. New York: Doubleday.
    A popular account of many of Boas's best-known students.
Lamphere, Louise. 1989. "Feminist Anthropology: The Legacy of Elsie Clews Parsons." *American Ethnologist* 16(3): 518–533.
    An essay describing the contribution of Elsie Clews Parsons, a key ally of Boas and a founding female anthropologist.
Lewis, H. S. 2001. "The Passion of Franz Boas." *American Anthropologist* 103: 447–467.
    An essay highlighting Boas's work to promote tolerance and racial equality.
Lucy, John A. 1992. *Language Diversity and Thought: A Reformulation of the Linguistic Relativity Hypothesis*. New York: Cambridge University Press.
    A historical overview of the linguistic work of Boas, Sapir, and Whorf and an introduction to Lucy's work on the Yucatec Maya.
Mead, Margaret. 1935. *Sex and Temperament in Three Primitive Societies*. New York: W. Morrow.
    Mead's pioneering work on gender describes three New Guinea societies: the Arapesh, the Mundugumor, and the Tchambuli.
Shankman, Paul. 2009. *The Trashing of Margaret Mead: Anatomy of an Anthropological Controversy*. Madison: University of Wisconsin Press.
    A summary and analysis of the Mead/Freeman debate over *Coming of Age in Samoa*.
Silverman, Sydel, ed. 2004. *Totems and Teachers: Key Figures in the History of Anthropology*. 2nd ed. New York: AltaMira Press.
    Essays about key figures in American anthropology, written by their students (an important source for many notes in this book).
Stocking, George W., ed. 1974. *The Shaping of American Anthropology, 1883–1911: A Franz Boas Reader*. Chicago: University of Chicago Press.
    An important collection of essays by Boas, presented with brief introductory material.
Whorf, Benjamin L. 1956. *Language, Thought, and Reality: Selected Writings of Benjamin Lee Whorf*. Cambridge, MA: MIT Press.
    A collection of essays by Whorf with a biographical and analytical introduction by John B. Carroll.
Zumwalt, Rosemary L. 2019. *Franz Boas: The Emergence of the Anthropologist*. Lincoln: University of Nebraska Press.
    A masterful biography of Franz Boas, from his childhood to the beginning of his career at Columbia University.

8. The Methods of Ethnology

Franz Boas (1858–1942)

URING THE LAST TEN YEARS the methods of inquiry into the historical development of civilization have undergone remarkable changes. During the second half of the last century evolutionary thought held almost complete sway and investigators like Spencer, Morgan, Tylor, Lubbock, to mention only a few, were under the spell of the idea of a general, uniform evolution of culture in which all parts of mankind participated. The newer development goes back in part to the influence of Ratzel, whose geographical training impressed him with the importance of diffusion and migration. The problem of diffusion was taken up in detail particularly in America, but was applied in a much wider sense by Foy and Graebner, and finally seized upon in a still wider application by Elliot Smith and Rivers, so that at the present time, at least among certain groups of investigators in England and also in Germany, ethnological research is based on the concept of migration and dissemination rather than upon that of evolution.[1]

A critical study of these two directions of inquiry shows that each is founded on the application of one fundamental hypothesis. The evolutionary point of view presupposes that the course of historical changes in the cultural life of mankind follows definite laws which are applicable everywhere, and which bring it about that cultural development is, in its main lines, the same among all races and all peoples. This idea is clearly expressed by Tylor in the introductory pages of his classic work "Primitive Culture." As soon as we admit that the hypothesis of a uniform evolution has to be proved before it can be accepted, the whole structure loses its foundation. It is true that

---

From *American Anthropologist* (1920)

1. In this essay, Boas attacks evolutionary theorists such as Lewis Henry Morgan and Edward Burnett Tylor as well as diffusionists like W. H. R. Rivers (1864–1922). Boas spent much of his career demonstrating the logical inconsistencies of evolutionism and diffusionism. This essay was published in *American Anthropologist* in 1920. However, the outlines of the argument he was later to use so effectively are evident in an article he wrote for *Science* in 1887. In "Museums of Anthropology and Their Classification," Boas attacked Otis Mason's display of ethnological material in the United States National Museum (today the Smithsonian). According to Boas, Mason had ordered the ethnological collection in an evolutionary sequence by objects, based on an erroneous analogy with biological classification, rather than organizing them according to the people to whom the objects belonged. Boas wrote, "We have to study each ethnological specimen individually in its history and in its medium. . . . By regarding a single implement outside of its surroundings, outside of the other inventions of the people to whom it belongs, and outside of other phenomena affecting that people and its productions, we cannot understand its meaning. Our objection to Mason's idea is that classification is not explanation" (Boas 1974b: 62).

Boas mentions some particularly eminent diffusionists. Fritz Graebner (1877–1934) and cultural geographer Friedrich Ratzel (1844–1904) were founders of the German *Kulturkreis* ("culture circle") school of diffusionism. *Kulturkreis* members were tightly linked to the Catholic Church, and in much of their work, they attempted to make newly available ethnographic data correspond with prevailing biblical interpretation (Harris 1968: 379). In Cologne, Graebner worked as an assistant to museum director Willy Foy (1873–1929). Graebner and Foy collaborated on Graebner's book *Die Methode der Ethnologie* (1911), which Boas brutally critiqued in an essay in *Science* that same year. Grafton Elliot Smith (1871–1937) and Rivers were English radical diffusionists who believed that all civilization had diffused from Egypt.

there are indications of parallelism of development in different parts of the world, and that similar customs are found in the most diverse and widely separated parts of the globe. The occurrence of these similarities, which are distributed so irregularly that they cannot readily be explained on the basis of diffusion, is one of the foundations of the evolutionary hypothesis, as it was the foundation of Bastian's psychologizing treatment of cultural phenomena. On the other hand, it may be recognized that the hypothesis implies the thought that our modern Western European civilization represents the highest cultural development towards which all other more primitive cultural types tend, and that, therefore, retrospectively, we construct an **orthogenetic** development towards our own modern civilization. It is clear that if we admit that there may be different ultimate and coexisting types of civilization, the hypothesis of one single general line of development cannot be maintained.[2]

Opposed to these assumptions is the modern tendency to deny the existence of a general evolutionary scheme which would represent the history of the cultural development the world over. The hypothesis that there are inner causes which bring about similarities of development in remote parts of the globe is rejected and in its place it is assumed that identity of development in two different parts of the globe must always be due to migration and diffusion. On this basis historical contact is demanded for enormously large areas. The theory demands a high degree of stability of cultural traits such as is apparently observed in many primitive tribes,

and it is furthermore based on the supposed correlation between a number of diverse and mutually independent cultural traits which reappear in the same combinations in distant parts of the world. In this sense, modern investigation takes up anew Gerland's theory of the persistence of a number of cultural traits which were developed in one center and carried by man in his migrations from continent to continent.[3]

It seems to me that if the hypothetical foundations of these two extreme forms of ethnological research are broadly stated as I have tried to do here, it is at once clear that the correctness of the assumptions has not been demonstrated, but that arbitrarily the one or the other has been selected for the purpose of obtaining a consistent picture of cultural development. These methods are essentially forms of classification of the static phenomena of culture according to two distinct principles, and interpretations of these classifications as of historical significance, without, however, any attempt to prove that this interpretation is justifiable. To give an example: It is observed that in most parts of the world there are resemblances between decorative forms that are representative and others that are more or less geometrical. According to the evolutionary point of view, their development is explained in the following manner: the decorative forms are arranged in such order that the most representative forms are placed at the beginning. The other forms are so placed that they show a gradual transition from representative forms to purely conventional geometric forms. This

---

2. Boas's attack on the evolutionists rested on a logical flaw in their argument. Boas showed that their argument assumed what it was trying to prove: that historical changes in human culture follow general laws. Boas supported the Darwinian model of biological evolution but was hostile to the application of Darwinian or Spencerian evolution to society. The evolutionary theories of Morgan and Tylor were strongly teleological, based on their belief that all of humanity moved along a single, invariable line of progress. This was neither Darwinian nor Spencerian.

Adolf Bastian (1826–1905) was a German theorist of psychic unity who believed that a few fundamental ideas, common to humankind, were the building blocks of culture. In 1873, Bastian became the first director of the Ethnological Museum of Berlin. Boas worked for Bastian at the museum in late 1885 and early 1886 (Zumwalt 2019 153).

"Orthogenetic": evolution along definite, predetermined lines

3. Above, Boas focused his assault on cultural evolutionists. In this paragraph, he begins his attack on the diffusionists.

Georg Gerland (1833–1919) was a German geographer/ethnologist. Whereas Bastian believed that cross-cultural similarities were due to shared elementary ideas, Gerland proposed that these were the result of a common inheritance from an earlier stage of cultural development.

order is then interpreted as meaning that geometric designs originated from representative designs which gradually degenerated. This method has been pursued, for instance, by Putnam, Stolpe, Balfour, and Haddon, and by Verworn and, in his earlier writings, by von den Steinen. While I do not mean to deny that this development may have occurred, it would be rash to generalize and to claim that in every case the classification which has been made according to a definite principle represents an historical development. The order might as well be reversed and we might begin with a simple geometric element which, by the addition of new traits, might be developed into a representative design, and we might claim that this order represents an historical sequence. Both of these possibilities were considered by

Holmes as early as 1885. Neither the one nor the other theory can be established without actual historical proof.[4]

The opposite attitude, namely, origin through diffusion, is exhibited in Heinrich Schurtz's attempt to connect the decorative art of Northwest America with that of Melanesia. The simple fact that in these areas elements occur that may be interpreted as eyes, induced him to assume that both have a common origin, without allowing for the possibility that the pattern in the two areas—each of which shows highly distinctive characteristics—may have developed from independent sources. In this attempt Schurtz followed Ratzel, who had already tried to establish connections between Melanesia and Northwest America on the basis of other cultural features.[5]

---

4. This paragraph is typical of Boas's method of attack: He does not attack particular examples but looks for flaws in methodology. Trained in physics, mathematics, and geography, Boas brought a striving for a meticulous scientific methodology to anthropology. Essentially, he faults his opponents for sloppy thinking. Writing in this way, he seems to imply that a rigorously scientific presentation of the data might allow the construction of an evolutionary model of human society. In fact, Boas staunchly opposed evolutionary explanations.

Notice Boas's passing reference to William Henry Holmes (1846–1933). Holmes was John Wesley Powell's successor at the Bureau of American Ethnology. In 1910, Holmes became chairman of the Division of Anthropology of the Smithsonian's US National Museum, and in 1920, he was appointed director of the National Gallery of Art (now the Smithsonian American Art Museum). In 1919, the year before this essay was published, Holmes led the American Anthropological Association's successful effort to censure Boas after Boas published a bitter letter to the editor in *The Nation* in which he criticized anthropologists who had used their scientific credentials to spy for the United States in World War I. Boas wrote, "A person, however, who uses science as a cover for political spying, who demeans himself to pose before a foreign government as an investigator and asks for assistance in his alleged researches in order to carry on, under this cloak, his political machinations, prostitutes science in an unpardonable way and forfeits the right to be classed as a scientist" (1919: 797). Boas did not mention the spies by name but his accusations were accurate and the spies were Samuel K. Lothrup (1892–1965), Sylvanus Morley (1883–1948), Herbert Spinden (1879–1967), and John Mason (1885–1967). All were archaeologists and ethnographers who specialized in the Caribbean and Central and South America. The first three voted for Boas's censure. The fourth, Mason, did not and sent Boas an apologetic letter (Price 2000 [anthropologists as spies]).

Other important scholars mentioned in this passage are Frederic W. Putnam (1839–1915), Hjalmar Stolpe (1841–1905), Henry Balfour (1863–1939), Alfred Cort Haddon (1855–1940), Max Verworn (1863–1921), and Karl von den Steinen (1855–1929). Putnam was a prominent nineteenth-century American archaeologist. He was curator of the Peabody Museum at Harvard University from 1874 to 1909 and head of the anthropology program for the World's Columbian Exposition held in Chicago in 1893. Putnam was a strong supporter of Boas and was distantly related to him through marriage. Stolpe was a Swedish archaeologist and ethnographer. Henry Balfour was the founding curator of the Pitt-Rivers Museum at Oxford University, a post he held for over forty years. Haddon was a British ethnologist who is best known for his fieldwork with W. H. R. Rivers and C. G. Seligman on the Torres Strait expedition in 1898. Verworn was a professor at the University of Göttingen. Von den Steinen was a German ethnologist and explorer who specialized in the study of indigenous cultures of Central Brazil.

5. While Boas recognized that diffusion occurred, he insisted that cultural traits had to be studied in the cultural context in which they were located, and diffusion had to be historically demonstrated, not just assumed.

Heinrich Schurtz (1863–1903) was a German ethnologist and historian. Schurtz was a student of Ratzel's.

While ethnographical research based on these two fundamental hypotheses seems to characterize the general tendency of European thought, a different method is at present pursued by the majority of American anthropologists. The difference between the two directions of study may perhaps best be summarized by the statement that American scholars are primarily interested in the dynamic phenomena of cultural change, and try to elucidate cultural history by the application of the results of their studies; and that they relegate the solution of the ultimate question of the relative importance of parallelism of cultural development in distant areas, as against worldwide diffusion, and stability of cultural traits over long periods to a future time when the actual conditions of cultural change are better known. The American ethnological methods are analogous to those of European, particularly of Scandinavian, archaeology, and of the researches into the prehistoric period of the eastern Mediterranean area.[6]

It may seem to the distant observer that American students are engaged in a mass of detailed investigations without much bearing upon the solution of the ultimate problems of a philosophic history of human civilization. I think this interpretation of the American attitude would be unjust because the ultimate questions are as near to our hearts as they are to those of other scholars, only we do not hope to be able to solve an intricate historical problem by a formula.[7]

First of all, the whole problem of cultural history appears to us as an historical problem. In order to understand history it is necessary to know not only how things are, but how they have come to be. In the domain of ethnology, where, for most parts of the world, no historical facts are available except those that may be revealed by archaeological study, all evidence of change can be inferred only by indirect methods. Their character is represented in the researches of students of comparative **philology**. The method is based on the comparison of static phenomena combined with the study of their distribution. What can be done by this method is well illustrated by Dr. Lowie's investigations of the military societies of the Plains Indians, or by the modern investigation of American mythology. It is, of course, true that we can never hope to obtain incontrovertible data relating to the chronological sequence of events, but certain general broad outlines can be ascertained with a high degree of probability, even of certainty.[8]

As soon as these methods are applied, primitive society loses the appearance of absolute

---

6. When Boas speaks here of American anthropologists, he is referring to himself and the many students he trained. The particular issue of cultural change with which they were primarily concerned involved Native American groups. Boas and his students were deeply concerned that Native American cultures were disappearing, largely as the result of intentional efforts of the United States Government to destroy them and assimilate native people (without granting them equality or compensating them for their land or cultural loss). Boasians often understood themselves as on a salvage mission to preserve what they could of native culture. They focused on trying to describe these cultures at their moment of contact with Euro-Americans. Current anthropologists have often criticized Boas for this salvage approach.

7. Boas was concerned with methodology rather than building grand theories of humanity, history, or social organization. European anthropologists often accused Boas and his students of producing atheoretical anthropology concerned only with the collection of data. In the following paragraphs, he attempts to answer this charge.

8. The studies Boas mentions here are marked by their reporting of the nature and distribution of cultural phenomena without any attempt to place these phenomena on an evolutionary scale or show their ultimate origin.

Robert Lowie (1883–1957), a student of Boas's and, later, a professor of anthropology at Berkeley, was an influential voice in American anthropology in the 1930s and 1940s. Boas's reference here is to Lowie's 1913 article "Military Societies of the Crow Indians."

"Philology": the study of the history of language. Comparative philology is the historical comparison of different languages. In Boas's day this was considered a method for estimating the time elapsed since a group split from their parent culture.

stability which is conveyed to the student who sees a certain people only at a certain given time. All cultural forms rather appear in a constant state of flux and subject to fundamental modifications.

It is intelligible why in our studies the problem of dissemination should take a prominent position. It is much easier to prove dissemination than to follow up developments due to inner forces, and the data for such a study are obtained with much greater difficulty. They may, however, be observed in every phenomenon of acculturation in which foreign elements are remodeled according to the patterns prevalent in their new environment, and they may be found in the peculiar local developments of widely spread ideas and activities. The reason why the study of inner development has not been taken up energetically is not due to the fact that from a theoretical point of view it is unimportant, it is rather due to the inherent methodological difficulties. It may perhaps be recognized that in recent years attention is being drawn to this problem as is manifested by the investigations on the processes of acculturation and of the interdependence of cultural activities which are attracting the attention of many investigators.[9]

The further pursuit of these inquiries emphasizes the importance of a feature which is common to all historic phenomena. While in natural sciences we are accustomed to consider a given number of causes and to study their effects, in historical happenings we are compelled to consider every phenomenon not only as effect but also as cause. This is true even in the particular application of the laws of physical nature, as, for instance, in the study of astronomy in which the position of certain heavenly bodies at a given moment may be considered as the effect of gravitation, while, at the same time, their particular arrangement in space determines future changes. This relation appears much more clearly in the history of human civilization. To give an example: a surplus of food supply is liable to bring about an increase of population and an increase of leisure, which gives opportunity for occupations that are not absolutely necessary for the needs of everyday life. In turn the increase of population and of leisure, which may be applied to new inventions, gives rise to a greater food supply and to a further increase in the amount of leisure, so that a cumulative effect results.[10]

Similar considerations may be made in regard to the important problem of the relation of the individual to society, a problem that has to be considered whenever we study the dynamic conditions of change. The activities of the individual are determined to a great extent by his social environment, but in turn his own activities influence the society in which he lives, and may bring about modifications in its form. Obviously, this problem is one of the most important ones to be taken up in a study of cultural changes. It is also beginning to attract the attention of students who are no longer satisfied with the systematic enumeration of standardized beliefs and customs of a tribe, but who begin to be interested in the question of the way in which the individual reacts to his whole social environment, and to the differences of opinion and of mode of action that occur in primitive society and which are the causes of far-reaching changes.[11]

---

9. Boas argues that although the existence of cultural elements like mythology and their diffusion over contiguous geographical areas are observable, "inner forces" such as the flowering of germs of thought described by Morgan (see essay 3), are not. Note that Boas does not claim his opponents' conclusions are necessarily wrong, simply that they are not supported by competent research.

10. Boas here points out that unlike the natural sciences where cause and effect may be straightforward, in the social sciences the cause-effect relationships in human activities may be much more complex. Cultures are *sui generis* (that is, they create themselves or are created by their histories). Consequently, whereas the natural sciences are based on universal principles (for example, the relationship between elements in the Periodic Table does not change), cultures can only be understood with reference to their specific circumstances.

11. Boas states here that while individuals are the product of their cultures, individuals can have enough influence to modify the culture in which they live. This focus on the influence of individuals in a society split

In short then, the method which we try to develop is based on a study of the dynamic changes in society that may be observed at the present time. We refrain from the attempt to solve the fundamental problem of the general development of civilization until we have been able to unravel the processes that are going on under our eyes.[12]

Certain general conclusions may be drawn from this study even now. First of all, the history of human civilization does not appear to us as determined entirely by psychological necessity that leads to a uniform evolution the world over. We rather see that each cultural group has its own unique history, dependent partly upon the peculiar inner development of the social group, and partly upon the foreign influences to which it has been subjected. There have been processes of gradual differentiation as well as processes of leveling down differences between neighboring cultural centers, but it would be quite impossible to understand, on the basis of a single evolutionary scheme, what happened to any particular people. An example of the contrast between the two points of view is clearly indicated by a comparison of the treatment of Zuñi civilization by Frank Hamilton Cushing on the one hand, on the other by modern students, particularly by Elsie Clews Parsons, A. L. Kroeber and Leslie Spier. Cushing believed that it was possible to explain Zuñi culture entirely on the basis of the reaction of the Zuñi mind to its geographical environment, and that the whole of Zuñi culture could be explained as the development which followed necessarily from the position in which the people were placed. Cushing's keen insight into the Indian mind and his thorough knowledge of the most intimate life of the people gave great plausibility to his interpretations. On the other hand, Dr. Parsons' studies prove conclusively the deep influence which Spanish ideas have had on Zuñi culture, and, together with Professor Kroeber's investigations, give us one of the best examples of acculturation that have come to our notice. The psychological explanation is entirely misleading, notwithstanding its plausibility; and the historical study shows us an entirely different picture, in which the unique combination of ancient traits (which in themselves are undoubtedly complex) and of European influences has brought about the present condition.[13]

Boas and his followers. A. L. Kroeber (1876–1960), for example, argued that individuals had little importance (see essay 9). Ruth Benedict (1887–1948) spent decades examining the relationship between culture and individual personality. Others such as Paul Radin (1883–1959) contended that anthropology should concentrate on individual life histories.

12. In other words, Boas's approach was to be purely inductive. Theoretical claims, he believed, could not be supported without the collection of large amounts of data. He is generally understood to have believed that the attempt to formulate general theories was not wrong, just extremely premature. However, Boas insisted that cultures could only be understood with respect to their unique historical development, whereas building theory necessarily involves comparison and generalization. Thus, it seems unlikely that anthropology as Boas practiced it could ever generate broad theoretical propositions.

13. Note that Boas's conclusions are largely negative. He proposes that evolutionary theory cannot explain the differences in human societies. These can only be explained by examining the specific history of each society. This suggests the impossibility of any single theory of human social development.

Frank Hamilton Cushing (1857–1900) spent five years with the Zuni people between 1879 and 1884 and was initiated into their Bow Priest Society. He wrote extensively on Zuni religion and technology. Here, Boas critiques Cushing's work as ahistorical and juxtaposes it with the ethnographic research conducted by Elsie Clews Parsons (1875–1941). Parsons was one of the most prominent folklorists and anthropologists of her generation. In anthropology, she is primarily known for her work among the Hopi, Tewa, and Zuni and as one of the founders of the New School for Social Research in New York City. However early in her career, after receiving her PhD in Sociology at Columbia University in 1899, she wrote about the repression of women, publishing several books using the pseudonym John Main to protect her husband's political career (he was Herbert Parsons (1869–1925), a three-term congressman and close associate of President Teddy Roosevelt).

Studies of the dynamics of primitive life also show that an assumption of long continued stability such as is demanded by Elliot Smith is without any foundation in fact. Wherever primitive conditions have been studied in detail, they can be proved to be in a state of flux, and it would seem that there is a close parallelism between the history of language and the history of general cultural development. Periods of stability are followed by periods of rapid change. It is exceedingly improbable that any customs of primitive people should be preserved unchanged for thousands of years. Furthermore, the phenomena of acculturation prove that a transfer of customs from one region into another without concomitant changes due to acculturation is very rare. It is, therefore, very unlikely that ancient Mediterranean customs could be found at the present time practically unchanged in different parts of the globe, as Elliot Smith's theory demands.[14]

While on the whole the unique historical character of cultural growth in each area stands out as a salient element in the history of cultural development, we may recognize at the same time that certain typical parallelisms do occur. We are, however, not so much inclined to look for these similarities in detailed customs but rather in certain dynamic conditions which are due to social or psychological causes that are liable to lead to similar results. The example of the relation between food supply and population to which I referred before may serve as an example. Another type of example is presented in those cases in which a certain problem confronting man may be solved by a limited number of methods only. When we find, for instance, marriage as a universal institution, it may be recognized that marriage is possible only between a number of men and a number of women; a number of men and one woman; a number of women and one man; or one man and one woman. As a matter of fact, all these forms are found the world over and it is, therefore, not surprising that analogous forms should have been adopted quite independently in different parts of the world, and, considering both the general economic conditions of mankind and the character of sexual instinct in the higher animals, it also does not seem surprising that group marriage and polyandrous marriages should be comparatively speaking rare. Similar considerations may also be made in regard to the philosophical views held by mankind. In short, if we look for laws, the laws relate to the effects of physiological, psychological, and social conditions, not to sequences of cultural achievement.[15]

By 1910 Parsons became interested in folklore and at the suggestion of Franz Boas, she turned to the study of African American culture. She became Associate Editor of the *Journal of American Folklore* in 1916 and was elected president of the American Folklore Society in 1919 and 1920. Parsons was also elected president of the American Ethnological Society (1923–1925) and was the first female president of the American Anthropological Association (1941).

In the final phase of her career, Parsons studied Pueblo Indian culture in the American southwest and worked with Zuni, Navajo, Hopi, and Tewa. She had a particular interest in the lives of women and the matrilineal kin structure of the Hopi and Zuni.

In addition to her own research, Parsons, the daughter of the immensely wealthy financier Henry Clews (1834–1923), was a major financial supporter of anthropology. Through The Southwest Society, which she founded and funded, Parsons financed the fieldwork of many of Boas's students, paid for secretarial help for Boas, and underwrote the cost of numerous publications including the *Journal of American Folklore*. Parsons's funding was critical to anthropology's survival, especially since many major funding organizations, such as the National Research Council, were controlled by eugenicists and white supremacists who were actively hostile to Boasian anthropology (Deacon 1997: 244–245).

14. As mentioned in note 1, Grafton Elliot Smith was an English diffusionist who proposed that all complex cultural traits originated in ancient Egypt. The radical diffusionists believed that humans were not inherently inventive, and as a result, societies remained static for long periods. Boas disagreed with this contention.

15. Equifinality is a key aspect of Boas's theoretical position. He argues that the presence of similar traits in many societies is not necessarily evidence either for psychic unity or large-scale diffusion. They may be

In some cases a regular sequence of these may accompany the development of the psychological or social status. This is illustrated by the sequence of industrial inventions in the Old World and in America, which I consider as independent. A period of food gathering and of the use of stone was followed by the invention of agriculture, of pottery and finally of the use of metals. Obviously, this order is based on the increased amount of time given by mankind to the use of natural products, of tools and utensils, and to the variations that developed with it. Although in this case parallelism seems to exist on the two continents, it would be futile to try to follow out the order in detail. As a matter of fact, it does not apply to other inventions. The domestication of animals, which, in the Old World must have been an early achievement, was very late in the New World, where domesticated animals, except the dog, hardly existed at all at the time of discovery. A slight beginning had been made in Peru with the domestication of the llama, and birds were kept in various parts of the continent.[16]

A similar consideration may be made in regard to the development of rationalism. It seems to be one of the fundamental characteristics of the development of mankind that activities which have developed unconsciously are gradually made the subject of reasoning. We may observe this process everywhere. It appears, perhaps, most clearly in the history of science which has gradually extended the scope of its inquiry over an ever-widening field and which has raised into consciousness human activities that are automatically performed in the life of the individual and of society.[17]

I have not heretofore referred to another aspect of modern ethnology which is connected with the growth of psycho-analysis. Sigmund Freud has attempted to show that primitive thought is in many respects analogous to those forms of individual psychic activity which he has explored by his psycho-analytical methods. In many respects his attempts are similar to the interpretation of mythology by symbolists like Stucken. Rivers has taken hold of Freud's suggestion as well as of the interpretations of Graebner and Elliot Smith, and we find, therefore, in his new writings a peculiar disconnected application of a psychologizing attitude and the application of the theory of ancient transmission.[18]

---

the result of convergent evolution and independent invention. Note also a key point in this passage: Boas says that one reason for the development of similar institutions is that logically, certain things can only be done in a limited number of ways. Thus, in his example here, one reason for similarities in marriage patterns is the low number of ways it is possible to construct an institution such as marriage. This idea, known as the principle of limited possibilities, is primarily associated with Boas's student, Alexander Goldenweiser (1880–1940). In 1913, Goldenweiser published "The Principle of Limited Possibilities in the Development of Culture" in which he described this idea and gave numerous examples.

16. This paragraph is an attack on unilineal evolutionists such as Morgan (see essay 3), who used the presence of specific technologies or items of material culture to mark developmental eras in his scheme of cultural evolution.

17. It is curious that having shown the weakness of arguments based on the principle of psychic unity, Boas here relies on a statement about the universal nature of the development of reasoning. Morgan, Tylor, and other evolutionists made statements very similar to this.

18. Freud's psychoanalytic theory was extremely popular in the 1920s. Sigmund Freud (1856–1939) argued that the evolutionary development of society mirrored the psychosexual development of individuals. One key implication of this was the idea that adult members of "primitive" cultures were similar to children in "civilized" societies. Boas and his students entirely rejected this theory, however, for many of them, some of Freud's other insights were critical. Margaret Mead (1901–1978) and Benedict developed their views on culture and personality partially in reaction to Freud's ideas. Others, such as Cora Du Bois (1903–1991) and Abram Kardiner (1891–1981), attempted to apply Freudian psychology to anthropology.

While I believe some of the ideas under-lying Freud's psycho-analytic studies may be fruitfully applied to ethnological problems, it does not seem to me that the one-sided exploitation of this method will advance our understanding of the development of human society. It is certainly true that the influence of impressions received during the first few years of life has been entirely underestimated and that the social behavior of man depends to a great extent upon the earliest habits which are established before the time when connected memory begins, and that many so-called racial or hereditary traits are to be considered rather as a result of early exposure to a certain form of social conditions. Most of these habits do not rise into consciousness and are, therefore, broken with difficulty only. Much of the differ-ence in the behavior of adult male and female may go back to this cause. If, however, we try to apply the whole theory of the influence of suppressed desires to the activities of man liv-ing under different social forms, I think we extend beyond their legitimate limits the infer-ences that may be drawn from the observation of normal and abnormal individual psychology. Many other factors are of greater importance. To give an example: The phenomena of lan-guage show clearly that conditions quite differ-ent from those to which psycho-analysts direct their attention determine the mental behavior of man. The general concepts underlying lan-guage are entirely unknown to most people. They do not rise into consciousness until the scientific study of grammar begins. Never-

theless, the categories of language compel us to see the world arranged in certain defi-nite conceptual groups which, on account of our lack of knowledge of linguistic processes, are taken as objective categories and which, therefore, impose themselves upon the form of our thoughts. It is not known what the ori-gin of these categories may be, but it seems quite certain that they have nothing to do with the phenomena which are the subject of psy-cho-analytic study.[19]

The applicability of the psycho-analytic the-ory of symbolism is also open to the greatest doubt. We should remember that symbolic interpretation has occupied a prominent posi-tion in the philosophy of all times. It is present not only in primitive life, but the history of phi-losophy and of theology abounds in examples of a high development of symbolism, the type of which depends upon the general mental atti-tude of the philosopher who develops it. The theologians who interpreted the Bible on the basis of religious symbolism were no less cer-tain of the correctness of their views, than the psycho-analysts are of their interpretations of thought and conduct based on sexual symbol-ism. The results of a symbolic interpretation depend primarily upon the subjective attitude of the investigator who arranges phenomena according to his leading concept. In order to prove the applicability of the symbolism of psycho-analysis, it would be necessary to show that a symbolic interpretation from other entirely different points of view would not be equally plausible, and that explanations that

---

Eduard Stucken (1865–1936) was a German specialist in Near Eastern Studies, particularly Egyptology. He also wrote novels, short stories, poems, and plays. He was best known for his four-volume romantic novel *Die weißen Götter* (translated as *The Great White Gods* [1934]) about the Spanish conquest of the Aztec Empire.

19. This fascinating paragraph identifies ideas that became critically associated with some of Boas's stu-dents. Boas first notes that some critical social differences, including gender, may be linked to early childhood experiences. This is a subject explored in depth by Mead in *Sex and Temperament in Three Primitive Societies* (1935). Boas then turns to language, a subject of particular interest for him and his students. He suggests that language is an unconscious classification system that compels people to see the world in particular ways. This idea, known today as the *Sapir-Whorf hypothesis*, is associated with Boas's student Edward Sapir (1884–1939), and Sapir's student and colleague, Benjamin Lee Whorf (1897–1941).

leave out symbolic significance or reduce it to a minimum would not be adequate.[20]

While, therefore, we may welcome the application of every advance in the method of psychological investigation, we cannot accept as an advance in ethnological method the crude transfer of a novel, one-sided method of psychological investigation of the individual to social phenomena the origin of which can be shown to be historically determined and to be subject to influences that are not at all to those that control the psychology of the individual.[21]

---

20. The particular attacks Boas makes in this essay are repeated frequently in anthropology. For example, Boas's criticism of psychology as dependent on "[the] subjective attitude of the investigator who arranges phenomena according to his leading concept" is repeated almost word for word by ethnoscientists and cognitive anthropologists in the 1950s and 1960s in their critique of other forms of anthropology and in a slightly different form by postmodernists as well.

21. Boas's criticism of psychoanalysis is similar to his attack on evolutionists and diffusionists: He faults psychoanalysis on methodological grounds. All of Boas's criticisms are intended to reinforce his call for an inductive methodology in anthropology. He insisted that it was only through the meticulous collection of empirical data that anthropologists could hope to understand cultures.

9. On the Principle of Order in Civilization as Exemplified by Changes of Fashion

A. L. Kroeber (1876–1960)

THE IDEA HAS NO DOUBT often been held which the talented dogmatist Le Bon voiced in the assertion that most social phenomena are expressible by nearly similar and presumably simple geometrical curves.[a] The rise and fall of national arts and of national fortunes certainly seem to bear out such a conception, even though definite proof has apparently never been attempted. Historians frequently allude to the development and degeneration of a state, or of some aspect of its civilization, as if such symmetrical growths and declines were familiar and normally recurring events; but they beware rather consistently from formulating the assumption into a principle, or proclaiming it as an abstract and accurate law.[1]

If one considers the story of the Elizabethan drama from its stiffly archaic inceptions through the awakening in Greene and Marlowe, the Shakespearian glory, the slackening to the level of Fletcher, Webster, Ford, and Massinger, to the close of the playhouses by the civil war, the picture of an even-sided curve rises in the mind. The masterpieces of the greatest member of the school fall in the first decade of the seventeenth century. His more **prolix** and less intense tragedies and comedies, and the plays of contemporaries nearest him in achievement, precede and follow by a few years. Each **quinquennium** more distant from the culmination is marked by greater crudity in recession, more extended laxity in progression of time; and the total duration before and after the **acme** is substantially equal.[b, 2]

If such a surge stood unique, it would be meaningless. But it is so often repeated in

---

From *American Anthropologist* (1919)

1. Kroeber's conception of culture, like that of Émile Durkheim, was superorganic. This implied that individual humans had little if any effect on culture. He believed that culture had an existence outside of humans and that it compelled us to conform to patterns that could be statistically demonstrated. Kroeber believed these patterns could be studied and the basic theoretical principles governing culture change could be outlined. Kroeber wrote this article to illustrate how patterns of culture change could be discovered. He chose the subject of fashion to illustrate that cyclical patterns of change have occurred beyond the influence or understanding of any given individual.

Gustave Le Bon (1841–1931) was a French social psychologist and sociologist, best known for his 1895 study of crowd psychology *The Crowd: A Study of the Popular Mind.*

2. Although his article focuses on cyclical changes in fashion, Kroeber believed that this pattern, which could be statistically illustrated by a curve, applied to all manner of cultural phenomena. For example, he begins by talking about the florescence and decay of great works of the Elizabethan theater and goes on to discuss the rise and fall of civilizations.

Note that Kroeber is willing to apply value judgments in ways that might strike current-day readers as odd. In this paragraph, Shakespeare is better than Fletcher and other playwrights of the late sixteenth and early seventeenth centuries. Shakespeare has greater and lesser plays. Kroeber provides a long footnote explaining exactly what he means and which plays are best. This is typical of his work. Kroeber divided culture into "utility culture" and "value culture." Utility culture included subsistence and survival techniques that Kroeber did not find particularly interesting. Value culture included artistic production in all fields and was Kroeber's primary area of study. Kroeber conceived of value culture as waxing and waning in time, following a curve like the one he describes here. The best and most numerous artistic productions were created at the highest points of such

the history of aesthetics, that something of a generic principle must be involved. The classic French drama, that of Spain, of ancient Athens; the briefly great literatures of Rome, Portugal, and Germany; the so-called romantic poetry of England—even the minor stirring known as American literature; Italian art of the Renaissance; the Dutch and Flemish schools of painting; Greek sculpture—and, we might add, philosophy—each of these isolable movements has been traced through a similar course of origin, growth, climax, decline, and either death or petrifaction, analogous to the life stories of organisms.[3]

While however we are obviously hovering above a latent principle embodied in these phenomena, its expression in exact form, capable of successful application in the resolution of other events of human history, is difficult; chiefly because the variability of the phenomena is qualitative, whereas a workable law or deterministic principle must be quantitative in its nature. It would indeed be possible to assemble comparative ratings of the degrees of achievement attained by each participant in any of these movements, to convert these ratings into numbers, and to trust to the averaging of opinions to efface, to a greater or less extent, the subjectivity of the individual judgments used. But such a procedure is too loose to promise much real advance of understanding. After all, it would rest on a series or composite photographs of verdicts as to qualities, and not on verifiable measurements.

The field of political history is also rich in data that point in the same direction. As a boy it seemed to me possible to express numerically the relative strength and prestige of the several Greek city states at intervals of equal duration, and thus to outline sharply the varying course of Hellenic history; and I remember computations actually entered in the attempt, which has very likely been made at one time or another by others. Everyone will recall in this connection the comment on the fall of Rome under Romulus Augustulus, whose name combined that of the founder and that of the exponent of the greatest success of the eternal city; and how, as at the laying of the walls first six and then twelve vultures flew overhead, the state grew, and then declined, for a total existence of an equal number of centuries. The anecdote is a play of symbolic fancy primarily, or perhaps a mnemonic device; but it also appeals dimly to a sense of historic necessity, of rhythmic inevitability, such as the later middle ages were fond of dwelling on in allusions to the wheel of fortune which revolved for nations as well as persons.[4]

There is no need of citing at length similar cyclical growths familiar from more modern

---

curves, which Krober referred to as culture climaxes. In 1936, Kroeber listed some indicators of culture climaxes as developments in "cults" (religions), kinship units, and music (https://digitalassets.lib.berkeley.edu/anthpubs/ucb/text/ucp037-001.pdf).

"Prolix": wordy, tedious.

"Quinquennium": a period of five years.

"Acme": the highest point or stage, or representing perfection.

3. Although Kroeber here describes periods of art and literature as having "life cycles" analogous to living organisms, he wrote extensively against the notion that cultural evolution was analogous to biological evolution.

4. Since Kroeber has told us that "everyone will recall . . . ," we are certain that you do not require this explanation. However, we will provide it anyway. Romulus Augustulus (461–c. 510) was the last emperor of the Roman Empire in the West. His name references Romulus, who was one of Rome's two (semi-)mythological founders, and Augustus (63 BCE–14 CE), the first, and perhaps greatest Roman emperor. The vultures refer to the omens Romulus and Remus (Rome's other [semi]mythological founder) claimed to have seen in their dispute over the proper place to build Rome. Remus saw six birds, but Romulus saw twelve. Remus claimed that his sighting was more important because he had seen the birds first. Shortly thereafter Romulus killed Remus, and the rest is history.

Knowledge of the classics was a basic part of Kroeber's anthropology. The index to his 1948 anthropology textbook includes extensive entries for ancient Greece and Rome.

times: the rise and flourishing and decay of Venice, Florence, Poland, Portugal, Spain, and Holland.[c] There are even cases of repetition, as of the acmes reached by France under Louis XIV, Napoleon I, and Napoleon III—the three crests themselves constituting an ascending and descending climax of a higher order. LanePoole, in his diagrammatic representations of the history of the Mohammedan chalifates and kingdoms, although operating solely with the elements of geography and time, gives several figures that approach closely to a **polygon of frequency** or normal curve such as the statistical sciences employ.[d, 5]

Political fortunes have this advantage over the fluctuations of the arts: they are readily expressible, and with substantial accuracy, in such quantitative terms as square miles of territory or drachmas or pounds of tribute and revenue. On the other hand, they suffer, as a medium for analysis, through their complexity. Any one of a number of factors, or any combination of them, may make or unmake a nation: a change of political institutions, a military invention, an economic alteration, a new demand or utilization of natural resources, a wave of religious fervor. The resultant of these variables being a composite, would in many cases show little regularity. Then, too, where a concentrated political organization has been achieved, opportunities are put in the hand of an occasional genius, or even of the man of unusual talent, for much more spectacular accomplishment, perhaps, than in the fields of artistic and intellectual endeavor. An Aristotle or Goethe needs predecessors, a Genghis Khan or Napoleon only a constellation.[6]

The fields of religion and society are not so open to these objections, but suffer from lack of statistics. Census data are less common, except in the most recent years, than records of territories and dynasties. In the matter of religion, also, they necessarily relate chiefly to its organizational aspects, which, being **crystallizations**, do not keep pace with inward movements, and change by distorting jerks instead of fluidly.[7]

Manufactured objects offer an approach which no other class of civilizational data presents: they can be accurately and easily measured. Yet often there are difficulties in this domain also. The series of articles preserved from the past are often insufficiently large, or from interrupted periods, or of uncertain date. Then, utilitarian pieces do not modify freely. Their purpose is likely to impose definite and narrow limits on their variability of form. A new material, or an added invention, may bring about a modification as sudden as it is radical; after which a new era of comparative stability ensues. Material objects whose chief end is ornament—jewelry, for instance—are much more free from the last mentioned defect. Still more promising are decorative or semi-decorative things of which satisfactory illustrations are available in numbers, in place of the concrete specimens themselves: articles of dress, for instance, as represented in fashion magazines. Such journals have existed for over a century; they are exactly dated; and they bring

---

5. Stanley Lane-Poole (1854–1931), a British archaeologist, was a Middle East specialist. Kroeber refers to his 1894 work *The Mohammedan Dynasties*.
   "Polygon of frequency": a line graph of frequencies with straight lines connecting the data points.

6. Note that Kroeber rejects the importance of the individual in society. However, he seems to make exceptions. In this passage, Genghis Khan and Napoleon stand out as individuals who determined the course of history (but not Aristotle or the German author and statesman Johann Wolfgang von Goethe [1749–1832]).

7. **"Crystallizations"**: Kroeber used the term crystallizations to refer to complex patterns of cultural traits underlying social, political, and economic organization and systems of religion that persisted for long periods of time. For example, Kroeber thought monotheism was a crystallization. In his paper "Culture: A Critical Review of Concepts and Definitions," he says the concept can be compared to "the clustering of steel filings around a magnet. This analogy might be pursued further: as a magnet is a point of reference, so are the key concepts centers of symbolic crystallization in each culture" (1952: 41).

together in each volume a considerable number of examples to which rule or calipers can be applied without hindrance. That the actual wear of average men and women lags somewhat ineffectually behind the incisive styles of models or pictures, is immaterial. A knowledge of the course followed by ideals of dress is quite as valuable, as a contribution to the understanding of civilization, as knowledge of real dress; and this both per se and as an exemplification of the processes involved.[8]

Twenty years ago the project of inquiring into the principles that guide fashion arose in my mind, and I went so far as to turn the leaves of volume after volume of a Parisian journal devoted to dress. But the difficulties were discouraging. Pivotal points seemed hard to find in the eternal flux. One might measure collars or sleeves or ruffles for some years, and then collars and sleeves and ruffles disappeared. One lady in a plate was seated, another erect, a third in profile, the fourth elevated her arms. If one took as a base the total length of the figure, coiffures fell and rose by inches from time to time, or were entirely concealed by hats or nets. I abandoned the plan as infeasible.

In 1918 I renewed the endeavor, this time with less ambitious scope and greater readiness to seize on any opening. I decided to attempt only eight measurements, four of length and four of width, all referring to the figure or dress as a whole, and to disregard all superficial parts or trimmings. Strict comparability of data being essential, it was necessary to confine observations to clothing of a single type. Women's **full evening toilette** was selected. This has served the same definite occasions for more than a century; does not therefore vary in purpose as does day dress, nor seasonally like street clothing. The material always remains silk, and there have been no totally new fundamental concepts introduced, such as the shirtwaist and tailored suit. The variations are therefore purely stylistic. And while this range promised to be perhaps somewhat narrower than those of certain other types of women's wear, this was of little moment. If any principle could be determined, it would apply **a fortiori** to the more changeable kinds of clothing.[9]

MEASUREMENTS

The measurements made were the following:

1. Total length of figure from the center of the mouth to the tip of the toe. If the shoe was covered, the lowest point of the skirt edge was chosen. The selection of the mouth obviated all difficulties arising from alteration of hairdress.
2. Distance from the mouth to the bottom of the skirt. This equals the last measurement less the height of the skirt from the ground.
3. Distance from the mouth to the minimum diameter across the waist. This serves as some sort of indication of the length of the waist or corsage, that is, of the upper part of the figure. The true waist line of the dress has been disregarded. It would have been much more significant stylistically and probably shown more decided variations; but there are periods when it vanishes. When the waist line is visible and below the minimum diameter of the waist, the distance between the two was also noted.

---

8. Kroeber is setting the stage for his choice of fashion as the subject for measurement in his study. Kroeber has suggested that there is a "latent principle" of development in the historical rise and fall of art styles, literature, and polities. Kroeber's goal is to demonstrate this latent principle. One can see the rise and fall of art, he says, but it is difficult to scientifically measure because artistic judgment is subjective. Political history is rich in examples of the cyclical rise and fall of civilizations, he tells us, but political power has too many complex factors to make a good example. Religion and society are poor examples because they are not easily quantified. However, manufactured objects, particularly those that are not utilitarian, can be easily measured.

9. **"Full evening toilette"**: a floor-length gown with a low neck and short sleeves.
"*a fortiori*": Latin, "with even greater force."

4. Depth or length of **decolletage**, measured from the mouth to the middle of the corsage edge in front. [10]
5. Diameter of the skirt at its hem or base.
6. Maximum diameter of the skirt at any point above the base. In some cases this exceeds the diameter at the bottom. Ordinarily it is smaller, but in some instances nevertheless definitely visible: that is, the skirt swells, constricts, and flares again. This diameter did not prove a generally useful measurement. Whenever it could be taken, the distance from its middle to the mouth was also recorded as a supplementary datum.
7. Minimum diameter in the region of the waist.
8. Width of shoulders, or more accurately, width of the decolletage across the shoulders. In the earlier years of the period covered, the upper edge of the dress frequently passes below the point of the shoulder, across the uppermost part of the arm, as a bertha or slight sleeve. In such cases the measurement was recorded. Of recent years, the corsage often really ends under the arms, being held up in appearance by straps over the shoulders. Here it seemed best to measure the distance between the straps. When however the strap is pushed off the shoulder to fall loosely down the arm, or is wholly wanting, the present measurement had to be omitted.

Ten figures were measured for each calendar year, the first ten suitable for measurement being taken from each volume, so as to ensure random instead of subjective selection. Fashion journals of the middle of the nineteenth century contain fewer illustrations than recent ones. It sometimes happened therefore that only seven or eight toilettes were represented in the numbers from the first of January until summer, when full dress styles suspend seasonally. In such cases the rear end of the volume for the preceding year was drawn upon to supplement the deficiency. An entry like 1857 is thus normally based on plates issued from January to March or April or May of that year, but occasionally would begin in December or even November of 1856. Even at that, insufficiency of material or oversight has resulted in a few years being represented by only nine sets of measurements. Unfortunately also, there is scarcely a year for which ten illustrations could be found in each of which all eight measurements were recordable. A gown may be shown very completely in full face except for one corner of the skirt, which is hidden behind the chair of a seated companion. The basal skirt width can often be pretty well guessed in such cases, and an estimate was generally made; but only actual measurements have been included in the averages discussed. If in the taking of the observations such a deficient figure had been passed over, the next picture might have indeed exhibited the desired skirt width, but failed to show two or three other features; and too firm an insistence on all eight traits would often have yielded only three or four instead of ten measurable illustrations in a year. For instance, there are periods when it was overwhelmingly fashionable to hold the forearm horizontal, or to bring out the convexity of the bust by drawing it in semi-profile. In such years waist diameters are mostly obscured by the arm, and full shoulder widths very hard to get. The consequence of all these little circumstances is that the majority of the eight features observed are represented, year by year, by less than ten measurements, sometimes only by four or five. On the whole, preference was given to observations of the entire figure length, which was to be used as a norm for computations; and to the two next greatest measures, skirt length and width. For these, then, the series of data are fullest. [11]

---

10. **"Décolletage"**: neckline.

11. At the time he was writing this essay, Kroeber was also studying the relationship between sixty-seven dialects of Native American languages in California, and he had recently completed an analysis of pottery shards collected at sites near Zuni Pueblo. Kroeber believed that the history of a culture could be understood using comparative linguistics, and by mapping the distribution and change of important cultural traits. Here

It must be admitted that ten measures is not a very large maximum from which to derive reasonably true averages in so variable thing as fashionable dress, where each design strives almost as keenly after distinctiveness as after conformity to the prevailing style. I was conscious of this slenderness of basis. But the measurements as well as the reductions to percentages and averages are time consuming; and for a preliminary investigation it seemed wiser to obtain a comparatively long series of small groups of measurements than to operate with measurement groups of a size more reliable for averages but covering fewer years. Ten cases from each of seventy-five years would give a better surveying perspective than twenty-five cases continued for thirty years; in addition to which the ten or approximately ten illustrations were rather readily obtainable, whereas it would have been bibliographically exacting to find twenty-five for most of the earlier years.

The outcome vindicated the hazard. The smallness of the series is unquestionably the cause of many of the fluctuating irregularities that appear in the chronologically arranged results. But in the case of every dimension the irregularities are not so great as to prevent recognition of the underlying drifts and tendencies; whereas the period of these tendencies is mostly so long that they would have been very imperfectly determinable, and often not at all, within a compass of only thirty years. In fact it would have been desirable if the range of investigation could have been extended from 75 years to 125. The net result of a larger series of cases would therefore have been a probable smoothing and increased regularity of the plotted curves expressive of the course of fashion; and some segregation of the present irregularities into historically true ones and others that represent only statistical inadequacy. But presumably nothing more would have eventuated from the increase of data.[12]

I may here express my conviction that any farther quantitative investigations that may be undertaken as to the course of stylistic changes should be planned to cover if possible a period of from one to two centuries, whether they concern fashions of dress or of jewelry, silverware, or furniture.

[*In a three-thousand-word section titled "The Data Obtained," Kroeber describes the fashion magazines from which he took his data and the elements of dress he measured. He presents his findings in a series of tables and charts, and discusses these measurements. Kroeber uses six elements of fashion that he believed could be accurately measured from drawings and photos. These were width of skirt, length of skirt, diameter of waist, length of waist, décolletage, and width of décolletage. He tries to show that each of these increases and decreases in regular patterns that he describes as waves having particular periodicity (the periodicity of a wave is the distance in time between its maximal or minimal points). He argues that apparent changes in style, such as the move from hoop skirts to dresses with trains, fit (more or less) neatly into these patterns.*]

---

he tries to apply the same form of quantitative analysis here to understand changing patterns of fashion through time.

Remember that he is not really interested in fashion. Kroeber believed he could identify "super organic" patterns of culture change and that these operated according to patterns that existed outside of individual consciousness or agency. In "The Superorganic" (1917) he argued that simultaneous instances of independent invention proved that culture operated according to its own rules. Here he is trying to demonstrate this principle statistically by showing that changes in elements of women's fashion follow rules of which neither clothing designers nor their customers are aware. Kroeber returned to this topic in 1940 with Jane Richardson, with "Three Centuries of Women's Dress Fashions, a Quantitative Analysis," and in his 1957 book *Style and Civilizations,* where he tried to correlate changing women's styles with periods of political and social unrest (Darnell 2001: 96).

12. It is a measure of Kroeber's status in anthropology at this time that he could discuss all the flaws in his data and get away with concluding that if his case study had been longer it would have probably just smoothed out the distribution of his data.

COMPARISON OF THE SEVERAL RHYTHMS

We have, I think, now found reasonable evidence of an underlying pulsation in the width of civilized women's skirts, which is symmetrical and extends in its up and down beat over a full century; of an analogous rhythm in skirt length, but with a period of only about a third the duration; some indication that the position of the waist line may completely alter, also following a "normal" curve, in a seventy-year period; and a possibility that the width of shoulder exposure varies in the same manner, but with the longest rhythm of all, since the continuity of tendency in one direction for seventy years establishes a periodicity of about a century and a half, if the change in this feature of dress follows a symmetrically recurrent plan.[13]

There is something impressive in the largeness of these lapses of time. We are all in the habit of talking glibly of how this year's fashion upsets that of last year. Details, trimmings, pleats and ruffles, perhaps colors and materials, all the conspicuous externalities of dress, do undoubtedly alter rapidly; and it is in the very nature of fashion to bring these to the fore. They are driven into our attention, and soon leave a blurred but overwhelming impression of incalculably chaotic fluctuations, of reversals that are at once bewildering and meaningless, of a sort of lightning-like prestidigitation to which we bow in dumb recognition of its uncontrollability. But underneath this glittering maze, the major proportions of dress change with a slow majesty, in periods often exceeding the duration of human life, and at least sometimes with the even regularity of the swing of an enormous pendulum. The child whose braids hang down her back may be reasonably sure that in the years when her daughters are being born she will wear longer dresses than her mother now goes about in; and that her skirts promise to be wider each successive decade until she is a grandmother. There is something in these phenomena, for all their reputed arbitrariness, that resembles what we call law: a scheme, an order on a scale not without a certain grandeur. Not that the fashion of a future date can be written now. Every style is a component of far too many elements, and in part uniquely entering elements, to make true prediction possible. But it does seem that some forecast can be made for any one basic element whose history has been sufficiently investigated; and that, when the event arrives, if the anticipation be proved to have been more or less erroneous, the source of the aberration may be clear, and the disturbingly injected forces stand revealed as subject to an order of their own.[14]

It is not to be expected that the development and decline of every trait of dress or civilization should follow a normal curve, that is, a symmetrical course. For an element of civilization wholly unrelated to all others, such symmetry could perhaps be anticipated. But completely integral elements are an idea rather than a fact. There must always be some interaction with other factors in the same and cognate phases of culture, and occasional interferences from more remote domains. A certain proportion of features should therefore follow irregular courses, or asymmetrical curves; and in this class it seems that diameter of the waist and depth of decolletage should be placed.[e, 15]

---

13. Franz Boas was trained in the physical sciences, and the resulting emphasis he placed on anthropology as a science led many of his students to the collection of quantifiable data. It was common practice to gather data in the form of cultural trait lists, lists of hundreds of possible cultural traits whose presence could be checked off. These lists could then be tabulated, graphed, and statistically analyzed as Kroeber does here. This form of analysis is one of the hallmarks of Kroeber's research, and some of his most famous pieces of work, such as his 1939 book *Cultural and Natural Areas of Native North America,* are based on this method.

14. Kroeber believed that through statistical analysis of historical data, one could discover laws that governed culture change. Readers can see this conviction expressed here as he says that changes in fashion are not arbitrary, but occur in long-term identifiable patterns.

15. The Boasians critiqued the evolutionists and radical diffusionists for errors in their method. Kroeber's argument in this essay is open to a similar critique. He predicts the future of some elements of fashion based on minimal evidence. He seems to assume that cultural forms move in wavelike patterns and tries to force his

Secondary tremors ruffling the evenness of the great pulsations are at first sight disturbing to the concept of orderliness, but on analysis confirmatory, in that they reveal an increase of the intricacy of the operative forces without diminishing their regularity. In this manner the long range curves for width of skirt and shoulders, each bearing about three superimposed but symmetrical minor crests, add substance to the generic conclusions reached.

Finally, while it would make for the greater simplicity of historical causality if it were found that acmes of fashion came in recurrences of equal periodicity, such regularity can hardly be expected. There is no conceivable reason why there should be anything inherent in the nature of dress tending toward a change from full to narrow and back to full skirts in a century. All historical phenomena are necessarily unique in some degree, in the field of nature as well as of human activity; and a similar rhythm of fashion might well extend over a thousand, a hundred, or ten years in different eras or among separate nations. Again, therefore, there is if not support for the idea of "law," at least no disconcertion in the fact that the past quarter century on the whole evinces distinctly more rapid and extreme variations of fashion than the half century preceding. This is the case for every feature examined except shoulder width.[16]

CONCLUSIONS AS TO CHANGE IN CIVILIZATION

The fact of regularity in social change is the primary inference from our phenomena. The amplitude of the periodicities is of hardly less importance. Their very magnitude dwarfs the influence which any individual can possibly have exerted in an alteration of costume. Were each rhythm confined to a few years, it might be thought that a mind, a particular genius, was its motivating impulse; and the claim would certainly be asserted by those who like to see history as only a vast complex of biographies. But when a swing of fashion requires a century for its satisfaction, a minimum of at least several personalities is involved. No matter how isolating one's point of view, how resistant to a social or super-individual interpretation, how much inclined to explain the general from the particular and to derive the fashions of a world from the one focus of Paris, the fact remains that a succession of human beings have contributed successively to the same end. Once the existence of tendencies or forces transcending the limits of organically inherited personality is thus admitted, the entire field of the history of civilization becomes disputable ground for the two conflicting interpretations. If the major swing of skirt proportions during the nineteenth century is the product, wholly or partly, of superindividual causes, it becomes a valid speculation whether the smaller developments are not also due to similar mechanisms. The reintroduction of the train in 1863, the invention of the **Grecian bend** in 1872, may now be looked upon as the product of the dress styles that preceded them, or of other cultural factors affecting style, more justifiably than they can be attributed to the talent of a specially gifted mind and hand. The wedge has entered.[17]

It is also evident how little even the intensest individual faculty can have added to the outcome of the greater revolutions, how little hastened their momentum. When a tide sets one

data to take that shape. Like a Ptolemaic astronomer invoking epicycles and deferents to explain the retrograde motion of the planets, Kroeber proposes additional crosscutting waves to explain the forms he observes. However, mathematically, enough of these can explain any pattern. The evidence he presents does not provide strong support for the patterns he claims to have found.

16. Note Kroeber's statement that similar rhythms of fashion may take different lengths among separate nations. Kroeber's argument for a "law" of changes in fashion is modified by his Boasian training. Although long-term patterns exist, their characteristics are unique to their specific context.

17. **"Grecian Bend":** a fashion style of the 1860s and 1870s that involved skirts gathered at the back with a bustle. This required the wearer to lean forward.

way for fifty years, men float with it, or thread their course across it; those who breast the vast stream condemn themselves in advance to futility of accomplishment. A designer born with an inextinguishable talent for emphasizing what we may call the horizontal as opposed to the vertical lines of the figure, and maturing twenty-five years ago, might have possessed ten times the genius of a Poiret or Worth: he would yet have been compelled to curb it into the channels which they followed, or waste it on unworn and unregarded creations. What it is that causes fashions to drive so long and with ever increasing insistence toward the consummation of their ends, we do not know; but it is clear that the forces are social, and not the fortuitous appearance of personalities gifted with this taste or that faculty. Again the principle of civilizational determinism scores as against individualistic randomness.[18]

It would be extravagant to infer that these conclusions deny the validity of superior minds, or even that they tend to minimize the differences between genius and mediocrity. There can be no questioning the universal experience that there are competent individuals and incompetent ones, and that the gulf between their extremes is vast. The existence of varying degrees of intellectual quality does not touch, one way or the other, the finding that there operate super-individual principles which determine the course of social events.

The content of history as a sum and in its parts, so far as these have civilizational meaning, is the product of such principles. Whether individual X or individual Y is to have the larger share in bringing one particular product of his culture to fruition, depends on their respective native endowments, plus a greater or less modification by their educations, personal environments, and settings of circumstance. For the career of X, it is obviously of the greatest importance that his heredity and opportunities be more favorable than those of other individuals. On the contrary, given this advantage, it will very little affect his success in life whether his society be moving from polytheism to monotheism, from monarchy to democracy or democracy to tyranny, from bronze to iron, from the wearing of wide skirts to narrow, or the reverse.

Conversely, so far as these social changes are concerned, it can well be argued on theoretical grounds that the greater or less innate capacity of this or that individual, or of any limited number of individuals, is of negligible consequence. That this factor is actually negligible from the aspect of civilization, the analysis of the data here presented, goes to show. In short, monotheism arises, an iron technique is discovered, institutions change, or dresses become full at a given period and place—subsequent to other cultural events and as the result of them, in other words—because, they must.[19]

---

18. Paul Poiret (1879–1944), one of the most important French fashion designers of the 1900s and 1910s. Charles Frederick Worth (1825–1895), founder of the House of Worth, one of the most prominent British fashion houses between 1858–1956. Worth is sometimes considered the father of haute couture.

19. In these passages, Kroeber asserts a superorganic theory of culture that denies the importance of individual genius in culture change. He says first that the patterns of culture change are not the product of individual effort because they occur over time spans much longer than human lives. He then compares culture to a tide within which humans float. Those who fight the tide, whose genius is too far out of step with their time, are condemned to futility while those who succeed do so within a certain cultural and historical context. For example, if Albert Einstein had not formulated his theory of relativity, someone else would have, because the cultural circumstances were right for it. It was the result of the scientific culture of the turn of the twentieth century, not Einstein's particular genius. Had Einstein been born an Australian Aborigine in the sixteenth century, he might well have been recognized as an intelligent individual, but he would not have discovered relativity. Einstein's genius was recognized and fulfilled because of the cultural context in which he lived and worked. Culture is the driving force behind cultural change in Kroeber's eyes, not individual achievement. This is in direct contrast to Boas's view of history and was a lifelong source of conflict between the two.
Rejection of the importance of the individual was an important theme in some American anthropological thought. For example, Leslie White (1900–1975), who was deeply influenced by Kroeber's ideas (Barrett 1989: 990), writes in "Ikhnaton: The Great Man vs. The Culture Process":

Historians may have been chary of asserting such a principle; but the greatest minds among them have time and again accepted it implicitly, though vaguely. This is as true of Thucydides as of Gibbon, and explains why Herodotus was as much interested in ethnology as in anecdotes, and Tacitus could place a Germania beside his Annals.

Among the commonality of men, such a recognition has not obtained, and does not now hold. What above all they are interested in, is their own lives and fortunes, their own feelings and acts, their competitions with other individuals and personal relations to them. Therefore, when they listen to history, or tell it, they look for what history can reflect that is similar; and what it offers of psychology and morality in its biographies, or those of its parts which can be distorted into dramatic crises or romantic tales, they seize with avidity.

The satisfaction of these interests has its justifiable function; only it prevents instead of cultivating an understanding of the workings of civilization. The individualistic view of historical phenomena is in its nature subjective, and its treatment must always remain subjective. To find "law" in the infinite intricacy of millions of inter-playing personalities is hopeless. We cannot even begin to get the facts as they happened. A geologist could as usefully set himself the task of explaining the size and shape of each pebble in a gravel bed. We are but such stones. Being human, we cannot however divest ourselves of inquisitiveness about other human beings as human beings, nor of inquisitiveness into their morality and psychology and of the desire for an aesthetic

representation of their actions. Only, the pursuit of such impulses does not lead to knowledge that is scientifically applicable; nor to a comprehension of what lies beyond ourselves as individuals; of that which touches and permeates our lives at all moments, which is the material on which our energies are released, which could not be if we did not exist, but which yet endures before and after, and grows and changes into forms that are not of our making but of its own definite unfolding. Our minds instinctively resist the first shock of the recognition of a thing so intimately woven into us and yet so far above and so utterly uncontrollable by our wills. We feel driven to deny its reality, to deny even the validity of dealing with it as an entity; just as men at large have long and bitterly resented admitting the existence of purely automatic forces and system in the realm that underlies and carries and makes possible the existence of our personalities: the realm of nature. The center of our interests must always be personal. Yet this pivoting has not prevented an increasing realization of objectivity; nor will it prevent the realization that objectivity is to be found on levels beyond us in both directions, instead of one only. The superorganic or super-psychic or super-individual that we call civilization appears to have an existence, an order, and a causality as objective and as determinable as those of the subpsychic or inorganic. At any rate, no insistence on the subjective aspects of personality can refute this objectivity, nor hinder its ultimate recognition; just as no advance in objective understanding has ever cramped the activity of personality.[20]

We must conclude that history is still the irresistible flow of the stream of culture and that all men are but chips floating on that stream. . . . We can come to no other conclusion than that the *general trend* of events would have been the same had Ikhnaton [an Egyptian Pharaoh said by some to have been a revolutionary figure] been but a sack of sawdust. (1948: 113, emphasis in the original)

The belief that individuals cannot affect the patterns of culture is deeply fatalistic. In Kroeber's case, it may be related to a rejection of political action. Eric Wolf (1923–1999) writes that we find in Kroeber's work a strong sense of distaste for anything that smacked of politics, for involvement in non-science, and . . . all those enterprises that had to do, he thought, with trying to improve the world. (2004: 36)

20. The final paragraph in this article is a criticism of the work of anthropologists like Boas and Paul Radin (1883–1959), who believed that individuals were an important factor in the study of culture. Kroeber compares anthropologists trying to build models of culture by studying individuals to geologists attempting to explain the size and shape of each pebble in a bed of gravel. He says the pursuit of individual biographical data does not yield scientific data or knowledge of what lies beyond people as individuals, that is, culture. He

AUTHOR'S NOTES

a. *The Psychology of Peoples*, London, 1898 (New York 1912), page 12, footnote.

b. *Ralph Roister Doister*, published 1566; *Gammer Gurton's Needle*, 1575; Lyly, wrote 1580–93; Greene died 1592, Kyd 1594, Peele 1598; blank verse in *Tamburlaine*, 1587; Shakspere's first period, 1589–1594; Marlowe died 1593; Shakspere's second period, 1594–1601; third period "Hamlet," "Othello," "Lear," "Macbeth"; Jonson wrote chiefly 1598–1614; Shakspere's fourth period, 1608–13; Webster's best plays, 1612, 1616; Beaumont died 1616; Fletcher died 1625; Ford's best plays, 1629–34; Massinger, first play 1620, died 1639; closing of the playhouses, 1642. [spelling of Shakespeare in the original].

c. Compare Quetelet's bold attempt in Du Systeme Social, 1848, to determine a normal duration of empires and cities.

d. S. Lane-Poole, The Mohammedan Dynasties, 1894. See especially "Growth" and "Decline of the Ottoman Empire," pages 190, 191; also "Mogul Emperors" on diagram facing page xx.

e. Clark Wissler, *American Anthropologist*, N.S., vol. XVIII, pp. 190–197, 1916, points out that the distribution of sherds of certain decorative styles in the successive levels of the refuse heap at the ancient New Mexican pueblo of San Cristobal, as excavated and reported on by N. C. Nelson, follows typical curves, these curves each representing "the rise and decline of a culture trait." Each foot of debris may be taken as representing an approximately equal duration of deposition, as indicated by the fairly steady number of sherds of all types found at each depth. The figures are, for black-on-white painted ware, (103), 107, 118, 40, 8, 2, 6, 10, 2, 2; and for black or brown glazed yellow ware, 0, 3, 45, 91, 192, 128, 52, 68, 64, 24. The latter series may be skew.

---

describes culture as that "which could not be if we did not exist, but which yet endures before and after, and grows and changes into forms that are not of our making but of its own definite unfolding."

Consistent with Boasian scholarship, Kroeber tries to show the sweeping patterns of culture but remains silent on their origin or purpose. Kroeber's student, Julian Steward (1902–1972) was to argue that certain elements of culture were evolutionary adaptive devices (essay 17). Kroeber, however, paid little attention to his student's work. Through his long and active career, Kroeber remained true to this aspect of his Boasian heritage. Eric Wolf describes him as a "natural historian of culture," trying to perform Linnean style taxonomy and classification but without any underlying theory of causality (2004: 39–40).

10. The Science of Custom: The Bearing of Anthropology on Contemporary Thought

Ruth Benedict (1887–1948)

ANTHROPOLOGY IS THE STUDY of primitive peoples—a statement which helps us to understand its bearing on contemporary thought as little as if, in the time of Copernicus, we had defined astronomy as the study of the stars, or biology in the time of Darwin, as the science of bugs. It was not facts about stars that made astronomy suddenly of first-class importance, but that—quite casually, as it were—the Copernican scheme placed the earth, this planetary scene of human life, in a perspective of such infinitesimal insignificance. In much the same way the significance of anthropology to modern thought does not lie in any secrets that the primitive has saved for us from a simple world, with which to solve the perplexities of this existence. Anthropology is not a search for the philosopher's stone in a vanished and golden age. What anthropologists find in the study of primitive people is a natural and well-nigh inexhaustible laboratory of custom, a great workshop in which to explore the major role it has played in the life-history of the world.[1]

Now custom has not been commonly regarded as a subject of any great moment. It is not like the inner workings of our own brains, which we feel to be uniquely worthy of investigation. Custom, we have a way of thinking, is behavior at its most commonplace. As a matter of fact, it is the other way around. Traditional custom, taken the world over, is a mass of detailed behavior more astonishing than any one person can ever evolve in personal acts no matter how aberrant. Yet that is a rather trivial aspect of the matter. The fact of first-rate importance is the predominant role that custom plays in experience and in belief. No man ever looks at the world with pristine eyes. He sees it edited by a definite set of customs and institutions and ways of thinking. Even in his philosophical probings he cannot go behind these stereotypes; his very concepts of the true and the false will still have reference to the structure of his particular traditional customs. John Dewey has said in all seriousness that the part played by custom in shaping the behavior of the individual as over against any way in which he can affect traditional custom, is as the proportion of the total vocabulary of his mother tongue over against those words of his own baby talk that are taken up into the vernacular of his family. There is no social problem it is more incumbent upon us to understand than that of the role of custom in our total life. Until we are intelligent as to the laws and the varieties of customs, the main complicating facts of human life will remain to us an unintelligible book.[2]

From *The Century Magazine* (1929)

1. Since the eighteenth century, there has been a strain of romantic thought in European philosophy that has imagined indigenous people as "noble savages" untouched by the corrupting influences of civilization. Here in the initial paragraph, Benedict tries to dispel that myth, saying that anthropology "is not a search for the philosopher's stone in a vanished and golden age." Anthropology's strength according to Benedict is that it is a worldwide workshop in which to examine the role culture has played in world history. Note that Benedict uses the word "custom," instead of "culture."

2. In this paragraph, Benedict says "No man ever looks at the world with pristine eyes." In several works, but especially his 1911 book *The Mind of Primitive Man*, Franz Boas argued that culture was autonomous, not a product of race, geography, or mentality. This notion was developed further by Benedict's friend and col-

The first concern of the anthropologist is always for an understanding of this affair of custom: how each society comes to be possessed of whole systems of it, how it is stabilized, cross-fertilized, how it is inculcated into all the members of the group among whom it flourishes. In other words, the business of the anthropologist is with the great ideational systems of language, social organization and religion of which every people on earth finds itself possessed, and which are passed on to every child as it is born into the group, but of which no child born in any other territory could ever achieve the thousandth part.

This matter of culture, to give it its anthropological term—that complex whole which includes all the habits acquired by man as a member of society—has been late in claiming scientific attention. There are excellent reasons for this. Any scientific study requires first of all that there be no preferential weighting of one or another of the items in the series it selects for its consideration. Anthropology was therefore by definition impossible as long as those old distinctions between ourselves and the barbarian, ourselves and the pagan, held sway over people's minds. It was necessary first to arrive at that degree of sophistication where one no longer set his belief over against his neighbor's superstition, and it is worth considering that it is barely one hundred years ago that any one took his superstitious neighbors seriously enough to include them in any general purview of serious belief.[3]

In the second place, custom did not challenge the attention of social theorists, because it was the very stuff of their own thinking. We do not see the lens through which we look. Precisely in proportion as it was fundamental, it was automatic, and had its existence outside the field of conscious attention. The custom of greeting a guest by an array of weeping women who sit in his lap and embrace him, may not need more or less psychological elu-

---

league A. L. Kroeber in his 1917 article "The Superorganic." There, Kroeber claimed that culture, while being carried by humans, transcends them. Here Benedict argues that humans are cultural beings whose ways of thinking are influenced by their cultural backgrounds. In the final chapter of *Patterns of Culture,* she writes, "Society in its full sense . . . is never an entity separable from the individuals who compose it. No individual can arrive at even the threshold of his potential without a culture in which he participates. Conversely, no civilization has in it any element which in the last analysis is not the contribution of an individual" (1935: 182).

Benedict paraphrases the psychologist and educational reformer John Dewey (1859–1952) on the role of custom in shaping individuals. Dewey was president of the American Psychological Association in 1899 and of the American Philosophical Association in 1905. He was a close colleague of Boas at Columbia. They taught a seminar together in the 1914–1915 academic year. Benedict and other Boasians also took classes with Dewey. G. A. Torres Colón and C. A. Hobbs (2015) report that Dewey's *Human Nature and Conduct* (1922) was an important source for Benedict's groundbreaking *Patterns of Culture* (1934).

3. Boas spent his career establishing anthropology as a university-based discipline. Consequently, most of the anthropologists he trained primarily published in academic journals such as *American Anthropologist.* Benedict however, published this essay in *The Century Magazine,* which was produced for a non-academic audience. You can see this in her definition of culture, paraphrased from the definition offered by E. B. Tylor at the opening of his book *Primitive Culture* (see essay 2).

Note how deeply optimistic Benedict is in this paragraph. She suggests that we no longer consider our beliefs to be superior to those of others. This essay was published in April 1929, before the stock market crash and the start of The Great Depression. As economic problems deepened and fascism rose in Europe, Benedict and the other Boasians became both increasingly disturbed and skeptical of both progress and optimism. In 1934, Benedict rewrote this essay as the first chapter of *Patterns of Culture.* However, that version does not include this passage. Instead, in roughly the same place in the essay she says, "So that today, whether it is a question of imperialism, or of race prejudice . . . we are still preoccupied with the uniqueness, not of the human institutions of the world at large, which no one has ever cared about anyway, but of our own institutions, and achievements, our own civilization" (1934b: 5).

Benedict, who studied English literature at Vassar College, was a more artful writer than most of her colleagues, and many of her works are still in print today. Additionally, Benedict wrote poetry under the pen name Anne Singleton.

cidation than the handshake, but it communicates the necessary shock, and the subject of the handshake will remain unexplored long after we have mustered our efforts toward the understanding of the tears-greeting. We have only to admit alien customs to the same rank in regulating human nature that our customs have for us, and we are perpetually galvanized into attention.[4]

It is not fair to lay our blindness to custom wholly to the fact that it is closer to us than breathing. Primitive people are sometimes far more conscious of the role of cultural traits than we are, and for good reason. They have had intimate experience of different cultures, and we have not. White civilization has standardized itself over most of the globe. We have never seen an outsider unless he is already Europeanized. The uniformity of custom, of outlook, seems convincing enough, and conceals from us the fact that it is after all an historical accident. All our observation reinforces the testimony of our easy assent to the familiar, and we accept without any ado the equivalence of human nature and of our own cultural standards. But many primitives have a different experience. They have seen their religion go down before the white man's, their economic system, their marriage prohibitions. They have laid down the one and taken up the other, and are quite clear and sophisticated about variant arrangements of human life. If they talk about human nature, they do it in plurals, not in the absolute singular, and they will derive dominant characteristics of the white man from his commercial institutions, or from his conventions of warfare, very much after the fashion of the anthropologist. If civilized Europeans have been especially dense to the scientific implications of custom, it has been not only because their own customs were too familiar to be discernible, and because they resisted the implication that their culture belonged to a series that included the customs of lesser people, but also because the standardization of their own culture over the globe has given an illusion of a world-wide uniform human behavior.[5]

—⁂—

What is it that anthropologists have to say about this matter of custom? In the first place, it is man's distinguishing mark in the animal kingdom. Man is the culture-making animal. It is not that insects, for instance, do not have

---

4. Benedict was interested in the relationship between culture and personality. Here she is addressing the power of culture to mold the way we understand the world. While she does not reference him, this passage strongly parallels a claim by the German historian and philosopher Wilhelm Dilthey (1833–1911) who argued that human understanding was historical, not objective, and was based on life experience. Dilthey is also known for his work with the notion of *weltanshauungen* or worldview, which he defined as the framework of ideas and beliefs through which an individual or group interprets the world.

The "tears-greeting" refers to a practice of Amazonian natives whose custom is to cry when they greet an old friend or acquaintance. In 2011, this practice was involved in an interesting controversy. Chief Raoni of the Kayapo (a Brazilian indigenous group) was photographed crying at a protest against the Belo Monte Dam. Outsiders imagined Raoni was crying because of the destruction that would be done by the dam. Raoni, however, reported that he was crying because he was greeting a family member (Salazar-Lopez 2011).

Benedict paraphrases John Dewey (1859–1952) on the role of custom in shaping a person. Dewey was an American psychologist and educational reformer. He was elected president of the American Psychological Association in 1899 and of the American Philosophical Association in 1905. Dewey was a close colleague of Boas at Columbia. They taught a seminar together in the 1914–1915 academic year. Benedict and other Boasians also took classes with Dewey. G. A. Torres Colón and C. A. Hobbs (2015) report that Dewey's *Human Nature and Conduct* (1922) was an important source for Benedict's groundbreaking *Patterns of Culture* (1934).

5. Between 1922 and 1926 Benedict conducted fieldwork with Native American peoples of the southwest, primarily the Serrano, Zuni, and the Pima. This essay, written just three years after the conclusion of her Pima research, shows her awareness of the importance of looking at culture and culture change from a historical perspective. Anthropology has come late to the sciences, she says, because the dominance of Western culture has hindered social scientists from recognizing the cultural processes that operate in their society. Native Americans, forced to accommodate to Anglo culture, have no such illusions.

complex cultural traits like the domestication of plants and animals, political organization, division of labor. But the mechanism of transmission makes them contrast sharply with man's particular contribution of traditionally *learned* behavior. Insect society takes no chances; the pattern of the entire social structure is carried in the cell structure of each individual ant, so that one isolated individual can automatically reproduce the entire social order of its own colony just as it reproduces the shape of antennae or of abdomen. For better or worse, man's solution has been at the opposite pole. Not one item of his tribal social organization, of language, of his local religion, is carried in his germ-cell. His whole centuries-evolved civilization is at the mercy of any accident of time and space. If he is taken at birth to another continent, it will be the entire set of cultural traits of the adopted society that he will learn, and the set that was his by heredity will play no part. More than this, whole peoples in one generation have shaken off their patterns, retaining hardly a residual vestige, and have put on the customs of an alien group.[6]

What is lost in nature's guarantee of safety, is made up in the advantage of greater plasticity. The human animal does not, like the bear, have to wait to grow himself a polar coat before he can adapt himself to the arctic; he learns to sew himself a coat and put up a snow house. It is a direct corollary of this difference

in the mechanism of human culture that, as Professor W. M. Wheeler tells us, ant societies have been stable for sixty-five million years, and human societies are never to-morrow what they are to-day.[7]

Anthropology has no encouragement to offer to those who would trust our spiritual achievements to the automatic perpetuation of any selected hereditary germ-plasms. Culture, it insists, is not carried in that fashion for the human race. We cannot trust any program of racial purity. It is a significant fact that no anthropologist has ever taught, along with so many popular theorists, that high civilization is bound up with the biological homogeneity of its carriers. Race is a classification based on bodily form, and the particular cultural behavior of any group is strikingly independent of its racial affiliations. We must accept all the implications of our human inheritance, one of the most important of which is the small scope of biologically transmitted behavior, and the enormous role of the cultural process of the transmission of tradition.[8]

There is another analogy with the animal world which has to be laid aside in the study of culture: no less than the idea of evolution. The modern anthropologist at this point is only throwing in his lot with the psychologist and the historian, emphasizing the fact that the

---

6. This discussion of the differences between the genetically programmed social behavior of insects versus the learned behavior of humans replicates the argument made by Kroeber in his 1917 article "The Superorganic."

7. When Benedict says humans have the advantage of greater "plasticity," she means that humans are changeable or adaptable.

William M. Wheeler (1865–1937) was curator of invertebrate zoology at the American Museum of Natural History and Professor at Harvard University. He was a leading authority on the behavior of social insects.

8. Throughout his career, Boas and many of his students, including Benedict, devoted significant time and energy to fighting racism. Much of Boas's "The Mind of Primitive Man" is devoted to proving that race is unrelated to culture. This paragraph goes far beyond the simple statement that culture is not hereditary. Benedict is stating that race has nothing to do with cultural achievement.

Benedict and fellow Boas student Gene Weltfish (1902–1980) elaborated on this in a 1943 pamphlet called "The Races of Mankind" intended for distribution to the US Army. The claim of equality contained in the pamphlet proved controversial to some. Kentucky congressman and chair of the House Military Affairs Committee, Andrew J. May (1875–1959), prohibited its distribution to the army. However, the resulting publicity led to the sale of almost a million copies in the next decade (Price 2004: 113–14). A short animated film, *The Brotherhood of Man*, was made based on the pamphlet. You can see the film at https://bit.ly/weltfish-brotherhood.

order of events in which they all deal in common is best studied without the complications of any attempted evolutionary arrangement. The psychologist is not able to demonstrate any evolutionary series in the sensory or emotional reactions of the individuals he studies, and the historian is not helped in the reconstruction of Plantagenet England by any concept of the evolution of government; just as superfluous for him also, the anthropologist insists, is any scheme of cultures arranged according to an ascending scale of evolution.

Since the science of anthropology took shape in the years when the "Origin of Species" was still new, it was inevitable that there should have been this attempt to arrange human societies from this point of view. It was simplicity itself. At the summit of the ascent was placed our own culture, to give meaning and plan to all that had preceded; to the lowest rungs was relegated by hypothesis all that was most different from this consummation; and the intermediate steps were arranged as these two fixed points suggested. It is important to insist that there was never any argument from actual chronology; even in cases where it could have been ascertained, it was not considered of such importance that it could compete with the a priori hypothesis. In this way the development of art, religion and marriage institutions was classically charted. It is a monument to the force of a theory that asked no proof other than its own conviction.[9]

Now if there is no positive correlation between culture and an evolutionary scheme, is there any order and arrangement of any kind in the diversity of human customs? To answer this question it is necessary to go back to fundamentals, to man's equipment of basic responses to environment. These responses, as anthropologists see them, are mere rough sketches, a list of bare facts; but they are hints that may be illimitably fertile. They are focal centers which any peoples may ignore, or which they may make the starting points of their most elaborated concepts. Let us take, for instance, the example of adolescence. Adolescence is a necessary biological fact for man and for his animal forebears, but man has used it as a spring-board. It may be made the occasion for the major part of the ritual the group practises; it may be ignored as completely as Margaret Mead has recently shown that it is in Samoa. It may be seen, as among the African Masai, as one item of an elaborate crisis ceremonialism that institutionalizes not only adolescence but provides, for instance, a ceremony for putting the father on the shelf after his son has attained young manhood. It may be, on the other hand, a magic occasion that will, in after life, give back as from a mirror every technique that is practised at this time. So a girl will pick each needle carefully from a pine-tree that she may be industrious, or a boy will race a stone down the mountain that he may be swift of foot. The rites may be limited to the young girls, or, it may be, to the boys; the period may be marked with horror and with torture, it may be a consecration to the gods. It is obvious that the physical fact of adolescence is only the touch to the ball of custom, which then follows grooves of thought not implied in the original impetus.[10]

---

9. *On the Origin of Species* by Charles Darwin (1809–1882) was first published in November 1859. However, Benedict's comment here is misleading; *On the Origin of Species* was not influential in most nineteenth-century cultural-evolutionary thinking. Evolutionists like Tylor and Lewis Henry Morgan conceived of cultural evolution as a mental process, not one based on natural selection. However, Darwin's work was influential in the development of the eugenics movement whose members argued that to protect the genetic quality of superior populations, inferior people should be prevented from breeding by sterilization or euthanasia.

10. Benedict's comments about cultural-evolutionary thinking echoes Boas's argument in "The Limitations of the Comparative Method of Anthropology" (1896). The rejection of social evolutionism and the nineteenth-century comparative method was a touchstone of Boasian anthropology. Many of Boas's students wrote essays attacking evolutionary schemes in general and L. H. Morgan's work in particular.

Benedict mentions Mead and Samoa. Margaret Mead's (1901–1978) study, *Coming of Age in Samoa*, was published in 1928, one year before this essay. Benedict and Mead were extremely close collaborators, and many of Benedict's ideas informed Mead's book (see essay 11).

What these grooves are we can sometimes account for out of the cultural history of a people; more often we can only record the facts. We know that traits that have once found themselves in company are likely to maintain that association quite apart from any intrinsic fitness in their nature. So bone head scratchers and the pursuit of a supernatural vision may go hand in hand over a continent, and the absence of footgear may coincide with carved door-posts.[11]

What we do know is that there is no one of the bare reactions of the human animal that may not be selected by some people for a position in the very forefront of its attention and be elaborated past belief. It may be that the economic facts of life, as for instance the buffalo herds of the Todas of India, may be singled out, and the whole life of the people may turn on the ritual of perpetuating and renewing the sacred pep, the soured milk saved by the Todas from day to day as the continuum of their culture, and used to hasten the next day's souring. The dairymen are the priests, annointed and sacrosanct, the holy of holies is the sacred cow bell. Most of the taboos of the people have to do with the infinite sacredness of the milk.[12]

Or a culture may, instead, elaborate an item of the social organization. All people over the earth recognize some forbidden degrees within which marriage may not take place. These are alike only in the common idea of incest; the degrees themselves differ entirely. In a large part of the world you may marry only one variety of own cousin, say your mother's brother's daughter, and it is incest to marry the other variety, say your father's sister's daughter. But however unreasonable the distinctions may seem from our point of view, some concept of forbidden degrees all men have, and animals, it seems, have not. Now this idea has been taken up by the aborigines of Australia and made the basis of a social system that knows no restraint in the elaboration of its favorite pattern. Not satisfied with stipulating one cousin group within which, and no other, one must find a mate, certain of these tribes have heaped the incest taboos on lineages, on local groups; on all who participate with them in certain ceremonies, until even in the specified cousin group there is no one who is not touched by some one of the taboos. Quite in keeping with the violence of their obsession with this detail of social organization, they are accustomed to visit death upon any one who transgresses the fantastic rules. Do they pull themselves together before they have reached the point of tribal suicide and reject their overgrown antisocial rulings? No, they get by with a subterfuge. Young men and women may escape together to an island which is regarded as asylum. If they succeed in remaining in seclusion until the birth of a child, they may return with no more than a formalized drubbing. So the tribe is enabled to maintain its ethics without acknowledged revision, and still avoid extinction.[13]

---

11. Here Benedict mentions culture history. A historical perspective of culture was vital to Boas and his students. Because they studied societies without written histories, studying the diffusion of culture traits was the primary way to estimate the history of contact between societies.

Note that Benedict emphasizes the random nature of the association of culture traits. For Boas and his students, cultural associations were largely the result of the accidents of history rather than any evolutionary or ecological necessity. In 1920, Boas's student Robert Lowie (1883–1957) famously described civilization (culture) as "that planless hodge-podge, that thing of shreds and patches" (1947: 441). Though later Lowie complained that he had been misunderstood, his description seemed to fit the Boasian understanding of culture.

12. The Todas had been studied by W. H. R. Rivers (1864–1922), a member of the Torres Straits expedition and founding British anthropologist. His 1906 book of the same name was widely cited.

13. In the previous paragraphs, Benedict is emphasizing the power and diversity of culture. In each example, Benedict argues that specific characteristics of culture have been emphasized at the expense of others. She elaborates on this theme in *Patterns of Culture* (1934). There, she connects these cultural emphases with personality, arguing that each culture has a particular personality that is related to cultural traits that are either emphasized or ignored. In *Patterns of Culture* Benedict identifies the Pueblo peoples as Apollonian, the Kwakiutl (Kwakwaka'wakw) as Dionysian, and the Dobuan as paranoid. She argues for a holistic connection between these personality traits and the rituals, attitudes, and beliefs emphasized in these cultures.

———ᴍ———

But it need not be incest that has run away with itself in the culture of a group; it may be some trick of ritualism, or love of display, or passion of acquisitiveness. It may be fishhooks. In a certain island of Oceania fish-hooks are currency, and to have large fish-hooks came gradually to be the outward sign of the possession of great wealth. Fish-hooks therefore are made very nearly as large as a man. They will no longer catch fish, of course. In proportion as they have lost their usefulness they are supremely coveted. After a long experience of such cultural facts anthropologists have made up their minds on two points. In the first place, it is usually beside the point to argue from its important place in behavior, the social usefulness of a custom. Man can get by with a mammoth load of useless lumber, and he has a passion for extremes. Once his attention is engaged upon one trait of behavior, he will juggle his customs till they perforce accommodate themselves to the outward manifestations of his obsession. After all, man has a fairly wide margin of safety, and he will not be forced to the wall even with a pitiful handicap. Our own civilization carries its burden of warfare, of the dissatisfaction and frustration of wage earners, of the overdevelopment of acquisitiveness. It will continue to bear them. The point is that it is more in line with the evidence to regard them as our equivalents of the fish-hooks or of the Australian marriage rules, and to give over the effort to prove their natural social utility.[14]

For every people will always justify their own folkways. Warfare, as long as we have it, will be for our moralists the essential school in which justice and valor are to be learned; the desire for possessions similarly will be the one motive power to which it is safe to trust the progress of the world. In the same way, China relied upon reverence for one's ancestors. There are too many of these folkways. They cannot all be the **sine qua non** of existence, and we shall do better to concentrate our attention upon an objective appreciation of different schemes, and to give our enthusiasms to those special values we can always discern in the most diverse civilizations.[15]

The second point on which anthropologists have made up their minds in this connection— and this holds true for all customs whether or not they have been carried to extremes—is that in any study of behavior it is these cultural patternings that turn out to be compulsive, not any original instincts with which we are born equipped. Even the basic emotions of fear and love and rage by the time they have been shaped over the different **cultural lasts** are well-nigh unrecognizable. Is there a jealousy of the mate innate in our sexual organization? Perhaps, but it will not dictate behavior except according to a cultural permit. Over a large part of the world, the woman is aggrieved if her husband does not take other wives—it may be to aid her in the duties of the household, or to relieve her of child-bearing, or to make plain her husband's social importance. And in other parts of the world, the male's virtues of generosity and of dignity are chiefly summed up in his practice of sharing his wife, and his calm acceptance of her desertion. Is there a maternal instinct? It will always be operative according

---

Australian kinship and incest customs had long been of interest to anthropologists. Information about them was collected by the Anglo Australian anthropologists Alfred W. Howitt (1830–1908) and Lorimer Fison (1832–1907) and used by Morgan in his analysis of kinship and social evolution.

14. Cultural relativism is a powerful and recurring theme in most of Benedict's work. Here, after describing Australian aboriginal incest taboos and oversized fishhooks in Oceania, she contrasts them with Western practices familiar to her readers: warfare, worker dissatisfaction, and conspicuous consumption. How prescient are these examples (or how persistent our problems)? More than ninety years after this article was published, we are still concerned with warfare, sustainable consumption, and paying workers a living wage. In the following paragraphs, she argues that rather than trying to defend our cultural practices, we should develop an aesthetic appreciation for the practices of others.

15. **"sine qua non":** Latin, "without which, nothing;" something indispensable or absolutely essential.

to the conventions of the group. If there is great emphasis upon rank, women may voluntarily kill their children to raise their own status, as among the Natchez, or the Polynesian Tonga. If there is a pattern of seemingly meaningless adoption, most families will place their infants in other households, sometimes assigning them before birth. And how often have different apologists tried to give reasons for infanticide, when all the reasons they list are just as operative outside as within the region where this cultural compulsion rests upon the women.[16]

Man evolves always elaborate traditional ways of doing things, great superstructures of the most varying design, and without very striking correlations with the underpinnings on which they must each and all eventually rest. It is only in a fundamental and non-spectacular sense that these superstructures are conditioned by their foundation in man's original endowment. And it is the superstructure in which man lives, not the foundation. The compulsion of folkways in a well-knit culture is just as strong as the compulsion of a style in architecture, Gothic, or Renaissance, or Egyptian. It fashions as it will the instincts of the people who live within it, remaking them in conformity with its own requirements. So it is that the cultural patterns are themselves creative; they take the raw material of experience and mold it into fifty different shapes among fifty different peoples. The traditional patterns of behavior set the mold and human nature flows into it.[17]

It follows that man's established folkways are also his morals. Judgments of right and wrong and of the glory of God grow up within the field of group behavior and attach themselves to those traits that have become automatic in the group. Interference with automatic behavior is always unpleasant, and it is rationalized as evil. No people have any truly empirical ethics; they uphold what they find themselves practising. Even our own literature of ethics is far from being a detached survey of different possible solutions; it is a system of apologetics for the well-known scheme of our own culture. It is not that the anthropologist would subtract a jot or tittle from this preference for one's own customs; there are values in any way of living that can be plumbed only by those who have been born and bred in them, and in an ideal world every man would love best his own culture. What the anthropologist would have us add to our understanding is that all cultures have alike grown up blindly, the useful and cumbersome together, and not one of them is so good that it needs no revision, and not one is so bad that it cannot serve, just as ours can, the ideal ends of society and of the individual.[18]

—m—

And how is it with regard to religion? All peoples have been religious; it is only what consti-

---

16. Here Benedict provides a striking argument for the cultural rather than biological origins of human behavior. She views humans as blank slates, their characteristics determined entirely by culture. This view was held by many Boasians, particularly A.L. Kroeber and Margaret Mead.

"cultural lasts": a last is a mechanical form shaped like a human foot used in the construction and repair of shoes. The last sets the pattern for the shoe.

17. In much of Benedict's later work such as *Patterns of Culture* (1934), she elaborated on the theme of cultural determinism presented here, arguing that cultures had "configurations" that molded the behavior and basic personality characteristics of members of a society. Here she argues that cultures develop almost entirely without regard to biology or environment. Instinct itself is fashioned by culture. In this, she closely follows Boas. Boas's student and his close friend Gladys Reichard (1893–1955) reported Boas told her and his daughter Helena Boas Yampolsky that his early experiences among the Eskimo had taught him that "they did things in spite of rather than because of environment" (in Herskovits 1957: 115).

As the many references to Boas in our notes suggest, Benedict was extremely close to Boas, as were Mead and Reichard. In the 1920s, all three of them referred to him as "Papa Franz." (Lamphere 1992: 83).

18. In this paragraph, Benedict argues against an ethnocentric perspective. She says that no people have truly empirical ethics, that all cultures could benefit from revision, but also that all cultures serve their societies equally well.

tuted religion that has varied. There is no item of experience, from the orientation of a house, to sleight of hand or foretelling the future, that has not been somewhere, it seems, the distinguishing matter of religion. Surely it is not this heterogeneous content of religion that is its essence. The role of religion is its slow and halting exploration of the spiritual life. Often it has wedged itself into blind alleys and wasted generations of experiment. It made a mistake and included within its scope not only its proper field, but also all that area of existence that is better handled in secular fashion. Its special field of the spiritual life is still in the process of delimitation. In that field it shares with art and with abstract thought and with all enthusiastic dedications of the self, the spiritual rewards of life. What the future holds we do not know, but it is not too much to hope that it will include a reinstating and reshaping of the spiritual values of existence that will balance the present immense unfolding of the material values.[19]

—⁓—

What is the upshot of this analysis of custom for our contemporary thinking? Is it subversive? Certainly not, except in the sense in which Copernicus's demonstration of the stellar series to which this earth belonged, was subversive. The culture we are born into, according to anthropology, is also—as the earth is in the solar scheme—one of a series of similar phenomena all driven by the same compulsions. What we give up, in accepting this view, is a dogged attachment to absolutes; what we gain is a sense of the intriguing variety of possible forms of behavior, and of the social function that is served by these communal patternings. We become culture-conscious.[20]

We perceive with new force the ties that bind us to those who share our culture. Ways of thinking, ways of acting, goals of effort, that we tend so easily to accept as the order of the universe, become rather the precious and special symbols we share together. Institutions that were massive Juggernauts demanding their toll become instead a world of the imagination to which all those of common culture have common access. For the social function of custom is that it makes our acts intelligible to our neighbors. It binds us together with a common symbolism, a common religion, a common set of values to pursue. In the past these groups have been geographical, and

---

19. In the previous two paragraphs, Benedict comments on morality and spirituality, and what she obviously considers the overemphasis on materialism in American life. This article was published in 1929. Perhaps it is an observation about American life in the Roaring Twenties, right before the start of the Great Depression initiated by the crash of the stock market in October 1929.

Benedict's vision of religion is extremely intellectual. She sees the history of religion as the "slow and halting exploration of the spiritual life." Benedict came from a deeply religious background and though she rejected orthodoxy, spirituality remained important to her throughout her life. Boas and many of his circle were involved with the New York Society for Ethical Culture (Opler 1967: 741), a nontheistic religious movement centered on ethics, whose mission is to encourage respect for humanity and nature and create a better world (New York Society for Ethical Culture [henceforth NYSFEC]: n.d.). The Society was founded by fellow Columbia University professor Felix Adler (1851–1933).

20. Throughout this essay, Benedict has argued for valuing diversity and for a culturally relativistic perspective. Although she does not say it outright, the cultural relativity of Benedict, and other Boasians was based on an analogy with Albert Einstein's theory of relativity, which was the dominant scientific discovery of her generation. Boas and Einstein knew one another and their papers, at the American Philosophical Society and the Hebrew University of Jerusalem respectively, include numerous letters between them. Einstein showed that time, matter, and space are linked in a continuum, but that time and motion are relative to an observer's location, and thus there is no fixed frame of reference. Correspondingly, Benedict repeatedly suggests that there are no cultural absolutes; what is common in one culture may be taboo in another.

Note that Benedict is having some fun with her audience. She declares that the understanding of culture she promotes is no more subversive than Copernicus's ideas. But the idea of a sun-centered solar system was profoundly subversive when first introduced. Galileo was convicted of heresy in 1633 for supporting it. It took the Catholic Church more than 350 years to reverse his conviction.

there has been little individual difference of choice among the members of a group. In the future there will be less geographical differentiation, more differentiation perhaps of voluntary groups. But though it will change the picture of civilization, it will not change the necessity in every sort of complicated human behavior of the cultural symbol, the framework within which alone our acts have meaning. The most individualistic rebel of us all would play a foolish role stripped of the conventions of his culture. Why should he make wholesale attack upon its institutions? They are the epic of his own people, written not in **rime** but in stone and currency and merchant marines and city colleges. They are the massive, creation of the imaginations of generations, given a local habitation and a name.[21]

We do not stand to lose by this tolerant and objective view of man's institutions and morals and ways of thought. On the one hand we shall value the bold imagination that is written in all great systems of behavior; on the other, we shall not fear for the future of the world because some item in that system is undergoing contemporary change. We know all culture changes. It is one of its claims upon our interest. We hope, a little, that whereas change has hitherto been blind, at the mercy of unconscious patternings, it will be possible gradually, in so far as we become genuinely culture-conscious, that it shall be guided by intelligence.

For what is the meaning of life except that by the discipline of thought and emotion, by living life to its fullest, we shall make of it always a more flexible instrument, accepting new relativities, divesting ourselves of traditional absolutes? To this end we need for our scientific equipment something of the anthropologist's way of looking at human behavior, something of respect for the epic of our own culture, something of fine tolerance for the values that have been elaborated in other cultures than our own.[22]

---

21. Note again the optimism of Benedict's vision. She imagines a future world culture based on voluntary association. She does not repeat these words in the version of this essay that appears in *Patterns of Culture* published five years later in a much changed, much harsher world.

There is no way Benedict could have predicted computers and the World Wide Web. However, the internet and social media today certainly bridge geographical barriers. Overall, do you think the internet has reduced cultural barriers, or does it create new types of divisions?

"Rime": a frost or coating of ice.

22. Benedict ends her essay with a plea for cultural tolerance, proposing that if we become more "culture conscious" both to other cultures and our own, we may be better able to direct culture change. Benedict appreciated cultural diversity both for its own sake and out of respect for other people. However, Boas and many of his students, particularly Benedict, were concerned with changing America. Benedict was deeply concerned with promoting racial equality and tolerance for diversity. Accepting the 1946 Annual Achievement Award of the American Association of University Women, she said, "I have the faith of a humanist in the advantages of mutual understanding among men" (in Mead 1959: 431).

11. Introduction to *Coming of Age in Samoa*

Margaret Mead (1901–1978)

URING THE LAST hundred years parents and teachers have ceased to take childhood and adolescence for granted. They have attempted to fit education to the needs of the child, rather than to press the child into an inflexible educational mould. To this new task they have been spurred by two forces, the growth of the science of psychology, and the difficulties and maladjustments of youth. Psychology suggested that much might be gained by a knowledge of the way in which children developed, of the stages through which they passed, of what the adult world might reasonably expect of the baby of two months or the child of two years. And the fulminations of the pulpit, the loudly voiced laments of the conservative social philosopher, the records of juvenile courts and social agencies all suggested that something must be done with the period which science had named adolescence. The spectacle of a younger generation diverging ever more widely from the standards and ideals of the past, cut adrift without the anchorage of respected home standards or group religious values, terrified the cautious reactionary, tempted the radical propagandist to missionary crusades among the defenseless youth, and worried the least thoughtful among us.[1]

In American civilisation, with its many immigrant strains, its dozens of conflicting standards of conduct, its hundreds of religious sects, its shifting economic conditions, this unsettled, disturbed status of youth was more apparent than in the older, more settled civilisation of Europe. American conditions challenged the psychologist, the educator, the social philosopher, to offer acceptable explanations of the growing children's plight. As today in post-war Germany, where the younger generation has even more difficult adjustments to make than have our own children, a great mass of theorising about adolescence is flooding the book shops; so the psychologist in America tried to account for the restlessness of youth. The result was works like

From *Coming of Age in Samoa* (1928)

1. *Coming of Age in Samoa* was published in 1928. Nonetheless, it is striking how the adolescent issues with which Mead starts this essay, including education, child psychology, juvenile crime, rebellion against home and parents, etc., sound so timely to a modern reader. *Coming of Age in Samoa* was meant to be a study comparing the influences of biology (in the form of puberty) and culture on adolescence. It challenged the popular American notion that adolescence was a troubled period because of biological/hormonal changes. Although Franz Boas assigned Mead the topic, it is easy to see how Mead, always unconventional, would have been drawn to it and illustrates how little these issues have changed in American popular culture since Mead's time. Although elders have complained about the decadence of the young from at least the time of ancient Greece, the 1920s were truly a time of radical cultural change, given radio, jazz, flappers, modern art, etc.

The passage also reflects Mead's interest in psychology. She mentions Stanley Hall below and she was interested in Sigmund Freud (1856–1939). However, Robert LeVine (1932–2019) argues that the conception of childhood experience held by Ruth Benedict (1887–1948), Mead, and other Culture and Personality theorists derived from the "neo-Freudian" psychoanalysis of Harry Stack Sullivan (1892–1949), Karen Horney (1885–1952), and Erich Fromm (1900–1980). Freudians focused on libidinal or psychosexual stages. Neo-Freudians focused on the quality of the child's interpersonal experience with parents and siblings during the early years. Unlike the orthodox Freudians, the neo-Freudians were open to the study of cultural variation, and their theory could be related to social relationships as ethnographers observed them (Levine 2007: 251).

that of Stanley Hall on "Adolescence," which ascribed to the period through which the children were passing, the causes of their conflict and distress. Adolescence was characterised as the period in which idealism flowered and rebellion against authority waxed strong, a period during which difficulties and conflicts were absolutely inevitable.[2]

The careful child psychologist who relied upon experiment for his conclusions did not subscribe to these theories. He said, "We have no data. We know only a little about the first few months of a child's life. We are only just learning when a baby's eyes will first follow a light. How can we give definite answers to questions of how a developed personality, about which we know nothing, will respond to religion?" But the negative cautions of science are never popular. If the experimentalist would not commit himself, the social philosopher, the preacher and the pedagogue tried the harder to give a short-cut answer. They observed the behaviour of adolescents in our society, noted down the omnipresent and obvious symptoms of unrest, and announced these as characteristics of the period. Mothers were warned

that "daughters in their teens" present special problems. This, said the theorists, is a difficult period. The physical changes which are going on in the bodies of your boys and girls have their definite psychological accompaniments. You can no more evade one than you can the other; as your daughter's body changes from the body of a child to the body of a woman, so inevitably will her spirit change, and that stormily. The theorists looked about them again at the adolescents in our civilisation and repeated with great conviction, "Yes, stormily."[3]

Such a view, though unsanctioned by the cautious experimentalist, gained wide currency, influenced our educational policy, paralysed our parental efforts. Just as the mother must brace herself against the baby's crying when it cuts its first tooth, so she must fortify herself and bear with what equanimity she might the unlovely, turbulent manifestations of the "awkward age." If there was nothing to blame the child for, neither was there any programme except endurance which might be urged upon the teacher. The theorist continued to observe the behaviour of American adolescents and each year lent new justification to his hypothesis, as the difficulties

---

2. Mead's reference to the difficult adjustments facing postwar children in Germany refers to the terrible economic and social conditions faced by Germans during the collapse of German society after World War I.

Granville Stanley Hall (1844–1924) was the founder of the *American Journal of Psychology* and first president of the American Psychological Association. In the late nineteenth and early twentieth centuries, he was one of the leading psychologists in the United States and a pioneer of educational psychology. Hall earned his doctorate in 1878 under the supervision of the pioneering American psychologist William James (1842–1910), brother of the novelist Henry James. He then visited Germany to study experimental psychology with Wilhelm Wundt (1832–1920) and, while there, was introduced to German biologist Ernst Haeckel's recapitulation theory (see Essay 1, Note 11). Following Haeckel, Hall proposed that children developed through psychological stages that reflected the evolutionary history of humankind and that educational curricula for children should be developed to track with these stages.

Hall's most famous work was *Adolescence*, published in 1904. There, he popularized the notion that adolescence was a time of stress characterized by conflict with one's parents, mood swings, and risk-taking. An ardent supporter of eugenics, Hall believed in forced sterilization and was against helping those who were socially, physically, or mentally impaired because this would slow the improvement of humanity. He proposed that the purpose of high schools should be to indoctrinate students with the ideals of military discipline, patriotism, and love of authority.

Mead's work helped show that the experience of adolescence was not universally stressful or conflict-ridden. By the time Mead wrote *Coming of Age in Samoa*, Hall's influence in psychology was declining. However, his view of adolescence (and the role of high schools) is still popular today.

3. Mead became one of the best-known social scientists of her day after the publication of this book. Reading these first paragraphs it is easy to see why. She discussed socially controversial topics in a reasonable and often lighthearted tone. Here she makes fun of "the social philosopher, the preacher and the pedagogue." You can just see old guys with beards and monocles saying, "Yes, stormily."

of youth were illustrated and documented in the records of schools and juvenile courts.

But meanwhile another way of studying human development had been gaining ground, the approach of the anthropologist, the student of man in all of his most diverse social settings. The anthropologist, as he pondered his growing body of material upon the customs of primitive people, grew to realise the tremendous role played in an individual's life by the social environment in which each is born and reared. One by one, aspects of behaviour which we had been accustomed to consider invariable complements of our humanity were found to be merely a result of civilisation, present in the inhabitants of one country, absent in another country, and this without a change of race. He learned that neither race nor common humanity can be held responsible for many of the forms which even such basic human emotions as love and fear and anger take under different social conditions.

So the anthropologist, arguing from his observations of the behaviour of adult human beings in other civilisations, reaches many of the same conclusions which the **behaviourist** reaches in his work upon human babies who have as yet no civilisation to shape their malleable' humanity.[4]

With such an attitude towards human nature the anthropologist listened to the current comment upon adolescence. He heard attitudes which seemed to him dependent upon social environment—such as rebellion against authority, philosophical perplexities, the flowering of idealism, conflict and struggle—ascribed to a period of physical development. And on the basis of his knowledge of the determinism of culture, of the plasticity of human beings, he

doubted. Were these difficulties due to being adolescent or to being adolescent in America?[5]

For the biologist who doubts an old hypothesis or wishes to test out a new one, there is the biological laboratory. There, under conditions over which he can exercise the most rigid control, he can vary the light, the air, the food, which his plants or his animals receive, from the moment of birth throughout their lifetime. Keeping all the conditions but one constant, he can make accurate measurement of the effect of the one. This is the ideal method of science, the method of the controlled experiment, through which all hypotheses may be submitted to a strict objective test.

Even the student of infant psychology can only partially reproduce these ideal laboratory conditions. He cannot control the pre-natal environment of the child whom he will later subject to objective measurement. He can, however, control the early environment of the child, the first few days of its existence, and decide what sounds and sights and smells and tastes are to impinge upon it. But for the student of the adolescent there is no such simplicity of working conditions. What we wish to test is no less than the effect of civilisation upon a developing human being at the age of puberty. To test it most rigorously we would have to construct various sorts of different civilisations and subject large numbers of adolescent children to these different environments. We would list the influences the effects of which we wished to study. If we wished to study the influence of the size of the family, we would construct a series of civilisations alike in every respect except in family organisation. Then if we found differences in the behaviour of our

---

4. **"Behaviorist"**: Behaviorism is a theory of learning that proposes that all behaviors are acquired through a process of conditioning in which actions are reinforced or punished. While B. F. Skinner (1904–1990) was the most famous behaviorist of the twentieth century, John B. Watson (1878–1958) was the best-known behaviorist of Mead's era.

5. In the previous paragraphs, Mead has been questioning Hall and the popular wisdom concerning the supposed turmoil of adolescence. As a devoted disciple of Boas, she looked to cultural explanations for human behavior. Like Boas, she argued that race and culture are not connected with each other. Also, like Boas, she rejected the idea that "common humanity" (psychic unity) can explain the diversity of forms that culture takes. Here she proposes that the experience of adolescence is a cultural phenomenon. Based on her work in Samoa, she argued that the stress psychologists associated with adolescence is a product of American society, not human-developmental biology.

adolescents we could say with assurance that size of family had caused the difference, that, for instance, the only child had a more troubled adolescence than the child who was a member of a large family. And so we might proceed through a dozen possible situations—early or late sex knowledge, early or late sex experience, pressure towards precocious development, discouragement of precocious development, segregation of the sexes or coeducation from infancy, division of labour between the sexes or common tasks for both, pressure to make religious choices young or the lack of such pressure. We would vary one factor, while the others remained quite constant, and analyse which, if any, of the aspects of our civilisation were responsible for the difficulties of our children at adolescence.[6]

Unfortunately, such ideal methods of experiment are denied to us when our materials are humanity and the whole fabric of a social order. The **test colony of Herodotus**, in which babies were to be isolated and the results recorded, is not a possible approach. Neither is the method of selecting from our own civilisation groups of children who meet one requirement or another. Such a method would be to select five hundred adolescents from small families and five hundred from large families, and try to discover which had experienced the greatest difficulties of adjustment at adolescence. But we could not know what were the other influences brought to bear upon these children, what effect their knowledge of sex or their neighbourhood environment may have had upon their adolescent development.[7]

What method then is open to us who wish to conduct a human experiment but who lack the power either to construct the experimental conditions or to find controlled examples of those conditions here and there throughout our own civilisation? The only method is that of the anthropologist, to go to a different civilisation and make a study of human beings under different cultural conditions in some other part of the world. For such studies the anthropologist chooses quite simple peoples, primitive peoples, whose society has never attained the complexity of our own. In this choice of primitive peoples like the Eskimo, the Australian, the South Sea Islander, or the Pueblo Indian, the anthropologist is guided by the knowledge that the analysis of a simpler civilisation is more possible of attainment.

In complicated civilisations like those of Europe, or the higher civilisations of the East,

---

6. In this paragraph and the next, Mead discusses the difficulty of controlling variables in social science research and in both paragraphs she mentions knowledge of sex as a possible factor in a person's emotional growth and development. This is a nod to Freud and his theory of psychoanalysis. Freud proposed that all humans evolved through a series of psychosexual phases he named the oral, anal, genital, latency, and genital primacy stages of development. Early childhood trauma could impede one's psychosexual development resulting in neurotic behavior. Freud was extremely popular in the 1920s. Psychoanalytic theory, with its emphasis on unconscious psychological processes such as repression, projection, and sublimation, captured the popular imagination of his day and became an important part of anthropological thought in the first decades of the twentieth century.

7. Here, Mead confronts one of the most fundamental shortcomings of trying to conduct experimental science in the social sciences. Because social scientists cannot control the variables in the lives of humans as they can for laboratory animals, it is not possible to set up the same kind of experimental situations or test hypotheses with the same scientific rigor found in the physical sciences. For Mead and the other students of Boas, the answer to this issue was conducting fieldwork in other societies.

"Test colony of Herodotus" refers to the account by the ancient Greek historian Herodotus (c. 484–c. 425 BCE) of an experiment supposedly performed by the Pharaoh Psammetichus I (now called Psamtik I, reigned 664–610 BCE). In an effort to discover the oldest language, Psamtik ordered two infants raised for two years in acoustic isolation. Psamtik believed that the language infants raised under these conditions first spoke would indicate the first language. According to Herodotus, Psamtik believed the children in his experiment spoke Phrygian, proving that this was the first language and that the Phrygians (from West Central Turkey) were the world's most ancient people. Herodotus's account is the only record of this experiment and Psamtik I died more than 125 years before Herodotus's birth.

years of study are necessary before the student can begin to understand the forces at work within them. A study of the French family alone would involve a preliminary study of French history, of French law, of the Catholic and Protestant attitudes towards sex and personal relations. A primitive people without a written language present a much less elaborate problem and a trained student can master the fundamental structure of a primitive society in a few months.[8]

Furthermore, we do not choose a simple peasant community in Europe or an isolated group of mountain whites in the American South, for these people's ways of life, though simple, belong essentially to the historical tradition to which the complex parts of European or American civilisation belong. Instead, we choose primitive groups who have had thousands of years of historical development along completely different lines from our own, whose language does not possess our Indo-European categories, whose religious ideas are of a different nature, whose social organisation is not only simpler but very different from our own. From these contrasts, which are vivid enough to startle and enlighten those accustomed to our own way of life and simple enough to be grasped quickly, it is possible to learn many things about the effect of a civilisation upon the individuals within it.[9]

So, in order to investigate the particular problem, I chose to go not to Germany or to Russia, but to Samoa, a South Sea island about thirteen degrees from the Equator, inhabited by a brown Polynesian people. Because I was a woman and could hope for greater intimacy in working with girls rather than with boys, and because owing to a paucity of women ethnologists our knowledge of primitive girls is far slighter than our knowledge of boys, I chose to concentrate upon the adolescent girl in Samoa.[10]

But in concentrating, I did something very different from what I would do if I concentrated upon a study of the adolescent girl in Kokomo, Indiana. In such a study, I would go right to the crux of the problem; I would not have to linger long over the Indiana language, the table manners or sleeping habits of my subjects, or make an exhaustive study of how they learned to dress themselves, to use the telephone, or what the concept of conscience meant in Kokomo. All these things are the general fabric of American life, known to me as investigator, known to you as readers.

But with this new experiment on the primitive adolescent girl the matter was quite otherwise. She spoke a language the very sounds of which were strange, a language in which nouns became verbs and verbs nouns in the most sleight-of-hand fashion. All of her habits of life were different. She sat cross-legged on the ground, and to sit upon a chair made her stiff and miserable. She ate with her fingers from a woven plate; she slept upon the floor. Her

---

8. Mead had a long-standing interest in French culture. In 1955, she and her collaborator Rhoda Métraux (1914–2003) published *Themes in French Culture: A Preface to a Study of French Community.*

9. The Boasian perspective that each society is the result of its own unique historical circumstances is sometimes called *historical particularism.* Because this viewpoint emphasized cultural relativism and the incommensurability of different cultures, it was a potent counterpoint to the evolutionary and diffusionist theories of the late nineteenth century. Here Mead expresses the view that Samoan culture is an anthropological laboratory because it developed on its own, uninfluenced by the Western world. Today, however, this notion that a society could exist in a "pure" form is considered naive. Archaeological evidence indicates that Samoa was settled around 1500 BCE and had a relationship with the polities of Fiji and Tonga. Europeans first arrived in the Samoan islands in the early 1700s, and missionaries a hundred years later. In other words, despite Mead's observations about the importance of working in non-Western societies, she was working among people influenced by European colonialism for almost two hundred years.

10. Although Mead's statement about working with young women because she was a woman and little research had been done with indigenous women seems obvious today, the anthropology of her day was male-dominated and largely oblivious to the importance of gender in anthropological fieldwork. In 1928, highlighting gender was innovative.

house was a mere circle of pillars, roofed by a cone of thatch, carpeted with water-worn coral fragments. Her whole material environment was different. Cocoanut palm, breadfruit, and mango trees swayed above her village. She had never seen a horse, knew no animals except the pig, dog and rat. Her food was taro, breadfruit and bananas, fish and wild pigeon and half-roasted pork, and land crabs. And just as it was necessary to understand this physical environment, this routine of life which was so different from ours, so her social environment in its attitudes towards children, towards sex, towards personality, presented as strong a contrast to the social environment of the American girl.[11]

I concentrated upon the girls of the community. I spent the greater part of my time with them. I studied most closely the households in which adolescent girls lived. I spent more time in the games of children than in the councils of their elders. Speaking their language, eating their food, sitting barefoot and cross-legged upon the pebbly floor, I did my best to minimise the differences between us and to learn to know and understand all the girls of three little villages on the coast of the little island of Tau, in the Manu'a Archipelago.

Through the nine months which I spent in Samoa, I gathered many detailed facts about these girls, the size of their families, the position and wealth of their parents, the number of their brothers and sisters, the amount of sex experience which they had had. All of these routine facts are summarised in a table in the appendix. They are only the barest skeleton, hardly the raw materials for a study of family situations and sex relations, standards of friendship, of loyalty, of personal responsibility, all those impalpable storm centres of disturbances in the lives of our adolescent girls. And because these less measurable parts of their lives were so similar, because one girl's life was so much like another's, in an uncomplex, uniform culture like Samoa, I feel justified in generalising although I studied only fifty girls in three small neighbouring villages.

In the following chapters I have described the lives of these girls, the lives of their younger sisters who will soon be adolescent, of their brothers with whom a strict taboo forbids them to speak, of their older sisters who have left puberty behind them, of their elders, the mothers and fathers whose attitudes towards life determine the attitudes of their children. And through this description I have tried to answer the question which sent me to Samoa: Are the disturbances which vex our adolescents due to the nature of adolescence itself or to the

---

11. Read the last two paragraphs again and think about Mead's comments concerning the "culture" of teenage girls in Kokomo, Indiana, and her description of the life of a teenage girl in Samoa. The simplicity of Mead's concept of culture is striking. For Mead, culture is the language, food, customs, and material culture of the people. This definition is little different than the definition of culture first published by E. B. Tylor in *Primitive Culture* in 1871 (see essay 2). However, work by many scholars challenged this static view of culture (most essays in the last third of this book are examples of this). Moreover, it is always easy to assume the past was a simpler time. The cultural homogeneity assumed in Mead's description may not really have existed in the Samoan villages she visited or in Kokomo, Indiana, in 1928. It is an artifact of the understanding of culture of her era.

It's worth stopping a moment to think about Kokomo in the 1920s. Our guess is that Mead chose Kokomo because it is midwestern and she liked the sound of the name. In Mead's mind Kokomo probably represented the typical American. However, this is a problem. When Mead said "Kokomo" she meant White and middle class. And, Kokomo had a lot of such people. But it also had other communities and was a particular hotspot of hatred. We know a good deal about it because, in 1923, Kokomo hosted one of the largest Ku Klux Klan rallies in American history. In the 1920s about 85 percent of Kokomo's population were White Anglo Saxon Protestants (WASPs) and as many as half of the adult males were Klan members) but there were other communities: The Italian and Slavic communities were "confined to an industrial district." Kokomo's Black population was deeply segregated. Some of the spirit of the town can be gauged from a 1925 editorial in the local newspaper that said, "Marriages in which American-born girls become wives of foreign born men are fruitful not only of unhappiness but of tragedy" (Safianow 1988: 337). Our points here are two: First, Mead's vision of Kokomo and Samoan cultures overlooks the complexity of both. Second, when Mead thinks of "normal" American culture, she thinks of WASP culture.

civilisation? Under different conditions does adolescence present a different picture?

Also, by the nature of the problem, because of the unfamiliarity of this simple life on a small Pacific island, I have had to give a picture of the whole social life of Samoa, the details being selected always with a view to illuminating the problem of adolescence. Matters of political organisation which neither interest nor influence the young girl are not included. Minutiae of relationship systems or ancestor cults, genealogies and mythology, which are of interest only to the specialist, will be published in another place. But I have tried to present to the reader the Samoan girl in her social setting, to describe the course of her life from birth until death, the problems she will have to solve, the values which will guide her in her solutions, the pains and pleasures of her human lot cast on a South Sea island.[12]

Such a description seeks to do more than illuminate this particular problem. It should also give the reader some conception of a different and contrasting civilisation, another way of life, which other members of the human race have found satisfactory and gracious. We know that our subtlest perceptions, our highest values, are all based upon contrast; that light without darkness or beauty without ugliness would lose the qualities which they now appear to us to have. And similarly, if we would appreciate our own civilisation, this elaborate pattern of life which we have made for ourselves as a people and which we are at such pains to pass on to our children, we must set our civilisation over against other very different ones. The traveller in Europe returns to America, sensitive to nuances in his own manners and philosophies which have hitherto gone unremarked, yet Europe and America are parts of one civilisation. It is with variations within one great pattern that the student of Europe today or the student of our own history sharpens his sense of appreciations. But if we step outside the stream of Indo-European culture, the appreciation which we can accord our civilisation is even more enhanced. Here in remote parts of the world, under historical conditions very different from those which made Greece and Rome flourish and fall, groups of human beings have worked out patterns of life so different from our own that we cannot venture any guess that they would ever have arrived at our solutions. Each primitive people has selected one set of human gifts, one set of human values, and fashioned for themselves an art, a social organisation, a religion, which is their unique contribution to the history of the human spirit.[13]

Samoa is only one of these diverse and gracious patterns, but as the traveller who has been once from home is wiser than he who has never left his own door step, so a knowledge of one other culture should sharpen our ability

12. In this paragraph Mead makes clear she is writing for a popular (White, middle-class) American audience. She says descriptions of aspects of culture "which are of interest only to the specialist" are not dealt with in this book because they are not of interest to the girls she studied. Aspects she mentions, such as political organization and kinship, were precisely the topics that were the focus of much of the anthropology of previous decades. Her study is among the first to focus on women and their lives. By announcing that she will publish accounts of politics and genealogy, Mead burnishes her credentials as a scientist, rather than simply a popular author.

Note also how deeply romantic the paragraphs you've just read are. Mead paints an idyllic picture of her time on "the little island of Tau." Portraits like this may not have accurately captured the difficulties of working in places like Tau, but they certainly increased interest in anthropology.

13. In this paragraph Mead pays tribute to her mentors Boas and Benedict. She notes that the culture of Samoa would not, in time, become more like our own culture, thus joining Boas's critique of evolutionism. Mead and Benedict were working closely together at the time Mead wrote *Coming of Age*. Benedict's *Patterns of Culture* would not appear until 1934. However, Benedict had published many of its key concepts in the 1920s. *Patterns of Culture* stresses the idea that each cultural group has its own "personality" built from a unique and consistent constellation of values. The book opens with a Digger Indian proverb that reflects what Mead says here: "In the beginning God gave to every people a cup of clay, and from this cup they drank their life."

to scrutinise more steadily, to appreciate more lovingly, our own.

And, because of the particular problem which we set out to answer, this tale of another way of life is mainly concerned with education, with the process by which the baby, arrived cultureless upon the human scene, becomes a full-fledged adult member of his or her society.

The strongest light will fall upon the ways in which Samoan education, in its broadest sense, differs from our own. And from this contrast we may be able to turn, made newly and vividly self-conscious and self-critical, to judge anew and perhaps fashion differently the education we give our children.[14]

---

14. Mead's cultural relativity and appreciation for other cultures shine through in these final paragraphs. One reason she was such a popular figure was her ability to make her readers appreciate the lifestyles of other peoples. Note, too, her argument that in learning about other cultures we are better able to understand and appreciate our own. Mead was raised in an unconventional household. Her father, Edward Sherwood Mead (1874–1956), was a professor of finance at the University of Pennsylvania. Her mother, Emily Fogg Mead (1871–1950), had been a teacher and, during Margaret's childhood, studied Italian immigrants in Hammonton, New Jersey, while working on a master's degree in sociology that she never completed. Growing up, Margaret was encouraged to explore her interests and have a career at a time before women were even allowed to vote. In these last paragraphs, she invites us all to open our minds, broaden our horizons, and value the diversity of cultures in the world as she had learned to do.

Note further that Mead's ultimate purpose is a critique of American culture and American education. Mead's work appeared at a time when the social and sexual mores of the late nineteenth and early twentieth century were increasingly under attack. In 1928, as *Coming of Age* appeared, Hollywood's most popular star was Clara Bow (1905–1965), "the 'It' girl." "It," of course, was sex, and Bow was considered scandalous. The implication of Mead's work was that the psychological problems of American teens were the result of repressive American education. Americans would do better to follow the sexually liberating practices of Samoans.

Mead's analysis has been both scientifically and politically controversial. In 1983 Derek Freeman (1916–2001) attacked Mead's analysis, arguing that she had misunderstood Samoan sexuality. Freeman argued that Samoan adolescents were even more anxious about sexuality than their Western counterparts. Controversy about Freeman's claims raged for years. Although scholars have been critical of both Mead and Freeman, most favor Mead's interpretation of Samoan sexuality (see Shankman 2009).

12. *Mules and Men*, Chapter 4

Zora Neale Hurston (1891–1960)

[*Before beginning this essay, readers should be aware that Hurston presents this work in her own voice and the voices of those with whom she was conversing. These latter make frequent use of the "N word." We comment on the context of her usage of this word in note 13.*]

TWELVE MILES BELOW KISSIMMEE I passed under an arch that marked the Polk County line. I was in the famed Polk County.

How often had I heard "Polk County Blues."[1]
"You don't know Polk County lak Ah do.
Anybody been dere, tell you de same thing too."[2]

The asphalt curved deeply and when it straightened out we saw a huge smoke-stack blowing smut against the sky. A big sign said, "Everglades Cypress Lumber Company, Loughman, Florida."[3]

We had meant to keep on to Bartow or Lakeland and we debated the subject between us until we reached the opening, then I won. We went in. The little Chevrolet was all against it. The thirty odd miles that we had come, it argued, was nothing but an appetizer. Lakeland was still thirty miles away and no telling what the road held. But it sauntered on down the bark-covered road and into the quarters just as if it had really wanted to come.[4]

From *Mules and Men* (1935)

1. If you would like to hear "Polk County Blues" for yourself, you can find a recording of it https://bit.ly/polk-county.

2. Hurston's first-person narrative as well as her use of the Black vernacular speech of her day stood out compared to her contemporaries such as Ruth Benedict or Margaret Mead. Today first-person writing is accepted, even encouraged, but this was uncommon until the 1970s and 1980s.

3. Hurston visited Polk County, Florida, several times in the late 1920s and early 1930s. Polk County is located Southwest of Orlando and has a violent history which forms the background of the lives of Hurston's interlocutors. African Americans settled in Polk County following the Civil War. Between reconstruction and 1950, there were twenty lynchings of Black people there, making it the twenty-first most violent county in the Southern states during this period. The story of Fred Rochelle is typical of the violence in Polk County: In 1901, Rochelle, a 16-year-old African American teen, was accused of the rape and murder of Rena Smith Taggart. After Rochelle was taken into custody, a white mob took him from the local sheriff and burned him alive (2015 Equal Justice Initiative; Moore 2018).
   The Ocoee massacre of Nov. 2–3, 1920 occurred just a few miles away in Orange County. On that occasion, after Moses Norman, a prominent member of the black community, was denied his right to vote, a mob of 250 whites, led by members of the Ku Klux Klan (KKK), rioted, burning twenty-two homes, two churches, and a lodge. At least thirty Black people were killed, but the death toll may have been as high as sixty. After the riot all African Americans left the town and did not return until the 1980s (Hoffman, Hoffman, and Storm 2014: 25–26).
   The KKK remained active in Polk County and surrounding areas through much of the twentieth century. They held a public march there as recently as 1979.

4. Boas recruited students from many different backgrounds. He was particularly fond of Hurston and believed that as an "insider," she was uniquely suited to collect disappearing African American folklore.

We halted beside two women walking to the commissary and asked where we could get a place to stay, despite the signs all over that this was private property and that no one could enter without the consent of the company.

One of the women was named "Babe" Hill and she sent me to her mother's house to get a room. I learned later that Mrs. Allen ran the boarding-house under patronage of the company. So we put up at Mrs. Allen's.[5]

That night the place was full of men—come to look over the new addition to the quarters. Very little was said directly to me and when I tried to be friendly there was a noticeable disposition to fend me off. This worried me because I saw at once that this group of several hundred Negroes from all over the South was a rich field for folklore, but here was I figuratively starving to death in the midst of plenty.

Babe had a son who lived at the house with his grandmother and we soon made friends. Later the sullen Babe and I got on cordial terms. I found out afterwards that during the Christmas holidays of 1926 she had shot her husband to death, had fled to Tampa where she had bobbed her hair and eluded capture for several months but had been traced thru letters to her mother and had been arrested and lodged in Bartow jail. After a few months she had been allowed to come home and the case was forgotten. Negro women are punished in these parts for killing men, but only if they exceed the quota. I don't remember what the quota is. Perhaps I did hear but I forgot. One woman had killed five when I left that turpentine still where she lived. The sheriff was thinking of calling on her and scolding her severely.[6]

James Presley used to come every night and play his guitar. Mrs. Allen's temporary brother-in-law could play a good second but he didn't have a **box** so I used to lend him mine. They would play. The men would crowd in and buy soft drinks and **woof** at me, the stranger, but I knew I wasn't getting on. The ole feather-bed tactics.[7]

Then one day after Cliffert Ulmer, Babe's son, and I had driven down to Lakeland together he felt close enough to tell me what was the trouble. They all thought I must be a revenue officer or a detective of some kind. They were accustomed to strange women dropping into the quarters, but not in shiny gray Chevrolets. They usually came plodding down the big road or counting railroad ties. The car made me look too prosperous. So they set me aside as different. And since most of them were fugitives from justice or had done plenty time,

---

Hurston bought the Chevrolet in the spring of 1927 using Boas as a character reference for the car loan (Salamone 2014: 219)

5. The mention of the company commissary and boardinghouse is a reference to a labor system in southern states initiated after the Civil War that maintained people in a state of semi-slavery. Under the "Black Codes," African Americans were required by law to sign annual labor contracts with plantation, mill, or mine owners. If a man refused, he would be arrested, fined, and jailed until an employer paid his fine thus buying the man's labor (Anderson 2016: 19). A company like Everglades Cypress Lumber provided housing, a grocery store, and other necessities for its workers but charged them exorbitant prices, thus keeping poor Black and white workers in debt. Workers could not leave a company while in debt, and if they ran away the debt was passed on to their remaining families.

6. Here Hurston, a Black woman working in the era of Jim Crow laws and lynching, openly criticizes White authorities for the lack of justice in the Black community but does this with humor so attracts less attention.

7. In the introduction to *Mules and Men*, Hurston describes what she calls "feather-bed resistance." She says that when white people question Black people, "We smile and tell him or her something that satisfies the white person because, knowing so little about us, he doesn't know what he is missing. . . . Questions are "smothered under a lot of laughter and pleasantries."

"box" in this paragraph, a guitar.

"woof" and **"woofing"**: verbally nimble teasing, and name-calling.

a detective was just the last thing they felt they needed on that "job."[8]

I took occasion that night to impress the job with the fact that I was also a fugitive from justice, "bootlegging." They were hot behind me in Jacksonville and they wanted me in Miami. So I was hiding out. That sounded reasonable. Bootleggers always have cars. I was taken in.

The following Saturday was pay-day. They paid off twice a month and pay night is big doings. At least one dance at the section of the quarters known as the Pine Mill and two or three in the big Cypress Side. The company works with two kinds of lumber.

You can tell where the dances are to be held by the fires. Huge bonfires of faulty logs and slabs are lit outside the house in which the dances are held. The refreshments are parched[a] peanuts, fried rabbit, fish, chicken and chitterlings.

The only music is guitar music and the only dance is the ole square dance. James Presley is especially invited to every party to play. His pay is plenty of **coon dick**, and he *plays*.[9]

Joe Willard is in great demand to call figures. He rebels occasionally because he likes to dance too.

But all of the fun isn't inside the house. A group can always be found outside about the fire, standing around and woofing and occasionally telling stories.

The biggest dance on this particular pay-night was over to the Pine Mill. James Presley and Slim assured me that they would be over there, so Cliffert Ulmer took me there. Being the reigning curiosity of the "job" lots of folks came to see what I'd do. So it was a great dance.

The guitars cried out "Polk County," "Red River" and just instrumental hits with no name, that still are played by all good box pickers. The dancing was hilarious to put it mildly. Babe, Lucy, Big Sweet, East Coast Mary and many other of the well-known women were there. The men swung them lustily, but nobody asked me to dance. I was just crazy to get into the dance, too. I had heard my mother speak of it and praise square dancing to the skies, but it looked as if I was doomed to be a wallflower and that was a new role for me. Even Cliffert didn't ask me to dance. It was so jolly, too. At the end of every set Joe Willard would trick the men. Instead of calling the next figure as expected he'd bawl out, "Grab yo' partners and march up to de table and treat." Some of the men did, but some would bolt for the door and stand about the fire and woof until the next set was called.

I went outside to join the woofers, since I seemed to have no standing among the dancers. Not exactly a hush fell about the fire, but a lull came. I stood there awkwardly, knowing that the too-ready laughter and aimless talk was a window-dressing for my benefit. The brother in black puts a laugh in every vacant place in his mind. His laugh has a hundred meanings. It may mean amusement, anger, grief, bewil-

---

8. Hurston visited Florida in 1928 under the patronage of Charlotte Osgood Mason (1854–1946). Mason was a patron of many Harlem Renaissance figures, including the poet and playwright Langston Hughes (1901–1967). She provided the financial support that allowed Hurston to collect folklore in Florida but also made her sign a contract that made Hurston Mason's employee, doing work on her behalf, and unable to share the material she collected without Mason's approval (Boyd 2003). Mason insisted on being called "Godmother" by those who received her funds.

Hurston's support from Mason included a monthly payment of $200 and a car. In 1928, $200 a month was close to the average union wage for all employees nationally (Monthly Labor Review 1928: 10). However, Black lumber workers in Florida made far less. The average wage for laborers in the Florida lumber industry in 1928 was about $12 a week (Bureau of Labor Statistics 1929: 35). So, Hurston was much wealthier than the people she was living with.

Osgood's patronage of Hughes, Hurston, and others was tied to her belief in the importance of what she thought was primitive spirituality and her additional belief that, in America, Black people were the carriers of this spirituality (Booth 2006). Recipients of Mason's largesse sometimes played to her beliefs. In one letter, Hurston addresses Mason as "dearest, little mother of the primitive world" (Hurston and Kaplan 2002: 123).

9. **"coon dick"**: moonshine. The penis bone of a raccoon was often placed in the outlet of a still to help the alcohol flow.

derment, chagrin, curiosity, simple pleasure or any other of the known or undefined emotions. Clardia Thornton of Magazine Point, Alabama, was telling me about another woman taking her husband away from her. When the showdown came and he told Clardia in the presence of the other woman that he didn't want her- could never use her again, she tole me "Den, Zora, Ah wuz so outdone, Ah just opened mah mouf an laffed."[10]

The folks around the fire laughed and boisterously shoved each other about, but I knew they were not tickled. But I soon had the answer. A pencil-shaped fellow with a big Adam's apple gave me the key.

"Ma'am, whut might be yo' entrimmins?" he asked with what was supposed to be a killing bow.

"My whut?"

"Yo entrimmins? Yo entitlum?"

The "entitlum" gave me the cue, "Oh, my name is Zora Hurston. And whut may be yours?" More people came closer quickly. "Mah name is Pitts and Ah'm sho glad to meet yuh. Ah asted Cliffert tuh knock me down tuh yuh but he wouldn't make me 'quainted. So Ah'm makin' mahseff 'quainted."

"Ah'm glad you did, Mr. Pitts."

"Sho nuff?" archly.

"Yeah. Ah wouldn't be sayin' it if Ah didn't mean it."

He looked me over shrewdly. "Ah see dat las' crap you shot Miss, and Ah fade yuh."[11]

I laughed heartily. The whole fire laughed at his quick come-back and more people came out to listen. "Miss, you know uh heap uh dese hard heads wants to woof at you but dey skeered."

"How come, Mr. Pitts? Do I look like a bear or panther?"

"Naw, but dey say youse rich and dey ain't got de nerve to open dey mouf."

I mentally cursed the $12.74 dress from Macy's that I had on among all the $1.98 mail-order dresses. I looked about and noted the number of bungalow aprons and even the rolled down paper bags on the heads of several women. I did look different and resolved to fix all that no later than the next morning.

"Oh, Ah ain't got doodley squat,"[b] I countered. "Mah man brought me dis dress de las' time he went to Jacksonville. We wuz

---

10. Notice the way that Hurston switches between standard American English and a form of Black Vernacular English. Like other Boasians, Hurston was deeply concerned with the relationship between language, thought, and culture. In her 1934 essay "The Characteristics of Negro Expression" Hurston argued that Black culture was characterized by a "will to adorn." This was particularly evident in language. Hurston says that "the American Negro has done wonders to the English Language." She says that the greatest contributions are the use of metaphor and simile, the use of double descriptives (such as "high-tall," "low-down," and "kill-dead"), and the use of verbal nouns (such as "funeralize," "I wouldn't friend with her," and "uglying away.").

Not everyone appreciated Hurston's use of dialect. In his 1937 review of Hurston's *Their Eyes Were Watching God*, The African American novelist and poet Richard Wright (1908–1960) wrote that Hurston "*voluntarily* continues her novel in the tradition which was *forced* upon the Negro . . . swing like a pendulum eternally in that safe and narrow orbit in which America likes to see the Negro live: between laughter and tears. [emphasis in the original]"

Hurston and the people with whom she talked grew up in an era of intense white-on-Black violence and repression. Hurston's comment about laughing is poignant, for it also is a comment on white violence against Blacks. She says the brother in Black's laugh has a hundred meanings. Laughter often covered other feelings since it was dangerous for a Black man or woman to be perceived as belligerent, angry, or demanding. Hurston was writing at a time when a Black man insisting on voting or whistling at a white woman might be killed. So, he laughs and appears nonthreatening.

11. Mr. Pitts's comments are slang from the dice game of craps. To fade when shooting craps is to bet against the shooter. Mr. Pitts is saying "I see what you are doing and I am calling you on it."

sellin' plenty stuff den and makin' good money. Wisht Ah had dat money now."[12]

Then Pitts began woofing at me and the others stood around to see how I took it. "Say, Miss, you know nearly all dese niggers is after you. Dat's all dey talk about out in de swamp."[13]

"You don't say. Tell 'em to make me know it."
"Ah ain't tellin' nobody nothin'. Ah ain't puttin' out nothin' to no ole hard head but ole folks eyes and Ah ain't doin' dat till they dead. Ah talks for Number One. Second stanza: Some of 'em talkin' 'bout marryin' you and dey wouldn't know whut to do wid you if they had you. Now, dat's a fack."
"You reckon?"
"Ah know dey wouldn't. Dey'd 'spect you tuh git out de bed and fix dem some breakfus' and a bucket. Dat's 'cause dey don't know no better. Dey's thin-brainded. Now me, Ah wouldn't let you fix me no breakfus'. Ah git up and fix mah own and den, whut make it so cool, Ah'd fix you some and set it on de back of de cook-stove so you could git it when you wake up. Dese mens don't even know how to talk to nobody lak you. If you wuz tuh ast dese niggers somethin' dey' d answer you 'yeah' and 'naw.' Now, if you wuz some ole gator-black 'oman dey'd be tellin' you jus' right. But dat ain't

de way tuh talk tuh nobody lak you. Now you ast me somethin' and see how Ah'll answer yuh."
"Mr. Pitts, are you havin' a good time?"
(In a prim falsetto) "Yes, Ma'am. See, dat's de way tuh talk tuh *you.*"

I laughed and the crowd laughed and Pitts laughed. Very successful woofing. Pitts treated me and we got on. Soon a boy came to me from Cliffert Ulmer asking me to dance. I found out that that was the social custom. The fellow that wants to broach a young woman doesn't come himself to ask. He sends his friend. Somebody came to me for Joe Willard and soon I was swamped with bids to dance. They were afraid of me before. My laughing acceptance of Pitts' woofing had put everybody at his ease.

James Presley and Slim spied noble at the orchestra. I had the chance to learn more about "John Henry" maybe. So I strolled over to James Presley and asked him if he knew how to play it.

"Ah'll play it if you sing it," he countered. So he played and I started to sing the verses I knew. They put me on the table and everybody urged me to **spread my jenk**,[c]* so I did the best I could. Joe Willard knew two verses and sang them. Eugene Oliver knew one; Big Sweet knew one. And how James Presley can make his box cry out the accompaniment![14]

---

12. Hurston is providing the reader with a tale of entry. That is, she is explaining to us how she established her position and her credibility in the community. This was unusual in the era in which this book was written but became almost universal in anthropology after the 1980s (see the famous example of it in Geertz's Deep Play essay, Number 26 in this book)

Note also that Huston lies to her interlocutors several times in this passage. She claims that she is a bootlegger and claims that she is poor and that her dress was given to her. By the way, Hurston was probably very well dressed. Her $12.74 dress, adjusted for inflation, would have been $225 in 2023.

13. The "n-word" appears for the first time in this passage. It appears an additional twenty times in this selection from Hurston. In using the word, Hurston is almost certainly being true to the way her interlocutors spoke. Consider the ways and contexts in which the word is used throughout the selection. Here it is used as a putdown of other speakers. But later, it is associated with the culture hero High John the Conqueror. The association of the N word with a culture hero may, in some sense, be a reclaiming of it: an insult becomes a word associated with power.

14. **"spread my jenk"** In a footnote to her essay Hurston defines spread my jenk as to have a good time. Hurston is saying that her companions at the dance asked her to sing, lifted her onto a table, and urged her to have a good time.

By the time that the song was over, before Joe Willard lifted me down from the table I knew that I was in the inner circle. I had first to convince the "job" that I was not an enemy in the person of the law; and, second, I had to prove that I was their kind. "John Henry" got me over my second hurdle.[15]

After that my car was everybody's car. James Presley, Slim and I teamed up and we had to do "John Henry" wherever we appeared. We soon had a reputation that way. We went to Mulberry, Pierce and Lakeland.

After that I got confidential and told them all what I wanted. At first they couldn't conceive of anybody wanting to put down "lies." But when I got the idea over we held a lying contest and posted the notices at the Post Office and the commissary. I gave four prizes and some tall lying was done. The men and women enjoyed themselves and the contest broke up in a square dance with Joe Willard calling figures.

The contest was a huge success in every way. I not only collected a great deal of material but it started individuals coming to me privately to tell me stories they had no chance to tell during the contest.

Cliffert Ulmer told me that I'd get a great deal more by going out with the swamp-gang. He said they lied a plenty while they worked. I spoke to the quarters boss and the swamp boss and both agreed that it was all right, so I strowed it all over the quarters that I was going out to the swamp with the boys next day. My own particular crowd, Cliffert, James, Joe Willard, Jim Allen and Eugene Oliver were to look out for me and see to it that I didn't get snake-bit nor 'gator-swallowed. The watchman, who sleeps out in the swamps and gets up steam in the **skitter** every morning before the men get to the cypress swamp, had been killed by a panther two weeks before, but they assured me that nothing like that could happen to me; not with the help I had.[16]

Having watched some members of that swamp crew handle axes, I didn't doubt for a moment that they could do all that they said. Not only do they chop rhythmically, but they do a beautiful double twirl above their heads with the ascending axe before it begins that accurate and bird-like descent. They can hurl their axes great distances and behead moccasins or sink the blade into an alligator's skull. In fact, they seem to be able to do everything with their instrument that a blade can do. It is a magnificent sight to watch the marvelous co-ordination between the handsome black torsos and the twirling axes.

So next morning we were to be off to the woods. It wasn't midnight dark and it wasn't day yet. When I awoke the saw-mill camp was a dawn gray. You could see the big saw-mill but you couldn't see the smoke from the chimney. You could see the congregation of shacks and the dim outlines of the scrub oaks among the houses, but you couldn't see the grey quilts of Spanish Moss that hung from the trees.

Dick Willie was the only man abroad. It was his business to be the first one out. He was the shack-rouser. Men are not supposed to oversleep and Dick Willie gets paid to see to it that they don't. Listen to him singing as he goes down the line.

---

15. "John Henry" is an important character in African American folklore and the subject of a well-known song. In the folk tale, John Henry is described as a steel driving man: that is, he works driving a steel drill into rock to make holes for dynamite in the construction of railway tunnels. In the song, John Henry, using a steel bar and hammer, races workers with a steam-powered rock drill. John Henry wins the race but dies from the stress of doing so. Many artists have recorded the John Henry folk song and there have been numerous presentations of the story in film and literature (and even *Wasteland 2*, a video game). Several scholars have tried to locate the historical John Henry but disagree on who he was.

In this passage, Hurston claimed that she had to prove that she was "one of their kind," something that, in many ways, she was not. Maria Cotera (2008: 96) notes that Hurston "mobilized key signifiers of authority and authenticity from within her community of informants to open up an ethnographic exchange with them." Hurston's lies are short lived. She tells us in the next passage that she soon told them the truth and even arranged a "lie telling" contest.

16. **"skitter** (skidder)": a piece of heavy logging equipment used to pull cut trees out of the forest.

Wake up, bullies, and git on de rock. 'Tain't quite day-light but it's four o'clock.

Coming up the next line, he's got another song.

Wake up, Jacob, day's a breakin'. Git yo' hoe-cake a bakin' and yo' shirt tail shakin'.

What does he say when he gets to the **jook** and the long-house?[d] I'm fixing to tell you right now what he says. He raps on the floor of the porch with a stick and says:

"Ah ha! What make de rooster crow every morning at sun-up? Dar's to let de pimps and rounders know de workin' man is on his way."[17]

About that time you see a light in every shack. Every kitchen is scorching up fat-back and hoe-cake. Nearly every skillet is full of corn-bread. But some like biscuit-bread better. Break your hoe-cake half in two. Half on the plate, half in the dinner-bucket. Throw in your black-eyed peas and fat meat left from supper and your bucket is fixed. Pour meat grease in your plate with plenty of cane syrup. Mix it and sop it with your bread. A big bowl of coffee, a drink of water from the tin dipper in the pail. Grab your dinner-bucket and hit the grit. Don't keep the straw-boss[e] waiting.[18]

This morning when we got to the meeting place, the foreman wasn't there. So the men squatted along the railroad track and waited.

Joe Willard was sitting with me on the end of a cross-tie when he saw Jim Presley coming in a run with his bucket and jumper-jacket.

"Hey, Jim, where the swamp boss? He ain't got here yet."
"He's ill-sick in the bed Ah hope, but Ah bet he'll git here yet."
"Aw, he ain't sick. Ah bet you a fat man he ain't," Joe said.
"How come?" somebody asked him and Joe answered:[19]
"Man, he's too ugly. If a spell of sickness ever tried to slip up on him, he'd skeer it into a three weeks' spasm."

Blue Baby[f] stuck in his oar and said: "He ain't so ugly. Ye all jus' ain't seen no real ugly man. Ah seen a man so ugly till he could get behind a jimpson weed and hatch monkies."

Everybody laughed and moved closer together. Then Officer Richardson said: "Ah seen a man so ugly till they had to spread a sheet over his head at night so sleep could slip up on him."

They laughed some more, then Clifford Ulmer said:

"Ah'm goin' to talk with my mouth wide open. Those men y'all been talkin' 'bout wasn't ugly at all. Those was pretty men. Ah knowed one so ugly till you could throw him in the Mississippi river and skim ugly for six months."

"Give Cliff de little dog," Jim Allen said. "He done tole the biggest lie."

---

17. **"jook"** In her notes Hurston defines "jook" as a bawdy house.

18. Consider the way that Hurston's tone and language use change from passage to passage. In most of this selection, she speaks in the first or third person. Here, she provides lyrical descriptions of the Florida countryside and speaks directly to the reader in the second person. This is different from most ethnographic writing of its era. Hurston was a very close friend of the poet Langston Hughes and was deeply influenced by him. She sometimes recited Hughes's poetry "to ease her way into the rough society of the work camps and lumber mills she visited" (Cotera 2008: 95). Hurston and Hughes wrote a play together (*Mule Bone: A Comedy of Negro Life*) but fell into disputes about the work which contributed to the ending of their friendship.

19. In the rest of this essay, and throughout *Mules and Men,* Hurston offers a series of stories presented as she says she heard them, with no interpretation. Critics have often taken her to task for this (Cotera 2008: 94). However, this was both true to Boas's emphasis on the objectively accurate recording of cultural information and typical of many publications of the era. The pages of *American Anthropologist* from the 1920s are full of essays that simply present folktales and other bits of ethnographic data.

"He ain't lyin'," Joe Martin tole them. "Ah knowed dat same man. He didn't die-he jus' uglied away."

They laughed a great big old kah kah laugh and got closer together.

"Looka here, folkses," Jim Presley exclaimed. "Wese a half hour behind schedule and no swamp boss and no log train here yet. What yo' all reckon is the matter sho' 'nough?"

"Must be something terrible when white folks get slow about putting us to work."

"Yeah," says Good Black. "You know back in slavery Ole Massa was out in de field sort of lookin' things over, when a shower of rain come up. The field hands was glad it rained so they could knock off for a while. So one slave named John says:

"More rain, more rest."

"Ole Massa says, 'What's dat you say?'"

"John says, 'More rain, more grass.'"[20]

"There goes de big whistle. We ought to be out in the woods almost."

The big whistle at the saw-mill boomed and shrilled and pretty soon the log-train came racking along. No flats for logs behind the little engine. The foreman dropped off the tender as the train stopped.

"No loggin' today, boys. Got to send the train to the Everglades to fetch up the track gang and their tools."

"Lawd, Lawd, we got a day off," Joe Willard said, trying to make it sound like he was all put out about it. "Let's go back, boys. Sorry you won't git to de swamp, Zora."

"Aw, naw," the Foreman said. "Y'all had better g'wan over to the mill and see if they need you over there."

And he walked on off, chewing his tobacco and spitting his juice.

The men began to shoulder jumper-jackets and grab hold of buckets.

Allen asked: "Ain't dat a mean man? No work in the swamp and still he won't let us knock off."

"He's mean all right, but Ah done seen meaner men than him," said Handy Pitts.

"Where?"

"Oh, up in Middle Georgy. They had a straw boss and he was so mean dat when the boiler burst and blowed some of the men up in the air, he docked 'em for de time they was off de job."

Tush Hawg up and said: "Over on de East Coast Ah used to have a road boss and he was so mean and times was so hard till he laid off de hands of his watch."

Wiley said: "He's almost as bad as Joe Brown. Ah used to work in his mine and he was so mean till he wouldn't give God an honest prayer without snatching back 'Amen.'"

Ulmer says: "Joe Wiley, youse as big a liar as you is a man! Whoo-wee. Boy, you molds 'em. But lemme tell y'all a sho nuff tale 'bout Ole Massa."

"Go 'head and tell it, Cliff," shouted Eugene Oliver. "Ah love to hear tales about Ole Massa and John. John sho was one smart nigger."

So Cliff Ulmer went on.[21]

---

20. In Hurston's work, the name "John" (as distinct from John Henry) usually refers to High John the Conqueror, an African American folk hero and trickster spirit. In an essay about John, Hurston (1943: 450) writes: "High John de Conquer came to be a man, and a mighty man at that. But he was not a natural man in the beginning. First off, he was a whisper, a will to hope, a wish to find something worthy of laughter and song. Then the whisper put on flesh. His footsteps sounded across the world in a low but musical rhythm as if the world he walked on was a singing-drum. The black folks had an irresistible impulse to laugh. High John de Conquer was a man in full and had come to live and work on the plantations, and all the slave folks knew him in the flesh." Lori Jirousek (2004: 425) writes: "High John represents a spirit of inevitable justice, the painstaking but undeniable defeat of racial and ethnic oppression."

21. The John the Conqueror story that Ulmer tells now was one of Hurston's favorites. She wrote the story as a play called *The Fiery Chariot* in 1932. The reference is to the biblical story of Elijah, who, in the second chapter of the second book of Kings, is taken to heaven in a fiery chariot.

You know befo' surrender Ole Massa had a nigger name John and John always prayed every night befo' he went to bed and his prayer was for God to come git him and take him to Heaven right away. He didn't even want to take time to die. He wanted de Lawd to come git him just like he was-boot, sock and all. He'd git down on his knees and say: "O Lawd, it's once more and again yo' humble servant is knee-bent and body-bowed-my heart beneath my knees and my knees in some lonesome valley, crying for mercy while mercy kin be found. O Lawd, Ah'm astin' you in de humblest way I know how to be so pleased as to come in yo' fiery chariot and take me to yo' Heben and its immortal glory. Come Lawd, you know Ah have such a hard time. Old Massa works me so hard, and don't gimme no time to rest. So come, Lawd, wid peace in one hand and pardon in de other and take me away from this sin-sorrowing world. Ah'm tired and Ah want to go home."

So one night Ole Massa passed by John's shack and heard him beggin' de Lawd to come git him in. his fiery chariot and take him away; so he made up his mind to find out if John meant dat thing. So he goes on up to de big house and got hisself a bed sheet and come on back. He throwed de sheet over his head and knocked on de door.[22]

John quit prayin' and ast: "Who dat?"

Ole Massa say: "It's me, John, de Lawd, done come wid my fiery chariot to take you away from this sin-sick world."

Right under de bed John had business. He told his wife: "Tell Him Ah ain't here, Liza."

At first Liza didn't say nothin' at all, but de Lawd kept right on callin' John: "Come on, John, and go to Heben wid me where you won't have to plough no mo' furrows and hoe no mo' corn. Come on, John."

Liza says: "John ain't here, Lawd, you hafta come back another time."

Lawd says: "Well, then Liza, you'll do."

Liza whispers and says: "John, come out from underneath dat bed and g'wan wid de Lawd. You been beggin' him to come git you. Now g'wan wid him."

John back under de bed not saying a mumblin' word. De Lawd out on de door step kept on callin'.

Liza says: "John, Ah thought you was so anxious to get to Heben. Come out and go on wid God."

John says: "Don't you hear him say 'You'll do'? Why don't you go wid him?"

"Ah ain't a goin' nowhere. Youse de one been whoopin' and hollerin' for him to come git you and if you don't come out from under dat bed Ah'm gointer tell God youse here."

Ole Massa makin' out he's God, says: "Come on, Liza, you'll do."

Liza says: "O, Lawd, John is right here underneath de bed."

"Come on John, and go to Heben wid me and its immortal glory."

John crept out from under de bed and went to de door and cracked it and when he seen all dat white standin' on de door-steps he jumped back. He says: "O, Lawd, Ah can't go to Heben wid you in yo' fiery chariot in dese ole dirty britches; gimme time to put on my Sunday pants."

"All right, John, put on yo Sunday pants."

John fooled around just as long as he could, changing them pants, but when he went back to de door, de big white glory was still standin' there. So he says agin: "O, Lawd, de Good Book says in Heben no filth is found and I got on dis dirty sweaty shirt. Ah can't go wid you in dis old nasty shirt. Gimme time to put on my Sunday shirt."

"All right, John, go put on yo' Sunday shirt."

John took and fumbled around a long time changing his shirt, and den he went back to de door, but Ole Massa was still on de door step. John didn't had nothin' else to change so he opened de door a little piece and says:

"O, Lawd, Ah'm ready to go to Heben wid you in yo' fiery chariot, but de radiance of yo' countenance is so bright, Ah can't come out by you. Stand back jus' a li'l way please."

---

22. In throwing a sheet over his head, Ole Massa makes himself look like a Klansman.

Ole Massa stepped back a li'l bit.

John looked out agin and says: "O, Lawd, you know dat po' humble me is less than de dust beneath yo' shoe soles. And de radiance of yo countenance is so bright Ah can t come out by you. Please, please, Lawd, in yo' tender mercy, stand back a li'l bit further."

Ole Massa stepped back a li'l bit mo'. John looked out agin and he says: "O, Lawd, Heben is so high and wese so low; youse so great and Ah'm so weak and yo' strength is too much for us poor sufferin' sinners. So once mo' and agin yo' humber servant is knee-bent and body-bowed askin' you one mo' favor befo' Ah step into yo' fiery chariot to go to Heben wid you and wash in yo' glory -be so pleased in yo' tender mercy as to stand back jus' a li'l bit further."

Ole Massa stepped back a step or two mo' and out dat door John come like a streak of lightning. All across de punkin patch, thru de cotton over de pasture-John wid Ole Massa right behind him. By de time dey hit de cornfield John was way ahead of Ole Massa.

Back in de shack one of de children was cryin' and she ast Liza: "Mama, you reckon God's gointer ketch papa and carry him to Heben wid him?"

"Shet yo' mouf, talkin' foolishness!" Liza clashed at de chile. "You know de Lawd can't outrun yo' pappy-specially when he's barefooted at dat."[23]

Kah, Kah, Kah! Everybody laughing with their mouths wide open. If the foreman had come along right then he would have been good and mad because he could tell their minds were not on work.

Joe Willard says: "Wait a minute, fellows, wese walkin' too fast. At dis rate we'll be there befo' we have time to talk some mo' about Ole Massa and John. Tell another one, Cliffert."

"Aw, naw," Eugene Oliver hollered out.

Let *me* talk some chat. Dis is de real truth 'bout Ole Massa 'cause my grandma told it to my mama and she told it to me.

During slavery time, you know, Ole Massa had a nigger named John and he was a faithful nigger and Ole Massa lakted John a lot too.

One day Ole Massa sent for John and tole him, says: "John, somebody is stealin' my corn out de field. Every mornin' when I go out I see where they done carried off some mo' of my roastin' ears. I want you to set in de corn patch tonight and ketch whoever it is."

So John said all right and he went and hid in de field.

Pretty soon he heard somethin' breakin' corn So John sneaked up behind him wid a short stick in his hand and hollered: "Now, break another ear of Ole Massa's corn and see what Ah'll do to you."

John thought it was a man all dis time, but it was a bear wid his arms full of roastin' ears. He throwed down de corn and grabbed John. And him and dat bear!

John, after while got loose and got de bear by the tail wid de bear tryin' to git to him all de time. So they run around in a circle all night long. John was so tired. But he couldn't let go of de bear's tail, do de bear would grab him in de back.

After a stretch they quit runnin' and walked. John swingin' on to de bear's tail and de bear's nose 'bout to touch him in de back.

---

23. Much has been written about Hurston's retelling of this tale. Analysts note its "complex ambiguity" (Meisenhelder 1996: 272). On the one hand, superficially the story seems to make fun of John, who first, is only getting what he has been praying for, and second, is the subject of a series of racist stereotypes. However, on the other, it's John who, both verbally outwits and physically outruns Ole Massa.

Robert Hemenway takes the analysis further. He points out that John's tenacity and his will to survive are clearly more important than his religious faith. In this story, the promise of a reward in heaven for suffering on earth, a trope much beloved by apologists for slavery and racism, is exposed as a sham. The "Lawd" is just Ole Massa with a sheet reminiscent of a KKK member. Seen this way, the story is a brutal indictment of racism in general and Christian support for white supremacy in particular. Hemenway writes that "the white sheet represents fraud, with no capability to clothe with either power or divinity" (Hemenway 1977: 226).

Daybreak, Ole Massa come out to see 'bout John and he seen John and de bear walkin' 'round in de ring. So he run up and says: "Lemme take holt of 'im, John, whilst you run git help!"

John says: "All right, Massa. Now you run in quick and grab 'im just so."

Ole Massa run and grabbed holt of de bear's tail and said: "Now, John you make haste to git somebody to help us."

John staggered off and set down on de grass and went to fanning hisself wid his hat.

Ole Massa was havin' plenty trouble wid dat bear and he looked over and seen John settin' on de grass and he hollered

"John, you better g'wan git help or else I'm gwinter turn dis bear aloose!"

John says: "Turn 'im loose, then. Dat's whut Ah tried to do all night long but Ah couldn't."[24]

Jim Allen laughed just as loud as anybody else and then he "We better hurry on to work befo' de buckra[g] get in behind us.

"Don't never worry about work," says Jim Presley. "There's more work in de world than there is anything else. God made de world and de white folks made work."

"Yeah, dey made work but they didn't make us do it," Joe Willard put in. "We brought dat on ourselves." "Oh, yes, de white folks did put us to work too," said Jim Allen.

Know how it happened? After God got thru makin' de world and de varmints and de folks, he made up a great big bundle and let it down in de middle of de road. It laid dere for thousands of years, then Ole Missus said to Ole Massa: "Go pick up dat box, Ah want to see whut's in it." Ole Massa look at de box and it look so heavy dat he says to de nigger, "Go fetch me dat big ole box out dere in de road." De nigger been stumblin' over de box a long time so he tell his wife:

"'Oman, go git dat box." So de nigger 'oman she runned to git de box. She says:

"Ah always lak to open up a big box 'cause there's nearly always something good in great big boxes." So she run and grabbed a-hold of de box and opened it up and it was full of hard work.

Dat's de reason sister in black works harder than anybody else in de world. De white man tells de nigger to work and he takes and tells his wife.

"Aw, now, dat ain't de reason niggers is working so hard," Jim Presley objected.

Dis is de way dat was.

God let down two bundles 'bout five miles down de road. So de white man and de nigger raced to see who would git there first. Well, de nigger out-run de white man and grabbed de biggest bundle. He was so skeered de white man would git it away from him he fell on top of de bundle and hollered back: "Oh, Ah got here first and dis biggest bundle is mine." De white man says: "All right, Ah'll take yo' leavings," and picked up de li'l tee-ninchy bundle layin' in de road. When de nigger opened up his bundle he found a pick and shovel and a hoe and a plow and chop-axe and then de white man opened up his bundle and found a writin' -pen and ink. So ever since then de nigger been out in de hot sun, usin' his tools and de white man been sittin' up figgerin', ought's a ought, figger's a figger; all for de white man, none for de nigger.

"Oh lemme spread my mess. Dis is Will Richardson doin' dis lyin'."

You know Ole Massa took a nigger deer huntin' and posted him in his place and told him, says: "Now you wait right here and keep yo' gun reformed and ready. Ah'm goin' 'round de hill and skeer up de deer and head him dis way. When he come past, you shoot."

De nigger says: "Yessuh Ah sho' will Massa."

---

24. Here again, Hurston provides a profoundly subversive story. Massa's wealth is based on agriculture and the bear steals his corn. Massa orders John to solve the problem, but in the end, it's Massa who ends up holding the bear by the tail, knowing that should he let go, the beast will attack him. We might read the ending as an allegory of white supremacy. Should white people ever let go. . . . Or, at least, that was what Ole Massa and his like believed.

He set there and waited wid de gun all cocked and after a while de deer come tearin' past him He didn't make a move to shoot de deer so he went on 'bout his business. After while de white man come on 'round de hill and ast de nigger:

> "Did you kill de deer?"
>
> De nigger says: "Ah ain't seen no deer pass here yet."
>
> Massa says: "Yes, you did. you couldn't help but see him He come right dis way."
>
> Nigger says: "Well Ah sho' ain't seen none. All Ah seen was a white man come along here wid a pack of chairs on his head and Ah tipped my hat to him and waited for de deer."[25]
>
> "Some colored folks ain't got no sense, and when Ah see 'em like dat," Ah say, "My race but not my taste."[26]

AUTHOR'S NOTES

a. Roasted

b. Nothing

c. Have a good time

d. See Glossary. In Glossary: Long House. Another name for jook. Sometimes means a mere bawdy house. A long low building cut into rooms that all open on a common porch. A woman lives in each of the rooms.

e. The low-paid poor white section boss on a railroad; similar to swamp boss who works the gang that gets the timber to the sawmill.

f. See glossary. In Glossary: Blue Baby. Nicknames such as this one given from appearances or acts, that is "Blue Baby" was so black he looked blue. "Tush Hawg," a rough man; full of fight like a wild boar

g. West African word meaning white people.

---

25. Hemenway argues that context is key to understanding this story. The story is told when the men are delaying and avoiding work. They've been told to report to the sawmill but are doing so as slowly as possible. In the story, the slave outwits the master using the "feather-bed" tactics Hurston mentioned at the start of the chapter. The slave claims to have only seen "a white man with a pack of chairs on his head." Hemenway says that this "is effective because the white man's racism disables him; to believe that the black man is intelligent enough to trick him would destroy his presumption of superiority" (1977: 169).

26. You've just read a series of humorous, well-told stories and we hope you've enjoyed them. However, partly because the stories are funny, and told in dialect, Huston's work has always been controversial. We pointed out Richard Wright's critique in note 10. Others in Hurston's era were also disparaging. For example, the white civil rights activist Herold Preece (1906–1992) was deeply critical of Hurston's work, and that of other collectors of black folklore. Preece described such tales as "syrupy folklore" and argued that writers should focus on African Americans' lack of political and economic power (Preece 1936: 364, 374). Defenders such as Hemenway argue that to the contrary, Hurston was radical and that her portrait of black culture showed the independence and strength of African Americans. We'll give the last line to Zora Neale Hurston herself. In her 1928 essay "How it Feels to be Colored Me" she wrote: "I do not belong to the sobbing school of Negrohood. . . . I am too busy sharpening my oyster knife."

13. The Relation of Habitual Thought and Behavior to Language

Benjamin L. Whorf (1897–1941)

Human beings do not live in the objective world alone, nor alone in the world of social activity as ordinarily understood, but are very much at the mercy of the particular language which has become the medium of expression for their society. It is quite an illusion to imagine that one adjusts to reality essentially without the use of language and that language is merely an incidental means of solving specific problems of communication or reflection. The fact of the matter is that the "real world" is to a large extent unconsciously built up on the language habits of the group . . . We see and hear and otherwise experience very largely as we do because the language habits of our community predispose certain choices of interpretation.

—EDWARD SAPIR[1]

THERE WILL PROBABLY be general assent to the proposition that an accepted pattern of using words is often prior to certain lines of thinking and forms of behavior, but he who assents often sees in such a statement nothing more than a platitudinous recognition of the hypnotic power of philosophical and learned terminology on the one hand or of catchwords, slogans, and rallying cries on the other. To see only thus far is to miss the point of one of the important interconnections which Sapir saw between language, culture, and psychology, and succinctly expressed in the introductory quotation. It is not so much in these special uses of language as in its constant ways of arranging data and its most ordinary everyday analysis of phenomena that we need to recognize the influence it has on other activities, cultural and personal.[2]

From *Language, Culture, and Personality* (1941)

1. Whorf opens this essay with a quote from his friend and mentor Edward Sapir (1884–1939) that is a strong statement of linguistic relativity and determinism, the principles underlying the Sapir-Whorf hypothesis. This essay, written in 1939, was first published in *Language, Culture, and Personality*, a 1941 memorial volume dedicated to Sapir, who died in 1939. The fundamental point of the essay is to demonstrate some ways in which grammatical categories in language unconsciously influence the ways people interpret the world around them and thus direct their behavior, a position called *linguistic determinism*. Whorf argues that speakers of different languages think and act differently because their languages create different conceptual worlds, a position called *linguistic relativity*.

2. Whorf begins this essay with an ambiguous statement. Is he saying that learning the grammatical categories of language comes before thinking, or language causes us to think in certain patterns? The first interpretation may reflect Sapir and Whorf's reading of philosopher Immanuel Kant's (1724–1804) *Critique of Pure Reason* (1781). There, Kant argues that for people to think, they must have certain categories of understanding that come before experience. Almost all current-day linguists reject the second idea and understand language and thought as separate processes. The psychologist Steven Pinker (1994) asks rhetorically, have you ever known what you wanted to say but not quite the words to use? If so, you've provided good evidence that

THE NAME OF THE SITUATION AS AFFECTING BEHAVIOR

I came in touch with an aspect of this problem before I had studied under Dr. Sapir, and in a field usually considered remote from linguistics. It was in the course of my professional work for a fire insurance company, in which I undertook the task of analyzing many hundreds of reports of circumstances surrounding the start of fires, and in some cases, of explosions. My analysis was directed toward purely physical conditions, such as defective wiring, presence or lack of air spaces between metal flues and woodwork, etc., and the results were presented in these terms. Indeed it was undertaken with no thought that any other significances would or could be revealed. But in due course it became evident that not only a physical situation *qua* physics, but the meaning of that situation to people, was sometimes a factor, through the behavior of the people, in the start of the fire. And this factor of meaning was clearest when it was a *linguistic meaning*, residing in the name or the linguistic description commonly applied to the situation. Thus, around a storage of what are called "gasoline drums," behavior will tend to a certain type, that is, great care will be exercised; while around a storage of what are called "empty gasoline drums," it will tend to be different—careless, with little repression of smoking or of tossing cigarette stubs about. Yet the "empty" drums are perhaps the more dangerous, since

they contain explosive vapor. Physically the situation is hazardous, but the linguistic analysis according to regular analogy must employ the word "empty," which inevitably suggests lack of hazard. The word "empty" is used in two linguistic patterns: (1) as a virtual synonym for "null and void, negative, inert," (2) applied in analysis of physical situations without regard to, e.g., vapor, liquid vestiges, or stray rubbish, in the container. The situation is named in one pattern (2) and the name is then "acted out" or "lived up to" in another (1), this being a general formula for the linguistic conditioning of behavior into hazardous forms.[3]

In a wood distillation plant the metal stills were insulated with a composition prepared from limestone and called at the plant "spun limestone." No attempt was made to protect this covering from excessive heat or the contact of flame. After a period of use, the fire below one of the stills spread to the "limestone," which to everyone's great surprise burned vigorously. Exposure to acetic acid fumes from the stills had converted part of the limestone (calcium carbonate) to calcium acetate. This when heated in a fire decomposes, forming inflammable acetone. Behavior that tolerated fire close to the covering was induced by use of the name "limestone," which because it ends in "-stone" implies noncombustibility.

A huge iron kettle of boiling varnish was observed to be overheated, nearing the temperature at which it would ignite. The operator moved it off the fire and ran it on its wheels to a distance, but did not cover it. In a min-

---

language and thought are different processes. Further, if Whorf's intent was to show the effects of language on thought, he seems to begin by assuming what he is trying to prove.

3. Whorf is an unusual figure in the history of anthropology in that he is a widely known theorist who never held a regular academic position. Although he was an honorary research fellow at Yale in the mid-1930s, he was educated as a chemical engineer, and spent his career working as an investigator for the Hartford Fire Insurance Company. Whorf began his studies in anthropology with Sapir in 1931 during the Great Depression, at a time when academic jobs were difficult to find and did not pay well. Whorf considered himself lucky to have a lucrative job that allowed him time to pursue his intellectual interests.

Whorf provides a series of examples from his work as an insurance inspector investigating the causes of fires. He claims that in the cases he discusses, fires started because the language that people used did not adequately describe physical reality. He notes that the "empty" gasoline drums were not really empty, and the "spun limestone" was not stone. Fires happened, Whorf claims, because people used the words "empty" and "limestone" to describe things that were neither factually empty nor made of stone. The implication is that the language we use can affect our actions because it influences the way we think about things.

ute or so the varnish ignited. Here the linguistic influence is more complex; it is due to the metaphorical objectifying (of which more later) of "cause" as contact or the spatial juxtaposition of "things"—to analyzing the situation as "on" versus "off" the fire. In reality, the stage when the external fire was the main factor had passed; the overheating was now an internal process of convection in the varnish from the intensely heated kettle, and still continued when "off" the fire.

An electric glow heater on the wall was little used, and for one workman had the meaning of a convenient coat hanger. At night a watchman entered and snapped a switch, which action he verbalized as "turning on the light." No light appeared, and this result he verbalized as "light is burned out." He could not see the glow of the heater because of the old coat hung on it. Soon the heater ignited the coat, which set fire to the building.

A tannery discharged waste water containing animal matter into an outdoor settling basin partly roofed with wood and partly open. This situation is one that ordinarily would be verbalized as "pool of water." A workman had occasion to light a blowtorch near by, and threw his match into the water. But the decomposing waste matter was evolving gas under the wood cover, so that the setup was the reverse of "watery." An instant flare of flame ignited the woodwork, and the fire quickly spread into the adjoining building.

A drying room for hides was arranged with a blower at one end to make a current of air along the room and thence outdoors through a vent at the other end. Fire started at a hot bearing on the blower, which blew the flames directly into the hides and fanned them along the room, destroying the entire stock. This hazardous setup followed naturally from the term "blower" with its linguistic equivalence to "that which blows," implying that its function necessarily is to "blow." Also its function is verbalized as "blowing air for drying," overlooking that it can blow other things, e.g., flames and sparks. In reality, a blower simply makes a current of air and can exhaust as well as blow. It should have been installed at the vent end to *draw* the air over the hides, then through the hazard (its own casing and bearings), and thence outdoors. Beside a coal-fired melting pot for lead reclaiming was dumped a pile of "scrap lead"—a misleading verbalization, for it consisted of the lead sheets of old radio condensers, which still had paraffin paper between them. Soon the paraffin blazed up and fired the roof, half of which was burned off.[4]

Such examples, which could be greatly multiplied, will suffice to show how the cue to a certain line of behavior is often given by the analogies of the linguistic formula in which the situation is spoken of, and by which to some degree it is analyzed, classified, and allotted its place in that world which is "to a large extent unconsciously built up on the language habits of the group." And we always assume that the linguistic analysis made by our group reflects reality better than it does.

GRAMMATICAL PATTERNS AS INTERPRETATIONS OF EXPERIENCE

The linguistic material in the above examples is limited to single words, phrases, and patterns of limited range. One cannot study the behavioral compulsiveness of such material without suspecting a much more far-reaching compulsion from large-scale patterning of grammatical categories, such as plurality, gender and similar classifications (animate, inanimate, etc.), tenses, voices, and other verb

---

4. Some of Whorf's examples are troubling. We don't know what caused workers' behavior in many of these examples. Was as tossing a lit match into a pool of water in which there was also flammable gas for example, driven by the use of language? Or, could the behavior have been caused by carelessness or lack of knowledge of the flammability of gases produced by decomposition? Was the "spun limestone" allowed to catch fire because workers thought of it as stone, or did they and the owners who bought the metal stills simply assume that the manufacturer provided safe equipment? Did the workers know the name of the insulation at all? As you read the examples that follow, consider whether the problems were caused by linguistic confusion or are these examples merely how Whorf interpreted the situations.

forms, classifications of the type of "parts of speech," and the matter of whether a given experience is denoted by a unit morpheme, an inflected word, or a syntactical combination. A category such as number (singular vs. plural) is an attempted interpretation of a whole large order of experience, virtually of the world or of nature; it attempts to say how experience is to be segmented, what experience is to be called "one" and what "several." But the difficulty of appraising such a far-reaching influence is great because of its background character, because of the difficulty of standing aside from our own language, which is a habit and a cultural ***non est disputandum***, and scrutinizing it objectively. And if we take a very dissimilar language, this language becomes a part of nature, and we even do to it what we have already done to nature. We tend to think in our own language in order to examine the exotic language. Or we find the task of unraveling the purely morphological intricacies so gigantic that it seems to absorb all else. Yet the problem, though difficult, is feasible; and the best approach is through an exotic language, for in its study we are at long last pushed willy-nilly out of our ruts. Then we find that the exotic language is a mirror held up to our own.[5]

In my study of the Hopi language, what I now see as an opportunity to work on this problem was first thrust upon me before I was clearly aware of the problem. The seemingly endless task of describing the morphology did finally end. Yet it was evident, especially in the light of Sapir's lectures on Navaho, that the description of the *language* was far from complete. I knew for example the morphological formation of plurals, but not how to use plurals. It was evident that the category of plural in Hopi was not the same thing as in English, French, or German. Certain things that were plural in these languages were singular in Hopi. The phase of investigation which now began consumed nearly two more years. The work began to assume the character of a comparison between Hopi and western European languages. It also became evident that even the grammar of Hopi bore a relation to Hopi culture, and the grammar of European tongues to our own "Western" or "European" culture. And it appeared that the interrelation brought in those large subsummations of experience by language, such as our own terms "time," "space," "substance," and "matter." Since, with respect to the traits compared, there is little difference between English, French, German, or other European languages with the possible (but doubtful) exception of Balto-Slavic and non-Indo-European, I have lumped these languages into one group called SAE, or "Standard Average European."[6]

That portion of the whole investigation here to be reported may be summed up in two questions: (1) Are our own concepts of "time,"

---

5. Whorf is suggesting that it is very difficult to understand the effects of language on culture because people perceive the world through the filter of their languages, which are filled with fundamental assumptions about the nature of the world. Similarly, it is difficult to study the linguistic categories of another language because we must ultimately perceive these through the linguistic categories of our own. Whorf suggests the study of exotic languages is the best way around this problem. Additionally, such studies can give us a new point of view from which to examine our own.

"***Non est disputandum***": Latin, "is not disputable." Generally seen as *de gustibus non est disputandum*: "There is no accounting for taste."

6. European scholars have been speculating about the nature of language and cognition and the differences between languages since the late seventeenth century. Echoing the Boasian rejection of unilineal-evolutionary thinking and the related ranking of races that were common at the time, Sapir and Whorf rejected the ranking of cultures or languages. Here Whorf begins to use his concept of linguistic relativity, the notion that different languages reflect different cultural conceptions of reality. He aims to demonstrate that European concepts of time, space, and matter are not universal, but take different conceptual forms in various cultures and that these differences are the result of language.

Note that Whorf has decided to lump all European languages together. However, there are differences among these languages of the sort he has mentioned above. For example, the words business and darkness are singular in English but plural in French (*les affaires* and *les ténèbres,* respectively).

"space," and "matter" given in substantially the same form by experience to all men, or are they in part conditioned by the structure of particular languages? (2) Are there traceable affinities between (a) cultural and behavioral norms and (b) large-scale linguistic patterns? I should be the last to pretend that there is anything so definite as "a correlation" between culture and language, and especially between ethnological rubrics such as "agricultural, hunting," etc., and linguistic ones like "inflected," "synthetic," or "isolating."[a] When I began the study, the problem was by no means so clearly formulated, and I had little notion that the answers would turn out as they did.

PLURALITY AND NUMERATION IN SAE AND HOPI

In our language, that is SAE, plurality and cardinal numbers are applied in two ways: to real plurals and imaginary plurals. Or more exactly if less tersely: perceptible spatial aggregates and metaphorical aggregates. We say "ten men" and also "ten days." Ten men either are or could be objectively perceived as ten, ten in one group perception[b]—ten men on a street corner, for instance. But "ten days" cannot be objectively experienced. We experience only one day, today; the other nine (or even all ten) are something conjured up from memory or imagination. If "ten days" be regarded as a group it must be as an "imaginary," mentally constructed group. Whence comes this mental pattern? Just as in the case of the fire-causing errors, from the fact that our language confuses the two different situations, has but one

pattern for both. When we speak of "ten steps forward, ten strokes on a bell," or any similarly described cyclic sequence, "times" of any sort, we are doing the same thing as with "days." *Cyclicity* brings the response of imaginary plurals. But a likeness of cyclicity to aggregates is not unmistakably given by experience prior to language, or it would be found in all languages, and it is not.[7]

Our awareness of time and cyclicity does contain something immediate and subjective—the basic sense of "becoming later and later." But, in the habitual thought of us SAE people, this is covered under something quite different, which though mental should not be called subjective. I call it *objectified*, or imaginary, because it is patterned on the *outer* world. It is this that reflects our linguistic usage. Our tongue makes no distinction between numbers counted on discrete entities and numbers that are simply "counting itself." Habitual thought then assumes that in the latter the numbers are just as much counted on "something" as in the former. This is objectification. Concepts of time lose contact with the subjective experience of "becoming later" and are objectified as counted *quantities*, especially as lengths, made up of units as a length can be visibly marked off into inches. A "length of time" is envisioned as a row of similar units, like a row of bottles.[8] In Hopi there is a different linguistic situation. Plurals and cardinals are used only for entities that form or can form an objective group. There are no imaginary plurals, but instead ordinals used with singulars. Such an expression as "ten days" is not used. The equivalent statement is an operational one that reaches one day by a suitable count. "They stayed ten days" becomes "they stayed until the eleventh

---

7. In this section, Whorf argues that SAE speakers use the same grammatical construction for physical things that we can experience at a single time such as "ten men" and things that we can only experience as a sequence such as ten days. He refers to the first of these as "real" plurals and the second as "imaginary" plurals. Linguists never took up Whorf's idea of real versus imaginary plurals. JSTOR's database of more than 12 million journal articles contains no mention of "imaginary plurals" that is not also describing Whorf's work (or unrelated to linguistics).

8. Whorf claims that because SAE speakers treat the abstract concept of numbers, particularly numbers of days, as if they were physical objects, SAE speakers have constructed a linear concept of time as a line of units that stretches out before us into the future and behind us in the past. He makes this point because he is preparing readers for a discussion of the cyclical nature of time in Hopi thought.

day" or "they left after the tenth day." "Ten days is greater than nine days" becomes "the tenth day is later than the ninth." Our "length of time" is not regarded as a length but as a relation between two events in lateness. Instead of our linguistically promoted objectification of that datum of consciousness we call "time," the Hopi language has not laid down any pattern that would cloak the subjective "becoming later" that is the essence of time.[9]

NOUNS OF PHYSICAL QUANTITY IN SAE AND HOPI

We have two kinds of nouns denoting physical things: individual nouns, and mass nouns, e.g., water, milk, wood, granite, sand, flour, meat. Individual nouns denote bodies with definite outlines: a tree, a stick, a man, a hill. Mass nouns denote homogeneous continua without implied boundaries. The distinction is marked by linguistic form; e.g., mass nouns lack plurals,[c] in English drop articles, and in French take the partitive article *du, de la, des*. The distinction is more widespread in language than in the observable appearance of things. Rather few natural occurrences present themselves as unbounded extents; air of course, and often water, rain, snow, sand, rock, dirt, grass. We do not encounter butter, meat, cloth, iron, glass, or most "materials" in such kind of manifestation, but in bodies small or large with definite outlines. The distinction is somewhat forced upon our description of events by an unavoidable pattern in language. It is so inconvenient in a great many cases that we need some way of individualizing the mass noun by further linguistic devices. This is partly done by names of body-types: stick of wood, piece of cloth, pane of glass, cake of soap; also, and even more, by introducing names of containers though their

contents be the real issue: glass of water, cup of coffee, dish of food, bag of flour, bottle of beer. These very common container formulas, in which "of" has an obvious, visually perceptible meaning ("contents"), influence our feeling about the less obvious type-body formulas: stick of wood, lump of dough, etc. The formulas are very similar: individual noun plus a similar relator (English "of"). In the obvious case this relator denotes contents. In the inobvious one it "suggests" contents. Hence the lumps, chunks, blocks, pieces, etc., seem to contain something, a "stuff," "substance," or "matter" that answers to the water, coffee, or flour in the container formulas. So with SAE people the philosophic "substance" and "matter" are also the naïve idea; they are instantly acceptable, "common sense." It is so through linguistic habit. Our language patterns often require us to name a physical thing by a binomial that splits the reference into a formless item plus a form.

Hopi is again different. It has a formally distinguished class of nouns. But this class contains no formal subclass of mass nouns. All nouns have an individual sense and both singular and plural forms. Nouns translating most nearly our mass nouns still refer to vague bodies or vaguely bounded extents. They imply indefiniteness, but not lack, of outline and size. In specific statements, "water" means one certain mass or quantity of water, not what we call "the substance water." Generality of statement is conveyed through the verb or predicator, not the noun. Since nouns are individual already, they are not individualized by either type-bodies or names of containers, if there is no special need to emphasize shape or container. The noun itself implies a suitable type-body or container. One says, not "a glass of water" but kəˈyi "a water," not "a pool of water" but paˈhə,[d] not "a dish of corn flour" but ŋəmni "a (quantity of) corn flour," not "a piece of meat" but sikʷi "a meat." The language has neither need for nor

---

9. Whorf asserts that while speakers of SAE think of time as an imaginary plural—e.g., "ten days"—speakers of Hopi think of it as a series of concrete events, day following day, getting later. The idea of real and imaginary plurals is in McGee's experience, similar in Lacandon Maya. When speaking in Maya, many Lacandon talk of time in terms of phases of the moon. For example, if McGee is staying in a community for two weeks, they describe this as "half a moon." Two weeks is an imaginary plural, fourteen days lined up in front of us that we will experience one day at a time. However, the phases of the moon are something that can be concretely experienced. One can watch the moon through its cycle.

analogies on which to build the concept of existence as a duality of formless item and form. It deals with formlessness through other symbols than nouns.[10]

PHASES OF CYCLES IN SAE AND HOPI

Such terms as summer, winter, September, morning, noon, sunset are with us nouns, and have little formal linguistic difference from other nouns. They can be subjects or objects, and we say "at" sunset or "in" winter just as we say at a corner or in an orchard.[e] They are pluralized and numerated like nouns of physical objects, as we have seen. Our thought about the referents of such words hence becomes objectified. Without objectification, it would be a subjective experience of real time, that is of the consciousness of "becoming later and later"—simply a cyclic phase similar to an earlier phase in that ever-later-becoming duration. Only by imagination can such a cyclic phase be set beside another and another in the manner of a spatial (i.e., visually perceived) configuration. But such is the power of linguistic analogy that we do so objectify cyclic phasing. We do it even by saying "a phase" and "phases" instead of, e.g., "phasing." And the pattern of individual and mass nouns, with the resulting binomial formula of formless item plus form, is so general that it is implicit for all nouns, and hence our very generalized formless items like "substance," "matter," by which we can fill out the binomial for an enormously wide range of nouns. But even these are not quite generalized enough to take in our phase nouns. So for the phase nouns we have made a formless item, "time." We have made it by using "a time," i.e., an occasion or a phase, in the pattern of a mass noun, just as from "a summer" we make "summer" in the pattern of a mass noun. Thus with our binomial formula we can say and think "a moment of time," "a second of time," "a year of time." Let me again point out that the pattern is simply that of "a bottle of milk" or "a piece of cheese." Thus we are assisted to imagine that "a summer" actually contains or consists of such-and-such a quantity of "time."

In Hopi however all phase terms, like summer, morning, etc., are not nouns but a kind of adverb, to use the nearest SAE analogy. They are a formal part of speech by themselves, distinct from nouns, verbs, and even other Hopi "adverbs." Such a word is not a case form or a locative pattern, like "**des Abends**" or "in the morning." It contains no morpheme like one of "in the house" or "at the tree."[f] It means "when it is morning" or "while morning-phase is occurring." These "temporals" are not used as subjects or objects, or at all like nouns. One does not say "it's a hot summer" or "summer is hot"; summer is not hot, summer is only *when* conditions are hot, *when* heat occurs. One does not say "this summer," but "summer now" or "summer recently." There is no objectification, as a region, an extent, a quantity, of the subjective duration-feeling. Nothing is suggested about time except the perpetual "getting later" of it. And so there is no basis here for a formless item answering to our "time."[11]

---

10. In this section, Whorf says that SAE has mass nouns such as "glass" and "water" that require us to individualize them by adding a qualifier such as "pane of glass" or a container such as "glass of water." However, he claims that Hopi has no mass nouns; rather, Hopi nouns for indefinite objects such as water imply outline, size, or quantity. It is curious that Whorf chooses the example of "water" to illustrate this point because in the case of "water" in English, one can construct nouns in the same manner as Hopi. The nouns "puddle," "pond," and "lake" all imply a certain size and quantity of water. "Twig," "stick," and "board" are other examples in the case of "wood." Maybe the differences between SAE and Hopi noun construction are not as absolute as Whorf claims.

11. Building on his discussions of plurality and mass nouns, Whorf proposes here that SAE terminology for phases of time such as summer or morning treats these imaginary nouns as if they were a quantity of concrete, observable items. In fact, in the Western calendar, the seasons are specific series of days that disregard local environmental conditions. This is another example of the Western objectification of time. In contrast, Whorf says the Hopi use phase terms in the manner of adverbs. For example, summer is not hot (because summer

TEMPORAL FORMS OF VERBS IN SAE AND HOPI

The three tense system of SAE verbs colors all our thinking about time. This system is amalgamated with that large scheme of objectification of the subjective experience of duration already noted in other patterns—in the binomial formula applicable to nouns in general, in temporal nouns, in plurality and numeration. This objectification enables us in imagination to "stand time units in a row." Imagination of time as like a row harmonizes with a system of *three* tenses; whereas a system of two, an earlier and a later, would seem to correspond better to the feeling of duration as it is experienced. For if we inspect consciousness we find no past, present, future, but a unity embracing complexity. *Everything* is in consciousness, and everything in consciousness *is*, and is together. There is in it a sensuous and a nonsensuous. We may call the sensuous—what we are seeing, hearing, touching—the "present" while in the nonsensuous the vast image-world of memory is being labeled "the past" and another realm of belief, intuition, and uncertainty "the future"; yet sensation, memory, foresight, all are in consciousness together—one is not "yet to be" nor another "once but no more." Where real time comes in is that all this in consciousness is "getting later," changing certain relations in an irreversible manner. In this "latering" or "durating" there seems to me to be a paramount contrast between the newest, latest instant at the focus of attention and the rest—the earlier. Languages by the score get along well with two tense-like forms answering to this paramount relation of later to earlier. We can of course *construct and contemplate in thought* a system of past, present, future, in the objectified configuration of points on a line. This is what our general objectification tendency leads us to do and our tense system confirms.

In English the present tense seems the one least in harmony with the paramount temporal relation. It is as if pressed into various and not wholly congruous duties. One duty is to stand as objectified middle term between objectified past and objectified future, in narration, discussion, argument, logic, philosophy. Another is to denote inclusion in the sensuous field: "I *see* him." Another is for nomic, i.e., customarily or generally valid, statements: "We see with our eyes." These varied uses introduce confusions of thought, of which for the most part we are unaware.[12]

---

is not a concrete thing that contains heat). Summer for the Hopi is when conditions are hot. Whorf asserts that, unlike SAE, Hopi is a concrete language that reflects people's physical experiences. This is a point that is dealt with in greater detail in the next section in the discussion of verb forms.

"*des Abends*": German, "in the evening."

12. Here, Whorf focuses on an important, and very Boasian, debate: Are notions such as past, present, and future related to aspects of human physiology, or is human behavior virtually completely flexible? Are tenses learned, cultural phenomena?

Whorf points out that SAE requires one to think and speak in a three-tense system. However, there is no past, present, or future in our consciousness. We live in a continual present and experience our memories (past), sensations (present), and anticipation of things (future) all together in "real time." This is another example of the way that SAE steers its speakers toward the Western objectification of time. Hopi, however, is different, as Whorf claims later.

Besides outlining how he thinks Hopi speakers understand the world, Whorf's claim has much larger implications. Whorf is saying that the physical phenomenon of consciousness can be divided into two categories: the "sensuous," which is, what we are experiencing at this instant, and the "non-sensuous," everything else (memories, anticipations, anxieties, and so on). Because of the structure of our language, we carve three tenses out of this phenomenon: past, present, and future. In fact, as a physical phenomenon, the only thing that exists is the process of getting later. In this, Whorf understands consciousness in a fashion that is consistent with Boasian thinking. Consciousness is essentially undifferentiated, a blank slate. Understandings are created by culture and environment rather than by any pre-existing tendency of the brain to work in particular ways. However, Whorf is incorrect, the universality of the fundamental characteristics of language is a strong argument for its biological basis. Every human language has ways of expressing present, future, and past, and

Hopi, as we might expect, is different here too. Verbs have no "tenses" like ours, but have validity-forms ("assertions"), aspects, and clause-linkage forms (modes), that yield even greater precision of speech. The validity-forms denote that the speaker (not the subject) reports the situation (answering to our past and present) or that he expects it (answering to our future)[g] or that he makes a nomic statement (answering to our nomic present). The aspects denote different degrees of duration and different kinds of tendency "during duration." As yet we have noted nothing to indicate whether an event is sooner or later than another when both are *reported*. But need for this does not arise until we have two verbs: i.e., two clauses. In that case the "modes" denote relations between the clauses, including relations of later to earlier and of simultaneity. Then there are many detached words that express similar relations, supplementing the modes and aspects. The duties of our three-tense system and its tripartite linear objectified "time" are distributed among various verb categories, all different from our tenses; and there is no more basis for an objectified time in Hopi verbs than in other Hopi patterns; although this does not in the least hinder the verb forms and other patterns from being closely adjusted to the pertinent realities of actual situations.[13]

[*In a 590-word section titled "Duration, Intensity, and Tendency in SAE and Hopi," Whorf shows that these are expressed metaphorically in SAE. For example, an event that concludes quickly is "short." Prices "rise and fall." An injured person may suffer a "sharp" pain. Whorf concludes that this demonstrates the way that SAE objectifies or spatializes qualities and events that are not concrete or spatial. He says SAE speakers have difficulty referring to nonspatial situations without physical metaphors. For example, do you "grasp" this point, or is it "over your head"? Whorf concludes by saying that the Hopi language does not use these physical metaphors because Hopi has "tensors," a class of words that denotes intensity, tendency, and duration.*]

HABITUAL THOUGHT IN SAE AND HOPI

The comparison now to be made between the habitual thought worlds of SAE and Hopi speakers is of course incomplete. It is possible only to touch upon certain dominant contrasts that appear to stem from the linguistic differences already noted. By "habitual thought" and "thought world" I mean more than simply language, i.e., than the linguistic patterns themselves. I include all the analogical and suggestive value of the patterns (e.g., our "imaginary space" and its distant implications), and all the give-and-take between language and the culture as a whole, wherein is a vast amount that is not linguistic but yet shows the shaping influence of language. In brief, this "thought world" is the microcosm that each man carries about within himself, by which he measures and understands what he can of the macrocosm.[14]

---

many gradations of the three. However, they may not use verbs to do it. Chinese verbs, for example, do not have tense or conjugation. Time is conveyed by context and a grammatical element called "aspect."

13. As Whorf indicates, many languages like Hopi have two tense forms (past and present) and numerous aspect forms that indicate duration or whether an action is about to happen, is ongoing, or has been completed. Whorf has given us a series of examples of differences between SAE and Hopi including plurality, physical quantity, phases and cycles, and verb tenses. He asserts that these reflect differences in understanding rather than simply being simply different ways of expressing the same thing. This, however, is impossible to prove. Consider an example from plurality. In English, we say, "I wear a shirt and a pair of pants." Following Whorf, this should indicate that we experience and understand a shirt as one thing but pants as two. Yet English speakers understand that a pair of pants is one item.

14. Up to this point Whorf has spent his time (whoops, another metaphor objectifying time as a quantity) discussing how SAE and Hopi grammatical categories are different. In this section, he now turns his attention to the relationship between language, thought, and behavior. Whorf argues that cultural differences are not

The SAE microcosm has analyzed reality largely in terms of what it calls "things" (bodies and quasibodies) plus modes of extensional but formless existence that it calls "substances" or "matter." It tends to see existence through a binomial formula that expresses any existent as a spatial form plus a spatial formless continuum related to the form, as contents is related to the outlines of its container. Nonspatial existents are imaginatively spatialized and charged with similar implications of form and continuum.

The Hopi microcosm seems to have analyzed reality largely in terms of *events* (or better "eventing"), referred to in two ways, objective and subjective. Objectively, and only if perceptible physical experience, events are expressed mainly as outlines, colors, movements, and other perceptive reports. Subjectively, for both the physical and nonphysical, events are considered the expression of invisible intensity factors, on which depend their stability and persistence, or their **fugitiveness and proclivities**. It implies that existents do not "become later and later" all in the same way; but some do so by growing like plants, some by diffusing and vanishing, some by a procession of metamorphoses, some by enduring in one shape till affected by violent forces. In the nature of each existent able to manifest as a definite whole is the power of its own mode of duration: its growth, decline, stability, cyclicity, or creativeness. Everything is thus already "prepared" for the way it now manifests by earlier phases, and

what it will be later, partly has been, and partly is in act of being so "prepared." An emphasis and importance rests on this preparing or being prepared aspect of the world that may to the Hopi correspond to that "quality of reality" that "matter" or "stuff" has for us.[15]

HABITUAL BEHAVIOR FEATURES OF HOPI CULTURE

Our behavior, and that of Hopi, can be seen to be coordinated in many ways to the linguistically conditioned microcosm. As in my fire casebook, people act about situations in ways which are like the ways they talk about them. A characteristic of Hopi behavior is the emphasis on preparation. This includes announcing and getting ready for events well beforehand, elaborate precautions to insure persistence of desired conditions, and stress on good will as the preparer of right results. Consider the analogies of the day-counting pattern alone. Time is mainly reckoned "by day" (*taLk*, *-tala*) or "by night" (*tok*), which words are not nouns but tensors, the first formed on a root "light, day," the second on a root "sleep." The count is by *ordinals*. This is not the pattern of counting a number of different men or things, even though they appear successively, for, even then, they *could* gather into an assemblage. It is the pattern of counting successive reappearances of the *same* man or thing, incapable of forming

---

simply reflected in language. Rather, the cultural differences "stem from" linguistic differences. He proposes that each person carries a "thought world," shaped by language, internally, through which the person understands the surrounding world.

In the discussion that follows, Whorf proposes that language and culture are homogeneous phenomena. An individual is born into both, and they are largely responsible for shaping his or her worldview. This notion of the thought world is similar to the concept put forth by Ruth Benedict of a *cultural configuration*. Benedict's *Patterns of Culture* was published in 1934, just at the time Whorf was formulating his thoughts on the role of language in anthropology. It is clear here that Whorf was familiar with Benedict's work. Both Whorf and Benedict were close friends of Sapir and shared his interests in the relationship between psychology and culture.

15. In other words, whereas SAE is characterized by "being," Hopi is characterized by "becoming." This is an interesting point, because Whorf's concerns here dovetail key interests of philosophers of his era, particularly the phenomenologists. Edmund Husserl (1859–1938) and his student Martin Heidegger (1889–1976) had both published works on the nature of time in the 1920s. Heidegger published *Being and Time* in 1927 and Husserl *Lectures on the Phenomenology of Internal Time Consciousness* in 1928. These works explore various objective and subjective experiences of time.

"Fugitiveness and proclivities": in this context, instabilities and tendencies.

an assemblage. The analogy is not to behave about day-cyclicity as to several men ("several days"), which is what we tend to do, but to behave as to the successive visits of the *same man*. One does not alter several men by working upon just one, but one can prepare and so alter the later visits of the same man by working to affect the visit he is making now. This is the way the Hopi deal with the future—by working within a present situation which is expected to carry impresses, both obvious and occult, forward into the future event of interest. One might say that Hopi society understands our proverb "Well begun is half done," but not our "Tomorrow is another day." This may explain much in Hopi character.[16]

This Hopi preparing behavior may be roughly divided into announcing, outer preparing, inner preparing, covert participation, and persistence. Announcing, or preparative publicity, is an important function in the hands of a special official, the Crier Chief. Outer preparing is preparation involving much visible activity, not all necessarily directly useful within our understanding. It includes ordinary practicing, rehearsing, getting ready, introductory formalities, preparing of special food, etc. (all of these to a degree that may seem overelaborate to us), intensive sustained muscular activity like running, racing, dancing, which is thought to increase the intensity of development of events (such as growth of crops), mimetic and other magic, preparations based on esoteric theory involving perhaps occult instruments like prayer sticks, prayer feathers, and prayer meal, and finally the great cyclic ceremonies and dances, which have the significance of preparing rain and crops. From one of the verbs meaning "prepare" is derived the noun for "harvest" or "crop": *na'twani* "the prepared" or the "in preparation."[h]

Inner preparing is use of prayer and meditation, and at lesser intensity good wishes and good will, to further desired results. Hopi attitudes stress the power of desire and thought. With their "microcosm" it is utterly natural that they should. Desire and thought are the earliest, and therefore the most important, most critical and crucial, stage of preparing. Moreover, to the Hopi, one's desires and thoughts influence not only his own actions, but all nature as well. This too is wholly natural. Consciousness itself is aware of work, of the feel of effort and energy, in desire and thinking. Experience more basic than language tells us that, if energy is expended, effects are produced. *We* tend to believe that our bodies can stop up this energy, prevent it from affecting other things until we will our *bodies* to overt action. But this may be so only because we have our own linguistic basis for a theory that formless items like "matter" are things in themselves, malleable only by similar things, by more matter, and hence insulated from the powers of life and thought. It is no more unnatural to think that thought contacts everything and pervades the universe than to think, as we all do, that light kindled outdoors does this. And it is not unnatural to suppose that thought, like any other force, leaves everywhere traces of effect. Now, when we *think* of a certain actual rosebush, we do not suppose that our thought goes to that actual bush, and engages with it, like a searchlight turned upon it. What then do we suppose our consciousness is dealing with when we are thinking of that rosebush? Probably we think it is dealing with a "mental image" which is not the rosebush but a mental surrogate of it. But why should it be *natural* to think that our thought deals with a surrogate and not with the real rosebush? Quite possibly because we are dimly aware that we carry about with us

---

16. In this section Whorf seeks to make the connection between Hopi language and behavior. He says that as with the insurance cases he has investigated, the Hopi act in ways that are similar to the way they talk, and he provides several examples that contrast the Hopi point of view with that of SAE speakers.

Whorf is firmly Boasian in using Hopi language as a way of explaining the Hopi worldview. Boas first proposed this use of language in 1911 in the introduction to his *Handbook of American Indian Languages*. However, unlike Boas and following Sapir, Whorf believed that psychology (rather than history) provided the explanatory tools that anthropology needed to analyze the relationship between humans and culture, and he saw linguistics as the bridge between anthropology and psychology.

a whole imaginary space, full of mental surrogates. To us, mental surrogates are old familiar fare. Along with the images of imaginary space, which we perhaps secretly know to be imaginary only, we tuck the thought-of actually existing rosebush, which may be quite another story, perhaps just because we have that very convenient "place" for it. The Hopi thought-world has no imaginary space. The corollary to this is that it may not locate thought dealing with real space anywhere but in real space, nor insulate real space from the effects of thought. A Hopi would naturally suppose that his thought (or he himself) traffics with the actual rosebush—or more likely, corn plant—that he is thinking about. The thought then should leave some trace of itself with the plant in the field. If it is a good thought, one about health and growth, it is good for the plant; if a bad thought, the reverse.[17]

The Hopi emphasize the intensity-factor of thought. Thought to be most effective should be vivid in consciousness, definite, steady, sustained, charged with strongly felt good intentions. They render the idea in English as "concentrating," "holding it in your heart," "putting your mind on it," "earnestly hoping." Thought power is the force behind ceremonies, prayer sticks, ritual smoking, etc. The prayer pipe is regarded as an aid to "concentrating" (so said my informant). Its name, *na'twanpi*, means "instrument of preparing."

Covert participation is mental collaboration from people who do not take part in the actual affair, be it a job of work, hunt, race, or ceremony, but direct their thought and good will toward the affair's success. Announcements often seek to enlist the support of such mental helpers as well as of overt participants, and contain exhortations to the people to aid with their active good will.[i] A similarity to our concepts of a sympathetic audience or the cheering section at a football game should not obscure the fact that it is primarily the power of directed thought, and not merely sympathy or encouragement, that is expected of covert participants. In fact these latter get in their deadliest work before, not during, the game! A corollary to the power of thought is the power of wrong thought for evil; hence one purpose of covert participation is to obtain the mass force of many good wishers to offset the harmful thought of ill-wishers. Such attitudes greatly favor cooperation and community spirit. Not that the Hopi community is not full of rivalries and colliding interests. Against the tendency to social disintegration in such a small, isolated group, the theory of "preparing" by the power of thought, logically leading to the great power of the combined, intensified, and harmonized thought of the whole community, must help vastly toward the rather remarkable degree of cooperation that, in spite of much private bickering, the Hopi village displays in all the important cultural activities.[18]

Hopi "preparing" activities again show a result of their linguistic thought background in an emphasis on persistence and constant insistent repetition. A sense of the cumulative value of innumerable small momenta is dulled by an objectified, spatialized view of time like ours, enhanced by a way of thinking close to the subjective awareness of duration, of the ceaseless "latering" of events. To us, for whom time is a motion on a space, unvarying repetition seems to scatter its force along a row of units of that space, and be wasted. To the Hopi, for whom time is not a motion but a "getting later" of everything that has ever been done, unvarying repetition is not wasted but accumulated. It is

---

17. This section is a brilliant example of culturally relativistic writing, and we want to draw your attention to the skill with which Whorf explains how Hopi view their place in the world. Boas believed that one of the goals of anthropology was to understand the "native" worldview. Here Whorf not only explains the Hopi view of things, he does it in a way that highlights the contrasts between Hopi and SAE and makes Hopi seem reasonable. It is good to point out that the clarity of Whorf's presentation does not mean he was correct. Linguists and psychologists have been experimenting with different aspects of Whorf's ideas for over half a century without reaching any definitive conclusions.

18. Note the similarity between Hopi notions of thought and many current American notions of prayer, particularly among Evangelical Christians.

storing up an invisible change that holds over into later events.[j] As we have seen, it is as if the return of the day were felt as the return of the same person, a little older but with all the impresses of yesterday, not as "another day," i.e., like an entirely different person. This principle joined with that of thought-power and with traits of general Pueblo culture is expressed in the theory of the Hopi ceremonial dance for furthering rain and crops, as well as in its short, piston-like tread, repeated thousands of times, hour after hour.[19]

SOME IMPRESSES OF LINGUISTIC HABIT IN WESTERN CIVILIZATION

It is harder to do justice in few words to the linguistically conditioned features of our own culture than in the case of the Hopi, because of both vast scope and difficulty of objectivity—because of our deeply ingrained familiarity with the attitudes to be analyzed. I wish merely to sketch certain characteristics adjusted to our linguistic binomialism of form plus formless item or "substance," to our metaphoricalness, our imaginary space, and our objectified time. These, as we have seen, are linguistic.

From the form-plus-substance dichotomy the philosophical views most traditionally characteristic of the "Western world" have derived huge support. Here belong materialism, psychophysical parallelism, physics at least in its traditional Newtonian form—and dualistic views of the universe in general. Indeed here belongs almost everything that is "hard, practical common sense." **Monistic**, holistic, and relativistic views of reality appeal to philosophers and some scientists, but they are badly handicapped in appealing to the "common sense" of the Western average man—not because nature herself refutes them (if she did, philosophers could have discovered this much), but because they must be talked about in what amounts to a new language. "Common sense," as its name shows, and "practicality" as its name does not show, are largely matters of talking so that one is readily understood. It is sometimes stated that Newtonian space, time, and matter are sensed by everyone intuitively, whereupon relativity is cited as showing how mathematical analysis can prove intuition wrong. This, besides being unfair to intuition, is an attempt to answer offhand question (1) put at the outset of this paper, to answer which this research was undertaken. Presentation of the findings now nears its end, and I think the answer is clear. The offhand answer, laying the blame upon intuition for our slowness in discovering mysteries of the Cosmos, such as relativity, is the wrong one. The right answer is: Newtonian space, time, and matter are no intuitions. They are recepts [*sic*] from culture and language. That is where Newton got them.[20]

Our objectified view of time is, however, favorable to historicity and to everything connected with the keeping of records, while the Hopi view is unfavorable thereto. The latter is too subtle, complex, and ever-developing, supplying no ready-made answer to the question of when "one" event ends and "another"

---

19. Here Whorf uses his discussion of the Hopi conception of time and their views on the physical power of thought to make sense of Hopi ritual activity. He says that because their language treats time fundamentally differently than SAE, repetition, for the Hopi, is an essential part of ceremonies. However, Whorf claims that SAE speakers as a result of their language cannot conceive of time in this "becoming later" fashion and therefore do not see the same value to repetition as do the Hopi. We are not able to quibble with Whorf over his observations of the Hopi, but we feel that Whorf overlooked the history of traditional Christian religious ceremony all over Europe as well as contemporary religious practice. Much of Christian ritual activity involves repetition. It would be hard to look at the life of people in Catholic monastic orders, for example, and not see that the lives of monks and nuns are structured around a repetitive prayer and ritual cycle. Catholic penance may involve repeated sayings of specific prayers. The last line in this paragraph could apply equally well to Christian pilgrims, whose every footstep may be considered a prayer.

20. Because he studied engineering Whorf had a better background in the physical sciences than most of his colleagues, and he continued to follow developments in the sciences throughout his career. He was familiar with Albert Einstein's work on relativity and saw a link between relativity in physics and cultural relativity in

begins. When it is implicit that everything that ever happened still is, but is in a necessarily different form from what memory or record reports, there is less incentive to study the past. As for the present, the incentive would be not to record it but to treat it as "preparing." But *our* objectified time puts before imagination something like a ribbon or scroll marked off into equal blank spaces, suggesting that each be filled with an entry. Writing has no doubt helped toward our linguistic treatment of time, even as the linguistic treatment has guided the uses of writing. Through this give-and-take between language and the whole culture we get, for instance:

1. Records, diaries, bookkeeping, accounting, mathematics stimulated by accounting.
2. Interest in exact sequence, dating, calendars, chronology, clocks, time wages, time graphs, time as used in physics.

3. Annals, histories, the historical attitude, interest in the past, archaeology, attitudes of introjection toward past periods, e.g., classicism, romanticism.[21]

Just as we conceive our objectified time as extending in the future in the same way that it extends in the past, so we set down our estimates of the future in the same shape as our records of the past, producing programs, schedules, budgets. The formal equality of the spacelike units by which we measure and conceive time leads us to consider the "formless item" or "substance" of time to be homogeneous and in ratio to the number of units. Hence our **prorata** allocation of value to time, lending itself to the building up of a commercial structure based on time—prorata values: time wages (time work constantly supersedes piece work), rent, credit, interest, depreciation charges, and insurance premiums. No doubt this vast system, once built,

---

the study of human societies, namely, that "reality" depends on the positioning of the observer. Here, this leads him to an extremely radical claim: that we experience Newtonian physics (things such as the effects of gravity, the consistency of time, or mass) not because these things are "real" but because our language and culture cause us to perceive and believe them. By implication, if we had a different language and culture (like the Hopi) we might perceive what SAE speakers call time, gravity, and mass differently (see essay 10, note 20 for more on Boasians and Einstein). It's an intriguing notion, and one needs to be careful not to misunderstand his point. Whorf is not arguing here that the physical laws that govern the universe are different in different cultures because people speak differently, but that the cultural reality or how events are defined may be different. Whorf is arguing a linguistic version of cultural relativity. However, his work is closer than most Boasians to *hermeneutics*, the study of the interpretation of meaning. Hermeneutics was developed in Europe in the early twentieth century by philosophers such as Heidegger and Hans-Georg Gadamer (1900–2002). Hermeneuticists argued that one could not have objective knowledge about the world because people necessarily understood the world through their cultural, linguistic, and intellectual models.

In American anthropology Boas and his students used the notion of cultural relativity to argue against racism and discrimination and to support the notion of cultural equality. Unfortunately, in post–World War I Germany political leaders used ideas from hermeneutics to argue for German cultural superiority, which led to a rise in nationalism, anti-Semitism, and the ascendance of Hitler and the Nazi Party.

"Monistic": referring to monism, the philosophical principle that mind and matter are essentially the same.

21. Whorf mentions the relationship of writing to our objectified concept of time. He argued that SAE languages lent themselves to writing because of the way SAE speakers were compelled by language to understand time. Writing was encouraged by the structure of SAE but discouraged by the structure of Hopi. A generation later, scholars such as Walter J. Ong (1912–2003) and Jack Goody (1919–2015) argued the reverse: that the process of writing led to differences in understanding. In *Orality and Literacy* (1982) Ong argues that literacy transforms thought in ways possible only after the technology of writing has been adopted. Goody chides Whorf for failing to see that the features of SAE are shared in common in part because they are written languages (1977: 161).

Note that Whorf's notion of society is thoroughly idealist. It is entirely determined by thinking. Most current theorists link the development of record-keeping to commerce, taxation, and the emergence of state-level society. For Whorf, it is a function of language structure.

would continue to run under any sort of linguistic treatment of time; but that it should have been built at all, reaching the magnitude and particular form it has in the Western world, is a fact decidedly in consonance with the patterns of the SAE languages. Whether such a civilization as ours would be possible with widely different linguistic handling of time is a large question—in our civilization, our linguistic patterns and the fitting of our behavior to the temporal order are what they are, and they are in accord. We are of course stimulated to use calendars, clocks, and watches, and to try to measure time ever more precisely; this aids science, and science in turn, following these well-worn cultural grooves, gives back to culture an ever-growing store of applications, habits, and values, with which culture again directs science. But what lies outside this spiral? Science is beginning to find that there is something in the Cosmos that is not in accord with the concepts we have formed in mounting the spiral. It is trying to frame a NEW LANGUAGE by which to adjust itself to a wider universe.[22]

It is clear how the emphasis on "saving time" which goes with all the above and is very obvious objectification of time, leads to a high valuation of "speed," which shows itself a great deal in our behavior.

Still another behavioral effect is that the character of monotony and regularity possessed by our image of time as an evenly scaled limitless tape measure persuades us to behave as if that monotony were more true of events than it really is. That is, it helps to routinize us. We tend to select and favor whatever bears out this view, to "play up to" the routine aspects of existence. One phase of this is behavior evincing a false sense of security or an assumption that all will always go smoothly, and a lack in foreseeing and protecting ourselves against hazards. Our technique of harnessing energy does well in routine performance, and it is along routine lines that we chiefly strive to improve it—we are, for example, relatively uninterested in stopping the energy from causing accidents, fires, and explosions, which it is doing constantly and on a wide scale. Such indifference to the unexpectedness of life would be disastrous to a society as small, isolated, and precariously poised as the Hopi society is, or rather once was.

Thus our linguistically determined thought world not only collaborates with our cultural idols and ideals, but engages even our unconscious personal reactions in its patterns and gives them certain typical characters. One such character, as we have seen, is *carelessness*, as in reckless driving or throwing cigarette stubs into waste paper. Another of different sort is *gesturing* when we talk. Very many of the gestures made by English-speaking people at least, and probably by all SAE speakers, serve to illustrate, by a movement in space, not a real spatial reference but one of the nonspatial references that our language handles by metaphors of imaginary space. That is, we are more apt to make a grasping gesture when we speak of grasping an elusive idea than when we speak of grasping a doorknob. The gesture seeks to make a metaphorical and hence somewhat unclear reference more clear. But, if a language refers to nonspatials without implying a spatial analogy, the reference is not made any clearer by gesture. The Hopi gesture very little,

---

22. Here Whorf suggests that language directs our scientific thinking and that scientific thinking in turn reinforces our "well-worn cultural grooves." Although Whorf here is talking about SAE–speaking society and not the Hopi, following this reasoning implies that the Hopi could never have come up with ideas such as payment for hourly labor or either Einsteinian or Newtonian physics. Their language would have prevented them from seeing the world in the way necessary for these concepts.

At the time Whorf wrote, relativity was a fairly new concept (Whorf published this piece in 1941; Einstein published the theory of specific relativity in 1905). Whorf argues that language had not yet adapted to Einstein's discoveries. Relativity creates an interesting problem for Whorf. If language controls thought to the degree that Whorf suggests, then how could Einstein discover concepts for which there were no words (that required a "NEW LANGUAGE")? Whorf attempts to solve this problem by proposing a feedback loop. Language creates science, which, in turn, creates new vocabularies.

"Prorata": *pro rata*, on a proportional basis.

perhaps not at all in the sense we understand as gesture.[23]

It would seem as if kinesthesia, or the sensing of muscular movement, though arising before language, should be made more highly conscious by linguistic use of imaginary space and metaphorical images of motion. Kinesthesia is marked in two facets of European culture: art and sport. European sculpture, an art in which Europe excels, is strongly kinesthetic, conveying great sense of the body's motions; European painting likewise. The dance in our culture expresses delight in motion rather than symbolism or ceremonial, and our music is greatly influenced by our dance forms. Our sports are strongly imbued with this element of the "poetry of motion." Hopi races and games seem to emphasize rather the virtues of endurance and sustained intensity. Hopi dancing is highly symbolic and is performed with great intensity and earnestness, but has not much movement or swing.[24]

Synesthesia, or suggestion by certain sense receptions of characters belonging to another sense, as of light and color by sounds and *vice versa*, should be made more conscious by a linguistic metaphorical system that refers to nonspatial experiences by terms for spatial ones, though undoubtedly it arises from a deeper source. Probably in the first instance metaphor arises from synesthesia and not the reverse; yet metaphor need not become firmly rooted in linguistic pattern, as Hopi shows. Nonspatial experience has one well-organized sense, *hearing*—for smell and taste are but little organized. Nonspatial consciousness is a realm chiefly of thought, feeling, and *sound*. Spatial consciousness is a realm of light, color, sight, and touch, and presents shapes and dimensions. Our metaphorical system, by naming nonspatial experiences after spatial ones, imputes to sounds, smells, tastes, emotions, and thoughts qualities like the colors, luminosities, shapes, angles, textures, and motions of spatial experience. And to some extent the reverse transference occurs; for, after much talking about tones as high, low, sharp, dull, heavy, brilliant, slow, the talker finds it easy to think of some factors in spatial experience as like factors of tone. Thus we speak of "tones" of color, a gray "monotone," a "loud" necktie, a "taste" in dress: all spatial metaphor in reverse. Now European art is distinctive in the way it seeks deliberately to play with synesthesia. Music tries to suggest scenes, color, movement, geometric design; painting and sculpture are often consciously guided by the analogies of music's rhythm; colors are conjoined with feeling for the analogy to concords and discords. The European theater and opera seek a synthesis of many arts. It may be that in this way our metaphorical language that is in some sense a confusion of thought is producing, through art, a result of far-reaching value—a deeper esthetic sense leading toward a more direct apprehension of underlying unity behind the phenomena so variously reported by our sense channels.[25]

HISTORICAL IMPLICATIONS

How does such a network of language, culture, and behavior come about historically? Which was first: the language patterns or the cultural norms? In main they have grown up together,

---

23. Note that Whorf makes several testable assertions in this paragraph (SAE speakers gesture more under certain conditions than under others) but does not provide data to back them.

24. It is frankly difficult to understand why Whorf makes some claims. In this paragraph, he says that European sculpture is "kinesthetic," that it shows motion. However, even the most cursory review of European art reveals that this is true during some eras (such as the Renaissance) but false during others (such as the Gothic). The structure of SAE languages did not change between these eras.

25. Earlier in the essay Whorf pointed out that SAE speakers typically use physical metaphors to talk about nonphysical things: for example, the phrase "I take your point." Here Whorf makes the interesting suggestion that this phenomenon developed from synesthesia. Yet if we accept Whorf's idea, this raises an interesting (and presumably unsolvable) problem. Whorf says that linguistic metaphor perhaps arose from the experience of synesthesia, which, presumably, all humans are capable of having. If this is so, why do certain metaphors become "rooted" in one language but not others?

constantly influencing each other. But in this partnership the nature of the language is the factor that limits free plasticity and rigidifies channels of development in the more autocratic way. This is so because a language is a system, not just an assemblage of norms. Large systematic outlines can change to something really new only very slowly, while many other cultural innovations are made with comparative quickness. Language thus represents the mass mind; it is affected by inventions and innovations, but affected little and slowly, whereas to inventors and innovators it legislates with the decree immediate.[26]

The growth of the SAE language-culture complex dates from ancient times. Much of its metaphorical reference to the nonspatial by the spatial was already fixed in the ancient tongues, and more especially in Latin. It is indeed a marked trait of Latin. If we compare, say Hebrew, we find that, while Hebrew has some allusion to not-space as space, Latin has more. Latin terms for nonspatials, like *educo, religio, principia, comprehendo*, are usually metaphorized physical references: lead out, tying back, etc. This is not true of all languages—it is quite untrue of Hopi. The fact that in Latin the direction of development happened to be from spatial to nonspatial (partly because of secondary stimulation to abstract thinking when the intellectually crude Romans encountered Greek culture) and that later tongues were strongly stimulated to mimic Latin, seems a likely reason for a belief, which still lingers on among linguists, that this is the natural direction of semantic change in all languages, and for the persistent notion in Western learned circles (in strong contrast to Eastern ones) that objective experience is prior to subjective. Philosophies make out a weighty case for the reverse, and certainly the direction of development is sometimes the reverse. Thus the Hopi

word for "heart" can be shown to be a late formation within Hopi from a root meaning think or remember. Or consider what has happened to the word "radio" in such a sentence as "he bought a new radio," as compared to its prior meaning "science of wireless telephony." In the Middle Ages the patterns already formed in Latin began to interweave with the increased mechanical invention, industry, trade, and scholastic and scientific thought. The need for measurement in industry and trade, the stores and bulks of "stuffs" in various containers, the type-bodies in which various goods were handled, standardizing of measure and weight units, invention of clocks and measurement of "time," keeping of records, accounts, chronicles, histories, growth of mathematics and the partnership of mathematics and science, all cooperated to bring our thought and language world into its present form.

In Hopi history, could we read it, we should find a different type of language and a different set of cultural and environmental influences working together. A peaceful agricultural society isolated by geographic features and nomad enemies in a land of scanty rainfall; arid agriculture that could be made successful only by the utmost perseverance (hence the value of persistence and repetition), necessity for collaboration (hence emphasis on the psychology of teamwork and on mental factors in general), corn and rain as primary criteria of value, need of extensive *preparations* and precautions to assure crops in the poor soil and precarious climate, keen realization of dependence upon nature favoring prayer and a religious attitude toward the forces of nature, especially prayer and religion directed toward the ever-needed blessing, rain—these things interacted with Hopi linguistic patterns to mold them, to be molded again by them, and so little by little to shape the Hopi world outlook.[27]

---

26. Here Whorf outlines a view of language that parallels his Boasian colleagues' view of culture. He refuses to speculate on whether language or culture came first, saying only that they form a network of factors that developed together and influenced each other. One can also see Whorf's linguistic determinism in the conclusion of this paragraph, where he says that although language changes slowly and is little affected by inventions, it has an immediate power over the inventors.

27. Here Whorf summarizes how language and culture developed together and influenced each other to produce Western society as we know it, and how a different language and different set of cultural and environmental influences produced a very different type of culture among the Hopi. This is a classic statement of the

To sum up the matter, our first question asked in the beginning, p. [196] is answered thus: Concepts of "time" and "matter" are not given in substantially the same form by experience to all men but depend upon the nature of the language or languages through the use of which they have been developed. They do not depend so much upon *any one system* (e.g., tense, or nouns) within the grammar as upon the ways of analyzing and reporting experience which have become fixed in the language as integrated "fashions of speaking" and which cut across the typical grammatical classifications, so that such a "fashion" may include lexical, morphological, syntactic, and otherwise systemically diverse means coordinated in a certain frame of consistency. Our own "time" differs markedly from Hopi "duration." It is conceived as like a space of strictly limited dimensions, or sometimes as like a motion upon such a space, and employed as an intellectual tool accordingly. Hopi "duration" seems to be inconceivable in terms of space or motion, being the mode in which life differs from form, and consciousness *in toto* from the spatial elements of consciousness. Certain ideas born of our own time-concept, such as that of absolute simultaneity, would be either very difficult to express or impossible and devoid of meaning under the Hopi conception, and would be replaced by operational concepts. Our "matter" is the physical subtype of "substance" or "stuff," which is conceived as the formless extensional item that must be joined with form before there can be real existence. In Hopi there seems to be nothing corresponding to it; there are no formless extensional items; existence may or may not have form, but what it also has, with or without form, is intensity and duration, these being nonextensional and at bottom the same.

But what about our concept of "space," which was also included in our first question?

There is no such striking difference between Hopi and SAE about space as about time, and probably the apprehension of space is given in substantially the same form by experience irrespective of language. The experiments of the **Gestalt psychologists** with visual perception appear to establish this as a fact. But the *concept of space* will vary somewhat with language, because, as an intellectual tool,[k] it is so closely linked with the concomitant employment of other intellectual tools, of the order of "time" and "matter," which are linguistically conditioned. We see things with our eyes in the same space forms as the Hopi, but our idea of space has also the property of acting as a surrogate of nonspatial relationships like time, intensity, tendency, and as a void to be filled with imagined formless items, one of which may even be called "space." Space as sensed by the Hopi would not be connected mentally with such surrogates, but would be comparatively "pure," unmixed with extraneous notions.[28]

As for our second question, p. [197]: There are connections but not correlations or diagnostic correspondences between cultural norms and linguistic patterns. Although it would be impossible to infer the existence of Crier Chiefs from the lack of tenses in Hopi, or vice versa, there is a relation between a language and the rest of the culture of the society which uses it. There are cases where the "fashions of speaking" are closely integrated with the whole general culture, whether or not this be universally true, and there are connections within this integration, between the kind of linguistic analyses employed and various behavioral reactions and also the shapes taken by various cultural developments. Thus the importance of Crier Chiefs does have a connection, not with tenselessness itself, but with a system of thought in which categories different from our tenses are natural. These connections are to be found not so much by focusing attention on the typical

---

Boasian historical view of culture. However, it fails to consider the enormous variability of the environments and cultures of native English speakers.

28. **"Gestalt psychology"**: A school of psychology developed in Germany in the 1920s. A "gestalt" is an organized whole. Gestalt psychologists developed six universal principles of visual perception. For example, the principle of proximity states that objects placed close together will be perceived as belonging together. Other gestalt principles are similarity, common fate, closure, good continuation, and good form.

rubrics of linguistic, ethnographic, or sociological description as by examining the culture and the language (always and only when the two have been together historically for a considerable time) as a whole in which concatenations that run across these departmental lines may be expected to exist, and, if they do exist, eventually to be discoverable by study.[29]

AUTHOR'S NOTES

a. We have plenty of evidence that this is not the case. Consider only the Hopi and the Ute, with languages that on the overt morphological and lexical level are as similar as, say, English and German. The idea of "correlation" between language and culture, in the generally accepted sense of correlation, is certainly a mistaken one.

b. As we say, *"ten at the same time,"* showing that in our language and thought we restate the fact of group perception in terms of a concept "time," the large linguistic component of which will appear in the course of this paper.

c. It is no exception to this rule of lacking a plural that a mass noun may sometimes coincide in lexeme with an individual noun that of course has a plural; e.g., "stone" (no pl.) with "a stone" (pl. "stones"). The plural form denoting varieties, e.g., "wines" is of course a different sort of thing from the true plural; it is a curious outgrowth from the SAE mass nouns, leading to still another sort of imaginary aggregates, which will have to be omitted from this paper.

d. Hopi has two words for water quantities; *ke yi* and *pa he*. The difference is something like that between "stone" and "rock" in English, pa he implying greater size and "wildness"; flowing water, whether or not outdoors or in nature; is *pa he*; so is "moisture." But, unlike "stone" and "rock," the difference is essential, not pertaining to a connotative margin, and the two can hardly ever be interchanged.

e. To be sure, there are a few minor differences from other nouns, in English for instance in the use of the articles.

f. "Year" and certain combinations of "year" with name of season, rarely season names alone, can occur with a locative morpheme "at," but this is exceptional. It appears like historical detritus of an earlier different patterning, or the effect of English analogy, or both.

g. The expective and reportive assertions contrast according to the "paramount relation." The expective expresses anticipation existing *earlier* than objective fact, and coinciding with objective fact *later* than the status quo of the speaker, this status quo, including all

---

29. Whorf concludes by saying that he has demonstrated connections but not correlations between language and culture. This and other passages in the essay make it extremely difficult to determine exactly what Whorf intends. For example, Whorf has said that some of our own ideas may be "devoid of meaning" to the Hopi and that this results from the differences in the structure of SAE and Hopi. He has argued that factory fires happen because people use the term "empty" to describe barrels filled with flammable gas. However, here (and in endnotes, particularly endnote a) he seems to deny the correlation between language and culture.

Most anthropologists have interpreted Whorf's work as supporting *linguistic determinism*, the notion that language has a deep influence on thought. In the 1950s, Sapir's student Harry Hoijer (1904–1976) coined the term "Sapir-Whorf hypothesis" to indicate this. Scholars of the Sapir-Whorf hypothesis debate whether there is strong or weak linguistic determinism. This has led to a substantial but inconclusive body of scholarship. Important work in this area includes Brent Berlin and Paul Kay's work (1969) on the universality of color terms, John Lucy's work (2004) on Yucatec Maya, and Michael Silverstein's work (1993) on metalinguistic awareness. Many others reject any form of linguistic determinism, such as the linguist John McWhorter (2014), who published a polemical attack on the idea that there is any connection between language and culture at all.

It is also worth noting that Whorf's knowledge of Hopi has been questioned. In 1983, Ekkehart Malotki argued that Whorf simply got it wrong and that claims that Hopi do not use expressions such as "ten days" are incorrect. Malotki argued that the Hopi conception of time was not radically different from our own (1983: 529–530).

In the end, the degree to which Sapir and Whorf believed that language determined thought and culture remains unclear. Both died young: Sapir at 55 and Whorf at 44, so neither contributed to the debates about the role of language in ethnography of the 1950s and 1960s. They also died before the work of Noam Chomsky (b. 1928) and others revolutionized linguistics. Chomsky focused on the universal characteristics of language. He famously said "A rational Martian scientist would probably find the variation [among human languages] rather superficial . . . [and conclude] that there is one human language with minor variants" (1995: 13). Almost all current-day linguists are more focused on the commonalities among languages rather than the differences. However, the idea that there is a relationship between language, thought, and behavior retains a strong presence in some branches of popular culture and anthropological thinking.

the subsummation of the past therein, being expressed by the reportive. Our notion "future" seems to represent at once the earlier (anticipation) and the later (afterwards, what will be), as Hopi shows. This paradox may hint of how elusive the mystery of real time is, and how artificially it is expressed by a linear relation of past-present-future.

h. The Hopi verbs of preparing naturally do not correspond neatly to our "prepare"; so that *na'twani* could also be rendered "the practiced-upon," "the tried-for," and otherwise.

i. See, e.g., Ernest Beaglehole, *Notes on Hopi Economic Life* (Yale University Publications in Anthropology, no. 15, 1937), especially the reference to the announcement of a rabbit hunt, and on p. 30, description of the activities in connection with the cleaning of Toreva Spring—announcing, various preparing activities, and finally, preparing the continuity of the good results already obtained and the continued flow of the spring.

j. This notion of storing up power, which seems implied by much Hopi behavior, has an analog in physics: acceleration. It might be said that the linguistic background of Hopi thought equips it to recognize naturally that force manifests not as motion or velocity, but as cumulation or acceleration. Our linguistic background tends to hinder in us this same recognition, for having legitimately conceived force to be that which produces change, we then think of change by our linguistic metaphorical analog, motion, instead of by a pure motionless changingness concept, i.e., accumulation or acceleration. Hence it comes to our naive feeling as a shock to find from physical experiments that it is not possible to define force by motion, that motion and speed, as also "being at rest," are wholly relative, and that force can be measured only by acceleration.

k. Here belong "Newtonian" and "Euclidean" space, etc.

Functionalism

In the first thirty years of the twentieth century, Franz Boas (1858–1942) and his students were the dominant anthropological thinkers in America, and the evolutionary model was temporarily abandoned. In Britain, on the other hand, the reaction to cultural evolution did not occur with the same force. With no single figure comparable to Boas, British anthropologists were divided into two camps: the diffusionists and the functionalists. It is the latter group that concerns us here.

In the 1880s and 1890s, a new group of anthropological thinkers, led by Alfred Cort Haddon (1855–1940), emerged in Britain. Haddon was trained in anatomy and zoology but was deeply influenced by E. B. Tylor (1832–1917), James George Frazer (1854–1941), and Herbert Spencer (1820–1903). In the 1880s, he held a position at the Royal College of Science in Dublin. In 1888, dissatisfied with life in Dublin, Haddon journeyed to the Torres Straits, between New Guinea and Australia, in the hope that an important expedition might get him a better job (Stocking 1992: 21).

Haddon went primarily to study coral reefs, but he brought several works of anthropology along, including *Notes and Queries on Anthropology for the Use of Travelers and Residents in Uncivilized Lands*. This was a book-length questionnaire designed to help untrained observers collect information of use to anthropologists. *Notes and Queries* was a collaborative work by many anthropologists, but E. B. Tylor was the primary author of the nineteenth-century editions. Using *Notes and Queries*, Haddon collected information from the islanders, and by the time he returned, he was committed to anthropology.

Back in England, Haddon moved to Cambridge University, where he became the first lecturer in physical anthropology. He published some of the data he had collected in the Torres Straits but soon became convinced that another expedition was essential. He hoped to make a comprehensive study of native body types, psychology, language, and material culture. To this end, he enlisted an interdisciplinary team of scholars, including the physician Charles Seligman (1873–1940), the experimental psychologist W. H. R. (William Halse Rivers) Rivers (1864–1922), and his students William McDougall (1871–1938) and Charles Samuel Myers (1873–1946). Other team members included the linguist Sidney Herbert Ray (1858–1939) and Anthony Wilkin (1877?–1901), a promising student who served as a photographer and studied land tenure issues (and who died of dysentery). The team arrived in the Torres Straits in April 1898. Group members stayed for varying lengths of time, but all left within six months.

Despite its relative brevity, the Torres Straits expedition was a defining moment in the development of both anthropology and psychology in Britain. Most expedition members went on to hold important professorships in England and the United States. Haddon and Rivers were at Cambridge, Seligman at the London School of Economics. Myers worked first as an assistant to Rivers at Cambridge but then moved to London, founding the Institute of Industrial Psychology in 1921. McDougall taught at Oxford, then at Harvard and Duke.

When Haddon and his colleagues returned to England, they published extensive accounts of their research and began to attract students. Thus they became critical in training the next generation of British Commonwealth anthropologists. These included Bronislaw Malinowski (1884–1942), A. R. (Alfred Reginald) Radcliffe-Brown (1881–1955), Gregory Bateson (1904–1980), Winifred Hoernle (1885–1960), and numerous others. Relying on their Torres Straits experiences, they made fieldwork a critical component of British anthropology. Although Haddon, Rivers, and the others had worked by summoning people and speaking with them through translators, they encouraged their students to learn local languages and live in far closer proximity to those they studied.

Haddon and his colleagues were profoundly affected by Tylor and the evolutionism of the nineteenth century. However, their anthropology was primarily descriptive, and there was little attempt at theoretical analysis. Their students were more influenced by Herbert Spencer and Émile Durkheim, and their anthropology was more strongly theoretical. This first generation of students attempted to carry out the research agenda implied by Spencer's organic analogy and Durkheim's *Rules of Sociological Method*. If, as Spencer claimed, society was like an organism, anthropologists should be able to describe the different social "organs" that composed a society. If, as Durkheim claimed, a positivist science of society was possible, then anthropologists should be able to find social facts and discover the laws that determine how they operate. The functionalists set out to accomplish just these things.

Functionalism in anthropology is generally divided into two schools of thought: *psychological functionalism* and *structural functionalism*. Each of these is associated with a key personality. Psychological functionalism is linked to Bronislaw Malinowski. For the psychological functionalists, cultural institutions function to meet the basic physical and psychological needs of members of a society. Like Boas, Malinowski's method was based on extensive in-depth fieldwork during which he gathered evidence to support his theoretical position. Structural functionalism is associated with A. R. Radcliffe-Brown. Structural functionalists, who drew heavily on Durkheim's work, sought to understand how cultural institutions operated to maintain the equilibrium and cohesion of a society.

Though Malinowski was interested in religion and folklore and had read Frazer's *The Golden Bough* as a young man, he was trained in the physical sciences and received a PhD in physics and mathematics in 1908. The following year, he did advanced studies in Leipzig, where he, like Durkheim, was deeply influenced by Wilhelm Wundt (1832–1920) and took classes with Karl Bücher (1847–1930), an economist who specialized in gift-and-exchange economies. His time with Wundt and Bücher led him to an interest in folk psychology and, from there, to anthropology (Gross 1986). In 1910, Malinowski traveled to England and enrolled in the London School of Economics (LSE), where he studied anthropology under Charles Seligman but also developed close relationships with other central figures in British anthropology, particularly Sir James Frazer.

At the outbreak of World War I, Malinowski was traveling in the British-controlled South Pacific. He had intended that the trip, undertaken for ethnographic research, be relatively brief. However, Malinowski was from Krakow, located in a part of Polish Galicia that had been controlled by Austria since 1849. Consequently, Malinowski was considered an enemy national, and the British forbade his return to Europe. British authorities, however, did permit Malinowski relative liberty in Australia and nearby areas under British control. Between 1915 and 1918, he made two extensive trips to the Trobriand Islands, with a lengthy break in Melbourne between them.

Perhaps because he was unable to return to Europe, Malinowski was the first of the students of the Torres Straits scholars to practice intensive fieldwork. He learned the native language and made extensive records of the daily activities of members of the communities in which he lived. Although he was more of an interviewer and an observer than a participant in local culture, his work set a high standard for those who came after, and he became closely associated with participant-observation.

After the war, Malinowski returned to England and accepted a teaching position at the LSE, where he spent most of his career. He published a series of books on his work in the Trobriands, including *Argonauts of the Western Pacific* (1922), *Crime and Custom in Savage Society* (1926), *Coral Gardens and Their Magic* (1935), and many others. He also trained many of the finest English anthropologists of his era. These included E. E. Evans-Pritchard (1902–1973), Isaac Schapera (1905–2003), Audrey Richards (1899–1984), Raymond Firth (1901–2002), Meyer Fortes (1906–1983), Lucy Mair (1901–1986), and S. F. Nadel (1903–1956).

At the time functionalism emerged, anthropology did not have a particularly good reputation. Traveling to distant locations to study natives was exciting and exotic, but also uncouth. It probably didn't help that Seligman as well as many of his students (and those of Haddon and Rivers) were Jewish. As a result, in the early years of the century, anthropology languished at Oxford and Cambridge, the most prestigious universities in England. Cambridge anthropologists Haddon and Rivers were considered ungentlemanly by other members of the faculty (Leach 1984: 5). However, anthropology prospered at the LSE, an institution founded by members of the socialist Fabian Society. While Malinowski built the anthropology program at the LSE, at Cambridge, his books *Sex and Repression in Savage Society*, first published in 1927, and *The Sexual Life of Savages in Northwestern Melanesia* (1929b) were kept in a special section of the library and could only be read with the permission of a senior college official (Leach 1984: 8).

Malinowski was concerned with how individuals pursued their own ends within the constraints of their culture. He believed that culture existed to satisfy seven basic human needs: nutrition, reproduction, bodily comforts, safety, relaxation, movement, and growth (1939). He wished to demonstrate how various cultural beliefs and practices contributed to the smooth functioning of society while providing individual biological or psychological benefits. For example, in his 1925 essay "Magic, Science, and Religion," Malinowski discussed the nature of thought in primitive societies and demonstrated the psychological functions served by supernatural beliefs such as magic. By basing his theory on physiological and biopsychological needs, Malinowski gave his theory of culture a universal character.

Malinowski was famous for his ethnographic reporting, and he was skilled at weaving theoretical ideas into his ethnographic discussions. His concept of psychological functionalism is represented here in essay 14, "The Essentials of the Kula," which is the third chapter of his groundbreaking ethnography *Argonauts of the Western Pacific* (1922). In this chapter, Malinowski offers a description of the trade in *kula* valuables that has become a classic of anthropology. The essay showcases Malinowski's skill as an ethnographer but also illustrates many of his fundamental ideas.

A. R. Radcliffe-Brown studied anthropology at Cambridge under Haddon and Rivers. Radcliffe-Brown had a peripatetic career, rarely staying at any one location for more than a few years. He did fieldwork in the Andaman Islands between 1906 and 1908 and again in Australia between 1910 and 1912. However, he is not remembered as a particularly talented fieldworker. After two years in England, his academic and administrative career took him to Australia, Tonga, South Africa, Australia again, the United States (where he was chair of anthropology at the University of Chicago), England again, Brazil, Egypt, and South Africa again. In 1954, ill-health caused his return to England, and he died there the following year. Throughout his career, Radcliffe-Brown played a central role in establishing university departments of anthropology. He also developed a very dedicated group of students. Some of Radcliffe-Brown's best-known students were Max Gluckman (1911–1975), Fred Eggan (1906–1991), Sol Tax (1907–1995), and Isaac Schapera.

Radcliffe-Brown was interested in deriving social laws governing behavior from the comparative study of different cultures rather than in cultural description based on intensive fieldwork in one culture. He corresponded with both Durkheim and Marcel Mauss, and Durkheim's influence is evident in Radcliffe-Brown's attempts to illustrate how cultural systems function to maintain a society's equilibrium.

Although he used the term *culture* in his early work, Radcliffe-Brown rejected the concept later in his career. He believed that culture was an abstract concept and that, because the values and norms of a society could not be observed, a science of culture was impossible. Radcliffe-Brown preferred to limit his research to social structures—to the principles that organize persons in a society (such as kinship) and to the actual roles and relationships that can be observed firsthand. To illustrate this perspective, Radcliffe-Brown used Spencer's organic analogy. In 1935, he wrote,

An animal organism is an agglomeration of cells and interstitial fluids arranged in relation to one another not as an aggregate but as an integrated living whole. The system of relations by which these units are related is the organic structure. As the terms are here used the organism is not itself the structure; it is a collection of units (cells or molecules) arranged in a structure, i.e., in a set of relations; the organism has a structure. The structure is thus to be defined as a set of relations between entities. Over a period its constituent cells do not remain the same. But the structural arrangement of the constituent units does remain similar. (Radcliffe-Brown 1965b [1935]: 178–179)

Applying this analogy to anthropological data, Radcliffe-Brown argued that it is more useful to study kinship systems than it is to study the individuals in a society because, although people die, the kin structure remains the same from generation to generation. In Radcliffe-Brown's view, Malinowski's focus on individuals led nowhere. To use a cliché, Radcliffe-Brown thought that Malinowski did not see the forest for the trees.

Radcliffe-Brown referred to his approach as "social anthropology" and insisted that it was distinct from other approaches, particularly from the "cultural anthropology" of the Boasian scholars. In 1946, his followers elected him "president for life" of the newly founded Association of Social Anthropologists.

Radcliffe-Brown's work is represented by his essay "On Joking Relationships" (1940) (essay 15). He argues that structural relations between people in certain positions in kinship systems lead to conflicts of interest. Such conflict could threaten the stability of society. However, this problem is solved through ritualized joking or avoidance between people in such positions. Thus, when conflict threatens stability, society develops social institutions to mediate oppositions and preserve social solidarity.

We stated in the first section of this book that scientific theories are a product of the social and cultural contexts in which they are conceived. Functionalism was conceived and practiced largely by European anthropologists in territories that were European colonial possessions, such as the Trobriand Islands, Australia, India, and East Africa. Given this context, it is surely no accident that these thinkers studied the function of cultural institutions in relation to the maintenance of social order and the smooth working of society. This focus was precisely the aspect of non-Western societies in which colonial governments were most interested.

The nature of the relationship between anthropology and colonialism today is highly controversial. It is certain that British anthropologists often thought about their usefulness to colonial administrations. From the turn of the twentieth century until World War II, most anthropologists wanted to provide their expertise to governments. A. C. Haddon, for example, campaigned persistently (but unsuccessfully) for an "imperial bureau of ethnology," designed to help the state deal with "conflicts derived from racial and cultural variation that arose both in the colonies and at home" (Kuklick 1991: 44). Radcliffe-Brown held positions in Cape Town and Sydney in which he was responsible for training officials to govern indigenous peoples. Both Radcliffe-Brown and Malinowski often pointed out ways in which anthropology could be useful to the colonial enterprise.

Governments, however, were not particularly interested in either funding or listening to anthropologists. Most of the money that supported the functionalists came from the Rockefeller Foundation and other charitable organizations. The British government provided almost nothing (Goody 1995). Additionally, governments were deeply suspicious of anthropologists. Colonial officials were most often political conservatives, whereas anthropologists tended to be liberals. Officials generally believed that anthropologists were too close to the natives and were more likely to see their efforts as undermining than supporting colonialism.

One other observation about functionalism is warranted: The functionalists typically were only marginally interested in history. Whereas American anthropology at this time was based largely on reconstructing cultures from interviews with informants, British anthropologists were directly observing native societies in action (or thought they were). Under these circumstances, they believed that issues of the functioning of the current system were of primary importance. They asserted that historical reconstruction did little to clarify the current functioning of social institutions—indeed, they were deeply skeptical of historical reconstructions. Many functionalists held that since most of the societies they studied lacked writing, such reconstructions could be little more than fiction. As a result, they examined societies as if they were timeless, and thus they were not concerned with social change.

Functionalism lost its place of theoretical prominence after World War II. Because of the massive social, cultural, and political transformations that resulted from the war, interest in how societies maintained social stability declined, to be replaced by concern with cultural change. Despite this, the work of Malinowski, Radcliffe-Brown, and their students Fortes, Gluckman, Schapera, Richards, and others continues to be widely read and to provide inspiration for modern anthropologists. Although few people would refer to themselves as structural-functionalist anthropologists today, and virtually no explicitly functionalist theoretical papers are being published, key functionalist concepts are still implicit in a great deal of anthropology. Functionalism continues to be a powerful idea, and many anthropologists are probably more functionalist than they generally acknowledge.

SUGGESTED READINGS

Elkin, A. P. 1956. "A. R. Radcliffe-Brown." *Oceania* 26(4): 239–251.

A highly critical but fascinating obituary of Radcliffe-Brown.

Goody, Jack. 1995. *The Expansive Moment: The Rise of Social Anthropology in Britain and Africa, 1918–1970.* Cambridge: Cambridge University Press.

An account of Malinowski, Radcliffe-Brown, and their students in the political and social context of the first two thirds of the twentieth century.

Malinowski, Bronislaw. 1948. *Magic, Science, and Religion, and Other Essays.* Boston: Beacon Press.

A collection of some of Malinowski's best-known essays.

Radcliffe-Brown, A. R. 1952. *Structure and Function in Primitive Society: Essays and Addresses.* Glencoe, IL: Free Press.

Volume from which our essay 15 is taken. A collection of some of Radcliffe-Brown's best-known essays.

Stocking, George W., ed. 1984. *Functionalism Historicized: Essays on British Social Anthropology.* Madison: University of Wisconsin Press.

A collection of essential academic essays about functionalism and the functionalists.

Stewart, Zachary, and Kelly Thomson. 2012. *Savage Memory.* Jamaica Plain, MA: Sly Productions.

A documentary film about Malinowski, his work, and his family, made by his great-grandson.

Young, Michael W. 2004. *Malinowski: Odyssey of an Anthropologist, 1884–1920.* New Haven, CT: Yale University Press.

A comprehensive biography of Malinowski.

14. The Essentials of the Kula

Bronislaw Malinowski (1884–1942)

I

HAVING THUS described the scene, and the actors, let us now proceed to the performance. The Kula is a form of exchange, of extensive, intertribal character; it is carried on by communities inhabiting a wide ring of islands, which form a closed circuit. This circuit can be seen on Map V, where it is represented by the lines joining a number of islands to the North and East of the East end of New Guinea. Along this route, articles of two kinds, and these two kinds only, are constantly travelling in opposite directions. In the direction of the hands of a clock, moves constantly one of these kinds—long necklaces of red shell, called *soulava* (Plates XVIII and XIX). In the opposite direction moves the other kind—bracelets of white shell called *mwali* (Plates XVI and XVII). Each of these articles, as it travels in its own direction on the closed circuit, meets on its way articles of the other class, and

is constantly being exchanged for them. Every movement of the Kula articles, every detail of the transactions is fixed and regulated by a set of traditional rules and conventions, and some acts of the Kula are accompanied by an elaborate magical ritual and public ceremonies.[1]

On every island and in every village, a more or less limited number of men take part in the Kula—that is to say, receive the goods, hold them for a short time, and then pass them on. Therefore every man who is in the Kula, periodically though not regularly, receives one or several *mwali* (arm-shells), or a *soulava* (necklace of red shell discs), and then has to hand it on to one of his partners, from whom he receives the opposite commodity in exchange. Thus no man ever keeps any of the articles for any length of time in his possession. One transaction action does not finish the Kula relationship, the rule being "once in the Kula, always in the Kula," and a partnership between two men is a permanent and lifelong affair. Again, any given *mwali*

From *Argonauts of the Western Pacific* (1922)

1. "The Essentials of the Kula" is the third chapter of Malinowski's 1922 monograph *Argonauts of the Western Pacific*. In the introduction and first two chapters of the work, Malinowski discusses his research methods, the geography of the region, and the different "races" of people who inhabit it, as well as their notions of magic, sorcery, and power. Here he begins his discussion of the *kula*, perhaps the subject for which this book is best remembered.

Malinowski included sixty-five plates consisting of one or two photographs each in the original publication of *Argonauts of the Western Pacific* and he refers to these throughout the book. We do not include the plates in this essay however, we will briefly describe them when they are mentioned. Plates 16, consists of a single picture of bracelets. It is titled "Armshells" and captioned "This shows several varieties, differing in size and finish." Plate 17 consists of a single picture. It is titled "Two Men Wearing Armshells." The caption reads "This illustrates the manner in which the armshells are usually adorned with beads, pendants and ribbons of dried pandanus. I do not remember having seen more than once or twice men wearing armshells, and then they were in full dancing array." Plate 18 shows two necklaces. It is titled "Two Necklaces, Made of Red Spondylus Discs." Its caption reads: "On the left the *soulava* or *bagi,* the real Kula article. On the right, the *katudababile* (or *samkupa*, as it is called among the Southern Massim), made of bigger disks, manufactured in the villages of Sinaketa and Vakuta (Trobriand Islands). This latter article does not play any important part in the Kula." Plate 19 shows a single photo of a group. It is titled "Two Women Adorned With Necklaces" and captioned "This shows the manner in which a *soulava* is worn when used as a decoration."

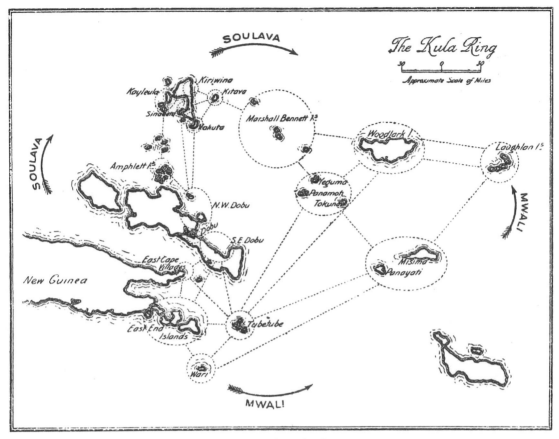

Map V   The Kula Ring

or *soulava* may always be found travelling and changing hands, and there is no question of its ever settling down, so that the principle "once in a Kula, always in a Kula" applies also to the valuables themselves.[2]

The ceremonial exchange of the two articles is the main, the fundamental aspect of the Kula. But associated with it, and done under its cover, we find a great number of secondary activities and features. Thus, side by side with the ritual exchange of arm-shells and necklaces, the natives carry on ordinary trade, bartering from one island to another a great number of utilities, often unprocurable in the district to which they are imported, and indispensable there. Further, there are other activities, preliminary to the Kula, or associated with it, such as the building of sea-going canoes for the expeditions, certain big forms of mortuary ceremonies, and preparatory taboos.[3]

---

2. Note that from the beginning of the essay, Malinowski builds the case for the social identification of people and objects. Malinowski's work on the kula was a key source for Marcel Mauss, who developed ideas about the social nature of gift exchange (see essay 6).

3. Malinowski's theoretical position is known as *psychological functionalism*. In a 1939 article "The Group and The Individual in Functionalist Analysis," Malinowski argued that there were seven universal biological and psychological needs. These individual needs were converted to cultural behavior through the use of symbols, which also served to mold individual behavior to group standards. The task of the psychological functionalist was to describe these symbols and demonstrate how social institutions operated to fill biological and psychological needs. However, it is not clear to what extent Malinowski had worked out these ideas when he wrote *Argonauts* and his other book-length accounts of the Trobriand Islands, most of which were published

The Kula is thus an extremely big and complex institution, both in its geographical extent, and in the manifoldness of its component pursuits. It welds together a considerable number of tribes, and it embraces a vast complex of activities, interconnected, and playing into one another, so as to form one organic whole.[4]

Yet it must be remembered that what appears to us an extensive, complicated, and yet well ordered institution is the outcome of ever so many doings and pursuits, carried on by savages, who have no laws or aims or characters definitely laid down. They have no knowledge of the *total outline* of any of their social structure. They know their own motives, know the purpose of individual actions and the rules which apply to them, but how, out of these, the whole collective institution shapes, this is beyond their mental range. Not even the most intelligent native has any clear idea of the Kula as a big, organized social construction, still less of its sociological function and implications. If you were to ask him what the Kula is, he would answer by giving a few details, most likely by giving his personal experiences and subjective views on the Kula, but nothing approaching the definition just given here. Not even a partial coherent account could be obtained. For the integral picture does not exist in his mind; he is in it, and cannot see the whole from the outside.[5]

The integration of all the details observed, the achievement of a sociological synthesis of all the various, relevant symptoms, is the task of the Ethnographer. First of all, he has to find out that certain activities, which at first sight might appear incoherent and not correlated, have a meaning. He then has to find out what is constant and relevant in these activities and what accidental and inessential, that is, to find out the laws and rules of all the transactions. Again, the Ethnographer has to *construct* the picture of the big institution, very much as the physicist constructs his theory from the experimental data, which always have been within reach of everybody but which needed a consistent interpretation. I have touched on this point of method in the Introduction (Divisions V and VI), but I have repeated it here, as it is necessary to grasp it clearly in order not to lose the right perspective of conditions as they really exist among the natives.

---

in the 1920s. In these, he seems far more interested in portraying the experiences of the Trobrianders in ways that make them comprehensible to audiences in Europe and America than in examining how institutions such as the kula fill specific needs. On the one hand, reading this work today, it is evident that the kula does serve at least some of the seven bio-psychological functions Malinowski enumerated in 1939. For example, it increases safety by setting up networks of trading partners and allies and may allow for movement and growth. On the other hand, Malinowski does not mention the needs anywhere in *Argonauts,* or draw attention to the specific ways institutions serve these needs.

4. Malinowski takes pains throughout this chapter to emphasize the size and complexity of the kula. His understanding of it was conditioned by Herbert Spencer's idea of society as an organism, a complex system of interrelated parts (see essay 1).

5. Notice Malinowski's characterization of the Trobriand Islanders in this and the next paragraph as aware of their individual actions and motives but unable to see their entire system. It takes an outsider, the ethnographer according to Malinowski, to conduct an objective analysis of a society and its institutions (a point echoed by the interpretive anthropologist Victor Turner [1920–1983] in essay 25). Malinowski is not denigrating the intelligence of the Trobriand Islanders, for he believed the same principle to be true for people in Western societies. The point that a person cannot objectively analyze the system in which they participate is a central tenet of psychoanalytic thought. A selection of the work of Sigmund Freud (1856–1939) was made available to Malinowski in the field by his professor Charles G. Seligman (1873–1940), and Malinowski's opinion on the issue may have been influenced by Freud's writings. Seligman, a medical doctor, was a member of the Torres Straits expedition and wrote the groundbreaking *The Melanesians of British New Guinea* (1910), which set the stage for Malinowski's research. Seligman found Freud useful in his work with victims of "shell shock" during World War I. On the other hand, Malinowski became a key critic of Freud and used data from the Trobriands to attack Freud's oedipal theory in *Sex and Repression in Savage Society* (1955 [1927]).

I I

In giving the above abstract and concise definition, I had to reverse the order of research, as this is done in ethnographic fieldwork, where the most generalised inferences are obtained as the result of long inquiries and laborious inductions. The general definition of the Kula will serve as a sort of plan or diagram in our further concrete and detailed descriptions. And this is the more necessary as the Kula is concerned with the exchange of wealth and utilities, and therefore it is an economic institution, and there is no other aspect of primitive life where our knowledge is more scanty and our understanding more superficial than in Economics. Hence misconception is rampant, and it is necessary to clear the ground when approaching any economic subject.

Thus in the Introduction we called the Kula a "form of trade," and we ranged it alongside other systems of barter. This is quite correct, if we give the word "trade" a sufficiently wide interpretation, and mean by it any exchange of goods. But the word "trade" is used in current Ethnography and economic literature with so many different implications that a whole lot of misleading, preconceived ideas have to be brushed aside in order to grasp the facts correctly. Thus the *a priori* current notion of primitive trade would be that of an exchange of indispensable or useful articles, done without much ceremony or regulation, under stress of dearth or need, in spasmodic, irregular intervals—and this done either by direct barter, everyone looking out sharply not to be done out of his due, or, if the savages were too timid and distrustful to face one another, by some customary arrangement, securing by means of heavy penalties compliance in the obligations incurred or imposed.[a] Waiving for the present the question how far this conception is valid or not in general—in my opinion it is quite misleading—we have to realise clearly that the Kula contradicts in almost every point the above definition of "savage trade." It shows us primitive exchange in an entirely different light.[6]

The Kula is not a surreptitious and precarious form of exchange. It is, quite on the contrary, rooted in myth, backed by traditional law, and surrounded with magical rites. All its main transactions are public and ceremonial, and carried out according to definite rules. It is not done on the spur of the moment, but happens periodically, at dates settled in advance, and it is carried on along definite trade routes, which must lead to fixed trysting places. Sociologically, though transacted between tribes differing in language, culture, and probably even in race, it is based on a fixed and permanent status, on a partnership which binds into couples some thousands of individuals. This partnership is a lifelong relationship, it implies various mutual duties and privileges, and constitutes a type of inter-tribal relationship on an enormous scale. As to the economic mechanism of the transactions, this is based on a specific form of credit, which implies a high degree of mutual trust and commercial honour—and

6. Malinowski is considered a founder of economic anthropology. One of his goals in *Argonauts* is to dispel what he considers misunderstandings of economics in primitive society. In his first footnote, Malinowski references the German economist Karl Bücher (1847–1930). Bücher's *Industrial Evolution*, first published in Germany in 1893, was enormously influential in Europe, and by 1901 had been translated into English, French, and Russian. Bücher developed a three-stage view of economic evolution, proposing that households led to towns, which led to national economies. The factor that differentiated these stages was the role of exchange. Bücher believed that contemporary primitive societies represented a pre-economic stage of society (Firth 1964: 210). He writes that "primitive man lives only for the present . . . shuns all regular work . . . has not the conception of duty, not of a vocation as a moral function in life" (1968 [1901]: 82). These views influenced the work of scholars such as Max Weber (see essay 7). Malinowski—though sympathetic to Bücher's attempts to understand primitive economy—wrote *Argonauts of the Western Pacific* as a reaction to this view of primitive humans, using the kula as a counterexample. Later in *Argonauts* he wrote, "Now I hope that whatever the meaning of the Kula might be for Ethnology, for the general science of culture, the meaning of the Kula will consist in being instrumental to dispel such crude, rationalistic conceptions of primitive mankind, and to induce both the speculator and the observer to deepen the analysis of economic facts" (1922: 516).

this refers also to the subsidiary, minor trade, which accompanies the Kula proper. Finally, the Kula is not done under stress of any need, since its main aim is to exchange articles which are of no practical use.

From the concise definition of Kula given at the beginning of this chapter, we see that in its final essence, divested of all trappings and accessories, it is a very simple affair, which at first sight might even appear tame and unromantic. After all it only consists of an exchange, interminably repeated, of two articles intended for ornamentation, but not even used for that to any extent. Yet this simple action—this passing from hand to hand of two meaningless and quite useless objects—has somehow succeeded in becoming the foundation of a big inter-tribal institution, in being associated with ever so many other activities. Myth, magic and tradition have built up around it definite ritual and ceremonial forms, have given it a halo of romance and value in the minds of the natives, have indeed created a passion in their hearts for this simple exchange.[7]

The definition of the Kula must now be amplified, and we must describe one after the other its fundamental characteristics and main rules, so that it may be clearly grasped by what mechanism the mere exchange of two articles results in an institution so vast, complex, and deeply rooted.

III

First of all, a few words must be said about the two principal objects of exchange, the arm-shells (*mwali*) and the necklaces (*soulava*). The arm-shells are obtained by breaking off the top and the narrow end of a big, cone-shaped shell (*Conus millepunctatus*) and then polishing up the remaining ring. These bracelets are highly coveted by all the Papuo-Melanesians of New Guinea, and they spread even into the pure Papuan district of the Gulf.[b] The manner of wearing the arm-shells is illustrated by Plate XVII, where the men have put them on on purpose to be photographed.[8]

The use of the small discs of red spondylus shell out of which the *soulava* are made, is also of very wide diffusion. There is a manufacturing centre of them in one of the villages

---

7. Malinowski believed that technologically primitive peoples were fully rational and just as intelligent as "civilized" people, but the point of the economic discussion in *Argonauts* is to critique the concept of "primitive economic man." The notion of economic man is that human beings rationally deploy limited resources to competing ends in such a way as to increase their personal benefit. This idea lies behind *Wealth of Nations* (1976 [1776]), by Adam Smith (1723–1790), and most of Western economics. Primitive economic man was a more extreme version of this: Since (economic theorists of the era argued) primitive people cannot delay gratification, they act only to achieve immediate and obvious rewards. Malinowski's attack at its most vitriolic is found in *Argonauts*, where he writes,

> Another notion which must be exploded, once and forever, is that of the Primitive Economic Man of some current economic textbooks. This fanciful, dummy creature, who has been very tenacious of existence in popular and semi-popular economic literature and whose shadow haunts even the minds of competent anthropologists, blighting their outlook with a preconceived idea, is an imaginary, primitive man, or savage, prompted in all his actions by a rationalistic concept of self-interest, and achieving his aims directly with the minimum of effort. (1922: 60)

Malinowski wanted "rational man" but not "economic man," and he needed to show that it was possible to have one without the other. In large part, this is the goal of the kula discussion. To Malinowski, the kula is a highly elaborate and rational system of exchange that has an economically irrational end: the distribution of goods that have no utilitarian value. It demonstrates that contrary to what Bücher said, the Trobrianders did not live for the present, engaged in regular work, had deep senses of duty, and were driven by morality as they understood it.

8. Unusually for the period in which this was written, Malinowski tells the reader about the conditions under which the photograph was taken. This is a level of ethnographic reporting that did not become common until the 1970s and 1980s.

Plate 17, mentioned in this paragraph has been described previously (in note 1).

in Port Moresby, and also in several places in Eastern New Guinea, notably in Rossell Island, and in the Trobriands. I have said "use" on purpose here, because these small beads, each of them a flat, round disc with a hole in the centre, coloured anything from muddy brown to carmine red, are employed in various ways for ornamentation. They are most generally used as part of earrings, made of rings of turtle shell, which are attached to the ear lobe, and from which hang a cluster of the shell discs. These earrings are very much worn, and, especially among the **Massim**, you see them on the ears of every second man or woman, while others are satisfied with turtle shell alone, unornamented with the shell discs. Another everyday ornament, frequently met with and worn, especially by young girls and boys, consists of a short necklace, just encircling the neck, made of the red spondylus discs, with one or more cowrie shell pendants. These shell discs can be, and often are, used in the make-up of the various classes of the more elaborate ornaments, worn on festive occasions only. Here however, we are more especially concerned with the very long necklaces, measuring from two to five metres, made of spondylus discs, of which there are two main varieties, one, much the finer, with a big shell pendant, the other made of bigger discs, and with a few cowrie shells or black banana seeds in the centre (see Plate XVIII).[9]

The arm-shells on the one hand, and the long spondylus shell strings on the other, the two main Kula articles, are primarily ornaments. As such, they are used with the most elaborate dancing dress only, and on very festive occasions such as big ceremonial dances, great feasts, and big gatherings, where several villages are represented, as can be seen in Plate VI. Never could they be used as everyday ornaments, nor on occasions of minor importance such as a small dance in the village, a harvest gathering, a love-making expedition, when facial painting, floral decoration and smaller though not quite everyday ornaments are worn (see Plates XII and XIII). But even though usable and sometimes used, this is not the main function of these articles. Thus, a chief may have several shell strings in his possession, and a few arm-shells. Supposing that a big dance is held in his or in a neighbouring village, he will not put on his ornaments himself if he goes to assist at it, unless he intends to dance and decorate himself, but any of his relatives, his children or his friends and even vassals, can have the use of them for the asking. If you go to a feast or a dance where there are a number of men wearing such ornaments, and ask anyone of them at random to whom it belongs, the chances are that more than half of them will answer that they themselves are not the owners, but that they had the articles lent to them. These objects are not owned in order to be used; the privilege of decorating oneself with them is not the real aim of possession.[10]

Indeed—and this is more significant—by far the greater number of the arm-shells, easily ninety percent, are of too small a size to be worn even by young boys and girls. A few are so big and valuable that they would not be worn at all, except once in a decade by a very important man on a very festive day. Though all the shell-strings can be worn, some of them are again considered too valuable, and are cumbersome for frequent use, and would be worn on very exceptional occasions only.

---

9. Plate 18 has been described in note 1.

"The Massim": It is not clear to whom Malinowski is referring here. The numerous different ethnic groups of the Milne Bay area of New Guinea are collectively referred to as the Massim.

10. This paragraph mentions plates 6, 12, and 13. Plate 6 is titled "Village Scenes During a So'I Fest." It consists of two photos showing groups of people. The caption reads: "These show types of Southern Massim and their decorations; again note the prominent part taken by women in the ceremonial actions." Plate 12 is titled "Boyowan Girls." It consists of two photos, one of three women. One shows eight women with additional people in the background. The caption reads: "Such facial painting and decorations are used when they go on a *katuyausi* expedition." Plate 13 is titled "Kaydebu Dance." It consists of a single picture showing many men doing a circular dance. The caption reads: "The circular dance with the carved shield on the *baku* of Omarakana. Note the plain, though picturesque headdress of cockatoo feathers."

This negative description leaves us with the questions: why, then, are these objects valued, what purpose do they serve? The full answer to this question will emerge out of the whole story contained in the following chapters, but an approximate idea must be given at once. As it is always better to approach the unknown through the known, let us consider for a moment whether among ourselves we have not some type of objects which play a similar role and which are used and possessed in the same manner. When, after a six years' absence in the South Seas and Australia, I returned to Europe and did my first bit of sight-seeing in Edinburgh Castle, I was shown the Crown Jewels. The keeper told many stories of how they were worn by this or that king or queen on such and such occasion, of how some of them had been taken over to London, to the great and just indignation of the whole Scottish nation, how they were restored, and how now everyone can be pleased, since they are safe under lock and key, and no one can touch them. As I was looking at them and thinking how ugly, useless, ungainly, even tawdry they were, I had the feeling that something similar had been told to me of late, and that I had seen many other objects of this sort, which made a similar impression on me.[11]

And then arose before me the vision of a native village on coral soil, and a small, rickety platform temporarily erected under a pandanus thatch, surrounded by a number of brown, naked men, and one of them showing me long, thin red strings, and big, white, worn-out objects, clumsy to sight and greasy to touch. With reverence he also would name them, and tell their history, and by whom and when they were worn, and how they changed hands, and how their temporary possession was a great sign of the importance and glory of the village. The analogy between the European and the Trobriand *vaygu'a* (valuables) must be delimited with more precision. The Crown Jewels, in fact, any heirlooms too valuable and too cumbersome to be worn, represent the same type as *vaygu'a* in that they are merely possessed for the sake of possession itself, and the ownership of them with the ensuing renown is the main source of their value. Also both heirlooms and *vaygu'a* are cherished because of the historical sentiment which surrounds them. However, ugly, useless, and—according to current standards—valueless an object may be, if it has figured in historical scenes and passed through the hands of historic persons, and is therefore an unfailing vehicle of important sentimental associations, it cannot but be precious to us. This historic sentimentalism, which indeed has a large share in our general interest in studies of past events, exists also in the South Seas. Every really good Kula article has its individual name, round each there is a sort of history and romance in the traditions of the natives. Crown Jewels or heirlooms are insignia of rank and symbols of wealth respectively, and in olden days with us, and in New Guinea up till a few years ago, both rank and wealth went together. The main point of difference is that the Kula goods are only in possession for a time, whereas the European treasure must be permanently owned in order to have full value.[12]

Taking a broader, ethnological view of the question, we may class the Kula valuables among the many "ceremonial" objects of wealth; enormous, carved and decorated weap-

---

11. Malinowski is considered one of the great ethnographers in anthropological history in part because of his gift for ethnographic reportage. The passages you have just read are notable for their clarity and a little bit of tongue-in-cheek humor. Malinowski believed it was important to understand how natives perceived their world and passed this understanding on to his readers by comparisons such as that presented here between *vaygu'a* and the crown jewels of Scotland. Like the jewels, *vaygu'a* do not have a practical utility; rather their value is symbolic, derived from their age and history. In making this comparison, Malinowski uses a nontechnical example easily accessible to a popular audience. *Argonauts,* like many of Malinowski's other works, was designed to be read by educated laypersons as well as professional anthropologists.

12. In the passage above, Malinowski tries to give us a native's perspective by explaining what the kula items mean to their recipients. Malinowski's writing style gave him a reputation as a man with great personal empathy for the people he studied. Admirers of Malinowski were greatly disillusioned when his sec-

ons, stone implements, articles of domestic and industrial nature, too well decorated and too clumsy for use. Such things are usually called "ceremonial," but this word seems to cover a great number of meanings and much that has no meaning at all. In fact, very often, especially on museum labels, an article is called "ceremonial" simply because nothing is known about its uses and general nature. Speaking only about museum exhibits from New Guinea, I can say that many so-called ceremonial objects are nothing but simply overgrown objects of use, which preciousness of material and amount of labour expended have transformed into reservoirs of condensed economic value. Again, others are used on festive occasions, but play no part whatever in rites and ceremonies, and serve for decoration only, and these might be called *objects of parade* (compare Chap. VI, Div. I). Finally, a number of these articles function actually as instruments of a magical or religious rite, and belong to the intrinsic apparatus of a ceremony. Such and such only could be correctly called *ceremonial*. During the *So'i* feasts among the Southern Massim, women carrying polished axe blades in fine carved handles, accompany with a rhythmic step to the beat of drums, the entry of the pigs and mango saplings into the village (see Plates V and VI). As this is part of the ceremony and the axes are an indispensable accessory, their use in this case can be legitimately called "ceremonial." Again, in certain magical ceremonies in the Trobriands, the *towosi* (garden magician) has to carry a mounted axe blade on his shoulders, and with it he delivers a ritual blow at a *kamkokola* structure (see Plate LIX; compare Chapter II Division IV).[13]

The *vaygu'a*—the Kula valuables—in one of their aspects are overgrown objects of use. They are also, however, *ceremonial* objects in the narrow and correct sense of the word. This will become clear after perusal of the following pages, and to this point we shall return in the last chapter.

It must be kept in mind that here we are trying to obtain a clear and vivid idea of what the Kula valuables are to the natives, and not to give a detailed and circumstantial description of them, nor to define them with precision. The comparison with the European heirlooms or Crown Jewels was given in order to show that this type of ownership is not entirely a fantastic South Sea custom, untranslatable into our ideas. For—and this is a point I want to stress—the comparison I have made is not based on purely external, superficial similarity. The psychological and sociological forces at work are the same, it is really the same mental attitude which makes us value our heirlooms, and makes the natives in New Guinea value their *vaygu'a*.

---

ond wife, the English painter and sculptor Valetta Swan (1904–1973) published his diaries in 1967, 25 years after his death (*A Diary in the Strict Sense of the Term*). Malinowski never intended for his diaries to be published (and it is unclear why Swan chose to do so). Using them as a therapeutic tool, he endlessly interrogates himself. In Malinowski biographer Michael Young's words, he "keeps on wanting to ransack the bottom of his soul" (2015 film). He records his intellectual and emotional frustrations and his loneliness. He obsesses about his sexual desires, his relationship with his mother, the idea of god, and his health. He expresses forbidden impulses. He often writes of anger and frustration with those around him and talks about the Trobrianders in very racist terms. At the time of its release, Malinowski's diaries caused a scandal. Now, more than half a century later, we are left to make of them what we will. On the one hand, Malinowski clearly had racist thoughts. But, on the other, he used his private diary to express them and rid himself of them, the written equivalent of going into an empty room and screaming.

13. Plate 5 consists of two photos and is titled "Scenes on the Beach of Silosilo (Southern Massim District)." Both show groups of people in the water. The caption reads "These represent phases of a big annual feast, the so'i. Note the prominent part taken by women in the proceedings; the use of the "ceremonial" axe handles; the manner of carrying pigs, and the canoes beached on the shore." Plate 6 has been described in note 10. Plate 59, which is placed much later in the book, is a single photo that shows men with piles of yams. It is titled "A Rite of Garden Magic" and the caption reads: "An offering of cooked food is exposed to the spirits for some time in the garden. The magician with the ceremonial axe on his arm, is seen squatting to the right. In the forefront, a big bundle of leaves which he will presently charm over."

I V

The exchange of these two classes of *vaygu'a*, of the arm-shells and the necklaces, constitutes the main act of the Kula. This exchange is not done freely, right and left, as opportunity offers, and where the whim leads. It is subject indeed to strict limitations and regulations. One of these refers to the sociology of the exchange, and entails that Kula transactions can be done only between partners. A man who is in the Kula—for not everyone within its district is entitled to carry it on—has only a limited number of people with whom he deals. This partnership is entered upon in a definite manner, under fulfillment of certain formalities, and it constitutes a life-long relationship. The number of partners a man has varies with his rank and importance. A commoner in the Trobriands would have a few partners only, whereas a chief would number hundreds of them. There is no special social mechanism to limit the partnership of some people and extend that of the others, but a man would naturally know to what number of partners he was entitled by his rank and position. And there would be always the example of his immediate ancestors to guide him. In other tribes, where the distinction of rank is not so pronounced, an old man of standing, or a headman of a hamlet or village would also have hundreds of Kula associates, whereas a man of minor importance would have but few.

Two Kula partners have to *kula* with one another, and exchange other gifts incidentally; they behave as friends, and have a number of mutual duties and obligations, which vary with the distance between their villages and with their reciprocal status. An average man has a few partners near by, as a rule his relations-in-law or his friends, and with these partners, he is generally on very friendly terms. The Kula partnership is one of the special bonds which unite two men into one of the standing relations of mutual exchange of gifts and services so characteristic of these natives. Again, the average man will have one or two chiefs in his or in the neighbouring districts with whom he

kulas. In such a case, he would be bound to assist and serve them in various ways, and to offer them the pick of his *vaygu'a* when he gets a fresh supply. On the other hand he would expect them to be specially liberal to him.

The overseas partner is, on the other hand, a host, patron and ally in a land of danger and insecurity. Nowadays, though the feeling of danger still persists, and natives never feel safe and comfortable in a strange district, this danger is rather felt as a magical one, and it is more the fear of foreign sorcery that besets them. In olden days, more tangible dangers were apprehended, and the partner was the main guarantee of safety. He also provides with food, gives presents, and his house, though never used to sleep in, is the place in which to foregather while in the village. Thus the Kula partnership provides every man within its ring with a few friends near at hand, and with some friendly allies in the far-away, dangerous, foreign districts. These are the only people with whom he can *kula*, but, of course, amongst all his partners, he is free to choose to which one he will offer which object.

Let us now try to cast a broad glance at the cumulative effects of the rules of partnership. We see that all around the ring of Kula there is a network of relationships, and that naturally the whole forms one interwoven fabric. Men living at hundreds of miles sailing distance from one another are bound together by direct or intermediate partnership, exchange with each other, know of each other, and on certain occasions meet in a large inter-tribal gathering (Plate XX). Objects given by one, in time reach some very distant indirect partner or other, and not only Kula objects, but various articles of domestic use and minor gifts. It is easy to see that in the long run, not only objects of material culture, but also customs, songs, art motives and general cultural influences travel along the Kula route. It is a vast, inter-tribal net of relationships, a big institution, consisting of thousands of men,—all bound together by one common passion for Kula exchange, and secondarily, by many minor ties and interests.[14]

---

14. Following Spencer's organic analogy, functionalists tended to see societies as collections of interrelated parts that worked together to promote the smooth functioning and equilibrium of the whole. Malinowski's emphasis on the kula as a mechanism for establishing ties between people on different islands is apparent in the previous few paragraphs. He characterizes the kula as a "vast, inter-tribal net of relationships."

Returning again to the personal aspect of the Kula, let us take a concrete example, that of *an average man* who lives, let us assume, in the village of Sinaketa, an important Kula centre in the Southern Trobriands. He has a few partners, near and far, but they again fall into categories, those who give him arm-shells, and those who give him necklaces. For it is naturally an invariable rule of the Kula that arm-shells and necklaces are never received from the same man, since they must travel in different directions. If one partner gives the arm-shells, and I return to him a necklace, all future operations have to be of the same type. More than that, the nature of the operation between me, the man of Sinaketa, and my partner, is determined by our relative positions with regard to the points of the compass. Thus I, in Sinaketa, would receive from the North and East only arm-shells; from the South and West, necklaces are given to me. If I have a near partner next door to me, if his abode is North or East of mine, he will always be giving me arm-shells and receiving necklaces from me. If, at a later time, he were to shift his residence within the village, the old relationship would obtain, but if he became a member of another village community on the other side of me the relationship would be reversed. The partners in villages to the North of Sinaketa, in the district of Luba, Kulumata, or Kiriwina all supply me with arm-shells. These I hand over to my partners in the South, and receive from them necklaces. The South in this case means the southern districts of Boyowa, as well as the Amphletts and Dobu.[15]

Thus every man has to obey definite rules as to the geographical direction of his transactions. At any point in the Kula ring, if we imagine him turned towards the centre of the circle, he receives the arm-shells with his left hand, and the necklaces with his right, and then hands them both on. In other words, he constantly passes the arm-shells from left to right, and the necklaces from right to left.

Applying this rule of personal conduct to the whole Kula ring, we can see at once what the aggregate result is. The sum total of exchanges will not result in an aimless shifting of the two classes of article, in a fortuitous come and go of the arm-shells and necklaces. Two continuous streams will constantly flow on, the one of necklaces following the hands of a clock, and the other, composed of the arm-shells, in the opposite direction. We see thus that it is quite correct to speak of the *circular* exchange of the Kula, of a ring or circuit of moving articles (comp. Map V). On this ring, all the villages are placed in a definitely fixed position with regard to one another, so that one is always on either the armshell or on the necklace side of the other.

Now we pass to another rule of the Kula, of the greatest importance. As just explained "the armshells and shell-strings always travel in their own respective directions on the ring, and they are never, under any circumstances, traded back in the wrong direction. Also, they never stop. It seems almost incredible at first, but it is the fact, nevertheless, that no one ever keeps any of the Kula valuables for any length of time. Indeed, in the whole of the Trobriands

---

Readers might also have noticed the frequent use of the term rule or rules in this section (it appears nine times). This shows the strong influence of Durkheim's ideas on Malinowski. Durkheim proposed that sociology was the study of social facts and the rules by which they operate. Although he does not use Durkheim's terminology, here, Malinowski has identified a social fact (the kula trade and its various valuables) and specifies the rules for participation in the trade.

Plate 20 is a single photograph. It is titled "A Kula Gathering on the Beach of Sinaketa" and shows many people and canoes. The caption reads: "Along about half a mile's length of shore, over eighty canoes are beached or moored, and in the village, on the beach, and in the surrounding country there are assembled some two thousand natives from several districts ranging from Kitava to Dobu. This illustrates the manner in which the Kula brings together large numbers of people belonging to different cultures; in this case, that of Kitava, Boyowa, the Amphletts, and Dobu."

15. The village of Sinaketa on Kiriwina Island, about 125 miles north-northeast of Milne Bay, Papua New Guinea, was a major site of Malinowski's fieldwork. In April 1918 he witnessed a major kula event near this village. He estimated that over one thousand people were involved. Malinowski took extensive photographs and made numerous sketches of the event (Young 2004: 541).

there are perhaps only one or two specially fine armshells and shell-necklaces permanently owned as heirlooms, and these are set apart as a special class, and are once and for all out of the Kula. 'Ownership,' therefore, in Kula, is quite a special economic relation. A man who is in the Kula never keeps any article for longer than, say, a year or two. Even this exposes him to the reproach of being niggardly, and certain districts have the bad reputation of being 'slow' and 'hard' in the Kula. On the other hand, each man has an enormous number of articles passing through his hands during his life time, of which he enjoys a temporary possession, and which he keeps in trust for a time. This possession hardly ever makes him use the articles, and he remains under the obligation soon again to hand them on to one of his partners. But the temporary ownership allows him to draw a great deal of renown, to exhibit his article, to tell how he obtained it, and to plan to whom he is going to give it. And all this forms one of the favourite subjects of tribal conversation and gossip, in which the feats and the glory in Kula of chiefs or commoners are constantly discussed and rediscussed."[c] Thus every article moves in one direction only, never comes back, never permanently stops, and takes as a rule some two to ten years to make the round.[16]

This feature of the Kula is perhaps its most remarkable one, since it creates a new type of ownership, and places the two Kula articles in a class of their own. Here we can return to the comparison drawn between the *vaygu'a* (Kiriwinian valuables) and the European heirlooms. This comparison broke down on one point: in the European objects of this class, permanent ownership, lasting association with the hereditary dignity or rank or with a family, is one of its main features.

In this the Kula articles differ from heirlooms, but resemble another type of valued object, that is, trophies, gauges of superiority, sporting cups, objects which are kept for a time only by the winning party, whether a group or an individual. Though held only in trust, only for a period, though never used in any utilitarian way, yet the holders get from them a special type of pleasure by the mere fact of owning them, of being entitled to them. Here again, it is not only a superficial, external resemblance, but very much the same mental attitude, favoured by similar social arrangements. The resemblance goes so far that in the Kula there exists also the element of pride in merit, an element which forms the main ingredient in the pleasure felt by a man or group holding a trophy. Success in Kula is ascribed to special, personal power, due mainly to magic, and men are very proud of it. Again, the whole community glories in a specially fine Kula trophy, obtained by one of its members.

All the rules so far enumerated—looking at them from the individual point of view—limit the social range and the direction of the transactions as well as the duration of ownership of the articles. Looking at them from the point of view of their integral effect, they shape the general outline of the Kula, give it the character of the double-closed circuit. Now a few words must be said about the nature of each individual transaction, in so far as its *commercial technicalities* are concerned. Here very definite rules also obtain.

---

16. Malinowski was concerned with differentiating his brand of functionalism from that of A. R. Radcliffe-Brown (1881–1955; see essay 15). Malinowski's theory was derived from his personal experiences in the field and was concerned with behavior within a cultural context, whereas Radcliffe-Brown studied social structure as an abstract representation that he believed existed independent of human beings. One of the most important differences between the two theorists was that Malinowski believed in the importance of individuals within a culture. Here he speaks of the kula as many individual transactions taking place simultaneously. He focuses, here and below, on the individual and group satisfactions derived from participating in the kula trade and possessing particularly fine kula objects. For Malinowski, the kula trade serves biopsychological functions for the individuals involved. Radcliffe-Brown, on the other hand, was concerned with how institutions functioned to create group solidarity and believed that the study of culture as individual human behavior was impossible.

Note that Malinowski's endnote c in this passage informs us that the quotes he uses in the rest of this text come from an article he published in the journal *Man* in the summer of 1920. In Malinowski's original, each of these is marked with the parenthetical Latin phrase "loc. cit.," meaning see previous citation. We have eliminated these phrases for ease of reading.

V

The main principle underlying the regulations of actual exchange is that the Kula consists in the bestowing of a ceremonial gift, which has to be repaid by an equivalent counter-gift, after a lapse of time, be it a few hours or even minutes, though sometimes as much as a year or more may elapse between payments.[d] But it can never be exchanged from hand to hand with the equivalence between the two objects discussed, bargained about and computed. The decorum of the Kula transaction is strictly kept, and highly valued. The natives sharply distinguish it from barter, which they practise extensively, of which they have a clear idea, and for which they have a settled term—in Kiriwinian: *gimwali*. Often, when criticising an incorrect, too hasty, or indecorous procedure of Kula, they will say: "He conducts his Kula as if it were *gimwali*."

The second very important principle is that the equivalence of the counter-gift is left to the giver, and cannot be enforced by any kind of coercion. A partner who has received a Kula gift is expected to give back fair and full value, that is, to give as good an arm-shell as the necklace he receives, or vice versa. Again, a very fine article must be replaced by one of equivalent value, and not by several minor ones, though intermediate gifts may be given to mark time before the real repayment takes place.[17]

If the article given as counter-gift is not equivalent, the recipient will be disappointed and angry, but he has no direct means of redress, no means of coercing his partner, or of putting an end to the whole transaction. What then are the forces at work which keep the partners to the terms of the bargain? Here we come up against a very important feature of the native's mental attitude towards wealth and value. The great misconception of attributing to the savage a pure economic nature, might lead us to reason incorrectly thus: "The passion of acquiring, the loathing to lose or give away, is the fundamental and most primitive element in man's attitude to wealth. In primitive man, this primitive characteristic will appear in its simplest and purest form. *Grab and never let go* will be the guiding principle of his life."[e] The fundamental error in this reasoning is that it assumes that "primitive man," as represented by the present-day savage, lives, at least in economic matters, untrammeled by conventions and social restrictions. Quite the reverse is the case. Although, like every human being, the Kula native loves to possess and therefore desires to acquire and dreads to lose, the social code of rules, with regard to give and take by far overrides his natural acquisitive tendency.[18]

This social code, such as we find it among the natives of the Kula is, however, far from weakening the natural desirability of possession; on the contrary, it lays down that to possess is to be great, and that wealth is the indispensable **appanage** of social rank and attribute of personal virtue. But the important point is that with them to possess is to give—and here the natives differ from us notably. A man who owns a thing is naturally expected to share it, to distribute it, to be its trustee and dispenser. And the higher the rank the greater the obligation. A chief will naturally be expected to give food to any stranger, visitor, even loiterer from another end of the village. He will be expected to share any of the betel-nut or tobacco he has about him. So that a man of rank will have to hide away any surplus of these articles which he wants to preserve for his further use. In the Eastern end of New Guinea a type of large

---

17. Malinowski's kula description is considered one of the seminal works in the development of economic anthropology and had a major impact on scholars of his day. Mauss, also considered a founder of economic anthropology, made extensive use of *Argonauts of the Western Pacific* in *The Gift*. For example, the first two principles of the kula outlined at the start of this section are fundamental elements of prestation discussed by Mauss (see essay 6). The kula, as Malinowski describes it, is what Mauss later calls a "total social fact."

18. Structural functionalists such as Radcliffe-Brown trace their intellectual descent directly from Durkheim. Malinowski was a bitter rival of Radcliffe-Brown, but he too was influenced by the French sociologist. However, there are critical differences. Durkheim emphasized the independent nature of the collective conscience, which he believed had an existence apart from any individual and operated by its own laws. Malinowski, on the other hand, believed that culture existed to serve human needs and that, ultimately, these needs were individual physiological and bio-psychological requirements.

basket, with three layers, manufactured in the Trobriands, was specially popular among people of consequence, because one could hide away one's small treasures in the lower compartments. Thus the main symptom of being powerful is to be wealthy, and of wealth is to be generous. Meanness, indeed, is the most despised vice, and the only thing about which the natives have strong moral views, while generosity is the essence of goodness.[19]

This moral injunction and ensuing habit of generosity, superficially observed and misinterpreted, is responsible for another wide-spread misconception, that of the *primitive communism of savages*. This, quite as much as the diametrically opposed figment of the acquisitive and ruthlessly tenacious native, is definitely erroneous, and this will be seen with sufficient clearness in the following chapters.[20]

Thus the fundamental principle of the natives' moral code in this matter makes a man do his fair share in Kula transaction and the more important he is, the more will he desire to shine by his generosity. **Noblesse oblige** is in reality the social norm regulating their conduct. This does not mean that people are always satisfied, and that there are no squabbles about the transactions, no resentments and even feuds. It is obvious that, however much a man may want to give a good equivalent for the object received, he may not be able to do so. And then, as there is always a keen competition to be the most generous giver, a man who has received less than he gave will not keep his grievance to himself, but will brag about his own generosity and compare it to his

partner's meanness; the other resents it, and the quarrel is ready to break out. But it is very important to realise that there is no actual haggling, no tendency to do a man out of his share. The giver is quite as keen as the receiver that the gift should be generous, though for different reasons. Then, of course, there is the important consideration that a man who is fair and generous in the Kula will attract a larger stream to himself than a mean one.[21]

The two main principles, namely, first that the Kula is a gift repaid after an interval of time by a counter-gift, and not a bartering; and second, that the equivalent rests with the giver, and cannot be enforced, nor can there be any haggling or going back on the exchange—these underlie all the transactions. A concrete outline of how they are carried on, will give a sufficient preliminary idea.

"Let us suppose that I, a Sinaketa man, am in possession of a pair of big arm-shells. An overseas expedition from Dobu in the d'Entrecasteaux Archipelago, arrives at my village. Blowing a conch shell, I take my arm-shell pair and I offer it to my overseas partner, with some words as 'This is a *vaga* (opening gift)—in due time, thou returnest to me a big *soulava* (necklace) for it!' Next year, when I visit my partner's village, he either is in possession of an equivalent necklace, and this he gives to me as *yotile* (return gift), or he has not a necklace good enough to repay my last gift. In this case he will give me a small necklace—avowedly not equivalent to my gift—and he will give it to me as *basi* (intermediary gift). This means that the main gift has to be repaid on a future

---

19. **"Appanage"**: necessary accompaniment.

20. Malinowski was writing just a few years after the Russian Revolution when communist rhetoric was fashionable in Europe and the United States. This comment on primitive communism is a critique of the Marxist five-stage theory of history. Marx suggested that European society had evolved through stages of primitive communism, ancient slave societies, feudalism, and capitalism. He believed that this evolution would end with the stages of socialism and finally communism. Many Marxists believed these stages could be found in all societies. Here, Malinowski argues that the generosity of Trobriand Islanders was not a form of primitive communism.

21. Notice how Malinowski acknowledges the presence of conflict but minimizes its effect. For him, conflict exists but does not drive the system; rather, it is an aberration in what is generally a smoothly functioning organism.

"Noblesse oblige": the idea that those of high social rank must act in accord with the social honor of their rank. In particular, those of high social rank must be benevolent to those of inferior rank.

occasion, and the *basi* is given in token of good faith—but it, in turn, must be repaid by me in the meantime by a gift of small arm-shells. The final gift, which will be given to me to clinch the whole transaction, would then be called *kudu* (clinching gift) in contrast to *basi*."[22]

Although haggling and bargaining are completely ruled out of the Kula, there are customary and regulated ways of bidding for a piece of *vaygu'a* known to be in the possession of one's partner. This is done by the offer of what we shall call solicitary gifts, of which there are several types. "If I, an inhabitant of Sinaketa, happen to be in possession of a pair of arm-shells more than usually good, the fame of it spreads, for it must be remembered that each one of the first-class arm-shells and necklaces has a personal name and a history of its own, and as they circulate around the big ring of the Kula, they are all well known, and their appearance in a given district always creates a sensation. Now, all my partners—whether from overseas or from within the district—compete for the favour of receiving this particular article of mine, and those who are specially keen try to obtain it by giving me *pokala* (offerings) and *kaributu* (solicitary gifts). The former (*pokala*) consist as a rule of pigs, especially fine bananas, and yams or taro; the latter (*kaributu*) are of greater value: the valuable, large axe blades (called *beku*), or lime spoons of whale bone are given." The further complication in the repayment of these solicitary gifts and a few more technicalities and technical expressions connected herewith will be given later on in Chapter IV [of *Argonauts of the Western Pacific*].

VI

I have enumerated the main rules of the Kula in a manner sufficient for a preliminary definition, and now a few words must be said about the associated activities and secondary aspects of the Kula. If we realise that at times the exchange has to take place between districts divided by dangerous seas, over which a great number of people have to travel by sail, and do so keeping to appointed dates, it becomes clear at once that considerable preparations are necessary to carry out the expedition. Many preliminary activities are intimately associated with the Kula. Such are, particularly, the building of canoes, preparation of the outfit, the provisioning of the expedition, the fixing of dates and social organisation of the enterprise. All these are subsidiary to the Kula, and as they are carried on in pursuit of it, and form one connected series, a description of the Kula must embrace an account of these preliminary activities. The detailed account of canoe building, of the ceremonial attached to it, of the incidental magical rites, of the launching and trial run, of the associated customs which aim at preparing the outfit—all this will be described in detail in the next few chapters.

Another important pursuit inextricably bound up with the Kula, is that of the *secondary trade*. Voyaging to far-off countries, endowed with natural resources unknown in their own homes, the Kula sailors return each time richly laden with these, the spoils of their enterprise. Again, in order to be able to offer presents to his partner, every outward bound canoe carries a cargo of such things as are known to be most desirable in the overseas district. Some of this is given away in presents to the partners, but a good deal is carried in order to pay for the objects desired at home. In certain cases, the visiting natives exploit on their own account during the journey some of the natural resources overseas. For example, the Sinaketans dive for the spondylus in Sanaroa Lagoon, and the Dobuans fish in the Trobriands on a beach on the southern end of the island. The second trade is complicated still more by the fact that such big Kula centres as, for instance, Sinaketa, are not efficient in any of the industries of special value to the Dobuans. Thus, Sinaketans have to procure the necessary store of goods from the inland villages of Kuboma, and this they do on minor trading expeditions preliminary to the Kula. Like the canoe-building, the secondary trading

---

22. Although Malinowski describes an idealized transaction, he has a real event in mind. The kula exchange he witnessed in Sinaketa (see note 14) was with people from Dobu, the Amphletts, and Kitava.

will be described in detail later on, and has only to be mentioned here.[23]

Here, however, these subsidiary and associated activities must be put in proper relation with regard to one another and to the main transaction. Both the canoe-building and the ordinary trade have been spoken of as secondary or subsidiary to the Kula proper. This requires a comment. I do not, by thus subordinating the two things in importance to the Kula mean to express a philosophical reflection or a personal opinion as to the relative value of these pursuits from the point of view of some social teleology. Indeed, it is clear that if we look at the acts from the outside, as comparative sociologists and gauge their real utility, trade and canoe-building will appear to us as the really important achievements, whereas we shall regard the Kula only as an indirect stimulus, impelling the natives to sail and to trade. Here, however, I am not dealing in sociological, but in pure ethnographical description and any sociological analysis I have given is only what has been absolutely indispensable to clear away misconceptions and to define terms.[f, 24]

By ranging the Kula as the primary and chief activity, and the rest as secondary ones, I mean that this precedence is implied in the institutions themselves. By studying the behaviour of the natives and all the customs in question, we see that the Kula is in all respects the main aim: the dates are fixed, the preliminaries settled, the expeditions arranged, the social organisation determined, not with regard to trade, but with regard to Kula. On an expedi-tion, the big ceremonial feast, held at the start, refers to the Kula; the final ceremony of reckoning and counting the spoil refers to Kula, not to the objects of trade obtained. Finally, the magic, which is one of the main factors of all the procedure, refers only to the Kula, and this applies even to a part of the magic carried out over the canoe. Some rites in the whole cycle are done for the sake of the canoe itself, and others for the sake of Kula. The construction of the canoes is always carried on directly in connection with a Kula expedition. All this, of course, will become really clear and convincing only after the detailed account is given. But it was necessary at this point to set the right perspective in the relation between the main Kula and the trade.

Of course not only many of the surrounding tribes who know nothing of the Kula do build canoes and sail far and daringly on trading expeditions, but even within the Kula ring, in the Trobriands for instance, there are several villages who do not *kula*, yet have canoes and carry on energetic overseas trade. But where the Kula is practiced, it governs all the other allied activities, and canoe-building and trade are made subsidiary to it. And this is expressed both by the nature of the institutions and the working of all the arrangements on the one hand, and by the behaviour and explicit statements of the natives on the other.

The Kula—it becomes, I hope, more and more clear—is a big, complicated institution, insignificant though its nucleus might appear. To the natives, it represents one of the most

---

23. Malinowski insisted that the kula was a rational system directed toward the exchange of items with only symbolic value. Because of this, he gives little weight to the fact that the offerings given to induce a partner to part with good *vaygu'a* are utilitarian items such as pigs, bananas, yams, and axe blades. The exchange of these items may be more purely utilitarian and more conventionally economic. Although this secondary trade is repeatedly mentioned, Malinowski spends little time analyzing it.

24. In Malinowski's endnote to this passage, he says that reconstructing history is an "unpardonable sin" and that he is unconcerned with searching for the origins of institutions, preferring to spend his time working out the interrelations of elements within a society. The endnote is a critique likely directed at European diffusionists, and possibly Boas. Malinowski dismissed popular diffusionists such as W. H. R. Rivers (1864–1922) and Grafton Elliot Smith (1871–1937), who tried to prove that all culture began in ancient Egypt and diffused from there. Malinowski and Franz Boas both stressed the importance of seeing cultures as integrated wholes and of firsthand observation. However, they disagreed on the importance of history. Boas believed that the current state of a culture could only be understood through the study of its history. Malinowski and other functionalists disagreed. They considered native accounts of history unreliable and were concerned with the current state of society.

vital interests in life, and as such it has a ceremonial character and is surrounded by magic. We can well imagine that articles of wealth might pass from hand to hand without ceremony or ritual, but in the Kula they never do. Even when at times only small parties in one or two canoes sail overseas and bring back *vay-gu'a*, certain taboos are observed, and a customary course is taken in departing, in sailing, and in arriving; even the smallest expedition in one canoe is a tribal event of some importance, known and spoken of over the whole district. But the characteristic expedition is one in which a considerable number of canoes take part, organised in a certain manner, and forming one body. Feasts, distributions of food and other public ceremonies are held, there is one leader and master of the expedition, and various rules are adhered to, in addition to the ordinary Kula taboos and observances.

The ceremonial nature of the Kula is strictly bound up with another of its aspects—magic. "The belief in the efficiency of magic dominates the Kula, as it does ever so many other tribal activities of the natives. Magical rites must be performed over the sea-going canoe when it is built, in order to make it swift, steady and safe; also magic is done over a canoe to make it lucky in the Kula. Another system of magical rites is done in order to avert the dangers of sailing. The third system of magic connected with overseas expeditions is the *mwasila* or the Kula magic proper. This system consists in numerous rites and spells, all of which act directly on the mind (*nanola*) of one's partner, and make him soft, unsteady in mind, and eager to give Kula gifts." [25]

It is clear that an institution so closely associated with magical and ceremonial elements, as is the Kula, not only rests on a firm, traditional foundation, but also has its large store of legend. "There is a rich mythology of the Kula in which stories are told about far-off times when mythical ancestors sailed on distant and daring expeditions. Owing to their magical knowledge they were able to escape dangers to conquer their enemies, to surmount obstacles, and by their feats they established many a precedent which is now closely followed by tribal custom. But their importance for their descendants lies mainly in the fact that they handed on their magic, and this made the Kula possible for the following generations."

The Kula is also associated in certain districts, to which the Trobriands do not belong, with the mortuary feasts called *so'i*. The association is interesting and important and in Chapter XX an account of it will be given.

The big Kula expeditions are carried on by a great number of natives, a whole district together. But the geographical limits, from which the members of an expedition are recruited, are well defined. Glancing at Map V, "we see a number of circles, each of which represents a certain sociological unit which we shall call a Kula community. A Kula community consists of a village or a number of villages, who go out together on big overseas expeditions, and who act as a body in the Kula transactions, perform their magic in common, have common leaders, and have the same outer and inner social sphere, within which they exchange their valuables. The Kula consists, therefore, first of the small, internal transac-

---

25. Magic plays an important role in Trobriand Island society, and Malinowski discusses the subject in other chapters of *Argonauts* and in his later works *Magic, Science, and Religion* (1954 [1925]) and *Coral Gardens and Their Magic* (1935). Malinowski was reacting against the theory of one of his mentors, Sir James Frazer (1854–1941). Frazer, a popular theorist of anthropology and religion, argued that people in primitive societies had magical beliefs and other superstitions because they had some form of primitive mentality and were incapable of scientific thought. Concerned with presenting people in simple societies as rational, Malinowski was careful to distinguish the contexts in which magic was used. He argued that the Trobrianders were just as intelligent and rational as European. They used magic in circumstances that were beyond rational control. Thus, magic filled the need for safety in situations that were intrinsically unpredictable. In a widely read essay, George Gmelch (b. 1944) applied Malinowski's insight to baseball. Gmelch (original 1971 but frequently updated) showed that professional baseball players were much more likely to have superstitions or do magic rituals for success at batting, which is highly unpredictable and potentially dangerous, than for success at out-fielding, which is very predictable.

tions within a Kula community or contiguous communities, and secondly, of the big overseas expeditions in which the exchange of articles takes place between two communities divided by the sea. In the first, there is a chronic, permanent trickling of articles from one village to another, and even within the village. In the second, a whole lot of valuables, amounting to over a thousand articles at a time, are exchanged in one enormous transaction, or, more correctly, in ever so many transactions taking place simultaneously." "The Kula trade consists of a series of such periodical overseas expeditions, which link together the various island groups, and annually bring over big quantities of *vaygu'a* and of subsidiary trade from one district to another. The trade is used and used up, but the *vaygu'a*—the arm-shells and necklaces—go round and round the ring."[26]

In this chapter, a short, summary definition of the Kula has been given. I enumerated one after the other its most salient features, the most remarkable rules as they are laid down in native custom, belief and behaviour. This was necessary in order to give a general idea of the institution before describing its working in detail. But no abridged definition can give to the reader the full understanding of a human social institution. It is necessary for this, to explain its working concretely, to bring the reader into contact with the people, show how they proceed at each successive stage, and to describe all the actual manifestations of the general rules laid down in abstract.

As has been said above, the Kula exchange is carried on by enterprises of two sorts; first there are the big overseas expeditions, in which a more or less considerable amount of valuables are carried at one time. Then there is the inland trade in which the articles are passed from hand to hand, often changing several owners before they move a few miles.

The big overseas expeditions are by far the more spectacular part of the Kula. They also contain much more public ceremonial, magical ritual, and customary usage. They require also, of course, more of preparation and preliminary activity. I shall therefore have a good deal more to say about the overseas Kula expeditions than about the internal exchange.

As the Kula customs and beliefs have been mainly studied in Boyowa, that is, the Trobriand Islands, and from the Boyowan point of view, I shall describe, in the first place, the typical course of an overseas expedition, as it is prepared, organized, and carried out from the Trobriands. Beginning with the construction of the canoes, proceeding to the ceremonial launching and the visits of formal presentation of canoes, we shall choose then the community of Sinaketa, and follow the natives on one of their overseas trips, describing it in all details. This will serve us as a type of a Kula expedition to distant lands. It will then be indicated in what particulars such expeditions may differ in other branches of the Kula, and for this purpose I shall describe an expedition from Dobu, and one between Kiriwina and Kitava. An account of inland Kula in the Trobriands, of some associated forms of trading and of Kula in the remaining branches will complete the account.[27]

---

26. The above paragraphs demonstrate Malinowski's belief that culture was a system of interrelated parts. One cannot study the kula alone, because it is interconnected with other aspects of Trobriand life such as canoe-building, magic, and family structure. Spencer's organic analogy can be seen behind Malinowski's model of the kula. The kula is a system in a physical sense; it can be diagrammed like the circulatory system of the body.

27. Malinowski is often considered to have originated participant observation. He was certainly one of its foremost early practitioners. Despite the knowledge of him that we gain from reading *A Diary in the Strict Sense* (see note 12), Malinowski still stands as an anthropologist who strove, and who taught others to strive, to approach understanding people with sympathy, compassion, and context. In the first chapter of *Argonauts of the Western Pacific* Malinowski says that ethnographers should never lose sight of the goal of grasping "the native's point of view, his relation to life, to realize *his* vision of *his* world" (1922: 25, emphasis in the original). Later in the same passage, he writes that to study native institutions, behaviors, and mentalities without striving to understand "the substances of their happiness . . . is, in my opinion, to miss the greatest reward which we can hope to obtain from the study of man" (1922: 25).

In the next chapter I pass, therefore, to the preliminary stages of the Kula, in the Trobriands, beginning with a description of the canoes.

AUTHOR'S NOTES

a. By "current view," I mean such as is to be found in textbooks and in passing remarks, scattered through economic and ethnological literature. As a matter of fact, Economics is a subject very seldom touched upon either in theoretical works or Ethnology, or in accounts of field-work. I have enlarged on this deficiency in the article on "Primitive Economics," published in the *Economic Journal*, March, 1921.

The best analysis of the problem of savage economy is to be found, in spite of its many shortcomings, in K. Bücher's "Industrial Evolution," English translation, 1901. On primitive trade, however, his views are inadequate. In accordance with his general view that savages have no national economy, he maintains that any spread of goods among natives is achieved by noneconomic means, such as robbery, tributes and gifts. The information contained in the present volume is incompatible with Bücher's views, nor could he have maintained them had he been acquainted with Barton's description of the Hiri (contained in Seligman's "Melanesians").

A summary of the research done on Primitive Economics, showing, incidentally, how little real, sound work has been accomplished, will be found in Pater W. Kopper's "Die Ethnologische Wirtschaftsforschung" in *Anthropos*, X–XI, 1915–16, pp. 611–651, and 971–1079. The article is very useful, where the author summarises the views of others.

b. Professor C. G. Seligman, op. cit., p. 93, states that arm-shells, toea, as they are called by the Motu, are traded from the Port Moresby district westward to the Gulf of Papua. Among the Motu and Koita, near Port Moresby, they are highly valued, and nowadays attain very high prices, up to £30, much more than is paid for the same article among the Massim.

c. This and the following quotations are from the Author's preliminary article on the Kula in Man, July, 1920. Article number 51, p. 100.

d. In order not to be guilty of inconsistency in using loosely the word "ceremonial" I shall define it briefly. I shall call an action ceremonial, if it is (1) public; (2) carried on under observance of definite formalities; (3) if it has sociological, religious, or magical import, and it carries with it obligations.

e. This is not a fanciful construction of what an erroneous opinion might be, for I could give actual examples proving that such opinions have been set forth, but as I am not giving here a criticism of existing theories of Primitive Economics, I do not want to overload this chapter with quotations.

f. It is hardly necessary perhaps to make it quite clear that all questions of origins of development or history of the institutions have been rigorously ruled out of this work. The mixing up of speculative or hypothetical views with an account of facts is, in my opinion an unpardonable sin against ethnographic method.

In the 2011 film *Savage Memory* filmmaker Zachery Stuart, explores Malinowski's legacy. He interviews Nukhala Khoubuli, then the heir apparent to the chieftaincy of one of the places Malinowski worked. On camera, Khoubuli says:

He made me a little upset when he came up with the title *The Sexual Life of the Savages*. [Malinowski's 1929 book *The Sexual Life of Savages in North-Western Melanesia*]. That's the only comment I have. Just that 'savages' made me a little bit upset. But when I read it, I believe. . . . He wasn't talking to us. He was talking to somebody, maybe, in the Western world. He was trying to prove to them, that's what I can gather, or maybe it was just my, sort of, self to justify his intention was good. But what I thought—maybe he was trying to convince those ones in the West that we are not really savages after all. I don't know. He's not alive so I wouldn't ask him.

15. On Joking Relationships

A. R. Radcliffe-Brown (1881–1955)

THE PUBLICATION OF Mr. F. J. Pedler's note[a] on what are called "joking relationships," following on two other papers on the same subject by Professor Henri Labouret[b] and Mademoiselle Denise Paulme,[c] suggests that some general theoretical discussion of the nature of these relationships may be of interest to readers of Africa.[d, 1]

What is meant by the term "joking relationship" is a relation between two persons in which one is by custom permitted, and in some instances required, to tease or make fun of the other, who in turn is required to take no offence. It is important to distinguish two main varieties. In one the relation is symmetrical; each of the two persons teases or makes fun of the other. In the other variety the relation is asymmetrical; A jokes at the expense of B and B accepts the teasing good humouredly but without retaliating; or A teases B as much as he pleases and B in return teases A only a little. There are many varieties in the form of this relationship in different societies. In some instances the joking or teasing is only verbal, in others it includes horse-play; in some the joking includes elements of obscenity, in others not.

Standardized social relationships of this kind are extremely widespread, not only in Africa but also in Asia, Oceania and North America. To arrive at a scientific understanding of the phenomenon it is necessary to make a wide comparative study. Some material for this now exists in anthropological literature, though by no means all that could be desired, since it is unfortunately still only rarely that such relationships are observed and described as exactly as they might be.[2]

The joking relationship is a peculiar combination of friendliness and antagonism. The behavior is such that in any other social context it would express and arouse hostility;

From *Africa* (1940)

1. Radcliffe-Brown begins his essay, which first appeared in the journal *Africa*, by mentioning several other anthropologists of his era. Frederick Johnson Pedler (1908–1991), later Sir Frederick Pedler, was a colonial administrator and diplomat who became the director of the United Africa Company and wrote several books on Africa. In the note referenced here, Pedler reports on a legal case involving a joking relationship called *utani*. We will return to that case below. Henri Labouret (1878–1959) was a soldier, colonial administrator, linguist, and ethnographer who played a critical role in West African ethnography in the early twentieth century. Denise Paulme (1909–1998) was a student of Marcel Mauss who became one of the leading French Africanist scholars. Her book *Femmes d'Afrique Noire* (1960), a volume of essays about African women written entirely by female anthropologists, is an early classic of feminist anthropology.

All the work cited by Radcliffe-Brown, as well as this essay itself, appeared in the journal *Africa: Journal of the International Africa Institute*. National traditions in anthropology tended to be located in specific places. Much American anthropology was done among Native American groups in the United States or among people living on American-controlled territories, particularly in the Pacific Islands. British and French anthropology tended to focus on Africa or Southeast Asia, where these nations had colonial possessions.

2. Note that Radcliffe-Brown says his goal is to provide a scientific understanding of joking relationships. He hoped to make anthropology a science and believed that it was possible to discover universal laws and principles underlying the structure of human society. These laws were to be found through the comparative analysis of social structure.

but it is not meant seriously and must not be taken seriously. There is a pretence of hostility and a real friendliness. To put it in another way, the relationship is one of permitted disrespect. Thus any complete theory of it must be part of, or consistent with, a theory of the place of respect in social relations and in social life generally. But this is a very wide and very important sociological problem; for it is evident that the whole maintenance of a social order depends upon the appropriate kind and degree of respect being shown towards certain persons, things and ideas or symbols.[3]

Examples of joking relationships between relatives by marriage are very commonly found in Africa and in other parts of the world. Thus Mademoiselle Paulme[e] records that among the Dogon a man stands in a joking relationship to his wife's sisters and their daughters. Frequently the relationship holds between a man and both the brothers and sisters of his wife. But in some instances there is a distinction whereby a man is on joking terms with his wife's younger brothers and sisters but not with those who are older than she is. This joking with the wife's brothers and sisters is usually associated with a custom requiring extreme respect, often partial or complete avoidance, between a son-in-law and his wife's parents.[f]

The kind of structural situation in which the associated customs of joking and avoidance are found may be described as follows. A marriage involves a readjustment of the social structure whereby the woman's relations with her family are greatly modified and she enters into a new and very close relation with her husband. The latter is at the same time brought into a special relation with his wife's family, to which, however, he is an outsider. For the sake of brevity, though at the risk of over-simplification, we will consider only the husband's relation to his wife's family. The relation can be described as involving both attachment and separation, both social conjunction and social disjunction, if I may use the terms. The man has his own definite position in the social structure, determined for him by his birth into a certain family, lineage or clan. The great body of his rights and duties and the interests and activities that he shares with others are the result of his position. Before the marriage his wife's family are outsiders for him as he is an outsider for them. This constitutes a social disjunction which is not destroyed by the marriage. The social conjunction results from the continuance, though in altered form, of the wife's relation to her family, their continued interest in her and in her children. If the wife were really bought and paid for, as ignorant persons say that she is in Africa, there would be no place for any permanent close relation of a man with his wife's family. But though slaves can be bought, wives cannot.[4]

Social disjunction implies divergence of interests and therefore the possibility of conflict and hostility, while conjunction requires the avoidance of strife. How can a relation which combines the two be given a stable, ordered form? There are two ways of doing this. One is to maintain between two persons so related an extreme mutual respect and a limitation of direct personal contact. This is exhibited in the very formal relations that are, in so many societies, characteristic of the behavior of a son-in-law on the one side and his wife's father and mother on the other. In its most extreme form there is complete avoidance of any social contact between a man and his mother-in-law.

This avoidance must not be mistaken for a sign of hostility. One does, of course, if one is wise, avoid having too much to do with one's enemies, but that is quite a different matter. I once asked an Australian native why he had to avoid his mother-in-law, and his reply was,

---

3. Following Émile Durkheim and using the concept of the organic analogy developed by Herbert Spencer, Radcliffe-Brown's key concern was the maintenance of social order. He understood society as composed of a series of institutions, each of which could be understood in terms of the role it played in maintaining social order. This was its function, hence functionalism.

4. Radcliffe-Brown sees a critical contradiction at the core of marriage. A husband does not become part of his wife's family, but neither is he entirely separate from them. A wife does not become part of her husband's family, and her family of origin continues to have an interest in her and her children. This contradiction creates the preconditions for conflict between the two families. For society to function smoothly there must be an institution to resolve this conflict.

"Because she is my best friend in the world; she has given me my wife." The mutual respect between son-in-law and parents-in-law is a mode of friendship. It prevents conflict that might arise through divergence of interest.[5]

The alternative to this relation of extreme mutual respect and restraint is the joking relationship, one, that is, of mutual disrespect and licence. Any serious hostility is prevented by the playful antagonism of teasing, and this in its regular repetition is a constant expression or reminder of that social disjunction which is one of the essential components of the relation, while the social conjunction is maintained by the friendliness that takes no offence at insult.[6]

The discrimination within the wife's family between those who have to be treated with extreme respect and those with whom it is a duty to be disrespectful is made on the basis of generation and sometimes of seniority within the generation. The usual respected relatives are those of the first ascending generation, the wife's mother and her sisters, the wife's father and his brothers, sometimes the wife's mother's brother. The joking relatives are those of a person's own generation; but very frequently a distinction of seniority within the generation is made; a wife's older sister or brother may be respected while those younger will be teased.

In certain societies a man may be said to have relatives by marriage long before he marries and indeed as soon as he is born into the world. This is provided by the institution of the required or preferential marriage. We will, for the sake of brevity, consider only one kind of such organisations. In many societies it is regarded as preferable that a man should marry the daughter of his mother's brother; this is a form of the custom known as cross-cousin marriage. Thus his female cousins of this kind, or all those women whom by the classificatory system he classifies as such, are potential wives for him, and their brothers are his potential brothers-in-law. Among the Ojibwa Indians of North America, the Chiga of Uganda, and in Fiji and New Caledonia, as well as elsewhere, this form of marriage is found and is accompanied by a joking relationship between a man and the sons and daughters of his mother's brother. To quote one instance of these, the following is recorded for the Ojibwa. "When cross-cousins meet they must try to embarrass one another. They 'joke' one another, making the most vulgar allegations, by their standards as well as ours. But being 'kind' relations, no one can take offence. Cross-cousins who do not joke in this way are considered boorish, as not playing the social game."[g]

The joking relationship here is of fundamentally the same kind as that already discussed. It is established before marriage and is continued, after marriage, with the brothers- and sisters-in-law.

In some parts of Africa there are joking relationships that have nothing to do with marriage. Mr. Pedler's note, mentioned above, refers to a joking relationship between two distinct tribes, the Sukuma and the Zaramu, and in the evidence it was stated that there was a similar relation between the Sukuma and the Zigua and between the Ngoni and the Bemba. The woman's evidence suggests that this custom of rough teasing exists in the Sukuma tribe between persons related by marriage, as it does in so many other African tribes.[h, 7]

---

5. In this passage, Radcliffe-Brown refers to asking a question of an Australian native. Radcliffe-Brown did fieldwork on the Andaman Islands from 1906 to 1908 and in Australia from 1910 to 1912. However, he did not enjoy fieldwork, and his work was far more in the style of the Torres Straits expedition (measuring people, recording their material culture, and asking them survey questions) than participant observation. He relied primarily on the fieldwork of others (Elkin 1956). Note that in this essay he mentions his own fieldwork anecdotally but gives data from a wide variety of sources.

6. Thus, society functions smoothly because the contradiction between the husband and the family of his wife is resolved either by avoidance or joking. Radcliffe-Brown shows that these are two related phenomena.

7. Be sure to read Radcliffe-Brown's original note located at the end of the essay. Pedler had reported a court case involving a joking relationship. Radcliffe-Brown uses this as a springboard to argue that anthropol-

While a joking relationship between two tribes is apparently rare, and certainly deserves, as Mr. Pedler suggests, to be carefully investigated, a similar relationship between clans has been observed in other parts of Africa. It is described by Professor Labouret and Mademoiselle Paulme in the articles previously mentioned, and amongst the Tallensi it has been studied by Dr. Fortes, who will deal with it in a forthcoming publication.[i, 8]

The two clans are not, in these instances, specially connected by intermarriage. The relation between them is an alliance involving real friendliness and mutual aid combined with an appearance of hostility.

The general structural situation in these instances seems to be as follows. The individual is a member of a certain defined group, a clan, for example, within which his relations to others are defined by a complex set of rights and duties, referring to all the major aspects of social life, and supported by definite sanctions. There may be another group outside his own which is so linked with his as to be the field of extension of jural and moral relations of the same general kind. Thus, in East Africa, as we learn from Mr. Pedler's note, the Zigua and the Zaramu do not joke with one another because a yet closer bond exists between them since they are ndugu (brothers). But beyond the field within which social relations are thus defined there lie other groups with which, since they are outsiders to the individual's own group, the relation involves possible or actual hostility. In any fixed relations between the members of two such groups the separateness of the groups must be recognised. It is precisely this separateness which is not merely recognised but emphasised when a joking relationship is established. The show of hostility, the perpetual disrespect, is a continual expression of that social disjunction which is an essential part of the whole structural situation, but over which, without destroying or even weakening it, there is provided the social conjunction of friendliness and mutual aid.

The theory that is here put forward, therefore, is that both the joking relationship which constitutes an alliance between clans or tribes, and that between relatives by marriage, are modes of organising a definite and stable system of social behaviour in which conjunctive and disjunctive components, as I have called them, are maintained and combined.[9]

ogy should be involved in colonial administration. He had been a colonial administrator, the director of education in Tonga from 1916 to 1920, and like other functionalists, saw service to the colonial administrations as one aim of their work. Bronislaw Malinowski argued, in an article entitled "Practical Anthropology" (1929a), that such service should be a key goal. Then (as today) access to funding was an important reason for stressing the applied aspects of anthropological research: Some of the money that funded research projects came from the Colonial Social Science Research Council. In general, functionalists did not question the basic fact of colonization or the subservient position of the colonized. Both paternalism and social evolutionism were implied in their writings. They believed that benevolent colonialism offered native societies the chance for progress. On the other hand, they considered themselves friends of those they studied and argued on their behalf before colonial administrations. Colonial administrations, for their part, were deeply suspicious of anthropologists, considering them too liberal and too close to the natives (Goody 1995). The same Malinowski who authored "Practical Anthropology" also authored the preface to Jomo Kenyatta's *Facing Mount Kenya: The Traditional Life of the Gikuyu* (1979 [1938]). Kenyatta (1897–1978), a student of Malinowski, is better remembered as a leader of Kenya's fight for independence and that nation's first president.

8. Meyer Fortes (1906–1983) was a member of the group of students who gathered around Malinowski and Radcliffe-Brown in the years between World Wars I and II. Fortes trained with Malinowski who wrote that "for sheer brilliancy and real capacity and intelligence [he is] the best pupil I ever had" (quoted in Goody 1995: 28). However, Fortes was ultimately more drawn to the structural side of functionalism than the psychological.

9. Thus, that which is true within a group is also true between groups. Just as the potential conflicts between the husband's and wife's families are resolved by avoidance and joking, so too potential conflicts between related tribes may be resolved by avoidance or joking. Notice Radcliffe-Brown's strong emphasis on structure in this paragraph. He locates relations of aid, joking, and hostility within a pattern of relationships among

To provide the full evidence for this theory by following out its implications and examining in detail its application to different instances would take a book rather than a short article. But some confirmation can perhaps be offered by a consideration of the way in which respect and disrespect appear in various kinship relations, even though nothing more can be attempted than a very brief indication of a few significant points.[10]

In studying a kinship system it is possible to distinguish the different relatives by reference to the kind and degree of respect that is paid to them.[j] Although kinship systems vary very much in their details there are certain principles which are found to be very widespread. One of them is that by which a person is required to show a marked respect to relatives belonging to the generation immediately preceding his own. In a majority of societies the father is a relative to whom marked respect must be shown. This is so even in many so called matrilineal societies, i.e. those which are organised into matrilineal clans or lineages. One can very frequently observe a tendency to extend this attitude of respect to all relatives of the first ascending generation and, further, to persons who are not relatives. Thus in those tribes of East Africa that are organised into age-sets a man is required to show special respect to all men of his father's age-set and to their wives.[11]

The social function of this is obvious. The social tradition is handed down from one generation to the next. For the tradition to be maintained it must have authority behind it. The authority is therefore normally recognised as possessed by members of the preceding generation and it is they who exercise discipline. As a result of this the relation between persons of the two generations usually contains an element of inequality, the parents and those of their generation being in a position of superiority over the children who are subordinate to them. The unequal relation between a father and his son is maintained by requiring the latter to show respect to the former. The relation is asymmetrical.[12]

When we turn to the relation of an individual to his grandparents and their brothers and sisters we find that in the majority of human

---

different groups. His implicit claim is that this structure of aid, joking, and hostility exists independently of both historical events and individual personalities. This claim owes much to Durkheim but stands in contrast to the emphasis Franz Boas places on both history and the individual.

10. Passages such as this are typical of Radcliffe-Brown's work. He frequently claims that the idea he wishes to demonstrate or the theory he wishes to prove would require a substantial body of work, which he never provides. Almost the whole of Radcliffe-Brown's written work consists of relatively brief pieces, such as this one, and addresses. He published one full-length ethnography *The Andaman Islanders,* his account of his 1906–1908 fieldwork, but even this was not published until 1922, well over a decade after his return from the field. *The Andaman Islanders* is noteworthy because it illustrates a shift from simple description to Durkheimian thinking rather than for the content of the ethnography itself.

11. Much of Radcliffe-Brown's work focused on kinship. He was guided in this in part by his mentor, W. H. R. Rivers (1864–1922). Rivers, a medical doctor who had joined the 1898 Torres Straits expedition, devised what he called the "genealogical method." In his 1910 article "The Genealogical Method of Anthropological Inquiry," Rivers proposed that a truly scientific anthropology could be achieved through the study of kinship.

12. Radcliffe-Brown glibly and without providing evidence claims that the "obvious" social function of respect to people one generation older than oneself is to provide for the continuity of the "social tradition." However, this is anything but obvious. For example, people might show respect to those a generation older because these determine whom their children marry, or whether or not they will inherit wealth and status. Radcliffe-Brown's work takes little account of economic possibilities such as this. Perhaps this is because they imply conflict and competition. Radcliffe-Brown's model is built around the idea of harmoniously functioning societies and mechanisms to smooth or eliminate conflict. Radcliffe-Brown concludes the paragraph by saying, "The unequal relation between a father and his son is maintained by requiring the latter to show respect to the former," but he doesn't explain how this asymmetry serves that purpose.

societies relatives of the second ascending generation are treated with very much less respect than those of the first ascending generation, and instead of a marked inequality there is a tendency to approximate to a friendly equality.

Considerations of space forbid any full discussion of this feature of social structure, which is one of very great importance. There are many instances in which the grandparents and their grandchildren are grouped together in the social structure in opposition to their children and parents. An important clue to the understanding of the subject is the fact that in the flow of social life through time, in which men are born, become mature and die, the grandchildren replace their grandparents.

In many societies there is an actual joking relationship, usually of a relatively mild kind, between relatives of alternate generations. Grandchildren make fun of their grandparents and of those who are called grandfather and grandmother by the classificatory system of terminology, and these reply in kind.

Grandparents and grandchildren are united by kinship; they are separated by age and by the social difference that results from the fact that as the grandchildren are in process of entering into full participation in the social life of the community the grandparents are gradually retiring from it. Important duties towards his relatives in his own and even more in his parents' generation impose upon an individual many restraints; but with those of the second ascending generation, his grandparents and collateral relatives, there can be, and usually is, established a relationship of simple friendliness relatively free from restraint. In this instance also, it is suggested, the joking relationship is a method of ordering a relation which combines social conjunction and disjunction.

This thesis could, I believe, be strongly supported if not demonstrated by considering the details of these relationships. There is space for only one illustrative point. A very common form of joke in this connection is for the grandchild to pretend that he wishes to marry the grandfather's wife, or that he intends to do so when his grandfather dies, or to treat her as already being his wife. Alternatively the grand-father may pretend that the wife of his grandchild is, or might be, his wife.[k] The point of the joke is the pretence at ignoring the difference of age between the grandparent and the grandchild.[13]

In various parts of the world there are societies in which a sister's son teases and otherwise behaves disrespectfully towards his mother's brother. In these instances the joking relationship seems generally to be asymmetrical. For example the nephew may take his uncle's property but not vice versa; or, as amongst the Nama Hottentots, the nephew may take a fine beast from his uncle's herd and the uncle in return takes a wretched beast from that of the nephew.[l]

The kind of social structure in which this custom of privileged disrespect to the mother's brother occurs in its most marked forms, for example the Thonga of South-East Africa, Fiji and Tonga in the Pacific, and the Central Siouan tribes of North America, is characterised by emphasis on patrilineal lineage and a marked distinction between relatives through the father and relatives through the mother.

In a former publication.[m] I offered an interpretation of this custom of privileged familiarity towards the mother's brother. Briefly it is as follows. For the continuance of a social system children require to be cared for and to be trained. Their care demands affectionate and unselfish devotion; their training requires that they shall be subjected to discipline. In the societies with which we are concerned there is something of a division of function between the parents and other relatives on the two

---

13. Once again, Radcliffe-Brown alludes to evidence but fails to present anything more than anecdotes. At this point, his thesis seems to be that joking is found in relationships where there is conjuncture and disjuncture. As with in-laws and in his examples of other groups, grandchildren are conjoined to their grandparents by being members of the same family but disjoined because they are separated by the generation of parents. This may be true but raises a problem: Because we are all individuals, no two human beings have exactly the same interests. Therefore, couldn't any two individuals be said to have both conjoined and disjoined interests? The question highlights the difficulties in trying to explain the behavior of groups of individuals through abstract and generalized theoretical constructs.

sides. The control and discipline are exercised chiefly by the father and his brothers and generally also by his sisters; these are relatives who must be respected and obeyed. It is the mother who is primarily responsible for the affectionate care; the mother and her brothers and sisters are therefore relatives who can be looked to for assistance and indulgence. The mother's brother is called "male mother" in Tonga and in some South African tribes.[14]

I believe that this interpretation of the special position of the mother's brother in these societies has been confirmed by further field work since I wrote the article referred to. But I was quite aware at the time it was written that the discussion and interpretation needed to be supplemented so as to bring them into line with a general theory of the social functions of respect and disrespect.

The joking relationship with the mother's brother seems to fit well with the general theory of such relationships here outlined. A person's most important duties and rights attach him to his paternal relatives, living and dead. It is to his patrilineal lineage or clan that he belongs. For the members of his mother's lineage he is an outsider, though one in whom they have a very special and tender interest. Thus here again there is a relation in which there is both attachment, or conjunction, and separation, or disjunction, between the two persons concerned.

But let us remember that in this instance the relation is asymmetrical.[n] The nephew is disrespectful and the uncle accepts the disre-

spect. There is inequality and the nephew is the superior. This is recognised by the natives themselves. Thus in Tonga it is said that the sister's son is a "chief" (eiki) to his mother's brother, and Junod[o] quotes a Thonga native as saying "The uterine nephew is a chief! He takes any liberty he likes with his maternal uncle." Thus the joking relationship with the uncle does not merely annul the usual relation between the two generations, it reverses it. But while the superiority of the father and the father's sister is exhibited in the respect that is shown to them the nephew's superiority to his mother's brother takes the opposite form of permitted disrespect.[15]

It has been mentioned that there is a widespread tendency to feel that a man should show respect towards, and treat as social superiors, his relatives in the generation preceding his own, and the custom of joking with, and at the expense of, the maternal uncle clearly conflicts with this tendency. This conflict between principles of behaviour helps us to understand what seems at first sight a very extraordinary feature of the kinship terminology of the Thonga tribe and the VaNdau tribe in SouthEast Africa. Amongst the Thonga, although there is a term malume (= male mother) for the mother's brother, this relative is also, and perhaps more frequently, referred to as a grandfather (kokwana) and he refers to his sister's son as his grandchild (ntukulu). In the VaNdau tribe the mother's brother and also the mother's brother's son are called "grandfather" (tetekulu, literally "great father") and their wives are called

---

14. The former publication is "Mother's Brother in South Africa" (1924). In that essay, in addition to making the point he just described, Radcliffe-Brown argues that matrilineal kinship systems are not survivals of earlier stages of human evolution, as E. B. Tylor and L. H. Morgan had argued, but fully functioning parts of current-day societies. In the present essay, Radcliffe-Brown attempts to place "Mother's Brother" in a more general theory of kin relations.

15. Henri Alexandre Junod (1863–1934) was a Swiss Protestant missionary, linguist and naturalist who worked in South Africa in the late nineteenth and early twentieth centuries. Junod was a multitalented scholar who wrote a grammar of the Tsonga-Shangaan language, several volumes of ethnography of the Tsonga, and numerous other works. In addition, he collected beetle and butterfly specimens for museums. Junod was deeply influenced by nineteenth-century theories of social evolution and believed that marriage among the Thonga had progressed from group marriage to matriarchy and then to patriarchy (Harries 1981: 38). Junod saw details such as the one just recounted by Radcliffe-Brown as evidence of an earlier matriarchal phase of society. Radcliffe-Brown rejects this explanation in favor of searching for the function of the custom in Thonga society. Junod was followed by his son, Henri Phillipe Junod (1897–1977) who also served as a missionary and also wrote on the Tsonga.

"grandmother" (mbiya), while the sister's son and the father's sister's son are called "grandchild" (muzukulu).[16]

This apparently fantastic way of classifying relatives can be interpreted as a sort of legal fiction whereby the male relatives of the mother's lineage are grouped together as all standing towards an individual in the same general relation. Since this relation is one of privileged familiarity on the one side, and solicitude and indulgence on the other, it is conceived as being basically the one appropriate for a grandchild and a grandfather. This is indeed in the majority of human societies the relationship in which this pattern of behaviour most frequently occurs. By this legal fiction the mother's brother ceases to belong to the first ascending generation, of which it is felt that the members ought to be respected.[17]

It may be worth while to justify this interpretation by considering another of the legal fictions of the VaNdau terminology. In all these south-eastern Bantu tribes both the father's sister and the sister, particularly the elder sister, are persons who must be treated with great respect. They are also both of them members of a man's own patrilineal lineage. Amongst the VaNdau the father's sister is called "female father" (tetadji) and so also is the sister.[p] Thus by the fiction of terminological classification the sister is placed in the father's generation, the one that appropriately includes persons to whom one must exhibit marked respect.

In the south-eastern Bantu tribes there is assimilation of two kinds of joking relatives, the grandfather and the mother's brother. It may help our understanding of this to consider an example in which the grandfather and the brother-in-law are similarly grouped together. The Cherokee Indians of North America probably numbering at one time about 20,000, were divided into seven matrilineal clans.[q] A man could not marry a woman of his own clan or of his father's clan. Common membership of the same clan connects him with his brothers and his mother's brothers. Towards his father and all his relatives in his father's clan of his own or his father's generation he is required by custom to show a marked respect. He applies the kinship term for "father" not only to his father's brothers but also to the sons of his father's sisters. Here is another example of the same kind of fiction as described above; the relatives of his own generation whom he is required to respect and who belong to his father's matrilineal lineage are spoken of as though they belonged to the generation of his parents. The body of his immediate kindred is included in these two clans, that of his mother and his father. To the other clans of the tribe he is in a sense an outsider. But with two of them he is connected, namely with the clans of his two grandfathers, his father's father and his mother's father. He speaks of all the members of these two clans, of whatever age, as "grandfathers" and "grandmothers." He stands in a joking relationship with all of them. When a man marries he must respect his wife's parents but jokes with her brothers and sisters.

The interesting and critical feature is that it is regarded as particularly appropriate that

---

16. Radcliffe-Brown's information on the VaNdau comes from several articles by Boas. Boas came to write about the VaNdau (or Vandau) through his association with Kamba Simango (1890–1966). Simango was born in Mozambique and, through an extraordinary series of adventures and sufferings, found his way to the Hampton School (today Hampton University), a historically black school in Virginia. He rose to prominence there and went on to Teachers College at Columbia University. Along with a member of the Hampton faculty, he wrote a book about the Ndau called *Songs and Tales from the Dark Continent* (1920). This brought him to the attention of Boas, his student Melville Herskovits (1895–1963), and key African American intellectuals, including W. E. B. Du Bois and Paul Robeson (Spencer 2013). Boas coauthored an essay about Vandau tales and proverbs with Simango (1922) and wrote several additional essays about the Vandau in both English and German. In 1923, Simango returned to Africa as a missionary. He died in Ghana in 1966.

17. Keep in mind that in kinship studies (particularly those by functionalist authors) kin names such as "grandfather" or "male mother" refer primarily to behavioral expectations rather than biological linkages. So, if a Thonga youth calls his mother's brother "grandfather," he behaves toward him as he behaves toward his father's father (whom he also calls "grandfather").

a man should marry a woman whom he calls "grandmother," i.e. a member of his father's father's clan or his mother's father's clan. If this happens his wife's brothers and sisters, whom he continues to tease, are amongst those whom he previously teased as his "grandfathers" and "grandmothers." This is analogous to the widely spread organisation in which a man has a joking relationship with the children of his mother's brother and is expected to marry one of the daughters.[18]

It ought perhaps to be mentioned that the Cherokee also have a one-sided joking relationship in which a man teases his father's sister's husband. The same custom is found in **Mota of the Bank Islands**. In both instances we have a society organised on a matrilineal basis in which the mother's brother is respected, the father's sister's son is called "father" (so that the father's sister's husband is the father of a "father"), and there is a special term for the father's sister's husband. Further observation of the societies in which this custom occurs is required before we can be sure of its interpretation. I do not remember that it has been reported from any part of Africa.[19]

What has been attempted in this paper is to define in the most general and abstract terms the kind of structural situation in which we may expect to find well-marked joking relationships. We have been dealing with societies in which the basic social structure is provided by kinship. By reason of his birth or adoption into a certain position in the social structure an individual is connected with a large number of other persons. With some of them he finds himself in a definite and specific jural relation, i.e. one which can be defined in terms of rights and duties. Who these persons will be and what will be the rights and duties depend on the form taken by the social structure. As an example of such a specific jural relation we may take that which normally exists between a father and son, or an elder brother and a younger brother. Relations of the same general type may be extended over a considerable range to all the members of a lineage or a clan or an age-set. Besides these specific jural relations which are defined not only negatively but also positively, i.e. in terms of things that must be done as well as things that must not there are general jural relations which are expressed almost entirely in terms of prohibitions and which extend throughout the whole political society. It is forbidden to kill or wound other persons or to take or destroy their property. Besides these two classes of social relations there is another, including many very diverse varieties, which can perhaps be called relations of alliance or consocation. For example, there is a form of alliance of very great importance in many societies, in which two persons or two groups are connected by an exchange of gifts or services.[r] Another example is provided by the institution of blood-brotherhood which is so widespread in Africa.[20]

---

18. In other words, in this example, a man jokes with his potential marriage partners and their families. He continues to joke with their families after his marriage.

19. If you're feeling a bit dizzy trying to keep track of all of these father's sister's sons and mother's brothers, rejoice that you were not studying anthropology in the 1950s. Kinship studies had an important role in anthropology from the days of L. H. Morgan but were a central focus of anthropology in the mid-twentieth century. College courses in kinship were common. However, starting in the 1970s, kin studies were increasingly critiqued. The work of David Schneider (1918–1995) was central to this. In *American Kinship: A Cultural Account* (1968) and *A Critique of the Study of Kinship* (1984) Schneider attacked the role of kinship in anthropology. Repudiating much of his own earlier work, Schneider charged that anthropological ideas about kinship incorrectly privileged biological connections between people. Further, he argued that kinship studies did not take local understandings of reproduction and local meanings of kin terms into account. Schneider also showed that kinship is not as central to many societies as the functionalists claimed. In the wake of Schneider's work, the importance of kin studies declined dramatically. Today it is rare for anthropology programs to teach courses specifically devoted to kinship studies.

"Mota of the Bank Islands": The Bank Islands are an archipelago of 10 islands and are part of the modern nation of Vanuatu in the South Pacific Ocean. Mota is one of the islands.

20. Notice Radcliffe-Brown's concern in this passage to associate kinship relations with law. Law was a central concern for colonial administrators. If they could understand native customs, they could govern

The argument of this paper has been intended to show that the joking relationship is one special form of alliance in this sense. An alliance by exchange of goods and services may be associated with a joking relationship, as in the instance recorded by Professor Labouret.[s] Or it may be combined with the custom of avoidance. Thus in the Andaman Islands the parents of a man and the parents of his wife avoid all contact with each other and do not speak; at the same time it is the custom that they should frequently exchange presents through the medium of the younger married couple.

But the exchange of gifts may also exist without either joking or avoidance, as in Samoa, in the exchange of gifts between the family of a man and the family of the woman he marries or the very similar exchange between a chief and his "talking chief."

So also in an alliance by blood-brotherhood there may be a joking relationship as amongst the Zande;[t] and in the somewhat similar alliance formed by exchange of names there may also be mutual teasing. But in alliances of this kind there may be a relation of extreme respect and even of avoidance. Thus in the Yaralde and neighbouring tribes of South Australia two boys belonging to communities distant from one another, and therefore more or less hostile, are brought into an alliance by the exchange of their respective umbilical cords. The relationship thus established is a sacred one; the two boys may never speak to one another. But when they grow up they enter upon a regular exchange of gifts, which provides the machinery for a sort of commerce between the two groups to which they belong.

Thus the four modes of alliance or consociation, (1) through intermarriage, (2) by exchange of goods or services, (3) by blood-brotherhood or exchanges of names or sacra, and (4) by the joking relationship, may exist separately or combined in several different ways. The comparative study of these combinations presents a number of interesting but complex problems. The facts recorded from West Africa by Professor Labouret and Mademoiselle Paulme afford us valuable material. But a good deal more intensive field research is needed before these problems of social structure can be satisfactorily dealt with.[21]

What I have called relations by alliance need to be compared with true contractual relations. The latter are specific jural relations entered into by two persons or two groups, in which either party has definite positive obligations towards the other, and failure to carry out the obligations is subject to a legal sanction. In an alliance by blood-brotherhood there are general obligations of mutual aid, and the sanction for the carrying out of these, as shown by Dr. Evans-Pritchard, is of a kind that can be called magical or ritual. In the alliance by exchange of gifts failure to fulfil the obligation to make an equivalent return for a gift received breaks the alliance and substitutes a state of hostility and may also cause a loss of prestige for the defaulting party. Professor Mauss[u] has argued that in this kind of alliance also there is a magical sanction, but it is very doubtful if such is

---

more effectively. In principle, anthropology could help administrators understand the nature of native law. However, this was problematic in practice. First, it assumed that native cultures had law in the sense that the colonizing countries had law. Second, as Radcliffe-Brown will note later in this essay, joking relations and the alliances they indicate are not laws in the sense that the prohibition of murder may be a law. But, if that is so, does calling them laws increase or diminish our understanding?

21. Radcliffe-Brown was deeply influenced by his reading of Durkheim and Durkheim's followers. This is evident in many ways in this essay. First, Radcliffe-Brown makes heavy use of the ideas of Mauss and Mauss's student, Paulme. Beyond this, his overriding concern is the same as Durkheim's. Durkheim was particularly concerned with the ways social solidarity is developed and maintained. In other words, he focused on the mechanisms that held societies together. He found these in notions of the collective conscience, social facts, and collective representations. Radcliffe-Brown has similar concerns. For him, kinship is the critical institution holding societies together (and this is consistent with his mentor Rivers's ideas as well as a general concern within Anglo American anthropology). Within kinship, the relations of law and alliance that he discusses here function to hold society together and maintain it. Notice that the system is very neat: Where there are possibilities of disjuncture and rupture, society creates institutions such as joking and avoidance relationships to smooth the disjunctures over and avoid conflict.

always present, and even when it is it may often be of secondary importance.[22]

The joking relationship is in some ways the exact opposite of a contractual relation. Instead of specific duties to be fulfilled there is privileged disrespect and freedom or even licence, and the only obligation is not to take offence at the disrespect so long as it is kept within certain bounds defined by custom, and not to go beyond those bounds. Any default in the relationship is like a breach of the rules of etiquette; the person concerned is regarded as not knowing how to behave himself.

In a true contractual relationship the two parties are conjoined by a definite common interest in reference to which each of them accepts specific obligations. It makes no difference that in other matters their interests may be divergent. In the joking relationship and in some avoidance relationships, such as that between a man and his wife's mother, one basic determinant is that the social structure separates them in such a way as to make many of their interests divergent, so that conflict or hostility might result. The alliance by extreme respect, by partial or complete avoidance, prevents such conflict but keeps the parties conjoined. The alliance by joking does the same thing in a different way.

All that has been, or could be, attempted in this paper is to show the place of the joking relationship in a general comparative study of social structure. What I have called, provisionally, relations of consociation or alliance are distinguished from the relations set up by common membership of a political society which are defined in terms of general obligations, of etiquette, or morals, or of law. They are distinguished also from true contractual relations, defined by some specific obligation for each contracting party, into which the individual enters of his own volition. They are further to be distinguished from the relations set up by common membership of a domestic group, a lineage or a clan, each of which has to be defined in terms of a whole set of socially recognised rights and duties. Relations of consociation can only exist between individuals or groups which are in some way socially separated.

This paper deals only with formalised or standardised joking relations. Teasing or making fun of other persons is of course a common mode of behaviour in any human society. It tends to occur in certain kinds of social situations. Thus I have observed in certain classes in English-speaking countries the occurrence of horse-play between young men and women as a preliminary to courtship, very similar to the way in which a Cherokee Indian jokes with his "grandmothers." Certainly these unformalised modes of behaviour need to be studied by the sociologist. For the purpose of this paper it is sufficient to note that teasing is always a compound of friendliness and antagonism.

The scientific explanation of the institution in the particular form in which it occurs in a given society can only be reached by an intensive study which enables us to see it as a particular example of a widespread phenomenon of a definite class. This means that the whole social structure has to be thoroughly examined in order that the particular form and incidence of joking relationships can be understood as part of a consistent system. If it be asked why that society has the structure that it does have, the only possible answer would lie in its history. When the history is unrecorded, as it is for the native societies of Africa, we can only indulge in conjecture, and conjecture gives us neither scientific nor historical knowledge.[v][23]

---

22. E. E. Evans-Pritchard (1901–1973) was a central member of the British Functionalist group. A student of both Malinowski and Radcliffe-Brown, he wrote extensively on the Azande and Nuer, two East African groups. In 1940, when this essay was written, Evans-Pritchard was one of Radcliffe-Brown's foremost followers. However, he became disillusioned with functionalism and in the 1950s began to promote a more historical, humanistic anthropology.

23. In this last paragraph, Radcliffe-Brown attacks Boasian anthropologists. The Boasians insisted that societies were the *sui generis* results of their own historical development. They had a strong distaste for general theories of society. To the contrary, Radcliffe-Brown argues that the histories of nonliterate societies

AUTHOR'S NOTES

a. "Joking Relationships in East Africa," *Africa*, Vol. XIII, p. 170.

b. "La Parentéà Plaisanteries en Afrique Occidentale," *Africa*, Vol. II, p. 244.

c. "Parentéà Plaisanteries et Alliance par le Sang en Afrique Occidentale," *Africa*, Vol. XII, p. 433.

d. Professor Marcel Mauss has published a brief theoretical discussion of the subject in the *Annuaire de l'École Pratique des Hautes Etudes, Section des Sciences religieuses*, 1927–8. It is also dealt with by Dr. F. Eggan in *Social Anthropology of North American Tribes*, 1937, pp. 75–81.

e. *Africa*, Vol. XII, p. 438.

f. Those who are not familiar with these widespread customs will find descriptions in Junod, *Life of a South African Tribe*, Neuchatel, Vol. I, pp. 220–37, and in *Social Anthropology of North American Tribes*, edited by F. Eggan, Chicago, 1937. pp. 55–7.

g. Ruth Landes in Mead, *Co-operation and Competition among Primitive Peoples*, 1937, p. 103.

h. Incidentally it may be said that it was hardly satisfactory for the magistrate to establish a precedent whereby the man, who was observing what was a permitted and may even have been an obligatory custom, was declared guilty of common assault, even with extenuating circumstances. It seems quite possible that the man may have committed a breach of etiquette in teasing the woman in the presence of her mother's brother, for in many parts of the world it is regarded as improper for two persons in a joking relationship to tease one another (particularly if any obscenity is involved) in the presence of certain relatives of either of them. But the breach of etiquette would still not make it an assault.

A little knowledge of anthropology would have enabled the magistrate, by putting the appropriate questions to the witnesses, to have obtained a fuller understanding of the case and all that was involved in it.

i. Fortes, M., *The Dynamics of Clanship among the Tallensi*. Oxford University Press, 1945.

j. See, for example, the kinship systems described in *Social Anthropology of North American Tribes*, edited by Fred Eggan, University of Chicago Press, 1937; and Margaret Mead, "Kinship in the Admiralty Islands," *Anthropological Papers of the American Museum of Natural History*, Vol. XXXIV, pp. 243–56.

k. For examples see Labouret, *Les Tribus du Rameau Lobi*, 1931, p. 248 and Sarat Chandra Roy, *The Oraons of Chota Nagpur*, Ranchi, 1915, pp. 352–54.

l. A. Winifred Hoernle, "Social Organisation of the Nama Hottentot," *American Anthropologist*, N.s., Vol. XXVII, 1925, pp. 1–24.

m. "The Mother's Brother in South Africa," *South African Journal of Science*, Vol. XXI, 1924. See Chapter I.

n. There are some societies in which the relation between a mother's brother and a sister's son is approximately symmetrical, and therefore one of equality. This seems to be so in the Western Islands of Torres Straits, but we have no information as to any teasing or joking, though it is said that each of the two relatives may take the property of the other.

o. *Life of a South African Tribe*, Vol. I, p. 255.

p. For the kinship terminology of the VaNdau see Boas, "Das Verwandtschafts system der Vandau," in *Zeitschrift für Ethnologie*. 1922, pp. 41–51.

q. For an account of the Cherokee see Gilbert, in *Social Anthropology of North American Tribes*, pp. 285–338.

---

are unknowable (and therefore, Boasian anthropology is essentially groundless). Earlier, he had written that those who hold that laws of human society do not exist (i.e., Boas and his followers) must hold that "in the field of social phenomena, in contradistinction to physical and biological phenomena, any attempt at the systematic testing of existing generalizations or toward the discovery and verification of new ones is, for some unexplained reason, futile, or as Dr. Radin puts it, 'crying for the moon'" (1965b [1935]: 187). He viewed this as a clearly irrational belief and suggested that arguing against such lack of logic was a waste of time. Radcliffe-Brown's goal was to create a science of society. Functionalist anthropology in general (and Radcliffe-Brown in particular) were scathingly critiqued by American anthropologists for their failure (so the Americans believed) to effectively do this. In 1951 George Peter Murdock (1897–1985) wrote an essay cataloging the sins of functionalism. Of Radcliffe-Brown's attempts at scientific theorizing, he says:

Radcliffe-Brown is responsible for two serious distortions of scientific method from which his followers have never freed themselves, namely (1) the notion that universal "laws" are discoverable from the intensive study of a few societies without reference to their representativeness and (2) the misconception that such laws can be adequately expressed by verbal statements which do not specify the concomitant behavior of variables (1951: 469).

Later in the same essay, he accuses functionalist anthropologists of having a "predilection" for "'sociologistic' verbalisms as a substitute for scientific laws" (1951: 472). None of this deterred Radcliffe-Brown's many ardent followers. They formed what their critics charged was a "cult" of Radcliffe-Brown (Elkin 1956: 246). In 1946 they founded the Association of Social Anthropologists to promote Radcliffe-Brown's style of anthropology and theoretical insights. They elected him president for life.

r. See Mauss, "Essai sur le Don," *Année Socio-logique*, Nouvelle Série, tome I, pp. 30–186.

s. *Africa*. Vol. II, p. 245.

t. Evans-Pritchard, "Zande Blood-brotherhood," *Africa*, Vol. VI, 1933, pp. 369–401.

u. "Essai sur le Don."

v. The general theory outlined in this paper is one that I have presented in lectures at various universities since 1909 as part of the general study of the forms of social structure. In arriving at the present formulation of it I have been helped by discussions with Dr. Meyer Fortes.

PART III

Theory in the Mid-Twentieth Century

The Reemergence of Evolutionary Thought

A major theoretical shift occurred in American anthropology in the late 1930s and the 1940s. For the first three decades of the century, the principal work in American anthropology was based on the Boasian tradition or the neo-Freudian approach of the culture and personality school. Beginning in the 1930s, the antievolutionary perspective of the Boasian tradition had once again to compete with new and more sophisticated evolutionary approaches such as those proposed by Leslie White (1900–1975) and Julian Steward (1902–1972).

White is best known for his formulation of a general evolutionary theory of culture, an approach that had been abandoned after Boas thrashed unilineal evolutionary theory at the turn of the century. Steward, on the other hand, developed a techno-environmental approach to cultural change that focused on adaptation as a consequence of the interaction between technology, environment, and social structure.

Additionally, George Peter Murdock (1897–1985) was influential in resurrecting the sort of large-scale cross-cultural comparisons that had been the basis of the work of nineteenth-century anthropologists such as Lewis Henry Morgan (1818–1881) and E. B. Tylor (1832–1917). Murdock is best known for his creation of the Human Relations Area Files, or HRAF. Marvin Harris (1968: 606) credits Murdock, Steward, and White's revival of cross-cultural comparison with the "mid-century collapse of historical particularism." Although Harris's eulogy for historical particularism was premature, the work of White and Steward especially set the foundation for the formulation of ecological anthropology and cultural materialism, two of the most influential forms of American anthropological analysis in the second half of the twentieth century.

Leslie White was the middle child of three, whose parents divorced in 1905 when he was five years old. White's father received custody of the children after his divorce and moved to rural Kansas, where White lived until 1914 when a family scandal (his sister's unplanned pregnancy) caused the family to move to Louisiana. White graduated from high school in 1916 at the age of sixteen. Although White was an outstanding student, he had a troubled relationship with his father, and on the day he graduated, White left home, working first as a bookkeeper but ultimately enlisting in the navy in 1918. Although he served for fewer than two years, White considered his time in the Navy to be a life-changing period. Upon his discharge in August 1919, he enrolled at Louisiana State University to study history. There, professors who recognized his ability recommended he transfer to Columbia. White took BA and MA degrees in psychology at Columbia but also took anthropology classes at the New School for Social Research, where he was exposed to the anthropology of Franz Boas by Boas's student Alexander Goldenweiser. At the urging of a friend, Leslie White then entered the PhD program in anthropology and sociology at the University of Chicago in 1924. With the help of Elsie Clews Parsons, he conducted his dissertation fieldwork in Acoma Pueblo in 1926 and received his degree in 1927. White accepted his first teaching post at the University of Buffalo in 1927, where he had access to L. H. Morgan's papers. Morgan had been vilified by Boas and was the target of attacks by many of Boas's students, but White argued that much of what Morgan wrote was correct. Specifically, White believed that cross-cultural studies demonstrated that cultural evolution existed, that it was empirically measurable, and that this evolution was in the direction of increasing complexity. The problem with the evolutionary thinkers of the nineteenth century, White argued, was that they failed to develop a nonethnocentric, scientific method of accurately assessing cultural complexity. Therefore, although their general idea was correct, many of their specific examples were in error. White proposed to remedy this by developing a quantifiable, universal standard of measurement. In his "Energy and the Evolution of Culture" (1943), reprinted here in essay 16, White proposed that the control of energy was a key factor in cultural evolution and could serve as the standard by which to measure evolutionary progress. In this essay he traces the history of human culture, arguing that changes in technology marked evolutionary stages. White understood culture as the means by which humans adapted to nature. As members of societies learned to capture energy, they were able to make their lives increasingly secure, and so culture advanced. Like Morgan, whom he cites in "Energy and the Evolution of Culture," White suggested a grand, universal law of cultural evolution: culture advances as the amount of energy harnessed per capita per year increases, or as the efficiency with which energy is utilized increases. While White understood that all the institutions of society contributed to the evolution of culture, inspired by his reading of Marx, he believed that technology played the primary role in social evolution and that changes in technology affected a society's institutions and value systems.

Julian Steward grew up in Washington, DC, but at age sixteen he went to the newly founded Deep Springs Preparatory School (today Deep Springs College) in California. Deep Springs almost surely had a profound effect on Steward. It was then, as today, an extremely small school (about twenty students), where intense study and debate were combined with strenuous physical labor. Deep Springs is also in a spectacular physical setting in the desert and mountains of eastern California. At Deep Springs, Steward became interested in the local Paiute and Shoshoni communities, and he may well have been impressed with how these groups survived in this beautiful but harsh environment. After completing his undergraduate education at the University of California, Berkeley, and Cornell University, Steward returned to Berkeley in 1925 to study anthropology as a student of A. L. Kroeber (1876–1960), Robert Lowie (1883–1957), and the geographer Carl Sauer (1889–1975). At this time, Kroeber was interested primarily in mapping culture areas and establishing the existence of long-term cultural cycles that existed independently of the people living through them (see essay 9). Steward conducted trait-list research for Kroeber, but collecting this comparative data led Steward to the conclusion that technology, social structure, and environment formed adaptive cultural systems, which Kroeber refused to consider. Consequently, they developed a contentious relationship, as Steward devoted most of his energy to the study of the cultural adaptations of specific societies. Although his first research was in archaeology, he soon moved to ethnography and worked with the Paiute, Shoshoni, Pueblo, and, later, the Carrier Indians in British Columbia.

In the second half of his career, Steward also devoted a great deal of energy to the investigation of parallel developmental sequences in the evolution of civilizations in the New and Old Worlds. He proposed that cultures in similar environments would tend to follow the same developmental sequences and formulate similar responses to their environmental challenges. He termed those cultural features most closely associated with subsistence practices the *cultural core*. Cultures that shared similar core features belonged to the same *culture type*. After identifying these culture types, Steward compared and ranked them into a hierarchy arranged by complexity. Steward's original ranking was family, multifamily, and state-level societies. His followers later refined these categories into the now familiar classifications of band, tribe, chiefdom, and state.

Steward did not believe that cultures followed a single universal sequence of development. He proposed instead that cultures could evolve in any number of distinct patterns depending on their environmental circumstances. He called this theory *multilinear evolution* to distinguish it from nineteenth-century unilineal-evolutionary theories. The methodology Steward outlined for multilinear evolution involved a field of study he called *cultural ecology*—that is, the examination of the cultural adaptations formulated by human beings to meet the challenges posed by their environments. The selection of Steward's work that we present in essay 17, "The Patrilineal Band," clearly shows how he viewed culture as an evolutionary adaptation to the environment.

Although not given an essay in this volume, George Peter Murdock was another important anthropologist deeply influenced by the work of Herbert Spencer and L. H. Morgan. He received his undergraduate and graduate degrees at Yale University and taught there for thirty-two years.

Like Leslie White, Murdock rejected the Boasian approach to anthropology. Murdock was interested in the statistical testing of cross-cultural hypotheses, in direct opposition to Boas's avoidance of cross-cultural generalizations. Toward this end, Murdock established the Cross-Cultural Survey in 1937, which a decade later formed the basis of the HRAF, a huge bank of ethnographic data on more than one thousand societies indexed according to standardized categories. The purpose of this data bank is to allow researchers to conduct cross-cultural quantitative analyses and test cultural hypotheses in a wide variety of societies.

In addition to creating the HRAF, Murdock is remembered for his 1949 book *Social Structure*, in which he proposed that a universal set of principles governed the relationship between family structure, kinship, and marriage practices. Using HRAF data, Murdock attempted to determine these principles through quantitative analysis and was able to analyze kinship structure and its relation to marriage and sexuality in 250 societies.

Murdock generally saw his work as deriving from the positivist approach of Spencer, but he recognized that Morgan's 1871 study of kinship was instrumental in shaping the quantitative-comparative approach he developed in *Social Structure*. On the opening page of his chapter on kinship, Murdock wrote, "The scientific significance of kinship systems was first appreciated by Morgan in what is perhaps the most original and brilliant single achievement in the history of anthropology" (1960: 61). Additionally, Morgan is one of the anthropologists to whom *Social Structure* is dedicated.

Although White, Steward, and Murdock were evolutionists, they had different ideas of what cultural evolution meant and how it happened. Steward's vision of evolution was specific and relativistic; he viewed a society's core features as cultural adaptations to its specific environment. On the other hand, White, like Morgan, looked at evolution as a general overall pattern of development and argued that cultural progress can be measured by specific, absolute standards and ranked on a universal scale. He proposed that the key factor driving evolutionary change was revolutionary change in technology. White and Steward were intellectual rivals, and in the 1960s, Marshall Sahlins (1930–2021) and Elman Service (1915–1996) attempted to reconcile their two approaches. Based on an analogy with biological evolution, they suggested that cultural evolution followed two paths. The first was general evolution, a grand movement from simple to complex represented by White's work. The second was specific evolution, the change of individual cultures in response to their particular environmental circumstances as proposed by Steward (Sahlins and Service 1960).

Murdock's cross-cultural comparisons of cultural traits in many ways paralleled Steward's theory of multilinear evolution, and his attempts to statistically demonstrate universal principles of kin relations resembled White's effort to formulate a universal theory of cultural evolution. However, Murdock focused his efforts on the evolution of aspects of social structure, such as kin terminology, family structure, and marriage patterns.

No theoretical viewpoint is immune to the political context in which it develops, and the neo-evolutionists were a particularly good example of this point. Steward and White relied heavily on the insights of Marxist analysis, but given the virulently anti-communist political climate of the United States at the time, they generally did not cite Marx openly. Steward made no reference at all to the influence of Marx in his work and was thus able to avoid controversy. White, on the contrary, often courted controversy.

Like many American scholars of the 1920s, White was drawn to Soviet communism. He visited the Soviet Union for eight weeks in the summer of 1929, and by the time he returned, he was convinced that "the Russian Revolution was the most significant event in modern history" (Peace 1998: 85). When the American Association for the Advancement of Science met in 1930, White gave an address, titled "An Anthropological Appraisal of the Russian Revolution," praising the Soviet Union and predicting disaster for capitalist nations. The address received front-page attention in the *New York Times* and *Pravda* (the official state newspaper of the Soviet Union) and created a firestorm. Burned by this experience, White became more cautious in expressing his political views. He concealed his political activities and avoided public statements of his attachment to either authors or individuals associated with the left. In the 1930s, as the nature of

Joseph Stalin's dictatorship became apparent, White became a fierce opponent and critic of Soviet communism, but he remained a committed socialist. He wrote articles and letters for the *Weekly People*, the newspaper of the Socialist Labor Party of America, under the pseudonym John Steel (Shankman and Dino 2001).

We should note that many anthropologists have paid a heavy price for their political activism. Boas, as you will recall, was censured for criticizing anthropologists who used the trust they had developed in the field to spy for the US government. Other anthropologists were followed and harassed by the FBI. These include Melville Jacobs (1902–1971), Paul Radin (1883–1959), Elman Service (1915–1996), Oscar Lewis (1914–1970), Margaret Mead, and Cora Du Bois (1903–1991). Ashley Montague (1905–1999) was fired from Rutgers University after giving a speech condemning Senator Joseph McCarthy (Price 2004). Boas's student Gene Weltfish (1902–1980) coauthored with Ruth Benedict (1887–1948) an extremely influential antiracist pamphlet, *The Races of Mankind*, distributed to troops during World War II (which was recalled because it suggested that northern blacks were intellectually superior to southern whites). Weltfish was called to testify before McCarthy and the House Committee on Un-American Activities. *The Races of Mankind* was declared subversive material, and Weltfish's teaching position at Columbia was not renewed (Pathe 1988; Shipp 1980).

Although White was pleased by the attention his views generated, he was also worried for his position at the University of Michigan. His ideas were repeatedly attacked, and attempts to have him fired were a recurring theme of his career. The University of Michigan denied him promotion and pay raises for thirteen years; nevertheless, White remained until the end of his career and felt that he owed a great debt to Michigan. He wrote that the university's "devotion to its own ideals made it possible for a nonconformist to stay there and keep being a nonconformist" (in Peace 1998: 89; see also Peace and Price 2001).

As the rehabilitation of cultural evolutionary ideas became accepted, White changed his focus from evolution to the concept of culture and the role of symbols in culture, proposing that the study of culture was a distinct scientific activity that deserved its own name, "culturology." While the term *culturology* was controversial, White was widely recognized for this work. In his 1959 article "The Concept of Culture," published in *American Anthropologist*, White defined *culture* as "a class of things and events, dependent on symboling, considered in an extrasomatic context" (1959a: 234). White's culturology did not easily accommodate his materialist views. For White the materialist, cultural traits were adaptive responses. However, White the culturologist believed that culture existed in its own right. In his last book, *The Concept of Cultural Systems*, White wrote, "We no longer think of culture as designed to serve the needs of man; culture goes on its own way in accordance with laws of its own" (1975: 159). Eventually White's work was widely acclaimed. In the late 1950s and the 1960s, he received numerous awards and two honorary degrees, and he was elected president of the American Anthropological Association.

Although a materialist, Murdock was at the opposite end of the political spectrum from White and thus avoided the kinds of public political controversies in which White became embroiled. However, in recent years, Murdock has come under scrutiny for his political activities during the 1940s and 1950s. Based on files recovered under the Freedom of Information Act, David Price discovered that Murdock was an informant for the FBI and reported on the activities of many of his professional colleagues. For example, in 1949, he corresponded directly with J. Edgar Hoover, naming a dozen anthropologists whom he was convinced were communists (Price 2004).

Murdock's research has also not escaped the critical appraisal of other anthropologists. One of the most telling criticisms of Murdock's work is the same as that which Boas leveled at the nineteenth-century evolutionists in his 1896 article "The Limitations of the Comparative Method in Anthropology." That is, the data on which Murdock's analyses were based were taken out of their appropriate cultural contexts, thus invalidating the reliability of the analysis. Murdock's popularity was largely limited to American anthropologists. Many British social anthropologists considered Murdock's work to be nothing more than classification of data.

SUGGESTED READINGS

Kerns, Virginia. 2003. *Scenes from the High Desert*. Urbana: University of Illinois Press.
An extensive and readable biography of Steward with an explanation of his theoretical positions.
Murdock, George Peter. 1949. *Social Structure*. New York: Macmillan.
Murdock's cross-cultural comparison of family, kinship, the regulation of sex, and incest taboos.
Peace, William. 2004. *Leslie A. White: Evolution and Revolution in Anthropology*. Lincoln: University of Nebraska Press.
An account of the tumultuous life of Leslie White that provides details of his anthropology, his politics, and his personal life.
Price, David. 2004. *Threatening Anthropology: McCarthyism and the FBI's Surveillance of Activist Anthropologists*. Durham, NC: Duke University Press.
Price examines the deep effects of McCarthysim on anthropology in the 1950s, and its role in the lives of the scholars featured in this section and many others.
Steward, Julian. 1955. *Theory of Culture Change*. Urbana: University of Illinois Press.
A collection of critical essays by Steward showcasing the relationship of environment and social form.
White, Leslie. 1949. *The Science of Culture*. New York: Grove Press.
A collection of critical essays by White tracing his thinking from the late 1930s to the late 1940s.

16. Energy and the Evolution of Culture

Leslie White (1900–1975)

EVERYTHING IN THE UNIVERSE may be described in terms of energy.[a] Galaxies, stars, molecules and atoms may be regarded as organizations of energy. Living organisms may be looked upon as engines which operate by means of energy derived directly or indirectly from the sun. The civilizations, or cultures of mankind, also, may be regarded as a form of organization of energy. Culture is an organization of phenomena—material objects, bodily acts, ideas, and sentiments—which consists of or is dependent upon the use of symbols. Man, being the only animal capable of symbol-behavior, is the only creature to possess culture.[b] Culture is a kind of behavior. And behavior, whether of man, mule, plant, comet or molecule, may be treated as a manifestation of energy. Thus we see, on all levels of reality,[c] that phenomena lend themselves to description and interpretation in terms of energy. Cultural anthropology is that branch of natural science[d] which deals with matter-and-motion, i.e., energy, phenomena in cultural form, as biology deals with them in cellular, and physics in atomic, form.[1]

The purpose of culture is to serve the needs of man. These needs are of two kinds: (1) those which can be served or satisfied by drawing upon resources within the human organism alone. Singing, dancing, myth-making, forming clubs or associations for the sake of companionship, etc., illustrate this kind of needs and ways of satisfying them. (2) The second class of needs can be satisfied only by drawing upon the resources of the external world, outside the human organism. Man must get his food from the external world. The tools, weapons, and other materials with which man provides himself with food, shelter from the elements, protection from his enemies, must likewise come from the external world. The satisfaction of spiritual and aesthetic needs through singing, dancing, myth-making, etc., is possible, however, only if man's bodily needs for food, shelter, and defense are met. Thus the whole cultural structure depends upon the material, mechanical means with which man articulates himself with the earth. Furthermore, the satisfaction of human needs from "inner resources" may be regarded as a constant,[e] the satisfaction of needs from the outer resources a variable. Therefore, in our discussion of cultural development we may omit consideration of the constant factor and deal only with the

---

From *American Anthropologist* (1943)

1. This arresting opening passage reveals an important aspect of White's thinking about culture at this stage of his career. Because he saw anthropology as a branch of science, he believed that the research methods used in the sciences, applied to anthropology, would reveal laws of culture.

White was trained in the Boasian tradition. He studied at the New School for Social Research under Alexander Goldenweiser (1880–1940), a student of Franz Boas and the mentor of Ruth Benedict. At the University of Chicago, where he received his PhD, he worked with Edward Sapir (1884–1939) and Fay-Cooper Cole (1881–1961), both students of Boas. His fieldwork in Acoma, a Native American Pueblo in New Mexico, was financially supported and mentored by Elsie Clews Parsons (1875–1941). White wrote, "Parsons . . . has advised and encouraged me at every step" (in Peace 2004:41). However, in this and other essays, White broke with the Boasians, modelling his theory on the work of nineteenth century evolutionists such as L. H. Morgan, E. B. Tylor, and Herbert Spencer.

variable—the material, mechanical means with which man exploits the resources of nature.[2]

The articulation-of-man-with-the-earth process may be analyzed and resolved into the following five factors: (1) the human organism, (2) the habitat, (3) the amount of energy controlled and expended by man, (4) the ways and means in which energy is expended, and (5) the human-need-serving product which accrues from the expenditure of energy. This is but another way of saying that human beings, like all other living creatures, exploit the resources of their habitat, in one way or another in order to sustain life and to perpetuate their kind.

Of the above factors, we may regard the organic factor as a constant. Although peoples obviously differ from each other physically, we are not able to attribute differences in culture to differences in physique (or "mentality"). In our study of culture, therefore, we may regard human race as of uniform quality, i.e., as a constant, and, hence, we eliminate it from our study.[3]

No two habitats are alike; every habitat varies in time. Yet, in a study of culture as a whole,[f] we may regard the factor of habitat as a constant: we simply reduce the need-serving, welfare-promoting resources of particular habitats to an average. (In a consideration of particular manifestations of culture we would of course have to deal with their respective particular habitats.) Since we may regard habitat as a constant, we exclude it, along with the human

organism, from our study of the development of culture.[4]

This leaves us, then, three factors to be considered in any cultural situation: (1) the amount of energy per capita per unit of time harnessed and put to work within the culture, (2) the technological means with which this energy is expended, and (3) the human-need-serving product that accrues from the expenditure of energy. We may express the relationship between these factors in the following simple formula: $E \times T = P$, in which E represents the amount of energy expended per capita per unit of time, T the technological means of its expenditure, and P the magnitude of the product per unit of time. This may be illustrated concretely with the following simple example: A man cuts wood with an axe. Assuming the quality of the wood and the skill of the workman to be constant, the amount of wood cut in a given period of time, say an hour, depends, on the one hand upon the amount of energy the man expends during this time: the more energy expended, the more wood cut. On the other hand, the amount of wood cut in an hour depends upon the kind of axe used. Other things being equal, the amount of wood cut varies with the quality of the axe: the better the axe the more wood cut. Our workman can cut more wood with an iron, or steel, axe than with a stone axe.[5]

The efficiency with which human energy is expended mechanically depends upon the bodily skills of the persons involved, and upon

---

2. In this essay, White provides a materialist and functionalist basis for the analysis of culture. His "functions and needs" approach is derived from Spencer, Bronislaw Malinowski, and A. R. Radcliffe-Brown. However, his emphasis on "material, mechanical means" reflects his grounding in the work of Karl Marx. White once said that he had read the first chapter of *Capital* sixteen times and had learned something from it each time (Carneiro 2004: 155).

3. As a child, White was interested in astronomy and intended to become a physicist. However, at Louisiana State University he majored in history, switching to psychology when he transferred to Columbia. White believed that anthropology was a science, and in this essay, he makes his argument in a scientific idiom—defining and eliminating variables and describing laws.

4. Like Spencer, White was concerned with culture as a general, pan-human phenomenon, thus he was uninterested in the effects of the environment on specific cultures. Here he says environment can be eliminated from the equation. This lack of concern for environment differentiates White from Julian Steward (1902–1972), whose work is featured in the next essay and to whom he is often compared.

5. Here and later, White refers to numbers and writes equations, suggesting that he is measuring attributes that can be quantified. However, White and his followers had great trouble actually providing agreed-on,

the nature of the tools employed. In the following discussion we shall deal with skill in terms of averages. It is obvious, of course, that, other things being equal, the product of the expenditure of human energy varies directly as the skill employed in the expenditure of this energy. But we may reduce all particular skills, in any given situation, to an average which, being constant, may be eliminated from our consideration of culture growth. Hereafter, then, when we concern ourselves with the efficiency with which human energy is expended mechanically, we shall be dealing with the efficiency of tools only.

With reference to tools, man can increase the efficiency of the expenditure of his bodily energy in two ways: by improving a tool, or by substituting a better tool for an inferior one. But with regard to any given kind of tool, it must be noted that there is a point beyond which it cannot be improved. The efficiency of various tools of a certain kind varies; some bows are better than others. A bow, or any other implement, may vary in efficiency between 0 per cent and 100 per cent. But there is a maximum, theoretically as well as actually, which cannot be exceeded. Thus, the efficiency of a canoe paddle can be raised or lowered by altering its length, breadth, thickness, shape, etc. Certain proportions or dimensions would render it useless, in which case its efficiency would be 0 per cent. But, in the direction of improvement, a point is reached, ideally as well as practically, when no further progress can be made—any further change would be a detriment. Its efficiency is now at its maximum (100 per cent). So it is with a canoe, arrow, axe, dynamo, locomotive, or any other tool or machine.[6]

We are now ready for some generalizations about cultural development. Let us return to our formula, but this time let us write it $E \times F = P$, in which E and P have the same values as before—E, the amount of energy expended; P the product produced—while F stands for the efficiency of the mechanical means with which the energy is expended. Since culture is a mechanism for serving human needs, cultural development may be measured by the extent to which, and the efficiency with which, need-serving goods or services are provided. P, in our formula, may thus stand for the total amount of goods or services produced in any given cultural situation. Hence P represents the status of culture, or, more accurately, the degree of cultural development. If, then, F, the efficiency with which human energy is expended, remains constant, then P, the degree of cultural development, will vary as E, the amount of energy expended per capita per year[8] varies:

$$\frac{E_1 \times F}{E_2 \times F} = \frac{P_1}{P_2}$$

Thus we obtain the first important law of cultural development: *Other things being equal, the degree of cultural development varies directly as the amount of energy per capita per year harnessed and put to work.*

Secondly, if the amount of energy expended per capita unit of time remains constant, then P varies as F:

$$\frac{E \times F_1}{E \times F_2} = \frac{P_1}{P_2}$$

and we get the second law of cultural development: *Other things being equal, the degree of cultural development varies directly as the efficiency of the technological means with which the harnessed energy is put to work.*

---

concrete, quantitative measures of the variables they discussed. As a result, critics considered their work pseudoscientific (for example Lowie 1949, Naroll 1961).

6. The concerns upon which White focuses in this essay, especially technology, reflect the influence of Marx on his work. Note that here he argues that there are limits to the degree that tools can be improved. The implication is that once this limit is reached, efficiency can only be improved by making a fundamental change in the tool itself. In other words, further changes are not only evolutionary but revolutionary!

White visited the Soviet Union in 1929 and, while there, was inspired by his reading of Marx and Engels. He later corresponded briefly with Leon Trotsky (1879–1940), one of the original leaders of the Bolshevik revolution in Russia (Beardsley 1976: 619). Trotsky opposed Joseph Stalin's rise to power in the 1920s and was assassinated in Mexico on Stalin's order, in 1940.

It is obvious, of course, that E and F may vary simultaneously, and in the same or in opposite directions. If E and F increase simultaneously P will increase faster, naturally, than if only one increased while the other remained unchanged. If E and F decrease simultaneously P will decrease more rapidly than if only one decreased while the other remained constant. If E increases while F decreases, or vice versa, then P will vary or remain unchanged, depending upon the magnitude of the changes of these two factors and upon the proportion of one magnitude to the other. If an increase in E is balanced by a decrease in F, or vice versa, then P will remain unchanged. But should E increase faster than F decreases or vice versa, then P would increase; if E decreases faster than F increases, or vice versa, then P would decrease.[7]

We have, in the above generalizations the law of cultural evolution: *culture develops when the amount of energy harnessed by man per capita per year is increased; or as the efficiency of the technological means of putting this energy to work is increased; or, as both factors are simultaneously increased.*[8]

All living beings struggle to live, to perpetuate their respective kinds. In the human species the struggle for survival assumes the cultural form. The human struggle for existence expresses itself in a never-ending attempt to make of culture a more effective instrument with which to provide security of life and survival of the species. And one of the ways of making culture a more powerful instrument is to harness and to put to work within it more energy per capita per year. Thus, wind, and water and fire are harnessed; animals are domesticated, plants cultivated; steam engines are built. The other way of improving culture as an instrument of adjustment and control is to invent new and better tools and improve old ones. Thus energy for culture-living and culture-building is augmented in quantity, is expended more efficiently, and culture advances.[9]

Thus we know, not only *how* culture evolves, but *why*, as well. The urge, inherent in all living species, to live, to make life more secure, more rich, more full, to insure the perpetuation of the species, seizes upon, when it does not produce, better[h] (i.e., more effective) means of living and surviving. In the case of man, the biological urge to live, the power to invent and to discover, the ability to select and use the better of two tools or ways of doing something—these are the factors of cultural evolution. Darwin could tell us the consequences of variations, but he could not tell us how these variations were produced. We know the motive force as well as the means of cultural evolution. The culturologist knows more about cultural evolution than the biologist, even today, knows about biological evolution.[i, 10]

---

7. White here equates energy capture with cultural development. The more energy a society uses and the more efficiently it uses that energy, the higher its level of development. White's idea implies a method of cross-cultural comparison that would allow cultures to be ranked against each other, at least in terms of energy usage. This places him in direct opposition to most Boasians, who held that comparing and ranking cultures was both logically and morally wrong.

These "laws" occasioned a dispute between White and Julian Steward. Steward's critique was that White's laws were so general as to be virtually self-evident and failed to consider the specifics of change within a culture. White responded that this, while true, was the fundamental nature of universal laws (White 1957: 540–542).

8. This famous statement is often known as "White's Law."

9. White's emphasis on life as a struggle reflects his reading of Spencer while the scheme he describes for the increasing capture of energy parallels Morgan. White first read Morgan in 1927 when he began teaching at the University of Buffalo. Over his career he published several works on Morgan, including a 1964 edition of Morgan's *Ancient Society*. White was probably the leading scholar on Morgan of his generation.

10. White called his work "culturology" rather than anthropology. He proposed that culturology was a science in its own right, distinct from human biology or psychology, and that culture followed its own laws. In this, he has clearly been influenced by Spencer and Kroeber's ideas about the superorganic as well as Durkheim's concept of the collective conscience. For White, individuals were placeholders for the superorganic culture

A word about man's motives with regard to cultural development. We do not say that man deliberately set about to improve his culture. It may well have been, as Morgan[j] suggested, decades before Lowie[k] emphasized the same point, that animals were first domesticated through whim or caprice rather than for practical, utilitarian reasons. Perhaps agriculture came about through accident. Hero's steam engine was a plaything. Gunpowder was first used to make pretty fireworks. The compass began as a toy. More than this, we know that peoples often resolutely oppose technological advances with a passionate devotion to the past and to the gods of their fathers. But all of this does not alter the fact that domesticated animals and cultivated plants have been used to make life more secure. Whatever may have been the intentions and motives (if any) of the inventors or discoverers of the bow and arrow, the wheel, the furnace and forge, the steam engine, the microscope, etc., the fact remains that these things have been seized upon by mankind and employed to make life more secure, comfortable, pleasant, and permanent. So we may disregard the psychological circumstances under which new cultural devices were brought into being. What is significant to the cultural evolutionist is that inventions and discoveries have been made, new tools invented, better ways of doing things found, and that these improved tools and techniques are kept and used until they are in turn replaced.[11]

So much for the laws, or generalizations, derived from our basic formula. Let us turn now to concrete facts and see how the history of culture is illuminated and made intelligible by these laws.

In the beginning of culture history, man had only the energy of his own body under his control and at his disposal for culture-living and culture-building. And for a very long period of time this was almost the only source of energy available to him. Wind, water, and fire were but rarely used as forms of energy. Thus we see that, in the first stage of cultural development, the only source of energy under man's control and at his disposal for culture-building was, except for the insignificant and limited use of wind, water and fire, his own body.

The amount of energy that could be derived from this source was very small. The amount of energy at the disposal of a community of 50, 100, 300 persons would be 50, 100, or 300 times the energy of the average member of the community, which, when infants, the sick, the

---

that flowed through them. One place this comes through is White's repeated critique of the idea that "great men" play important roles in shaping history. White once wrote that individuals were no more personally effective in shaping the general course of culture than a "sack of sawdust" (1949: 279, see essay 9 note 19 for a more complete account of this quote). William Peace (1993: 135) notes that White's particular insistence that individuals don't matter also served to distance himself from Soviet dictator Joseph Stalin (1878–1953), who surrounded himself with a cult of personality insisting on his individual greatness. Cults of personality had formed around other twentieth century dictators as well.

White's insistence that culture follows its own path independent of individual humans seems to contradict his notion that culture exists to make life more secure for humans. If culture truly followed its own path, there is no reason why it should lead to human betterment. At the end of his life, he confronted this problem. Evidence that culture was often maladaptive, particularly the threat of nuclear war and environmental threats, led him to reject the idea that culture exists to serve people's needs. In his last work, he wrote, "Man lives within the embrace of cultural systems, and enjoys or suffers whatever they mete out to him" (1975: 159).

11. White's thinking is modeled after the evolutionary scheme proposed by Morgan in *Ancient Society*. However, Morgan proposed that evolutionary advances in technology and social structure were driven by "germs of thought." All humans had these germs of thought but they were not expressed until triggered by advances in subsistence. This notion was a weak point in Morgan's theory. Here, White claims that the psychological circumstances in which cultural innovations are developed can be disregarded because humans just have an "inherent urge" to make their lives more secure. Are White's inherent urges any better than Morgan's germs of thought?

Hero of Alexandria (c. 10–70 CE) was a Greek mathematician and engineer, who described a steam-powered device called an aeolipile .

old and feeble are considered, would be considerably less than one "man-power" per capita. Since one "manpower" is about one-tenth of one horsepower, we see that the amount of energy per capita in the earliest stage of cultural development was very small indeed—perhaps 1/20th horsepower per person.

Since the amount of energy available for culture-building in this stage was finite and limited, the extent to which culture could develop was limited. As we have seen, when the energy factor is a constant, cultural progress is made possible only by improvements in the means with which the energy is expended, namely, the technology. Thus, in the human-energy stage of cultural development progress is achieved only by inventing new tools—the bow and arrow, harpoon, needle, etc., by improving old ones— new techniques of chipping flint implements, for example. But when man has achieved maximum efficiency in the expenditure of energy, and when he has reached the limits of his finite bodily energy resources, then his culture can develop no further. Unless he can harness additional quantities of energy—by tapping new sources—cultural development will come to an end. Man would have remained on the level of savagery[l] indefinitely if he had not learned to augment the amount of energy under his control and at his disposal for culture-building by harnessing new sources of energy. This was first accomplished by the domestication of animals and by the cultivation of plants.[12]

Man added greatly to the amount of energy under his control and at his disposal for cul-ture-building when he domesticated animals and brought plants under cultivation. To be sure, man nourished himself with meat and grain and clothed himself with hides and fibers long before animal husbandry and agriculture came into being. But there is a vast difference between merely exploiting the resources of nature and harnessing the forces of nature. In a wild food economy, a person, under given environmental conditions, expends a certain amount of energy (we will assume it is an average person so that the question of skill may be ignored) and in return he will secure, on the average, so much meat, fish, or plant food. But the food which he secures is itself a form and a magnitude of energy. Thus the hunter or wild plant-food gatherer changes one magnitude of energy for another: m units of labor for n calories of food. The ratio between the magnitude of energy obtained in the form of food and the magnitude expended in hunting and gathering may vary. The amount obtained may be greater than, less than (in which case the hunter-gatherer would eventually perish), or equal to, the amount expended. But although the ratio may vary from one situation to another, it is in any particular instance fixed: that is, the magnitude of energy-value of the game taken or plant-food gathered remains constant between the time that it is obtained and the time of its consumption. (At least it does not increase, it may in some instances decrease through natural deterioration.)[13]

In a wild food economy, an animal or a plant is of value to man only after it has ceased to

---

12. White's description of the relationship between technology and culture was heavily influenced by Marx's idea of a mode of production. Marxists understand different societies as being determined by particular combinations of relations of production and forces of production (see essay 4). White's analysis is similar but less complex. He sees different types of society as fundamentally conditioned by the different types of technology they use. But humans are more than the sum of their material possessions. Many of humanity's greatest achievements are intangible such as art, literature, philosophy, music, and so on. Comparing cultural achievement in these areas is perilous. White's scheme examines cultural development in terms of quantifiable criteria. Are there similar measurements with which to rank artistic achievement? Can we quantify the difference between a Lascaux cave painting and a Picasso?

13. In the first half of the twentieth century, the evolutionary perspective of nineteenth century anthropology had been largely abandoned by American cultural anthropologists, but after World War I it was rehabilitated by archaeologists and European anthropologists. In particular, White used the work of the Australian-born archaeologist V. Gordon Childe (1892–1957). This passage and much of White's later work show that influence. Childe was openly Marxist and is remembered for, among other things, coining the term "Neolithic Revolution." Childe had been conducting archaeological studies of cultural evolution for a number of years before

be an animal or a plant, i.e., a living organism. The hunter kills his game, the gatherer digs his roots and bulbs, plucks the fruit and seeds. It is different with the herdsman and the farmer. These persons make plants and animals work for them.[14]

Living plants and animals are biochemical mechanisms which, of themselves, accumulate and store up energy derived originally from the sun. Under agriculture and animal husbandry these accumulations can be appropriated and utilized by man periodically in the form of milk, wool, eggs, fruits, nuts, seeds, sap, and so on. In the case of animals, energy generated by them may be utilized by man in the form of work, more or less continuously throughout their lifetime. Thus, when man domesticated animals and brought plants under cultivation, he harnessed powerful forces of nature, brought them under his control, and made them work for him just as he has harnessed rivers and made them run mills and dynamos, just as he has harnessed the tremendous reservoirs of solar energy that are coal and oil. Thus the difference between a wild plant and animal economy and a domestic economy is that in the former the return for an expenditure of human energy, no matter how large, is fixed, limited, whereas in agriculture and animal husbandry the initial return for the expenditure of human labor, augments itself indefinitely. And so it has come about that with the development and perfection of the arts of animal husbandry and agriculture—selective breeding, protection from their competitors in the Darwinian struggle for survival, feeding, fertilizer, irrigation, drainage, etc.—a given quantity of human labor produces much more than it could before these forces were harnessed. It is true, of course, that a given amount of human labor will produce more food in a wild economy under exceptionally favorable circumstances,—such, e.g., as in the Northwest Coast of America where salmon could be taken in vast numbers with little labor, or in the Great Plains of North America where, after the introduction of the horse and in favorable circumstances, a large quantity of bison meat could be procured with but little labor,—than could be produced by a feeble development of agriculture in unfavorable circumstances. But history and archaeology prove that, by and large, the ability of man to procure the first necessity of life, food, was tremendously increased by the domestication of animals and by the cultivation of plants. Cultural progress was extremely rapid after the origin of agriculture.[m] The great civilizations of China, India, Mesopotamia, Egypt, Mexico, and Peru sprang up quickly after the agricultural arts had attained to some degree of development and maturity. This was due, as we have already observed, to the fact that, by means of agriculture man was able to harness, control, and put to work for himself powerful forces of nature. With greatly augmented energy resources man was able to expand and develop his way of life, i.e., his culture.[15]

White published this essay, and although White does not cite Childe here, White makes acknowledged use of Childe's work in a later book *The Evolution of Culture* (1959).

14. In these passages, White, following Childe—who followed Morgan—provides criteria for distinguishing savagery, barbarism, and civilization. Compare White's criteria with Childe's comment that "upper Paleolithic societies must be designated savage inasmuch as they relied for a livelihood on hunting, fishing, and collecting" (1942: 37) or his statement that the development of agriculture was the first step in the Neolithic Revolution and distinguishes barbarism from savagery (1942: 48).

15. As these passages illustrate, for White, human cultural evolution was best understood as a process of increasing human control over the natural environment. This is a teleological vision of evolution, much like that of the nineteenth-century evolutionists. For White, cultural evolution has a single goal: virtually complete human control of the environment. This vision accords well with the times in which White wrote. In the 1940s and (particularly) the 1950s, people foresaw a not-too-distant future of domed, climate-controlled cities and total human mastery of nature. Today, our understanding of human ability to exert control over nature, as well as its desirability, is considerably different. In 1942, Childe wrote that the development of agriculture turned humans into "active partners with nature instead of parasites on nature" (1942: 48). Fifty-five years later, Jared Diamond wrote that the advent of agriculture was "The worst mistake in the history of the human race." No

In the development of culture, agriculture is a much more important and powerful factor than animal husbandry.[n] This is because man's control over the forces of nature is more immediate and more complete in agriculture than in animal husbandry. In a pastoral economy man exerts control over the animals only, he merely harnesses solar energy in animal form. But the animals themselves are dependent upon wild plants. Thus pastoral man is still dependent to a great extent upon the forces and caprices of nature. But in agriculture, his control is more intimate, direct, and, above all, greater. Plants receive and store up energy directly from the sun. Man's control over plants is direct and immediate. Further independence of nature is achieved by means of irrigation, drainage, and fertilizer. To be sure, man is always dependent upon nature to a greater or less extent; his control is never complete. But his dependence is less, his control greater, in agriculture than in animal husbandry. The extent to which man may harness natural forces in animal husbandry is limited. No matter how much animals are improved by selective breeding, no matter how carefully they are tended—defended from beasts of prey, protected from the elements—so long as they are dependent upon wild plant food, there is a limit, imposed by nature, to the extent to which man can receive profitable returns from his efforts expended on his herds. When this limit has been reached no further progress can be made. It is not until man controls also the growth of the plants upon which his animals feed that progress in animal husbandry can advance to higher levels. In agriculture, on the other hand, while there may be a limit to the increase of yield per unit of human labor, this limit has not yet been reached, and, indeed it is not yet even in sight. Thus there appears to be a limit to the return from the

expenditure of a given amount of human labor in animal husbandry. But in agriculture this technological limit, if one be assumed to exist, lies so far ahead of us that we cannot see it or imagine where it might lie.

Added to all of the above, is the familiar fact that a nomadic life, which is customary in a pastoral economy, is not conducive to the development of advanced cultures. The sedentary life that goes with agriculture is much more conducive to the development of the arts and crafts, to the accumulation of wealth and surpluses, to urban life.[16]

Agriculture increased tremendously the amount of energy per capita available for culture-building, and, as a consequence of the maturation of the agricultural arts, a tremendous growth of culture was experienced. Cultural progress was very slow during Eolithic and Paleolithic times. But after a relatively brief period in the Neolithic age, during which the agricultural arts were being developed, there was a tremendous acceleration of culture growth and the great cultures of China, India, Mesopotamia, Egypt, Mexico, and Peru, came rapidly into being.

The sequence of events was somewhat as follows: agriculture transformed a roaming population into a sedentary one. It greatly increased the food supply, which in turn increased the population. As human labor became more productive in agriculture, an increasing portion of society became divorced from the task of food-getting, and was devoted to other occupations. Thus society becomes organized into occupational groups: masons, metal workers, jade carvers, weavers, scribes, priests. This has the effect of accelerating progress in the arts, crafts, and sciences (astronomy, mathematics, etc.), since they are now in the hands of specialists, rather than

---

modern anthropologist would refer to non-agricultural societies as parasitic. The theories produced today often emphasize the limits of human abilities and the impossibility of determining the direction of biological or cultural evolution. But our vision of the world is conditioned by the economics and politics of our day just as White's was by events of his era.

16. White's comment that nomadic life is not conducive to the development of advanced culture is a reminder of how firmly rooted in the nineteenth century was his concept of culture. In *The Evolution of Culture* White writes, "The theory of evolution set forth in this work does not differ one whit in principle from that expressed in Tylor's Anthropology in 1881" (1959b: ix).

jacks-of-all-trades. With an increase in manufacturing, added to division of society into occupational groups, comes production for exchange and sale (instead of primarily for use as in tribal society), mediums of exchange, money, merchants, banks, mortgages, debtors, slaves. An accumulation of wealth and competition for favored regions provoke wars of conquest, and produce professional military and ruling classes, slavery and serfdom. Thus agriculture wrought a profound change in the life-and-culture of man as it had existed in the human-energy stage of development.[17]

But the advance of culture was not continuous and without limit. Civilization had, in the main, reached the limit of its development on the basis of a merely agricultural and animal husbandry technology long before the next great cultural advance was initiated by the industrial revolution. As a matter of fact, marked cultural recessions took place in Mesopotamia, Egypt, Greece, Rome, perhaps in India, possibly in China. This is not to say that no cultural progress whatsoever was made; we are well aware of many steps forward from time to time in various places. But so far as general type of culture is concerned, there is no fundamental difference between the culture of Greece during the time of Archimedes and that of Western Europe at the beginning of the eighteenth century.

After the agricultural arts had become relatively mature, some six, eight or ten thousand years before the beginning of the Christian era, there was little cultural advance until the nineteenth century A.D. Agricultural methods in Europe and the United States in 1850 differed very little from those of Egypt of 2000 B.C. The Egyptians did not have an iron plow, but otherwise there was little difference in mode of production. Even today in many places in the United States and in Europe we can find agricultural practices which, the use of iron excepted, are essentially like those of dynastic Egypt. Production in other fields was essentially the same in western Europe at the beginning of the eighteenth (we might almost say nineteenth) century as in ancient Rome, Greece, or Egypt. Man, as freeman, serf, or slave, and beasts of burden and draft animals supplemented to a meager extent by wind and water power, were the sources of energy. The Europeans had gunpowder whereas the ancients did not. But gunpowder cannot be said to be a culture-builder.° There was no essential difference in type of social—political and economic—institutions. Banks, merchants, the political state, great land-owners, guilds of workmen, and so on were found in ancient Mesopotamia, Greece, and Rome.[18]

Thus we may conclude that culture had developed about as far as it could upon the basis of an agricultural-animal husbandry econ-

---

17. In this passage, White presents an evolutionary model that derives from Childe (1942: Chapters 3 and 4) but is ultimately based upon Spencer. He saw cultural evolution as a process of increasing differentiation and specialization. Additionally, the notion that production for exchange replaces production for use is from Marx.

White's evolutionism, like that of other twentieth-century thinkers, lacks the explicit ethnocentrism and racism of nineteenth-century evolutionists. Boas's cultural relativism was certainly influential in this shift. But the experience of World War I was also critical. It was, perhaps, easy for American and European intellectuals at the end of the nineteenth century to maintain that the Victorian Age represented the pinnacle of currently achieved evolution. To continue to hold this belief in European cultural superiority after the carnage of battles like the Somme, (fought from July 1 to November 18, 1916) where the British suffered 60,000 casualties on the first day of fighting, and during which there were a total of more than 1.2 million casualties, required considerable mental gymnastics.

18. White enlisted in the navy in 1918 and served until 1919. He saw no combat, but his navy experiences and the war clearly changed his life. He became opposed to all war. Of World War I he wrote, "I was awed and appalled by the war; I could not understand it. And I had the sickening feeling that our verbal explanations and professions did not really account for our behavior. I wanted to know *why* millions of men should murder and mangle each other, and why women and priests should urge them to do it." Of World War II he wrote, "This war sickens me. The lying, cheating, bragging; the nauseating hypocrisy, the parading of vicious hate, envy, greed, as holy and noble striving and idealism. Using the war and patriotism to shackle and enslave—to humiliate and discredit—the working class—while at the same time proclaiming that this is a war of the common man—is sickening" (quoted in Peace 2004: 9).

omy, and that there were recessions from peaks attained in Mesopotamia, Egypt, Greece and Rome long before the beginning of the eighteenth century A.D. We may conclude further, that civilization would never have advanced substantially beyond the levels already reached in the great cultures of antiquity if a way had not been found to harness a greater magnitude of energy per capita per unit of time, by tapping a new source of energy: fuel.[19]

The invention of the steam engine, and of all subsequent engines which derive power from fuels, inaugurated a new era in culture history. When man learned to harness energy in the form of fuel he opened the door of a vast treasure house of energy. Fuels and engines tremendously increased the amount of energy under man's control and at his disposal for culture-building. The extent to which energy has been thus harnessed in the modern world is indicated by the eminent physicist, Robert A. Millikan (1939:211) as follows:[p, 20]

In this country there is now expended about 13.5 horsepower hours per day per capita—the equivalent of 100 human slaves for each of us; in England the figure is 6.7, in Germany 6.0, in France 4.5, in Japan 1.8, in Russia 0.9, China, 0.5.

Let us return now, for a moment, to our basic principle—culture develops as (1) the amount of energy harnessed and put to work per capita per unit of time increases, and (2) as the efficiency of the means with which this energy is expended increases—and consider the evolution of culture from a slightly different angle. In the course of human history various sources of energy are tapped and harnessed by man and put to work at culture-living and culture-building. The original source of energy was, as we have seen, the human organism. Subsequently, energy has been harnessed in other forms—agriculture, animal husbandry, fire,[q] wind, water, fuel. Energy is energy, and from the point of view of technology it makes no difference whether the energy with which a bushel of wheat is ground comes from a free man, a slave,[r] an ox, the flowing stream or a pile of coal. But it makes a big difference to human beings where the energy comes from,[s] and an important index of cultural development is derived from this fact.

To refer once more to our basic equation: On the one hand we have energy expended; on the other, human-need-serving goods and services are produced. Culture advances as these two factors increase, hand in hand. But the energy component is resolvable into two factors: the human energy, and the non-human energy, factors. Of these, the human energy factor is a constant; the non-human energy factor, a variable. The increase in quantity of need-serving goods goes hand in hand with an

19. White's evolutionism was modified by his reading of Marx. Most nineteenth-century evolutionists saw evolution as a process of gradual change without major breaks, but Marx saw cultural evolution as proceeding by revolution: long periods of relative stasis broken by cataclysmic upheaval. White's vision in these passages is close to this understanding: He saw long epochs without change broken by quantum changes in energy production and consumption.

Note that in the passages you just read, part of White's point is to lump very different cultures together. Most anthropologists would view the cultures of seventeenth-century Europe and ancient Greece as extraordinarily different. White claims that the differences are trivial compared to the fact that the agricultural base of both was similar.

20. White had an interest in physics and would certainly have been aware of quantum mechanics which was conceived by the German physicist Max Planck (1858–1947) in 1900 and elaborated by Danish physicist Niels Bohr (1885–1962) in 1913. Although there is no direct link between White's theories here and quantum theory, the parallel is suggestive. Quantum mechanics described abrupt changes in the levels of energy of subatomic particles; White describes abrupt changes in the levels of energy available to cultures. He quotes Robert Millikan twice in this article. Millikan (1868–1953) won the Nobel Prize in 1923, primarily for his famous oil drop experiment which he performed with Harvey Fletcher (1884–1981) at the University of Chicago in 1909. Using a simple but ingenious apparatus, Millikan was able to determine the electrical charge of an electron and discovered that it was constant. The experiment demonstrated one of the fundamental insights of quantum mechanics, that is, the basic building blocks of all matter are electrically charged particles.

increase in the amount of non-human energy expended. But, since the human energy factor remains constant, an increase in amount of goods and services produced means more goods and services per unit of human labor. Hence, we obtain the law: *Other things being equal, culture evolves as the productivity of human labor increases.*[21]

In Savagery (wild food economy) the productivity of human labor is low; only a small amount of human-need-serving goods and services are produced per unit of human energy. In Barbarism (agriculture, animal husbandry), this productivity is greatly increased. And in Civilization (fuels, engines) it is still further increased.[22]

We must now consider another factor in the process of cultural development, and an important one it is, viz., *the social system within which energy is harnessed and put to work.*

We may distinguish two kinds of determinants in social organization, two kinds of social groupings. On the one hand we have social groupings which serve those needs of man which can be fed by drawing upon resources within man's own organism: clubs for companionship, classes or castes in so far as they feed the desire for distinction, will serve as examples. On the other hand, social organization is concerned with man's adjustment to the external world; social organization is the way in which human beings organize themselves for the three great processes of adjustment and

survival—food-getting, defense from enemies, protection from the elements. Thus, we may distinguish two factors in any social system, those elements which are ends in themselves, which we may call E; and elements which are *means to ends* (food, defense, etc.) which we may term M.[23]

In any social system M is more important than E, because E is dependent upon M. There can be no men's clubs or classes of distinction unless food is provided and enemies guarded against. In the development of culture, moreover, we may regard E as a constant: a men's club is a men's club whether among savage or civilized peoples. Being a constant, we may ignore factor E in our consideration of cultural evolution and deal only with the factor M.

M is a variable factor in the process of cultural evolution. It is, moreover, a dependent variable, dependent upon the technological way which energy is harnessed and put to work. It is obvious, of course, that it is the technological activities of hunting people that determine, in general, their form of social organization (in so far as that social organization is correlated with hunting rather than with defense against enemies). We of the United States have a certain type of social system (in part) because we have factories, railroads, automobiles, etc.; we do not possess these things as a consequence of a certain kind of social system. Technological systems engender social systems rather than the reverse. Disregarding the factor E,

---

21. In *Capital* (1930 [1867]), Marx argued that human labor gave value to goods and services, thus labor could be exploited. Here White is discussing labor but in the context of his equations $E \times T = P$ and $E \times F = P$. In White's equations human labor is a constant, so the source of the labor is irrelevant. In his footnote o, White writes, "Technologically a freeman and a slave are equal, both being energy in homo sapiens form." This is similar to Marx's idea of abstract labor. Nicholas Diaz (2021) writes: "Labor in the abstract is what produces the values of commodities and is their common social substance. Concrete labor, on the other hand, is the unique form of labor that produces a commodity's use-value or gives it utility." https://medium.com/@nicholasadiaz7/introduction-to-marxian-economics-part-3-abstract-and-concrete-labor-6ab6e86ba3cf.

22. Note White's use of *Savagery*, *Barbarism*, and *Civilization* in this paragraph. He draws these terms from Morgan and uses them to get the maximum possible reaction from Boasian anthropologists who specifically reject them.

23. White distinguished three components in the analysis of culture: technological, sociological, and ideational or attitudinal. He gave priority to the technological. He saw social organization and beliefs as arising primarily from the constraints and possibilities of technology (1959b: 18–28). These ideas are variations on Marx's analytical divisions: forces of production, relations of production, base, and superstructure.

social organization is to be regarded as the way in which human beings organize themselves to wield their respective technologies. Thus we obtain another important law of culture: *The social organization (E excluded) of a people is dependent upon and determined by the mechanical means with which food is secured, shelter provided, and defense maintained*. In the process of cultural development, *social evolution is [a] consequence of technological evolution*.[24]

But this is not the whole story. While it is true that social systems are engendered by, and dependent upon, their respective underlying technologies, it is also true that social systems condition the operation of the technological systems upon which they rest; the relationship is one of mutual, though not necessarily equal, interaction and influence. A social system may foster the effective operation of its underlying technology or it may tend to restrain and thwart it. In short, in any given situation the social system may play a progressive role or it may play a reactionary role.[25]

We have noted that after the agricultural arts had attained a certain degree of development, the great civilizations of China, India, Egypt, the Near East, Central America and Peru came rapidly into being as a consequence of the greatly augmented energy resources of the people of these regions. But these great civilizations did not continue to advance indefinitely. On the contrary they even receded from maximum levels in a number of instances. Why did they not continue progressively to advance? According to our law culture will advance, other things being equal, as long as the amount of energy harnessed and put to work per capita per unit of time increases. The answer to our question, Why did not these great cultures continue to advance? is, therefore, that the amount of energy per capita per unit of time, *ceased to increase*, and furthermore, the efficiency of the means with which this energy was expended *was not advanced beyond a certain limit*. In short, there was no fundamental improvement in the agricultural arts from say 2000 B.C. to 1800 A.D.

The next question is, Why did not the agricultural arts advance and improve during this time? We know that the agricultural arts are still capable of tremendous improvement, and the urge of man for plenty, security and efficiency was as great then as now. Why, then, did agriculture fail to progress beyond a certain point in the great civilizations of antiquity? The answer is, The social system, within which these arts functioned, curbed further expansion, thwarted progress.[26]

All great civilizations resting upon intensive agriculture are divided into classes: a ruling class and the masses who are ruled. The masses produced the means of life. But the distribution of these goods is in accordance with rules which are administered by the ruling class. By one method of control or another—by levies, taxes, rents, or some other means—the ruling class takes a portion of the wealth produced by the masses from them, and consumes it according to their liking or as the exigencies of the time dictate.[27]

---

24. Here, without crediting Marx, White describes the basic idea of a mode of production: the means of production and the social organization that results in the employment of those means. Marx wrote that the mode of production determines the general character of the social, political, and spiritual processes of life, and White uses American society as an example.

25. In other words, White sees a dialectical relationship between the social system and the technologies on which it rests. Society is not a simple result of the technology of production. Rather, it emerges in the conflict between social systems and technological systems.

26. Marx believed that the ultimate result of the thwarting of technology by society was revolution and the emergence of new social structures. In the passages below, White echoes this belief.

27. Notice, here and below, the direct use of class analysis. White does not quote Marx directly, but the Marxist view of history as class struggle is evident in these passages. In the midst of the Great Depression in 1930, during an address to the American Association for the Advancement of Science, White argued that

In this sort of situation cultural advancement may cease at a certain point for lack of incentive. No incentive to progress came from the ruling class in the ancient civilizations of which we are speaking. What they appropriated from their subjects they consumed or wasted. To obtain more wealth the ruling class merely increased taxes, rents, or other levies upon the producers of wealth. This was easier, quicker, and surer than increasing the efficiency of production and thereby augmenting the total product. On the other hand, there was no incentive to progress among the masses—if they produced more by increasing efficiency it would only mean more for the tax-gatherers of the ruling class. The culture history of China during the past few centuries, or indeed, since the Han dynasty, well illustrates situations of this sort.

We come then to the following conclusion: *A social system may so condition the operation of a technological system as to impose a limit upon the extent to which it can expand and develop. When this occurs, cultural evolution ceases.* Neither evolution nor progress in culture is inevitable (neither Morgan nor Tylor ever said, or even intimated, that they are). When cultural advance has thus been arrested, it can be renewed only by tapping some new source of energy and by harnessing it in sufficient magnitude to burst asunder the social system which binds it. Thus freed the new technology will form a new social system, one congenial to growth, and culture will again advance until, perhaps, the social system once more checks it.

It seems quite clear that mankind would never have advanced materially beyond the maximum levels attained by culture between 2000 B.C. and 1700 A.D. had it not tapped a new source of energy (fuel) and harnessed it in substantial magnitudes. The speed with which man could travel, the range of his projectiles, and many other things, could not have advanced beyond a certain point had he not learned to harness more energy in new forms. And so it was with culture as a whole.[28]

The steam engine ushered in a new era. With it, and various kinds of internal combustion engines, the energy resources of vast deposits of coal and oil were tapped and harnessed in progressively increasing magnitudes. Hydroelectric plants contributed a substantial amount from rivers. Populations grew, production expanded, wealth increased. The limits of growth of the new technology have not yet been reached; indeed, it is probably not an exaggeration to say that they have not even been foreseen, so vast are the possibilities and so close are we still to the beginning of this new era. But already the new technology has come into conflict with the old social system. The new technology is being curbed and thwarted. The progressive tendencies of the new technology are being held back by a social system that was adapted to pre-fuel technology. This fact has become commonplace today.

In our present society, goods are produced for sale at a profit. To sell one must have a market. Our market is a world market, but it is, nevertheless, finite in magnitude. When the limit of the market has been reached production ceases to expand: no market, no sale; no sale, no profit; no profit, no production. Drastic curtailment of production, wholesale destruction of surpluses follow. Factories, mills, and mines close; millions of men are divorced from industrial production and thrown upon relief.

---

the Russian Revolution had ushered in a new social order. Socialism would make the social system conform to technology and ensure that there was plenty for all members of society (Peace 2004: 72–79). But White rejected Stalinism and considered the members of the American Communist Party "a bunch of stooges for Stalin" (quoted in Peace 1998). White was a dedicated member of the non-Stalinist Socialist Labor Party and, under the pen name "John Steel," wrote many columns for its newspaper *The Weekly People*.

28. Note once again White's absolute faith in the desirability of technological progress. But also note that White seems to diverge from Marx. Marx viewed progress and the *eventual* triumph of communism as inevitable. White seems to say that it is not.

Population growth recedes. National incomes cease to expand. Stagnation sets in.[29]

When, in the course of cultural development, the expanding technology comes into conflict with the social system, one of two things will happen: either the social system will give way, or technological advance will be arrested. If the latter occurs, cultural evolution will, of course, cease. The outcome of situations such as this is not preordained. The triumph of technology and the continued evolution and progress of culture are not assured merely because we wish it or because it would be better thus. In culture as in mechanics, the greater force prevails. A force is applied to a boulder. If the force be great enough, the rock is moved. If the rock be large enough to withstand the force, it will remain stationary. So in the case of technology-institutions conflicts: if the force of the growing technology be great enough, the restraining institutions will give way; if this force is not strong enough to overcome institutional opposition, it must submit to it.

There was undoubtedly much institutional resistance to the expanding agricultural technology in late Neolithic times. Such staunch institutions as the tribe and clan which had served man well for thousands of years did not give way to the political state without a fight; the "liberty, equality and fraternity" of primitive society were not surrendered for the class-divided, serf and lord, slave and master, society of feudalism without a struggle. But the ancient and time-honored institutions of tribal society could not accommodate the greatly augmented forces of the agricultural technology. Neither could they successfully oppose these new forces. Consequently, tribal institutions gave way and a new social system came into being.

Similarly in our day, our institutions have shown themselves incapable of accommodating the vast technological forces of the Power Age. What the outcome of the present conflict between modern fuel technology and the social system of an earlier era will be, time alone will tell. It seems likely, however, that the old social system is now in the process of destruction. The tremendous forces of the Power Age are not to be denied. The great wars of the twentieth century derive their chief significance from this fact: they are the means by which an old social order is to be scrapped, and a new one to be brought into being. The First World War wiped out the old ruling families of the Hapsburgs, Romanoffs, and Hohenzollerns, hulking relics of Feudalism, and brought Communist and Fascist systems into being. We do not venture to predict the social changes which the present war will bring about. But we may confidently expect them to be as profound and as far-reaching as those effected by World War I.

Thus, in the history of cultural evolution, we have witnessed one complete cultural revolution, and the first stage of a second. The technological transition from a wild food economy to a relatively mature agricultural and animal husbandry economy was followed by an equally profound institutional change: from tribal society to civil society. Thus the first fundamental and all-inclusive cultural change, or revolution, took place. At the present time we are entering upon the second stage of the second great cultural revolution of human history. The Industrial Revolution was but the first stage, the technological stage, of this great cultural revolution. The Industrial Revolution has run its course, and we are now entering upon the second stage, one of profound institutional change, of social revolution. Barring collapse and chaos, which is of course possible, a new social order will emerge. It appears likely that the human race will occupy the earth for some million years to come. It seems probable, also, that man, after having won his way up through Savagery and Barbarism, is not likely to stop,

---

29. White's distaste for capitalism is evident in passages such as this. When White wrote this essay in 1943, World War II was raging, and the memory of the Great Depression was still fresh in people's minds. White believed that capitalism was a product of the "pre-fuel" era, and consequently, no longer fit the world that had been created by the technologies of the fuel age.

when at last he finds himself upon the very threshold of civilization.[30]

The key to the future, in any event, lies in the energy situation. If we can continue to harness as much energy per capita per year in the future as we are doing now, there is little doubt but that our old social system will give way to a new one, a new era of civilization. Should, however, the amount of energy that we are able to harness diminish materially, then culture would cease to advance or even recede. A return to a cultural level comparable to that of China during the Ming dynasty is neither inconceivable nor impossible. It all depends upon how man harnesses the forces of nature and the extent to which this is done.

At the present time "the petroleum in sight is only a twelve year supply, . . . and new discoveries are not keeping pace with use."[t] Coal is more abundant. Even so, many of the best deposits in the United States—which has over half of the world's known coal reserves—will some day be depleted. "Eventually, no matter how much we conserve, this sponging off past ages for fossil energy must cease . . . What then?"[u] The answer is, of course, that culture will decline unless man is able to maintain the amount of energy harnessed per capita per year by tapping new sources.

Wind, water, waves, tides, solar boilers, photochemical reactions, atomic energy, etc., are sources which might be tapped or further exploited. One of the most intriguing possibilities is that of harnessing atomic energy. When the nucleus of an atom of uranium (U235) is split it "releases 200,000,000 electron volts, the largest conversion of mass into energy that has yet been produced by terrestrial means."[v] Weight for weight, uranium (as a source of energy produced by nuclear fission) is 5,000,000 times as effective as coal.[w] If harnessing subatomic energy could be made a practical success, our energy resources would be multiplied a thousand fold. As Dr. R. M. Langer,[x] research associate in physics at California Institute of Technology, has put it:

> The face of the earth will be changed . . . Privilege and class distinctions will become relics because things that make up the good life will be so abundant and inexpensive. War will become obsolete because of the disappearance of those economic stresses that immemorially have caused it . . . The kind of civilization we might expect . . . is so different in kind from anything we know that even guesses about it are futile.

To be able to harness sub-atomic energy would, without doubt, create a civilization surpassing sober imagination of today. But not everyone is as confident as Dr. Langer that this advance is imminent. Some experts have their doubts, some think it a possibility. Time alone will tell.[31]

But there is always the sun, from which man has derived all of his energy, directly or indirectly, in the past. And it may be that it will become, directly, our chief source of power in the future. Energy in enormous amounts

---

30. Writing two years before the war's end, White saw the conflict as a clash between the "technological forces of the Power Age" and the outmoded social systems of the old European empires trying to hold on to power despite the tide of worldwide change. Notice the strong utopian thread in White's writing here and later. Provided enough energy can be found, the destiny of humanity is civilization and a new social order. It follows from White's logic that the new social order, since it is better matched to technology, will be superior to the old.

Note too that White subtly recasts the nineteenth-century evolutionary scheme. The evolutionists claimed that they were representatives of civilized society. White says that we are now at (but have not yet passed through) the threshold of civilization.

31. White wrote this before the atomic bomb and the generation of electricity by nuclear-fueled power plants, solar panels, and wind farms. In the 1950s, his writing seemed almost prescient. Many people then believed that nuclear energy would result in electric power so inexpensive it would not be worth metering. White, and others, pointed out that such a development would have profound effects on social structure.

Rudolph Meyer Langer (1899–1999), the Caltech physicist quoted here, is perhaps disingenuous when he writes that guesses are futile; the type of society he describes is precisely that predicted by Marx.

reaches the earth daily from the sun. "The average intensity of solar energy in this latitude amounts to about 0.1 of a horse power per square foot" (Furnas 1941: 426). "Enough energy falls on about 200 square miles of an arid region like the Mojave Desert to supply the United States" (Furnas 1941: 427). But the problem is, of course, to harness it effectively and efficiently.[y] The difficulties do not seem insuperable. It will doubtless be done, and probably before a serious diminution of power from dwindling resources of oil and coal overtakes us. From a power standpoint the outlook for the future is not too dark for optimism.[32]

We turn now to an interesting and important fact, one highly significant to the history of anthropology: The thesis set forth in the preceding pages is substantially the same as that advanced by Lewis H. Morgan and E. B. Tylor many decades ago. We have expounded it in somewhat different form and words; our presentation is, perhaps, more systematic and explicit. At one point we have made a significant change in their theoretical scheme: we begin the third great stage of cultural evolution with engines rather than with writing. But essentially our thesis is that of the Evolutionist school as typified by Morgan and Tylor.[33]

According to Morgan, culture developed as man extended and improved his control over his environment, especially with regard to the food supply. The "procurement of subsistence" is man's "primary need" (p. 525).[z, 34]

The important fact that mankind commenced at the bottom of the scale and worked up, is revealed in an expressive manner by their successive arts of subsistence. Upon their skill in this direction, the whole question of human supremacy on the earth depended. Mankind are the only beings who may be said to have gained an absolute control over the production of food; which at the outset they did not possess above other animals. Without enlarging the basis of subsistence, mankind could not have propagated themselves into other areas not possessing the same kinds of food, and ultimately over the whole surface of the earth; and, lastly, without obtaining an absolute control over

---

32. White here correctly anticipates the contemporary development of solar and wind power generation. However, he predicted these technologies would be the result of dwindling supplies of coal and oil rather than our need to develop more environmentally friendly and sustainable sources of energy. The environmental threats we face today with rising global temperatures, melting of the polar caps, and rising sea levels were not recognized in 1943.

33. You may have caught many references to Morgan's and Tylor's scheme of cultural evolution in the preceding passages. Here, White makes their contribution to his work explicit. White's detailed acknowledgment of Morgan and Tylor must be seen as an attack on most of American anthropology of his time in that much of Boasian anthropology was a reaction against these and other evolutionist scholars. Boas and his students dismissed their work as logically flawed, insufficiently scientific, and implicitly racist. White's rehabilitation of Morgan and Tylor in the pages of *American Anthropologist* (where this article first appeared) must have seemed audacious to his contemporaries. His repeated quotation of them in these passages was a goad to established anthropological opinion. White had presented similar ideas at the 1939 meeting of the American Anthropological Association. White later wrote of this presentation: "I was ridiculed and scoffed at. Everyone knew that evolutionism was dead." He quotes Ralph Linton (1893–1953), an eminent anthropologist of the time, as saying that he, White, "ought to be given the courtesy extended to suspected horse thieves and shady gamblers in the days of the Wild West, namely, to allow them to get out of town before sundown" (quoted in Carneiro 2004: 161). However, others remember the incident differently. According to one of Boas's students Esther Goldfrank (1896–1997), White "spoke with extreme passion, his tone strident and his language intemperate." Boas was unmoved by White's presentation (Peace 2004: 106).

34. White's interest in Morgan was related to his belief in Marxist theory. Marx thought that Morgan's *Ancient Society* provided ethnographic data in support of many of Marx's ideas. He made extensive notes on *Ancient Society* and, after his death, Engels expanded these. He published the result as *The Origins of Family, Private Property and the State* (1884).

both its variety and amount, they could not have multiplied into populous nations. It is accordingly probable that the great epochs of human progress have been identified, more or less directly, with the enlargement of the sources of subsistence (p. 19). When the great discovery was made that the wild horse, cow, sheep, ass, sow and goat might be tamed, and, when produced in flocks and herds, become a source of permanent subsistence, it must have given a powerful impulse to human progress (p. 534).

And

the acquisition of farinaceous food by cultivation must be regarded as one of the greatest events in human experience (p. 42).

Morgan is much concerned with the significance of technology and its development:

"The domestic animals supplementing human muscle with animal power, contributed a new factor of the highest value" (p. 26). The bow and arrow, "the first deadly weapon for the hunt, . . . must have given a powerful upward influence to ancient society," since it made man more effective in the food quest (pp. 21–22). "The plow drawn by animal power may be regarded as inaugurating a new art" (p. 26). The "production of iron gave the plow with an iron point and a better spade and axe" (p. 26). Many other inventions, such as pottery, adobe brick, metallurgy—when man "had invented the furnace, and produced iron from ore, nine tenths of the battle for civilization was won" (p. 43)—are emphasized as motive forces of cultural development. "The most advanced

portion of the human race were halted, so to express it, at certain stages of progress, until some great invention or discovery, such as the domestication of animals or the smelting of iron ore, gave a new and powerful impulse forward" (pp. 39–40).

Morgan shows how technological advance brings about social change: technological evolution produces social evolution. In many places, but particularly in Part IV of *Ancient Society*, he shows how property, which accumulates through "an enlargement of the means of subsistence" and through a development of the individual arts, affects and changes the constitution of society. "Property and office were the foundations upon which aristocracy planted itself" (p. 551). Also,

From . . . the increased abundance of subsistence through field agriculture, nations began to develop, numbering many thousands under one government . . . The localization of tribes in fixed areas and in fortified cities, with the increase of the numbers of the people, intensified the struggle for the possession of the most desirable territories. It tended to advance the art of war, and to increase the rewards of individual prowess. These changes of condition and of the plan of life indicate the approach of civilization which was to overthrow gentile and establish political society (p. 540).[35]

We find essentially the same ideas in Tylor. Like Morgan, Tylor declares that man's "first need is to get his daily food" (p. 206).[aa] Culture develops as man's control over his environment, especially over the food supply, increases. Mankind advanced from savagery to barbarism when they

---

35. In these passages, White emphasizes Morgan's work on the relationship between subsistence technologies and social organization. White was unquestionably inspired by Morgan's work. Marvin Harris (1927–2001), who was deeply influenced by White's ideas (see essay 18) wrote, "In every respect, White's *The Evolution of Culture* is the modern equivalent of Morgan's *Ancient Society*" (1968: 643). However, both White and Harris overstate the similarity between Morgan's and White's ideas, failing to mention critical aspects of Morgan's work White rejects. White believes that the overall pattern of evolution moves from simple to complex. Morgan (and Spencer) would have agreed. However, Morgan held that all humanity was on a single path of cultural development. Ultimately, people were propelled down this path by the flowering of germs of thought that were present (or would become present) in all human brains. White, on the other hand, gave priority to technology. Neither germs of thought nor an inevitable single path of cultural evolution are found in White's work. Morgan is concerned with the evolution of family forms and the supposed transition from matriarch to patriarch. Issues such as these are absent in White's writing.

took to agriculture: "With the certain supply of food which can be stored until next harvest, settled village and town life is established, with immense results in the improvement of arts, knowledge, manners and government" (p. 24). "Those edible grasses," says Tylor, "which have been raised by cultivation into the cereals, such as wheat, barley, rye, and by their regular and plentiful supply have become the mainstay of human life and the *great moving power of civilization*" (p. 215, emphasis ours).

A pastoral economy, according to Tylor, is superior to that of a hunting and gathering (wild food) economy, but inferior to an agricultural economy. A combination of agriculture and animal husbandry is superior to either way of life by itself (pp. 24, 220).

Social evolution comes as a consequence of technological development: To this "change of habit may be plainly in great part traced the expansion of industrial arts and the creation of higher social and political institutions" (p. 118; article "Anthropology," in *Encyclopaedia Britannica*, 11th ed.).

With the development of agriculture and the industrial arts comes a struggle for the most desirable territories (as Morgan puts it) and warfare "for gain" rather than "for quarrel or vengeance" (Tylor, p. 225). The consequences of this warfare for gain are tremendous: ". . . captives, instead of being slain, are brought back for slaves, and especially set to till the ground. By this agriculture is much increased, and also a new division of society takes place . . . Thus we see how in old times the original equality of men broke up, a nation dividing into an aristocracy of warlike freemen, and an inferior laboring caste" (p. 225). "It was through slave labor that agriculture and industry increased, that wealth accumulated, and leisure was given to priests, scribes, poets, philosophers, to raise the level of men's minds" (p. 435). Furthermore, according to Tylor, warfare, among culturally advanced peoples, produces "two of the greatest facts in history—the

organized army . . . and the confederation of tribes . . ." (pp. 432–433); tribes become states, primitive society gives way to civil society.

Tylor is much interested in the ways in which man harnesses the forces of nature and the extent to which energy is harnessed. "It was a great movement in civilization," he says, when man harnessed water power (p. 204). He speaks of the "civilized world . . . drawing an immense supply of power from a new source, the coal burnt in the furnace of the steam-engine, which is already used so wastefully that economists are uneasily calculating how long this stored-up fossil force will last, and what must be turned to next—tide force or sun's heat—to labor for us" (pp. 204–205).

Tylor clearly recognizes the problem we have dealt with in this essay when he speculates: "It is an interesting problem in political economy to reckon the means of subsistence in our country during the agricultural and pastoral period, and to compare them with the resources we now gain from coal, in doing homework and manufacturing goods to exchange for foreign produce. Perhaps the best means of realizing what coal is to us, will be to consider, that of three Englishmen now, one at least may be reckoned to live by coal, inasmuch as without it the population would have been so much less" (p. 272). The energy significance of modern civilization lies in the fact that "in modern times, man seeks more and more to change the laborer's part he played in early ages, for the higher duty of director or controller of the world's forces" (p. 205).[36]

Thus, we see that our essay is substantially a systematic exposition of the ideas of Morgan and Tylor. Man is an animal. His first and greatest need is food. Control over habitat in general and food supply in particular is effected by means of tools (of all kinds, weapons included). Through invention and discovery the technological means of control are extended and improved. Social evolution follows upon technological evolution.

---

36. White presents a very selective reading of Tylor to support his arguments. His connection with Tylor is more tenuous than with Morgan. The bulk of Tylor's work in *Primitive Culture* is an explanation of the origin and development of religion. For Tylor, people essentially reason their way to states of higher social and religious organization. Like Morgan, Tylor believed that all humanity was on a single, quite specific path of social evolution. This is very different than what White proposes.

At one point we have made an innovation. Both Morgan (p. 12) and Tylor (p. 24) use the origin of writing to mark the beginning of the third great era of cultural development, "Civilization." In our scheme, "civilization" begins with the invention of the steam engine as a practical means of harnessing energy.[37]

Although Morgan and Tylor both deal directly with the energy factor in cultural development, they lose sight of it when they consider writing. Writing is not a motive force. What change would writing have effected in the culture of the Arunta, or the Eskimo, or the Iroquois? It would not have altered their way of life in any essential respect. The culture of the ancient Peruvians, which lacked writing, was quite as advanced as that of the Aztecs who had writing. And in our own culture, writing has served to preserve and perpetuate—when it has not sanctified—the ignorance and superstitions of our barbaric ancestors quite as much as it has promoted progress and enlightenment.

But, if writing is not to be considered a motive force in cultural development, the human organism, domesticated animals, cultivated plants, water wheels, windmills, steam engines, etc., are motive forces (or the means of harnessing energy). What we have done is to reduce all specific, concrete motive forces in cultural development to a single, abstract, common term: energy. To classify cultures as "wild food, domestic food, and literate," as Morgan and Tylor did, is illogical; it is like classifying vehicles as "three-wheeled, four-wheeled, and pretty." We classify cultures according to the way, or ways, in which they harness energy and the manner in which it is put to work to serve human needs.[38]

In the foregoing we have, we believe, a sound and illuminating theory of cultural evolution. We have hold of principles, fundamental principles, which are operative in all cultures at all times and places. The motive force of cultural evolution is laid bare, the mechanisms of development made clear. The nature of the relationship between social institutions on the one hand and technological instruments on the other is indicated. Understanding that the function of culture is to serve the needs of man, we find that we have an objective criterion for evaluating culture in terms of the extent to which, and the efficiency with which, human needs are satisfied by cultural means. We can measure the amounts of energy expended; we can calculate the efficiency of the expenditure of energy in terms of measurable quantities of goods and services produced. And, finally, as we see, these measurements can be expressed in mathematical terms.

The theory set forth in the preceding pages was, as we have made clear, held by the foremost thinkers of the Evolutionist school of the nineteenth century, both in England and in America. Today they seem to us as sound as they did to Tylor and Morgan, and, if anything, more obvious. It seems almost incredible that anthropologists of the twentieth century could have turned their backs upon and repudiated such a simple, sound, and illuminating generalization, one that makes the vast range of tens of thousands of years of culture history intelligible. But they have done just this.[bb] The anti-evolutionists, led in America by Franz Boas, have rejected the theory of evolution in cultural anthropology—and have given us instead a philosophy of "planless hodge-podge-ism."[39]

---

37. Though White characterizes his work as a "systematic exposition of the ideas of Morgan and Tylor," he breaks with the two on the issue of writing as the mark of civilization. This highlights an important difference between White and the others. For Morgan and Tylor evolution is driven as much (or in the case of Tylor, more) by changes in thought than by changes in subsistence. For White it is the capture and more efficient use of energy that powers cultural evolution.

38. Boas and most of his students believed that universal laws of the evolution of human culture could not be formulated and that thinkers such as Morgan and Tylor were ethnocentric. However, Boas's specific criticism of the evolutionists was based on flaws in their method—he claimed that they were insufficiently scientific. Here, White answers this criticism by showing what he believes are objective, empirical criteria for the comparison of cultures.

39. The "planless hodge-podge-ism" refers to a frequently quoted passage by Robert Lowie. In the final paragraph of his widely read *Primitive Society*, Lowie wrote, "To that planless hodgepodge, that thing of shreds and patches called civilization, its historian can no longer yield superstitious reverence" (1920: 441).

It is not surprising, therefore, to find at the present time the most impressive recognition of the significance of technological progress in cultural evolution in the writings of a distinguished physicist, the Nobel prize winner, Robert A. Millikan:[cc]

The changes that have occurred within the past hundred years not only in the external conditions under which the average man, at least in this western world, passes life on earth, but in his superstitions . . . his fundamental beliefs, in his philosophy, in his conception of religion, in his whole world outlook, are probably greater than those that occurred during the preceding four thousand years all put together. Life seems to remain static for thousands of years and then shoot forward with amazing speed. The last century has been one of those periods of extraordinary change, the most amazing in human history. If, then, you ask me to put into one sentence the cause of that recent rapid and enormous change I should reply: "It is found in the discovery and utilization of the means by which heat energy can be made to do man's work for him."

Tucked away in the pages of Volume II of a manual on European archaeology, too, we find a similar expression from a distinguished American scholar, George G. MacCurdy:[dd]

The *degree of civilization* of any epoch, people, or group of peoples *is measured by ability to utilize energy for human advancement or needs*. Energy is of two kinds, internal and external or free. Internal energy is that of the human body or machine, and its basis is food. External energy is that outside the human body and its basis is fuel. Man has been able to tap the great storehouse of external energy. Through his internal energy and that acquired from external sources, he has been able to overcome the opposing energy of his natural environment. *The difference between these two opposing forces is the gauge of civilization* [emphasis ours].

Thus, this view is not wholly absent in anthropological theory in America today although extremely rare and lightly regarded. The time will come, we may confidently expect, when the theory of evolution will again prevail in the science of culture as it has in the biological and the physical sciences. It is a significant fact that in cultural anthropology alone among the sciences is a philosophy of anti-evolutionism respectable—a fact we would do well to ponder.[40]

AUTHOR'S NOTES

a. By "energy" we mean "the capacity for performing work."

b. Cf. Leslie A. White, *The Symbol: The Origin and Basis of Human Behavior* (Philosophy of Science, Vol. 7, October, 1940), pp. 451–463.

c. See Leslie A. White, *Science Is Sciencing* (Philosophy of Science, Vol. 5, October, 1938), pp. 369–389, for a discussion of this general point of view.

Although it stands at variance with much of Lowie's other work, this statement has often been used to caricature Boasian anthropology (see essay 10, note 11).

40. Tylor's famous definition of culture (see essay 2) does not mention subsistence and focuses instead on attributes such as morals and beliefs. Morgan's understandings were similar. White focuses only on passages in which they mention subsistence, implying that it is the central subject of their work. In so doing, he distorts their thinking. However, he also provides a useful corrective to the Boasian tendency to reject things simply because Morgan or Tylor claimed they were true.

Most American anthropologists of the 1940s and 1950s rejected White's ideas and continued to work in the Boasian tradition, following ideas more closely related to those of Boasians such as Kroeber, Benedict, and Whorf. However, White had a profound effect on many younger scholars. He spent almost all of his forty-year academic career at the University of Michigan and was known as a brilliant and challenging teacher. Through his students, he had a powerful impact not only on cultural anthropology but on archaeology and physical anthropology as well. His students include cultural anthropologists Marshall Sahlins (1930–2021), Robert Carneiro (1927–2020), Gertrude Dole (1915–2001), David Kaplan (1929–2012), and Napoleon Chagnon (1938–2019); archaeologists Louis Binford (1931–2011) and Jeffrey Parsons (1939–2021); and physical anthropologists Frank Livingston (1928–2005), George Armelagos (1936–2014), and Jack Kelso (1930–2019), as well as many others in each of these fields.

d. "Natural science" is a redundancy. All science is natural; if it is not natural it is not science.

e. Actually, of course, it is not wholly constant; there may be progress in music, myth-making, etc., regardless of technology. A men's club, however, is still a men's club, whether the underlying technology be simple and crude or highly developed. But, since the overwhelming portion of cultural development is due to technological progress, we may legitimately ignore that small portion which is not so dependent by regarding it a constant.

f. "There is only one cultural reality that is not artificial, to wit: the culture of all humanity at all periods and in all places," R. H. Lowie, *Cultural Anthropology: A Science* (American Journal of Sociology, Vol. 42, 1936), p. 305.

g. We say "per year" although "per unit of time" would serve as well, because in concrete cultural situations a year would embrace the full round of the seasons and the occupations and actions appropriate thereto.

h. The cultural evolutionists have been criticized for identifying progress with evolution by pointing out that these two words are not synonymous. It is as true as it is obvious that they are not synonymous—in the dictionary. But by and large, in the history of human culture, progress and evolution have gone hand in hand.

See Tylor, *Primitive Culture*, Vol. I, p. 14 (London, 1929 printing) for another respect in which, in the theory of evolution, "the student of the habits of mankind has a great advantage over the student of the species of plants and animals."

j. "Commencing probably with the dog . . . followed . . . by the capture of the young of other animals and rearing them, not unlikely, from the *merest freak of fancy*, it required time and experience to discover the utility of each . . . " (emphasis ours). Morgan, *Ancient Society*, p. 42 (Holt ed.).

k. *Introduction to Cultural Anthropology* (New York, 1940 ed.), pp. 51–52. In this argument Lowie leans heavily upon Eduard Hahn, whose work, incidentally, appeared many years after *Ancient Society* ("Subsistence," p. 303, in *General Anthropology*, F. Boas, ed., New York, 1938; *History of Ethnological Theory*, p. 112 ff., New York, 1937).

l. Following Morgan and Tylor, we use "savagery" to designate cultures resting upon a wild-food basis, "barbarism" for cultures with a domestic food basis. Our use of "civilization," however, differs from that of Tylor and Morgan (see p. 355).

m. "Finds in the Near East seem to indicate that the domestication of plants and animals in that region was followed by an extraordinary flowering of culture," Ralph Linton, *The Present Status of Anthropology* (Science, Vol. 87, 1938), p. 245.

n. But this does not mean that agriculture must be preceded by a pastoral economy in the course of cultural development. Contrary to a notion current nowadays, none of the major evolutionists ever maintained that farming *must be preceded* by herding.

o. It is true, of course, that powder is used in blasting in quarries, etc., and is to this extent a motive force in culture-building. But energy employed in this way is relatively insignificant quantitatively. The bow and arrow inaugurated cultural advance because in its economic context it provided man with food in greater quantity or with less effort. The gun, in its hunting context, has had the opposite effect, that of reducing the food supply by killing off the game. In their military contexts, neither the bow and arrow or the gun has been a culture-builder. The mere conquest or extermination of one tribe or nation by another, the mere change from one dynasty or set of office holders to another, is not culture-building.

p. *Science and the World Tomorrow* (Scientific Monthly, Sept. 1939) p. 211. These figures do not, however, tell the whole story for they ignore the vast amount of energy harnessed in the form of cultivated plants and domesticated animals.

q. We may be permitted thus to distinguish two different ways of harnessing energy although each involves fire and fuel. By "fire" we indicate such energy uses of fire which preceded the steam engine—clearing forests, burning logs to make dugout canoes, etc. By "fuel" we designate energy harnessed by steam, gasoline, etc., engines.

r. Technologically a freeman and a slave are equal, both being energy in homo sapiens form. Sociologically, there is, of course, a vast difference between them. Sociologically, a slave is not a human being; he is merely a beast of burden who can talk.

s. According to E. H. Hull, of the General Electric Research Laboratory, the power equivalent of "a groaning and sweating slave" is "75 watts of electricity, which most of us can buy at the rate of two-fifths of a cent an hour." *Engineering: Ancient and Modern* (Scientific Monthly, November, 1939), p. 463.

t. C. C. Furnas, *Future Sources of Power* (Science, Nov. 7, 1941), p. 425.

u. Ibid., p. 426.

v. Herbert L. Anderson, *Progress in Harnessing Power from Uranium* (Scientific Monthly, June 1940).

w. Robert D. Potter, *Is Atomic Power at Hand?* (Scientific Monthly, June, 1940), p. 573.

x. *Fast New World* (Collier's, July 6, 1940).

y. See C. C. Abbot, Utilizing Heat from the Sun (Smithsonian Miscellaneous Collections, Vol. 98, No. 5, March 30, 1939).

z. The page references are to Morgan's *Ancient Society*, Henry Holt edition.

aa. Page references are to Tylor's *Anthropology* (New York, Appleton & Co. edition of 1916).

bb. One distinguished anthropologist has gone so far as to declare that "the theory of cultural evolution to my mind the most inane, sterile, and pernicious theory ever conceived in the history of science . . . " B. Laufer, in a review of Lowie's *Culture and Ethnology* (American Anthropologist, Vol. 20, 1918), p. 90.

cc. Op. cit., p. 211.

dd. *Human Origins* (New York, 1933), Vol. II, pp. 134–135.

17. The Patrilineal Band[a]

Julian Steward (1902–1972)

LOOSE AGGREGATES of comparatively independent families such as those of the Shoshoni occur only rarely because in most parts of the world subsistence patterns required sufficient regularity of co-operation and leadership to give definite form and stability to multifamily social groups. There are many kinds of such multifamily groups of which the patrilineal band is but one.

The patrilineal band illustrates several concepts. First, it is a cultural type whose essential features—patrilineality, patrilocality, exogamy, land ownership, and lineage composition—constituted a cultural core which recurred cross-culturally with great regularity, whereas many details of technology, religion, and other aspects of culture represent independent variables, the nature of which was determined by diffusion or by unique local circumstances. Second, its cultural core resulted from ecological adaptations which, under the recurrent conditions of environment and subsistence technology, could vary only within minor limits. Third, it represents a level of sociocultural integration slightly higher than that of the Shoshoni family; for its multifamily aggregates found cohesion not only in kinship relations but in co-operative hunting, in common landownership, and to some extent in joint ceremonies.[1]

I shall analyze the cultures of these bands as they occurred among the Bushmen of South Africa, some of the Congo Negritos of Central Africa, some Philippine Negritos, the Australians, the Tasmanians, some southern California Shoshonean-speaking groups, and the Ona of Tierra del Fuego. Other tribes besides those covered in the present survey no doubt had the same pattern.

The essential features of these bands are most readily explained as the independent product of similar patterns of adaptation of technology and certain social forms to the environment. There are only two other possible explanations of the patrilineal band. First, that the pattern was borrowed from neighboring tribes. This explanation is untenable since their neighbors did not have the pattern. Second, that the pattern is the heritage of some archaic culture which developed at an early period of human history and has been preserved ever since. Perhaps some social patterns do have great persistence, but they must

---

From *Theory of Culture Change, the Methodology of Multilinear Evolution* (1955)

1. Steward's preoccupation with the causes of culture is immediately evident in this first passage. Unlike his Boas-trained colleagues, who focused on diffusion and psychology to explain culture, Steward searched for causal processes in the interaction between technology and environment and was interested in discovering cross-cultural patterns of adaptation.

Steward divided culture into core and secondary features. This notion was probably inspired by his professor A. L. Kroeber, who divided culture into utility and value components. For Kroeber, utility components were the things that people had to do to stay alive, such as food production. Value components were art, music, storytelling, and so on. Steward's culture core was similar to Kroeber's utility culture. Core features consisted of those cultural traits closest to subsistence activities and economic arrangements. A key difference between the two men is that Kroeber thought the value culture was more interesting and important than the utility culture, whereas Steward focused his studies on the latter.

Collections of elements of the culture core that regularly occur cross-culturally, such as the features of the patrilineal band described here, produced what Steward termed "culture types."

meet some need. It would be stretching credulity much too far to suppose that a pattern which is closely adapted to a special kind of subsistence had persisted for thousands of years among tribes who had wandered through dozens of unlike environments to the remotest corners of the earth, especially when other hunting and gathering tribes had lost these patterns and acquired types of society appropriate to their mode of life. Moreover, like most cultural historical theories, neither the hypothesis of diffusion nor of archaic heritage provides an explanation of how and why the patrilineal band developed in the first place. The cultural ecological hypothesis on the other hand is not only explanatory but it is by far the simplest and most consistent with the facts.[2]

The cultural ecological explanation of the patrilineal band hinges on an identity of exploitative patterns rather than of technology or environment. Technology and environment were similar in crucial respects, but they were not identical in their totality. Cultures do not exploit their entire environments, and it is, therefore, necessary to consider only those features which bear upon the productive patterns. The environments of the patrilineal bands were similar in that, first, they had limited and scattered food resources, which not only restricted

population to a low density but which prevented it from assembling in large, permanent aggregates. Second, the principal food resource was game, which unlike wild seeds, may be profitably taken collectively. Third, the game occurred in small, nonmigratory bands rather than in large, migratory herds. This kind of game can support only small aggregates of people, who remain within a restricted territory. Large herds, on the other hand, support much larger aggregates who can remain together as they follow the herds. These latter aggregates were bilateral or composite bands.

Dispersed and small game herds are, therefore, a condition of patrilineal bands, but this does not mean identity of environment, for deserts, jungles, and mountains tend to limit the number of game and the distance it could wander. Of the tribes examined here, the Bushmen, Australians, and southern California Shoshoneans lived in areas which had sparse game because of extreme aridity. Moreover, all were affected by the limited sources of water. In Tierra del Fuego, the habitat is one of wet plains but **guanaco** and small rodents, the principal foods, were scattered and nonmigratory. The Congo **Negritos** and the Philippine Negritos lived in the tropical rain forests, the former in lowlands and the latter in mountains.[3]

---

2. In this passage, Steward differentiates his cultural ecological approach from the historical approach of the Boasians, which he claims has little explanatory power. He further distinguished himself from nineteenth-century evolutionists such as L. H. Morgan and E. B. Tylor, who saw the existence of bands as survivals of a preexisting social form, precisely the second possibility that Steward mentions and discounts here. Unlike other Boasians, Steward's research emphasized cross-cultural comparison, but his rejection of the ideas of unilineal evolution and psychic unity separates his work from the comparative method of the nineteenth-century evolutionists.

3. Here and below, Steward focuses on the interplay between environment and technology. The idea that environment determined culture—a position known as *geographical determinism*—was not new. One prominent advocate was the British historian Henry Thomas Buckle (1821–1862), who believed history to be governed by laws of nature. For Buckle, the development of nations could be explained by the general effect of nature upon the human mind as well as the specific effects of climate, food, soil, and so on.

American anthropologist Clark Wissler (1870–1947) was also convinced that there was a relationship between environment and culture. In a series of works, including *The Relation of Nature to Man in Aboriginal America* (1926), Wissler attempted to map American cultural areas based on the principal modes of food production.

Steward was not a geographic determinist such as Buckle, and his environmental perspective was more sophisticated than that of Wissler. He believed that culture was a form of adaptation and certain cultural forms were likely to occur under particular conditions of technology and environment. His emphasis was on technology and the process of human labor within the environment and the ways these were related to different social structures. This emphasis derives from Steward's reading of Karl Marx.

"Guanaco": a wild South American camelid. Two domesticated varieties are the llama and alpaca.

Exploitative technology of these societies varied considerably in detail, but in all cases it included weapons of about equal efficiency and hunting patterns which entailed as much co-operation as circumstances permitted. The Bushmen used bows, poisoned arrows, clubs, pitfalls, poisoned springs, grass fires, dogs, and surrounds. The Congo Negritos employed bows, poisoned and nonpoisoned arrows, spears, knives, and long game nets. The Shoshoneans had bows, thrown clubs, traps, nets, surrounds, and drives. The Ona used bows, spears, clubs, slings, and spring pole nooses. Australian technology may have been less efficient in that it lacked the bow, but it included clubs, spears, and the spear-thrower. The sociological effect of hunting scattered game individually or collectively was the same everywhere.

The interaction between a bow-spear-club technology and a small, nonmigratory herd food resource tended to produce the patrilineal band. This type of band was the normal result of the adaptive processes of cultural ecology, and though various factors constantly operated to destroy the ideal pattern, as will be shown, interaction of technology and environment was such as to restore it. Only a basic change in environment or technology could have eliminated the patrilineal band. The inevitability of such bands under the given conditions is shown by its persistence along with clans, moieties, and other special patterns in the different groups, and, in the case of the Congo, an interdependence of the hunting Negritos and farming Bantu tribes who inhabited the same area.[4]

With a given population density, the size of the territory and of the band which owns it are direct variables. If the group is enlarged the territory must also be increased in order to support it. Among the ethnic groups in question, however, the population is sparse, ranging from a maximum which seldom exceeds one person per 5 square miles to one person per 50 or more square miles. This prevents indefinite enlargement of the band because there would be no means of transporting the food to the people or the people to the food. The area which the band can conveniently forage averages some 100 square miles and seldom exceeds 500 square miles, a tract roughly 20 miles to a side. Consequently, the band averages 50 individuals and seldom exceeds 100.[b] Only in regions of unusual resources—for example, where there are herds of migratory game—does the group size surpass these figures.

We now have to consider why these bands are patrilineal. First, it is characteristic of hunters in regions of sparse population for postmarital residence to be patrilocal. This has several causes. If human beings could be conceived stripped of culture, it is not unreasonable to suppose that innate male dominance would give men a commanding position.[c] If, in addition to native dominance, however, the position of the male is strengthened by his greater economic importance, as in a hunting culture,[d] or even if women are given greater economic importance than men, it is extremely probable that postmarital residence will be patrilocal.[5]

But in these small bands patrilocal residence will produce the fact or fiction that all

---

"Negrito": In Steward's day, the parlance of racial classification included the term Negrito, used for short, dark-skinned people. These included groups in Africa, India, the Philippines, and the Malay Peninsula.

4. This paragraph is an excellent summary of Steward's theoretical viewpoint. Here he argues that the patrilineal band is the adaptive result of the interaction between a certain type of technology and a particular type of food resource. The purpose of this essay is to describe how particular features of patrilineal bands are an adaptive response to the environment and demonstrate that the same constellation of cultural traits can be found wherever technological and environmental conditions are similar.

5. Up to this point, Steward's argument is based on purely material factors. However, in the case of patrilineality, he relies primarily on the supposition of innate male dominance. He backs this with a footnote about gorilla and baboon behavior. This is an unusual move because Boasians tended to see people as blank slates and rarely commented on the behavior of non-humans as an analog to human behavior. They saw the dominance of one group over another as a result of either the specific history of the group or childhood

members of the band are patrilineally related[e] and hence matrimonially taboo. Band exogamy—that is local exogamy—is therefore required. Probably at one time or another such bands have actually consisted of relatives with traceable connection. Genealogical data on the tribes of southern California, for example, show that more often than not the band comprises a true patrilineal lineage. Because life is so precarious that increase of the total population is impossible and budding collateral lineages often become extinct, the possibility is small that several independent families which have no traceable connection will develop in any band. Such families will occur only if the band is extraordinarily large. And even in this case, the fiction of relationship may be perpetuated after the connection is forgotten if group unity is reinforced by patronymy, myths, and other factors.[f, 6]

For these reasons, the bands of hunters who live in sparsely populated areas must ordinarily be patrilineal. But special factors may make them temporarily composite. Thus, if unrelated and hence intermarriageable families exist within a band, local exogamy and patrilocal residence with respect to the band are unnecessary. This will occur when parallel-cousin marriage is permitted or where bands have, for various reasons, become unusually large and lack any factor that would create or perpetuate a fiction of relationship between its members. Occasionally, matrilocal residence will introduce families which are not related patrilineally into a band. This will prevent strictly patrilineal inheritance of band territory and tend to weaken the fiction of relationship between band members. For these reasons, patrilineal bands at certain times or places deviate from the ideal pattern and consist of unrelated families. In this respect, they resemble composite bands, but whereas the latter normally must remain composite, patrilineal bands tend to return to their typical pattern. The factors which produce composite bands will be analyzed subsequently.[7]

Political unity in all bands is very similar. Centralized control exists only for hunting, for rituals, and for the few other affairs that are communal. Consequently, the leader has temporary and slight authority. In patrilineal bands, he is usually the head of the lineage, which, being a status based on kinship, is usually not formally institutionalized. The shaman, however, controls many collective activities, and he is feared and respected for his supernatural power, which often gives him more influence than the other leaders. Bands which are ordinarily autonomous may temporarily unite for special occasions such as Australian and Fuegian initiation ceremonies. Although the reason for this larger unity is religious and social, food supply strictly limits the duration of multiband gatherings.

The occurrence of clans among Australians, Ojibway, and others, of **moieties** in Australia and in southern California, and of other social forms in no way affects the cause-and-effect relationships involved in the formation of the patrilineal band. Such institutions are variables with respect to the pattern we have analyzed. Their presence or absence is to be explained by diffusion or by some special local factors and not by adaptations of technology to environment.[8]

---

enculturation. Here, Steward breaks with that tradition. However, his claim that males were "naturally" dominant was consistent with the consensus in the biological and social sciences of his day.

6. Steward worked with indigenous American groups like the Great Basin Shoshone, so he had firsthand experience with patrilineal communities and the practice of exogamy. However, in this paragraph, he is trying to justify his statement that patrilineality and band exogamy are in some manner adaptive responses to particular environmental conditions. This is the weakest portion of Steward's argument as he does not present any evidence that specific ecological conditions require patrilineality over matrilineality.

7. Steward's analysis of composite bands appears in *Theory of Culture Change* as the chapter following this one.

8. Critics of Steward's work point out that he explained away those things that did not fit the patterns he outlined by suggesting, as he does here, that they were secondary features resulting from diffusion or the specific history of the group under study.

"Moieties": When societies are split into two intermarrying groups, each group is referred to as a "moiety."

TRIBES WITH THE PATRILINEAL BAND

In the following pages some patrilineal bands will be discussed in detail, showing reasons in each case for departures from the ideal pattern.[9]

The Bushmen[g]

A hunting and gathering culture imposed upon an arid and unproductive native environment produced a sparse population among the Bushmen. Population aggregates were necessarily small[h] and the group that co-operated in various undertakings was a politically autonomous patrilineal lineage. Although the band or lineage split seasonally into smaller units, probably family groups, it owned and communally utilized a definite territory. Some hunting required joint effort of all band members, and game was often shared by all.

The bands of the Northwestern Bushmen, including the Heikum, were ordinarily patrilineal owing to patrilocal residence and local or band exogamy. The Naron bands, however, were sometimes composite because matrilocal residence, which was practiced occasionally in order that the wife's mother might help the wife with her children, introduced families which were not related patrilineally into the same band. This weakened patrilineal inheritance of the estate and tended to obviate the necessity of band exogamy, which, however, was preferred (Schapera 1930: 81–85). The Cape, Namib, and !Okung bands also tended to be composite because, although band exogamy was preferred, matrilocal residence, for a reason which has not been revealed, was sometimes practiced. Band endogamy, moreover, was facilitated by cousin marriage, parallel or cross, which was barred among the Northwestern groups (Schapera 1930: 82–83, 102–07).[10]

Schebesta (1931) reports what appears to be an identical pattern. The Bambuti, Efe, Bac'wa, and Batwa of the Belgian Congo had exogamous, patrilocal, and generally autonomous sibs ("sippe") or families of male relatives numbering sixty to sixty-five persons each. Apparently, the "totemic clans" of these people were the same as lineages, that is, they were localized clans or sibs.

Central African Negritos

Several scattered groups of Negritos or pygmies living in the dense tropical rain forests of the Congo in equatorial Africa also belonged to the patrilineal band type. The bands were predominantly hunters, and the exploitative patterns produced the features typical of the patrilineal band despite the fact that the pygmies lived in a close dependency relationship with the Bantu Negroes.[11]

In the Ituri Forest (Putnam 1948: 322–42), a Negro village and a pygmy band jointly owned about 100 square miles of country. The Negroes were largely farmers, and the pygmies were entirely hunters, the latter supplying the former with meat in exchange for vegetable foods. The dependence of the pygmy upon the Negro might account for the cohesion of the pygmy band and for the pattern of land-tenure, but it would not account for the patrilineality and exogamy, which must be explained by the low population density, the small band size, and the predominance of hunting.

---

9. In this section, Steward cites evidence from a wide variety of societies to support his claim that certain environmental and technological constraints lead to the formation of patrilineal bands.

10. Marvin Harris (1968: 667) claims that Steward's listing of factors responsible for patrilineal, complex, or matrilineal band formation are "fortuitous and quixotic." For example, note the reliance in this passage and later in this work on phrasing like "a reason which has not been revealed" and other such linguistic devices. Steward's model cannot explain why circumstances that produced a patrilineal band could also lead to matrilocal residence in the same band.

11. The fact that hunting bands of pygmies lived close to agricultural Bantus was critical for Steward. Traditional evolutionary schemes had placed agriculture far above hunting and gathering. If diffusion alone could account for cultural traits, and agriculture was superior to hunting and gathering, why had the pygmies not adopted it? Steward felt he could solve this problem using a cultural-ecological approach.

The bands ranged in size from 100 to 200 persons, 150 being the average. All families were normally related through the male line, and the band, therefore, constituted a locally exogamous and patrilocal group. The cohesion of the lineage or band was reinforced by the belief that a totemic animal was the ancestor of the band and by myths. The band contained unrelated families only when exceptional circumstances introduced a man from some other band, for example, when a man could not get along in his own band or when he had trouble with his Negro group. The patrilineal features resulted from the hunting pattern. The men spent all their time hunting for game which was normally scattered. They used nets in collective drives or else bows, spears, and knives in individual stalking. The game was varied and included turtles, rats, antelope, buffalo, and elephants. Hunting was restricted to the band's territory, the size of which must be interpreted as the optimum which can be exploited. Had the territory been substantially larger, the band would have surpassed a kin group in size and therefore ceased to be exogamous and patrilocal. However, the sparse population, the limitations upon the area which could be hunted, and the patrilocality after marriage produced localized lineages.

These bands sometimes tended to be composite for two reasons. First, it was customary at marriage for the husband's band to furnish a woman who married a member of his wife's band. When no woman was available, the man lived with his wife's people. Second, band endogamy, that, marriage between related members of the band, though felt to be a breach of incest laws, was often practiced when other bands were remote and inaccessible (Schmidt 1910: 173).

The Negritos of Gabon in French Equatorial Africa were grouped in some 100 or 150 villages, each of which usually comprised one family "rangée sous l'autorité d'un seul chef, le père du clan, généralement de 30 à 35 individus mâles." These seemed to be independent, patrilocal, and exogamous, and therefore true patrilineal bands. But they belonged to some kind of larger patrilineal totemic clans, which were preferably, but not always, exogamous (Trilles 1932: 20–23, 143–51, 409–18). [12]

Semang

The more or less inadequate information now available indicates that many of the Negritos of the Malay peninsula possessed the patrilineal band. Largely hunters and gatherers and more or less isolated in the sparsely settled mountain forests, the Semang groups were small, ranging, according to fragments of evidence recorded by Schebesta (1929), from individual families which were probably temporary subdivisions to groups of 50 or more persons. These seem to have been politically autonomous, landowning bands. Skeat and Blagden (1900: 495–97) say that the Kedah Semang band often amounted to an enlarged family and, somewhat obscurely, that the chief was practically "the head of a family, which in this case is represented by a larger family, the tribe." It may be, however, that band territory was sometimes further subdivided among bilateral families so that each owned an area for its durian trees. Schebesta says (1929: 83, 234, 279) that "the individual groups wander within the tribal boundaries but always return to their family territory, especially at the time of the durian crop" and that the trees are owned by men as family heads. These family tracts were, perhaps, comparable to the Algonkian and Althabaskan beaver-trapping territories.

That these bands were truly patrilineal is indicated by Schebesta's statement (1929) that the unit of society was the "sib" like that of the Congo Negritos, but he does not particularize its characteristics. Elsewhere he observes that there was considerable band exogamy and patrilocal residence, although he recorded one band that was composite. One reason for the occurrence of the latter among the Kenta Semang was that durian trees were sometimes inherited matrilineally. This would, of course,

---

12. **"rangée ... mâles"**: French, "placed under the authority of a single leader, usually the father [eldest] of the clan, and generally consisting of thirty to thirty-five men."

favor matrilocal residence and tend to set up a composite band.

Philippine Negritos

The predominantly hunting and gathering Philippine Negritos lived in comparative isolation from the Malaysians. They were clustered in bands which Vanoverbergh (1925: 430–33), says comprise "a certain group of families." These remained in the same portion of the forest and seasonally exploited different parts of an area which had a radius of not over twenty miles. Trespass on the land of neighboring bands was not forbidden but was avoided. The land was hunted communally by its owners, but cultivated trees and honey nests were privately owned. It is not recorded, however, how trees were inherited. Bands seem to have been politically autonomous, but the lack of an institutionalized band chief is implied by the somewhat vague statement that authority rested in the father of the family.

There is some indication that Philippine Negrito bands have recently changed from patrilineal to composite. Schmidt (1910: 72–73), quoting Blumentritt on the Zambales-Bataam, says that the bands are now endogamous but at the end of the eighteenth century were exogamous. Present-day endogamy is further shown by the presence of unrelated families in the same band.[i] Nevertheless, patrilocal residence is recorded, although it is not clear whether residence is patrilocal with respect to the band or the family.

There is, therefore, some doubt as to the frequency of the two types of bands and the customs concerning residence and other matters which would produce them. It appears, however, that some factor has tended to produce a change from patrilineal to composite bands during the past century. At least one important cause of composite bands today is the practice of marrying cousins. Although marriage was preferably between cross-cousins, parallel-cousins were eligible for matrimony (Vanoverbergh 1925: 425–28).[13]

Australians[j]

The relatively low productivity of Australia permitted but a sparse population which averaged only 1 person per 12 square miles for the entire continent.[k] The population was grouped into relatively small, autonomous bands which Radcliffe-Brown calls hordes. Each band comprised 20 to 50 individuals and owned 100 to 150 square miles of land. The male members of the band inherited and communally hunted their tract, which was definitely bounded and protected from trespass.[l]

These bands were truly patrilineal, and they approximated male lineages. They were almost universally exogamous and patrilocal. The idea of relationship between band members was further reinforced by kinship terminology. Even those ethnic groups which had moieties, sections (formerly called "marriage classes"), and matrilineal clans and totems had not, except in a portion of western Australia, lost the patrilineal band (Radcliffe-Brown 1931: 438).

Tasmanians

Information on the Tasmanians, though incomplete, indicates the aboriginal presence of the patrilineal band. The scant population[m] was divided into autonomous bands of 30 to 40 persons each. Each band owned a tract of land on which it wandered seasonally in search of food. It protected its hunting rights against trespass, which was a common cause of war (Roth 1899: 58–59, 104–107).

The Tasmanian band must have been patrilineal, for evidence assembled by Roth indicates, although it does not prove beyond

---

13. In assembling his cases, Steward relied on historical accounts as well as then-current ethnography. The use of these sources was important for him since his intellectual achievement was to explain the presence of the patrilineal band in very different and widely distributed locales. The use of historical accounts was problematic, however, since it led him to use sources that were not very reliable and to discuss groups, such as the Tasmanians, which anthropologists incorrectly believed had disappeared by his era. Further, much of the information he presents here, for example, his description of the Central African Negritos, has since been shown to be invalid, or, at best, only partially correct. Does this invalidate his argument?

question, that the band was exogamous and marriage patrilocal.

The Ona of Tierra Del Fuego

The Ona of Tierra del Fuego fall strictly into the patrilineal band pattern. The low subsistence level, based largely upon guanaco hunting, produced a population of only one individual to 4.5 or 5 square miles. This was grouped in politically independent bands of 40 to 120 persons, each owning an average of 410 square miles. Gusinde (1931) believes that the manner of life would not have supported larger aggregates. Each territory was named, band rights to it were sanctioned by myths, and hunting privileges were protected against trespass. Although each band was politically autonomous, there was no institution of chief.

The band was patrilineal because it was exogamous and patrilocal. Local exogamy was required even among the large bands in which relationship between members was not traceable, for native theory held that each band was a male lineage.

Tehuelche of Patagonia

The Tehuelche of Patagonia, although very incompletely known, are instructive when compared with the Ona. Also dependent largely upon herds of guanaco, their economic life appears formerly to have resembled that of the Fuegians. There is evidence that they were divided into bands, each having some degree of localization[n] and led in its travels, etc., by a patrilineal chief (Outes and Bruch 1910: 126; Beerbohm 1881: 93) who was called "father" (Musters 1873: 194). The band chief, however, acknowledged a general **cacique**, who, according to Musters, had very little authority. The institution of general or tribal cacique may

easily have developed subsequent to the arrival of the European.[14]

The introduction of the horse about a century and a half ago completely altered ecological conditions in Patagonia. It enabled people to move widely in pursuit of guanaco herds and to transport foods considerable distances. This would, of course, have tended to eliminate band ownership of small parcels of territory, even had it existed. It also permitted enlargement of population aggregates far beyond the size of the usual lineage. Further motivation for amalgamation of formerly separate bands was provided by internecine strife, which was stimulated by competition for foods and war against the white man. The political unit consequently increased in size and had a single, although not absolute, chief. Thus, in 1871, bands numbered as many as 400 or 500 persons, although they occasionally split into smaller groups (Musters 1873: 64, 70, 96–97, 117, 188). As there is no mention of exogamy of any form, it must be assumed that these bands were composite. This is common elsewhere in bands of such size.[15]

Southern Californians

The Shoshonean-speaking Serrano, Cahuilla, and Luiseño, and some of the Yuman-speaking Diegueño of southern California were divided into patrilineal bands. This region is exceptional in that abundance of acorns and other wild seeds permitted the unusually dense native population of one person per square mile. But this great density was accompanied by small territory size rather than large band size, probably because the very few and small sources of water prevented greater concentration of people. Therefore, bands averaged only fifty individuals and the territory only fifty square miles.

---

14. **"Cacique"**: Spanish term derived from the indigenous Taíno word for a community leader. Today, the word refers to a local political boss.

15. Here Steward gives an example of the effect of technological change on social structure: The introduction of the horse led to an increase in band size. Examples like this, linking technology and social structure were essential because they left traces in the archaeological record, which meant that archaeological data could be used to bolster Steward's theoretical position. Steward had begun his career as an archaeologist working in the Columbia River Valley, and this connection between theory in cultural anthropology and archaeology was one of the factors leading to the emergence of the new archaeology in the 1960s.

The other factors producing the patrilineal bands were those which operated elsewhere. Because of patrilocal residence coupled with the small size of the bands, most of them were actual patrilineal lineages so local exogamy was required. In addition, a band chief, "priest," ceremonies, ceremonial house and bundle, and myths contributed to group cohesion (Strong 1927, 1929; Gifford 1918, 1926, 1931; Kroeber 1925, 1934). This strongly fortified patrilineal pattern may also have served to maintain the band at lineage size.[16]

The culturally similar neighboring Cupeño provide an illuminating contrast to these groups. Because the local abundance of food and water permitted greater concentration, they were able to live in two permanent towns, each numbering some 250 persons. Each village contained several lineages and had a chief. Bands were, therefore, of the composite type (Gifford 1926: 394–96; Strong 1929: 188–90, 233).

CAUSAL FORMULATION FOR PATRILINEAL BANDS

In any society there are certain cultural factors which potentially give cohesion to aggregates of several families: marriage, extension of kinship ties and corollary extensions of incest taboos, group ceremonies, myths, games, and other features. These features may be derived from cultural heritage of the group or they may be borrowed from neighboring tribes. In each group they are integrated in a total sociocultural system, but the nature of this system is not explained merely by tracing the diversified history of the features or by describing the functional interdependency of the parts. These features must be adjusted to the subsistence patterns that are established through the exploitation of a particular habitat by means of a particular technology; and the subsistence patterns are only partly explainable in terms of culture history. The use of bows and arrows, traps, hunting nets, game drives, or grass firing can generally be traced to diffusion, but the hunting patterns and the social effect of these patterns are quite unlike in areas of sparse and scattered game and in areas of large herds of migratory game. Among societies which devote a very great portion of their time and energy to food-getting, these differences in hunting patterns will greatly affect the size, permanency, composition, and general behavior patterns of the group. The extent and degree to which subsistence patterns affect the total structure of the society and the functional integration of its various parts are questions to be answered by empirical procedure.[17]

The patrilineal band represents a social type the principal features of which are determined within exceedingly narrow limits by the cultural ecology—by the interaction of technology and environment. Other features, such as clans, moieties, age-grades, men's tribal societies,

16. Steward's most protracted fieldwork was among the Shoshoni in Utah, and here, as he describes southern California peoples, he is closest to his fieldwork interests. His fieldwork experiences were important for two reasons. First, working among the Shoshoni, he was struck by the small group size and the extremely demanding environment they inhabited. In the Great Basin Desert of Eastern California, Nevada and Western Utah, the powerful influences of the environment and technology might have been more evident than they were in many other places. Second, Steward was known for his fieldwork technique. He was highly critical of ethnographic studies that used material collected from people no longer engaged in aboriginal lifestyles. He encouraged an ethnography based on recording actual behavior rather than one based on what people said about past behavior. It is ironic that in developing his concept of multilinear evolution, he, of necessity, had to rely on secondhand data collected under conditions that were not well known, precisely the type of information he distrusted.

17. This passage outlines Steward's theoretical position and critiques Boasian and Functionalist anthropology. Staking out this position brought him into direct conflict with many other Boasians. For example, in this passage, Steward discards unique historically derived features as having no explanatory value. However, it was precisely these unique features that Kroeber and many other Boasians were interested in documenting. Unsurprisingly, the relationship between Kroeber and Steward was not close. Kroeber considered Steward a promising but not particularly interesting student. Steward respected Kroeber but was fundamentally at odds with most of what he stood for (Wolf 2004: 39).

group ceremonialism, totemism, and mythology may or may not also be present. If they do form part of the cultural inventory of the band, they are integrated to the patrilineal pattern. A causal formulation of the factors producing the patrilineal band may therefore omit these various historically-derived features, for the latter are of interest only when attention is shifted to the uniqueness of each culture and they do not help explain the patrilineal features which are the subject of inquiry.[18]

The factors which produce the patrilineal band are:

1. A population density of one person or less—usually much less—per square mile, which is caused by a hunting and gathering technology in areas of scarce wild foods;
2. An environment in which the principal food is game that is nonmigratory and scattered, which makes it advantageous for men to remain in the general territory of their birth;
3. Transportation restricted to human carriers;
4. The cultural-psychological fact, which cannot be explained by local adaptation, that groups of kin who associate together intimately tend to extend incest taboos from the biological family to the extended family thus requiring group exogamy.

These four factors interact as follows: The scattered distribution of the game, the poor transportation, and the general scarcity of the population make it impossible for groups that average over 50 or 60 persons and that have a maximum of about 100 to 150 persons to associate with one another frequently enough and to carry out sufficient joint activities to maintain social cohesion. The band consists of persons who habitually exploit a certain territory over which its members can conveniently range. Customary use leads to the concept of ownership. Were individual families to wander at will, hunting the game in neighboring areas, competition would lead to conflict. Conflict would call for alliance with other families, allies being found in related families. As the men tend to remain more or less in the territory in which they have been reared and with which they are familiar, patrilineally related families would tend to band together to protect their game resources. The territory would therefore become divided among these patrilineal bands.

It is worth noting that the nature of Great Basin Shoshonean land use precluded the banding together of patrilineal families and landownership. For two reasons, the pine nut, which was the principal food, had a very different sociological effect than game hunting. First, good crops were so abundant that there was never competition for it. Second, abundant crops occurred each year in very different localities and they brought different groups together each time.[19]

Among the patrilineal bands, the component biological families associated together sufficiently often to permit an extension of incest taboos to all members. Prohibition of marriage within the immediate biological family is uni-

---

18. Although Steward rejected much of what his professors believed, his work was not unprecedented in American anthropology. Earlier, members of the culture area school attempted to map North and South America into a series of areas of similar cultures, which, they noted, tended to overlap with ecological zones. Otis Mason (1838–1908) formulated one such version in the 1890s, but Franz Boas, his student Kroeber, and Wissler created a more definitive mapping in the teens and early twenties (see Mason 1895, Holmes 1914, Wissler 1917). The culture area theorists tended to see the environment as a passive factor placing broad restrictive limits on cultural possibilities. Steward saw the combination of technology and environment as playing a far more causal role in determining social systems.

19. Steward was also influenced by his work with Carl Sauer (1889–1975), a geographer interested in anthropology and archaeology who stressed an approach to geography based on the interaction of humans and the environment. Sauer, who was at Berkeley during Steward's time there, had an important impact on Kroeber and his students. Sauer, incidentally, also believed that Irish monks visited North America before the Vikings (Sauer 1968).

versal among mankind. There are generally extensions of marriage restrictions to collateral relatives of the second or third degree, though cross-cousins may marry in certain cultures. The patrilineal bands were so small that they usually consisted of known relatives who commonly fall within the prohibited degrees of relationship, and cross-cousins—the father's sister's daughter or the mother's brother's daughter—would normally be in another band. Band exogamy is therefore required.

The several features of the patrilineal band reinforce one another. Patrilocal residence after marriage because the male wishes to remain in country he knows causes an area to be habitually occupied, utilized, and defended by patrilineally-related families. Local exogamy prevents the introduction into the band of unrelated families, so that the band becomes in fact, a patrilineal lineage.[20]

The requirement that the band be exogamous may persist after traceable kinship relations in the group are forgotten if the patrilineal complex is reinforced by other features, such as names, kinship terminology, myths, ceremonies, totems, and the like. Thus, the bands of Australia, southern California, and Tierra del Fuego conform more rigidly to the pattern because they possess such supports.

Among the Bushmen and Negritos patrilineal bands may often temporarily become composite bands when special conditions exist.

A theory of the patrilineal band which sought its origin in purely cultural-historical terms would be confronted by insuperable difficulties. Such a theory would have to assume either that the band inherited the basic patrilineal pattern from some archaic world-wide culture or that it borrowed it from some neighboring tribes. As we have seen, primitive non-agricultural peoples in areas of seed resources, of fish, or of large game herds do not have the patrilineal band because these areas are not conducive to the exploitation of a certain restricted territory by small groups of men in the manner found among the patrilineal band peoples. It is inconceivable that this pattern could have survived the migrations of mankind over dozens of unlike environments during thousands of years. The theory of borrowing from neighbors will not stand up because the neighbors of these tribes simply do not have patrilineal bands.[21]

A holistic or functional explanation minimizes the importance of cultural ecology by insisting that all features of the culture are equally cause and effect. This simply evades the issue of causality. As we have seen, the clans,

---

20. Steward's approach is oriented toward technology and environment, but he frequently refers to psychology as an important factor (as here, where he discusses a male's wish to remain in territory he knows). Steward's work is contemporaneous with the culture and personality school whose supporters relied heavily on psychological explanations.

21. In this passage and later, Steward attacks the other prominent theoretical positions of his time. He first takes on the Boasian historical approach, then functionalism, and, in the next paragraph, diffusionism. When Steward presented the first version of this paper in 1936, functionalism was growing increasingly important in the United States. A. R. Radcliffe-Brown, then at the University of Chicago, was a loud and eloquent critic of the Boasians. Steward relies on Radcliffe-Brown for much of his information about Australians and Tasmanians. However, this passage critiques him. Radcliffe-Brown identified an ecological-adaptive aspect of social structure but assigned it no particular importance. Steward argues that because of this, Radcliffe-Brown's system describes but does not explain culture.

Tracing out the ways in which culture changed was to become one of Steward's key concerns. He is known as the creator of *multilinear evolutionism*, which he contrasted with nineteenth-century unilineal evolution and the universal evolution championed by his contemporary Leslie White. He argued that, unlike White and his nineteenth-century predecessors, he was not interested in formulating a general, universal plan of evolution but rather in showing how particular cultures changed and developed (1955: 11–19).

However, Steward's is an uneasy evolutionism. It is perhaps best seen as a compromise between his Boasian training and his goal of creating an anthropology based on the discovery of causal principles. He placed societies in a single evolutionary scheme from family to multifamily to state civilization. He then focused on the multiple pathways that societies may take between these evolutionary stages.

moieties, men's tribal societies, and other special features occur with only some of the patrilineal patterns and they also occur among quite different kinds of societies. There is a functional interrelationship between hunting in a restricted area, the male's continued residence in that area, patrilocality, and local exogamy. Exogamy within a localized patrilineal group causes the men to hunt scattered game in certain ways. The groups hunt what is available with devices at their command; men best remain in the territory where they were raised; their wives come to their territory after marriage; and the bands are so small that people are related and, given concepts of incest, local exogamy is practiced. It is not claimed that the cultural ecological factors explain everything about the patrilineal band. They explain why these bands differ from other bands which have a similar technology and similar potentialities for extending incest taboos outward from the biological family.

A common explanation of the patrilineal band is that it is merely a localized clan, and diffusionists seek to trace its source to clans elsewhere. Societies which have clans may influence patrilineal bands in two ways; first, borrowed clans may crosscut the bands but fail to change their basic patterns; second, clan myths, ceremonies, and other features may be borrowed by the band and reinforce its local unity. But diffused unilateral structure and exogamy cannot explain the adjustment of male lineages to exploitative activities. In fact, the concept of the patrilineal band has greater value in explaining the clan than vice versa. If,

for reasons stated here, a localized patrilineal group develops, it is in effect a localized clan. Whether it should properly be called a clan, however, would depend upon whether it is exogamous regardless of locality. Those groups which have reinforcing features, such as the southern California Shoshoneans, the Australians, and others, would be clans if exogamy continued after they were dislocated from their territories and the different bands mixed up. Evidently this has happened often in human history and clans have developed in many places. We shall subsequently show how the data of archaeology and ethnography support such an interpretation of the origin of clans among the Pueblo Indians of the Southwest.[22]

CULTURAL VARIABLES AND THE PATRILINEAL BAND

The features of the patrilineal band which must be explained by ecological factors are patrilineality, patrilocality, exogamy, landownership, and informal and limited leadership. Many other features however, were fairly variable in form despite this basic pattern. A substantial range of possible alternatives made diffusion a more direct explanation of their presence.[23]

Some of the technological traits secondary to the main hunting patterns were extremely variable. Containers used in transporting, preparing, and storing food, for example, could not be elaborate, heavy, or numerous because of the nomadic life, but the materials of which they were made, their specific forms, and their

---

22. Kroeber did important work in tracing the diffusion of cultural traits throughout the Southwest. Additionally, radical diffusionist theories claiming that all civilizations originated in Egypt or Greece and diffused from there were popular in Britain and Germany when Steward wrote. Steward's point is that although diffusion of traits can be shown to exist, the traits are always modified to fit the ecological conditions of the society accepting them.

23. In this section, Steward explores cultural variables that he considers secondary features, aspects of culture not closely tied to the cultural core and determined by purely cultural-historical factors such as innovation and diffusion. This section of Steward's text is fairly long (more than 1,300 words), but much of it is a simple cataloging of cultural traits with little or no analysis of them. This presentation reflects two factors: first, Steward's training in Boasian and Kroeberian anthropology (the collection and cataloging of cultural traits was precisely the sort of anthropology Kroeber urged on his followers), and second, the likelihood that Steward placed little importance on the information he presents here. From the lack of analysis and the fact that this section is only weakly articulated with the rest of the essay, it appears that Steward considered this material a collection of virtually random facts of no particular interest.

decorations were quite variable. The Congo Negritos, Semang, Shoshoneans, and Ona used basketry of various weaves, shapes, and ornamentation; the Bushmen and Congo Negritos employed some pottery; the other areas utilized skins, shells, bark, or other convenient materials. Fire was made with the wooden drill by the Bushmen and Shoshoneans, with the fire saw by the Semang, and with pyrite and stone by the Ona. The Congo Negritos had no means of making fire and were forced to borrow it if their own went out. Shelters were limited by the requirement that they be quickly and easily put together of materials available. These bands used natural shelters, such as caves, when possible. Otherwise, they built mere windbreaks, brush- or skin-covered conical lodges, or dome-shaped brush houses. Similar huts are found scattered throughout the world among primitive peoples, and it would be rather profitless to speculate as to whether they diffused or not, for they are so elementary that it would require no great ingenuity to invent them. Clothing was scant and made with simple skills, but styles varied locally: string skirts or aprons, wrap-around skin skirts, breechclouts, robes, and the like, or perhaps nothing but a few smudges of paint.

Musical instruments and games were generally simple, for extensive paraphernalia was out of the question. The former were generally learned from neighboring tribes. For example, the Semang used flutes, jew's-harps, guitars, and drums borrowed from their Malay neighbors; and the Bushmen had musical bows, flutes, cocoon rattles, and drums, all probably acquired from the Bantu; while the southern California Shoshoneans used only flutes and rattles; the Australians swung bull-roarers and pounded sticks on rolled-up hides; the Ona struck sticks together; and the African Negritos thumped hollow logs.

A certain distinctiveness is evident in many features of social organization. While the formal aspects of these are attributable to diffusion, their functional significance was very similar because of their role in the total culture. Several of the bands had men's tribal societies—religious organizations into which young men were initiated during rites from which women and children were barred. The neophytes were scarified, given hunting tests, and made to observe food taboos while religion was explained to them. The Australian societies used bull-roarers in their ceremonies, whereas the Ona used masks and special huts and had rites based on the concept of death and resurrection of the initiate. Southern California Shoshoneans lacked such societies, but their group fetish bundle, ritual, and ceremonial leader had a similar function in reinforcing group cohesion. These and other social features, however, were not necessary to existence of the patrilineal band pattern, and they can hardly constitute the primary basis of cultural typology. The Semang have no men's society.

The presence in any society of the patrilineal band and the tribal society must be "explained" in different terms. The secret society is scattered throughout the world in many kinds of cultures and there is little doubt that it represents a very ancient pattern which has fitted certain psychological-cultural needs as well as a variety of cultural functions so well that it has persisted in spite of tremendous cultural change and that it has even diffused from one type of culture to another. The secret society can in no way be considered a cause of the patrilineal pattern or of the type of land use that underlies this pattern.[24]

There were other social features which, from the point of view of the patrilineal pattern, were secondary or variable and which were found also among tribes lacking the patrilineal band. Some of the northern Australians had matrilineal moieties, which were probably diffused from Melanesia. The combination of these with localized patrilineal, exogamous groups created a very complex organization. The uniqueness of this organization—the fact that it consisted of functionally

---

24. Here and to the end of the essay, Steward attempts to demonstrate that the cultural features he believes are secondary have little causal significance for the cultural core which consists of subsistence resources, technology, and social structure. His explanation of secret societies is a nod to Bronislaw Malinowski and psychological functionalism.

interrelated parts—does not mean that the origin of its parts cannot be treated separately and in causal terms. The southern California Shoshoneans had moieties which cut across localized patrilineal bands, but these functioned primarily at death ceremonies.

The religious patterns of these tribes were affected by the ecological adjustments principally in a negative sense: they lacked complicated and institutionalized worship of the kinds found among more developed cultures, there being little ceremonialism dedicated to group purposes. Rites were concerned primarily with birth, puberty, sickness, death, and other crisis situations of individuals. The patterns of these crisis rites and of shamanism show certain general similarity to one another and very probably they represent in large part an ancient heritage which survived throughout the world in cultures of many kinds. That is, these rites show a great deal of stability, their basic patterns persisting in many cultural contexts which are quite dissimilar. This fact makes it obviously quite absurd to conceive that religion could be the starting point, the primary factor, in an investigation of the origin of social forms and economic patterns. Religion was a functional part of each culture, but from the point of view of the basic social types and cultural ecological determinants its form was a relatively independent variable.[25]

[*In the original publication, at this point Steward presents a table summarizing the data he presented earlier. The table's columns are: name of the group, number of persons per square mile, average size of band, average number of square miles in band ter-*

ritory, permanent residence patrilocal with respect to band (yes or no), exogamy of band, that is, locality, required (yes or no), band politically autonomous, weak chief (yes or no), and references.]

The local forms and functions of the puberty rites are an illustration of the considerable range of variations that could be woven into the basic pattern of the patrilineal band. We have already seen how puberty rites stressed the maturing of young men among the Northwest Bushmen, the Australians, and the Ona to the extent that the adult males constituted a secret organization. The Congo Negritos may also have had such societies; at least, it is clear that in the Ituri Forest young Pygmy men together with the sons of their Negro overlords were circumcised in groups every few years, each group becoming an age-grade society. The other tribes wholly lacked any such formal grouping of their males. Among the Semang, children of both sexes were merely inducted into the status of puberty by a simple rite at which they were painted, tattooed, scarified, and had their teeth filed. The Shoshoneans of southern California, like their nonpatrilineal neighbors, had observances for both sexes. Pubescent girls were "roasted" in a pit and required to race each day, to scratch themselves only with a stick, and to refrain from drinking cold water. Boys were drugged, lectured on tribal lore and morality, subjected to biting ants, and required to dance. Among the Semang both sexes were painted, scarified, and tattooed at adolescence.[26]

In all these tribes, as in hundreds of others throughout the world, the shaman's chief func-

---

25. Here Steward reaffirms his basic materialism: Material conditions condition ideas, not vice versa. This passage seems to be a direct attack on Tylor, who saw the progressive rationalization of religion as one of the fundamental processes driving cultural change (see essay 2). But why would Steward attack Tylor more than a half century after the publication of *Primitive Culture* and two decades after the latter's death? It is more likely that he was thinking of Max Weber. The English translation of Weber's highly influential *The Protestant Ethic and the Spirit of Capitalism* had been published in 1930, not many years before the first appearance of Steward's essay. In this book, Weber argued that Protestant theology was critical to the advent of capitalism in Europe.

26. Steward turns the Boasian practice of cataloging cultural traits against them. Here, his style of writing is significant. By presenting a seemingly random listing of traits, he draws the reader to the conclusion that such a presentation, and hence the Boasian research program, has little explanatory value.

tion was to cure disease by supernatural means, generally through singing and sucking out the supposed cause of disease. He had certain other functions, however, which varied with the special local patterning of religion. Among the Bushmen, for example, he officiated at puberty ceremonies, and among the Semang he mediated between mankind and the thunder god.

Death observances were matters of private ritual among most of these bands, but the Shoshoneans of southern California developed them into a ceremony which greatly strengthened group cohesion. An annual mourning ceremony was held under the direction of a special ceremonial leader, while images of the deceased were burned and myths were recited to commemorate the dying god. This ceremony seems to have contributed greatly to the cohesion of Shoshonean bands, and it may partly explain why the bands continued to regard themselves as kin groups and to practice exogamy after they became dislocated from their territories, scattered, and lost genealogical knowledge of their relationship to one another.[27]

REFERENCES

Beerbohn, Julius. 1881. *Wanderings in Patagonia or Life Among the Ostrich-Hunters*. London.

Dornan, S. S. 1925. *Pygmies and Bushmen of the Kahlahari*. London.

Dunn, E. J. 1931. *The Bushman*. London.

Gifford, E. W. 1918. "Clans and Moieties in Southern California." *University of California Publications in American Archaeology and Ethnology* XIV: 155–219.

———. 1926. "Miwok Lineages and the Political Unit in Aboriginal California." *American Anthropologist* n.s. XXVIII: 389–401.

———. 1931. "The Kamia of the Imperial Valley." *Bureau of American Ethnology Bulletin* 97.

Gusinde, Martin. 1931. "Die Feuerland Indianer. Bande I. Die Selk'nam. Verlag der Internationalen Zeitschrift." *Anthropos*: 302–306.

Kroeber, A. L. 1925. "Handbook of the Indians of California." *Bureau of American Ethnology Bulletin* 78.

———. 1934. "Native American Population." *American Anthropologist* n.s. XXXVI(1): 1–25.

Musters, George C. 1873. *At Home with the Patagonians. A Year's Wandering over Untrodden Ground from the Straits of Magellan to the Rio Negro*. London.

Outes, Felix, F., and Carlos Bruch. 1910. *Los Aborigenes de la Republica Argentina*. Buenos Aires.

Putnam, Patrick. 1948. "The Pygmies of the Ituri Forest," *In A General Reader in Anthropology*, ed. Carleton S. Coon, pp. 322–342. New York: H. Holt and Company.

Radcliffe-Brown, A. R. 1930. "Former Numbers and Distribution of the Australian Aborigines." *Official Yearbook of the Commonwealth of Australia* 23: 671–696.

———. 1931. "The Social Organization of Australian Tribes, III." *Oceania* I: 426–456.

Roth, H. Ling. 1899. *The Aborigines of Tasmania*. Halifax (England): F. King and Sons.

Schapera, I. 1926. "A Preliminary Consideration of the Relationship between the Hottentots and the Bushmen." *South African Journal of Science XXIII*: 833–866.

———. 1930. *The Khosian Peoples of South Africa*. London.

Schebesta, Paul. 1929. *Among the Forest Dwarfs of Malaya*. London.

———. 1931. "Erste Mitteilungen uber die Ergebnisse meiner Forschungsreise bei den Pygmaen in Belgische-Kongo." *Anthropos* XXVI: 1–17.

Schmidt, P. W. 1910. "Die Stellung der Pygmaenvolker in der Entwicklungsgeschichte des Menshen." *Studien u. Forschungen zur Menschen-u. Volkerkunde.* Stuttgart.

Skeat, W. W., and C. O. Blagden. 1900. *Pagan Races of the Malay Peninsula*. London and New York: The Macmillan Company.

Strong, W. D. 1927. "An Analysis of Southwestern Society." *American Anthropologist* n.s. XXIX: 1–61.

———. 1929. "Aboriginal Society in Southern California." *University of California Publications in American Archaeology and Ethnology* XXVI: 1–358.

Trilles, R. P. 1932. "Les Pygmées de la Forêt Equatorial." *Anthropos* III: 1–530.

Vanoverbergh, Morice. 1925. "Negritos of Northern Luzon." *Anthropos* XX: 148–199, 399–443.

---

27. Even though his focus is ecological, in this final paragraph Steward provides a structural functionalist explanation for continued Shoshone social cohesion after the loss of their lands and dispersion.

Steward's work had a profound effect on the anthropologists of his day. Although his career, unlike that of Boas or White, was characterized by many short stays at different universities, he was a charismatic professor and attracted an important following. Among the students of Steward who later became prominent anthropologists were Stanley Diamond (1922–1991), Morton H. Fried (1923–1986), Sidney Mintz (1922–2015), Robert Murphy (1924–1990), Elman Service (1915–1996), Elliott Skinner (1924–2007), and Eric Wolf (1923–1999).

AUTHOR'S NOTES

a. This is an adaptation and expansion of the article, "The Economic and Social Basis of Primitive Bands," in Essays in Honor of A. L. Kroeber (University of California Press, 1936), pp. 331–50.

b. Wilhelm Koppers observes that 15 to 20 individuals is common and about 100 the probable limit. See Wilhelm Koppers, Die Anfänge des menschlichen Gemeinschaftslebens (Vienna, 1921), p. 72.

c. Bingham observed gorillas in a state of nature in groups of eight to twenty-two individuals, each group under a dominant male; chimpanzees are said to be similar; and it is probable that the males among the baboons observed in nature by Zuckerman had a comparable dominance. See Harold C. Bingham, *Gorillas in a Native Habitat*. Report Joint Expedition of 1929–1932 by Yale University and Carnegie Institution of Washington for Psychobiological Study of Mountain Gorillas (Gorilla berengei) in Parc National Albert, Belgian Congo Africa (1932). Also see S. Zuckerman, *The Social Life of Monkeys and Apes* (New York: Harcourt, Brace and Company, 1932).

d. E.g., the extraordinarily low status of women in the arduous hunting area of northern Canada. Radcliffe-Brown has observed that Australian hunters would be much less successful in territory which was not known to them from childhood.

e. Relationship is seldom traced beyond three generations among these people.

f. I make no effort to solve the very difficult problem of why there are incest laws at all. Marriage with relatives to the third generation, i.e., cousins, is taboo in most of these cases, although cross-cousin and even parallel-cousin marriage is permitted among several.

g. This section is based on I. Schapera, "A Preliminary Consideration of the Relationship between the Hottentots and the Bushmen," *South African Journal of Science*, XXIII (1926), 833–66; I. Schapera, *The Khoisan Peoples of South Africa* (London, 1930); S. S. Dornan, *Pygmies and Bushmen of the Kalahari* (London, 1925); E. J. Dunn, *The Bushman* (London, 1931); George W. Stow, *The Native Races of South Africa* (New York, 1905); S. Passarge, *Die Buschmanner der Kalahari* (Berlin, 1907).

h. Schapera, *The Khoisan Peoples of South Africa*, pp. 67–81, has gleaned a few figures on band size from various sources: Cape Bushmen, who were seriously affected by foreign contacts, 100 to 150, according to one estimate, and 3 to 4 families each, according to a more recent figure; Heichware, 20; Kalahari, 30; !Okung, not exceeding 30; Northwestern Bushmen, ranging from 20 to 150 and probably averaging 50 to 60 each.

i. Morice Vanoverbergh, "Negritos of Northern Luzon," *Anthropos*, XXV (1930), 538–39, found that some bands contained related males and also that related males occurred in different bands.

j. This material is largely from A. R. Radcliffe-Brown, "Former Numbers and Distribution of the Australian Aborigines," *Official Yearbook of the Commonwealth of Australia*, No. 23 (1930), pp. 671–96, and Radcliffe-Brown, "The Social Organization of Australian Tribes, I–III," *Oceania* I (1930, 1931) 34–63, 204–46, 426–56 (especially pp. 436–39, 455).

k. Radcliffe-Brown, *Official Yearbook of the Commonwealth of Australia*, No. 23 (1930), p. 696. The population range was 1 person per 2 square miles in the most fertile section to 1 per 38 square miles in the more arid regions.

l. D. Sutherland Davidson, "The Family Hunting Territory in Australia," *American Anthropologist*, n.s., XXX (1928), 614–32. Davidson has collected evidence that in some localities the landowning group was the bilateral family. It is the opinion of Radcliffe-Brown, *Oceania*, I (1931), 438, however, that "the particularism of the family whereby it might tend to become an isolated unit is neutralized by the horde solidarity."

m. Radcliffe-Brown, *Official Yearbook of the Commonwealth of Australia*, No. 23 (1930), p. 695, gives the aboriginal total as probably 2,000 or 3,000, which is one person to 8 or 13 square miles.

n. Antonio Serrano, *Los Primitivos Habitantes del Territorio Argentina* (Buenos Aires, 1930), p. 157. Nuñoz, quoted by Serrano, says that among the Northern Tehuelche the head chief owned the land and that the lesser chiefs could not change their land without giving notice to him.

Neomaterialism

Julian Steward (1902–1972) and Leslie White (1900–1975) set the stage for ecological anthropology and materialist cultural analysis, but it was the next generation of anthropologists who developed these fields of inquiry. By the 1960s, two types of materialism were becoming popular in anthropology: ecological-materialist approaches and neo-Marxist approaches.

The ecological-materialist approach to anthropology was heavily influenced by the field of cybernetics, general systems theory, and the growing science of ecology. Ecological materialists commonly assumed that societies were *homeostatic*, that is, that cultural institutions functioned as feedback mechanisms (like thermostats) to maintain a balance between energy production and expenditure and the productive capacity of the environment. Typically, ecological materialists examined culture using an equilibrium model that traced energy flow within an ecosystem. For example, a society might be analyzed in terms of its food production and the caloric expenditure of human energy required to maintain the society in equilibrium.

In addition, ecological-materialist studies differed from those of Steward and White in that the former tended to take local populations rather than cultures as their units of analysis. Ecological materialists examined the interactions between populations and environments rather than treating the environment as a passive background that shapes culture but is not influenced by it.

Like the psychological and structural functionalists of the first half of the twentieth century, ecological materialists were interested in the function and purpose of institutions and beliefs. However, whereas the functionalists described institutions in terms of their contribution to individual needs or social stability, ecological materialists were interested in adaptation. They focused on the ways in which particular cultural beliefs, practices, and institutions allowed populations to maintain and reproduce themselves successfully within specific physical, political, and economic environments. The dominant perspective within ecological materialism is sometimes called *cultural materialism*, and Marvin Harris (1927–2001) was its leading proponent.

Harris did both his undergraduate and graduate training at Columbia University, where he also served as a professor from 1953 to 1980. His mentor was Charles Wagley (1913–1991), a student of Franz Boas. Harris took courses from Steward and was attracted by White's critique of the Boasians, but during his career as a student, these experiences did not have a very profound effect on him. He moved decisively toward materialism after his fieldwork in Mozambique. His experiences of Portuguese colonialism there convinced him that systems of production were fundamental to any understanding of culture (Harris 1994: 75–76). In 1980, Harris moved to the University of Florida, where he spent the remainder of his career.

Harris's work followed the Marxist perspective resurrected by White. Karl Marx was a dialectical materialist, believing that production played the primary role in social evolution but that it was in a dialectical relationship with ideology and superstructure (see essay 4). Harris rejected the dialectic while insisting on the primacy of modes of production and reproduction—what he called "infrastructure"—in determining behaviors and beliefs within a society (1979). Much of Harris's work was an attack on what he considered to be the obscurant and ideological explanations of symbolic and interpretive anthropology, as well as religion and the various "consciousness" movements of the 1960s and 1970s. Harris wrote that Americans have "been taught to value elaborate 'spiritualized' explanations of cultural phenomena." He, on the other hand, intended to show

that even the most bizarre-seeming beliefs and practices turn out on closer inspection to be based on ordinary, banal, one might say "vulgar" conditions, needs, and activities. What I mean by a banal or vulgar solution is that it rests on the ground and that it is built up out of guts, sex, energy, wind, rain, and other palpable and ordinary phenomena. (1974: 2–3)

From the 1970s to the 1990s, cultural materialism was a powerful theoretical position within modern American anthropology. This was partly because Harris himself was an extremely successful and indefatigable promoter of it. In the last quarter of the twentieth century, Harris's classic *The Rise of Anthropological Theory* (1968) was virtually required reading for graduate students. You may have noticed that we sometimes refer to it in this volume. Harris's book is a comprehensive analysis of the history of anthropology in the late nineteenth and the first half of the twentieth centuries, but it is also a polemic promoting cultural materialism.

In addition to copious work designed for professional consumption, Harris wrote many books for popular audiences, including *Cows, Pigs, Wars, and Witches: The Riddles of Culture* (1974), *Cannibals and Kings: The Origins of Culture* (1977), *Good to Eat: Riddles of Food and Culture* (1985), and many others. These books, which give cultural-materialist explanations of cultural phenomena, are written in an extremely accessible and engaging style and had enormous popular success.

Cultural-materialist analysis was extremely popular in the 1970s and 1980s, and materialist ideas continue to be popular. However, it was also frequently attacked as naive positivism "rooted in a mechanical, naturalistic mode that fails to reckon with the fact that the mind is more than a tabula rasa" (Murphy 1994: 58). Harris vehemently resisted such charges, while insisting that an objective, positivist science of society is not only possible but necessary. He was particularly incensed by the rise of postmodern thinking. His position is perhaps best summed up in the title of one of his essays, "Cultural Materialism Is Alive and Well and Won't Go Away until Something Better Comes Along" (1994).

A second orientation in neofunctionalist materialism is exemplified by the work of Roy Rappaport (1926–1997). Whereas Harris drew inspiration from Marx, Rappaport was more deeply affected by the work of ecological biologists. Like Harris, Rappaport was a student at Columbia. However, although influenced by Steward and White's notions concerning cultural evolution, Rappaport was more deeply affected by classes he took with Harold C. Conklin (1926–2016) and Conrad Arensberg (1910–1997) and by fieldwork seminars with Margaret Mead (Rappaport 1994: 166). His deep reading in biological ecology led to his dissertation under Andrew P. Vayda (1931–2022), an anthropologist vitally interested in ecology. Rappaport and Vayda believed that general laws of biological ecology could be used to study human populations, a belief they sought to substantiate in their fieldwork.

Rappaport and other neofunctionalist anthropologists adopted the concept of feedback from cybernetics to explain cultural stability. In his best-known work, *Pigs for the Ancestors* (1967), Rappaport proposed that the sacrifice of pigs in the *kaiko* ritual of the Tsembaga of New Guinea was a feedback mechanism that regulated the ecological relationship between men, pigs, local food supplies, and warfare.

For many reasons, *Pigs for the Ancestors* became a central work in the anthropology of the era. Robert Gardner's film *Dead Birds* about the Dani people of neighboring Irian Jaya had been released in 1963. Its importance was increased by the death of Michael Rockefeller (1938–1961). Rockefeller was killed after his boat sank off the New Guinea coast during the making of the film. He was the son of Nelson Rockefeller (1908–1979), a descendent of John D. Rockefeller (1839–1937), the founder of Standard Oil and one of the wealthiest men in late-nineteenth-century America. Nelson Rockefeller was the governor of New York at the time of his son's death (and later vice president of the United States, 1994–1997). The intense media coverage of his son's disappearance contributed to popular interest in violence in that region of the world. At this time, ideas of systems, ecology, and informatics became increasingly important in American culture, while debates about the war in Vietnam made work about peace and violence especially salient. These factors, combined with the virtuosity of the work itself, made Rappaport's ideas central to the anthropological debates of the era. Although, in general, *Pigs for the Ancestors* was very well received, many aspects of the work were critiqued. Rappaport responded in 1984, publishing a second edition of the book that included an appendix that was almost as long as the original work and in which he responded to his critics.

Although Rappaport and Vayda's original idea had been to try to understand human cultural activities in the same way in which ethologists understood the activities of nonhuman animals, he quickly began to reconsider this. Without dropping his emphasis on ecology, systems, and evolution, Rappaport began to consider how language and meaning make humans different. He began to work on the manuscript that eventually became the posthumously published *Ritual and Religion in the Making of Humanity*. There he combined ecological and semiotic thinking to comprehend religion and ritual as a method of maintaining and assuring group solidarity and coping with the multiplicity of meaning and indeterminacy inherent in language as well as the deceit that language enables. Hoey (2013: 688) writes that Rappaport often said that "humanity is a species living in terms of meaning in a world subject to law. [He] believed that it was our responsibility as humans not merely to think of the world but also to think on behalf of the world."

Our two selections for this section are Harris's "The Cultural Ecology of India's Sacred Cattle" and Rappaport's "Ritual Regulation of Environmental Relations among a New Guinea People." In "The Cultural Ecology," Harris argues that the Hindu prohibition on killing cattle should be understood in relation to the role that cattle play in the production of food crops, fuel, and fertilizer. He convincingly demonstrates the material and ecological importance of cattle to Indian society and argues that this, rather than Hindu religious doctrine, is the ultimate basis for the ban on killing and eating cattle. The essay was originally written for a professional audience. However, a version of it also appeared in *Cows, Pigs, Wars, and Witches*, and another in *Human Nature* (1978). An educational film version appeared in 1980. Harris's argument that the sacredness of cattle was based on economic factors rather than theology was radical when first introduced but today has become a standard interpretation of the Hindu veneration of cattle.

Rappaport's "Ritual Regulation of Environmental Relations among a New Guinea People" presents, in shortened form, the argument he makes at much greater length in *Pigs for the Ancestors*. In this essay, we see Rappaport's attempt to understand the Tsembaga Maring of New Guinea as a population from a systems perspective, as he traces how this population exchanges energy and information with its environment, and how religious ritual and warfare act as control mechanisms to maintain the Tsembaga Maring population's balance with its environment.

SUGGESTED READINGS

Greenough, Paul, and Anna Lowenhaupt Tsing. 2003. *Nature in the Global South.* Durham, NC: Duke University Press.
  An edited volume that explores the cultural construction of nature in South and Southeast Asia; it covers a wide range of topics from the role of cultural practices in the maintenance and transformation of landscape to the effects of colonialism and specific current government programs.
Harris, Marvin. 1974. *Cows, Pigs, Wars, and Witches: The Riddles of Culture.* New York: Random House.
  Harris's popular account of cultural-materialist explanations of phenomena from the Hindu ban on cattle killing to the rise of Christianity.
———. 1979. *Cultural Materialism: The Struggle for a Science of Society.* New York: Random House.
  Harris summarizes his theoretical position and attacks alternatives. Designed for a professional audience.
Hoey, Brian. 2013. "Roy Rappaport." In *Theory in Social and Cultural Anthropology*, ed. R. Jon McGee and Richard L. Warms, 2:685–688. Los Angeles, CA: Sage Reference.
  A brief overview of Rappaport's life and work.
Ingold, Tim. 1986. *The Appropriation of Nature: Essays on Human Ecology and Social Relations.* Manchester, UK: Manchester University Press.
  A collection of essays focused on the relations between humans and the environment in foraging and some pastoral societies.

Kottak, Conrad P. 1999. "The New Ecological Anthropology." *American Anthropologist* 101(1): 23–35.
  Examining the legacy of Rappaport, Kottak calls for a recognition of the role of culture in ecology rather than simply examining culture as adaptation to environment.
Lee, Richard B., and Irven DeVore. 1968. *Man the Hunter*. Chicago: Aldine.
  Critical collection of essays based on papers presented at a 1966 conference focusing on the practices of foraging groups and their relationship to environment.
Moran, Emilio F. 2006. *People and Nature: An Introduction to Human Ecological Relations*. Malden, MA: Blackwell.
  An examination of the role of humanity in the world's ecology that surveys archaeological and contemporary evidence for human nature interactions. Explores the role of culture in an increasing environmental crisis.
Netting, Robert M. 1986. *Cultural Ecology*. 2nd ed. Prospect Heights, IL: Waveland Press.
  A brief introduction to ecological thinking in anthropology.
Odum, Howard T., and Elisabeth C. Odum. 1976. *Energy Basis for Man and Nature*. New York: McGraw-Hill.
  An analysis of energy production and flow in a wide variety of societies with an emphasis on ways to diagram such flows. Written in the context of the energy crises of the 1970s.
Rappaport, Roy. 1984. *Pigs for the Ancestors: Ritual in the Ecology of a New Guinea People*. 2nd ed. New Haven, CT: Yale University Press.
  A description of the ecological role of ritual and warfare in New Guinea. The second edition includes an appendix responding to some criticisms of the original book.
Vayda, Andrew P. 1969. *Environment and Cultural Behavior*. Austin: University of Texas Press.
  An edited collection of classic essays relating cultural practices, particularly religion, to various aspects of the environment.

18. The Cultural Ecology of India's Sacred Cattle

Marvin Harris (1927–2001)

I N THIS PAPER I attempt to indicate certain puzzling inconsistencies in prevailing interpretations of the ecological role of bovine cattle in India. My argument is based upon intensive reading—I have never seen a sacred cow, nor been to India. As a non-specialist, no doubt I have committed blunders an Indianist would have avoided. I hope these errors will not deprive me of that expert advice and informed criticism which alone can justify so rude an invasion of unfamiliar territory.[1]

I have written this paper because I believe the irrational, non-economic, and exotic aspects of the Indian cattle complex are greatly overemphasized at the expense of rational, economic, and mundane interpretations.

My intent is not to substitute one dogma for another, but to urge that explanation of taboos, customs, and rituals associated with management of Indian cattle be sought in "positive functioned" and probably "adaptive" processes of the ecological system of which they are a part,[a] rather than in the influence of Hindu theology.[2]

Mismanagement of India's agricultural resources as a result of the Hindu doctrine of *ahimsa*,[b] especially as it applies to beef cattle, is frequently noted by Indianists and others concerned with the relation between values and behavior. Although different antirational, dysfunctional, and inutile aspects of the cattle complex are stressed by different authors, many agree that *ahimsa* is a prime example of how men will diminish their material welfare to obtain spiritual satisfaction in obedience to nonrational or frankly irrational beliefs.

A sample opinion on this subject is here summarized: According to Simoons (1961: 3), "irrational ideologies" frequently compel men "to overlook foods that are abundant locally and are of high nutritive value, and to utilize other scarcer foods of less value." The Hindu beef-eating taboo is one of Simoons' most important cases. Venkatraman (1938: 706) claims, "India is unique in possessing an enormous amount of cattle without making profit from its slaughter." The Ford Foundation (1959: 64) reports "widespread recognition not only among animal husbandry officials, but among citizens generally, that India's cattle population is far in excess of the available supplies of fodder and feed . . . At least 1/3,

---

From *Current Anthropology* (1966)

1. In the 1960s, ethnographic experience was the cornerstone of authority in American anthropology (and to some extent it still is today). Harris's upfront admission that he had never been to India was a challenge to this prevailing anthropological practice and is related to his views on the emic-etic debate that was raging within the profession at this time. (For more on emics and etics, see note 5.)

2. Harris makes his materialist and neofunctionalist positions clear in the opening paragraphs of this essay. As a materialist, Harris assumes that the Indian veneration of cattle has an explanation based in the realities of rural Indian agriculture. Indian theology surrounding cattle is the result, not the cause, of their production practices. Harris's statement that the explanation for Indian cattle management can be found in the "adaptive processes of the ecological system of which they are a part" demonstrates the influence of the cultural ecology of Julian Steward (see essay 17). His claim that he does not wish to substitute one dogma for another is disingenuous—Harris was one of the more polemic writers in anthropology. His career was devoted to publicizing and arguing for his theoretical position, which he called "cultural materialism."

298 Part III: Theory in the Mid-Twentieth Century

and possibly as many as 1/2, of the Indian cattle population may be regarded as surplus in relation to feed supply." Matson (1933: 227) writes it is a commonplace of the "cattle question that vast numbers of Indian cattle are so helplessly inefficient as to have no commercial value beyond that of their hides." Srinivas (1952: 222) believes "Orthodox Hindu opinion regards the killing of cattle with abhorrence, even though the refusal to kill the vast number of useless cattle which exist in India today is detrimental to the nation."

According to the Indian Ministry of Information (1957: 243), "The large animal population is more a liability than an asset in view of our land resources." Chatterjee (1960) calculates that Indian production of cow and buffalo milk involves a "heavy recurring loss of Rs 774 crores. This is equivalent to 6.7 times the amount we are annually spending on importing food grains." Knight (1954: 141) observes that because the Hindu religion teaches great reverence for the cow, "there existed a large number of cattle whose utility to the community did not justify economically the fodder which they consumed." Das and Chatterji (1962: 120) concur: "A large number of cattle in India are old and decrepit and constitute a great burden on an already impoverished land. This is due to the prejudice among the Hindus against cow killing." Mishra (1962) approvingly quotes Lewis (1955: 106): "It is not true that if economic and religious doctrines conflict the economic interest will always win. The Hindu cow has remained sacred for cen-

turies, although this is plainly contrary to economic interest." Darling (1934: 158) asserts, "By its attitude to slaughter Hinduism makes any planned improvement of cattle breeding almost impossible." According to Desai (1959: 36), "The cattle population is far in excess of the available fodder and feeds."[3]

[*In a four-hundred-word passage eliminated from this edition, Harris continues his catalog of experts and government agencies that have declared Indian cattle practices uneconomic.*]

In spite of the sometimes final and unqualified fashion in which "surplus," "useless," "uneconomic," and "superfluous" are applied to part or all of India's cattle, contrary conclusions seem admissible when the cattle complex is viewed as part of an *eco-system* rather than as a sector of a national price market. Ecologically, it is doubtful that any component of the cattle complex is "useless," i.e., the number, type, and condition of Indian bovines do not per se impair the ability of the human population to survive and reproduce. Much more likely the relationship between bovines and humans is symbiotic[c] instead of competitive. It probably represents the outcome of intense Darwinian pressures acting upon human and bovine population, cultigens, wild flora and fauna, and social structure and ideology. Moreover presumably the degree of observance of taboos against bovine slaughter and beef eating reflect the power of these ecological pressures rather than *ahimsa*; in other words, *ahimsa* itself derives power and

---

3. Harris's materialist point of view has been so successful in the last sixty years that it should be noted that Westerners used to think that the Hindu veneration of cattle was irrational. The view that non-Western people were irrational formed one of the cornerstones of colonial ethnocentrism. From the Western point of view, this irrationality was demonstrated in India by the failure of Indians to conform to European notions of animal husbandry, a failure that confirmed the British belief that they were bringing "civilization" to India. Harris is doing a cultural-materialist analysis, but, at the same time, he is also explaining the rationality of the apparently nonrational practices of non-Western people. In this, he is firmly in the tradition of both Franz Boas and Bronislaw Malinowski.

It is also worth noting that some of those critiqued by Harris in this passage fired back at him. For example, the geographer Frederick J. Simoons (1922–2022) pointed out that the words "irrational ideologies" do not appear in the section of his book on beef eating in India and charged that Harris's work was full of half-truths and outright errors (1979: 467). Harris responded to Simoons's attack by claiming that the errors Simoons cited were trivial and that Simoons continually "throw[s] up obstacles [to Harris's theory] based on non sequiturs and misinformation" (1979: 481). Elsewhere Simoons argued that "a proper understanding of India's cattle situation can only be gained by full awareness of the devout Hindu's views of the cow as reflected both in his religious behavior and round of daily activities" (1981: 121).

sustenance from the material rewards it confers upon both men and animals. To support these hypotheses, the major aspects of the Indian cattle complex will be reviewed under the following headings: (1) Milk Production, (2) Traction, (3) Dung, (4) Beef and Hides, (5) Pasture, (6) Useful and Useless Animals, (7) Slaughter, (8) Anti-Slaughter Legislation, (9) Old-Age Homes, and (10) Natural Selection.[4]

MILK PRODUCTION

In India the average yield of whole milk per Zebu cow is 413 pounds, compared with the 5,000-pound average in Europe and the U.S.[d] (Kartha 1936: 607; Spate 1954: 231). In Madhya Pradesh yield is as low as 65 pounds, while in no state does it rise higher than the barely respectable 1,445 pounds of the Punjab (Chatterjee 1960: 1347). According to the 9th Quinquennial Livestock Census (1961) among the 47,200,000 cows over 3 years old, 27,200,000 were dry and/or not calved (Chaudri and Giri 1963: 598).

These figures, however should not be used to prove that the cows are useless or uneconomic, since milk production is a minor aspect of the sacred cow's contribution to the *eco-system*. Indeed, most Indianists agree that it is the buffalo, not the Zebu, whose economic worth must be judged primarily by milk production. Thus, Kartha (1959: 225) writes, "the buffalo, and not the Zebu, is the dairy cow." This distinction is elaborated by Mamoria (1953: 255):

Cows in the rural areas are maintained for producing bullocks rather than for milk. She-buffaloes, on the other hand, are considered to be better dairy animals than cows. The male buffaloes are neglected and many of them die or are sold for slaughter before they attain maturity.

Mohan (1962: 47) makes the same point:

For agricultural purposes bullocks are generally preferred, and, therefore, cows in rural areas are primarily maintained for the production of male progeny and incidentally only for milk.

It is not relevant to my thesis to establish whether milk production is a primary or secondary objective or purpose of the Indian farmer. Failure to separate emics from etics (Harris 1964) contributes greatly to confusion surrounding the Indian cattle question. The significance of the preceding quotations lies in the agreement that cows contribute to human material welfare in more important ways than milk production. In this new context, the fact that U.S. cows produce 20 times more milk than Indian cows loses much of its significance. Instead, it is more relevant to note that, despite the marginal status of milking in the symbiotic syndrome, 46.7% of India's dairy products come from cow's milk (Chatterjee 1960: 1347). How far this production is balanced by expenditures detrimental to human welfare will be discussed later.[5]

---

4. Harris's debt to the cultural ecology of Steward is clear in this paragraph. His statement that the features of the cattle complex are the consequence of Darwinian pressures within an ecological system sounds very much like Steward's concept of the cultural core. However, the invocation of Darwin is problematic. Natural selection is fundamentally based on adaptation, sexual selection, and reproduction. Biological change is the result of an alteration in the frequency of genetically based traits. Harris is arguing that Hindu customs of cattle husbandry are somehow the result of a similar process of selection. However, it would be difficult to demonstrate how the philosophy of *ahimsa* is the result of genetically based selection.

5. The terms *emic* and *etic* were coined in 1954 by the missionary-linguist Kenneth Pike (1912–2000). Emic statements refer to meaning as it is perceived by the natives of a culture, and emic anthropologists tried to outline the models by which natives understood their society. By definition, emic understanding is culture bound. In contrast, etic meanings are those arrived at by empirical investigation by trained observers. Etic anthropologists aimed at producing generalizations that are cross-culturally valid using methods of investigation that can be verified and replicated by anyone using a similar investigative process. In the 1960s and 1970s, anthropologists doing etic analyses claimed their work was more scientific than emic anthropology. Harris's analysis of cattle in India is an etic study. Whether or not it is scientific we leave to your judgment.

TRACTION

The principal positive ecological effect of India's bovine cattle is in their contribution to production of grain crops, from which about 80% of the human calorie ration comes. Some form of animal traction is required to initiate the agricultural cycle, dependent upon plowing in both rainfall and irrigation areas. Additional traction for hauling, transport, and irrigation is provided by animals, but by far their most critical kinetic contribution is plowing.

Although many authorities believe there is an overall surplus of cattle in India, others point to a serious shortage of draught animals. According to Kothavala (1934: 122), "Even with . . . overstocking, the draught power available for land operations at the busiest season of the year is inadequate . . ." For West Bengal, the National Council of Applied Economic Research (1962: 56) reports:

> However, despite the large number of draught animals, agriculture in the State suffers from a shortage of draught power. There are large numbers of small landholders entirely dependent on hired animal labour.

Spate (1954: 36) makes the same point, "there are too many cattle in the gross, but most individual farmers have too few to carry on with." Gupta (1959: 42) and Lewis and Barnouw (1958: 102) say a pair of bullocks is the minimum technical unit for cultivation, but in a survey by Diskalkar (1960: 87), 18% of the cultivators had only 1 bullock or none. Nationally, if we accept a low estimate of 60,000,000 rural households (Mitra 1963: 298) and a high estimate of 80,000,000 working cattle and buffaloes (Government of India 1962: 76), we see at once that the allegedly excess number of cattle in India is insufficient to permit a large portion, perhaps as many as 1/3, of India's farmers to begin the agricultural cycle under conditions appropriate to their techno-environmental system.

Much has been made of India's having 115 head of cattle per square mile, compared with 28 per square mile for the U.S. and 3 per square mile for Canada. But what actually may be most characteristic of the size of India's herd is the low ratio of cattle to people. Thus, India has 44 cattle per 100 persons, while in the U.S. the ratio is 58 per 100 and in Canada, 90 (Mamoria 1953: 256). Yet, in India cattle are employed as a basic instrument of agricultural production.

Sharing of draught animals on a cooperative basis might reduce the need for additional animals. Chaudhri and Giri point out that the "big farmer manages to cultivate with a pair of bullock a much larger area than the small cultivators" (1963: 596). But, the failure to develop cooperative forms of plowing can scarcely be traced to *ahimsa*. If anything, emphasis upon independent, family-sized farm units follows intensification of individual land tenure patterns and other property innovations deliberately encouraged by the British (Bhatia 1963: 18 on). Under existing property arrangements, there is a perfectly good economic explanation of why bullocks are not shared among adjacent households. Plowing cannot take place at any time of the year, but must be accomplished within a few daylight hours in conformity with seasonal conditions. These are set largely by summer monsoons, responsible for about 90% of the total rainfall (Bhatia 1963: 4). Writing about Orissa, Bailey (1957: 74) notes:

> As a temporary measure, an ox might be borrowed from a relative, or a yoke of cattle and a ploughman might be hired . . . but during the planting season, when the need is the greatest, most people are too busy to hire out or lend cattle.

According to Desai (1948: 86):

> . . . over vast areas, sowing and harvesting operations, by the very nature of things, begin simultaneously with the outbreak of

---

Harris believes that many studies mix etic and emic data together, thus confounding the analysis. Here he says the same problem "contributes greatly to confusion surrounding the Indian cattle question." Harris claims that when the situation is examined from an etic perspective (energy contribution of cows versus energy expenditures of cows within an overall ecosystem), it is clear that the treatment of cattle in India is adaptive.

the first showers and the maturing of crops respectively, and especially the former has got to be put through quickly during the first phase of the monsoon. Under these circumstances, reliance by a farmer on another for bullocks is highly risky and he has got, therefore, to maintain his own pair.

Dube (1955: 84) is equally specific:

> The cultivators who depend on hired cattle or who practice cooperative lending and borrowing of cattle cannot take the best advantage of the first rains, and this enforced wait results in untimely sowing and poor crops.

Wiser and Wiser (1963: 62) describe the plight of the bullock-short farmer as follows, "When he needs the help of bullocks most, his neighbors are all using theirs." And Shastri (1960: 1592) points out, "Uncertainty of Indian farming due to dependence on rains is the main factor creating obstacles in the way of improvements in bullock labor."

It would seem, therefore, that this aspect of the cattle complex is not an expression of spirit and ritual, but of rain and energy.[6]

DUNG

In India cattle dung is the main source of domestic cooking fuel. Since grain crops cannot be digested unless boiled or baked, cooking is indispensable. Considerable disagreement exists about the total amount of cattle excrement and its uses, but even the lowest estimates are impressive. An early estimate by Lupton (1922: 60) gave the BTU equivalent of dung consumed in domestic cooking as 35,000,000 tons of coal or 68,000,000 tons of wood. Most detailed appraisal is by National Council of Applied Economic Research (1959: 3), which rejects H. J. Bhabha's estimate of 131,000,000 tons of coal and the Ministry of Food and Agriculture's 112,000,000 tons. The figure preferred by the NCAER is 35,000,000 tons anthracite or 40,000,000 tons bituminous, but with a possible range of between 35–45,000,000 of anthracite dung-coal equivalent. This calculation depends upon indications that only 36% of the total wet dung is utilized as fuel (p. 14), a lower estimate than any reviewed by Saha (1956: 923). These vary from 40% (Imperial Council on Agricultural Research) to 50% (Ministry of Food and Agriculture) to 66.6% (Department of Education, Health, and Lands). The NCAER estimate of a dung-coal equivalent of 35,000,000 tons is therefore quite conservative; it is nonetheless an impressive amount of BTU's to be plugged into an energy system.

Kapp (1963: 144 on), who discusses at length the importance of substituting tractors for bullocks, does not give adequate attention to finding cooking fuel after the bullocks are replaced. The NCAER (1959: 20) conclusion that dung is cheaper than coke seems an understatement. Although it is claimed that wood resources are potentially adequate to replace dung the measures advocated do not involve *ahimsa* but are again an indictment of a land tenure system not inspired by Hindu tradition (NCAER 1959: 20 on; Bansil 1958: 97 on). Finally, it should be noted that many observers stress the slow burning qualities of dung and its special appropriateness for preparation of **ghi** and deployment of woman-power

---

6. When Harris wrote this essay, he was arguing against some mainstream practices of American anthropology, therefore, he presents quotation after quotation supporting his views when one or two would suffice. Note that he relies almost exclusively on statistical rather than ethnographic data. The vast majority of the sources cited in this section come from economists, statisticians, and geographers. With the exception of the anthropologists, these are not sources with whom Harris's readers would be familiar. It is also instructive to examine Harris's writing style. Although not as polemical an author as Marx, whose work is full of in-jokes and snide comments about intellectual rivals, Harris undercuts his opponents through rhetorical style as well as logical argument. Throughout this section, Harris concludes points by referring to technological and environmental circumstances. The cumulative rhetorical effect is to overwhelm religious explanations.

in the household (Lewis and Barnouw 1958: 40; Mosher 1946: 153).[7]

As manure, dung enters the energy system in another vital fashion. According to Mujumdar (1960: 743), 300,000,000 tons are used as fuel, 340,000,000 tons as manure, and 160,000,000 tons "wasted on hillsides and roads." Spate (1954: 238) believes that 40% of dung production is spread on fields, 40% burned, and 20% "lost." Possibly estimates of the amount of dung lost are grossly inflated in view of the importance of "roads and hillsides" in the grazing pattern (see Pasture). Similarly artificial and culture- or even class-bound judgments refer to utilization of India's night soil. It is usually assumed that Chinese and Indian treatment of this resource are radically different, and that vast quantities of nitrogen go unused in agriculture because of Hindu-inspired definitions of modesty and cleanliness. However, most human excrement from Indian villages is deposited in surrounding fields; the absence of latrines helps explain why such fields raise 2 and 3 successive crops each year (Mosher 1946: 154, 33; Bansil 1958: 104). More than usual caution, therefore, is needed before concluding that a significant amount of cattle dung is wasted. Given the conscious premium set on dung for fuel and fertilizer, thoughtful control maintained over grazing patterns (see Pasture), and occurrence of specialized sweeper and gleaner castes, much more detailed evidence of wastage is needed than is now available. Since cattle graze on "hillsides and roads," dung dropped there would scarcely be totally lost to the *eco-system*, even with allowance for loss of nitrogen by exposure to air and sunlight. Also, if any animal dung is wasted on roads and hillsides it is not because of *ahimsa* but of inadequate pasturage suitable for collecting and processing animal droppings. The sedentary, intensive rainfall agriculture of most of the subcontinent is heavily dependent upon manuring. So vital is this that Spate (1954: 239) says substitutes for manure consumed as fuel "must be supplied, and lavishly, even at a financial loss to government." If this is the case, then old, decrepit, and dry animals might have a use after all, especially when, as we shall see, the dung they manufacture employs raw materials lost to the culture-energy system unless processed by cattle, and especially when many apparently moribund animals revive at the next monsoon and provide their owners with a male calf.[8]

BEEF AND HIDES

Positive contributions of India's sacred cattle do not cease with milk-grazing, bullock-producing, traction, and dung-dropping. There remains the direct protein contribution of 25,000,000 cattle and buffalo which die each year (Mohan 1962: 54). This feature of the ecosystem is reminiscent of the East African cattle area where, despite the normal taboo on slaughter, natural deaths and ceremonial occasions are probably frequent enough to maintain beef consumption near the ecological limit with dairying as the primary func-

---

7. Harris's statement about "a land tenure system not inspired by Hindu tradition" and his earlier statement that private ownership was intensified by British rule references the colonization of India. Despite these brief mentions of colonialism, Harris's analysis is essentially ahistorical. He does not consider the history of cattle slaughter prohibition in its relation to broader Indian or world history. As Jonathan Friedman points out in his 1974 critique of Harris, Harris never deals with the cultural context in which the traditions he analyzes take place—that is, centuries of British colonial rule.

Note also that in 1966 Harris didn't see a problem with citing authors who suggested that using cow manure as fuel was somehow particularly appropriate for women's household roles. It is hard to imagine anyone making a similar argument today.

"*Ghi*," or "ghee": clarified butter made from the butterfat of milk.

8. Since the 1943 publication of "Energy and the Evolution of Culture" by Leslie White, energy has had a significant role in American anthropology. Harris's discussion of dung as an energy source is an early example of the type of analysis that became a mainstay of the ecological and evolutionary approaches in cultural anthropology.

tion (Schneider 1957: 278 on). Although most Hindus probably do not consume beef, the *eco-system* under consideration is not confined to Hindus. The human population includes some 55,000,000 "scheduled" exterior or untouchable groups (Hutton 1961: vii), many of whom will consume beef if given the opportunity (Dube 1955: 68–69), plus several million more Moslems and Christians. Much of the flesh on the 25,000,000 dead cattle and buffalo probably gets consumed by human beings whether or not the cattle die naturally. Indeed, could it be that without the orthodox Hindu beef eating taboo, many marginal and depressed castes would be deprived of an occasional, but nutritionally critical, source of animal protein?

It remains to note that the slaughter taboo does not prevent depressed castes from utilizing skin, horns and hoofs of dead beasts. In 1956 16,000,000 cattle hides were produced (Randhawa 1962: 322). The quality of India's huge leather industry—the world's largest—leaves much to be desired, but the problem is primarily outmoded tanning techniques and lack of capital, not *ahimsa*.[9]

PASTURE

The principal positive-functioned or useful contributions of India's sacred cattle to human survival and well-being have been described. Final evaluation of their utility must involve assessment of energy costs in terms of resources and human labor input which might be more efficiently expended in other activities.

Direct and indirect evidence suggests that in India men and bovine cattle do not compete for existence. According to Mohan (1962: 43 on):

. . . the bulk of the food on which the animals subsist . . . is not the food that is required for human consumption, that is, fibrous fodders produced as incidental to crop production, and a large part of the crop residues or byproducts of seeds and waste grazing.

On the contrary, "the bulk of foods (straws and crop residues) that are ploughed into the soil in other countries are converted into milk" (p. 45).

The majority of the Indian cattle obtain their requirements from whatever grazing is available from straw and stalk and other residues from human foodstuffs, and are starved seasonally in the dry months when grasses wither.

In Bengal the banks and slopes of the embankments of public roads are the only grazing grounds and the cattle subsist mainly on paddy straw, paddy husks and . . . coarse grass . . . . (Mamoria 1953: 263–64)

According to Dube (1955:84, ". . . the cattle roam about the shrubs and rocks and eat whatever fodder is available there." This is confirmed by Moomaw (1949: 96): "Cows subsist on the pasture and any coarse fodder they can find. Grain is fed for only a day or two following parturition." The character of the environmental niche reserved for cattle nourishment is described by Gourou (1963: 123), based on data furnished by Dupuis (1960) for Madras:

Il faut voir clairement que le faible rendement du bétail indien n'est pas un gaspillage: ce bétail n'entre pas en concurrence avec la consommation de produits agricoles . . . ils ne leur sacrifient pas des surfaces agricoles, ou ayant un potential agricole.[10]

---

9. Notice the absence of statistical support in Harris's discussion of beef eating and the leather industry. This section is full of words like "probably" and "could be." Harris writes that the poor quality of India's leather industry results from a lack of capital rather than *ahimsa*. However, one could easily argue that it is precisely *ahimsa* that accounts for the lack of capital since no one with prestige or wealth will invest in tanning. This is typical of Harris's dogmatism: He will allow no explanatory power to *ahimsa* at all.

10. *"Il faut voir . . ."*: French for "It is clear that the low yield of Indian cattle is not waste: these beasts do not compete for the consumption of agricultural products . . . neither fields nor areas that could be used for agriculture are sacrificed to them."

NCAER (1961: 57) confines this pattern for Tripura: "There is a general practice of feeding livestock on agricultural by-products such as straw, grain wastes and husks"; for West Bengal (NCAER 1962: 59): "The state has practically no pasture or grazing fields, and the farmers are not in the habit of growing green fodders . . . livestock feeds are mostly agricultural by-products"; and for Andhra Pradesh (NCAER 1962: 52): "Cattle are stall-fed, but the bulk of the feed consists of paddy straw . . ."

The only exceptions to the rural pattern of feeding cattle on waste products and grazing them on marginal or unproductive lands involve working bullocks and nursing cows:

The working bullocks, on whose efficiency cultivation entirely depends, are usually fed with chopped bananas at the time of fodder scarcity. But the milch cows have to live in a semi-starved condition, getting what nutrition they can from grazing on the fields after their rice harvest (Gangulee 1935: 17). At present cattle are fed largely according to the season. During the rainy period they feed upon the grass which springs up on the *uncultivated* hillsides . . . But in the dry season there is hardly any grass, and cattle wander on the *cropless* lands in an often half-starved condition. True there is some fodder at these times in the shape of rice-straw and dried copra, but it is not generally sufficient, and is furthermore given mainly to the animals actually *working* at the time. (Mayer 1952: 70, italics added)

There is much evidence that Hindu farmers calculate carefully which animals deserve more food and attention. In Madras, Randhawa, et al. (1961: 117) report: "The cultivators pay more attention to the male stock used for ploughing and for draft. There is a general neglect of the cow and the female calf even from birth . . ." Similar discrimination is described by Mamoria (1953: 263 on):

Many plough bullocks are sold off in winter or their rations are ruthlessly decreased

whenever they are not worked in full, while milch cattle are kept on after lactation on poor and inadequate grazing . . . The cultivator feeds his bullocks better than his cow because it pays him. He feeds his bullocks better during the busy season, when they work, than during the slack season, when they remain idle. Further, he feeds his more valuable bullocks better than those less valuable . . . Although the draught animals and buffaloes are properly fed, the cow gets next to nothing of stall feeding. She is expected to pick up her living on the bare fields after harvest and on the village wasteland . . .

The previously cited NCAER report on Andhra Pradesh notes that "Bullocks and milking cows during the working season get more concentrates . . ." (1962: 52). Wiser and Wiser (1963: 71) sum up the situation in a fashion supporting Srinivas' (1958: 4) observation that the Indian peasant is "nothing if he is not practical":

Farmers have become skillful in reckoning the minimum of food necessary for maintaining animal service. Cows are fed just enough to assure their calving and giving a little milk. They are grazed during the day on lands which yield very little vegetation, and are given a very sparse meal at night.

Many devout Hindus believe the bovine cattle of India are exploited without mercy by greedy Hindu owners. *Ahimsa* obviously has little to do with economizing which produces the famous *phooka* and *doom dev* techniques for dealing with dry cows.[11] Not to Protestants but to Hindus did Gandhi (1954: 7) address lamentations concerning the cow:

How we bleed her to take the last drop of milk from her, how we starve her to emaciation, how we ill-treat the calves, how we deprive them of their portion of milk, how cruelly we treat the oxen, how we castrate them, how we beat them, how we overload them . . . I do not know that the condition of

---

11. The "famous" *phooka* and *doom dev* techniques are procedures Indians use to stimulate a cow's flow of milk. As described by Harris in *Cows, Pigs, Wars, and Witches* (1974), *phooka* is blowing air into the cow's uterus through a hollow pipe; *doom dev* refers to inserting the cow's tail into its vagina.

the cattle in any other part of the world is as bad as in unhappy India.

USEFUL AND
USELESS ANIMALS

How then, if careful rationing is characteristic of livestock management, do peasants tolerate the widely reported herds of useless animals? Perhaps "useless" means one thing to the peasant and quite another to the price-market-oriented agronomist. It is impossible at a distance to judge which point of view is ecologically more valid, but the peasants could be right more than the agronomists are willing to admit.

Since non-working and non-lactating animals are thermal and chemical factories which depend on waste lands and products for raw materials, judgment that a particular animal is useless cannot be supported without careful examination of its owner's household budget. Estimates from the cattle census which equate useless with dry or non-working animals are not convincing. But even if a given animal in a particular household is of less-than-marginal utility, there is an additional factor whose evaluation would involve long-range bovine biographies. The utility of a particular animal to its owner cannot be established simply by its performance during season or an animal cycle. Perhaps the whole system of Indian bovine management is alien to costing procedures of the West. There may be a kind of low-risk sweepstakes which drags on for 10 or 12 years before the losers and winners are separated.

As previously observed, the principal function of bovine cows is not their milk-producing but their bullock-producing abilities. Also established is the fact that many farmers are short of bullocks. Cows have the function primarily to produce male offspring, but when? In Europe and America, cows become pregnant under well-controlled, hence predictable, circumstances and a farmer with many animals can count on male offspring in half the births. In India, cows become pregnant under quite different circumstances. Since cows suffer from malnutrition through restriction to marginal pasture, they conceive and deliver in unpredictable fashion. The chronic starvation

of the inter-monsoon period makes the cow, in the words of Mamoria (1953: 263), "an irregular breeder." Moreover, with few animals, the farmer may suffer many disappointments before a male is born. To the agriculture specialist with knowledge of what healthy dairy stock look like, the hot weather herds of walking skeletons "roaming over the bare fields and dried up wastes" (Leake 1923: 267) must indeed seem without economic potential. Many of them, in fact, will not make it through to the next monsoon. However, among the survivors are an unknown number still physically capable of having progeny. Evidently neither the farmer nor the specialist knows which will conceive, nor when. To judge from Bombay city, even when relatively good care is bestowed on a dry cow, no one knows the outcome: "If an attempt is made to salvage them, they have to be kept and fed for a long time. Even then, it is not known whether they will conceive or not" (Nandra, *et al.* 1955: 9).

In rural areas, to judge a given animal useless may be to ignore the recuperative power of these breeds under conditions of erratic rainfall and unpredictable grazing opportunities. The difference of viewpoint between the farmer and the expert is apparent in Moomaw's (1949) incomplete attempt to describe the life history of an informant's cattle. The farmer in question had 3 oxen, 2 female buffaloes, 4 head of young cattle and 3 "worthless" cows (p. 23). In Moomaw's opinion, "the three cows . . . are a liability to him, providing no income, yet consuming feed which might be placed to better use." Yet we learn, "The larger one had a calf about once in three years"; moreover 2 of the 3 oxen were "raised" by the farmer himself. (Does this mean that they were the progeny of the farmer's cows?) The farmer tells Moomaw, "The young stock get some fodder, but for the most part they pasture with the village herd. The cows give nothing and I cannot afford to feed them." Whereupon Moomaw's *non sequitur:* "We spoke no more of his cows, for like many a farmer he just keeps them, without inquiring whether it is profitable or not" (p. 25). The difficulties in identifying animals that are definitely uneconomic for a given farmer are reflected in the varying estimates of the total of such animals. The Expert Committee on the Prevention of Slaughter of Cattle esti-mated 20,000,000 uneconomic cattle in India (Nandra, *et al.* 1953: 62). Roy (1955: 14) set-tles for 5,500,000, or about 3.5%. Mamoria (1953: 257), who gives the still lower estimate of 2,900,000, or 2.1%, claims most of these are males. A similarly low percentage—2.5%—is suggested for West Bengal (NCAER 1962: 56). None of these estimates appears based on bovine life histories in relation to household budgets; none appears to involve estimates of economic significance of dung contributions of older animals.[12]

Before a peasant is judged a victim of Ori-ental mysticism, might it not be well to indi-cate the devastating material consequences which befall a poor farmer unable to replace a bullock lost through disease, old age, or acci-dent? Bailey (1957: 73) makes it clear that in the economic life of the marginal peasantry, "Much the most devastating single event is the loss of an ox (or a plough buffalo)." If the farmer is unable to replace the animal with one from his own herd, he must borrow money at usurious rates. Defaults on such loans are the principal causes of transfer of land titles from peasants to landlords. Could this explain why the peasant is not overly perturbed that some of his animals might turn out to be only dung-providers? After all, the real threat to his existence does not arise from animals but from people ready to swoop down on him as soon as one of his beasts falters. Chapekar's (1960: 27) claim that the peasant's "stock serve as a great security for him to fall back on whenever he is in need" would seem to be appropriate only in reference to the unusually well-established minority. In a land where life expectancy at birth has only recently risen to 30 years (Black 1959: 2), it is not altogether appropriate to speak of security. The poorest farmers own insufficient stock. Farm manage-ment studies show that holdings below 2/3 of average area account for 2/5 of all farms, but maintain only 1/4 of the total cattle on farms. "This is so, chiefly because of their limited

resources to maintain cattle" (Chaudhri and Giri 1963: 598).

SLAUGHTER

Few, if any, Hindu farmers kill their cattle by beating them over the head, severing their jugular veins or shooting them. But to assert that they do not kill their animals when it is economically important for them to do so may be equally false. This interpretation escapes the notice of so many observers because the slaughtering process receives recognition only in euphemisms. People will admit that they "neglect" their animals, but will not openly accept responsibility for the *etic* effects, i.e., the more or less rapid death which ensues. The strange result of this euphemistic pattern is evidenced in the following statement by Moomaw (1949: 96): "All calves born, how-ever inferior, are allowed to live until they die of neglect." In the light of many similar but, by Hindu standards, more vulgar observations, it is clear that this kind of statement should read, "Most calves born are not allowed to live, but are starved to death."

This is roughly the testimony of Gourou (1963: 125), "Le paysan conserve seulement les veaux qui deviendront boeufs de labour ou vaches laitiè` res; les autres sont écartés . . . et meurent d'epuisement." Wiser and Wiser (1963: 70) are even more direct:

> Cows and buffaloes too old to furnish milk are not treated cruelly, but simply allowed to starve. The same happens to young male buffaloes . . . The males are unwanted and little effort is made to keep them alive.

Obviously, when an animal, undernourished to begin with, receives neither food nor care, it will not enjoy a long life (compare Gourou 1963: 124). Despite claims that an aged and decrepit cow "must be supported like an unproductive relative, until it dies a natural death" (Mosher

---

12. Harris's concern is for the economics of cattle at the level of the Indian peasant household, but the statistics he cites are national or state-level figures. Millions of starving cattle wandering around might pres-ent state-level problems not experienced by an individual farmer. The level at which a problem is examined affects one's analysis. Both Harris and the government figures he cites may be correct, but in different ways.

1946: 124), ample evidence justifies belief that "few cattle die of old age"[e] (Bailey 1957: 75). Dandekar (1964: 352) makes the same point: "In other words, because the cows cannot be fed nor can they be killed, they are neglected, starved and left to die a 'natural' death."[13]

The farmer culls his stock by starving unwanted animals and also, under duress, sells them directly or indirectly to butchers. With economic pressure, many Indians who will not kill or eat cows themselves:

> are likely to compromise their principles and sell to butchers who slaughter cows, thereby tacitly supporting the practice for other people. Selling aged cows to butchers has over the centuries become an accepted practice along side the *mos* that a Hindu must not kill cattle (Roy 1955: 15)

Determining the number of cattle slaughtered by butchers is almost as difficult as determining the number killed by starvation. According to Dandekar (1964: 351), "Generally it is the useless animals that find their way to the slaughter house." Lahiry (n.d.:140) says only 126,900 or .9% of the total cattle population is slaughtered per year. Darling (1934: 158) claims:

> All Hindus object to the slaughter and even to the sale of unfit cows and keep them indefinitely . . . rather than sell them to a cattle dealer, who would buy only for the slaughter house, they send them to a **gowshala** or let them loose to die. Some no doubt sell secretly, but this has its risks in an area where public opinion can find strong expression through the **panchayat**.[14]

Such views would seem to be contradicted by Sinha (1961: 95): "A large number of animals

are slaughtered privately and it is very difficult to ascertain their numbers." The difficulty of obtaining accurate estimates is also implied by the comment of the Committee on the Prevention of Slaughter that "90% of animals not approved for slaughter are slaughtered stealthily outside of municipal limits" (Nandra, *et al.* 1955: 11).[15]

An indication of the propensity to slaughter cattle under duress is found in connection with the food crisis of World War II. With rice imports cut off by Japanese occupation of Burma (Thirumalai 1954: 38; Bhatia 1963: 309 on), increased consumption of beef by the armed forces, higher prices for meat and foodstuffs generally, and famine conditions in Bengal, the doctrine of *ahimsa* proved to be alarmingly ineffectual. Direct military intervention was required to avoid destruction of animals needed for plowing, milking, and bullock-production:

> During the war there was an urgent need to reduce or to avoid the slaughter for food of animals useful for breeding or for agricultural work. For the summer of 1944 the slaughter was prohibited of: 1) Cattle below three years of age; 2) Male cattle between two and ten years of age which were being used or were likely to be used as working cattle; 3) All cows between three and ten years of age, other than cows which were unsuitable for bearing offspring; 4) All cows which were pregnant or in milk. (Knight 1954: 141)

Gourou (1963: 124–25), aware that starvation and neglect are systematically employed to cull Indian herds, nonetheless insists that destruction of animals through starvation amounts to an important loss of capital. This loss is attributed to the low price of beef caused

---

13. *"Le paysan conserve . . ."*: French for "The peasant only saves those calves that will become traction animals or milk cows. The others are taken away and die of starvation."

14. **"Gowshala"**: an "old age home" for cattle; **"Panchayat"**: "village council."

15. As you read these statements, keep in mind that the slaughter of cattle has been an extremely sensitive political topic in India for centuries.

by the beef-eating taboo, making it economically infeasible to send animals to slaughter. Gourou's appraisal, however, neglects deleterious consequences to the rural tanning and carrion-eating castes if increased numbers of animals went to the butchers. Since the least efficient way to convert solar energy into comestibles is to impose an animal converter between plant and man (Cottrell 1955), it should be obvious that without major technical and environmental innovations or drastic population cuts, India could not tolerate a large beef-producing industry. This suggests that insofar as the beef eating taboo helps discourage growth of beef producing industries, it is part of an ecological adjustment which maximizes rather than minimizes the calorie and protein output of the productive process.[16]

ANTI-SLAUGHTER LEGISLATION AND GOWSHALAS

It is evident from the history of anti-slaughter agitation and legislation in India that more than *ahimsa* has been required to protect Indian cattle from premature demise. Unfortunately, this legislation is misinterpreted and frequently cited as evidence of the anti-economic effect of Hinduism. I am unable to unravel all the tangled economic and political interests served by the recent anti-slaughter laws of the Indian states. Regardless of the ultimate ecological consequences of these laws, however, several points deserve emphasis. First it should be recalled that cow protection was a major political weapon in Gandhi's campaign against both British and Moslems. The sacred cow was the ideological focus of a successful struggle against English colonialism; hence the enactment of total anti-slaughter legislation obviously had a relational base, at least among politicians who seized and retained power on anti-English and anti-Moslem platforms. It is possible that the legislation will now backfire and upset the delicate ecological balance which now exists. The Committee on the Prevention of Slaughter claimed that it actually saw in Pepsu (where slaughter is banned completely) what a menace wild cattle can be. Conditions have become so desperate there, that the State Government have got to spend a considerable sum for catching and redomesticating wild animals to save the crops (Nandra, *et al.* 1955: 11).

According to Mayadas (1954: 29):

> The situation has become so serious that it is impossible in some parts of the country to protect growing crops from grazing by wandering cattle. Years ago it was one or two stray animals which could either be driven off or sent to the nearest cattle pound. Today it is a question of constantly being harassed day and night by herds which must either feed on one's green crops, or starve. How long can this state of affairs be allowed to continue?

Before the deleterious effects of slaughter laws can be properly evaluated, certain additional evolutionary and functional possibilities must be examined. For example, given the increasing growth rate of India's human population, the critical importance of cattle in the *eco-system,* and the absence of fundamental technical and environmental changes, a substantial increase in cattle seems necessary and predictable, regardless of slaughter legislation. Furthermore, there is some indication, admittedly incomplete but certainly worthy of careful inquiry, that many who protest most against destructiveness of marauding herds of useless beasts may perceive the situation from very special vantage points in the social hierarchy. The implications of the following newspaper editorial are clear:

---

16. On the other hand, in 2014, India was the world's largest beef exporter (water buffalo count as beef in this statistic) (Iyengar 2015). India's population is certainly greater now than when Harris wrote. About 16 percent of Indians, or about 200 million people, are Muslim or Christian and do not believe in *ahimsa*. However, they alone do not account for either this industry or the two million cows that are smuggled yearly from India to Bangladesh. Additionally, there are believed to be thirty thousand illegal slaughterhouses in India (Gopal 2015).

The alarming increase of stray and wild cattle over wide areas of Northern India is fast becoming a major disincentive to crop cultivation . . . Popular sentiment against cow slaughter no doubt lies at the back of the problem. People prefer to let their aged, diseased, and otherwise useless cattle live at the expense of *other people's crops*. (Indian Express, New Delhi, 7 February 1959, italics added)

Evidently we need to know something about whose crops are threatened by these marauders. Despite post-independence attempts at land reform, 10% of the Indian agricultural population still owns more than 1/2 the total cultivated area and 15,000,000, or 22%, of rural households own no land at all (Mitra 1963: 298). Thorner and Thorner (1962: 3) call the land reform program a failure, and point out how "the grip of the larger holder serves to prevent the lesser folk from developing the land . . ." Quite possibly, in other words, the anti-slaughter laws, insofar as they are effective, should be viewed as devices which, contrary to original political intent, bring pressure to bear upon those whose lands are devoted to cash crops of benefit only to narrow commercial, urban, and landed sectors of the population. To have one's cows eat other people's crops may be a very fine solution to the subsistence problem of those with no crops of their own. Apparently,

in the days when animals could be driven off or sent to the pound with impunity, this could not happen, even though *ahimsa* reigned supreme then as now.[17]

Some form of anti-slaughter legislation was required and actually argued for, on unambiguously rational, economic, and material grounds. About 4% of India's cattle are in the cities (Mohan 1962: 48). These have always represented the best dairy stock, since the high cost of feeding animals in a city could be offset only by good milking qualities. A noxious consequence of this dairy pattern was the slaughter of the cow at the end of its first urban lactation period because it was too expensive to maintain while awaiting another pregnancy. Similarly, and by methods previously discussed, the author calf was killed after it had stimulated the cow to "let down." With the growth of urban milk consumption, the best of India's dairy cattle were thus systematically prevented from breeding, while animals with progressively poorer milking qualities were preserved in the countryside (Mohan 1962: 48; Mayadas 1954: 29; Gandhi 1954: 13 on). The Committee on the Prevention of Slaughter of Cattle (Nandra, *et al.* 1955: 2) claimed at least 50,000 high-yielding cows and she-buffaloes from Madras, Bombay, and Calcutta were "annually sent to premature slaughter" and were "lost to the country." Given such evidence of waste and the political potential of Moslems being

---

17. Having discussed the utility of *ahimsa* to Indian peasant farmers, Harris turns to a discussion of the social and political ramifications of the practice. Here he injects an element of class conflict into his argument. However, while Harris sees conflict, he doesn't make it the engine of cultural change. The system he describes is essentially static. A true Marxist would bring this conflict to the center of the analysis.

When Harris wrote this essay, anti–cow slaughter legislation was an issue in India. It still is. In 2014, Narendra Modi (b. 1950) was elected prime minister of India. His campaign platform included a promise to ban the purchase of cows for slaughter nationwide, and legislation to enact this ban passed in 2017. Indian religious leaders and politicians have a long history of using beliefs about cows for political purposes. There were cow protection riots in the eighteenth century violence related to cattle killing happened repeatedly from the late 1860s through the 1920s. In many cases, this was rioting and violence by the Hindu community against the Muslim community. In 1966, the year this article came out, a mob of ten thousand supporters of anti-slaughter legislation rioted in New Delhi. From 2016 to 2020 over fifty people died in cow protection–related violence. Overwhelmingly the victims of these attacks are members of minority groups. According to Human Rights Watch, the rhetoric used by members of Modi's Bharatiya Janata Party (BJP) has encouraged violence and BJP politicians have publically justified the attacks (Maskara 2021, Human Rights Watch 2019). Regardless of any ecological considerations, *ahimsa* and the sacredness of cattle are profoundly emotional issues that mobilize the BJP's political base. India is an economically powerful, nuclear armed nation. Understanding the emotional and political implications of how cows are understood by many Indians is almost surely far more important than understanding their ecological role in the historic Indian countryside.

identified as cow-butchers and Englishmen as cow-eaters (Gandhi 1954: 16), the political importance of *ahimsa* becomes more intelligible. Indeed, it could be that the strength of Gandhi's *charisma* lay in his superior understanding of the ecological significance of the cow, especially in relation to the underprivileged masses, marginal low caste and out caste farmers. Gandhi (p. 3) may have been closer to the truth than many a foreign expert when he said:

> Why the cow was selected for apotheosis is obvious to me. The cow was in India the best companion. She was the giver of plenty. Not only did she give milk but she also made agriculture possible.

OLD-AGE HOMES

Among the more obscure aspects of the cattle complex are bovine old-age homes, variously identified as *gowshalas*, *pinjrapoles*, and, under the Five-Year Plans, as *gosadans*. Undoubtedly some of these are "homes for cows, which are supported by public charity, which maintain the old and derelict animals till natural death occurs" (Kothavala 1934: 123). According to Gourou (1963: 125), however, owners of cows sent to these religious institutions pay rent with the understanding that if the cows begin to lactate they will be returned. The economics of at least some of these "charitable" institutions is, therefore, perhaps not as quaint as usually implied. It is also significant that, although the 1st Five-Year Plan called for establishment of 160 *gosadans* to serve 320,000 cattle, only 22 *gosadans* servicing 8,000 cattle were reported by 1955 (Government of India Planning Commission 1956: 283).

NATURAL SELECTION

Expert appraisers of India's cattle usually show little enthusiasm for the typical undersized breeds. Much has been made of the fact that 1 large animal is a more efficient dung, milk, and traction machine than 2 small ones. "Weight for weight, a small animal consumes

a much larger quantity of food than a bigger animal" (Mamoria 1953: 268). "More dung is produced when a given quantity of food is consumed by one animal than when it is shared by two animals" (Ford Foundation 1959: 64). Thus it would seem that India's smaller breeds should be replaced by larger, more powerful, and better milking breeds. But once again, there is another way of looking at the evidence. It might very well be that if all of India's scrub cattle were suddenly replaced by an equivalent number of large, high-quality European or American dairy and traction animals, famines of noteworthy magnitude would immediately ensue. Is it not possible that India's cattle are undersized precisely because other breeds never could survive the atrocious conditions they experience most of the year? I find it difficult to believe that breeds better adapted to the present Indian *eco-system* exist elsewhere.

> By nature and religious training, the villager is unwilling to inflict pain or to take animal life. But the immemorial grind for existence has hardened him to an acceptance of survival of the fittest. (Wiser and Wiser 1963)

Not only are scrub animals well adapted to the regular seasonal crises of water and forage and general year-round neglect, but long-range selective pressures may be even more significant. The high frequency of drought-induced famines in India (Bhatia 1963) places a premium upon drought-resistance plus a more subtle factor: A herd of smaller animals, dangerously thinned by famine or pestilence, reproduces faster than an equivalent group of larger animals, despite the fact that the larger animal consumes less per pound than 2 smaller animals. This is because there are 2 cows in the smaller herd per equivalent large cow. Mohan (1962: 45) is one of the few authorities to have grasped this principle, including it in defense of the small breeds:

> Calculations of the comparative food conversion efficiency of various species of Indian domestic livestock by the writer has revealed, that much greater attention should be paid to small livestock than at present, not only because of their better conversion

efficiency for protein but also because of the possibilities of bringing about a rapid increase in their numbers.

CONCLUSION

The probability that India's cattle complex is a positive-functioned part of a naturally selected *eco-system* is at least as good as that it is a negative-functioned expression of an irrational ideology. This should not be interpreted to mean that no "improvements" can be made in the system, nor that different systems may not eventually evolve. The issue is not whether oxen are more efficient than tractors. I suggest simply that many features of the cattle complex have been erroneously reported or interpreted. That Indian cattle are weak and inefficient is not denied, but there is doubt that this situation arises from and is mainly perpetuated by Hindu ideology. Given the techno-environmental base, Indian property relationships, and political organization, one need not involve the doctrine of *ahimsa* to understand fundamental features of the cattle complex. Although the cattle population of India has risen by 38,000,000 head since 1940, during the same period, the human population has risen by 120,000,000. Despite the anti-slaughter legislation, the ratio of cattle to humans actually declined from 44:100 in 1941 to 40:100 in 1961 (Government of India 1962: 74; 1963: 6). In the absence of major changes in environment, technology or property relations, it seems unlikely that the cattle population will cease to accompany the rise in the human population. If *ahimsa* is negative-functioned, then we must be prepared to admit the possibility that all other factors contributing to the rapid growth of the Indian human and cattle populations, including the germ theory of disease, are also negative-functioned.[18]

AUTHOR'S NOTES

a. The author (1960) suggested that the term "adaptive" be restricted to traits, biological or cultural, established and diffused in conformity with the principle of natural selection. Clearly, not all "positive-functioned," i.e., useful, cultural traits are so established.

b. Ahimsa is the Hindu principle of unity of life, of which sacredness of cattle is principal sub-case and symbol.

c. According to Zeuner (1954:328), "Symbiosis includes all conditions of the living together of two different species, provided both derive advantages therefrom. Cases in which both partners benefit equally are rare." In the symbiosis under consideration, men benefit more than cattle.

d. The U.S. Census of Agriculture (1954) showed milk production averaging from a low of 3,929 pounds per cow in the Nashville Basin sub-region to 11,112 pounds per cow in the Southern California sub-region.

e. Srinivas (1962:126) declared himself properly skeptical in this matter: "It is commonly believed that the peasant's religious attitude to cattle comes in the way of the disposal of useless cattle. Here again, my experience of Rampura makes me skeptical of the general belief. I am not denying that cattle are regarded as in some sense sacred, but I doubt whether the belief is as powerful as it is claimed to be. I have already mentioned that bull-buffaloes are sacrificed to village goddesses. And in the case of the cow, while the peasant does not want to kill the cow or bull himself he does not seem to mind very much if someone else does the dirty job out of his sight."

---

18. Harris was one of the most colorful and polemical figures in anthropology from the 1960s until his death in 2001. He was a vociferous supporter of materialist approaches to anthropology and his advocacy of this position took on moral and ideological dimensions. For example, in the introduction to *Cows, Pigs, Wars, and Witches: The Riddles of Culture,* Harris wrote:

> I shall show that even the most bizarre-seeming beliefs and practices turn out . . . to be based on ordinary, banal . . . conditions needs and activities. [They] rest on the ground that is built up out of guts, sex, energy wind, rain, and other palpable ordinary phenomena. . . .
>
> Some anthropologists and historians . . . argue that the [cultural] participants' explanation constitutes an irreducible reality. They warn that . . . the scientific framework appropriate to the study of physics or chemistry has no relevance when applied to the study of lifestyles. . . . Nothing could be more absurd. (1974: 5–6)

This is powerful rhetoric, but the scientific framework appropriate to physics and chemistry involves highly specified variables, controlled experimentation, and hypothesis testing. Has Harris demonstrated these?

19. Ritual Regulation of Environmental Relations among a New Guinea People[a]

Roy A. Rappaport (1926–1997)

MOST FUNCTIONAL STUDIES of religious behavior in anthropology have as an analytic goal the elucidation of events, processes, or relationships occurring within a social unit of some sort. The social unit is not always well defined, but in some cases it appears to be a church, that is, a group of people who entertain similar beliefs about the universe, or a congregation, a group of people who participate together in the performance of religious rituals. There have been exceptions. Thus Vayda, Leeds, and Smith (1961) and O. K. Moore (1957) have clearly perceived that the functions of religious ritual are not necessarily confined within the boundaries of a congregation or even a church. By and large, however, I believe that the following statement by Homans (1941:172) represents fairly the dominant line of anthropological thought concerning the functions of religious ritual:

> Ritual actions do not produce a practical result on the external world—that is one of the reasons why we call them ritual. But to make this statement is not to say that ritual has no function. Its function is not related to the world external to the society but to the internal constitution of the society. It gives the members of the society confidence, it dispels their anxieties, it disciplines their social organization.[1]

No argument will be raised here against the sociological and psychological functions imputed by Homans, and many others before

---

From *Ethnology* (1967)

1. In the opening passage of this essay, Rappaport critiques functionalism in much the same way Julian Steward did almost thirty years previously. That is, holistic functional explanations do not generally show causes, only interrelations among parts within a system. Before Julian Steward, functionalists typically supposed that social systems were only weakly connected with their environments. Rappaport, following the cultural-ecology model, wishes to show that ritual, at least among those he studies, is articulated with, and has a profound effect on, the natural world.

Andrew P. Vayda (1931–2022) was Rappaport's dissertation advisor at Columbia and was in New Guinea with Rappaport when the fieldwork that formed the basis for this essay was done.

Vayda, Anthony Leeds (1925–1989), Rappaport, as well as Harris, and many others were students at Columbia in the late 1940s and 1950s. Julian Steward taught at Columbia from 1946 to 1953. Although neither Rappaport nor Harris were direct students of Steward (he had moved to the University of Illinois by the time Rappaport arrived at Columbia), his cultural ecological thinking had a deep effect on many anthropologists who trained there (see also essay 31, Wolf, note 8).

Omar Khayyam Moore (1920–2006) was a Yale sociologist known for arguing that the Naskapi practice of scapulimancy (divination using reindeer scapula) had the ecological effect of randomizing their hunting patterns. Moore was a true polymath who, in addition to publications in mathematics, pedagogy, sociology, and philosophy, held more than thirty patents.

George C. Homans (1910–1989) whom Rappaport quotes here, was a behavioral sociologist and a president of the American Sociological Association (1963–1964). Homans was particularly inspired by the behavioral psychology of B. F. Skinner (1904–1990). Skinner's approach treated humans as a blank slate whose behavior was almost completely shaped by reward and punishment. You can see evidence of this in the quote that Rappaport selects. For Homans, people do ritual because they receive specific rewards for engaging in it.

him, to ritual. They seem to me to be plausible. Nevertheless, in some cases at least, ritual does produce, in Homans' terms, "a practical result on the world" external not only to the social unit composed of those who participate together in ritual performances but also to the larger unit composed of those who entertain similar beliefs concerning the universe. The material presented here will show that the ritual cycles of the Tsembaga, and of other local territorial groups of Maring speakers living in the New Guinea interior, play an important part in regulating the relationships of these groups with both the nonhuman components of their immediate environments and the human components of their less immediate environments, that is, with other similar territorial groups. To be more specific, this regulation helps to maintain the biotic communities existing within their territories, redistributes land among people and people over land, and limits the frequency of fighting. In the absence of authoritative political statuses or offices, the ritual cycle likewise provides a means for mobilizing allies when warfare may be undertaken. It also provides a mechanism for redistributing local pig surpluses in the form of pork throughout a large regional population while helping to assure the local population of a supply of pork when its members are most in need of high quality protein.[2]

Religious ritual may be defined, for the purposes of this paper, as the prescribed performance of conventionalized acts manifestly directed toward the involvement of nonempirical or supernatural agencies in the affairs of the actors. While this definition relies upon the formal characteristics of the performances and upon the motives for undertaking them, attention will be focused upon the empirical effects of ritual performances and sequences of ritual performances. The religious rituals to be discussed are regarded as neither more nor less than part of the behavioral repertoire employed by an aggregate of organisms in adjusting to its environment.[3]

---

2. One of the principal influences on Rappaport and many other social scientists of the 1960s was General Systems Theory. This approach developed primarily by Austrian biologist Ludwig von Bertalanffy (1901–1972), was a way of providing a mathematical description of a physical system that examined the flow of energy, a chemical, a hormone, or some other attribute through the system.

Systems theory provided anthropologists a way to examine cultures as systems composed of both human and nonhuman elements. Bertalanffy, writing in 1968, says that "*Social science is the science of social systems. For this reason, it will have to use the approach of general systems theory*" (emphasis in the original) (1968: 195).

Systems theorists presumed that the normal state of a system was equilibrium and described the various methods by which systems out of balance were returned to equilibrium. In this essay, Rappaport describes Tsembaga culture as just such a system, highlighting the role of religious practices as mechanisms that maintain the cultural stability of a system. In its emphasis on the close integration of various elements of society and stability, Rappaport's analysis strongly resembles structural functionalism.

3. Notice Rappaport's style, he writes in a scientific trope, frequently referring to those he studies as "biological organisms" rather than people or individuals. Rappaport went into the field with a background in Steward's cultural ecology. Once there, his experiences compelled him to take a position in some ways more extreme than the classic cultural ecologists. Steward had supposed that, though the environment had an impact on human society, humans were, in fundamental ways, so different from other creatures that the natural laws that applied to populations of other animals could not be applied to them. This view was consistent with his Boasian training. Rappaport, on the other hand, came to believe that while human culture does separate us from other animals, as biological organisms we are subject to the same fundamental ecological laws. In this essay, he repeatedly compares humans to other species.

Ethology, the study of animal behavior, was becoming an increasingly important field within biology at this time. Austrian ethologist Konrad Lorenz (1901–1989) published his popular account of animal behavior *King Solomon's Ring* in 1952. This had an important impact on many scholars of the era. Rappaport's view is that ritual is an adaptive behavior just like a bird's song or a dog circling a space before lying down (Melina 2011).

Note Rappaport's use of the term "formal." A formal analysis seeks to find the structural and logical elements of a thing. It is not concerned with the emotional, symbolic, or experiential aspects of its subject (except

The data upon which this paper is based were collected during fourteen months of field work among the Tsembaga, one of about twenty local groups of Maring speakers living in the Simbai and Jimi Valleys of the Bismarck Range in the Territory of New Guinea. The size of Maring local groups varies from a little over 100 to 900. The Tsembaga, who in 1963 numbered 204 persons, are located on the south wall of the Simbai Valley. The country in which they live differs from the true highlands in being lower, generally more rugged, and more heavily forested. Tsembaga territory rises, within a total surface area of 3.2 square miles, from an elevation of 2,200 feet at the Simbai river to 7,200 feet at the ridge crest. Gardens are cut in the secondary forests up to between 5,000 and 5,400 feet, above which the area remains in primary forest. Rainfall reaches 150 inches per year.

The Tsembaga have come into contact with the outside world only recently; the first government patrol to penetrate their territory arrived in 1954. They were considered uncontrolled by the Australian government until 1962, and they remain unmissionized to this day.[4]

The 204 Tsembaga are distributed among five putatively patrilineal clans, which are, in turn, organized into more inclusive groupings on two hierarchical levels below that of the total local group.[b] Internal political structure is highly egalitarian. There are no hereditary or elected chiefs nor are there even "big men" who can regularly coerce or command the support of their clansmen or coresidents in economic or forceful enterprises.

It is convenient to regard the Tsembaga as a population in the ecological sense, that is, as one of the components of a system of **trophic exchanges** taking place within a bounded area. Tsembaga territory and the biotic community existing upon it may be conveniently viewed as an ecosystem. While it would be permissible arbitrarily to designate the Tsembaga as a population and their territory with its biota as an ecosystem, there are also nonarbitrary reasons for doing so. An ecosystem is a system of material exchanges, and the Tsembaga maintain against other human groups exclusive access to the resources within their territorial borders. Conversely, it is from this territory alone that the Tsembaga ordinarily derive all of their foodstuffs and most of the other materials they require for survival. Less anthropocentrically, it may be justified to regard Tsembaga territory with its biota as an ecosystem in view of the rather localized nature of cyclical material exchanges in tropical rainforests.[5]

---

as these bear directly on its structural and logical elements). For example, art critic Roger Fry (1866–1934) wanted to separate the visual appearance of a work of art from any emotion the art generated in its viewers. Rappaport tries to do something similar with the Tsembaga, that is, to separate the symbolic, ideological, and emotional aspects of their ceremonies from the ecological relationships that were regulated by their rituals. The idea of formal analysis played a strong role in the anthropology of the 1950s and 1960s. In addition to being found in ecologically based work like this (and see especially Marvin Harris's work as described in Bourdieu (essay 27 note 20), it was also part of ethnoscience and cognitive anthropology.

4. A criticism sometimes made of this essay (and this style of analysis) is that it makes very little reference to context and history. This brief paragraph is virtually the only reference to the history of the Tsembaga or their relations with outside (European) powers. Rappaport seems to assume that what he sees among the Tsembaga is natural behavior that has evolved in a bounded system. Rappaport notes that the first government patrol penetrated Tsembaga territory in 1954, but that doesn't mean this was the first time the Tsembaga were affected by the outside world. Trade and colonial policies affected those around the Tsembaga, and most likely, this, in turn, affected them. In the era when Rappaport wrote this essay, anthropologists tended to assume that cultures like the Tsembaga were relatively isolated and minimally influenced by Western societies. Today anthropologists tend to assume the opposite. However, does the lack of a historical context change Rappaport's argument? Does knowing whether a ritual is old or new change that ritual's adaptive function within a cultural system?

5. Notice that Rappaport again speaks of humans simply as organisms within an ecosystem, and he implies the valley in which the Tembaga live is a closed system. Consequently, the Tembaga's rituals must be adap-

As they are involved with the nonhuman biotic community within their territory in a set of trophic exchanges, so do they participate in other material relationships with other human groups external to their territory. Genetic materials are exchanged with other groups, and certain crucial items, such as stone axes, were in the past obtained from the outside. Furthermore, in the area occupied by the Maring speakers, more than one local group is usually involved in any process, either peaceful or warlike, through which people are redistributed over land and land redistributed among people.[6]

The concept of the ecosystem, though it provides a convenient frame for the analysis of inter-specific trophic exchanges taking place within limited geographical areas, does not comfortably accommodate intraspecific exchanges taking place over wider geographic areas. Some sort of geographic population model would be more useful for the analysis of the relationship of the local ecological population to the larger regional population of which it is a part, but we lack even a set of appropriate terms for such a model. Suffice it here to note that the relations of the Tsembaga to the total of other local human populations in their vicinity are similar to the relations of local aggregates of other animals to the totality of their species occupying broader and more or less continuous regions. This larger, more inclusive aggregate may resemble what geneticists mean by the term population, that is, an aggregate of interbreeding organisms persisting through an indefinite number of generations and either living or capable of living in isolation from similar aggregates of the same species. This is the unit which survives through long periods of time while its local ecological (***sensu stricto***) subunits, the units more or less independently involved in interspecific trophic exchanges such as the Tsembaga, are ephemeral.[7]

Since it has been asserted that the ritual cycles of the Tsembaga regulate relationships within what may be regarded as a complex system, it is necessary, before proceeding to the ritual cycle itself, to describe briefly, and where

---

tive responses to living in this environment. If this is true, what is the role of culture and culture change? Rappaport's answer is somewhat obscure. In the epilogue to the second edition of Rappaport's book-length treatment of this material, *Pigs for the Ancestors* (1984: 371–403) Rappaport writes: "cultures . . . constitute the major and most distinctive means by which human populations maintain common sets of material relations with other components of the ecosystems in which they participate" (1984: 384). However, a paragraph later he tells us that "If the concept of culture as adaptation is the truth, it is not the whole truth." Once cultures are established, "It becomes no longer clear whether culture is a symbolic means to organic ends or organisms living means to cultural ends" (1984: 385).

"**Trophic exchange**" refers to the movement of nutrients between different levels in a food chain (from producers, through herbivores, and then different types of carnivores and omnivores).

6. Did you catch Rappaport's use of the phrase "genetic materials are exchanged" to discuss sex? This is a good example of the use of an extremely simplified formal vocabulary to describe an extraordinarily complicated human activity.

7. When Rappaport says the Tsembaga are ephemeral, he means that as a named group they may not persist very long. If you came back two hundred years later there might be another group that called themselves the Agabmest, but they would still have similar practices.

Rappaport ignores an important distinction between humans and animals in that humans have history. The Tsembaga in this valley are not isolated at all. They intermarry with other Maring-speaking groups, they trade for tools, hold reciprocal feasts, and make alliances in times of war. Rappaport imagines the Tsembaga who live in this valley as inhabiting an ecological niche in which the rituals discussed here have evolved. But do humans only occupy a particular ecological niche or have they always moved among many possible niches? Does Rappaport's argument only hold together if societies like the Tsembaga are stable, without history, and occupy a single ecological niche?

"***Sensu stricto***": Latin strictly speaking or in a narrow sense.

possible in quantitative terms, some aspects of the place of the Tsembaga in this system.[8]

All gardens are mixed, many of them containing all of the major root crops and many greens. Two named garden types are, however, distinguished by the crops which predominate in them. "Taro-yam gardens" were found to produce, on the basis of daily harvest records kept on entire gardens for close to one year, about 5,300,000 calories[c] per acre during their harvesting lives of 18 to 24 months; 85 percent of their yield is harvested between 24 and 76 weeks after planting. "Sugar-sweet potato gardens" produce about 4,600,000 calories per acre during their harvesting lives, 91 percent being taken between 24 and 76 weeks after planting. I estimated that approximately 310,000 calories per acre is expended on cutting, fencing, planting, maintaining, harvesting, and walking to and from taro-yam gardens. Sugar-sweet potato gardens required an expenditure of approximately 290,000 calories per acre.[d] These energy ratios, approximately 17:1 on taro-yam gardens and 16:1 on sugar-sweet potato gardens, compare favorably with figures reported for swidden cultivation in other regions.[e]

Intake is high in comparison with the reported dietaries of other New Guinea populations. On the basis of daily consumption records kept for ten months on four households numbering in total sixteen persons, I estimated the average daily intake of adult males to be approximately 2,600 calories, and that of adult females to be around 2,200 calories. It may be mentioned here that the Tsembaga are small and short-statured. Adult males average 101 pounds in weight and approximately 58.5 inches in height; the corresponding averages for adult females are 85 pounds and 54.5 inches.[f, 9]

Although 99 percent by weight of the food consumed is vegetable, the protein intake is high by New Guinea standards. The daily protein consumption of adult males from vegetable sources was estimated to be between 43 and 55 grams, of adult females 36 to 48 grams. Even with an adjustment for vegetable sources, these values are slightly in excess of the recently published WHO/FAO daily requirements (Food and Agriculture Organization of the United Nations 1964). The same is true of the younger age categories, although soft and discolored hair, a symptom of protein deficiency, was noted in a few children. The WHO/FAO protein requirements do not include a large "margin for safety" or allowance for stress; and, although no clinical assessments were undertaken, it may be suggested that the Tsembaga achieve nitrogen balance at a low level. In other words, their protein intake is probably marginal.[10]

---

8. Rappaport's description focuses on those aspects of Tsembaga life that are of direct concern to his theoretical approach, particularly gardening. Within this framework, he discusses the Tsembaga as calorie producers and consumers. Note also Rappaport's quantification of data, which reflects his desire to make his work scientifically rigorous. Subsistence activities form the basis of his analysis. Other cultural features arise as a secondary result of subsistence or are historically particular and of less analytic importance. Rappaport's treatment is similar to Steward's idea of the culture core and secondary cultural features (see essay 17, Steward, note 1).

9. Rappaport gives many figures, but they are based on observation of only sixteen people in four families. In most studies in biology or ecology, this would be a very small sample. What sort of questions does this raise about his conclusions? Despite the small numbers, at the time this essay was published, it was probably the most detailed and comprehensive body of data ever collected on swidden agriculturalists. In keeping with the biological model on which he based this work, Rappaport makes his data available in the appendices to *Pigs for the Ancestors* (1967).

Rappaport mentions the short stature of the Tsembaga. In *Pigs for the Ancestors* (1967), a picture shows the five-foot, ten-inch Rappaport towering over a group of Tsembaga men.

10. Rappaport's analysis, although clearly materialist, is not Marxist. This essay contains neither references to the evolution of culture nor the notion that cultures are characterized by conflict that drives change, both hallmarks of Marxist thinking. Although war is a central feature of Rappaport's analysis, it functions as

Measurements of all gardens made during 1962 and of some gardens made during 1963 indicate that, to support the human population, between .15 and .19 acres are put into cultivation per capita per year. Fallows range from 8 to 45 years. The area in secondary forest comprises approximately 1,000 acres, only 30 to 50 of which are in cultivation at any time. Assuming calories to be the limiting factor, and assuming an unchanging population structure, the territory could support—with no reduction in lengths of fallow and without cutting into the virgin forest from which the Tsembaga extract many important items—between 290 and 397 people if the pig population remained minimal. The size of the pig herd, however, fluctuates widely. Taking Maring pig husbandry procedures into consideration, I have estimated the human carrying capacity of the Tsembaga territory at between 270 and 320 people.[11]

Because the timing of the ritual cycle is bound up with the demography of the pig herd, the place of the pig in Tsembaga adaptation must be examined.

First, being omnivorous, pigs keep residential areas free of garbage and human feces. Second limited numbers of pigs rooting in secondary growth may help to hasten the development of that growth. The Tsembaga usually permit pigs to enter their gardens one and a half to two years after planting, by which time **second-growth** trees are well established there. The Tsembaga practice selective weeding; from the time the garden is planted, herbaceous species are removed, but tree species are allowed to remain. By the time cropping is discontinued and the pigs are let in, some of the trees in the garden are already ten to fifteen feet tall. These well-established trees are relatively impervious to damage by the pigs, which, in rooting for seeds and remaining tubers, eliminate many seeds and seedlings that, if allowed to develop, would provide some competition for the established trees. Moreover, in some Maring-speaking areas swiddens are planted twice, although this is not the case with the Tsembaga. After the first crop is almost exhausted, pigs are penned in the garden, where their rooting eliminates weeds and softens the ground, making the task of planting for a second time easier. The pigs, in other words, are used as cultivating machines.[12]

Small numbers of pigs are easy to keep. They run free during the day and return home at night to receive their ration of garbage and substandard tubers, particularly sweet potatoes. Supplying the latter requires little extra work, for the substandard tubers are taken from the ground in the course of harvesting the daily ration for humans. Daily consumption records kept over a period of some months show that the ration of tubers received by the

---

an element in a system designed to preserve equilibrium rather than promote change. The results of Tsembaga warfare do not result in changes in the mode of production.

11. Rappaport again uses a concept borrowed from biology—carrying capacity, the number of individuals of a species that a given ecosystem can support without suffering degradation. However, it is good to keep in mind that for humans, the technology of food production must be considered. The carrying capacity of land exploited by foraging is different from that of the same land exploited by horticulture, a point discussed by Steward. Additionally, for nonhuman animals, carrying capacity can be scientifically calculated. However, for humans, carrying capacity depends not only on technology but on other aspects of culture, such as the prestige value of different foods. For humans carrying capacity is a political and social issue rather than an ecological one.

Rapport's use of carrying capacity illustrates how thoroughly his thinking is guided by systems theory and the ecological thinking of his day. It places him squarely in the mainstream of the scientific approaches of the 1960s.

12. Rappaport's description of pigs very closely matches the argument Marvin Harris (another Columbia student) made for cows in essay 18, published a year earlier. In both cases, animals are described as a kind of agricultural machinery.

"Primary growth" is the original growth on a piece of ground. **"Secondary growth"** occurs after a cultivated piece of ground is left fallow. Herbaceous species refers to plants that have nonwoody stems, like flowers.

pigs approximates in weight that consumed by adult humans, i.e., a little less than three pounds per day per pig.

If the pig herd grows large, however, the substandard tubers incidentally obtained in the course of harvesting for human needs become insufficient, and it becomes necessary to harvest especially for the pigs. In other words, people must work for the pigs and perhaps even supply them with food fit for human consumption. Thus, as Vayda, Leeds, and Smith (1961:71) have pointed out, there can be too many pigs for a given community.

This also holds true of the sanitary and cultivating services rendered by pigs. A small number of pigs is sufficient to keep residential areas clean, to suppress superfluous seedlings in abandoned gardens, and to soften the soil in gardens scheduled for second plantings. A larger herd, on the other hand, may be troublesome; the larger the number of pigs, the greater the possibility of their invasion of producing gardens, with concomitant damage not only to crops and young secondary growth but also to the relations between the pig owners and garden owners.

All male pigs are castrated at approximately three months of age, for boars, people say, are dangerous and do not grow as large as barrows. Pregnancies, therefore, are always the result of unions of domestic sows with feral males. Fecundity is thus only a fraction of its potential. During one twelve-month period only fourteen litters resulted out of a potential 99 or more pregnancies. Farrowing generally takes place in the forest and mortality of the young is high. Only 32 of the offspring of the above mentioned fourteen pregnancies were alive six months after birth. This number is barely sufficient to replace the number of adult animals which would have died or been killed during most years without pig festivals.

The Tsembaga almost never kill domestic pigs outside of ritual contexts. In ordinary times, when there is no pig festival in progress, the rituals are almost always associated with misfortunes or emergencies, notably warfare, illness, injury, or death. Rules state not only the contexts in which pigs are to be ritually slaughtered, but also who may partake of the flesh of the sacrificial animals. During warfare it is only the men participating in the fighting who eat the pork. In cases of illness or injury, it is only the victim and certain near relatives, particularly his co-resident agnates and spouses, who do so.

It is reasonable to assume that misfortune and emergency are likely to induce in the organisms experiencing them a complex of physiological changes known collectively as "stress." Physiological stress reactions occur not only in organisms which are infected with disease or traumatized, but also in those experiencing rage or fear (Houssay et al. 1955:1096), or even prolonged anxiety (National Research Council 1963:53). One important aspect of stress is the increased catabolization of protein (Houssay et al. 1955:451; National Research Council 1963:49), with a net loss of nitrogen from the tissues (Houssay et al. 1955:450). This is a serious matter for organisms with a marginal protein intake. Antibody production is low (Berg 1948:311), healing is slow (Large and Johnston 1948:352), and a variety of symptoms of a serious nature are likely to develop (Lund and Levenson 1948:349; Zintel 1964:1043). The status of a protein-depleted animal, however, may be significantly improved in a relatively short period of time by the intake of high quality protein, and high protein diets are therefore routinely prescribed for surgical patients and those suffering from infectious diseases (Burton 1959:231; Lund and Levenson 1948:350; Elman 1951:85ff.; Zintel 1964:1043ff.).[13]

It is precisely when they are undergoing physiological stress that the Tsembaga kill and consume their pigs, and it should be noted that they limit the consumption to those likely to be experiencing stress most profoundly.[8] The

---

13. One element of Rappaport's argument is that pig consumption is driven by exceptional demand for protein. Rappaport reconsidered the protein issue in the appendix of the 1984 edition of *Pigs for the Ancestors* and suggested that he was probably mistaken about protein intake. Further fieldwork revealed that the stressed person generally does not get to eat much of the pig sacrificed for him. In any event, it would be exceedingly difficult to prove that pork was consumed for metabolic reasons.

Tsembaga, of course, know nothing of physiological stress. Native theories of the etiology and treatment of disease and injury implicate various categories of spirits to whom sacrifices must be made. Nevertheless, the behavior which is appropriate in terms of native understandings is also appropriate to the actual situation confronting the actors. We may now outline in the barest of terms the Tsembaga ritual cycle. Space does not permit a description of its ideological correlates. It must suffice to note that the Tsembaga do not necessarily perceive all of the empirical effects which the anthropologist sees to flow from their ritual behavior. Such empirical consequences as they may perceive, moreover, are not central to their rationalizations of the performances. The Tsembaga say that they perform the rituals in order to rearrange their relationships with the supernatural world. We may only reiterate here that behavior undertaken in reference to their "cognized environment"—an environment which includes as very important elements the spirits of ancestors—seems appropriate in their "operational environment," the material environment specified by the anthropologist through operations of observation, including measurement.[14]

Since the rituals are arranged in a cycle, description may commence at any point. The operation of the cycle becomes clearest if we begin with the rituals performed during warfare. Opponents in all cases occupy adjacent territories, in almost all cases on the same valley wall. After hostilities have broken out, each side performs certain rituals which place the opposing side in the formal category of "enemy." A number of taboos prevail while hostilities continue. These include prohibitions on sexual intercourse and on the ingestion of certain things—food prepared by women, food grown on the lower portion of the territory, marsupials, eels, and while actually on the fighting ground, any liquid whatsoever.[15]

One ritual practice associated with fighting which may have some physiological consequences deserves mention. Immediately before proceeding to the fighting ground, the warriors eat heavily salted pig fat. The ingestion of salt, coupled with the taboo on drinking, has the effect of shortening the fighting day, particularly since the Maring prefer to fight only on bright sunny days. When everyone gets unbearably thirsty, according to informants, fighting is broken off.

There may formerly have been other effects if the native salt contained sodium (the production of salt was discontinued some years previous to the field work, and no samples were obtained). The Maring diet seems to be deficient in sodium. The ingestion of large amounts of sodium just prior to fighting would have permitted the warriors to sweat normally without a lowering of blood volume and consequent weakness during the course of the fighting. The pork belly ingested with the salt would have provided them with a new burst of energy two hours or so after the commencement of the engagement. After fighting was finished for the day, lean pork was consumed,

---

14. The focus of much of Rappaport's work is the relationship between the cognized and operational environments, that is, the environment as the Tsembaga understand it and the environment as depicted by science. This distinction is similar to the one Marvin Harris and others have made between etic and emic analysis (see essay 18, footnote 5). In *Pigs for the Ancestors* Rappaport says that a population's cognized model of the environment can never truly accurately represent the real world because it must always mask some material relations. Rappaport continues: "The cognized model of the environment, then, is understood by the functional anthropologist to be part of a population's means of adjusting to its environment . . . the place of the cognized model . . . is analogous to that of the 'memory' of a computer control in an automated system of material exchanges and transformations" (1968: 239–240). Note Rappaport's confidence that the science of his era is capable of accurately describing the operational environment.

15. The idea of a cycle is important and again relates to developments in biology in the 1960s. Biologists viewed ecosystems in terms of nutrient cycles. Rappaport applies the same sort of logic to the system he describes here.

Rappaport was in the field for only fourteen months, from October 1962 to December 1963. He was thus unable to observe a single complete cycle, which takes place over a decade or more.

off-setting, at least to some extent, the nitrogen loss associated with the stressful fighting (personal communications from F. Dunn, W. McFarlane, and J. Sabine, 1965).[16]

Fighting could continue sporadically for weeks. Occasionally it terminated in the rout of one of the antagonistic groups, whose survivors would take refuge with kinsmen elsewhere. In such instances, the victors would lay waste to their opponents' groves and gardens, slaughter their pigs, and burn their houses. They would not, however, immediately annex the territory of the vanquished. The Maring say that they never take over the territory of an enemy for, even if it has been abandoned, spirits of their ancestors remain to guard it against interlopers. Most fights, however, terminated in truces between the antagonists.

With the termination of hostilities a group which has not been driven off its territory performs a ritual called "planting the *rumbim*." Every man puts his hand on the ritual plant, *rumbim* (*Cordyline fruticosa* (L.), A. Chev; *C. terminalis*, Kunth), as it is planted in the ground. The ancestors are addressed, in effect, as follows:

> We thank you for helping us in the fight and permitting us to remain on our territory. We place our souls in this *rumbim* as we plant it on our ground. We ask you to care for this *rumbim*. We will kill pigs for you now, but they are few. In the future, when we have many pigs, we shall again give you pork and uproot the *rumbim* and stage a *kaiko* (pig festival). But until there are sufficient pigs to repay you the *rumbim* will remain in remain the ground.[17]

This ritual is accompanied by the wholesale slaughter of pigs. Only juveniles remain alive. All adult and adolescent animals are killed, cooked, and dedicated to the ancestors. Some are consumed by the local group, but most are distributed to allies who assisted in the fight.

Some of the taboos which the group suffered during the time of fighting are abrogated by this ritual. Sexual intercourse is now permitted, liquids may be taken at any time, and food from any part of the territory may be eaten. But the group is still in debt to its allies and ancestors. People say it is still the time of the *bamp ku*, or "fighting stones," which are actual objects used in the rituals associated with warfare. Although the fighting ceases when *rumbim* is planted, the concomitant obligations, debts to allies and ancestors, remain outstanding; and the fighting stones may not be put away until these obligations are fulfilled. The time of the fighting stones is a time of debt and danger which lasts until the *rumbim* is uprooted and a pig festival (*kaiko*) is staged.

Certain taboos persist during the time of the fighting stones. Marsupials, regarded as the pigs of the ancestors of the high ground, may not be trapped until the debt to their masters has been repaid. Eels, the "pigs of the ancestors of the low ground," may neither be caught nor consumed. Prohibitions on all intercourse with the enemy come into force. One may not touch, talk to, or even look at a member of the enemy group, nor set foot on enemy ground. Even more important, a group may not attack another group while its ritual plant remains in the ground, for it has not yet fully rewarded its ancestors and allies for their assistance in the last fight. Until the debts to them have been

---

16. Since the publication of this essay, the role of nutrition in human evolution has been widely explored (see for example Johns 1999; Wrangham 2010). Analysis of the kind Rappaport does here, linking the biology of specific events of food consumption to specific cultural activities is unusual in anthropology.

17. Notice that Rappaport does not report what people said on a particular occasion, but rather the kind of thing they are likely to say. He cannot report verbatim because he was not present at a *rumbim* planting. Anthropologists who view culture in primarily mentalistic terms, such as structuralists and symbolic and interpretive analysts would have trouble with such a reconstruction. They would most likely be concerned with the specifics of *rumbim* symbolism and would see Rappaport's technique as doing violence to the data. Because Rappaport's view of culture is materialist, the reconstruction adds a bit of ethnographic interest and is largely irrelevant to his argument.

paid, further assistance from them will not be forthcoming. A kind of "truce of god" thus prevails until the rumbim is uprooted and a *kaiko* completed.[18]

To uproot the rumbim requires sufficient pigs. How many pigs are sufficient, and how long does it take to acquire them? The Tsembaga say that, if a place is "good," this can take as little as five years; but if a place is "bad," it may require ten years or longer. A bad place is one in which misfortunes are frequent and where, therefore, ritual demands for the killing of pigs arise frequently. A good place is one where such demands are infrequent. In a good place, the increase of the pig herd exceeds the ongoing ritual demands, and the herd grows rapidly. Sooner or later the substandard tubers incidentally obtained while harvesting become insufficient to feed the herd, and additional acreage must be put into production specifically for the pigs.

The work involved in caring for a large pig herd can be extremely burdensome. The Tsembaga herd just prior to the pig festival of 1962–63, when it numbered 169 animals, was receiving 54 percent of all the sweet potatoes and 82 percent of all the manioc harvested. These comprised 35.9 percent by weight of all root crops harvested. This figure is consistent with the difference between the amount of land under cultivation just previous to the pig festival, when the herd was at maximum size, and that immediately afterwards, when the pig herd was at minimum size. The former was 36.1 percent in excess of the latter.[19]

I have estimated, on the basis of acreage yield and energy expenditure figures, that about 45,000 calories per year are expended in caring for one pig 120–150 pounds in size. It is upon women that most of the burden of pig keeping falls. If, from a woman's daily intake of about 2,200 calories, 950 calories are allowed for basal metabolism, a woman has only 1,250 calories a day available for all her activities, which include gardening for her family, child care, and cooking, as well as tending pigs. It is clear that no woman can feed many pigs; only a few had as many as four in their care at the commencement of the festival; and it is not surprising that agitation to uproot the *rumbim*

---

18. Rappaport's description of the relationship between ritual and environment is heavily influenced by cybernetics, which was considered an important new field at the time the essay was written. Cybernetics had begun in the 1940s and was concerned with systems of environmental feedback in automatic devices. By the time Rappaport was writing, the principles of cybernetics were being applied to a variety of mechanical systems from computers to air conditioning and the human nervous system. Think of the thermostat where you live. It measures the temperature and sends a signal to turn a heater or air conditioner on. When the temperature reaches a selected point, the thermostat sends a signal to turn the equipment off. The function of the thermostat is to keep the air temperature in your space in equilibrium. Not too hot, not too cold. Here, the ritual planting of the *rumbim* is understood as a switch, or thermostat that turns hostilities off, keeping the system in equilibrium. Rappaport makes this analogy explicit in his 1971 essay "Ritual, Sanctity, and Cybernetics."

19. Rappaport goes to lengths to prove that the Tsembaga hold festivals when the burden of caring for pigs becomes excessive. Critics ask why the Tsembaga don't control herd size simply by killing and eating pigs when they are too numerous. Rappaport does not address these issues here, preferring to concentrate on the functioning of the *kaiko* rather than its origin. However, he did respond to this, and a great many other issues raised by critics of his work in the second edition of *Pigs for the Ancestors* published in 1984. There he presents an epilogue that runs to nearly 200 pages (almost as long as the original book) and covers topics such as ecology as vulgar materialism; fallacy, final cause, and formal cause, and the ecology of explanation. That Rappaport felt compelled to elaborate on his work at such length is a good index of both how influential and how widely critiqued it was.

Functionalism had important effects on Steward and other key thinkers in cultural ecology. Like functionalists, ecological anthropologists looked for what different aspects of culture did. And, like functionalists, they tended to assume that, in the main, cultural institutions and traditions increased social stability. However, they criticized functionalism because it did not give enough attention to the relation between people and their environment and because it did not produce empirically testable hypotheses. Rappaport's work is, in part, a functional analysis that attempts to respond to these problems.

and stage the *kaiko* starts with the wives of the owners of large numbers of pigs.[20]

A large herd is not only burdensome as far as energy expenditure is concerned; it becomes increasingly a nuisance as it expands. The more numerous pigs become, the more frequently are gardens invaded by them. Such events result in serious disturbances of local tranquility. The garden owner often shoots, or attempts to shoot, the offending pig; and the pig owner commonly retorts by shooting, or attempting to shoot, either the garden owner, his wife, or one of his pigs. As more and more such events occur, the settlement, nucleated when the herd was small, disperses as people try to put as much distance as possible between their pigs and other people's gardens and between their gardens and other people's pigs. Occasionally this reaches its logical conclusion, and people begin to leave the territory, taking up residence with kinsmen in other local populations.

The number of pigs sufficient to become intolerable to the Tsembaga was below the capacity of the territory to carry pigs. I have estimated that, if the size and structure of the human population remained constant at the 1962–1963 level, a pig population of 140 to 240 animals averaging 100 to 150 pounds in size could be maintained perpetually by the Tsembaga without necessarily inducing environmental degradation. Since the size of the herd fluctuates, even higher cyclical maxima could be achieved. The level of toleration, however, is likely always to be below the carrying capacity, since the destructive capacity of the pigs is dependent upon the population density of both people and pigs, rather than upon population size. The denser the human population, the fewer pigs will be required to disrupt social life. If the carrying capacity is exceeded, it is likely to be exceeded by people and not by pigs. The *kaiko* or pig festival, which commences with the planting of stakes at the boundary and the uprooting of the *rumbim*, is thus triggered by either the additional work attendant upon feeding pigs or the destructive capacity of the pigs themselves. It may be said, then, that there are sufficient pigs to stage the *kaiko* when the relationship of pigs to people changes from one of mutualism to one of parasitism or competition.[21]

A short time prior to the uprooting of the rumbim, stakes are planted at the boundary. If the enemy has continued to occupy its territory, the stakes are planted at the boundary which existed before the fight. If, on the other hand, the enemy has abandoned its territory, the victors may plant their stakes at a new boundary which encompasses areas previously occupied by the enemy. The Maring say, to be sure, that they never take land belonging to an enemy, but this land is regarded as vacant, since no *rumbim* was planted on it after the last fight. We may state here a rule of land redistribution in terms of the ritual cycle: *If one of a pair of antagonistic groups is able to uproot its* rumbim *before its opponents can plant their* rumbim, *it may occupy the latter's territory.*[22]

Not only have the vanquished abandoned their territory; it is assumed that it has also been abandoned by their ancestors as well. The surviving members of the erstwhile enemy group have by this time resided with other groups for a number of years, and most if not all of them have already had occasion to sacrifice pigs to their ancestors at their new residences. In so

---

20. Rappaport is writing in the mid 1960s, before the advent of feminist anthropology. His analysis of Tsembaga ritual and warfare focuses almost entirely on the activities of men. In this essay, women's activities are limited to those listed here and, critically, nagging the men so that they will take action to kill the pigs.

21. Here Rappaport again relies on the vocabulary of biology. Mutualism is a relationship between any two species in which both species benefit. Parasitism is a relationship in which only one benefits.

22. In this paragraph and below, Rappaport builds a formal model (or part of one) by stating a series of rules. This is similar to White's style of writing (see essay 16). Unlike White, whose rules are evolutionary and intended to apply to all cultures, Rappaport's are specific to Tsembaga culture and say nothing about the long-term direction of cultural change. Rules and principles like the ones found in this essay are relatively rare in anthropology.

doing they have invited these spirits to settle at the new locations of the living, where they will in the future receive sacrifices. Ancestors of vanquished groups thus relinquish their guardianship over the territory, making it available to victorious groups. Meanwhile, the **de facto** membership of the living in the groups with which they have taken refuge is converted eventually into **de jure** membership. Sooner or later the groups with which they have taken up residence will have occasion to plant *rumbim*, and the refugees, as co-residents, will participate, thus ritually validating their connection to the new territory and the new group. A rule of population redistribution may thus be stated in terms of ritual cycles: *A man becomes a member of a territorial group by participating with it in the planting of rumbim.*[23]

The uprooting of the *rumbim* follows shortly after the planting of stakes at the boundary. On this particular occasion the Tsembaga killed 32 pigs out of their herd of 169. Much of the pork was distributed to allies and affines outside of the local group.

The taboo on trapping marsupials was also terminated at this time. Information is lacking concerning the population dynamics of the local marsupials, but it may well be that the taboo which had prevailed since the last fight—that against taking them in traps—had conserved a fauna which might otherwise have become extinct.[24]

The *kaiko* continues for about a year, during which period friendly groups are entertained from time to time. The guests receive presents of vegetable foods, and the hosts and male guests dance together throughout the night.

These events may be regarded as analogous to aspects of the social behavior of many non-human animals. First of all, they include massed epigamic, or courtship, displays (Wynne-Edwards 1962:17). Young women are presented with samples of the eligible males of local groups with which they may not otherwise have had the opportunity to become familiar. The context, moreover, permits the young women to discriminate amongst this sample in terms of both endurance (signaled by how vigorously and how long a man dances) and wealth (signaled by the richness of a man's shell and feather finery).[25]

More importantly, the massed dancing at these events may be regarded as **epideictic** display, communicating to the participants information concerning the size or density of the group (Wynne-Edwards 1962:16). In many species such displays take place as a prelude to actions which adjust group size or density, and such is the case among the Maring. The massed dancing of the visitors at a *kaiko* entertainment communicates to the hosts, while the *rumbim* truce is still in force, information concerning the amount of support they may expect from the visitors in the bellicose enterprises that they are likely to embark upon soon after the termination of the pig festival.[26]

Among the Maring there are no chiefs or other political authorities capable of com-

---

23. In a personal communication Rappaport noted that participating in the planting of a *rumbim* is how the Tsembaga themselves understand becoming a member of a territorial group. What is important for Rappaport's approach, however, is that participation in this ceremony provides a clear operational and behavioral way of determining group membership, *whether* perceived that way by the Tsembaga or not.
"**De facto**": in actuality, "**de jure**": in law.

24. Notice that Rappaport suggests that other aspects of the system he has identified also serve ecological functions.

25. Rappaport here suggests that the entertaining of allied groups during the *kaiko* provides courtship displays; young men show off their endurance and wealth to young women who are potential mates. He describes the dancing and shell and feather decorations in terms of Darwinian-style sexual selection; as if the dancers were peacocks spreading their tail plumage to attract females.

26. "**Epideictic**": Biologist Vero Copner Wynne-Edwards (1906–1997) used the word epideictic to refer to very intense displays by members of a population that indicate population density. He worked with birds and argued that these displays were related to the regulation of population. The intensity of the display

manding the support of a body of followers, and the decision to assist another group in warfare rests with each individual male. Allies are not recruited by appealing for help to other local groups as such. Rather, each member of the groups primarily involved in the hostilities appeals to his cognatic and affinal kinsmen in other local groups. These men, in turn, urge other of their co-residents and kinsmen to "help them fight." The channels through which invitations to dance are extended are precisely those through which appeals for military support are issued. The invitations go not from group to group, but from kinsman to kinsman, the recipients of invitations urging their co-residents to "help them dance."

Invitations to dance do more than exercise the channels through which allies are recruited; they provide a means for judging their effectiveness. Dancing and fighting are regarded as in some sense equivalent. This equivalence is expressed in the similarity of some pre-fight and pre-dance rituals, and the Maring say that those who come to dance come to fight. The size of a visiting dancing contingent is consequently taken as a measure of the size of the contingent of warriors whose assistance may be expected in the next round of warfare.[27]

In the morning the dancing ground turns into a trading ground. The items most frequently exchanged include axes, bird plumes, shell ornaments, an occasional baby pig, and,

in former times, native salt. The *kaiko* thus facilitates trade by providing a market-like setting in which large numbers of traders can assemble. It likewise facilitates the movement of two critical items, salt and axes, by creating a demand for the bird plumes which may be exchanged for them.

The *kaiko* concludes with major pig sacrifices. On this particular occasion the Tsembaga butchered 105 adult and adolescent pigs, leaving only 60 juveniles and neonates alive. The survival of an additional fifteen adolescents and adults was only temporary, for they were scheduled as imminent victims. The pork yielded by the Tsembaga slaughter was estimated to weigh between 7,000 and 8,500 pounds, of which between 4,500 and 6,000 pounds were distributed to members of other local groups in 163 separate presentations. An estimated 2,000 to 3,000 people in seventeen local groups were the beneficiaries of the redistribution. The presentations, it should be mentioned, were not confined to pork. Sixteen Tsembaga men presented bridewealth or childwealth, consisting largely of axes and shells, to their affines at this time.

The *kaiko* terminates on the day of the pig slaughter with the public presentation of salted pig belly to allies of the last fight. Presentations are made through the window in a high ceremonial fence built specially for the occasion at one end of the dance ground.

---

provides a standard by which members can assess how many matings can take place. The idea was part of a famous debate between Wynne-Edwards and David Lambert Lack (1910–1973), another evolutionary biologist. Wynne-Edwards argued that natural selection operated at the level of the group, Lack that it operated at the level of the individual. Because the regulation of total population levels is usually a concern of the group rather than the individual epideictic displays were part of Wynne-Edwards group selection argument; they supplied information for the homeostatic regulation of population density (Borrello 2018: 69). Group versus individual selection remains a controversial topic in biology.

27. Notice that the flow of information is important in Rappaport's description. Information theory, first developed by Claude Shannon (1916–2001) in the late 1940s and 1950s, provided a way of expressing the transmission of certain types of information in energy terms. It was useful because, in principle, when combined with nutritional analysis, it provided a way of measuring the flow of both food and information through a cultural system in terms of energy. In practice, it proved extremely difficult to apply.

Rappaport proposes that rituals like the *kaiko* not only convey information but are adaptive mechanisms for populations in particular environments, keeping the societies in equilibrium. Although Rappaport's argument is convincing and impressive in how thoroughly he arranges so many elements into a neat evolutionary package, it rests in large part on the assumption that human behavior can be studied like ethologists study animal behavior. The inconvenient truth ignored here though is that humans act within a cultural context that they create. Most nonhuman animals do not.

The name of each honored man is announced to the assembled multitude as he charges to the window to receive his hero's portion. The fence is then ritually torn down, and the fighting stones are put away. The pig festival and the ritual cycle have been completed, demonstrating, it may be suggested, the ecological and economic competence of the local population. The local population would now be free, if it were not for the presence of the government, to attack its enemy again, secure in the knowledge that the assistance of allies and ancestors would be forthcoming because they have received pork and the obligations to them have been fulfilled.[28]

Usually fighting did break out again very soon after the completion of the ritual cycle. If peace still prevailed when the ceremonial fence had rotted completely—a process said to take about three years, a little longer than the length of time required to raise a pig to maximum size—*rumbim* was planted as if there had been a fight, and all adult and adolescent pigs were killed. When the pig herd was large enough so that the rumbim could be uprooted, peace could be made with former enemies if they were also able to dig out their *rumbim*. To put this in formal terms: *If a pair of antagonistic groups proceeds through two ritual cycles without resumption of hostilities their enmity may be terminated.*[h]

The relations of the Tsembaga with their environment have been analyzed as a complex system composed of two subsystems. What may be called the "local subsystem" has been derived from the relations of the Tsembaga with the nonhuman components of their immediate or territorial environment. It corresponds to the ecosystem in which the Tsembaga participate. A second subsystem, one which corresponds to the larger regional population of which the Tsembaga are one of the constituent units and which may be designated as the "regional subsystem," has been derived from the relations of the Tsembaga with neighboring local populations similar to themselves.

It has been argued that rituals, arranged in repetitive sequences, regulate relations both within each of the subsystems and within the larger complex system as a whole. The timing of the ritual cycle is largely dependent upon changes in the states of the components of the local subsystem. But the *kaiko*, which is the culmination of the ritual cycle, does more than reverse changes which have taken place within the local subsystem. Its occurrence also affects relations among the components of the regional subsystem. During its performance, obligations to other local populations are fulfilled, support for future military enterprises is rallied, and land from which enemies have earlier been driven is occupied. Its completion, furthermore, permits the local population to initiate warfare again. Conversely, warfare is terminated by rituals which preclude the reinitiation of warfare until the state of the local subsystem is again such that a *kaiko* may be staged and completed. Ritual among the Tsembaga and other Maring, in short, operates as both transducer, "translating" changes in the state of one subsystem into information which can effect changes in a second subsystem, and homeostat, maintaining a number of variables which in sum comprise the total system within ranges of viability. To repeat an earlier assertion, the operation of ritual among the Tsembaga and other Maring helps to maintain an undegraded environment, limits fighting to frequencies which do not endanger the existence of the regional population, adjusts man-land ratios, facilitates trade, distributes

---

28. The Tsembaga were under the colonial administration of the Australian government when Rappaport worked with them, and the government had suppressed fighting among the different groups. Rappaport describes a *kaiko* festival he witnessed. However, he was unable to witness the cycle of warfare that led to it, which took place before his arrival. This element of his description is thus reconstructed from the memories of informants he interviewed.

Rappaport visited Papua New Guinea during an era that when the Australian administration was effective in suppressing tribal warfare. However, by the late 1960s, warfare, and violence was beginning to return, often in new and more deadly forms. For example, by the 1990s, Enga youth were fighting old wars with shotguns and M16s. Anthropologists have been critical in helping to mediate these disputes (see Wiessner and Pupu 2012; Roscoe 2014).

local surpluses of pig throughout the regional population in the form of pork, and assures people of high quality protein when they are most in need of it.[29]

Religious rituals and the supernatural orders toward which they are directed cannot be assumed a priori to be mere **epiphenomena**. Ritual may, and doubtless frequently does, do nothing more than validate and intensify the relationships which integrate the social unit, or symbolize the relationships which bind the social unit to its environment. But the interpretation of such presumably sapiens-specific phenomena as religious ritual within a framework which will also accommodate the behavior of other species shows, I think, that religious ritual may do much more than symbolize, validate, and intensify relationships. Indeed, it would not be improper to refer to the Tsembaga and the other entities with which they share their territory as a "ritually regulated ecosystem," and to the Tsembaga and their human neighbors as a "ritually regulated population."[30]

REFERENCES

Berg, C. 1948. Protein Deficiency and its Relation to Nutritional Anemia, Hypoproteinemia, Nutritional Edema, and Resistance to Infection. In *Protein and Amino Acids in Nutrition*, ed. M. Sahyun, pp. 290–317. New York: Reinhold.

Burton, B. T., ed. 1959. *The Heinz Handbook of Nutrition*. New York: McGraw-Hill.

Elman, R. 1951. *Surgical Care*. New York: Appleton-Century-Crofts.

Food and Agriculture Organization of the United Nations. 1964. *Protein: At the Heart of the World Food Problem*. World Food Problems 5. Rome: FAO.

Hipsley, E., and N. Kirk. 1965. *Studies of the Dietary Intake and Energy Expenditure of New Guineans*. South Pacific Commission, Technical Paper 147. Noumea: South Pacific Commission.

Homans, G. C. 1941. Anxiety and Ritual: The Theories of Malinowski and Radcliffe-Brown. *American Anthropologist* 43:164–172.

Houssay, B. A., et al. 1955. *Human Physiology*, 2nd ed. New York: McGraw-Hill.

Large, A., and C. G. Johnston. 1948. Proteins as Related to Burns. In *Proteins and Amino Acids in Nutrition*, ed. M. Sahyun, pp. 386–396. New York: Reinhold.

Lund, C. G., and S. M. Levenson. 1948. Protein nutrition in surgical patients. In *Proteins and amino acids in nutrition*, ed. M. Sahyun, pp. 349–363. New York: Reinhold.

Moore, O. K. 1957. Divination—A New Perspective. *American Anthropologist* 59:69–74.

National Research Council. 1963. *Evaluation of protein quality*. National Academy of Sciences—National Research Council Publication 1100. Washington: NAS/NRC.

---

29. With all the details of the *kaiko*, pig populations, and rumbin planting and uprooting it is easy to forget that Rappaport is using systems theory as it was applied to cybernetics at the beginning of the computer age. Notice here Rappaport returns to the language of electrical engineering.

When Rappaport's work on the Tsembaga was published, it fell on fertile ground. It seemed to demonstrate the ecological soundness and wisdom of traditional society. This idea was appealing in the late 1960s and the 1970s, when many in academia were concerned with ecology and the value of traditional communities and folks were busy developing communes. Criticism of his work grew as these ideas fell out of popularity and political conservatism became increasingly dominant.

30. Here Rappaport closes by returning to his criticism of the Homans quote with which he began the article. Homans provided a psychological behaviorist explanation for ritual. Because Rappaport's theory is evolutionary and ecological, he claims that it can also be used to explain the behavior of other species.

By the 1970s, Rappaport was moving away from analyses that focused on treating human populations the same as ethologists treat nonhuman populations. By the early 1980s he had begun to develop his final book, *Ritual and Religion in the Making of Humanity*, which was published posthumously in 1999. There he argued that the kind of religious ritual he witnessed among the Tsembaga was not only uniquely human, but that such rituals were critical to the development of human society. Rappaport preserved the evolutionary and ecological aspects of his work and it continued to be informed by systems theory and information theory. However, Rappaport's analysis also centered on language. Rappaport argued that when humans acquired language, they also acquired the ability to lie. Religion, and its encoding in ritual, is a way to control the effects of lying and disorder that are inherent in language. By participating in religious rituals, people demonstrate their commitment to ultimate sacred postulates that are, by their nature, unprovable. This, along with the consistent nature of ritual, fosters community and acts as an imperfect bulwark against falsehood and disorder.

"Epiphenomena": secondary events that arise from but do not cause a process.

Rappaport, R. A. 1966. *Ritual in the Ecology of a New Guinea people.* Unpublished doctoral dissertation. Columbia University, New York.

Vayda, A. P., A. Leeds, and D. B. Smith. 1961. The Place of Pigs in Melanesian Subsistence. In *Proceedings of the 1961 Annual Spring Meeting of the American Ethnological Society,* ed. V. E. Garfield, pp. 69–77. Seattle: University of Washington Press.

Wynne-Edwards V. C. 1962. *Animal Dispersion in Relation to Social Behavior.* Edinburgh and London: Oliver & Boyd.

Zintel, Harold A. 1964. Nutrition in the Care of the Surgical Patient. In *Modern Nutrition in Health and Disease,* ed. M. G. Wohl and R. S. Goodhart, pp. 1043–1064, 3rd ed. Philadelphia: Lea and Febiger.

AUTHOR'S NOTES

a. The field work upon which this paper is based was supported by a grant from the National Science Foundation, under which Professor A. P. Vayda was principal investigator. Personal support was received by the author from the National Institutes of Health. Earlier versions of this paper were presented at the 1964 annual meeting of the American Anthropological Association in Detroit, and before a Columbia University seminar on Ecological Systems and Cultural Evolution. I have received valuable suggestions from Alexander Alland, Jacques Barrau, William Clarke, Paul Collins, C. Glen King, Marvin Harris, Margaret Mead, M. J. Meggitt, Ann Rappaport, John Street, Marjorie Whiting, Cherry Vayda, A. P. Vayda and many others, but I take full responsibility for the analysis presented herewith.

b. The social organization of the Tsembaga will be described in detail elsewhere.

c. Because the length of time in the field precluded the possibility of maintaining harvest records on single gardens from planting through abandonment, figures were based, in the case of both "taro-yam" and "sugar-sweet potato" gardens, on three separate gardens planted in successive years. Conversions from the gross weight to the caloric value of the yield were made by reference to the literature. The sources used are listed in Rappaport (1966: Appendix VIII).

d. Rough time and motion studies of each of the tasks involved in making, maintaining, harvesting, and walking to and from gardens were undertaken. Conversion to energy expenditure values was accomplished by reference to energy expenditure tables prepared by Hipsley and Kirk (1965:43) on the basis of gas exchange measurements made during the performance of garden tasks by the Chimbu people of the New Guinea highlands.

e. Marvin Harris, in an unpublished paper, estimates the ratio of energy return to energy input on Dyak (Borneo) rice swiddens at 10:1. His estimates of energy ratios on Tepoltzlan (Meso-America) swiddens range from 13:1 on poor land to 29:1 on the best land.

f. Heights may be inaccurate. Many men wear their hair in large coiffures hardened with pandanus grease, and it was necessary in some instances to estimate the location of the top of the skull.

g. The possible significance of pork consumption by protein-short people during periods of physiological stress was unknown to me while I was in the field. I did not, therefore, investigate this matter in full detail. Georgeda Bick and Cherry Vayda, who visited the Maring area in 1966, have investigated the circumstances surrounding pork consumption further, and will publish their more detailed materials elsewhere.

h. After this article had gone to press in *Ethnology,* where it was originally published, I learned from A. P. Vayda, who spent the summer of 1966 in the Maring area, that he received somewhat different accounts of peace-making mechanisms, both from informants in other Maring local groups and from the Tsembaga man who had supplied me with the only full account which I was able to obtain (details of his account were, however, corroborated by information obtained from other Tsembaga men). According to Vayda's account, when the ceremonial fence had rotted away completely, some, but not all, adult and adolescent pigs were slain and offered to certain ancestral spirits to insure the health and fecundity of the remaining pigs, and no *rumbim* was planted. When the herds of the erstwhile antagonists again reached maximum size peace could be made.

It is important to note here that the other rituals treated in this paper were either observed by me or described by a number of informants who had participated in them, but none of either Vayda's informants or mine had ever participated in peace-making procedures, for none had taken place during the adult life of any of them. They were only reporting what they remembered from their childhood or what they had heard from their fathers or grandfathers. It is likely, therefore, that none of the informants are particularly well versed in the details of the procedure. However, it is also important to note that all of the informants are in basic agreement upon what is in the present context the most important aspects of peace-making: that the rituals were not performed until pig herds of the erstwhile antagonists had reached maximum size. The rule which I have proposed would seem to stand if it is understood that the second ritual cycle of the sequence may differ from the first in that *rumbim* might not be planted, and if it is understood that the truce may not be sanctified during the second cycle of the sequence.

Structure, Language, and Cognition

By the middle of the twentieth century, American anthropology was largely dominated by the students of Franz Boas, practicing *Culture and Personality*–inspired fieldwork, and others who followed materialist approaches. Marxism and structural functionalism were the primary approaches in Europe. However, in the 1950s and 1960s, the United States and Europe each produced influential perspectives that focused on language and cognition. The American approach was heavily influenced by the cultural relativistic ethos promoted by Franz Boas and his students, while European theory was influenced by the nineteenth-century emphasis on cultural similarities and psychic unity.

The concept of psychic unity was deeply entrenched in the evolutionary thinking of nineteenth-century scholars. The German ethnologist Adolf Bastian (1826–1905) was particularly influential at this time, and his concept of *elementargedanke* (hereditary elementary ideas) was widely adopted in evolutionary reasoning and was fundamental to the notion of psychic unity. Bastian also proposed that geographic and historical circumstances created different local variations of these elementary ideas that he called *Völkergedanken* (folk ideas). For Bastian, cofounder and first director of the Museum of Ethnology in Berlin, the discovery of these elementary ideas was one of the primary objectives of anthropology. This perspective found its way into late-nineteenth-century French thinking in the work of Émile Durkheim, who studied in Germany from 1885 to 1887. The work of Bastian and Durkheim provides the background to help us understand the thinking of Lévi-Strauss and his search for the universal structures of human thought.

Claude Lévi-Strauss (1908–2009) almost single-handedly founded the field of French structuralism. Lévi-Strauss was born in Brussels and grew up in Paris. He studied law and philosophy at the Sorbonne, graduating with a degree in philosophy in 1931. In 1935, he accepted a position as a visiting professor of sociology at the University of São Paulo, while his wife, Dina Dreyfus (1911–1999), served as a visiting professor of ethnology. The couple lived in Brazil from 1935 to 1939, and Lévi-Strauss conducted his only fieldwork during this period.

Though Lévi-Strauss rarely mentioned her, Dreyfus was an accomplished scholar in her own right. She was born in Milan in 1911 and emigrated with her family to France when she was thirteen. Dreyfus graduated from the Sorbonne with a degree in philosophy that included a certificate in anthropology. While at the University of São Paolo, she founded the first ethnological society in Brazil with Mário de Andrade (1893–1945), an important Brazilian poet and ethnomusicologist. In 1936 and 1938, she conducted fieldwork with Lévi-Strauss and a Brazilian colleague, Luiz de Castro Faria (1913–2004), who became a critical figure in the development of anthropology in Brazil. In 1938, she left the field because of an eye infection and returned to São Paolo and then to Paris.

When war broke out in 1939, Dreyfus separated from Lévi-Strauss, but they did not divorce until 1945. Before the Nazi occupation of France, Lévi-Strauss moved to New York City while Dreyfus participated in the Resistance under the name of Denise Roche. After the war, she became a professor of philosophy. She taught at Versailles, at Lycée Moliere, at Lycée Fenelon, and at the Sorbonne. She was the first female member of the Inspection Générale de Philosophie (the IG evaluates all aspects of philosophy education in French schools at all levels). Dreyfus was particularly interested in education and in popularizing philosophy, and in the 1960s she produced television and radio programs that featured conversations with famous philosophers. She died in 1999.

In 1948, Lévi-Strauss returned to France to pursue his PhD at the Sorbonne. His first book, *The Elementary Structure of Kinship* (1949), was part of his thesis work.

Lévi-Strauss's structuralism begins with the assumption that culture is, first and foremost, a product of the mind. Following Bastian and Durkheim, he reasoned that since all human brains were biologically similar, there must be deep-seated concepts or ways of thinking that are the same in all cultures. Although he did not use a term similar to Bastian's *elementary ideas*, the goal Lévi-Strauss set for anthropology was to discover the fundamental structures of human thought. Pursuing this quest, he spent his career conducting cross-cultural studies of kinship, myth, and religion. The titles of his early works—*The Elementary Structures of Kinship* (1949), *Structural Anthropology* (1959), *The Savage Mind* (1962)—show the trajectory of his thinking. In particular, *The Elementary Structures of Kinship* echoes the title of Durkheim's great work on religion, *The Elementary Forms of the Religious Life* (orig. 1912).

Lévi-Strauss believed that there were underlying cognitive processes tying cultures together and that these could be discovered in bits of information that provide messages about the structure of society. However, each culture was also the product of its history and its technological adaptation to the world. These processes combined, altered, transfigured, and modified the original elementary ideas. For Lévi-Strauss, transmitting culture was rather like playing "telephone" or "whispering down the alley" in a crowded bus station. Messages are apt to get jumbled. Lévi-Strauss hoped that by breaking down cultural elements like folktales into their elemental parts, he could get beyond this "noise" and recover these original messages.

The Prague School of structural linguistics (organized in 1926) also played a supporting role in the development of Lévi-Strauss's theory. Up to this time, the most influential area within linguistics was historical linguistics and Ferdinand de Saussure's (1857–1913) work in semiotics. However, the Prague School scholars, led by the linguists Roman Jakobson (1896–1982) and Nikolai Trubetzkoy (1890–1938), emphasized the phonemic study of languages and promoted the theory that linguistic meaning was built upon binary contrasts between phonemes. This work, and his study of Durkheim, provided Lévi-Strauss with the concept of binary contrasts that was fundamental to his formulation of structural analysis. Following this linguistic model, Lévi-Strauss proposed that the fundamental patterns of human thought were encoded in binary contrasts such as black–white, night–day, and hot–cold. This insight dovetailed nicely with Durkheim's and Hertz's proposition that distinctions such as sacred–profane and right–left were fundamental manifestations of the *l'ame collective* (collective conscience), or what an English-speaking anthropologist would call *culture*.

Lévi-Strauss first applied the notion of the binary structure of human thought to analyze kinship. In *The Gift* (1967, orig. 1925), Marcel Mauss had tried to demonstrate that exchange in primitive societies was driven not by economic motives but by rules of reciprocity upon which the solidarity of society depended. In *Elementary Structures of Kinship* (1969, orig. 1949), Lévi-Strauss took Mauss's concept of reciprocity and applied it to marriage in undeveloped societies. He argued that in those societies, women were commodities who were exchanged between kin groups. Lévi-Strauss contended that one of the first and most important distinctions people make is between self and others. This "natural" binary opposition led to the formation of the incest taboo. In this fashion, Lévi-Strauss claimed that the binary distinction between kin and non-kin was resolved in primitive societies by the reciprocal exchange of women and the formation of kin networks.

Lévi-Strauss is best known today for his analysis of myth. His interest in mythology was founded in his belief that studying the mythologies of Indigenous peoples allowed him to examine the unconscious patterning of human thought in its least contaminated form. Much of Lévi-Strauss's work was on the folktales of aboriginal people of South America such as the Nambikuara. Lévi-Strauss had visited the Nambikuara in 1938, but he also relied on ethnographic material on the Nambikuara collected by Karl von den Steinen (1855–1929), a German ethnologist and physician who was a colleague of Bastian's at the National Museum in Berlin. Because he believed that binary oppositions were the basis of human cognition, Lévi-Strauss sorted elements of indigenous stories into sets of oppositions. He also proposed that a fundamental characteristic of human thought was the desire to find a midpoint between such oppositions, a category that transcends and somehow resolves them. In Lévi-Strauss's view, the elements of myth, like the phonemes of a language, acquire meaning only as a consequence of certain structural relations. Therefore, to uncover the unconscious meaning of myth, the structuralist must break myth into its constituent elements and examine the rules that govern their relationships. In this way, the hidden structural elements could be revealed.

Structural analysis was very popular in Europe, but in the United States, beginning in the 1950s, some ethnographers proposed a different methodology for conducting fieldwork that they called *ethnoscience*. Ethnoscientists claimed that up to that time, ethnography had been unscientific. They complained that there was no single way of doing ethnography. Each anthropologist studied and wrote in his or her own idiosyncratic way. As a result, ethnographies contained different sorts of information and were not analytically comparable to each other. Furthermore, ethnographers tried to describe native society and native understandings, but they did so using the conceptual categories of Western society. Ethnoscientists claimed that this distorted the results.

To make anthropology more scientific and ethnographic descriptions more accurate, ethnoscientists argued that anthropologists should attempt to reproduce cultural reality as it was perceived and lived by members of society. To this end, they urged that descriptions of culture be couched in terms of native thought. Understanding native conceptual categories was key to this task.

The ideal ethnoscientific ethnography would include all the rules, principles, and categories that natives must know to understand and act appropriately in social situations within their cultures. The underlying theoretical assumption of ethnoscience was that cultures were sets of mental models. It was the job of ethnographers to duplicate the features of those cognitive models so that they could think like a native. An ethnographer's model was presumed correct if it allowed them to replicate the way a native categorized phenomena.

Because no one has direct access to another person's mind, the cognitive principles and models drawn by ethnoscientists were based on what informants told them. Thus the new ethnography drew heavily on the techniques of linguistic analysis. Like Lévi-Strauss, ethnoscientists drew on the methodology developed in the 1920s by members of the Prague School of linguistics. Members of the Prague School studied the phonetic structure of languages by contrasting sounds to analyze the features that made sounds distinct. Ethnoscientists incorporated this idea into their research, but rather than contrasting sounds, they created diagrams in which contrasts of meaning could be outlined and the features of native conceptual categories distinguished.

Another set of linguistic principles upon which ethnoscience was based can be traced to the 1930s and the work of Edward Sapir and Benjamin L. Whorf. As one can see in essay 13, Sapir and Whorf were interested in the relationship between language and thought. In numerous papers and essays, they proposed that language was not just a means of communication but that it also shaped people's perceptions of the world, an idea later called the Sapir-Whorf hypothesis. Whorf wrote:

> We dissect nature along lines laid down by our native languages. . . . We cut nature up, organize it into concepts, and ascribe significances as we do, largely because we are parties to an agreement to organize it in this way—an agreement that holds throughout our speech community and is codified in the patterns of our language. (1956: 213)

Sapir and Whorf's emphasis on the interrelationship of language and perception was one element that led ethnoscientists to see a close connection between culture and language. They reasoned that replicating the classification system of any language would give them the ability to view the world in the same way as native speakers of that language. William Sturtevant outlined the fundamental principles of this new approach in his 1964 article "Studies in Ethnoscience." However, other ethnoscientists were already outlining the new research methodologies. In particular, Ward Goodenough (1919–2013) and Charles O. Frake (1930–2021) discussed ways to conduct fieldwork and analyze data in this new approach (Frake 1962; Goodenough 1956). The key research instrument was the highly structured interview, aimed specifically at eliciting native conceptual categories, which ethnoscientists called *domains* or *taxa*. They then used a technique called *componential analysis* to determine the definitive characteristics by which the objects and ideas in each domain were sorted. Using this information, ethnoscientists believed they could classify information according to native conceptual categories. In theory, data collection in this manner was more systematic and replicable and thus, followers claimed, more scientific.

Early attempts at ethnoscientific analysis, such as Floyd Lounsbury's (1914–1998) 1956 analysis of Pawnee kin terminology, concentrated on kinship, but the methodology was easily applicable to other areas and was soon applied in a variety of research situations. Notable examples of this are Harold C. Conklin's 1954 study of Hanunóo ethnobotany, Frake's 1961 study of disease categories among the Subanun, Ralph Bulmer's 1967 study of zoological taxonomy in the highlands of New Guinea, and Brent Berlin, Dennis E. Breedlove, and Peter H. Raven's 1974 analysis of Tzeltal Maya plant classification.

The ethnoscientists' focus on understanding the native point of view was not new. In the introduction to *Argonauts of the Western Pacific*, Bronislaw Malinowski had written that the final goal of ethnography was "to grasp the native's point of view, his relation to life, to realize *his* vision of *his* world" (1922: 25, emphasis in original). The search for the native viewpoint also had strong resonances with Boasian anthropology. Franz Boas and his students insisted on the uniqueness of each culture. They collected masses of physical data on the material and behavioral existence of the people they studied and made the doctrine of cultural relativism an item of faith among American anthropologists. Ethnoscientists continued the Boasian insistence on culture being sui generis and extended the search for data from the material to the mental, something Boas had first suggested half a century previously.

Ethnoscience, like Boasian anthropology, implied extreme cultural relativism—an approach that presented problems. Critics maintained that this approach made cross-cultural comparison impossible. If each culture had a unique way of conceptualizing the world and could only be described in its own terms, how could cultures be compared? Lévi-Strauss's structuralism was seen by some as the answer to this dilemma, but skeptics argued that it was impossible for either ethnoscientists or structuralists to get inside another's head and see how they thought or what they believed.

A further problem concerned individual variation within society. When ethnoscientists said they were trying to re-create cultural reality from a native's point of view, an obvious question to ask was, which native? Despite these criticisms, ethnoscience was an important factor in the development of at least two other theoretical approaches—cognitive anthropology and symbolic anthropology—that both achieved major prominence in the following decades.

In the late 1960s and early 1970s, the focus of ethnoscientific work began to diverge onto different paths. First, instead of simply outlining native categories of thought, anthropologists proposed that by analyzing these categories, one could learn how the human mind functioned. Using models developed in linguistics, researchers proposed that there were universal cognitive processes that were a product of brain structure. In particular, a 1969 book by Brent Berlin and Paul Kay, *Basic Color Terms: Their Universality and Evolution*, galvanized research in language and cognition. Berlin and Kay proposed that color perception was innate, thus challenging the linguistic relativism of Sapir and Whorf. Berlin and Kay's work encouraged further research in areas like ethnobotany and ethnozoology. In this work, researchers focused on the way people classified their environments in an attempt to discover other universal patterns of human perception.

A second approach is called *cognitive anthropology* and is closely related to psychology and neurology. By the mid-1970s, advances in anthropology, psychology, and the field of artificial intelligence had made it apparent that human cognition was much more complex than the models of native classification derived from componential analysis suggested. The earlier focus on domains and taxonomies gave way to schema theory.

A fundamental part of ethnoscience and the basis for componential analysis was the idea that people classified objects in their world by checking off a mental list of essential features (apple

= red, round, stem). Rejecting this, cognitive anthropologists argued that people conceptualize by reference to general mental prototypes called *schemas*, or *schemata*. Schemas are neurological pathways that humans build through life experience. When an athlete practices a skill over and over again until it is automatic, it is called building "muscle memory." However, a muscle cannot remember. To a cognitive anthropologist, the athlete has created a schema, a special neurological pathway for that skill. Another way to think of schemas is that they are loci for neural processing that enable us to act quickly and without conscious thought. Thinking about where you want to go for lunch is a conscious process. However, a "lunch schema" is activated when you crave a hamburger but are repulsed by the idea of a cricket sandwich. Crickets are not part of the neurological "lunch" pattern you have created.

To explain nonsequential thought processes in areas where thinking is nonlinguistic, cognitive anthropologists and psychologists turned to the concept of connectionism. Those who follow connectionist theory suggest that knowledge is linked, networked, and widely distributed by mental processing units and that we access and analyze information through these mechanisms. Because these units are connected and work simultaneously, we can process information much faster than any computer (Strauss and Quinn 1994: 286). Notable scholars in this area are Claudia Strauss (b. 1953), Naomi Quinn (1939–2019), and Roy D'Andrade (1931–2016).

The essays chosen for this section reflect the development of theory based on structural and cognitive models through the last half century. In the first article, "Four Winnebago Myths: A Structural Sketch," published in 1960, Lévi-Strauss demonstrates basic aspects of his theory and methodology by comparing four Native American myths collected by Paul Radin.

The second essay is an example of structural analysis by Sherry Ortner published in 1972, but written while she was a doctoral student at the University of Chicago. In this essay, Ortner conducts a structural analysis of gender inequality. Ortner has had a long and distinguished career in anthropology. She has held academic positions at Sarah Lawrence College, the University of Michigan, and Columbia University. She is currently a professor of anthropology at the University of California, Los Angeles. Her fieldwork and research have focused on the Sherpas of Nepal (her books about them include *High Religion* [1989] and *Life and Death on Mt. Everest* [1999]), gender studies (*Sexual Meanings: The Cultural Construction of Gender and Sexuality* [1981] and *Making Gender: The Politics and Erotics of Culture* [1996]), her high school classmates (*New Jersey Dreaming: Capital, Culture, and the Class of '58* [2003]), and independent film directors and producers in New York and Los Angeles (*Not Hollywood: Independent Film at the Twilight of the American Dream* [2013]).

SUGGESTED READINGS

Berlin, B. O., D. Breedlove, and P. Raven. 1974. *Principles of Tzeltal Plant Classification.* New York: Academic Press.
  An ethnobotanical study of the Tzeltal Maya classification of plants.
D'Andrade, Roy. 1995. *The Development of Cognitive Anthropology.* Cambridge: Cambridge University Press.
  A summary of the history of ethnoscience and cognitive anthropology and its principal theoretical tenets from the 1950s to the 1990s.
Goodenough, W. H. 1967. "Componential Analysis and the Study of Meaning." *Language* 32(2): 195–216.
  One of the defining essays on the use of componential analysis in ethnoscience.
Harkin, Michael E. 2013. "Claude Lévi-Strauss." In *Theory in Social and Cultural Anthropology: An Encyclopedia,* ed. R. Jon McGee and Richard L. Warms, 473–477. Thousand Oaks, CA: Sage.
  An overview of the life and career of Claude Lévi-Strauss.
Hénaff, Marcel. 1998. *Claude Lévi-Strauss and the Making of Structural Anthropology.* Minneapolis: University of Minnesota Press.
  A comprehensive review of the work of Lévi-Strauss.
Kronenfeld, David, Giovanni Bennardo, Victor de Munck, and Michael Fischer, eds. 2011. *A Companion to Cognitive Anthropology.* Malden, MA: Wiley-Blackwell.

A collection of twenty-nine essays exploring the history, methodologies, and theoretical precepts of cognitive anthropology, along with examples of research from the 2000s.

McGee, R. Jon. 2013. "Ethnoscience/New Ethnography." In *Theory in Social and Cultural Anthropology: An Encyclopedia*, ed. R. Jon McGee and Richard L. Warms, 232–234. Thousand Oaks, CA: Sage.
    A brief overview of the basic elements of ethnoscience.

Sturtevant, William C. 1964. "Studies in Ethnoscience." *American Anthropologist* 66(2): 99–131.
    An overview of the theory and basic concepts of ethnoscience.

Wilcken, Patrick. 2010. *Claude Lévi-Strauss: The Father of Modern Anthropology*. New York: Penguin.
    A biography of Lévi-Strauss.

20. Four Winnebago Myths: A Structural Sketch

Claude Lévi-Strauss (1908–2009)

AMONG THE MANY TALENTS which make him one of the great anthropologists of our time, Paul Radin has one which gives a singular flavor to his work. He has the authentic esthetic touch, rather uncommon in our profession. This is what we call in French *flair*: the gift of singling out those facts, observations, and documents which possess an especially rich meaning, sometimes undisclosed at first, but likely to become evident as one ponders the implications woven into the material. A crop harvested by Paul Radin, even if he does not choose to mill it himself, is always capable of providing lasting nourishment for many generations of students.[1]

This is the reason why I intend to pay my tribute to the work of Paul Radin by giving some thought to four myths which he has published under the title *The Culture of the Winnebago: As Described by Themselves*.[a]

Although Radin himself pointed out in the Preface: "In publishing these texts I have only one object in view, to put at the disposal of students, authentic material for the study of Winnebago culture," and although the four myths were each obtained from different informants, it seems that, on a structural level, there was good reason for making them the subject of a single publication. A deep unity underlies all four, notwithstanding the fact that one myth, as Radin has shown in his introduction and notes, appears to differ widely in content, style, and structure from the other three. My purpose will be to analyze the structural relationships between the four myths and to suggest that they can be grouped together not only because they are part of a collection of ethnographic and linguistic data referring to one tribe, which Radin too modestly claimed as his sole purpose, but because they are of the same genre, i.e., their meanings logically complement each other.[2]

The title of the first myth is "The Two Friends Who Became Reincarnated: The Origin of the Four Nights' Wake." This is the story of two friends, one of them a chief's son, who decide to sacrifice their lives for the welfare of the community. After undergoing a series of

From *Culture in History: Essays in Honor of Paul Radin* (1960)

1. This article first appeared in a volume edited by the anthropologist and poet Stanley Diamond (1922–1991) called *Culture in History: Essays in Honor of Paul Radin* (1960), published soon after Radin's death in 1959. Radin was born in the Polish city of Lodz in 1883 and immigrated to New York in 1884. He graduated from the College of the City of New York (today The City College of New York, the City University of New York's founding institution) in 1902 and started graduate school at Columbia University, intending to study the biology of fish. However, between 1905 and 1907, Radin studied in Europe, where he was introduced to anthropology at the University of Berlin. When he returned to Columbia he became a student of Franz Boas and received his PhD in 1911. Radin is best known for his ethnographic work among the Winnebago, whom he lived with from 1908 to 1912.

2. "Four Winnebago Myths" is a short example of Lévi-Strauss's structural analysis of myth. Lévi-Strauss's goal was to understand the unconscious structure of the human mind. He believed that myths of indigenous peoples were the perfect vehicles for that endeavor because such mythology had less "cultural interference" to filter out than stories in Western industrial societies. For Lévi-Strauss, the outward storyline of the myth is irrelevant. The logical relationships between its elements are critical. By analyzing these, Lévi-Strauss believed he could arrive at universal unconscious messages conveyed by myth.

ordeals in the underworld, they reach the lodge of Earthmaker, who permits them to become reincarnated and to resume their previous lives among their relatives and friends.

As explained by Radin in his commentary,[b] there is a native theory underlying the myth: every individual is entitled to a specific quota of years of life and experience. If a person dies before his time, his relatives can ask the spirits to distribute among them what he has failed to utilize. But there is more in this theory than meets the eye. The unspent life-span given up by the hero, when he lets himself be killed by the enemies, will be added to the capital of life, set up in trust for the group. Nevertheless, his act of dedication is not entirely without personal profit: by becoming a hero an individual makes a choice, he exchanges a full life-span for a shortened one, but while the full life-span is unique, granted once and for all, the shortened one appears as a kind of lease taken on eternity. That is, by giving up one full life, an indefinite succession of half-lives is gained. But since all the unlived halves will increase the life expectancy of the ordinary people, everybody gains in the process: the ordinary people whose average life expectancy will slowly but substantially increase generation after generation, and the warriors with shortened but indefinitely renewable lives, provided their minds remain set on self-dedication.

It is not clear, however, that Radin pays full justice to the narrator when he treats as a "secondary interpretation" the fact that the expedition is undertaken by the heroes to show their appreciation of the favors of their fellow villagers.[c] My contention is that this motive of the heroes deserves primary emphasis, and it is supported by the fact that there are two war parties. The first one is undertaken by the warriors while the heroes are still in their adolescent years, so they are neither included in, nor even informed of it; they hear about the party only as a rumor[d] and they decide to join it uninvited. We must conclude then that the heroes have no responsibility for the very venture wherein they distinguish themselves, since it has been instigated and led by others. Moreover, they are not responsible for the second war party, during which they are killed, since this latter foray has been initiated by the enemy in revenge for the first.

The basic idea is clear: the two friends have developed into successful social beings;[e] accordingly, they feel obliged to repay their fellow tribesmen who have treated them so well.[f] As the story goes, they set out to expose themselves in the wilderness; later they die in an ambush prepared by the enemy in revenge for the former defeat. The obvious conclusion is that the heroes have willingly died for the sake of their people. And because they died without responsibility of their own, but instead that of others, those will inherit the unspent parts of their lives, while the heroes themselves will be permitted to return to earth and the same process will be repeated all over again. This interpretation is in agreement with information given elsewhere by Radin: i.e., in order to pass the test of the Old Woman who rids the soul of all the recollections belonging to its earthly life, each soul must be solicitous not of its own welfare but of the welfare of the living members of the group.

Now at the root of this myth we find—as the phonologist would say—a double opposition. First there is the opposition between *ordinary life* and *heroic life*, the former realizing a full lifespan, not renewable, the latter gambling with life for the benefit of the group. The second opposition is between two kinds of death, one "straight" and final, although it provides a type of unearthly immortality in the villages of the dead; the other "undulating," and swinging between life and death. Indeed one is tempted to see the reflection of this double fate in the Winnebago symbol of the ladder of the afterworld as it appears in the Medicine Rite. One side is "like a frog's leg, twisted and dappled with light-and-life. The other [is] like a red cedar, blackened from frequent usage and very smooth and shiny."[g, 3]

---

3. Lévi-Strauss believed in the general notion shared by Émile Durkheim and the Prague School linguists that, for reasons that are ultimately biological, human perception is segmented into binary oppositions. However, Lévi-Strauss also believed that human minds were not satisfied with binary oppositions, but searched for a mediating category: something that transcended the binary. Lévi-Strauss believed that humans uni-

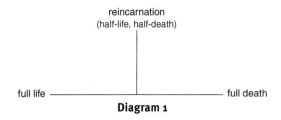

Diagram 1

To sum up the meaning of the myth so far: if one wants a full life one gets a full death; if one renounces life and seeks death, then one increases the full life of his fellow-tribesmen, and, moreover, secures for oneself a state composed of an indefinite series of half-lives and half-deaths. Thus we have a triangular system:

The second myth, entitled "The Man Who Brought His Wife Back from Spiritland," is a variation on the same theme, although there is a significant difference involved. Here too, we find a hero—the husband—ready to sacrifice his unspent life-span; not, as in the first myth, for the benefit of the group, but rather for the benefit of only one individual, his beloved wife. Indeed, the hero is not aware at first that by seeking death he will secure a new lease on life for both his dead wife and himself. Had he been

so aware, and this holds equally for the protagonists in the first myth, the essential element of sacrifice would have been missing. In both cases the result is similar: an altruistic loss of life means life regained, not only for the self-appointed victim, but also for the one or more persons to whom the sacrifice was consecrated.

The third myth, "The Journey of the Ghost to Spiritland, as Told in the Medicine Rite," belongs, as the title suggests, to a religious society. It explains how the members of the Medicine Rite, after death, undergo (as do the protagonists of the other myths) several tests in Spiritland, which they overcome, thus gaining the right to become reincarnated.[4]

At first sight this situation seems to differ from the others, since nobody sacrificed his life. However, the members of the Medicine Rite actually spend their lives in symbolic sacrifice. As Radin has shown, in *The Road of Life and Death* and elsewhere, the Medicine Rite follows the familiar pattern of letting oneself be "killed" and then "revived." Thus the only departure consists in the fact that whereas in the first and second myths the heroes are willing to die once and, so they anticipate, permanently, the heroes

---

versally experienced satisfaction when they could impose this mediated binary structure on the world. Stories, classification systems, and experiences that followed this pattern were "good to think" in a sense analogous to something that is good to eat. That is, human beings are particularly satisfied by this pattern, regardless of the content of the elements it contained.

In his structural analyses of myth, Lévi-Strauss looked for binary oppositions within the elements of the story and the factors that mediated them. For example, in the Winnebago myth described here, the opposition between life and death is mediated by reincarnation. The myth is satisfying because it fits the mediated binary pattern. According to Lévi-Strauss, its message is not about the friends nor about what Winnebago men should do but rather about the nature of life and death themselves.

The phrase "as the phonologist would say—a double opposition" refers to Prague School linguists who proposed that the phonemes in a language could be found by identifying the minimal pairs where sounds stand in opposition to each other. When such oppositions are found and they cause a change in meaning, it is clear that the sound is recognized as distinctive. For example, in English, *l* and *r* are in opposition, so the word "led" is different from "red." In Japanese, however, *l* and *r* are heard as the same. Consequently, someone from Japan who speaks English does not hear a distinction between *l* and *r*. Thus, "led" may be pronounced "red." For Japanese speakers, these two sounds, *l* and *r*, are not in opposition.

4. Notice that Lévi-Strauss wrote in the tradition of the French sociological school that preceded him. Because he believed he was uncovering universal elementary ideas, his method was comparative and he was not concerned with historical or cultural context. He chose those pieces of traditions or beliefs from different societies that fit his view regardless of the context in which these elements were found.

Lévi-Strauss interpreted these Winnebago myths for his readers without giving them the full text of the stories or providing any background information about Winnebago society. This is a typical French structuralist approach: Because the unconscious structure of human thought is universal, the cultural context of the myths is superficial and irrelevant to the myths' underlying message. American anthropologists, as inheritors of the Boasian tradition, are inclined to place more emphasis on the specific cultural contexts in which events occur.

of the third myth (the members of the Rite) repeatedly, though symbolically, have trained themselves to self-sacrifice. They have, so to speak, **mithridatized** themselves against a full death by renouncing a full ordinary life which is replaced, in ritual practice, by a life-long succession of half-lives and half-deaths. Therefore we are entitled to assume that, in this case too, the myth is made up of the same elements, although Ego—and not another person, nor the group as a whole—is conceived as the primary beneficiary.[5]

Let us now consider the fourth myth, "How an Orphan Restored the Chief's Daughter to Life," a tale which has given Radin some concern. This myth, he says, is not only different from the other three, its plot appears unusual relative to the rest of Winnebago mythology. After recalling that in his book *Method and Theory of Ethnology*[h] he suggested that this myth was a version, altered almost beyond recognition, of a type which he then called village-origin myths, he proceeds to explain in *The Culture of the Winnebago*[i] why he can no longer support his earlier interpretation.

It is worthwhile to follow closely Radin's new line of reasoning. He begins by recapitulating the plot—such a simple plot, he says, that there is practically no need for doing so: "The daughter of a tribal chief falls in love with an orphan, dies of a broken heart and is then restored to life by the orphan who must submit to and overcome certain tests, not in spiritland but here, on earth, in the very lodge in which the young woman died."[j]

If this plot is "simplicity itself," where do the moot points lie? Radin lists three which he says every modern Winnebago would question: (1) the plot seems to refer to a highly stratified society; (2) in order to understand the plot one should assume that in that society women occupied a high position and that, possibly, descent was reckoned in the matrilineal line; (3) the tests which in Winnebago mythology

take place, as a rule, in the land of ghosts occur, in this instance, on earth.

After dismissing two possible explanations—that we are dealing here with a borrowed European tale or that the myth was invented by some Winnebago radical—Radin concludes that the myth must belong to "a very old stratum of Winnebago history." He also suggests that two distinct types of literary tradition, divine tales on the one hand and human tales on the other, have merged while certain primitive elements have been reinterpreted to make them fit together.[k]

I am certainly not going to challenge this very elegant reconstruction backed by an incomparable knowledge of Winnebago culture, language, and history. The kind of analysis I intended to offer is no alternative to Radin's own analysis. It lies on a different level, logical rather than historical. It takes as its context the three myths already discussed, not Winnebago culture, old or recent. My purpose is to explicate the structural relationship—if any—which prevails between this myth and the other three.

First, there is a theoretical problem which should be noted briefly. Since the publication of Boas' *Tsimshian Mythology*, anthropologists have often simply assumed that a full correlation exists between the myths of a given society and its culture. This, I feel, is going further than Boas intended. In the work just referred to, he did not suppose that myths automatically reflect the culture, as some of his followers seem always to anticipate. Rather, he tried to find out how much of the culture actually did pass into the myths, if any, and he convincingly showed that *some* of it does. It does not follow that whenever a social pattern is alluded to in a myth this pattern must correspond to something real which should be attributed to the past if, under direct scrutiny, the present fails to offer an equivalent.[6]

There must be, and there is, a correspondence between the unconscious meaning of a

---

5. **"Mithridatize"**: to develop a tolerance or immunity to poison by taking small doses of it, from Mithridates VI of Pontus (135–63 BCE), who, after the assassination of his father by arsenic poisoning, tried to protect himself from poisoning in this way.

6. Boas was an ardent proponent of cultural relativism. Here Lévi-Strauss tries to reconcile French structuralism with Boasian particularism.

myth—the problem it tries to solve—and the conscious content it makes use of to reach that end, i.e., the plot. However, this correspondence should not always be conceived as a kind of mirror-image, it can also appear as a *transformation*. If the problem is presented in "straight" terms, that is, in the way the social life of the group expresses and tries to solve it, the overt content of the myth, the plot, can borrow its elements from social life itself. But should the problem be formulated, and its solution sought for, "upside down," that is **ab absurdo**, then the overt content will become modified accordingly to form an inverted image of the social pattern actually present to the consciousness of the natives.[7]

If this hypothesis is true, it follows that Radin's assumption that the pattern of social life referred to in the fourth myth must belong to a past stage of Winnebago history, is not inescapable.

We may be confronted with the pattern of a nonexistent society, contrary to the Winnebago traditional pattern, only because the structure of that particular myth is itself inverted, in relation to those myths which use as overt content the traditional pattern. To put it simply, if a certain correspondence is assumed between A and B, then if A is replaced by 2A, B must be replaced by 2B, without implying that, since B corresponds to an external object, there should exist another external object 2B, which must exist somewhere: either in another society (borrowed element) or in a past stage of the same society (survival).

Obviously the problem remains: why do we have three myths of the A type and one of the 2A type? This could be the case because 2A is older than A, but it can also be because 2A is one of the transformations of A which is already

known to us under three different guises: $A_1 A_2$, A_3, since we have seen that the three myths of the assumed A type are not identical.

We have already established that the group of myths under consideration is based upon a fundamental opposition: on the one hand, the lives of ordinary people unfolding towards a natural death, followed by immortality in one of the spirit villages; and, on the other hand, heroic life, self-abridged, the gain being a supplementary life quota for the others as well as for oneself. The former alternative is not envisaged in this group of myths which, as we have seen, is mostly concerned with the latter. There is, however, a secondary difference which permits us to classify the first three myths according to the particular end assigned to the self-sacrifice in each. In the first myth the group is intended to be the immediate beneficiary, in the second it is another individual (the wife), and in the third it is oneself.

When we turn to the fourth myth, we may agree with Radin that it exhibits "unusual" features in relation to the other three. However, the difference seems to be of a logical more than of a sociological or historical nature. It consists in a new opposition introduced within the first pair of opposites (between "ordinary" life and "extraordinary" life). Now there are two ways in which an "extraordinary" phenomenon may be construed as such; it may consist either in a *surplus* or in a *lack*. While the heroes of the first three myths are all overgifted, through social success, emotions or wisdom, the heroes of the fourth myth are, if one may say so, "below standard," at least in one respect.

The chief's daughter occupies a high social position; so high, in fact, that she is cut off from the rest of the group and is therefore paralyzed when it comes to expressing her feelings. Her

---

7. In his first book, *The Elementary Structures of Kinship* (1949), Lévi-Strauss postulated that there was a universal psychological need to give and receive gifts. He believed that this was based on a fundamental dialectic of the human mind—the distinction between self and others—and he devoted an entire chapter to child psychology in an attempt to justify this claim (1967: 84–97). Here Lévi-Strauss once again resorts to psychological theory, in this case, psychoanalysis, to justify his point of view. He states that there must be some agreement between a myth's underlying meaning and its plot. However, the correspondence between meaning and plot may appear as a "transformation," or an "upside down" version of the apparent meaning. There is no question that this is an important insight for both psychology and myth analysis, but it offers dangers as well. If used carelessly, this concept can be used to justify any flight of imagination that may occur to the interpreter.

"Ab absurdo": Latin, reasoning or an interpretation that leads to an absurd conclusion.

exalted position makes her a defective human being, lacking an essential attribute of life. The boy is also defective, but socially, that is, he is an orphan and very poor. May we say, then, that the myth reflects a stratified society? This would compel us to overlook the remarkable symmetry which prevails between our two heroes, for it would be wrong to say simply that one is high and the other low: as a matter of fact, structures, wherein the two terms are inverted relative to each other, belongs to the realm of ideological constructs rather than of sociological systems. We have just seen that the girl is "socially" above and "naturally" below. The boy is undoubtedly very low in the social scale; however, he is a miraculous hunter, i.e., he entertains privileged relations with the natural world, the world of animals. This is emphasized over and over again in the myth.[l]

Therefore may we not claim that the myth actually confronts us with a polar system consisting in two individuals, one male, the other female, and both exceptional insofar as each of them is overgifted in one way (+) and undergifted in the other (−).[8]

	Nature	Culture
Boy	+	−
Girl	−	+

Diagram 2

The plot consists in carrying this disequilibrium to its logical extreme; the girl dies a *natural* death, the boy stays alone, i.e., he also dies, but in a *social* way. Whereas during their ordinary lives the girl was overtly above, the boy overtly below, now that they have become segregated (either from the living or from society) their positions are inverted: the girl is below (in her grave), the boy above (in his lodge). This, I think, is clearly implied in a detail stated by the narrator which seems to have puzzled Radin:

"On top of the grave they then piled loose dirt, placing everything in such a way that nothing could seep through."[m] Radin comments: "I do not understand why piling the dirt loosely would prevent seepage. There must be something else involved that has not been mentioned."[n] May I suggest that this detail be correlated with a similar detail about the building of the young man's lodge: ". . . the bottom was piled high with dirt so that, in this fashion, they could keep the lodge warm."[o] There is implied here, I think, not a reference to recent or past custom but rather a clumsy attempt to emphasize that, relative to the earth's surface, i.e., dirt, the boy is now above and the girl below.

This new equilibrium, however, will be no more lasting than the first. *She who was unable to live cannot die;* her ghost lingers "on earth." Finally she induces the young man to fight the ghosts and take her back among the living. With a wonderful symmetry, the boy will meet, a few years later, with a similar, although inverted, fate; "Although I am not yet old, he says to the girl (now his wife), I have been here (lasted) on earth as long as I can. . . ."[p] *He who overcame death, proves unable to live.* This recurring antithesis could develop indefinitely, and such a possibility is noted in the text (with an only son surviving his father, he too an orphan, he too a sharpshooter) but a different solution is finally reached. The heroes, equally unable to die or to live, will assume an intermediate identity, that of twilight creatures living under the earth but also able to come up on it; they will be neither men nor gods, but wolves, that is, ambivalent spirits combining good and evil features. So ends the myth.

If the above analysis is correct, two consequences follow: first, our myth makes up a consistent whole wherein the details balance and fit each other nicely; secondly, the three problems raised by Radin can be analyzed in terms of the myth itself; and no hypothetical past stage of Winnebago society need be invoked.

---

8. The opposition of nature and culture and its association with gender illustrated in the figure and explained later is one of the fundamental principles in French structuralist thought and finds expression in a variety of forms. (See, for example, Lévi-Strauss's book *The Raw and the Cooked* [1969]). In essay 21, Sherry Ortner explores precisely this issue and its relationship to the oppression of women.

Let us, then, try to solve these three problems, following the pattern of our analysis.

1. The society of the myth appears stratified, only because the two heroes are conceived as a pair of opposites, but they are such both from the point of view of nature *and* of culture. Thus, the so-called stratified society should be interpreted not as a sociological vestige but as a projection of a logical structure wherein everything is given both in opposition and correlation.

2. The same answer can be given to the question of the assumed exalted position of the women. If I am right, our myths state three propositions, the first by implication, the second expressly stated in myths 1, 2 and 3, the third expressly stated in myth 4.

These propositions are as follows:
   a. -Ordinary people live (their full lives) and die (their full deaths).
   b. -Positive extraordinary people die (earlier) and live (more).
   c. -Negative extraordinary people are able neither to live nor to die.

Obviously proposition c offers an inverted demonstration of the truth of a and b. Hence, it must use a plot starting with protagonists (here, man and woman) in inverted positions. This leads us to state that a plot and its component parts should neither be interpreted by themselves nor relative to something outside the realm of the myth proper, but as *substitutions* given in, and understandable only with reference to *the group made up of all the myths of the same series.*

3. We may now revert to the third problem raised by Radin about myth 4, that is, the contest with the ghosts takes place on earth instead of, as was usually the case, in spiritland. To this query I shall suggest an answer along the same lines as the others.

It is precisely because our two heroes suffer from a state of *under-life* (in respect either to culture or nature) that, in the narrative, the ghosts become a kind of *super-dead.* It will be recalled that the whole myth develops and is resolved on an intermediary level, where humans become underground animals and ghosts linger on earth. It tells about people who are, from the start, half-alive and half-dead while, in the preceding myths, the opposition between life and death is strongly emphasized at the beginning, and overcome only at the end. Thus, the integral meaning of the four myths is that, in order to be overcome the opposition between life and death should be first acknowledged, or else the ambiguous state will persist indefinitely.[9]

I hope to have shown that the four myths under consideration all belong to the same *group* (understood as in *group theory*) and that Radin was even more right than he supposed in publishing them together. In the first place, the four myths deal with extraordinary, in opposition to ordinary, fate. The fact that ordinary fate is not illustrated here and thus is reckoned as an "empty" category, does not imply, of course, that it is not illustrated elsewhere. In the second place, we find an opposition between two types of extraordinary fate, positive and negative. This

---

9. Lévi-Strauss presents his analysis with unquestioned skill, but is erudition the same as accuracy? One of the principal criticisms of Lévi-Strauss's structuralism is that although his analyses are masterful, their believability rests primarily on Lévi-Strauss's rhetorical skill rather than empirically grounded, step-by-step reasoning. Lévi-Strauss hoped to make anthropology more scientific. He believed that the Prague School linguists, in describing phonemes, had uncovered scientifically verifiable basic elements of language. He hoped to do the same for culture. However, culture has no units that can be described as accurately and consistently as phonemes. There is no agreed-upon way to determine the elementary units of culture. Phonemes turn out to be a lot more complicated than Lévi-Strauss thought as well. How many phonemes are there in English? Scientifically speaking, anywhere from 35 to 48, depending on whom you ask (Bizzocchi 2017).

new dichotomy which permits us to segregate myth 4 from myths 1, 2 and 3 corresponds, on a logical level, to the discrimination that Radin makes on psychological, sociological, and historical grounds. Finally, myths 1, 2 and 3 have been classified according to the purpose of the sacrifice which is the theme of each.[10]

Thus the four myths can be organized in a dichotomous structure of correlations and oppositions. But we can go even further and try to order them on a common scale. This is suggested by the curious variations which can be observed in each myth with respect to the kind of test the hero is put to by the ghosts. In myth 3 there is no test at all, so far as the ghosts are concerned. The tests consist in overcoming material obstacles while the ghosts themselves figure as indifferent fellow travelers. In myth 1 they cease to be indifferent without yet becoming hostile. On the contrary, the tests result from their overfriendliness, as inviting women and infectious merry-makers. Thus, from *companions* in myth 3 they change to seducers in myth 1. In myth 2 they still behave as human beings, but they now act as *aggressors*, and permit themselves all kinds of rough play. This is even more evident in myth 4, but here the human element vanishes; it is only at the end that we know that ghosts, not crawling insects, are responsible for the trials of the hero. We have thus a twofold progression, from a peaceful attitude to an *aggressive* one, and from *human* to *nonhuman* behavior.

This progression can be correlated with the kind of relationship which the hero (or heroes) of each myth entertain with the social group. The hero of myth 3 belongs to a ritual brotherhood: he definitely assumes his (privileged) fate as a member of a group, he acts with and in his group.

The two heroes of myth 1 have resolved to part from the group, but the text states repeatedly that this is in order to find an opportunity to achieve something beneficial for their fellow tribesmen. They act, therefore, for the group. But in myth 2 the hero is only inspired by his love for his wife. There is no reference to the group. The action is undertaken independently for the sake of another individual. Finally, in myth 4, the negative attitude toward the group is clearly revealed; the girl dies of her "uncommunicativeness," if one may say so. Indeed she prefers to die rather than speak; death is her "final" exile. As for the boy, he refuses to follow the villagers when they decide to move away and abandon the grave. The segregation is thus willfully sought on all sides; the action unrolls against the group.

The accompanying chart summarizes our discussion. I am quite aware that, in order to be fully convincing, the argument should not be limited to the four myths considered here, but include more of the invaluable Winnebago mythology which Radin has given us. But I hope that by integrating more material the basic structure outlined has become richer

---

10. Lévi-Strauss has done anthropology a tremendous service by outlining a methodology for the sorting of anthropological data. Structuralism can lead to valuable interpretive insights where other theoretical perspectives may fail. But as a means for proving the binary structure of the mind, structuralism has failed. Lévi-Strauss was no closer to proving his hypothesis about the unconscious structure of human thought in 1960 than Sigmund Freud more than half a century earlier.

Despite the dialectical nature of Lévi-Strauss's theory and his self-professed allegiance to Marxist thought, materialists have provided some of the most telling critiques of structuralism. Those who view anthropology as a science generally discount Lévi-Strauss's structuralism because the reality he claims to present is unconscious and thus unverifiable (Malefijt 1974: 330). Marvin Harris, for example, says that a "paralysis of reality" spreads over his entire work (1968: 497). Even one of Lévi-Strauss's greatest admirers, Edmund Leach, says,

I am ready to concede that the structures which he displays are products of an unconscious mental process, but I can see no reason to believe that they are human universals. Bereft of Lévi-Strauss's resourceful special pleading they appear to be local, functionally determined attributes of particular individuals or of particular cultural groups. (Leach 1976: 126)

and more complex, without being impaired. By singling out one book which its author would perhaps consider a minor contribution, I have intended to emphasize, in an indirect way, the fecundity of the method followed by Radin, and the lasting value of the problems he poses for the anthropologist.[11]

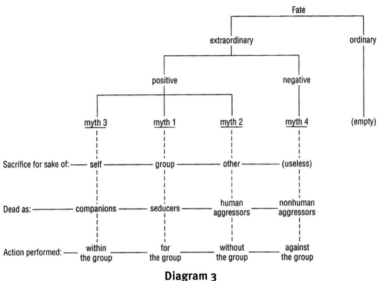

Diagram 3

AUTHOR'S NOTES

a. Paul Radin, The Culture of the Winnebago: As Described by Themselves Special Publication of the Bollingen Foundation (also published as Memoir 2 of the International Journal of American Linguistics, 1949, pp. iv, 1–119).

b. Ibid., p. 41, para. 32.

c. Ibid., p. 37, para. 2.

d. Ibid., paras. 11–14.

e. Ibid., paras. 66–70.

f. Ibid., para. 72.

g. Ibid., p. 71, paras. 91–93; see also Paul Radin, *The Road of Life and Death*, Bollingen Series, Vol. V

(New York, 1945), especially the author's illuminating comments on pp. 63–65.

h. Paul Radin, *Method and Theory of Ethnology* (New York, 1933), pp. 238–45.

i. Radin, *The Culture of the Winnebago*, pp. 74 ff.

j. Ibid., p. 74.

k. Ibid., pp. 74–77.

l. Ibid., see paras. 10–14, 17–18, 59–60, 77–90.

m. Ibid., p. 87, para. 52.

n. Ibid., p. 100, n. 40.

o. Ibid., p. 87, para. 74.

p. Ibid., p. 4, para. 341.

---

11. It is ironic that in the last paragraph of this text Lévi-Strauss states he intended to emphasize the "fecundity of the method followed by Radin." Radin was the quintessential Boasian who spent much of his career studying the Winnebago in extensive detail. With its emphasis on universal structures of the mind and large-scale cross-cultural comparisons, nothing could be further from Radin's approach than Lévi-Strauss's structuralism. Lévi-Strauss was perhaps aware of this irony.

21. Is Female to Male as Nature Is to Culture?

SHERRY ORTNER (b. 1941)

MUCH OF THE CREATIVITY of anthropology derives from the tension between two sets of demands: that we explain human universals, and that we explain cultural particulars. By this canon, woman provides us with one of the more challenging problems to be dealt with. The secondary status of woman in society is one of the true universals, a pan-cultural fact. Yet within that universal fact, the specific cultural conceptions and symbolizations of woman are extraordinarily diverse and even mutually contradictory. Further, the actual treatment of women and their relative power and contribution vary enormously from culture to culture, and over different periods in the history of particular cultural traditions. Both of these points—the universal fact and the cultural variation—constitute problems to be explained.[1]

My interest in the problem is of course more than academic: I wish to see genuine change come about, the emergence of a social and cultural order in which as much of the range of human potential is open to women as is open to men. The universality of female subordination, the fact that it exists within every type of social and economic arrangement and in societies of every degree of complexity, indicates to me that we are up against something very profound, very stubborn, something we cannot rout out simply by rearranging a few tasks and roles in the social system, or even by reordering the whole economic structure. In this paper I try to expose the underlying logic of cultural thinking that assumes the inferiority of women; I try to show the highly persuasive nature of the logic, for if it were not so persuasive, people would not keep subscribing to it. But I also try to show the social and cultural sources of that logic, to indicate wherein lies the potential for change.[2]

From *Feminist Studies* (1972)

1. Early feminist critiques assumed the universal subordination of women. For instance, in her opening paragraph, Ortner states that the secondary status of women is a "pan-cultural fact." The purpose of the essay is to formulate a theory that explains this universal gender asymmetry. Feminist scholars dealt with this issue in a variety of ways. Ortner's turns inward. Rather than examining the material bases of society, she looks for the answer in the structure of human thought.

Structuralists believe that cultural phenomena are the products of universal logical processes that organize human thought. According to them, a fundamental characteristic of human thought is to sort data into binary oppositions. Therefore, one should be able to identify cross-cultural patterns of these oppositions associated with men and women. This is what Ortner sets out to do in this essay. A decade later, theorists abandoned the view that women were everywhere and always subordinate to men in favor of a more sophisticated view that examined the cultural construction of relationships between men and women. But in the 1970s, within the political context of the women's movement, the domination of women by men was an accepted doctrine for feminist anthropologists.

Ortner modified her position on the universality of male dominance in several subsequent articles—"Gender Hegemonies" (1989) and "So, Is Female to Male as Nature Is to Culture?" (1996)—both available in Ortner's *Making Gender* (1996) collection.

2. Most anthropological theory, though influenced by prevailing political events or philosophies, is not written with an openly political objective. With rare exceptions, it was not until the 1970s, when college

It is important to sort out the levels of the problem. The confusion can be staggering. For example, depending on which aspect of Chinese culture we look at, we might extrapolate any of several entirely different guesses concerning the status of women in China. In the ideology of Taoism, *yin,* the female principle, and *yang,* the male principle, are given equal weight; "the opposition, alternation, and interaction of these two forces give rise to all phenomena in the universe" (Siu, 1968:2). Hence we might guess that maleness and femaleness are equally valued in the general ideology of Chinese culture.[a] Looking at the social structure, however, we see the strongly emphasized patrilineal descent principle, the importance of sons, and the absolute authority of the father in the family. Thus we might conclude that China is the archetypal patriarchal society. Next, looking at the actual roles played, power and influence wielded, and material contributions made by women in Chinese society—all of which are, upon observation, quite substantial—we would have to say that women are allotted a great deal of (unspoken) status in the system. Or again, we might focus on the fact that a goddess, Kuan Yin, is the central (most worshiped, most depicted) deity in Chinese Buddhism, and we might be tempted to say, as many have tried to say about goddess-worshiping cultures in prehistoric and early historical societies, that China is actually a sort of matriarchy. In short, we must be absolutely clear about *what* we are trying to explain before explaining it.

We may differentiate three levels of the problem:

1. The universal fact of culturally attributed second-class status of women in every society. Two questions are important here. First, what do we mean by this; what is our evidence that this is a universal fact? And second, how are we to explain this fact, once having established it?

2. Specific ideologies, symbolizations, and socio-structural arrangements pertaining to women that vary widely from culture to culture. The problem at this level is to account for any particular cultural complex in terms of factors specific to that group—the standard level of anthropological analysis.

3. Observable on-the-ground details of women's activities, contributions, powers, influence, etc., often at variance with cultural ideology (although always constrained within the assumption that women may never be officially preeminent in the total system). This is the level of direct observation, often adopted now by feminist-oriented anthropologists.

This paper is primarily concerned with the first of these levels, the problem of the universal devaluation of women. The analysis thus depends not upon specific cultural data but rather upon an analysis of "culture" taken generically as a special sort of process in the world. A discussion of the second level, the problem of cross-cultural variation in conceptions and relative valuations of women, will entail a great deal of cross-cultural research and must be postponed to another time. As for the third level, it will be obvious from my approach that I would consider it a misguided endeavor to focus only upon women's actual though culturally unrecognized and unvalued powers in any given society, without first understanding the overarching ideology and

---

campuses were extremely politicized, that anthropologists such as Ortner started writing politically charged work. Note Ortner's strong rejection of Marxist materialism. She insists that even a complete reordering of the economic system would not solve the problem of female subordination.

Ortner talks about exposing the "underlying logic of cultural thinking." The notion that a hidden logic underlies human thought is basic to structuralism. The fundamental dichotomy she has constructed for analysis is male power versus female subordination. Ortner's argument is based directly on the work of Lévi-Strauss, whose books *The Elementary Structures of Kinship* (1969) [1949] and *The Raw and the Cooked* (1969) are cited in her paper. The title of one section of her essay ("Nature and Culture") is a direct reference to Lévi-Strauss's proposition that a fundamental opposition through which humans conceptualize the world is between nature and culture.

deeper assumptions of the culture that render such powers trivial.[3]

THE UNIVERSALITY OF FEMALE SUBORDINATION

What do I mean when I say that everywhere, in every known culture, women are considered in some degree inferior to men? First of all, I must stress that I am talking about *cultural* evaluations; I am saying that each culture, in its own way and on its own terms, makes this evaluation. But what would constitute evidence that a particular culture considers women inferior?

Three types of data would suffice: (1) elements of cultural ideology and informants' statements that *explicitly* devalue women, according them, their roles, their tasks, their products, and their social milieux less prestige than are accorded men and the male correlates; (2) symbolic devices, such as the attribution of defilement, which may be interpreted as *implicitly* making a statement of inferior valuation; and (3) social structural arrangements that exclude women from participation in or contact with some realm in which the highest powers of the society are felt to reside.[b] These three types of data may all of course be interrelated in any particular system, though they need not necessarily be. Further, any one of them will usually be sufficient to make the point of female inferiority in a given culture. Certainly,

female exclusion from the most sacred rite or the highest political council is sufficient evidence. Certainly, explicit cultural ideology devaluing women (and their tasks, roles, products, etc.) is sufficient evidence. Symbolic indicators such as defilement are usually sufficient, although in a few cases in which, say, men and women are equally polluting to one another, a further indicator is required—and is, as far as my investigations have ascertained, always available.[4]

On any or all of these counts, then, I would flatly assert that we find women subordinated to men in every known society. The search for a genuinely egalitarian, let alone matriarchal, culture has proved fruitless. An example from one society that has traditionally been on the credit side of this ledger will suffice. Among the matrilineal Crow, as Lowie (1956) points out, "Women had highly honorific offices in the Sun Dance; they could become directors of the Tobacco Ceremony and played, if anything, a more conspicuous part in it than the men; they sometimes played the hostess in the Cooked Meat Festival; they were not debarred from sweating or doctoring or from seeking a vision" (p. 61). Nonetheless, "Women [during menstruation] formerly rode inferior horses and evidently this loomed as a source of contamination, for they were not allowed to approach either a wounded man or men starting on a war party. A taboo still lingers against their coming near sacred objects at these times" (p. 44). Fur-

---

3. In a very brief catalog of Chinese society, Ortner gives us an example of the complexity of the relationship between gender and power. But then she declares that female subordination is universal, and the ideology of such subordination will be her focus. This choice follows from her structuralist theoretical position. A basic principle of structuralism is that all individual cultures are built on a foundation of universal cultural patterns. Therefore, structuralism should be a good method for explaining universal cultural characteristics. It would be less effective at explaining the specifics of cultural symbols (Ortner's second level). Structuralists do not generally consider the meanings of individual symbols important. It is the pattern of symbols that is critical. The third level is of even less interest to structuralists. Since they believe that culture is a mental model, structuralists are much more concerned with what people think and say than what they do. But is this a danger? Does real power lie in the ways in which people think about society or in their actions?

4. In this paragraph, Ortner sets out the basic criteria that she believes prove a culture considers women inferior. Below, she provides examples of these different classes of evidence from different societies. She argues that the existence of any of these is sufficient evidence of female subordination. However, does this statement assume a level of cultural agreement that may not exist? Do people agree on what the most powerful offices and objects in their society are? If an anthropologist finds "elements of cultural ideology and informants' statements that *explicitly* devalue women," does that mean that elements explicitly devaluing men do not exist?

ther, just before enumerating women's rights of participation in the various rituals noted above, Lowie mentions one particular Sun Dance Doll bundle that was not supposed to be unwrapped by a woman (p. 60). Pursuing this trail we find: "According to all Lodge Grass informants and most others, the doll owned by Wrinkled-face took precedence not only of other dolls but of all other Crow medicines whatsoever. This particular doll was not supposed to be handled by a woman" (p. 229).[c, 5]

In sum, the Crow are probably a fairly typical case. Yes, women have certain powers and rights, in this case some that place them in fairly high positions. Yet ultimately the line is drawn: menstruation is a threat to warfare, one of the most valued institutions of the tribe, one that is central to their self-definition; and the most sacred object of the tribe is taboo to the direct sight and touch of women.

Similar examples could be multiplied ad infinitum, but I think the onus is no longer upon us to demonstrate that female subordination is a cultural universal; it is up to those who would argue against the point to bring forth counter examples. I shall take the universal secondary status of women as a given, and proceed from there.[6]

NATURE AND CULTURE[d]

How are we to explain the universal devaluation of women? We could of course rest the case on biological determinism. There is something genetically inherent in the male of the species, so the biological determinists would argue, that makes them the naturally dominant sex; that "something" is lacking in females, and as a result women are not only naturally subordinate but in general quite satisfied with their position, since it affords them protection and the opportunity to maximize maternal pleasures, which to them are the most satisfying experiences of life. Without going into a detailed refutation of this position, I think it fair to say that it has failed to be established to the satisfaction of almost anyone in academic anthropology. This is to say, not that biological facts are irrelevant, or that men and women are not different, but that these facts and differences only take on significance of superior/inferior within the framework of culturally defined value systems.[7]

If we are unwilling to rest the case on genetic determinism, it seems to me that we have only one way to proceed. We must attempt to interpret female subordination in light of other universals, factors built into the structure of the most generalized situation in which all human beings, in whatever culture, find themselves. For example, every human being has a physical body and a sense of nonphysical mind, is part of a society of other individuals and an inheritor of a cultural tradition, and must engage in some relationship, however mediated, with "nature," or the non-human realm in order to survive. Every human being is born (to a mother) and ultimately dies, all are assumed to have an interest in personal survival, and society/culture has its own interest in (or at least momentum toward) continuity and sur-

---

5. Austrian-born anthropologist Robert Lowie (1883–1957) was a student of Franz Boas. Lowie wrote extensively on the Crow as well as other Plains Indians. Be sure to read Ortner's footnote c about Lowie and his doll.

6. Ortner says that even in societies in which women may hold high status and powerful positions, one can still find evidence indicating that they are inferior to men. She declares her case to be proven and places the burden of disproof on those who disagree. Are you convinced? Does the Crow example she provides bear this out?

7. The reference to biological determinism in this paragraph is an allusion to theories current at the time this essay was written. Popular books such as Robert Ardrey's 1961 *African Genesis*, Konrad Lorenz's 1966 (orig. 1963) *On Aggression*, and Desmond Morris's 1967 *The Naked Ape: A Zoologist's Study of the Human Animal* promoted the idea that male domination was rooted in genetics and thus inevitable. Anthropologists rejected these works, but *The Naked Ape* sold over ten million copies worldwide.

vival, which transcends the lives and deaths of particular individuals. And so forth. It is in the realm of such universals of the human condition that we must seek an explanation for the universal fact of female devaluation.

I translate the problem, in other words, into the following simple question. What could there be in the generalized structure and conditions of existence, common to every culture, that would lead every culture to place a lower value upon women? Specifically, my thesis is that woman is being identified with—or, if you will, seems to be a symbol of—something that every culture devalues, something that every culture defines as being of a lower order of existence than itself. Now it seems that there is only one thing that would fit that description, and that is "nature" in the most generalized sense. Every culture, or, generically, "culture," is engaged in the process of generating and sustaining systems of meaningful forms (symbols, artifacts, etc.) by means of which humanity transcends the givens of natural existence, bends them to its purposes, controls them in its interest. We may thus broadly equate culture with the notion of human consciousness, or with the products of human consciousness (i.e., systems of thought and technology), by means of which humanity attempts to assert control over nature.[8]

Now the categories of "nature" and "culture" are of course conceptual categories—one can find no boundary out in the actual world between the two states or realms of being. And there is no question that some cultures articulate a much stronger opposition between the two categories than others—it has even been argued that primitive peoples (some or all) do not see or intuit any distinction between the human cultural state and the state of nature at all. Yet I would maintain that the universality of ritual betokens an assertion in all human cultures of the specifically human ability to act upon and regulate, rather than passively move with and be moved by, the givens of natural existence. In ritual, the purposive manipulation of given forms toward regulating and sustaining order, every culture asserts that proper relations between human existence and natural forces depend upon culture's employing its special powers to regulate the overall processes of the world and life.[9]

One realm of cultural thought in which these points are often articulated is that of concepts of purity and pollution. Virtually every culture has some such beliefs, which seem in large part (though not, of course, entirely) to be concerned with the relationship between culture and nature (see Ortner, 1973, n.d.). A well-known aspect of purity/pollution beliefs cross-culturally is that of the natural "contagion" of pollution; left to its own devices, pollution (for these purposes grossly equated with the unregulated operation of natural energies) spreads and overpowers all that it comes in contact with. Thus a puzzle—if pollution is

---

8. The idea that all humans make a fundamental distinction between culture and nature and that in every society, culture is believed to be superior to nature, is basic to the work of Lévi-Strauss. In the two paragraphs you have just read, Ortner paraphrases him. In *The Elementary Structures of Kinship*, Lévi-Strauss wrote:

> It is easy to recognize universality as the criterion of nature, for what is constant in man falls necessarily beyond the scope of customs, techniques, and institutions. . . . Let us suppose that everything universal in man relates to the natural order . . . and that everything subject to a norm is cultural and is both relative and particular. (quoted in Boyne 1966: 200)

Ortner's comments here directly reflect Lévi-Strauss's statement. She reasons from this passage that if everything universal relates to nature, and if female subordination is universal, then female subordination must relate to nature.

9. A critical element of structuralist thought is expressed in this passage. Ortner notes that there is no boundary in the physical world between nature and culture. The boundary is a product of human thinking. Structuralists believe that the human mind imposes order by parsing, or breaking down, the world into culturally meaningful bits. Structuralists try to discover the fundamental principles by which humans accomplish this parsing.

so strong, how can anything be purified? Why is the purifying agent not itself polluted? The answer, in keeping with the present line of argument, is that purification is effected in a ritual context; purification ritual, as a purposive activity that pits self-conscious (symbolic) action against natural energies, is more powerful than those energies.[10]

In any case, my point is simply that every culture implicitly recognizes and asserts a distinction between the operation of nature and the operation of culture (human consciousness and its products); and further, that the distinctiveness of culture rests precisely on the fact that it can under most circumstances transcend natural conditions and turn them to its purposes. Thus culture (i.e., every culture) at some level of awareness asserts itself to be

not only distinct from but superior to nature, and that sense of distinctiveness and superiority rest precisely on the ability to transform—to "socialize" and "culturalize"—nature.[11]

Returning now to the issue of women, their pan-cultural second-class status could be accounted for, quite simply, by postulating that women are being identified or symbolically associated with nature, as opposed to men, who are identified with culture. Since it is always culture's project to subsume and transcend nature, if women were considered part of nature, then culture would find it "natural" to subordinate, not to say oppress, them. Yet although this argument can be shown to have considerable force, it seems to oversimplify the case. The formulation I would like to defend and elaborate on in the following section,

---

10. Ideas about purity and pollution were popularized by Mary Douglas, who published *Purity and Danger* in 1966 (see essay 24).

Having rejected biological foundations for the universal subordination of women, Ortner must formulate a cultural explanation. Following Lévi-Strauss, she chooses ritual as the focus of her analysis, as the place where cultures attempt to regulate and sustain order. Lévi-Strauss authored two studies of mythology—*The Raw and the Cooked* (1969) and *From Honey to Ashes* (1973)—based on what he claimed to be a fundamental opposition between nature and culture. Following Lévi-Strauss, Ortner states that humans transcend and control nature through the use of symbols. We distinguish ourselves from the natural world and regulate it through the use of rituals. It is through rituals that the natural, dangerous, and unacceptable are transformed into the cultural, acceptable, and safe.

Ortner has been an enduring force in anthropology partly because she has written from a variety of theoretical perspectives. This essay is structuralist, but other essays from this era focused on symbolic and interpretive anthropology. In 1973, the year before this essay's publication, Ortner published "On Key Symbols," in which she discusses how symbols operate in ritual thought and action. Then in 1975, she published another analysis titled "Gods' Bodies, Gods' Food: A Symbolic Analysis of Sherpa Ritual," which was inspired by the work of Clifford Geertz (see essay 26). By the mid-1980s, with the publication of her critical essay "Theory in Anthropology since the Sixties" (1984), Ortner began moving toward the structure and agency approaches associated with Pierre Bourdieu (see essay 27) and Anthony Giddens.

11. Anthropologist Carol MacCormack (1934–1997) criticized Lévi-Strauss's nature-culture formulation. Whereas Lévi-Strauss saw the nature-culture contrast as timeless and value free, MacCormack concluded that such ideas were culturally specific. She wrote:

> There is no way to absolutely verify that the nature-culture opposition exists as an essential feature of universal unconscious structure, and there is ethnographic evidence to suggest that in the form in which Europeans now conceive it, the contrast is not a universal feature of consciously-held folk models. (1980: 10)

To what degree was the concern with culture as superior to nature a product of the mid-twentieth century? Leslie White (see essay 16) imagined culture as conquering nature to make life secure for humankind. People of his era imagined domed cities where everything was controlled and built public buildings with small windows that couldn't be opened since they were confident that human-built environments were superior to natural ones. In a famous 1966 essay, historian Lynn White (1907–1987) proclaimed that the idea that humans must achieve dominion over nature was at the root of many of the world's evils. Is Lévi-Strauss's and Ortner's focus on nature-culture part of this same complex of ideas?

then, is that women are seen "merely" as being *closer* to nature than men. That is, culture (still equated relatively unambiguously with men) recognizes that women are active participants in its special processes, but at the same time sees them as being more rooted in, or having more direct affinity with, nature.

The revision may seem minor or even trivial, but I think it is a more accurate rendering of cultural assumptions. Further, the argument cast in these terms has several analytic advantages over the simpler formulation; I shall discuss these later. It might simply be stressed here that the revised argument would still account for the pan-cultural devaluation of women, for even if women are not equated with nature, they are nonetheless seen as representing a lower order of being, as being less transcendental of nature than men are. The next task of the paper, then, is to consider why they might be viewed in that way.[12]

WHY IS WOMAN SEEN AS CLOSER TO NATURE?

It all begins of course with the body and the natural procreative functions specific to women alone. We can sort out for discussion three levels at which this absolute physiological fact has significance: (1) woman's *body and its functions,* more involved more of the time with "species life," seem to place her closer to nature, in contrast to man's physiology, which frees him more completely to take up the projects of culture; (2) woman's body and its functions place her in *social roles* that in turn are considered to be at a lower order of the cultural process than man's; and (3) woman's traditional social roles, imposed because of her body and its functions, in turn give her a different *psychic structure,* which, like her physiological nature and her social roles, is seen as being closer to nature. I shall discuss each of these points in turn, showing first how in each instance certain factors strongly tend to align woman with nature, then indicating other factors that demonstrate her full alignment with culture, the combined factors thus placing her in a problematic intermediate position. It will become clear in the course of the discussion why men seem by contrast less intermediate, more purely "cultural" than women. And I reiterate that I am dealing only at the level of cultural and human universals. These arguments are intended to apply to generalized humanity; they grow out of the human condition, as humanity has experienced and confronted it up to the present day.

1. *Woman's physiology seen as closer to nature.* This part of my argument has been anticipated, with subtlety, cogency, and a great deal of hard data, by de Beauvoir (1953). De Beauvoir reviews the physiological structure, development, and functions of the human female and concludes that "the female, to a greater extent than the male, is the prey of the species" (p. 60). She points out that many major areas and processes of the woman's body serve no apparent function for the health and stability of the individual; on the contrary, as they perform their specific organic functions, they are often sources of discomfort, pain, and danger. The breasts are irrelevant to personal health; they may be excised at any time of a woman's life. "Many of the ovarian secretions function for the benefit of the egg, promoting its maturation and adapting the uterus to its requirements; in respect to the organism as a whole, they make for disequilibrium rather than for regulation—the woman is

---

12. Ortner's distinction between women as identified with nature and women as "merely" closer to nature is subtle and performs two tasks in this essay. First, it makes her case more compelling but less amenable to testing. If Ortner said that women were identified wholly with nature, one or two counterexamples could easily disprove her point. However, since she suggests that women are merely closer to nature than men, in every case where anthropologists find women associated with culture rather than nature, they must ask, "Well, are men even more associated with culture?" This is a difficult proposition to test. Second, it opens the possibility that women mediate between culture and nature. Recall that for Lévi-Strauss, the mediated binary is a unit of human thought. Humans, for reasons that are ultimately biological, tend to arrange the categories of their world into something, its opposite, and a third category that lies between and transcends these two. Things in the mediating third category tend to have a special status for good or ill.

adapted to the needs of the egg rather than to her own requirements" (p. 24). Menstruation is often uncomfortable, sometimes painful; it frequently has negative emotional correlates and in any case involves bothersome tasks of cleansing and waste disposal; and—a point that de Beauvoir does not mention—in many cultures it interrupts a woman's routine, putting her in a stigmatized state involving various restrictions on her activities and social contacts. In pregnancy many of the woman's vitamin and mineral resources are channeled into nourishing the fetus, depleting her own strength and energies. And finally, childbirth itself is painful and dangerous (pp. 24–27 *passim*). In sum, de Beauvoir concludes that the female "is more enslaved to the species than the male, her animality is more manifest" (p. 239).[13]

While de Beauvoir's book is ideological, her survey of woman's physiological situation seems fair and accurate. It is simply a fact that proportionately more of woman's body space, for a greater percentage of her lifetime, and at some—sometimes great—cost to her personal health, strength, and general stability, is taken up with the natural processes surrounding the reproduction of the species.

De Beauvoir goes on to discuss the negative implications of woman's "enslavement to the species" in relation to the projects in which humans engage, projects through which culture is generated and defined. She arrives thus at the crux of her argument (pp. 58–59):

> Here we have the key to the whole mystery. On the biological level a species is maintained only by creating itself anew; but this creation results only in repeating the same Life in more individuals. But man assures the repetition of Life while transcending

Life through Existence [i.e., goal-oriented, meaningful action]; by this transcendence he creates values that deprive pure repetition of all value. In the animal, the freedom and variety of male activities are vain because no project is involved. Except for his services to the species, what he does is immaterial. Whereas in serving the species, the human male also remodels the face of the earth, he creates new instruments, he invents, he shapes the future.

In other words, woman's body seems to doom her to mere reproduction of life; the male, in contrast, lacking natural creative functions, must (or has the opportunity to) assert his creativity externally, "artificially," through the medium of technology and symbols. In so doing, he creates relatively lasting, eternal, transcendent objects, while the woman creates only perishables—human beings.

This formulation opens up a number of important insights. It speaks, for example, to the great puzzle of why male activities involving the destruction of life (hunting and warfare) are often given more prestige than the female's ability to give birth, to create life. Within de Beauvoir's framework, we realize it is not the killing that is the relevant and valued aspect of hunting and warfare; rather, it is the transcendental (social, cultural) nature of these activities, as opposed to the naturalness of the process of birth: "For it is not in giving life but in risking life that man is raised above the animal; that is why superiority has been accorded in humanity not to the sex that brings forth but to that which kills" (ibid.).[14]

Thus if male is, as I am suggesting, everywhere (unconsciously) associated with culture and female seems closer to nature, the ratio-

---

13. Simone de Beauvoir (1908–1986) was a French existentialist author of plays, novels, and works of philosophy. She was the companion of the philosopher Jean-Paul Sartre (1905–1980). The reference is to her book *The Second Sex* (1952), which analyzes women's inferior positions in society. In *The Second Sex*, de Beauvoir used existential argument and ethnographic data to compare women to oppressed minorities. De Beauvoir cataloged women's biological differences but proposed that women's status was the result of social conditions and argued for complete equality. Today, *The Second Sex* is considered a fundamental document of feminism.

14. Pause for a moment to consider how counterintuitive de Beauvoir's ideas are. Is hunting valued because it is culturally transcendental or because it feeds people? Is hunting more cultural than gathering? Is warfare valued because it is cultural or for other reasons?

nale for these associations is not very difficult to grasp, merely from considering the implications of the physiological contrast between male and female. At the same time, however, woman cannot be consigned fully to the category of nature, for it is perfectly obvious that she is a full-fledged human being endowed with human consciousness just as a man is; she is half of the human race, without whose cooperation the whole enterprise would collapse. She may seem more in the possession of nature than man, but having consciousness, she thinks and speaks; she generates, communicates, and manipulates symbols, categories, and values. She participates in human dialogues not only with other women but also with men. As Lévi-Strauss says, "Woman could never become just a sign and nothing more, since even in a man's world she is still a person, and since insofar as she is defined as a sign she must [still] be recognized as a generator of signs" (1969a:496).[15]

Indeed, the fact of woman's full human consciousness, her full involvement in and commitment to culture's project of transcendence over nature, may ironically explain another of the great puzzles of "the woman problem"—woman's nearly universal unquestioning acceptance of her own devaluation. For it would seem that, as a conscious human and member of culture, she has followed out the logic of culture's arguments and has reached culture's conclusions along with the men. As de Beauvoir puts it (p. 59):

For she, too, is an existent, she feels the urge to surpass, and her project is not mere repetition but transcendence towards a different future—in her heart of hearts she finds confirmation of the masculine pretensions. She joins the men in the festivals that celebrate the successes and victories of the males. Her misfortune is to have been biologically destined for the repetition of Life, when even in her own view Life does not carry within itself its reasons for being, reasons that are more important than life itself.

In other words, woman's consciousness—her membership, as it were, in culture—is evidenced in part by the very fact that she accepts her own devaluation and takes culture's point of view.

I have tried here to show one part of the logic of that view, the part that grows directly from the physiological differences between men and women. Because of woman's greater bodily involvement with the natural functions surrounding reproduction, she is seen as more a part of nature than man is. Yet in part because of her consciousness and participation in human social dialogue, she is recognized as a participant in culture. Thus she appears as something intermediate between culture and nature, lower on the scale of transcendence than man.[16]

2. *Woman's social role seen as closer to nature.* Woman's physiological functions, I have argued, may tend in themselves to motivate[e] a view of woman as closer to nature, a view she herself, as an observer of herself and the world, would tend to agree with. Woman creates naturally from within her own being,

---

15. Lévi-Strauss's comments on women and signs are from his 1949 book *The Elementary Structures of Kinship*. There, he uses the notion of sign taken from the turn-of-the-century Swiss structural linguist Ferdinand de Saussure (1857–1913). Contrary to the popular views of his time, Saussure argued that the meanings of the majority of words in a language are derived from the arbitrary association of sound and meaning. Each idea in a language is arbitrarily associated with a set of sounds. The sounds, Saussure called the *signifier*; the associated idea, the *signified*. Together they form, in Saussure's terminology, a linguistic *sign*.

16. Although Lévi-Strauss proposed that human thinking always parsed the world into binary oppositions, he also believed that the mind was dissatisfied with such oppositions and always searched for a mediator for them. This mediator was a category that was not subsumed by either part of the binary but somehow transcended them. He argued that the mediator was always problematic. It was privileged, special, or ambiguous. In positioning women as "merely" closer to nature than men, and in insisting that women, while identified with nature, are in truth part of society's cultural project, Ortner is beginning to build a case that women are the mediating element in the culture-nature binary.

whereas man is free to, or forced to, create artificially, that is, through cultural means, and in such a way as to sustain culture. In addition, I now wish to show how woman's physiological functions have tended universally to limit her social movement, and to confine her universally to certain social contexts which *in turn* are seen as closer to nature. That is, not only her bodily processes but the social situation in which her bodily processes locate her may carry this significance. And insofar as she is permanently associated (in the eyes of culture) with these social milieux, they add weight (perhaps the decisive part of the burden) to the view of woman as closer to nature. I refer here of course to woman's confinement to the domestic family context, a confinement motivated, no doubt, by her lactation processes.

Woman's body, like that of all female mammals, generates milk during and after pregnancy for the feeding of the newborn baby. The baby cannot survive without breast milk or some similar formula at this stage of life. Since the mother's body goes through its lactation processes in direct relation to a pregnancy with a particular child, the relationship of nursing between mother and child is seen as a natural bond, other feeding arrangements being seen in most cases as unnatural and makeshift. Mothers and their children, according to cultural reasoning, belong together. Further, children beyond infancy are not strong enough to engage in major work, yet are mobile and unruly and not capable of understanding various dangers; they thus require supervision and constant care. Mother is the obvious person for this task, as an extension of her natural nursing bond with the children, or because she has a new infant and is already involved with child-oriented activities. Her own activities are

thus circumscribed by the limitations and low levels of her children's strengths and skills:[f] she is confined to the domestic family group; "woman's place is in the home."[17]

Woman's association with the domestic circle would contribute to the view of her as closer to nature in several ways. In the first place, the sheer fact of constant association with children plays a role in the issue; one can easily see how infants and children might themselves be considered part of nature. Infants are barely human and utterly unsocialized; like animals they are unable to walk upright, they excrete without control, they do not speak. Even slightly older children are clearly not yet fully under the sway of culture. They do not yet understand social duties, responsibilities, and morals; their vocabulary and their range of learned skills are small. One finds implicit recognition of an association between children and nature in many cultural practices. For example, most cultures have initiation rites for adolescents (primarily for boys; I shall return to this point below), the point of which is to move the child ritually from a less than fully human state into full participation in society and culture; many cultures do not hold funeral rites for children who die at early ages, explicitly because they are not yet fully social beings. Thus children are likely to be categorized with nature, and woman's close association with children may compound her potential for being seen as closer to nature herself. It is ironic that the rationale for boys' initiation rites in many cultures is that the boys must be purged of the defilement accrued from being around mother and other women so much of the time, when in fact much of the woman's defilement may derive from her being around children so much of the time.[18]

---

17. Ortner, like all authors, writes within a historical and political context. Her remarks on mother-child bonds and mothers' nursing are an interesting reflection of this. American middle-class women "rediscovered" breastfeeding in the 1970s. Nursing became part of a political movement that included campaigns against corporations such as Nestlé, which sold infant formula, especially in poor nations. There was also much popular writing on the importance of mother-infant bonding.

18. Ortner has constructed an elegant argument, but like Lévi-Strauss before her, she has based her logic on a set of unproven assumptions. Why, for example, is the link between women and nature assumed as fact? As she herself states, women socialize children into cultural beings and turn raw substances into edible meals. So why are women not closer to culture? She answers by saying that socialization activities are

The second major problematic implication of women's close association with the domestic context derives from certain structural conflicts between the family and society at large in any social system. The implications of the "domestic/public opposition" in relation to the position of women have been cogently developed by Rosaldo (1974), and I simply wish to show its relevance to the present argument. The notion that the domestic unit—the biological family charged with reproducing and socializing new members of the society—is opposed to the public entity—the superimposed network of alliances and relationships that is the society—is also the basis of Lévi-Strauss's argument in the *Elementary Structures of Kinship* (1969a). Lévi-Strauss argues not only that this opposition is present in every social system, but further that it has the significance of the opposition between nature and culture. The universal incest prohibition[g] and its ally, the rule of exogamy (marriage outside the group), ensure that "the risk of seeing a biological family become established as a closed system is definitely eliminated; the biological group can no longer stand apart, and the bond of alliance with another family ensures the dominance of the social over the biological, and of the cultural over the natural" (p. 479). And although not every culture articulates a radical opposition between the domestic and the public as such, it is hardly contestable that the domestic is always subsumed by the public; domestic units are allied with one another through the enactment of rules that are logically at a higher level than the units themselves; this creates an emergent unit—society—that is logically at a higher level than the domestic units of which it is composed.[19]

Now, since women are associated with, and indeed are more or less confined to, the domestic context, they are identified with this lower order of social/cultural organization. What are the implications of this for the way they are viewed? First, if the specifically biological (reproductive) function of the family is stressed, as in Lévi-Strauss's formulation, then the family (and hence woman) is identified with nature pure and simple, as opposed to culture. But this is obviously too simple; the point seems more adequately formulated as follows: the family (and hence woman) represents lower-level, socially fragmenting, particularistic sort of concerns, as opposed to interfamilial relations representing higher-level, integrative, universalistic sorts of concerns. Since men lack a "natural" basis (nursing, generalized to child care) for a familial orientation, their sphere of activity is defined at the level of interfamilial relations. And hence, so the cultural reasoning seems to go, men are the "natural" proprietors of religion, ritual, politics, and other realms of cultural thought and action in which universalistic statements of spiritual and social synthesis are made. Thus men are identified not only with culture, in the sense of all human creativity, as opposed to nature; they are identified in particular with culture in the old-fashioned sense of the finer and higher aspects of human thought—art, religion, law, etc.[20]

---

taken over by men in adolescence. But why should this time period be inherently more important than earlier childhood in determining the relation of men and women to culture? Ortner takes up the ambiguity of identifying particular actions with culture or nature below.

19. Ortner is referring here to Lévi-Strauss's contention that one of the most basic of binary oppositions is between us and them, kin and non-kin. This relates to the nature-culture opposition because of the universal rules of incest.

Ortner mentions Michelle Rosaldo's (1944–1981) article on gender inequality. There, Rosaldo presented a structuralist argument, but one that relied on a sociocultural rather than a biological explanation. She focused on the domestic-public opposition between men and women. She argued that men are typically associated with higher-prestige public activities, while women, because they raise children, are limited to less prestigious domestic tasks.

Michelle Rosaldo, the wife of Renato Rosaldo, died in an accident during field research in October 1981. Renato Rosaldo's attempt to deal with his wife's death forms the core of his essay "Grief and a Headhunter's Rage" (essay 29).

20. When Ortner talks of culture in the old-fashioned sense, she is referring to Tylor's nineteenth-century definition of culture (arts, laws, morals, etc.; see essay 2) as opposed to a Boasian notion of culture.

Here again, the logic of cultural reasoning aligning woman with a lower order of culture than man is clear and, on the surface, quite compelling. At the same time, woman cannot be fully consigned to nature, for there are aspects of her situation, even within the domestic context, that undeniably demonstrate her participation in the cultural process. It goes without saying, of course, that except for nursing newborn infants (and artificial nursing devices can cut even this biological tie), there is no reason why it has to be mother—as opposed to father, or anyone else—who remains identified with child care. But even assuming that other practical and emotional reasons conspire to keep woman in this sphere, it is possible to show that her activities in the domestic context could as logically put her squarely in the category of culture.

In the first place, one must point out that woman not only feeds and cleans up after children in a simple caretaker operation; she in fact is the primary agent of their early socialization. It is she who transforms newborn infants from mere organisms into cultured humans, teaching them manners and the proper ways to behave in order to become full-fledged members of the culture. On the basis of her socializing functions alone, she could not be more a representative of culture. Yet in virtually every society there is a point at which the socialization of boys is transferred to the hands of men. The boys are considered, in one set of terms or another, not yet "really" socialized; their entree into the realm of fully human (social, cultural) status can be accomplished only by men. We still see this in our own schools, where there is a gradual inversion in the proportion of female to male teachers up through the grades: most kindergarten teachers are female; most university professors are male.[h]

Or again, take cooking. In the overwhelming majority of societies cooking is the woman's work. No doubt this stems from practical considerations—since the woman has to stay home with the baby, it is convenient for her to perform the chores centered in the home. But if it is true, as Lévi-Strauss has argued (1969b), that transforming the raw into the cooked may represent, in many systems of thought, the transition from nature to culture, then here we have woman aligned with this important culturalizing process, which could easily place her in the category of culture, triumphing over nature. Yet it is also interesting to note that when a culture (e.g., France or China) develops a tradition of *haute cuisine*—"real" cooking, as opposed to trivial ordinary domestic cooking—the high chefs are almost always men. Thus the pattern replicates that in the area of socialization—women perform lower-level conversions from nature to culture, but when the culture distinguishes a higher level of the same functions, the higher level is restricted to men.

In short, we see once again some sources of woman's appearing more intermediate than man with respect to the nature/culture dichotomy. Her "natural" association with the domestic context (motivated by her natural lactation functions) tends to compound her potential for being viewed as closer to nature, because of the animal-like nature of children, and because of the **infrasocial** connotation of the domestic group as against the rest of society. Yet at the same time her socializing and cooking functions within the domestic context show her to be a powerful agent of the cultural process, constantly transforming raw natural resources into cultural products. Belonging to culture, yet appearing to have stronger and more direct connections with nature, she is once again seen as situated between the two realms.[21]

[*We have omitted most of the last two sections of Ortner's article, about 3,000 words, called "Woman's Psyche Seen as Closer to Nature" and "The Implications of Intermediacy." In the first section she argues that women not only have a different body and a different social importance than men but also a different psychic structure. To support this view, she relies mainly on an argument developed by the sociologist Nancy Chodorow (b. 1944) (1974), who claimed that men are more objective than women and communicate in terms of relatively abstract categories whereas women are subjective and relate in terms of relatively concrete phenomena. She argued that these differences are not innate but happen because "women, universally, are largely*

---

21. **"Infrasocial"**: below the level of society, solitary.

responsible for early care and for (at least) later female socialization" (1974:43).

The last section, "The Implications of Intermediacy," summarizes the essay's main points and discusses the implications of women's mediation between nature and culture. Ortner says that women are universally seen as occupying a middle status on a hierarchy of being from culture to nature. As a result, they are lower than men and less capable of achieving transcendence of nature. Ortner believes that this position assigns them greater symbolic ambiguity. She says,

"Thus we can account easily for both the subversive feminine symbols (witches, evil eye, menstrual pollution, castrating mothers) and the feminine symbols of transcendence (mother goddesses, merciful dispensers of salvation, female symbols of justice, and the strong presence of feminine symbolism in the realms of art, religion, ritual, and law). Feminine symbolism, far more often than masculine symbolism, manifests this propensity toward polarized ambiguity—sometimes utterly exalted, sometimes utterly debased, rarely within the normal range of human possibilities."

Ortner concludes this section as follows:]

In short, the postulate that woman is viewed as closer to nature than man has several implications for further analysis, and can be interpreted in several different ways. If it is viewed simply as a *middle* position on a scale from culture down to nature, then it is still seen as lower than culture and thus accounts for the pan-cultural assumption that woman is lower than man in the order of things. If it is read as a *mediating* element in the culture-nature relationship, then it may account in part for the cultural tendency not merely to devalue woman but to circumscribe and restrict her functions, since culture must maintain control over its (pragmatic and symbolic) mechanisms for the conversion of nature into culture. And if it is read as an *ambiguous* status between culture and nature, it may help account for the fact that, in specific cultural ideologies and symbolizations, woman can occasionally be aligned with culture, and in any event is often

assigned polarized and contradictory meanings within a single symbolic system. Middle status, mediating functions, ambiguous meaning—all are different readings, for different contextual purposes, of woman's being seen as intermediate between nature and culture.

CONCLUSIONS

Ultimately, it must be stressed again that the whole scheme is a construct of culture rather than a fact of nature. Woman is not "in reality" any closer to (or further from) nature than man—both have consciousness, both are mortal. But there are certainly reasons why she appears that way, which is what I have tried to show in this paper. The result is a (sadly) efficient feedback system: various aspects of woman's situation (physical, social, psychological) contribute to her being seen as closer to nature, while the view of her as closer to nature is in turn embodied in institutional forms that reproduce her situation. The implications for social change are similarly circular: a different cultural view can only grow out of a different social actuality; a different social actuality can only grow out of a different cultural view.

It is clear, then, that the situation must be attacked from both sides. Efforts directed solely at changing the social institutions—through setting quotas on hiring, for example, or through passing equal-pay-for-equal-work laws—cannot have far-reaching effects if cultural language and imagery continue to purvey a relatively devalued view of women. But at the same time efforts directed solely at changing cultural assumptions—through male and female consciousness-raising groups, for example, or through revision of educational materials and mass-media imagery—cannot be successful unless the institutional base of the society is changed to support and reinforce the changed cultural view. Ultimately, both men and women can and must be equally involved in projects of creativity and transcendence. Only then will women be seen as aligned with culture, in culture's ongoing dialectic with nature.[22]

---

22. In the final paragraph, Ortner seems to be caught on the horns of a dilemma. She advocates political action to end what she considers the universal subordination of women but cannot accommodate this notion within structuralism. Structuralism is designed to find consistencies within different cultures in order

REFERENCES

Carlson, Rae. 1971. "Sex Differences in Ego Functioning: Exploratory Studies of Agency and Communion," *Journal of Consulting and Clinical Psychology* 37:267–277.

De Beauvoir, Simone. 1953. *The Second Sex.* New York.

Lévi-Strauss, Claude. 1969a. *The Elementary Structures of Kinship.* Trans. J. H. Bell and J. R. von Sturmer; ed. R. Needham. Boston.

———. 1969b. *The Raw and the Cooked.* Trans. J. and D. Weightman. New York.

Lowie, Robert. 1956. *The Crow Indians.* New York. Originally published in 1935.

Ortner, Sherry B. 1973. "Sherpa Purity," *American Anthropologist* 75:49–63.

———. N.d. "Purification Beliefs and Practices." *Encyclopedia Britannica,* forthcoming.

Pitt-Rivers, Julian. 1961. *People of the Sierra.* Chicago.

Rosaldo, Michelle. 1974. "Women, Culture, and Society: A Theoretical Overview." In *Women, Culture, and Society,* ed. Michelle Rosaldo and Louise Lamphere, 14–42. Palo Alto, CA: Stanford University Press.

Siu, R. G. H. 1968. *The Man of Many Qualities.* Cambridge, MA.

Ullman, Stephen. 1963. "Semantic Universals." In *Universals of Language,* ed. Joseph H. Greenberg. Cambridge, MA (1952).

Author's Notes

The first version of this paper was presented in October 1972 as a lecture in the course "Women: Myth and Reality" at Sarah Lawrence College. I received helpful comments from the students and from my co-teachers in the course: Joan Kelly Gadol, Eva Kollisch, and Gerda Lerner. A short account was delivered at the American Anthropological Association meetings in Toronto, November 1972. Meanwhile, I received excellent critical comments from Karen Blu, Robert Paul, Michelle Rosaldo, David Schneider, and Terence Turner, and the present version of the paper, in which the thrust of the argument has been rather significantly changed, was written in response to those comments.

I, of course, retain responsibility for its final form. The paper is dedicated to Simone de Beauvoir, whose book *The Second Sex* (1953), first published in French in 1949, remains in my opinion the best single comprehensive understanding of "the woman problem."

a. It is true of course that *yin,* the female principle, has a negative valence. Nonetheless, there is an absolute complementarity of *yin* and *yang* in Taoism, a recognition that the world requires the equal operation and interaction of both principles for its survival.

b. Some anthropologists might consider this type of evidence (social-structural arrangements that exclude women, explicitly or de facto, from certain groups, roles, or statuses) to be a subtype of the second type of evidence (symbolic formulations of inferiority). I would not disagree with this view, although most social anthropologists would probably separate the two types.

c. While we are on the subject of injustices of various kinds, we might note that Lowie secretly bought this doll, the most sacred object in the tribal repertoire, from its custodian, the widow of Wrinkled-face. She asked $400 for it, but this price was "far beyond [Lowie's] means," and he finally got it for $80 (p. 300).

d. With all due respect to Lévi-Strauss (1969a, b, and *passim*).

e. Semantic theory uses the concept of motivation of meaning, which encompasses various ways in which a meaning may be assigned to a symbol because of certain objective properties of that symbol, rather than by arbitrary association. In a sense, this entire paper is an inquiry into the motivation of the meaning of woman as a symbol, asking why woman may be unconsciously assigned the significance of being closer to nature. For a concise statement on the various types of motivation of meaning, see Ullman (1963).

f. A situation that often serves to make her more childlike herself.

g. David M. Schneider (personal communication) is prepared to argue that the incest taboo is not universal, on the basis of material from Oceania. Let us say at this point, then, that it is virtually universal.

h. I remember having my first male teacher in the fifth grade, and I remember being excited about that—it was somehow more grown up.

to reconstruct fundamental patterns of human thought. Because of this, culture change is irrelevant in a structuralist analysis. Additionally, Ortner has located the source of female oppression in the fact that members of societies universally parse their worlds into nature and culture and universally assign women to a mediating category between them. One can easily imagine political action designed to improve the conditions of women in a society, but how does one change a culturally universal pattern of thought?

PART IV

Late-Twentieth-Century Developments

Feminist Anthropology

Anthropology has long been a male-dominated field. In 1900, Franz Boas at Columbia and Frederic W. Putnam at Harvard were among the very few anthropology professors accepting women graduate students. However, from this inauspicious beginning, women in anthropology quickly reached high levels of professional achievement and gained popular recognition for their work. In the twentieth century, women such as Ruth Benedict and Margaret Mead became household names. Many others, including Mary Douglas (1921–2007), Laura Bohannan (1922–2002), Sherry Ortner (b. 1941), Michelle Rosaldo (1944–1981), Peggy Reeves Sanday (b. 1937), Louise Lamphere (b. 1940), Lila Abu-Lughod (b. 1952), Marilyn Strathern (b. 1941), and Nancy Scheper-Hughes (b. 1944), are widely known to scholars outside of anthropology.

Despite the achievements of women within anthropology, as Lamphere (2004: 127) notes, even such seminal figures as Mead, Benedict, and Elsie Clews Parsons (1875–1941) were marginalized, pigeonholed, and excluded from important aspects of the discipline. Until the mid-twentieth century, discussions of women in the anthropological literature were usually limited to introductory textbook chapters on marriage, family, and kinship. In the 1960s and 1970s, this situation began to change.

In the United States, it is common, if somewhat contentious, to speak of feminism as a series of waves, an idea credited to Martha Weinman Lear (b. 1932). The first wave of feminism was the period beginning in the nineteenth century and ending with the achievement of certain aspects of legal equality, such as voting rights. The modern feminist movement in anthropology had its beginnings in the second wave of feminism that accompanied the social upheavals of the 1960s—the civil rights movement, anti–Vietnam War activism, and various consciousness-raising experiments. By the early 1970s, women anthropologists were documenting the discipline's neglect of women and questioning anthropological assumptions they considered male centered. They increasingly focused their research on recording women's lives and their roles in societies around the world.

Virtually all studies of women of this era assumed that women played a subordinate role in almost every society. They attempted to analyze this situation using various theoretical perspectives. For example, Ernestine Friedl (1920–2015) endeavored to explain the position of women from a materialist perspective by focusing on women's subsistence roles (1975). Nancy Chodorow (b. 1944) examined the issue of subordination from a psychological view, emphasizing the role of childhood socialization in the formation of sex roles (1974). M. Rosaldo and Lamphere's 1974 volume *Women, Culture, and Society* and Reyna Reiter's 1975 anthology *Toward an Anthropology of Women*, both collections of essays from a variety of feminist thinkers, were two of the defining works in this era of feminist anthropology.

At the same time that feminist cultural anthropologists focused on gender inequality, research on women and gender by feminist archaeologists and physical anthropologists challenged the "man the hunter" version of human evolution. The 1975 essay by Sally Slocum (b. 1939) is a good example of this. Slocum is in many ways the most unusual scholar represented in this volume. She wrote the essay printed here while she was a graduate student at the University of Colorado. She finished her PhD and taught for a time at the University of Montana, then later at the University of Nevada, Las Vegas, and at various community colleges. However, she spent most of her career working with charitable organizations and, from 1985 to 1997, as a Foreign Service officer for the US Department of State. Other unusual aspects of her career include work as an exotic dancer (she presented a paper on her experiences at the American Anthropological Association meeting in 1975 [Associated Press and *Daytona Beach Morning Journal*, December 9, 1975]), in a plywood mill, and playing oboe in two symphony orchestras.

In essay 22, Slocum charges that women's roles in human evolution have been ignored because scholars focused on hunting rather than gathering. For instance, she challenges the popular idea that hunting by men, because it implied tool making, communication, and the development of complex cognitive skills (Washburn and Lancaster 1968), played a pivotal role in our evolutionary past. She stresses that women's gathering and child care also demanded complex communication, cooperation, and tool making. Slocum argues that evidence indicates foraging, not hunting, was the principal economic strategy throughout most of human evolutionary history. This "woman the gatherer" approach inspired scholars to reexamine human evolution. Most current reconstructions of human evolution give a more prominent place to women.

The materialist perspective was another prominent direction in gender research. Materialist scholars used cross-cultural analysis to explain differences in the roles and power of different gender groups. They concentrated on research that analyzed gender-related activities using measures of social, economic, and political power (Morgen 1989: 4). Many scholars in this area focused on gender as it relates to class, the social relations of power, and changes in modes of production. The work of Eleanor Leacock (1922–1987) in essay 23 fits this category of study. Leacock was the daughter of the literary theorist Kenneth D. Burke (1897–1993). Burke, influenced by Karl Marx, developed a critical technique of analysis he called "dramatism." Burke wrote: "If *action* then *drama*. . . . But if *drama*, then *conflict*. And if *conflict*, then *victimage*" (1989: 125). His daughter absorbed lessons such as this. Leacock received her doctorate from Columbia University in 1952. She was part of the same group of scholars that included Eric Wolf (1923–1999), Sidney Mintz (1922–2015), and numerous others who were deeply influenced by Marx and by the work of Julian Steward. Because she was a political radical and a woman, Leacock struggled to get support as a graduate student, and it took her eleven years to get her first full-time teaching job. However, she was ultimately very successful, working first at Brooklyn Polytechnical Institute and then, from 1972 until her death, chairing the anthropology department at the City University of New York. There she worked particularly with her colleague June Nash (1927–2019) to revitalize Marxist anthropology. Leacock published ten books and eighty-one articles and became one of the foremost interpreters of Marx of her generation. She is particularly remembered for her 1972 edition of *Origin of the Family, Private Property, and the State* by Friedrich Engels (1820–1895).

The essay selected for this volume first appeared in 1983; in it, Leacock claims that prior to Western contact, gender relations in Native American and Australian Aboriginal societies were typically egalitarian because men and women participated equally in the processes of production. She argues that the unequal place of women in these societies today is the result of the subjugation of these societies by Europeans and the imposition of capitalist forms of production.

Feminist anthropology and women's studies in general gained strength at universities through the 1980s. However, in the 1990s, the field began to change. The tendency of the 1970s and 1980s was for scholars to view all women as somewhat similar and differentiate them from all men. However, in the 1990s, the paradigm shifted, and scholars began to focus on different understandings of gender, on the ways that these were enacted in different societies, and the effects this had on ideas of personhood.

SUGGESTED READINGS

Babb, Florence E. 2013. "Feminist Anthropology." In *Theory in Social and Cultural Anthropology: An Encyclopedia*, ed. R. Jon McGee and Richard L. Warms, 258–262. Los Angeles, CA: Sage.
    A brief overview of the development of feminist anthropology.
Behar, Ruth, and Gordon D. Behar, eds. 1995. *Women Writing Culture*. Berkeley: University of California Press.
    A collection of essays by feminist scholars that explore new forms of ethnography and challenge the prevailing forms of male-biased anthropology.

Di Leonardo, M., ed. 1991. *Gender at the Crossroads of Knowledge: Feminist Anthropology in the Postmodern Era.* Berkeley: University of California Press.

A collection of feminist contributions to a wide range of anthropological concerns, including biological anthropology, political economy, reproductive technologies, race, and gender.

Lewin, Ellen. 2006. *Feminist Anthropology: A Reader.* Hoboken, NJ: Wiley.

A survey of the history of feminist anthropology using a wide range of classic and recent feminist ethnography.

Reiter, Rayna R., ed. 1975. *Toward an Anthropology of Women.* New York: Monthly Review Press.

An anthology of essays examining gender inequality from a variety of theoretical perspectives.

22. Woman the Gatherer: Male Bias in Anthropology

Sally Slocum (b. 1939)

LITTLE SYSTEMATIC attention has been given in our discipline to an "anthropology of knowledge." While some anthropologists have concerned themselves with knowledge in general, as seen through the varieties of human cultures, few have examined anthropological knowledge itself. An anthropology of knowledge would have several parts. First is what Peter Berger (1967: 1–18) has called "philosophical anthropology": a study of the nature of the human species. This has always been a legitimate concern of anthropology, but too often we become so concerned with minute differences that we forget we are studying a single species. Second is how we "know" anything—what is accepted as "proof," what is reality, what are the grounds for rationality (Garfinkel 1960), what modes are used in gathering knowledge, what are the effects of differences in culture and world view on what we "know." Third is a close examination of the questions asked in anthropology, for questions always determine and limit answers.[1]

It is the third point, the nature of anthropological questions, to which I wish to speak in this paper. We are human beings studying other human beings, and we cannot leave ourselves out of the equation. We choose to ask certain questions, *and not others*. Our choice grows out of the cultural context in which anthropology and anthropologists exist. Anthropology, as an academic discipline, has been developed primarily by white Western males, during a specific period in history. Our questions are shaped by the particulars of our historical situation, and by unconscious cultural assumptions.[2]

Given the cultural and ethnic background of the majority of anthropologists, it is not surprising that the discipline has been biased. There are signs, however, that this selective blindness is beginning to come under scrutiny. For example, in the exchange in the journal *Current Anthropology* (1968), anthropologists like Kathleen Gough and Gerald Berreman point out the unconscious efforts of American political and economic assumptions on our selection of problems and populations to be studied. Restive minority groups in this country are pointing to the bias inherent in anthropological studies of themselves through books such as Vine Deloria's *Custer Died for Your Sins*. We have always encouraged members of American minority groups, and other "foreigners," to take

From *Toward an Anthropology of Women* (1975)

1. The 1960s and 1970s were an era of radical rethinking within anthropology, with many strands contributing to a broad critique of positivist anthropology. The feminist critique was one of the most powerful since it attacked what feminists viewed as fundamental biases in a field that prided itself on being relatively bias free. This essay is taken from *Toward an Anthropology of Women*, edited by Rayna Reiter (the pen name of Rayna Rapp, b. 1946), one of several groundbreaking anthologies of feminist essays in anthropology to appear in the 1970s.

2. Anthropology is generally done by college-educated Americans and Europeans who have had a specific kind of training. At the time Slocum wrote this essay, most anthropologists were men. One of the key philosophical questions of anthropology from the 1970s to the current day is whether the fact that anthropology is done by a specific group of people with specific backgrounds fundamentally prejudices its results. Feminists were among the first to pose the question in these terms, as Slocum does in this second paragraph.

up anthropology because of the perspective on the world that they can supply. The invitation is increasingly being accepted. As we had both hoped and feared, repercussions from this new participation are being felt in theory, method, interpretation, and problem choice, shaking anthropology to the roots.[3]

The perspective of women is, in many ways, equally foreign to an anthropology that has been developed and pursued primarily by males. There is a strong male bias in the questions asked, and the interpretations given. This bias has hindered the full development of our discipline as "the study of the human animal" (I don't want to call it "the study of man" for reasons that will become evident). I am going to demonstrate the Western male bias by reexamining the matter of evolution of Homo sapiens from our nonhuman primate ancestors. In particular, the concept of "Man the Hunter" as developed by Sherwood Washburn and C. Lancaster (1968) and others is my focus. This critique is offered in hopes of transcending the male bias that limits our knowledge by limiting the questions we ask.[4]

Though male bias could be shown in other areas, hominid evolution is particularly convenient for my purpose because it involves speculations and inferences from a rather small amount of data. In such a case, hidden assumptions and premises that lie behind the speculations and inferences are more easily demonstrated. Male bias exists not only in the ways in which the scanty data are interpreted,

but in the very language used. All too often the word "man" is used in such an ambiguous fashion that it is impossible to decide whether it refers to males or to the human species in general, including both males and females. In fact, one frequently is led to suspect that in the minds of many anthropologists, "man," supposedly meaning the human species, is actually exactly synonymous with "males."

This ambiguous use of language is particularly evident in the writing that surrounds the concept of Man the Hunter. Washburn and Lancaster make it clear that it is specifically males who hunt, that hunting is much more than simply an economic activity, and that most of the characteristics which we think of as specifically human can be causally related to hunting. They tell us that hunting is a whole pattern of activity and way of life: "The biology, psychology, and customs that separate us from the apes—all these we owe to the hunters of time past" (1968: 303). If this line of reasoning is followed to its logical conclusion, one must agree with Jane Kephart when she says

> Since only males hunt, and the psychology of the species was set by hunting, we are forced to conclude that females are scarcely human, that is, do not have built-in the basic psychology of the species: to kill and hunt and ultimately to kill others of the same species. The argument implies built-in aggression in human males, as well as the assumed passivity of human females

---

3. The feminist critique was part of a broader revision of the social sciences and humanities that has continued in American intellectual culture. This change was powerfully influenced by popular politics, especially the civil rights and women's movements of the 1960s. Several books aimed at popular rather than scholarly audiences were crucial. These included Vine Deloria's *Custer Died for Your Sins* (1969), Dee Brown's *Bury My Heart at Wounded Knee* (1971), and David Wallechinsky and Irving Wallace's *The People's Almanac* (1975). All became best sellers. *Bury My Heart*, first published in January 1971, went through thirteen printings by October of that year.

4. It may seem curious that anthropology should be accused of male bias. After all, several key early figures in anthropology had been women, and the best-known anthropologist in America in the 1960s was Margaret Mead. However, statistically, anthropology was overwhelmingly dominated by men. Mead, Benedict, and other prominent women in anthropology were systematically discriminated against in their careers. Moreover, the topics anthropologists frequently considered most worthy of study such as politics, warfare, and religion tended to be dominated by men. Studies of activities dominated by women such as child-rearing tended to be rarer.

and their exclusion from the mainstream of human development. (1970: 5)[5]

To support their argument that hunting is important to human males, Washburn and Lancaster point to the fact that many modern males still hunt, though it is no longer economically necessary. I could point out that many modern males play golf, play the violin, or tend gardens: these, as well as hunting, are things their culture teaches them. Using a "survival" as evidence to demonstrate an important fact of cultural evolution can be accorded no more validity when proposed by a modern anthropologist than when proposed by Tylor.

Regardless of its status as a survival, hunting, by implication as well as direct statement, is pictured as a male activity to the exclusion of females. This activity, on which we are told depends the psychology, biology, and customs of our species, is strictly male. A theory that leaves out half the human species is unbalanced. The theory of Man the Hunter is not only unbalanced; it leads to the conclusion that the basic human adaptation was the desire of males to hunt and kill. This not only gives too much importance to aggression, which is after all only one factor of human life, but it derives culture from killing.

I am going to suggest a less biased reading of the evidence, which gives a more valid and logical picture of human evolution, and at the same time a more hopeful one. First I will note the evidence, discuss the more traditional reading of it, and then offer an alternative reconstruction.[6]

The data we have to work from are a combination of fossil and archaeological materials, knowledge of living nonhuman primates, and knowledge of living humans. Since we assume that the proto-hominid ancestors of Homo sapiens developed in a continuous fashion from a base of characteristics similar to those of living nonhuman primates, the most import-

---

5. The feminist critique of the specific language used by anthropologists was particularly powerful because it referenced the Sapir-Whorf hypothesis that language shaped worldview (see Whorf, essay 13, particularly note 29).

The idea of primitive "man" and "man" the hunter was a particularly apt target. Sherwood Washburn (1911–2000) and Chet Lancaster theorized that hunting was the most critical activity for early humans and that the most important human adaptations, bipedalism and language, arose as a result of it. This idea found its way into popular culture. However, research on hunter-gatherers in the 1960s demonstrated that hunting by males played a relatively small role in supplying the nutritional needs of people in those communities. Thus, doubt was cast on the evolutionary primacy of hunting.

6. In addition to Washburn and Lancaster, popular thinking in ethology and evolution in the 1960s gave a very important place to aggression. *On Aggression* (1966) by ethologist Konrad Lorenz (1903–1989) and *African Genesis* (1961) by Robert Ardrey (1908–1980) were popular works that promoted this viewpoint. They argued for the primacy of hunting and aggression in the evolutionary formation of humanity and more or less ignored the role played by women.

It is interesting to note that most of the primate ethology of the 1960s, particularly that on which Ardrey's popular works were based, was fundamentally flawed. It was derived largely from the work of Raymond Dart (1893–1988) and Sir Solly Zuckerman (1904–1993). Dart, an Australian, was an anatomy professor and fossil hunter who is most famous for his part in the discovery of the first fossils of *Australopithecus africanus*. On the basis of minimal evidence (damaged fossil bones), Dart proposed the "killer ape" hypothesis, that aggression was a driving force in early hominid evolution. This idea was later developed and popularized by Robert Ardrey in *African Genesis*.

Zuckerman studied medicine at the University of Cape Town, in South Africa (Dart was one of his professors), and his first position was as a research anatomist at the London Zoological Society. Zuckerman drew his conclusions from watching an artificially assembled colony of Hamadryas baboons in the London Zoo in the 1920s. However, the behavior of these animals in the wild is different from the high levels of aggression shown by the more than 100 baboons crowded together on the London Zoo's "monkey hill," a 60 by 100 foot oval with a central rockwork surrounded by a deep mote (https://zoologyweblog.blogspot.com/2016/05/london-zoos-monkey-hill-1925-1955.html). As a result, Zuckerman greatly overestimated the role of aggression among baboons.

ant facts seem to be the ways in which humans differ from nonhuman primates, and the ways in which we are similar. The differences are as follows: longer gestation period; more difficult birth; neoteny, in that human infants are less well developed at birth; long period of infant dependency; absence of body hair; year-round sexual receptivity of females, resulting in the possibility of bearing a second infant while the first is still at the breast or still dependent; erect bipedalism; possession of a large and complex brain that makes possible the creation of elaborate symbolic systems, languages, and cultures, and also results in most behavior being under cortical control; food sharing; and finally, living in families. (For the purposes of this paper I define families as follows: a situation where each individual has defined responsibilities and obligations to a specific set of others of both sexes and various ages. I use this definition because, among humans, the family is a *social* unit, regardless of any biological or genetic relationship which may or may not exist among its members.)[7]

In addition to the many well-known close physiological resemblances, we share with nonhuman primates the following characteristics: living in social groups; close mother-infant bonds; affectional relationships; a large capacity for learning and a related paucity of innate behaviors; ability to take part in dominance hierarchies; a rather complex nonsymbolic communication system which can handle with considerable subtlety such information as the mood and emotional state of the individual, and the attitude and status of each individual toward the other members of the social group. The fossil and archaeological evidence consists of various bones labeled Ramapithecus, Aus-

tralopithecus, Homo habilis, Homo erectus, etc.; and artifacts such as stone tools representing various cultural traditions, evidence of use of fire, etc. From this evidence we can make reasonable inferences about diet, posture and locomotion, and changes in the brain as shown by increased cranial capacity, ability to make tools, and other evidences of cultural creation. Since we assume that complexity of material culture requires language, we infer the beginnings of language somewhere between Australopithecus and Homo erectus.

Given this data, the speculative reconstruction begins. As I was taught anthropology, the story goes something like this. Obscure selection pressures pushed the protohominid in the direction of erect bipedalism—perhaps the advantages of freeing the hands for food carrying or for tool use. Freeing the hands allowed more manipulation of the environment in the direction of tools for gathering and hunting food. Through a hand-eye-brain feedback process, coordination, efficiency, and skill were increased. The new behavior was adaptive, and selection pressure pushed the protohominid further along the same lines of development. Diet changed as the increase in skill allowed the addition of more animal protein. Larger brains were selected for, making possible transmission of information concerned with tool making, and organizing cooperative hunting. It is assumed that as increased brain size was selected for, so also was neoteny—immaturity of infants at birth with a corresponding increase in their period of dependency, allowing more time for learning at the same time as this learning became necessary through the further reduction of instinctual behaviors and their replacement by symbolically invented ones.[8]

---

7. Part of Slocum's argument comes from her focus on developmental differences between humans and nonhuman primates. In traditional anthropology and popular culture, the key differences between the two were brain size and language, but by 1975 it was well established that apes were capable of rudimentary tool use and had some basic linguistic abilities. Consequently, the old evolutionary model based on bipedalism, tool use, and hunting became less relevant in differentiating between hominids and other primates. Notice that the first factors mentioned by Slocum in the previous paragraph all concern women exclusively. She places brain size and language well down the list.

8. Despite the popular interest in the social and behavioral aspects of early humans, palaeoanthropology was, at the time this article was written, relatively unconcerned with it. Most paleoanthropologists focused on recovering and identifying fossils. Reconstructing behavior from such finds is notoriously speculative. Even

Here is where one may discover a large logical gap. From the difficult-to-explain beginning trends toward neoteny and increased brain size, the story jumps to Man the Hunter. The statement is made that the females were more burdened with dependent infants and could not follow the rigorous hunt. Therefore they stayed at a "home base," gathering what food they could, while the males developed cooperative hunting techniques, increased their communicative and organizational skills through hunting and brought the meat back to the dependent females and young. Incest prohibitions, marriage, and the family (so the story goes) grew out of the need to eliminate competition between males for females. A pattern developed of a male hunter becoming the main support of "his" dependent females and young (in other words, the development of the nuclear family for no apparent reason). Thus the peculiarly human social and emotional bonds can be traced to the hunter bringing back the food to share. Hunting, according to Washburn and Lancaster, involved "cooperation among males, planning, knowledge of many species and large areas, and technical skill" (1968: 296). They even profess to discover the beginnings of art in the weapons of the hunter. They point out that the symmetrical Acheulian biface tools are the earliest beautiful man-made objects. Though we don't know what these tools were used for, they argue somewhat tautologically that the symmetry indicates they may have been swung, because symmetry only makes a difference when irregularities might lead to deviations in the line of flight. "It may well be that it was the

attempt to produce efficient high-speed weapons that first produced beautiful, symmetrical objects" (1968: 298).

So, while the males were out hunting, developing all their skills, learning to cooperate, inventing language, inventing art, creating tools and weapons, the poor dependent females were sitting back at the home base having one child after another (many of them dying in the process), and waiting for the males to bring home the bacon. While this reconstruction is certainly ingenious, it gives one the decided impression that only half the species—the male half—did any evolving. In addition to containing a number of logical gaps, the argument becomes somewhat doubtful in the light of modern knowledge of genetics and primate behavior.

The skills usually spoken of as being necessary to, or developed through, hunting are things like coordination, endurance, good vision, and the ability to plan, communicate, and cooperate. I have heard of no evidence to indicate that these skills are either carried on the Y chromosome, or are triggered into existence by the influence of the Y chromosome. In fact, on just about any test we can design (psychological, aptitude, intelligence, etc.) males and females score just about the same. The variation is on an individual, not a sex, basis.

Every human individual gets half its genes from a male and half from a female; genes sort randomly. It is possible for a female to end up with all her genes from male ancestors, and for a male to end up with all his genes from female ancestors. The logic of the hunting argument

---

sexing fossil hominid remains is based on modern anatomical differences between men and women that may not be accurate for early humans two to three million years ago (Hager 1997: 10–12).

The version of evolution Slocum describes here was the prevailing view in part because it mirrored popular American gender stereotypes of the 1950s and 1960s, that is, men went out hunting to support their mates while women stayed home with the kids. The women the gatherer hypothesis advanced by Slocum and others such as Nancy Tanner (1933–1989) and Adrienne Zihlman (b. 1940) in their 1976 essay "Women in Evolution." met with a lot of resistance. Other alternatives more palatable to paleoanthropologists at the time were the food-sharing hypothesis (1978) formulated by South African archaeologist Glynn Isaac (1937–1985) and the "Man the Provisioner" model (1981) offered by C. Owen Lovejoy (b. 1943) that simply reversed Slocum's argument. In Lovejoy's scheme, gathering was the primary subsistence activity but it was conducted by men.

Slocum here is intentionally drawing a caricature of Washburn and Lancaster's position by describing the theory with phrases such as "the story goes something like this," "obscure selection pressures," and "poor dependent females." Although Slocum's language was polemic, it highlighted the untested assumptions of the Washburn-Lancaster model and reinforced her point about bias in the literature.

would have us believe that all the selection pressure was on the males, leaving the females simply as drags on the species. The rapid increase in brain size and complexity was thus due entirely to half the species; the main function of the female half was to suffer and die in the attempt to give birth to their large-brained male infants. An unbiased reading of the evidence indicates there was selection pressure on both sexes, and that hunting was not in fact the basic adaptation of the species from which flowed all the traits we think of as specifically human. Hunting does not deserve the primary place it has been given in the reconstruction of human evolution, as I will demonstrate by offering the following alternate version.

Picture the primate band: each individual gathers its own food, and the major enduring relationship is the mother-infant bond. It is in similar circumstances that we imagine the evolving protohominids. We don't know what started them in the direction of neoteny and increased brain size, but once begun the trends would prove adaptive. To explain the shift from the primate individual gathering to human food sharing, we cannot simply jump to hunting. Hunting cannot explain its own origin. It is much more logical to assume that as the period of infant dependency began to lengthen, *the mothers would begin to increase the scope of their gathering to provide food for their still dependent infants.* The already strong primate mother-infant bond would begin to extend over a longer time period, increasing the depth and scope of social relationships, and giving rise to the first sharing of food.[9]

It is an example of male bias to picture these females with young as totally or even mainly dependent on males for food. Among modern hunter-gatherers, even in the marginal environments where most live, the females can usually gather enough to support themselves and their families. In these groups gathering provides the major portion of the diet, and there is no reason to assume that this was not also the case in the Pliocene or early Pleistocene. In the modern groups women and children both gather and hunt small animals, though they usually do not go on the longer hunts. So, we can assume a group of evolving protohominids, gathering and perhaps beginning to hunt small animals, with the mothers gathering quite efficiently both for themselves and for their offspring.

It is equally biased, and quite unreasonable, to assume an early or rapid development of a pattern in which one male was responsible for "his" females(s) and young. In most primate groups when a female comes into estrus she initiates coitus or signals her readiness by presenting. The idea that a male would have much voice in "choosing" a female, or maintain any sort of individual, long-term control over her or her offspring, is surely a modern invention which could have had no place in early hominid life. (Sexual control over females through rape or the threat of rape seems to be a modern human invention. Primate females are not raped because they are willing throughout estrus, and primate males appear not to attempt coitus at other times, regardless of physiological ability.) In fact, there seems to me no reason for suggesting the development of male-female adult pair-bonding until much later. Long-term monogamy is a fairly rare pattern even among modern humans—I think it is a peculiarly Western male bias to suppose its existence in protohuman society. An argument has been made (by Morris 1967, and others) that traces the development of male-female pair-bonding to the shift of sexual character-

---

9. The picture of the primate band that Slocum draws here is much closer to that held by current biological anthropologists than the version she ridiculed above. It was, however, only one of several feminist versions of human evolution offered in the early 1970s. The version that was probably most popular with nonprofessionals at that time was the aquatic hypothesis, presented by the Welsh popular author Elaine Morgan (1920–2013) in her 1972 book *The Descent of Woman*. Morgan published a more technical version of the same theory called *The Aquatic Ape* in 1982. The aquatic hypothesis enjoyed great popularity among feminists and some cultural anthropologists, but it was rejected by physical anthropologists as incompatible with existing fossil evidence. Unlike Morgan or Ardrey, Slocum was a biological anthropologist; she did her doctoral research on rhesus monkeys. Thus, her argument demonstrates a much greater technical command of the field than Morgan's or Ardrey's.

istics to the front of the body, the importance of the face in communication, and the development of face-to-face coitus. This argument is insufficient in the first place because of the assumption that face-to-face coitus is the "normal," "natural," or even the most common position among humans (historical evidence casts grave doubt on this assumption). It is much more probable that the coitus position was invented *after* pair-bonding had developed for other reasons.

Rather than adult male-female sexual pairs, a temporary consort-type relationship is much more logical in hominid evolution. It is even a more accurate description of the modern human pattern: the most dominant males (chief, headman, brave warrior, good hunter, etc.), mate with the most dominant females (in estrus, young and beautiful, fertile, rich, etc.), for varying periods of time. Changing sexual partners is frequent and common. We have no way of knowing when females began to be fertile year-round, but this change is not a necessary condition for the development of families. We need not bring in any notion of paternity, or the development of male-female pairs, or any sort of marriage in order to account for either families or food sharing.

The lengthening period of infant dependency would have strengthened and deepened the mother-infant bond; the earliest families would have consisted of *females and their children*. In such groups, over time, the sibling bond would have increased in importance also. The most universal, and presumably oldest, form of incest prohibition is between mother and son. There are indications of such avoidance even among modern monkeys. It could develop logically from the mother-children family: as the period of infant dependency lengthened, and the age of sexual maturity advanced, a mother might no longer be capable of childbearing when her son reached maturity. Another factor which may have operated is the situation found in many primates today where only the most dominant males have access to fertile females. Thus a young son, even after reaching sexual maturity, would still have to spend time working his way up the male hierarchy before gaining access to females. The length of time it would take him increases the possibility that his mother would no longer be fertile.[10]

Food sharing and the family developed from the mother-infant bond. The techniques of hunting large animals were probably much later developments, after the mother-children family pattern was established. When hunting did begin, and the adult males brought back food to share, the most likely recipients would be first their mothers, and second their siblings. In other words, a hunter would share food *not* with a wife or sexual partner, but with those who had shared food with him: his mother and siblings.[11]

It is frequently suggested or implied that the first tools were, in fact, the weapons of the hunters. Modern humans have become so accustomed to the thought of tools and weapons that it is easy for us to imagine the first manlike creature who picked up a stone or club. However, since we don't really know what the early stone tools such as hand-axes were used for, it is equally probable that they were not weapons at all, but rather *aids in gathering*.

---

10. Here, in passing, Slocum makes a stab at the origins of the incest taboo, one of the oldest problems in anthropology and one that is still not solved to general satisfaction. The case she presents here is weak since human females do not have to be in estrus to have sex. However, just as theorists such as Washburn tried to link the evolution of an enormous number of traits to hunting by males, Slocum tries to link a wide range of characteristics to particular aspects of female-led evolution.

11. Most theories of Slocum's day proposed that food sharing was the basis for the formation of families among early humans. However, based on primate studies of the time, Slocum concludes that it was more likely that mothers and siblings shared food rather than sexual partners. Female chimpanzees, for example, are receptive to most males when in estrus. Thus, sexual partners do not form stable family units. In particular, mothers and daughters remain close in primate troops. Recent studies indicate that food sharing among chimpanzees and bonobos is far more common than previously thought (Samuni et al. 2018, Silk et al. 2013, Crick et al. 2013).

We know that gathering was important long before much animal protein was added to the diet, and continued to be important. Bones, sticks, and hand-axes could be used for digging up tubers or roots, or to pulverize tough vegetable matter for easier eating. If, however, instead of thinking in terms of tools and weapons, we think in terms of *cultural inventions,* a new aspect is presented. I suggest that two of the *earliest and most important* cultural inventions were containers to hold the products of gathering, and some sort of sling or net to carry babies. The latter in particular must have been extremely important with the loss of body hair and the increasing immaturity of neonates, who could not cling and had less and less to cling to. Plenty of material was available—vines, hides, human hair. If the infant could be securely fastened to the mother's body, she could go about her tasks much more efficiently. Once a technique for carrying babies was developed, it could be extended to the idea of carrying food, and eventually to other sorts of cultural inventions—choppers and grinders for food preparation, and even weapons. Among modern hunter-gatherers, regardless of the poverty of their material culture, food carriers and baby carriers are always important items in their equipment.[12]

A major point in the Man the Hunter argument is that cooperative hunting among males demanded more skill in social organization and communication, and thus provided selection pressure for increased brain size. I suggest that longer periods of infant dependency, more difficult births, and longer gestation periods also demanded more skills in social organization and communication—creating selective pressure for increased brain size without look-

ing to hunting as an explanation. The need to organize for feeding after weaning, learning to handle the more complex social-emotional bonds that were developing, the new skills and cultural inventions surrounding more extensive gathering—all would demand larger brains. Too much attention has been given to the skills required by hunting, and too little to the skills required for gathering and the raising of dependent young. The techniques required for efficient gathering include location and identification of plant varieties, seasonal and geographical knowledge, containers for carrying the food, and tools for its preparation. Among modern hunting-gathering groups this knowledge is an extremely complex, well-developed, and important part of their cultural equipment. Caring for a curious, energetic, but still dependent human infant is difficult and demanding. Not only must the infant be watched, it must be taught the customs, dangers, and knowledge of its group. For the early hominids, as their cultural equipment and symbolic communication increased, the job of training the young would demand more skill. Selection pressure for better brains came from many directions.

Much has been made of the argument that cooperation among males demanded by hunting acted as a force to reduce competition for females. I suggest that competition for females has been greatly exaggerated. It could easily have been handled in the usual way for primates—according to male status relationships already worked out—and need not be pictured as particularly violent or extreme. The seeds of male cooperation already exist in primates when they act to protect the band from predators. Such dangers may well have increased with a shift to savannah living, and the longer

---

12. As Slocum attacked male bias in beliefs about evolution, she took on many commonly accepted themes in popular culture. The idea that early tools were offensive weapons came from Dart's work. Compare Slocum's analysis here to the story presented in *2001: A Space Odyssey* by Stanley Kubrick (1928–1999), an extremely popular film that appeared in 1968. The opening scenes of the film show the discovery of tools. One apeman picks up a large bone, stares at it, and then uses it to beat a companion over the head. Again, recent studies show that the actual situation is more complex. Bonobos, chimpanzees and some monkeys are known to use stones as tools to break open nuts and seeds. Jill Pruetz and Paco Bertolani (2007) observed groups of chimpanzees hunting cooperatively, using sharpened sticks to impale bush babies (small nocturnal primates). The researchers also noted that females were more successful hunters than males. The oldest stone tools date to about 3.3 million years ago. As with modern chimpanzees, these tools appear to have been used to crack nuts and tubers, not as weapons.

dependency of infants. If biological roots are sought to explain the greater aggressiveness of males, it would be more fruitful to look toward their function as protectors, rather than any supposedly basic hunting adaptation. The only division of labor that regularly exists in primate groups is the females caring for infants and the males protecting the group from predators. The possibilities for both cooperation and aggression in males lies in this protective function.[13]

The emphasis on hunting as a prime moving factor in hominid evolution distorts the data. It is simply too big a jump to go from the primate individual gathering pattern to a hominid cooperative hunting-sharing pattern without some intervening changes. Cooperative hunting of big game animals could only have developed *after* the trends toward neoteny and increased brain size had begun. Big game hunting becomes a more logical development when it is viewed as growing out of a complex of changes which included sharing the products of gathering among mothers and children, deepening social bonds over time, increase in brain size, and the beginnings of cultural invention for purposes such as baby carrying, food carrying, and food preparation. Such hunting not only needed the prior development of some skills in social organization and communication, it probably also had to await the development of the "home base." It is difficult to imagine that most or all of the adult primate males in a group would go off on a hunting expedition, leaving the females and young exposed to the danger of predators, without some way of communicating to arrange for their defense, or at least a way of saying, "Don't worry, we'll be back in two days." Until that degree of com-

municative skill developed, we must assume either that the whole band traveled *and hunted* together, or that the males simply did not go off on large cooperative hunts.[14]

The development of cooperative hunting requires, as a prior condition, an increase in brain size. Once such a trend is established, hunting skills would take part in a feedback process of selection for better brains just as would other cultural inventions and developments such as gathering skills. By itself, hunting fails to explain any part of human evolution and fails to explain itself.

Anthropology has always rested on the assumption that the mark of our species is our ability to *symbol*, to bring into existence forms of behavior and interaction, and material tools with which to adjust and control the environment. To explain human nature as evolving from the desire of males to hunt and kill is to negate most of anthropology. Our species survived and adapted through the invention of *culture*, of which hunting is simply a part. It is often stated that hunting *must* be viewed as the "natural" species' adaptation because it lasted as long as it did, nine-tenths of all human history. However:

Man the Hunter lasted as long as "he" did from no natural propensity toward hunting any more than toward computer programming or violin playing or nuclear warfare, but because that was what the historical circumstances allowed. We ignore the first premise of our science if we fail to admit that "man" is no more natural a hunter than "he" is naturally a golfer, for after symboling became possible our species left forever the

---

13. Early theories about protohuman social organization tended to emphasize violent competition among males for essentially passive females. John F. McLennan (1827–1881) described marriage by capture in his 1865 work *Primitive Marriage*. The popular image of the caveman dragging the cavewoman off by the hair has been around since at least 1924 when the comic actor Buster Keaton (1895–1966) did this in his first feature film *The Three Ages* (Ruddick 2007). There is little evidence to support these images of male violence. More modern theory tends to emphasize the role of females in sexual selection, diminishing the importance of male aggression.

14. If the analogy between ancient hominids and modern chimpanzees is accurate then Slocum was exactly correct. Research on wild chimpanzees in Senegal has shown that male and female chimpanzees hunt together (Pruetz and Bertolani 2007).

ecological niche of the necessity of any one adaptation, and made all adaptations possible for ourselves. (Kephart 1970: 23).[15]

That the concept of Man the Hunter influenced anthropology for as long as it did is a reflection of male bias in the discipline. This bias can be seen in the tendency to equate "man," "human," and "male"; to look at culture almost entirely from a male point of view; to search for examples of the behavior of males and assume that this is sufficient for explanation, ignoring almost totally the female half of the species; and to filter this male bias through the "ideal" modern Western pattern of one male supporting a dependent wife and minor children.[16]

The basis of any discipline is not the answers it gets, but the questions it asks. As an exercise in the anthropology of knowledge, this paper stems from asking a simple question: what were the females doing while the males were out hunting? It was only possible for me to ask this question after I had become politically conscious of myself as a woman. Such is the prestige of males in our society that a woman, in anthropology or any other profession, can only gain respect or be attended to if she deals with questions deemed important by men. Though there have been women anthropologists for years, it is rare to be able to discern any difference between their work and that of male anthropologists. Learning to be an anthropologist has involved learning to think from a male perspective, so it should not be surprising that women have asked the same kinds of questions as men. But political consciousness, whether among women, blacks, American Indians, or any other group, leads to reexamination and reevaluation of taken-for-granted assumptions. It is a difficult process, challenging the conventional wisdom, and this paper is simply a beginning. The male bias in anthropology that I have illustrated here is just as real as the white bias, the middle-class bias, and the academic bias that exist in the discipline. It is our task, as anthropologists, to create a "study of the human species" in spite of, or perhaps because of, or maybe even by means of, our individual biases and unique perspectives.

REFERENCES

Berger, Peter, and T. Luckmann. 1967. *The Social Construction of Reality*. Garden City, NY: Doubleday Anchor.

Current Anthropology. 1968. Social Responsibilities Symposium. Reprint from December 1968 issue.

Garfinkel, Harold. 1960. "The Rational Properties of Scientific and Common Sense Activities." *Behavioral Science* 5, no. 1: 72–83.

Kephart, Jane. 1970. "*Primitive Woman as Nigger, or, The Origin of the Human Family as Viewed Through the Role of Women.*" M.A. Dissertation, University of Maryland.

Morris, Desmond. 1967. *The Naked Ape*. New York: McGraw-Hill.

Washburn, Sherwood, and Lancaster, C. 1968. "The Evolution of Hunting." In *Man the Hunter*, edited by R. B. Lee and Irven DeVore. Chicago: Aldine.

15. As you read these passages, recall again that this essay first appeared in 1971, close to the height of the movement protesting the Vietnam War. Slocum's suggestion that the hunting hypothesis negates most anthropology seems rash, but the idea that humans did not innately desire to kill was extremely popular in this era and, whether it followed logically or not, increased the emotional appeal of Slocum's argument.

16. Slocum's suggestion that, even within anthropology, there was a tendency to equate man and human was certainly no exaggeration. Consider C. F. Hockett's 1973 introductory anthropology text called Man's Place in Nature, with chapters titled "Man the Tinkerer," "Man the Chatterer," "Man the Worshiper," "Man the Owner," and so on.

23. Interpreting the Origins of Gender Inequality: Conceptual and Historical Problems

Eleanor Leacock (1922–1987)

FOR SOME TIME I have argued that the analysis of women's oppression and its origins calls for clarification along two lines, historical and conceptual.* The historical dimension requires that the myth of the "ethnographic present" be totally eradicated, and that anthropologists deal fully with the fact that the structure of gender relations among the people they study does not follow from precapitalist production relations as such, but from the ways in which these have been affected by particular histories of colonization. The conceptual dimension requires a complete break with the tendency to interpret all cultures in terms of categories derived from capitalist society. Such categories distort the structure of primitive communist relations and thereby obscure the sources of hierarchy. Equally critical, as consistently pointed out by feminist scholars, is the need to root out the pervasive assumption that women are not actors on the scene of human history to the same degree as are men. There is still a wide-spread failure to recognize that correcting the anthropological distortion of women's roles in society has profound implications for the interpretation of social structure generally. In particular, the fact that the French Marxists have not launched a thorough-going criticism of Lévi-Strauss' assumption that the exchange of women by men inaugurated human society has served to weaken their analyses of pre-capitalist production modes.[1]

ANTHROPOLOGY AND HISTORY

The importance of paying constant attention to history was impressed upon me as a graduate student at Columbia University when I was fortunate enough to take part in Wm. Duncan Strong's seminar on "Time Perspective and the Plains." Strong drew on archaeology and ethnohistory to demonstrate that "typical" Plains

---

From *Dialectical Anthropology* (1983)

1. Leacock's feminist Marxist perspective is immediately apparent in this opening paragraph. Here, she touches on a number of issues that were central to feminists and Marxists in the late 1970s and early 1980s. These included a critique of the notion of the ethnographic present (see this essay, note 3) as well as colonialism and the reproduction of race, class, and gender inequality.

The notion of primitive communism is very important in this essay. Karl Marx and Friedrich Engels proposed that early societies were close to communism, an idea given force by Lewis Henry Morgan's description of early societies as having communal living arrangements and possessing liberty and equality (1871, 1985 [1877]). Engels, in *The Origin of the Family, Private Property, and the State* (1884) wrote "Everything runs smoothly without soldiers, gendarmes, or police. . . . There can be no poor and needy—the communistic household and the gens know their obligations toward the aged, the sick, and those disabled in war. All are free and equal—including the women" (2004: 97–98; https://readingfromtheleft.com/PDF/EngelsOrigin.pdf).

In the last sentence of the paragraph, Leacock refers to *The Elementary Structures of Kinship* by Claude Lévi-Strauss (1955, orig. 1949). There, Lévi-Strauss argues that one of the fundamental patterning elements of society is that women are commodities exchanged by men. You can find a more thorough discussion of Lévi-Strauss's theory in the introduction to the section "Structure, Language, and Cognition" in this book.

"*" Leacock's original text contained ninety-six notes. Space limitations prevent us from reproducing them here, but asterisks have been included to show where they were placed.

culture, as then conceived, was not aboriginal, but had developed in the 18th century when formerly diverse tribes, some agricultural, some hunting-gathering, took advantage of the horse and either moved out onto, or spent more of the year on the prairies. I would add that a greatly expanded market for buffalo hides plus land pressure resulting from European intrusion to the east and south were also important reasons for the move out onto the plains. In a fairly short time, social, ritual, and material traits were borrowed, developed, and/or elaborated upon by different peoples who integrated them into a relatively uniform culture.[2]

Strong's ethnohistorical orientation influenced a number of dissertations, some on Plains peoples,* and some on other areas.* Subsequently, extensive studies of native American social-economic organization and land use were undertaken in connection with the Indian Claims actions initiated in the 1950s.* This work revealed a fact of major significance for understanding the unstratified societies that existed in most of what was to become the United States: bands, villages, and towns were only loosely grouped into what are called tribes; politically, however, they functioned as fully autonomous units. The point was made explicit by Kroeber,* and it has been elaborated upon by Fried in his critique of the concept "tribe."* Kroeber wrote:

> The more we review aboriginal America, the less certain does any consistently recurring phenomenon become that matches our usual conventional concept of tribe; and the more largely does this concept appear to be a White man's creation of convenience for talking about Indians, negotiation with them, administering them . . . It was infinitely more convenient and practicable

for us to deal with representatives of one large group than with these of ten, twenty, or thirty tiny and shifting ones whose very names and precise habitat often were not known. This was equally so whether treaties were being negotiated for trade, traverse, settlement or resettlement, land cession, peace, subsidy or rationing, administration on a reservation, or abrogating and opening up a reservation. Generally we treated the nationality "tribes" as if they were sovereign state-tribes, and by sheer pressure of greater strength forced the Indians to submit to our classification of them.*

Kroeber's point that tribes as commonly defined were a product of colonization requires the qualification that tribal organization and leadership were not only imposed from without. They also arose among Native Americans as necessary for resisting white invasion. Such warfare as had existed in pre-colonial times usually took the form of petty raiding by young men (and such women as occasionally chose to participate) who tested their mettle in a coup counting system that deemed it more prestigious to touch enemies than kill them. When warfare for survival became necessary, strong leaders emerged to unite one or more tribes and meet the need.

In any case, Kroeber wrote that the "larger nationalities," i.e., the culturally affiliated groups known as tribes, were "ethnic" but "non-political" in the sense that they held no power over their constituents. It was the "smaller units, whether they be called villages, bands, towns, tribelets, lineages, or something else . . . that were independent, sovereign, and held and used a territory."* However, these smaller units should not be considered miniature tribes in the sense of stable, bonded

---

2. The archaeologist William Duncan Strong (1899–1962) was a student of A. L. Kroeber and a classmate of Julian Steward. Strong was Leacock's dissertation advisor during her years at Columbia. He conducted extensive archaeological research in southern California and the Great Plains, Labrador, and, with his student Gordon R. Wiley (1913–2002), in Peru. Although not a Marxist, Strong emphasized the role of history in anthropology. He was one of the leading proponents of the direct historical approach in archaeology (by which one would analyze the archaeological record by extrapolating from historical sources) in the 1920s and 1930s.

After Strong's death, Leacock edited the journals he kept during his fieldwork among the Naskapi, indigenous people of Northern Quebec and Labrador. Although she began this project in the early 1960s, the resulting book, *Labrador Winter: The Ethnographic Journals of William Duncan Strong, 1927–1928*, was not published until 1994, seven years after her death.

groups subject to the authority of a chief and/or council. Such a formulation violates the reality of communally organized societies, in which movement among groups was easy and frequent; rights to lands were not viewed as exclusive; decisions about individual activities were made by those who would carry them out; and decisions about group activities, arrived at through consensus, did not bind those who did not agree.* Such a formulation also distorts the working structure of relations among bands and villages and the complex social and ceremonial forms that affirmed cooperation and friendship or ritualized and contained potential animosity.

Kroeber's and Fried's discussions of changing political forms demonstrate how unjustifiable it is to consider the cultures that have been reconstructed from the memories of late 19th and early 20th century elders as "traditional" in the sense of pre-Columbian. To do so is to gloss over the active participation of native Americans in almost 500 years of post-colonial history. It is to present them as cardboard figures, living according to a congeries of "culture traits" within "culture areas," traits that did not change but were "lost" through "acculturation."*3

GENDER IN NATIVE NORTH AMERICA

With regard to the position of women, it is equally unjustifiable to make generalizations about one or another Indian culture without consideration of the historical dimension. During the colonial period, male authority was being encouraged by Euro-Americans in their political and military dealings with native Americans at the same time as Indian women were becoming dependent in individual households on wage-earning and trading husbands. For example, after documenting the full social equality of Cherokee women revealed by colonial accounts, Reid, an historian of law, wrote:

The decline of hunting and the adoption of American ways during the nineteenth century, with the substitution of factory-made for home-made goods . . . freed the Cherokee woman from outdoor labor, placing her in the kitchen and her husband in the fields, but it also deprived her of economic independence, making her politically and legally more like her white sisters.*4

---

3. Throughout this section, Leacock shows her concern with the historical background of Native America and attacks the notion of the ethnographic present. Through the first half of the twentieth century, most ethnographies did not pay any attention to broad patterns of history, particularly conquest and colonization. Societies were described either in their current state or as they were remembered by their elder members. For the purposes of their writing, many anthropologists assumed that the societies they studied were relatively isolated from external forces of change, and internally driven change was extremely slow. Thus, notions of history were largely irrelevant to ethnography. Leacock's focus on history derives from the influence of her mentor Strong, however, this paragraph is a criticism of his direct historical approach and Kroeber's culture area work. The "Fried" Leacock refers to at the beginning of the paragraph is Morton Fried (1923–1986). Fried was Leacock's contemporary at Columbia and one member of a core group of Columbia students and professors deeply influenced by Marx. In addition to Fried and Leacock, the group included Stanley Diamond (1922–1991), Eric Wolf (1923–1999), Sidney Mintz (1922–2015), and Elman Service (1915–1996). Fried is best known for his book *The Evolution of Political Society* (1967).

Two prominent schools of thought in the 1950s and 1960s were structuralism and ethnoscience. Members of these schools focused on what they believed to be the fundamental ways in which the members of a society understood their world. They held that the effects of history on such understandings were of little importance. Marxism, on the other hand, is fundamentally concerned with history: Marxists see societies developing as their internal contradictions are worked out. Thus, a feminist Marxist approach must be vitally concerned with showing the importance of history for understanding the position of women in society.

4. In this section Leacock begins to build the case that the gender relations reported in most twentieth century ethnographies are the result of contact with Europeans rather than structural elements of non-European society. Some of the important names Leacock mentions in this section are the Wyandot, Powell, and Lafitau. The Wyandot are an indigenous group also known as the Huron. Originally from the Georgian Bay region of

A second example of changes in women's position following the colonization of native North America is afforded by the contrast between Lafitau and Morgan on the Iroquois. In his 18th century account, Lafitau stated that Iroquois and/or Huron women were "the souls of the Councils, the arbiters of peace and war," in whom "all real authority is vested."* In Morgan's description, despite reference to women's decision-making powers in Iroquois households, he wrote that Iroquois men considered women as "inferior, the dependent, and the servant of men," and that a woman, "from nurture and habit, . . . actually considered herself to be so."* Although the flatness of the latter statement can well be questioned, it was written at the time when Iroquois women had lost their role as major producers and the control over the products of their labor that had insured them personal autonomy and public authority. Their situation was no longer that of 1791, when elder Seneca women informed Colonel Proctor, an envoy from George Washington, you ought to hear and listen to what we, women, shall speak, as well as to the sachems; for we are the owners of this land—and it is ours. It is we that plant it for our and their use. Hear us, therefore, for we speak of things that concern us while our men shall say more to you; for we have told them.*

The changing relationship between women's economic role and their decision-making powers among the Iroquois and the Huron is further illuminated by a little known paper on the Wyandot by the early anthropologist Powell. Powell wrote:

> Cultivation is communal; that is, all of the able-bodied women of the gens take part in the cultivation of each household tract in the following manner:
> The head of the household sends her brother or son into the forest or to the stream to bring in game or fish for a feast; then the able-bodied women of the gens are invited to assist in the cultivation of the land, and when this work is done a feast is given.*

Powell stated that women were family heads among the Wyandot, and that four family heads, plus a man of their choosing, made up the clan council. The clan councils together made up the tribal council that was responsible for dividing Wyandot lands among the clans. The women councilors of each clan were in turn responsible for dividing it among the clan households, as well as for matters such as giving personal names and discussing and consenting to marriages. Apparently the entire council, that is, including the male member, handled certain transgressions while others were brought before the tribal council. Warfare was the responsibility of the men; all "able-bodied men" made up what Powell called a "military council" headed by a "military chief." The fact that women were not members of these councils has led to a serious underestimation of their authority in societies organized, as many North American societies were, along lines roughly similar to the Wyandot Huron. First, accounts of military negotiations between the outsiders and "military councils" and "military chiefs" do not recognize the formal structure of women's power which can therefore be interpreted as indirect and "behind the scene."* Second, the imminence of conquest increased the responsibility and power of "military councils." Subsequent economic developments, along with policies such as the Dawes (General Allotment) Act of 1887 (designed to divide all Indian lands into family-owned plots), undercut the collective economic activities traditionally controlled by women. As among the Cherokee and the Iroquois, the egalitarian and reciprocal structure of decision-making among the Huron was destroyed.

Lake Huron, the Wyandotte nation is now located in Northeastern Oklahoma. Powell refers to John Wesley Powell (1834–1902), the founder of the Bureau of American Ethnology. Powell is also mentioned in our introduction to "The Boasians." Joseph-François Lafitau (1681–1746), author of *American Savages Compared with Those of Earliest Times* (1724), was a Jesuit missionary who worked among the Iroquois from 1711 to 1717. He wrote about Iroquois kinship systems 150 years before Morgan.

CONCEPTUALIZING PRIMITIVE COMMUNISM AND ITS TRANSFORMATION

As the above discussion suggests, the egalitarian relations that obtained in most foraging and many horticultural societies around the world at the time of European expansion rested on the fact that all mature individuals participated directly in the full process of production. By "full process" I refer to Marx's concept of production, distribution, exchange, and consumption as "members of one entity, different aspects of one unit,"* as opposed to formulations that limit their emphasis to either work processes or the allocation of produce. The control that all individuals had over the conditions of their labor, over the skills as well as the resources necessary to perform it, and over the disposition and use of its products, distinguishes egalitarian from hierarchically ordered structures.[5]

A Marxist conceptual baseline for analysing egalitarian society, interpreted in these terms, sharpens the fact that the transformation from egalitarian to hierarchical relations was qualitative and not merely quantitative. Such a view contrasts with the common practice of describing egalitarian society in terms of the same features that characterize class society. In formulations of this type, differential access to land and other resources, hereditary authority, and social-economic hierarchies are treated as incipient—as weakly developed tendencies that only needed strengthening to become predominant. Despite caveats to the contrary, history is thereby implied to be unilineal and teleological, with Western society as its ultimate purpose and measure. Alternatives for the future are obscured by the implication that there was no real alternative in the past.[6]

The widely held assumption that female subordination is a universal of human society derives from, and in turn supports, the assumption that primitive communal society was ultimately ordered by the same constraints and compulsions that order class society.* Where institutionalized hostility between the sexes exists, it is interpreted as a variant of a universal battle between the sexes, rather than as evidence of emerging status differentiations among men and among women, as well as between men and women. The critical relationship between the development of ranking and the attempt to subvert women's public and autonomous status (such as in the so-called big men societies of Melanesia) is seldom recognized. In sum, gender hierarchy is all too often taken for granted, and both the structure of primitive communism and the basis for its transformation are thereby mystified.[7]

There is much talk of paradigms these days, and much emphasis on process. Nonetheless, cross-cultural analyses still rely heavily on states or essences as categories, rather than processes or relationships. The mid-century admission that the regularities of social evolution as broadly outlined by Engels and Morgan approximated historical reality, opened the way in anthropology for a dialectical analysis of human history in terms of basic trans-

---

5. In Marxist thought, there is a close link between production and power. Since social relations flow primarily from relations of production, the greater control of production an individual (or class) exercises, the greater their power should be. Leacock is arguing that her reading of history shows that women and men exercised equal control of production before their societies were profoundly affected by Europeans. If so then, from a Marxist viewpoint, both would likely participate fully in the political life of their societies as well.

6. Although Leacock does not provide any references for what she describes as a common practice—seeing egalitarian societies as incipient states—she is probably thinking of Fried's *The Evolution of Political Society* (1967) which was published several years before this essay.

7. Many 1970s feminists understood female subordination as a human universal (see essay 21). When a practice is universal, there is at least a strong suspicion that it is rooted in human nature. However, for a Marxist, there can be no such thing. Human nature is not fixed and universal but created in the process of production. Therefore, explanations that rely upon human nature cannot be sustained. Leacock makes this point repeatedly in the next several paragraphs.

formations in the ways people interrelated as they reproduced themselves and their social structures. In particular, given the focus on relations between individual and society that characterized the personality and culture school, and its successors in psychological anthropology, the significance of Marx's sixth thesis on Feuerbach could have been explored in terms of how individual behavior and societal processes interrelate.[8]

"The essence of man is no abstraction inherent in each separate individual," Marx wrote. "In its reality it is the *ensemble* (aggregate) of social relations."* To Marx and Engels people did not have an intrinsic nature apart from society, but neither were they mere reflections of their society. In a number of oft-quoted passages, Marx and Engels stressed that "men make their own history,"* although the circumstances under which they do so are inherited from the past. Furthermore, the independent unfolding of social forces means that people's actions do not necessarily lead to the intended results. Instead the "simplest determinations," the relations of production, ways people relate to one another as they produce, distribute, exchange, and consume the necessities of life, set processes in motion that lie beyond the wills of the actors.* On the one hand, social structures are created by the behavior of individuals; "the social structure and the State are continually evolving out of the life-processes of

definite individuals." On the other hand, however, these life-processes are themselves structured by production relations, as people "are effective, produce materially, and are active under definite material limits, presuppositions and conditions independent of their will."*[9]

Marxist dialectics, then, opened the way for examining the series of interlocking processes—the different levels of integration—that constitute human history. At the individual physiological level, human nature is not a given but a mix of potentials and propensities that are expressed differently under different conditions; at the societal level, social-historical processes are of an altogether different order; in between, mediating the two, at the individual psycho-social or behavioral level, the person operates as a nexus of social-economic relationships; and at the ideological level, people's perceptions of their relations to each other and to nature are patterned by traditional concepts, in part spontaneous and in part manipulated, and with a certain lawfulness of their own that arises from the nature of language as a symbol system.*

Such a line of thinking has been followed through only minimally. Instead, anthropology has been plagued by ever more radically reductionist and anti-historical formulations. In structuralist theory, and more recently in sociobiology, social determinants are defined in terms of behavioral outcomes and ultimately reduced

---

8. When Leacock refers to the mid-century admission that Engels and Morgan were approximately correct, she is probably thinking of work by Leslie White on cultural evolution and his editing of Morgan's work (see essay 16).

Marx's *Theses on Feuerbach* is a short work written in 1845. It was published as an appendix to Engels's *Ludwig Feuerbach and the End of Classical German Philosophy* (1949 [1888]). It consists of eleven brief points that, in Marx's opinion, separated his own work from Feuerbach's. The sixth thesis, in its entirety, is:

> Feuerbach resolves the religious essence into the human essence. But the human essence is no abstraction inherent in each single individual. In its reality it is the ensemble of the social relations. Feuerbach, who does not enter upon a criticism of this real essence, is consequently compelled: 1) To abstract from the historical process and to fix the religious sentiment as something by itself and to presuppose an abstract—isolated—human individual. 2) Essence, therefore, can be comprehended only as "genus," as an internal, dumb generality which naturally unites the many individuals.

In the following paragraph, Leacock explains the significance of Marx's point for her own argument.

9. In this and the following paragraph, Leacock is describing a Marxist dialectic. She is saying that society is not simply a reflection of the structure of production (that is, a position that Marxists call "vulgar materialism") but rather emerges from the relations of production and how people think about these relations.

to psycho-biologically fixed entities. Whether these be such grotesque notions as Wilson's "conformer" and other behavior-specific genes, or Lévi-Strauss's more elegant, since undefined, deep structures, or Laughlin and d'Aquili's more scientifically couched, if less euphonious "neuroanatomical-neurophysiological relationships," their inventors all reduce human history and society to mere projections of individual biological propensities, with the environment the only independently interacting factor.*[10]

The result of ruling out a level of societal process entirely separate from individual propensities is like attempting to explain the movements of the solar system as flowing from the properties of the atomic particles (or processes) that make it up. To be sure, planetary movements are in a superficial sense the sum total of all movements of subatomic particles, just as social processes are in a trivial sense the sum total of individual behaviors. Scientifically, however, it would be absurd not to recognize that the lawful movements of planetary bodies have their own history of development, and operate at a level of integration independent from the internal processes that characterize their constituent parts. With respect to society, few would argue directly that social processes do not also operate at a level of their own. In effect, however, this is precisely what reductionist formulations imply.

Anthropologists have long been sensitive to biological reductionism with regard to physical variations of a racial order, and somewhat aware that reductionist formulations serve as ideological rationalizations of oppression. Unfortunately, this is not the case with respect to physical variations of a sexual order. Although the fact that physiological sex and social gender are far from **isometric** is well established and documented in anthropology, cross-cultural discussions of sex roles commonly fall into reductionism in their formulations. Many Marxists, as well as other scholars, translate the gender structure of the hierarchical exploitative society with which they are familiar into innate predispositions and the practice is encouraged by the recent worldwide spread of Western norms, at least on a superficial level. The assumption remains prevalent that physiological differences between the sexes embody hints of female subordination only slightly expressed in egalitarian cultures but that come to full flower in class-based state-organized urban societies. Instead of being treated as an historical development, hierarchy becomes written into human physiology. Despite much citation from Marx and Engels on the part of those who do this, they contradict a fully Marxist view of human nature as informed by the last hundred years of social science research. Their entanglement with male supremacist ideology feeds into and is fed by the failure to deal rigorously with both history and theory in the interpretation of primitive communist society and the source of its transformation.[11]

---

10. When this essay was written, French structuralism and sociobiology were extremely popular in the United States. In this paragraph, Leacock takes aim at both, particularly at *Sociobiology: The New Synthesis* (1975) by sociobiologist E. O. Wilson. Wilson's notion that genes were responsible for much of human nature was anathema to most anthropologists. Wilson claimed that "human beings are absurdly easy to indoctrinate." Since he believed that human characteristics were genetically based he hypothesized that humans must have "conformer genes." (1975: 562).

Behind the notion of the "conformer gene" is the idea that hunting required a high degree of coordination. The physical anthropologist William. S. Laughlin (1919–2001, mentioned in this paragraph) called hunting the "master behavior pattern of the human species" (cited in Barash 1979: 186). Thus, according to this view, the tendency of humans to conform is genetically based—the result of the fact that, over the millennia, the key human survival tactic was hunting and it demanded high levels of conformity.

Leacock criticizes French structuralism as reductionist and antihistorical. For Lévi-Strauss, the underlying meaning of myths and other cultural phenomena involves a few universal themes such as resolving humans' relations to nature. The outward form of the stories and the historical circumstances that produced them have no meaning. Leacock rejects this perspective.

11. In this paragraph Leacock takes aim at unnamed Marxists who fail to fully apply Marxist analysis to their subject because they accept the Western ideology of male supremacy. Leacock says that although sex

THE ORIGINS OF HIERARCHY

The two sets of relations defined by Marx and Engels as critical to the emergence of exploitation are: first, the loss of control over the production process (i.e., production, exchange, distribution, and consumption) through the division of labor beyond that by sex; and second, the emergence of **dyadic** relations of dependency within individual families as a public/private dichotomy developed in economic and political life, making families separate economic units rather than parts of encompassing communal groups. The fundamental historical development analysed at length in Marx's opening section of *Capital* and central to Engels' reworking of Morgan's evolutionary hypothesis in *The Origin of the Family, Private Property and the State*, was the transformation from production for use to production for exchange. The emergence of production for exchange meant that value as an attribute of goods began to supersede use as the feature of primary social significance. As a consequence "abstract labor," the labor time represented in an exchangeable object, became separable from concrete work, a development that eventually made it possible for those who controlled exchange to regulate and exploit the productivity of others. Finally, money developed in various forms as a medium of exchange, as a pure commodity. Marx stressed that the money form allowed the fetishistic absurdity whereby relations among people appeared to them as relations among things; thus the structure of exploitation was mystified and the existence of class differences rationalized.[12]

In *The Evolution of Political Society,* Fried raised the question why people accepted control by others over the products of their work and allowed the loss of their independence. Whatever the answer, Fried stated, people did not realize the magnitude of the changes they were bringing about.* To be sure, they did not, since, through exchange and the division of labor, people were simply enriching their lives and cementing interpersonal and intergroup bonds, innocent of the processes thereby set in motion. As Engels put it, "the more a social activity, a series of social processes . . . appears a matter of pure chance, then all the more surely within this chance the laws peculiar to it and inherent in it assert themselves." Commodity production and the division of labor that accompanied it slowly but inexorably led to class stratification; they

---

and gender are not equivalent, many scholars still believe that the physiological differences between men and women are the basis for gender inequality. Instead of analyzing gender hierarchies as historical developments, they accept the view that hierarchy is the result of human physiology.

"Isometric": of equal measure.

12. In this paragraph, Leacock is trying to briefly recount Marx's theory of the origins of hierarchy. The first step is a movement from producing things simply to use them (for their "use value") to producing things as commodities that can be sold. Marx argues that this shift allows people in capitalist societies to think of the amount of labor that goes into the production of an object as equivalent to the value of that object. However, capitalist society makes a fetish of the commodity, valuing it over the labor that produced it. Marx's notion is that the value of an object is equivalent to the labor that goes into it. This is sometimes referred to as the labor theory of value and is found in the work of both Marx and Adam Smith. Most modern economists reject it.

The private/public dyadic relationship Leacock refers to here is that households become individual economic units with men working outside the home and women relegated to domestic tasks. This she argues ended the practice of extended families or kin groups working together as a communal unit.

The Origin of the Family, Private Property, and the State (1972 [1884]) is a book that Engels wrote after Marx's death based on notes Marx had taken as he read Morgan's *Ancient Society* (1985 [1877]). Engels's analysis is based on Morgan's notion that families were originally matrilineal. He ties the historic shift from matrilineality to patrilineality to the emergence of private property. Leacock was very familiar with this work. She wrote an introduction to the 1972 edition.

A **"dyadic"** relationship is one with two parts.

raised up "incorporeal alien powers . . . too powerful for men's conscious control."*[13]

Simple barter does not separate the producer from control over exchange and distribution. As barter develops in importance, however, it leads to a contradiction between the material benefits to be derived from specialized production for trade and the structure of full egalitarianism. Fried suggested that the elaboration of redistribution was important to the emergence of ranking, the first form of stratification.* The focus should be sharpened and emphasis placed on the significance of redistribution for the emergence of commodity production with all its consequences. Goods produced for exchange rather than for use create new interest groups. For a long time, egalitarian relationships prevent persons in pivotal positions in networks of exchange and redistribution from exploiting the economic possibilities of their position. Nonetheless, the conflict between egalitarian relations sharpens and, in what are called ranking societies, people begin to accept dependent positions in relation to "big men" and other chiefly people in order to benefit from the handouts associated with them. Eventually, unequal appropriation among and within competitively structured lineages is institutionalized, and the conflict between egalitarian distribution and consumption on the one hand, and the potential afforded by exchange and increasing specialization of labor on the other, is partially resolved. New contradictions are already crystallizing, however, between the potentials created by increasingly far flung economic ties and social forms attuned to autonomous kin and village groupings, in turn to be resolved by full stratification and political organization and the familiar conflicts of class society.[14]

To return to the second component of exploitation and stratification, it is in conjunction with the above developments that a public/private dichotomy emerges and dyadic relations of dependence within families as economic units begin to take shape. Lévi-Strauss posits to the contrary, in egalitarian societies, women are not exchanged by men; instead they exchange goods and services with men.* Direct exchange between the sexes, like single barter, does not separate either sex from control over its own production. Instead, alienation develops in tandem with the development of exchange systems, as individuals use lineage and extended family units to compete for ranking positions in relation to control over the production and distribution of valued goods. Gender responsibilities for marketing and exchange vary according to how different environments and histories have patterned the sex division of labor, and women's position in decision-making structures varies correspondingly.* Yet the question remains: when ranking begins to undermine the equal prerogatives of people generally, why is it that the autonomy and authority of women as a sex are threatened rather than those of men? Aside from various formulations of male superiority, it is usually argued that the physical limitations of childbirth and suckling are critical. Yet these do not hinder women in egalitarian societies.* In

---

13. In this section, Leacock leans heavily on the theory of stratification advanced by Morton Fried in *The Evolution of Political Society* (1967).

Further, Leacock points out that the actions of individuals are qualitatively different from social processes. Individuals simply pursue activities for their own benefit, but the net result is a social shift to hierarchy that results in their loss of independence. She argues that this same shift also results in the emergence of gender hierarchy. Recall that Adam Smith proposed that taken collectively, individual decisions led to public good. Here, Leacock, following Marx, argues that this is not necessarily the case.

14. In Marxist thinking, the resolution of conflict through revolution creates change between social forms. However, each such resolution contains the germs of a new conflict and, hence, progress to new social forms. In this paragraph, Leacock points first to a conflict between egalitarian social forms and specialization. Since no two specializations are likely to be entirely equal, it is impossible to maintain egalitarian social relations once specialization begins. This problem is resolved in rank societies through a hierarchical ordering of kin groups. Such ranking, however, creates new contradictions because non-kin relations are now available through trade with distant people.

keeping with my reading of dialectical materialist theory as outlined above, I would say that the significance of women's childbearing ability is transformed by new social relations when they become the producers, not only of people as individuals, but also of what is becoming "abstract"—i.e., exploitable—labor. The origins of gender hierarchy, then, are inextricably meshed with the origins of exploitation and class stratification.[*15]

Engels posed a sharp contrast between the status of women among the egalitarian Iroquois and that in the patriarchal societies of the classical Middle East and Mediterranean where control over female sexuality was important for the inheritance of status and property. In his view, the family as an economic unit was of primary importance within the upper class although it had ramifications throughout society. It remained for mid-20th century Marxist feminist scholarship to add a further dimension to these ramifications. Female subordination within the family as an economic unit also enabled an upper class to squeeze more surplus from workers, serfs and slaves. The fact that domestic work could be separated from a public sphere and assigned to women as the wards of men assured to an upper class the reproduction and maintenance of workers through socially unremunerated—i.e., slave—labor. This is not to say that the arrangement was thought through in advance any more than other major historical developments of the past. However, given the records of women's steady decline in legal and social rights in classical antiquity, it remains to trace some of the steps whereby the household subordination of women was buttressed by ideological and social sanctions as its economic advantages were realized.[*16]

All of this, however, pertains to the final stages of women's subordination. The majority of societies with which anthropology deals involve the most preliminary stages—points at which women's autonomy began to be threatened and a certain hostility between the sexes began to be institutionalized, but that were very far indeed from the legal and political reduction of women to the status of ward that accompanied full-scale stratification. I am suggesting that the structure of gender in such societies needs to be interpreted in relation to: the structure of exchange and the division of labor; the structure of ranking and the degree to which some sections of the society are gaining control over the labor of others; the structure of kinship and the extent to which lineages have become competing sodalities rather than the means for organizing production and distribution in communal villages; the degree to which the well-being of one segment of a society is not merely relative but is actually at the expense of other segments; and, in the light of all this, the structure of marriage in relation to

---

15. Leacock argues that in egalitarian societies based on barter economics, gender relations are relations of equality. Making a fetish of commodities and making labor a commodity are part of the formation of hierarchical societies, and it is only when egalitarian societies become rank societies that women lose rights and men gain them. This leaves her with a difficult question: Why are women, rather than men, the ones who lose the rights? She rejects explanations rooted in either biology or "human nature" and instead asserts that women are disadvantaged because they are associated with the production of labor power rather than of commodities themselves. Thus, women produce labor, and men produce commodities. Commodities are more valued in hierarchical societies than is labor. Therefore, men are more highly valued than women. Note that the accuracy of this claim rests on acceptance of Marx's notion of the labor theory of value and the notion of making a fetish of the commodity. Without these ideas, there is no reason why producing labor should be intrinsically more or less valuable than producing commodities.

16. Leacock is arguing that men were able to reproduce their superior social position by relying on the unpaid domestic work of women. Her argument comes substantially from Engels's *Origin of the Family*. In that work, Engels argues that property was key to marriage among the bourgeoisie, and he likened marriage to prostitution. Women in such marriages traded domestic and sexual service for economic support. Engels was a strong advocate for gender equality. However, he saw this in terms of the massive entry of women into jobs previously held by men and the socialization of domestic chores. Marriage would be egalitarian since each partner would be equally involved in production.

control over children as exploitable labor or as exploiters of labor.[17]

In what are called ranking societies, women's position begins to shift from valued people who cement networks of reciprocal relations and who have access to various publically recognized mechanisms for adjudicating their interests as women, into that of service workers in the households of husbands and their kin groups. Bride wealth begins to take the form of purchasing a woman's children, rather than of gift exchange. Sacks has explored the relation of such developments to the emergence of status difference among women as well as between women and men.* She has demonstrated the usefulness of separating the status of women as wives from that as sisters in order to appreciate the extent to which women exercise publically recognized authority through the manipulation of kin ties in societies where economic stratification and gender hierarchy are emerging. Sanday has stressed the fact that women may protect and maintain their public authority well into the conditions of stratification, a fact attested to by extensive data on West African societies and suggested by the case of ancient Crete.* All told, a focus on the above developments and the particularities of their unfolding in different historical, cultural and environmental contexts, makes clear that changes in women's position are neither secondary phenomena, as some imply, nor prior to economic hierarchy, as argued by others. They are at the core of, and inseparable from, profound transformations that take place in conjunction with the development of exchange and the division of labor.

The social and economic subordination of women was established in some parts of the world millenia ago; it was unfolding in other parts of the world at the time of European exploration and conquest; and it has been developing in yet others in the context of Western colonialism and imperialism.* I am here arguing that in order to interpret this development correctly, it is essential, first: to have a clear concept of primitive communism, divested of stereotypical assumptions that female subordination is a natural rather than historical phenomenon, and second: to place any society under study clearly in the context of its particular history, pre and post-colonial. I now return to the second point.

THE HISTORICAL CONTEXT OF ANTHROPOLOGICAL ANALYSIS

The actual people contemporary anthropologists study are not autonomous gatherer-hunters or horticulturalists or whatever. In one way or another the relations of capitalism have impinged upon them for a long time. Whatever the specific nature of a people's involvement with capitalism, the *ultimate* direction of change is the same: the individualization and alienation of labor, the individualization of the nuclear family, and the relegation of women both to unrecompensed domestic labor and to public labor as an unstable and underpaid work force. People lose what control over the process and products of their labor they previously had, and their labor itself becomes increasingly transformed into a commodity to be bought, if not outright commandeered. The responsibility for rearing the new generation is progressively transferred from some larger kin or band grouping to individual families. Idealized by missionary teachings as loving care for husband and children, women's labor in the household becomes for all practical purposes a gift to the plantation or mine owner, manufacturer or trader, who draws profits from the work

---

17. In this passage, Leacock cites two other prominent feminist anthropologists: Peggy Sanday (b. 1937) and Karen Sacks (b. 1941). When this essay was written, Sanday had recently published *Female Power and Male Dominance: On the Origins of Sexual Inequality* (1981). There, she argued that in "inner oriented" societies—those with abundant food supplies and little threat of outside aggression—people lived in harmony with nature and each other. Gender relations were egalitarian. But in "outer oriented" societies, characterized by food scarcity and warfare, men dominated women. She reported that the number of "outer oriented" societies increased with colonialism. Karen Sacks is also concerned with issues of gender equality and, at the time this essay was written, had recently published *Sisters and Wives: The Past and Future of Sexual Equality* (1979).

of husbands and sons and then buys women's additional labor at a marginal price.*[18]

Untidy details like plantation labor and commercial transactions have too commonly been ignored when data on so-called traditional societies are codified and punched on IBM cards for cross-cultural comparison. Not surprisingly, a recent analysis concludes that there are no consistent correlations between women's position in a society and other factors.* Luckily, however, ethnohistorical and archaeological reconstruction of pre-colonial and colonial culture histories is proceeding apace, and it is possible to throw light on puzzling cases where there seems to be little relation between female subordination and economic inequality.[19]

I have already made reference to North America, which, north of Mexico, constitutes the largest world area that was inhabited by egalitarian peoples at the time of European expansion. Ranking was elaborated in coastal areas, especially along the Gulf of Mexico and

---

18. Leacock's critical point is that women's domestic labor is essential to the reproduction of the workforce. Without domestic labor, families cannot be maintained, and workers cannot be produced. However, the owners of capital (the factory owners or mine owners) pay their workers (usually male) but do not pay the women, whose work enables the production of these workers. Thus, from Leacock's perspective, women's domestic work is a gift to capitalists.

19. Note that in the first sentence of the paragraph Leacock talks about information "punched on IBM cards for cross-cultural comparison." She is attacking the Human Relations Area Files (HRAF) project undertaken by George Peter Murdock (1897–1985; see the introduction to the section "The Reemergence of Evolutionary Thought"). Murdock's project was a descendant of the large-scale cross-cultural studies started by Herbert Spencer and has a history that places it squarely in the anti-Marxist camp.

Cultural data in the HRAF was indexed according to a system Murdock created and published as *Outline of Cultural Materials* (1961). The data was coded on punch cards that could be read by the computers of the era. Researchers could then discover mathematical correlations between the characteristics of different cultures. Such a system can only analyze that which had been indexed and the "Outline" is decidedly non-Marxist. For example, in the 1965 edition of the *Outline* social stratification has seven entries, entertainment has nine. Recreation is its own category distinct from entertainment with an additional nine categories.

Leacock makes the point in the second half of this essay that European expansion, from the fifteenth century on, had critical effects on people throughout the world. In particular, as capitalist relations of production were imposed on indigenous groups, the social and political position of women suffered. Previously egalitarian societies, in which women enjoyed either full equality with men or very substantial rights, were subverted, and men came to dominate women. Leacock argues that most ethnographic writing simply fails to take the effects of European colonialism into account. Thus, ethnographies that showed the oppression of women among indigenous peoples were generally in error. The authors of these monographs, writing in the ethnographic present, fail to realize that the practices they assume to be "traditional" date only from the transformation of these societies by capitalism. If these societies could be seen before the advent of European expansion, the equality of gender relations in egalitarian and early ranked societies would be apparent. In making this argument Leacock is strongly influenced by world systems theory, a popular neo-Marxist position of the 1960s and 1970s. Although notions of dependency have been around for a long time, world systems theory was promoted by the work of Andre Gunder Frank (1929–2005) and Immanuel Wallerstein (1930–2019). In his most famous essay, "The Development of Underdevelopment" (1966), Frank argued that the nations of Latin America were not poor because they failed to industrialize. Rather, the processes of the expansion of capitalism in the wealthy nations, particularly in North America and northern Europe, had drawn wealth out of Latin America. Thus, the poverty of southern nations was directly linked to the wealth of northern capitalist societies. In 1974 Wallerstein published *The Modern World-System,* in which he traced the development of global capitalism from its origins in the early seventeenth century, emphasizing its deleterious effects on noncapitalist cultures around the world. Like Frank, the principal thesis Wallerstein advanced was that the wealth of nations and the poverty of nations are interlinked. Today's wealthy nations became rich by expropriating the wealth of today's poor nations. You'll find more about Frank and Wallerstein in the Introduction to Globalization section of this book. Although Leacock focuses on gender relations rather than wealth, the fundamental argument is the same. She insists that it was the expansion of capitalist power that undermined the position of women in society after society.

the northern Pacific, but the vast majority of native North Americans had retained egalitarian socio-economic structures. The Iroquois are the best known example of the gender equality common in North America, and, contrary to the opinion of Lévi-Strauss,* are not an anomaly. Instead, they afford a well-documented example of the economic and political reciprocity that accompanied the matrilineal/matrilocal organization widespread among North American horticulturalists.* Among hunting-gathering peoples, the Inuit (Eskimo) are commonly cited as an example of masculine brutality toward women in an otherwise egalitarian society, an example seemingly paralleled by accounts of female subordination among the Chipewyan.* However, ethnographic accounts of women's independence and assertiveness among the Inuit indicate that ethnohistorical analysis, long overdue, will reveal the latter-day character of male abusiveness as following from the demoralization and drunkenness suffered in many Inuit communities.* As for the Chipewyan case, it is based on an account of middlemen in the fur trade, the "gang" that collected around the unusually dedicated worker for the Hudson's Bay Company, and not on independent Chipewyan hunters. The quality of relations therein described contrasts sharply with the 17th century Jesuit accounts of gender equality among the Montagnais-Naskapi.*

AUSTRALIA

Aboriginal Australia has furnished ample grounds for arguments that male dominance is a psychosocial or psychobiological universal rather than an historical development. Male control of women's marriage, male inheritance of land, virilocal residence, male brutality towards women, and male exclusion of women from important rituals in a non-stratified society form an imposing package and have been documented again and again. To be sure, data modifying these generalizations are beginning to assert themselves. Older women have a say in marriages along with older men, while young men, like young women, have little say. Just as young women are commonly married the first time to elder men, so are young men often married to elder women. Women have clubs

with which they not only defend themselves, but with which they beat men for misbehavior; they are not cowed by men. Furthermore, if wrongfully hit, a woman may simply leave, or may take up residence in the women's section of the camp, taboo to men. Women are important in the conduct of some male rituals, and are indifferent to their exclusion from others; their own, from which men are excluded, hold more interest for them.* Tindale has pointed out that among the Pitjandara of western Australia, women call male rituals to a close if they find themselves walking too far for food and wish to move camp.* Bell worked in a north-central Australian settlement where "the maintenance of law and order . . . is still a cooperative venture between men and women who turn to each other for assistance on some issues and assert their independent rights on others."*

However, while such data qualify the picture of male dominance claimed for Australian gatherer-hunters, the historical setting in which 20th century Aboriginal society has been functioning must be understood if this image is to be contradicted in its entirety. First and foremost, not to evaluate the effects of the brutal genocide native Australians have suffered is as unscientific as it is unethical. Brutality against native Australians has been practiced from the earliest forays by Malays; to the sporadic explorations by Europeans and the 1788 convict settlement at what is now Sydney; through the steady encroachment on Australian lands and the accompanying shooting, poisoning, beating and enslaving, along with disastrous disease; into the brutal policing and racist restrictions of the present. One cannot talk of men hitting women as if apart from a pattern of frontier violence where demoralization is compounded by alcohol.*

Second, it is—or should be—inexcusable to analyse land rights in Australia without considering the impact of forced movements away from coastal areas and the resulting land pressure in interior regions to which many Aborigines fled. Some early meetings between Europeans and Australians were friendly, but the Europeans were over-ready to use their guns, and apparently the Australians sometimes retaliated with the unambiguous act of treating their foes as food. For the most part, therefore, early explorers from Europe were glad to leave the Australians alone, once it was decided that there was no ready gold or other easy wealth on their lands. Then the arrival of the first merino sheep in New South Wales in 1797 was followed in 1813 by the discovery, west of the Blue Mountains, of the immense grasslands that were to make Australia the largest producer of fine wool in the world.* The push was on. The rich southeast, where 400 to 600 people were wont to gather at certain seasons to socialize and live on seafood and crayfish, was soon depopulated of Aborigines. Some were killed, some moved west, and a few married into the white community. The herders too pushed west, enslaving the Aborigines, or pressing them into labor, and brutally suppressing their resistance.* Driven westward and inland, away from expanding centers of white settlement and onto each other's traditional homelands, different peoples turned against each other, fighting and quarrelling. As among native Americans, the recognition of a common identity as Aborigines, with a common history and common struggle, took time to emerge. White Australians of course took advantage of and exacerbated divisiveness among the Aborigines, favoring "pacified" groups and using them to enslave or control others.

The demoralization found among displaced Aboriginal survivors is documented by Daisy Bates, who over a period of some forty years publicized the Aboriginal condition from her isolated camp in South Australia.* Despite the patronization and misinterpretations of her account, many incidents she reports parallel the macabre bitterness of collective suicide described by Turnbull for the Ik.* A particularly bizarre scene ensues when Bates accompanied Radcliffe-Brown to the grim hospital island where sick and fearful Aborigines, sep-

arated from their own people, are taken only to die. She describes Radcliffe-Brown asking the old men to sing ritual songs into his phonograph and playing them Tannhauser and Egmont in return.*[20]

By the 20th century, disease and genocide in its various forms had reduced an estimated 300,000 or more people of aboriginal Australia to less than 40,000.* By mid-century, with the "stabilization" of native reserves, and the dispensation of minimal food supplies and medical care by government or mission stations, the Aboriginal population began to rise again. Ritual life, too, began to revive and expand, although serving a new function as a focus for the assertion of identity and self-respect by a people robbed of their independence. Anthropologists also expanded in numbers, typically wishing to study the lives of pristine hunter-gatherers. They usually took care to interview people living a distance from mission stations or cattle ranches, rather than the service workers directly attached to such enterprises. Seldom, however, did they inquire deeply into a people's history, nor even inquire about existing official regulations for Aborigines, such as those that prohibit marriage off of a reserve.*

The point should be clear. To ignore the historical, economic, and political realities of Aboriginal life is to gloss over the effects of conquest and oppression, and therefore to misconstrue the social relations that obtained when Aborigines were autonomous gatherers and hunters in control of their own social world. With respect to relations between the sexes, when one scrapes the surface of ethnohistorical materials, one finds suggestions of women's former importance, such as Howitt's reference to influential elder women in south-

---

20. This paragraph contains references to several notorious characters. Daisy Bates (1861–1951) was an Irishwoman who lived among the Aborigines for thirty years, beginning in about 1913. Bates wrote several books about her experience. It is impossible to doubt that horrific things happened to the Aborigines, but for their history Daisy Bates might not be the best source. Julia Blackburn, author of *Daisy Bates in the Desert: A Woman's Life among the Aborigines* (1994), writes that Bates fabricated her life history and that she was unable to separate her experiences from her imagination.

Colin Turnbull (1924–1994) was the author of *The Forest People* (1961) and *The Mountain People* (1972). The first of these describes the idyllic life of the Mbuti of the Ituri Forest and the second the horrific life of the Ik of Uganda. Both portraits have been heavily critiqued as romantic (or antiromantic).

A. R. Radcliffe-Brown lived in Australia from 1926 to 1931. The image Bates and Leacock present here is a compelling one, and it may well have happened. It is clear that Radcliffe-Brown had little interest in history and believed that the social structures he studied had been relatively little affected by colonialism.

eastern Australia. Only recently, however, have these begun to be followed up.* As long ago as a hundred years, Spencer and Gillin note a three-day women's section of an initiation ceremony among the Arunta and comment that "there was a time when women played a more important part in regard to such ceremonies than they do at the present time."* Unfortunately, they give no further information except that they personally find the ceremony boring. In his recently republished *Australian Religion*, Mircea Eliade makes ample reference to male high gods, but nowhere mentions the important mythological personage who keeps reappearing in the pages of Spencer and Gillin, the female Sun. Eliade writes that initiation for Australian girls is simpler than for boys, and flatly contradicts ethnographic fact by stating, "as everywhere in the world."*[21]

Hart and Pilling raise the need for ethnohistorical work in their account of the Tiwi.* They describe how missionary influences as well as prostitution encouraged male control over women's sexuality in the early 20th century, and then go on to consider earlier influences on the politics of wife-trading. Archival research is needed, they write, to determine the extent of slave raiding by the Portuguese in the 18th century. Since it was probably the younger men who were taken off to Timor, they suggest the slaving may have encouraged the dominance of old Tiwi men and their monopolization of wives.

[*Leacock provides three additional ethnographic examples, but space considerations prevent us from reprinting them here. We summarize them below.*

In a 1,100-word section with twelve notes entitled "The Amazon," Leacock first divides Amazonian history into five periods. The first of these is precolonial, but in the others she dwells on the effects of colonization. She then moves to a discussion of the Yanomamo, asserting that their portrayal as "the fierce people" serves to rationalize the destruction of the Amazon forests. Citing geographer William J. Smole (1976), Leacock argues that the Yanomamo studied by Napoleon Chagnon were made fierce by their contacts with Portuguese and Spanish invaders. Smole also reports that the position of women among the highland Yanomamo he studied was very much better than that reported by Chagnon. Leacock concludes this section by claiming that Chagnon's failure to deal with the Yanomamo history and politics cast doubt on his portrayal of the male aggressiveness and dominance among a virtually pristine egalitarian people.

In an 830-word section with six notes entitled "Melanesia," Leacock suggests that the societies of New Guinea are often used as evidence for the subordination of women in egalitarian societies. This portrayal, however, is incorrect since ancient irrigation works and trade connections suggest that stratification had already begun in this area. Further, trade connections with Malays, Chinese, and Europeans may have badly compromised egalitarian relations. The hostility often expressed between men and women is highly suggestive of a society in which rank is being asserted and women are losing control over their production. The fact that in New Guinea women often respond to their subordination with open anger rather than passive acceptance is strongly suggestive of societies in which the process of stratification is only beginning. These relations may have been further exacerbated by European conquest, which increased conflict between tribes.

A two-thousand-word section with nineteen notes titled "Africa" includes a substantial

---

21. Alfred William Howitt (1830–1908) was an Englishman who studied the culture of indigenous Australians. He is best known for his 1904 book *The Native Tribes of South East Australia* and his collaboration with the missionary and ethnographer Lorimer Fison (1832–1907).

Between about 1890 and 1912 Walter Baldwin Spencer (1860–1929) and Francis James Gillin (1885–1912) gathered extensive collections of indigenous Australian ethnographic materials. They published *The Native Tribes of Central Australia* in 1899.

Mircea Eliade (1907–1986) was a historian of religion and professor at the University of Chicago. He is known to anthropologists primarily because of his work on shamanism.

critique of the work of French neo-Marxists Claude Meillassoux and Emmanuel Terray. Their work was critical in the development of Marxist thought in anthropology during the 1960s and 1970s, and both worked in Africa. The French neo-Marxists broke from Soviet-style Marxist anthropology. Soviet ethnographers insisted on the primacy of the modes of production outlined by Marx and Morgan's scheme for the evolution of society. The French neo-Marxists expanded the notion of mode of production to include new modes germane to the societies anthropologists studied. They were also largely trained by Lévi-Strauss and were deeply influenced by his notions on exchange and the role of women.

Leacock begins by noting that African history is extremely complex but often ignored. Despite some exceptions, the ethnography of African societies portrays women as firmly under male authority. Ethnohistorical work, however, shows that the position of African women deteriorated with the advent of colonial rule. Before colonialism, they often had important public political roles. Although in African hierarchical societies, women's autonomy was undermined, it was not destroyed, except in later Muslim states. Leacock faults the French neo-Marxists for failing to use Engels's notion that the subjugation of women was central to the development of hierarchy in analyzing the emergence of ranked societies in Africa. Because they agree with Lévi-Strauss on the universal subjugation of women, they tend to condense egalitarian and beginning rank societies into a single mode of production. This obscures the critical processes of the emergence of hierarchy. The problem is evident in Terray's work on the Gayman. Terray sees kin relations among the Gayman as exploiting women and youth. These relations were eventually dominated by relations based on slavery. Terray does not, however, look for a reason

why women are exploited in the first place. Leacock, however, finds the answer in Terray's own work. She notes that he says the lineage structure is related to the political structure and did not come before it; further, "youth" was a rank that could include older men. Finally, captive labor was used in the lineage mode of production. Thus, Terray fails to realize that the exploitation of women and youth in the lineage mode of production is integral to the existence of hierarchical society and did not precede it. Terray also fails to consider that the ranked urban portion of society could have affected the more egalitarian rural part of society. His analysis is also weakened by failure to consider changes brought about by exposure to European slaving.]

CONCLUSION

Across the disciplines, research on the economic and social activities of women has been shaking up some established assumptions about society and history. I have argued that only when gender hierarchy is taken as an historical problematic, rather than a psycho-biological given, can the structure of primitive communist relations be properly understood, and the part played by exchange in the transformation of these relations clearly formulated. The need for an effective theory of exchange in pre-capitalist societies is well recognized by Marxist anthropologists,* but ironically it is associated, especially for those working in the structuralist tradition, with the wholly anti-Marxist concept of woman exchange as basic in primitive communist society. Only when such a formulation is stringently challenged can the first phases of the process whereby women actually became exchanged be understood, for these were inseparable from initial steps in the transformation of use to value, work to abstract labor, and cooperative production to exploitation.[22]

---

22. Here, Leacock sums up the basic points of her essay and provides an excellent summary of the Marxist/historical view of how social hierarchy was created. First, the formation of gender hierarchy is a historical process. It is not based on biological differences between men and women. Second, in indigenous egalitarian societies women typically had strong social positions and were not objects of exchange as proposed by Lévi-Strauss. Third, gender relations in indigenous societies can only be understood in the context of Western capitalism and colonialism.

An effective theory of exchange is necessary both for analysing pre-capitalist societies and for interpreting the effects on these societies of colonization and imperialism. Only when the genders in primitive communist societies are understood as economically independent exchangers of goods and services, can the full force of capitalist relations in subverting the labor of women, and therefore transforming the entire structure of relationships in such societies, be appreciated. Until such time, the myth of the ethnographic present will continue to support the assumption, so prevalent in pop science and the mass media, that the widespread normative ideal of men as household heads who provision dependent women and children reflects some human need or drive. And until such time, the unique and valued culture history and tradition of each Third World people will continue to be distorted, twisted to fit the interests of capitalist exploitation.

Symbolic and Interpretive Anthropology

Beginning in the 1960s and reaching its fullest expression in the 1970s, symbolic or interpretive anthropology was part of a general reevaluation of cultural anthropology as a scientific enterprise. Materialists insisted that the analysis of culture focus on empirical material phenomena. Ethnoscientists and cognitive anthropologists argued that culture was a mental phenomenon that could be scientifically modeled following principles similar to mathematics or formal logic. Symbolic anthropologists agreed with the ethnoscientists and cognitive anthropologists that culture was a mental phenomenon but rejected the notion that culture could be modeled like mathematics or logic. Instead, they used a variety of analytical tools drawn from psychology, history, and literature to study symbolic action within culture. Their fundamental interest was in examining how people formulated their reality. Janet Dolgin et al. (1977: 5), for example, wrote, "Our concern is not with whether or not the views a people hold are accurate in any 'scientific' sense of the term. . . . In social action, that which is thought to be real is treated as real."

The development of symbolic analysis was influenced by the work of Benjamin L. Whorf and Edward Sapir in linguistics and ethnoscientific studies, which gained popularity in the 1950s. Symbolic anthropologists argued that, like language, symbols were a shared system of meaning that could only be understood within a particular historical and social context. Culture, they believed, was embedded in people's interpretations of the events and the things around them. In other words, symbolic anthropologists argued that we construct our cultural reality. Consequently, they took a semiotic approach focusing on the analysis of meaning. As Clifford Geertz (1926–2006) writes,

> Believing, with Max Weber, that man is an animal suspended in webs of significance he himself has spun, I take cultures to be those webs, and the analysis of it to be therefore not an experimental science in search of law but an interpretive one in search of meaning. (1973: 5)

The term *symbolic anthropology* covers a variety of forms of analysis, but two dominant trends in the field are represented by the work of Geertz and Victor Turner (1920–1983). Although both were concerned with the interpretation of symbolic action, their approaches are very different. Geertz's emphasis on culture as an organized collection of symbolic systems is typically American in flavor. Turner's work, on the other hand, was in the British structural-functionalist style and is concerned with the operation of symbols in the maintenance of society, a process that Turner referred to as *communitas* (Turner 1969).

Geertz studied philosophy at Antioch College but moved to anthropology after a chance encounter with Margaret Mead. He studied with Talcott Parsons (1902–1979) at Harvard. Parsons hoped to create a science of society by combining the insights of sociology, psychology, and anthropology and was particularly influenced by Weber. Geertz's early work hewed closely to Weberian themes. His early fieldwork in Java, Indonesia, was based around the idea that Muslims in Java were socially and economically similar to Protestants in Reformation Europe. Although Geertz's work in the 1960s moved sharply away from Parsons's scientism, it retained a strongly Weberian flavor.

In addition to his fieldwork in Java, Geertz and his wife, the anthropologist Hildred Geertz (1927–2022), also worked in Bali and Morocco. Hildred Geertz published books and essays both on her own account and in coauthorship with her husband. In 1960, the Geertzes took positions at the University of Chicago, and in 1970 they moved to Princeton, where Clifford Geertz became the first director of the school of social science at the Institute for Advanced Studies, a position he held until his death. Clifford and Hildred Geertz divorced in 1981, after which he married the anthropologist Karen Blu (b. 1945).

To Geertz, symbols were means of transmitting meaning. His focus was on how symbols affected the way people think about their world, how "symbols operate as vehicles of culture" (Ortner 1984: 129). For example, in "Deep Play: Notes on the Balinese Cockfight" (essay 26), Geertz described and analyzed the various symbolic meanings of the cockfight for the Balinese who engaged in the sport and discussed how these various levels of meaning influenced their lives. Ultimately, he argued that the cockfight does not have any function in the sense of maintaining social solidarity, reinforcing societal norms, or filling Malinowskian biopsychological needs. Instead, the cockfight enables the Balinese to share experiences and create meaning from their lives, much in the same way that sports or religious rituals may be organizing experiences for those in the West.

Geertz's type of analysis was focused at the level of the individual participant in society. Although he acknowledged that it was impossible to get inside the head of native informants, he wanted to provide his readers with a sense of what it might feel like to be a member of the culture he was describing. He did this using a technique borrowed from the philosopher Gilbert Ryle called "thick description." Geertz assumed that important symbols and actions had many layers of meaning and that their power derived from this fact. In thick description, the anthropologist attempts to analyze each layer of meaning. Geertz compared doing thick description to peeling an onion. There is layer after layer after layer, but no reward at the center. The onion *is* its layers; similarly, culture is its meanings (see Geertz 1973: 6–10).

Victor Turner was the son of an electrical engineer and an actress who was a founding member of the Scottish National Theater. His family background as well as his undergraduate studies of poetry and classical literature had a profound influence on his later anthropological work. He studied under Max Gluckman (1911–1975) at the University of Manchester, completing his doctorate in 1955, based on research conducted among the Ndembu in East Africa. His academic career started with a position at Manchester but took him to Cornell, the Center for Advanced Studies at Stanford, the University of Chicago, and the University of Virginia. Turner worked with his wife, Edith Turner (1921–2016), who, according to his student Barbara Babcock, was heavily involved in all aspects of Turner's research and academic life (in addition to being the mother of the couple's five children) (St. John 2008: 27). After Victor Turner's death, Edith Turner authored numerous books and essays in anthropology, including *Heart of Lightness: The Life Story of an Anthropologist* (2006) and *Communitas: The Anthropology of Collective Joy* (2012).

Victor Turner examined symbols as mechanisms for the maintenance of society. He viewed symbols as "operators in the social process, things that, when put together in certain arrangements in certain contexts (especially rituals), produce essentially social transformations" (Ortner 1984: 131). Turner argued that social solidarity had to be continually maintained. Ritual symbols, in his view, were the primary tools through which social order was renewed. Turner also made a major contribution to the conceptual vocabulary of symbolic analysis by outlining various properties of symbols, such as multivocality, condensation, the unification of disparate significata, and polarization of meaning (Turner 1967b: 28). These terms are discussed in essay 25.

Unlike Geertz's "thick description," Turner followed a more formal program of symbolic analysis. He believed that the interpretation of ritual symbols could be derived from three classes of data: (1) external form and observable characteristics, (2) the interpretations of specialists and laypeople within the society, and (3) deduction from specific contexts by the anthropologist.

Turner viewed his work as a contrast to the structuralism of Claude Lévi-Strauss and to the psychoanalytic analysis of cultural symbols. In particular, he emphasized study of the context in which symbols were expressed. He wrote,

> I found that I could not analyze ritual symbols without studying them in a time series in relation to other "events," for symbols are essentially involved in social process. I came to see performances of rituals as distinct phases in the social process whereby groups became adjusted to

internal changes and adapted to their external environment. From this standpoint the ritual symbol becomes a factor in social action, a positive force in an activity field. (Turner 1967b: 20)

One of the great shortcomings of symbolic analysis is that it is primarily descriptive and does not lend itself to general theoretical or methodological formulations. Symbolic anthropologists claim to search for universals of human understanding through the collection of locally particular data. However, much of what symbolic anthropologists know is derived through imaginative insight into particular cultures or events within those cultures. As a result, their knowledge does not provide a theoretical basis for understanding culture as a universal phenomenon.

Mary Douglas (born Mary Tew) (1921–2007) was one symbolic anthropologist whose work defied this generalization. Douglas was born in Italy to English parents. She was a boarding student at a Catholic secondary school in London, and Catholicism remained an important influence in her life. She took both her undergraduate and graduate degrees at Oxford and was particularly influenced by E. E. Evans-Pritchard (1902–1973). She did her doctoral fieldwork among the Lele in Central Africa and received her PhD in 1952. Her academic career included appointments at the University of London, the Russell Sage Foundation in New York City, Northwestern University, and Princeton. Her intellectual achievements were widely recognized, and she became a Dame Commander of the Order of the British Empire in 2007 (the equivalent of a knighthood). *The Guardian* called her the most widely read British social anthropologist of her generation (2007). Mary Douglas's husband, James Douglas (1919–2004), was a conservative politician and onetime head of the Conservative Party research department. He played an important intellectual role for her. In the dedication to her book *Risk and Blame* (1992), she wrote that he had been critical in helping her "relate the discourse of anthropology to the discourse in economics and political theory."

Douglas attempted to analyze universal patterns of symbolism, focusing on beliefs about pollution and hygiene as they were expressed in religions. In her two most famous works—*Purity and Danger* (1966) and *Natural Symbols* (1970)—Douglas contended that universal patterns of purity/pollution symbolism existed and were based on reference to the human body. She argued her case from a Durkheimian perspective, suggesting that shared symbols "create a unity in experience" (1966: 2) and that religious ideas about purity and pollution symbolized beliefs about social order. In the introduction to *Purity and Danger*, an excerpt from which is the subject of essay 24, she wrote,

> I believe that some pollutions are used as analogies for expressing a general view of the social order. For example, there are beliefs that each sex is a danger to the other through contact with sexual fluids. . . . Such patterns of sexual danger can be seen to express symmetry or hierarchy. It is implausible to interpret them as suggesting something about the actual relation of the sexes. I suggest that many ideas about sexual dangers are better interpreted as symbols of the relation between parts of society, as mirroring designs of hierarchy or symmetry which apply in the larger social system. . . . Sometimes bodily orifices seem to represent points of entry or exit to social units, or bodily perfection can symbolise an ideal theocracy. (1966: 3–4)

Symbolic anthropology is concerned with studying the process by which people give meaning to their world and how this world is expressed in cultural symbols. Geertz wrote that "cultural analysis is (or should be) guessing at meanings, assessing the guesses, and drawing explanatory conclusions from the better guesses" (1973: 20). However, symbolic anthropologists have never specifically explained a methodology for "guessing at meaning." Anthropologists who do not share Geertz's views often believe that this is a fundamental flaw. Critics claim that the credibility of symbolic interpretation is based on the explanatory skills of the anthropologist and argue that such anthropology often seems closer to literary criticism than social science. In fact, much of the work that characterized the symbolic analyses of the 1970s and 1980s was incorporated into the postmodern movement of the 1990s. Today it is rare to see analytical work such as that conducted by Turner and Geertz. Rather than being concerned with what a symbol "means," contemporary symbolic analyses are much more likely to be concerned with the postmodern issues of agency, power, and positioning.

SUGGESTED READINGS

Douglas, Mary. 1966. *Purity and Danger: An Analysis of the Concepts of Pollution and Taboo.* London: Routledge.
Douglas's classic work on the relationship of the body, classification, dirt, and pollution.
———. 1986. *How Institutions Think.* London: Routledge.
Douglas relates her symbolic work to political science and the analysis of the relationship between institutions and thought across cultures.
Geertz, Clifford. 1973. *The Interpretation of Cultures.* New York: Basic Books.
A seminal collection of essays focusing on the role of symbols in constructing public meaning.
———. 2001. *Available Light: Anthropological Reflections on Philosophical Topics.* Princeton, NJ: Princeton University Press.
Part autobiography, part analysis, in this series of essays, Geertz comments on the work of a wide variety of intellectuals and considers their impact on ideas about nation, identity, and multiculturalism.
Ortner, Sherry. 1973. "On Key Symbols." *American Anthropologist* 75(5): 1338–1346.
A brief essay that describes a method for identifying symbols and using them in analysis.
Schneider, David. 1968. *American Kinship: A Cultural Account.* Englewood Cliffs, NJ: Prentice Hall.
Schneider's analysis critiques functionalist accounts of kinship, focusing on the symbolic meanings of kin rather than the interrelated roles.
Turner, Victor. 1969. *The Ritual Process: Structure and Anti-Structure.* Chicago: Aldine.
Using material from the Ndembu, Turner analyzes the stages of ritual emphasizing the complementarity of order and disorder.

24. External Boundaries

Mary Douglas (1921–2007)

THE IDEA OF SOCIETY is a powerful image. It is potent in its own right to control or to stir men to action. This image has form; it has external boundaries, margins, internal structure. Its outlines contain power to reward conformity and repulse attack. There is energy in its margins and unstructured areas. For symbols of society any human experience of structures, margins or boundaries is ready to hand.[1]

Van Gennep shows how thresholds symbolise beginnings of new statuses. Why does the bridegroom carry his bride over the lintel? Because the step, the beam and the door posts make a frame which is the necessary everyday condition of entering a house. The homely experience of going through a door is able to express so many kinds of entrance. So also are cross roads and arches, new seasons, new clothes and the rest. No experience is too lowly to be taken up in ritual and given a lofty meaning. The more personal and intimate the source of ritual symbolism, the more telling its message. The more the symbol is drawn from the common fund of human experience, the more wide and certain its reception.[2]

The structure of living organisms is better able to reflect complex social forms than door posts and lintels. So we find that the rituals of sacrifice specify what kind of animal shall be used, young or old, male, female or neutered, and that these rules signify various aspects of the situation which calls for sacrifice. The way the animal is to be slaughtered is also laid down. The Dinka cut the beast longitudinally through the sexual organs if the sacrifice is intended to undo an incest; in half across the middle for celebrating a truce; they suffocate it for some occasions and trample it to death for others. Even more direct is the symbolism worked upon the human body. The body is a model which can stand for any bounded system. Its boundaries can represent any boundaries which are threatened or precarious. The body is a complex

---

From *Purity and Danger* (1966)

1. Trained in structural functionalism at Oxford by E. E. Evans-Pritchard (1902–1973), a student of both Malinowski and Radcliffe-Brown, Mary Douglas was influenced by Émile Durkheim's ideas about society and social cohesion. Durkheim argued that religion was a model of society that served to promote social cohesion (see essay 5); Douglas believed that shared symbols promote social solidarity and provide mechanisms for social control. She opens this article with a powerful image of society as a coherently organized whole. Her comment that human experiences of structures or boundaries can serve as symbols of society hints at one of her fundamental ideas—that the human body is a symbol of society.

Note also the poetry of Douglas's opening passage. Douglas's background was in the social sciences and humanities. She studied philosophy, politics, and economics at Oxford before turning to anthropology.

2. Douglas, interested in discovering universals of symbolism, suggests that the most potent symbols are found in the realm of the mundane. In this paragraph, she mentions folklorist Arnold van Gennep (1873–1957). In his best-known work, *Rites of Passage* (1960 [1909]), Van Gennep argued that rites of passage marked a person's change from one status to another, and were characterized by three stages: separation, transition, and incorporation. Van Gennep believed that the transition phase of rites of passage was particularly important since during this time individuals were outside the margins of society, no longer one thing but not yet another. Van Gennep referred to this state as "liminality," which Douglas references in her comment about the lintel and door frame. As Douglas later points out, states of liminality may be ritually impure or dangerous.

structure. The functions of its different parts and their relation afford a source of symbols for other complex structures. We cannot possibly interpret rituals concerning excreta, breast milk, saliva and the rest unless we are prepared to see in the body a symbol of society, and to see the powers and dangers credited to social structure reproduced in small on the human body.[3]

It is easy to see that the body of a sacrificial ox is being used as a diagram of a social situation. But when we try to interpret rituals of the human body in the same way the psychological tradition turns its face away from society, back towards the individual. Public rituals may express public concerns when they use inanimate door posts or animal sacrifices: but public rituals enacted on the human body are taken to express personal and private concerns. There is no possible justification for this shift of interpretation just because the rituals work upon human flesh. As far as I know the case has never been methodically stated. Its protagonists merely proceed from unchallenged assumptions, which arise from the strong similarity between certain ritual forms and the behavior of psychopathic individuals. The assumption is that in some sense primitive cultures correspond to infantile stages in the development of the human psyche. Consequently such rites are interpreted as if they express the same preoccupations which fill the mind of psychopaths or infants.[4]

Let me take two modern attempts to use primitive cultures to buttress psychological insights. Both stem from a long line of similar discussions, and both are misleading because the relation between culture and individual psyche are not made clear.

Bettelheim's *Symbolic Wounds* is mainly an interpretation of circumcision and initiation rites. The author tries to use the set rituals of Australians and Africans to throw light on psychological phenomena. He is particularly concerned to show that psychoanalysts have overemphasized girls' envy of the male sex and overlooked the importance of boys' envy of the female sex. The idea came to him originally in studying groups of schizophrenic children approaching adolescence. It seems very likely that the idea is sound and important. I am not at all claiming to criticize his insight into schizophrenia. But when he argues that rituals which are explicitly designed to produce genital bleeding in males are intended to express male envy of female reproductive processes, the anthropologist should protest that this is an inadequate interpretation of a public rite. It is inadequate because it is merely descriptive. What is being carved in human flesh is an image of society. And in the moiety- and section-divided tribes he cites, the Murngin and Arunta, it seems more likely that the public rites are concerned to create a symbol of the symmetry of the two halves of society.[5]

---

3. Because the form of the human body may be the most common human experience, Douglas's analysis centers on the body and its products. Douglas treats blood, breast milk, and other substances produced by the body as symbols of society. Ultimately, this argument is based on the organic analogy, a nineteenth-century model of society generally associated with Herbert Spencer. But whereas Spencer argued by direct analogy— telegraph wires are the nerves of society, Douglas's argument is symbolic—society is not a body, but it can be symbolically represented by a body. In the next essay, on Ndembu symbolism, Victor Turner (1920–1983) makes a similar point.

Douglas refers to the Dinka. The Dinka and Nuer, two closely related groups living in what was then Anglo-Egyptian Sudan, were studied by Evans-Pritchard, Douglas's mentor.

4. Douglas here criticizes psychological interpretations of symbolism, particularly psychoanalytic interpretations, which have tended to treat non-Western peoples as childlike or mentally ill. For example, in his book *Totem and Taboo* (1913), Sigmund Freud (1856–1939) famously equated the behavior of adults in non-Western society with children in European society. A second line of psychoanalytic thought equates the trancing of shamans or other religious specialists in primitive societies with the acts of psychiatric patients in Western hospitals. See, for example, "Psychotic Factors in Shamanism" (1940) by A. L. Kroeber or the French ethnographer and psychoanalyst George Devereux's (1908–1985) "Shamans as Neurotics" (1961).

5. Bruno Bettelheim (1903–1990) was an Austrian student of Sigmund Freud. Imprisoned at Dachau and Buchenwald concentration camps, Bettelheim was freed in 1939 and emigrated to the United States. He

The other book is *Life Against Death,* in which Brown outlines an explicit comparison between the culture of "archaic man" and our own culture, in terms of the infantile and neurotic fantasies which they seem to express. Their common assumptions about primitive culture derive from Roheim (1925): primitive culture is autoplastic, ours is alloplastic. The primitive seeks to achieve his desires by self manipulation, performing surgical rites upon his own body to produce fertility in nature, subordination in women or hunting success. In modern culture we seek to achieve our desires by operating directly on the external environment, with the impressive technical results that are the most obvious distinction between the two types of cultures. Bettelheim adopts this summing up of the differences between the ritual and the technical bias in civilization. But he supposes that the primitive culture is produced by inadequate, immature personalities, and even that the psychological shortcomings of the savage accounts for his feeble technical achievements:

If preliterate peoples had personality structures as complex as those of modern man, if their defenses were as elaborate and their consciences as refined and demanding; if the dynamic interplay between ego, superego and id were as intricate and if

their egos were as well adapted to meet and change external reality—they would have developed societies equally complex, though probably different. Their societies have, however, remained small and relatively ineffective in coping with the external environment. It may be that one of the reasons for this is their tendency to try to solve problems by autoplastic rather than alloplastic manipulation. (p. 87)[6]

Let us assert again, as many anthropologists have before, that there are no grounds for supposing that primitive culture as such is the product of a primitive type of individual whose personality resembles that of infants or neurotics. And let us challenge the psychologists to express the syllogisms on which such a hypothesis might rest. Underlying the whole argument is the assumption that the problems which rituals are intended to solve are personal psychological problems. Bettelheim actually goes on to compare the primitive ritualist with the child who hits his own head when frustrated. This assumption underlies his whole book.

[We have omitted a 1,500-word discussion in which Douglas refutes a psychoanalytic interpretation made by Norman O. Brown (1913–2002) of body magic in indigenous societies. Brown was an Oxford-educated

---

spent virtually his whole career at the University of Chicago. Bettelheim was best known for his work with emotionally disturbed children. He was also recognized for his psychoanalytic analysis of ethnographic material, particularly his 1955 work *Symbolic Wounds.* Bettelheim is also often remembered for popularizing the incorrect idea that autism resulted from the behavior of mothers who were cold, distant, and uncaring. Scholars have little regard for Bettelheim today. His biographer, Richard Pollak, calls him a pathological liar (1997: 16–17), and there are many reports that he brutalized the schizophrenic children he treated.

6. Geza Roheim (1892–1953) was a Hungarian anthropologist. Early in his career, he became a follower of Freud. Roheim spent several years conducting fieldwork in Australia, Africa, and Melanesia and was one of the leading proponents of the psychoanalytic analysis of ethnographic material. When Bronislaw Malinowski attacked Freud's excursions into anthropology, Roheim was one of Freud's staunchest defenders. In *Australian Totemism* (1925), he characterized primitive cultures as *autoplastic* and Western society as *alloplastic.* These are terms that originated in medicine but are often used in psychology. In medicine "Autoplastic" refers to the surgical repair of defects with tissue from another part of the patient's body. "Alloplasty" refers to replacing a diseased or damaged body part with synthetic material. Using Bettelheim's example from *Symbolic Wounds* cited by Douglas in the paragraph above, Australian Aborigines are autoplastic because a man performs a ritual subincision of his penis to simulate the flow of a woman's menstrual blood. Ritual use of a blood substitute, say, a red vegetable dye, would be considered alloplastic.

Note how deeply idealistic (and deeply racist) the quote from Bettelheim is. He argues that complexity of society results from complexity of thinking and that primitive people are incapable of complex thought.

American scholar best known for his book Life Against Death *(1959), a psychoanalytic reinterpretation of human history. Brown argues that the ritual use of body substances such as excrement means that indigenous people are in a cultural evolutionary stage comparable to infantile anal eroticism. Today, Brown's (and Bettelheim's) works are usually considered artifacts of a bygone era; even at the time of publication these works were never widely popular among American anthropologists. But Douglas was English, and Freudian theory was taken much more seriously by European anthropologists. Douglas exposes Brown's bias in his discussion of a Winnebago Indian trickster myth and also cites an ethnographic example of how body substances such as blood and spittle may be considered as both polluting and sacred substances. Douglas concludes her discussion of what she calls "body dirt" with a reference to the ritual use of royal corpses. We rejoin the text at the beginning of her discussion of why products of the body are symbols of danger and power.]*

But now we are ready to broach the central question. Why should bodily refuse be a symbol of danger and of power? Why should sorcerers be thought to qualify for initiation by shedding blood or committing incest or **anthropophagy**. Why, when initiated, should their art consist largely of manipulating powers thought to inhere in the margins of the human body? Why should bodily margins be thought to be specially invested with power and danger?[7]

First, we can rule out the idea that public rituals express common infantile fantasies. These erotic desires which it is said to be the infant's dream to satisfy within the body's bounds are presumably common to the human race. Consequently body symbolism is part of the common stock of symbols, deeply emotive because of the individual's experience. But rituals draw on this common stock of symbols selectively. Some develop here, others there. Psychological explanations cannot of their nature account for what is culturally distinctive.

Second, all margins are dangerous. If they are pulled this way or that the shape of fundamental experience is altered. Any structure of ideas is vulnerable at its margins. We should expect the orifices of the body to symbolise its specially vulnerable points. Matter issuing from them is marginal stuff of the most obvious kind. Spittle, blood, milk, urine, faeces or tears by simply issuing forth have traversed the boundary of the body. So also have bodily parings, skin, nail, hair clippings and sweat. The mistake is to treat bodily margins in isolation from all other margins. There is no reason to assume any primacy for the individual's attitude to his own bodily and emotional experience, any more than for his cultural and social experience. This is the clue which explains the unevenness with which different aspects of the body are treated in the rituals of the world. In some, menstrual pollution is feared as a lethal danger; in others not at all. In some, death pollution is a daily preoccupation; in others not at all. In some, excreta is dangerous, in others it is only a joke. In India cooked food and saliva are pollution-prone, but Bushmen collect melon seeds from their mouths for later roasting and eating (Marshall-Thomas, p. 44).[8]

Each culture has its own special risks and problems. To which particular bodily margins its beliefs attribute power depends on what situation the body is mirroring. It seems that our deepest fears and desires take expression with a kind of witty aptness. To understand body pollution we should try to argue back from the known dangers of society to the known selection of bodily themes and try to recognize what **appositeness** is there.[9]

---

7. **"Anthropophagy"**: the eating of human flesh.

8. In this passage, Douglas applies Van Gennep's ideas about liminality to the body. Just as liminal states are dangerous because people in them are neither one thing nor another, so too the margins of the body are potentially dangerous because they are neither one thing nor another. Material such as hair, menstrual blood, and feces are both of the body and not of the body.

9. **"Appositeness"**: suitability or pertinence.

In pursuing a last-ditch reduction of all behavior to personal preoccupations of individuals with their own bodies the psychologists are merely **sticking to their last**.[10]

The derisive remark was once made against psychoanalysis that the unconscious sees a penis in every convex object and a vagina or anus in every concave one. I find that this sentence well characterises the facts. (Ferenczi, *Sex in Psychoanalysis*, p. 227, quoted by Brown)

It is the duty of every craftsman to stick to his last. The sociologists have the duty of meeting one kind of reductionism with their own. Just as it is true that everything symbolizes the body, so it is equally true (and all the more so for that reason) that the body symbolizes everything else. Out of this symbolism, which in fold upon fold of interior meaning leads back to the experience of the self with its body, the sociologist is justified in trying to work in the other direction to draw out some layers of insight about the self's experience in society.[11]

If anal eroticism is expressed at the cultural level we are not entitled to expect a population of anal erotics. We must look around for whatever it is that has made appropriate any cultural analogy with anal eroticism. The procedure in a modest way is like Freud's analysis of jokes. Trying to find a connection between the verbal form and the amusement derived from it he laboriously reduced joke interpretation to a few general rules. No comedian script-writer could use the rules for inventing jokes, but they help us to see some connections between laughter, the unconscious, and the structure of stories. The analogy is fair for pollution is like an inverted form of humour. It is not a joke for it does not amuse. But the structure of its symbolism uses comparison and double meaning like the structure of a joke.[12]

Four kinds of social pollution seem worth distinguishing. The first is danger pressing on external boundaries; the second, danger from transgressing the internal lines of the system; the third, danger in the margins of the lines. The fourth is danger from internal contradiction, when some of the basic postulates are denied by other basic postulates, so that at certain points the system seems to be at war with itself. In this chapter I show how the symbolism of the body's boundaries is used in this kind of unfunny wit to express danger to community boundaries.

The ritual life of the Coorgs (Srinivas) gives the impression of a people obsessed by the fear of dangerous impurities entering their system. They treat the body as if it were a beleaguered town, every ingress and exit guarded for spies and traitors. Anything issuing from the body is never to be re-admitted, but strictly avoided. The most dangerous pollution is for anything which has once emerged gaining re-entry. A little myth, trivial by other standards, justifies so much of their behavior and system of thought that the ethnographer has to refer to it three or four times. A Goddess in every trial of strength or cunning defeated her two brothers. Since future precedence depended on the outcome of these contests, they decided to defeat her by a ruse. She was tricked into taking out of her mouth the betel that she was chewing to

---

10. **"Sticking to their last"**: A last is a form in the shape of a foot that a shoemaker uses to make or repair shoes. Douglas means that psychologists tend to derive explanatory theories from their study of an individual's behavior

11. Note the centrality of Douglas's idea of the body. Also, consider the relationship between this and Durkheim's idea that religious classification systems such as totemism symbolize society. If such systems are society writ large, Douglas is saying that the body is society writ small.
  Sandor Ferenczi (1873–1933) was a professor of psychoanalysis and a colleague of Freud.

12. Douglas is referring to Freud's *Jokes and Their Relation to the Unconscious* (1960 [1905]), which explored the relationship between dreams and jokes. In this book, Freud outlined different types of jokes and the literary and psychological mechanisms that he believed made them amusing.
  Note that Douglas's argument is literary rather than scientific. She urges us to understand society in terms of metaphors rather than environmental adaptations or calorie counts.

see if it was redder than theirs and into popping it back again. Once she had realized she had eaten something which had once been in her own mouth and was therefore defiled by saliva, though she wept and bewailed she accepted the full justice of her downfall. The mistake canceled all her previous victories, and her brothers' eternal precedence over her was established as of right.[13]

The Coorgs have a place within the system of Hindoo castes. There is good reason to regard them as not exceptional or aberrant in Hindoo India (Dumont and Peacock). Therefore they conceive status in terms of purity and impurity as these ideas are applied throughout the regime of castes. The lowest castes are the most impure and it is they whose humble services enable the higher castes to be free of bodily impurities. They wash clothes, cut hair, dress corpses and so on. The whole system represents a body in which by the division of labour the head does the thinking and praying and the most despised parts carry away waste matter. Each sub-caste community in a local region is conscious of its relative standing in the scale of purity. Seen from ego's position the system of caste purity is structured upwards. Those above him are more pure. All the positions below him, be they ever so intricately distinguished in relation to one another, are to him polluting. Thus for any ego within the system the threatening non-structure against

which barriers must be erected lies below. The sad wit of pollution as it comments on bodily functions symbolizes descent in the caste structure by contact with faeces, blood and corpses.[14]

The Coorgs shared with other castes this fear of what is outside and below. But living in their mountain fastness they were also an isolated community, having only occasional and controllable contact with the world around. For them the model of the exits and entrances of the human body is a doubly apt symbolic focus of fears for their minority standing in the larger society. Here I am suggesting that when rituals express anxiety about the body's orifices the sociological counterpart of this anxiety is a care to protect the political and cultural unity of a minority group. The Israelites were always in their history a hard-pressed minority. In their beliefs all the bodily issues were polluting, blood, pus, excreta, semen, etc. The threatened boundaries of their body politic would be well mirrored in their care for the integrity, unity and purity of the physical body.

The Hindoo caste system, while embracing all minorities, embraces them each as a distinctive, cultural sub-unit. In any given locality, any sub-caste is likely to be a minority. The purer and higher its caste status, the more of a minority it must be. Therefore the revulsion from touching corpses and excreta does not merely express the order of caste in the system

---

13. Douglas bases her analysis on the Coorgs, an Indian ethnic group now called the Kodava who live in Southwestern India. The Coorgs were studied by M. N. Srinivas (1916–1999), a student of A. R. Radcliffe-Brown. Srinivas presented a structural-functionalist analysis of food taboos in *Religion and Society among the Coorgs of South India* (1952).

14. In the caste system of India, people are ranked by ritual purity. The purest individuals are leaders and priests; those who are most polluted have tasks dealing with the disposal of human waste and refuse. This association of pollution with human refuse is an extension of body symbolism, a key metaphor in Hindu belief. In the Vedas (sacred Hindu texts), the creation of the world is described as the result of the gods sacrificing a divine being named Purusha, with the caste divisions created by the division of Purusha's body. From Purusha's mouth came the priests, his arms the warriors, his thighs the merchants, and from his feet the laborers. This Hindu myth is a poetic example of the body-society symbolism with which Douglas began the essay. Note that the fifth major division of the caste system is the Dalit caste, which accounts for as much as 25 percent of India's population. Dalits occupy the lowest, most polluted position in the caste system. There are numerous accounts of their origin but they do not have as direct a theological connection with Purusha as the other castes.

Douglas cites a work here by Louis Dumont (1911–1998). Dumont was a French anthropologist who wrote a classic analysis of the Indian caste system called *Homo Hierarchicus* which was published in 1966, the same year as *Purity and Danger*. Dumont, like Douglas, was strongly influenced by Durkheim.

as a whole. The anxiety about bodily margins expresses danger to group survival.[15]

That the sociological approach to caste pollution is much more convincing than a psychoanalytic approach is clear when we consider what the Indian's private attitudes to defecation are. In the ritual we know that to touch excrement is to be defiled and that the latrine cleaners stand in the lowest grade of the caste hierarchy. If this pollution rule expressed individual anxieties we would expect Hindoos to be controlled and secretive about the act of defecation. It comes as a considerable shock to read that slack disregard is their normal attitude, to such an extent that pavements, verandahs and public places are littered with faeces until the sweeper comes along.

> Indians defecate everywhere. They defecate, mostly, beside the railway tracks. But they also defecate on the beaches—they defecate on the streets; they never look for cover . . . These squatting figures—to the visitor, after a time, as eternal and emblematic as Rodin's Thinker—are never spoken of; they are never written about; they are not mentioned in novels or stories; they do not appear in feature films or documentaries. This might be regarded as part of a permissible prettifying intention. But the truth is that Indians do not see these squatters and might even with complete sincerity, deny that they exist. (Naipaul, Chapter 3)

Rather than oral or anal eroticism it is more convincing to argue that caste pollution represents only what it claims to be. It is a symbolic system, based on the image of the body, whose primary concern is the ordering of a social hierarchy.

It is worth using the Indian example to ask why saliva and genital excretions are more pollution-worthy than tears. If I can reverently drink his tears, wrote Jean Genet, why not the so **limpid** drop on the end of his nose? To this we can reply: first that nasal secretions are not so limpid as tears. They are more like **treacle** than water. When a thick **rheum** oozes from the eye it is no more apt for poetry than nasal rheum. But admittedly clear, fast-running tears are the stuff of romantic poetry: they do not defile. This is partly because tears are naturally preempted by the symbolism of washing. Tears are like rivers of moving water. They purify, cleanse, bathe the eyes, so how can they pollute? But more significantly tears are not related to the bodily functions of digestion or procreation. Therefore their scope for symbolizing social relations and social processes is narrower. This is evident when we reflect on caste structure. Since place in the hierarchy of purity is biologically transmitted, sexual behavior is important for preserving the purity of caste. For this reason, in higher castes, boundary pollution focuses particularly on sexuality. The caste membership of an individual is determined by his mother, for though she may have married into a higher caste, her children take their caste from her. Therefore women are the gates of entry to the caste. Female purity is carefully guarded and a woman who is known to have had sexual intercourse with a man of lower caste is brutally punished. Male sexual purity does not carry this responsibility. Hence male promiscuity is a lighter matter. A mere ritual bath is enough to cleanse a man from sexual contact with a low caste woman. But his sexuality does not entirely escape the burden of worry which boundary pollution attaches to the body. According to Hindoo belief a sacred quality inheres in semen, which should not be wasted. In a penetrating essay on female purity in India (1963) Yalman says:

> While caste purity must be protected in women and men may be allowed much greater freedom, it is, of course, better for

---

15. Douglas's central theme is that the boundaries of the body are the metaphorical equivalent of the boundaries of society. Concern for the boundaries of society is mirrored by concern for the boundaries of the body. Douglas makes two related points: first, this is likely to be a particular concern of minority groups. Second, the structure of Hindu society creates many minority groups. The higher the caste of such groups, the smaller their membership and the greater their concern with policing their borders. The care taken to avoid pollution to their physical bodies is a symbolic manifestation of their desire to protect their political and social integrity.

the men not to waste the sacred quality contained in their semen. It is well-known that they are exhorted not merely to avoid low caste women, but all women (Carstairs 1956, 1957; Gough 1956). For the loss of semen is the loss of this potent stuff . . . it is best never to sleep with women at all.

Both male and female physiology lend themselves to the analogy with the vessel which must not pour away or dilute its vital fluids. Females are correctly seen as, literally, the entry by which the pure content may be adulterated. Males are treated as pores through which the precious stuff may ooze out and be lost, the whole system being thereby enfeebled.[16]

A double moral standard is often applied to sexual offenses. In a patrilineal system of descent wives are the door of entry to the group. In this they hold a place analogous to that of sisters in the Hindoo caste. Through the adultery of a wife impure blood is introduced to the lineage. So the symbolism of the imperfect vessel appropriately weighs more heavily on the women than on the men.[17]

If we treat ritual protection of bodily orifices as a symbol of social preoccupations about exits and entrances, the purity of cooked food becomes important. I quote a passage on the capacity of cooked food to be polluted and to carry pollution (in an unsigned review article on Pure and Impure, *Contributions to Indian Sociology*, III, July 1959, p. 37).

When a man uses an object it becomes part of him, participates in him. Then, no doubt, this appropriation is much closer in the case of food, and the point is that appropriation precedes absorption, as it accompanies the cooking. Cooking may be taken to imply a complete appropriation of the food by the household. It is almost as if, before being "internally absorbed" by the individual, food was, by cooking, collectively predigested. One cannot share the food prepared by people without sharing in their nature. This is one aspect of the situation. Another is that cooked food is extremely permeable to pollution.

This reads like a correct transliteration of Indian pollution symbolism regarding cooked food. But what is gained by proffering a descriptive account as if it were explanatory? In India

---

16. Note the connection Douglas makes between her earlier invocation of doorways, Van Gennep's idea of the liminal, and women as the gateway into caste. In so doing, she connects the physical body, symbolism, and social structure. Note also the heavy emphasis on simile in this passage. Women are like gates; tears are like rivers; bodies are like vessels. This type of argument is characteristic of symbolic anthropology.

Jean Genet (1910–1986) was a French novelist, playwright, and protégé of the existentialist philosopher Jean-Paul Sartre. Genet was best known for his plays. His works are contributions to the theater of the absurd, a form of drama in which the impossible routinely happens in order to make philosophical points. Much of Genet's work was designed to raise questions by shocking and offending.

Nur Yalman (b. 1931), a Turkish anthropologist, also studied with the British functionalists. His advisor was Edmund Leach (1910–1989).

In this paragraph, Douglas makes references to three works that she does not include in her bibliography: two of the psychiatrist and anthropologist George Morris Carstairs's (1916–1991) works on high-caste Hindus and an essay by anthropologist Kathleen Gough (1925–1990) on Brahmin kinship. Curious readers will find complete references for these in the References Cited section of this book. Both Carstairs and Gough were trained by British structural functionalist mentors. Gough became well known for her analysis of the relationship between anthropology and colonialism.

"Limpid": clear or transparent; **"treacle"**: molasses or syrup; **"rheum"**: a watery mucous discharge from the eyes or nose.

17. Douglas says that rules of body purity and pollution are symbolic of a group's place in society as well as the preservation of that group. It follows that because caste membership is transmitted through women, the rules of sexual purity and pollution are stricter for women than for men. Just as sexual restrictions can be symbolic of anxiety about caste membership, the polluting qualities of menstrual blood, semen, or other body products can be symbolic of lineage membership.

the cooking process is seen as the beginning of ingestion, and therefore cooking is susceptible to pollution, in the same way as eating. But why is this complex found in India and in parts of Polynesia and in Judaism and other places, but not wherever humans sit down to eat? I suggest that food is not likely to be polluting at all unless the external boundaries of the social system are under pressure. We can go further to explain why the actual cooking of the food in India must be ritually pure. The purity of the castes is correlated with an elaborate hereditary division of labour between castes. The work performed by each caste carries a symbolic load: it says something about the relatively pure status of the caste in question. Some kinds of labour correspond with the excretory functions of the body, for example that of washermen, barbers, sweepers, as we have seen. Some professions are involved with bloodshed or alcoholic liquor, such as tanners, warriors, toddy tappers. So they are low in the scale of purity in so far as their occupations are at variance with Brahminic ideals. But the point at which food is prepared for the table is the point at which the interrelation of the purity structure and the occupational structure needs to be set straight. For food is produced by the combined efforts of several castes of varying degrees of purity: the blacksmith, carpenter, ropemaker, the peasant. Before being admitted to the body some clear symbolic break is needed to express food's separation from necessary but impure contacts. The cooking process, entrusted to pure hands, provides this ritual break. Some such break we would expect to find whenever the production of food is in the hands of the relatively impure.[18]

These are the general lines on which primitive rituals must be related to the social order and the culture in which they are found. The examples I have given are crude, intended to exemplify a broad objection to a certain current treatment of ritual themes. I add one more, even cruder, to underline my point. Much literature has been expended by psychologists on Yurok pollution ideas (Erikson, Posinsky). These North Californian Indians who lived by fishing for salmon in the Klamath River, would seem to have been obsessed by the behavior of liquids, if their pollution rules can be said to express an obsession. They are careful not to mix good water with bad, not to urinate into rivers, not to mix sea and fresh water, and so on. I insist that these rules cannot imply obsessional neuroses, and they cannot be interpreted unless the fluid formlessness of their highly competitive social life be taken into account (Du Bois).

To sum up. There is unquestionably a relation between individual preoccupations and primitive ritual. But the relation is not the simple one which some psychoanalysts have assumed. Primitive ritual draws upon individual experience, of course. This is a truism. But it draws upon it so selectively that it cannot be said to be primarily inspired by the need to solve individual problems common to the human race, still less explained by clinical research. Primitives are not trying to cure or prevent personal neuroses by their public rituals. Psychologists can tell us whether the public expression of individual anxieties is likely to solve personal problems or not. Certainly we must suppose that some interaction of the kind is probable. But that is not at issue. The analysis of ritual symbolism cannot begin until we recognize ritual as an attempt to create and maintain a particular culture, a particular set of assumptions by which experience is controlled. Any culture is a series of related structures which comprise social forms, values, cosmology, the whole of knowledge and through which all experience is mediated. Certain cultural themes are expressed by rites of bodily manipulation. In this very general sense primitive culture can be said to be autoplastic. But the objective of these rituals is not negative withdrawal from reality. The assertions they make are not usefully to be compared to the withdrawal of the infant into thumb-sucking and masturbation.

---

18. Douglas refers to the prohibition on eating beef in India, the principles of mana and taboo in traditional Polynesian societies, and the dietary rules about kosher food in Judaism. She suggests that rules about food and its preparation symbolize the need for a society or class to protect itself from outsiders or foreign influences. According to Douglas, protecting the body from pollution by guarding the orifices, in this case restricting the diet, symbolizes the protection of traditional beliefs.

The rituals enact the form of social relations and in giving these relations visible expression they enable people to know their own society. The rituals work upon the body politic through the symbolic medium of the physical body.[19]

REFERENCES

Bettelheim, B. 1955. *Symbolic Wounds*. Glencoe, IL.

Brown, Norman O. 1959. *Life Against Death*. London.

Du Bois, Cora. 1936. "The Wealth Concept as an Integrative Factor in Tolowa-Tututni Culture." Chapter in *Essays in Anthropology, Presented to A. L. Kroeber*.

Dumont, L. and Peacock, D. 1959. *Contributions to Indian Sociology*. Vol. III.

Marshall-Thomas, E. 1959. *The Harmless People*. New York.

Naipaul, V. S. 1964. *An Area of Darkness*. London.

Posinky. 1956. *Psychiatric Quarterly* XXX, p. 598.

Roheim, G. 1925. *Australian Totemism*.

Yalman, N. 1963. "The Purity of Women in Ceylon and Southern India." *Journal of the Royal Anthropological Institute*.

---

19. In this last paragraph, Douglas makes one final objection to the psychological explanation of ritual. Instead, Douglas's conclusion reflects the strong influence of Durkheim on her work. Durkheim was concerned with demonstrating that a society was more than the sum of the psychological makeup of its citizens. In other words, he tried hard to separate sociology from psychology. Douglas attempts to do the same thing. She insists that the rules of ritual and pollution are what Durkheim called *social facts*. They are not reducible to manifestations of individual psychology. Whatever effects they may have on the individual, they reflect the ways society maintains its structure and solidarity. Douglas's work is profoundly symbolic—a materialist's analysis of the caste system, for example, would have focused on the political and economic inequalities inherent in Indian society, which Douglas ignores. With some modification, we could imagine this essay appearing as a chapter in Durkheim's *Elementary Forms of the Religious Life* (orig. 1912). For example, in the last sentences of this final paragraph, she characterizes ritual as the attempt to create and maintain a particular culture.

25. Symbols in Ndembu Ritual

Victor Turner (1920–1983)

AMONG THE NDEMBU OF ZAMBIA (formerly Northern Rhodesia), the importance of ritual in the lives of the villagers in 1952 was striking. Hardly a week passed in a small neighborhood without a ritual drum being heard in one or another of its villages.

By "ritual" I mean prescribed formal behavior for occasions not given over to technological routine having reference to beliefs in mystical beings or powers. The symbol is the smallest unit of ritual which still retains the specific properties of ritual behavior; it is the ultimate unit of specific structure in a ritual context. Since this essay is in the main a description and analysis of the structure and properties of symbols, it will be enough to state here, follow-

ing the *Concise Oxford Dictionary*, that a "symbol" is a thing regarded by general consent as naturally typifying or representing or recalling something by possession of analogous qualities or by association in fact or thought. The symbols I observed in the field were, empirically, objects, activities, relationships, events, gestures, and spatial units in a ritual situation.[1]

Following the advice and example of Professor Monica Wilson, I asked Ndembu specialists as well as laymen to interpret the symbols of their ritual. As a result, I obtained much **exegetic** material. I felt that it was methodologically important to keep observational and interpretative materials distinct from one another. The reason for this will soon become apparent.[2]

From *The Forest of Symbols* (1967)

1. This essay, first presented as a paper at a professional meeting in 1958, is one of Turner's most famous works. In it, he outlines some basic properties of symbols and contrasts his method of symbolic analysis with psychoanalytic thought using examples from his fieldwork with the Ndembu. Freudian theory had been popular in anthropology since the 1930s. However, by the 1960s, critiques in works such as this and the previous essay by Mary Douglas were instrumental in anthropologists turning away from psychoanalytic concepts in social analysis.

In this passage, Turner identifies the symbol as the smallest unit of ritual and hence the primary unit of analysis. There was much interest in the 1950s and 1960s in trying to find the smallest units of social behavior. It is an issue that connects Claude Lévi-Strauss, ethnoscientists such as Harold C. Conklin (1926–2016), and symbolic anthropologists such as Turner. The materialist Marvin Harris also proposed a basic unit of culture, the "actone," which he defined as "a behavioral bit consisting of body motion and environmental effect" (1964: 37).

2. Turner was a student of Monica H. Wilson (1908–1982), a Cambridge-educated South African social anthropologist, and a student of Bronislaw Malinowski. In the 1930s, functionalist anthropologists were writing about African societies as if they were static. Wilson, however, focused on economic, political, and social change in African societies, particularly among the Nyakyusa of southern Tanzania and northern Malawi. She is best known for her detailed fieldwork and ethnographies.

Turner speaks of keeping observational and interpretive materials separate from one another because he wrote this article at a time when symbolic interpretation was controversial and because of the training he received from Wilson. The care with which he outlines his argument is in part a reaction to the controversy caused by Freudian interpretations of ethnographic material. Psychoanalytic analysis relies heavily on the interpreter's explication of the unconscious meaning of a ritual or other symbols. In the British structural

405

I found that I could not analyze ritual symbols without studying them in a time series in relation to other "events," for symbols are essentially involved in social process. I came to see performances of ritual as distinct phases in the social processes whereby groups became adjusted to internal changes and adapted to their external environment. From this standpoint the ritual symbol becomes a factor in social action, a positive force in an activity field. The symbol becomes associated with human interests, purposes, ends, and means, whether these are explicitly formulated or have to be inferred from the observed behavior. The structure and properties of a symbol become those of a dynamic entity, at least within its appropriate context of action.[3]

STRUCTURE AND PROPERTIES OF RITUAL SYMBOLS

The structure and properties of ritual symbols may be inferred from three classes of data: (1) external form and observable characteristics; (2) interpretations offered by specialists and by laymen; (3) significant contexts largely worked out by the anthropologist.[4]

Here is an example. At *Nkang'a*, the girl's puberty ritual, a novice is wrapped in a blanket and laid at the foot of a *mudyi* sapling. The *mudyi* tree *Diplorrhyncus condylocarpon* is conspicuous for its white latex, which exudes in milky beads if the thin bark is scratched. For Ndembu this is its most important observable characteristic, and therefore I propose to call it "the milk tree" henceforward. Most Ndembu women can attribute several meanings to this tree. In the first place, they say that the milk tree is the "senior" (*mukulumpi*) tree of the ritual. Each kind of ritual has this "senior" or, as I will call it, "dominant" symbol. Such symbols fall into a special class which I will discuss more fully later. Here it is enough to state that dominant symbols are regarded not merely as means to the fulfillment of the avowed purposes of a given ritual, but also and more importantly refer to values that are regarded as ends in themselves, that is, to axiomatic values. Secondly, the women say with reference to its observable characteristics that the milk tree

---

functionalist tradition, Turner considers symbols to be empirically verifiable units and is interested in the laws by which they are used.

"Exegetic": interpretive or explanatory.

3. Contrary to the psychoanalytic approach, Turner maintains that because ritual symbols are a part of social action they must be analyzed within the social and temporal contexts in which they are expressed. Turner's structural-functionalist roots are also apparent in this paragraph in that he sees rituals as the mechanism by which groups adjust to changes in their social and external environment.

Note Turner's use of the phrase "activity field." He will build on this concept throughout the essay, referring to action fields and total field situations. Turner's notion of a "field" is derived from the work of Kurt Lewin (1890–1947), a German psychologist who, after fleeing the Nazis, made his career in the United States. Lewin believed that understanding behavior required considering an individual and their context as a single "field." He argued that behavior is a function of the field as it exists at a particular moment, that an analysis should begin with the entire situation and move toward an understanding of the component parts, and that this could be mathematically represented (Hall and Lindzey 1978: 386).

4. In this short paragraph Turner lays out his position on the *emic* and *etic* debate that was raging in anthropology in the 1960s. Rather than arguing the validity of one perspective over the other, Turner presents three perspectives that he believes are equally important and valid. He proposes that observed data, informants' interpretations, and the anthropologist's analysis are all legitimate. In the following paragraph, he demonstrates how the symbolism of the *mudyi* tree can be viewed from all three perspectives. Turner makes numerous references to emics and etics throughout this essay (though never using those words). He repeatedly attacks the (emic) notion that anthropologists should limit themselves to faithfully recording the worldview and interpretations of their subjects. He considers such explanations important but only alongside other forms of interpretive work.

stands for human breast milk and also for the breasts that supply it. They relate this meaning to the fact that *Nkang'a* is performed when a girl's breasts begin to ripen, not after her first menstruation, which is the subject of another and less elaborate ritual. The main theme of *Nkang'a* is indeed the tie of nurturing between mother and child, not the bond of birth. This theme of nurturing is expressed at *Nkang'a* in a number of supplementary symbols indicative of the act of feeding and of foodstuff. In the third place, the women describe the milk tree as "the tree of a mother and her child." Here the reference has shifted from description of a biological act, breast feeding, to a social tie of profound significance both in domestic relations and in the structure of the widest Ndembu community. This latter meaning is brought out most clearly in a text I recorded from a male ritual specialist. I translate literally.

> The milk tree is the place of all mothers of the lineage (*ivumu,* literally "womb" or "stomach"). It represents the ancestress of women and men. The milk tree is where our ancestress slept when she was initiated. To initiate here means the dancing of women round and round the milk tree where the novice sleeps. One ancestress after another slept there down to our grandmother and our mother and ourselves the children. That is the place of our tribal custom (*muchidi*)[a] where we began, even men just the same, for men are circumcised under a milk tree.[5]

This text brings out clearly those meanings of the milk tree which refer to principles and values of social organization. At one level of abstraction the milk tree stands for matriliny, the principle on which the continuity of Ndembu society depends. Matriliny governs succession to office and inheritance of property, and it vests dominant rights of residence in local units. More than any other principle of social organization it confers order and structure on Ndembu social life. Beyond this, however, "*mudyi*" means more than matriliny, both according to this text and according to many other statements I have collected. It stands for tribal custom (*muchidi wetu*) itself. The principle of matriliny, the backbone of Ndembu social organization, as an element in the semantic structure of the milk tree, itself symbolizes the total system of interrelations between groups and persons that makes up Ndembu society. Some of the meanings of important symbols may themselves be symbols, each with its own system of meanings. At its highest level of abstraction, therefore, the milk tree stands for the unity and continuity of Ndembu society. Both men and women are components of that spatiotemporal continuum. Perhaps that is why one educated Ndembu, trying to cross the gap between our cultures, explained to me that the milk tree was like the British flag above the administrative headquarters. "*Mudyi* is our flag," he said.[6]

When discussing the milk tree symbolism in the context of the girls' puberty ritual, informants tend to stress the harmonizing, cohesive aspects of the milk tree symbolism. They also stress the aspect of dependence. The child depends on its mother for nutriment; similarly, say the Ndembu, the tribesman drinks from

---

5. Turner says Ndembu women attribute several symbolic meanings to the *mudyi* tree. The fact that a single symbol can represent many things is called *multivocality,* and it is one of Turner's key ideas. He first defined the term in his article "Ritual Symbolism, Morality, and Social Structure among the Ndembu" (1967c). Turner also uses the phrase "dominant symbol" for the first time. This is a symbol that represents axiomatic values in a society. The *mudyi* tree is a Ndembu example, the American flag is a good example in the United States.

6. Like Douglas, Turner inherited the Durkheimian perspective implicit in British structural functionalism. Here you see this perspective expressed in his statement that the *mudyi* tree represents not only breast milk but at its most abstract level of meaning, Ndembu society. Thus, in Durkheimian terms, it is a collective representation. Turner was also influenced by Raymond Firth (1901–2002). A student of Malinowski, Firth was interested in linking the interpretation of symbolism to social structures and social events (Firth 1973: 25). Note the symbolic tie between the *mudyi* tree and matrilineality. Here Turner shows the link between kinship and symbolism.

the breasts of tribal custom. Thus nourishment and learning are equated in the meaning content of the milk tree. I have often heard the milk tree compared to "going to school"; the child is said to swallow instruction as a baby swallows milk and *kapudyi,* the thin cassava gruel Ndembu liken to milk. Do we not ourselves speak of "a thirst for knowledge"? Here the milk tree is a shorthand for the process of instruction in tribal matters that follows the critical episode in both boys' and girls' initiation—circumcision in the case of the boys and the long trial of lying motionless in that of the girls. The mother's role is the archetype, of protector, nourisher, and teacher. For example, a chief is often referred to as the "mother of his people," while the hunter-doctor who initiates a novice into a hunting cult is called "the mother of huntsmanship *(mama dawuyang'a).*" An apprentice circumciser is referred to as "child of the circumcision medicine" and his instructor as "mother of the circumcision medicine." In all the senses hitherto described, the milk tree represents harmonious, benevolent aspects of domestic and tribal life.

However, when the third mode of interpretation, contextual analysis, is applied, the interpretations of informants are contradicted by the way people actually behave with reference to the milk tree. It becomes clear that the milk tree represents aspects of social differentiation and even opposition between the components of a society which ideally it is supposed to symbolize as a harmonious whole. The first relevant context we shall examine is the role of the milk tree in a series of action situations within the framework of the girls' puberty ritual. Symbols, as I have said, produce action, and dominant symbols tend to become focuses in interaction. Groups mobilize around them, worship before them, perform other symbolic activities near them, and add other symbolic objects to them, often to make composite shrines. Usually these groups of participants themselves stand for important components of the secular social system, whether these components consist of corporate groups, such as families and lineages, or of mere categories of persons possessing similar characteristics, such as old men, women, children, hunters, or widows. In each kind of Ndembu ritual a different group or category becomes the focal social element. In *Nkang'a* this focal element is the unity of Ndembu women. It is the women who dance around the milk tree and initiate the recumbent novice by making her the hub of their whirling circle. Not only is the milk tree the "flag of the Ndembu"; more specifically, in the early phases of *Nkang'a,* it is the "flag" of Ndembu women. In this situation it does more than focus the exclusiveness of women; it mobilizes them in opposition to the men. For the women sing songs taunting the men and for a time will not let men dance in their circle. Therefore, if we are to take account of the operational aspect of the milk tree symbol, including not only what Ndembu say about it but also what they do with it in its "meaning," we must allow that it distinguishes women as a social category and indicates their solidarity.[7]

The milk tree makes further discriminations. For example, in certain action contexts it stands for the novice herself. One such context is the initial sacralization of a specific milk

7. Max Gluckman (1911–1975) was Turner's mentor, dissertation advisor, and a major influence on him. Gluckman was the recipient of the first doctorate in anthropology awarded by Oxford University. His dissertation was supervised by the evolutionary anthropologist Robert Marett (1866–1943) but he was more deeply influenced by Radcliffe-Brown and Malinowski, whose seminar at the London School of Economics he attended. Gluckman focused on the socially integrative effects of ritual expressions of conflict. Famous for his formulation of the concept of "rituals of rebellion," Gluckman proposed that the ritual enactment of conflict (such as that between women and men in the *Nkang'a* rite) allows the expression of hostility while actually reinforcing the established social order. Having discussed the role that *mudyi* tree symbolism plays in tribal life, Turner tells us that the milk tree also represents differentiation and opposition in a situation that should be harmonious. In the *Nkang'a* ritual the *mudyi* is the "flag" of Ndembu women as they highlight their opposition to men, taunting them and denying them access to their dance circle. This contradiction is explained in Gluckman's terms.

tree sapling. Here the natural property of the tree's immaturity is significant. Informants say that a young tree is chosen because the novice is young. A girl's particular tree symbolizes her new social personality as a mature woman. In the past and occasionally today, the girl's puberty ritual was part of her marriage ritual, and marriage marked her transition from girlhood to womanhood. Much of the training and most of the symbolism of *Nkang'a* are concerned with making the girl a sexually accomplished spouse, a fruitful woman, and a mother able to produce a generous supply of milk. For each girl this is a unique process. She is initiated alone and is the center of public attention and care. From her point of view it is *her Nkang'a,* the most thrilling and self-gratifying phase of her life. Society recognizes and encourages these sentiments, even though it also prescribes certain trials and hardships for the novice, who must suffer before she is glorified on the last day of the ritual. The milk tree, then, celebrates the coming-of-age of a new social personality, and distinguishes her from all other women at this one moment in her life. In terms of its action context, the milk tree here also expresses the conflict between the girl and the moral community of adult women she is entering. Not without reason is the milk tree site known as "the place of death" or "the place of suffering," terms also applied to the site where boys are circumcised, for the girl novice must not move a muscle throughout a whole hot and **clamant** day. [8]

In other contexts, the milk tree site is the scene of opposition between the novice's own mother and the group of adult women. The mother is **debarred** from attending the ring of dancers. She is losing her child, although later

she recovers her as an adult co-member of her lineage. Here we see the conflict between the matricentric family and the wider society which, as I have said, is dominantly articulated by the principle of matriliny. The relationship between mother and daughter persists throughout the ritual, but its content is changed. It is worth pointing out that, at one phase in *Nkang'a,* mother and daughter interchange portions of clothing. This may perhaps be related to the Ndembu custom whereby mourners wear small portions of a dead relative's clothing. Whatever the interchange of clothing may mean to a psychoanalyst—and here we arrive at one of the limits of our present anthropological competence—it seems not unlikely that Ndembu intend to symbolize the termination for both mother and daughter of an important aspect of their relationship. This is one of the symbolic actions—one of very few—about which I found it impossible to elicit any interpretation in the puberty ritual. Hence it is legitimate to infer, in my opinion, that powerful unconscious wishes, of a kind considered illicit by Ndembu, are expressed in it. [9]

Opposition between the tribeswomen and the novice's mother is **mimetically** represented at the milk tree towards the end of the first day of the puberty ritual. The girl's mother cooks a huge meal of cassava and beans—both kinds of food are symbols in *Nkang'a,* with many meanings—for the women visitors, who eat in village groups and not at random. Before eating, the women return to the milk tree from their eating place a few yards away and circle the tree in procession. The mother brings up the rear holding up a large spoon full of cassava and beans. Suddenly she shouts: "Who wants the cassava of *chipwampwilu?*" All the

---

8. **"Clamant"**: noisy.

9. Elements of both Gluckman and Sigmund Freud (1856–1939) appear in this paragraph. First, Turner explains that the ritual allows the symbolic expression of hostility between the initiate's mother and the larger group of adult women in this matrilineal society. Then, because Turner was unable to elicit any explanation for a mother and daughter's exchange of apparel during the *Nkang'a* rite, he assumes the symbolism of the exchange indicates unconscious feelings that the Ndembu censor from conscious expression. However, is Turner's inference legitimate? A famous quip apocryphally attributed to Freud has it that "sometimes a cigar is just a cigar." Do actions such as exchanging portions of clothing have to have meaning?

"Debarred": prohibited.

women rush to be first to seize the spoon and eat from it. "*Chipwampwilu*" appears to be an archaic word and no one knows its meaning. Informants say that the spoon represents the novice herself in her role of married woman, while the food stands both for her reproductive power (*lusemu*) and her role as cultivator and cook. One woman told my wife: "It is lucky if the person snatching the spoon comes from the novice's own village. Otherwise, the mother believes that her child will go far away from her to a distant village and die there. The mother wants her child to stay near her." Implicit in this statement is a deeper conflict than that between the matricentric family and mature female society. It refers to another dominant articulating principle of Ndembu society, namely virilocal marriage according to which women live at their husbands' villages after marriage. Its effect is sometimes to separate mothers from daughters by considerable distances. In the episode described, the women symbolize the matrilineal cores of villages. Each village wishes to gain control through marriage over the novice's capacity to work. Its members also hope that her children will be raised in it, thus adding to its size and prestige. Later in *Nkang'a* there is a symbolic struggle between the novice's matrilineal kin and those of her bridegroom, which makes explicit the conflict between virilocality and matriliny.[10]

Lastly, in the context of action situation, the milk tree is sometimes described by informants as representing the novice's own matrilineage. Indeed, it has this significance in the competition for the spoon just discussed, for women of her own village try to snatch the spoon before members of other villages. Even if such women do not belong to her matrilineage but are married to its male members, they are thought to be acting on its behalf. Thus, the milk tree in one of its action aspects represents the unity and exclusiveness of a single matrilineage with a local focus in a village against other such corporate groups. The conflict between yet another subsystem and the total system is given dramatic and symbolic form.

By this time, it will have become clear that considerable discrepancy exists between the interpretations of the milk tree offered by informants and the behavior exhibited by Ndembu in situations dominated by the milk tree symbolism. Thus, we are told that the milk tree represents the close tie between mother and daughter. Yet the milk tree separates a daughter from her mother. We are also told that the milk tree stands for the unity of Ndembu society. Yet we find that in practice it separates women from men, and some categories and groups of women from others. How are these contradictions between principle and practice to be explained?[11]

---

10. Turner mentions the presence of his wife in this paragraph. Although she accompanied him into the field and helped him conduct research, Edith Turner (1921–2016) is rarely mentioned in his works. She was an accomplished anthropologist in her own right and with her husband the coauthor of a book on Christian pilgrimage (1978). After her husband's death in 1983, she published numerous books including *The Spirit and the Drum: A Memoir of Africa* (1987), *Experiencing Ritual: A New Interpretation of African Healing* (1992), and *Heart of Lightness: The Life Story of an Anthropologist* (2005).

Turner's mention of his wife raises another interesting question. Turner has chosen to focus his study on a women's ritual, not an easy task for a male anthropologist. James Anthony Pritchett (1948–2019), an anthropologist who studied the Ndembu more than thirty years after Turner's fieldwork there notes that the society is "highly segregated by gender." Pritchett reports that, as a male anthropologist, he would "produce tension" if he worked with women and that therefore he chose to work with men (2007: 12). Given the gender segregation in Ndembu society, it is likely that Edith Turner's contribution to her husband's work was substantial but little acknowledged by her husband.

"**Mimetic**": Relating to mimicking or imitating.

11. Turner's analysis owes much to the work of both A. R. Radcliffe-Brown and Max Gluckman. Compare the works by Turner and Radcliffe-Brown in this volume (essay 15). Both essays uncover disjunctures in the social structure of society. In Radcliffe-Brown's essay, disjuncture between a husband and his wife's family is dealt with through a joking relationship. For Turner, ritual and symbolism mark the disjunction between mothers and daughters and between matrilineality and virilocality.

SOME PROBLEMS OF INTERPRETATION

I am convinced that my informants genuinely believed that the milk tree represented only the linking and unifying aspects of Ndembu social organization. I am equally convinced that the role of the milk tree in action situations where it represents a focus of specified groups in opposition to other groups, forms an equally important component of its total meaning. Here the important question must be asked, "meaning for whom?" For if Ndembu do not recognize the discrepancy between their interpretation of the milk tree symbolism and other behavior in connection with it, does this mean that the discrepancy has no relevance for the social anthropologist? Indeed some anthropologists claim, with Nadel (1954: 108), that "uncomprehended symbols have no part in social enquiry, their social effectiveness lies in their capacity to indicate, and if they indicate nothing to the actors, they are, from our point of view, irrelevant, and indeed no longer symbols (whatever their significance for the psychologist or psychoanalyst)." Professor Monica Wilson (1957: 6) holds a similar point of view. She writes that she stresses "Nyakyusa interpretations of their own rituals, for anthropological literature is bespattered with symbolic guessing, the ethnographer's interpretations of the rituals of other people." Indeed, she goes so far as to base her whole analysis of Nyakyusa ritual on "the Nyakyusa translation or interpretation of the symbolism." In my view, these investigators go beyond the limits of salutary caution and impose serious, and even arbitrary, limitations on themselves. To some extent, their difficulties derive from their failure to distinguish the concept of symbol from that of a mere sign. Although I am in complete disagreement with his fundamental postulate that the collective unconscious is the main formative principle in ritual symbolism, I consider that Carl Jung (1949: 601) has cleared the way for further investigation by making just this distinction. "A sign," he says, "is an analogous or abbreviated expression of a *known* thing. But a symbol is always the best possible expression of a relatively *unknown* fact, a fact, however, which is none the less recognized or postulated as existing." Nadel and Wilson, in treating most ritual symbols as signs, must ignore or regard as irrelevant some of the crucial properties of such symbols.[12]

FIELD SETTING AND STRUCTURAL PERSPECTIVE

How, then, can a social anthropologist justify his claim to be able to interpret a society's ritual symbols more deeply and comprehensively than the actors themselves? In the first place, the anthropologist, by the use of his special techniques and concepts, is able to view the performance of a given kind of ritual as "occurring in, and being interpenetrated by, a total-

---

12. Here Turner attempts to deal with the argument that symbolic meaning not recognized by native informants is invalid. This is an idea parallel to the emic-etic debate. Emic anthropologists argued that an explanation of a social phenomenon cannot be true unless it is recognized by native informants.

There is a profound epistemological issue here. On the one hand, as Turner points out, part of the meaning of symbols is that they express that which cannot easily be articulated. On the other, how can we rely on anthropologists to differentiate symbols from bits of culture that exist for historic or idiosyncratic reasons?

Note also that Turner uses the term "social anthropologist" for the first of many times in this essay. Radcliffe-Brown insisted on the use of the term "social anthropology" to differentiate his approach, based on the analysis of social structure and the search for natural laws of society, from other anthropological approaches (such as Boasian ideas about the description of culture) which he termed ethnology.

S. F. Nadel (1903–1956) received a doctoral degree in psychology and philosophy from the University of Vienna and studied anthropology at the London School of Economics with Malinowski and Seligman. He is best known for his work with the Nupe in northern Nigeria and the Nuba in Sudan.

Carl Jung (1875–1961) was a Swiss psychiatrist and close associate of Freud. Jung proposed (among many other things) that there were certain symbols that were inherited by all humans. These symbols, called *archetypes*, resided in the unconscious and were expressed in ritual, art, and literature. Turner (and almost all anthropologists) rejects this idea.

ity of coexisting social entities such as various kinds of groups, sub-groups, categories, or personalities, and also barriers between them, and modes of interconnexion" (Lewin 1949: 200). In other words, he can place this ritual in its significant field setting and describe the structure and properties of that field. On the other hand, each participant in the ritual views it from his own particular corner of observation. He has what Lupton has called his own "structural perspective." His vision is circumscribed by his occupancy of a particular position, or even of a set of situationally conflicting positions, both in the persisting structure of his society, and also in the role structure of the given ritual. Moreover, the participant is likely to be governed in his actions by a number of interests, purposes, and sentiments, dependent upon his specific position, which impair his understanding of the total situation. An even more serious obstacle against his achieving objectivity is the fact that he tends to regard as axiomatic and primary the ideals, values, and norms that are overtly expressed or symbolized in the ritual. Thus, in the *Nkang'a* ritual, each person or group in successive contexts of action, sees the milk tree only as representing her or their own specific interests and values at those times. However, the anthropologist who has previously made a structural analysis of Ndembu society, isolating its organizational principles, and distinguishing its groups and relationships, has no particular bias and can observe the real interconnections and conflicts between groups and persons, in so far as these receive ritual representation. What is meaning-

less for an actor playing a specific role may well be highly significant for an observer and analyst of the total system.[13]

On these grounds, therefore, I consider it legitimate to include within the total meaning of a dominant ritual symbol, aspects of behavior associated with it which the actors themselves are unable to interpret, and indeed of which they may be unaware, if they are asked to interpret the symbol outside its activity context. Nevertheless, there still remains for us the problem of the contradiction between the expressed meanings of the milk tree symbol and the meaning of the stereotyped forms of behavior closely associated with it. Indigenous interpretations of the milk tree symbolism in the abstract appear to indicate that there is no incompatibility or conflict between the persons and groups to which it refers. Yet, as we have seen, it is between just such groups that conflict is mimed at the milk tree site.

THREE PROPERTIES OF RITUAL SYMBOLS

Before we can interpret, we must further classify our descriptive data, collected by the methods described above. Such a classification will enable us to state some of the properties of ritual symbols. The simplest property is that of *condensation*. Many things and actions are represented in a single formation. Secondly, a dominant symbol is a *unification of disparate significata*. The disparate *significata* are interconnected by virtue of their com-

---

13. Turner says that, as observers, anthropologists have an advantage over a ritual's participants because they can examine the ritual from a broader context than the participants. This is precisely the same claim that Malinowski makes in his analysis of the kula trade (see essay 14).

Turner also says that anthropologists have no particular bias and argues that they are objective observers of interconnections and conflicts. Thus, Turner positions anthropologists as social scientists who can report accurately and objectively. In the 1980s and 1990s, many anthropologists attacked this idea, arguing that anthropologists (and everyone else) always have their own positions and biases and that anthropological observations can never be considered objective.

While Turner does not question the view that an anthropologist is an impartial, objective observer, his use of the concept of action fields leads him to a different conclusion about the participants in a ritual. He says that participants in a ritual view it from their own particular corner of observation and that their vision is circumscribed by their occupancy of a particular social position. This is a crucial insight that Turner does not recognize as equally true of anthropologists. However, this idea is central to the work of postmodernists such as Renato Rosaldo (b. 1941) in the 1980s (see essay 29).

mon possession of analogous qualities or by association in fact or thought. Such qualities or links of association may in themselves be quite trivial or random or widely distributed over a range of phenomena. Their very generality enables them to bracket together the most diverse ideas and phenomena. Thus, as we have seen, the milk tree stands for, *inter alia*, women's breasts, motherhood, a novice at *Nkang'a,* the principle of matriliny, a specific matrilineage, learning, and the unity and persistence of Ndembu society. The themes of nourishment and dependence run through all these diverse *significata.*[14]

The third important property of dominant ritual symbols is *polarization of meaning.* Not only the milk tree but all other dominant Ndembu symbols possess two clearly distinguishable poles of meaning. At one pole is found a cluster of *significata* that refer to components of the moral and social orders of Ndembu society, to principles of social organization, to kinds of corporate grouping, and to the norms and values inherent in structural relationships. At the other pole, the *significata* are usually natural and physiological phenomena and processes. Let us call the first of these the "ideological pole," and the second the "sensory pole." At the sensory pole, the meaning content is closely related to the outward form of the symbol. Thus one meaning of the milk tree—breast milk—is closely related to the exudation of milky latex from the tree. One sensory meaning of another dominant symbol, the *mukula* tree, is blood; this tree secretes a dusky red gum.[15]

At the sensory pole are concentrated those *significata* that may be expected to arouse desires and feelings; at the ideological pole one finds an arrangement of norms and values that guide and control persons as members of social groups and categories. The sensory, emotional *significata* tend to be "gross" in a double sense. In the first place, they are gross in a general way, taking no account of detail or the precise qualities of emotion. It cannot be sufficiently stressed that such symbols are social facts, "collective representations," even though their appeal is to the lowest common denominator of human feeling. The second sense of "gross" is "frankly, even flagrantly, physiological." Thus, the milk tree has the gross meanings of breast milk, breasts, and the process of breast feeding. These are also gross in the sense that they represent items of universal Ndembu experience. Other Ndembu symbols, at their sensory poles of meaning, represent such themes as blood, male and female genitalia, semen, urine, and feces. The same symbols, at their ideological poles of meaning, represent the unity and con-

---

14. The distinction between condensation and the unification of disparate significata can be difficult to grasp. In *The Forest of Symbols*, Turner discussed dominant symbols and claimed they had three main properties: condensation, the unification of disparate significata, and the polarization of meaning. Deflem (1991) explains these as follows: Condensation is polysemy or multivocality. Symbols do not have a single meaning. Instead, they simultaneously have many possible and actual meanings and represent different things or actions. Significata are the underlying meanings of the symbol. The unification of disparate significata occurs when these meanings are interconnected by virtue of their common analogous qualities, or by association in fact or thought. Turner's discussion of the mudyi or "milk" tree is a good illustration of both these properties of symbols. The mudyi tree is called the milk tree because it has a thick white sap, and this sap can take on a variety of meanings in a single ritual and across multiple rituals. But the sap is also a sign that points to numerous underlying meanings around the general theme of motherhood and lineage continuity. These include. breast milk, women who produce the milk, and Ndembu matrilineages. The sap, as a single symbol, thus unifies these disparate meanings.

"***Inter alia***": among other things.

15. Turner here imposes a scheme of classification that strongly resembles Lévi-Strauss's nature-culture binary opposition. The poles of meaning that Turner labels ideological and sensory could almost as easily be labeled culture and nature. Other anthropologists trained in the British Functionalist tradition such as Edmund Leach (1910–1989) and Rodney Needham (1923–2006) found Lévi-Strauss's structuralism attractive. However, Turner chose to derive his symbolic meanings from Freud.

tinuity of social groups, primary and associational, domestic, and political.[16]

[*A 569-word section of Turner's article called "Reference and Condensation" has been omitted. In this section, Turner discusses the analysis by Edward Sapir (1884–1939) of the means by which ritual symbols stimulate emotional responses.*]

DOMINANT AND INSTRUMENTAL SYMBOLS

Certain ritual symbols, as I have said, are regarded by Ndembu as dominant. In rituals performed to propitiate ancestor spirits who are believed to have afflicted their living kin with reproductive disorders, illness, or bad luck at hunting, there are two main classes of dominant symbols. The first class is represented by the first tree or plant in a series of trees or plants from which portions of leaves, bark, or roots are collected by practitioners or adepts in the curative cult. The subjects of ritual are marked with these portions mixed with water, or given them, mixed in a potion, to drink. The first tree so treated is called the "place of greeting" (*ishikenu*), or the "elder" (*mukulumpi*). The adepts encircle it several times to sacralize it. Then the senior practitioner prays at its base, which he sprinkles with powdered white clay. Prayer is made either to the named spirit, believed to be afflicting the principal subject of ritual, or to the tree itself, which is in some way identified with the afflicting spirit. Each *ishikenu* can be allotted several meanings by adepts. The second class of dominant symbols in curative rituals consists of shrines where the subjects of such rituals sit while the practitioners wash them with vegetable substances mixed with water and perform actions on their behalf of a symbolic or ritualistic nature. Such shrines are often composite, consisting of several objects

in configuration. Both classes of dominant symbols are closely associated with nonempirical beings. Some are regarded as their repositories; others, as being identified with them; others again, as representing them. In life-crisis rituals, on the other hand, dominant symbols seem to represent not beings but nonempirical powers or kinds of efficacy. For example, in the boys' circumcision ritual, the dominant symbol for the whole ritual is a "medicine" (*yitumbu*), called "*nfunda*," which is compounded from many ingredients, e.g., the ash of the burnt lodge which means "death," and the urine of an apprentice circumciser which means "virility." Each of these and other ingredients have many other meanings. The dominant symbol at the camp where the novices' parents assemble and prepare food for the boys is the *chikoli* tree, which represents, among other things, an erect phallus, adult masculinity, strength, hunting prowess, and health continuing into old age. The dominant symbol during the process of circumcision is the milk tree, beneath which novices are circumcised. The dominant symbol in the immediate postcircumcision phase is the red *mukula* tree, on which the novices sit until their wounds stop bleeding. Other symbols are dominant at various phases of seclusion. Each of these symbols is described as "*mukulumpi*" (elder, senior). Dominant symbols appear in many different ritual contexts, sometimes presiding over the whole procedure, sometimes over particular phases. The meaning-content of certain dominant symbols possesses a high degree of constancy and consistency throughout the total symbolic system, exemplifying Radcliffe-Brown's proposition that a symbol recurring in a cycle of rituals is likely to have the same significance in each. Such symbols also possess considerable autonomy with regard to the aims of the rituals in which they appear. Precisely because of these properties, dominant symbols are readily analyzable in a cultural framework of reference. They may be regarded

---

16. Turner is concerned not only with interpreting symbols, but also with explaining how they affect people, and to do this he draws heavily on Durkheim and Freud. When Turner argues that symbols represent ideas such as the continuity of social groups and the principle of matrilineal descent, he is drawing directly on Durkheim's ideas. When Turner argues about the importance of milk, blood, semen, etc., he draws on Freud, who believed that such symbolism was universal because the experience of these bodily functions was universal.

for this purpose as what Whitehead would have called "eternal objects."[b] They are the relatively fixed points in both the social and cultural structures, and indeed constitute points of junction between these two kinds of structure. They may be regarded irrespective of their order of appearance in a given ritual as ends in themselves, as representative of the axiomatic values of the widest Ndembu society. This does not mean that they cannot also be studied, as we have indeed studied them, as factors of social action, in an action frame of reference, but their social properties make them more appropriate objects of morphological study than the class of symbols we will now consider.[17]

These symbols may be termed "instrumental symbols." An instrumental symbol must be seen in terms of its wider context, i.e., in terms of the total system of symbols which makes up a given kind of ritual. Each kind of ritual has its specific mode of interrelating symbols. This mode is often dependent upon the ostensible purposes of that kind of ritual. In other words, each ritual has its own teleology. It has its explicitly expressed goals, and instrumental symbols may be regarded as means of attaining those goals. For example, in rituals performed for the overt purpose of making women fruitful, among the instrumental symbols used are portions of fruit-bearing trees or of trees that possess innumerable rootlets. These fruits and rootlets are said by Ndembu to represent children. They are also thought of as having efficacy to make the woman fruitful. They are means to the main end of the ritual. Perhaps such symbols could be regarded as mere signs or referential symbols, were it not for the fact that the meanings of each are associated with powerful conscious and unconscious emotions and wishes. At the psychological level of analysis, I suspect that these symbols too would approximate to the condition of condensation symbols, but here we touch upon the present limits of competence of anthropological explanation, a problem we will now discuss more fully.[18]

THE LIMITS OF ANTHROPOLOGICAL INTERPRETATION

We now come to the most difficult aspect of the scientific study of ritual symbolism: analysis. How far can we interpret these enigmatic formations by the use of anthropological concepts? At what points do we reach the frontiers of our explanatory competence? Let us first consider the case of dominant symbols. I have suggested that these have two poles of meaning, a sensory and an ideological pole. I have also suggested that dominant symbols have the property of unifying disparate *significata*. I would go so far as to say that at both poles of meaning are clustered disparate and even contradictory *significata*. In the course of its historical development, anthropology

---

17. Turner refers here to the British philosopher Alfred North Whitehead (1861–1947) and his idea of "eternal objects." Turner's ideas on both symbols and states of *communitas* were informed by Whitehead's philosophy. However, Whitehead is extremely abstract and there is much debate on exactly what ideas such as "eternal object" mean. One commentator defines "eternal object" as "a possibility for an actuality that is comprehensible without reference in the comprehension to some one particular occasion of experience (Henry 1993: 88).

The idea of dominant symbols and instrumental symbols was to play an important role in American symbolic anthropology. In 1973 Sherry Ortner (b. 1941), referencing Turner and David Schneider's work, introduced the idea of a key symbol as well as a methodology for finding, describing, and analyzing such symbols. Following Ortner's essay, the analysis of key symbols became popular in American anthropology.

Clifford Geertz (1926–2006) also builds on the concept of dominant symbols in his discussion of rituals that have "depth" in his 1973 essay "Deep Play: Notes on a Balinese Cockfight" (essay 26).

18. When Turner says each ritual has its "own teleology" he means that each ritual has its own design and purpose. An instrumental symbol must be analyzed in terms of the specific ritual context in which it occurs. Dominant symbols are "axiomatic," that is, self-evidently true. The implication here is that, within a culture, dominant symbols are constant in meaning, whereas the meaning of instrumental symbols is dependent on their context.

has acquired techniques and concepts that enable it to handle fairly adequately the kind of data we have classified as falling around the ideological pole. Such data, as we have seen, include components of social structure and cultural phenomena, both ideological and technological. I believe that study of these data in terms of the concepts of three major subdivisions of anthropology—cultural anthropology, structuralist theory, and social dynamics—would be extremely rewarding. I shall shortly outline how I think such analyses might be done and how the three frameworks might be interrelated, but first we must ask how far and in what respects is it relevant to submit the sensory pole of meaning to intensive analysis, and, more importantly, how far are we, as anthropologists, qualified to do so? It is evident, as Sapir has stated, that ritual symbols, like all condensation symbols, "strike deeper and deeper roots in the unconscious." Even a brief acquaintance with depth psychology is enough to show the investigator that ritual symbols, with regard to their outward form, to their behavioral context, and to several of the indigenous interpretations set upon them, are partially shaped under the influence of unconscious motivations and ideas. The interchange of clothes between mother and daughter at the *Nkang'a* ritual; the belief that a novice would go mad if she saw the milk tree on the day of her separation ritual; the belief that if a novice lifts up the blanket with which she is covered during seclusion and sees her village her mother would die; all these are items of symbolic behavior for which the Ndembu themselves can give no satisfactory interpretation. For these beliefs suggest an element of mutual hostility in the mother-daughter relationship which runs counter to orthodox interpretations of the milk tree symbolism, in so far as it refers to the mother-daughter relationship.

One of the main characteristics of ideological interpretations is that they tend to stress the harmonious and cohesive aspect of social relationships. The exegetic idiom feigns that persons and groups always act in accordance with the ideal norms of Ndembu society.[19]

[*We have omitted a seven-hundred-word section of Turner's article called "Depth Psychology and Ritual Symbolism," in which he discusses the psychoanalytic interpretation of ritual symbols such as the work of Bruno Bettelheim, which was discussed in the previous essay, by Mary Douglas. In this section, Turner claims that psychoanalysts generally reject the ideological pole of meaning and focus on the sensory meanings. They regard indigenous explanations of symbols as identical to the justifications that neurotics provide for their behavior. Turner disagrees with this point of view. He agrees that symbols are partly influenced by unconscious motivations and ideas, but his is not a psychoanalytic interpretation. He ends the section in an almost comic manner, referring to "hapless anthropologists" having to choose between competing psychoanalytic interpretations.*]

PROVINCES OF EXPLANATION

I consider that if we conceptualize a dominant symbol as having two poles of meaning, we can more exactly demarcate the limits within which anthropological analysis may be fruitfully applied. Psychoanalysts, in treating most indigenous interpretations of symbols as irrelevant, are guilty of a naive and one-sided approach. For those interpretations that show how a dominant symbol expresses important components of the social and moral orders are by no

---

19. Turner here refers to Edward Sapir's (1884–1939) influential 1934 essay on symbolism, written for the *Encyclopedia of Social Sciences*. In that essay, Sapir distinguishes two types of symbols: referential symbols and condensation symbols.

Depth psychology refers to psychological approaches deriving primarily from Freud and Jung that seek to uncover the relationship between unconscious and conscious thought and action. Turner here paraphrases Sapir saying it is evident that condensation symbols strike deep roots into the unconscious. Ideas about the effect of the unconscious on everyday life were common in mid-century America and Britain. Today, few scholars would accept that statement as self-apparent.

means equivalent to the "rationalizations," and the "secondary elaborations" of material deriving from **endopsychic** conflicts. They refer to social facts that have an empirical reality exterior to the psyches of individuals. On the other hand, those anthropologists who regard only indigenous interpretations as relevant, are being equally one-sided. This is because they tend to examine symbols within two analytical frameworks only, the cultural and the structural. This approach is essentially a static one, and it does not deal with processes involving temporal changes in social relations. [20]

Nevertheless, the crucial properties of a ritual symbol involve these dynamic developments. Symbols instigate social action. In a field context they may even be described as "forces," in that they are determinable influences inclining persons and groups to action. It is in a field context, moreover, that the properties we have described, namely, polarization of meanings, transference of affectual quality, discrepancy between meanings, and condensations of meanings, become most significant. The symbol as a unit of action, possessing these properties, becomes an object of study both for anthropology and for psychology. Both disciplines, in so far as they are concerned with human actions must conceptualize the ritual symbol in the same way.

The techniques and concepts of the anthropologist enable him to analyze competently the interrelations between the data associated with the ideological pole of meaning. They also enable him to analyze the social behavior directed upon the total dominant symbol. He cannot, however, with his present skills, discriminate between the precise sources of unconscious feeling and wishing, which shape much of the outward form of the symbol; select some natural objects rather than others to serve as symbols; and account for certain aspects of the behavior associated with symbols. For him,

it is enough that the symbol should evoke emotion. He is interested in the fact that emotion is evoked and not in the specific qualities of its constituents. He may indeed find it situationally relevant for his analysis to distinguish whether the emotion evoked by a specific symbol possesses the gross character, say, of aggression, fear, friendliness, anxiety, or sexual pleasure, but he need go no further than this. For him the ritual symbol is primarily a factor in group dynamics, and, as such, its references to the groups, relationships, values, norms, and beliefs of a society are his principal items of study. In other words, the anthropologist treats the sensory pole of meaning as a constant, and the social and ideological aspects as variables whose interdependencies he seeks to explain.[21]

The psychoanalyst, on the other hand, must, I think, attach greater significance than he now does to social factors in the analysis of ritual symbolism. He must cease to regard interpretations, beliefs, and dogmas as mere rationalizations when, often enough, these refer to social and natural realities. For, as Durkheim wrote (1954: 2–3), "primitive religions hold to reality and express it. One must learn to go underneath the symbol to the reality which it represents and which gives it its meaning. No religions are false, all answer, though in different ways, to the given conditions of human existence." Among those given conditions, the arrangement of society into structured groupings, discrepancies between the principles that organize these groupings, economic collaboration and competition, schism within groups and opposition between groups—in short, all those things with which the social aspect of ritual symbolism is concerned—are surely of at least equal importance with biopsychical drives and early conditioning in the elementary family. After all, the ritual symbol has, in common with the dream symbol, the characteristic, discovered by Freud, of being a compromise

---

20. **"Endopsychic"**: existing within the mind.

21. Here Turner distinguishes between cultural symbols and individual psychological symbols. He argues that cultural symbols are the province of anthropology, the latter that of psychology. This concern with distinguishing anthropology and sociology from psychology is similar to that expressed by Durkheim. Both Turner and Durkheim argued that collective phenomena are the subjects of anthropology and that individual consciousness belongs in psychology.

formation between two main opposing tendencies. It is a compromise between the need for social control, and certain innate and universal human drives whose complete gratification would result in a breakdown of that control.[22]

Ritual symbols refer to what is normative, general, and characteristic of unique individuals. Thus, Ndembu symbols refer among other things, to the basic needs of social existence (hunting, agriculture, female fertility, favourable climatic conditions, and so forth), and to shared values on which communal life depends (generosity, comradeship, respect for elders, the importance of kinship, hospitality, and the like). In distinguishing between ritual symbols and individual psychic symbols, we may perhaps say that while ritual symbols are gross means of handling social and natural reality, psychic symbols are dominantly fashioned under the influence of inner drives. In analyzing the former, attention must mainly be paid to relations between data external to the psyche; in analyzing the latter, to endopsychic data.

For this reason, the study of ritual symbolism falls more within the province of the social anthropologist than that of the psychologist or psychoanalyst, although the latter can assist the anthropologist by examining the nature and interconnections of the data clustered at the sensory pole of ritual symbolism. He can also, I believe, illuminate certain aspects of the stereotyped behavior associated with symbols in field contexts, which the actors themselves are unable to explain. For as we have seen, much of this behavior is suggestive of attitudes that differ radically from those deemed appropriate in terms of traditional exegesis. Indeed, certain conflicts would appear to be so basic that they totally block exegesis.

THE INTERPRETATION OF OBSERVED EMOTIONS

Can we really say that behavior portraying conflict between persons and groups, who are rep-resented by the symbols themselves as being in harmony, is in the full Freudian sense unconscious behavior? The Ndembu themselves in many situations outside *Nkang'a,* both secular and ritual, are perfectly aware of and ready to speak about hostility in the relationships between particular mothers and daughters, between particular sublineages, and between particular young girls and the adult women in their villages. It is rather as though there existed in certain precisely defined public situations, usually of a ritual or ceremonial type, a norm obstructing the verbal statement of conflicts in any way connected with the principle and rules celebrated or dramatized in those situations. Evidences of human passion and frailty are just not spoken about when the occasion is given up to the public commemoration and reanimation of norms and values in their abstract purity.

Yet, as we have seen, recurrent kinds of conflict may be acted out in the ritual or ceremonial form. On great ritual occasions, common practice, as well as highest principle, receives its symbolic or stereotyped expression, but practice, which is dominantly under the sway of what all societies consider man's "lower nature," is rife with expressions of conflict. Selfish and factional interests, oath breaking, disloyalty, sins of omission as well as sins of commission, pollute and disfigure those ideal prototypes of behavior which in precept, prayer, formula, and symbol are held up before the ritual assembly for its exclusive attention. In the orthodox interpretation of ritual it is pretended that common practice has no efficacy and that men and women really are as they ideally should be. Yet, as I have argued above, the "energy" required to reanimate the values and norms enshrined in dominant symbols and expressed in various kinds of verbal behavior is "borrowed," to speak metaphorically in lieu at the moment of a more rigorous language, from the miming of well-known and normally mentionable conflicts. The raw energies of conflict are domesticated into the service of social order.[23]

---

22. The quote Turner uses is from Durkheim's last major work *The Elementary Forms of the Religious Life* (orig. 1912).

23. For Turner, apparent conflict reinforces social order, once again illustrating Gluckman's perspective. Although he does not specifically call the *Nkang'a* a ritual of rebellion, it is clear that he has this in mind. Ritu-

I should say here that I believe it possible, and indeed necessary, to analyze symbols in a context of observed emotions. If the investigator is well acquainted with the common idiom in which a society expresses such emotions as friendship, love, hate, joy, sorrow, contentment, and fear, he cannot fail to observe that these are experienced in ritual situations. Thus, in *Nkang'a* when the women laugh and jeer at the men, tease the novice and her mother, fight one another for the "porridge of *chipwamp-wilu*," and so on, the observer can hardly doubt that emotions are really aroused in the actors as well as formally represented by ritual custom. ("What's Hecuba to him or he to Hecuba, that he should weep for her?").[24]

These emotions are portrayed and evoked in close relation to the dominant symbols of tribal cohesion and continuity, often by the performance of instrumentally symbolic behavior. However, since they are often associated with the **mimesis** of interpersonal and intergroup conflict, such emotions and acts of behavior obtain no place among the official, verbal meanings attributed to such dominant symbols.[25]

THE SITUATIONAL SUPPRESSION OF CONFLICT FROM INTERPRETATION

Emotion and **praxis**, indeed, give life and coloring to the values and norms, but the connection between the behavioral expression of conflict and the normative components of each kind of ritual, and of its dominant symbols, is seldom explicitly formulated by believing actors. Only if one were to personify a society, regarding it

as some kind of supra-individual entity, could one speak of "unconsciousness" here. Each individual participant in the *Nkang'a* ritual is well aware that kin quarrel most bitterly over rights and obligations conferred by the principle of matriliny, but that awareness is situationally held back from verbal expression: the participants must behave as if conflicts generated by matriliny were irrelevant.[26]

[Several paragraphs totaling about 560 words were omitted from the text. These contain a discussion of the situational suppression of conflict in the ritual expression of dominant symbols that continues below.]

For example, in the frequently performed *Nkula* ritual, the dominant symbols are a cluster of red objects, notably red clay (*mukundu*) and the *mukula* tree mentioned previously. In the context of *Nkula*, both of these are said to represent menstrual blood and the "blood of birth," which is the blood that accompanies the birth of a child. The ostensible goal of the ritual is to coagulate the patient's menstrual blood, which has been flowing away in menorrhagia, around the fetus in order to nourish it. A series of symbolic acts are performed to attain this end. For example, a young *mukula* tree is cut down by male doctors and part of it is carved into the shape of a baby, which is then inserted into a round calabash medicated with the blood of a sacrificed cock, with red clay, and with a number of other red ingredients. The red medicines here, say the Ndembu, represent desired coagulation of the patient's menstrual blood, and the calabash is a symbolic womb. At the ideological pole of meaning, the *mukula* tree and the medicated calabash both

---

alized conflict does not reject the social order, rather it focuses on the difference between what people are supposed to be and what they actually are.

24. Turner says that it is important for one to analyze symbols in the context of observed emotions. The quotation is from *Hamlet*, Act II, scene 2, where Hamlet, writing a play in which his father's murder will be re-created, comments on the power of emotion that can be expressed by an actor. Hecuba was the wife of King Priam of Troy and plays an important role in Homer's *Iliad*. Shakespeare frequently refers to Hecuba.

25. **"Mimesis"**: imitation.

26. **"Praxis"**: practice guided by the application of a specific theory.

represent (as the milk tree does) the patient's matrilineage and, at a higher level of abstraction, the principle of matriliny itself. This is also consistent with the fact that *ivumu*, the term for "womb," also means "matrilineage." In this symbolism the procreative, rather than the nutritive, aspect of motherhood is stressed. However, Ndembu red symbolism, unlike the white symbolism of which the milk tree symbolism is a species, nearly always has explicit reference to violence, to killing, and, at its most general level of meaning, to breach, both in the social and natural orders. Although informants, when discussing this *Nkula* ritual specifically, tend to stress the positive, feminine aspects of parturition and reproduction, other meanings of the red symbols, stated explicitly in other ritual contexts, can be shown to make their influence felt in *Nkula*. For example, both red clay and the *mukula* tree are dominant symbols in the hunter's cult, where they mean the blood of animals, the red meat of game, the inheritance through either parent of hunting prowess, and the unity of all initiated hunters. It also stands for the hunter's power to kill. The same red symbols, in the context of the *Wubanji* ritual performed to purify a man who has killed a kinsman or a lion or leopard (animals believed to be reincarnated hunter kin of the living), represent the blood of homicide. Again, in the boys' circumcision ritual, these symbols stand for the blood of circumcised boys. More seriously still, in divination and in antiwitchcraft rituals, they stand for the blood of witches' victims, which is exposed in **necrophagous** feasts.[27]

Most of these meanings are implicit in *Nkula*. For example, the female patient, dressed in skins like a male hunter and carrying a bow and arrow, at one phase of the ritual performs a special hunter's dance. Moreover, while she does this, she wears in her hair, just above the brow, the red feather of a lourie bird. Only shedders of blood, such as hunters, man-slayers, and circumcisers, are customarily entitled to wear this feather. Again, after the patient has been given the baby figurine in its symbolic womb, she dances with it in a style of dancing peculiar to circumcisers when they brandish aloft the great *nfunda* medicine of the circumcision lodge. Why then is the woman patient identified with male blood spillers? The field context of these symbolic objects and items of behavior suggests that the Ndembu feel that the woman, in wasting her menstrual blood and in failing to bear children, is actively renouncing her expected role as a mature married female. She is behaving like a male killer, not like a female nourisher. The situation is analogous, though modified by matriliny, to the following pronouncement in the ancient Jewish **Code of Qaro**: "Every man is bound to marry a wife in order to beget children, and he who fails of this duty is as one who sheds blood."[28]

---

27. Earlier in the essay, Turner stated that psychoanalytic interpretations typically focus on the sensory pole of meaning. Here, in his description of the *Nkula* ritual, the sensory symbolism of the calabash as womb and red clay as menstrual blood is very Freudian and psychoanalytic. At the ideological pole of meaning the same symbols refer to the patient's matrilineage. The ideological meanings reflect Radcliffe-Brown's Structural Functionalism. The characteristics of symbols that Turner described earlier in this article—condensation, the polarization of meaning, and the unification of disparate significata—allow him to reconcile the contradictions between the sensory-Freudian and ideological-Functionalist interpretations.

Earlier, Turner characterized instrumental symbols as those that have a meaning that depends on their ritual context. Here he gives an example. The *mukula* tree represents menstrual blood and the matrilineage in the women's *Nkula* rite, but it also represents the blood of animals and the hunter's power to kill, among other meanings, in men's hunting rites.

"Necrophagy": the eating of the dead.

28. The role reversals in the *Nkula* ceremony—women dressing in hunter's garb and dancing a hunter's dance—are other aspects of the rituals of rebellion that Gluckman described in his research. Gluckman's central idea was that while the ritualized reversing of established roles (the poor mock the wealthy, women dress as men) seemed to challenge the established order, these symbolic reversals actually reinforced it. Similarly, Turner identifies Ndembu women's ceremonial cross-dressing as a demonstration of male and female roles.

One does not need to be a psychoanalyst, one only needs sound sociological training, acquaintance with the total Ndembu symbolic system, plus ordinary common sense, to see that one of the aims of the ritual is to make the woman accept her lot in life as a childbearer and rearer of children for her lineage. The symbolism suggests that the patient is unconsciously rejecting her female role, that indeed she is guilty; indeed, "*mbayi,*" one term for menstrual blood, is etymologically connected with "*ku-baya*" (to be guilty). I have not time here to present further evidence of symbols and interpretations, both in *Nkula* and in cognate rituals, which reinforce this explanation. In the situation of *Nkula,* the dominant principles celebrated and reanimated are those of matriliny, the mother-child bond, and tribal continuity through matriliny. The norms in which these are expressed are those governing the behavior of mature women, which ascribe to them the role appropriate to their sex. The suppressed or submerged principles and norms, in this situation, concern and control the personal and corporate behavior deemed appropriate for man.

The analysis of *Nkula* symbolism throws into relief another major function of ritual. Ritual adapts and periodically readapts the biopsychical individual to the basic conditions and axiomatic values of human social life. In redressive rituals, the category to which *Nkula* belongs, the eternally rebellious individual is converted for a while into a loyal citizen. In the case of *Nkula,* a female individual whose behavior is felt to demonstrate her rebellion against, or at least her reluctance to comply with, the biological and social life patterns of her sex, is both induced and coerced by means of precept and symbol to accept her culturally prescribed destiny.

MODES OF INFERENCE IN INTERPRETATION

Each kind of Ndembu ritual, like *Nkula,* has several meanings and goals that are not made explicit by informants, but must be inferred by the investigator from the symbolic pattern and from behavior. He is able to make these inferences only if he has previously examined the symbolic configurations and the meanings attributed to their component symbols by skilled informants, of many other kinds of ritual in the same total system. In other words, he must examine symbols not only in the context of each specific kind of ritual, but in the context of the total system. He may even find it profitable, where the same symbol is found throughout a wide culture area, to study its changes of meaning in different societies in that area.[29]

There are two main types of contexts, irrespective of size. There is the action-field context, which we have discussed at some length. There is also the cultural context in which symbols are regarded as clusters of abstract meanings. By comparing the different kinds and sizes of contexts in which a dominant symbol occurs, we can often see that the meanings "officially" attributed to it in a particular kind of ritual may be mutually consistent. However, there may be much discrepancy and even contradiction between many of the meanings given by informants, when this dominant symbol is regarded as a unit of the total symbolic

---

He sees the ritual as a symbolic means of forcing women to accept their place as bearers of children and not challenge male gender roles.

"The Code of Qaro": refers to the Shulchan Aruch, a code of Jewish law written by Joseph B. Ephraim Caro (1488–1575).

29. Note again Turner's view of the anthropologist as neutral omniscient observer. Turner's work belongs to a period of modernism when the notion of science and scholarly authority was important even in symbolic interpretation, a discipline that seems to owe more to literary criticism than scientific methodology. Additionally, the functionalist lack of historical context is much evident in Turner's analysis. While he recognizes that symbolic meaning can change, he does not discuss Ndembu symbols or society as the products of a historical process.

system. I do not believe that this discrepancy is the result of mere carelessness and ignorance or variously distributed pieces of insight. I believe that discrepancy between *significata* is a quintessential property of the great symbolic dominants in all religions. Such symbols come in the process of time to absorb into their meaning-content most of the major aspects of human social life, so that, in a sense, they come to represent "human society" itself. In each ritual they assert the situational primacy of a single aspect or of a few aspects only, but by their mere presence they suffuse those aspects with the awe that can only be inspired by the human total. All the contradictions of human social life, between norms, and drives, between different drives and between different norms, between society and the individual, and between groups, are condensed and unified in a single representation, the dominant symbols. It is the task of analysis to break down this amalgam into its primary constituents.[30]

[*The 350-word section called "The Relativity of Depth" was omitted from this text. In it, Turner criticizes the notion that psychoanalytic interpretations of symbolism are "deeper" than anthropological analyses and characterizes symbols as a "force in a field of social action."*]

CONCLUSION: THE ANALYSIS OF SYMBOLS IN SOCIAL PROCESSES

Let me outline briefly the way in which I think ritual symbols may fruitfully be analyzed. Performances of ritual are phases in broad social processes, the span and complexity of which are roughly proportional to the size and degree of differentiation of the groups in which they occur. One class of ritual is situated near the apex of a whole hierarchy of redressive and regulative institutions that correct deflections and deviations from customarily prescribed behavior. Another class anticipates deviations and conflicts. This class includes periodic rituals and life-crisis rituals. Each kind of ritual is a patterned process in time, the units of which are symbolic objects and serialized items of symbolic behavior.[31]

The symbolic constituents may themselves be classed into structural elements, or "dominant symbols," which tend to be ends in themselves, and variable elements, or "instrumental symbols," which serve as means to the explicit or implicit goals of the given ritual. In order to give an adequate explanation of the meaning of a particular symbol, it is necessary first to examine the widest action-field context, that, namely, in which the ritual itself is simply a phase. Here one must consider what kinds of circumstances give rise to a performance of ritual, whether these are concerned with natural phenomena, economic and technological processes, human life-crises, or with the breach of crucial social relationships. The circumstances will probably determine what sort of ritual is performed. The goals of the ritual will have overt and implicit reference to the antecedent circumstances and will in turn help to determine the meaning of the symbols. Symbols must now be examined within the context of the specific ritual. It is here that we enlist the aid of indigenous informants. It is here also that we may be able to speak legitimately of "levels" of interpretation, for laymen will give the investigator simple and esoteric meanings, while specialists will give him esoteric explanations and more elaborate texts. Next, behavior directed towards each symbol should be noted, for such behavior is an important component of its total meaning.

We are now in a position to exhibit the ritual as a system of meanings, but this system

---

30. In *The Elementary Forms of the Religious Life* Durkheim argued that Australian Aboriginal religious beliefs were a model of their society. Here Turner makes a similar claim, not just for Ndembu symbolism, but for the dominant symbols of any society.

31. In this section Turner summarizes the social situations in which different types of rituals occur, and he reviews his discussion of dominant symbols, instrumental symbols, and action fields.

acquires additional richness and depth if it is regarded as itself constituting a sector of the Ndembu ritual system, as interpreted by informants and as observed in action. It is in comparison with other sectors of the total system, and by reference to the dominant articulating principles of the total system, that we often become aware that the overt and ostensible aims and purposes of a given ritual conceal unavowed, and even "unconscious," wishes and goals. We also become aware that a complex relationship exists between the overt and the submerged, and the manifest and latent patterns of meaning. As social anthropologists we are potentially capable of analyzing the social aspect of this relationship. We can examine, for example, the relations of dependence and independence between the total society and its parts, and the relations between different kinds of parts, and between different parts of the same kind. We can see how the same dominant symbol, which in one kind of ritual stands for one kind of social group or for one principle of organization, in another kind of ritual stands for another kind of group or principle, and in its aggregate of meanings stands for unity and continuity of the widest Ndembu society, embracing its contradictions.

THE LIMITS OF CONTEMPORARY ANTHROPOLOGICAL COMPETENCE

Our analysis must needs be incomplete when we consider the relationship between the normative elements in social life and the individual. For this relationship, too, finds its way into the meaning of ritual symbols. Here we come to the confines of our present anthropological competence, for we are now dealing with the structure and properties of psyches, a scientific field traditionally studied by other disciplines than ours. At one end of the symbol's spectrum of meanings we encounter the individual psychologist and the social psychologist, and even beyond them (if one may make a friendly tilt at an envied friend), brandishing his Medusa's head, the psychoanalyst, ready to turn to stone the foolhardy interloper into his caverns of terminology. We shudder back thankfully into the light of social day. Here the significant elements of a symbol's meaning are related to what it does and what is done to it by and for whom. These aspects can only be understood if one takes into account from the beginning, and represents by appropriate theoretical constructs, the total field situation in which the symbol occurs. This situation would include the structure of the group that performs the ritual we observe, its basic organizing principles and perdurable relationships, and, in addition, its extant division into transient alliances and factions on the basis of immediate interest and ambitions, for both abiding structure and recurrent forms of conflict and selfish interest are stereotyped in ritual symbolism. Once we have collected informants' interpretations of a given symbol, our work of analysis has indeed just begun. We must gradually approximate to the action-meaning of our symbol by way of what Lewin calls (1949: 149) "a stepwise increasing specificity" from widest to narrowest significant action context. Informants' "meanings" only become meaningful as objects of scientific study in the course of this analytical process.[32]

REFERENCES

Bettelheim, Bruno. 1954. *Symbolic Wounds: Puberty Rites and the Envious Male*. Glencoe, IL: Free Press.
Durkheim, E. 1954. *Elementary Forms of the Religious Life*. London: Allen & Unwin.

---

32. In the two paragraphs above, Turner provides an outline of his methods of analysis. The role of symbols in culture and individual psychology is a complex question that has defied definitive explication since it first arose at the turn of the twentieth century. The sophistication that Turner brought to symbolic analysis becomes apparent when you compare his work with studies of ritual or religion from the first part of the century such as *The Golden Bough* (1911–1915 [1890]) by Sir James Frazer (1854–1941) and Freud's *Moses and Monotheism* (1939). Turner's analysis of the different types of symbols and their properties stands today as one of the seminal works in symbolic anthropology.

Fenichel, Otto. 1946. *The Psychoanalytic Theory of Neuroses*. London: Routledge and Kegan Paul.

Jung, Carl G. 1949. *Psychological Types*. London: Routledge and Kegan Paul.

Lewin, K. 1949. *Field Theory in Social Science*. London: Tavistock Publications.

Nadel, S. F. 1954. *Nupe Religion*. London: Routledge and Kegan Paul.

Sapir, E. "Symbols," *Encyclopedia of the Social Sciences*, XIV. New York: Macmillan.

Wilson, M. 1957. *Rituals of Kinship Among the Nyakyusa*. London: Oxford University Press, for the International African Institute.

AUTHOR'S NOTES

Read at a meeting of the Association of Social Anthropologists of the Commonwealth in London, March 1958. First published in *Closed Systems and Open Minds: The Limits of Naivety in Social Science*, M. Gluckman, ed. (Edinburgh: Oliver and Boyd, 1964).

a. *Muchidi* also means "category," "kind," "species," and "tribe" itself.

b. i.e., objects not of indefinite duration but to which the category of time is not applicable.

26. Deep Play: Notes on the Balinese Cockfight

Clifford Geertz (1926–2006)

THE RAID

EARLY IN APRIL OF 1958, my wife and I arrived, malarial and diffident, in a Balinese village we intended, as anthropologists, to study. A small place, about five hundred people, and relatively remote, it was its own world. We were intruders, professional ones, and the villagers dealt with us as Balinese seem always to deal with people not part of their life who yet press themselves upon them: as though we were not there. For them, and to a degree for ourselves, we were nonpersons, specters, invisible men.[1]

We moved into an extended family compound (that had been arranged before through the provincial government) belonging to one of the four major factions in village life. But except for our landlord and the village chief, whose cousin and brother-in-law he was, everyone ignored us in a way only a Balinese can do. As we wandered around, uncertain, wistful, eager to please, people seemed to look right through us with a gaze focused several yards behind us on some more actual stone or tree. Almost nobody greeted us; but nobody scowled or said anything unpleasant to us either, which would have been almost as satisfactory. If we ventured to approach someone (something one is powerfully inhibited from doing in such an atmosphere), he moved, negligently but definitely, away. If, seated or leaning against a wall, we had him trapped, he said nothing at all, or mumbled what for the Balinese is the ultimate nonword—"yes." The indifference, of course, was studied; the villagers were watching every move we made, and they had an enormous amount of quite accurate information about who we were and what we were going to be doing. But they acted as if we simply did not exist, which, in fact, as this behavior was designed to inform us, we did not, or anyway not yet.

This is, as I say, general in Bali. Everywhere else I have been in Indonesia, and more latterly in Morocco, when I have gone into a new

From *Daedalus* (1972)

1. The work of symbolic anthropologists like Victor Turner and Mary Douglas was concerned with demonstrating what the economist Ely Devons (1913–1967) and Max Gluckman called in 1964 the "logic of the irrational." One motive underlying their work was to demonstrate how institutions that seemed irrational to the observer are actually rational, even if the natives themselves are unaware of the cultural logic behind their behavior. Turner and Douglas accounted for this hidden rationality by penetrating the surface behavior and explanations to look for concealed layers of meaning. This form of inquiry ultimately led analysts to resort to psychological explanations of behavior, or semi-metaphysical concepts such as social facts or the collective conscience. Geertz, although he too is concerned with the interpretation of cultural symbolism, follows a different approach. Geertz believes that culture is acted out in public symbols such as the cockfight and is the mechanism by which members of a society understand and think about the meaning of their actions and social world. He is not trying to uncover the hidden psychological meaning of the Balinese cockfight, for he believes the Balinese understand the symbolism of the contest as well as anyone. Instead, in this essay Geertz attempts to situate readers within the Balinese system to facilitate the reader's understanding of the meaning of the cockfight. This is not, in any sense, a scientific goal. His observations are not replicable. Someone else trying to do the same work might well have a different set of insights.

Geertz's original article is accompanied by forty-three voluminous footnotes, which space limitations do not allow us to reprint. Asterisks have been used to show readers the placement of his footnotes in the text.

village, people have poured out from all sides to take a very close look at me, and, often an all-too-probing feel as well. In Balinese villages, at least those away from the tourist circuit, nothing happens at all. People go on pounding, chatting, making offerings, staring into space, carrying baskets about while one drifts around feeling vaguely disembodied. And the same thing is true on the individual level. When you first meet a Balinese, he seems virtually not to relate to you at all; he is, in the term Gregory Bateson and Margaret Mead made famous, "away."* Then—in a day, a week, a month (with some people the magic moment never comes)—he decides, for reasons I have never quite been able to fathom, that you *are* real, and then he becomes a warm, gay, sensitive, sympathetic, though, being Balinese, always precisely controlled, person. You have crossed, somehow, some moral or metaphysical shadow line. Though you are not exactly taken as a Balinese (one has to be born to that), you are at least regarded as a human being rather than a cloud or a gust of wind. The whole complexion of your relationship dramatically changes to, in the majority of cases, a gentle, almost affectionate one—a low-keyed, rather playful, rather mannered, rather bemused geniality.[2]

My wife and I were still very much in the gust-of-wind stage, a most frustrating, and even, as you soon begin to doubt whether you are really real after all, unnerving one, when, ten days or so after our arrival, a large cockfight was held in the public square to raise money for a new school.

Now, a few special occasions aside, cockfights are illegal in Bali under the Republic (as, for not altogether unrelated reasons, they were under the Dutch), largely as a result of the pretensions to puritanism radical nationalism tends to bring with it. The elite, which

is not itself so very puritan, worries about the poor, ignorant peasant gambling all his money away, about what foreigners will think, about the waste of time better devoted to building up the country. It sees cockfighting as "primitive," "backward," "unprogressive," and generally unbecoming an ambitious nation. And, as with those other embarrassments—opium smoking, begging, or uncovered breasts—it seeks, rather unsystematically, to put a stop to it.

Of course, like drinking during Prohibition or, today, smoking marihuana, cockfights, being a part of "The Balinese Way of Life," nonetheless go on happening, and with extraordinary frequency. And, as with Prohibition or marihuana, from time to time the police (who, in 1958 at least, were almost all not Balinese but Javanese) feel called upon to make a raid, confiscate the cocks and spurs, fine a few people, and even now and then expose some of them in the tropical sun for a day as object lessons which never, somehow, get learned, even though occasionally, quite occasionally, the object dies.

As a result, the fights are usually held in a secluded corner of a village in semisecrecy, a fact which tends to slow the action a little—not very much, but the Balinese do not care to have it slowed at all. In this case, however, perhaps because they were raising money for a school that the government was unable to give them, perhaps because raids had been few recently, perhaps, as I gathered from subsequent discussion, there was a notion that the necessary bribes had been paid, they thought they could take a chance on the central square and draw a larger and more enthusiastic crowd without attracting the attention of the law.

They were wrong. In the midst of the third match, with hundreds of people, including, still transparent, myself and my wife, fused into a single body around the ring, a super-

---

2. Geertz mentions Indonesia and Morocco in this passage. These were two important field sites for him. His first field research location was in Java and in 1960 Geertz published *The Religion of Java*. Additional books based on both Java and work in Bali were *Agricultural Involution: The Process of Ecological Change in Indonesia* (1963) and *Peddlers and Princes: Social Change and Economic Modernization in Two Indonesian Towns* (1963). As the titles show, Geertz at this time was interested in ecology, change, and economic development. Geertz worked in Morocco in the mid-1960s, publishing *Islam Observed: Religious Development in Morocco and Indonesia* (1971). Geertz wrote numerous other works on both Indonesia and Morocco. In 1996, he published a broad review of his work in both places: *After the Fact: Two Countries, Four Decades, One Anthropologist*.

organism in the literal sense, a truck full of policemen armed with machine guns roared up. Amid great screeching cries of "pulisi! pulisi!" from the crowd, the policemen jumped out, and, springing into the center of the ring, began to swing their guns around like gangsters in a motion picture, though not going so far as actually to fire them. The superorganism came instantly apart as its components scattered in all directions. People raced down the road, disappeared headfirst over walls, scrambled under platforms, folded themselves behind wicker screens, scuttled up coconut trees. Cocks armed with steel spurs sharp enough to cut off a finger or run a hole through a foot were running wildly around. Everything was dust and panic.

On the established anthropological principle, "When in Rome," my wife and I decided, only slightly less instantaneously than everyone else, that the thing to do was run too. We ran down the main village street, northward, away from where we were living, for we were on that side of the ring. About halfway down another fugitive ducked suddenly into a compound—his own, it turned out—and we, seeing nothing ahead of us but rice fields, open country, and a very high volcano, followed him. As the three of us came tumbling into the courtyard, his wife, who had apparently been through this sort of thing before, whipped out a table, a tablecloth, three chairs, and three cups of tea, and we all, without any explicit communication whatsoever, sat down, commenced to sip tea, and sought to compose ourselves.

A few moments later, one of the policemen marched importantly into the yard, looking for the village chief. (The chief had not only been at the fight, he had arranged it. When the truck drove up he ran to the river, stripped off his sarong, and plunged in so he could say, when at length they found him sitting there pouring water over his head, that he had been away bathing when the whole affair had occurred and was ignorant of it. They did not believe him and fined him three hundred rupiah, which the village raised collectively.) Seeing me and my wife, "White Men," there in the yard, the policeman performed a classic double take. When he found his voice again he asked, approximately, what in the devil did we think

we were doing there. Our host of five minutes leaped instantly to our defense, producing an impassioned description of who and what we were, so detailed and so accurate that it was my turn, having barely communicated with a living human being save my landlord and the village chief for more than a week, to be astonished. We had a perfect right to be there, he said, looking the Javanese upstart in the eye. We were American professors; the government had cleared us; we were there to study culture; we were going to write a book to tell Americans about Bali. And we had all been there drinking tea and talking about cultural matters all afternoon and did not know anything about any cockfight. Moreover, we had not seen the village chief all day; he must have gone to town. The policeman retreated in rather total disarray. And, after a decent interval, bewildered but relieved to have survived and stayed out of jail, so did we.

The next morning the village was a completely different world for us. Not only were we no longer invisible, we were suddenly the center of all attention, the object of a great outpouring of warmth, interest, and most especially, amusement. Everyone in the village knew we had fled like everyone else. They asked us about it again and again (I must have told the story, small detail by small detail, fifty times by the end of the day), gently, affectionately, but quite insistently teasing us: "Why didn't you just stand there and tell the police who you were?" "Why didn't you just say you were only watching and not betting?" "Were you really afraid of those little guns?" As always, kinesthetically minded and, even when fleeing for their lives (or, as happened eight years later, surrendering them), the world's most poised people, they gleefully mimicked, also over and over again, our graceless style of running and what they claimed were our panic stricken facial expressions. But above all, everyone was extremely pleased and even more surprised that we had not simply "pulled out our papers" (they knew about those too) and asserted our Distinguished Visitor status, but had instead demonstrated our solidarity with what were now our covillagers. (What we had actually demonstrated was our cowardice, but there is fellowship in that too.) Even the Brahmana priest, an old, grave, halfway-to-heaven type who because of its associations with the underworld would never be involved, even distantly, in a cockfight, and was difficult to approach even to other Balinese, had us called into his courtyard to ask us about what had happened, chuckling happily at the sheer extraordinariness of it all.

In Bali, to be teased is to be accepted. It was the turning point so far as our relationship to the community was concerned, and we were quite literally "in." The whole village opened up to us, probably more than it ever would have otherwise (I might actually never have gotten to that priest, and our accidental host became one of my best informants), and certainly very much faster. Getting caught, or almost caught, in a vice raid is perhaps not a very generalizable recipe for achieving that mysterious necessity of anthropological field work, rapport, but for me it worked very well. It led to a sudden and unusually complete acceptance into a society extremely difficult for outsiders to penetrate. It gave me the kind of immediate, inside-view grasp of an aspect of "peasant mentality" that anthropologists not fortunate enough to flee headlong with their subjects from armed authorities normally do not get. And, perhaps most important of all, for the other things might have come in other ways, it put me very quickly on to a combination emotional explosion, status war, and philosophical drama of central significance to the society whose inner nature I desired to understand. By the time I left I had spent about as much time looking into cockfights as into witchcraft, irrigation, caste, or marriage.[3]

OF COCKS AND MEN

Bali, mainly because it is Bali, is a well-studied place. Its mythology, art, ritual, social organization, patterns of child rearing, forms of law, even styles of trance, have all been microscopically examined for traces of that elusive substance Jane Belo called "The Balinese Temper."* But, aside from a few passing remarks, the cockfight has barely been noticed, although as a popular obsession of consuming power it is at least as important a revelation of what being a Balinese "is really like" as these more celebrated phenomena.* As much of America surfaces in a ball park, on a golf links, at a race track, or around a poker table, much of Bali surfaces in a cock ring. For it is only apparently cocks that are fighting there. Actually, it is men.

To anyone who has been in Bali any length of time, the deep psychological identification of Balinese men with their cocks is unmistakable. The double entendre here is deliberate. It works in exactly the same way in Balinese as it does in English, even to producing the same tired jokes, strained puns, and uninventive obscenities. Bateson and Mead have even

---

3. You've just read one of the most famous tales of entry in anthropology. In the late twentieth century, you could have asked almost any American anthropologist, "How do you arrive in a Balinese village?" and they would have responded, "Malarial and diffident." Why is the story so famous? First, it is an adventure tale and a fieldworker's fantasy: Confused anthropologists find empathy and acceptance. Second, it highlights the strength of Geertz's writing style. It's not only fun to read, but Geertz's writing helps a reader visualize the events. He addresses the reader directly: "*You* have crossed, somehow, some oral or metaphysical shadow line. Though *you* are not exactly taken as Balinese . . . *you* are at least regarded as a human being."

Interestingly, this essay was first published in *Daedalus,* a literary journal. It is aimed at a highly educated audience but not one composed exclusively of anthropologists.

Although it has become much more common, Geertz's self-revelatory style was unusual for ethnographic writing at this time. (See the introduction to *The Nuer* [1940] by E. E. Evans-Pritchard (1902–1973) for an early example of self-revelatory ethnographic writing.) Can you imagine A. L. Kroeber or Radcliffe-Brown writing an account of their escape from the police?

The story is crucial to Geertz's analysis because it gives him authority. We should believe Geertz, we are told, because these events gave him excellent access to Balinese informants (he tells us, for example, that without them he might never have been able to meet the priest). Due to a more or less chance event, Geertz claimed to have gained a particular place in the village that enabled him to make certain kinds of observations and reach certain kinds of understandings. Later anthropologists would refer to this as *positioning*. In a 1986 analysis, Vincent Crapanzano (b. 1939) challenged both Geertz's story and his claims of authority.

suggested that, in line with the Balinese conception of the body as a set of separately animated parts, cocks are viewed as detachable, self-operating penises, ambulant genitals with a life of their own.* And while I do not have the kind of unconscious material either to confirm or disconfirm this intriguing notion, the fact that they are masculine symbols par excellence is about as indubitable, and to the Balinese about as evident, as the fact that water runs downhill.[4]

The language of everyday moralism is shot through, on the male side of it, with roosterish imagery. *Sabung,* the word for cock (and one which appears in inscriptions as early as a.d. 922), is used metaphorically to mean "hero," "warrior," "champion," "man of parts," "political candidate," "bachelor," "dandy," "lady killer," or "tough guy." A pompous man whose behavior presumes above his station is compared to a tailless cock who struts about as though he had a large, spectacular one. A desperate man who makes a last, irrational effort to extricate himself from an impossible situation is likened to a dying cock who makes one final lunge at his tormentor to drag him along to a common destruction. A stingy man, who promises much, gives little, and begrudges that, is compared to a cock which, held by the tail, leaps at another without in fact engaging him. A marriageable young man still shy with the opposite sex or someone in a new job anxious to make a good impression is called "a fighting cock caged for the first time."* Court trials, wars, political contests, inheritance disputes, and street arguments are all compared to cockfights.* Even the very island itself is perceived from its shape as a small, proud cock, poised, neck extended, back taut, tail raised, in eternal challenge to large, feckless, shapeless Java.*

But the intimacy of men with their cocks is more than metaphorical. Balinese men, or anyway a large majority of Balinese men, spend an enormous amount of time with their favorites, grooming them, feeding them, discussing them, trying them out against one another, or just gazing at them with a mixture of rapt admiration and dreamy self-absorption. Whenever you see a group of Balinese men squatting idly in the council shed or along the road in their hips down, shoulders forward, knees up fashion, half or more of them will have a rooster in his hands, holding it between his thighs, bouncing it gently up and down to strengthen its legs, ruffling its feathers with abstract sensuality, pushing it out against a neighbor's rooster to rouse its spirit, withdrawing it toward his loins to calm it again. Now and then, to get a feel for another bird, a man will fiddle this way with someone else's cock for a while, but usually by moving around to squat in place behind it, rather than just having it passed across to him as though it were merely an animal.[5]

In the houseyard, the high-walled enclosures where the people live, fighting cocks are kept in wicker cages, moved frequently about so as to maintain the optimum balance of sun and shade. They are fed a special diet, which varies somewhat according to individual theories but which is mostly maize, sifted for impurities with far more care than it is when mere humans are going to eat it, and offered to the animal kernel by kernel. Red pepper is stuffed down their beaks and up their anuses to give them spirit. They are bathed in the same ceremonial preparation of tepid water, medicinal herbs, flowers, and onions in which infants are bathed, and for a prize cock just about as often. Their combs are cropped, their plumage dressed, their spurs trimmed, and their legs massaged, and they are inspected for flaws with the squinted concentration of a diamond merchant. A man who has a passion for cocks, an enthusiast in the literal sense of the term, can spend most of his life with them, and even those, the overwhelming majority, whose passion though intense has not entirely run away with them, can and do spend what seems not only to an outsider, but also to themselves, an inordinate amount of time with them. "I am cock crazy," my landlord, a quite

---

4. In a lengthy footnote, Geertz tells us that the cockfight is also unusual in being an exclusively male event. Women are rarely excluded from Balinese social events. Geertz describes Bali as a "unisex" society.

5. Be sure to pause for a moment to consider the sexual innuendo in this passage. Geertz's essay is full of puns and double entendre, mostly around the word "cock." In 1973, this was funny stuff. Do you think it still holds up today? Would an essay that engaged in this sort of humor be publishable today?

ordinary *afficionado* by Balinese standards, used to moan as he went to move another cage, give another bath, or conduct another feeding. "We're all cock crazy."

The madness has some less visible dimensions, however, because although it is true that cocks are symbolic expressions or magnifications of their owner's self, the narcissistic male ego writ out in **Aesopian terms**, they are also expressions—and rather more immediate ones—of what the Balinese regard as the direct inversion, aesthetically, morally, and metaphysically, of human status: animality.[6]

The Balinese revulsion against any behavior regarded as animal-like can hardly be overstressed. Babies are not allowed to crawl for that reason. Incest, though hardly approved, is a much less horrifying crime than bestiality. (The appropriate punishment for the second is death by drowning, for the first being forced to live like an animal.)* Most demons are represented—in sculpture, dance, ritual, myth—in some real or fantastic animal form. The main puberty rite consists in filing the child's teeth so they will not look like animal fangs. Not only defecation but eating is regarded as a disgusting, almost obscene activity, to be conducted hurriedly and privately, because of its association with animality. Even falling down or any form of clumsiness is considered to be bad for these reasons. Aside from cocks and a few domestic animals—oxen, ducks—of no emotional significance, the Balinese are aversive to animals and treat their large number of dogs not merely callously but with a phobic cruelty. In identifying with his cock, the Balinese man is identifying not just with his ideal self, or even his penis, but also, and at the same time, with what he most fears, hates, and ambivalence being what it is, is fascinated by—"The Powers of Darkness."

The connection of cocks and cockfighting with such Powers, with the animalistic demons that threaten constantly to invade the small, cleared-off space in which the Balinese have so carefully built their lives and devour its inhabitants, is quite explicit. A cockfight, any cockfight, is in the first instance a blood sacrifice offered, with the appropriate chants and oblations, to the demons in order to pacify their ravenous, cannibal hunger. No temple festival should be conducted until one is made. (If it is omitted, someone will inevitably fall into a trance and command with the voice of an angered spirit that the oversight be immediately corrected.) Collective responses to natural evils—illness, crop failure, volcanic eruptions—almost always involve them. And that famous holiday in Bali, "The Day of Silence" (*Njepi*), when everyone sits silent and immobile all day long in order to avoid contact with a sudden influx of demons chased momentarily out of hell, is preceded the previous day by large-scale cockfights (in this case legal) in almost every village on the island.

In the cockfight, man and beast, good and evil, ego and id, the creative power of aroused masculinity and the destructive power of loosened animality fuse in a bloody drama of hatred, cruelty, violence, and death. It is little wonder that when, as is the invariable rule, the owner of the winning cock takes the carcass of the loser—often torn limb from limb by its enraged owner—home to eat, he does so with a mixture of social embarrassment, moral satisfaction, aesthetic disgust, and cannibal joy. Or that a man who has lost an important fight is sometimes driven to wreck his family shrines and curse the gods, an act of metaphysical (and social) suicide. Or that in seeking earthly analogues for heaven and hell the Balinese compare the former to the mood of a man whose cock has just won, the latter to that of a man whose cock has just lost.[7]

---

6. **"Aesopian terms"**: communications that seem trivial to outsiders but have important meanings to members of society who understand the cultural coding in their language.

7. Although Geertz is attempting a very different kind of symbolic analysis than Sigmund Freud (1856–1939), Émile Durkheim, or Claude Lévi-Strauss, the influence of their work is apparent here. The symbolic link between the fighting birds, genitals, and male status is Freudian. The binary constructions—man-beast, good-evil, creation-destruction—are based on Durkheim's ideas of the sacred and profane and Lévi-Strauss's

THE FIGHT

Cockfights (*tetadjen; sabungan*) are held in a ring about fifty feet square. Usually they begin toward late afternoon and run three or four hours until sunset. About nine or ten separate matches (*sehet*) comprise a program. Each match is precisely like the others in general pattern: there is no main match, no connection between individual matches, no variation in their format, and each is arranged on a completely ad hoc basis. After a fight has ended and the emotional debris is cleaned away—the bets have been paid, the curses cursed, the carcasses possessed—seven, eight, perhaps even a dozen men slip negligently into the ring with a cock and seek to find there a logical opponent for it. This process, which rarely takes less than ten minutes, and often a good deal longer, is conducted in a very subdued, oblique, even dissembling manner. Those not immediately involved give it at best but disguised, sidelong attention; those who, embarrassedly, are, attempt to pretend somehow that the whole thing is not really happening.[8]

A match made, the other hopefuls retire with the same deliberate indifference, and the selected cocks have their spurs (*tadji*) affixed—razor-sharp, pointed steel swords, four or five inches long. This is a delicate job which only a small proportion of men, a half-dozen or so in most villages, know how to do properly. The man who attaches the spurs also provides them, and if the rooster he assists wins, its owner awards him the spur-leg of the victim. The spurs are affixed by winding a long length of string around the foot of the spur and the leg of the cock. For reasons I shall come to presently, it is done somewhat differently from case to case, and is an obsessively deliberate affair. The lore about spurs is extensive—they are sharpened only at eclipses and the dark of the moon, should be kept out of the sight of women, and so forth. And they are handled, both in use and out, with the same curious combination of fussiness and sensuality the Balinese direct toward ritual objects generally.

The spurs affixed, the two cocks are placed by their handlers (who may or may not be their owners) facing one another in the center of the ring.* A coconut pierced with a small hole is placed in a pail of water, in which it takes about twenty-one seconds to sink, a period known as a *tjeng* and marked at beginning and end by the beating of a slit gong. During these twenty-one seconds the handlers (*pengangkeb*) are not permitted to touch their roosters. If, as sometimes happens, the animals have not fought during this time, they are picked up, fluffed, pulled, prodded, and otherwise insulted, and put back in the center of the ring and the process begins again. Sometimes they refuse to fight at all, or one keeps running away, in which case they are imprisoned together under a wicker cage, which usually gets them engaged.[9]

Most of the time, in any case, the cocks fly almost immediately at one another in a wing-beating, head-thrusting, leg-kicking explosion of animal fury so pure, so absolute, and in its own way so beautiful, as to be almost abstract, a **Platonic concept of hate**. Within moments one or the other drives home a solid blow with his spur. The handler whose cock has delivered the blow immediately picks it up so that it will not get a return blow, for if he does not the match is likely to end in a mutu-

---

nature-culture dichotomy. The human cultural world is repulsed by the animal-natural world, but the two spheres of existence meet in the cockfight.

8. Geertz describes cockfighting and patterns of betting in great detail. He attempts to re-create the context in which the action takes place so that the reader may understand how Balinese cultural meaning is created. Geertz used British philosopher Gilbert Ryle's (1900–1976) concept of *thick description* to describe this form of analysis, which he identifies as uncovering the layers of meaning surrounding an event. Part of Geertz's point is that, as the cliché has it, the devil truly is in the details. Understanding exactly what happens, and exactly who does what allows us to penetrate the Aesopian language of social action in general and the cockfight in particular.

9. In a long footnote, Geertz tells us that whether or not an owner "handles his own cock" is a matter of skill. When he does not, the handler and spur affixer are usually relatives or very close friends.

ally mortal tie as the two birds wildly hack each other to pieces. This is particularly true if, as often happens, the spur sticks in its victim's body, for then the aggressor is at the mercy of his wounded foe. [10]

With the birds again in the hands of their handlers, the coconut is now sunk three times after which the cock which has landed the blow must be set down to show that he is firm, a fact he demonstrates by wandering idly around the ring for a coconut sink. The coconut is then sunk twice more and the fight must recommence.

During this interval, slightly over two minutes, the handler of the wounded cock has been working frantically over it, like a trainer patching a mauled boxer between rounds, to get it in shape for a last, desperate try for victory. He blows in its mouth, putting the whole chicken head in his own mouth and sucking and blowing, fluffs it, stuffs its wounds with various sorts of medicines, and generally tries anything he can think of to arouse the last ounce of spirit which may be hidden somewhere within it. By the time he is forced to put it back down he is usually drenched in chicken blood, but, as in prize fighting, a good handler is worth his weight in gold. Some of them can virtually make the dead walk, at least long enough for the second and final round.

In the climactic battle (if there is one; sometimes the wounded cock simply expires in the handler's hands or immediately as it is placed down again), the cock who landed the first blow usually proceeds to finish off his weakened opponent. But this is far from an inevitable outcome, for if a cock can walk, he can fight, and if he can fight, he can kill, and what counts is which cock expires first. If the wounded one can get a stab in and stagger on until the other drops, he is the official winner, even if he himself topples over an instant later.

Surrounding all this melodrama—which the crowd packed tight around the ring follows in near silence, moving their bodies in kinesthetic sympathy with the movement of the animals, cheering their champions on with wordless hand motions, shiftings of the shoulders, turnings of the head, falling back en masse as the cock with the murderous spurs careens toward one side of the ring (it is said that spectators sometimes lose eyes and fingers from being too attentive), surging forward again as they glance off toward another—is a vast body of extraordinarily elaborate and precisely detailed rules. [11]

These rules, together with the developed lore of cocks and cockfighting which accompanies them, are written down in palm-leaf manuscripts (*lontar; rontal*) passed on from generation to generation as part of the general legal and cultural tradition of the villages. At a fight, the umpire (*saja komong; djuru kembar*)—the man who manages the coconut—is in charge of their application and his authority is absolute. I have never seen an umpire's judgment questioned on any subject, even by the more despondent losers, nor have I ever heard, even in private, a charge of unfairness directed against one, or, for that matter, complaints about umpires in general. Only exceptionally well trusted, solid, and, given the complexity of the code, knowledgeable citizens perform this job, and in fact men will bring their cocks only to fights presided over by such men. It is also the umpire to whom accusations of cheating, which, though rare in the extreme, occasionally arise, are referred; and it is he who in the not infrequent cases where the cocks expire virtually together decides which (if either, for, though the Balinese do not care for such an outcome, there can be ties) went first. Likened to a judge, a king, a priest, and a policeman, he is all of these, and under his assured direction the animal passion of the fight proceeds within the civic certainty of the law. In the dozens of cockfights I saw in Bali, I never once saw an altercation about rules. Indeed, I never saw an open altercation, other than those between cocks, at all.

This crosswise doubleness of an event which, taken as a fact of nature, is rage untram-

---

10. **"Platonic notion of hate"**: hate perfected.

11. One criticism of Geertz's work is that his interpretation is intuitive, making it difficult for others to replicate. Indeed, one could say that the power of Geertz's analysis is based on his compelling writing style. For example, you may not have noticed that Geertz is not presenting us with a description of one cockfight but rather with a composite cockfight of his own creation based on his experience of at least fifty-seven matches.

meled and, taken as a fact of culture, is form perfected, defines the cockfight as a sociological entity. A cockfight is what, searching for a name for something not vertebrate enough to be called a group and not structureless enough to be called a crowd, Erving Goffman has called a "focused gathering"—a set of persons engrossed in a common flow of activity and relating to one another in terms of that flow.* Such gatherings meet and disperse; the participants in them fluctuate; the activity that focuses them is discrete—a particulate process that reoccurs rather than a continuous one that endures. They take their form from the situation that evokes them, the floor on which they are placed, as Goffman puts it; but it is a form, and an articulate one, nonetheless. For the situation, the floor is itself created, in jury deliberations, surgical operations, block meetings, sit-ins, cockfights, by the cultural preoccupations—here, as we shall see, the celebration of status rivalry—which not only specify the focus but, assembling actors and arranging scenery, bring it actually into being.[12]

In classical times (that is to say, prior to the Dutch invasion of 1908), when there were no bureaucrats around to improve popular morality, the staging of a cockfight was an explicitly societal matter. Bringing a cock to an important fight was, for an adult male, a compulsory duty of citizenship; taxation of fights, which were usually held on market day, was a major source of public revenue; patronage of the art was [the] stated responsibility of princes; and the cock ring, or *wantilan*, stood in the center of the village near those other monuments of Balinese civility—the council house, the origin temple, the marketplace, the signal tower, and the banyan tree. Today, a few special occasions aside, the newer rectitude makes so open a statement of the connection between the excitements of collective life and those of blood sport impossible, but, less directly expressed, the connection itself remains intimate and intact. To expose it,

however, it is necessary to turn to the aspect of cockfighting around which all the others pivot, and through which they exercise their force, an aspect I have thus far studiously ignored. I mean, of course, the gambling.

[*We have omitted a 2,200-word section with 7 footnotes, some quite extensive, called "Odds and Even Money," in which Geertz gives a detailed explanation of cockfight betting patterns. The high level of detail in this section is a good example of thick description. Geertz explains that his analysis is based on "exact and reliable data" from 57 matches.*

Geertz identifies two types of bets in a cockfight, the "axial" or center bet between the principals who own the fighting cocks and peripheral bets between members of the audience. Center bets are large collective wagers involving coalitions of bettors; they are quietly arranged with the umpire in the center of the ring. The peripheral bets are typically small and are arranged impulsively by individuals shouting back and forth across the ring.

Because center bets are always for even money, participants typically arrange fair matches. The more evenly matched the cocks, the higher the center bets. The peripheral bets vary wildly according to the odds individual bettors are willing to give. The larger the center bet, the more frenzied the peripheral betting. Fights with high center bets are considered more interesting because more is at stake in them. In a high-stakes fight, men are risking money and social prestige, as well as valuable fighting cocks. When a match ends, all bets are immediately paid.

The Balinese want to create interesting matches with high center bets. Geertz refers to these as "deep" matches and contrasts them with "shallow" relatively trivial matches. High center bets are a device for creating "deep" matches, but not the real reason they

---

12. In this paragraph, you get a sense of Geertz's definition of culture: a shared code of meaning that is acted out in public. Geertz believed that culture is not a mental model, but exists between people, created by their social actions. His reference to Erving Goffman (1922–1982), an important sociologist of the 1960s, gives a clue to the sociological influence on his work. Goffman viewed individual actions as performances and was concerned with delineating the rules governing nonverbal interaction. You can see Goffman's influence in these paragraphs, as Geertz describes people's actions at cockfights.

are deep. This, Geertz implies, is what he will explore in the next section.]

PLAYING WITH FIRE

Bentham's concept of "deep play" is found in his *The Theory of Legislation*.* By it he means play in which the stakes are so high that it is, from his utilitarian standpoint, irrational for men to engage in it at all. If a man whose fortune is a thousand pounds (or ringgits) wages five hundred of it on an even bet, the marginal utility of the pound he stands to win is clearly less than the marginal disutility of the one he stands to lose. In genuine deep play, this is the case for both parties. They are both in over their heads. Having come together in search of pleasure they have entered into a relationship which will bring the participants, considered collectively, net pain rather than net pleasure. Bentham's conclusion was, therefore, that deep play was immoral from first principles and, a typical step for him, should be prevented legally.[13]

But more interesting than the ethical problem, at least for our concerns here, is that despite the logical force of Bentham's analysis men do engage in such play, both passionately and often, and even in the face of law's revenge. For Bentham and those who think as he does (nowadays mainly lawyers, economists, and a

few psychiatrists), the explanation is, as I have said, that such men are irrational—addicts, fetishists, children, fools, savages, who need only to be protected against themselves. But for the Balinese, though naturally they do not formulate it in so many words, the explanation lies in the fact that in such play, money is less a measure of utility, had or expected, than it is a symbol of moral import, perceived or imposed.

It is, in fact, in shallow games, ones in which smaller amounts of money are involved, that increments and decrements of cash are more nearly synonyms for utility and disutility, in the ordinary, unexpanded sense—for pleasure and pain, happiness and unhappiness. In deep ones, where the amounts of money are great, much more is at stake than material gain: namely, esteem, honor, dignity, respect—in a word, though in Bali a profoundly freighted word, status.* It is at stake symbolically, for (a few cases of ruined addict gamblers aside) no one's status is actually altered by the outcome of a cockfight; it is only, and that momentarily, affirmed or insulted. But for the Balinese, for whom nothing is more pleasurable than an affront obliquely delivered or more painful than one obliquely received—particularly when mutual acquaintances, undeceived by surfaces, are watching—such appraisive drama is deep indeed.[14]

This, I must stress immediately, is *not* to say that the money does not matter, or that the

---

13. Jeremy Bentham (1748–1832) was an English philosopher and social theorist best known for his doctrine of utilitarianism, the principles of which are outlined in his 1789 book *An Introduction to the Principles of Morals and Legislation*. Utilitarianism is the belief that the aim of society should be to create the greatest level of happiness for the greatest number of people. Bentham believed that correct conduct was determined by the balance of pleasure over pain that an act would produce and that pain and pleasure could be quantitatively measured. Thus, legislative decision-making could be reduced to a quasimathematical science. Bentham rejected "deep play" since the result must be more bad than good. However, Bentham's formula seems to miss something essential about humanity. For example, dangerous sports are examples of deep play. Base jumping, mountain climbing, sky diving and so on cannot fit Bentham's utilitarian model since the benefits that one accrues by participating in these can never exceed the possible cost of death. Yet, these and many other dangerous sports are popular in many cultures. Among Bentham's best known intellectual followers were John Stuart Mill (1806–1873) and Herbert Spencer.

In his will of 1832, Jeremy Bentham directed his friend the physician and public health advocate Thomas Southwood Smith (1788–1861) to take charge of his body and have his skeleton put together and displayed in a favorite chair. The skeleton, padded out with straw and cloth and clad in Bentham's clothes, with a wax head, was placed on display at University College, London, where it remains to this day.

14. This passage includes a critical aspect of Geertz's analysis: Cockfights do not actually change people's status. You might compare this to American professional sports. If the Detroit Tigers beat the New York Yankees, there is no meaningful change in the real status of the cities of Detroit and New York. Whatever you may feel about those two cities (and baseball), their relative status is set by economic, historical, environmental, and demographic factors that have nothing to do with sports and are not changed by baseball wins and losses.

Balinese is no more concerned about losing five hundred ringgits than fifteen. Such a conclusion would be absurd. It is because money *does*, in this hardly unmaterialistic society, matter and matter very much that the more of it one risks, the more of a lot of other things, such as one's pride, one's poise, one's dispassion, one's masculinity, one also risks, again only momentarily but again very publicly as well. In deep cockfights an owner and his collaborators, and, as we shall see, to a lesser but still quite real extent also their backers on the outside, put their money where their status is.

It is in large part *because* the marginal disutility of loss is so great at the higher levels of betting that to engage in such betting is to lay one's public self, allusively and metaphorically, through the medium of one's cock, on the line. And though to a Benthamite this might seem merely to increase the irrationality of the enterprise that much further, to the Balinese what it mainly increases is the meaningfulness of it all. And as (to follow Weber rather than Bentham) the imposition of meaning on life is the major end and primary condition of human existence, that access of significance more than compensates for the economic costs involved.* Actually, given the even-money quality of the larger matches, important changes in material fortune among those who regularly participate in them seem virtually nonexistent, because matters more or less even out over the long run. It is, actually, in the smaller, shallow fights, where one finds the handful of more pure, addict-type gamblers involved—those who *are* in it mainly for the money—that "real" changes in social position, largely downward, are affected. Men of this sort, plungers, are highly dispraised by "true cockfighters" as fools who do not understand what the sport is all about, vulgarians who simply miss the point of it all. They are, these addicts, regarded as fair game for the genuine enthusiasts, those who do understand, to take a little money away from—something

that is easy enough to do by luring them, through the force of their greed, into irrational bets on mismatched cocks. Most of them do indeed manage to ruin themselves in a remarkably short time, but there always seems to be one or two of them around, pawning their land and selling their clothes in order to bet, at any particular time.*[15]

This graduated correlation of "status gambling" with deeper fights and, inversely, "money gambling" with shallower ones is in fact quite general. Bettors themselves form a sociomoral hierarchy in these terms. As noted earlier, at most cockfights there are, around the very edges of the cockfight area, a large number of mindless, sheer-chance-type gambling games (roulette, dice throw, coin-spin, pea-under-the-shell) operated by concessionaires. Only women, children, adolescents, and various other sorts of people who do not (or not yet) fight cocks—the extremely poor, the socially despised, the personally idiosyncratic—play at these games, at, of course, penny ante levels. Cockfighting men would be ashamed to go anywhere near them. Slightly above these people in standing are those who though they do not themselves fight cocks, bet on the smaller matches around the edges. Next, there are those who fight cocks in small, or occasionally medium matches, but have not the status to join in the large ones, though they may bet from time to time on the side in those. And finally, there are those, the really substantial members of the community, the solid citizenry around whom local life revolves, who fight in the larger fights and bet on them around the side. The focusing element in these focused gatherings, these men generally dominate and define the sport as they dominate and define the society. When a Balinese male talks, in that almost venerative way, about "the true cockfighter," the *bebatoh* ("bettor") or *djuru kurung* ("cage keeper"), it is this sort of person, not those who bring the mentality of the pea-and-shell game

15. Geertz claims Max Weber as one of the major influences in his intellectual development. He was first exposed to Weber by the sociologist Talcott Parsons (1902–1979), while a graduate student at Harvard University (see Handler 1991 for more about Geertz's career and academic life). Geertz invokes Weber in explaining his concept of culture and, simultaneously, introducing the essays in *The Interpretation of Cultures* (1973): "The concept of culture I espouse . . . is essentially a semiotic one. Believing, with Max Weber that man is an animal suspended in webs of significance he himself has spun, I take culture to be those webs, and the analysis of it to be therefore not an experimental science in search of law but an interpretive one in search of meaning" (1973: 5).

into the quite different, inappropriate context of the cockfight, the driven gambler (*potét*, a word which has the secondary meaning of thief or reprobate), and the wistful hanger-on, that they mean. For such a man, what is really going on in a match is something rather closer to an ***affaire d'honneur*** (though, with the Balinese talent for practical fantasy, the blood that is spilled is only figuratively human) than to the stupid, mechanical crank of a slot machine. [16]

What makes Balinese cockfighting deep is thus not money in itself, but what, the more of it that is involved the more so, money causes to happen: the migration of the Balinese status hierarchy into the body of the cockfight. Psychologically an Aesopian representation of the ideal/demonic, rather narcissistic, male self, sociologically it is an equally Aesopian representation of the complex fields of tension set up by the controlled, muted, ceremonial, but for all that deeply felt, interaction of those selves in the context of everyday life. The cocks may be surrogates for their owners' personalities, animal mirrors of psychic form, but the cockfight is—or more exactly, deliberately is made to be—a simulation of the social matrix, the involved system of cross-cutting, overlapping, highly corporate groups—villages, kin groups, irrigation societies, temple congregations, "castes"—in which its devotees live.* And as prestige, the necessity to affirm it, defend it, celebrate it, justify it, and just plain bask in it (but not, given the strongly ascriptive character of Balinese stratification, to seek it), is perhaps the central driving force in the society, so also—ambulant penises, blood sacrifices, and monetary exchanges aside—is it of the cockfight. This apparent amusement and seeming sport is, to take another phrase from Erving Goffman, "a status bloodbath."*[17]

The easiest way to make this clear, and at least to some degree to demonstrate it, is to invoke the village whose cockfighting activities I observed the closest—the one in which the raid occurred and from which my statistical data are taken.

Like all Balinese villages, this one—Tihingan, in the Klungkung region of southeast Bali—is intricately organized, a labyrinth of alliances and oppositions. But, unlike many, two sorts of corporate groups, which are also status groups, particularly stand out, and we may concentrate on them, in a part-for-whole way, without undue distortion.

First, the village is dominated by four large, patrilineal, partly endogamous descent groups which are constantly vying with one another and form the major factions in the village. Sometimes they group two and two, or rather the two larger ones versus the two smaller ones plus all the unaffiliated people; sometimes they operate independently. There are also subfactions within them, subfactions within the subfactions, and so on to rather fine levels of distinction. And second, there is the village itself, almost entirely endogamous, which is opposed to all the other villages round about in its cockfight circuit (which, as explained, is the market region), but which also forms alliances with certain of these neighbors against certain others in various supravillage political and social contexts. The exact situation is thus, as everywhere in Bali, quite distinctive; but the general pattern of a tiered hierarchy of status rivalries between highly corporate but various based groupings (and, thus, between the members of them) is entirely general.

Consider, then, as support of the general thesis that the cockfight, and especially the deep cockfight, is fundamentally a dramatization of status concerns, the following facts, which to avoid extended ethnographic description I shall simply pronounce to be facts though the concrete evidence, examples, statements, and num-

---

16. ***Affaire d'honneur***: literally "affair of honor," but usually used to refer to a duel.

17. For Geertz, the cockfight is an interpretive key to Balinese society because it is the ritual through which the Balinese express their values. Geertz uses the phrase "the migration of the Balinese status hierarchy into the body of the cockfight" to characterize his idea that one can observe the stratification of Balinese society in the organization of people within and around the cockfight area. The implication is that in this example of deep play is that the cockfight is a simulation of the Balinese system of status and ranking.

bers that could be brought to bear in support of them, is both extensive and unmistakable[18]

1. A man virtually never bets against a cock owned by a member of his own kin group. Usually he will feel obliged to bet for it, the more so the closer the kin tie and the deeper the fight. If he is certain in his mind that it will not win, he may just not bet at all, particularly if it is only a second cousin's bird or if the fight is a shallow one. But as a rule he will feel he must support it and, in deep games, nearly always does. Thus the great majority of the people calling "five" or "speckled" so demonstratively are expressing their allegiance to their kinsman, not their evaluation of his bird, their understanding of probability theory, or even their hopes of unearned income.[19]

2. This principle is extended logically. If your kin group is not involved you will support an allied kin group against an unallied one in the same way, and so on through the very involved networks of alliances which, as I say, make up this, as any other, Balinese village.

3. So, too, for the village as a whole. If an outsider cock is fighting any cock from your village, you will tend to support the local one. If, what is a rarer circumstance but occurs every now and then, a cock from outside your cockfight circuit is fighting one inside it, you will also tend to support the "home bird."

4. Cocks which come from any distance are almost always favorites, for the theory is the man would not have dared to bring it if it was not a good cock, the more so the further he has come. His followers are, of course, obliged to support him, and

when the more grand-scale legal cockfights are held (on holidays, and so on) the people of the village take what they regard to be the best cocks in the village, regardless of ownership, and go off to support them, although they will almost certainly have to give odds on them and to make large bets to show that they are not a cheapskate village. Actually, such "away games," though infrequent, tend to mend the ruptures between village members that the constantly occurring "home games," where village factions are opposed rather than united, exacerbate.

5. Almost all matches are sociologically relevant. You seldom get two outsider cocks fighting, or two cocks with no particular group backing, or with group backing which is mutually unrelated in any clear way. When you do get them, the game is very shallow, betting very slow, and the whole thing very dull, with no one save the immediate principals and an addict gambler or two at all interested.

6. By the same token, you rarely get two cocks from the same group, even more rarely from the same subfaction, and virtually never from the same sub-subfaction (which would be in most cases one extended family) fighting. Similarly, in outside village fights two members of the village will rarely fight against one another, even though, as bitter rivals, they would do so with enthusiasm on their home grounds.

7. On the individual level, people involved in an institutionalized hostility relationship, called *puik,* in which they do not speak or otherwise have anything to do with each other (the causes of this formal breaking of relations are many:

---

18. Geertz's discussion is reminiscent of the analysis of the potlatch by Marcel Mauss (see essay 6). The potlatch was a competition for status between individuals representing their kin groups and communities. In the same way, the Balinese cockfight is a competition for status, with men always betting on the birds owned by kinsmen or men of their communities who are competing with people from other communities. A major difference between Geertz and Mauss, however, is that Mauss described the potlatch as a real competition for status—a defeat in a potlatch meant the loss of a position of leadership. Geertz however, makes it clear that the cockfight does not really change anything because status in Bali is determined by birth and cannot change.

19. Calling "five" or "speckled" refers to the betting on birds that Geertz detailed earlier.

wife-capture, inheritance arguments, political differences) will bet very heavily, sometimes almost maniacally, against one another in what is a frank and direct attack on the very masculinity, the ultimate ground of his status, of the opponent.

8. The center bet coalition is, in all but the shallowest games, *always* made up by structural allies—no "outside money" is involved. What is "outside" depends upon the context, of course, but given it, no outside money is mixed in with the main bet; if the principals cannot raise it, it is not made. The center bet, again especially in deeper games, is thus the most direct and open expression of social opposition, which is one of the reasons why both it and matchmaking are surrounded by such an air of unease, furtiveness, embarrassment, and so on.

9. The rule about borrowing money—that you may borrow *for* a bet but not *in* one—stems (and the Balinese are quite conscious of this) from similar considerations: you are never at the *economic* mercy of your enemy that way. Gambling debts, which can get quite large on a rather short-term basis, are always to friends, never to enemies, structurally speaking.

10. When two cocks are structurally irrelevant or neutral so far as *you* are concerned (though, as mentioned, they almost never are to each other) you do not even ask a relative or a friend whom he is betting on, because if you know how he is betting and he knows you know, and you go the other way, it will lead to strain. This rule is explicit and rigid; fairly elaborate, even rather artificial precautions are taken to avoid breaking it. At the very least you must pretend not to notice what he is doing, and he what you are doing.

11. There is a special word for betting against the grain, which is also the word for "pardon me" (*mpura*). It is considered a bad thing to do, though if the center bet is small it is sometimes all right as long as you do not do it too often. But the larger the bet and the more frequently you do it, the more the "pardon me" tack will lead to social disruption.

12. In fact, the institutionalized hostility relation, *puik*, is often vformally initiated (though its causes always lie elsewhere) by such a "pardon me" bet in a deep fight, putting the symbolic fat in the fire. Similarly, the end of such a relationship and resumption of normal social intercourse is often signalized (but, again, not actually brought about) by one or the other of the enemies supporting the other's bird.

13. In sticky, cross-loyalty situations, of which in this extraordinarily complex social system there are of course many, where a man is caught between two more or less equally balanced loyalties, he tends to wander off for a cup of coffee or something to avoid having to bet, a form of behavior reminiscent of that of American voters in similar situations.*

14. The people involved in the center bet are, especially in deep fights, virtually always leading members of their group—kinship, village, or whatever. Further, those who bet on the side (including these people) are, as I have already remarked, the more established members of the village—the solid citizens. Cockfighting is for those who are involved in the everyday politics of prestige as well, not for youth, women, subordinates, and so forth.

15. So far as money is concerned, the explicitly expressed attitude toward it is that it is a secondary matter. It is not, as I have said, of no importance; Balinese are no happier to lose several weeks' income than anyone else. But they mainly look on the monetary aspects of the cockfight as self-balancing, a matter of just moving money around, circulating it among a fairly well-defined group of serious cockfighters. The really important wins and losses are seen mostly in other terms, and the general attitude toward wagering is not any hope of cleaning up, of making a killing (addict gamblers again

excepted), but that of the horse-player's prayer: "Oh, God, please let me break even." In prestige terms, however, you do not want to break even, but, in a momentary, punctuate sort of way, win utterly. The talk (which goes on all the time) is about fights against such-and-such a cock of So-and-So which your cock demolished, not on how much you won, a fact people, even for large bets, rarely remember for any length of time, though they will remember the day they did in Pan Loh's finest cock for years.

16. You must bet on cocks of your own group aside from mere loyalty considerations, for if you do not people generally will say, "What! Is he too proud for the likes of us? Does he have to go to Java or Den Pasar [the capital town] to bet, he is such an important man?" Thus there is a general pressure to bet not only to show that you are important locally, but that you are not so important that you look down on everyone else as unfit even to be rivals. Similarly, home team people must bet against outside cocks or the outsiders will accuse them—a serious charge—of just collecting entry fees and not really being interested in cockfighting, as well as again being arrogant and insulting.

17. Finally, the Balinese peasants themselves are quite aware of all this and can and, at least to an ethnographer, do state most of it in approximately the same terms as I have. Fighting cocks, almost every Balinese I have ever discussed the subject with has said, is like playing with fire only not getting burned. You activate village and kin group rivalries and hostilities, but in "play" form, coming dangerously and entrancingly close to the expression of open and direct interpersonal and intergroup aggression (something which, again, almost never happens in the normal course of ordinary life), but not quite, because, after all, it is "only a cockfight."[20]

More observations of this sort could be advanced, but perhaps the general point is, if not made, at least well-delineated, and the whole argument thus far can be usefully summarized in a formal paradigm:

The more a match is . . .

1. Between near status equals (and/or personal enemies)
2. Between high status individuals

. . . *the deeper the match.*
The deeper the match . . .

1. The closer the identification of cock and man (or, more properly, the deeper the match the more the man will advance his best, most closely-identified-with cock).
2. The finer the cocks involved and the more exactly they will be matched.
3. The greater the emotion that will be involved and the more the general absorption in the match.
4. The higher the individual bets center and outside, the shorter the outside bet odds will tend to be, and the more betting there will be overall.
5. The less an "economic" and the more a "status" view of gaming will be involved, and the "solider" the citizens who will be gaming.*

---

20. Much of this may sound quite familiar to students with a detailed knowledge of ethnography. The system that Geertz describes here is strikingly similar to the "segmentary lineage" system that Evans-Pritchard described for the Nuer and that has become a standard example of a political system in an acephalous society. In a segmentary lineage, people are organized into small units allied in a specific manner. Allied units join together when threatened by outsiders. Who joins together and how many people are involved depends on the specific kin position of those involved in the conflict. Evans-Pritchard was a student of Radcliffe-Brown and the author of *The Nuer,* a classic of structural-functionalist ethnography. This is important because, to this point, Geertz's essay sounds much like a structural functionalist analysis: Society is divided into different status, kin, and village groups, and these groups interact in specified ways to promote social solidarity. However, Geertz is no structural functionalist.

Inverse arguments hold for the shallower the fight, culminating, in a reversed-signs sense, in the coin-spinning and dice-throwing amusements. For deep fights there are no absolute upper limits, though there are of course practical ones, and there are a great many legend like tales of great Duel-in-the-Sun combats between lords and princes in classical times (for cockfighting has always been as much an elite concern as a popular one), far deeper than anything anyone, even aristocrats, could produce today anywhere in Bali.

Indeed, one of the great culture heroes of Bali is a prince, called after his passion for the sport, "The Cockfighter," who happened to be away at a very deep cockfight with a neighboring prince when the whole of his family—father, brothers, wives, sisters—were assassinated by commoner usurpers. Thus spared, he returned to dispatch the upstart, regain the throne, reconstitute the Balinese high tradition, and build its most powerful, glorious, and prosperous state. Along with everything else that the Balinese see in fighting cocks—themselves, their social order, abstract hatred, masculinity, demonic power—they also see the archetype of status virtue, the arrogant, resolute, honor-mad player with real fire, the *ksatria* prince.*

FEATHERS, BLOOD, CROWDS, AND MONEY

"Poetry makes nothing happen," Auden says in his elegy of Yeats, "it survives in the valley of its saying . . . a way of happening, a mouth." The cockfight too, in this colloquial sense, makes nothing happen. Men go on allegorically humiliating one another and being allegorically humiliated by one another, day after day, glorying quietly in the experience if they have triumphed, crushed only slightly more openly by it if they have not. *But no one's status really changes.* You cannot ascend the status ladder by winning cockfights; you cannot, as an individual, really ascend it at all. Nor can you descend it that way.* All you can do is enjoy and savor, or suffer and withstand, the concocted sensation of drastic and momentary movement along an aesthetic semblance of that ladder, a kind of behind-the-mirror status jump which has the look of mobility without its actuality.[21]

Like any art form—for that, finally, is what we are dealing with—the cockfight renders ordinary, everyday experience comprehensible by presenting it in terms of acts and objects which have had their practical consequences removed and been reduced (or, if you prefer, raised) to the level of sheer appearances, where their meaning can be more powerfully articulated and more exactly perceived. The cockfight is "really real" only to the cocks—it does not kill anyone, castrate anyone, reduce anyone to animal status, alter the hierarchical relations among people, or refashion the hierarchy; it does not even redistribute income in any significant way. What it does is what, for other peoples with other temperaments and other conventions, *Lear* and *Crime and Punishment* do; it catches up these themes—death, masculinity, rage, pride, loss, beneficence, chance—and, ordering them into an encompassing structure, presents them in such a way as to throw into relief a particular view of their essential nature. It puts a construction on them, makes them, to those historically positioned to appreciate the construction, meaningful—visible, tangible, graspable—"real," in an ideational sense. An image, fiction, a model, a metaphor, the cockfight is a means of expression; its function is neither to assuage social passions nor to heighten them (though, in its playing-with-fire way it does a bit of both), but,

---

21. In a 1991 interview (Handler 1991), Geertz stated that a weakness of anthropology before the 1960s was that anthropologists read only other anthropologists. His point was that intellectual development in anthropology should be based on knowledge in a wide range of fields. As you read, look at the diversity of literature that Geertz ties into his work: Balinese sources, poetry, sociology, psychology, mythology, art, and philosophy, to name just a few, all have a place in his thought. Conversely, Geertz is one of the few anthropological theorists widely read by scholars of literature and history.

W. H. Auden (1907–1973) was a British-born American poet. William Butler Yeats (1865–1939) was an Irish poet and nationalist.

in a medium of feathers, blood, crowds, and money, to display them.

The question of how it is that we perceive qualities in things—paintings, books, melodies, plays—that we do not feel we can assert literally to be there has come, in recent years, into the very center of aesthetic theory.* Neither the sentiments of the artist, which remain his, nor those of the audience, which remain theirs, can account for the agitation of one painting or the serenity of another. We attribute grandeur, wit, despair, exuberance to strings of sounds; lightness, energy, violence, fluidity to blocks of stone. Novels are said to have strength, buildings eloquence, plays momentum, ballets repose. In this realm of eccentric predicates, to say that the cockfight, in its perfected cases at least, is "disquietful" does not seem at all unnatural, merely, as I have just denied it practical consequence, somewhat puzzling.[22]

The disquietfulness arises, "somehow," out of a conjunction of three attributes of the fight: its immediate dramatic shape; its metaphoric content; and its social context. A cultural figure against a social ground, the fight is at once a convulsive surge of animal hatred, a mock war of symbolical selves, and a formal simulation of status tensions, and its aesthetic power derives from its capacity to force together these diverse realities. The reason it is disquietful is not that it has material effects (it has some, but they are minor); the reason that it is disquietful is that, joining pride to selfhood, selfhood to cocks, and cocks to destruction, it brings to imaginative realization a dimension of Balinese experience normally well-obscured from view. The transfer of a sense of gravity into what is in itself a rather blank and unvarious spectacle, a commotion of beating wings and throbbing

legs, is effected by interpreting it as expressive of something unsettling in the way its authors and audience live, or, even more ominously, what they are.[23]

As a dramatic shape, the fight displays a characteristic that does not seem so remarkable until one realizes that it does not have to be there: a radically atomistical structure.* Each match is a world unto itself, a particulate burst of form. There is the matchmaking, there is the betting, there is the fight, there is the result—utter triumph and utter defeat—and there is the hurried, embarrassed passing of money. The loser is not consoled. People drift away from him, look around him, leave him to assimilate his momentary descent into nonbeing, reset his face, and return, scarless and intact, to the fray. Nor are winners congratulated, or events rehashed; once a match is ended the crowd's attention turns totally to the next, with no looking back. A shadow of the experience no doubt remains with the principals, perhaps even with some of the witnesses of a deep fight, as it remains with us when we leave the theater after seeing a powerful play well performed; but it quite soon fades to become at most a schematic memory—a diffuse glow or an abstract shudder—and usually not even that. Any expressive form lives only in its own present—the one it itself creates. But, here, that present is severed into a string of flashes, some more bright than others, but all of them disconnected, aesthetic quanta. Whatever the cockfight says, it says in spurts.

But, as I have argued lengthily elsewhere, the Balinese live in spurts.* Their life, as they arrange it and perceive it, is less a flow, a directional movement out of the past, through the present, toward the future than an on-off pul-

22. Having identified the cockfight as a form of art analogous to the plays of Shakespeare (*Lear*) or the novels of Dostoyevsky (*Crime and Punishment*) Geertz begins to present an analysis of the cockfight using the same sorts of language and ideas that a reviewer might use analyzing a new novel or play. In a footnote to the next passage, Geertz writes, perhaps somewhat tongue in cheek, that "as a genre, the cockfight has perhaps less compositional flexibility than, say, Latin comedy [the comic plays of ancient Rome], but it is not entirely without any."

23. Geertz views culture as shared codes of meaning that are publicly acted out, which makes his style of analysis a method of dramatic interpretation. The cockfight is like a play the Balinese perform for themselves, and its importance is artistic. Geertz says it has "aesthetic power" because it forces layers of significance, what he calls "diverse realities," together. It expresses in poignant ways what it means to be Balinese.

sation of meaning and vacuity, an arrhythmic alternation of short periods when "something" (that is, something significant) is happening, and equally short ones where "nothing" (that is, nothing much) is between what they themselves call "full" and "empty" times, or, in another idiom, "junctures" and "holes." In focusing activity down to a burning-glass dot, the cockfight is merely being Balinese in the same way in which everything from the monadic encounters of everyday life, through the clanging pointillism of **gamelan** music, to the visiting-day-of-the-gods temple celebrations are. It is not an imitation of the punctuateness of Balinese social life, nor a depiction of it, nor even an expression of it; it is an example of it, carefully prepared.*[24]

If one dimension of the cockfight's structure, its lack of temporal directionality, makes it seem a typical segment of the general social life, however, the other, its flat-out, head-to-head (or spur-to-spur) aggressiveness, makes it seem a contradiction, a reversal, even a subversion of it. In the normal course of things, the Balinese are shy to the point of obsessiveness of open conflict. Oblique, cautious, subdued, controlled, masters of indirection and dissimulation—what they call *alus,* "polished," "smooth"—they rarely face what they can turn away from, rarely resist what they can evade. But here they portray themselves as wild and murderous, with manic explosions of instinctual cruelty. A powerful rendering of life as the Balinese most deeply do not want it (to adapt a phrase Frye has used of Gloucester's blinding) is set in the context of a sample of it as they do in fact have it.* And, because the context suggests that the rendering, if less than a straightforward description, is nonetheless more than an idle fancy; it is here that the disquietfulness—the disquietfulness of the *fight,* not (or, anyway, not necessarily) its patrons, who seem in fact rather thoroughly to enjoy it—emerges. The slaughter in the cock ring is not a depiction of how things literally are among men, but, what is almost worse, of how, from a particular angle, they imaginatively are.*[25]

The angle, of course, is stratificatory. What, as we have already seen, the cockfight talks most forcibly about is status relationships, and what it says about them is that they are matters of life and death. That prestige is a profoundly serious business is apparent everywhere one looks in Bali—in the village, the family, the economy, the state. A peculiar fusion of Polynesian title ranks and Hindu castes, the hierarchy of pride is the moral backbone of the society. But only in the cockfight are the sentiments upon which that hierarchy rests revealed in their natural colors. Enveloped elsewhere in a haze of etiquette, a thick cloud of euphemism and ceremony, gesture and allusion, they are here expressed in only the thinnest disguise of an animal mask, a mask which in fact demonstrates them far more effectively than it conceals them. Jealousy is as much a part of Bali as poise, envy as grace, brutality as charm; but without the cockfight the Balinese would have a much less certain understanding of them, which is, presumably, why they value it so highly.

---

24. Geertz has led us back from the details of the cockfight to his definition of culture. He stresses that culture does not exist apart from individuals; instead, it is created in people's interpretations of events around them and bound up in public symbols and communication (Applebaum 1987: 485). Here he says the cockfight is not a depiction, expression, or example of Balinese life; rather, it *is* Balinese life.

"*Gamelan*": a type of Southeast Asian music using chimes and gongs.

25. Northrop Frye (1912–1991) was an influential literary critic who was particularly concerned with the relationship of literature to myth and society. Geertz quotes Frye extensively in the remainder of his essay. Gloucester's blinding occurs in Shakespeare's play *King Lear,* when the Earl of Gloucester is punished for aiding Lear by having his eyes gouged out. Frye says that the audience does not want to see a real experience (a man's eyes put out); they want a vicarious experience from the point of view of the imagination. The fact that the blinding does not really happen is crucial to the psychological experience (Frye 1964: 98–99). Similarly, the audience at a cockfight doesn't really want to see men viciously attack each other. They want the vicarious experience of violence.

Any expressive form works (when it works) by disarranging semantic contexts in such a way that properties conventionally ascribed to certain things are unconventionally ascribed to others, which are then seen actually to possess them. To call the wind a cripple, as Stevens does, to fix tone and manipulate timbre, as Schoenberg does, or, closer to our case, to picture an art critic as a dissolute bear, as Hogarth does, is to cross conceptual wires; the established conjunctions between objects and their qualities are altered, and phenomena—fall weather, melodic shape, or cultural journalism—are clothed in signifiers which normally point to other referents.* Similarly, to connect—and connect, and connect—the collision of roosters with the divisiveness of status is to invite a transfer of perceptions from the former to the latter, a transfer which is at once a description and a judgment. (Logically, the transfer could, of course, as well go the other way; but, like most of the rest of us, the Balinese are a great deal more interested in understanding men than they are in understanding cocks.)[26]

What sets the cockfight apart from the ordinary course of life, lifts it from the realm of everyday practical affairs, and surrounds it with an aura of enlarged importance is not, as functionalist sociology would have it, that it reinforces status discriminations (such reinforcement is hardly necessary in a society where every act proclaims them), but that it provides a metasocial commentary upon the whole matter of assorting human beings into fixed hierarchical ranks and then organizing the major part of collective existence around that assortment. Its function, if you want to call it that, is interpretive: it is a Balinese reading of Balinese experience, a story they tell themselves about themselves.[27]

SAYING SOMETHING OF SOMETHING

To put the matter this way is to engage in a bit of metaphorical refocusing of one's own, for it shifts the analysis of cultural forms from an endeavor in general parallel to dissecting an organism, diagnosing a symptom, deciphering a code, or ordering a system—the dominant analogies in contemporary anthropology—to one in general parallel with penetrating a literary text. If one takes the cockfight, or any other collectively sustained symbolic structure, as a means of "saying something of something" (to invoke a famous Aristotelian tag), then one is faced with a problem not in social mechanics but social semantics.* For the anthropologist, whose concern is with formulating sociological principles, not with promoting or appreciating cockfights, the question is, what does one learn about such principles from examining culture as an assemblage of texts?[28]

---

26. In this paragraph, Geertz describes how the Balinese cockfight communicates a message about status in the same way that poetry, music, and art convey messages to their audiences. Geertz uses terminology developed by the Swiss linguist Ferdinand de Saussure (1857–1913) in his semiotics (the study of signs and symbols).

Wallace Stevens (1879–1955) was an American poet. The citation is to "The Motive for Metaphor." Stevens writes: "The wind moves like a cripple among the leaves/And repeats words without meaning." Arnold Schoenberg (1874–1951) was an Austrian composer, and William Hogarth (1697–1764) was an English painter and lithographer.

27. Up to this point, Geertz has performed an analysis that could have come straight from the pen of a British structural functionalist ethnographer. In the last few sections, however, he turns the structural functionalist position upside down, saying that functionalist conclusions are meaningless for the Balinese. The Balinese live in a world where they are constantly reminded of status. Status is "overdetermined." There is no social need for the cockfight to support it. Rather than contributing to social solidarity, Geertz argues that the cockfight allows them to play with status in ways that interrogate what it means to be human in Bali.

28. "Saying something of something," the quote from Aristotle that forms the chapter title, references Aristotle's ideas about the nature of knowledge. Aristotle argues that there are three ways to say something

444 *Part IV: Late-Twentieth-Century Developments*

Such an extension of the notion of a text beyond written material, and even beyond verbal, is, though metaphorical, not, of course, all that novel. The *interpretatio naturae* tradition of the middle ages, which, culminating in Spinoza, attempted to read nature as Scripture, the Nietzschean effort to treat value systems as glosses on the will to power (or the Marxian one to treat them as glosses on property relations), and the Freudian replacement of the enigmatic text of the manifest dream with the plain one of the latent, all offer precedents, if not equally recommendable ones.* But the idea remains theoretically undeveloped; and the more profound corollary, so far as anthropology is concerned, that cultural forms can be treated as texts, as imaginative works built out of social materials, has yet to be systematically exploited.*29

In the case at hand, to treat the cockfight as a text is to bring out a feature of it (in my opinion, the central feature of it) that treating it as a rite or a pastime, the two most obvious alternatives, would tend to obscure: its use of emotion for cognitive ends. What the cockfight says it says in a vocabulary of sentiment—the thrill of risk, the despair of loss, the pleasure of triumph. Yet what it says is not merely that risk is exciting, loss depressing, or triumph gratifying, banal tautologies of affect, but that it is of these emotions, thus exampled, that society is built and individuals are put together. Attending cockfights and participating in them is, for

the Balinese, a kind of sentimental education. What he learns there is what his culture's ethos and his private sensibility (or, anyway, certain aspects of them) look like when spelled out externally in a collective text; that the two are near enough alike to be articulated in the symbolics of a single such text; and—the disquieting part—that the text in which this revelation is accomplished consists of a chicken hacking another mindlessly to bits.

Every people, the proverb has it, loves its own form of violence. The cockfight is the Balinese reflection on theirs: on its look, its uses, its force, its fascination. Drawing on almost every level of Balinese experience, it brings together themes—animal savagery, male narcissism, opponent gambling, status rivalry, mass excitement, blood sacrifice—whose main connection is their involvement with rage and the fear of rage, and, binding them into a set of rules which at once contains them and allows them play, builds a symbolic structure in which, over and over again, the reality of their inner affiliation can be intelligibly felt. If, to quote Northrop Frye again, we go to see *Macbeth* to learn what a man feels like after he has gained a kingdom and lost his soul, Balinese go to cockfights to find out what a man, usually composed, aloof, almost obsessively self-absorbed, a kind of moral **autocosm**, feels like when, attacked, tormented, challenged, insulted, and driven in result to the extremes of fury, he has totally triumphed or been brought

---

of something: the universal, the particular, and the indefinite (Byrne 1997: 32). In this final section, Geertz summarizes his argument and explains how the cockfight attains personal significance for Balinese participants. Up to now, the analysis has been very particular, but his conclusions try to say something universal about the nature of culture: that cultures are a form of text.

29. The "interpretatio naturae" or "interpretation of nature" tradition is linked to Francis Bacon (1561–1626) who argued for an inductive methodology in the observation of nature. The "interpretatio naturae" tradition is, in some sense, the opposite of the Aristotelian deductive "saying something of something" tradition mentioned in the previous paragraph.

Baruch Spinoza (1632–1677) was an influential philosopher in the rationalist tradition. In one of his best-known works, *Ethics,* first published in 1677, he set out a geometrical program of definitions, axioms, postulates, and theorems that he proposed was a systematic procedure for the perfection of human nature. His work influenced many later scholars, including Georg Wilhelm Friedrich Hegel (1770–1831).

Geertz's comment concerning the "will to power" refers to a concept Friedrich Nietzsche (1844–1900) developed in *Thus Spake Zarathustra* (1954 [1883–1885]) and several other places. Nietzsche sees "will to power" as a critical force animating many, if not all human actions. Nietzsche's ideas were deeply influential for anthropologists and other social thinkers. In this book references to Nietzsche also occur in essays by Max Weber (7) and Pierre Bourdieu (27).

totally low. The whole passage, as it takes us back to Aristotle (though to the *Poetics* rather than the *Hermeneutics*), is worth quotation:

But the poet [as opposed to the historian], Aristotle says, never makes any real statements at all, certainly no particular or specific ones. The poet's job is not to tell you what happened, but what happens: not what did take place, but the kind of thing that always does take place. He gives you the typical, recurring, or what Aristotle calls universal event. You wouldn't go to *Macbeth* to learn about the history of Scotland—you go to it to learn what a man feels like after he's gained a kingdom and lost his soul. When you meet such a character as **Micawber** in Dickens, you don't feel that there must have been a man Dickens knew who was exactly like this: you feel that there's a bit of Micawber in almost everybody you know, including yourself. Our impressions of human life are picked up one by one, and remain for most of us loose and disorganized. But we constantly find things in literature that suddenly coordinate and bring into focus a great many such impressions, and this is part of what Aristotle means by the typical or universal human event.*[30]

It is this kind of bringing of assorted experiences of everyday life to focus that the cockfight, set aside from that life as "only a game" and reconnected to it as "more than a game," accomplishes, and so creates what, better than typical or universal, could be called a paradigmatic human event—that is, one that tells us less what happens than the kind of thing that would happen if, as is not the case, life were art and could be as freely shaped by styles of feeling as *Macbeth* and *David Copperfield* are.

Enacted and re-enacted, so far without end, the cockfight enables the Balinese, as, read and reread, *Macbeth* enables us, to see a dimension of his own subjectivity. As he watches fight after fight, with the active watching of an owner and a bettor (for cockfighting has no more interest as a pure spectator sport than does croquet or dog racing), he grows familiar with it and what it has to say to him, much as the attentive listener to string quartets or the absorbed viewer of still life grows slowly more familiar with them in a way which opens his subjectivity to himself.*[31]

Yet, because—in another of those paradoxes, along with painted feelings and unconsequenced acts, which haunt aesthetics—that subjectivity does not properly exist until it is thus organized, art forms generate and regenerate the very subjectivity they pretend only to display. Quartets, still lifes, and cockfights are not merely reflections of a pre-existing sensibility analogically represented; they are positive agents in the creation and maintenance of such a sensibility. If we see ourselves as a pack of Micawbers, it is from reading too much Dickens (if we see ourselves as unillusioned realists, it is from reading too little); and similarly for Balinese, cocks, and cockfights. It is in such a way, coloring experience with the light they cast it in, rather than through whatever material effects they may have, that the arts play their role, as arts, in social life.*

In the cockfight, then, the Balinese forms and discovers his temperament and his society's temper at the same time. Or, more exactly, he forms and discovers a particular facet of them. Not only are there a great many other cultural texts providing commentaries on status hierarchy and self-regard in Bali, but there are a great many other critical sectors of Balinese life besides the stratificatory and the agonistic

---

30. **"Autocosm"**: private world.

   "Micawber": a character in Charles Dickens's novel *David Copperfield*. Micawber, despite his frequent difficulties, lives in hopeful expectation that "something will turn up." He is relentlessly optimistic.

31. Geertz here uses "subjectivity" to refer to the ways the consciousness of each individual is shaped by the structures and values of their society. Such socially shaped subjectivities are often linked to status within a hierarchy, as is the case in Bali. But, as Geertz points out below, the cockfight not only allows the Balinese to reflect on their subjectivity (drawing back the curtain on the rage and violence that lies under the surface of Balinese society); cockfights also help to shape that subjectivity.

that receive such commentary. The ceremony consecrating a Brahmana priest, a matter of breath control, postural immobility, and vacant concentration upon the depths of being, displays a radically different, but to the Balinese equally real, property of social hierarchy—its reach toward the **numinous** transcendent. Set not in the matrix of the kinetic emotionality of animals, but in that of the static passionlessness of divine mentality, it expresses tranquility not disquiet. The mass festivals at the village temples, which mobilize the whole local population in elaborate hostings of visiting gods— songs, dances, compliments, gifts—assert the spiritual unity of village mates against their status inequality and project a mood of amity and trust.* The cockfight is not the master key to Balinese life, any more than bullfighting is to Spanish. What it says about that life is not unqualified nor even unchallenged by what other equally eloquent cultural statements say about it. But there is nothing more surprising in this than in the fact that Racine and Moliere were contemporaries, or that the same people who arrange chrysanthemums cast swords.*[32]

The culture of a people is an ensemble of texts, themselves ensembles, which the anthropologist strains to read over the shoulders of those to whom they properly belong. There are enormous difficulties in such an enterprise, methodological pitfalls to make a Freudian quake, and some moral perplexities as well. Nor is it the only way that symbolic forms can be sociologically handled. Functionalism lives, and so does psychologism. But to regard such forms as "saying something of something," and saying it to somebody, is at least to open up the possibility of an analysis which attends to their substance rather than to reductive formulas professing to account for them.

As in more familiar exercises in close reading, one can start anywhere in a culture's repertoire of forms and end up anywhere else. One can stay, as I have here, within a single, more or less bounded form, and circle steadily within it. One can move between forms in search of broader unities or informing contrasts. One can even compare forms from different cultures to define their character in reciprocal relief. But whatever the level at which one operates, and however intricately, the guiding principle is the same: societies, like lives, contain their own interpretations. One has only to learn how to gain access to them.[33]

---

32. In this critical paragraph Geertz notes that although the cockfight interpreted as a text tells us something powerful about the nature of society in Bali, society does not speak with one voice. Other public rituals in Balinese culture present other contradictory texts about the nature of Balinese subjectivity. Geertz argues that this is not surprising, that culture, by its nature, is full of competing voices and messages that are at odds with each other. This statement marks a significant trend in American anthropology toward culture as a field where competing views and interests collide.

In an important footnote, Geertz notes that to someone who understood Bali only "through the medium of its dances, its shadow-plays, its sculpture, and its girls," the extraordinary violence that accompanied the Indonesian military coup of 1965–1966, in which eighty thousand Balinese were killed, would be incomprehensible. The cockfight, of course, did not cause the massacre. However, understanding the rage inherent in the cockfight makes the violence less surprising if no less horrific. Geertz concludes that "sometimes people actually get life precisely as they most deeply do not want it."

Jean Racine (1639–1699) and Jean-Baptiste Molière (1622–1673) were French playwrights: the first a great writer of tragedies, the latter famous for his comedies. The last line of the paragraph refers to Benedict's study of the Japanese national character, *The Chrysanthemum and the Sword* (1946).

"Numinous": mysterious, surpassing comprehension.

33. The notion that culture is a collection of texts that anthropologists read over the shoulders of those who live them had a powerful impact on the generation of anthropological theorists that earned their doctorates in the 1970s and 1980s. In particular, this idea led anthropologists to borrow some of the tools of textual analysis from literary criticism. Geertz's work provided part of the foundation for postmodernism, which is dealt with in the following sections.

This essay was published at a time when the works of modern French critical thinkers such as Roland Barthes (1915–1980) and Jacques Derrida (1930–2004) were becoming available in English. Among their critical insights is the notion that texts are systems of symbols that reveal the assumptions of particular cultures at particular times. As Geertz was writing this article, the whole idea of deconstructing texts, or culture, was transforming the field of literary criticism. This selection is a critical bridge between literature and anthropological theory.

French Social Thought: Postmodernism and Practice

In 1917, Marcel Duchamp submitted his work *The Fountain* to a show organized by the Society of Independent Artists in New York City, but his work was not exhibited. In 2004, the BBC reported that five hundred art experts had voted *The Fountain* as the most influential work of modern art. In case you're not familiar with it, *The Fountain* is a urinal that Duchamp signed with the name "R. Mutt, 1917." The original of *The Fountain* was lost, but Duchamp made as many as eleven replicas in the mid-1960s. One of these was purchased for $1.76 million at a Sotheby's auction in New York in 1999. In its origin, *The Fountain* cannot be considered a postmodern work. Duchamp is generally associated with a school of art called Dada. However, the current-day appreciation of works like *The Fountain* definitely portrays a postmodern sensibility. *The Fountain* is postmodern because, for viewers and critics in the late twentieth and early twenty-first centuries, it raises all the right questions. It disorients the viewer and makes the viewer ask what makes something art. It raises questions about the nature of authorship and the control of the author or artist over the works and objects they create. It plays with signs and symbols. It raises questions about authority and power (it is art because the powerful—in this case the curators of major museums and the "experts"—use their authority to declare it art). For the postmodernist, questions of Duchamp's intentions or the life history that led to the work are irrelevant. We have only the object, and we have only our reactions now.

Postmodernism is a movement that began sometime after World War II; it has affected art, music, and literature as well as all of the social sciences. To some degree, who counts as postmodern is in the eye of the beholder, but some postmodern visual artists include Jenny Holzer (b. 1950) and Barbara Kruger (b. 1945). Laurie Anderson (b. 1947) might be considered a postmodern musician. Postmodern novelists include David Foster Wallace (1962–2008) and Ray Federman (1928–2009). The kinds of questions raised and the play of signs and significance found in *The Fountain* are also found in the works of these artists.

In this book, we are most concerned with postmodernism as it affects the social sciences and humanities, particularly philosophy, literature, history, sociology, and anthropology. Although the postmodern influence in these subjects has many sources, much of it can be traced to developments in France in the 1950s and early 1960s. There, a group of mostly young scholars challenged existing orthodoxies and created new understandings of history, literature, and society.

In postwar France, leading intellectuals were drawn both to the philosophy of existentialism and to communism. The French communism of that era was heavily influenced both by its desire to play an active role in the French government and by its ties to the Soviet Union. In the 1950s, this left French communist intellectuals vulnerable on two fronts: Since it generally backed the government, the French Communist Party found itself in support of French colonial wars in both Indochina and Algeria. Since it was tied to the Soviets, it also supported Soviet actions, such as the suppression of the Hungarian Revolution of 1956. The issues of colonialism and Soviet domination of Eastern Europe left many French intellectuals disillusioned with the Communist Party. Although most remained staunch leftists, they broke with the party. At the same time, leading French thinkers were also becoming disillusioned with existentialism. The existentialist doctrine that existence precedes essence suggested that humans were created by the choices they made. In an era of decolonization and liberation movements, a philosophy centered on human experience and individual freedom seemed less vital than theories that foregrounded structure. Marxism, as well as the anthropology of Durkheim and Lévi-Strauss drew scholars' attention to the social structures and systems of classification that undergirded oppression and determined the range of choices available to people.

Disenchanted with both Soviet-style communism and existentialism, French scholars of the 1950s looked for new ways to understand the world. They created these by reinterpreting both Marx and the writings of key twentieth-century philosophers such as Martin Heidegger (1889–1976), Edmund Husserl (1859–1938), and Ludwig Wittgenstein (1889–1951). They combined these with the linguistics of Ferdinand de Saussure (1857–1913) and the anthropology of Durkheim and Lévi-Strauss.

In the 1960s, a relatively close-knit group of scholars formed in Paris. Most were about the same age and shared a variety of connections. Pierre Bourdieu (1930–2002), Michel Foucault (1926–1984), and Jacques Derrida (1930–2004) were all students of Louis Althusser (1918–1990). Gilles Deleuze (1925–1995) was a friend of Foucault. Paul de Man (1919–1983) was a close friend of Derrida (and Derrida published a book in memory of de Man). Other critical postmodern thinkers working in France at this time included Jean-François Lyotard (1924–1998), Jacques Lacan (1901–1981), and Jean Baudrillard (1929–2007). With the exception of de Man, who taught at Yale, all of these thinkers held university positions in and around Paris. The University of Paris has thirteen numbered branches as well as several elite institutions designated as Écoles. Althusser taught at the École Normale Supérieure. Foucault, Lyotard, and Deleuze taught at University of Paris VIII; Baudrillard taught at University of Paris X; and Derrida, Bourdieu, and Lacan (along with Lévi-Strauss) taught at the École Pratique des Hautes Etudes (later the École Pratique des Hautes Etudes en Sciences Sociales). Although many of them moved from institution to institution (e.g., Foucault was at the University of Tunis from 1965 to 1968), they developed their ideas in contact with one another, and their work bears the imprint of this.

Many elements tie the work of the postmodernist scholars together. However, among the most important of these are an emphasis on the relationships between language and power, in particular the perspective of hermeneutics and the philosophy of Paul Ricoeur (1913–2005). Some have referred to this as the "linguistic turn" in the social sciences and philosophy (Rorty 1967 and many others). Building on the work of Wittgenstein and Saussure, the postmodernists held that languages were systems of signs and symbols that took their meanings from relationships with each other rather than relationships with the empirical world. The empirical world itself remained ineffable, that is, beyond our direct understanding. These ideas articulated nicely with developments in hermeneutic philosophy in the first half of the twentieth century. *Hermeneutics* is the study of theories of interpretation. Hermeneuticists, particularly Heidegger and Hans-Georg Gadamer (1900–2002), argued that it is impossible for people to separate ways of knowing from language and culture.

Paul Ricoeur (1913–2005), a philosopher deeply influenced by Heidegger, had a more direct influence on the development of postmodernism. Ricoeur taught at the Sorbonne and was an administrator at Nanterre (University of Paris X) in the 1950s and 1960s. Derrida was sometimes his assistant and frequently debated with him. Ricoeur focused on the "double nature" of human beings: at once metaphysical entities and material beings with physical bodies. He held that our self-understandings and our understandings of history are created through imagination and interpretations. However, these understandings are anchored in our physical bodies and in the material world.

In the work of the French postmodernists, the elements we have been describing come together in several prominent themes. The first is an emphasis on understanding society as created and held together through discourse: Society is, somehow, a series of narratives through which we understand how to interpret the world and behave in it. However, because of the nature of language and interpretation, these narratives can never accurately represent the world. Instead, they are made up of signs and symbols that reference each other and can be substituted for each other.

A second element is that such discourses are set within power relationships and are reflective of them. Language is never neutral, never a clear window through which we can perceive the world.

Discourses promote ways of understanding and interpreting the world to the favor or disadvantage of particular individuals or groups. Postmodernists have been particularly skeptical of grand narratives—totalizing stories that argue for the progress of all humanity or the ultimate triumph of science. For example, in *The Postmodern Condition*, Lyotard argues, "The grand narrative has lost its credibility, regardless of what mode of unification it uses, regardless of whether it is a speculative narrative or a narrative of emancipation" (1984: 37). He declares that postmodernism is most simply defined as "incredulity toward metanarratives" (xxiv). Lyotard's attack on science is particularly instructive. Rather than a way to understand the world or create a better life for people, Lyotard understands science as simply a discourse, and one that, backed by the power of states, corporations, and the wealthy, is particularly effective at extending the domination of these forces over others. However, if science, which claims to be an objective way of determining material truth, is simply a discourse, then there can be no agreed-upon method of determining material truth. Since no appeal to an external reality can ever determine truth, all that is left are competing discourses. In such a competition, the truths of the wealthy, the powerful, the social elites, will in most cases triumph over those of the poor, oppressed, or marginalized. Thus, postmodernists claim, power decides what is true. Althusser's ideas were particularly influential in this regard. You will recall that many key postmodern thinkers were among his students. Althusser was a Marxist thinker particularly concerned with social reproduction. He argued that societies had at their disposal both a repressive state apparatus (RSA) and an ideological state apparatus (ISA). While RSA were institutions of violence through which the state enforced its dominion, ISA were institutions, such as religion, education, family, law, politics, trade unions, communication, and culture, through which the state promulgates its understandings of truth and the nature of the world.

One response of postmodernists to these issues is the idea of deconstruction. Deconstruction is most closely connected with the work of Jacques Derrida. Derrida argued that narratives, both literary texts and cultural understandings, are incapable of accurately representing reality. Instead, they create particularistic understandings of reality by allowing readers or cultural participants to hear some voices and interpretations while at the same time suppressing (or "delicensing") others. However, Derrida argued that this practice created ruptures: zones of conflict or logical inconsistency. Deconstruction is the practice of finding and interpreting such ruptures to reveal underlying cultural assumptions or repressed voices. In *Of Grammatology* (1976), for example, Derrida argues that the work of Lévi-Strauss as well as several other writers shows a valuing of speech over written communication. First, Derrida explores a variety of reasons why speech might be so valued (writing is only a substitute for speech, speech communicates intention more immediately than writing, etc.). However, he then goes on to show that none of these really makes any sense. All of writing's problems can logically be applied to speech, too. He concludes that the privileging of speech cannot be supported by logic but actually reflects the biases and assumptions of Western thought.

In this section, we explore the work of two critical thinkers associated with postmodernism: Michel Foucault and Pierre Bourdieu. Foucault was born in 1926 in Poitiers, France. Educated at the prestigious École Normale Supérieure in Paris, he held a series of university positions. In the early 1950s he was a member of the French Communist Party but, like many of his generation, became rapidly disillusioned with it, although he remained a political radical throughout his life. In 1960, Foucault met Daniel Defert (1937–2023), then a philosophy student with a deep political engagement with the left. Foucault and Defert lived together openly from 1963 until Foucault's death in 1984. In a 1981 interview, Foucault described his relationship with Defert as a state of passion beyond love and reason (Miller and Miller 2000: 186). When Defert went to Tunisia in 1966 to fulfill his French national service obligations, Foucault followed him, taking a position at the University of Tunis. Foucault and Defert returned to France in 1968. They were important figures in the students' movements of 1968–1969 and were associated with Maoist political parties in the early 1970s. However, by the end of that decade, Foucault's direct political involvement had diminished and he began to spend increasing time in the United States, becoming a visiting professor at Berkeley in 1980. He was also increasingly involved with the gay liberation movement. Foucault died of AIDS in 1984. Until the end of his life in 2023, Defert remained a prominent sociologist and AIDS activist as well as the executor of Foucault's literary estate.

Foucault published a series of books, lectures, and interviews, beginning with *Madness and Civilization* in 1961. His other well-known works include *The Order of Things* (1966), *Discipline and Punish* (1977), and the multivolume *History of Sexuality* (originally published 1976–1984). In these works, Foucault explored the development of certain kinds of knowledge and institutions. He was particularly concerned with the period starting in the mid-seventeenth century and continuing to the twentieth century, and he focused on the development of the discourses and institutions of medicine, prisons, and understandings of sexuality in this period. He wished to understand the relationships between these ways of speaking and thinking and the power of the government and institutions to intervene in the lives of people and mobilize their labor. In particular, Foucault was interested in the ways in which certain kinds of knowledge become dominant and institutionalized, and the way these forms of knowledge are used to dominate and delicense alternative understandings. The Foucault selection reprinted in essay 28 of this volume comes from the first chapter of volume 1 of *The History of Sexuality*. Foucault had planned for *The History of Sexuality* to be a six-volume work, and the first three volumes were published in his lifetime. The manuscript of a fourth volume is held in Foucault's estate and cannot be published. The last two volumes were never completed. In volume 1, Foucault attempted to analyze the emergence of a new discourse about sexuality starting in the late seventeenth century. He tried to show how this new discourse became a key way of controlling individuals and populations (Pollis 1987). Foucault's original plan called for additional volumes on specific groups of people and historical periods. Volume 2 was intended to cover sexuality in early Christian thinking. Volume 3 was to discuss the sexuality of children. Additional volumes were planned on the female body, "perverts," and race. However, Foucault's ideas changed after the publication of the first volume, and he revised his study to focus on ethics as it developed in ancient Roman and Greek thought (Davidson 2005).

One of the best-known concepts to come out of Foucault's work is his concept of power. Foucault had a complex understanding of power. He thought about it in terms of "regimes of truth" that were the product of scientific discourse and social institutions and were reinforced through the education system, media, and political ideologies (Lorenzini 2015). In Foucault's view, a regime of truth was not an accepted absolute but rather was a struggle over the rules according to which the true and false were decided and power attached to the true.

Pierre Bourdieu was born in southwestern France and, like Foucault, studied at prestigious Parisian schools, including the École Normale Supérieure. Also, like Foucault, he spent time in North Africa. Beginning in the early 1960s, he held increasingly prestigious academic positions at major institutions in and around Paris. In 1968 he was named director of the Centre de Sociologie Européenne, a position he held for the rest of his life. Like Foucault, Bourdieu was always a "Man of the Left" (Wacquant 2004). Unlike Foucault, Bourdieu distrusted party politics and throughout the first half of his career was not engaged in public politics. However, in the 1980s and 1990s, he became increasingly visible and increasingly outspoken until, by the time of his death, he was one of the most easily recognized public intellectuals in France. In his public political pronouncements, he was harshly critical of left-leaning French governments (first of the government of François Mitterand and later of the government of Lionel Jospin) and argued that the Socialist Party was both corrupt and co-opted by the right. He also spoke frequently and powerfully against neoliberalism, free trade, and globalization, considering that these were merely cover for the expansion of wealthy capitalist powers. He railed against the fatalism with which he believed the left accepted these developments.

Bourdieu was very heavily influenced by the linguistic turn in philosophy and anthropological theory. However, more than other postmodern thinkers, he continued both to focus on material aspects of the world and to believe in the possibility of a scientific anthropology. Bourdieu created critical new frameworks for exploring social phenomena, and much of the vocabulary that he pioneered has become standard in social science. Among his critical concepts are structural violence; cultural, social, and symbolic capital; field; *habitus*; and *doxa*. The Bourdieu selection we have reprinted in essay 27 is a chapter from his *The Logic of Practice* (1980). In this book, Bourdieu lays out key aspects of his theory, including ideas about *habitus*, symbolic capital, and modes of domination. He then applies these to matrimonial strategies and kinship among the Kabyle, a North African group among whom he did ethnographic fieldwork in the late 1950s. In our selection, Bourdieu explains the idea of *habitus*, which are social norms and ways of thinking that people internalize and which then guide their thinking and behavior. Meenakshi Thapan (2002: 826) has written that Bourdieu "attempted to solve the eternal problem created by the opposing forces of essentialism and determinism primarily through the concept of 'habitus' which mediates between the subject and the object and is therefore crucial to theory."

The work of Foucault, Bourdieu, Derrida, and other scholars associated with postmodernism has been deeply controversial in anthropology. In the introduction to the next section, we describe some of this controversy and the effect it had on the academic organization of anthropology in the United States. Despite this, there is no doubt that the work of the postmodernists forms a touchstone for many, if not most, anthropologists working today.

SUGGESTED READINGS

Bouissac, Paul. 2010. *Saussure: A Guide for the Perplexed*. London: Continuum.
  An introduction to Saussure's thinking written in an accessible style.
Bourdieu, Pierre. 1990. *In Other Words: Essays toward a Reflexive Sociology*. Stanford, CA: Stanford University Press.
  A collection of essays by Bourdieu and interviews with him that present his ideas in an accessible format.
Derrida, Jacques. 1976. *Of Grammatology*. Baltimore, MD: Johns Hopkins University Press.
  Derrida's key work on the relationship of spoken to written language.
Foucault, Michel. 1972. *The Archaeology of Knowledge*. New York: Pantheon.
  Foucault argues in favor of a system of rules governing the structure and development of systems of thought.
———. 1977. *Discipline and Punish: The Birth of the Prison*. New York: Vintage.
  Foucault's classic work on the emergence of the prison as the expression of the power of the state over the bodies of its subjects.
Gutting, Gary. 2005. *Foucault: A Very Short Introduction*. New York: Oxford University Press.
  A beginner's guide to Foucault's thinking with chapters covering his key works.
Jenkins, Richard. 1992. *Pierre Bourdieu*. New York: Routledge.
  An often critical introduction to Bourdieu's contributions to anthropology.

27. Structures, *Habitus*, Practices

Pierre Bourdieu (1930–2002)

OBJECTIVISM CONSTITUTES the social world as a spectacle offered to an observer who takes up a "point of view" on the action and who, putting into the object the principles of his relation to the object, proceeds as if it were intended solely for knowledge and as if all the interactions within it were purely symbolic exchanges. This viewpoint is the one taken from high positions in the social structure, from which the social world is seen as a representation (as the word is used in idealist philosophy, but also as in painting) or a performance (in the theatrical or musical sense), and practices are seen as no more than the acting-out of roles, the playing of scores or the implementation of plans. The theory of practice as practice insists, contrary to positivist materialism, that the objects of knowledge are constructed, not passively recorded, and, contrary to intellectualist idealism, that the principle of this construction is the system of structured, structuring dispositions, the *habitus*, which is constituted in practice and is always oriented towards practical functions. It is possible to step down from the sovereign viewpoint from which objectivist idealism orders the world, as Marx demands in the *Theses on Feuerbach*, but without having to abandon to it the "active aspect" of apprehension of the world by reducing knowledge to a mere recording. To do this, one has to situate oneself *within* "real activity as such," that is, in the practical relation to the world, the preoccupied, active presence in the world through which the world imposes its presence, with its urgencies, its things to be done and said, things made to be said, which directly govern words and deeds without ever unfolding as a spectacle. One has to escape from the realism of the structure, to which objectivism, a necessary stage in breaking with primary experience and constructing the objective relationships, necessarily leads when it hypostatizes these relations by treating them as realities already constituted outside of the history of the group—without falling back into subjectivism, which is quite incapable of giving an account of the necessity of the social world. To do this, one has to return to practice, the site of the dialectic of the **opus operatum** and the **modus operandi**; of the objectified products and the incorporated products of historical practice; of structures and *habitus*.[1]

From *The Logic of Practice* (1980)

1. In this opening passage, Bourdieu explores the relationship between *objectivism*, the idea that the actions of individuals and groups can be understood as the direct result of the external relations and forces that impinge upon them, and *subjectivism*, the notion that the actions of individuals are the result of their interpretations and understandings of the world around them. Bourdieu finds both of these positions inadequate and proposes the idea of *habitus* as, in part, a way to resolve the conflict between objectivism and subjectivism.

Bourdieu refers to "practice theory" the general term for his ideas. *Practice theory* focuses on the relationship between the social, political, economic, and ecological structures within which people live, and "agency," the ability of people, guided by their life experiences, to pursue their own interests. In the United States, Sherry Ortner (b. 1941) is among the best-known anthropologists associated with practice theory. Her essay (36) in this volume explores issues of agency in greater detail.

The bringing to light of the presuppositions inherent in objectivist construction has paradoxically been delayed by the efforts of all those who, in linguistics as in anthropology, have sought to "correct" the structuralist model by appealing to "context" or "situation" to account for variations, exceptions and accidents (instead of making them simple variants, absorbed into the structure, as the structuralists do). They have thus avoided a radical questioning of the objectivist mode of thought, when, that is, they have not simply fallen back on to the free choice of a rootless, unattached, pure subject. Thus, the method known as "situational analysis," which consists of "observing people in a variety of social situations" in order to determine "the way in which individuals are able to exercise choices within the limits of a specified social structure" (Gluckman 1961; cf. also Van Velsen 1964), remains locked within the framework of the rule and the exception, which Edmund Leach (often invoked by the exponents of this method) spells out explicitly: "I postulate that structural systems in which all avenues of social action are narrowly institutionalized are impossible. In all viable systems, there must be an area where the individual is free to make choices so as to manipulate the system to his advantage" (Leach 1962: 133).[2]

The conditionings associated with a particular class of conditions of existence produce *habitus,* systems of durable, transposable dispositions, structured structures predisposed to function as structuring structures, that is, as principles which generate and organize practices and representations that can be objectively adapted to their outcomes without presupposing a conscious aiming at ends or an express mastery of the operations necessary in order to attain them. Objectively "regulated" and "regular" without being in any way the product of obedience to rules, they can be collectively orchestrated without being the product of the organizing action of a conductor.[a, 3]

It is, of course, never ruled out that the responses of the *habitus* may be accompanied by a strategic calculation tending to perform in a conscious mode the operation that the *habitus* performs quite differently, namely an estimation of chances presupposing transformation of the past effect into an expected objective. But these responses are first defined, without any calculation, in relation to objective potentialities, immediately inscribed in the present, things to

---

Bourdieu refers to Karl Marx's *Theses on Feuerbach,* of 1845, a short document summarizing essential points of his thinking at that time. Marx and Feuerbach are more fully discussed in essay 4 of this volume.

"*Opus operatum*": Latin for "the work wrought." In Catholicism, this refers to the virtue inherent in a ritual. This can include the spiritual effect inherent in a religious ritual, regardless of those who do the ritual or for whom the ritual is done.

"*Modus operandi*": Latin, "mode of operation" the manner of working or habits of an individual or group.

2. Here Bourdieu attacks the "objectivist" mode of thought represented by the structural-functionalist approaches of anthropologists such as Max Gluckman, and to a lesser extent the approach of Claude Lévi-Strauss (see essay 20), because he believes these are merely ways of supporting objectivist thought. He quotes Edmund Leach (1910–1989) a student of Bronislaw Malinowski who was critical of the rigidity of functionalist thinking and became an avid proponent of Lévi-Strauss's structuralism.

Bourdieu wishes to differentiate his ideas from the situational analysis proposed by Gluckman. This is important since there is a strong overlap. Gluckman argued that analysis should be based on a detailed recording of events as they happen on the ground, the larger historical context in which these events occur, and theoretical generalization that compares these with other events (Kapferer 2006: 123).

3. This paragraph defining *habitus* is notoriously difficult to understand. Bourdieu's student Loïc Wacquant defines *habitus* as the system of durable and transposable *dispositions* through which we perceive, judge, and act in the world and notes that the word was not original with Bourdieu but used by Aristotle, Aquinas, Hegel, and others. *Habitus* overlaps with both Durkheim's idea of the collective conscience and the American anthropological notion of culture. However, it is clearly different from both. For Bourdieu, *habitus* is encoded into the physical bodies and mental structures of individuals. However, *habitus* also interacts with the physical and social structures of the world external to individuals. On the one hand, *habitus* organizes how individuals perceive and act in the world. However, people's *habitus* change as a result of their experiences. Thus, *habitus* both structures and is structured by the encounter of the individual with external reality.

do or not to do, things to say or not to say, in relation to a probable, "upcoming" future (***un a venir***), which—in contrast to the future seen as "absolute possibility" (***absolute Moglichkeit***) in Hegel's (or Sartre's) sense, projected by the pure project of a **"negative freedom"**—puts itself forward with an urgency and a claim to existence that excludes all deliberation. Stimuli do not exist for practice in their objective truth, as conditional, conventional triggers, acting only on condition that they encounter agents conditioned to recognize them.[b] The practical world that is constituted in the relationship with the *habitus*, acting as a system of cognitive and motivating structures, is a world of already realized ends—procedures to follow, paths to take—and of objects endowed with a "permanent **teleological** character," in Husserl's phrase, tools or institutions. This is because the regularities inherent in an arbitrary condition ("arbitrary" in Saussure's and Mauss's sense) tend to appear as necessary, even natural, since they are the basis of the schemes of perception and appreciation through which they are apprehended.[4]

If a very close correlation is regularly observed between the scientifically constructed objective probabilities (for example, the chances of access to a particular good) and agents' subjective aspirations ("motivations" and "needs"), this is not because agents consciously adjust their aspirations to an exact evaluation of their chances of success, like a gambler organizing his stakes on the basis of perfect information about his chances of winning. In reality, the dispositions durably inculcated by the possibilities and impossibilities, freedoms and necessities, opportunities and prohibitions inscribed in the objective conditions (which science apprehends through statistical regularities such as the probabilities objectively attached to a group or class) generate dispositions objectively compatible with these conditions and in a sense pre-adapted to their demands. The most improbable practices are therefore excluded, as unthinkable, by a kind of immediate submission to order that inclines agents to make a virtue of necessity, that is, to refuse what is anyway denied and to will the inevitable. The very conditions of

---

4. In this passage, Bourdieu notes that although actions influenced by *habitus* may become the focus of rational and conscious calculation, the *habitus* itself is more like a system of automatic actions rather than a system of deliberate, logical analysis.

This paragraph is extremely dense, filled with references and wordplay. Following is a guide to help unpack some of it.

"Un a venir": The translator has preserved wordplay from the French here. Bourdieu draws the reader's attention to the contrast between the word *"l'avenir"* literally "the future" and *"a venir"* literally "to come" (with the word "come" in the infinitive).

Hegel and Sartre: Bourdieu was deeply influenced by both Georg Wilhelm Friedrich Hegel (1770–1831) and the French Existentialist philosopher Jean-Paul Sartre (1905–1980).

Absolute Möglichkeit is from Hegel. It is directly translated as "absolute possibility." In *The Science of Logic* (originally published between 1812 and 1816) Hegel wrote, "There is as good reason for taking everything to be impossible as to be possible: for every content (a content is always concrete) includes not only diverse but even opposite characteristics." By contrast, Bourdieu notes that individuals do not perceive everything as possible.

"Negative freedom" usually refers to freedom from interference from other people. This concept is often associated with the political and philosophical traditions of Thomas Hobbes (1588–1679), John Locke (1632–1704), and Adam Smith (1723–1790).

Edmund Husserl (1859–1938) is considered one of the founders of the philosophical school of phenomenology, which focused on experience as the source of knowledge.

"Teleology" refers to the assumption of purpose or end goal in design and function.

Ferdinand de Saussure (1857–1913) was a Swiss linguist and a critical thinker both in linguistics and in social sciences more generally. Saussure noted that the relationship between a signifier (such as a word) and the signified (such as an object) was arbitrary but conventional. Thus, there was no objective relationship between a word such as "table" and the object table, but communication depends on the notion shared by members of a linguistic community that the word "table" refers to the object.

production of the *habitus*, a virtue made of necessity, mean that the anticipations it generates tend to ignore the restriction to which the validity of calculation of probabilities is subordinated, namely that the experimental conditions should not have been modified. Unlike scientific estimations, which are corrected after each experiment according to rigorous rules of calculation, the anticipations of the *habitus*, practical hypotheses based on past experience, give disproportionate weight to early experiences. Through the economic and social necessity that they bring to bear on the relatively autonomous world of the domestic economy and family relations, or more precisely, through the specifically familial manifestations of this external necessity (forms of the division of labour between the sexes, household objects, modes of consumption, parent-child relations, etc.), the structures characterizing a determinate class of conditions of existence produce the structures of the *habitus*, which in their turn are the basis of the perception and appreciation of all subsequent experiences.[5]

The *habitus*, a product of history, produces individual and collective practices—more history—in accordance with the schemes generated by history. It ensures the active presence of past experiences, which, deposited in each organism in the form of schemes of perception, thought and action, tend to guarantee the "correctness" of practices and their constancy over time, more reliably than all formal rules and explicit norms.[c] This system of dispositions—a present past that tends to perpetuate itself into the future by reactivation in similarly structured practices, an internal law through which the law of external necessities, irreducible to immediate constraints,

is constantly exerted—is the principle of the continuity and regularity which objectivism sees in social practices without being able to account for it; and also of the regulated transformations that cannot be explained either by the extrinsic, instantaneous determinisms of mechanistic sociologism or by the purely internal but equally instantaneous determination of spontaneist subjectivism. Overriding the spurious opposition between the forces inscribed earlier state of the system, outside the body, and the internal forces arising instantaneously as motivations springing from free will, the internal dispositions—the internalization of externality—enable the external forces to exert themselves, but in accordance with the specific logic of the organisms in which they are incorporated, i.e. in a durable, systematic and non-mechanical way. As an acquired system of generative schemes, the *habitus* makes possible the free production of all the thoughts, perceptions and actions inherent in the particular conditions of its production—and only those. Through the *habitus*, the structure of which it is the product governs practice, not along the paths of a mechanical determinism, but within the constraints and limits initially set on its inventions. This infinite yet strictly limited generative capacity is difficult to understand only so long as one remains locked in the usual antinomies—which the concept of the *habitus* aims to transcend—of determinism and freedom, conditioning and creativity, consciousness and the unconscious, or the individual and society. Because the *habitus* is an infinite capacity for generating products—thoughts, perceptions, expressions and actions—whose limits are set by the historically and socially situated conditions of its production, the conditioned and conditional freedom it provides is

---

5. Note two aspects of Bourdieu's thinking expressed here. First, the *habitus* is generated by the social and personal situation in which one lives, and in turn, generates a person's assumptions and expectations about the world that are compatible with those situations. The *habitus* thus predisposes individuals to think only about certain possibilities and ignore others. In this regard *habitus* is similar to the concept of hegemony discussed in the work of the Italian Marxist Antonio Gramsci (1891–1937). See Bourgois, essay 35, note 10, for more information on Gramsci.

Second, although Bourdieu is "relentless in his attempts to get rid of psychoanalysis and psychology" (Frère 2004), the idea of *habitus* shows a Freudian influence both in the fact that it is unconscious and in the fact that, like Sigmund Freud, Bourdieu believes in the particular importance of childhood experience in molding adult responses.

as remote from creation of unpredictable novelty as it is from simple mechanical reproduction of the original conditioning.[6]

Nothing is more misleading than the illusion created by hindsight in which all the traces of a life, such as the works of an artist or the events at a biography, appear as the realization of an essence that seems to preexist them. Just as a mature artistic style is not contained, like a seed, in an original inspiration but is continuously defined and redefined in the dialectic between the objectifying intention and the already objectified intention, so too the unity of meaning which, after the event, may seem to have preceded the acts and works announcing the final significance, retrospectively transforming the various stages of the temporal series into mere preparatory sketches, is constituted through the confrontation between questions that only exist in and for a mind armed with a particular type of schemes and the solutions obtained through application of these same schemes. The genesis of a system of works or practices generated by the same *habitus* (or homologous *habitus*, such as those that underlie the unity of the life-style of a group or a class) cannot be described either as the autonomous development of a unique and always self-identical essence, or as a continuous creation of novelty, because it arises from the necessary yet unpredictable confrontation between the *habitus* and an event that can exercise a pertinent incitement on the *habitus* only if the latter snatches it from the contingency of the accidental and constitutes it as a problem by applying to it the very principles of its solution; and also because the *habitus*, like every "art of inventing," is what makes it possible to produce an infinite number of practices that are relatively unpredictable (like the corresponding situations) but also limited in their diversity. In short, being the product of a particular class of objective regularities, the *habitus* tends to generate all the "reasonable," "common-sense"[d] behaviours (and only these) which are possible within the limits of these regularities, and which are likely to be positively sanctioned because they are objectively adjusted to the logic characteristic of a particular field, whose objective future they anticipate. At the same time, "without violence, art or argument," it tends to exclude all "extravagances" ("not for the likes of us"), that is, all the behaviours that would be negatively sanctioned because they are incompatible with the objective conditions.[7]

---

6. Bourdieu argues that the *habitus* obviates the conflict between objectivism and subjectivism by creating a set of dispositions that are both created by action within a social and physical world and generates action in that world. He notes that the *habitus* is not a cookbook-like series of rules that are simply applied to the world in a highly predictive fashion (he may have been critiquing ethnoscience and cognitive anthropology) and characterizes this approach as "mechanistic sociologism": the inappropriate application of sociological technique. *Habitus* has the quality of being strictly constrained by social structures and unconscious principles (what Bourdieu calls *doxa*), but at the same time being able to generate an infinity of forms within those structures.

7. In this paragraph, Bourdieu argues that the *habitus* consists of flexible, generative principles that produce more or less consistent effects as they interact with the world. He attacks the notion that individuals or groups have any transcendent essence that can be determined from their lives or works. Rather individuals and groups are the products of ongoing interaction between the individuals and their society as this society is apprehended through the structures of *habitus*.

This is also the first time that Bourdieu uses the critical concept of a field. For Bourdieu, social space is composed of fields. Fields are distinct social spaces with their own rules, regularities, and forms of authority (Wacquant 2008). Fields are realms in which people with differing positions struggle for control of different types of capital (see this essay, note 9). For example, going to the theater under normal circumstances is not a field. But appearing on the red carpet at the Oscars, a venue in which individuals use fashion and style to compete for prestige, very much is. Examples of fields include education, religion, art, and so on.

Notice Bourdieu's use of quotation marks throughout this essay. These serve different purposes in different locations. For example, in this paragraph, Bourdieu puts the words "reasonable" and "common sense" in quotation marks to suggest that these are not self-evident and transcendent characteristics. There is no uni-

Because they tend to reproduce the regularities immanent in the conditions in which their generative principle was produced while adjusting to the demands inscribed as objective potentialities in the situation as defined by the cognitive and motivating structures that constitute the *habitus*, practices cannot be deduced either from the present conditions which may seem to have provoked them or from the past conditions which have produced the *habitus*, the durable principle of their production. They can therefore only be accounted for by relating the social conditions in which the *habitus* that generated them was constituted, to the social conditions in which it is implemented, that is, through the scientific work of performing the interrelationship of these two states of the social world that the *habitus* performs, while concealing it, in and through practice. The "unconscious," which enables one to dispense with this interrelating, is never anything other than the forgetting of history which history itself produces by realizing the objective structures that it generates in the quasi-natures of *habitus*. As Durkheim (1977: 11) puts it:[8]

In each one of us, in differing degrees, is contained the person we were yesterday, and indeed, in the nature of things it is even

true that our past personae predominate in us, since the present is necessarily insignificant when compared with the long period of the past because of which we have emerged in the form we have today. It is just that we don't directly feel the influence of these past selves precisely because they are so deeply rooted within us. They constitute the unconscious part of ourselves. Consequently we have a strong tendency not to recognize their existence and to ignore their legitimate demands. By contrast, with the most recent acquisitions of civilization we are vividly aware of them just because they are recent and consequently have not had time to be assimilated into our collective unconscious.

The *habitus*—embodied history, internalized as a second nature and so forgotten as history—is the active presence of the whole past of which it is the product. As such, it is what gives practices their relative autonomy with respect to external determinations of the immediate present. This autonomy is that of the past, enacted and acting, which, functioning as accumulated capital, produces history on the basis of history and so ensures the permanence in change that makes the individual agent a world within the world. The *habitus* is

---

versal "common sense," only the "common sense" of a particular field. On the other hand, the use of quotation marks around "art of inventing" or "without violence, art, or argument" indicates quotes from particular sources. Frequently these quotes are too general for most people to identify. However, in these two cases, the first probably refers to the German philosopher and mathematician Gottfried Wilhelm Leibniz (1646–1716) whom Bourdieu discusses extensively in the pages to come. The second certainly refers to a passage in Blaise Pascal's *Pensées,* first published in 1662. Pascal (1623–1662) was a French philosopher and mathematician. In *Pensées* he wrote, "We have to acquire an easier credence,—that of habit,—which without violence, art, or argument, makes us believe things and inclines all our powers to this belief, so that our mind falls into it naturally." https://archive.org/stream/pascalspenseesoroopasc/pascalspenseesoroopasc_djvu.txt.

8. When Bourdieu talks about the forgetting of history, he is not necessarily referring to our lack of knowledge of the past. Rather he is insisting that the social structures in which we live and our experience of them are present in every decision we make but they are unconscious. Thus we "forget our history" because we are unaware of the dispositions that guide our choice of what to have for lunch or what music we listen to in the car.

Note the use of the word "scientific" as well as the long quotations from Durkheim in this paragraph. You will recall that most of Durkheim's students perished during World War I and that, apart from Marcel Mauss and Georges Davy (1883–1976), few in France followed Durkheim's lead. Instead, social thinking was dominated by the Marxist analysis promoted by the Soviet Communist Party and, particularly after World War II, existentialism. In the early 1960s, Bourdieu as well as others broke with these political and philosophical schools and moved to rehabilitate Durkheim, reinterpret Marx, and reestablish "the scientific and civic legitimacy of sociology" (Wacquant 2008).

a spontaneity without consciousness or will, opposed as much to the mechanical necessity of things without history in mechanistic theories as it is to the reflexive freedom of subjects "without inertia" in rationalist theories.[9]

Thus the dualistic vision that recognizes only the self-transparent act of consciousness or the externally determined thing has to give way to the real logic of action, which brings together two objectifications of history, objectification in bodies and objectification in institutions or, which amounts to the same thing, two states of capital, objectified and incorporated, through which a distance is set up from necessity and its urgencies. This logic is seen in paradigmatic form in the dialectic of expressive dispositions and instituted means of expression (morphological, syntactic and lexical instruments, literary genres, etc.) which is observed in the intentionless invention of regulated improvisation. Endlessly overtaken by his own words, with which he maintains a relation of "carry and be carried," as Nicolai Hartmann put it, the virtuoso finds in his discourse the triggers for his discourse, which goes along like a train laying its own rails (Ruyer 1966: 136). In other words, being produced by a *modus operandi* which is not consciously mastered,

the discourse contains an "objective intention," as the Scholastics put it, which outruns the conscious intentions of its apparent author and constantly offers new pertinent stimuli to the *modus operandi* of which it is the product and which functions as a kind of "spiritual automaton." If witticisms strike as much by their unpredictability as by their retrospective necessity, the reason is that the *trouvaille* that brings to light long buried resources presupposes a *habitus* that so perfectly possesses the objectively available means of expression that it is possessed by them, so much so that it asserts its freedom from them by realizing the rarest of the possibilities that they necessarily imply. The dialectic of the meaning of the language and the "sayings of the tribe" is a particular and particularly significant case of the dialectic between *habitus* and institutions, that is, between two modes of objectification of past history, in which there is constantly created a history that inevitably appears, like witticisms, as both original and inevitable.[10]

This durably installed generative principle of regulated improvisations is a practical sense which reactivates the sense objectified in institutions. Produced by the work of inculcation and appropriation that is needed in order for

---

9. In this paragraph, Bourdieu continues to examine the *habitus* as a way of resolving conflicts between different theoretical positions. Elsewhere, Bourdieu and Jean-Claude Passeron write, "The 'choices' which constitute culture ('choices' which no one makes) appear as arbitrary when related to . . . the universe of possible cultures; they reveal their necessity as soon as they are related to the social conditions of their emergence and perpetuation" (1990 [1970]: 8).

Bourdieu also mentions one of his most influential ideas: capital. For Bourdieu, capital is any resource that allows one access to position and the ability to benefit within a field (recall that for Bourdieu, fields are microcosms with their own rules, regularities, and forms of authority). Capital comes in three varieties: financial (money), cultural (access to scarce symbolic goods or particular forms of knowledge), and social (status resulting from membership in particular groups).

10. In this paragraph, Bourdieu focuses on the interaction between the *habitus*, which is somehow encoded in the physical body and consciousness of the individual, and the institutional setting in which the individual exists. The emphasis is on the actual actions of individuals constrained by the workings of both institutions and *habitus*. Bourdieu referred to his work as a "theory of practice" because he hoped to focus on the physical actions of people in light of *habitus* and the fields in which *habitus* operates.

Nicolai Hartmann (1882–1950) was a German philosopher, probably best known for the idea of *emergence*, the notion that highly complex systems can be produced by many relatively simple, separate interactions. The work of Hartmann's student, Hans-Georg Gadamer (1900–2002), was a key source of postmodern thought.

Scholasticism ("the Scholastics") was the strongest intellectual tradition in the European Middle Ages and was based on reconciling seemingly contradictory texts. "Objective intention" is the notion that one can infer people's intentions from their actions. A "trouvaille" is a lucky find or a sudden insight (but also something of a pun since "trou" means hole).

objective structures, the products of collective history, to be reproduced in the form of the durable, adjusted dispositions that are the condition of their functioning, the *habitus*, which is constituted in the course of an individual history, imposing its particular logic on incorporation, and through which agents partake of the history objectified in institutions, is what makes it possible to inhabit institutions, to appropriate them practically, and so to keep them in activity, continuously pulling them from the state of dead letters, reviving the sense deposited in them, but at the same time imposing the revisions and transformations that reactivation entails. Or rather, the *habitus* is what enables the institution to attain full realization: it is through the capacity for incorporation, which exploits the body's readiness to take seriously the performative magic of the social, that the king, the banker or the priest are hereditary monarchy, financial capitalism or the Church made flesh. Property appropriates its owner, embodying itself in the form of a structure generating practices perfectly conforming with its logic and its demands. If one is justified in saying, with Marx that "the lord of an entailed estate, the first-born son, belongs to the land," that "it inherits him," or that the "persons" of capitalists are the "personification" of capital, this is because the purely social and quasi-magical process of socialization, which is inaugurated by the act of marking that institutes an individual as an eldest son, an heir, a successor, a Christian, or simply as a man (as opposed to a woman), with all the corresponding privileges and obligations, and which is prolonged, strengthened and confirmed by social treatments that tend to transform instituted difference into natural distinction, produces quite real effects, durably inscribed in the body and in belief. An institution, even an economy, is complete and fully viable only if it is durably objectified not only in things, that is, in the logic, transcending individual agents, of a particular field, but also in bodies, in durable dispositions to recognize and comply with the demands immanent in the field.[11]

In so far—and only in so far—as *habitus* are the incorporation of the same history, or more concretely, of the same history objectified in *habitus* and structures, the practices they generate are mutually intelligible and immediately adjusted to the structures, and also objectively concerted and endowed with an objective meaning that is at once unitary and systematic, transcending subjective intentions and conscious projects, whether individual or collective. One of the fundamental effects of the harmony between practical sense and objectified meaning (*sens*) is the production of a common-sense world, whose immediate self-evidence is accompanied by the objectivity provided by consensus on the meaning of practices and the world, in other words the harmonization of the agents' experiences and the constant reinforcement each of them receives from expression—individual or collective (in festivals, for example), improvised or programmed (commonplaces, sayings)—of similar or identical experiences.[12]

The homogeneity of *habitus* that is observed within the limits of a class of conditions of existence and social conditionings is what causes practices and works to be immediately intelligible and foreseeable, and hence taken for granted. The *habitus* makes questions of intention superfluous, not only in the production but also in the deciphering of practices and works.[e] Automatic and impersonal, significant without a signifying intention, ordinary practices lend themselves to

---

11. Bourdieu here quotes from Marx's *Economic and Philosophic Manuscripts of 1844*.

12. To the degree that the *habitus* of different individuals is the product of similar personal histories, the practices they generate are mutually intelligible. Because such practices are set within shared dispositions and assumptions, they transcend individual intention and consciousness. The result of this is an idea of "common sense" shared by members of a culture and reinforced in institutions and rituals.

The word *sens* is of interest. Richard Nice (the translator) has rendered it as "objectified meaning" (but left us the French original). The simplest translation is "sense." But note that the French title of the book from which this selection is taken (*The Logic of Practice* in English) is *Le sens pratique*.

an understanding that is no less automatic and impersonal. The picking up of the objective intention they express requires neither "reactivation" of the "lived" intention of their originator, nor the "intentional transfer into the Other" cherished by the phenomenologists and all advocates of a "participationist" conception of history or sociology, nor tacit or explicit inquiry ("What do you *mean*?") as to other people's intentions. "Communication of consciousnesses" presupposes community of "unconsciouses" (that is, of linguistic and cultural competences). Deciphering the objective intention of practices and works has nothing to do with "reproduction" (*Nachbildung*, as the early Dilthey puts it) of lived experiences and the unnecessary and uncertain reconstitution of an "intention" which is not their real origin.[13]

The objective homogenizing of group or class *habitus* that results from homogeneity of conditions of existence is what enables practices to be objectively harmonized without any calculation or conscious reference to a norm and mutually adjusted in the absence of any direct interaction or, *a fortiori*, explicit coordination. The interaction itself owes its form to the objective structures that have produced the dispositions of the interacting agents, which continue to assign them their relative positions in the interaction and elsewhere.[f] "Imagine," Leibniz suggests (1866c: 548), "two clocks or watches in perfect agreement as to the time. This may occur in one of three ways. The first consists in mutual influence; the second is to appoint a skillful workman to correct them and synchronize constantly; the third is to construct these two clocks with such art and precision that one can be assured of their subsequent agreement." So long as one ignores the true principle of the conductorless orchestration which gives regularity, unity and systematicity to practices even in the absence of any spontaneous or imposed organization of individual projects, one is condemned to the naive artificialism that recognizes no other unifying principle than conscious coordination.[g] The practices of the members of the same group or, in a differentiated society, the same class, are always more and better harmonized than the agents know or wish, because, as Leibniz again says, "following only (his) own laws," each "nonetheless agrees with the other." The *habitus* is precisely this immanent law, **lex insita**, inscribed in bodies by identical histories, which is the precondition not only for the coordination of practices but also for practices of coordination.[h] The corrections and adjustments the agents themselves consciously carry out presuppose mastery of a common code; and undertakings of collective mobilization cannot succeed without a minimum of concordance between the *habitus* of the mobilizing agents (prophet, leader, etc.) and the dispositions of those who recognize themselves in their practices or words, and, above all, without the inclination towards grouping that springs from the spontaneous orchestration of dispositions.[14]

It is certain that every effort at mobilization aimed at organizing collective action

---

13. This passage, set off from the rest of the text, is a critique of other philosophical approaches, particularly "participationism," the notion that participation in collective activities is prior to the development of individual consciousness and individual capacity to complete an activity by oneself. Bourdieu also emphasizes the automatic and unconscious nature of much of the action of the *habitus*.

Wilhelm Dilthey (1833–1911) was a German sociologist and philosopher. For Dilthey, *Nachbildung* (literally analog, emulation, or replica) is a conscious process by which an individual experiences someone else's mental process thus making it possible for one person to understand another's reality (Jha 1995).

14. Like Bourdieu, Leibniz was interested in transcending the dualistic philosophical approaches of his day, particularly the mind/body dualism of René Descartes (1596–1650). His solution was to understand the universe, humans, and God as "monads," indivisible entities that contain within themselves all the properties they currently exhibit and will exhibit in any conceivable future. Leibniz used the example of the two clocks several times, the first in 1696. For Leibniz, the example points to the superiority of preestablished harmony over other explanations because he believed that it provides evidence of God and of the wholeness and uniformity of the universe. Bourdieu also argues that the third explanation is the best, but for him, this

has to reckon with the dialectic of dispositions and occasions that takes place in every agent, whether he mobilizes or is mobilized (the **hysteresis** of *habitus* is doubtless one explanation of the structural lag between opportunities and the dispositions to grasp them which is the cause of missed opportunities and, in particular, of the frequently observed incapacity to think historical crises in categories of perception and thought other than those of the past, however revolutionary). It is also certain that it must take account of the objective orchestration established among dispositions that are objectively co-ordinated because they are ordered by more or less identical objective necessities. It is, however, extremely dangerous to conceive collective action by analogy with individual action, ignoring all that the former owes to the relatively autonomous logic of the institutions of mobilization (with their own history, their specific organization, etc.) and to the situations, institutionalized or not, in which it occurs.

Sociology treats as identical all biological individuals who, being the products of the same objective conditions, have the same *habitus*. A social class (in-itself)—a class of identical or similar conditions of existence and conditionings—is at the same time a class of biological individuals having the same *habitus*, understood as a system of dispositions common to all products of the same conditionings. Though it is impossible for all (or even two) members of the same class to have had the same experiences, in the same order, it is certain that each member of the same class is more likely than any member of another class to have been confronted with the situations most frequent for members of that class. Through the always convergent experiences that give a social environment its physiognomy, with its "closed doors," "dead ends" and "limited prospects," the objective structures that sociology apprehends in the form of probabilities of access to goods, services and powers, inculcate the "art of assessing likelihoods," as Leibniz put it, of anticipating the objective future, in short, the "sense of reality," or realities, which is perhaps the best-concealed principle of their efficacy.[15]

To define the relationship between class *habitus* and individual *habitus* (which is inseparable from the organic individuality that is immediately given to immediate perception— *intuitus personae* and socially designated and recognized—name, legal identity, etc.), class (or group) *habitus*, that is, the individual *habitus* in so far as it expresses or reflects the class (or group), could be regarded as a subjective but non-individual system of internalized structures, common schemes of perception, conception and action, which are the precondition of all objectification and apperception; and the objective co-ordination of practices and the sharing of a world-view could be founded on the perfect impersonality and interchangeability of singular practices and views. But this would amount to regarding all the practices or representations produced in accordance with

---

is evidence of the workings of the *habitus* which is not universal but must rather be a characteristic of a specific group of people acting in a specific time and place.

"A fortiori": with greater reason.

"Lex insita": underlying principle.

15. In this passage, Bourdieu moves from presenting *habitus* as a characteristic of the individual to presenting it as a characteristic of a class. Bourdieu acknowledges the differences in lived experiences of the individuals composing a class but argues that class is still a useful unit of analysis since the overall pattern of life experiences themselves tend to follow class lines. Thus, two levels of *habitus* emerge, the *habitus* generated by individual life experiences and the *habitus* generated by membership in a social class.

Note also the critical role that Bourdieu assigns the *habitus* in creating the reality of experience for members of a class.

"Hysteresis": the lagging of an event behind its cause (most frequently used in chemistry and the physics of magnetism). Bourdieu uses it to describe the time lapse between changing field conditions and *habitus* or the "persistence of elements within the *habitus* that endured beyond the social context(s) of their production" (Barrett 2018: 36).

identical schemes as impersonal and interchangeable, like individual intuitions of space which, according to Kant, reflect none of the particularities of the empirical ego. In fact, the singular *habitus* of members of the same class are united in a relationship of homology, that is, of diversity within homogeneity reflecting the diversity within homogeneity characteristic of their social conditions of production. Each individual system of dispositions is a structural variant of the others, expressing the singularity of its position within the class and its trajectory. "Personal" style, the particular stamp marking all the products of the same *habitus*, whether practices or works, is never more than a deviation in relation to the style of a period or class, so that it relates back to the common style not only by its conformity—like **Phidias**, who, for Hegel, had no "manner"—but also by the difference that makes the "manner."[16]

The principle of the differences between individual *habitus* lies in the singularity of their social trajectories, to which there correspond series of chronologically ordered determinations that are mutually irreducible to one another. The *habitus* which, at every moment, structures new experiences in accordance with the structures produced by past experiences, which are modified by the new experiences within the limits defined by their power of selection, brings about a unique integration, dominated by the earliest experiences, of the experiences statistically common to members of the same class.[i] Early experiences have particular weight because the *habitus* tends to ensure its own constancy and its defense against

change through the selection it makes within new information by rejecting information capable of calling into question its accumulated information, if exposed to it accidentally or by force, and especially by avoiding exposure to such information. One only has to think, for example, of **homogamy**, the paradigm of all the "choices" through which the *habitus* tends to favour experiences likely to reinforce it (or the empirically confirmed fact that people tend to talk about politics with those who have the same opinions). Through the systematic "choices" it makes among the places, events and people that might be frequented, the *habitus* tends to protect itself from crises and critical challenges by providing itself with a milieu to which it is as pre-adapted as possible, that is, a relatively constant universe of situations tending to reinforce its dispositions by offering the market most favourable to its products. And once again it is the most paradoxical property of the *habitus*, the unchosen principle of all "choices," that yields the solution to the paradox of the information needed in order to avoid information. The schemes of perception and appreciation of the *habitus* which are the basis of all the avoidance strategies are largely the product of a non-conscious, unwilled avoidance, whether it results automatically from the conditions of existence (for example, spatial segregation) or has been produced by a strategic intention (such as avoidance of "bad company" or "unsuitable books") originating from adults themselves formed in the same conditions.[17]

Even when they look like the realization of explicit ends, the strategies produced by

---

16. In this and other passages, Bourdieu tries to balance individual agency with the structures of society. Bourdieu understands *habitus* as something particular to the individual: Each individual has their own *habitus*. However, he also believes that there is class *habitus*, the high degree of consistency among individuals who are members of a social class or other social group. In such a group, individuals are variations on a common theme.

Phidias, who had no "manner": Phidias (c. 480–430 BCE) is commonly regarded as the greatest sculptor of ancient Greece. None of his original statues remain and his work is known through Roman copies produced long after his lifetime. In the introduction to *Elements of the Philosophy of the Right* (1820), Hegel writes, "When a great artist finishes a work we say: 'It must be so.' The particularity of the artist has wholly disappeared and the work shows no mannerism. Phidias has no mannerism: the statue itself lives and moves."

"*Intuitus personae*": taking the personality and personal qualities of the individual into account.

17. In other words, people tend to associate with and listen to those people and institutions that support their understanding of the world. This situation results either from social structure (such as laws or traditions forbidding certain classes of individuals from associating with one another) or from enculturation

the *habitus* and enabling agents to cope with unforeseen and constantly changing situations are only apparently determined by the future. If they seem to be oriented by anticipation of their own consequences, thereby encouraging the **finalist illusion**, this is because, always tending to reproduce the objective structures that produced them, they are determined by the past conditions of production of their principle of production, that is, by the already realized outcome of identical or interchangeable past practices, which coincides with their own outcome only to the extent that the structures within which they function are identical to or homologous with the objective structures of which they are the product. Thus, for example, in the interaction between two agents or groups of agents endowed with the same *habitus* (say A and B), everything takes place as if the actions of each of them (say a_1 for A) were organized by reference to the reactions which they call forth from any agent possessing the same *habitus* (say b_1 for B). They therefore objectively imply anticipation of the reaction which these reactions in turn call forth (a_2, A's reaction to b_1). But the ideological description, the only one appropriate to a "rational actor" possessing perfect information as to the preferences and competences of the other actors, in which each action has the purpose of making possible the reaction to the reaction it induces (individual A performs an action a_1, a gift for example, in order to make individual B produce action b_1, so that he can then perform

action a_1, a stepped-up gift), is quite as naive as the mechanistic description that presents the action and the riposte as so many steps in a sequence of programmed actions produced by a mechanical apparatus.[18]

To have an idea of the difficulties that would be encountered by a mechanistic theory of practice as mechanical reaction, directly determined by the antecedent conditions and entirely reducible to the mechanical functioning of pre-established devices—which would have to be assumed to exist in infinite number, like the chance configurations of stimuli capable of triggering them from outside—one only has to mention the grandiose, desperate undertaking of the anthropologist, fired with positivist ardour, who recorded 480 elementary units of behaviour in 20 minutes' observation of his wife in the kitchen: "Here we confront the distressing fact that the sample episode chain under analysis is a fragment of a larger segment of behavior which in the complete record contains some 480 separate episodes. Moreover, it took only twenty minutes for these 480 behavior stream events to occur. If my wife's rate of behavior is roughly representative of that of other actors, we must be prepared to deal with an inventory of episodes produced at the rate of some 20,000 per sixteen-hour day per actor . . . In a population consisting of several hundred actor-types, the number of different episodes in the total repertory

---

(our kind of people don't read those kinds of books, watch that sort of TV, go to those sorts of sporting events, eat that kind of food). Paradoxically, Bourdieu argues that by making a "choice" to associate with those similar to themselves, people choose to avoid choice! The algorithms that govern social media have made Bourdieu's observation common knowledge.

"Homogamy": the marriage of individuals who have similar characteristics such as nationality, ethnicity, religious background, education, and socioeconomic status.

18. Bourdieu argues that actions that seem to be based on rational calculation of future events are based on past understandings, particularly those developed early in life, and that such understandings are not explicitly matters of conscious thought. However, since current conditions are never exactly the same as past conditions, practice plays out in ways that are not predictable. The conditions of life-as-lived feed back into the continuing change and development of the *habitus*.

Note that at the end of this passage, Bourdieu is critiquing Mauss's description of gift giving. He argues that changing conditions and the specific life experiences of the individuals involved in gift exchanges make gifting and counter-gifting more than a mechanical response and counter response.

"Finalist": finalism is the philosophical position that the world (life, society, etc.) is moving toward a specific goal.

must amount to many millions in the course of an annual cycle" (Harris 1964: 74–75).[19]

The *habitus* contains the solution to the paradoxes of objective meaning without subjective intention. It is the source of these strings of "moves" which are objectively organized as strategies without being the product of a genuine strategic intention—which would presuppose at least that they be apprehended as one among other possible strategies.[j] If each stage in the sequence of ordered and oriented actions that constitute objective strategies can appear to be determined by anticipation of the future, and in particular, of its own consequences (which is what justifies the use of the concept of strategy), it is because the practices that are generated by the *habitus* and are governed by the past conditions of production of their generative principle are adapted in advance to the objective conditions whenever the conditions in which the *habitus* functions have remained identical, or similar, to the conditions in which it was constituted. Perfectly and immediately successful adjustment to the objective conditions provides the most complete illusion

of finality, or—which amounts to the same thing—of self-regulating mechanism.[20]

The presence of the past in this kind of false anticipation of the future performed by the *habitus* is, paradoxically, most clearly seen when the sense of the probable future is belied and when dispositions ill-adjusted to the objective chances because of a hysteresis effect (Marx's favourite example of this was Don Quixote) are negatively sanctioned because the environment they actually encounter is too different from the one to which they are objectively adjusted.[k] In fact the persistence of the effects of primary conditioning, in the form of the *habitus*, accounts equally well for cases in which dispositions function out of phase and practices are objectively ill-adapted to the present conditions because they are objectively adjusted to conditions that no longer obtain. The tendency of groups to persist in their ways, due ***inter alia*** to the fact that they are composed of individuals with durable dispositions that can outlive the economic and social conditions in which they were produced, can be the source of misadaptation as well as adaptation, revolt as well as resignation.[21]

---

19. Bourdieu refers here to *The Nature of Cultural Things* (1964) by Marvin Harris (1927–2001). In this work, Harris proposed an anthropology that "precludes the need to know the actor's goals, meanings, and motives" that is "operationally equivalent to the physical sciences" (Metzger 1965). Harris's system is based on units he called "actones." An actone is a specific motion of a body part and the effect of that motion on the environment. Actones were to be grouped into classes called actonemes. These in turn were grouped into higher-level patterns of organization called episodes, nodes, scenes, and serials.

Harris became one of the best-known anthropologists of his era but rapidly abandoned this scheme. It gained no support and is largely forgotten. Here, Harris serves as a foil for Bourdieu. Although Bourdieu also wishes to create a scientific anthropology, he believes that the subjective experiences and dispositions of social actors are keys to understanding society. A purely objective anthropology is not possible.

20. Here Bourdieu continues to criticize neo-functionalist models such as Harris's (see essay 18). Bourdieu suggests that the self-regulating, homeostatic mechanism of culture that such theorists perceive is an illusion, an artifact of the operation of the *habitus*.

21. A strength of Bourdieu's analysis, compared with functionalist and neo-functionalist analyses is that it can account for maladaptation and conflict. Functionalists of all varieties tended to interpret all forms of social action as promoting social solidarity. Bourdieu clearly shows that the *habitus* at the individual level can also be a source of discord.

Don Quixote, a fictional character created by Spanish author Miguel de Cervantes (1547–1616) is the paradigmatic example of a person living out of context. Don Quixote, a man living in the sixteenth or seventeenth century, imagines himself to be a knight errant of the twelfth century. Marx makes extensive use of Cervantes's work, particularly in chapter 3 of *The German Ideology* (the selection "Feuerbach" in this book is chapter 1 of that work) where, among other things, he imagines a duet sung by Bruno Bauer (whom he calls Saint Bruno) and Sancho Panza (whom he calls Saint Sancho).

"Inter alia": among other things.

One only has to consider other possible forms of the relationship between dispositions and conditions to see that the pre-adjustment of the *habitus* to the objective conditions is a "particular case of the possible" and so avoid unconsciously universalizing the model of the near-circular relationship of near-perfect reproduction, which is completely valid only when the conditions of production of the *habitus* and the conditions of its functioning are identical or homothetic. In this particular case, the dispositions durably inculcated by the objective conditions and by a pedagogic action that is tendentially adjusted to these conditions, tend to generate practices objectively compatible with these conditions and expectations pre-adapted to their objective demands (***amor fati***) (for some psychologists' attempts at direct verification of this relationship, see Brunswik 1949; Preston and Barrata 1948; Attneave 1953). As a consequence, they tend, without any rational calculation or conscious estimation of the chances of success, to ensure immediate correspondence between the ***a priori*** or ***ex ante*** probability conferred on an event (whether or not accompanied by subjective experiences such as hopes, expectation, fears, etc.) and the ***a posteriori*** or ***ex post*** probability that can be established on the basis of past experience. They thus make it possible to understand why economic models based on the (tacit) premise of a "relationship of intelligible causality," as Max Weber (1922) calls it, between generic ("typical") chances "objectively existing as an average" and "subjective expectations," or, for example, between investment or the propensity to invest and the rate of return expected or really obtained in the past, fairly exactly account for practices which do not arise from knowledge of the objective chances.[22]

By pointing out that rational action, "judiciously" oriented according to what is "objectively valid" (1922), is what "would have happened if the actors had had knowledge of all the circumstances and all the participants' intentions" (1968: 6), that is, of what is "valid in the eyes of the scientist," who alone is able to calculate the system of objective chances to which perfectly informed action would have to be adjusted, Weber shows clearly that the pure model of rational action cannot be regarded as an anthropological description of practice. This is not only because real agents only very exceptionally possess the complete information, and the skill to appreciate it, that rational action would presuppose. Apart from rare cases which bring together the economic and cultural conditions for rational action oriented by knowledge of the profits that can be obtained in the different markets, practices depend not on the average chances of profit, an abstract and unreal notion, but on the specific chances that a singular agent or class of agents possesses by virtue of its capital, this being understood, in this respect, as a means of appropriation of the chances theoretically available to all.

Economic theory which acknowledges only the rational "responses" of an indeterminate, interchangeable agent to "potential opportunities," or more precisely to average chances (like the "average rates of profit" offered by the different markets), converts the immanent law of the economy into a universal norm of proper economic behavior. In so doing, it conceals the fact that the "rational"

---

22. "Particular case of the possible": The reference here is to Gaston Bachelard (1884–1962), a French philosopher of science who had a strong influence on French scholars of Bourdieu's generation. Bachelard is best known for the idea that the progress of science is not continuous but rather is blocked by certain patterns of thinking. Such patterns must be transcended in an epistemological break for progress to occur.

"***Amor fati***": literally, "love of fate," or "love of one's fate"; a Latin expression coined by the German philosopher Friedrich Nietzsche (1844–1900).

"***A priori***": Latin for "from the former," that is, reasoning from a general law to a particular instance, a conclusion not based on prior study.

"***Ex ante***": Latin for "from before," that is, based on assumption.

"***A posteriori***": Latin for "from the latter," a conclusion arrived at by reasoning from observed facts or reasoning from particular instances to a general principle.

"***Ex post***": Latin for "after the fact."

habitus which is the precondition for appropriate economic behaviour is the product of particular economic condition, the one defined by possession of the economic and cultural capital required in order to seize the "potential opportunities" theoretically available to all; and also that the same dispositions, by adapting the economically most deprived to the specific condition of which they are the product and thereby helping to make their adaptation to the generic demands of the economic cosmos (as regards calculation, forecasting, etc.) lead them to accept the negative sanctions resulting from this lack of adaptation, that is, their deprivation. In short, the art of estimating and seizing chances, the capacity to anticipate the future by a kind of practical induction or even to take a calculated gamble on the possible against the probable, are dispositions that can only be acquired in certain social conditions, that is, certain social conditions. Like the entrepreneurial spirit or the propensity to invest, economic information is a function of one's power over the economy. This is, on the one hand, because the propensity to acquire it depends on the chances of using it successfully, and the chances of acquiring it depend on the chances of successfully using it; and also because economic competence, like all competence (linguistic, political, etc.), far from being a simple technical capacity acquired in certain conditions, is a power tacitly conferred on those who have power over the economy or (as the very ambiguity of the word "competence" indicates) an attribute of status.[23]

Only in imaginary experience (in the folk tale, for example), which neutralizes the sense of social realities, does the social world take the form of a universe of possibles equally possible for any possible subject. Agents shape their aspirations according to concrete indices of the accessible and the inaccessible, of what is and is not "for us," a division as fundamental and as fundamentally recognized as that between the sacred and the profane. The pre-emptive rights on the future that are defined by law and by the monopolistic right to certain possibles that it confers are merely the explicitly guaranteed form of the whole set of appropriated chances through which the power relations of the present project themselves into the future, from where they govern present dispositions, especially those towards the future. In fact, a given agent's practical relation to the future, which governs his present practice, is defined in the relationship between, on the one hand, his *habitus* with its temporal structures and dispositions towards the future, constituted in the course of a particular relationship to a particular universe of probabilities, and on the other hand a certain state of the chances objectively offered to him by the social world. The relation to what is possible is a relation to power; and the sense of the probable future is constituted in the prolonged relationship with a world structured according to the categories of the possible (for us) and the impossible (for us), of what is appropriated in advance by and for others and what one can reasonably expect for oneself. The *habitus* is the principle of a selective perception of the indices tending to confirm and reinforce it rather than transform it, a matrix generating responses adapted in advance to all objective conditions identical to or homologous with the (past) conditions of its production; it adjusts itself to a probable future which it anticipates and helps to bring about because it reads it directly in the present of the presumed world, the only one it can ever know.[1] It is thus the basis of what Marx (1975: 378) calls "effective demand" (as opposed to "demand without effect," based on need and desire), a realistic relation to what is

---

23. In this passage, Bourdieu critiques economic theory which, he argues, presupposes the existence of a universal economic logic and is based on analyzing and predicting the actions of individuals assumed to be identical. However, for Bourdieu, the logic of the market is not universal but tied to the assumptions and dispositions of individuals in particular times and places. Individuals do not come to the market as random and identical. Because they exist within history, and within cultural and social systems, people are endowed with different sorts and quantities of capital (see this essay, note 10). Therefore they face different potential outcomes in the market. These outcomes are strongly tied to social class. It might be helpful to note that Bourdieu came from a lower-class background ("the only child of a peasant sharecropper turned postman" [Ollion 2012]) but, by the time of his death, was among France's best-known intellectuals and moved in the highest social circles.

possible, founded on and therefore limited by power. This disposition, always marked by its (social) conditions of acquisition and realization, tends to adjust to the objective chances of satisfying need or desire, inclining agents to "cut their coats according to their cloth," and so to become the accomplices of the processes that tend to make the probable a reality.[24]

REFERENCES

Attneave, F. 1953: Psychological probability as a function of experienced frequency. *Journal of Experimental Psychology*, 46, 81–6.

Brunswik, E. 1949: Systematic and representative design of psychological experiments. In J. Neymen (ed.), *Proceedings of the Berkeley Symposium on Mathematical Statistics and Probability*. Berkeley, Calif.: University of California Press, 143–202.

Cournot, A. 1922: *Essai sure les fondements de la connaissance et sure les caracte` res de la critique philosophique*. Paris: Hachette (1st edn 1851).

Durkheim, E. 1977: *The Evolution of Educational Thought*. London: Routledge & Kegan Paul. (*L'Évolution pédagogique en France*. 1938).

Gluckman, M. 1961. Ethnographic data in British social anthropology. *Sociological Review*. 9, 5–17.

Harris, M. 1964. *The Nature of Cultural Things*. New York: Random House.

Leach, E. 1962: On certain unconsidered aspects of double descent systems. *Man*, 62.

Le Ny, J. F. 1979: *La Sémantique psychologique*. Paris: PUF.

Leibniz, G. W. 1866: *Second éclaircissement du syste` me de la communication des substances*. (first pub. 1696). In Leibniz *Oeuvres philosophiques*. Ed. P. Janet. Paris: Ladrange.

Marx, K. 1975: *Econonomic and Philosophic Manuscripts of 1844*. In K. Marx, *Early Writings*, Harmondsworth: Penguin.

Preston, M. G. and Barrata, P. 1948: An experimental study of the action-value of an uncertain income. *American Journal of Psychology*, 61, 183–93.

Ruyer, R. 1966: *Paradoxes de la conscience et limites de l'automatisme*. Paris: Albin Michel.

Van Velsen, J. 1964: *The Politics of Kinship: A Study in Social Manipulation Among the Lakeside Tonga*. Manchester: Manchester University Press.

Weber, M. 1922: *Gesammelte Aufsätze zur Wissenschaftslehre*. Tübingen: J. C. Mohr.

———. 1968. *Economy and Society*, vol I. New York: Bedminster.

AUTHOR'S NOTES

a. Ideally, one would like to be able completely to avoid talking about concepts for their own sake and so running the risk of being both schematic and formal. Like all dispositional concepts, the concept of the *habitus*, which is predisposed by its range of historical uses to designate a system of acquired, permanent, generative dispositions, is justified above all by the false problems and false solutions that it eliminates, the questions it enables one to formulate better or to resolve, and the specifically scientific difficulties to which it gives rise.

b. The notion of the *structural relief* of the attributes of an object, i.e. the character that causes an attribute (e.g. colour or shape) "to be more easily taken into account in any semantic treatment of the signified which contains it" (Le Ny 1979: 190ff.), like the Weberian notion of "average chances" which is its equivalent in another context, is an abstraction, since relief varies according to dispositions. However, it enables one to escape from pure subjectivism by taking note of the existence of objective determinations of perceptions. The illusion of the free creation of the properties of a situation and, therefore, of the ends of action, no doubt finds an apparent justification in the circle, characteristic of all conditional stimulation, whereby the *habitus* can produce the response objectively inscribed in its "formula" only to the extent that it confers a triggering efficacy on the situation

---

24. In this final paragraph, Bourdieu refers directly to two of the most powerful influences on him: Durkheim and Marx. He begins with Durkheim's notion of the sacred and profane. Durkheim believed that the tendency of people to divide their world into sacred and profane was a universal social fact. Bourdieu juxtaposes this with the idea that one of the most basic elements of the *habitus* is to think in terms of things that are appropriate to us or not appropriate to us. Although he does not use the term here, Bourdieu generally characterizes such shared sets of opinions and unquestioned beliefs that bind members of a community to one another as *doxa* (Wacquant 2008).

Bourdieu also refers to Marx's discussion of the power of money in *The Economic and Philosophic Manuscripts of 1844*. There Marx says, "The difference between effective demand based on money and ineffective demand based on my need, my passion, my wish, etc., is the difference between *being* and *thinking*, between that which *exists* within me merely as an idea and the idea which exists as a *real object* outside of me." Bourdieu thus combines elements of Durkheim's concept of the collective conscious with an understanding of history, political, and economic structures, and power relationships that characterize Marx's work.

by constituting it according to its own principles, i.e. making it exist as a pertinent question in terms of a particular way of questioning reality.

c. In social formations in which the reproduction of relations of domination (and economic or cultural capital) is not performed by objective mechanisms, the endless work required to maintain relations of personal dependence would be condemned to failure if it could not count on the permanence of *habitus*, socially constituted and constantly reinforced by individual or collective sanctions. In this case, the social order rests mainly on the order that reigns in people's minds, and the *habitus*, i.e. the organism as appropriated by the group and attuned to the demands of the group, functions as the materialization of the collective memory, reproducing the acquisitions of the predecessors in the successors. The group's resulting tendency to persist in its being works at a much deeper level than that of "family traditions," the permanence of which presupposes a consciously maintained loyalty and also guardians. These traditions therefore have a rigidity alien to the strategies of the *habitus*, which, in new situations, can invent new ways of fulfilling the old functions. It is also deeper than the conscious strategies through which agents seek expressly to act on their future and shape it in the image of the past, such as testaments, or even explicit norms, which are simple calls to order, i.e. to the probable, which they make doubly potent.

d. "We call this subjective, variable probability—which sometimes excludes doubt and engenders a certainty *sui generis* and which at other times appears as no more than a vague glimmer—*philosophical probability*, because it refers to the exercise of the higher faculty whereby we comprehend the order and the rationality of things. All reasonable men have a confused notion of similar probabilities: this then determines, or at least justifies, those unshakeable beliefs we call *common sense*" (Cournot 1922: 70).

e. One of the virtues of subjectivism and of the "moralism of consciousness" (or the examination of conscience) which it often disguises is that, in the analyses that condemn actions subject to the pressures of the world as "inauthentic" (cf. Heidegger on everyday existence and "das Man" or Sartre on "serious-mindedness"), it shows, *per absurdum*, the impossibility of the "authentic" existence that would absorb all pre-given meanings and objective determinations in a project of freedom. The purely ethical pursuit of "authenticity" is the privilege of those who have the leisure to think and can afford to dispense with the economy of thought that "inauthentic" conduct allows.

f. Contrary to all forms of the occasionalist illusion which inclines one to relate practices directly to properties inscribed in the situation, it has to be pointed out that "interpersonal" relations are only apparently person-to-person relations and that the truth of the interaction never lies entirely in the interaction. This is forgotten when the objective structure of the relationship between the assembled individuals or the groups they belong to—that is, distances and hierarchies—is reduced to the momentary structure of their interaction in a particular situation and group, and when everything that occurs in an experimental situation is explained in terms of the experimentally controlled characteristics of the situation, such as relative positions in space or the nature of the channels used.

g. Thus ignorance of the surest but best-hidden basis of the integration of groups or classes can lead some people to deny the unity of the dominant class with no other proof than the impossibility of empirically establishing that the members of the dominant class have an explicit policy, expressly imposed by concertation or even conspiracy; while it can lead others to see the only possible basis for the unity of the dominated class in the awakening of consciousness, a kind of revolutionary cogito that is supposed to bring the working class into existence by constituting it as a "class in itself."

h. It can be understood why dancing, a particular and spectacular case of synchronization of the homogeneous and orchestration of the heterogeneous, is everywhere predisposed to symbolize and reinforce group integration.

i. It is easy to see that the infinite possible combinations of the variables associated with the trajectories of each individual and of the lineages from which he comes can account for the infinity of individual differences.

j. The most profitable strategies are usually those produced, without any calculation, and in the illusion of the most absolute "sincerity," by a *habitus* objectively fitted to the objective structures. These strategies without strategic calculation procure an important secondary advantage for those who can scarcely be called their authors: the social approval accruing to apparent disinterestedness.

k. Generation conflicts oppose not age-classes separated by natural properties, but *habitus* which have been produced by different modes of generation, that is, by conditions of existence which, by imposing different definitions of the impossible, the possible and the probable, cause one group to experience practices or aspirations that another group finds unthinkable or scandalous as natural or reasonable, and vice versa.

l. Emotion, the extreme case of such anticipation, is a hallucinatory "presenting" of the impending future, which, as bodily reactions identical to those of the real situation bear witness, leads a person to live a still suspended future as already present, or even already past, and therefore necessary and inevitable—"I'm a dead man," "I'm done for."

28. The Incitement to Discourse

Michel Foucault (1926–1984)

THE SEVENTEENTH CENTURY, then, was the beginning of an age of repression emblematic of what we call the bourgeois societies, an age which perhaps we still have not completely left behind. Calling sex by its name thereafter became more difficult and more costly. As if in order to gain mastery over it in reality, it had first been necessary to subjugate it at the level of language, control its free circulation in speech, expunge it from the things that were said, and extinguish the words that rendered it too visibly present. And even these prohibitions, it seems, were afraid to name it. Without even having to pronounce the word, modern prudishness was able to ensure that one did not speak of sex, merely through the interplay of prohibitions that referred back to one another: instances of muteness which, by dint of saying nothing, imposed silence. [1]

CENSORSHIP

Yet when one looks back over these last three centuries with their continual transformations, things appear in a very different light: around and apropos of sex, one sees a veritable discursive explosion. We must be clear on this point, however. It is quite possible that there was an **expurgation**—and a very rigorous one—of the authorized vocabulary. It may indeed be true that a whole rhetoric of allusion and metaphor was codified. Without question, new rules of propriety screened out some words: there was a policing of statements. A control over enunciations as well: where and when it was not possible to talk about such things became much more strictly defined; in which circumstances, among which speakers, and within which social relationships. Areas were thus established, if not of utter silence, at least of tact and discretion: between parents and children, for instance, or teachers and pupils, or masters and domestic servants. This almost certainly constituted a whole restrictive economy, one that was incorporated into that politics of language and speech—spontaneous on the one hand, concerted on the other—which accompanied the social redistributions of the classical period. [2]

From *The History of Sexuality*, Volume 1 (1976)

1. In this opening paragraph, Foucault makes it clear that he intends to discuss the historical development of the discourse concerning sexuality in Western Europe. His central thesis is that beginning sometime in the seventeenth century, the discourse about sexuality began to change from general and open to increasingly specific and confined. This was coincident with other changes including the development of capitalism, increases in social control, and increases in specialization of all kinds. The discourse around sexuality, as Foucault understands it, includes both the words we use to describe sexuality and the ways we think about it. A critical point for Foucault is that discourse is always related to the expression of power. In other words, discourse concerns not only what is said, but what one is prohibited from saying due to law or social pressure.

2. By "the social redistributions of the classical period" Foucault refers to "the class divisions and other social relationships developed and defined during the Eighteenth Century" (Roughley 2003). Foucault sees the control and regulation of sexual discourse as fundamental to the project of class division and specialization that he believes forms the basis of capitalism.
"Expurgation": cleansing.

At the level of discourses and their domains, however, practically the opposite phenomenon occurred. There was a steady proliferation of discourses concerned with sex—specific discourses, different from one another both by their form and by their object: a discursive ferment that gathered momentum from the eighteenth century onward. Here I am thinking not so much of the probable increase in "illicit" discourses, that is, discourses of infraction that crudely named sex by way of insult or mockery of the new code of decency; the tightening up of the rules of decorum likely did produce, as a countereffect, a valorization and intensification of indecent speech. But more important was the multiplication of discourses concerning sex in the field of exercise of power itself: an institutional incitement to speak about it, and to do so more and more; a determination on the part of the agencies of power to hear it spoken about, and to cause it to speak through explicit articulation and endlessly accumulated detail.[3]

Consider the evolution of the Catholic pastoral and the sacrament of penance after the Council of Trent. Little by little, the nakedness of the questions formulated by the confession manuals of the Middle Ages, and a good number of those still in use in the seventeenth century, was veiled. One avoided entering into that degree of detail which some authors, such as Sanchez or Tamburini, had for a long time believed indispensable for the confession to be complete: description of the respective positions of the partners, the postures assumed, gestures, places touched, caresses, the precise moment of pleasure—an entire painstaking review of the sexual act in its very unfolding. Discretion was advised, with increasing emphasis. The greatest reserve was counseled when dealing with sins against purity: "This matter is similar to pitch, for, however one might handle it, even to cast it far from oneself, it sticks nonetheless, and always soils."[a] And later, Alfonso de'Liguori prescribed starting—and possibly going no further, especially when dealing with children—with questions that were "roundabout and vague."[b, 4]

But while the language may have been refined, the scope of the confession—the confession of the flesh—continually increased. This was partly because the Counter-Reformation busied itself with stepping up the rhythm of the yearly confession in the Catholic countries, and because it tried to impose meticulous rules of self-examination; but above all, because it attributed more and more importance in penance—and perhaps at the expense of some other sins—to all the insinuations of the flesh: thoughts, desires, voluptuous imag-

---

3. Foucault argues that although where one could speak about sex and what one could say were diminished, new specific and controlled styles and venues for discourse about sexuality emerged. The new ways of speaking about sexuality were fundamentally linked to new expressions of power. To prohibit speaking of sex in certain ways and valorize speaking of it in others was related to the emergence and legitimization of new forms and divisions of power in the state.

4. In this passage, Foucault argues that the language the Catholic Church required priests to use in the ritual of confession (the "Catholic Pastoral") was gradually restricted between the Middle Ages and the nineteenth century.

The Council of Trent (1545–1563) was a series of meetings of Catholic Church officials held in response to the emergence of Protestantism. The Council reaffirmed the centrality and efficacy of the sacrament of Confession and specified that "all the mortal crimes into which the faithful may have fallen should be revealed" (Sess. XIV, c. v).

"Tamburini" refers to Thomas Tamburini (1591–1675), who wrote a five-volume manual on the proper ways for priests to receive confessions (*Methodus expeditæ confessionis* [1647]).

Tomás Sanchez (1550–1610) wrote in great detail about practices such as fondling, unusual mating positions, coitus interruptus, and female masturbation (Hurteau 1993).

Alphonsus Maria de' Liguori (1696–1787), later canonized, was the founder of the Redemptorists, a society of missionary priests. De' Liguori preached exhaustive confession for adults but a much more moderate form for children. Foucault discusses de' Liguori in greater detail in *Abnormal: Lectures at the Collège de France, 1974–1975*.

inings, delectations, combined movements of the body and the soul; henceforth all this had to enter, in detail, into the process of confession and guidance. According to the new pastoral, sex must not be named imprudently, but its aspects, its correlations, and its effects must be pursued down to their slenderest ramifications: a shadow in a daydream, an image too slowly dispelled, a badly exorcised complicity between the body's mechanics and the mind's complacency: everything had to be told. A twofold evolution tended to make the flesh into the root of all evil, shifting the most important moment of transgression from the act itself to the stirrings—so difficult to perceive and formulate—of desire. For this was an evil that afflicted the whole man, and in the most secret of forms: "Examine diligently, therefore, all the faculties of your soul: memory, understanding, and will. Examine with precision all your senses as well . . . Examine, moreover, all your thoughts, every word you speak, and all your actions. Examine even unto your dreams, to know if, once awakened, you did not give them your consent. And finally, do not think that in so sensitive and perilous a matter as this, there is anything trivial or insignificant."[c] Discourse, therefore, had to trace the meeting line of the body and the soul, following all its meanderings: beneath the surface of the sins, it would lay bare the unbroken **nervure** of the flesh. Under the authority of a language that had been carefully expurgated so that it was no longer directly named, sex was taken charge of, tracked down as it were, by a discourse that aimed to allow it no obscurity, no respite.[5]

It was here, perhaps, that the injunction, so peculiar to the West, was laid down for the first time, in the form of a general constraint. I am not talking about the obligation to admit to violations of the laws of sex, as required by traditional penance; but of the nearly infinite task of telling—telling oneself and another, as often as possible, everything that might concern the interplay of innumerable pleasures, sensations, and thoughts which, through the body and the soul, had some affinity with sex. This scheme for transforming sex into discourse had been devised long before in an ascetic and monastic setting. The seventeenth century made it into a rule for everyone. It would seem in actual fact that it could scarcely have applied to any but a tiny elite; the great majority of the faithful who only went to confession on rare occasions in the course of the year escaped such complex prescriptions. But the important point, no doubt, is that this obligation was decreed, as an ideal at least, for every good Christian. An imperative was established: Not only will you confess to acts contravening the law, but you will seek to transform your desire, your every desire, into discourse. Insofar as possible, nothing was meant to elude this dictum, even if the words it employed had to be carefully neutralized. The Christian pastoral prescribed as a fundamental duty the task of passing everything having to do with sex through the endless mill of speech.[d] The forbidding of certain words, the decency of expressions, all the censorings of vocabulary, might well have been only secondary devices compared to that great subjugation: ways of rendering it morally acceptable and technically

---

5. Foucault argues that although the vocabulary of sex was restricted, the idea of sex became all encompassing. In medieval Europe, confession focused on the particular physical acts of sex. More modern confession expanded the idea of sex (and the need for confession) to all aspects of the body and soul. For Foucault, this expansion of the meaning of sex is linked to the idea of "biopower," a term he introduces in the last section of *History of Sexuality,* Volume 1 (1978: 139). Biopower refers to the extension of state power over the bodies of its subjects and citizens. Foucault makes a distinction between biopower as disciplinary power over "the body as a machine" (the regulation of peoples' space, time, and activities through institutions such as prisons, hospitals, asylums, and schools) and biopower over the body as "species" (the management of populations through institutional administration of birth, death, sex, and illness).

The Counter-Reformation was a move toward increased piety and rigor of practice within the Catholic Church that occurred in the hundred years following the Council of Trent. Thus, Foucault is arguing that the Protestant Reformation and the Catholic response to it were among the key early sources of the increasingly detailed verbal accounting of different types and practices of sexuality.

"Nervure": the vein of an insect's wing or a leaf. Here, the smallest part.

useful. One could plot a line going straight from the seventeenth-century pastoral to what became its projection in literature, "scandalous" literature at that. "Tell everything," the directors would say time and again: "not only consummated acts, but sensual touchings, all impure gazes, all obscene remarks . . . all consenting thoughts."[e] Sade takes up the injunction in words that seem to have been retranscribed from the treatises of spiritual direction: "Your narrations must be decorated with the most numerous and searching details; the precise way and extent to which we may judge how the passion you describe relates to human manners and man's character is determined by your willingness to disguise no circumstance; and what is more, the least circumstance is apt to have an immense influence upon the procuring of that kind of sensory irritation we expect from your stories."[f] And again at the end of the nineteenth century, the anonymous author of *My Secret Life* submitted to the same prescription; outwardly, at least, this man was doubtless a kind of traditional libertine; but he conceived the idea of complementing his life—which he had almost totally dedicated to sexual activity—with a scrupulous account of every one of its episodes. He sometimes excuses himself by stressing his concern to educate young people, this man who had eleven volumes published, in a printing of only a few copies, which were devoted to the least adventures, pleasures, and sensations of his sex. It is best to take him at his word when he lets into his text the voice of a pure imperative: "I recount the facts, just as they happened, insofar as I am able to recollect them; this is all that I can do"; "a secret life must not leave out anything; there is nothing to be ashamed of . . . one can never know too much concerning human nature."[g] The solitary

author of *My Secret Life* often says, in order to justify his describing them, that his strangest practices undoubtedly were shared by thousands of men on the surface of the earth. But the guiding principle for the strangest of these practices, which was the fact of recounting them all, and in detail, from day to day, had been lodged in the heart of modern man for over two centuries. Rather than seeing in this singular man a courageous fugitive from a "Victorianism" that would have compelled him to silence, I am inclined to think that, in an epoch dominated by (highly prolix) directives enjoining discretion and modesty, he was the most direct and in a way the most naive representative of a **plurisecular** injunction to talk about sex. The historical accident would consist, rather, of the reticences of "Victorian Puritanism"; at any rate, they were a digression, a refinement, a tactical diversion in the great process of transforming sex into discourse.[6]

This nameless Englishman will serve better than his queen as the central figure for a sexuality whose main features were already taking shape with the Christian pastoral. Doubtless, in contrast to the latter, for him it was a matter of augmenting the sensations he experienced with the details of what he said about them; like Sade, he wrote "for his pleasure alone," in the strongest sense of the expression; he carefully mixed the editing and rereading of his text with erotic scenes which that writer's activities repeated, prolonged, and stimulated. But, after all, the Christian pastoral also sought to produce specific effects on desire, by the mere fact of transforming it—fully and deliberately—into discourse: effects of mastery and detachment, to be sure, but also an effect of spiritual reconversion, of turning back to God, a physical effect of blissful suffering

---

6. In this spectacular passage, Foucault draws a rhetorical line connecting changes in the Catholic practice of confession with the work of the Marquis de Sade (1740–1814), and the author of *My Secret Life*. Thus, he argues that the requirement to detail the physical actions of sex has become a requirement to make public every aspect of one's life, especially one's innermost thoughts. Foucault sees these eighteenth and nineteenth-century figures as unconsciously ahead of their time, sensing the discursive move to lives that can be fully controlled by power because they are fully open to power.

My Secret Life is a series of books authored by "Walter," chronicling the details of his extremely active sex life. Controversy remains over the identity of the author but the best candidate seems to be Henry Spencer Ashbee (1834–1900), also known for writing bibliographies of pornographic works.

"Plurisecular": long term, over the centuries.

from feeling in one's body the pangs of temptation and the love that resists it. This is the essential thing: that Western man has been drawn for three centuries to the task of telling everything concerning his sex; that since the classical age there has been a constant optimization and an increasing valorization of the discourse on sex; and that this carefully analytical discourse was meant to yield multiple effects of displacement, intensification, reorientation, and modification of desire itself. Not only were the boundaries of what one could say about sex enlarged, and men compelled to hear it said; but more important, discourse was connected to sex by a complex organization with varying effects, by a deployment that cannot be adequately explained merely by referring it to a law of prohibition. A censorship of sex? There was installed, rather, an apparatus for producing an ever greater quantity of discourse about sex, capable of functioning and taking effect in its very economy.[7]

This technique might have remained tied to the destiny of Christian spirituality if it had not been supported and relayed by other mechanisms. In the first place, by a "public interest." Not a collective curiosity or sensibility; not a new mentality; but power mechanisms that functioned in such a way that discourse on sex—for reasons that will have to be examined—became essential. Toward the beginning of the eighteenth century, there emerged a political, economic, and technical incitement to talk about sex. And not so much in the form of a general theory of sexuality as in the form of analysis, stocktaking, classification, and specification, of quantitative or causal studies. This need to take sex "into account," to pronounce a discourse on sex that would not derive from morality alone but from rationality as well, was sufficiently new that at first it wondered at itself and sought apologies for its own existence. How could a discourse based on reason speak

of that? "Rarely have philosophers directed a steady gaze to these objects situated between disgust and ridicule, where one must avoid both hypocrisy and scandal."[h] And nearly a century later, the medical establishment, which one might have expected to be less surprised by what it was about to formulate, still stumbled at the moment of speaking: "The darkness that envelops these facts, the shame and disgust they inspire, have always repelled the observer's gaze . . . For a long time I hesitated to introduce the loathsome picture into this study."[i] What is essential is not in all these scruples, in the "moralism" they betray, or in the hypocrisy one can suspect them of, but in the recognized necessity of overcoming this hesitation. One had to speak of sex; one had to speak publicly and in a manner that was not determined by the division between licit and illicit, even if the speaker maintained the distinction for himself (which is what these solemn and preliminary declarations were intended to show): one had to speak of it as of a thing to be not simply condemned or tolerated but managed, inserted into systems of utility, regulated for the greater good of all, made to function according to an optimum. Sex was not something one simply judged; it was a thing one administered. It was in the nature of a public potential; it called for management procedures; it had to be taken charge of by analytical discourses. In the eighteenth century, sex became a "police" matter—in the full and strict sense given the term at the time: not the repression of disorder, but an ordered maximization of collective and individual forces: "We must consolidate and augment, through the wisdom of its regulations, the internal power of the state; and since this power consists not only in the Republic in general, and in each of the members who constitute it, but also in the faculties and talents of those belonging to it, it follows that the police must concern themselves with these means and make them serve the public

---

7. Note the emphasis in this passage on the relationship between discourse (the act of recounting as well as the words and phrases we use), the body, and society. Foucault argues that for the author of *My Secret Life,* the act of writing and the physical pleasure of sex were intertwined. For Foucault, this intimate connection between speech and body was already implicit in the ritual of confession. Foucault believes it is axiomatic that the way we talk about things is related to the ways we experience them and how that experience can be modified and controlled by others. Thus, speech is ultimately related to the development of institutions that promote, control, and regulate both discourse and actions.

welfare. And they can only obtain this result through the knowledge they have of those different assets."ʲ A policing of sex: that is, not the rigor of a taboo, but the necessity of regulating sex through useful and public discourses.[8]

A few examples will suffice. One of the great innovations in the techniques of power in the eighteenth century was the emergence of "population" as an economic and political problem: population as wealth, population as manpower or labor capacity, population balanced between its own growth and the resources it commanded. Governments perceived that they were not dealing simply with subjects, or even with a "people," but with a "population," with its specific phenomena and its peculiar variables: birth and death rates, life expectancy, fertility, state of health, frequency of illnesses, patterns of diet and habitation. All these variables were situated at the point where the characteristic movements of life and the specific effects of institutions intersected: "States are not populated in accordance with the natural progression of propagation, but by virtue of their industry, their products, and their different institutions . . . . Men multiply like the yields from the ground and in proportion to the advantages and resources they find in their labors."ᵏ At the heart of this economic and political problem of population was sex: it was necessary to analyze the birth rate, the age of marriage, the legitimate and illegitimate births, the precocity and frequency of sexual relations, the ways of making them fertile and sterile, the effects of unmarried life or of the prohibitions, the impact of contraceptive practices—of those notorious "deadly secrets" which demographers on the eve of the Revolution knew were already familiar to the inhabitants of the countryside.[9]

Of course, it had long been asserted that a country had to be populated if it hoped to be rich and powerful; but this was the first time that a society had affirmed, in a constant way, that its future and its fortune were tied not only to the number and the uprightness of its citizens, to their marriage rules and family organization, but to the manner in which each individual made use of his sex. Things went from ritual lamenting over the unfruitful debauchery of the rich, bachelors, and libertines to a discourse in which the sexual conduct of the population was taken both as an object of analysis and as a target of intervention; there was a progression from the crudely populationist arguments of the mercantilist epoch to the much more subtle and calculated attempts at regulation that tended to favor or

---

8. Here Foucault proposes that at the beginning of the eighteenth century, the discussion of sexuality moved from the domain of the Church to the domain of the state, and that sex became something to be administered and managed. Foucault says sex became a "police matter." Sex was rationalized and put in the service of state goals. The scholars he quotes are models of rationalist, Enlightenment thinking. In order, they are the eighteenth-century rational progressivist Condorcet (see the introduction to "Nineteenth-Century Evolutionism" in this volume), Auguste Ambroise Tardieu (1818–1879), a pioneer in forensic medicine and author of the first medical text on child sexual abuse (the symptoms characteristic of battered children are often called *Tardieu's syndrome* in recognition of his work), and Johann Heinrich Gottlob von Justi (1717–1771), another key Enlightenment figure who, writing on a wide variety of subjects, argued for the rationalization of the economic and social systems of Prussia and other states of the Holy Roman Empire. Thus, Foucault understands the changes in discourses concerning sexuality to be part of larger changes attempting to rationalize and reform European societies.

9. Here Foucault links the expansion of state power to the idea of a population. In other words, people begin to be understood as a particular kind of resource that can be grown, controlled, and utilized in certain ways.

"Deadly secrets" is how the eighteenth-century demographer Jean-Baptiste Moheau (1745–1794) refers to contraceptives and possibly abortion. Moheau was concerned with depopulation and wrote an essay on the French population (1778). In a commonly cited phrase, Moheau wrote, "Rich women . . . are not the only ones who regard the propagation of the species as an old-fashioned foolishness. . . . already the deadly secrets unknown to every other animal except man have penetrated the countryside: even in the villages nature is deceived" (cited in McLaren 1974: 611).

The revolution refers to the French Revolution of 1789.

discourage—according to the objectives and exigencies of the moment—an increasing birth rate. Through the political economy of population there was formed a whole grid of observations regarding sex. There emerged the analysis of the modes of sexual conduct, their determinations and their effects, at the boundary line of the biological and the economic domains. There also appeared those systematic campaigns which, going beyond the traditional means—moral and religious exhortations, fiscal measures—tried to transform the sexual conduct of couples into a concerted economic and political behavior. In time these new measures would become anchorage points for the different varieties of racism of the nineteenth and twentieth centuries. It was essential that the state know what was happening with its citizens' sex, and the use they made of it, but also that each individual be capable of controlling the use he made of it. Between the state and the individual, sex became an issue, and a public issue no less; a whole web of discourses, special knowledges, analyses, and injunctions settled upon it.[10]

The situation was similar in the case of children's sex. It is often said that the classical period consigned it to an obscurity from which it scarcely emerged before the *Three Essays* or the beneficent anxieties of Little Hans. It is true that a longstanding "freedom" of language between children and adults, or pupils

and teachers, may have disappeared. No seventeenth-century pedagogue would have publicly advised his disciple, as did Erasmus in his *Dialogues*, on the choice of a good prostitute. And the boisterous laughter that had accompanied the precocious sexuality of children for so long—and in all social classes, it seems—was gradually stifled. But this was not a plain and simple imposition of silence. Rather, it was a new regime of discourses. Not any less was said about it; on the contrary. But things were said in a different way; it was different people who said them, from different points of view, and in order to obtain different results. Silence itself—the things one declines to say, or is forbidden to name; the discretion that is required between different speakers—is less the absolute limit of discourse, the other side from which it is separated by a strict boundary, than an element that functions alongside the things said, with them and in relation to them within overall strategies. There is no binary division to be made between what one says and what one does not say; we must try to determine the different ways of not saying such things, how those who can and those who cannot speak of them are distributed, which type of discourse is authorized, or which form of discretion is required in either case. There is not one but many silences, and they are an integral part of the strategies that underlie and permeate discourses.[11]

---

10. Once populations are understood as among the most central of resources, it follows that sex becomes a topic of state intervention. Later in *The History of Sexuality,* Volume 1, Foucault refers to this as *"a biopolitics of the population"* (1978: 139, emphasis in the original).

11. In this passage, Foucault develops the idea that a discourse consists not only of what is said but also of strategic silences: what is not said, or not said by certain people or in certain places. He also considers authorization: the idea that institutions of power authorize or de-authorize certain types of discourses. Ultimately, what concerns Foucault is not specific ideas about sexuality but the ways the discourse about sexuality is used by institutions of power, and the ways in which such usage is resisted and subverted.

Three Essays and Little Hans both refer to the work of Sigmund Freud (1856–1939). Freud published the book *Three Essays on the Theory of Sexuality* in 1905. The second of the three focused on the sexuality of infants and children. There, Freud advanced the theory that infantile sucking was the prototype of future sexual gratification. Little Hans refers to Freud's 1909 paper "Analysis of a Phobia in a Five Year Old Boy," about a young boy's fear of horses. Freud argued that for Little Hans, horses were symbolic of his father and he feared that he would be bitten, and thus castrated by the horses. This paper is considered an important step in the development of Freud's theory of the Oedipus complex. Little Hans was Freud's pseudonym for Herbert Graf (1903–1973). Graf became a well-known opera producer in Europe and the United States.

Desiderius Erasmus (1466–1526) was a key Renaissance figure, a priest, and social critic. His widely read *Colloquies* or dialogues first appeared in 1518.

Take the secondary schools of the eighteenth century, for example. On the whole, one can have the impression that sex was hardly spoken of at all in these institutions. But one only has to glance over the architectural layout, the rules of discipline, and their whole internal organization: the question of sex was a constant preoccupation. The builders considered it explicitly. The organizers took it permanently into account. All who held a measure of authority were placed in a state of perpetual alert, which the fixtures, the precautions taken, the interplay of punishments and responsibilities, never ceased to reiterate. The space for classes, the shape of the tables, the planning of the recreation lessons, the distribution of the dormitories (with or without partitions, with or without curtains), the rules for monitoring bedtime and sleep periods—all this referred, in the most prolix manner, to the sexuality of children.[l] What one might call the internal discourse of the institution—the one it employed to address itself, and which circulated among those who made it function—was largely based on the assumption that this sexuality existed, that it was precocious, active, and ever-present. But this was not all: the sex of the schoolboy became in the course of the eighteenth century—and quite apart from that of adolescents in general—a public problem. Doctors counseled the directors and professors of educational establishments, but they also gave their opinions to families; educators designed projects which they submitted to the authorities; schoolmasters turned to students, made recommendations to them, and drafted for their benefit books of exhortation, full of moral and medical examples. Around the schoolboy and his sex there proliferated a whole literature of precepts, opinions, observations, medical advice, clinical cases, outlines for reform, and plans for ideal institutions. With Basedow and the German "philanthropic" movement, this transformation of adolescent sex into discourse grew to considerable dimensions. Salzmann even organized an experimental school which owed its exceptional character to a supervision and education of sex so well thought out that youth's universal sin would never need to be practiced there. And with all these measures taken, the child was not to be simply the mute and unconscious object of attentions prearranged between adults only; a certain reasonable, limited, canonical, and truthful discourse on sex was prescribed for him—a kind of discursive orthopedics. The great festival organized at the Philanthropinum in May of 1776 can serve as a vignette in this regard. Taking the form of an examination, mixed with floral games, the awarding of prizes, and a board of review, this was the first solemn communion of adolescent sex and reasonable discourse. In order to show the success of the sex education given students, Basedow had invited all the dignitaries that Germany could muster (Goethe was one of the few to decline the invitation). Before the assembled public, one of the professors, a certain Wolke, asked the students selected questions concerning the mysteries of sex, birth, and procreation. He had them comment on engravings that depicted a pregnant woman, a couple, and a cradle. The replies were enlightened, offered without shame or embarrassment. No unseemly laughter intervened to disturb them—except from the very ranks of an adult audience more childish than the children themselves, and whom Wolke severely reprimanded. At the end, they all applauded these cherub-faced boys who, in front of adults, had skillfully woven the garlands of discourse and sex.[m, 12]

---

12. Here Foucault discusses the way the concerns of the educators of the Philanthropinism movement were translated into architecture and physical space. The relationship between ideology and the use of space is a common concern in Foucault's work. In a widely read chapter of his book *Discipline and Punish* (1975), Foucault considers Jeremy Bentham's (1748–1832) idea of a panopticon, a prison designed so that prisoners would believe they were always being observed. Bentham originally described the panopticon in a series of letters written while he was visiting his brother the mechanical engineer and naval architect Samuel Bentham (1757–1832) in Belarus in 1787. Jacques-Alain Miller (1987: 3) paraphrasing Bentham describes the panopticon as a circular building "There are cells around the circumference, on each floor. In the center, a tower. Between the center and the circumference is a neutral intermediate zone. Each cell has a window to the outside so

It would be less than exact to say that the pedagogical institution has imposed a ponderous silence on the sex of children and adolescents. On the contrary, since the eighteenth century it has multiplied the forms of discourse on the subject; it has established various points of implantation for sex; it has coded contents and qualified speakers. Speaking about children's sex, inducing educators, physicians, administrators, and parents to speak of it, or speaking to them about it, causing children themselves to talk about it, and enclosing them in a web of discourses which sometimes address them, sometimes speak about them, or impose canonical bits of knowledge on them, or use them as a basis for constructing a science that is beyond their grasp—all this together enables us to link an intensification of the interventions of power to a multiplication of discourse. The sex of children and adolescents has become, since the eighteenth century, an important area of contention around which innumerable institutional devices and discursive strategies have been deployed. It may well be true that adults and children themselves were deprived of a certain way of speaking about sex, a mode that was disallowed as being too direct, crude, or coarse. But this was only the counterpart of other discourses, and perhaps the condition necessary in order for them to function; discourses that were interlocking, hierarchized, and all highly articulated around a cluster of power relations.[13]

One could mention many other centers which in the eighteenth or nineteenth century began to produce discourses on sex. First, there was medicine, via the "nervous disorders"; next psychiatry, when it set out to discover the etiology of mental illnesses, focusing its gaze first on "excess," then onanism, then frustration, then "frauds against procreation," but especially when it annexed the whole of the sexual perversions as its own province; criminal justice, too, which had long been con-

---

constructed that air and light can enter, but the view outside is blocked; each cell also has a grilled door that opens toward the inside so that air and light can circulate to the central core. The cells can be viewed from the rooms in the central tower, but a system of shutters prevents those rooms or their inhabitants being seen from the cells. . . . The building is completely closed."

Bentham and his brother tried unsuccessfully for years to have their plans for a panoptical prison built. They purchased land for it that is now the site of the Tate Modern, a famous art museum in London. Milbank prison, which operated from 1816–1890, was eventually built on the site, but it did not follow the Bentham's plans (Cottell and Mueller 2020). Numerous prisons with designs similar to or influenced by Bentham's panopticon were built in Europe and the United States. Bentham's idea of the panopticon has become a touchstone in current-day discourse in the social sciences and humanities.

Johann Bernhard Basedow (1724–1790) was the founder of an eighteenth-century German educational movement called *Philanthropinism*. The Philanthropinists hoped to create a rational and scientific form of education. Strongly influenced by Rousseau's key work on education, *Emile* (see Durkheim, essay 5, note 6), the Philanthropinists conceived education to be less a direct imparting of information and more of a setting of rules and structures in which a child's personality and potential could develop.

The Philanthropinists had idiosyncratic views concerning the importance of semen, which they linked to manliness, strength, and courage. They were extremely concerned with preventing masturbation ("youth's universal sin"), which they considered dangerous, and they had a wide repertoire of tactics designed to eliminate it, including the architectural elements Foucault discusses here (Sumser 1992).

Philanthropist ideas about masturbation have not survived, and Basedow's Philanthropinum in Dessau closed in 1793. However, other elements of their educational program continue to exert a strong influence over education today.

13. Discussions of the sexuality of children follow the same pattern Foucault identified earlier in the essay. That is, certain kinds of discourse about sex are prohibited among certain kinds of people (particularly the children themselves). At the same time, the subjugation of sexuality to scrutiny by the institutions of the state greatly increased other kinds of discussion of sex. This permitted a discourse embedded in specific power relationships. The ordering and cataloging of sexuality became a method for an increasingly powerful state as well as a growing world of professionals such as educators and doctors to impose their control on children and other members of society.

cerned with sexuality, particularly in the form of "heinous" crimes and crimes against nature, but which, toward the middle of the nineteenth century, broadened its jurisdiction to include petty offenses, minor indecencies, insignificant perversions; and lastly, all those social controls, cropping up at the end of the last century, which screened the sexuality of couples, parents and children, dangerous and endangered adolescents—undertaking to protect, separate, and forewarn; signaling perils everywhere; awakening people's attention; calling for diagnoses; piling up reports; organizing therapies. These sites radiated discourses aimed at sex, intensifying people's awareness of it as a constant danger, and this in turn created a further incentive to talk about it.[14]

One day in 1867, a farmhand from the village of Lapcourt, who was somewhat simpleminded, employed here then there, depending on the season, living hand-to-mouth from a little charity or in exchange for the worst sort of labor, sleeping in barns and stables, was turned in to the authorities. At the border of a field, he had obtained a few caresses from a little girl, just as he had done before and seen done by the village urchins round about him; for, at the edge of the wood, or in the ditch by the road leading to Saint-Nicolas, they would play the familiar game called "curdled milk." So he was pointed out by the girl's parents to the mayor of the village, reported by the mayor to the gendarmes, led by the gendarmes to the judge, who indicted him and turned him over first to a doctor, then to two other experts who not only wrote their report but also had it published.[n]

What is the significant thing about this story? The pettiness of it all; the fact that this everyday occurrence in the life of village sexuality, these inconsequential bucolic pleasures, could become, from a certain time, the object not only of a collective intolerance but of a judicial action, a medical intervention, a careful clinical examination, and an entire theoretical elaboration. The thing to note is that they went so far as to measure the brain span, study the facial bone structure, and inspect for possible signs of degenerescence the anatomy of this personage who up to that moment had been an integral part of village life; that they made him talk; that they questioned him concerning his thoughts, inclinations, habits, sensations, and opinions. And then, acquitting him of any crime, they decided finally to make him into a pure object of medicine and knowledge—an object to be shut away till the end of his life in the hospital at Mareville, but also one to be made known to the world of learning through a detailed analysis. One can be fairly certain that during this same period the Lapcourt schoolmaster was instructing the little villagers to mind their language and not talk about all these things aloud. But this was undoubtedly one of the conditions enabling the institutions of knowledge and power to overlay this everyday bit of theater with their solemn discourse. So it was that our society—and it was doubtless the first in history to take such measures—assembled around these timeless gestures, these barely furtive pleasures between simpleminded adults and alert children, a whole machinery for speechifying, analyzing, and investigating.[15]

---

14. The alert reader might consider Mead's discussion of typical American attitudes toward adolescents in the introduction to *Coming of Age in Samoa* (essay 11) as well as the publication of that book, as part of the discourse that Foucault describes in this passage.

15. The important part of this passage is Foucault's claim that in the nineteenth century, the "inconsequential bucolic pleasures" of an earlier time were systematized, categorized, and regulated. Rather than simply being ignored or punished, the farmhand becomes the subject of medicine, analysis, research, and governmental control.

Many current readers may object to the notion that the game of "curdled milk," presumably involving semen, could be described as an "inconsequential bucolic pleasure." On the one hand, this may be the result of our acceptance of the dominant discourse of control and regulation of sexuality. On the other, Foucault's sexuality, and his beliefs about sexuality, may have had a strong influence both on his decision to write about sex and the attitudes he presents in his work.

Foucault lived much of his adult life as a more-or-less openly gay man. He was involved in the gay sadomasochist scene in San Francisco in the late 1970s and early 1980s, and he died of an AIDS-related illness in 1984. His own position on the borders of the sexual landscape may have given him a particular concern with

Between the licentious Englishman, who earnestly recorded for his own purposes the singular episodes of his secret life, and his contemporary, this village halfwit who would give a few pennies to the little girls for favors the older ones refused him, there was without doubt a profound connection: in any case, from one extreme to the other, sex became something to say, and to say exhaustively in accordance with deployments that were varied, but all, in their own way, compelling. Whether in the form of a subtle confession in confidence or an authoritarian interrogation, sex—be it refined or rustic—had to be put into words. A great polymorphous injunction bound the Englishman and the poor Lorrainese peasant alike. As history would have it, the latter was named Jouy.°

Since the eighteenth century, sex has not ceased to provoke a kind of generalized discursive **erethism**. And these discourses on sex did not multiply apart from or against power, but in the very space and as the means of its exercise. Incitements to speak were orchestrated from all quarters, apparatuses everywhere for listening and recording, procedures for observing, questioning, and formulating. Sex was driven out of hiding and constrained to lead a discursive existence. From the singular imperialism that compels everyone to transform his sexuality into a perpetual discourse, to the manifold mechanisms which, in the areas of economy, pedagogy, medicine, and justice, incite, extract, distribute, and institutionalize the sexual discourse, an immense verbosity is what our civilization has required and organized. Surely no other type of society has ever accumulated—and in such a relatively short span of time—a similar quantity of discourses concerned with sex. It may well be that we talk about sex more than anything else; we set our minds to the task; we convince ourselves that we have never said enough on the subject, that, through inertia or submissiveness, we conceal from ourselves the blinding evidence, and that what is essential always eludes us, so that we must always start out once again in search of it. It is possible that where sex is concerned, the most long-winded, the most impatient of societies is our own.[16]

But as this first overview shows, we are dealing less with a discourse on sex than with a multiplicity of discourses produced by a whole series of mechanisms operating in different institutions. The Middle Ages had organized around the theme of the flesh and the practice of penance a discourse that was markedly unitary. In the course of recent centuries, this relative uniformity was broken apart, scattered, and multiplied in an explosion of distinct discursivities which took form in demography, biology, medicine, psychiatry, psychology, ethics, pedagogy, and political criticism. More precisely, the secure bond that held together the moral theology of **concupiscence** and the obligation of confession (equivalent to the theoretical discourse on sex and its first-person formulation) was, if not broken, at least loosened and diversified: between the objectification of sex in rational discourses, and the movement by which each individual was set to the task of recounting his own sex, there has occurred, since the eighteenth century, a whole

---

the relations between power and sexual actions and led him to positions that some may consider both radical and disturbing. For example, he argued that "the criminality of rape is overrated because sexuality is, and that it should be juridically restricted to the element of bodily harm, any genital transactions being neither here nor there and any denial of this being itself phallocentric" (Rawson 1994: 473, see Foucault 1988 *Politics, Philosophy, Culture*).

Foucault may have considered HIV a threat based on discourse rather than biology, a means of the state extending control over unruly populations. The novelist, playwright, and literary scholar Edmond White (b. 1940) reported that Foucault and Gilles Barbedette (1956–1992), a French author and translator, "had both laughed when [in the early 1980s] I'd told them about this mysterious new disease that was killing gay men and blacks and addicts. "Oh no" they said, "you're so gullible, A disease that kills gays and blacks and drug addicts? Why not child molesters too? That's too perfect!" (White 2014: 20)]. Barbedette also died of AIDS.

16. Much of Foucault's general argument in this essay is summarized in this and the following paragraph. **"Erethism"**: abnormal sensitivity of a body part or organ to stimulation.

series of tensions, conflicts, efforts at adjustment, and attempts at retranscription. So it is not simply in terms of a continual extension that we must speak of this discursive growth; it should be seen, rather, as a dispersion of centers from which discourses emanated, a diversification of their forms, and the complex deployment of the network connecting them. Rather than the uniform concern to hide sex, rather than a general prudishness of language, what distinguishes these last three centuries is the variety, the wide dispersion of devices that were invented for speaking about it, for having it be spoken about, for inducing it to speak of itself, for listening, recording, transcribing, and redistributing what is said about it: around sex, a whole network of varying, specific, and coercive transpositions into discourse. Rather than a massive censorship, beginning with the verbal proprieties imposed by the Age of Reason, what was involved was a regulated and polymorphous incitement to discourse.[17]

The objection will doubtless be raised that if so many stimulations and constraining mechanisms were necessary in order to speak of sex, this was because there reigned over everyone a certain fundamental prohibition; only definite necessities—economic pressures, political requirements—were able to lift this prohibition and open a few approaches to the discourse on sex, but these were limited and carefully coded; so much talk about sex, so many insistent devices contrived for causing it to be talked about—but under strict conditions: Does this not prove that it was an object of secrecy, and more important, that there is still an attempt to keep it that way? But this oft-stated theme, that sex is outside of discourse and that only the removing of an obstacle, the breaking of a secret, can clear the way leading to it, is precisely what needs to be examined. Does it not partake of the injunction by which discourse is provoked? Is it not with the aim of inciting people to speak of sex that it is made to mirror, at the outer limit of every actual discourse, something akin to a secret whose discovery is imperative, a thing abusively reduced to silence, and at the same time difficult and necessary, dangerous and precious to divulge? We must not forget that by making sex into that which, above all else, had to be confessed, the Christian pastoral always presented it as the disquieting enigma: not a thing which stubbornly shows itself, but one which always hides, the insidious presence that speaks in a voice so muted and often disguised that one risks remaining deaf to it. Doubtless the secret does not reside in that basic reality in relation to which all the incitements to speak of sex are situated—whether they try to force the secret, or whether in some obscure way they reinforce it by the manner in which they speak of it. It is a question, rather, of a theme that forms part of the very mechanics of these incitements: a way of giving shape to the requirement to speak about the matter, a fable that is indispensable to the endlessly proliferating economy of the discourse on sex. What is peculiar to modern societies, in fact, is not that they consigned sex to a shadow existence, but that they dedicated themselves to speaking of it ad infinitum, while exploiting it as the secret.[18]

---

17. Note that this passage includes the title of the essay. Foucault explains that rather than being silenced, the discourse of sexuality has been expanded. However, this has not been a simple process. Because it has become an arena of power, different groups have vied with each other to interpret and control sexuality.
   "Concupiscence": in Catholic theology, a desire of the lower appetite (organic needs) contrary to reason; also, overwhelming desires, particularly of a sexual nature.

18. This final paragraph expresses one of Foucault's central themes but also presents the reader with a dilemma. Foucault is concerned with the fundamental conditions of discourse. He is less concerned with whether various syndromes diagnosed by psychiatrists and government officials are "real" than with the ways power and control are exerted and people are classified through both the silences and the specifications of a discourse.
   The dilemma is that Foucault here sets a logical model that is impossible to prove or disprove. If we discuss sex in detail, that shows the elaboration of an increasingly complex system of sexual identification and control. However, if we urge people to be silent on the subject of sex, Foucault tells us that our principal aim is to cause people to speak of sex.

AUTHOR'S NOTES

a. Paolo Segneri, *L'Instruction du penitent* (French trans. 1695), p. 301.

b. Alfonso de' Liguori, *Practique des confesseurs* (French trans. 1854), p. 140.

c. Segneri, *L'Instruction du penitent*, pp 301–2.

d. The reformed pastoral also laid down rules, albeit in a more discreet way, for putting sex into discourse. This notion will be developed in the next volume, *The Body and the Flesh*.

e. Alfonso de' Liguori, *Préceptes sur le sixie`me commandement* (French trans. 1835), p. 5.

f. Donatien-Alphonse de Sade, *The 120 Days of Sodom*, trans. Austryn Wainhouse and Richard Seaver (New York: Grove Press, 1966), p. 271.

g. Anonymous, *My Secret Life* (New York: Grove Press, 1966).

h. Condorcet, cited by Jean-Louis Flandrin, *Familles: parenté, maison, sexualité dans l'ancienne société* (Paris: Hachette, 1976).

i. Auguste Tardieu, Étude medico-légale sur les attentats aux moeurs (1857), p. 114.

j. Johann von Justi, *Éléments généraux de police* (French trans. 1769), p. 20.

k. Claude-Jacques Herbert, *Essai sur la police general des grains* (1753), pp 320–1.

l. *Réglement des police pour les lycées* (1809), art. 67: "There shall always be, during class and study hours, an instructor watching the exterior, so as to prevent students who have gone out to relieve themselves from stopping and congregating."

art. 68: "After the evening prayer, the students will be conducted back to the dormitory, where the schoolmasters will put them to bed at once."

art. 69: "The masters will not retire except after having made certain that every student is in bed."

art. 70: "The beds shall be separated by partitions two meters in height. The dormitories shall be illuminated during the night."

m. Johann Gottlieb Schummel, *Fritzens Reise nach Dessau* (1776) cited by August Pinloche, *La Réform de l'éducation in Allemagn au XVIII e siècle* (1889), pp. 125–9.

n. Bonnet and J. Bulard, *Rapport medico-légal sur l'état mental de Ch. J. Jouy,* Janaury 4, 1968.

o. Jouy sounds like the past participle of *jouir* the French verb meaning to enjoy, to delight in (something), but also to have an orgasm, to come. (Translator's note)

Postmodernism

McGee. "I'm having trouble getting started on this introduction to postmodernism."

Warms. "Why don't you write about the process of writing the introduction?"

Rich Warms responded to Jon McGee's difficulty starting this introduction in a classic postmodernist fashion, trying to convince him to write it in a postmodern style. We hope that what makes Warms's (unsuccessful) response postmodern will become clear as you read.

Modernism is a term drawn from the study of literature and art as well as the history of science. In general, it reflects the epistemological notion that the world is knowable. People can use the techniques of science, philosophy, and rational inquiry to analyze and understand their world. Proper use of these tools can lead us to a thorough understanding of any subject material to which they are applied. In anthropology, *modernism* broadly refers to the time period stretching from the early twentieth century until the mid-1970s. Common attributes of modernist writing in anthropology include detachment, the assumption of a position of scientific neutrality, and rationalism.

Postmodernists challenge the assertion that science and rationalism can lead to full and accurate knowledge of the world. They argue that these are specific historically constituted ways of understanding. Therefore, they can create only specific historically constituted sorts of knowledge. Since the ideas and practices that we usually refer to when we talk about science and rationality had their historical origin at a certain time and among a certain class within Western European and North American society, the truths they generate are appropriate to (or empowering of) that group. Although science makes transcendent claims, postmodernists argue that the truths generated by science or any other system of knowledge are limited. Furthermore, the methods of science and rationality, when applied to other cultures (or other groups within Western culture), are very likely to produce distortions of knowledge. Postmodernists assert that other peoples have their own ways of knowing and, since all knowledge is historically constituted, these are just as valid (or just as invalid) as any other.

In the 1980s, the postmodernist challenge led many anthropologists to examine some of the basic assumptions of their discipline. For example, anthropologists have historically positioned themselves as authorities on other cultures. They fortified this claim by providing convincing written descriptions of other cultures and emphasizing their individual experiences of fieldwork. However, postmodern approaches encouraged anthropologists to examine the ways in which their authority and that of the discipline of anthropology were established and maintained. Such analysis focused on several areas, including the conduct of fieldwork, the literary techniques used in writing ethnographies, and the validity of the author's interpretations over competing alternatives.

The conduct of fieldwork is a critical issue to postmodernists because, traditionally, most ethnography has contained little information on the actual process of field research. Postmodernists argue that it is precisely these practices that are crucial in the creation of ethnographic texts. Fieldworkers must, of necessity, be in specific places at specific times. As a result, they see some things and not others. The particular circumstances of fieldwork—the political context in which it occurs, the investigator's interests and education, and the people met by chance or design—all critically condition the understanding of society that results. Consequently, postmodern theorists believe that anthropology can never be purely objective.

Literary style is a second issue of importance to postmodern anthropologists. Modernist ethnographies were written as if the anthropologist were a neutral, omniscient observer. In this text, ethnographies from Émile Durkheim to Victor Turner are all modernist. Postmodernists claim, however, that because the collection of anthropological data is subjective, it is not possible to be a neutral observer.

Writing ethnography is the primary means by which anthropologists convey their interpretations of other cultures, and ethnographies have usually followed some basic literary conventions, which George Marcus and Dick Cushman (1982) have described in detail. Even if you are not a student of ethnographic writing, you will immediately recognize several of these forms in the essays of this volume. One of the most obvious characteristics of ethnographic writing is that authors claim to represent the native point of view. Of course, an anthropologist cannot possibly present the point of view of everyone in a society; they work with selected informants. So, the anthropologist chooses who speaks for the society and, in his or her translation of the native language, decides what words are presented to the audience.

Another common rhetorical device of European and American ethnography is that writers claim to completely describe other cultures or societies even though anthropologists actually know only the part of a culture that they personally experience. One of the techniques through which this is commonly accomplished is the use of the omniscient narrator, the authoritative third-person observer who replaces the fallible first person. Instead of writing a direct statement of what the anthropologist actually observed, such as "I saw a student pour ketchup on his ice cream," many ethnographies contain statements like "Texas State students pour ketchup on their ice cream." Postmodern critics argue that the use of the omniscient narrator heightens the sense of scientific objectivity projected by the text and improperly severs the relationship between what the ethnographer knows and how they came to know it (Marcus and Cushman 1982: 32).

One result of the postmodern critique of ethnography was the more revealing style in which some anthropologists began to write. There has always been some self-revelation in ethnography, but in the late 1960s and the 1970s, anthropologists such as Jean Briggs (1929–2016), Clifford Geertz, and Paul Rabinow (1944–2021) began to write ethnographies in which the recounting of their own experiences and feelings took a prominent role (see Briggs 1970; Geertz 1973; Rabinow 1977). For postmodern writers in the 1980s and 1990s, this self-reflexiveness was not simply a more straightforward form of reportage. The recounting of field experiences became a narrative device by which personal goals as well as anthropological understanding were conveyed. Renato Rosaldo (b. 1941), for example, says that the writing of his article (essay 29) was an act of catharsis that helped him deal with his grief as well as gain new insight into the custom of headhunting.

A third issue that underlies almost all postmodern writing concerns the question of whose voice gets heard. Postmodernists maintain that a text is necessarily an author's interpretation. If that author's work is taken as an authoritative account, then other voices and differing interpretations are dismissed. In the postmodern view, writing ethnography is an assertion of power because the way authors generate an interpretation that is accepted as true is to "delicense" all others. But can one person's interpretation be more valid than another's? Postmodernists maintain that it cannot. They insist that the acceptance of an interpretation is ultimately an issue of power and wealth. Historically, they say, the interpretations voiced by white males in Western industrialized nations have delicensed and silenced all others. They ask why this view of events is the only acceptable interpretation and claim that deconstructing the work of this mainstream allows other opinions to be expressed. Postmodernists assert that in history, literature, and politics, the voices of women, minorities, and the poor have long been suppressed. It is only through recognizing and combating "epistemic violence," the subtle forms of oppression that legitimate and enforce the discourses of the wealthy and powerful, that the voices of the oppressed can be heard. You may have heard about one example of this form of subtle violence in 2015. A student in a ninth-grade geography class in Pearland, Texas, noticed that his textbook described American slaves as "workers." The passage in a McGraw-Hill textbook said, "The Atlantic slave trade between the 1500s and the 1800s brought millions of workers from Africa to the southern United States to work on agricultural plantations." To call slaves "workers" is a grotesque distortion of the brutal nature of American slavery, and it mocks the millions of people who had to live and die being treated like beasts of burden. That one of the largest textbook publishing companies in the nation thought it was appropriate to call slaves "workers" as if they were hired staff in a business is an example of how the discourse of a certain class of people can be heard at the expense of those less powerful. It was only after a huge public outcry that McGraw-Hill promised to revise the passage in new books, although it did not recall those textbooks already distributed.

A final form of postmodern scholarship deals with textual analysis (and this, in fact, informs most other sorts of postmodern thinking). Postmodernists argue that data are, of themselves, mute. Data are just data. Anthropologists participate in the flow of events around them, interpret what they observe, and construct meaning from those observations through the process of writing. Because one must write according to certain literary conventions (tense, voice, and so on), the finished text is of necessity a literary construction of its author. Readers in turn impose their own interpretation on the author's text. In other words, the written word can never be adequate to represent reality. Instead, writing involves the piling up of layer upon layer of convention and interpretation. Similarly, reading involves its own conventions, and each reader brings personal history and understanding to the act of reading. Thus, a finished text is a thing unto itself. It cannot be an accurate representation of the reality it claims to portray, for this is impossible. So, what's a postmodernist to do when a text can tell us very little of the "reality" of its purported subject? The answer is that a postmodernist may deconstruct the ways in which the devices and conventions of writing and reading are exploited in the text, explore the sorts of meanings that are promoted by the text as well as those that are delegitimized, and examine what this may tell us about the current or historical nature of the society in which the text is written and read. Furthermore, since any form of deconstruction and analysis is itself a literary process, all deconstruction is subject to further deconstruction. Jacques Derrida (1930–2004), the father of deconstruction, did not argue that his analysis of texts was authoritative. It was implicit in the process he outlined that deconstruction changed with the subject of analysis and the person who conducted it. In Derrida's view, no authoritative reading is possible.

The issues of fieldwork, literary style, interpretation, and deconstruction are all important elements that inform the work of authors featured in this section. The first author is Renato Rosaldo, who received his PhD from Harvard University in 1971 and has served as president of the American Ethnological Society and chair of the Stanford University Department of Anthropology. He is an emeritus professor at Stanford and New York University. In addition to his work in anthropology, Rosaldo has published four books of poetry.

"Grief and a Headhunter's Rage" is one of Rosaldo's best-known works and is a classic example of postmodern writing. It deals directly with issues of fieldwork, literary style, and the question of who has the right to interpret. In this essay, Rosaldo describes his failed attempts to find a logical explanation for Ilongot headhunting. However, Rosaldo describes his almost unbearable sorrow after the accidental death of his wife, the anthropologist Michelle Zimbalist Rosaldo (1944–1981), while doing fieldwork, and how this experience led him to a visceral understanding of why Ilongot men go headhunting after the death of loved ones. He argues that it was only this gut-wrenching personal experience, not the study of Ilongot custom or society, that allowed him insight into Ilongot society. Written in a highly reflexive style, Rosaldo's description of his wife's accidental death is excruciatingly personal, probably unlike any ethnography you have read. Rosaldo claims that what you know and how you know it is based on your positioning, that is, on factors such as your ethnicity, sex, education, and personal history. Furthermore, he characterizes ethnographic information as a negotiation between what an ethnographer wants to know and what the people in the field want to tell you. Everyone involved in the interaction is a positioned subject. Someone in a different position, say, of the opposite sex, with a different ethnic background or of a different generation, is positioned to understand the same information differently.

Rosaldo's text is also a critique of Geertz's notions of depth and thick description (see essay 26), countering these with his concept of force. Geertz argued that cultural analysis was intrinsically incomplete. Socially important acts have depth to the actors and many layers of meaning. Anthropological analysis operates by exposing these layers, but there are always more layers to expose. Rosaldo argues that frequently this is not true. Sometimes events just are. There are no deeper layers of meaning to be uncovered.

The second author, Michel-Rolph Trouillot (1949–2012), was a Haitian American anthropologist who taught at the University of Chicago. Trouillot was born into a prestigious Haitian family. His father (1922–1987) was a lawyer and professor who hosted a Haitian television show on Haitian history. Trouillot's uncle was a prominent historian and the director of the Haitian National Archives. All three of his siblings became well-known authors. Trouillot was pursuing an elite education when in 1968 he was forced into exile by the dictatorial regime of François "Papa Doc" Duvalier (1907–1971). He, and several hundred other Haitian students, fled to New York City. There he lived in poverty, supporting himself by driving a cab and doing odd jobs. However, he also began to write history, poetry, journalism, and music. He was the founder of Tanbou Libèrté, an activist music and theater group opposed to the Duvalier regime. He also pursued his undergraduate degree at Brooklyn College, from which he graduated in 1978. By that time, he had already published a book that analyzed the Haitian revolution from a Marxist position that was written in Haitian Creole called *Ti dife boule sou istoua Ayiti*, or Stirring the Pot of Haitian History (1977). Sidney Mintz and Richard Price recruited him as a graduate student at Johns Hopkins. Both Mintz and Price were focused on understanding the Caribbean in the context of global history and colonialism. Mintz had been a Columbia University student with Eric Wolf and was deeply interested in Marxist interpretations of culture. He was the first director of the Johns Hopkins Institute for Global Studies in Culture, History, and Power. In 1998, Trouillot moved from Johns Hopkins to the University of Chicago. However, his career there was tragically cut short. In early 2002, at the age of fifty-two, Trouillot suffered a series of aneurysms that left him mentally alert but unable to complete his academic projects. He died in 2012.

Trouillot was deeply influenced by his experience of dictatorship and exile, his reading of Marx, and the work of Sidney Mintz and Eric Wolf, and he developed a multidisciplinary approach in his work that integrated history, philosophy, political economy, and ethnography. "The Savage Slot" is an example of this approach. In the essay, Trouillot examines the historical development of anthropology and its political consequences, in particular the origins of the notion of "the savage," and how this concept influenced the course of the discipline's development and predisposed it to certain kinds of study and analysis. The title refers to the treatment of "otherness" in the development of anthropology, specifically in the context of the triad of savage-utopia-order. Trouillot argues that postmodern attempts to analyze anthropological techniques and writing are both incomplete and misdirected. Rather than focusing their attention on the history of anthropology and the structure of its practice, anthropologists need to focus on the larger historical-discursive field within which anthropology arose and the ways in which its claim to knowledge interacts with European and American structures of power.

Postmodernism has been extensively critiqued within anthropology. Many scholars vigorously defend the idea that anthropology is or should be an empirical science. They argue that although some aspects of ethnographic data collection are subjective, anthropologists can accurately observe and record what happens in the field and build useful theories based on this information. They point out that an anthropology that can only make very specific claims about the actions of particular individuals would have little of value to say. Consider our example from earlier in this introduction: If the only thing an anthropologist can say is "I saw one of Jon McGee's students pour ketchup on his ice cream," why should anyone care about anthropology? What is the importance of one of McGee's students if his actions can never be generalized? Additionally, some have claimed that there are critical logical flaws in postmodern arguments (e.g., see O'Meara 1989).

Postmodernists argue that power constructs truth. They use this argument, they claim, to recover the voices and agendas of the powerless. In recent years, this has generally been true. Many works by postmodern thinkers attempt to find the voices and represent the interests of those who have historically been oppressed. Throughout the 1990s, postmodernists generally positioned themselves as those who "speak truth to power." However, opponents of postmodernism note that, pushed to its logical extreme, the postmodern idea that truth is determined by power must result in nihilism. If all voices should be heard, they say, then are fascist voices, the voices of white supremacists or neo-Nazis, less worthy of respect than others? In the past, some whose work was fundamental in the development of postmodernism chose to side with the powerful. Indeed, during World War II, hermeneuticist Martin Heidegger (1889–1976) was an apologist for the Nazis, and the literary critic Paul de Man (1919–1983), who later became a prominent deconstructionist, was a Nazi journalist (Lehman 1992). Today, people representing all shades of the political spectrum seem to struggle to control the discourse and determine how individuals, groups, and history will be represented.

No doubt, taken to its logical extreme, postmodernism can seem nihilistic. Furthermore, if all anthropologists took radical postmodern positions, then cultural anthropology might become just another genre of literature. However, the postmodern critique has been of enduring value. Few ethnographies today use the device of an omniscient narrator. Describing something of the personal history of the author and the conditions of fieldwork is now virtually a requirement for publication. Beyond this, postmodernism encouraged anthropologists to be aware of issues of rhetoric, power, voice, and perspective. And this awareness continues to enrich our fieldwork and our writing. It helps us to evaluate both our own and others' claims to objectivity. And, since it encouraged anthropologists to be explicit about the specific sources of knowledge for the claims they make, postmodernism may have had the ironic effect of making anthropology more objective. Postmodernists remind us that cultures are never static and that power, conflict, and politics are always present. The postmodern critique of anthropology requires us to remember that these issues are expressed in the cultural structures within which people live and that they influence peoples' actions, language, and, ultimately, the stories they tell.

SUGGESTED READINGS

Clifford, James, and George Marcus, eds. 1986. *Writing Culture: The Poetics and Politics of Ethnography*. Berkeley: University of California Press.
>	Scholars from different backgrounds bring together interpretive anthropology, travel writing, discourse theory, and textual criticism in an analysis of ethnography.

Hanson, Allan, 1989. "The Making of the Maori: Cultural Invention and Its Logic." *American Anthropologist* 91(4): 890–902.
>	This essay discusses the role of invention in ethnographic analysis. Hanson uses Derrida's concept of logocentrism to argue that the notion of cultural authenticity in ethnography is an invention of the ethnographer and that culture is reinvented every generation.

Lukas, Scott A. 2013. "Postmodernism." In *Theory in Social and Cultural Anthropology: An Encyclopedia*, ed. R. Jon McGee and Richard L. Warms, 639–645. Los Angeles, CA: Sage.
>	A brief and good overview and introduction to postmodernism, including postmodern theory and some of the influential scholars in this area.

Marcus, George, and Michael M. J. Fischer. 1996. *Anthropology as Cultural Critique: An Experimental Moment in the Human Sciences*. Chicago: University of Chicago Press.
>	Marcus and Fischer explore the theory that the social sciences are in an experimental period where the once dominant modernist paradigm has lost its hold and scholars are experimenting with new interdisciplinary approaches.

Rosaldo, Renato. 1993. *Culture and Truth: The Remaking of Social Analysis*. Boston: Beacon Press.
>	A postmodern critique of modernist anthropology, especially the notions of detachment and objectivity in social science. Based on his own experiences in the field, Rosaldo calls for a more subjective, emotional, and engaged anthropology.

Wolf, Margery. 1992. *A Thrice Told Tale: Feminism, Postmodernism, and Ethnographic Responsibility*. Stanford, CA: Stanford University Press.
>	Wolf explores issues raised by feminist and postmodern critics. Based on her own research, and focusing on experimental ethnography, reflexivity, and the differences between fiction and ethnography, Wolf analyzes the same set of events as short story, field notes, and scholarly article.

29. Grief and a Headhunter's Rage

Renato Rosaldo (b. 1941)

IF YOU ASK AN OLDER Ilongot man of northern Luzon, Philippines, why he cuts off human heads, his answer is brief, and one on which no anthropologist can readily elaborate: He says that rage, born of grief, impels him to kill his fellow human beings. He claims that he needs a place "to carry his anger." The act of severing and tossing away the victim's head enables him, he says, to vent and, he hopes, throw away the anger of his bereavement. Although the anthropologist's job is to make other cultures intelligible, more questions fail to reveal any further explanation of this man's pithy statement. To him, grief, rage, and headhunting go together in a self-evident manner. Either you understand it or you don't. And, in fact, for the longest time I simply did not.

In what follows, I want to talk about how to talk about the cultural force of emotions.[a] The *emotional force* of a death, for example, derives less from an abstract brute fact than from a particular intimate relation's permanent rupture. It refers to the kinds of feelings one experiences on learning, for example, that the child just run over by a car is one's own and not a stranger's. Rather than speaking of death in general, one must consider the subject's position within a field of social relations in order to grasp one's emotional experience.[b, 1]

My effort to show the force of a simple statement taken literally goes against anthropology's classic norms, which prefer to explicate culture through the gradual thickening of symbolic webs of meaning. By and large, cultural analysts use not *force* but such terms as *thick description, multivocality, polysemy, richness,* and *texture.* The notion of force, among other things, opens to question the common anthropological assumption that the greatest human import resides in the densest forest of symbols and that analytical detail, or "cultural depth," equals enhanced explanation of a culture, or "cultural elaboration." Do people always in fact describe most thickly what matters most to them?[2]

From *Culture and Truth* (1989)

1. From the opening, it is evident that Rosaldo is writing a different sort of anthropology than most of the authors in this book. Most anthropological writing has been built on a scientific model. Works are usually written as reports, almost always in the third person. This essay, on the other hand, is conversational in tone, and much of it is in the first and second person. Beyond this, Rosaldo seems, in his opening, to deny the possibility of an empirical explanation of Ilongot headhunting. The idea of emotional *force* which he elaborates below, is not so much explanation as a statement that no further description or explanation is possible.

Rosaldo also introduces the idea of *positionality* in this paragraph. He argues throughout this work that an observer's position, that is, the observer's personal history, experiences, and location in the class, racial, and ethnic hierarchy of their society and the society that they are studying, plays a critical role in what is observed and how it is interpreted. The idea of positionality has some historical depth in anthropology (see Rosaldo's endnote j). It became increasingly popular after the publication of this essay. Indeed, the importance of positionality is a critical insight of postmodern anthropology. However, it also raises fundamental questions: Is objective knowledge possible if what you observe and the conclusions you draw from it depend on your positioning?

2. By invoking the concepts of thick description and multivocality, Rosaldo is referring to Clifford Geertz and Victor Turner. The term "thick description" is associated with Geertz and the phrase "forest of symbols"

THE RAGE IN ILONGOT GRIEF

Let me pause a moment to introduce the Ilongots, among whom my wife, Michelle Rosaldo, and I lived and conducted field research for thirty months (1967–69, 1974). They number about 3,500 and reside in an upland area some 90 miles northeast of Manila, Philippines.[c] They subsist by hunting deer and wild pig and by cultivating rain-fed gardens (swiddens) with rice, sweet potatoes, manioc, and vegetables. Their (bilateral) kin relations are reckoned through men and women. After marriage, parents and their married daughters live in the same or adjacent households. The largest unit within the society, a largely territorial descent group called the *bertan,* becomes manifest primarily in the context of feuding. For themselves, their neighbors, and their ethnographers, headhunting stands out as the Ilongots' most salient cultural practice.

When Ilongots told me, as they often did, how the rage in bereavement could impel men to headhunt, I brushed aside their one-line accounts as too simple, thin, opaque, implausible, stereotypical, or otherwise unsatisfying. Probably I naively equated grief with sadness. Certainly no personal experience allowed me to imagine the powerful rage Ilongots claimed to find in bereavement. My own inability to conceive the force of anger in grief led me to seek out another level of analysis that could provide a deeper explanation for older men's desire to headhunt.

Not until some fourteen years after first recording the terse Ilongot statement about grief and a headhunter's rage did I begin to grasp its overwhelming force. For years I thought that more verbal elaboration (which was not forthcoming) or another analytical level (which remained elusive) could better explain older men's motives for headhunting. Only after being repositioned through a devastating loss of my own could I better grasp that Ilongot older men mean precisely what they say when they describe the anger in bereavement as the source of their desire to cut off human heads. Taken at face value and granted its full weight, their statement reveals much about what compels these older men to headhunt.

In my efforts to find a "deeper" explanation for headhunting, I explored exchange theory, perhaps because it had informed so many classic ethnographies. One day in 1974, I explained the anthropologist's exchange model to an older Ilongot man named Insan. What did he think, I asked, of the idea that headhunting resulted from the way that one death (the beheaded victim's) canceled another (the next of kin). He looked puzzled, so I went on to say that the victim of a beheading was exchanged for the death of one's own kin, thereby balancing the books, so to speak. Insan reflected a moment and replied that he imagined somebody could think such a thing (a safe bet, since I just had), but that he and other Ilongots did not think any such thing. Nor was there any indirect evidence for my exchange theory in ritual, boast, song, or casual conversation.[d, 3]

---

refers to the title of Turner's book which includes essay 25 in this volume . An important difference between Rosaldo and Geertz can be seen by comparing Geertz's concept of depth with Rosaldo's idea of force. Geertz argues that critical aspects of culture are complex and have many layers. Anthropologists doing thick description of a ritual such as a funeral try to explain those layers of complexity. Rosaldo argues that some critical aspects of culture have force but do not lend themselves to deep explanations. There are no deeper layers of meaning. Instead, it's their simplicity that gives them meaning and power.

3. The "deeper" explanation of headhunting Rosaldo searched for was some sort of accounting modeled on natural law (here, the formula one death cancels another). However, in describing this theory to the Ilongot, Rosaldo faced a problem: Even if the theory explained observed behavior, how could Rosaldo grant it any explanatory power when the idea is utterly unintelligible to the Ilongot themselves? Note that in this passage, Rosaldo implies that for a model to be satisfying, it must be recognized as accurate by the people whose behavior it purports to describe. Consider how different this position is from that of Marvin Harris, who, in essay 18, argues that what Hindus think of his explanation of the taboo on killing cattle is irrelevant to its accuracy. Consider as well that we usually do not accept Rosaldo's claim in thinking about our own soci-

In retrospect, then, these efforts to impose exchange theory on one aspect of Ilongot behavior appear feeble. Suppose I had discovered what I sought? Although the notion of balancing the ledger does have a certain elegant coherence, one wonders how such bookish dogma could inspire any man to take another man's life at the risk of his own.[4]

My life experience had not as yet provided the means to imagine the rage that can come with devastating loss. Nor could I, therefore, fully appreciate the acute problem of meaning that Ilongots faced in 1974. Shortly after Ferdinand Marcos declared martial law in 1972, rumors that firing squads had become the new punishment for headhunting reached the Ilongot hills. The men therefore decided to call a moratorium on taking heads. In past epochs, when headhunting had become impossible, Ilongots had allowed their rage to dissipate, as best it could, in the course of everyday life. In 1974, they had another option; they began to consider conversion to evangelical Christianity as a means of coping with their grief. Accepting the new religion, people said, implied abandoning their old ways, including headhunting.

It also made coping with bereavement less agonizing because they could believe that the deceased had departed for a better world. No longer did they have to confront the awful finality of death.[5]

The force of the dilemma faced by the Ilongots eluded me at the time. Even when I correctly recorded their statements about grieving and the need to throw away their anger, I simply did not grasp the weight of their words. In 1974, for example, while Michelle Rosaldo and I were living among the Ilongots, a six-month-old baby died, probably of pneumonia. That afternoon we visited the father and found him terribly stricken. "He was sobbing and staring through glazed and bloodshot eyes at the cotton blanket covering his baby."[e] The man suffered intensely, for this was the seventh child he had lost. Just a few years before, three of his children had died, one after the other, in a matter of days. At the time, the situation was murky as people present talked both about evangelical Christianity (the possible renunciation of taking heads) and their grudges against lowlanders (the contemplation of headhunting forays into the surrounding valleys).[6]

---

ety. For example, in holiness churches in Appalachia worshipers dance with poisonous snakes. They say they do so because God and the Bible tell them they must. Would analysts say that therefore, that is the only possible explanation? Or would they point to economic and ethnic factors, whether the members of the churches recognized these or not?

4. Rosaldo and other postmodern authors are concerned about privileged positions. In social science, to privilege a position is to give special credence to certain explanations and discount others. Postmodernists argue that Western social science has privileged explanatory models used in the physical sciences. The closer an explanation is to this model, the "truer" the information it generates, and the higher the prestige of the field that uses it. The exchange theory Rosaldo has described here sounds like science; therefore, it is privileged (but, Rosaldo insists, incorrect). Part of the reason Rosaldo claims that he misunderstood Ilongot headhunting is that he attempted to apply a Western scientific model to it.

5. Although postmodern anthropology draws on ethnoscience, it is critically different in many ways, one of which is shown here. Ethnoscientists viewed culture as a more or less unchanging mental template. For postmodernists, culture is always historically contingent. The actions of individuals and the derivation of meaning within cultures cannot be explained without reference to specific sociohistorical circumstances.

Ferdinand Marcos (1917–1989) was president of the Philippines from 1965 to 1986. Elected in 1965, he declared martial law in 1972 and ruled as a dictator until 1986. The Marcos regime was noted for its corruption, extravagance, and brutality (Litonjua 2001). Ferdinand Marcos's son, Ferdinand "Bongbong" Romualdez Marcos Jr. (b. 1957) was elected president of the Philippines in 2022.

6. A key source of the emphasis on history in postmodernism is Marxism, particularly as filtered by the French Marxist anthropologists and political radicals of the 1960s and 1970s (when many postmodernists were doing their graduate training). Marxists, of course, see culture as part of a historical process that will

Through subsequent days and weeks, the man's grief moved him in a way I had not anticipated. Shortly after the baby's death, the father converted to evangelical Christianity. Altogether too quick on the inference, I immediately concluded that the man believed that the new religion could somehow prevent further deaths in his family. When I spoke my mind to an Ilongot friend, he snapped at me, saying that I had missed the point: what the man in fact sought in the new religion was not the denial of our inevitable deaths but a means of coping with his grief. With the advent of martial law, headhunting was out of the question as a means of venting his wrath and thereby lessening his grief. Were he to remain in his Ilongot way of life, the pain of his sorrow would simply be too much to bear.[f] My description from 1980 now seems so apt that I wonder how I could have written the words and nonetheless failed to appreciate the force of the grieving man's desire to vent his rage.

Another representative anecdote makes my failure to imagine the rage possible in Ilongot bereavement all the more remarkable. On this occasion, Michelle Rosaldo and I were urged by Ilongot friends to play the tape of a headhunting celebration we had witnessed some five years before. No sooner had we turned on the tape and heard the boast of a man who had died in the intervening years than did people abruptly tell us to shut off the recorder. Michelle Rosaldo reported on the tense conversation that ensued:

> As Insan braced himself to speak, the room again became almost uncannily electric. Backs straightened and my anger turned to nervousness and something more like fear

as I saw that Insan's eyes were red. Tukbaw, Renato's Ilongot "brother," then broke into what was a brittle silence, saying he could make things clear. He told us that it hurt to listen to a headhunting celebration when people knew that there would never be another. As he put it: "The song pulls at us, drags our hearts, it makes us think of our dead uncle." And again: "It would be better if I had accepted God, but I still am an Ilongot at heart; and when I hear the song, my heart aches as it does when I must look upon unfinished bachelors whom I know that I will never lead to take a head." Then Wagat, Tukbaw's wife, said with her eyes that all my questions gave her pain, and told me: "Leave off now, isn't that enough? Even I, a woman, cannot stand the way it feels inside my heart."[g, 7]

From my present position, it is evident that the tape recording of the dead man's boast evoked powerful feelings of bereavement, particularly rage and the impulse to headhunt. At the time I could only feel apprehensive and diffusely sense the force of the emotions experienced by Insan, Tukbaw, Wagat, and the others present.

The dilemma for the Ilongots grew out of a set of cultural practices that, when blocked, were agonizing to live with. The cessation of headhunting called for painful adjustments to other modes of coping with the rage they found in bereavement. One could compare their dilemma with the notion that the failure to perform rituals can create anxiety.[h] In the Ilongot case, the cultural notion that throwing away a human head also casts away the anger creates a problem of meaning when the headhunting rit-

---

ultimately result in communism. Postmodernists do not see any end to history, but they do view cultural action as dependent on historical circumstances. It is, for example, critical to the story Rosaldo is telling here that the action takes place in 1974 when headhunting was made impossible and evangelical Christianity was available as an alternative.

7. This extended quotation, from Michelle Rosaldo's *Knowledge and Passion* (1980) is typical of the self-revealing style of postmodernism. Michelle Rosaldo (1944–1981) makes extensive use of such quotations. In traditional ethnography, information from the field is presented in an abstract, scientific fashion. Names are rarely mentioned; in fact, pains are sometimes taken to ensure the anonymity of the speakers. Here the opposite is done. Since all knowledge is contingent on the positioning of observers and informants, the fact that specific people are speaking is critical.

ual cannot be performed. Indeed, Max Weber's classic problem of meaning in *The Protestant Ethic and the Spirit of Capitalism* is precisely of this kind.[i] On a logical plane, the Calvinist doctrine of predestination seems flawless: God has chosen the elect, but his decision can never be known by mortals. Among those whose ultimate concern is salvation, the doctrine of predestination is as easy to grasp conceptually as it is impossible to endure in everyday life (unless one happens to be a "religious virtuoso"). For Calvinists and Ilongots alike, the problem of meaning resides in practice, not theory. The dilemma for both groups involves the practical matter of how to live with one's beliefs, rather than the logical puzzlement produced by abstruse doctrine.[8]

HOW I FOUND THE RAGE IN GRIEF

One burden of this introduction concerns the claim that it took some fourteen years for me to grasp what Ilongots had told me about grief, rage, and headhunting. During all those years I was not yet in a position to comprehend the force of anger possible in bereavement, and now I am. Introducing myself into this account requires a certain hesitation both because of the discipline's taboo and because of its increasingly frequent violation by essays laced with trendy amalgams of continental philosophy and autobiographical snippets. If classic ethnography's vice was the slippage from the ideal of detachment to actual indifference, that of present-day reflexivity is the tendency for the self-absorbed Self to lose sight altogether of the culturally different Other. Despite the risks involved, as the ethnographer I must enter the discussion at this point to elucidate certain issues of method.[9]

The key concept in what follows is that of the positioned (and repositioned) subject.[j] In routine interpretive procedure, according to the methodology of hermeneutics, one can say that ethnographers reposition themselves as they go about understanding other cultures. Ethnographers begin research with a set of questions, revise them throughout the course of inquiry, and in the end emerge with different questions than they started with. One's surprise at the answer to a question, in other words, requires one to revise the question until lessening surprises or diminishing returns indicate a stopping point. This interpretive approach has been most influentially articulated within anthropology by Clifford Geertz.[k]

Interpretive method usually rests on the axiom that gifted ethnographers learn their trade by preparing themselves as broadly as possible. To follow the meandering course of ethnographic inquiry, field-workers require wide-ranging theoretical capacities and finely

---

8. Another aspect of Marxist theory absorbed by postmodernists is the emphasis on conflict. Functionalists and ethnoscientists looked for logically consistent systems. Postmodernists believe society is beset by conflict between social groups (here, the Ilongot versus the government) or between theory and practice (the Calvinist example that follows). The contradictions are not abnormalities that would be eliminated in a smoothly functioning society, but rather a fundamental part of any social system.

Max Weber's 1905 book *The Protestant Ethic and the Spirit of Capitalism* to which Rosaldo refers in this paragraph was extremely influential in anthropology and sociology. In it, Weber argued that the beliefs encouraged by Calvinist theology, particularly individualism and the moral value of work contributed directly to the rise of capitalism.

9. The fundamental implication of Rosaldo's position is that the accounts produced by ethnographers depend upon their positioning, that is, the vantage point from which they view and analyze society. Their positioning is, in turn, contingent on their life experiences rather than being derived from any uniform application of the scientific method. The logical extension of this is that postmodern ethnographies are often highly introspective. They become tales about the ethnographer's experiences. The subject of such work is generally the ethnographer's increasing understanding of themselves and the people with whom they are living. Rather than writing conventional anthropological reports, postmodernists tend to write about the process of doing fieldwork. Although Rosaldo criticizes the worst excesses of this sort of ethnography, he uses this approach himself.

tuned sensibilities. After all, one cannot predict beforehand what one will encounter in the field. One influential anthropologist, Clyde Kluckhohn, even went so far as to recommend a double initiation: first, the ordeal of psychoanalysis, and then that of fieldwork. All too often, however, this view is extended until certain prerequisites of field research appear to guarantee an authoritative ethnography. Eclectic book knowledge and a range of life experiences, along with edifying reading and self-awareness, supposedly vanquish the twin vices of ignorance and insensitivity.[10]

Although the doctrine of preparation, knowledge, and sensibility contains much to admire, one should work to undermine the false comfort that it can convey. At what point can people say that they have completed their learning or their life experience? The problem with taking this mode of preparing the ethnographer too much to heart is that it can lend a false air of security, an authoritative claim to certitude and finality that our analyses cannot have. All interpretations are provisional; they are made by positioned subjects who are prepared to know certain things and not others. Even when knowledgeable, sensitive, fluent in the language, and able to move easily in an alien cultural world, good ethnographers still have their limits, and

their analyses always are incomplete. Thus, I began to fathom the force of what Ilongots had been telling me about their losses through my own loss, and not through any systematic preparation for field research.[11]

My preparation for understanding serious loss began in 1970 with the death of my brother, shortly after his twenty-seventh birthday. By experiencing this ordeal with my mother and father, I gained a measure of insight into the trauma of a parent's losing a child. This insight informed my account, partially described earlier, of an Ilongot man's reactions to the death of his seventh child. At the same time, my bereavement was so much less than that of my parents that I could not then imagine the overwhelming force of rage possible in such grief. My former position is probably similar to that of many in the discipline. One should recognize that ethnographic knowledge tends to have the strengths and limitations given by the relative youth of fieldworkers who, for the most part, have not suffered serious losses and could have, for example, no personal knowledge of how devastating the loss of a long-term partner can be for the survivor.

In 1981 Michelle Rosaldo and I began field research among the Ifugaos of northern Luzon, Philippines. On October 11 of that year, she

---

10. Anthropologists in the 1960s were very concerned with the methodology of data gathering. Structuralists searched for mediated binaries, ethnoscientists prescribed structured interviews and neo-functionalists counted calories people produced. All wanted to create scientifically valid, replicable results. However, if anthropology is dependent on the life experiences of the anthropologist, no training or field methodology can produce the sorts of replicability and validity that anthropologists following these theories desire. Postmodernists insist on good training in language and ethnography, but they do not believe that such skills will result in a more scientific anthropology.

Clyde Kluckhohn (1905–1960) was a Harvard-based anthropologist with a long-term interest in the Navajo. In 1931 and 1932 Kluckhohn studied at the University of Vienna and became interested in psychoanalysis. He used a psychoanalytical approach in *Navajo Witchcraft* (1944) and many other papers.

11. Rosaldo argues that interpretation changes with positioning. To understand Ilongot headhunting, he had to experience grief and loss himself. In this paragraph and later, he describes those personal experiences. Personal revelation is rare in ethnography before 1970 but has become commonplace in the last half century. Some historical ethnographies contain occasional glimpses of the fieldworker. For example, E. E. Evans-Pritchard, in the introduction to *The Nuer* (1940), tells about his experience of Nuerland and his problems living there. However, the reader learns nothing of his background or family life. The difference is that Evans-Pritchard did not believe that his background had a critical bearing on his understanding of the Nuer. Rosaldo is convinced that only his personal experiences allow him to understand the Ilongot. Here and later, Rosaldo touches on experiences that are so personal they may make the reader uneasy (because of our own positioning, Michelle Rosaldo might seem like a real person to us in a way that the dead Ilongot uncle described earlier does not).

was walking along a trail with two Ifugao companions when she lost her footing and fell to her death some 65 feet down a sheer precipice into a swollen river below. Immediately on finding her body I became enraged. How could she abandon me? How could she have been so stupid as to fall? I tried to cry. I sobbed, but rage blocked the tears. Less than a month later I described this moment in my journal: "I felt like in a nightmare, the whole world around me expanding and contracting, visually and viscerally heaving. Going down I find a group of men, maybe seven or eight, standing still, silent, and I heave and sob, but no tears." An earlier experience, on the fourth anniversary of my brother's death, had taught me to recognize heaving sobs without tears as a form of anger. This anger, in a number of forms, has swept over me on many occasions since then, lasting hours and even days at a time. Such feelings can be aroused by rituals, but more often they emerge from unexpected reminders (not unlike the Ilongots' unnerving encounter with their dead uncle's voice on the tape recorder).

Lest there be any misunderstanding, bereavement should not be reduced to anger, neither for myself nor for anyone else.[l] Powerful visceral emotional states swept over me, at times separately and at other times together. I experienced the deep cutting pain of sorrow almost beyond endurance, the cadaverous cold of realizing the finality of death, the trembling beginning in my abdomen and spreading through my body, the mournful keening that started without my willing, and frequent tearful sobbing. My present purpose of revising earlier understandings of Ilongot headhunting, and not a general view of bereavement, thus focuses on anger rather than on other emotions in grief.

Writings in English especially need to emphasize the rage in grief. Although grief therapists routinely encourage awareness of anger among the bereaved, upper-middle-class Anglo-American culture tends to ignore the rage devastating losses can bring. Paradoxically, this culture's conventional wisdom usually denies the anger in grief at the same time that therapists encourage members of the invisible community of the bereaved to talk in detail about how angry their losses make them feel. My brother's death in combination with what I learned about anger from Ilongots (for them, an emotional state more publicly celebrated than denied) allowed me immediately to recognize the experience of rage.[m, 12]

Ilongot anger and my own overlap, rather like two circles, partially overlaid and partially separate. They are not identical. Alongside striking similarities, significant differences in tone, cultural form, and human consequences distinguish the "anger" animating our respective ways of grieving. My vivid fantasies, for example, about a life insurance agent who refused to recognize Michelle's death as job-related did not lead me to kill him, cut off his head, and celebrate afterward. In so speaking, I am illustrating the discipline's methodological caution against the reckless attribution of one's own categories and experiences to members of another culture. Such warnings against facile notions of universal human nature can, however, be carried too far and harden into the equally pernicious doctrine that, my own group aside, everything human is alien to me. One hopes to achieve a balance between recognizing wide-ranging human differences and the modest truism that any two human groups must have certain things in common.

Only a week before completing the initial draft of an earlier version of this introduction, I rediscovered my journal entry, written some six weeks after Michelle's death, in which I made a vow to myself about how I would return to writing anthropology, if I ever did so, "by writing Grief and a Headhunter's Rage . . ." My journal went on to reflect more broadly on death, rage, and headhunting by speaking of my "wish for the Ilongot solution; they are much more in touch with reality than Christians. So, I need a place to carry my anger—

---

12. Rosaldo's understanding is conditioned by his culture as well his experiences. Here, he points to the "Anglo-American" understanding of grief. However, note that Rosaldo is a Chicano. One of the principal motivations for postmodern interpretive anthropology is culture critique. For the postmodernist, anthropology allows the opportunity to reflect upon and analyze the culture of our own society as much as it allows for the analysis of the other. Here and later, in order for Rosaldo to examine and explain Ilongot practices, he must also examine and explain American practices. Anthropology then becomes a dialogue—a negotiation of interpretation between ethnographers, their interlocutors, and the cultures they study.

and can we say a solution of the imagination is better than theirs? And can we condemn them when we napalm villages? Is our rationale so much sounder than theirs?" All this was written in despair and rage.[13]

Not until some fifteen months after Michelle's death was I again able to begin writing anthropology. Writing the initial version of "Grief and a Headhunter's Rage" was in fact cathartic, though perhaps not in the way one would imagine. Rather than following after the completed composition, the catharsis occurred beforehand. When the initial version of this introduction was most acutely on my mind, during the month before actually beginning to write, I felt diffusely depressed and ill with a fever. Then one day an almost literal fog lifted and words began to flow. It seemed less as if I were doing the writing than that the words were writing themselves through me.[14]

My use of personal experience serves as a vehicle for making the quality and intensity of the rage in Ilongot grief more readily accessible to readers than certain more detached modes of composition. At the same time, by invoking personal experience as an analytical category one risks easy dismissal. Unsympathetic readers could reduce this introduction to an act of mourning or a mere report on my discovery of the anger possible in bereavement. Frankly, this introduction is both and more. An act of mourning, a personal report, *and* a critical analysis of anthropological method, it simultaneously encompasses a number of distinguishable processes, no one of which cancels out the others. Similarly, I argue in what follows that ritual in general and Ilongot headhunting in particular form the intersection of multiple coexisting social processes. Aside from revising the ethnographic record, the paramount claim made here concerns how my own mourning and consequent reflection on Ilongot bereavement, rage, and headhunting raise methodological issues of general concern in anthropology and the human sciences.[15]

DEATH IN ANTHROPOLOGY

Anthropology favors interpretations that equate analytical "depth" with cultural "elaboration." Many studies focus on visibly bounded arenas where one can observe formal and repetitive events, such as ceremonies, rituals, and games. Similarly, studies of word play are more likely to focus on jokes as programmed monologues than on the less scripted, more free-wheeling improvised interchanges of witty banter. Most ethnographers prefer to study events that have definite locations in space with marked centers and outer edges. Temporally, they have middles and endings. Historically, they appear to repeat identical structures by seemingly doing things today as they were done yesterday. Their qualities of fixed definition liberate such events from the untidiness of everyday life so that they can be "read" like articles, books, or, as we now say, *texts*.[16]

---

13. Notice the important role that empathy plays in Rosaldo's analysis. He warns against false attribution of our character traits to the other, but his essential insight into Ilongot headhunting occurs only after he has personal experiences that allow him to identify with the Ilongot in a visceral way. Also consider that although the passages cited by Rosaldo were written in grief and anger, he is suggesting that "a solution of the imagination" is no better than assuaging one's grief by taking the life of a random, innocent person—a radical statement of cultural relativism indeed.

14. Postmodernists remind us that most of what anthropologists do, we do for our own purposes. Here, Rosaldo's anthropological insights come either as revelation or therapy. As he reports later, writing this piece was a cathartic act and an enormously personal one.

15. Turner's idea of multivocality runs deeply through Rosaldo's work. Just as symbols do not necessarily have single meanings, cultural action does not have discrete, unique causes. Instead, causation is always multiple. This essay is no exception: For Rosaldo, it is an "act of mourning, a personal report, and an analysis of anthropological method."

16. Rosaldo's analysis of anthropological interpretations of mourning is a critique of historical ways of doing ethnography. Rosaldo suggests that the way ethnography is written—the way it delimits events by time,

Guided by their emphasis on self-contained entities, ethnographies written in accord with classic norms consider death under the rubric of ritual rather than bereavement. Indeed, the subtitles of even recent ethnographies on death make the emphasis on ritual explicit. William Douglas's *Death in Murelaga* is subtitled *Funerary Ritual in a Spanish Basque Village;* Richard Huntington and Peter Metcalf's *Celebrations of Death* is subtitled *The Anthropology of Mortuary Ritual;* Peter Metcalf's *A Borneo Journey into Death* is subtitled *Berawan Eschatology from Its Rituals.*[n] Ritual itself is defined by its formality and routine; under such descriptions, it more nearly resembles a recipe, a fixed program, or a book of etiquette than an open-ended human process.

Ethnographies that in this manner eliminate intense emotions not only distort their descriptions but also remove potentially key variables from their explanations. When anthropologist William Douglas, for example, announces his project in *Death in Murelaga,* he explains that his objective is to use death and funerary ritual "as a heuristic device with which to approach the study of rural Basque society."[o] In other words, the primary object of study is social structure, not death, and certainly not bereavement. The author begins his analysis by saying, "Death is not always fortuitous or unpredictable."[p] He goes on to describe how an old woman, ailing with the infirmities of her age, welcomed her death. The description largely ignores the perspective of the most bereaved survivors, and instead vacillates between those of the old woman and a detached observer.

Undeniably, certain people do live a full life and suffer so greatly in their decrepitude that they embrace the relief death can bring. Yet the problem with making an ethnography's major case study focus on "a very easy death"[q] (I use Simone de Beauvoir's title with irony, as she did) is not only its lack of representativeness but also that it makes death in general appear as routine for the survivors as this particular one apparently was for the deceased. Were the old woman's sons and daughters untouched by her death? The case study shows less about how people cope with death than about how death can be made to appear routine, thereby fitting neatly into the author's view of funerary ritual as a mechanical programmed unfolding of prescribed acts. "To the Basque," says Douglas, "ritual is order and order is ritual."[r, 17]

Douglas captures only one extreme in the range of possible deaths. Putting the accent on the routine aspects of ritual conveniently conceals the agony of such unexpected early deaths as parents losing a grown child or a mother dying in childbirth. Concealed in such descriptions are the agonies of the survivors who muddle through shifting, powerful emotional states. Although Douglas acknowledges the distinction between the bereaved members of the deceased's domestic group and the more public ritualistic group, he writes his account primarily from the viewpoint of the latter. He masks the emotional force of bereavement by reducing funerary ritual to orderly routine.[18]

---

actors, physical location, and so on—is, in itself, the imposition of a certain sort of reality upon ethnographic material. To postmodernists, such boundaries are artificial, the products of specific observers or specific individuals involved. To report on an event, the ethnographer draws discrete boundaries around it. The type of boundary drawn around the event critically influences its interpretation.

17. Rosaldo here shows an example of how the preconceptions of the investigator can exert a powerful influence over the ethnography produced. Notice that Rosaldo is not accusing William Douglas (b. 1939) of misreporting but rather of choosing a point of view within Basque society that confirms his own understanding of that society.

In *A Very Easy Death* (1966), the French philosopher and pioneering feminist Simone de Beauvoir (1908–1986) describes the death of her mother from cancer and her reaction to it. De Beauvoir wrote, "For me, my mother had always existed and I had never seriously thought that some day, that soon I should see her go."

18. One element of Rosaldo's critique of anthropology is a recurring theme first expressed by Franz Boas in his attack on the evolutionists. According to Rosaldo, Douglas is not producing ethnography driven by observation but using specific case examples to back his theoretical position. To some degree, this is also true of the

Surely, human beings mourn both in ritual settings *and* in the informal settings of everyday life. Consider the evidence that willy-nilly spills over the edges in Godfrey Wilson's classic anthropological account of "conventions of burial" among the Nyakyusa of South Africa:

That some at least of those who attend a Nyakyusa burial are moved by grief it is easy to establish. I have heard people talking regretfully in ordinary conversation of a man's death; I have seen a man whose sister had just died walk over alone towards her grave and weep quietly by himself without any parade of grief; and I have heard of a man killing himself because of his grief for a dead son.[5, 19]

Note that all the instances Wilson witnesses or hears about happen outside the circumscribed sphere of formal ritual. People converse among themselves, walk alone and silently weep, or more impulsively commit suicide. The work of grieving, probably universally, occurs both within obligatory ritual acts and in more everyday settings where people find themselves alone or with close kin.

In Nyakyusa burial ceremonies, powerful emotional states also become present in the ritual itself, which is more than a series of obligatory acts. Men say they dance the passions of their bereavement, which includes a complex mix of anger, fear, and grief:

"This war dance (*ukukina*)," said an old man, "is mourning, we are mourning the dead man. We dance because there is war in our hearts. A passion of grief and fear exasperates us (*ilyyojo likutusila*)." . . . *Elyojo* means a passion or grief, anger or fear; *ukusila* means to annoy or exasperate beyond endurance. In explaining *ukusila* one man put it like this: "If a man continually insults me then he exasperates me (*ukusila*) so that I want to fight him." Death is a fearful and grievous event that exasperates those [men] nearly concerned and makes them want to fight.[1]

Descriptions of the dance and subsequent quarrels, even killings, provide ample evidence of the emotional intensity involved. The articulate testimony by Wilson's informants makes it obvious that even the most intense sentiments can be studied by ethnographers.

Despite such exceptions as Wilson, the general rule seems to be that one should tidy things up as much as possible by wiping away the tears and ignoring the tantrums. Most anthropological studies of death eliminate emotions by assuming the position of the most detached observer.[u] Such studies usually conflate the ritual process with the process of mourning, equate ritual with the obligatory, and ignore the relation between ritual and everyday life. The bias that favors formal ritual risks assuming the answers to questions that most need to be asked. Do rituals, for example, always reveal cultural depth?[20]

Most analysts who equate death with funerary ritual assume that rituals store encapsulated wisdom as if it were a microcosm of its encompassing cultural macrocosm. One recent

---

symbolic anthropologists, with whom Rosaldo has great sympathy. Symbolic anthropologists tended to concentrate on the analysis of ceremony and other symbolically complex behavior. They saw these events as the points at which culture displays its greatest richness, therefore making interpretive analysis more productive.

19. Godfrey Wilson (1908–1944), whom Rosaldo quotes here, was the husband of Monica Wilson (1908–1982). The Wilsons worked together in Tanganyika (now Tanzania) and Northern Rhodesia (now Zambia) in the 1930s and 1940s. For more on the Wilsons, see Turner, essay 25, note 2.

20. The notion that great symbolic complexity does not necessarily indicate great meaning to the people involved is critical to Rosaldo's concept of force. If this is true, exhaustive interpretive treatments of ceremonies may not aid much in understanding culture. Great cultural depth may be present in the Nyakyusa ceremonies described in this passage, but as Rosaldo notes later, despite great symbolism, there was little depth in the ceremonies he attended for his brother and wife. The notion of force stands in opposition to the symbolic and interpretive anthropology of Geertz and Turner. These anthropologists propose that anthropologists should analyze society by finding complex rituals and exploring their layers of meaning as one might peel an onion. For Rosaldo, complexity is not necessarily a good index of meaning.

study of death and mourning, for example, confidently begins by affirming that rituals embody "the collective wisdom of many cultures."[v] Yet this generalization surely requires case-by-case investigation against a broader range of alternative hypotheses.[21]

At the polar extremes, rituals either display cultural depth or brim over with platitudes. In the former case, rituals indeed encapsulate a culture's wisdom; in the latter instance, they act as catalysts that precipitate processes whose unfolding occurs over subsequent months or even years. Many rituals, of course, do both by combining a measure of wisdom with a comparable dose of platitudes.

My own experience of bereavement and rituals fits the platitudes and catalyst model better than that of microcosmic deep culture. Even a careful analysis of the language and symbolic action during the two funerals for which I was a chief mourner would reveal precious little about the experience of bereavement.[w] This statement, of course, should not lead anyone to derive a universal from somebody else's personal knowledge. Instead, it should encourage ethnographers to ask whether a ritual's wisdom is deep or conventional, and whether its process is immediately transformative or but a single step in a lengthy series of ritual and everyday events.

In attempting to grasp the cultural force of rage and other powerful emotional states, both formal ritual and the informal practices of everyday life provide crucial insight. Thus, cultural descriptions should seek out force as well as thickness, and they should extend from well-defined rituals to myriad less circumscribed practices.

GRIEF, RAGE, AND ILONGOT HEADHUNTING

When applied to Ilongot headhunting, the view of ritual as a storehouse of collective wisdom aligns headhunting with expiatory sacrifice. The raiders call the spirits of the potential victims, bid their ritual farewells, and seek favorable omens along the trail. Ilongot men vividly recall the hunger and deprivation they endure over the days and even weeks it takes to move cautiously toward the place where they set up an ambush and await the first person who happens along. Once the raiders kill their victim, they toss away the head rather than keep it as a trophy. In tossing away the head, they claim by analogy to cast away their life burdens, including the rage in their grief.[22]

Before a raid, men describe their state of being by saying that the burdens of life have made them heavy and entangled, like a tree with vines clinging to it. They say that a successfully completed raid makes them feel light of step and ruddy in complexion. The collective energy of the celebration with its song, music, and dance reportedly gives the participants a sense of well-being. The expiatory ritual process involves cleansing and catharsis.

The analysis just sketched regards ritual as a timeless, self-contained process. Without denying the insight in this approach, its limits must also be considered. Imagine, for example,

---

21. Cultural force, though it may not be present in ritual, frequently appears where powerful emotional states such as rage, anger, fear, or love are expressed. However, traditional ethnography, modeled on scientific writing, deals poorly with these. The scientific trope in writing demands that reporting be dispassionate and that writers adopt an emotionally neutral stance toward their subjects. Paul Stoller (b. 1947) contends that "vivid descriptions of the sensoria of ethnographic situations have been largely overshadowed by a dry analytic prose" (1989: 8). Although it may be relatively easy to describe a ritual in such prose, Stoller claims that characterizations of others as they lead their social lives are lost in this sort of writing. He argues for an anthropology that relies more on descriptions of nonvisual sensory information.

22. In this relatively brief section of the essay, Rosaldo gives an analysis of Ilongot headhunting that is sensitive to the issues he raises throughout the paper. Rosaldo attempts to break through the boundaries imposed by the act of analysis. For many postmodernists, anthropology is, above all, the acts of observing and writing, which necessarily impose boundaries upon events. Because of this, anthropologists tend to write about self-contained events. To escape from this type of analysis, Rosaldo proposes instead that Ilongot headhunting results from the intersection of three more or less independent processes.

exorcism rituals described as if they were complete in themselves, rather than being linked with larger processes unfolding before and after the ritual period. Through what processes does the afflicted person recover or continue to be afflicted after the ritual? What are the social consequences of recovery or its absence? Failure to consider such questions diminishes the force of such afflictions and therapies for which the formal ritual is but a phase. Still other questions apply to differently positioned subjects, including the person afflicted, the healer, and the audience. In all cases, the problem involves the delineation of processes that occur before and after, as well as during, the ritual moment.

Let us call the notion of a self-contained sphere of deep cultural activity the *microcosmic view,* and an alternative view *ritual as a busy intersection.* In the latter case, ritual appears as a place where a number of distinct social processes intersect. The crossroads simply provides a space for distinct trajectories to traverse, rather than containing them in complete encapsulated form. From this perspective, Ilongot headhunting stands at the confluence of three analytically separable processes.

The first process concerns whether or not it is an opportune time to raid. Historical conditions determine the possibilities of raiding, which range from frequent to likely to unlikely to impossible. These conditions include American colonial efforts at pacification, the Great Depression, World War II, revolutionary movements in the surrounding lowlands, feuding among Ilongot groups, and the declaration of martial law in 1972. Ilongots use the analogy of hunting to speak of such historical vicissitudes. Much as Ilongot huntsmen say they cannot know when game will cross their path or whether their arrows will strike the target, so certain historical forces that condition their existence remain beyond their control. My book *Ilongot Headhunting, 1883–1974*

explores the impact of historical factors on Ilongot headhunting.[23]

Second, young men coming of age undergo a protracted period of personal turmoil during which they desire nothing so much as to take a head. During this troubled period, they seek a life partner and contemplate the traumatic dislocation of leaving their families of origin and entering their new wife's household as a stranger. Young men weep, sing, and burst out in anger because of their fierce desire to take a head and wear the coveted red hornbill earrings that adorn the ears of men who already have, as Ilongots say, arrived *(tabi).* Volatile, envious, passionate (at least according to their own cultural stereotype of the young unmarried man [*buintaw*]), they constantly lust to take a head. Michelle and I began fieldwork among the Ilongots only a year after abandoning our unmarried youths; hence our ready empathy with youthful turbulence. Her book on Ilongot notions of self explores the passionate anger of young men as they come of age.

Third, older men are differently positioned than their younger counterparts. Because they have already beheaded somebody, they can wear the red hornbill earrings so coveted by youths. Their desire to headhunt grows less from chronic adolescent turmoil than from more intermittent acute agonies of loss. After the death of somebody to whom they are closely attached, older men often inflict on themselves vows of abstinence, not to be lifted until the day they participate in a successful headhunting raid. These deaths can cover a range of instances from literal death, whether through natural causes or beheading, to social death where, for example, a man's wife runs off with another man. In all cases, the rage born of devastating loss animates the older men's desire to raid. This anger at abandonment is irreducible in that nothing at a deeper level explains it. Although certain analysts argue against the dreaded last analysis, the

---

23. The idea of positioning is again crucial. Rosaldo has spoken earlier of the positioning of the anthropologist; here the positioning of the Ilongot becomes the main object of analysis. Rosaldo does not see Ilongot society as timeless, harmonious, and undifferentiated (as Émile Durkheim, for example, might) but as fixed in historical time and composed of diverse individuals and groups with different interests. Headhunting happens when historical circumstances make it possible and when the emotional states of young and old men coincide.

linkage of grief, rage, and headhunting has no other known explanation,[24]

My earlier understandings of Ilongot head-hunting missed the fuller significance of how older men experience loss and rage. Older men prove critical in this context because they, not the youths, set the processes of headhunting in motion. Their rage is intermittent, whereas that of youths is continuous. In the equation of headhunting, older men are the variable and younger men are the constant. Culturally speaking, older men are endowed with knowl-edge and stamina that their juniors have not yet attained, hence they care for (*saysay*) and lead (*bukur*) the younger men when they raid.

In a preliminary survey of the literature on headhunting, I found that the lifting of mourn-ing prohibitions frequently occurs after taking a head. The notion that youthful anger and older men's rage lead them to take heads is more plausible than such commonly reported "explanations" of headhunting as the need to acquire mystical "soul stuff" or personal names.[x] Because the discipline correctly rejects stereo-types of the "bloodthirsty savage," it must inves-tigate how headhunters create an intense desire to decapitate their fellow humans. The human sciences must explore the cultural force of emo-tions with a view to delineating the passions that animate certain forms of human conduct.

SUMMARY

The ethnographer, as a positioned subject, grasps certain human phenomena better than others. He or she occupies a position or struc-tural location and observes with a particular angle of vision. Consider, for example, how age, gender, being an outsider, and association with a neocolonial regime influence what the ethnographer learns. The notion of position also refers to how life experiences both enable and inhibit particular kinds of insight. In the case at hand, nothing in my own experience equipped me even to imagine the anger possible in bereavement until after Michelle Rosaldo's death in 1981. Only then was I in a position to grasp the force of what Ilongots had repeatedly told me about grief, rage, and headhunting. By the same token, so-called natives are also positioned subjects who have a distinctive mix of insight and blindness. Consider the struc-tural positions of older versus younger Ilongot men, or the differing positions of chief mourn-ers versus those less involved during a funeral. My discussion of anthropological writings on death often achieved its effects simply by shift-ing from the position of those least involved to that of the chief mourners.[25]

Cultural depth does not always equal cul-tural elaboration. Think simply of the speaker who is filibustering. The language used can sound elaborate as it heaps word on word, but surely it is not deep. Depth should be separated from the presence or absence of elaboration. By the same token, one-line explanations can be vacuous or pithy. The concept of force calls attention to an enduring intensity in human conduct that can occur with or without the dense elaboration conventionally associated with cultural depth. Although relatively without elaboration in speech, song, or ritual, the rage of older Ilongot men who have suffered devas-tating losses proves enormously consequential in that, foremost among other things, it leads them to behead their fellow humans. Thus, the notion of force involves both affective intensity and significant consequences that unfold over a long period of time.

Similarly, rituals do not always encapsulate deep cultural wisdom. At times they instead

24. In analyzing the headhunting of the older men, Rosaldo applies his notion of force. He insists that there is no meaningful way to analyze Ilongot rage other than to record it. His insistence that there can be no other explanation for the linkage between grief, rage, and headhunting is extremely provocative. Many anthro-pologists find it difficult to accept. Rosaldo has, after all, provided other explanations including the exchange theory that appears earlier in this selection and the "soul stuff" mentioned below. Rosaldo and his Ilongot informants reject these explanations. Are you convinced that no other explanations are possible?

25. Postmodern anthropology collapses many of the distinctions upon which more traditional anthropol-ogy is based. There is no longer an observer and an observed. Instead, there are individuals prepared to know certain things and not others. These are both anthropologists and members of the cultures the anthropolo-gists are analyzing. Accepting Rosaldo's critique renders the distinction between emic and etic meaningless.

contain the wisdom of **Polonius**. Although certain rituals both reflect and create ultimate values, others simply bring people together and deliver a set of platitudes that enable them to go on with their lives. Rituals serve as vehicles for processes that occur both before and after the period of their performance. Funeral rituals, for example, do not "contain" all the complex processes of bereavement. Ritual and bereavement should not be collapsed into one another because they neither fully encapsulate nor fully explain one another. Instead, rituals are often but points along a number of longer processual trajectories; hence, my image of ritual as a crossroads where distinct life processes intersect.[y, 26]

The notion of ritual as a busy intersection anticipates the critical assessment of the concept of culture developed in the following chapters. In contrast with the classic view, which posits culture as a self-contained whole made up of coherent patterns, culture can arguably be conceived as a more porous array of intersections where distinct processes crisscross from within and beyond its borders. Such heterogeneous processes often derive from differences of age, gender, class, race, and sexual orientation.

This book argues that a sea change in cultural studies has eroded once-dominant conceptions of truth and objectivity. The truth of objectivism—absolute, universal, and timeless—has lost its monopoly status. It now competes, on more nearly equal terms, with the truths of case studies that are embedded in local contexts, shaped by local interests, and colored by local perceptions. The agenda for social analysis has shifted to include not only eternal verities and lawlike generalizations but also political processes, social changes, and human differences. Such terms as *objectivity, neutrality,* and *impar-*

tiality refer to subject positions once endowed with great institutional authority, but they are arguably neither more nor less valid than those of more engaged, yet equally perceptive, knowledgeable social actors. Social analysis must now grapple with the realization that its objects of analysis are also analyzing subjects who critically interrogate ethnographers—their writings, their ethics, and their politics.[27]

AUTHOR'S NOTES

a. In contrasting Moroccan and Javanese forms of mysticism, Clifford Geertz found it necessary to distinguish the "force" of cultural patterning from its "scope" (Clifford Geertz, *Islam Observed* [New Haven, Conn: Yale University Press, 1968]). He distinguished force from scope in this manner: "By 'force' I mean the thoroughness with which such a pattern is internalized in the personalities of the individuals who adopt it, its centrality or marginality in their lives" (p. 111). "By 'scope,' on the other hand, I mean the range of social contexts within which religious considerations are regarded as having more or less direct relevance" (p. 112). In his later works, Geertz developed the notion of scope more than that of force. Unlike Geertz, who emphasizes processes of internalization within individual personalities, my use of the term force stresses the concept of the positioned subject.

b. Anthropologists have long studied the vocabulary of the emotions in other cultures (see, e.g., Hildred Geertz, "The Vocabulary of Emotion: A Study of Javanese Socialization Processes," *Psychiatry* 22 [1959]: 225–37). For a recent review essay on anthropological writings on emotions, see Catherine Lutz and Geoffrey M. White, "The Anthropology of Emotions," *Annual Review of Anthropology* 15 (1986):405–36.

c. The two ethnographies on the Ilongots are Michelle Rosaldo, *Knowledge and Passion: Ilongot Notions of Self and Social Life* (New York: Cambridge University Press, 1980), and Renato Rosaldo, *Ilongot Headhunting, 1883–*

---

26. **"Polonius"**: a character in *Hamlet,* is Ophelia's father and a minister to the king. He dispenses greeting-card wisdom.

27. Rosaldo makes several important points in closing. He refers to the fact that in a world where education in Western languages is increasingly widespread, people who were traditionally the subjects of ethnography are reading ethnographies and sometimes writing their own. Anthropologists of an earlier age such as Evans-Pritchard did not have to worry about how the Nuer were going to react to his description of them. Current anthropologists write with the knowledge that members of the group they are studying will read and critique their work. This approach has changed the nature of anthropology.

More controversially, Rosaldo asserts that the interpretations of anthropologists must be judged as neither more nor less valid than those of other astute observers. By extension, this implies that anthropological training confers no particular authority. If this is the case, what should be the role of the "human sciences," among which Rosaldo has included anthropology?

1974: A Study in Society and History (Stanford, Calif: Stanford University Press, 1980). Our field research among the Ilongots was financed by a National Science Foundation predoctoral fellowship, National Science Foundation Research Grants GS–1509 and GS–40788, and a Mellon Award for junior faculty from Stanford University. A Fulbright Grant financed a two-month stay in the Philippines during 1981.

d. Lest the hypothesis Insan rejected appear utterly implausible, one should mention that at least one group does link a version of exchange theory to headhunting. Peter Metcalf reports that, among the Berawan of Borneo, "Death has a chain reaction quality to it. There is a considerable anxiety that, unless something is done to break the chain, death will follow upon death. The logic of this is now plain: The unquiet soul kills, and so creates more unquiet souls" (Peter Metcalf, *A Borneo Journey into Death: Berawan Eschatology from Its Rituals* [Philadelphia: University of Pennsylvania Press, 1982], p. 127).

e. R. Rosaldo, *Ilongot Headhunting, 1883–1974*, p. 286.

f. Ibid., p. 288.

g. M. Rosaldo, *Knowledge and Passion*, p. 33.

h. See A. R. Radcliffe-Brown, *Structure and Function in Primitive Society* (London: Cohen and West, Ltd., 1952), pp. 133–52. For a broader debate on the "functions" of ritual, see the essays by Bronislaw Malinowski, A. R. Radcliffe-Brown, and George C. Homans, in *Reader in Comparative Religion: An Anthropological Approach* (4th ed.), ed. William A. Lessa and Evon Z. Vogt (New York: Harper & Row, 1979), pp. 37–62.

i. Max Weber, *The Protestant Ethic and the Spirit of Capitalism* (New York: Charles Scribner's Sons, 1958).

j. A key antecedent to what I have called the "positioned subject" is Alfred Schutz, *Collected Papers*, vol. 1, *The Problem of Social Reality*, ed. and intro. Maurice Natanson (The Hague: Martinus Nijhoff, 1971). See also, e.g., Aaron Cicourel, *Method and Measurement in Sociology* (Glencoe, Ill.: The Free Press, 1964) and Gerald Berreman, *Behind Many Masks: Ethnography and Impression Management in a Himalayan Village*, Monograph No. 4 (Ithaca, N.Y.: Society for Applied Anthropology, 1962). For an early anthropological article on how differently positioned subjects interpret the "same" culture in different ways, see John W. Bennett, "The Interpretation of Pueblo Culture," *Southwestern Journal of Anthropology* 2 (1946): 361–74.

k. Clifford Geertz, *The Interpretation of Cultures* (New York: Basic Books, 1974) and *Local Knowledge: Further Essays in Interpretive Anthropology* (New York: Basic Books, 1983).

l. Although anger appears so often in bereavement as to be virtually universal, certain notable exceptions do occur. Clifford Geertz, for example, depicts Javanese funerals as follows: "The mood of a Javanese funeral is not one of hysterical bereavement, unrestrained sobbing, or even of formalized cries of grief for the deceased's departure. Rather, it is a calm, undemonstrative, almost languid letting go, a brief ritualized relinquishment of a relationship no longer possible" (Geertz, *The Interpretation of Cultures*, p. 153). In cross-cultural perspective, the anger in grief presents itself in different degrees (including zero), in different forms, and with different consequences.

m. The Ilongot notion of anger (*liget*) is regarded as dangerous in its violent excesses, but also as life enhancing in that, for example, it provides energy for work. See the extensive discussion in M. Rosaldo, *Knowledge and Passion*.

n. William Douglas, *Death in Murelaga: Funerary Ritual in a Spanish Basque Village* (Seattle: University of Washington Press, 1969); Richard Huntington and Peter Metcalf, *Celebrations of Death: The Anthropology of Mortuary Ritual* (New York: Cambridge University Press, 1979); Metcalf, *A Borneo Journey into Death*.

o. Douglas, *Death in Murelaga*, p. 209.

p. Ibid., p. 19.

q. Simone de Beauvoir, *A Very Easy Death* (Harmondsworth, United Kingdom: Penguin Books, 1969).

r. Douglas, *Death in Murelaga*, p. 75.

s. Godfrey Wilson, *Nyakyusa Conventions of Burial* (Johannesburg: The University of Witwatersrand Press, 1939), pp. 22–23. (Reprinted from Bantu Studies.)

t. Ibid., p. 13.

u. In his survey of works on death published during the 1960s, for example, Johannes Fabian found that the four major anthropological journals carried only nine papers on the topic, most of which "dealt only with the purely ceremonial aspects of death" (Johannes Fabian, "How Others Die: Reflections on the Anthropology of Death," in *Death in American Experience*, ed. A. Mack [New York: Schocken, 1973], p. 178).

v. Huntington and Metcalf, *Celebrations of Death*, p. 1.

w. Arguably, ritual works differently for those most afflicted by a particular death than for those least so. Funerals may distance the former from overwhelming emotions whereas they may draw the latter closer to strongly felt sentiments (see T. J. Scheff, *Catharsis in Healing, Ritual, and Drama* [Berkeley: University of California Press, 1979]). Such issues can be investigated through the notion of the positioned subject.

x. For a discussion of cultural motives for headhunting, see Robert McKinley, "Human and Proud of It! A Structural Treatment of Headhunting Rites and the Social Definition of Enemies," in *Studies in Borneo Societies: Social Process and Anthropological Explanation*, ed. G. Appell (DeKalb, Ill.: Center for Southeast Asian Studies, Northern Illinois University, 1976), pp. 92–126; Rodney Needham, "Skulls and Causality," *Man* 11 (1976): 71–88; Michelle Rosaldo, "Skulls and Causality," *Man* 12 (1977): 168–170.

y. Pierre Bourdieu, *Outline of a Theory of Practice* (New York: Cambridge University Press, 1977), p. 1.

30. Anthropology and the Savage Slot: The Poetics and Politics of Otherness[1]

Michel-Rolph Trouillot (1949–2012)

ANTHROPOLOGY faces an unprecedented wave of challenges that require an archaeology of the discipline and a careful examination of its implicit premises. The postmodernist critique of anthropology, which is now the most vocal and direct response to these challenges in the United States, falls short of building that archaeology because it tends to treat the discipline as a closed discourse. In contradistinction, I contend that the internal tropes of anthropology matter much less than the larger discursive field within which anthropology operates and upon whose existence it is premised. A cultural critique of anthropology requires a historicization of that entire field. New directions will come only from the new vantage points discovered through such a critique.[2]

CHALLENGES AND OPPORTUNITIES

Academic disciplines do not create their fields of significance, they only legitimize particular organizations of meaning. They filter and rank—and in that sense, they truly *discipline*—contested arguments and themes that often precede them. In doing so, they continuously expand, restrict or modify in diverse ways their distinctive arsenals or tropes, the types of statements they deem acceptable. But the poetics and politics of the "slots" within which disciplines operate do not dictate the enunciative relevance of these slots. There is no direct correlation between the "electoral politics" of a discipline and its political relevance. By "electoral politics," I mean the set of institu-

---

From *Recapturing Anthropology: Working in the Present* (1991)

1. This essay was originally prepared for a 1989 seminar at the School for American Studies in Santa Fe, New Mexico. The seminar brought a group of eminent anthropologists together to consider the impact of postmodernism on anthropology. Members of the seminar group included Lilia Abu-Lughod, Sherry Ortner, and Arjun Appadurai, whose essays appear in this book. Trouillot first published this essay in 1991. He published a revised version in 2003. We present the 1991 version since it appeared contemporaneously with the Rosaldo essay that also appears in this section. There are few differences between his two versions. We will mention important differences in our notes.

Due to space limitations, we have not included Trouillot's many references. Readers will find them in the original publication.

2. Trouillot's opening paragraph reflects the influence of Michel Foucault. In the 1960s, Foucault referred to his historical method as archaeology. He uses this term first in *Madness and Civilization* (1961). For Foucault, all thinking involved implicit rules that determine what it is possible to think. People are largely unaware of such rules. Foucault hoped to use literary and historical works to unearth the "general structure of the system in which [their authors] thought and wrote" (Gutting 2005: 32). Thus, Trouillot's "archaeology of the discipline" does not attempt to determine the specific direct history of anything but rather the unconscious terms of understanding and discourse that conditioned how people of an era understood themselves, each other, and the world around them.

tionalized practices and relations of power that influence the production of knowledge from within academe: academic filiations, the mechanisms of institutionalization, the organization of power within and across departments, the market value of publish-or-perish prestige, and other worldly issues that include, but expand way beyond, the maneuvering we usually refer to as "academic politics." Changes in the types of statements; produced as "acceptable" within a discipline, regulated as they are—if only in part—by these "electoral politics," do not necessarily modify the larger field of operation, and especially the enunciative context of that discipline. Changes in the explicit criteria of acceptability do not automatically relieve the historical weight of the field of significance that the discipline inherited at birth. More likely, the burden of the past is alleviated when the sociohistorical conditions that obtained at the time of emergence have changed so much that practitioners face a choice between complete oblivion and fundamental redirection. At one point in time alchemists become chemists or cease to be—but the transformation is one that few alchemists can predict and even fewer would wish.[3]

Anthropology is no exception to this scenario. Like all academic disciplines, it inherited a field of significance that preceded its formalization. Like many of the human sciences it now faces dramatically new historical conditions of performance. Like any discourse, it can find new directions only if it modifies the boundaries within which it operates. . . . These boundaries not only predated the emergence of anthropology as a discipline, but they also prescribed anthropology's role (and ethnography's ultimate relevance) to an extent not yet unveiled. Anthropology fills a preestablished compartment within a wider symbolic field: the "savage" slot of a thematic trilogy that helped to constitute the West as we know it. A critical and reflexive anthropology requires, beyond the self-indulgent condemnation of traditional techniques and tropes, a reappraisal of this symbolic organization upon which anthropological discourse is premised.[4]

---

3. Here, Trouillot uses *discipline* both in the sense of academic field and in a Foucauldian sense. For Foucault, discipline is one of the ways in which power regulates the behavior of individuals in society. Foucault's famous example of discipline is the panopticon (see essay 28, note 12). However, for Foucault, the term refers to more than just the structure of space. Discipline uses the techniques of hierarchical observation, a process of normalizing judgment that compares individuals to each other, and systems of examination. The effect of the application of these is to produce "docile bodies." Academic disciplines, such as anthropology, are systems of power that use these techniques (both in the evaluation of students and in the evaluation of colleagues). Trouillot argues that the use of such discipline structures individual prestige as well as acceptable research and results within anthropology (and by extension all other academic fields). This action of discipline is independent of the value of any findings or results produced.

4. In the section "Challengers and Opportunities," Trouillot lays out the points that are critical to understanding this essay. First, he claims that academic disciplines legitimize "particular organizations of meaning." Because disciplines filter and rank the information that precedes them, they determine what is considered acceptable information, creating the "slot" within which they operate. Trouillot argues that anthropology, like other disciplines, has inherited a slot, the "savage slot," that is comprised of three themes (the "thematique") that have helped create Westerners' understandings of themselves. However, anthropology risks slipping into irrelevance if anthropologists do not understand and contest this thematique.

To many, anthropology seemed to be in crisis in the late 1980s. There were multiple reasons people felt this way, but three were widely shared. First, many felt that, if the subject matter of anthropology was isolated groups of people living "traditional" lifestyles, anthropology was simply running out of people to study. It was increasingly obvious that there were few places that modernity had not reached. Second, natives were increasingly talking back to anthropologists, and many had unpleasant things to say. Third, the postmodern critique challenged the meaning, accuracy, and importance of much of what anthropologists had written. *Writing Culture: The Poetics and Politics of Culture*, a collection of essays edited by James Clifford (b. 1945) and George Marcus (b. 1946), was a key work of postmodern criticism and was particularly influential. Trouillot refers to it numerous times in this essay. Like the book in which this essay first appeared, *Writing Culture* was the product of a seminar at the School for American Studies in Santa Fe.

Anthropology's future depends much on its ability to contest the savage slot and the *thematique* that constructs this slot. The times are ripe for such questioning. More important, solutions that fall short of this challenge can only push the discipline toward irrelevance, however much they may reflect serious concerns. In that light, current calls for reflexivity in the United States are not products of chance, the casual convergence of individual projects. Neither are they a passing fad, the accidental effect of debates that stormed philosophy and literary theory.[a] Rather, they are timid, spontaneous—and in that sense genuinely American—responses to major changes in the relations between anthropology and the wider world, provincial expressions of wider concerns, allusions to opportunities yet to be seized. What are those changes? What are these concerns? What are the opportunities?

On sheer empirical grounds, the differences between Western and non-Western societies are blurrier than ever before. Anthropology's answer to this ongoing transformation has been typically ad hoc and haphazard. The criteria according to which certain populations are deemed legitimate objects of research continue to vary with departments, with granting agencies, with practitioners, and even with the mood shifts of individual researchers. Amid the confusion, more anthropologists reenter the West cautiously, through the back door; after paying their dues elsewhere. By and large this reentry is no better theorized than were previous departures for faraway lands.[b]

While some anthropologists are rediscovering the West without ever naming it, what "the West" stands for is itself an object of debate, within and outside the gates of academe. The reactionary search for a fundamental Western corpus of "great texts" by many intellectuals and bureaucrats in the English-speaking world is both the reflection of a wider conflict and a particular response to the uncertainties stirred by this conflict. Interestingly, few anthropologists have intervened in that debate. Fewer even among those thought to be at the forefront of the discipline have deigned to address directly the issue of Western monumentalism, with one or two exceptions (e.g., Rosaldo 1989). Even more interestingly, anthropological theory remains irrelevant to—and unused by—either side of the "great texts" debate, rhetorical references notwithstanding. Today, the statement that any canon necessarily eliminates an unspecified set of experiences need not come only from anthropology—thanks, of course, to the past diffusion of anthropology itself, but thanks especially to changes in the world and to the experiences that express and motivate these changes. Minorities of all kinds can and do voice their cultural claims, not on the basis of explicit theories of culture but in the name of historical authenticity. They enter the debate not as academics—or not only as academics—but as situated individuals with rights to historicity. They speak in the first person, signing their arguments with an "I" or a "we," rather than invoking the ahistorical voice of reason, justice, or civilization.[5]

Trouillot will return to the idea of a thematic trilogy numerous times throughout the essay. He does not tell you precisely what the three parts are until much later; however, we think it is useful to have them now. Trouillot's trilogy is order-utopia-savagery. Order refers to the Western belief in reason as constructed by the philosophers of the Enlightenment. Utopia denotes the creation of a genre of literature during the Enlightenment (based on imaginary understandings of indigenous societies) describing the rational creation of an ideal society. Finally, the theme of savages is linked to utopia. Depending on the writer, savages lived in utopias because they were not polluted by European ideas, or savages needed Europeans to show them how to improve their lives.

5. Here Trouillot is referring to the twentieth-century attempts to selectively rank works and authors considered to best represent the highest level of human knowledge. This movement was associated first with Harvard University president Charles W. Eliot (1834–1926), whose 1909–1910 "five-foot shelf" consisted of fifty books that he believed provided the basis of a liberal education. Later, great books programs were promoted by the University of Chicago, its president (then chancellor) Robert M. Hutchins (1899–1977), and the philosopher Morton J. Adler (1902–2001). Although it included a few works such as the Bhagavad Gita, The Sayings of Confucius, and various Buddhist writings, the great books were overwhelmingly dominated

Anthropology is caught off guard by this reformulation. Traditionally, it approached the issue of cultural differences with a monopoly over native discourse, hypocritically aware that this discourse would remain a quote. It is too liberal to accept either the radical authenticity of the first person or the conservative reversion to canonical truths—hence, its theoretical silence.

Here again, silence seems to me a hasty abdication. At the very least, anthropology should be able to illuminate the myth of an unquestioned Western canon upon which the debate is premised.[c] In doing so, it would certainly undermine some of its own premises; but that risk is an inherent aspect of the current wave of challenges: its numerous opportunities are inseparable from its multiple threats. Nowhere is this combination of threats and opportunities as blatant as in the postmodern admission that the metanarratives of the West are crumbling.

THE FALL OF THE HOUSE OF REASON

Whatever else postmodernism means, it remains inseparable from the acknowledgment of an ongoing collapse of **metanarratives** in a world where reason and reality have become fundamentally destabilized (Lyotard 1979, 1986).[d] To be sure, the related claim (Tyler 1986: 123) that "the world that made science, and that science made, has disappeared" is somewhat premature. The growing awareness among literati that rationality has not fulfilled its promises to uncover the absolute becoming of the spirit does not alter the increasing institutionalization of rationality itself (Godzich 1986:xvii–xix). Indeed, one could argue that the spectacular failure of science and reason, judged on the universal grounds that scholars love to emphasize, serves to mask success on more practical and localized terrains into which academics rarely venture.[6]

But if the world that science made is very much alive, the world that made science is now shaky. The crisis of the nation-state, the crisis of the individual, the crisis of the parties of order (liberal, authoritarian, or communist), terrorism, the crisis of "late capitalism"—all contribute to a Western malaise and, in turn, feed upon it (Aronowitz 1988; Jameson 1984). Philosophers reportedly asked: can one think after Auschwitz? But it took some time for Auschwitz to sink in, for communism to reveal its own nightmares, for structuralism to demonstrate its magisterial impasse, for North and South to

---

by male European and American authors. As people who were not straight, white, and male began to gain increasing representation in universities in the 1980s, the idea that there was a core of "great books" that was the essential canon of Western literature came increasingly under attack. Attempts to broaden what was considered great books or to eliminate the idea entirely were met with conservative reaction. Defending "Western literature" became a political issue in the 1980s and 1990s. Several universities offer great books programs. One of the best known (and the one that first adopted the program in 1937) is St. John's College. You can see their current curriculum at https://www.sjc.edu/academic-programs/undergraduate/great-books-reading-list. Trouillot points out that the great books idea is repeatedly contested by people whose cultural, ethnic, racial, and gender perspectives have not been included.

6. A **metanarrative** is a theory or story that explains the world, the forces by which it operates, and its ultimate destiny (though it need not do all of these). Examples include the neoliberal idea that societies move toward individual liberty and free market capitalism, the Marxist idea that societies are driven by class conflict and move toward communism, and the Christian idea that the world unfolds according to God's plan and moves toward salvation and the end of time.

Jean-François Lyotard (1924–1998) was a French philosopher and the author of *The Postmodern Condition* (1979), which is considered one of the founding texts of postmodernism. After the French uprisings of 1968, Lyotard rejected the Marxism dominant in French philosophical thought of the era. This led to his eventual abandonment of all metanarratives. In the introduction to *The Postmodern Condition*, he wrote: "I will use the term *modern* to designate any science that legitimates itself with reference to a metadiscourse . . . making an explicit appeal to some grand narrative. . . . I define *postmodern* as an incredulity toward metanarratives" (1979, xxiii–xxiv).

admit the impossibility of dialogue, for fundamentalists of all denominations to desacralize religion, and for reenlightened intellectuals to question all foundational thought. As the walls crumbled—North and South and East and West—intellectuals developed languages of postdestruction. It is this mixture of negative intellectual surprise, this postmortem of the metanarratives, that situates the postmodernist mood as primarily Western and primarily petit bourgeois.

These words are not inherently pejorative, but they are meant to historicize the phenomenon—an important exercise if we intend to have cross-cultural relevance. First, it is not self-evident that all past and present cultures required metanarratives up to their current entry into postmodernity. Second, if only the collapse of metanarratives characterized the postmodern condition, then some of the non-Western cultures that have been busily deconstructing theirs for centuries, or that have gone through megacollapses of their own, have long been "postmodern," and there is nothing new under the sun. Things fell apart quite early on the southern shores of the Atlantic, and later in the hinterlands of Africa, Asia, and the Americas. Third, even if we concede, for the sake of argument, that metanarratives once were a prerequisite of humankind and are now collapsing everywhere at equal rates (two major assumptions, indeed), we cannot infer identical reactive strategies to this collapse.

Thus, we must distinguish between postmodernism, as a mood, and the recognition of a situation of postmodernity. The acknowledgment that there is indeed a crisis of representation, that there is indeed an ongoing set of qualitative changes in the international

organization of symbols (Appadurai 1991), in the rhythms of symbolic construction (Harvey 1989), and in the ways symbols relate to localized, subjective experience, does not in itself require a postmortem. In that light, the key to the dominant versions of postmodernism is an ongoing destruction lived as shock and revelation. Postmodernism builds on this revelation of the sudden disappearance of established rules, foundational judgments, and known categories (Lyotard 1986: 33) But the very fact of revelation implies a previous attitude toward such rules, judgments, and categories for instance, that they have been taken for granted or as immutable. The postmortem inherent in the postmodernist mood implies a previous "world of universals" (Ross 1988a:-xii-xiii) It implies a specific view of culture and or culture change. It implies at least in part, the Enlightenment and nineteenth-century Europe.

In cross-cultural perspective, the dominant mood of postmodernism thus appears as a historically specific phenomenon, a reaction provoked by the revelation that the Enlightenment and its conflicting tributaries may have run their course. This mood is not inherent in the current world situation, but neither is it a passing ambience, as many of the postmodernists' detractors would have—even though it ushers in fads of its own. It is a mood in the strong sense in which Geertz (1973b:90) defines religious moods: powerful, persuasive, and promising endurance. But contrary to religions, it rejects both the pretense of factuality and the aspiration to realistic motivations. It seeks a "psychoanalytic therapeutic" from the "modern neurosis," the "Western schizophrenia, paranoia, etc., all the sources of misery we have known for two centuries" (Lyotard 1986: 125–26).[7]

---

7. It's worth pausing to reflect, as Trouillot does, on the emergence of postmodernism in anthropology. From our perspective, many of the ideas of the postmodern era of the mid-1980s to mid-1990s seem optimistic, innocent, and naive. As Trouillot notes, Stephen Tyler's 1986 declaration that science has failed, coming as it did on the eve of scientific discoveries and technological changes that affect virtually every aspect of life today and make the world of the 1980s difficult for current-day people to remember or understand, was "premature." But beyond that, most of the attacks on metanarratives, science, and the possibility of objectivity of that era came from the political left. For many, these things were implicated in colonialism, oppression, and the perpetuation of white supremacy. They hoped that in destabilizing these critical ideas, they would open spaces for the voices of the oppressed and impoverished. They seemingly did not understand, consider, or care that ideas such as the linkage of power and truth, the denial of objectivity, and the rejection of science had historically been tools of reaction and most effectively used by some of the most oppressive regimes in

"We" here, is the West, as in Michael Jackson and Lionel Ritchie's international hit, "We Are the World." This is not "the West" in a genealogical or territorial sense. The postmodern world has little space left for genealogies, and notions of territoriality are being redefined right before our eyes (Appadurai 1991). It is a world where black American Michael Jackson starts an international tour from Japan and imprints cassettes that mark the rhythm of Haitian peasant families in the Cuban Sierra Maestra; a world where Florida speaks Spanish (once more); where a Socialist prime minister in Greece comes by way of New England and an imam of fundamentalist Iran by way of Paris. It is a world where a political leader in reggae-prone Jamaica traces his roots to Arabia, where U.S. credit cards are processed in Barbados, and Italian designer shoes made in Hong Kong. It is a world where the Pope is Polish, where the most orthodox Marxists live on the western side of a fallen iron curtain. It is a world where the most enlightened are only part-time citizens of part-time communities of imagination.[8]

But these very phenomena—and their inherent connection with the expansion of what we conveniently call the West—are part of the text that reveals the dominant mood as eventuating from a Western **problematique**. The perception of a collapse as revelation cannot be envisioned outside of the trajectory of thought that has marked the West and spread unevenly outside of its expanding boundaries. Its conditions of existence coalesce within the West. The stance it spawns is unthinkable outside of the West, and has significance only within the boundaries set by the West.[9]

If the postmodern mood is fundamentally Western in the global sense delineated above, what does this mean for an anthropology of the present? First, it means that the present that anthropologists must confront is the product of a particular past that encompasses the history and the prehistory of anthropology itself. Second and consequently, it means that the postmodernist critique within North American anthropology remains, so far, within the very thematic field that it claims to challenge. Third, it means that a truly critical and reflexive anthropology needs to contextualize the Western metanarratives and read critically the place of the discipline in the field so discovered. In

---

history. By the late 2010s, the use of these tools by right-wing and nationalist parties was pervasive. The (metaphorical, left-leaning) children of Stephen Tyler ended up putting up yard signs that proclaimed, "In This House, We Believe Science Is Real," and arguing (or hoping) that "the arc of the moral universe is long but it bends toward justice."

8. Here, and in many other places, Trouillot refers to people and events of the 1980s and early 1990s. By the time the essay was revised for its 2003 publication, some of these were passing from public memory, and Trouillot provided notes to identify them. "We Are the World" is one of these. In the 2003 essay, Trouillot in a footnote explains that "We Are the World," written by Michael Jackson (1959–2009) and Lionel Ritchie (b. 1949), was part of a fundraising effort for a relief organization called "U.S.A. for Africa." The song was recorded in 1985 at a time that ensured thirty-five of the most popular musicians of the era could participate in it. It, and the album of the same name, won Grammys for song and record of the year. Throughout the essay, we will identify other cultural references as well as many of the authors that Trouillot mentions. The Cuban Sierra Maestra is a mountain range in southwestern Cuba. Greece's first socialist prime minister was Andreas Papandreou (1919–1996) who held a PhD from MIT and had taught at Harvard, the University of Minnesota, and Berkeley. The fundamentalist imam was Ayatollah Ruhollah Khomeini (1900–1989), who briefly lived in exile in a suburb of Paris before returning to Iran to lead the 1979 revolution. The Jamaican political leader was probably Edward Seaga (1930–2019), prime minister from 1980 to 1989. Seaga's father, Philip George Seaga (1900–1977), was from the Lebanese Jamaican community, but Edward Seaga was born in Boston. The Polish pope was Karol Józef Wojtyla, Pope John Paul II (1920–2005).

9. The word **"problematique"** refers to "an intricate and dynamic maze of situations, mechanisms, phenomena, and dysfunctions, which, even when they are apparently disjointed, interfere and interact with one another" (https://uia.org/archive/ency-problems-comm-1-1). The term, in this sense of its usage, was probably coined by the Turkish American philosopher and systems scientist Hasan Özbekhan (1921–2007).

short, anthropology needs to turn the apparatus elaborated in the observation of non-Western societies on itself and, more specifically, on the history from which it sprang. That history does not start with the formalization of the discipline, but with the emergence of the symbolic field that made this formalization possible.[10]

THE SAVAGE AND
THE INNOCENT

In 1492, Christopher Columbus stumbled upon the Caribbean. The admiral's mistake would later be heralded as "The Discovery of America," the quincentennial of which two worlds will soon celebrate. To be sure, it took Balboa's sighting of the Pacific in 1513 to verify the existence of a continental mass, and Vespucci's insistence on a *mundus novus* for Christendom to acknowledge this "discovery." Then it took another fifty years to realize its symbolic significance. Yet 1492 was, to some extent, a discovery even then, the first material step in a continuously renewed process of invention (Ainsa 1988). Abandoning one lake for another, Europe confirmed the sociopolitical fissure that was slowly pushing the Mediterranean toward northern and southern shores. In so doing, it created itself, but it also discovered America, its still unpolished alter ego, its elsewhere, its other. The Conquest of America stands as Europe's model for the constitution of the Other (Todorov 1982; Ainsa 1988).

Yet from the beginning, the model was **Janus-faced**. The year 1516 saw the publication of two anthropological precursors: the Alcala edition of the *Decades* of Pietro Martire d'Anghiera (a paraethnographic account of the Antilles, and in many ways one of Europe's earliest introductions to a "state of nature" elsewhere) and one more popular edition of Amerigo Vespucci's epistolary travel accounts. In that same year too, Thomas More published his fictional account of an "ideal state" on the island of Utopia, the prototypical nowhere of European imagination.[11]

The chronological coincidence of these publications, fortuitous as it may be, symbolizes a thematic correspondence now blurred by intellectual specialization and the abuse of categories. We now claim to distinguish clearly between travelers' accounts, colonial surveys, ethnographic reports, and fictional utopias. Such cataloging is useful, but only to some extent. In the early sixteenth century, European descrip-

---

10. This critical paragraph identifies Trouillot's goal in this essay. He wants to turn the tools of postmodernism, particularly Foucauldian archaeology, on the discipline of anthropology in a new way, providing a history of the intellectual and ideological context that made it possible, perhaps necessary, to think the discipline of anthropology into being. That it was thought into being in a specific historical and ideological context gave anthropology form and predisposed it to certain kinds of study and analysis.

11. **Janus-faced**: In ancient Rome, Janus was the god of time, doorways, and transitions and was depicted with two faces, one looking forward or to the future, one backward or to the past. However, *Janus-faced* can also be a synonym for hypocritical or untrustworthy. Trouillot will refer to Janus several times in this essay.

Pietro Martire d'Anghiera (also Peter Martyr d'Anghiera) (1457–1526) was an Italian historian and diplomat employed by the Spanish Crown. His *Decades* are essays that describe the travels and actions of key European adventurers including Vasco Núñez de Balboa, Hernán Cortés, and Ferdinand Magellan.

Amerigo Vespucci (1451–1512) was an Italian merchant. He claimed to have made numerous voyages of exploration; to have understood that the Americas were, from the European perspective, a new continent; and to have made rudimentary maps showing this continent. Almost all of this is disputed. However, booklets published under his name and describing his alleged voyages were extremely popular in Europe, and this resulted in his name being given to the new continents. An epistolary travel account is one in the form of a series of letters.

Thomas More (1478–1535) was an English lawyer, statesman, philosopher, and author. More served as Lord High Chancellor of England under Henry VIII. However, More was a devout Catholic and was imprisoned and executed when he refused to join others in asking Pope Clement VII to support Henry's divorce from Catherine of Aragon. In *Utopia* (1516), More imagines a perfectly governed society. More, canonized in 1935, is the patron saint of statesmen and politicians. Trouillot refers to More frequently in this essay.

tions of an alleged state of nature in the realist mode filled the writings of colonial officers concerned with the immediate management of the Other The realist mode also pervaded travelers' accounts of the sixteenth and seventeenth centuries, before settling in the privileged space of learned discourse with eighteenth-century philosophers and the nineteenth-century rise of armchair anthropology. Even then, the line between these genres was not always clear-cut (Thornton 1983; Weil 1984). The realist mode also pervaded fiction—so much so that some twentieth-century critics distinguish between utopias and "extraordinary voyages," or trips to the lands of nowhere with the most "realistic" geographical settings. On the other hand, fantasies about an ideal state increased in fiction, but they also found their way into theater, songs, and philosophical treatises.

In short, classifications notwithstanding, the connection between a state of nature and an ideal state is, to a large extent, in the symbolic construction of the materials themselves. The symbolic transformation through which Christendom became the West structures a set of relations that necessitate both utopia and the savage. What happens within the slots so created—and within the genres that condition their historical existence—is not inconsequential. But the analysis of these genres cannot explain the slots nor even the internal tropes of such slots. To wit, "utopia" has been the most studied form of this ensemble, yet there is no final agreement on which works to include in the category (Atkinson 1920, 1922; Andrews 1937; Trousson 1975; Manuel and Manuel 1979; Eliav-Feldon 1982; Kamenka 1987). Further, when reached, agreement is often ephemeral. Even if one could posit a continuum from realist ethnography to fictional utopias, works move in and out of these categories, and categories often overlap on textual and nontextual grounds. Finally, textuality is rarely the final criterion of inclusion or exclusion. From the 200-year-long controversy about the *Voyage et aventures de Franrois Leguat* (a 1708 best-seller believed by some to be a true account and by others, a work of fiction) to the Castañeda embarrassment to professional anthropology and the more recent debates on *Shabono* or the existence of the Tasaday, myriad cases indicate the ultimate relevance of issues outside of "the text" proper (Atkinson 1922; Weil 1984; Pratt 1986).[12]

---

12. François Leguat (1637–1735), whom Trouillot does not further describe, was a French traveler and naturalist. In 1691, Leguat along with nine Huguenot refugees from France attempted to settle on the then uninhabited island of Rodrigues in the Indian Ocean. Their attempt to form a utopian community there foundered after two years. Leguat returned to Europe and, a decade later, wrote the account of his travels that Trouillot mentions. Leguat's account accurately describes Rodrigues Island plants and animals, many of which are now extinct, and is now considered largely factual (https://www.jstor.org/stable/jj.4256600.17).

In the 2003 edition of this essay, Trouillot provided footnotes on Carlos Castaneda, Shabono, and the Tasaday. Our comments on them differ somewhat from Trouillot's. Carlos Castaneda (1925–1998) was the author of a series of best-selling books between 1965 and 1999. Most of these purported to describe his experiences as an apprentice to the Yaqui shaman Don Juan Matus. The books include many vivid descriptions of hallucinogenic experiences. Castaneda was awarded a doctorate in anthropology from UCLA (the third book in the series was based on his dissertation). Most anthropologists and literary critics today consider the series fictional (https://www.salon.com/2007/04/12/castaneda, The Don Juan Papers, many other sources).

Florinda Donner (1944–1998, disappeared), the author of *Shabono: A Visit to a Remote and Magical World in the South American Rainforest* (1982), was one of several women supporters and students who were part of an inner circle that surrounded Carlos Castaneda. Castaneda bought a house in Los Angeles in 1973 that he called "the witches' house," and numerous female followers including Donner lived there with him (and were sometimes referred to as Castaneda's witches). They taught shamanic spirituality workshops in what Castaneda called "Tensegrity." However, according to numerous sources, Castaneda also became the abusive leader of a cult of devotees, including Donner (https://laist.com/news/la-history/carlos-castanedas-sinister-legacy-witches-of-westwood). Donner, and four other women of Castaneda's inner circle, disappeared the day after his death. The remains of one have been found. The others are presumed dead (https://www.seanmunger.com/blog/disappeared-the-women-of-tensegrity-missing-since-1998). Today, Donner's *Shabono* is considered a work of fiction, much of it plagiarized. Tensegrity goes on and is promoted by a company called Cleargreen.

That the actual corpus fitting any of these genres at any given period has never been unproblematic underscores a thematic correspondence that has survived the increasingly refined categorizations. In the 1500s, readers could not fail to notice the similarities between works such as Jacques Cartier's *Bref Recit*, which features paraethnographic descriptions of Indians, and some of Rabelais's scenes in Gargantua. Montaigne, an observant traveler himself within the confines of Europe, used descriptions of America to set for his readers issues in philosophical anthropology—and in the famous essay "Des cannibales," he is quick to point out the major difference between his enterprise and that of his Greek predecessors, including Plato: the Greeks had no realistic database (Montaigne 1952). Early in the seventeenth century, Tommaso Campanella produced his *Citta del sole* (1602), informed by descriptions that Portuguese missionaries and Dutch mercenaries were bringing back from Ceylon and by Jesuit reports of socialism within the Inca kingdom.[13]

Utopias were both rare and inferior—by earlier and later standards—during the seventeenth century. Few are now remembered other than those of Campanella, Bacon, and Fenelon. But the search for an exotic ideal had not died, as some authors (Trousson 1975) seem to suggest. Fenelon's *Aventures de Telemaque* went into twenty printings. The *History of the Sevarites* of Denis Vairasse d'Alais (1677–79) was published originally in English, then in a French version that spurred German, Dutch, and Italian translations (Atkinson 1920). Utopias did not quench the thirst for fantasy lands, but only because relative demand had increased unexpectedly.[14]

Travel accounts, of which the numbers kept multiplying, helped fill this increased demand

---

The Tasaday are a supposed group of indigenous people in the Philippines contacted in 1971. The Tasaday were alleged to be unusually cooperative, peaceful, and "primitive." However, controversy over their existence erupted almost immediately, and it is still not fully resolved. At issue is whether they were truly an uncontacted group or members of other far larger groups.

13. Jacques Cartier (1491–1557) was a French explorer who mapped the Gulf of St. Lawrence and some of the St. Lawrence River. The *Bref récet* describes reports of his travels and his encounters with indigenous people.

Trouillot also refers to two key authors of the French Renaissance: François Rabelais (c. 1490–1553) and Michel de Montaigne (1533–1592). Both authors blend fictional and factual accounts of "primitive" people to comment on European society. Rabelais is best known for his series of comic novels *Gargantua* and *Pantagruel* in which he used caustic wit, irony, satire, and very often vulgarity to comment on society. Montaigne was a philosopher, statesman, and essayist (he arguably invented the essay as a form of writing, and he was the first to use the word in its modern sense). He was known for introspection and questioning of the assumptions of his society. His essays ranged over an extremely wide range of topics. "Of Cannibals" is an early statement of cultural relativism. Montaigne writes: "I find that there is nothing barbarous and savage in this nation, by anything that I can gather, excepting, that every one gives the title of barbarism to everything that is not in use in his own country."

Tommaso Campanella (1568–1639) was an Italian philosopher and theologian. A key defender of Galileo, he spent much of his life in prison. There, among other works, he wrote *City of the Sun* (orig. 1602), in which he imagined a theocratic utopia in which men held property, women, and children in common.

14. **Bacon:** Sir Francis Bacon (1561–1626), English statesman and philosopher, sometimes known as the father of empiricism. Bacon's *The New Atlantis*, published posthumously in 1626, is a brief, incomplete novel that describes the utopian Island of Bensalem where experimental science is used to better humanity.

Fénelon: François Fénelon (1651–1715) was a French theologian and archbishop of Cambrai. His *Adventures of Telemachus* of 1699 is a novel that depicts the education of Telemachus, the son of Odysseus, by the goddess Minerva. In it, Fénelon argues for a world of peace, simplicity, and relative equality.

Denis Vairasse (c. 1630–1672) was a French Protestant who spent much of his life in exile in England. *History of Sevarambes* imagines a utopia in Australia. The crew of a European ship bound for India is shipwrecked in Australia and discovers a European-like society but with communal ownership (and both polyandry and polygyny).

for the elsewhere. Some did so with reports of unicorns and floating isles, then accepted as reality by their public, including some of the most respected scholars of the time. But most did so with what were "realist" pictures of the savage, pictures that would pass twentieth-century tests of accuracy and are still being used by historians and anthropologists. Du Tertre (1667), Labat (1722), and Gage (1648) to take only a few recognizable authors writing on one hemisphere familiarized readers with the wonders of the Antilles and the American mainland.[15]

Outside of a restricted group of overzealous scholars and administrators, it mattered little to the larger European audience whether such works were fictitious or not. That they presented an elsewhere was enough. That the elsewhere was actually somewhere was a matter for a few specialists. The dream remained alive well into the next century. Montesquieu was so much aware of this implicit correspondence that he gambled on reversing all the traditions at the same time, with considerable aesthetic and didactic effect, in his *Lettres persanes* (1721). The elsewhere became Paris; the Other became French; the utopia became a well-known state of affairs. It worked, because everyone recognized the models and understood the parody.[16]

The thematic correspondence between utopias and travel accounts or paraethnographic descriptions was not well camouflaged until the end of the eighteenth century. The forms continued to diverge, while the number of publications within each category kept increasing. Utopias filled the century that gave us the Enlightenment, from Swift's parodic *Gulliver's Travels* (1702) to Bernadin de Saint-Pierre's unfinished *L'amazone* (1795). But so did realistic descriptions of faraway peoples, and so did, moreover, cross-national debates in Europe on what exactly those descriptions meant for the rational knowledge of humankind. In the single decade or the 1760s, England alone sent expeditions like those of Commodore Byron, Captains Cartwright, Bruce, Furneaux, and Wallis, and Lieutenant Cook to savage lands all over the world. Bruce, Wallis, and Cook brought home reports from Abyssinia, Tahiti, and Hawaii. Byron and his companions carried back accounts "of a race of splendid giants", from Patagonia. Cartwright returned with five living Eskimos who caused a commotion in the streets of London (Tinker 1922: 5–25).[17]

---

15. **Du Tertre:** Jean-Baptiste Du Tertre (1610–1687) was a French Dominican friar and botanist. He lived in the Caribbean for eighteen years and wrote numerous books describing indigenous people, flora, and fauna. He is known for coining the phrase *bon sauvage*, or "noble savage," further elaborated a century later by the Swiss/French Enlightenment philosopher Jean-Jacques Rousseau (1712–1778).

Labat: Jean-Baptiste Labat (1663–1738) was a French Dominican friar, botanist, and sugar plantation and slave owner. He lived in the Caribbean in the 1690s, holding positions in the Catholic Church and making several innovations in growing and processing sugar. He wrote *Nouveau voyage aux îles Francoises de L'Amérique*, a description of people, plants, animals, customs, and government in the French Caribbean.

Gage: Thomas Gage (1603–1656) was yet another Dominican friar who traveled in Mexico and Central America in the first half of the seventeenth century. He wrote and compiled (and plagiarized) a book about the West Indies, *The English-American, or a New Survey of the West Indies* (1648).

16. Trouillot has mentioned a wide range of authors, and we've provided simple background information on them. He will continue to provide more, as will we. However, pausing for a moment, Trouillot contends that modern genres of writing had not yet emerged and most people perceived fictional, travel, scientific, and philosophical accounts as equally realistic. However, his list includes works that contain detailed botanical descriptions and those that are fanciful imaginations of ancient Greece or elaborate European societies in Australia.

Montesquieu: Charles Louis de Secondat, Baron de Montesquieu (1689–1755), usually just Montesquieu, was a French noble, judge, historian, and philosopher. His *Persian Letters* (1721) is a satire of French society. Montesquieu imagines two Persian noblemen, Usbek and Rica, visiting France. He uses their imagined perspectives to analyze and critique French society.

17. Jonathan Swift (1667–1745) was an Anglo-Irish satirist. Most readers will be familiar with some of the fanciful imagined worlds depicted in *Gulliver's Travels* as well as his essay "A Modest Proposal."

Scholars devoured such "realistic" data on the savage with a still unsurpassed interest, while writing didactic utopias and exploring in their philosophical treatises the rational revelation behind the discoveries or the travelers. Voltaire, who read voraciously the travel descriptions of his time, gave us *Candide* and "Zadig." But he also used paraethnographic descriptions to participate in anthropological debates of his time, siding for instance with the Gottingen school on polygenesis (Duchet 1971). Diderot, who may have read more travel accounts than anyone then alive, and who turned many of them in paraethnographic descriptions for the *Encyclopedie*, wrote two utopias true to form.[e] Rousseau, whom Lévi-Strauss called "the father of eth-nology," sought the most orderly link between "the state of nature" first described by Martire d'Anghiera and the "ideal commonwealth" envisioned by More and his followers. He thus formalized the myth of the "noble savage," renewing a theme that went back not only to Pope and Defoe, but to obscure travelers of the sixteenth and seventeenth centuries. Long before Rousseau's *Social Contract*, Pietro Martire already thought that the Arawak of the Antilles were sweet and simple. Magellan's companion, Pigafetta, claimed in 1522 that the Indians of Brazil were "**creduli e boni**" by instinct. And Pierre Boucher, writing of the Iroquois in 1664, had confirmed that "tous les Sauuages ont l'esprit bon" (Gonnard 1946: 36; Atkinson 1920: 65–70).[18]

Bernadin de Saint-Pierre (Jacques-Henri Bernardin de Saint-Pierre, 1737–1814) was a French writer and botanist. His 1788 *Paul et Virginie*, a classic of French literature, is a romance set in Mauritius. *L'Amazone* is a fragment of a novel set in a fictional hidden settlement in South America founded by benevolent Europeans on unoccupied land (Howells 2017; https://doi.org/10.5699/modelangrevi.112.2.0341).

We leave readers to look up the expedition leaders Trouillot mentions except for George Cartwright (1739–1819), an English trader and adventurer in Newfoundland and Labrador. In 1772, Cartwright returned to England with five Inuit people. As Trouillot says, they were a sensation in London and were seen by many well-known figures of the era including the king. Cartwright's relationship with the Inuit was complex, and it's not clear whether their voyage to England was undertaken freely. It had a tragic conclusion. Four of them died of smallpox on the return journey, the fifth shortly thereafter (Stopp and Mitchell 2010).

18. This paragraph includes references to many key Enlightenment thinkers. They recur numerous times in the essay, so it's worth taking a moment to reacquaint yourself with them. In order of their appearance:

Voltaire (François-Marie Arouet, 1694–1778): one of the best-known philosophers of the French Enlightenment, Voltaire is remembered for his critiques of society in his era, his support of civil liberties, his scathing critique of religion, and his attack on slavery, as well as his wit. He wrote in an extraordinary number of genres, producing novels, plays, essays, and scientific tracts. Trouillot refers to *Candide* (1759), his most famous novel, a comedic send-up of the idea that this is the best of all possible worlds. *Zadig* (1747), an earlier novella, tells a similar story but set in ancient Babylon. Both books are ruthless attacks on illogical practices and inhumane institutions.

Diderot: Denis Diderot (1713–1784) was a key French Enlightenment figure, best remembered as the creator of the *Encyclopedia*, an attempt to catalog all the knowledge of his era and the ancestor of all modern encyclopedias. He shared many of Voltaire's ideas and, like Voltaire, he wrote in many different genres. Trouillot makes a joke about Diderot, calling it "true to form" that he wrote two utopias. This is because Diderot was extraordinarily prolific. He wrote seven thousand articles for his Encyclopedia as well as many, many other works.

The Göttingen school was a group of historians based at the University of Göttingen, in Lower Saxony, in the eighteenth century. Members of the school contributed to the discussion of race. However, Trouillot mischaracterizes Göttingen. Members of the school included advocates of polygenesis such as Christoph Meiners (1747–1810, see below) and of monogenesis such as Johann Friedrich Blumenbach (1752–1840). Voltaire (alas) was a believer in polygenesis. That is, he thought that different races had different biological origins.

Information about Martire d'Anghiera is in note 11, and Thomas More is found in note 12.

Alexander Pope (1688–1733) was an English poet and satirist. In "An Essay on Man," a long poem published in the 1730s, Pope contemplates "primitive" people: "Lo! The poor Indian, whose untutor'd mind / Sees God in clouds, or hears him in the wind; / . . . To be, contents his natural desire." You might recognize

The myth of the noble savage is not a creation of the Enlightenment. Ever since the West became the West, Robinson has been looking for Friday. The eighteenth century was not even the first to see arguments on or around that myth (Gonnard 1946). The verbal duel between las Casas and Sepulveda on the "nature" of the Indians and the justice of their enslavement, fought at Valladolid in the early 1550s in front of Spain's intellectual nobility, was as spectacular as anything the Enlightenment could imagine (Andre-Vincent 1980; Pagden 1982). Rather, the specificity of eighteenth-century anthropological philosophers was to dismiss some of the past limitations of this grandiose controversy and to claim to resolve it not on the basis of the Scriptures, but on the open grounds of rationality and experience. But the debate was always implicit in the thematic concordance that had tied the observation of the savage and the hopes of utopia since at least 1516. Swiss writer Isaac Iselin, a leading voice of the Gottingen school of anthropology, criticized Rousseau's ideals and the state of savagery as "disorderly fantasy" (Rupp-Eisenreich 1984: 99). The fact that the Gottingen school did not much bother to verify its own "ethnographic" bases, or that it used travelers' accounts for other purposes than Rousseau's (Rupp-Eisenreich 1985) matters less than the fact that Rousseau, Iselin, Meiners, and De Gerando shared the same premises on the relevance of savagery. For Rousseau, as for More and Defoe, the savage is an argument for a particular kind of utopia. For Iselin and Meiners, as for Swift and Hobbes in other times and contexts, it is an argument against it. Given the tradition of the genre being used, the formal terrain of battle, and the personal taste of the author, the argument was either tacit or explicit and the savage's face either sketched or magnified. But argument there was.[19]

---

many famous lines from Pope's "Essay." For example, in the stanza before "Lo! . . . ," you'll find "Hope springs eternal in the human breast."

Daniel Defoe (c. 1660–1731) was another extraordinarily prolific writer. He was the author of numerous political pamphlets and reports but is best remembered for his novels *Robinson Crusoe* (1719), one of the most popular books of its era, and *Moll Flanders* (1722).

Pierre Boucher (1622–1717) was a French colonial settler, and then governor of Trois-Rivières in what is now Canada. Boucher married an indigenous woman, but she died in childbirth. Boucher wrote a book of the natural history and social customs of New France.

Creduli e boni: ingenuous and good. *Tous les Sauvages ont l'esprit bon*: All wild people have good dispositions. Boucher's quote continues, "Among them, it is rare to see coarse dispositions like we see among French peasants."

19. "Robinson has been looking for Friday." In *Robinson Crusoe*, the title character frees an indigenous person from captivity by other indigenous people. The freed individual, whom Crusoe names Friday, becomes Crusoe's servant.

The debate between Bartolomé de las Casas (1484–1566), the first bishop of Chiapas, and the philosopher Juan Ginés de Sepúlveda (1490–1573) was a critical but inconclusive moment in Spanish colonialism. It was held in 1550 and 1551 at the Colegio de San Gregorio in Valladolid, Spain. Las Casas defended indigenous people as fully human and having intrinsic rights. Sepúlvada spoke for the property rights of Spanish colonists and argued that native practices disqualified them from full inclusion in humanity. The debate was held before a panel of judges, but these failed to declare a winner.

Isaak Iselin (1728–1782) was a Swiss historian and philosopher and one of the leading scholars of the German-speaking world of his era. Whereas Rousseau glorified nature and called for a return to simplicity indirectly based on the idea of the noble savage, Iselin, following Thomas Hobbes (1588–1679), saw nature as a battle of all against all. He called for a moderate monarchy based on the British model (Kapossy 2006).

Christoph Meiners (1747–1810) was a member of the Göttingen school, a historian, and a prolific author. Meiners was a champion of racist thinking and slavery. He was a key influence on later racists such as Arthur de Gobineau (1816–1882), and his work proved a key inspiration for Nazi racial theories in the twentieth century (Michael 2021). https://www.academia.edu/49757945/The_Race_Supremacist_Anthropology_of_Christoph_Meiners_its_Origins_and_Reception.

The nineteenth century blurred the most visible signs of this thematic correspondence by artificially separating utopia and the savage. To schematize a protracted and contested process: it is as if that century of specialization subdivided the Other that the Renaissance had set forth in creating the West. From then on, utopia and the savage evolved as two distinguishable slots. Kant had set the philosophical grounds for this separation by laying his own teleology without humor or fiction while moving away from the *Naturinstink*. Nineteenth-century French positivists, in turn, derided utopias as chimeric utopianisms (Manuel and Manuel 1979).

The growing fictional literature in the United States also modified the forms of utopia (Pfaelzer 1984). To start with, America had been the imagined site of traditional utopias, Tocqueville's *feuille blanche*, the land of all (im)possibilities. Defining an elsewhere from this site was a dilemma. Ideally, its Eden was within itself (Walkover 1974). Not surprisingly, William Dean Howells brings *A Traveler from Altruria* to the United States before sending his readers back to utopia. Edward Bellamy chose to look "backward." More important, America's savages and its colonized were also within itself: American Indians and black Americans, only one of whom white anthropologists dared to study before the latter part of this century (Mintz 1971, 1990). With two groups of savages to pick from, specialization set in, and Indians (especially "good" Indians) became the preserve of anthropologists.[20]

At the same time, a black utopia was unthinkable, given the character or North American racism and the fabric of black/white imagery in American literature (Levin 1967). Thus the black pastoral (the unmatched apex of which is Uncle Tom's Cabin [1851]—but note that the flavor is also in Faulkner) played the role that *Paul et Virginie* had played earlier in European imagination.[f] But true-to-form utopia writers in North America moved away from the specter of savagery.[21]

Other factors were at play. The nineteenth century was America's century of concreteness, when its utopias became reachable. Of the reported 52 million migrants who left Europe between 1824 and 1924, more than ninety percent went to the Americas, mostly to the United States. In the United States, and in Europe as well, decreasing exchange among writers, who were involved in different forms of discourse and seeking legitimacy on different grounds, contributed even more to giving each group of practitioners the sentiment that they were carrying on a different enterprise. As they believed their practice and practiced their beliefs, the enterprises indeed became separated, but only to a certain extent. By the end of the nineteenth century, utopian novelists accentuated formal interests while utopianisms

---

De Gerando: Joseph Marie, Baron de Gérando (1772–1842) was a French statesman, writer, and educator. De Gérando was a key inspiration for the American Transcendentalists such as Ralph Waldo Emerson.

20. **Tocqueville's feuille blanch:** Alexis de Tocqueville (1805–1859) was a French aristocrat and politician best known for his 1835 account of his 1831 trip to the United States, *De la démocratie en Amérique* (Democracy in America). *Feuille blanch* is French for "blank page."

William Dean Howells (1837–1920) was an American novelist, editor, and politician. *A Traveler from Alturia* (1894) is a utopian novel in which a traveler from the hidden island of Alturia visits the United States and finds it backward in every way. The book is a critique of late-nineteenth-century capitalism.

Edward Bellamy (1850–1898) was an American novelist and socialist political activist. His utopian novel *Looking Backwards* (1889) is set in an imaginary Boston in 2000 in which industry has been nationalized and the United States has become a socialist utopia.

21. William Faulkner (1897–1962) wrote a famous series of novels set in the fictional Yoknapatawpha County, Mississippi, that describe the lives of white and black characters. Most of Faulkner's novels were written in the 1930s.

Paul et Virginie, as has already been mentioned, was a widely read novel by Bernadin de Saint-Pierre (see note 18). Be sure to read Trouillot's endnote about it.

were acknowledged primarily as doctrines couched in non-fictional terms: Saint-Simonism, **Fabian Socialism**, Marxism (Gonnard 1946). Travel accounts came to pass as a totally separate genre, however Robinson-like some remained. The "scientific" study of the savage qua savage became the privileged field of academic anthropology, soon to be anchored in distinguished chairs, but already severed from its imaginary counterpart.[22]

The rest of the story is well known, perhaps too well known, inasmuch as the insistence on the methods and tropes of anthropology as a discipline may obscure the larger discursive order that made sense of its institutionalization. Histories that fail to problematize this institutionalization—and critiques premised on that naive history—necessarily fall short of illuminating the enunciative context of anthropological discourse. To be sure, anthropologists to this day keep telling both undergraduates and lay readers that their practice is useful to better understand "ourselves," but without ever spelling exactly the specifics of this understanding, the utopias behind this curiosity turned profession.

It has often been said that the savage or the primitive was the alter ego the West constructed for itself. What has not been emphasized enough is that this Other was a Janus, of whom the savage was only the second face.[8] The first face was the West itself, but the West fancifully constructed as a utopian projection and meant to be, in that imaginary correspondence, the condition of existence of the savage.

This thematic correspondence preceded the institutionalization of anthropology as a specialized field of inquiry. Better said, *the constitutive moment of ethnography as metaphor antedates the constitution of anthropology as discipline* and even precedes its solidification as specialized discourse. The dominant metamorphosis, the transformation of savagery into sameness by way of utopia as positive or negative reference, is not the outcome of a textual exercise within the anthropological practice, but part of anthropology's original conditions of existence. Anthropology came to fill the savage slot of a larger thematic field, performing a role played, in different ways, by literature and travel accounts—and soon to be played, perhaps, by unexpected media, if one takes the success of "Roots," "Miami Vice," or "China Beach" on North American television, or the international sales of Saddam Hussein punching balls during the Gulf War, as indications of a future. That the discipline was positivist in a positivist age, structuralist in a context dominated by structuralism, is not very intriguing; and as Tyler (1986: 128) notes acutely, the more recent "textualization of pseudo-discourse" can accomplish "a terrorist alienation more complete than that of the positivists." Thus, attempts at disciplinary reflexivity cannot stop at the moment of institutionalization, or emphasize the internal tropes of late modern ethnographies, even though some rightly allude to the correspondence between savagery and utopia or to the use of the pastoral mode in anthropology (e.g., Tyler 1986; Clifford 1986; Rosaldo 1986). Such attempts are not wrong. But the primary focus on the textual construction of the Other in anthropology may turn our attention away from the construction of otherness upon which anthropology is premised, and further mask a correspondence already well concealed by increasing specialization since the nineteenth century.[23]

---

22. Saint-Simonism, after Henri de Saint-Simon (1760–1825), was a political movement centered on the recognition and development of an industrial working class. Saint-Simon supported meritocracy but is also considered a utopian socialist.

Fabian socialism: the Fabian Society was a British political organization founded 1884 to promote democratic socialism achieved by gradual reform. They were critical to the founding of the British Labour Party and remain affiliated with it.

23. Trouillot once again returns to Clifford and Marcus's 1986 *Writing Culture: The Poetics and Politics of Ethnography*, which includes all of the essays referenced in this paragraph. Trouillot's critical point is that in *Writing Culture*, anthropologists examined the tropes and truth-making techniques of anthropological

Indeed, the savage-utopia correspondence tends to generate false candor. It rarely reveals its deepest foundations or its inherent inequality, even though it triggers claims of reciprocity. From Pietro Martire and Rousseau to the postmodernist contingent(s) of North American anthropology, the savage has been an occasion to profess innocence. We may guess at some of the reasons behind this recurrent tendency to exhibit the nude as nakedness. Let me just say this much: in spite of such old claims, the utopian West dominated the thematic correspondence. It did so from behind the scene, at least most of the time. It showed itself in least equivocal terms on just a few occasions, most notably in the philosophical jousts over American colonization in sixteenth-century Spain (Pagden 1982) and in the anthropological debates of the eighteenth century (Duchet 1971).[24]

But visible or not, naive or cynical, the West was always first, as utopia or as challenge to it—

that is, as a universalist project, the boundaries of which were no-where, u-topous, non-spatial. And that, one needs to repeat, is not a product of the Enlightenment, but part and parcel of the horizons set by the Renaissance and its simultaneous creation of Europe and otherness, without which the West is inconceivable. Thomas More did not have to wait for ethnographic reports on the Americas to compose his Utopia. Similarly, eighteenth-century readers of travel accounts did not wait for verification. Even today, there is a necessary gap between the initial acceptance of the most fanciful "ethnographies" and the "restudies" or "reassessments" that follow. The chronological precedence reflects a deeper inequality in the two faces of Janus: the utopian West is first in the construction of this complementarity. It is the first observed face of the figure, the initial projection against which the savage becomes a reality. The savage makes sense only in terms of utopia.[25]

---

writing. However, they do not consider the place of the discipline of anthropology in the larger tropes and truth-making techniques of European society, exactly what he has been examining in this essay.

The 2003 version of this essay eliminates these cultural and political references or moves them to a footnote. *Roots* was a famous 1977 TV miniseries based on a novel by Alex Haley (1921–1992) that followed a black family from slavery in colonial America through the Civil War. *Miami Vice* was a popular TV show that ran for five seasons in the 1980s. *China Beach* was a less-known TV show about the Vietnam War that ran between 1988 and 1991. Saddam Hussein (1937–2006) was president of Iraq during the 1990–1991 Gulf War that occurred while Trouillot was preparing this essay for publication.

24. Trouillot uses the phrase "the nude as nakedness" twice in critical passages in this essay. We believe this is a metaphorical way to express the idea of the savage as a cultural innocent. Or perhaps it means to clinically examine something that should be appreciated as art. What do you think it means?

In the last sentence of the paragraph, Trouillot refers back to the Las Casas–Sepúlveda debate described in note 20.

25. In this section, Trouillot has argued that beginning in the Renaissance, European discourse separated Europeans from non-Europeans in new ways. This was expressed in fictional utopias, accounts of exploration, travel writing, and philosophy. Trouillot argues that in each case, the savage, non-European acted as a counterbalance in understanding what European civilization meant to Europeans. However, all of these forms were undifferentiated. In the nineteenth century, greater systematization began, and utopian fiction was differentiated from scientific writing and philosophy. This resulted in the emergence of two "slots" or categories of thought: the utopian and the savage. This history of this discourse forms the background for the emergence of anthropology, which assumed the science role in the already established savage slot. Trouillot cites an extraordinarily wide variety of sources without really delving into any of them. The main thing these have in common is that they make some use of the idea of non-European societies in their arguments. Some imagine non-European societies as ideals that Europeans should strive for, others as exemplars of depravity that Europeans have escaped. Some are celebratory of European culture, but many are highly critical of it. For Trouillot, this is beside the point. All demonstrate the existence and importance of the savage slot in European thinking from the Renaissance to the current day. Further, the savage slot exists within an overall framework of European/white supremacy. Trouillot seems to suggest, for example, that Voltaire's biting critique of European

THE MEDIATION OF ORDER

Utopia itself made sense only in terms of the absolute order against which it was projected, negatively or not.[h] Utopias do not necessarily advance foundational propositions, but they feed upon foundational thought. Fictional "ideal states," presented as novels or treatises, suggest a project or a counterproject. It is this very projection, rather than their alleged or proven fanciful characteristics, that makes them utopias. Here again, we need to go back to the Renaissance, that fictional rebirth through which Christendom became the West, where two more snapshots may clarify the issue.

From the point of view of contemporaries, the most important event of the year 1492 was not Columbus's landing in the Antilles, but the conquest of the Muslim kingdom of Granada and its incorporation into Castile (Trouillot 1990). The gap between the three religions of Abraham had paralleled the sociopolitical fissure that split the Mediterranean, but because of that fissure, religious intolerance increasingly expressed itself in ways that intertwined religion, ethnicity, territory, and matters of state control. To put it simply, as Christendom became Europe, Europe itself became Christian. It is no accident that the fall of Muslim Granada was immediately followed by the expulsion of the Jews from the now Christian territory. It is no accident either that the very same individual who signed the public order against the Jews also signed Ferdinand and Isabella's secret instructions to Columbus. Indeed, nascent Europe could turn its eyes to the Atlantic only because the consolidation of political borders and the concentration of political power in the name of the Christian God presaged the advent of internal order.[26]

Order—political and ideological—was high on the agenda, both in theory and in practice: and the increased use of the printing press stimulated the interchange between theory and practice. Thus, in 1511, three years before Thomas More's *Utopia*, Niccolò Machiavelli wrote *The Prince*. In retrospect, that work signified a threshold: some leaders of the emerging Western world were ready to phrase the issue of control in terms of realpolitik long before the word was coined. The Machiavelli era encompassed Erasmus's *Education of a Christian Prince*, Bude's *Education of a Prince* and other treatises that shared an "emphasis on the workable rather than the ideal," a belief that men's destinies were to some extent within their own control and that this control depended upon self-knowledge" (Hale 1977:305).[27]

---

society relies fundamentally on ideas of utopia, savagery, and European supremacy and could not exist without them. Are you convinced by his argument?

Trouillot discusses his thematic trilogy of discourse in the formation of anthropology: utopia, savagery, and order. In this section you have just read, he showed the development of the utopia and savagery division. In the next section he will focus on ideas and meanings of order.

26. Christian control of Spain was consolidated in 1492, but in Eastern Europe, the Ottoman Turks had captured Constantinople in 1453 and would continue to threaten Christian Europe until the twentieth century. Additionally, European voyages to other parts of the world had begun decades previously. Prince Henry the Navigator of Portugal (1394–1460) died when Columbus was only nine.

The individual whom Trouillot refers to as signing Columbus's secret instructions and the order against Jews was presumably Tomás de Torquemada (1420–1498), the Inquisition's first and most notorious Grand Inquisitor. Torquemada's name has become synonymous with rigidity and cruelty.

27. Niccolò Machiavelli (1469–1527) was a Florentine diplomat, philosopher, and author most famous for his 1532 work *The Prince*, essentially a how-to guide for aristocracy. *The Prince* is primarily about how power is maintained and manipulated. Machiavelli is known for justifying immoral actions to maintain and increase power.

Desiderius Erasmus (1466–1536) was among the best-known humanist thinkers of the fifteenth and sixteenth centuries. He was a close friend of Thomas More.

Guillaume Budé (1468–1540) was another well-known humanist and a friend of Erasmus. Like Erasmus, his book of instruction for princes urged scholarship, particularly the study of Greek and Latin.

The seminal writings that inscribed savagery, utopia, and order were conceived in the same era. This simultaneity is but one indication that these slots were created against the backdrop of one another. In the context of Europe, the works that set up these slots were part of an emerging debate that tied order to the quest for universal truths, a quest that gave savagery and utopia their relevance. Looming above the issue of the ideal state of affairs, and tying it to that of the state of nature, was the issue of order as both a goal and a means, and of its relation with reason and justice. Campanella's *City*, the runner-up to *Utopia* in the critics' view, clearly engaged some of Machiavelli's proposals and those of contemporary Spanish philosophers (Manuel and Manuel 1979 261–88). Campanella, like More, also wrote in nonfiction modes. He commented on European political regimes, in terms of their ultimate justification. He proposed to various European monarchs a nonfictional plan of rule based on his religious and philosophical views. Indeed, the opinions expressed in his treatises got him thrown into a Spanish jail, where he wrote his fictionalized utopia (Manuel and Manuel 1979: Trousson 1975: 39, 72–78). Sir Thomas More, in turn, was executed.[28]

The relation between fictionalized utopias and matters of political power goes way back to the ancestral forms of the genre in ancient Greece (Trousson 1975:39). So do debates on the nature of otherness. But we need not take the naive history of the West at face value: Greece did not beget Europe. Rather, Europe claimed Greece. The revisionist historiography through which the Renaissance turned Christendom into Europe and gave it its Greek heritage is itself a phenomenon that needs to be placed in history. The distinctiveness of the Renaissance was, in part, the invention of a past for the West.[i] It was also, in part, an emerging claim to universality and to an absolute order inconceivable without that claim. As Las Casas, Montesquieu, and Montaigne were quick to point out in different terms and times, a major difference between Europe and ancient Greece was the reality of the savage as experienced by Europe after 1492. Unlike that of Greece and Rome, or that of the Islamic world, the West's vision of order implied from its inception two complementary spaces, the here and the elsewhere, which premised one another and were conceived as inseparable.[29]

In imaginary terms that elsewhere could be Utopia; but in the concrete terms of conquest, it was a space of colonization peopled by others who would eventually become "us"—or at the very least who should—in a project of assimilation antithetic to the most liberal branches of Greek philosophy. In that sense, order had become universal, absolute—both in the shape of the rising absolutist state (quite opposed, indeed, to Greek democracy), and in the shape of a universal empire stretching the limits of Christendom out into nowhere. Colonization became a mission, and the savage became absence and negation.[j] The symbolic process through which the West created itself thus involved the universal legitimacy of power— and order became, in that process, the answer to the question of legitimacy. To put it other-

---

Note that here, Trouillot merges very different sorts of work. Machiavelli's *The Prince* is about power. Much of it concerns how to engage in warfare. It is famous for the dictum that though it is best to be both loved and feared, it is better to be feared than loved. Erasmus's *The Education of a Christian Prince* emphasizes pacifism and that the proper prince rules only over free and willing subjects. Erasmus is far more concerned with promoting and maintaining a peaceful, orderly society than Machiavelli.

28. For More and Campanella, see notes 12 and 14, respectively.

29. Trouillot does not reference Benedict Anderson's *Imagined Communities* or Eric Hobsbawm and Terence Ranger's *The Invention of Tradition*, but he may well have both in mind. Here, he suggests an imagined community of Christian Europe poised in contrast to the rest of the world. He argues that this community was created by an act of imagination: ancient Greece, part of the Mediterranean and Eastern world, is reimagined as European. The ability to read Greek had been lost in Europe by the early Middle Ages. It was revived by scholars such as Petrarch (1304–1374) and Boccaccio (1312–1375) in the fourteenth century.

wise, the West is inconceivable without a met-anarrative, for since their common emergence in the sixteenth century, both the modern state and colonization posed—and continue to pose—to the West the issue of the philosophical base of order. As Edouard Glissant (1989: 2) phrases it "The West is not in the West. It is a project, not a place," a multilayered enterprise in transparent universality.[30]

Chronological convergences again illustrate the point. At about the time Machiavelli wrote *The Prince*, the Spanish Crown made known its supplementary laws on American colonization. And the Medici clan in 1513 secured the papacy with the nomination of Leo X—the same Leo, bishop of Rome, to whom Pietro Martire dedicated parts of his ethnography. Two years later, the accession of Francis I as king of France signaled the self-conscious invention of the traditions constitutive of the French nation-state—a self-consciousness manifested in the imposed use of the French dialect and the creation of the College de France.[k] One year after Francis's advent, Charles I (later Charles V) became king of Castile and of its New World possessions, and Martin Luther published the theses of Wittenberg. The second decade of the new century ended quite fortuitously with a semblance of victory on the side of order, that is, with Charles's "election" to the imperial crown in 1519. But the condemnation of Luther (1520), rural agitation

within Castile itself, and the so-called Oriental menace (culminating with the 1529 siege of Vienna by the Turks) kept reminding a nascent Europe that its self-delivery was not to happen without pains. The notion of a universal empire that would destroy, through its ineluctable expansion, the borders of Christendom became both more attractive in thought and more unattainable in practice.[31]

The fictionalized utopias that immediately followed More's and overlapped with the practical reshaping of power in a newly defined Europe were by and large reformist rather than revolutionary, hardly breaking new imaginary ground (Trousson 1975:62–72). This is not surprising, for, just as the savage is in an unequal relationship with utopia, so is utopia in an uneven relation with order. Just as the savage is a metaphorical argument for or against utopia, so is utopia (and the savage it encompasses) a metaphorical argument for or against order, conceived of as an expression of legitimate universality. It is the mediation of universal order as the ultimate signified of the savage-utopia relation, that gives the triad its full sense. In defense of a particular vision of order the savage became evidence for a particular type of utopia. That the same ethnographic source could be used to make the opposite point did not matter, beyond a minimal requirement for verisimilitude. To be sure, Las Casas had been there, Sepulveda had not;

---

30. Édouard Glissant (1928–2011) was a poet, philosopher, and literary critic. He was a key member of the Négritude movement, a twentieth-century political movement of black intellectuals, based in Africa and throughout the African diaspora, aimed at raising black consciousness and dedicated to the end of colonialism. Glissant was from Martinique.

31. Supplementary laws on American colonization, probably the 1542 "New Laws of the Indies for the Good Treatment and Preservation of the Indians." These laws theoretically recognized the humanity of indigenous people, limited their exploitation, and made them subject to the Spanish Crown.

Pope Leo X (1513–1521), born Giovani di Lorenzo de' Medici, was the son of Lorenzo de' Medici (1449–1492), who was also known as Lorenzo the Magnificent. The Medici were the leading banking and political family of Florence of that era. Leo X was a controversial pope. He was a patron of the arts and education, a hedonist, and a clever and cynical politician.

Francis I (1494–1547, reigned 1515–1547), like Leo X, is remembered as a patron of the arts. Among many other things, Francis declared French the official language of his kingdom and insisted on the use of French rather than Latin in official documents.

Charles I of Spain, and also Charles V, Holy Roman Emperor (1500–1558), was the grandson of Ferdinand and Isabella of Spain. He became ruler of Spain, the Netherlands, and the Holy Roman Empire. Holy Roman Emperors were chosen by a small group of electors, some representing the church, some representing secular states.

and this helped the cause of the **procurador**. To be sure, the Rousseauists were right and Gottingen was wrong about cranial sizes. To be sure, the empirical verdict is not yet in on the Tasaday. But now as before, the savage is only evidence within a debate, the importance of which surpasses not only his understanding but his very existence.[32]

Just as utopia itself can be offered as a promise or as a dangerous illusion the savage can be noble, wise, barbarian, victim, or aggressor, depending on the debate and the aims of the interlocutors. The space within the slot is not static, and its changing contents are not predetermined by its structural position. Regional and temporal variants of the savage figure abound, in spite of recurring tendencies that suggest geographical specialization.[l]

Too often, anthropological discourse modifies the projection of nonacademic observers only to the extent that it "disciplines" them.[m] At other times, anthropologists help create and buttress images that can question previous permutations.[n] Thus, what happens within the slot is neither doomed nor inconsequential (Fox 1991; Vincent 1991)). The point is, rather, that a critique of anthropology cannot skirt around this slot. The direction of the discipline now depends upon an explicit attack on that slot itself and the symbolic order upon which it is premised (fig 2.1) For as long as the slot remains, the savage is at best a figure of speech, a metaphor in an argument about nature and the universe, about being and existence—in short, an argument about foundational thought.[33]

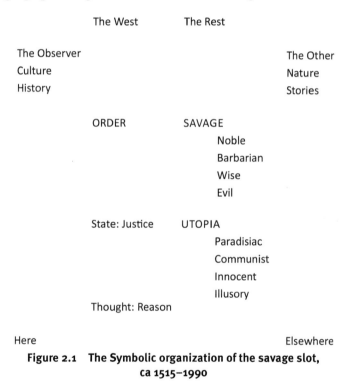

	The West	The Rest
	The Observer	The Other
	Culture	Nature
	History	Stories
	ORDER	SAVAGE
		Noble
		Barbarian
		Wise
		Evil
	State: Justice	UTOPIA
		Paradisiac
		Communist
		Innocent
		Illusory
	Thought: Reason	
Here		Elsewhere

Figure 2.1 The Symbolic organization of the savage slot, ca 1515–1990

32. Note the strong influence of Lévi-Strauss in this passage. Savage–utopia presents a binary of the same sort as nature–culture. This is mediated by the idea of order. As in Lévi-Strauss, the content (whether the savage is pictured positively or negatively, whether the utopia is paradise or dystopic) matters less than the structure, which is maintained despite the positive or negative connotations of savages and utopias.

The procurador: Las Casas was the *procurador*, or the protector, of the Indians.

33. Here, Trouillot both announces his most important point and runs into a dilemma. He has said that the binary utopia–savage mediated by the idea of universal order is foundational to Western thinking. Real non-European peoples, both as written about by Europeans and in the policies of European governments, are

PORTRAIT OF THE ARTIST AS A BUBBLE

This brings us right back to the present. I have argued so far that to historicize the West is to historicize anthropology and vice versa. I have further suggested that the postmodern condition makes that two-pronged historicization both urgent and necessary. If these two arguments are correct, together they expose the unspoken assumptions of postmodernist anthropology in North America and reveal its inherent limitations. For the portrait of the postmodernist anthropologist that emerges from this dual exercise is not a happy one indeed. Camera and notebooks in hand he is looking for the savage, but the savage has vanished.[34]

The problem starts with the fated inheritance of the moderns themselves. The world that the anthropologist inherits has wiped out the empirical trace of the savage-object: Coke bottles and cartridges now obscure the familiar tracks. To be sure, one could reinvent the savage, or create new savages within the West itself—solutions of this kind are increasingly appealing. The very notion of a pristine savagery, however, is now awkward, irrespective of the savage-object. Lingering conditions or modernity make the notion a hard one to evoke in imagination, now that hordes of savages have joined the slums of the Third World or touched the shores of the West. We are far from the days when five Eskimos caused an uproar in London. The primitive has become terrorist, refugee, freedom fighter, opium and coca grower, or parasite. He can even play anthropologist at times. Televised documentaries show his "real" conditions of existence; underground newspapers expose his dreams of modernity. Thanks to modernity, the savage has changed, the West has changed, and the West knows that both have changed empirically.[35]

But modernity is only part of the anthropologist's difficulty. Modern obstacles have modern (technical) answers, or so we used to think. The more serious issue is that technical solutions do not suffice anymore. At best, they can solve the problem of the empirical object by removing the Cokes and cartridges. At worst, they can fabricate an entire new face for savagery. But they cannot remedy the loss of the larger thematic field, especially since the savage never dominated this field. He was only one of the requisite parts of a tripartite relation, the mask of a mask. The problem is not simply that the masks are torn, that true cannibals are now rare. The problem is that now—as in Norman Mailer's *Cannibals and Christians* (1966)—both are equally good, or equally evil (Walkover 1974), if evil itself can be defined (Lyotard 1986).[36]

---

incidental tokens used to make whatever arguments the European authors desire. He has traced the origins of this kind of thinking back to political and intellectual patterns of the fifteenth and sixteenth centuries. He argues that these patterns form a kind of Lévi-Straussian pattern of thought buried deep in the cultural consciousness of European-dominated societies. The dilemma is that Trouillot has proposed that anthropology's continued existence depends on overcoming this centuries-old way of thinking. However, one of the elements of foundational structures of thought is that they are very resistant to change. If the savage–utopia–order structure underlies the logic of our society, it may be impossible to change.

34. Trouillot continues to argue that anthropologists need to critique not only anthropological writing but also the fundamental elements of thought that make anthropological writing possible.

35. The five Eskimos in London were those brought by English merchant George Cartwright (1739–1819) in 1772. Historian Coll Thrush (2014: 67) writes that "from the moment they arrived, the Inuit family was both subjected to the spectacle of Georgian London and cast as one of that spectacle's attractions."

36. **Norman Mailer's *Cannibals and Christians***: Norman Mailer (1923–2007) was an extremely successful mid-twentieth-century novelist, journalist, and playwright. *Cannibals and Christians* (1967) was a collection of essays and poems. It was not well received but is remembered mostly for its devastating analyses of both the 1964 Republican Presidential Convention and the War in Vietnam. Mailer writes, "In a modern world which produces mediocrities at an accelerating rate . . . in a civilization where compassion is of political use and is stratified in welfare programs which do not build a better society but shore up a worse; in a world whose ultimate logic is war. . . . A world of such hypercivilization is . . . a world of whirlpools and formlessness where

This is altogether a postmodern quandary. It is part of the world or constructs and relations revealed by our juxtaposed snapshots, and it is an intrinsic dilemma of postmodern anthropology. For if indeed foundational thoughts are seen as collapsing, if indeed utopias are arguments about order and foundational thoughts, and if indeed the savage exists primarily within an implicit correspondence with utopia, the specialist in savagery is in dire straits. He does not know what to aim at. His favorite model has disappeared or, when found, refuses to pose as expected. The fieldworker examines his tools and finds his camera inadequate. Most importantly, his very field of vision now seems blurred. Yet he needs to come back home with a picture. It's pouring rain out there, and the mosquitoes are starting to bite. In desperation,. the baffled anthropologist burns his notes to create a moment of light, moves his face against the flame, closes his eyes, and hands grasping the camera, takes a picture of himself.[37]

TACTICS AND STRATEGY

Lest this portrait be taken to characterize the postmodernist anthropologist as the epitome of self-indulgence (as many critics, indeed, imply), let me say that narcissist labels characterize postmodernist anthropologists, as individuals no better than they typify their predecessors or adversaries. Intellectuals as a group claimed and gained socially sanctioned self-indulgence long before postmodernism.

Individual intent is secondary here. At any rate, anthropology's postmodern situation warrants more sober reflection than petty accusations of egomania across theoretical camps.

I may end up being both more lenient and more severe—thus risking the condemnation of foes and proponents alike—by saying that the perceived self-indulgence of the postmodernist anthropologists inheres in the situation itself. That is what makes it so obvious and such an easy target for opponents. If we take seriously the perception of an ongoing collapse of the Western metanarratives, the vacuum created by the fall of the house of reason in the once fertile fields of utopian imagination, and the empirical destruction of the savage-object, then the anthropologist who is aware of the postmodern situation has no target outside of himself (as witness) and his text (as pretext), within the thematic universe he inherits.

Once phrased in these terms, the dilemma becomes manageable. One obvious solution is to confront and change the thematic field itself and claim new grounds for anthropology— which is just what some anthropologists have been doing, though without explicit programs. But the dilemma as lived by the postmodernists, is no less real, and the epiphany of textuality cannot be reduced to a mere aggregate of individual tactics of self-aggrandizement or preservation.° If electoral politics may explain either overstatements or the craving for new fads in North American anthropology and elsewhere, they say little of the mechanisms leading to specific choices among myriad pos-

two huge groups begin to reemerge, types there at the beginning of it all: Cannibals and Christians" (1967: 3). In other words, Mailer is using the ideas of cannibals and Christians as metaphors for political attitudes in the United States, precisely as Trouillot suggests.

37. Trouillot is suggesting (in very clever language) that the reflexive turn in postmodern anthropology is in part a result of the disappearance of the anthropological subject, the "savage." But the disappearance of the "savage" in the sense of the untouched society of Trouillot's imagery was not a problem for most working anthropologists. Anthropologists have been documenting and analyzing the effects of colonialism, industrialization, and capitalism since the 1940s (for example, Gluckman [1940], Mead [1956], Steward [1955], and many, many others). (This isn't to say that work in so-called traditional cultures didn't exist. It did but was increasingly supplemented by work that positioned its subjects as fully part of the modern world. McGee and Warms's ethnographic work in the 1980s is a good example of this contrast. In that era, McGee's worked with the Lacandon Maya, who were a subject of anthropological interest precisely because at that time they lived in ways that were similar to how they had lived for generations. Warms, on the other hand, worked with the merchants in West Africa who were busy importing goods from China and Europe and constructing distribution networks. They had little interest in how previous generations had behaved.]

sibilities. Why the text? Why the sudden (for anthropologists, to some extent) rediscovery of literature, and of some literature at that? However much the (re)discovery of textuality and authorial legitimation may be associated with midterm maneuvers, it also must be seen in another context. In that context—the thematic field delineated by order, utopia, and the savage—this emphasis on textuality represents a strategic retreat triggered by the perception of ongoing destruction. In other words, electoral politics alone cannot explain postmodernist anthropology. To propose viable alternatives, one needs to take the ideological and theoretical context of postmodernism seriously, more seriously than the postmodernists do themselves. One needs also to take more seriously both literary criticism and philosophy.

METAPHORS IN ETHNOGRAPHY AND ETHNOGRAPHY AS METAPHOR

The recent discovery of textuality by North American anthropologists is, based on a quite limited notion of the text. The emphasis on "the independent importance of ethnographic writing as a genre" (Marcus 1980: 507), the dismissal of pre-text, con-text, and content, all contribute to reading the anthropological product as isolated from the larger field in which its conditions of existence are generated. Passing references aside, the course of inquiry on the relations among anthropology, colonialism, and political "neutrality," which opened in the late 1960s and early 1970s (e.g., Asad 1973),

is now considered closed, because it allegedly revealed all its partial truths. Passing mentions of gender aside, feminism—as a discourse that claims the specificity of (some) historical subjects—is bypassed because it is said to deal only with "content."[P] Passing references to the Third World notwithstanding, the issues raised by Wolf's historicization of the Other (1982), an inquiry that inherently makes anthropology part of this changing world, are considered moot. Mentions of relations of textual production notwithstanding, the mechanisms and processes emphasized are those that singularize the voice of anthropology, as if anthropological discourse was "either self-enclosed or self-sufficient."[38]

Not surprisingly, the archaeological exploration that underpins the North American exercise in reflexivity tends to stop at the institutionalization of anthropology as a discipline in the Anglophone world, or at best at the delineation of a specialized anthropological discourse in the Europe of the Enlightenment. In spite of the professed renunciation of labels, boundaries are set in modern terms to produce a history of the discipline, albeit one with different emphases. The construction exposed is a discursive order within anthropology, not the discursive order within which anthropology operates and makes sense—even though, here again, this larger field seems to warrant passing mention. The representational aspect of ethnographic discourse is attacked with a vigor quite disproportionate to the referential value of ethnographies in the wider field within which anthropology finds its significance. In short, to use a language that still has its validity, the object of inquiry is the

---

38. Be sure to read Trouillot's endnote p. James Clifford was widely criticized for writing in the introduction to *Writing Culture* that although "feminism clearly has contributed to anthropological theory . . . feminist ethnography has focused either on setting the record straight about women or on revising anthropological categories. . . . It has not produced either unconventional forms of writing or a developed reflection on ethnographic textuality as such" (1986: 20–21).

Trouillot refers to Eric Wolf's 1982 *Europe and the People without History*. Wolf and Sidney Mintz (1922–2015) both had deep impacts on Trouillot. Wolf is mentioned and thanked several times in this essay. Mintz was the chair of anthropology at Johns Hopkins, where Trouillot did his graduate work. Both Wolf and Mintz were 1950s graduates of Columbia, deeply affected by both Julian Steward and Marxist thinking. Both focused their studies around world history, colonialism, and culture change. Although the authors in *Writing Culture* did not explore this work, it is widely considered one of the most influential anthropology books of the 1980s. A JSTOR search for "Europe and the People without History" in summer 2023 returns over two thousand results.

"simple" rather than the "enlarged" reproduction of anthropological discourse. Terminology and citations notwithstanding, the larger thematic field on which anthropology is premised is barely scratched.

But if we take seriously the proposition to look at anthropology as metaphor—as I think we can, given the thematic field outlined—we cannot just look at metaphors in anthropology. The study of "ethnographic allegory" (Clifford 1986; Tyler 1986) cannot be taken to refer primarily to allegorical forms in ethnography without losing site [*sic*] of the larger picture. Our starting point cannot be "a crisis in anthropology" (Clifford 1986a: 3), but in the histories of the world.[q] We need to go out of anthropology to see the construction of "ethnographic authority" not as a late requirement of anthropological discourse (Clifford 1983b) but as an early component of this wider field that is itself constitutive of anthropology. Would that the power of anthropology hinged upon the academic success of genial immigrants such as Franz Boas and Bronislaw Malinowski! It would allow us to find new scapegoats without ever looking back at the Renaissance. But the exercise in reflexivity must go all the way and examine fully the enlarged reproduction of anthropological discourse.[r]

Observers may wonder why the postmodernist experiment in U.S. anthropology has not encouraged a surge of substantive models. The question of time aside, the difficulty of passing from criticism to substance is not simply due to a theoretical aversion to content or an instinctive suspicion of exemplars. After all, the postmodernist wave has revitalized substantive production in other academic fields. It has stimulated architects and political theorists alike. At the very least, it has provoked debates on and of substance. Further, some political radicals advocate the possibility of militant practices rooted in postmodernism—although not without controversies (Laclau and Mouffe 1985; Arne 1986; Ross 19886). More important, the implicit awareness of an expanding situation of postmodernity continues to motivate grass-roots movements all over the world, with their partial truths and partial results. In fact, an anthropologist could well read postmodernism, or at the very least the postmodern situation, as a case for the specificity of otherness, for the destruction of the savage slot.[39]

To claim the specificity of otherness is to suggest a residual of historical experience that always escapes universalisms exactly because history itself always involves irreducible subjects. It is to reserve a space for the subject, not the existential subject favored by the early Sartre and who keeps creeping back into the mea culpa anthropology, but the men and women who are the subjects of history.[s] It is to acknowledge that this space of the historical subject is out of reach of all metanarratives, not because all metanarratives are created equal and are equally wrong (which is the claim of nihilism and always ends up favoring some subjects and some narratives), but because metanarrative claims to universality necessarily imply the muting of first persons, singular or plural, deemed marginal. To say that otherness is always specific and historical is to reject this marginality. The Other cannot be encompassed by a residual category: there is no savage slot. The "us and all of them" binary, implicit in the symbolic order that creates the West, is an ideological construct, and the many forms of Third-World-ism that reverse its terms are its mirror images. There is no Other, but multitudes of others who are all others for different reasons, in spite of totalizing narratives, including that of capital.[40]

---

39. See again our footnote 7 in this essay. Trouillot imagines postmodernism as energizing political movements on the left and destroying the savage slot. However, postmodernism also energized the right. Far from eliminating the savage slot, it related to its reinvigoration in the form of xenophobic nationalist movements worldwide. Postmodernism served as a whipping boy for right-wing attacks on left-leaning intellectuals. But critically, it also provided the right with methods to attack all truth claims and supported the linkage of power and ability to determine what can count as fact.

40. *Mea culpa*, Latin for "my fault." The existential subject favored by the early Sartre. Jean-Paul Sartre (1905–1980) was a key existential philosopher. The early Sartre, probably best represented by his works

Many propositions follow from this statement not the least of which is that a discipline whose object is the Other may in fact have no object—which may lead us to take a much needed look at the methodological specificity of anthropology. It also follows that the authenticity of the historical subject may not be fully captured from the outside even by way of direct quotes; there may be something irreducible in the first person singular. This, in turn, raises two related issues: that of the epistemological status of native discourse;[t] and that of the theoretical status of ethnography. I will turn to these issues, not so much in a purely abstract mode (though this may be also necessary), but as entwined with specific research projects.

First, anthropology needs to evaluate its gains and losses in light of these issues, with a fair tally of the knowledge anthropologists have produced in the past, sometimes in spite of themselves and almost always in spite of the savage slot. We owe it to ourselves to ask what remains of anthropology and of specific monographs when we remove this slot—not to revitalize disciplinary tradition through cosmetic surgery, but to build both an epistemology and a semiology of what anthropologists have done and can do. We cannot simply assume that modernism has exhausted all its potential projects. Nor can we assume that "realist ethnography" has produced nothing but empty figures of speech and shallow claims to authority.[41]

Second, armed with this renewed arsenal, we can recapture domains of significance by creating strategic points of "reentry" into the discourse on otherness: areas within the discourse where the introduction of new voices or new combinations of meaning perturbate the entire field and open the way to its (partial) recapture.[u] This chapter is not the place to expand in the directions of these many queries, so I can only tease the reader. But a few tasks seem to me urgent in this new context: an epistemological reassessment of the historical subject (the first person singular that has been overwhelmed by the voice of objectivity or by that of the narrator and that is so important to many feminists, especially Afro-American feminists); a similar reassessment of nativeness and native discourse, now barely conceptualized; and a theory of ethnography, now repudiated as the new "false consciousness." And for the time being, at least, we need more ethnographies that raise these issues through concrete cases. Not so much ethnographies that question the author/native dichotomy by exposing the nude as nakedness but ethnographies (ethno-historio-semiologies?) that offer new points of reentry by questioning the Symbolic world upon which "nativeness" is premised At the very least, anthropologists can show that the Other, here and elsewhere, is indeed a product—symbolic and material—of the same process that created the West.[v] In short, the time is ripe for substantive propositions that aim explicitly at the destruction of the savage slot.

That it has not been so among the postmodernists of North American anthropology is thus a matter of choice. In spite of a terminology that intimates a decoding of "anthropology as metaphor," we are barely reading anthropology itself. Rather, we are reading anthropological pages, and attention remains focused primarily on the metaphors in anthropology. This recur-

---

Nausea (1938) and *Being and Nothingness* (1943) saw each individual as ultimately free and therefore responsible for their life and their choices, even though these were limited by history and circumstance. Later Sartre was more directly political.

41. Trouillot makes a critical point in this paragraph. He is not attacking the validity of all previous anthropology but pointing out that the way that ethnography fits into Western semiotics is separate from its accuracy. For example, it is easy to see how Margaret Mead's *Coming of Age in Samoa* employs a utopian vision of savagery to comment on the psychological, sexual, and gender order of the United States. It fits Trouillot's trilogy well. It describes a positive savage utopia that implies a change in the order of Western psychological and gender conceptions. However, this is a different question from whether it accurately describes Samoan society of the late 1920s. But Trouillot also begs the question of how we are to assess the quality and validity of anthropology. The facticity of *Coming of Age* has been repeatedly questioned, but no definitive answer has been determined (Shankman 2009).

ring refusal to pursue further the archaeological exercise obscures the asymmetrical position of the savage-other in the thematic field upon which anthropology was premised. It negates the specificity of otherness, subsuming the Other in the sameness of the text perceived as liberating cooperation. "We are the world"?

Anthropology did not create the savage. Rather, the savage was the raison d'etre of anthropology. Anthropology came to fill the savage slot in the trilogy order-utopia-savagery, a trilogy which preceded anthropology's institutionalization and gave it continuing coherence in spite of intradisciplinary shifts. This trilogy is now in jeopardy. Thus the time is ripe—and in that sense, it is postmodern—to attack frontally the visions that shaped this trilogy, to uncover its ethical roots and its consequences, and to find better anchor for an anthropology of the present, an anthropology of the changing world and its irreducible histories. But postmodernist anthropologists pass near this opportunity looking for the savage in the text. They want us to read the internal tropes of the savage slot, no doubt a useful exercise in spite of its potential for self-indulgence. But they refuse to address directly the thematic field (and thus the larger world) that made (makes) this slot possible, morosely preserving the empty slot itself.

Times have changed since the sixteenth century: one now is innocent until proven guilty. Thus, claims of innocence can take the shape of silence. Somehow, to my surprise, I miss the faithful indignation of a Las Casas.[42]

AUTHOR'S NOTES

My thanks to all those who commented on earlier versions of this paper, the participants at the Santa Fe Seminar, graduate students and faculty at Johns Hopkins University and at the New School for Social Research, and the readers for the School of American Research. Personal thanks to Karman Ali, Talal Asad, Lanfranco Blanchetti, Ashraf Ghani, Ananta Giri, Richard G. Fox, Richard Kagan, and Eric Wolf, none of whom should be held responsible for the final product. An early version of this paper, "Anthropology as Metaphor: The Savage's Legacy and the Post-Modern World," appeared in Review, a Journal of the Fernand Braudel Center, vol. XIV, no. 1, Winter 1991.

a. For reasons of space, I cannot retrace here all the connections between recent debates in philosophy and literary theory and recent critiques of anthropology. Our readings are too parochial, anyway—to the point that any major thinker needs to be translated into the discipline by an insider. Anthropology has much more to learn from other disciplines, notably history, literary criticism, and philosophy, than the reflexivist interpreters assume. There are blanks to be filled by the reader with proper use of the bibliographical references.

b. Other reasons aside, long-term fieldwork in the so-called Third World, after the initial dissertation, is becoming more difficult and less rewarding for a majority of anthropologists. Unfortunately, issues such as the increased competition for funds to do fieldwork abroad or the growing proportion of two-career families in and out of academe only make good conversation. Practitioners tend to dismiss them in written (and therefore "serious") assessments of trends in the discipline. The sociology of our practice is perceived as taboo, but see Wolf (1969), whose early appeal for such a sociology fell on dead ears and Rabinow (this volume).

c. In that sense, I take exception to Renato Rosaldo's formulation that the conservative domination "has distorted a once-healthy debate" (Rosaldo 1989: 223). What a certain kind of anthropology can demonstrate is exactly that the debate was never as healthy as we were led to believe.

d. See Graff (1977), Jameson (1984), Arac (1986), Lyotard (1986). Ross (1988b), and Harvey (1989) on conflicting definitions of postmodernism I am not qualified to settle this debate. But if postmodernism only means a style, a bundle of expository devices, characterized (or not) by "double coding" (Jencks 1986), then it does not much matter to anthropologists—as long as they note that double coding has been part of the cultural arsenal of many non-Western cultures for centuries. On the connection between postmodernism and metanarratives, see Lyotard (1979, 1986), Eagleton (1987). and Harvey (1989)

e. The first consists of two chapters in *Les Bijoux indiscrets*. The second is the fantastic *Supplement au voyage du Bougainville*, a primitivist utopia where Tahiti is the Other in more than one way, being both savage and female (Trousson 1975: 140; Brewer 1985).

---

42. In these last paragraphs, Trouillot summarizes his critique of postmodernism in general and *Writing Culture* in particular. He calls for a reevaluation of anthropology that places both its assumptions and presumptions in broader historical context. He faults postmodernists for overconcentration on the internal techniques of anthropology and failing to grapple with the ways of thinking that made anthropology possible.

f. I owe my ideas on the black or plantation pastoral to conversations with Professor Maximilien Laroche and access to his unpublished paper on the subject. In Bernadin Saint-Pierre's successful *Paul et Virginie* (1787), whose setting is a plantation island, a group of maroon slaves surprises the two lovers. But to the heroes' amazement, the chief of the runaway slaves says, "Good little whites, don't be afraid; we saw you pass this morning with a negro woman from Riviere-Noire; you went to ask her grace to her bad master; in gratitude, we will carry you back home on our shoulders."

g. Some writers have made this point. Others have assembled the necessary information to make it, without always drawing the same conclusion from their juxtapositions. I have read over the shoulders of so many of them, and imposed my reading on so many others that credits for this section and the next were sometimes difficult to attribute in the main text; but see Atkinson (1920, 1922, 1924), Baudet (1959), Chinard (1934). Duchet (1971), De Certeau (1975), Gonnard (1946). Todorov (1982). Trousson (1975). Rupp-Eisenreich (1984), and Droixhe and Gossiaux (1985).

h. My phrasing of this issue in terms of order owes to conversations with Ashraf Ghani. I remain responsible for its use here and its possible shortcomings. Empirical elements of an analysis of the role of order within the symbolic horizons of the Renaissance are plentiful in Hale's *Renaissance Europe: Individual and Society, 1480–1520* (Hale 1977).

i. Genealogies that trace the beginnings of anthropology to Herodotus (why not Ibn Battuta?) partake of that naive history. They serve the guild interests of the "discipline," its construction of tradition, authorship, and authority and the reproduction of the savage slot upon which it builds its legitimacy. Note, however, that it was only in the eighteenth and nineteenth centuries that Romantics and racists abandoned the ancient Greeks' own version of their cultural origins, denying the contributions of Africans and Semites to "civilization." Classical studies then invented a new past for Greece with an Aryan model (Bernal 1987).

j. From then on, descriptions of savagery would inscribe grammatically the absence in a way now all too familiar (and unquestioned) by anthropologists. The savage is what the West is not: "no manner of traffic, no knowledge of letters, no science of numbers . . . no contracts, no successions, no dividends, no properties . . ." (Montaigne 1952:94). This language is quite different from that of Polo (1958) or even from that of Pliny. But its immediate antecedents are in the very first descriptions of the Americas: Columbus, for instance, thought the "Indians" had "no religion"-by which he probably meant "none of the three religions of Abraham."

k. One cannot suggest that Francis I consciously foresaw a French nation-state in the modem sense, but the absolutist order he envisioned revealed itself historically untenable without the invented tradition necessary for the symbolic construction of the nation.

It is only by one of those ironies of which history is full that this tradition became fully alive at the time of the Revolution and as solidified by a Corsican mercenary with no claim to Frankish nobility, namely, Napoleon Buonaparte.

l. One suspects that the savage as wise is more often than not Asiatic, the savage as noble is often a Native American. and the savage as barbarian is often African or African American. But neither roles nor positions are always neat, and the structural dichotomies do not always obtain historically. Jews and Gypsies, for instance, are savages "within" the West—an awkward position not accounted by the here/elsewhere dichotomy, but resolved in practice by persecution.

m. Anthropological insistence on, say, rebellion and resistance in Latin America, economic qua material survival in Africa, or ritual expression in Southeast Asia partakes of a symbolic distribution that predates chronologically and precedes epistemologically the division of labor within the discipline. A major limitation of the work of Edward Said is the failure to read "Orientalism" as one set of permutations within the savage slot.

n. My greater familiarity with Caribbean anthropology may explain why I find most of my positive examples in this corner of the world, but it is obvious to Caribbeanists that anthropology helped challenge the vision of the Antilles as islands in the sun peopled by indolent natives—a view popularized since the nineteenth century by racist yet celebrated writers such as Anthony Trollope (1859). How successful was the challenge is another issue, but forty years before "voodoo economics" became a pejorative slogan in North American political parlance, some North American and European anthropologists took Haitian popular religion quite seriously (e.g., Herskovits 1937b).

o. To be sure, in its current form, the alleged discovery of the text provokes transient hyperboles. We all knew that ethnography was also text if only because of the ABDs relegated to driving cabs when their lines could not see the light of day, or because of the careers destroyed when dissertations failed to sprout "publishable" books (the text/test par excellence?). That Marcus and Cushman (1982: 27) "for simplicity . . . do not consider the very interesting relationship between the production of a published ethnographic text and its intermediate written versions" is not novel. Tenure committees have been doing the same for years, also "for simplicity," while we all continued to ignore politely the electoral politics that condition academic success.

p. See Clifford's (1986a:21) indulgent neglect of feminism on purely textual grounds: "It has not produced either unconventional forms of writing or a developed reflection on ethnographic textuality as such." Never mind that feminism now sustains one of the most potent discourses on the specificity of the historical subject and, by extension, on the problem of "voice." To be sure, some white middle-class women, especially in the United States, want to make that newfound "voice" universal, and their feminist enterprise threatens to become a new metanarrative, akin to Fanon's Third-World-ism, or Black Power a la 1960. But it is at the very least awkward for Clifford to dismiss feminist and "non-Western writings" for having made their impact on issues of content alone.

q. In fact, I doubt that there is a crisis in anthropology as such; rather, there is a crisis in the world that anthropology assumes.

r. The limited exercises of the postmodernists would take on new dimensions if used to look at the enlarged reproduction of anthropology. For example, were we to rekindle the notion of genre to read ethnography (Marcus 1980), we would need to speculate either a metatext (the retrospective classification of a critic), or the sanction of a receiving audience of nonspecialists, or a thematic and ideological framework in the form of an archi-textual field (Genette, Jauss, and Schaffer, 1986). To speak of any of these in relation to ethnography as genre would illustrate enlarged reproduction and reexamine anthropology's own grounds.

s. I thank Eric Wolf for forcing me to make this important distinction.

t. The matter of the status of "halfies" (approached by Abu-Lughod in this volume) can be further analyzed in these terms. We need not fall into nativism in order to raise epistemological questions about the effect of historically accumulated experience, the "historical surplus value" that specific groups of subjects-as-practitioners bring to a discipline premised on the existence of the savage slot and the commensurability of otherness. At the same time, for philosophical and political reasons, I am profoundly opposed to the formulas of the type "add native, stir. and proceed as usual," so successful in electoral politics in and out of academe. Anthropology needs something more fundamental than reconstitutive surgery, and halfies, women, people of color. etc., deserve something better than a new slot.

u. The symbolic reappropriation that Christianity imposed on Judaism, or that liberation theology is imposing on Christianity in some areas of the world; the reorientation that the ecology movement has injected into notions of "survival"; the redirection that feminism has imposed on issues of gender; and Marx's perturbation of classical political economy from within are all unequal examples of "reentry" and recapture.

v. The anthropology of agricultural commodities as material and symbolic boundaries between human groups (along the lines opened by Mintz 1985b); the anthropology of the categories and institutions that reflect and organize power-such as "peasants," "nation," "science," (Trouillot 1988. 1989, 1990;

Martin 1987) or the "West" itself (to renew with both Benveniste [1969] and Foucault); the anthropology of the transnational media and other forms of communication shaping the international organization of symbols-all can be fruitfully conceptualized within such a scheme.

Globalization

When Napoleon Chagnon (1938–2019) went to do research among the Yanomamo in 1964, he could be excused if he believed that he was seeing people who were relatively untouched by the outside world and living in more or less the same way they had for countless generations. The Yanomamo had relatively few material goods from outside, had only rarely seen others who did not look like them, and behaved in ways clearly alien to Venezuelan and Brazilian societies.

No one visiting the Yanomamo today could make such a mistake. In the half century since Chagnon's first fieldwork among the Yanomamo, Yanomamo land has been invaded by gold miners, and the Yanomamo have been at the center of disputes about national parks and the rights of native peoples. They have been the subject of both documentary and fiction films. Their leaders have made frequent appearances at universities and government hearings. Yanomamo crafts can be purchased on the internet, and individual Yanomamo have become laborers in the mines and oil fields of Venezuela and Brazil. Between January 1, 1970, and January 1, 1976, the only coverage of the Yanomamo in the *New York Times* was a note announcing the showing of an anthropological film. However, "Yanomamo" (and "Yanomami," an alternate spelling) appeared in more than forty *New York Times* articles between January 1, 2010, and January 1, 2016. Whatever you can say about the Yanomamo, you can't say they have been isolated from the rest of the world.

The Yanomamo are an extreme (and largely tragic) example of an indigenous culture being overwhelmed by international economic and political forces. However, what is true of the Yanomamo is also the case just about everywhere else in the world. Almost anywhere you go, you can see the influence of the international movement of information, money, and people. Television is ubiquitous, and it no longer feels terribly strange to be sitting in a small African village watching American sitcoms. By 2014, cell phone ownership was almost as common in Ghana, Senegal, and Nigeria as in the United States (though Americans owned more smartphones) (Pew Research Center 2015). No doubt, the distribution of these phones is affected by geography, class, ethnicity, and many other factors, but the numbers are impressive nonetheless. The trappings of consumer society are visible virtually everywhere, and this makes globalization one of the most obvious and powerful phenomena in the world. This is particularly clear to anthropologists who (like McGee) have worked in a single location for several decades.

On one hand, interest in contact between cultures and the movement of ideas, technologies, and artifacts among them is one of the oldest areas of study in anthropology. For example, German and British diffusionists proposed (often unrealistic) patterns of cultural exchange in the late nineteenth century. Otis T. Mason (1838–1908), Clark Wissler (1870–1947), and A. L. Kroeber all wrote about culture areas and diffusion in North America in the late nineteenth and the first half of the twentieth centuries. However, current-day interest in culture exchange on a global scale increased greatly with the work of Immanuel Wallerstein (1930–2019) in the 1970s and Eric Wolf (1923–1999) in the 1980s.

In his 1974 work *The Modern World System: Capitalist Agriculture and the Origins of the European World Economy in the Sixteenth Century*, Wallerstein argued that European conquests in the early sixteenth century began to establish a capitalist world economy that superseded the national and ethnic boundaries of feudal Europe. This new world economy differed from earlier systems because capitalism enabled this new economy to extend beyond the political boundaries of any one European empire. Wallerstein sorted this new world economic system into regions he called core, semi-periphery, periphery, and external. These categories described each region's relative position within the world economy.

Core regions (primarily northern Europe) benefited the most from this new system. These states developed strong central governments and large armies that permitted them to control commerce and trade for their own profit. The peripheral areas were on the other end of this system. These areas were controlled by states in the core and exported raw materials to the core using coercive labor practices like slavery. Between the two extremes of core and periphery lie regions Wallerstein called semi-peripheries. These are areas that are core regions in decline or periphery regions attempting to advance their position in the world economic system. Finally, Wallerstein described a fourth region, external areas, which are those regions that maintained their own economic systems and remained outside of this world system.

The value of Wallerstein's analysis is that it shows how political and economic conditions in the sixteenth century transformed northwestern Europe into a world commercial and political power and how the expansion of their economies altered political systems and labor conditions all around the globe. These core countries have been the centers of economic power, technological development, and the manufacture of complex products for centuries, while the peripheries, in contrast, supplied raw materials, agricultural products, and cheap labor.

A similar study is Eric Wolf's *Europe and the People without History* (1982), in which Wolf, strongly influenced by Karl Marx, traces the expansion of Europe as a global power in the fifteenth century, the European establishment of colonies that became tributary networks, and how European countries transformed those networks into global capitalism. Unlike Wallerstein, whose focus was on how core nations subjugated the periphery, Wolf's emphasis is on the "people without history," that is, the organization and modes of subsistence of indigenous societies before European conquest and how European capitalism replaced indigenous modes of existence. In short, Wolf examines the expansion of the power of Europe over the last several hundred years and the incorporation of societies across the globe in an economic system dominated by European capitalism.

Many globalization theorists do not generally share Wolf's interest in the long-term history of the societies they study. And this brings up a key question in theories of globalization. On one hand, anthropologists, following Wolf, Wallerstein, and others, have promoted the idea that global connections among societies are critically important and that these must be understood as operating over centuries, or perhaps millennia. On the other, there is little doubt that the sheer speed and volume of the international exchange of information and material goods are unprecedented. So, does the current era represent merely a quantitative change from the past, or is there a more dramatic qualitative change as well?

Most anthropologists of globalization focus on the present and the past two or three decades in analyzing the ways in which societies are articulated with the world economy in general and with capitalist enterprises in particular. Critical foci of their studies include the effects of the expansion of multinational corporations, the outsourcing of production and labor, and the ability to move goods and information around the globe. Influenced by the work of Antonio Gramsci (1897–1931) and Michel Foucault (1926–1984) (both of whom have been discussed earlier in this book), they seek to understand the ways in which both the powerful and the powerless perceive and manipulate symbols and comprehend their position in the world, how they choose which objects and activities are desirable, and how they view the goals of society.

The two works in this section capture much of the flavor of the different approaches to globalization. The first selection is by Eric Wolf. Wolf was one of the most influential neo-Marxist thinkers in the United States. Born in Vienna, he emigrated first to England, then, in 1940, to New York. After service in World War II, during which he was decorated for bravery, he went on to earn his PhD at Columbia, where he studied with Ruth Benedict, Stanley Diamond (1922–1991), Sidney Mintz (1922–2015), Morton Fried (1923–1986), and Julian Steward. Steward was his mentor, and when, in 1952, Steward moved to the University of Illinois, Wolf followed. Subsequent moves took Wolf to the University of Virginia, the University of Michigan, and then, finally, the City University of New York (CUNY).

Because of his contact with Fried, Steward, and others, Wolf's work was informed by Marx's notion of society as a historical and material process. His first book, *Sons of the Shaking Earth* (1959), explored the rise of Mesoamerican cultures in relation to the geography, ecology, and ethnic diversity of the area and examined effects of the Spanish conquest.

Wolf began to conduct cultural analysis in openly Marxist terms in his 1966 book *Peasants*. In *Peasants* Wolf examines the structure of peasant societies and their relation to industrialized states. *Peasants* was followed in 1969 by *Peasant Wars of the Twentieth Century*, a book that applied Marxist thinking to a series of conflicts in Mexico, Russia, China, Algeria, and Cuba.

In the 1960s and 1970s, Wolf was a strong critic of the war in Vietnam. Along with Marshall Sahlins, he helped start the "teach-in" movement at the University of Michigan (Wolf and Jorgensen 1970). Teach-ins were developed as a protest against the Vietnam War and soon spread to many universities. Students and faculty would meet to debate, question, challenge assumptions, and learn about the Vietnam War. Wolf intended *Peasant Wars* to be a text used at such meetings. As a result of their activism, Wolf and Sahlins both came under FBI scrutiny in the late 1960s (Price 2004).

As mentioned previously, Wolf's most influential book was *Europe and the People without History* (1982). Wolf was deeply influenced by the economist Andre Gunder Frank (1929–2005) and the sociologist Immanuel Wallerstein, who were leading thinkers of dependency theory and world systems theory. In the 1960s, economists such as W. W. Rostow proposed that poor nations could become wealthy by repeating the historical experience of wealthy nations—the premise of what came to be called *modernization theory*. Frank and others argued that modernization in undeveloped nations could not succeed because their wealth and labor had been systematically siphoned from them by Europe and the United States. Poor nations had not simply failed to modernize and develop; they had been systematically underdeveloped by wealthy nations.

In *Europe and the People without History*, Wolf took the expansion of European capitalism as his central subject. He showed how the mercantile and capitalist expansion of Europe affected and undermined indigenous cultural systems throughout the Third World and how this process produced great wealth and great suffering. The book is critical because it moved American neo-Marxists and neofunctionalists away from the study of small-scale, isolated systems to large-scale social analysis. However, Wolf's analysis had effects well beyond neo-Marxist circles. His revisionist approach to world history championed the voices of the poor and oppressed. He cast doubt on the coherence of ethnic groupings and identities, pointing out that these were often created by the forces of capital. He reminded readers that the dominant narrative of history was generally told only from the point of view of the wealthy and powerful, which was a very biased perspective. Wolf attempted to give voice to the poor and oppressed in his telling of history.

Wolf's work was particularly influential because it combined the concern for the downtrodden that was an important element of Boasian thinking with a powerful neo-Marxist analysis. At a time when postmodernism was emerging as an important force within anthropology, Wolf drew attention to the issue of voice, of who has the authority to tell history and how that authority is constituted, and to the historical and contingent nature of identity.

Wolf's essay is called "Facing Power: Old Insights, New Questions" and was first presented as the Distinguished Lecture at the 1989 meeting of the American Anthropological Association. In this essay, Wolf discusses the different ways that anthropologists have studied power by examining three ethnographic projects: the People of Puerto Rico led by Julian Steward in 1948–1949, the Rhodes-Livingstone Institute's study of social change in southern Africa between 1937 and 1947, and Richard Adams's study of social change in Guatemala from 1963 to 1966. He argues that these three studies are important because they remind us that events unfold over time on a macro scale as well as of the micro settings on which most anthropologists focus. The essay is also important because it presents an alternative perspective to the view of anthropology at that time being promoted by interpretive and postmodern anthropologists like Clifford Geertz, George Marcus, and James Clifford.

The second essay is by Arjun Appadurai (b. 1949). Appadurai was born and raised in Mumbai, India, but pursued university education in the United States. He received his PhD from the University of Chicago in 1976, studying under the Committee on Social Thought, an interdisciplinary program. He has held university appointments at the University of Pennsylvania, the University of Chicago, New York University, and the New School. With anthropologist Carol Breckenridge (1942–2009), he is also cofounder of the journal *Public Culture*.

"Disjuncture and Difference in the Global Cultural Economy" is among the best-known anthropology articles published in the last few decades, and it shows a particularly deep debt to French postmodern scholars. In addition to the work of Foucault and Pierre Bourdieu (1930–2002), Appadurai refers to the work of Jacques Lacan (1901–1981) and Jacques Derrida (1930–2004), among others. Appadurai argues that the movement of people, capital, and information that has been enabled by new technologies has created a world qualitatively different than that described in traditional ethnographies. The world, he argues, is probably best described as a series of *scapes*, a term he has made famous. For Appadurai, a scape is designed to capture the ways in which people immersed in globalized cultures and economies understand and act in their world. Appadurai identifies five scapes, composed of ethnicity, media, technology, finance, and ideas. These are not hierarchical. Although they intersect and overlap, the relations among them are characterized by difference and rupture rather than unity. Using these terms, Appadurai attempts to capture the notion of culture as a changing flow of people, information, money, and technology. Much of Appadurai's essay, written in 1990, seems to capture a sense of the experience of current-day life as it is lived by many people (but perhaps not everyone). Appadurai's vision of globalization is broadly (though not entirely) optimistic. Globalization is not a universalizing juggernaut. Rather, it enables people to use the disjunctive forces now at their disposal to pursue their own, frequently innovative cultural projects.

To some degree, globalization theory represents a synthesis between the materialism and attempted empiricism of the neofunctionalists and neo-Marxists and the more idealist approaches of the cognitive and the symbolic and interpretive anthropologists. Like materialists, they are concerned with people's behaviors and choices. They see these as influenced by economic pressures and economic rationales and set within systems of relations of production. Like symbolic and interpretive anthropologists, they are particularly concerned with the ways in which people create and contest meaning and morality within these structures.

SUGGESTED READINGS

Appadurai, Arjun. 1996. *Modernity at Large: Cultural Dimensions of Globalization.* Minneapolis: University of Minnesota Press.
   A collection of Appadurai's essays (including the essay published in this book) that focuses on the end of the nation-state, international flows, and the production of locality.
Bestor, Theodore. 2004. *Tsukiji: The Fish Market at the Center of the World.* Berkeley: University of California Press.
   Bestor's ethnography of the central Tokyo fish market focuses on the complexity of social institutions and global flows that characterize the Japanese seafood trade.
Friedman, Jonathan, and Kajsa Ekholm Friedman. 2013. "Globalization as a Discourse of Hegemonic Crisis: A Global Systemic Analysis." *American Ethnologist* 40(2): 244–257.
   A critique that places the discourse of globalization in long-term historical context.
Hannerz, Ulf. 1996. *Transnational Connections: Culture, People, Places.* London: Routledge.
   A collection of essays by one of the key theorists (and celebrators) of globalization.
Mintz, Sidney. 1986. *Sweetness and Power: The Place of Sugar in Modern History.* New York: Penguin.
   An account of the central role of sugar in globalization from the sixteenth to the twentieth century.
Wolf, Eric. 1983. *Europe and the People without History.* Berkeley: University of California Press.
   One of the founding documents of globalization studies in anthropology, Wolf's highly readable account of the history of European expansion is a must for those interested in globalization.

31. Facing Power—Old Insights, New Questions

Eric R. Wolf (1923–1999)

IN THIS ESSAY I engage the problem of power and the issues that it poses for anthropology. I argue that we actually know a great deal about power, but have been timid in building upon what we know. This has implications for both theory and method, for assessing the insights of the past and for raising new questions.[1]

The very term makes many of us uncomfortable. It is certainly one of the most loaded and polymorphous words in our repertoire. The Romance, Germanic, and Slavic languages, at least, conflate a multitude of meanings in speaking about *pouvoir* or *potere*, *Macht*, or *mogushchestvo*. Such words allow us to speak about power as if it meant the same thing to all of us. At the same time, we often speak of power as if all phenomena involving it were somehow reducible to a common core, some inner essence. This conjures up monstrous images of power, Hobbes's Leviathan or Bertrand de Jouvenel's Minotaur, but it leads away from specifying different kinds of power implicated in different kinds of relationships.[2]

I argue instead that it is useful to think of four different modes of power. One is power as the attribute of the person, as potency or capability, the basic Nietzschean idea of power (Kaufmann 1968). Speaking of power in this sense draws attention to the endowment of persons in the play of power, but tells us little about the form and direction of that play. The second kind of power can be understood as the ability of an ego to impose its will on an alter,

---

From *American Anthropologist* (1990)

1. This essay was the Distinguished Lecture at the 1989 meeting of the American Anthropological Association. AAA Distinguished Lectures are currently given every other year. Lecturers are chosen by a panel of AAA past presidents. An invitation to deliver a Distinguished Lecture is a high honor. Other recipients include Faye Harrison (2021), Emily Martin (2018), Bruno Latour (2014), Fredrik Barth (2002), Marvin Harris (1991), Mary Douglas (1988), and Clifford Geertz (1983). The text of each lecture is published in *American Anthropologist* therefore many anthropologists either hear or read these lectures.

2. It is impossible to know the effect of any one presentation or essay. What is certainly true is that in the years since Wolf gave this lecture, issues of power have become central in anthropology. A JSTOR search shows that in the ten years before the lecture (1980–1989) the word power appeared 370 times in the titles of essays in anthropology,. However, in the ten years after the lecture (1990–1999) the word power appears 738 times.

Thomas Hobbes (1588–1679), was an English political philosopher whose best-known work is *Leviathan* (orig. 1651). In *Leviathan* Hobbes discussed the structure and legitimacy of different types of government. He argued that the natural state of humankind was a war of all against all (Chapter XIII, available online at https://www.bartleby.com/34/5/13.html). This could only be avoided through the power of a strong central authority that could suppress and control rivalries between people.

Bertrand de Jouvenel (1903–1987), was a French philosopher and political economist. In the 1930s and 1940s Jouvenel associated with leading European fascists. In his 1944 work, *On Power, Its Nature and the History of Its Growth* (1948 Eng trans), Jouvenel describes power as "the minotaur," "an ever-expanding, ever-greedy creature, bent on usurping all authority within society" (Rosenberg 2017: 121). Jouvenel believed that the unrestrained growth of power in modern states was linked with the rise of the ideas of equality and individualism.

in social action, in interpersonal relations. This draws attention to the sequences of interactions and transactions among people, but it does not address the nature of the arena in which the interactions go forward. That comes into view more sharply when we focus on power in the third mode, as power that controls the settings in which people may show forth their potentialities and interact with others. I first came across this phrasing of power in anthropology when Richard Adams sought to define power not in interpersonal terms, but as the control that one actor or "operating unit" (his term) exercises over energy flows that constitute part of the environment of another actor (Adams 1966, 1975). This definition calls attention to the instrumentalities of power and is useful for understanding how "operating units" circumscribe the actions of others within determinate settings. I call this third kind of power tactical or organizational power.[3]

But there is still a fourth mode of power, power that not only operates within settings or domains but that also organizes and orchestrates the settings themselves, and that specifies the distribution and direction of energy flows. I think that this is the kind of power that Marx addressed in speaking about the power of capital to harness and allocate labor power, and it forms the background of Michel Foucault's notion of power as the ability "to structure the possible field of action of others" (Foucault 1984:428). Foucault called this "to govern," in the 16th-century sense of governance, an exercise of "action upon action"

(1984:427–428). Foucault himself was primarily interested in this as the power to govern consciousness, but I want to use it as power that structures the political economy. I will refer to this kind of power as structural power. This term rephrases the older notion of "the social relations of production," and is intended to emphasize power to deploy and allocate social labor. These governing relations do not come into view when you think of power primarily in interactional terms. Structural power shapes the social field of action so as to render some kinds of behavior possible, while making others less possible or impossible. As old Georg Friedrich Hegel argued, what occurs in reality has first to be possible.[4]

What capitalist relations of production accomplish, for example, is to make possible the accumulation of capital based on the sale of marketable labor power in a large number of settings around the world. As anthropologists we can follow the flows of capital and labor through ups and downs, advances and retreats, and investigate the ways in which social and cultural arrangements in space and time are drawn into and implicated in the workings of this double whammy. This is not a purely economic relation, but a political one as well: it takes clout to set up, clout to maintain, and clout to defend; and wielding that clout becomes a target for competition or alliance building, resistance or accommodation.

This is the dimension that has been stressed variously in studies of imperialism, dependency, or world-systems. Their questions are

---

3. For the German philosopher Friedrich Nietzsche (1844–1900) human actions were motivated by the desire to increase the feeling of power. In *The Gay Science* Nietzsche wrote that the fundamental instinct of life "aims at *the expansion of power*" (Nietzsche 1974: 291 orig. 1882 emphasis in the original).

Richard Adams (1924–2018) was an archaeologist who worked primarily in Guatemala. He was president of the American Anthropological Association in 1977. Adams argued that social power increases and becomes more centralized as people increase control over energy resources (Adams 1977, Chambers 1977). This idea is derived from the cultural ecology of Julian Steward and Leslie White and relates closely to White's ideas in essay 16 in this book.

4. Wolf was deeply influenced by Marx. He said that Marxist analysis provided "a sense of the principal strategic relations that make things move" (Friedman 1987: 113) and was a key tool missing from much of anthropological analysis.

Wolf mentions Foucault in this passage. However, his emphasis on the ways that structures shape social fields is more reminiscent of Bourdieu. Richard Fox (1995: 277) writes that "the 'anthropology of practice' the 'construction of culture' and the 'invention of tradition'" are all ways of talking about some of the ways Wolf urged anthropologists to consider culture.

why and how some sectors, regions, or nations are able to constrain the options of others, and what coalitions and conflicts occur in the course of this interplay. Some have said that these questions have little relevance to anthropology, in that they don't have enough to say about "real people doing real things," as Sherry Ortner put it (Ortner 1984:114); but it seems to me that they do touch on a lot of what goes on in the real world, that constrains, inhibits, or promotes what people do, or cannot do, within the scenarios we study. The notion of structural power is useful precisely because it allows us to delineate how the forces of the world impinge upon the people we study, without falling back into an anthropological nativism that postulates supposedly isolated societies and uncontaminated cultures, either in the present or in the past. There is no gain in a false romanticism that pretends that "real people doing real things" inhabit self-enclosed and self-sufficient universes.[5]

I address here primarily the relation between tactical (or organizational) power and structural power. I do this because I believe that these concepts can help us to explain the world we inhabit. I think that it is the task of anthropology—or at least the task of some anthropologists—to attempt explanation, and not merely description, descriptive integration, or interpretation. Anthropology can be

different things to different people (entertainment, exotic ***frisson***, a "show-and-tell" of differences), but it should not, I submit, be content with James Boon's "shifting collage of contraries threatening (promising) to become unglued" (Boon 1982:237). Writing culture may require literary skill and genre, but a search for explanation requires more: it cannot do without naming and comparing things, and formulating concepts for naming and comparison. I think we must move beyond Geertz's "experience-near" understandings to analytical concepts that allow us to set what we know about X against what we know about Y, in pursuit of explanation. This means that I subscribe to a basically realist position. I think that the world is real, that these realities affect what humans do and that what humans do affects the world, and that we can come to understand the whys and wherefores of this relationship. We need to be professionally suspicious of our categories and models; we should be aware of their historical and cultural contingencies; we can understand a quest for explanation as approximations to truth rather than the truth itself. But I also believe that the search for explanation in anthropology can be cumulative; that knowledge and insights gained in the past can generate new questions, and that new departures can incorporate the accomplishments of the past.[6]

---

5. The central argument of much of Wolf's work is that historical and technological forces have created a world economic system that reaches even very remote places. Anthropology should be focused on this historical process and the exploration and analysis of its effect on cultures. He explores this theme at length in his best-known book, *Europe and the People without History* (1982), written, in part, as a response to evolutionism. For Wolf, the band, tribe, chiefdom, state model has important uses, but is greatly complicated by economic history.

The idea that the communities often thought of as isolated and untouched by outsiders are, in fact, deeply affected by (and in some cases created by) global economic and historical forces is central to Wolf's work. Communities are not self-enclosed or self-sufficient but rather integrated into world history and economy in specific ways. This sometimes shows up in tourism. For example, the Garifuna People live on the North Coast of Honduras and operate Garifuna Tours (www.garifunatours.com). You can visit Miami, a relatively isolated village of thatched huts that the company says is the most interesting and unique of the villages. There, you can "experience the lifestyle of the Garifuna." You can buy crafts and watch and participate in indigenous dances. However, you should note that the Garifuna are an Afro-Caribbean people. Garifuna villages exist only because of the slave trade.

6. When Wolf gave this presentation in 1989, much of the most influential thinking in anthropology centered around postmodernism. George Marcus and James Clifford's anthology *Writing Culture* (1986) had recently appeared. Many of the essays in that volume were aimed at discrediting the notion of a stable reality that could be described in a meaningful way. For example, in a widely read essay from that volume, Stephen

In anthropology we are continuously slaying paradigms, only to see them return to life, as if discovered for the first time. The old-time evolutionism of Morgan and Engels reappeared in ecological guise in the forties and fifties. The Boasian insistence that we must understand the ways "that people actually think about their own culture and institutions" (Goldman 1975:15) has resurfaced in the anthropology of cognition and symbolism, now often played as a dissonant quartet in the format of deconstructionism. Diffusionism grew exhausted after biting too deeply into the seductive apple of trait-list collecting, but sprang back to life in the studies of acculturation, interaction spheres, and world-systems. Functionalism overreached itself by claiming to depict organic unities, but returned in systems theory as well as in other disguises. Culture-and-personality studies advanced notions of "basic personality structure" and "national character," without paying heed to history, cultural heterogeneity, or the role of hegemony in shaping uniformities; but suspiciously similar characterizations of modern nations and "ethnic groups" continue to appear. The varieties of ecological anthropology and the various Marxisms are being told by both user-friendly and unfriendly folk that what they need is "the concept of culture." We are all familiar, I trust, with Robert Lowie's image of "diffusionism laying the axe to evolutionism." As each successive approach carries the ax to its predecessors, anthropology comes to resemble a project in intellectual deforestation.[7]

A. Tyler declared that "the world that made science, and that science made, has disappeared, and scientific thought is now an archaic mode of consciousness surviving for a while yet in degraded form" (Tyler 1986: 123). Wolf writes powerfully against this idea. While acknowledging the difficulties in the way anthropologists understand and classify things, Wolf insists that there are meaningful relationships that can be objectively discovered and used to understand history and society.

James Boon (b. 1946) is professor and dean emeritus at Princeton. The quote Wolf mentions here is Boon's description of writing in anthropology.

Clifford Geertz (see essay 26), referencing the psychoanalyst Heinz Kohut (1913–1981) discusses "experience-near" and "experience-distant" concepts. He says: "An experience-near concept is, roughly, one which an individual . . . might himself naturally and effortlessly use to define what he or his fellows see, feel, think, imagine, and so on, and which he would readily understand when similarly applied by others. An experience-distant concept is one which various types of specialists . . . employ to forward their scientific, philosophical, or practical aims. 'Love' is an experience-near concept; 'object cathexis' is an experience distant one" (Geertz 1974: 28).

"*Frisson*": a momentary feeling of excitement

7. Wolf in one paragraph has captured the central intent of this volume: to look at the trajectories of theoretical perspectives in anthropology and show their relationships to each other. If we had started this book with an epigraph (a short quote), it might well have been this paragraph. We think that Wolf here captures an essential truth of our field (and perhaps most others as well). The theories of past eras do not disappear. Instead, they return again and again with new modifications and in new guises. Sometimes these are improvements (for example, the return of evolution in the work of Steward and White). Sometimes, perhaps, not so much (as in the return of Culture and Personality in Hofstede's cultural dimensions (1991)).

Robert Lowie (1883–1957) was a prominent student of Franz Boas and a leader in both Native American ethnography and Culture and Personality. Like other Boasians, Lowie stressed cultural relativism and argued strongly against evolutionism in any form. The passage Wolf mentions comes from Lowie's 1920 work *Primitive Society*. It reads: "Thus, neither the examples of independent evolution from like causes nor those of convergent evolution from unlike causes establish an innate law of social progress. One fact, however, encountered at every stage and in every phase of society, by itself lays the axe to the root of any theory of historical laws—the extensive occurrence of diffusion" (1920: 434).

One reason Wolf trusts that his audience will be familiar with the Lowie passage is that it was used by Leslie White (see essay 16) to open his polemical 1945 essay "'Diffusionism Vs. Evolution': An Anti-Evolutionist Fallacy," supporting an evolutionary position (and in Lowie's vitriolic 1946 reply to that essay in which he says that he is convinced of White's good faith but, quoting Voltaire, in the original French suggests that White is "*privé de la raison*," (deprived of reason) (Lowie 1946b).

I do not think that this is either necessary or desirable. I think that anthropology can be cumulative, that we can use the work of our predecessors to raise new questions.

THREE PROJECTS

Some of anthropology's older insights into power can be the basis for new inquiry. I want to briefly review three projects that sought to understand what happens to people in the modern world and in the process raised questions about power, both tactical and structural. These projects yielded substantial bodies of data and theory; they opened up perspectives that reached beyond their scope of inquiry; and all were criticized in their time and subjected to reevaluation thereafter. All three were efforts toward an explanatory anthropology.

The first of these projects is the study of Puerto Rico in 1948–49, directed by Julian Steward; the results are in the collective work, *The People of Puerto Rico* (Steward et al. 1956). The original thrust of the project stemmed from Steward's attack on the assumptions of a unitary national culture and national character which then dominated the field of culture-and-personality. The project aimed instead at exhibiting the heterogeneity of a national society. It was also a rejection of the model in which a single community was made to stand for an entire nation. It depicted Puerto Rico as a structure of varied localities and regions, clamped together by island wide institutions and the activities of an insular upper class, a system of heterogeneous parts and levels. The project was especially innovative in trying to find out how this complex arrangement developed historically, by tracing out the historical causes and courses of crop production on the island, and then following out the differential implications of that development in four representative communities. It promised to pay attention to the institutions connecting localities, regions, and nation, but actually confined itself to looking at these institutions primarily in terms of their local effects. It did carry out a study of the insular upper class, which was conceived as occupying the apex of linkages to the level of the nation. The project's major shortfall, in terms of its own undertaking, was its failure to take proper account of the rapidly intensifying migration to the nearby U.S. mainland. Too narrow a focus on agricultural ecology prevented it from coming to grips with issues already then becoming manifest on the local level, but prompted and played out upon a much larger stage.[8]

While the Puerto Rico project averted its eyes from the spectacle of migration, another research effort took labor migration to the towns and burgeoning mines of Central Africa as its primary point of reference. This research was carried out under the auspices of the Rhodes-Livingstone Institute, set up in 1937 in what was then Northern Rhodesia and is now Zambia. Its research goal was defined by the first director, Godfrey Wilson, whose own outlook has been characterized as an unconscious effort to combine Marx and Malinowski (Brown 1973:195). Wilson under-

---

Lowie's quote laying the axe to theories of historical laws comes just four pages before his famous description of civilization as a "thing of shreds and patches" (see Benedict, essay 10, note 11).

8. Julian Steward (essay 17) was Wolf's doctoral advisor and had a profound effect on him. Wolf's 1951 doctoral dissertation, "Culture Change and Culture Stability in a Puerto Rican Coffee Community" was done as part of Steward's People of Puerto Rico project that Wolf describes here. Steward's anthropology originally focused on the relationship between culture and ecology. However, by the late 1940s, he had begun to place increasing emphasis on the political and social as well as the physical environment.

Wolf was one of a group of students that coalesced around Steward, who taught at Columbia from 1946–1953). Many of these would go on to have important influences on anthropology from the 1950s through the 1980s. They included Sidney Mintz (1922–2015), Stanley Diamond (1922–1991), Elman Service (1915–1996), Morton Fried (1923–1986), Robert Manners 1913–1996), and Robert F. Murphy (1934–1990). All of these were close friends. They called themselves the "Mundial [or Mundiana] Upheaval Society" (Friedman 1987: 109). Eleanor Leacock was part of Wolf's circle but not part of the society.

stood the processes affecting Central Africa as an industrial revolution connected to the workings of the world economy. The massive penetration of the mining industry was seen as causal in generating multiple conflicts on the local and regional scene. Then Max Gluckman, the director from 1942 to 1947, drew up a research plan for the Institute which outlined a number of problem-oriented studies, and enlisted a stellar cast of anthropologists to work on such problems as the intersections of native and colonial governance, the role of witchcraft, the effects of labor migration on domestic economy, and the conflicts generated by the tension-ridden interplay of matrilineal descent and patrilocal residence. Dealing with an area of considerable linguistic and cultural diversity, the researchers were able to compare their findings to identify what was variable and what was common in local responses to general processes. But where the project was at its most innovative was in looking at rural locations, mining centers, and towns not as separate social and cultural entities but as interrelated elements caught up in one social field. It thus moved from Wilson's original concern with detribalization as anomic loss toward a more differentiated scenario of variegated responses to the new behavior settings of village, mine, and urban township. In doing so, it opened perspectives that the Puerto Rico project did not address. Its major failing lay in not taking systematic

and critical account of the colonial structure in which these settings were embedded.[9]

The third project I want to mention was directed by Richard Adams between 1963 and 1966, to study the national social structure of Guatemala. It is described in the book *Crucifixion by Power* (Adams 1970). The project took account of the intense growth of agricultural production for the market, and placed what was then known about life in localities within that context. Its specific innovation, however, lies in the fact that it engaged the study of national institutions in ways not broached by the two other projects I have referred to. Adams showed how local, regional, and supranational elites contested each other's power, and how regional elites stabilized their command by forging ties at the level of the nation. At that level, however, their power was subject to competition and interference by groups operating on the transnational and international plane. The study of elites was followed by accounts of the development of various institutions: the military, the renascent Guatemalan Church, the expanding interest organizations of the upper sector, and the legal system and legal profession. Adams then showed how these institutions curtailed agrarian and labor demands in the countryside, and produced individualized patron-client ties between the urban poor and their political sponsors in the capital. What the project did not do was to bring together

---

9. The Rhodes-Livingstone Institute was the first anthropological institute in Sub-Saharan Africa. Founded (as Wolf notes) in 1937, the Institute existed until Northern Rhodesia gained independence (as Zambia) in 1964. The institute was associated with some of the most important anthropological thinkers of its era. Godfrey Wilson (1908–1944) and Max Gluckman (1911–1975) were among these. Wilson was the Institute's first director, Gluckman its second.

Much of the work of the Institute focused on social change in Southern Africa. Wilson was particularly interested in analyzing the effect of mining companies on African society. Working with his wife Monica Wilson (1908–1982 see Turner, essay 25, note 2), he described a social reality at odds with colonial settler policy and was harshly critical of the mining companies. This led to his replacement by Gluckman. Wilson was a pacifist but joined the South African Medical Corps in 1942. Suffering from depression, bored, and distraught, Wilson took his own life in 1944 (Marsland 2013: 134–135; Hansen 2015).

Gluckman proved more radical than Wilson. He not only continued Wilson's critique but, at odds with official Governmental understandings, insisted on analyzing the region as a single complex social system that included Blacks, Whites, Indians, and others as well as urban and rural areas. Gluckman left the Rhodes-Livingstone in 1947, and after spending two years at Oxford, in 1949 founded the anthropology department at The University of Manchester. There he trained and worked with many anthropologists who became prominent in the 50s, 60s, and 70s, including Fredrik Barth (1928–2016), F. G. Bailey (1925–2020), and Victor Turner. Together, Gluckman and his students became known as the "Manchester School."

this rich material into a synthesis that might have provided a theoretical model of the nation for further work.

It seems clear now that the three projects all stood on the threshold of a promising new departure in anthropological inquiry, but failed to cross it. They were adventurous, but not adventurous enough. First, in my view, they anticipated a move toward political economy, while not quite taking that next step. The Puerto Rico project, in its concentration on agriculture, failed to come to grips with the political and economic forces that established that agriculture in the first place, and that were already at work in "Operation Bootstrap" to transform the agricultural island into an industrial service station. We did not understand the ways in which island institutions, supposedly "national" but actually interlocked with mainland economics and politics, were battlegrounds for diverse contending interests. Thus, the project also missed an opportunity to deal with the complex interplay of hegemonic and subaltern cultural stances in the Puerto Rican situation. In fact, no one has done so to date; the task remains for the doing.[10]

The Central Africa project was similarly confined by its own presuppositions. Despite its attention to conflicts and contradictions, it remained a captive of the prevailing functionalism, especially when it interpreted disjunctions as mere phases in the restoration of continuity. There was a tendency to take the colonial system as a given and thus to mute both the historical implications of conquest and the cumulative confrontations between Africans and Europeans. New questions now

enable us to address these issues. Colonialism overrode the kin-based and tributary polities it encountered. Their members were turned into peasants in the hinterland and into workers in mine and town; peasantization and proletarianization were concomitant processes, often accompanied by force and violence. New ethnic and class identities replaced older, now decentered ties (Sichone 1989). Yet research has also uncovered a multiplicity of African responses in labor and political organization (Epstein 1958; Ranger 1970), in dance societies (Mitchell 1957; Ranger 1975), in a proliferation of religious movements (Van Binsbergen and Schofeleers 1985; Werbner 1989), in rebellion and resistance (Lan 1985). These studies have reemphasized the role of cultural understandings as integral ingredients of the transformation of labor and power.[11]

Adams's project came very close to a new opening. It embodied an historical perspective, it understood the relations among groups as conflict-ridden processes, and it included the operations of multinational and transnational powers in this dynamic. It did not, however, move toward a political economic model of the entire ensemble—perhaps because Adams's own specific interests lay in developing an evolutionary theory of power. It thus also neglected the complex interplay of cultures in the Guatemalan case. Such a move toward synthesis still awaits the future.

The significance of these three projects lies not only in their own accomplishments but in the new questions they lead us to ask. First, they all call attention to history, but not history as "one damned thing after another," as

---

10. "Operation Bootstrap" was the name given to a series of economic changes to Puerto Rican economic policy devised by Luis Muñoz Marín (1898–1980), Governor of Puerto Rico from 1949 to 1965. The goal of the program was to move Puerto Rico from a primarily agricultural economy to a primarily industrial one. This demanded outside investment. To encourage this, the government granted tax exemptions to many corporations (particularly those from the US mainland). The government also made critical industrial investments (Toro n.d)

11. The members of the Rhodes-Livingstone Institute had deep connections to British Functionalist anthropology. Wilson was a student of Malinowski. Gluckman was a student of Robert Marett (1866–1943), who was one of the first British anthropologists to be influenced by Durkheim (Stocking 1995: 169). However, Gluckman also studied with and was deeply influenced by Radcliffe-Brown. The idea that cultures should be smoothly running integrated systems is a background assumption of functionalism. Because of this, functionalists tended to treat conflict as a kind of dysfunction that would, in time, be smoothed out. Wolf (and probably most current-day anthropologists), inspired by Marx, saw conflict as inherent in all societies: conflict is a feature of social systems, not a glitch.

Leslie White used to say. "History," says Maurice Godelier, "does not explain: it has to be explained" (1977:6). What attention to history allows you to do is to look at processes unfolding, intertwining, spreading out, and dissipating over time. This means rethinking the units of our inquiries—households, localities, regions, national entities—seeing them not as fixed entities, but as problematic: shaped, reshaped, and changing over time. Attention to processes unfolding over time foregrounds organization—the structuring arrangements of social life—but requires us to see these in process and change. Second, the three projects point us to processes operating on a macro-scale, as well as in micro-settings. Puerto Rico was located first in the Hispanic orbit, then in the orbit of the United States. Central Africa was shaped by worldwide industrialization, as well as by the policies of colonial governance. Guatemala has been crucified by external connections and internal effects at the same time. The point continues an older anthropology which spoke first of "culture areas," then of oikumenes, interaction spheres, interethnic systems, and symbiotic regions, and that can now entertain "world-systems." Macroscopic history and processes of organization thus become important elements of a new approach. Both involve considerations of power tactical and structural.[12]

ORGANIZATION

Organization is key, because it sets up relationships among people through allocation

---

12. Leslie White, Maurice Godelier (b. 1934) and Wolf were all deeply influenced by Marx. Godelier was one of the strongest advocates of Marxist anthropology in the 1960s and 1970s. Marxist philosophy is sometimes called "historical materialism." A fundamental tenet of historical materialism is that history is NOT just one damn thing after another, but is driven by specific social, intellectual, and economic processes. It is these that make history the thing to be explained. White wrote that anthropologists had an unfortunate tendency to see history and science as opposed. He argued that, to the contrary, "History is one way of 'sciencing'" (1945: 248). William Peace, White's biographer, writes that White accepted the materialist conception of history as fact (1993: 141).

In this section, Wolf discusses three different large-scale ethnographic projects and their shortcomings. He says, "What attention to history allows you to do is to look at processes unfolding." For American readers, Guatemala provides a tragic and timely example. Wolf says Guatemala was crucified by "external connections and internal effects at the same time." This process continues today. At the time he was giving this talk, the country was embroiled in a 36-year-long civil war. In this war, the Guatemalan government, backed by the United States, sought to eliminate an indigenous leftist insurgency through a scorched-earth campaign. More than 200,000 died in the conflict, mostly at the hands of military and paramilitary forces (Comisión para Esclarecimiento Histórico 1998).

The war ended in 1996. However, according to a 2022 report issued by the organization Human Rights Watch, the prosecution of those who committed crimes against civilians during the war has stalled because of attacks upon prosecutors and judges. This report also claims that there is widespread corruption among elected officials in the Guatemalan government, businessmen, and drug dealers. The Council on the Americas has ranked Guatemala thirteenth out of 15 Latin American countries in the government's ability to detect and punish corruption (https://www.hrw.org/world-report/2023/country-chapters/guatemala#:~:text=Guatemala%20has%20no%20comprehensive%20civil,people%20from%20violence%20and%20discrimination). According to the US State Department's Bureau of International Narcotics and Law Enforcement Affairs, many areas of the country are under the influence of drug trafficking organizations. An array of transnational criminal organizations are involved in migrant smuggling, human and weapons trafficking, and money laundering (https://www.state.gov/bureau-of-international-narcotics-and-law-enforcement-affairs-work-by-country/guatemala-summary). One consequence of the failure of the Guatemalan state is that many people, mostly families with children, are fleeing to seek sanctuary elsewhere. As a proportion of total Guatemalan apprehensions, family units grew from less than 5 percent to 70 percent between 2012 and 2019—from just 340 to 185,134 individuals (https://www.brookings.edu/articles/rural-poverty-climate-change-and-family-migration-from-guatemala). Other Central American countries such as El Salvador Honduras, and Nicaragua have similar histories, levels of violence, and concomitant refugee problems (https://www.migrationpolicy.org/article/refugees-and-asylees-united-states).

and control of resources and rewards. It draws on tactical power to monopolize or share out liens and claims, to channel action into certain pathways while interdicting the flow of action into others. Some things become possible and likely; others are rendered unlikely. At the same time, organization is always at risk. Since power balances always shift and change, its work is never done; it operates against entropy (Balandier 1970). Even the most successful organization never goes unchallenged. The enactment of power always creates friction—disgruntlement, foot-dragging, escapism, sabotage, protest or outright resistance, a panoply of responses well documented with Malaysian materials by James Scott (1985) in *Weapons of the Weak*.[13]

Granted the importance of the subject, one might ask why anthropology seems to have relinquished the study of organization, so that today you can find the topic more often discussed in the manuals of business management than in our publications. We structure and are structured, we transact, we play out

metaphors, but the whole question of organization has fallen into abeyance.

Many of us entered anthropology when there were still required courses in something called "social organization." It dealt with principles of categorization like gender, generation, and rank, and with groupings, such as lineages, clans, age sets, and associations. We can now see in retrospect that this labeling was too static, because organization was then grasped primarily as an outcome, a finished product responding to a cultural script, and not visualized in the active voice, as process, frequently a difficult and conflict-ridden process at that. When the main emphasis was on organizational forms and principles, it was all too easy to understand organization in architectural terms, as providing the building blocks for structure, a reliable edifice of regular and recurrent practices and ideas that rendered social life predictable, and could thus be investigated in the field. There was little concern with tactical power in shaping organizations, maintaining them, destabilizing them, or undoing them.[14]

---

13. Without mentioning Bourdieu, Wolf here begins an argument that is strongly reminiscent of Bourdieu's agency and structure approach (see essays 35–37). In 1984, Sherry Ortner published "Anthropology Since the Sixties" an article in which she detailed some of the major trends in anthropology and brought Bourdieu and practice theory to the attention of many anthropologists. Ortner's essay opens by referring to Wolf (and Wolf has returned the favor by referring to Ortner early in this essay).

James Scott (b. 1936) is an anthropologist and political scientist based at Yale. Scott's work was critical in the anthropological reappraisal of the lives of oppressed peoples that began in the 1980s. Rather than focusing solely on how elites used the power of the state and ideology to subdue the oppressed, Scott focused on the ways oppressed people engaged in small, daily acts of resistance. *Weapons of the Weak* published in 1985 was based on Scott's research in Malaysia. It was followed in 1990 by *Domination and the Arts of Resistance: Hidden Transcripts*. There, Scott expanded his analysis to include many cultures. He focused on the idea of public and hidden "transcripts;" culturally prescribed ways of behaving and speaking. Scott shows how oppressed people fight an "undeclared ideological guerilla war" using "rumor, gossip, disguises, linguistic tricks, metaphors, euphemisms, folktales, ritual gestures" (1990: 137) to contest elite understandings and assert their dignity within them.

14. The ideas Wolf mentions in this paragraph were mainstays of British Structural Functionalism (see the introduction to Functionalism in this volume). However, an emphasis on understanding kinship systems was also a critical part of American anthropology. Until the 1970s, anthropology students were usually expected to take courses in kinship and to know their bifurcate collateral from their bifurcate merging, lineal, and generational (according to a famous 1928 paper by Robert Lowie). These understandings of kinship were strongly critiqued by David Schneider and others (see Radcliffe-Brown, essay 15, note 19).

Wolf's critique here is extremely important. Anthropological concepts are often understood and taught as static. For example, Radcliffe-Brown in this book describes the VaNdau (today Nadu) as patrilineal (see essay 15), and Malinowski discusses the Trobriand Islanders practicing reciprocity (see essay 14). But cultural traits are fluid and respond to changing circumstances like colonialism and tourism. That is why authors like Wolf and Leacock argue that historical context is so important. Anthropologists study a subject that is constantly shifting.

If an idea is judged by its fruitfulness, then the notion of social structure proved to be a very good idea. It yielded interesting work and productive insights. It is now evident that it also led us to reify organizational results into the building blocks of **hypostatized** social architectures, for example, in the concept of "the unilineal descent group." That idea was useful in leading us to think synoptically about features of group membership, descent, jural-political solidarity, rights and obligations focused on a common estate, injunctions of "prescriptive altruism," and norms of encompassing morality. Yet it is one thing to use a model to think out the implications of organizational processes, and another to expect unilineal descent groups with all these features to materialize in these terms, as dependably shaped bricks in a social-structural edifice.[15]

How do we get from viewing organization as product or outcome to understanding organization as process? For a start, we could do worse than heed Conrad Arensberg's advice (1972:10-11) to look at "the flow of action," to ask what is going on, why it is going on, who engages in it, with whom, when, and how often. Yet we would now add to this behavior-centered approach a new question: For what and for whom is all this going on, and—indeed—against whom? This question should not be posed merely in interactionist terms. Asking why something is going on and for whom requires a conceptual guess about the forces and effects of the structural power that drives organization and to which organization on all levels must respond. What are the dominant relations through which labor is deployed? What are the organizational impli-

cations of kinship alliances, kin coalitions, chiefdoms, or forms of state? Not all organizations or articulations of organization answer to the same functional requisites, or respond to the same underlying dynamic.[16]

Furthermore, it behooves us to think about what is entailed in conceiving organization as a process. This is an underdeveloped area in anthropological thinking. Clearly dyadic contracts, networks of various sizes and shapes, kinship systems, political hierarchies, corporations, and states possess very different organizational potentials. Understanding how all these sets of people and instrumentalities can be aggregated, hooked together, articulated under different kinds of structural power remains a task for the future.

In the pursuit of this task we can build upon the past by using our concepts and models as discovery procedures, not as fixed representations, universally applicable. For example, Michel Verdon developed a strong critique of lineage theory in his book on the Abutia Ewe (Verdon 1983). Yet the critique itself is informed by the questions raised by that theory and by the demands for evidence required for its corroboration. Verdon investigated the characteristics and distribution of domestic units, residential entities, and matrimonial practices, treating these as prerequisites for defining linkages by kinship. He then used the model of lineage theory to pose further queries about the relation of kinship to political synchronization, taking this connection as a problem, rather than an assumption a priori. The model served as a method of inquiry, rather than an archetype.[17]

---

15. The phrase "prescriptive altruism" comes from the Structural Functionalist anthropologist Meyer Fortes (1906–1983). Fortes argued that rather than being part of human nature, altruism is a social rule that connects people in particular statuses within a kinship structure. Thus, altruism is "not spontaneous but obligatory" (Ingold 1986: 285). Wolf references several structural functionalists here in part because structural functionalist studies assumed that cultures were static. Wolf proposes here that cultural features are part of a historical process.
Hypostatize: to make something abstract into a concrete reality.

16. Note that Wolf is asking a fundamentally Marxist question here: what are the relations of production?
Conrad Arensberg (1910–1997) was a mid-twentieth-century American anthropologist best known for his studies of Ireland. Arensberg was known as one of the founders of applied anthropology. He served as president of the American Anthropological Association in 1980.

17. For an analysis of the history and development of lineage theory (the analysis of society based on kinship) see Adam Kuper (b. 1941). He concludes that "the lineage model, its predecessors, and its analogs, have no value for anthropological analysis" (1982: 92).

A similar redefinition of the problem has taken place in the study of chiefdoms, where interest, as Timothy Earle has said, "has shifted from schemes to classify societies as chiefdoms or not, towards consideration of the causes of observed variability" (Earle 1987:279). Social constellations that can be called chiefdoms not only come in many sizes and shapes (Feinman and Neitzel 1984), but they are now understood as "fragile negotiated institutions," both in securing compliance within and in competition with rivals outside. Emphasis in research now falls on the mixes of economic, political, and ideological strategies that chiefdoms employ to these ends, as well as on their variable success in shaping their different historical trajectories (Earle 1989:87). Similarly, where people once simply spoke of "the state," the state is now seen less as a thing than as "a process" (Gailey 1987). A new emphasis on state-making processes takes account both of the "diversity and fluidity of form, function and malfunction" and of "the extent to which all states are internally divided and subject to penetration by conflicting and usually contradictory forces" (Bright and Harding 1984:4).[18]

SIGNIFICATION

Finally, I want to address the issue of power in signification. Anthropology has treated signification mainly in terms of encompassing cultural unities, such as patterns, configurations, ethos, eidos, epistemes, paradigms, cultural structures. These unities, in turn, have been conceptualized primarily as the outcomes of processes of logico-aesthetic integration. Even when the frequently incongruous and disjointed characteristics of culture are admitted,

the hope has been—and I quote Geertz—that identifying significant symbols, clusters of such symbols, and clusters of clusters would yield statements of "the underlying regularities of human experience implicit in their formation" (Geertz 1973:408). The appeal is to the efficacy of symbols, to the workings of logics and aesthetics in the movement toward integration or reintegration, as if these cognitive processes were guided by a **telos** all their own.[19]

I call this approach into question on several grounds. First, I draw on the insight of Anthony Wallace, who in the late 1950s contrasted views of culture that emphasize "the replication of uniformity" with those that acknowledge the problem of "the organization of diversity." He argued that

all societies are, in a radical sense, plural societies. . . How do societies ensure that the diverse cognitions of adults and children, males and females, warriors and shamans, slaves and masters articulate to form the equivalence structures that are the substance of social life? (Wallace 1970:110)

This query of Wallace's continues to echo in many quarters: in a feminist anthropology that questions the assumption that men and women share the same cultural understandings; in ethnography from various areas, where "rubbish-men" in Melanesia and "no account people" on the Northwest Coast do not seem to abide by the norms and ideals of Big Men and chiefs; in studies of hierarchical systems in which different strata and segments exhibit different and contending models of logico-aesthetic integration (India furnishes a telling case). We have been told that such divergences are ultimately kept in check and on track by

---

18. Timothy Earle (b. 1946) is Professor Emeritus at Northwestern. Earle is an archaeologist and anthropologist whose work focuses on complex societies and social inequality. Earle's 1987 essay "Chiefdoms in Archaeological and Ethnohistorical Perspective" was critical in reevaluating chiefdoms as a type of society. Earle argued that the ideas of chiefdoms in the band, tribe, chiefdom, state model of the 1960s were overly deterministic. As Wolf notes, chiefdoms are variable in many dimensions.

19. The Geertz quote comes from "Person, Time, and Conduct in Bali," originally published in 1966. Geertz continues: "A workable theory of culture is to be achieved, if it is to be achieved at all, by building up from directly observable modes of thought" (1973: 408). In other words, for Geertz, culture is a mental model. This fits closely with work in cognitive anthropology and ethnoscience as well as symbolic anthropology of the 1960s.

"Telos": end purpose.

cultural logic, pure and simple. This seems to me unconvincing. It is indeed the case that our informants in the field invoke metaphoric polarities of purity and pollution, well-being and malevolence, yin and yang, life and death. Yet these metaphors are intrinsically polysemic, so abundant in possible signifiers that they can embrace any and all situations. To put them to work in particular scenarios requires that their range be constricted and narrowed down to but a small set of referents. What Levi Strauss called "the surplus of signifiers" must be subjected to parsimonious selection before the logic of cultural integration can be actualized. This indexing, as some have called it, is no automatic process, but passes through power and through contentions over power, with all sorts of consequences for signification.[20]

Wallace's insights on the organization of diversity also raise questions about how meaning actually works in social life. He pointed out that participants in social action do not need to understand what meanings lie behind the behavior of their partners in interchange. All they have to know is how to respond appropriately to the cues signaled by others. Issues of meaning need not ever rise into consciousness. This is often the concern only of certain specialists, whose specific job or interest it is to explore the plenitude of possible meanings: people such as shamans, *tohunga*, or academics. Yet there are also situations in which the mutual signaling of expectations is deranged, where opposite and contradictory interests come to the fore, or where cultural schemata come under challenge. It then becomes apparent that beyond logic and aesthetics, it is power that guarantees—or fails.[21]

Power is implicated in meaning through its role in upholding one version of significance as true, fruitful, or beautiful, against other possibilities that may threaten truth, fruitfulness, or beauty. All cultures, however conceived, carve out significance and try to stabilize it against possible alternatives. In human affairs, things might be different, and often are. Roy Rappaport, in writing on sanctity and ritual (Rappaport 1979), has emphasized the basic arbitrariness of all cultural orders. He argues that they are anchored in postulates that can neither be verified nor falsified, but that must be treated as unquestionable: to make them unquestionable, they are surrounded with sacredness. I would add that there is always the possibility that they might come unstuck. Hence, symbolic work is never

---

20. Anthony F. C. Wallace (1923–2015) was an ethnohistorian and specialist in Native American societies. He is best known today for his studies of Native Americans and religion. Wallace was interested in connections between culture and psychology and used psychological testing as a method for investigating the relationship between the two. For his PhD research, Wallace administered Rorschach tests to 103 Tuscarora Indians in an effort to identify a Tuscarora modal personality.

The concept of *mazeway* was central to Wallace's study of culture, personality, and religion. Wallace used mazeway to refer to the mental map by which people understood their world. In his 1956 article "Mazeway Resynthesis: A Biocultural Theory of Religious Inspiration" Wallace proposed that prophets of new religious movements often found willing followers among people whose mazeways had been disrupted by social collapse or rapid and dramatic social change. In these circumstances, people were receptive to new understandings of the world. Although Wallace was a key figure in Psychological and Cognitive Anthropology, he was also drawn to materialist and economic explanations of culture.

Lévi-Strauss's most direct statement of the idea of a surplus of signifiers is found in his *Introduction to Marcel Mauss*. There, in a discussion of *mana*, Lévi-Strauss says: "there is always a non-equivalence or 'inadequation' between [the signifier-totality and the signified], a non-fit and overspill which divine understanding alone can soak up; this generates a signifier-surfeit relative to the signifieds to which it can be fitted. So, in man's effort to understand the world, he always disposes of a surplus of signification" (Lévi-Strauss 1987: 62 orig. 1950).

For Wolf, "divine understanding" comes down to the power to require and enforce certain ways of thinking and not others.

21. In Maori culture, a *tohunga* is an expert practitioner, usually a healer. Tohunga were described in a 1925 essay by the Structural Functionalist anthropologist Raymond Firth (1901–2002).

done, achieves no final solution. The cultural assertion that the world is shaped in this way and not in some other has to be repeated and enacted, lest it be questioned and denied. The point is well made by Valerio Valeri in his study of *Kingship and Sacrifice* in Hawaii. Ritual, he says, produces sense

> by creating contrasts in the continuum of experience. This implies suppressing certain elements of experience in order to give relevance to others. Thus the creation of conceptual order is also, constitutively, the suppression of aspects of reality. [Valeri 1985:xi][22]

The Chinese doctrine of "the rectification of names" also speaks to this point of the suppressed alternatives. Stipulating that the world works in one way and not in another requires categories to order and direct experience. According to this doctrine, if meanings multiplied so as to transcend established boundaries, social consensus would become impossible—people would harm each other "like water and fire." Hence, a wise government would have to restore things to their proper definitions, in clear recognition that the maintenance of categories upholds power, and power maintains the order of the world (see Pocock 1971:42–79).[23]

I have spoken of different modes of structural power, which work through key relations of governance. Each such mode would appear to require characteristic ways of conceptualizing and categorizing people. In social formations that deploy labor through relations glossed at [sic, as?] kinship, people are assigned to networks or bodies of kin that are distinguished by criteria of gender, distinct substances or essences of descent, connections with the dead, differential distributions of myths, rituals, and emblems. Tributary formations hierarchize these criteria and set up distinct social strata, each stratum marked by a distinctive inner substance that also defines its positions and privileges in society. Capitalist formations peel the individual out of encompassing ascriptive bodies and install people as separate actors, free to exchange, truck, or barter in the market, as well as in other provinces of life. The three modes of categorizing social actors, moreover, imply quite different relations to "nature" and cosmos. When one mode enters into conflict with another, it also challenges the fundamental categories that empower its dynamics. Power will then be invoked to assault rival categorical claims. Power is thus never external to signification—it inhabits meaning and is its champion in stabilization and defense.[24]

---

22. Valerio Valeri (1944–1998) was a University of Chicago anthropology professor who argued for religion as a fundamental means of organizing political life (Breslin 1998).
   For detailed information about Roy Rappaport see essay 19.

23. In Chinese culture, the doctrine of rectification of names means that the name of an office (or by extension, a person, or further extension the name of anything at all) should correspond to its reality. The primary source for the rectification of names is the Analects of Confucius. In Book 13, Confucius is asked by his disciple Zuli what would be the first thing that he would do if he were to become the ruler. Confucius replies that he would "rectify names." After insulting his disciple, Confucius explains: "If names are not right then speech does not accord with things; if speech is not in accord with things then affairs cannot be successful" (Eno 2015). Of course, Confucius claims that rectification brings names into correspondence with reality. However, Wolf's point is that the variable nature of reality means that the effect of Confucius's idea is to exert power to bring reality into conformity with names rather than the reverse.

24. Wolf provides an extensive discussion of the kinship, tributary, and capitalist modes of production in *Europe and the People without History* (1982). In the kinship mode, labor is organized through lineages and other kin structures. In the tributary mode, people own the means of production but much of what they produce is expropriated in the form of tribute. And, in capitalism, capitalists own the means of production and workers sell their labor. Wolf does not believe that kinship, tributary, and capitalist modes of production represent an evolutionary sequence. Rather, they are contingent on large-scale historic and economic forces.

We owe to social anthropology the insight that the arrangements of a society become most visible when they are challenged by crisis. The role of power also becomes most evident in instances where major organizational transformations put signification under challenge. Let me offer some examples. In their study of the Plains Vision Experience, Patricia Albers and Seymour Parker (1971) contrast the individualized visions of the egalitarian foragers of the Plains periphery with the standardized kin-group-controlled visions of the horticultural village dwellers. Still a third kind of vision, oriented toward war and wealth, emerged among the buffalo-hunting nomads who developed in response to the introduction of horse and gun. As horse pastoralism proved increasingly successful, the horticulturalists became riven by conflicts between the personal-private visions of young men involved in buffalo hunting, and the visions controlled by hereditary groups of kin.[25]

The development of the Merina state in Madagascar gives us another example (see, for example, Berg 1986; Bloch 1986). As the state became increasingly powerful and centralized around an intensified agriculture and ever more elaborate social hierarchy, the royal center also emerged as the hub of the ideational system. Local rites of circumcision, water sprinkling, offerings to honor superiors, and rituals ministering to group icons and talismans were increasingly synchronized and fused with rituals of state.

The royal rituals of Hawaii furnish a third case. Their development was linked to major transformations that affected Hawaii after 1400, when agriculture and aquaculture were extended and intensified (see, for example, Earle 1978; Kirch 1985; Spriggs 1988). Local communities were reorganized; lineages were deconstructed; commoners lost the right to keep genealogies and to attend temples, and were assigned as quasi-tenants to nonlocal subaltern chiefs. Chiefs and aristocrats were raised up, godlike, into a separate endogamous stratum. Conflicts within the elite brought on endemic warfare and attempts at conquest: both fed the cult of human sacrifice. Innovations in myth and ritual portrayed the eruption of war and violence by the coming of outsiders, "sharks upon the land." Sahlins (1985) has offered the notion of a cultural structure to interpret how Hawaiians understood such changes and re-valued their understandings in the course of change. But reference to a cultural structure alone, or even to a dialectic of a structure of meaning with the world, will not yet explain how given forms of significance relate to transformations of agriculture, settlement, sociopolitical organization, and relations of war and peace. To explain what happened in Hawaii or elsewhere, we must take the further step of understanding the consequences of the exercise of power.[26]

I have put forward the case for an anthropology that is not content merely to translate, interpret, or play with a kaleidoscope of cul-

---

The phrase "exchange, truck, or barter" is a reference to Adam Smith's *The Wealth of Nations* (orig. 1776). In the opening paragraph of chapter 2 of that work, Smith famously declares that the "propensity" of humans "to truck, barter, and exchange one thing for another" is either a fundamental part of human nature or "a necessary consequence of the faculties of reason and speech."

25. Wolf states above that "Power is implicated in meaning through its role in upholding one version of significance as true, fruitful, or beautiful," and he says here that the role of power becomes visible where organizational transformations challenge signification. While Wolf's work is typically about as far as one can get from postmodern thought, his comments on power and meaning parallel Michel Foucault's theory of the discourse of power (see essay 28). In the following examples, Wolf shows how elites used the intensification of subsistence to redefine their status and power.

26. The issue of the ways that Hawaiians understood the coming of outsiders became the subject of a significant debate in anthropology several years after the publication of this essay. In *Islands of History* (1985), Marshal Sahlins (1930–2021) argued that a particular Hawaiian religious and historical understanding led to the death of Captain James Cook (1728–1779) when, in 1779, he returned to Hawaii after briefly leaving. Gananath Obeyesekere (b. 1930) in his 1992 book *The Apotheosis of Captain Cook* argued to the contrary, that Cook's death was the result of the natives' rational calculation of the threat he posed.

tural fragments, but that seeks explanations for cultural phenomena. We can build upon past efforts and old insights, but we must also find our way to asking new questions. I understand anthropology as a cumulative undertaking, as well as a collective quest that moves in ever expanding circles, a quest that depends upon the contributions of each of us, and for which we are all responsible.

REFERENCES

Adams, Richard N. 1966 Power and Power Domains. *America Latina* 9: 3–5, 8–11.

——. 1970 *Crucifixion by Power: Essays on Guatemalan Social Structure, 1944–1966.* Austin: University of Texas Press.

——. 1975 *Energy and Structure: A Theory of Social Power.* Austin: University of Texas Press.

Albers, Patricia, and Seymour Parker 1971 The Plains Vision Experience: A Study of Power and Privilege. *Southwestern journal of Anthropology* 27:203–233.

Arensberg, Conrad M. 1972 Culture as Behavior: Structure and Emergence. *Annual Review of Anthropology* I:1–26. Palo Alto, CA: Annual Reviews.

Balandier, Georges 1970 *Political Anthropology.* New York: Random House.

Berg, Gerald M. 1986 Royal Authority and the Protector System in Nineteenth-Century Imerina. In *Madagascar: Society and History.* Conrad P. Kottak et al., eds. Pp. 175–192. Durham, NC: Carolina Academic Press.

Bloch, Maurice 1986 *From Blessing to Violence: History and Ideology in the Circumcision Ritual of the Merina of Madagascar.* Cambridge: Cambridge University Press.

Boon, James A. 1982 *Other Tribes, Other Scribes: Symbolic Anthropology in the Comparative Study of Cultures, Histories, Religions, and Texts.* Cambridge: Cambridge University Press.

Bright, Charles, and Susan Harding, eds. 1984 *State Making and Social Movements: Essays in History and Theory.* Ann Arbor: University of Michigan Press.

Brown, Richard 1973 Anthropology and Colonial Rule: Godfrey Wilson and the Rhodes-Livingstone Institute, Northern Rhodesia. In *Anthropology and the Colonial Encounter.* Talal Asad, ed. Pp. I 73–197. London: Ithaca Press.

Earle, Timothy K. 1978 *Economic and Social Organization of a Complex Chiefdom: The Halelea District, Kauai, Hawaii. Anthropological Papers,* No. 63. Ann Arbor: Museum of Anthropology, University of Michigan.

——. 1987 Chiefdoms in Archaeological and Ethnohistorical Perspective. *Annual Review of Anthropology* 16: 279–308. Palo Alto, CA: Annual Reviews.

——. 1989 The Evolution of Chiefdoms. *Current Anthropology* 30:84–88.

Epstein, A. L. 1958 *Politics in an Urban African Community.* Manchester: Manchester University Press.

Feinman, Gary M., and Jill Neitzel 1984 Too Many Types: An Overview of Sedentary Prestate Societies in the Americas. In *Advances in Archaeological Method and Theory,* Vol. 7. Michael B. Schiffer, ed. Pp. 39–102. New York: Academic Press.

Foucault, Michel 1984 The Subject and Power. In *Art after Modernism: Rethinking Representation.* Brian Wallis, ed. Pp. 417–432. Boston/New York: David R. Godine/New Museum of Contemporary Art.

Gailey, Christine Ward 1987 *Kinship to Kingship: Gender Hierarchy and State Formation in the Tongan Islands.* Austin: University of Texas Press.

Geertz, Clifford 1973 *The Interpretation of Cultures.* New York: Basic Books.

Godelier, Maurice 1977 *Perspectives in Marxist Anthropology. Cambridge Studies in Social Anthropology,* No. 18. Cambridge: Cambridge University Press.

Goldman, Irving 1975 *The Mouth of Heaven: An Introduction to Kwakiutl Religious Thought.* New York: Wiley Interscience.

Kaufmann, Walter 1968 *Nietzsche: Philosopher, Psychologist, Antichrist.* Princeton, NJ: Princeton University Press.

Kirch, Patrick V. 1985 *Feathered Gods and Fishhooks: An Introduction to Hawaiian Archaeology and Prehistory.* Honolulu: University of Hawaii Press.

Lan, David 1985 *Guns and Rain: Guerillas and Spirit Mediums in Zimbabwe.* Berkeley/Los Angeles: University of California Press.

Mitchell, Clyde 1957 *The Kalela Dance. Aspects of Social Relationships among Urban Africans in Northern Rhodesia. Rhodes-Livingstone Paper No. 27.* Manchester: Manchester University Press for Rhodes-Livingstone Institute.

Ortner, Sherry B. 1984 Theory in Anthropology since the Sixties. *Comparative Studies in Society and History* 26:126–166.

Pocock, John G. A. 1971 *Politics, Language and Time: Essays in Political Thought and History.* New York: Atheneum.

Ranger, Terence O. 1970 *The African Voice in Southern Rhodesia, 1898–1930.* London: Heinemann.

——. 1975 *Dance and Society in Eastern Africa, 1890–1970: The Beni Ngoma.* Berkeley/Los Angeles: University of California Press.

Rappaport, Roy A. 1979 *Ecology, Meaning, and Religion.* Richmond, CA: North Atlantic Books.

Sahlins, Marshall D. 1985 *Islands of History.* Chicago, IL: University of Chicago Press.

Scott, James 1985 *Weapons of the Weak: Everyday Forms of Peasant Resistance*. New Haven, CT: Yale University Press.

Sichone, Owen B. 1989 The Development of an Urban Working-Class Culture on the Rhodesian Copperbelt. In *Domination and Resistance*. Daniel Miller, Michael Rowlands, and Christopher Tilley, eds. Pp. 290–298. London: Unwin Hyman.

Spriggs, Mathew 1988 The Hawaiian Transformation of Ancestral Polynesian Society: Conceptualizing Chiefly States. In *State and Society: The Emergence and Development of Social Hierarchy and Political Centralization*. John Gledhill, Barbara Bender, and Mogens Trolle-Larsen, eds. Pp. 57–73. London: Unwin Hyman.

Steward, Julian H., et al. 1956 *The People of Puerto Rico*. Urbana: University of Illinois Press.

Valeri, Valerio 1985 *Kingship and Sacrifice: Ritual and Society in Ancient Hawaii*. Chicago, IL: University of Chicago Press.

Van Binsbergen, Wim M.J., and Matthew Schofeleers, eds. 1985 *Theoretical Explorations in African Religion*. London: Kegan Paul International.

Verdon, Michel 1983 *The Abutia Ewe of West Africa: A Chiefdom that Never Was. Studies in the Social Sciences, No. 38*. Berlin/New York: Mouton.

Wallace, Anthony F. C. 1970 [1961] *Culture and Personality*. New York: Random House.

Werbner, Richard P. 1989 *Ritual Passage, Sacred journey: The Form, Process and Organization of Religious Movement*. Washington, DC: Smithsonian Institution Press.

32. Disjuncture and Difference in the Global Cultural Economy

Arjun Appadurai (b. 1949)

IT TAKES ONLY THE merest acquaintance with the facts of the modern world to note it is now an interactive system in a sense that is strikingly new. Historians and sociologists, especially those concerned with translocal processes (Hodgson 1974) and the world systems associated with capitalism (Abu-Lughod 1989; Braudel 1981–4; Curtin 1984; Wallerstein 1974; Wolf 1982), have long been aware that the world has been a **congerie** of largescale interactions for many centuries. Yet today's world involves interactions of a new order and intensity. Cultural transactions between social groups in the past have generally been restricted, sometimes by the facts of geography and ecology, and at other times by active resistance to interactions with the Other (as in China for much of its history and in Japan before the Meiji Restoration). Where there have been sustained cultural transactions across large parts of the globe, they have usually involved the long-distance journey of commodities (and of the merchants most concerned with them) and of travelers and explorers of every type (Helms 1988; Schafer 1963). The two main forces for sustained cultural interaction before this century have been warfare (and the large-scale political systems sometimes generated by it) and religions of conversion, which have sometimes, as in the case of Islam, taken warfare as one of the legitimate instruments of their expansion. Thus, between travelers and merchants, pilgrims and conquerors, the world has seen much long-distance (and long-term) cultural traffic. This much seems self-evident.[1]

But few will deny that given the problems of time, distance, and limited technologies for the command of resources across vast spaces, cultural dealings between socially and spatially separated groups have, until the past few centuries, bridged at great cost and sustained over time only with great effort. The forces of cultural gravity seemed always to pull away from the formation of large-scale **ecumenes**, whether religious, commercial, or political, toward smaller-scale accretions of intimacy and interest.[2]

From *Public Culture* (1990)

1. In the nineteenth and twentieth centuries, anthropologists tended to understand the object of their study as more or less bounded tribes, ethnic groups, or communities. Though they often studied patterns of diffusion among communities, this rarely included the movement of goods or ideas from industrialized societies. The anthropologists' job was to see beyond change to the precontact community that was assumed to be pristine and change very slowly. In the 1970s and 1980s, world systems theorists such as Eric Wolf and Immanuel Wallerstein, cited in Appadurai's opening paragraph, argued that this perception was incorrect. The communities anthropologists studied were not bounded and traditional but rather connected to and conditioned by international flows of trade and wealth. Appadurai follows and extends this argument. In this paragraph and below, he points out that although interaction between cultures has been the rule rather than the exception, the difficulty and expense of communication historically militated against a world system. Over the past several centuries, these factors have steadily diminished in importance, until, by the end of the twentieth century (when this piece was written), the transmission of information and transportation of people were both low cost and relatively simple. This has important implications for cultures and how they are studied.
"**Congerie**": a collection or assemblage.

2. "**Ecumene**": a civilization or worldwide organization. In Appadurai's use, a grouping larger than a society that is tied together by several commonalities.

Sometime in the past few centuries, the nature of this gravitational field seems to have changed. Partly because of the spirit of the expansion of western maritime interests after 1500, and partly because of the relatively autonomous developments of large and aggressive social formations in the Americas (such as the Aztecs and the Incas), in Eurasia (such as the Mongols and their descendants, the Mughals and Ottomans), in island Southeast Asia (such as the Buginese), and in the kingdoms of pre-colonial Africa (such as Dahomey), an overlapping set of ecumenes began to emerge, in which congeries of money, commerce, conquest, and migration began to create durable cross-societal bonds. This process was accelerated by the technology transfers and innovations of the late eighteenth and nineteenth centuries (e.g., Bayly 1989), which created complex colonial orders centered on European capitals and spread throughout the non-European world. This intricate and overlapping set of Eurocolonial worlds (first Spanish and Portuguese, later principally English, French, and Dutch) set the basis for a permanent traffic in ideas of peoplehood and selfhood, which created the imagined communities (Anderson 1983) of recent nationalisms throughout the world.[3]

With what Benedict Anderson has called "print capitalism," a new power was unleashed in the world, the power of mass literacy and its attendant large-scale production of projects of ethnic affinity that were remarkably free of the need for face-to-face communication or even of indirect communication between persons and groups. The act of reading things together

set the stage for movements based on a paradox—the paradox of constructed primordialism. There is, of course, a great deal else that is involved in the story of colonialism and its dialectically generated nationalisms (Chatterjee 1986), but the issue of constructed ethnicities is surely a crucial strand in this tale.[4]

But the revolution of print capitalism and the cultural affinities and dialogues unleashed by it were only modest precursors to the world we live in now. For in the past century, there has been a technological explosion, largely in the domain of transportation and information, that makes the interactions of a print-dominated world seem as hard-won and as easily erased as the print revolution made earlier forms of cultural traffic appear. For with the advent of the steamship, the automobile, the airplane, the camera, the computer, and the telephone, we have entered into an altogether new condition of neighborliness, even with those most distant from ourselves. Marshall McLuhan, among others, sought to theorize about this world as a "global village," but theories such as McLuhan's appear to have overestimated the communitarian implications of the new media order (McLuhan and Powers 1989). We are now aware that with media, each time we are tempted to speak of the global village, we must be reminded that media create communities with "no sense of place" (Meyrowitz 1985). The world we live in now seems **rhizomic** (Deleuze and Guattari 1987), even schizophrenic, calling for theories of rootlessness, alienation, and psychological distance between individuals and groups on the one hand, and fantasies (or

---

3. Benedict Anderson (1936–2015) was a scholar of international studies. In his influential 1983 book *Imagined Communities,* he argued nations were socially constructed by relatively recent and ongoing processes rather than "natural" social organizations. In particular, Anderson argued that the technology of print and the use of vernacular language rather than Latin were essential to the idea of nationhood in Europe. The printing of works in vernacular languages allowed people to conceive of themselves as members of specific language communities. This became one of the building blocks of nationalism. Because nations are composed of large and diverse bodies of people most of whom do not know each other but imagine themselves to be united by shared ideals, common language, etc. Anderson proposed they are "imagined communities." Anderson's notion that nations are the results of very particular—rather than natural and inevitable—historical processes and types of understandings is an important foundation for the theory Appadurai proposes in this essay.

4. Appadurai uses the phrase "constructed primordialism" to argue that the idea that particular nations (e.g., "the German people" or "the French") have great antiquity or are the original inhabitants of a territory is false. Following Anderson, all nations are social constructions.

nightmares) of electronic **propinquity** on the other. Here, we are close to the central problematic of cultural processes in today's world.[5]

Thus, the curiosity that recently drove Pico Iyer to Asia (1988) is in some ways the product of a confusion between some ineffable McDonaldization of the world and the much subtler play of indigenous trajectories of desire and fear with global flows of people and things. Indeed, Iyer's own impressions are testimony to the fact that, if a global cultural system is emerging, it is filled with ironies and resistances, sometimes camouflaged as passivity and a bottomless appetite in the Asian world for things western.[6]

Iyer's own account of the uncanny Philippine affinity for American popular music is rich testimony to the global culture of the hyperreal, for somehow Philippine renditions of American popular songs are both more widespread in the Philippines, and more disturbingly faithful to their originals, than they are in the United States today. An entire nation seems to have learned to mimic Kenny Rogers and the Lennon sisters, like a vast Asian Motown chorus. But Americanization is certainly a pallid term

to apply to such a situation, for not only are there more Filipinos singing perfect renditions of some American songs (often from the American past) than there are Americans doing so, there is also, of course, the fact that the rest of their lives is not in complete synchrony with the referential world that first gave birth to these songs.[7]

In a further globalizing twist on what Fredric Jameson has recently called "nostalgia for the present" (1989), these Filipinos look back to a world they have never lost. This is one of the central ironies of the politics of global cultural flows, especially in the arena of entertainment and leisure. It plays havoc with the hegemony of Euro-chronology. American nostalgia feeds on Filipino desire represented as a hypercompetent reproduction. Here, we have nostalgia without memory. The paradox, of course, has its explanations, and they are historical; unpacked, they lay bare the story of the American missionization and political rape of the Philippines, one result of which has been the creation of a nation of make-believe Americans, who tolerated for so long a leading lady who played the piano while the

---

5. Marshall McLuhan (1911–1980) was a seminal thinker in media studies. In his 1962 book *The Gutenberg Galaxy,* McLuhan argued that advances in communications technology were turning the world into a "global village" in which all people were connected, and the transfer of information was instantaneous. McLuhan promoted a theory of technological determinism, arguing that changes in culture are driven by changes in the technology of communication. Although McLuhan's ideas have been very influential, they are also frequently criticized and deeply controversial. Appadurai clearly appreciates McLuhan's work but argues that the global village is a gross oversimplification.

"Rhizome": In botany an underground stem that sends out shoots. Gilles Deleuze (1925–1995) and Félix Guattari (1930–1992) use the idea of rhizomes as a metaphor for the spread and working of culture. Rhizomes can connect any point to any other point.

"Propinquity": an appearance of closeness or relatedness.

6. Pico Iyer (b. 1957) is a travel writer and journalist. A multicultural individual himself (British born of Indian descent), Iyer's writing focuses on the ironies and paradoxes of globalization. An oft-cited quote from him is "I am a multinational soul on a multinational globe on which more and more countries are as polyglot and restless as airports" (in London 1996).

McDonaldization is a term popularized by the sociologist George Ritzer (b. 1940). Ritzer, strongly influenced by Max Weber, identifies the principles of McDonaldization as predictability, calculability, efficiency, and control.

7. Kenny Rogers (1938–2020) was a popular American country music artist of the 1970s and 1980s. The Lennon Sisters, a pop music group that included four sisters, were popular from the mid-1950s to the mid-1960s.

Appadurai's point here is that with modern media, information is spread around the world and often takes root in vastly different cultural circumstances. For example, he says Kenny Rogers's songs are more popular in the Philippines than in the United States.

slums of Manila expanded and decayed. Perhaps the most radical postmodernists would argue that this is hardly surprising because in the peculiar chronicities of late capitalism, pastiche and nostalgia are central modes of image production and reception. Americans themselves are hardly in the present anymore as they stumble into the mega-technologies of the twenty-first century garbed in the film-noir scenarios of sixties' chills, fifties' diners, forties' clothing, thirties' houses, twenties' dances, and so on *ad infinitum*.[8]

As far as the United States is concerned, one might suggest that the issue is no longer one of nostalgia but of a social *imaginaire* built largely around reruns. Jameson was bold to link the politics of nostalgia to the postmodern commodity sensibility, and surely he was right (1983). The drug wars in Colombia recapitulate the tropical sweat of Vietnam, with Ollie North and his succession of masks—Jimmy Stewart concealing John Wayne concealing Spiro Agnew and all of them transmogrifying into Sylvester Stallone, who wins in Afghanistan—thus simultaneously fulfilling the secret American envy of Soviet imperialism and the rerun (this time with a happy ending) of the Vietnam War. The Rolling Stones, in their fifties, gyrate before eighteen-year-olds who do not appear to need the machinery of nostalgia to be sold on their parents' heroes. Paul McCartney is selling the Beatles to a new audience by hitching his oblique nostalgia to their desire for the new that smacks of the old. *Dragnet* is back in nineties drag, and so is *Adam-12,* not to speak of *Batman* and *Mission Impossible,* all dressed up technologically but remarkably faithful to the atmospherics of their originals.[9]

---

8. In this passage, Appadurai refers to Fredric Jameson (b. 1934), an American philosopher and literary critic. He is known for his Marxist critique of postmodernism, which he argues is a feature of corporate capitalism. Jameson's best-known work is *Postmodernism: Or the Cultural Logic of Late Capitalism* (1991). Jameson is particularly concerned with "pastiche," which the dictionary defines as a style imitating and celebrating the work of other artists. Jameson, however, says that pastiche is part of the postmodern condition and that "Pastiche is, like parody, the imitation of a peculiar or unique style . . . but it is a neutral practice of such mimicry, without parody's ulterior motive . . . without laughter" (1991: 17).

The "leading lady who played the piano" is Imelda Marcos (b. 1929), wife of former Philippine dictator Ferdinand Marcos (1917–1989). Imelda Marcos was known for her extravagance while in power, which included, among other things, her collection of 2,700 pairs of shoes. In a perfectly postmodern twist that Appadurai would appreciate, in 2001, Marcos opened a shoe museum in Marikina, a Philippine city with a large shoe industry.

"Ad infinitum": Latin, "to infinity," or "forever."

9. Appadurai's use of *imaginaire* refers to the work of the French psychoanalytic Marxist Jacques Lacan (1901–1981). Lacan argued that a critical realization for children is their existence as an entity seen by others (he calls this the mirror stage). This gives children a way of understanding and imagining themselves. To create this understanding, children begin to assemble a story of what it is they are like. But ultimately, they cannot truly see themselves. Rather, they compose their self-image out of partial glimpses of themselves, understandings of other children, stories they are told, pictures they see, and so on. This collection is the *imaginaire,* and, by definition, it is not accurate. Lacan had a genius for and love of puns. *Imaginaire* is an example, connoting both "imaginary" and "made up of images." In another wonderful pun (that doesn't translate as easily), Lacan calls the child with an *imaginaire* an *homme-lette.* In French, this has the connotation of both a "little man" and an omelet—something made out of broken eggs. Appadurai in this passage speaks of America as an *imaginaire,* an idea composed of bits and pieces, of images that are other than reality, and he provides a plethora of cultural references (many now dated) to illustrate this idea. Some you may not be familiar with are:

Oliver North (b. 1943) was a US Marine Corps officer who was implicated in the Iran-Contra political scandal of the late 1980s. North was a member of President Ronald Reagan's National Security Council who organized the illegal sale of weapons to Iran to secretly finance rebel groups (called the Contras) who opposed Nicaragua's leftist government because it was supported by Cuba.

Spiro Agnew (1918–1996), vice president under Richard Nixon, and forced to resign in 1973 after being charged with extortion and tax fraud.

The past is now not a land to return to in a simple politics of memory. It has become a synchronic warehouse of cultural scenarios, a kind of temporal central casting, to which recourse can be taken as appropriate, depending on the movie to be made, the scene to be enacted, the hostages to be rescued. All this is par for the course, if you follow Jean Baudrillard or Jean-François Lyotard into a world of signs wholly unmoored from their social signifiers (all the world's a Disneyland). But I would like to suggest that the apparent increasing substitutability of whole periods and postures for one another, in the cultural styles of advanced capitalism, is tied to larger global forces, which have done much to show Americans that the past is usually another country. If your present is their future (as in much modernization theory and in many self-satisfied tourist fantasies), and their future is your past (as in the case of the Filipino virtuosos of American popular music), then your own past can be made to appear as simply a normalized modality of your present. Thus, although some anthropologists may continue to relegate their Others to temporal spaces that they do not themselves occupy (Fabian 1983), postindustrial cultural productions have entered a post-nostalgic phase.[10]

The crucial point, however, is that the United States is no longer the puppeteer of a world system of images but is only one node of a complex transnational construction of imaginary landscapes. The world we live in today is characterized by a new role for the imagination in social life. To grasp this new role, we need to bring together the old idea of images, especially mechanically produced images (in the Frankfurt School sense); the idea of the imagined community (in Anderson's sense); and the French idea of the imaginary (*imaginaire*) as a constructed landscape of collective aspirations, which is no more and no less real than the collective representations of Emile Durkheim, now mediated through the complex prism of modern media.[11]

The image, the imagined, the imaginary— these are all terms that direct us to something critical and new in global cultural processes: the imagination as a social practice. No longer mere fantasy (opium for the masses whose real work is elsewhere), no longer simple escape (from a world defined principally by more concrete purposes and structures), no longer elite pastime (thus not relevant to the lives of ordinary people), and no longer mere contemplation (irrelevant for new forms of desire and subjectivity), the imagination has become an organized field of social practices, a form of work (in the sense of both labor and culturally organized practice), and a form of negotiation between sites of agency (individuals) and globally defined fields of possibility. This unleashing of the imagination links the play of pastiche

---

Stallone in Afghanistan, refers to the movie *Rambo 3* (1988) in which the fictional character John Rambo, played by Sylvester Stallone, rescues a friend from an Afghan warlord. Appadurai's essay was written a decade before the US military involvement in Afghanistan.

Dragnet, Adam-12, Batman, and *Mission Impossible* were all television shows of the 1950s, 1960s, and 1970s. Readers may be familiar with recent movies reprising characters of the original television shows. As of 2024, the Rolling Stones and Paul McCartney are still performing.

10. Jean Baudrillard (1929–2007) and Jean-François Lyotard (1924–1998) are both well-known postmodern theorists.

11. The Frankfurt school was a group of scholars who examined the Western philosophical tradition and Marxism in light of twentieth-century history. One influential member was Walter Benjamin (1892–1940). In "The Work of Art in the Age of Mechanical Reproduction," originally published in 1936, Benjamin argued that in traditional societies art had an "aura"; that is, its originality and creativity inspired feelings of awe and respect in those who viewed it. In the modern era, mechanical reproduction has subverted the uniqueness of works of art, and therefore their power is diminished. Benjamin looked upon this as an ambiguous but generally positive development. It meant that people could observe and analyze art free from the mysticism of power. Benjamin believed that media such as radio and film had the potential to liberate, creating alternatives to the high culture of elites. Appadurai refers again to Benjamin later in this essay.

(in some settings) to the terror and coercion of states and their competitors. The imagination is now central to all forms of agency, is itself a social fact, and is the key component of the new global order. But to make this claim meaningful, we must address some other issues.

HOMOGENIZATION AND HETEROGENIZATION

The central problem of today's global interactions is the tension between cultural homogenization and cultural heterogenization. A vast array of empirical facts could be brought to bear on the side of the homogenization argument, and much of it has come from the left end of the spectrum of media studies (Hamelink 1983; Mattelart 1983; Schiller 1976), and some from other perspectives (Gans 1985; Iyer 1988). Most often, the homogenization argument sub-speciates into either an argument about Americanization or an argument about commoditization, and very often the two arguments are closely linked. What these arguments fail to consider is that at least as rapidly as forces from various metropolises are brought into new societies they tend to become indigenized in one or another way: this is true of music and housing styles as much as it is true of science and terrorism, spectacles and constitutions. The dynamics of such indigenization have just begun to be explored systemically (Barber 1987; Feld 1988; Hannerz 1987, 1989; Ivy 1988; Nicoll 1989; Yoshimoto 1989), and much more needs to be done. But it is worth noticing that for the people of Irian Jaya, Indonesianization may be more worrisome than Americanization, as Japanization may be for Koreans, Indianization for Sri Lankans, Vietnamization for the Cambodians, and Russianization for the people of Soviet Armenia and the Baltic republics. Such a list of alternative fears to Americanization could be greatly expanded, but it is not a shapeless inventory: for polities of smaller scale, there is always a fear of cultural absorption by polities of larger scale, especially those that are nearby. One man's imagined community is another man's political prison.

This scalar dynamic, which has widespread global manifestations, is also tied to the relationship between nations and states, to which I shall return later. For the moment let us note that the simplification of these many forces (and fears) of homogenization can also be exploited by nation-states in relation to their own minorities, by posing global commoditization (or capitalism, or some other such external enemy) as more real than the threat of its own hegemonic strategies.

The new global cultural economy has to be seen as a complex, overlapping, disjunctive order that cannot any longer be understood in terms of existing center-periphery models (even those that might account for multiple centers and peripheries). Nor is it susceptible to simple models of push and pull (in terms of migration theory), or of surpluses and deficits (as in traditional models of balance of trade), or of consumers and producers (as in most neo-Marxist theories of development). Even the most complex and flexible theories of global development that have come out of the Marxist tradition (Amin 1980; Mandel 1978; Wallerstein 1974; Wolf 1982) are inadequately quirky and have failed to come to terms with what Scott Lash and John Urry have called disorganized capitalism (1987). The complexity of the current global economy has to do with certain fundamental disjunctures between economy, culture, and politics that we have only begun to theorize.[12]

---

12. Here Appadurai introduces a critical element of his thinking: that the patterns of economy and culture in the world are far more complex than the modernization and global systems theories of the 1970s and 1980s suggested. He introduces the term *disjuncture* to characterize this complexity. A disjuncture is a separation, a disconnection, a disunion. Appadurai uses the term to signify ideas that are in some sort of relationship to one another but where that relationship cannot be specified because it is characterized by gaps and irregularities.

Much of anthropological theory from the time of Herbert Spencer envisioned societies and cultures as more or less organic systems. That is, theorists understood societies as being composed of a series of elements that stood in certain relations to each other. Together, these elements created an integrated pattern of culture. A.

I propose that an elementary framework for exploring such disjunctures is to look at the relationship among five dimensions of global cultural flows that can be termed (a) *ethnoscapes,* (b) *mediascapes,* (c) *technoscapes,* (d) *financescapes,* and (e) *ideoscapes.* The suffix -scape allows us to point to the fluid, irregular shapes of these landscapes, shapes that characterize international capital as deeply as they do international clothing styles. These terms with the common suffix scape also indicate that these are not objectively given relations that look the same from every angle of vision but, rather, that they are deeply perspectival constructs, inflected by the historical, linguistic, and political situatedness of different sorts of actors: nation-states, multinationals, diasporic communities, as well as subnational groupings and movements (whether religious, political, or economic), and even intimate face-to-face groups, such as villages, neighborhoods, and families. Indeed, the individual actor is the last locus of this perspectival set of landscapes, for these landscapes are eventually navigated by agents who both experience and constitute larger formations, in part from their own sense of what these landscapes offer.[13]

These landscapes thus are the building blocks of what (extending Benedict Anderson) I would like to call imagined worlds, that is, the multiple worlds that are constituted by the historically situated imaginations of persons and groups spread around the globe. An important fact of the world we live in today is that many persons on the globe live in such imagined worlds (and not just in imagined communities) and thus are able to contest and sometimes even subvert the imagined worlds of the official mind and of the entrepreneurial mentality that surround them.[14]

By *ethnoscape,* I mean the landscape of persons who constitute the shifting world in which we live: tourists, immigrants, refugees, exiles, guest workers, and other moving groups and individuals constitute an essential feature of the world and appear to affect the politics of (and between) nations to a hitherto unprecedented degree. This is not to say that there are no relatively stable communities and networks of kinship, friendship, work, and leisure, as well as of birth, residence, and other filial forms. But it is to say that the warp of these stabilities is everywhere shot through with the woof of human motion, as more persons and groups deal with the realities of having to move or the fantasies of wanting to move. What is more, both these realities and fantasies now function on larger scales, as men and women from villages in India think not just of moving to Poona or Madras but of moving to Dubai and Houston, and refugees from Sri Lanka find themselves in South India

---

R. Radcliffe-Brown, for example, also uses the term "disjuncture" (see Radcliffe-Brown, essay 15, especially notes 13 and 20), but for him, a disjuncture is something to be resolved (in that case, by the joking relationship). For Appadurai, disjuncture is the unresolvable nature of life in the current day. Culture is characterized by elements that combine, conflict, cooperate, and separate in ways that seem largely chaotic.

13. Appadurai coined the term "scape" in this essay. Within a quarter century, it became a common usage in anthropology, sociology, and economics. Its usage has been extended in various ways, for example, brandscapes (Klingmann 2007), experiencescapes (O'Dell and Billing 2005), heritagescapes (Di Giovine 2008), and many others.
This passage draws the reader to a critical aspect of the essay. Appadurai is describing phenomena that exist at many different levels of scale. We can talk of financescape and ideoscape at the level of the nation, the village, or perhaps the individual. This is an idea he returns to again in his conclusion.

14. Appadurai owes a critical debt to the Italian Marxist Antonio Gramsci (1897–1931) and notions of hegemony and counter-hegemony. Gramsci focused on understanding ideology within a Marxist framework. He emphasized that power elites set the general rules of understanding and debate within a society. He referred to this as the *hegemony* of the ruling classes. However, hegemony is negotiated as intellectuals and oppressed classes create counter-hegemonies to challenge elite ideas. In this passage, Appadurai notes that individuals can challenge and subvert the "official mind." Additional information on Gramsci can be found in Bourgois, essay 35, note 10.

as well as in Switzerland, just as the Hmong are driven to London as well as to Philadelphia. And as international capital shifts its needs, as production and technology generate different needs, as nation-states shift their policies on refugee populations, these moving groups can never afford to let their imaginations rest too long, even if they wish to.[15]

By *technoscape,* I mean the global configuration, also ever fluid, of technology and the fact that technology, both high and low, both mechanical and informational, now moves at high speeds across various kinds of previously impervious boundaries. Many countries now are the roots of multinational enterprise: a huge steel complex in Libya may involve interests from India, China, Russia, and Japan, providing different components of new technological configurations. The odd distribution of technologies, and thus the peculiarities of these technoscapes, are increasingly driven not by any obvious economies of scale, of political control, or of market rationality but by increasingly complex relationships among money flows, political possibilities, and the availability of both un and highly skilled labor. So, while India exports waiters and chauffeurs to Dubai and Sharjah, it also exports software engineers to the United States—indentured briefly to Tata-Burroughs[16] or the World Bank, then laundered through the State Department to become wealthy resident aliens, who are in turn objects of seductive messages to invest their money and know-how in federal and state projects in India.

The global economy can still be described in terms of traditional indicators (as the World Bank continues to do) and studied in terms of traditional comparisons (as in Project Link at the University of Pennsylvania), but the complicated technoscapes (and the shifting ethnoscapes) that underlie these indicators and comparisons are further out of the reach of the queen of social sciences than ever before. How is one to make a meaningful comparison of wages in Japan and the United States or of real estate costs in New York and Tokyo, without taking sophisticated account of the very complex fiscal and investment flows that link the two economies through a global grid of currency speculation and capital transfer?[17]

Thus it is useful to speak as well of *financescapes,* as the disposition of global capital is now a more mysterious, rapid, and difficult landscape to follow than ever before, as currency markets, national stock exchanges, and commodity speculations move megamonies through national turnstiles at blinding speed, with vast, absolute implications for small differences in percentage points and time units. But the critical point is that the global relationship among ethnoscapes, technoscapes, and financescapes is deeply disjunctive and profoundly unpredictable because each of these landscapes is subject to its own constraints and incentives (some political, some informational, and some technoenvironmental), at the same time as each acts as a constraint and a parameter for movements in the others. Thus, even an elementary model of global political economy must take into account the deeply disjunctive relationships among human movement, technological flow, and financial transfers.

Further refracting these disjunctures (which hardly form a simple, mechanical global infrastructure in any case) are what I call *mediascapes* and *ideoscapes,* which are closely related landscapes of images. Mediascapes refer both

---

15. We note that the world refugee population has climbed steadily since Appadurai wrote this essay. At the end of 2023, the United Nations High Commission for Refugees put the number of forcibly displaced people worldwide at 117.3 million, the highest number since World War II (https://unhcr.org).

16. Tata-Burroughs, now Tata Group, is an international corporation headquartered in India.

17. Founded in 1968 by Nobel Prize–winning economist Lawrence Klein (1920–2013) and supported by the United Nations, Project LINK attempts to create a comprehensive global econometric model. From relatively small beginnings, LINK now includes more than seventy different models. It has moved from the University of Pennsylvania to the University of Toronto and the United Nations in New York.
The "queen of the social sciences" refers to economics.

to the distribution of the electronic capabilities to produce and disseminate information (newspapers, magazines, television stations, and film-production studios), which are now available to a growing number of private and public interests throughout the world, and to the images of the world created by these media. These images involve many complicated inflections, depending on their mode (documentary or entertainment), their hardware (electronic or pre-electronic), their audiences (local, national, or transnational), and the interests of those who own and control them. What is most important about these mediascapes is that they provide (especially in their television, film, and cassette forms) large and complex repertoires of images, narratives, and ethnoscapes to viewers throughout the world, in which the world of commodities and the world of news and politics are profoundly mixed. What this means is that many audiences around the world experience the media themselves as a complicated and interconnected repertoire of print, celluloid, electronic screens, and billboards. The lines between the realistic and the fictional landscapes they see are blurred, so that the farther away these audiences are from the direct experiences of metropolitan life, the more likely they are to construct imagined worlds that are chimerical, aesthetic, even fantastic objects, particularly if assessed by the criteria of some other perspective, some other imagined world.

Mediascapes, whether produced by private or state interests, tend to be image-centered, narrative-based accounts of strips of reality, and what they offer to those who experience and transform them is a series of elements (such as characters, plots, and textual forms) out of which scripts can be formed of imagined lives, their own as well as those of others living in other places. These scripts can and do get disaggregated into complex sets of metaphors by which people live (Lakoff and Johnson 1980) as they help to constitute narratives of the Other and protonarratives of possible lives, fantasies that could become **prolegomena** to the desire for acquisition and movement. [18]

Ideoscapes are also concatenations of images, but they are often directly political and frequently have to do with the ideologies of states and the counter ideologies of movements explicitly oriented to capturing state power or a piece of it. These ideoscapes are composed of elements of the Enlightenment worldview, which consists of a chain of ideas, terms, and images, including freedom, welfare, rights, sovereignty, representation, and the master term democracy. The master narrative of the Enlightenment (and its many variants in Britain, France, and the United States) was constructed with a certain internal logic and presupposed a certain relationship between reading, representation, and the public sphere. (For the dynamics of this process in the early history of the United States, see Warner 1990.) But the diaspora of these terms and images across the world, especially since the nineteenth century, has loosened the internal coherence that held them together in a Euro-American master narrative and provided instead a loosely structured **synopticon** of politics, in which different nation-states, as part of their evolution, have organized their political cultures around different keywords (e.g., Williams 1976).[19]

As a result of the differential diaspora of these keywords, the political narratives that govern communication between elites and followers in different parts of the world involve problems of both a semantic and pragmatic nature: semantic to the extent that words (and their lexical equivalents) require careful trans-

---

18. **"Prolegomena"**: an introduction or introductory comments.

19. **"Synopticon"**: Synoptic, from the Greek for "seen together" is a term derived from religious studies. Matthew, Mark, and Luke are the "synoptic gospels" because they seem to be slightly different versions of the same story of the ministry of Jesus (whereas the Gospel of John is distinctly different). Jeremy Bentham (1748–1832) proposed the "panopticon," a system in which many prisoners could be seen by a single guard (see Foucault, essay 28, note 12), an idea used by Michel Foucault. Writing later than Appadurai but providing insight into his meaning, Thomas Mathiesen in *The Viewer Society* (1997) used "synopticon" to refer to the capacity of radio and television to allow the many to see the few.

lation from context to context in their global movements, and pragmatic to the extent that the use of these words by political actors and their audiences may be subject to very different sets of contextual conventions that mediate their translation into public politics. Such conventions are not only matters of the nature of political rhetoric: for example, what does the aging Chinese leadership mean when it refers to the dangers of hooliganism? What does the South Korean leadership mean when it speaks of discipline as the key to democratic industrial growth?

These conventions also involve the far more subtle question of what sets of communicative genres are valued in what way (newspapers versus cinema, for example) and what sorts of pragmatic genre conventions govern the collective readings of different kinds of text. So, while an Indian audience may be attentive to the resonances of a political speech in terms of some keywords and phrases reminiscent of Hindi cinema, a Korean audience may respond to the subtle codings of Buddhist or neo-Confucian rhetoric encoded in a political document. The very relationship of reading to hearing and seeing may vary in important ways that determine the morphology of these different ideoscapes as they shape themselves in different national and transnational contexts. This globally variable **synaesthesia**

has hardly even been noted, but it demands urgent analysis. Thus democracy has clearly become a master term, with powerful echoes from Haiti and Poland to the former Soviet Union and China, but it sits at the center of a variety of ideoscapes, composed of distinctive pragmatic configurations of rough translations of other central terms from the vocabulary of the Enlightenment. This creates ever new terminological kaleidoscopes, as states (and the groups that seek to capture them) seek to pacify populations whose own ethnoscapes are in motion and whose mediascapes may create severe problems for the ideoscapes with which they are presented. The fluidity of ideoscapes is complicated in particular by the growing diasporas (both voluntary and involuntary) of intellectuals who continuously inject new meaning streams into the discourse of democracy in different parts of the world.[20]

This extended terminological discussion of the five terms I have coined sets the basis for a tentative formulation about the conditions under which current global flows occur: they occur in and through the growing disjunctures among ethnoscapes, technoscapes, financescapes, mediascapes, and ideoscapes. This formulation, the core of my model of global cultural flow, needs some explanation. First, people, machinery, money, images, and ideas now follow increasingly **nonisomorphic**

---

20. Appadurai here employs a fundamental element of postmodern thinking particularly shaped by the work of Jacques Derrida (1930–2004). Derrida argued that after publication, authors lose control of their texts. Readers understand text based on their own histories and contexts. Thus, meaning can never be fixed. Here, Appadurai notes that the lexicon of modern political debate was largely generated by the historical experiences and meanings of Enlightenment Europe. It is now used freely throughout the world and, because of this, takes on meanings its authors could not have imagined let alone controlled. So, for example, the authors of the Declaration of Independence did not intend for any of its wording to resonate with either a Buddhist or Confucian audience. Yet, passages of that document may take on special meaning for individuals in those traditions because, by chance, they do so resonate. These meanings may or may not have anything to do with what the authors intended. From a postmodern perspective, loss of authorial control is an aspect of all text. Appadurai points out that this is much more the case when text (and movies, advertisements, and all other forms of communication) move among people of radically different cultures and histories.

Let us also take a moment to consider how prescient Appadurai was. The trends that he identified in the section you have just read greatly increased in the decades that followed. We have already noted the vast number of refugees. To this, we must add the development of new forms of technology, finance and currency, new forms of media, and new forms of ideology all spreading in patterns that escape centralized control. We also note something that Appadurai did not anticipate: the countering of the Enlightenment rhetoric of democracy with a widespread and frequently totalitarian rhetoric.

"Synesthesia": the association of unrelated sensations, such as touch and hearing. In this case Appadurai refers to the association of reading, with hearing and seeing.

paths; of course, at all periods in human history, there have been some disjunctures in the flows of these things, but the sheer speed, scale, and volume of each of these flows are now so great that the disjunctures have become central to the politics of global culture. The Japanese are notoriously hospitable to ideas and are stereotyped as inclined to export (all) and import (some) goods, but they are also notoriously closed to immigration, like the Swiss, the Swedes, and the Saudis. Yet the Swiss and the Saudis accept populations of guest workers, thus creating labor diasporas of Turks, Italians, and other circum-Mediterranean groups. Some such guest-worker groups maintain continuous contact with their home nations, like the Turks, but others, like high-level South Asian migrants, tend to desire lives in their new homes, raising anew the problem of reproduction in a **deterritorialized** context.[21]

Deterritorialization, in general, is one of the central forces of the modern world because it brings laboring populations into the lower class sectors and spaces of relatively wealthy societies, while sometimes creating exaggerated and intensified senses of criticism or attachment to politics in the home state. Deterritorialization, whether of Hindus, Sikhs, Palestinians, or Ukrainians, is now at the core of a variety of global fundamentalisms, including Islamic and Hindu fundamentalism. In the Hindu case, for example, it is clear that the overseas movement of Indians has been exploited by a variety of interests both within and outside India to create a complicated network of finances and religious identifications, by which the problem of cultural reproduction for Hindus abroad has become tied to the politics of Hindu fundamentalism at home.

At the same time, deterritorialization creates new markets for film companies, art impresarios, and travel agencies, which thrive on the need of the deterritorialized population for contact with its homeland. Naturally, these invented homelands, which constitute the mediascapes of deterritorialized groups, can often become sufficiently fantastic and one-sided that they provide the material for new ideoscapes in which ethnic conflicts can begin to erupt. The creation of Khalistan, an invented homeland of the deterritorialized Sikh population of England, Canada, and the United States, is one example of the bloody potential in such mediascapes as they interact with the internal colonialisms of the nation-state (e.g., Hechter 1975). The West Bank, Namibia, and Eritrea are other theaters for the enactment of the bloody negotiation between existing nation-states and various deterritorialized groupings.[22]

It is in the fertile ground of deterritorialization, in which money, commodities, and persons are involved in ceaselessly chasing each other around the world, that the mediascapes and ideoscapes of the modern world find their fractured and fragmented counterpart. For the ideas and images produced by mass media often are only partial guides to the goods and experiences that deterritorialized populations transfer to one another. In Mira Nair's brilliant film *India Cabaret,* we see the multiple loops of this fractured deterritorialization as young women, barely competent in Bombay's metropolitan glitz, come to seek their fortunes as cabaret dancers and prostitutes in Bombay, entertaining men in clubs with dance formats derived wholly from the prurient dance sequences of Hindi films. These scenes in turn cater to ideas about western and foreign women and their

---

21. **"Nonisomorphic"**: having a different form or appearance.
 "Deterritorialized": To separate people or practices from their original location or context. For example, an online university course is deterritorialized from its campus context.

22. Khalistan is the name of a proposed Sikh homeland in the Punjab in India. Separatists demanding a Sikh state were most active in the 1970s and 1980s. Between 1980 and 1992 the Punjab was convulsed by a series of rebellions that left almost twenty-five thousand dead, most of them Sikhs (Van Dyke 2009). Numerous famous incidents of terrorism were linked to this movement including the assassination of Indian Prime Minister Indira Gandhi (1917–1984) in 1984 and, most likely, the destruction of Air India Flight 182 off the coast of Ireland in 1985, in which 329 died. The decades of the 1960s through the 1980s also saw bloody wars of independence in Namibia (1966–1990) and Eritrea (1961–1991), as well as many other places.

looseness, while they provide tawdry career alibis for these women. Some of these women come from Kerala, where cabaret clubs and the pornographic film industry have blossomed, partly in response to the purses and tastes of Keralites returned from the Middle East, where their diasporic lives away from women distort their very sense of what the relations between men and women might be. These tragedies of displacement could certainly be replayed in a more detailed analysis of the relations between the Japanese and German sex tours to Thailand and the tragedies of the sex trade in Bangkok, and in other similar loops that tie together fantasies about the Other, the conveniences and seductions of travel, the economics of global trade, and the brutal mobility fantasies that dominate gender politics in many parts of Asia and the world at large.[23]

While far more could be said about the cultural politics of deterritorialization and the larger sociology of displacement that it expresses, it is appropriate at this juncture to bring in the role of the nation-state in the disjunctive global economy of culture today. The relationship between states and nations is everywhere an embattled one. It is possible to say that in many societies the nation and the state have become one another's projects. That is, while nations (or more properly groups with ideas about nationhood) seek to capture or coopt states and state power, states simultaneously seek to capture and monopolize ideas about nationhood (Baruah 1986; Chatterjee 1986; Nandy 1989). In general, separatist

transnational movements, including those that have included terror in their methods, exemplify nations in search of states. Sikhs, Tamil Sri Lankans, Basques, Moros, Quebecois—each of these represents imagined communities that seek to create states of their own or carve pieces out of existing states. States, on the other hand, are everywhere seeking to monopolize the moral resources of community, either by flatly claiming perfect coevality between nation and state, or by systematically museumizing and representing all the groups within them in a variety of heritage politics that seems remarkably uniform throughout the world (Handler 1988; Herzfeld 1982; McQueen 1988).[24]

Here, national and international mediascapes are exploited by nation-states to pacify separatists or even the potential **fissiparousness** of all ideas of difference. Typically, contemporary nation-states do this by exercising taxonomic control over difference, by creating various kinds of international spectacle to domesticate difference, and by seducing small groups with the fantasy of self-display on some sort of global or cosmopolitan stage. One important new feature of global cultural politics, tied to the disjunctive relationships among the various landscapes discussed earlier, is that state and nation are at each other's throats, and the hyphen that links them is now less an icon of conjuncture than an index of disjuncture. This disjunctive relationship between nation and state has two levels: at the level of any given nation-state, it means that there is a battle of

---

23. *India Cabaret* (1985) is a made-for-TV documentary that details the lives and expectations of two aging strippers at a run-down Bombay nightclub.

24. Americans tend to think of "nation" and "state" as synonyms. However, most social scientists regard the two as different. The nation refers to a group of people tied together by real or imagined historical ties of affinity and emotion. The state is a political formation. Historically, states included many different national groups. Particularly in the past 150 years, a wide variety of political, economic, and social forces have promoted the emergence of the nation-state: a political formation in which the state and nation are identical. This has been done by states suppressing or exiling alternative national identities within their borders or by groups with national identities demanding statehood.

In this passage Appadurai identifies several national groups that seek their own states: Sikhs are a group located primarily in Northwest India, Tamils are the largest minority group in Sri Lanka, Basques are a minority group in Spain, Moros are a Muslim minority group in Mindanao in the Philippines, and the Quebecois are of Quebec, a province of Canada. Each of these groups have a land base but also a large community of members spread across the globe. Appadurai points out that millions of people have become displaced (or deterritorialized). These pose an important challenge to nation-state identity.

the imagination, with state and nation seeking to cannibalize one another. Here is the seedbed of brutal separatisms—majoritarianisms that seem to have appeared from nowhere and microidentities that have become political projects within the nation-state. At another level, this disjunctive relationship is deeply entangled with the global disjunctures discussed throughout this chapter: ideas of nationhood appear to be steadily increasing in scale and regularly crossing existing state boundaries, sometimes, as with the Kurds, because previous identities stretched across vast national spaces or, as with the Tamils in Sri Lanka, the dormant threads of a transnational diaspora have been activated to ignite the micropolitics of a nation-state.[25]

In discussing the cultural politics that have subverted the hyphen that links the nation to the state, it is especially important not to forget the mooring of such politics in the irregularities that now characterize disorganized capital (Kothari 1989; Lash and Urry 1987). Because labor, finance, and technology are now so widely separated, the volatilities that underlie movements for nationhood (as large as transnational Islam on the one hand, or as small as the movement of the Gurkhas for a separate state in Northeast India) grind against the vulnerabilities that characterize the relationships between states. States find themselves pressed to stay open by the forces of media, technology, and travel that have fueled consumerism throughout the world and have increased the craving, even in the non-western world, for new commodities and spectacles. On the other hand, these very cravings can become caught up in new ethnoscapes, mediascapes, and, eventually, ideoscapes, such as democracy in China, that the state cannot tolerate as threats to its own control over ideas of nationhood and peoplehood. States throughout the world are under siege, especially where contests over the ideoscapes of democracy are fierce and fundamental, and where there are radical disjunctures between ideoscapes and technoscapes (as in the case of very small countries that lack contemporary technologies of production and information); or between ideoscapes and financescapes (as in countries such as Mexico or Brazil, where international lending influences national politics to a very large degree); or between ideoscapes and ethnoscapes (as in Beirut, where diasporic, local, and translocal filiations are suicidally at battle); or between ideoscapes and mediascapes (as in many countries in the Middle East and Asia) where the lifestyles represented on both national and international TV and cinema completely overwhelm and undermine the rhetoric of national politics. In the Indian case, the myth of the law-breaking hero has emerged to mediate this naked struggle between the pieties and realities of Indian politics, which has grown increasingly brutalized and corrupt (Vachani 1989).[26]

The transnational movement of the martial arts, particularly through Asia, as mediated by the Hollywood and Hong Kong film industries (Zarilli 1995) is a rich illustration of the ways in which long-standing martial arts traditions, reformulated to meet the fantasies of contemporary (sometimes **lumpen**) youth populations, create new cultures of masculinity and violence, which are in turn the fuel for increased violence in national and international politics. Such violence is in turn the spur to an increasingly rapid and amoral arms trade that penetrates the entire world. The worldwide spread of the AK-47 and the Uzi, in films, in corporate and state security, in terror, and in police and military activity, is a reminder that apparently simple technical uniformities often conceal an increasingly complex set of loops,

---

25. **"Fissiparousness"**: the tendency of things to break into pieces.

26. When this essay was published in 1990, many states seemed to be collapsing. The Soviet Union was in the process of disintegrating. China had recently put down a mass pro-democracy movement with substantial loss of life. Yugoslavia was about to break into seven states. Additionally, violent separatist movements were active in many states, including Spain and Northern Ireland. In the years since, many of these conflicts have been at least partially resolved but new threats to state integrity have appeared, particularly in the Middle East.

linking images of violence to aspirations for community in some imagined world.[27]

Returning then to the ethnoscapes with which I began, the central paradox of ethnic politics in today's world is that primordia (whether of language or skin color or neighborhood or kinship) have become globalized. That is, sentiments, whose greatest force is in their ability to ignite intimacy into a political state and turn locality into a staging ground for identity, have become spread over vast and irregular spaces as groups move yet stay linked to one another through sophisticated media capabilities. This is not to deny that such primordia are often the product of invented traditions (Hobsbawm and Ranger 1983) or retrospective affiliations, but to emphasize that because of the disjunctive and unstable interplay of commerce, media, national policies, and consumer fantasies, ethnicity, once a genie contained in the bottle of some sort of locality (however large), has now become a global force, forever slipping in and through the cracks between states and borders.

But the relationship between the cultural and economic levels of this new set of global disjunctures is not a simple one-way street in which the terms of global cultural politics are set wholly by, or confined wholly within, the vicissitudes of international flows of technology, labor, and finance, demanding only a modest modification of existing neo-Marxist models of uneven development and state formation. There is a deeper change, itself driven by the disjunctures among all the landscapes I have discussed and constituted by their continuously fluid and uncertain interplay, that concerns the relationship between production and consumption in today's global economy. Here, I begin with Marx's famous (and often mined) view of the fetishism of the commodity and suggest that this fetishism has been replaced in the world at large (now seeing the world as one large, interactive system, composed of many complex subsystems) by two mutually supportive descendants, the first of which I call production fetishism and the second, the fetishism of the consumer.[28]

---

27. Over the past several paragraphs Appadurai has presented a powerful historical argument. Until perhaps the time of World War II, the various *scapes* that Appadurai characterizes existed in greater or lesser synchrony. Nation-states, capital, media, and so on, overlapped. Firms were tied to national interests and the result was a world characterized by the hegemony of Western wealth, power, and ideas. However, Appadurai argues that since then, these ties have come loose from their moorings, radically affecting the interests of nations and capitalist firms. The result is a profoundly disjunctive world. Appadurai's ideas have been very productive in inspiring research about the ways in which nationalism, capitalism, the media, and other aspects of modernity are articulated.

On the other hand, Appadurai may be extending his argument a bit too far. In the paragraph you just read, he argues that the international popularity of kung-fu films is related to the rise of an international arms trade. Although a causal relationship between martial arts films and international violence seems unlikely, terrorist groups today use sophisticated media to recruit new members to their cause. In 2015 the FBI arrested six young men in Minnesota for trying to join the Islamic State terrorist organization. That propaganda from terrorist organizations in the Middle East can inspire teenage boys in the American Midwest to try to join their movement is an example of what Appadurai is talking about.

"*Lumpen*": is a term from Marxist vocabulary. It generally refers to the underclass, particularly dispossessed and displaced individuals, the very lowest social strata. See also Bourgois, essay 35, note 10, where the Marxist term *lumpenproletariat* is discussed.

28. Commodity fetishism is a critical idea introduced by Marx in *Capital* (1930 [1867]). Marx argues that in capitalism (as distinct from other modes of production) commodities are removed from the conditions of their production through the medium of money. This disjuncture makes it possible to think of a market consisting only of items that are traded against each other and especially against money. Economists focus on this market, but in doing so, they fetishize commodities, making them magical items that seem to have wills and values of their own, separate from either their uses or their conditions of production. Because of this fetishism, Marx argues, bourgeois economists misunderstand value (which is tied to the amount of labor in things) and economic relations themselves. Fetishizing commodities thus acts to disguise or obscure the true nature of the relation of production that created them. In the next paragraph, Appadurai argues that a similar process

By *production fetishism* I mean an illusion created by contemporary transnational production loci that masks translocal capital, transnational earning flows, global management, and often faraway workers (engaged in various kinds of high-tech putting-out operations) in the idiom and spectacle of local (sometimes even worker) control, national productivity, and territorial sovereignty. To the extent that various kinds of free-trade zones have become the models for production at large, especially of high-tech commodities, production has itself become a fetish, obscuring not social relations as such but the relations of production, which are increasingly transnational. The locality (both in the sense of the local factory or site of production and in the extended sense of the nation-state) becomes a fetish that disguises the globally dispersed forces that actually drive the production process. This generates alienation (in Marx's sense) twice intensified, for its social sense is now compounded by a complicated spatial dynamic that is increasingly global.[29]

As for the *fetishism of the consumer*, I mean to indicate here that the consumer has been transformed through commodity flows (and the mediascapes, especially of advertising, that accompany them) into a sign, both in **Baudrillard's sense of a simulacrum** that only asymptotically approaches the form of a real social agent, and in the sense of a mask for the real seat of agency, which is not the consumer but the producer and the many forces that constitute production. Global advertising is the key technology for the worldwide dissemination of a plethora of creative and culturally well-chosen ideas of consumer agency. These images of agency are increasingly distortions of a world of merchandising so subtle that the consumer is consistently helped to believe that he or she is an actor, where in fact he or she is at best a chooser.[30]

The globalization of culture is not the same as its homogenization, but globalization involves the use of a variety of instruments of homogenization (armaments, advertising techniques, language hegemonies, and clothing styles) that are absorbed into local political and cultural economies, only to be repatriated as heterogeneous dialogues of national sovereignty, free enterprise, and fundamentalism in which the state plays an increasingly delicate

---

has happened for both production and consumption and that this is a deeper-level change driven by the disjunctures among all the scapes he has discussed. Production and consumption have become terms that mask rather than reveal processes and understanding.

29. Alienation in Marx's sense refers to removal. Recall that Marx believed that workers were alienated to the extent that ownership of the means of production was taken away from them. Here they are doubly alienated because not only are the means of production (the factory) removed from the worker but, despite its physical presence, it is removed from the nation as well. The factory may be physically located nearby, but virtually all aspects of its control, operation, and economic benefits may be managed from afar. Alternatively (and more commonly since the publication of this essay), brands may be identified with one nation, but their products may be produced by companies in other places. Apple is a well-known example. It is closely associated with the United States (and with California in particular), but its products are manufactured mostly in China and mostly by another company, Foxconn.

30. **"Baudrillard's sense of a simulacrum"**: A simulacrum is an image or a representation. In Baudrillard's 1994 book *Simulacra and Simulation*, the French sociologist and philosopher argued that advanced capitalism and, in particular, the media have detached the image from the real. As we are bombarded with images, we are exposed to models of objects and behaviors that have no counterparts in our actual lives. The notions of masculinity and femininity seen on TV, the homes portrayed on TV and in glossy magazines, and so on, are frequently held up as consummately desirable. Thus, consumerism is fired by an attempt to purchase and create a simulacrum or model that has no origin in reality. Efforts to model reality on such a simulacrum are ultimately doomed and lead to a collapse of meaning. Appadurai, following Baudrillard, argues for a fetishism of the consumer. He claims that analysts focus on consumer behavior, but such a focus misunderstands the true dynamics of the situation. The consumer is buffeted and controlled by elements of capitalism that structure the nature of desire and the possibilities available to satisfy it.

role: too much openness to global flows, and the nation-state is threatened by revolt, as in the China syndrome; too little, and the state exits the international stage, as Burma, Albania, and North Korea in various ways have done. In general, the state has become the arbitrageur of this *repatriation of difference* (in the form of goods, signs, slogans, and styles). But this repatriation or export of the designs and commodities of difference continuously exacerbates the internal politics of majoritarianism and homogenization, which is most frequently played out in debates over heritage.[31]

Thus the central feature of global culture today is the politics of the mutual effort of sameness and difference to cannibalize one another and thereby proclaim their successful hijacking of the twin Enlightenment ideas of the triumphantly universal and the resiliently particular. This mutual cannibalization shows its ugly face in riots, refugee flows, state sponsored torture, and ethnocide (with or without state support). Its brighter side is in the expansion of many individual horizons of hope and fantasy, in the global spread of oral rehydration therapy and other low-tech instruments of well-being, in the susceptibility even of South Africa to the force of global opinion, in the inability of the Polish state to repress its own working classes, and in the growth of a wide range of progressive, transnational alliances. Examples of both sorts could be multiplied. The critical point is

that both sides of the coin of global cultural process today are products of the infinitely varied mutual contest of sameness and difference on a stage characterized by radical disjunctures between different sorts of global flows and the uncertain landscapes created in and through these disjunctures.[32]

THE WORK OF REPRODUCTION IN AN AGE OF MECHANICAL ART

I have inverted the key terms of the title of Walter Benjamin's famous essay (1969) to return this rather high-flying discussion to a more manageable level. There is a classic human problem that will not disappear however much global cultural processes might change their dynamics, and this is the problem today typically discussed under the rubric of reproduction (and traditionally referred to in terms of the transmission of culture). In either case, the question is, how do small groups, especially families, the classical loci of socialization, deal with these new global realities as they seek to reproduce themselves and, in so doing, by accident reproduce cultural forms themselves? In traditional anthropological terms, this could be phrased as the problem of enculturation in a period of rapid culture change. So the problem is hardly novel. But it does take on some

---

31. In this passage Appadurai plays with a double meaning of the phrase "the China Syndrome." He refers both to the Chinese state's brutal suppression of a pro-democracy movement and to the title of a 1979 American movie *The China Syndrome* about the possible meltdown of the core of a nuclear reactor. The movie title refers to the idea that a melting nuclear core in America would pass through the earth until it reaches China. The notion of meltdown fits nicely with Appadurai's ideas in this paragraph.

When this essay was written, both Albania and Burma (now Myanmar) were nations almost entirely closed to outsiders. Neither Albania or Myanmar are closed today (but North Korea still is).

32. Appadurai, referring to South Africa and Poland here, is commenting on the politics of the 1980s. Between the early years of the twentieth century and the early 1990s, South Africa had a legal system of obligatory racial discrimination called apartheid. It was eventually dismantled by a combination of civil disobedience in South Africa and sanctions and diplomatic pressure from the rest of the world. In Poland, a communist nation after World War II, an anticommunist trade union, Solidarity, was founded in 1980. Despite several attempts, the government was unable to suppress the union and by 1989, a Solidarity-led government was in place and union leader Lech Walesa (b. 1943) had been elected president. The collapse of apartheid, the success of Solidarity, and the fall of communism in Eastern Europe and Russia were titanic events that had just happened when Appadurai wrote this essay.

novel dimensions under the global conditions discussed so far in this chapter.[33]

First, the sort of transgenerational stability of knowledge that was presupposed in most theories of enculturation (or, in slightly broader terms, of socialization) can no longer be assumed. As families move to new locations, or as children move before older generations, or as grown sons and daughters return from time spent in strange parts of the world, family relationships can become volatile; new commodity patterns are negotiated, debts and obligations are recalibrated, and rumors and fantasies about the new setting are maneuvered into existing repertoires of knowledge and practice. Often, global labor diasporas involve immense strains on marriages in general and on women in particular, as marriages become the meeting points of historical patterns of socialization and new ideas of proper behavior. Generations easily divide, as ideas about property, propriety, and collective obligation wither under the siege of distance and time. Most important, the work of cultural reproduction in new settings is profoundly complicated by the politics of representing a family as normal (particularly for the young) to neighbours and peers in the new locale. All this is, of course, not new to the cultural study of immigration.

What is new is that this is a world in which both points of departure and points of arrival are in cultural flux, and thus the search for steady points of reference, as critical life choices are made, can be very difficult. It is in this atmosphere that the invention of tradition (and of ethnicity, kinship, and other identity markers) can become slippery, as the search for certainties is regularly frustrated by the fluidities of transnational communication. As group pasts become increasingly parts of museums, exhibits, and collections, both in national and transnational spectacles, culture becomes less what Pierre Bourdieu would have called a habitus (a tacit realm of reproducible practices and dispositions) and more an arena for conscious choice, justification, and representation, the latter often to multiple and spatially dislocated audiences.[34]

The task of cultural reproduction, even in its most intimate arenas, such as husband-wife and parent-child relations, becomes both politicized and exposed to the traumas of deterritorialization as family members pool and negotiate their mutual understandings and aspirations in sometimes fractured spatial arrangements. At larger levels, such as community, neighborhood, and territory, this politicization is often the emotional fuel for more explicitly violent politics of identity, just as these larger politics sometimes penetrate and ignite domestic politics. When, for example, two offspring in a household split with their father on a key matter of political identification in a transnational setting, preexisting localized norms carry little force. Thus a son who has joined the Hezbollah group in Leba-

---

33. Though he phrases it partially as the anthropological issue of enculturation, Appadurai also locates his argument squarely in neo-Marxist thought. For Marx, every society both produces and reproduces. It produces its livelihood, and it reproduces the mode of production. Societies provide their members with sufficient resources to reproduce their own living conditions and relations of production as they promulgate ideologies that justify these conditions and relations. Social reproduction is the force that drives society forward in time. Appadurai, punning on the title of Walter Benjamin's most famous essay "The Work of Art in the Age of Mechanical Reproduction," points to the difficulties of social reproduction in an age of global flow. See note 11 for more information about Walter Benjamin.

34. The idea of *habitus* is most frequently associated with the work of Pierre Bourdieu. *Habitus* refers to the common daily practices and beliefs of an individual as a member of a social group that form their basic assumptions about the nature of social life and the world. Two key characteristics of *habitus* are, first, that its elements are so basic to individuals' understandings that it is difficult to think of them directly. They are the things that not only go without saying but are extremely difficult to say. Second, in at least some of its expressions, *habitus* is a physical thing. It is expressed in people's bodies and the ways they are held and used in social interaction. Appadurai here points out that the global economy has the effect of making culture a conscious attribute and a series of choices rather than a *habitus*, something that is inscribed in our consciousness and our bodies in ways that we can only partially recognize.

non may no longer get along with parents or siblings who are affiliated with Amal or some other branch of Shi'i ethnic political identity in Lebanon. Women in particular bear the brunt of this sort of friction, for they become pawns in the heritage politics of the household and are often subject to the abuse and violence of men who are themselves torn about the relation between heritage and opportunity in shifting spatial and political formations.[35]

The pains of cultural reproduction in a disjunctive global world are, of course, not eased by the effects of mechanical art (or mass media), for these media afford powerful resources for counternodes of identity that youth can project against parental wishes or desires. At larger levels of organization, there can be many forms of cultural politics within displaced populations (whether of refugees or of voluntary immigrants), all of which are inflected in important ways by media (and the mediascapes and ideoscapes they offer). A central link between the fragilities of cultural reproduction and the role of the mass media in today's world is the politics of gender and violence. As fantasies of gendered violence dominate the B-grade film industries that blanket the world, they both reflect and refine gendered violence at home and in the streets, as young men (in particular) are swayed by the macho politics of self-assertion in contexts where they are frequently denied real agency, and women are forced to enter the labor force in new ways on the one hand, and continue the maintenance of familial heritage on the other. Thus the honor of women becomes not just an armature of stable (if inhuman) systems of cultural reproduction but a new arena for the formation of sexual identity and family politics, as men and women face new pressures at work and new fantasies of leisure.[36]

Because both work and leisure have lost none of their gendered qualities in this new global order but have acquired ever subtler fetishized representations, the honor of women becomes increasingly a surrogate for the identity of embattled communities of males, while their women in reality have to negotiate increasingly harsh conditions of work at home and in the nondomestic workplace. In short, deterritorialized communities and displaced populations, however much they may enjoy the fruits of new kinds of earning and new dispositions of capital and technology, have to play out the desires and fantasies of these new ethnoscapes, while striving to reproduce the family-as-microcosm of culture. As the shapes of cultures grow less bounded and tacit, more fluid and politicized, the work of cultural reproduction becomes a daily hazard. Far more could, and should, be said about the work of reproduction in an age of mechanical art: the preceding discussion is meant to indicate the contours of the problems that a new, globally informed theory of cultural reproduction will have to face.

SHAPE AND PROCESS IN GLOBAL CULTURAL FORMATIONS

The deliberations of the arguments that I have made so far constitute the bare bones of an approach to a general theory of global cultural processes. Focusing on disjunctures, I have employed a set of terms (*ethnoscape, financescape, technoscape, mediascape,* and *ideoscape*) to stress different streams or flows along which cultural material may be seen to be moving across national boundaries. I have also sought to exemplify the ways in which these various flows (or landscapes, from the stabilizing per-

---

35. Hezbollah and Amal were two rival political groups involved in bitter warfare in Lebanon in the 1980s. Amal was (mostly) defeated. Amal still exists but is now in alliance with Hezbollah, which is still a potent military and political power in Lebanon.

36. In this passage, Appadurai modifies Benjamin's argument. Benjamin was optimistic about mass culture because he saw it as demystifying art and giving it as a tool to the masses. Appadurai, however, sees the media as providing images of violence and sexuality that encourage street and household-level violence by individuals (particularly men) who are denied any meaningful agency in the world at large. Thus, mechanical art becomes not a tool of the people but an avenue to power and profit by the capitalist elite at the expense of the disempowered.

spectives of any given imagined world) are in fundamental disjuncture with respect to one another. What further steps can we take toward a general theory of global cultural processes based on these proposals?

The first is to note that our very models of cultural shape will have to alter, as configurations of people, place, and heritage lose all semblance of **isomorphism**. Recent work in anthropology has done much to free us of the shackles of highly localized, boundary-oriented, holistic, primordialist images of cultural form and substance (Hannerz 1989; Marcus and Fischer 1986; Thornton 1988). But not very much has been put in their place, except somewhat larger if less mechanical versions of these images, as in Eric Wolf's work on the relationship of Europe to the rest of the world (1982). What I would like to propose is that we begin to think of the configuration of cultural forms in today's world as fundamentally fractal, that is, as possessing no Euclidean boundaries, structures, or regularities. Second, I would suggest that these cultural forms, which we should strive to represent as fully fractal, are also overlapping in ways that have been discussed only in pure mathematics (in set theory, for example) and in biology (in the language of polythetic classifications). Thus we need to combine a fractal metaphor for the shape of cultures (in the plural) with a polythetic

account of their overlaps and resemblances. Without this latter step, we shall remain mired in comparative work that relies on the clear separation of the entities to be compared before serious comparison can begin. How are we to compare fractally shaped cultural forms that are also polythetically overlapping in their coverage of terrestrial space?[37]

Finally, in order for the theory of global cultural interactions predicated on disjunctive flows to have any force greater than that of a mechanical metaphor, it will have to move into something like a human version of the theory that some scientists are calling chaos theory. That is, we will need to ask not how these complex, overlapping, fractal shapes constitute a simple, stable (even if large-scale) system, but to ask what its dynamics are: Why do ethnic riots occur when and where they do? Why do states wither at greater rates in some places and times than in others? Why do some countries flout conventions of international debt repayment with so much less apparent worry than others? How are international arms flows driving ethnic battles and genocides? Why are some states exiting the global stage while others are clamoring to get in? Why do key events occur at a certain point in a certain place rather than in others? These are, of course, the great traditional questions of causality, contingency, and prediction in the human sciences, but in

---

37. In this last section, Appadurai refers to ideas from mathematics and biology. Chaos mathematics was an extremely popular notion in the late 1980s and 1990s. Enthusiasm for it was fired, in part, by James Gleick's popular 1987 account *Chaos: Making a New Science*. The notion of a fractal is central to chaos theory. A fractal is, technically, a complex figure that can be represented by a mathematical equation. The key characteristic of a fractal is that its pattern repeats itself on both larger and smaller scales. For example, the pattern of a coastline is repeated in the pattern of a smaller section of that coastline, and repeated again in a still smaller section, and so on and so on. Thus, fractals are said to be self-referential. It is not clear that this definition is quite the same as "as possessing no Euclidean boundaries, structures, or regularities," which raises at least two interesting questions: First, is Appadurai simply using *fractal* as a synonym for *chaotic* (and thus mischaracterizing both fractals and the idea of chaos math, which does both seek and find complex patterns)? Second, is the nature of culture properly fractal—that is, are the patterns of global culture reiterated at many different levels: the state, nation, community, and individual?

Appadurai also invokes the idea of *polythetic set*. A group is polythetic if all its members share at least one element of a set of traits but there is no single trait that is shared by all members. The philosopher Ludwig Wittgenstein (1889–1951) provides an example. He challenges us to come up with a single trait shared by all games. This is an impossible task, but Wittgenstein (2001) argues that our failure at it is not because we lack understanding of the true nature of games, but rather indicates that games form a polythetic set and have a family resemblance rather than one or more defining characteristics.

"Isomorphism": sharing the same or similar form.

a world of disjunctive global flows, it is perhaps important to start asking them in a way that relies on images of flow and uncertainty, hence chaos, rather than on older images of order, stability, and systematicness. Otherwise, we will have gone far toward a theory of global cultural systems but thrown out process in the bargain. And that would make these notes part of a journey toward the kind of illusion of order that we can no longer afford to impose on a world that is so transparently volatile.[38]

Whatever the directions in which we can push these macrometaphors (fractals, polythetic classifications, and chaos), we need to ask one other old-fashioned question out of the Marxist paradigm: is there some pre-given order to the relative determining force of these global flows? Because I have postulated the dynamics of global cultural systems as driven by the relationships among flows of persons, technologies, finance, information, and ideology, can we speak of some structural-causal order linking these flows by analogy to the role of the economic order in one version of the Marxist paradigm? Can we speak of some of these flows as being, for a priori structural or historical reasons, always prior to and formative of other flows? My own hypothesis, which can only be tentative at this point, is that the relationship of these various flows to one another as they constellate into particular events and social forms will be radically context-dependent. Thus, while labor flows and their loops with financial flows between Kerala and the Middle East may account for the shape of media flows and ideoscapes in Kerala, the reverse may be true of Silicon Valley in California, where intense specialization in a single technological sector (computers) and particular flows of capital may well profoundly determine the shape that ethnoscapes, ideoscapes, and mediascapes may take.[39]

This does not mean that the causal-historical relationship among these various flows is random or meaninglessly contingent but that our current theories of cultural chaos are insufficiently developed to be even parsimonious models at this point, much less to be predictive theories, the golden fleeces of one kind of social science. What I have sought to provide in this chapter is a reasonably economical technical vocabulary and a rudimentary model of disjunctive flows, from which something like a decent global analysis might emerge. Without some such analysis, it will be difficult to construct what John Hinkson calls a "social theory of postmodernity" that is adequately global (1990: 84).

REFERENCES

Abu-Lughod, J. L. 1989. *Before European Hegemony: The World System AD 1250–1350*. New York: Oxford University Press.

Ahmad, A. 1987. "Jameson's Rhetoric of Otherness and the 'National Allegory,'" *Social Text* 17: 3–25.

Amin, S. 1980. *Class and Nation: Historically and in the Current Crisis*. New York and London: Monthly Review Press.

Anderson, B. 1983. *Imagined Communities: Reflections on the Origin and Spread of Nationalism*. London: Verso.

Appadurai, A. 1996. *Modernity at Large: Cultural Dimensions of Globalization*. Minneapolis: University of Minnesota Press.

---

38. In this passage, Appadurai seems to call for a global theory that creates a predictive science of anthropology. Invoking chaos mathematics seems to suggest that we could apply some sort of mathematical formula to either predict or explain major geopolitical events with a degree of certainty. Although Appadurai does seem to many anthropologists to have captured many essential aspects of the current world, his call for an overarching theory has not been successful. A critical problem is that ideas such as ethnoscapes are powerful metaphors and useful tools for thinking about the nature of modernity. However, it is not apparent how such ideas could be quantified in ways that might make rigorous prediction or explanation possible.

39. In Marxist thought, production and ideology both play important roles, but forces and relations of production are held to be prior to and more important than ideology. Here, Appadurai suggests that this relationship will not hold true for the *scapes* he identifies. Rather, their relationships will need to be determined afresh for each instance of analysis. Thus, Appadurai calls for global theory on the one hand, but something far closer to Boasian relativism and particularism, on the other.

Barber, K. 1987. "Popular Arts in Africa," *African Studies Review* 30(3) (September): 1–78.

Baruah, S. 1986. "Immigration, Ethnic Conflict and Political Turmoil, Assam 1979–1985," *Asian Survey* 26(11) (November): 1184–1206.

Bayly, C. A. 1989. *Imperial Meridian: The British Empire and the World, 1780–1830*. London and New York: Longman.

Benjamin, W. 1969. "The Work of Art in the Age of Mechanical Reproduction [1936]." In H. Arendt (ed.) *Illuminations*. H. Zohn (trans.). New York: Schocken Books.

Braudel, F. 1981–84. *Civilization and Capitalism, Fifteenth–Eighteenth Century* (3 vols.). London: Collins.

Chatterjee, P. 1986. *Nationalist Thought and the Colonial World: A Derivative Discourse?* London: Zed Books.

Curtin, P. 1984. *Cross-Cultural Trade in World History*. Cambridge: Cambridge University Press.

Deleuze, G., and F. Guattari. 1987. *A Thousand Plateaus: Capitalism and Schizophrenia*. B. Massumi (trans.). Minneapolis: University of Minnesota Press.

Fabian, J. 1983. *Time and the Other. How Anthropology Makes Its Object*. New York: Columbia University Press.

Feld, S. 1988. "Notes on World Beat," *Public Culture* 1(1): 31–7.

Gans, E. 1985. *The End of Culture: Toward a Generative Anthropology*. Berkeley: University of California Press.

Hamelink, C. 1983. *Cultural Autonomy in Global Communications*. New York: Longman.

Handler, R. 1988. *Nationalism and the Politics of Culture in Quebec*. Madison: University of Wisconsin Press.

Hannerz, U. 1987. "The World in Creolization," *Africa* 57(4): 546–559.

———. 1989. "Notes on the Global Ecumene," *Public Culture* 1(2) (Spring): 66–75.

Hechter, M. 1975. *Internal Colonialism: The Celtic Fringe in British National Development, 1536–1966*. Berkeley: University of California Press.

Helms, M. W. 1988. *Ulysses' Sail: An Ethnographic Odyssey of Power, Knowledge, and Geographical Distance*. Princeton, NJ: Princeton University Press.

Herzfeld, M. 1982. *Ours Once More: Folklore, Ideology and the Making of Modern Greece*. Austin: University of Texas Press.

Hinkson, J. (1990). "Postmodernism and Structural Change," *Public Culture* 2(2) (Spring): 82–101.

Hobsbawm, E., and T. Ranger (eds.) 1983. *The Invention of Tradition*. New York: Cambridge University Press.

Hodgson, M. 1974. *The Venture of Islam. Conscience and History in a World Civilization* (3 vols.). Chicago: University of Chicago Press.

Ivy, M. 1988. "Tradition and Difference in the Japanese Mass Media." *Public Culture* 1(1): 21–9.

Iyer, P. 1988. *Video Night in Kathmandu*. New York: Knopf.

Jameson, F. 1983. "Postmodernism and Consumer Society," In H. Foster (ed.) *The Anti-Aesthetic: Essays on Postmodern Culture*. Port Townsend, WA: Bay Press.

———. 1986. "Third World Literature in the Era of Multi-National Capitalism," *Social Text* 1 (Fall): 65–88.

———. 1989. "Nostalgia for the Present," *South Atlantic Quarterly* 88(2) (Spring): 517–537.

Kothari, R. 1989. *State against Democracy: In Search of Humane Governance*. New York: New Horizons.

Lakoff, G., and M. Johnson 1980. *Metaphors We Live By*. Chicago and London: University of Chicago Press.

Lash, S., and J. Urry 1987. *The End of Organized Capitalism*. Madison: University of Wisconsin Press.

Mandel, E. 1978. *Late Capitalism*. London: Verso.

Marcus, G., and M. Fischer 1986. *Anthropology as Cultural Critique: An Experimental Moment in the Human Sciences*. Chicago: University of Chicago Press.

Mattelart, A. 1983. *Transnational and the Third World: The Struggle for Culture*. South Hadley, MA: Bergin and Garvey.

McLuhan, M., and B. R. Powers 1989. *The Global Village: Transformations in World Life and Media in the 21st Century*. New York: Oxford University Press.

Mc-Queen, H. 1988. "The Australian Stamp: Image, Design and Ideology," *Arena* 84 (Spring): 78–96.

Meyrowitz, J. 1985. *No Sense of Place: The Impact of Electronic Media on Social Behavior*. New York: Oxford University Press.

Nandy, A. 1989. "The Political Culture of the Indian State," *Daedalus* 118(4): 1–26.

Nicoll, F. 1989. "My Trip to Alice," *Criticism, Heresy and Interpretation* 3: 21–32.

Schafer, E. 1963. *Golden Peaches of Samarkand: A Study of T'ang Exotics*. Berkeley: University of California Press.

Schiller, H. 1976. *Communication and Cultural Domination*. White Plains, NY: International Arts and Sciences.

Thornton, R. 1988. "The Rhetoric of Ethnographic Holism," *Cultural Anthropology* 3(3) (August): 285–303.

United Nations High Commission for Refugees (UNHCR). 2019. Figures at a Glance. Available at: https://www.unhcr.org/en-us/figures-at-a-glance.html Retrieved September 16, 2019.

Vachani, L. 1989. *Narrative, Pleasure and Ideology in the Hindi Film: An Analysis of the Outsider Formula*. MA thesis, Annenberg School of Communication, University of Pennsylvania.

Wallerstein, L. 1974. *The Modern World System* (2 vols.). New York and London: Academic Press.

Warner, M. 1990. *The Letters of the Republic: Publication and the Public Sphere in Eighteenth-Century America*. Cambridge, MA: Harvard University Press.

Williams, R. 1976. *Keywords*. New York: Oxford University Press.

Wolf, E. 1982. *Europe and the People without History*. Berkeley: University of California Press.

Yoshimoto, M. 1989. "The Postmodern and Mass Images in Japan," *Public Culture* 1 (2): 8–25.

Zarilli, P. 1995. "Repositioning the Body: An Indian Martial Art and its Pan-Asian Publics," In C. A. Breckenridge (ed.), *Consuming Modernity: Public Culture in a South Asian World*. Minneapolis: University of Minnesota Press.

AUTHOR'S NOTE

a. One major exception is Fredric Jameson, whose work on the relationship between postmodernism and late capitalism has in many ways inspired this essay. The debate between Jameson and Aijaz Ahmad in *Social Text*, however, shows that the creation of a globalizing Marxist narrative in cultural matters is difficult territory indeed (Ahmad 1987; Jameson 1986). My own effort in this context is to begin a restructuring of the Marxist narrative (by stressing lags and disjunctures) that many Marxists might find abhorrent. Such a restructuring has to avoid the dangers of obliterating difference within the Third World, eliding the social referent (as some French postmodernists seem inclined to do), and retaining the narrative authority of the Marxist tradition, in favor of greater attention to global fragmentation, uncertainty, and difference.

PART V

Trends in Contemporary Anthropology

Gender

Samuel Goldwyn or Yogi Berra or Casey Stengel once said, "Never make predictions, especially about the future." In true postmodern fashion, the quote is attributed to all three, and many others besides. We'll never know who really said it first, and there is a website dedicated to tracking claims for its authorship: http://www.larry.denenberg.com/predictions.html. It's impossible to know the directions in which anthropological theory will move in the next ten years. However, based on the tendencies of the last decade or so, it seems that work having to do with gender, power, and agency will probably play an important role in the discipline.

As we saw earlier in this book, feminist anthropology was largely associated with the second wave of feminism, a social and political movement that occurred from the mid-1960s until the late 1980s. However, by the early 1980s, voices critical of second-wave feminists began to emerge. They questioned not only the assumptions of second-wave feminism but also the very idea of waves of feminism (Hewitt 2010). One charge made against the second-wave feminists was that they were largely white, middle- and upper-middle-class women who took their condition as representative of the condition of all women. In her 1981 book *Ain't I a Woman: Black Women and Feminism*, scholar, activist, and poet bell hooks (1952–2021) argued that not only had white feminists ignored women of color but their actions had often worked to further oppress them.

By the late 1980s and 1990s, additional critical works appeared. Among the most important of these was the 1990 book *Gender Trouble: Feminism and the Subversion of Identity* by philosopher Judith Butler (b. 1956). There, Butler critiqued feminists for understanding the world in terms of a gender binary. Instead, she argued for an understanding of gender as "a relation among socially constituted subjects in specifiable contexts . . . [that] suggest that what the person 'is' and, indeed, what gender 'is' is always relative to the constructed relations in which it is determined" (1990: 10). The work of Michel Foucault (1926–1984) (described more fully in the "French Social Thought: Postmodernism and Practice" section) was particularly influential in helping people understand sexuality (and gender identities) as historically constituted and variable. Other works, such as the 1987 book *Intercourse* by Andrea Dworkin (1946–2005), questioned the meaning of the act of sex itself and its role in maintaining male domination. Anthropologist Gayle Rubin (b. 1949) in particular revitalized discussion of the relationship between gender and sex. Her examination of lesbian and gay sexualities called for the identification, description, and denunciation of "erotic injustice and sexual oppression" (1984: 9).

In anthropology, these intellectual trends broadened research and theory from a relatively narrow approach based primarily around ideas of the gender binary and oppression to a far broader understanding of the meaning and role of gender in different cultures (and among different groups in the same culture). Micaela di Leonardo writes that feminist scholars were forced to confront "the question of 'difference'—the multiple racial, ethnic, class, sexual, age, regional, and national identities of women—as they noted their own restricted demographic representation and research interests" (1991: 18). In the 1990s, "the question of difference" expanded to include LGBTQ issues as studies began to explore the links between sexuality, identity, and social positioning and power. In particular, anthropologists focused on the social construction of gender and the ways in which gender intersects with a wide variety of forces linked to power and inequality including race, politics, economics, and history.

Anthropologists writing about gender also developed new, experimental forms of ethnographic writing. They tended to emphasize multivocality—that is, giving voice to a variety of viewpoints in their ethnographic writing. They encouraged members of marginalized groups to write about their cultures for themselves and challenged anthropologists to take into account "the discriminations of racism, homophobia, sexism, and classism" (Behar and Gordon 1995: 7). Claiming that all ways of knowing are subjective, some authors have offered works of poetry and fiction as new forms of ethnography. Others experiment with the epistemological assumptions of anthropology by introducing their own thoughts and experiences into their research.

Our two choices for this section illustrate various facets of research in gender. The first essay is by Lila Abu-Lughod (b. 1952). Abu-Lughod is the daughter of Palestinian scholar Ibrahim Abu-Lughod (1929–2001) and urban sociologist Janet Lippman Abu-Lughod (1928–2013). She received her PhD from Harvard University in 1984 and soon became known for her research on the Bedouin in Egypt. As of 2016, she is a professor at Columbia University.

Abu-Lughod's work is an answer to the critics of second-wave feminism who called for the recognition of class, ethnic, and economic differences between women. She explores issues of gender, power, and identity and refers to herself as living a "hybrid" life, balancing Middle Eastern and American influences. Abu-Lughod called for new forms of ethnographic writing in her 1991 work titled "Writing against Culture." There, she argued that the writing of ethnography is inherently an expression of Western power because it is based on the textual construction of the "other" and removed from the reality of the particulars of individually lived lives. Instead, Abu-Lughod proposed that anthropologists write "ethnographies of the particular" (1991: 149). By this she means that instead of writing broad generalizations about a whole group, anthropologists should write ethnographies of particular people in specific times and places.

Abu-Lughod's "A Tale of Two Pregnancies," reprinted here in essay 33, is an example of "autoethnography"—work that combines autobiographical information with anthropological analyses. Abu-Lughod discusses her experience of pregnancy and contrasts it with the experience of Kareema, an Egyptian Bedouin woman who had been pregnant during Abu-Lughod's fieldwork. There is little Bedouin "other" in the text, most of which consists of descriptions of specific events during Abu-Lughod's fieldwork related to her eventually successful attempt to become pregnant.

While Abu-Lughod is interested in issues surrounding the writing of ethnographies, Tom Boellstorff's 2004 essay "The Emergence of Political Homophobia in Indonesia: Masculinity and National Belonging" illustrates how changing political ideologies have placed LGBT citizens in the center of debates over national identity in Indonesia. Indonesia has typically been portrayed as a country whose people are tolerant of diversity in gender expression and sexuality, and gay Indonesians have used their society's existing gender diversity to claim legitimacy. However, in the last few decades, there have been increasing levels of violence against gay and lesbian Indonesians at public rallies and events, and Boellstorff argues that the rise in violence corresponds to the rise in popularity of a new national discourse of masculinity that is promoted by the Indonesian government. In this discourse, heterosexual marriage is identified as being the essential characteristic of a modern citizen. Consequently, the attacks on gay and lesbians are more about the country's increasing heterosexism in which nonnormative sexuality is perceived as a threat to proper masculinity.

The past forty years (1980–2020) have seen enormous growth in gender studies. Almost all major universities now have gender studies programs. However, despite the success of these programs in the academy, after almost eight decades of work in the areas of gender and sexuality, anthropologists have not successfully translated their findings to the wider culture beyond an academic audience. The cultural clashes over women in the workplace, what bathrooms transgender individuals should use, marriage of same-sex couples, and workplace and legal discrimination against homosexuals, to name a few, continue unabated in the United States more than eighty years after the groundbreaking studies of gender conducted by Margaret Mead. However, we find that students today overall are much more open-minded than students of the past. They don't care who someone marries or what bathroom they use, and they are for the most part accepting of nonnormative gender expression. It appears that generational changes in attitudes may finally catch up to where Mead tried to lead us in 1935.

SUGGESTED READINGS

Boellstorff, Tom. 2005. *The Gay Archipelago: Sexuality and Nation in Indonesia*. Princeton, NJ: Princeton University.
An important book in queer studies, Boellstorff analyzes the ways in which gay and lesbian identities articulate with nationalism and globalization.

Butler, Judith. 1990. *Gender Trouble*. New York: Routledge.
Butler's critique of the feminism of the 1970s and 1980s. A founding text of queer theory.

Di Leonardo Micaela. 1991. *Gender at the Crossroads of Knowledge: Feminist Anthropology in the Postmodern Era*. Berkeley: University of California Press.
A collection of essays by different authors assessing feminist anthropology in the early 1990s.

Ginsberg, Faye, and Anna Lowenhaupt Tsing. 1990. *Uncertain Terms: Negotiating Gender in American Culture*. Boston: Beacon Press.
A collection of essays by different authors focusing on gender stereotypes, feminism and conservative politics, gender in the workplace, female identity, and marginality.

Lewin, Ellen, and William L. Leap. 2002. *Out in Theory: The Emergence of Lesbian and Gay Anthropology*. Urbana: University of Illinois Press.
This collection of essays by leading scholars attempts to examine the scope of LGBTQ studies in anthropology. It includes essays by Gayle Rubin, David Valentine, and Esther Newton, as well as the editors.

Nanda, Serena. 2014. *Gender Diversity: Crosscultural Variations*. 2nd ed. Long Grove, IL: Waveland Press.
An introduction to gender and a survey of some gender ideas among Native Americans and other populations in America as well as in India, Bangladesh, Brazil, Polynesia, Thailand, the Philippines, Indonesia, and Europe.

Rubin, Gayle. 2011. *Deviations: A Gayle Rubin Reader*. Durham, NC: Duke University Press.
A collection of essays that traces the evolution of Rubin's thinking from the 1970s to the early 2010s.

33. A Tale of Two Pregnancies

Lila Abu-Lughod (b. 1952)

ENTERING MY twenty-fourth week. Heartburn woke me up this morning, and I turned to my favorite of the three pregnancy guidebooks I keep near my bed—the one organized around anxieties. In the section titled "Heartburn and Indigestion," sandwiched between "Losing Your Figure" and "Food Aversions and Cravings," I read: "It's nearly impossible to have an indigestion-free nine months; it's just one of the less pleasant facts of pregnancy."[1]

I closed my eyes. This was, I thought, what my friend Kareema must have felt.[a] She was the mother of eleven whom I'd seen through two pregnancies in the 1980s. Like all but one of her others, her last pregnancy, at an age closer to my current age than I liked to imagine, had proceeded without the benefit of medical care. She had suffered terrible indigestion, and I remembered those many evenings when, by the light of a kerosene lantern, I had prepared her the fizzy orange drink she swore relieved the pain: effervescent tablets of vitamin C purchased at the local pharmacy, dissolved in a glass of water.[2]

In those days I understood little about what Kareema and the other Awlad 'Ali Bedouin women I lived with in Egypt were experiencing. Caught up in my own world and my research, first in my mid-twenties and later in my thirties, I claimed to be, and was, very interested in women's experiences. But I barely noticed anything about their pregnancies except protruding bellies artfully hidden by large red belts. The women worked hard, lifting heavy cooking pots, carrying their other children on their backs, washing clothes, and walking long distances to visit friends and relatives. Pregnancy hardly seemed to interfere. At the end, with the help of a local midwife, their mothers, or their mothers-in-law, these women suddenly produced infants who, by the time I would see them, were lovingly swaddled and lying close to them. Or so it seemed. Except that every older woman who told me her life story mentioned a miscarriage or a stillbirth.

My pregnancy, in contrast, was the ultimate late-capitalist U.S. achievement: assisted by the most recent advances in reproductive technology, monitored from egg production to fetal

---

From *Women Writing Culture* (1995)

1. Like the opening of the analysis by Clifford Geertz of the Balinese cockfight, Abu-Lughod starts with a personal account that immediately draws the reader into her story. Unlike Geertz, who abandons his personal account for a more formal analysis, Abu-Lughod focuses on her pregnancy experience and writes in a personal, reflexive, style throughout the essay. She embraces the postmodern view that ethnography is the creation of the writer, arguing that because ethnographers know things within a personal context, what they write are partial and positioned truths (Abu-Lughod 1991: 141). Consequently, in writing about her pregnancy, Abu-Lughod tries to place the reader within her frame of reference as an anthropologist and a woman pregnant with twins.

2. In her critique of ethnography, "Writing Against Culture," Abu-Lughod criticizes the practice of making ethnographic generalizations. She says that generalization is part of a language of power used by those who stand apart from and outside of those they study (1991: 150). She argues that one way to combat generalization is to write "ethnographies of the particular" (1991: 149), and indeed this text is an outstanding example of the approach. She is writing about her pregnancy and her experiences with one specific Egyptian Bedouin woman; she does not try to discuss Bedouin women in general.

heartbeats with the help of ultrasound and hormonal analysis, and expensive. I was one of the fortunate women in her late thirties for whom in vitro fertilization had succeeded on the first try. I began the pregnancy with a mix of scientific knowledge, common sense, and holistic medical advice: warned by my books about **preeclampsia**, prevented from carrying heavy objects by my husband, pampering myself by lying down to allow blood to flow to my placenta, counting my calcium milligrams, balancing my green and yellow vegetables, and studying with some despair the undecipherable diagrams that promise to guide pregnant women through proper exercise regimens.[3]

If I had not known Kareema and the other women in Egypt who had shared their lives with me, I would not have been able to shake my head and laugh at myself for the fuss I was making. I also might not have felt so lucky. My personal experience of the pregnancy was shaped by the double (or hybrid, in Kirin Narayan's view) life I lived as an anthropologist.[b] I moved between the world of "home" in the United States, with my network of friends and family and the resources of feminist scholarship on reproduction to help me think about the facts

of life, and "the field" in Egypt, where I was surrounded by women who became pregnant, gave birth, lived with children, and talked to me and to each other about why things sometimes went wrong. I looked to both places for help in understanding what was happening to me, just as I had sought this pregnancy in both places.[4]

SEARCHING FOR CHILDREN

Living in what is known as the Western Desert of Egypt, with only a substandard clinic not close enough for easy access, the Bedouin women I knew could not take advantage of the superb doctors and excellent hospital facilities available in Egypt's major cities, Cairo and Alexandria. They gave each other advice, told stories about their pregnancies and those of others, and complained—of headaches, fevers, aches, swelling. That did not stop them from feeling sorry for me, their anthropologist friend, still childless long after their own daughters, who had kept me company on the long winter evenings of my first stay in the late 1970s, had married and given birth to one, two, sometimes three children.[5]

---

3. In "Grief and a Headhunter's Rage" (essay 29), published just two years before this piece, Renato Rosaldo argues that how one understands events depends on one's position and that interpretations change as one's positioning changes. Although Abu-Lughod noticed that women were pregnant and had babies, when she became pregnant these events took on new significance for her. In Rosaldo's terminology, as Abu-Lughod's position changed, her Egyptian friends' pregnancies became events with "force." McGee had a similar experience. It was not until McGee's wife, pregnant with their first child, went with him into the field that he thought to ask Lacandon Maya women about pregnancy and childbirth. Like Abu-Lughod, he discovered that most women had lost babies or their daughters had died in childbirth (McGee 2002: 67–70).

"Preeclampsia": a condition that occurs in 5 to 8 percent of pregnancies. It is characterized by high blood pressure and the presence of protein in the urine. It can be fatal to both mother and child.

4. Abu-Lughod's viewpoint was created by the intersection of her multiple identities as a woman, anthropologist, wife, mother, and person of Palestinian descent (Abu-Lughod is the daughter of the sociologist Janet Lippman Abu-Lughod [1928–2013] and the political scientist Ibrahim Abu-Lughod [1929–2001]), as well as years she spent as a child in Egypt. Through the course of the essay, she shows us some of these identities, as an anthropologist, a patient in an IVF clinic, Kareema's friend and confidante, and a mother.

Kirin Narayan (b. 1959) an anthropologist at the Australian National University, is the daughter of an American-born Indian mother and an Indian-born father. Her book *My Family and Other Saints* (2007) describes her childhood and focuses on the complex, multicultural life of her older brother Rahoul.

5. Much of the work in the anthropology of gender has occurred after the rise of postmodern theory in anthropology in the 1980s and 1990s. One of the many insights that postmodern anthropologists have contributed to anthropology is a concern with generalization. Avoiding generalizations may help anthropologists to avoid making claims that are beyond their knowledge. Note Abu-Lughod's wording in this paragraph. She

Even though I did not yet want children, they sympathetically told me stories about women who were "searching for children" too. They explained the theory of "blocking"—how conception could be blocked by a sudden fright, by being confronted with someone who has come back from a funeral, or by a donkey who has just given birth. They scared me by offering to take me to healers to have a string sewn through my back or an amulet made. They told me how a second fright could undo a blockage, or how bathing on successive Fridays with water in which a gold necklace had been soaked might counteract a different kind of blockage.

I eagerly scribbled all this in my notebooks; mostly it was material for my book on Bedouin women's stories. I wondered, occasionally, how these notions about flows and blockages fit with our medical narratives about hormones, eggs, sperm, and fallopian tubes. I had long been skeptical of images of how our bodies worked that relied on biological entities whose existence I had to take on faith. Emily Martin's analysis of the mechanical metaphors and bizarre implications of these scientific stories about women's bodies had confirmed my own ambivalence.[c, 6]

Later, when I was back in Egypt in 1990 with my husband, I felt it was time to get pregnant. I did not yet know there was a serious problem, but other friends were generous with remedies for infertility. After appointments with the quiet and serious doctor at the Cairo Motherhood Center—where the equipment was sterilized, the sheets clean and white, the ultrasound machine shiny, and the receipts computer generated—I would fly south to the palm-draped village in Upper Egypt where my husband and I were then doing research. My new friend Zaynab, mother of five children conceived on annual visits of her migrant husband, took time from her busy schedule of working her small fields, collecting fodder for her animals, and pressing land claims against her paternal relatives to try to help me.

Zaynab knew of three treatments. First she took me to the ruins of the Pharaonic temple that dominated the small hamlet in which her mud-brick house stood. Calling out to the local guard that we were just going to the well, she saw to it that he waved us on, ignoring the fact that we had no entrance tickets. She took me around the temple and then down some steep steps to a pool of stagnant water. "It is good to bathe with this water," she said. Anticipating my modesty, she had brought with her an empty tin container. "You can do it back at the hotel," she explained as she filled the can with the water.

When we came out of the cool, dark shaft she steered me away from the entrance to the temple. "You have to leave by a different path from the one you used to enter," she said. Later, another old village woman told my husband that Zaynab should have had another woman there, hiding above the shaft, to drop a stone into the water just when I was looking in. This would have frightened me. Although they lived hundreds of miles from the Bedouin and shared little of their way of life, these village women seemed to be working with the same theory of blocking: a second fright undoes the effect of a first, and leaving by a different route

---

is not making a claim to describe the behavior of all Bedouin women; rather, she claims to present information from only "the Bedouin women I knew."

6. Scholars of gender are especially concerned with issues of power, and in this selection, Abu-Lughod frequently speaks of the ways in which the power imbalance between medical practitioners and their patients results in the dehumanization of the latter. She mentions Emily Martin's book *The Woman in the Body: A Cultural Analysis of Reproduction* (1987), in which Martin examines some American women's views of the medical science model of pregnancy and reproduction. Martin (b. 1944) is a professor emerita of sociocultural anthropology at New York University. Her research interests focus on religion, the anthropology of science and medicine, gender, and the history of psychiatry and psychology. In addition to *The Woman in the Body*, Martin is also known for her 2007 book *Bipolar Expeditions: Mania and Depression in American Culture* in which, relying in part on her own experience of bipolar disorder, she explores the interconnections of popular culture and psychiatry.

literally opens up, or unblocks, a path to conception and birth.[d]

The next time I came to the village, still not pregnant, Zaynab decided to take me to the Coptic monastery nearby. "It's good," this Muslim woman explained, "to look at those Christian priests with their beards." When we had been admitted by a gentle nun, Zaynab whispered in the hush of the monastery, "Just look at the beautiful things, the velvet curtains, the pictures. The older things are, the better."

Next we went to the monastery's cemetery. Zaynab kept calling out for someone. She seemed agitated and finally hailed a young boy who was riding by on his donkey. "Where is your father?" she asked. "Go get him. Tell them there's a woman here who wants him." Eventually a burly man with a huge grey mustache appeared. He was the undertaker. He led me around the cemetery, explaining so much that I couldn't tell if this was a guided tour meant for a tourist or something special to induce pregnancy.

I realized that he knew why I was there when he took me to a cloth-draped coffin, its cover half on, empty inside. He instructed me to take off my shoes and step back and forth over the casket seven times, using my right foot first each time. Later he took me down to some dusty vaults. Reaching inside, he tore a strip of green cloth off the top of another unused coffin. Zaynab had gone off. "Wrap it under your breasts and bathe three times with it," he said conspiratorially. "But don't tell the woman you're with about this."

Then he told me to climb into the vault. I started in but jumped back in fear as a lizard darted out. Scolding me for being afraid when he was there, he then instructed me to tear another strip of cloth from the cover of the empty coffin in the far corner. He wadded this up and told me to stuff it inside me when I had sex with my husband.

Just then Zaynab returned and reminded him that it was important for me to see the well. So we all walked on. With a key he opened a small structure housing a very old brick well. He told me to look down until I could see my own eye. It was a long way down and there was very little water at the bottom. He explained that the monastery had an electric pump for irrigation and that tanks of water were brought in from the pipeline for drinking. Zaynab and I finally left, she apologetically giving him a small sum (all I had brought with me), he saying he hoped God would grant me what I wanted.

A few weeks later Zaynab decided, with some encouragement from me, that she should take me to visit the local Muslim woman curer. This was an old woman who had married and had five children, spent years in Cairo, and returned to her father's village when her husband died. Her father, himself a religious figure with powers of healing, had appointed her his successor, and she was now famous throughout the area. It was rumored that people came from as far away as Kuwait to seek her help. I had heard about her and was curious.

We waited until the heat of the day had passed and then set off to her hamlet. In her courtyard we saw other women leaving. The healer herself sat in a dark room, a small and wrinkled blind woman with her knees drawn up and her feet tucked neatly under her black dress. Women with children in their laps sat waiting their turn to speak to her. After listening to them, she would talk quickly in a kind of rhyme while deftly winding green thread into small objects they were to take with them. When our turn came, Zaynab first discussed her land dispute. Then she explained my problem and answered questions for me. The old curer prescribed a concoction that my husband was to drink. Zaynab and I pressed some money into her hand and then walked home.

In the end the recipe was too complicated. I didn't know where to get many of the ingredients. I didn't even know what these spices and powders were. Their Arabic names meant nothing to me. And though surely I could have arranged to put the bowl of liquid out on the balcony to catch the starlight, as instructed, where would we get the glowing rod to douse in it, in our Cairo apartment?

The problem, of course, was that my husband and I didn't believe it would work. I had half-heartedly bathed with the water from the Pharaonic temple, wary enough of the dead insects floating in it not to splash sensitive parts of my body—the very parts that were supposed to receive this healing treatment. I had also dutifully stepped over the coffins in the Christian cemetery, feeling silly and hypocritical, but I never wrapped the cloth strips around my chest or stuffed them inside me. Oddly, though, I still have the strips of cloth in my dresser drawer, somehow unable to bring myself to simply throw them away. I also don't quite know what to do with an old amulet I acquired from my Bedouin friends. I had wanted to see what was inside and had even photographed the contents. But then I could not help being awed by people's insistence that amulets were powerful and should never touch the ground or be thrown away. In matters mysterious, like religion and reproduction, one finds oneself uncertain enough about the truth to be half willing to "go native."[7]

INSIDE AND OUTSIDE THE BODY

When I returned home after a year in Egypt, I entered that new world that has become familiar to so many women of my generation and class in the U.S.—the world of laparoscopies, tubal adhesions, endometriosis, amniocentesis, and other such unpronounceables; the world of busy doctors in white coats who inspect and prod and shine lights at parts of you that you cannot see; the world of procedures that, they inform you absentmindedly, might cause slight cramping. I finally was allowed to graduate into the world of IVF, as in vitro fertilization is known. I joined well-dressed women with bags under their eyes who spent the early morning hours waiting their turn to have blood drawn from bruised veins and to lie back in darkened rooms with their legs in stirrups so their ovaries could be scanned on grainy black-and-white screens.

It was a world of sitting by the phone, waiting for your daily instructions. Of injections that quickly cured you of any squeamishness about large hypodermic needles. Sometimes, as you expertly drew from the small vials the correct dosages of Pergonal or Metrodin, or later, progesterone in a viscous base of sesame oil, you wondered if someone watching outside the apartment window might take you for a drug addict. This was, after all, New York.

"Our goal is to make you pregnant," the doctor had explained in our first visit. "Our success rates are the highest in the city. We average about thirty-three percent per three-month cycle." This kind of talk leads to a world of uneasy comparison. You look around the waiting room and wonder who will make the statistics. The woman next to you tells you she has fifteen eggs; yesterday you'd been told that you had five but that one was bigger than the others. "What does that mean?" you ask the busy doctor. "We'll see how they come along. If the others don't catch up, we'll have to cancel the cycle." You beg those little ones to grow.

Another woman tells you that this is her third try; last time she had to be hospitalized for ovarian enlargement. The next day someone tells you about her friend who had so many eggs she froze some. She became pregnant and had twins. Then her husband was killed in a car accident. Now she wants to thaw her other eggs and have another child by him. A tough young woman in blue jeans cheerfully jokes with the nurses as they take her blood. She's been coming for a year. You listen in dismay as another recounts how she got pregnant after four tries and then lost her triplets. She and her husband couldn't stand the strain, so they took a break for two years. You also look around at some of the women and think they're just too old.

All these women are surely bringing down the percentages. You think, with some secret pleasure, that this means your own odds as a first-timer are that much better. You keep

---

7. In this essay Abu-Lughod describes herself as a "hybrid," with one foot in the Arab world and another in the West. She writes about how she tried the folk remedies of her Egyptian friends to get pregnant and then describes some of her experiences undergoing IVF procedures in New York City. She writes, "In matters mysterious, like religion and reproduction, one finds oneself uncertain enough about the truth to be half willing to 'go native.'" Consider how the last few pages of Abu-Lughod's essay reflect Boasian anthropology. It is a classic telling of folklore much like articles by Paul Radin (1883–1959) in the 1920s on Ojibwa folklore, but more personal.

talking to your friend and colleague, the one who told you about this clinic and who became pregnant on the first try. She barely seems to remember the anger and frustration you feel, or the uncertainty. She encourages you and tells you what will happen next. You compare notes about the waiting-room experience and tell her what an interesting anthropological study it would make, if only you didn't feel so much hostility to the money-making production line the clinic creates that all you want to do is escape—as soon as you no longer need their services so helplessly.

Retrieval is the clinical term for the procedure of removing your ripe eggs from the ovary to be fertilized outside your body. You go to the hospital for this, feeling perfectly healthy and afraid that when you wake up you won't be anymore. After being kept waiting, as usual, you are walked in your oversized nonskid slippers down corridors, into elevators, and then into an operating room. The room looks familiar from the slide show the nurse gave a few weeks earlier, and you feel less resentful at that two hours wasted in a session of elementary talk about IVF. (The session protects the IVF program by covering in simple language the complex material contained in the pile of consent forms you must sign.) The lights in the room are bright. It's a little cold. An intravenous feeder is put in your wrist, and the nurses talk to you reassuringly. You disappear. You wake up in the recovery room, people groaning all around you, some quite frightening with tubes in their noses. You want to get away but are too groggy to move.

As we were leaving the hospital, my husband and I bumped into one of the doctors. She asked how it had gone. I said no one had told us. Surprised, she went off to telephone the lab. She gave us the first good news: they had retrieved six eggs. She insisted that some-

one must have come to tell me in the recovery room but I had forgotten. I didn't believe her.

Then we waited for the telephone call our typed instructions said would come as soon as they knew the results. Five eggs had fertilized. One more success. As Sarah Franklin, one of the few feminist anthropologists to study IVF, has noted, the cultural narrative of conception has been rewritten by the infertility specialists so that conception is no longer the natural result of intercourse but a scientific and technological achievement. The road to pregnancy is a complex obstacle course in which hurdles are overcome, one by one.[e, 8]

The next step was what they call "the transfer"—from dish to womb. Back at the hospital, I sat on a simple wooden bench with the same women who had been in the surgical waiting room on the day of the retrieval. Everyone was a little nervous, but cheerful. This part wasn't supposed to hurt. To pass the time we chatted. One of the women asked if I remembered the blonde woman who had been there with us three days earlier. Yes. "Well," she whispered, "her husband was in there for an hour and a half and couldn't do it. So they had to rush me ahead of her in line for the retrieval." We giggled in a mixture of relief that our husbands had performed efficiently and embarrassment at the others' humiliation.

Finally, my turn. I entered the familiar operating room and climbed onto the table. The doctor was joking with the embryologist in the adjoining room. It had been a long day. Suddenly I saw something come into focus on the elevated television screen to my right. My name was typed on the screen, and there were my four fertilized eggs. The fifth, the doctor explained, had disintegrated. An assistant printed out the image on two Polaroid snapshots, a general view and a close-up. I had imagined test-tube babies as little fetuses

---

8. Comparing the descriptions of the IVF procedures with the treatments she received from her Egyptian friends it is clear that Abu-Lughod found the IVF procedures unpleasant. In this paragraph, she cites work by Sarah Franklin (b. 1960) on IVF. Franklin is a prominent American sociologist in England, who has made extensive contributions in the fields of feminism, gender studies, cultural studies, and the social study of reproductive and genetic technology. She is currently a professor of sociology at Cambridge. Franklin has written extensively about IVF, kinship, and medical technology. In numerous papers, Franklin explores the culture of assisted reproduction and shows the way patients are subjected to an unpleasant technological regime in which their lives are scheduled by doctors and medical technicians.

in jars, but these were just cells, clusters of overlapping circles sitting in a petri dish, like illustrations from a biology textbook.

The transfer only took a minute, with some joking about not dropping the catheter as the embryologist rushed from the lab to the table. I was moved onto a trolley and wheeled out, like the women who went before me, clutching my Polaroids.

Abandoned together in a small, otherwise empty ward, we made conversation. One woman's companion helped us exchange our "baby pictures," all we might get for the $8,000 we had had to pay up front (I was counting the days until my insurance company would reimburse me; most of the women had no insurance coverage for IVF). The doctor had told us we could leave after fifteen minutes, but we all insisted on staying for forty-five—superstitious that if we stood up our precious embryos might slide out. One by one, we gingerly climbed out of bed and dressed. I took a taxi home, not wanting to risk the subway.

The month during which I underwent IVF was also the month in which the copyedited manuscript of my book on Bedouin women's stories arrived in the mail.[f] I read over the chapter called "Reproduction," written before I'd entered that strange world of reproductive technology. I could have longed for the more natural character of these women's experiences of becoming pregnant and having babies. I could have viewed pregnancy as an alienation of my body by the medical establishment. But I thought of Donna Haraway, the feminist historian of science, who keeps insisting that it is dangerous for feminists, nostalgic for an organic wholeness, to condemn and reject science and technology. Such associations of the natural with the feminine have been essential to women's confinements to the body and the home; and such rejections of science leave it in the hands of others who may not have women's interests at heart.[g] In the late twentieth century the boundaries between inside and outside our bodies are more fluid. Are glasses to be rejected because they are not our natural eyes? So what if for two days a petri dish served as my fallopian tubes?[9]

Still, I refused to believe the nurse who telephoned twelve days later to say my blood test was positive. I thought the IVF staff would fudge the results so they could publish articles in the medical journals and claim to be the best clinic in the city. Then they'd accuse you, the incompetent female body, of having lost the baby. I didn't believe I was pregnant until two weeks later, when I saw, on that familiar black and-white television screen, the image of those tiny sacs, each with a twinkling star in it. Fetal heartbeats. Multiple gestation, as they call it in the business.

Kareema, on the other hand, knew the other signs of pregnancy. Her period stopped. She began to feel sick. She threw up. She felt fatigued. She couldn't bear to smoke. Some women have cravings; others have aversions to certain foods. Some Bedouin women claim to have aversions to their husbands.

My menstrual cycle had been suppressed by drugs, and it was too early for the other signs. I was dependent on the ultrasound scanner for my knowledge of pregnancy. I recalled Rosalind Petchesky's classic work on fetal imaging and the politics of reproduction. Rather than condemning, along with other feminists, the **panoptic** gaze the ultrasound technologies afford the male medical establishment or even the disembodiment of the fetus from the mother, demoted to a mere environment for this rights-bearing entity, she drew attention to the possibility that women might experience this technology positively. "How different women," she wrote, "see fetal images depends on the context of the looking and the relationship of the viewer to the image

---

9. Donna Haraway's argument that if women reject science, they leave it in the hands of people who may not have women's interests at heart seems prescient. IVF has increasingly become a political, legal, and cultural flash point in the United States far beyond what Abu-Lughod could have imagined in 1995. In February 2024, the Alabama Supreme Court ruled that in vitro fertilized embryos were legally unborn children. In June 2024, the Southern Baptist Convention, representing 13 million church members, voted to oppose IVF as conflicting with their understanding of the right to life of embryos (Graham 2024).

Donna J. Haraway (b. 1944) is a professor emerita at the University of California–Santa Cruz. She studies the relationship of science and culture, frequently from a feminist perspective.

and what it signifies."[h] I couldn't help finding it reassuring to see on the screen to my right what was supposed to be inside me. I was so unsure of my babies that I worried about their having disappeared if I didn't see them every two weeks or so.[10]

COMMUNITIES OF WOMEN

Now, months later, when I have heartburn and the amazement of feeling the babies move in a part of me that had never even existed before, I feel closer to Kareema. The belly I rub with almond oil and look down at is here, not on the screen. It looks the way Kareema's did. My pregnancy book had told me I'd first feel the babies' movements as butterflies or fish swimming around, but the book was wrong. It was a definite thumping—like a heartbeat in the wrong place. I wondered what else the book might be wrong about and instead tried to remember every detail of what the Bedouin women had said and done. How would I cope when the babies came? I tried to remember how these women had managed. How had they breastfed? It had all seemed so natural and easy. How had they coped at night? I don't remember Kareema's babies crying. I realized I hadn't paid much attention to things that now mattered enormously to me. I also understood now that Kareema had probably been feeling that same thumping inside her as she kindly told me folktales to record for my book.

When you are pregnant for the first time, you suddenly see other women you know in a different light. My mother began to tell stories about her pregnancies, and I loved seeing her soften as she reminisced about how exquisite it was to hold an infant. My mother-in-law seemed remarkable for having had seven children. I asked my sister about her experience of giving birth alone in India. She said she had never read a book on the subject and had no idea what was going on. My friends with children began to seem more important. I felt I was crossing a threshold I hadn't noticed before.

This experience of recognizing a commonality among women led me to think back to an article I had begun writing five years earlier about the possibilities for feminist ethnography.[i] I had argued that women ethnographers who studied women unsettled the central divide between Self and Other on which anthropology usually rested. This was not because of any essential, cross-cultural sameness of women but because feminist anthropologists had to recognize that womanhood was only a partial identity. In the abstract language of academic life I wrote, "By working with the assumption of difference in sameness, of a self that participates in multiple identifications, and an other that is also partially the self, we might be moving beyond the impasse of the fixed self/other or subject/object divide."[j] I also noted, however, that there was often a perceived kinship, albeit limited, between women anthropologists and their women subjects that made seeking knowledge of their situations more of a political project that had implications for "home." The kinship Zaynab and other women in Egypt felt for me was apparent in their sisterly concerns about my childless state and their efforts to help me. My feelings for them had led me both to friendships there and to explorations in my anthropological work back home about ways to represent them that might make the complexity of their lives and individual person-

10. **"Panoptic"**: all-encompassing. When Abu-Lughod refers to the "panoptic gaze" that the ultrasound technology provided the medical professionals caring for her, she means that her fetuses were completely revealed inside her. However, she is also referring to Michel Foucault's "Panopticism," (1975) a critical essay in postmodern thinking. Foucault writes about the idea of a society organized around surveillance (see essay 28, especially note 12).

Rosalind Petchesky (b. 1942) is a professor of political science at Hunter College, City University of New York. Abu-Lughod's mention of Petchesky's work on fetal imaging and the comment that how people see the images depends on the context is a restatement of the postmodern notion of positioning and knowledge. What that image means to a viewer is conditioned by whether the viewer is female or male, whether the pregnancy was planned, and many other factors. For Abu-Lughod the image meant the fulfillment of her dreams. For others, it might be a personal disaster.

alities—forms of complexity we recognize in the Self, not the Other—more apparent.[11]

What I did not explore then was another process that could occur: that one's own constructions of personal experience would be shaped by knowledge of these women's lives and even by particular women one had come to know.[k] In being pregnant, I was finding that the cultural resources I had at my disposal to think about what I was experiencing and to fill in gaps in my knowledge of an uncertain terrain included both those from "home" and those from "the field," often juxtaposed. From "home" I had my own family background, the biomedical discourse with which so many white middle-class women feel comfortable, feminist critiques of this same discourse as well as of the popular cultural representations in media and books, and a patchy familiarity with women who had given birth.[l] From Kareema and the other women I knew in Egypt I had notebooks full of beliefs about reproduction, stories about reproduction, and, most important of all, years' worth of vivid memories of an everyday world rich in pregnancies, births, and children. I now thought and felt with all these resources.[12]

As I begin to gain confidence that the pregnancy really will last, I have started to worry about the birth. I sometimes skip ahead to the later chapters of my pregnancy books and frighten myself with those glossy photographs that seem to have nothing to do with the reassuring text about positions, helpers, and water births. I look at my husband and wonder about my new dependency—will he mop my brow as they show husbands doing in the photographs, will he comfort me, will he find the birth disgusting, will he help me? When I dare look beyond the birth, I am excited. My husband, always more optimistic than I am, reminds me that this is a new adventure for us. When he compliments me for being so brave I swell with pride.

Yet when I think ahead to the days and weeks just after the birth, I envy Kareema. Like most professional women I have good friends, but they don't live nearby. My family too is scattered. My sister, whom I saw every day for more than a month because she gave me my injections, won't be around. I look forward to the new intimacy with my husband, and I'm counting on him; but I've been warned about the strains. As an academic I think of books as companions, but will they really give me the advice I need? So much is unknown: I don't know how long I'll be in the hospital; whether I'll have a caesarian section; who will deliver me; whether the babies will be in incubators.

When Kareema gave birth, as usual the women in her community dropped everything to come help. She had her baby in the room she likes best for this—a warm room away from the rest of the house. Her cousin and her best friend, women she has known nearly all her life, were there to hold her. Along with some other women and all her children, they stayed with her for a week, busily cooking, doing her laundry for her, and talking. They had all been through this experience. They knew she would be there when it was their turn. They joked and gossiped and told stories late into the night. They made her soothing teas. No men came near, and few demands were made on them. It was a sort of holiday. Kareema's only responsi-

---

11. This essay, published in 1995, is in many ways the companion of one that Abu-Lughod wrote in 1991, called "Writing Against Culture." In the earlier piece, Abu-Lughod writes at length about the divide between self and other, or between writers and their subjects, on which ethnography rests. She says "[A]nthropology's avowed goal may be "the study of man [*sic*], but it is a discipline built on the historically constructed divide between the West and the non-West. It has been and continues to be primarily the study of the non-Western other by the Western self. . . . And the relationship between the West and the non-West, at least since the birth of anthropology, has been constituted by Western domination" (1991: 139 bracketed *sic* in the original. However, she implies here that feminist anthropologists (who she assumes will be women) working with women in other cultures can begin to move beyond this self-other divide.

12. Many anthropologists have discovered that lessons they learned in the field can have unexpected applications at home. Although Abu-Lughod makes the point more eloquently, anthropologists who spend long times in the field might be considered hybrid people.

bility was to rest, to nurse and change her new infant, and to receive her women visitors, who came bringing chickens, eggs, bars of soap, and little hand-sewn dresses.

At my wedding four years ago, I missed my Bedouin friends. To bring them in, I recited some songs they would have sung to celebrate my wedding had they been there. It will be harder to find a substitute for the busy companionship they provide to the mother of a newborn. They say a new mother should not be left alone. I expect I will be, from time to time. They say she is vulnerable. We call it postpartum depression. Perhaps I'll wear my Bedouin silver bracelet. They say it is good for a new mother to wear silver; it protects her.[13]

AUTHOR'S NOTES

I am grateful to the women like Kareema and Zaynab in Egypt who taught me about infertility, among other things. A fellowship from the National Endowment for the Humanities through the American Research Center in Egypt enabled me to come to know Zaynab in 1990. Since 1978 I have had generous support for my research among the Awlad 'Ali Bedouin; my most recent extended stay with Kareema and her family was made possible by a Fulbright award. Ruth Behar's insightful suggestions made the essay richer.

a. All the names used in this essay are pseudonyms.

b. In a sensitive and sensible rethinking of the misnomer of "native" or "indigenous" anthropologist, Kirin Narayan has drawn attention to the complex and shifting identifications all anthropologists have and has proposed hybridity as a more appropriate characterization of anthropologists' identities. She has also suggested that their texts should embody the enactment of that hybridity. See Kirin Narayan, "How Native Is a 'Native' Anthropologist?" *American Anthropologist* 95 (1993): 671–86.

c. Emily Martin, *The Woman in the Body: A Cultural Analysis of Reproduction* (Boston: Beacon Press, 1987).

d. For more on Awlad 'Ali theories of infertility, see Lila Abu-Lughod, *Writing Women's Worlds: Bedouin Stories* (Berkeley: University of California Press, 1993), Chapter 3. See also Marcia Inhorn, *Quest for Conception: Gender, Infertility, and Egyptian Medical Traditions* (Philadelphia: University of Pennsylvania Press, 1994), especially its rich descriptions of Egyptian infertility treatments.

e. Sarah Franklin, "Making Sense of Missed Conceptions: Anthropological Perspectives on Unexplained Infertility," in *Changing Human Reproduction*, ed. Meg Stacey (London: Sage Publications, 1992), 75–91; and "Postmodern Procreation: A Cultural Account of Assisted Reproduction," in *Conceiving the New World Order: The Global Politics of Reproduction*, ed. Faye D. Ginsburg and Rayna Rapp (Berkeley: University of California Press, 1995), 323–45.

f. Abu-Lughod, *Writing Women's Worlds*.

g. Among the articles in which Donna Haraway makes this sort of argument, "A Cyborg Manifesto," in her *Simians, Cyborgs, and Women* (New York: Routledge, 1991), 149–81, is probably the most powerful.

h. Rosalind Pollack Petchesky, "Fetal Images: The Power of Visual Culture in the Politics of Reproduction," *Feminist Studies* 13, no. 2 (Summer 1987): 280.

i. Lila Abu-Lughod, "Can There Be a Feminist Ethnography?" *Women and Performance* 5, no. 1 (1990): 7–27.

j. Ibid., 25.

k. It is difficult for anthropologists to reflect on the ways their sense of self or their experience of life events might have been shaped by the people and ideas encountered in the field. It can be done, however, as exemplified by Dorinne Kondo, "Dissolution and Reconstitution of Self: Implications for Anthropological Epistemology," *Cultural Anthropology* I (1986): 74–88; Renato Rosaldo, "Introduction: Grief and a Headhunter's Rage," in his *Culture and Truth* (Boston: Beacon Press, 1989), 1–21; and Paul Riesman, *Freedom in Fulani Life: An Introspective Ethnography* (Chicago: University of Chicago Press, 1977).

l. This greater acceptance by middle-class women of the biomedical discourse on reproduction is documented by Martin, *Woman in the Body*, and by Rayna Rapp, "Constructing Amniocentesis: Maternal and Medical Discourses," in *Uncertain Terms: Negotiating Gender in American Culture*, ed. Faye Ginsburg and Anna Lowenhaupt Tsing (Boston: Beacon Press, 1990), 28–42.

---

13. You have now completed Abu-Lughod's story about pregnancy. The subject is interesting, and her writing style engaging; but stop for a moment and reflect on the topic, how the story was written, and what you have learned. This essay is a wonderful example of postmodern writing and the postmodern perspective on ethnography. Contrary to a modernist approach as seen, for example, in essay 18 by Marvin Harris, Abu-Lughod doesn't claim to speak for Bedouin women. She instructs her readers by describing her interactions with Bedouin women she knows well and contrasts that with her personal experience with in vitro fertilization procedures. This is a subtle but important difference in how ethnographic information is reported.

34. The Emergence of Political Homophobia in Indonesia: Masculinity and National Belonging

Tom Boellstorff (b. 1969)

ON NOVEMBER 11, 2000, about 350 *gay* and male-to-female transvestite (*waria, banci, béncong*) Indonesians gathered in the resort town of Kaliurang in Central Java for an evening of artistic performances and comedy skits.[a] The event, in observance of National Health Day, was sponsored by several health organizations as well as the local France-Indonesia Institute: many heterosexual or *normal* Indonesians also attended. Events like this have been held across Indonesia since the early 1990s, and those present had no reason to suspect this night would be any different.[1]

However, at around 9:30 p.m. about 150 men who later claimed to be members of the *Gerakan Pemuda Ka'bah* (Ka'bah Youth Movement) burst into the Wisma Hastorenggo hall where the celebration was underway.[b] Arriving in a mass of motorcycles and jeeps, many wore the white hats or robes associated with political Islam. Shouting "God is Great" and "look at these men done up like women. Get out, *banci!*"[c] they assaulted those present with knives, machetes, and clubs. Sounds of shattering glass filled the air as the attackers smashed windows and destroyed chairs, tables, and equipment. No one was killed but at least twenty-five were injured; witnesses spoke of persons "bathed in blood" from severe wounds. At least three persons were hospitalized, including the local director of the France-Indonesia Institute, who among other injuries was struck in the head by a sword; another victim suffered injuries near his right eye after being hit with clubs and a chair; yet another was struck over the head with a bottle until the bottle broke.[d] Others were hurt while fleeing; one *gay* man was injured when leaping from a window to escape. The attackers also robbed and verbally abused their victims, vandalizing the vehicles used to transport participants to the site. These male attackers displayed a high state of emotion throughout the incident; one *gay* witness described them as filled with cruel anger (*bengis*), possessed by anger (*kalap*), hot-tempered and wild (*beringas*), and shouting sadistically (*bentakan-bentakan sadis*).[e] Fifty-seven men were arrested following the event but all were soon released without charges being filed.[2]

This incident was foreshadowed by another one year earlier. For two decades in Indone-

---

From *Ethos* (2004)

1. Boellstorff begins with a news account of a violent incident . . . a sort of tale of entry. Note Boellstorff's careful attention to the specific vocabulary of gender used by Indonesians. Boellstorff has had a long interest in language. He trained at Stanford in the 1990s when linguistic analysis and, particularly deconstruction and the relationships between language and power were at the forefront of anthropology there.

2. In his footnotes, Boellstorff comments on some of the terms he uses and on his use of italics for "gay" and "lesbi." Some additional information will put these terms and Boellstorff's use of italics in context.

Waria is a broadly used term that blends the Indonesian words for women and man. Kathy Huang notes that waria are a diverse group and encompass what Americans "might call cross-dressers, transsexuals, drag queens, and effeminate gay men." She says these are united by "an irrepressible feminine spirit" (Huang 2016). The terms *banci* and *bencong* are also used to describe this group. Boellstorff provides an extensive discussion of the differences between the terms in *A Coincidence of Desires: Anthropology, Queer Studies, Indonesia* (2007).

sia a series of groups—ranging from formally structured entities to small clusters of persons in rural areas or even single correspondents—have worked to link together *gay* men and *lesbi* women in a national network.[f] Dedé Oetomo, an anthropologist and linguist based in Surabaya (East Java), has been a major figure in this movement and in the mid-1990s became involved with the Education and Propaganda division of the People's Democratic Party (*Partai Rakyat Demokratik* or PRD), which includes a call for *lesbi* and *gay* rights in its platform. In 1998 Oetomo even stood as a candidate for national parliament under the PRD banner.[3]

Through the efforts of Oetomo and many others, plans were hatched in the early 1990s to hold a meeting that could strengthen the national network. In December 1993, the first National Gay and Lesbian Congress was held without any negative consequences at Kaliurang, the very location where the violence described above would take place seven years later. From this meeting was born the Indonesian *Lesbi* and *Gay* Network (*Jaringan Lesbi dan Gay Indonesia* or JLGI). The JLGI successfully staged a Second National Congress in Bandung (West Java) in 1995 and a third in Denpasar (Bali) in 1997. Like the first National Congress, these events attracted from fifty to one hundred participants from Java, Bali, and Sulawesi (persons from other islands rarely attended because there was no money for scholarships). At no time did these events draw unfavorable public attention. The 1997 Denpasar Congress, which I attended, was covered extensively by the local newspaper *Nusa* in a five-day series of feature articles (November 24–28, 1997); much of the coverage repeated stereotypes of *gay* men and *lesbi* women as obsessed with sex, but it also included statements by public figures calling for Indonesian society to "embrace" *lesbi* women and *gay* men.

Fig. 1 (not included in this edition) is a political cartoon. Two men are shown with their arms linked. In their other arms, they carry magazines. They look over their shoulders as they run from an angry crowd that stands, fists raised, and carries a banner reading Sodom and Gemorah. The caption reads: "Cartoon from Gatra magazine, September 19, 1999," commenting on the Solo incident. Note the angry men in the background as well as the magazines held by the two men, arms linked in flight, that read "Rakernas [RApat KERja NASional or 'national working meeting'] Lesbian & Gay Solo." One of the shirts reads "JLGI."

In the wake of these successes, plans were soon underway for a fourth meeting in 1999—the first to follow Soeharto's fall.[g] That September, members of twenty-one organizations and groups came from Java and Bali to the city of Solo in Central Java to participate in the meeting, which was to take place at the Dana Hotel on the 9th and 10th, with a press conference to follow. Such a press conference had never taken place before, and represented a substantial move to claim public recognition in a post-Soeharto civil society. By at least September 7, however, several Muslim organizations in Solo had learned of the meeting and, in sharp contrast to the indifference that greeted the previous Congresses, declared that it should not take place. Moreover, this rejection took the form of threatened violence—specifically, to burn down the Dana Hotel and kill anyone found there.[h] The Secretary of the local Indonesian Muslim Cleric's Council, Muhammad Amir, stated that the meeting would be "very embarrassing [*sangat memalukan*]. As if we

---

Boellstorff's use of italics for the words "gay" and "lesbi" emphasizes the cultural, gender role dimensions of these terms. Indonesians are not gay in the American sense. The American term "gay" classifies a particular gender role and a particular type of gender performance. Indonesian notions of what "gay" means and what performing this role involves are different. The use of italics acknowledges this difference.

3. Dédé Oetomo (b. 1953), as Boellstorff notes is a scholar and LGBT rights campaigner. He founded Lambda Indonesia (now called GAYA Nusantara) in 1982 and is, in 2023 its national coordinator. In Indonesia, he is often the public face of Indonesia's gay rights movement. Oetomo studied linguistics at Cornell where he was strongly influenced by Benedict Anderson who wrote the introduction to his first book. Oetomo has run several times for public office but has never won.

are legalizing the practice of such sexual deviations." Once these threats became known the meeting was canceled, but the Muslim organizations soon learned of a backup plan to hold a press conference at the local PRD office; on September 10, group of youths from these organizations surrounded the office and threatened to burn it down. Death threats were made against Oetomo and a mobilization took place across the city based on rumors that the meeting would be moved to an undisclosed location. H. Sadili, member of the governing board for the Solo Muslim Youth Front, said that "if they become known, they'll definitely become the target of masses running *amok*."[4]

MASCULINITY
AND THE NATION

From one perspective, these incidents appear as further cases of the dreary efflorescence of violence following the 1998 fall of Soeharto's "New Order," violence whose genealogy stretches back through the New Order (1967–1998) to the colonial state. From another perspective, however, they are bluntly novel: historically, violence against non-normative men in Indonesia has been rare to a degree unimaginable in many Euro-American societies, where assaults on homosexual and transgendered men are familiar elements of the social world.[i] What is in particular need of explanation is the cultural logic that makes this new genre of violence comprehensible to Indonesians (*gay* or not, Muslim or not) so that these two events could have a continuing, generalized impact. In a recent review of anthropological writing on violence in Southeast Asia, Mary Steedly cautions against either essentializing violence (as an inevitable dimension of human sociality) or culturalizing it (as necessary element of a particular social system). The third alternative Steedly proposes is

---

4. An understanding of the Indonesian political context in the twentieth century is critical to this essay. In the early twentieth century, Indonesia was a colony of the Netherlands. By the 1920s Sukarno (1901–1970 most Javanese people do not use family names) had become the leader of an independence movement. In the 1930s, he served jail time for his politics. In 1942, combined Japanese and Indonesian revolutionary forces defeated the Dutch and forced them from the archipelago. After Japan's defeat in 1945, the Indonesian independence movement declared national independence and made Sukarno president. The Dutch tried but failed to reestablish their rule and Indonesia instituted a parliamentary democracy. However, by the mid-1950s, Sukarno undercut democracy and moved the country toward communism, receiving substantial aid from both Russia and China.

The United States encouraged and backed several unsuccessful coup attempts in the late 1950s and early 1960s. In 1965, in a complex series of moves backed by the US and Britain, Suharto (1921–2008), one of the leaders of the Indonesian Army, staged a right-wing coup d'état. This was followed by an extraordinarily violent wave of repression against leftists. At least half a million people were killed and possibly as many as a million. The CIA was almost certainly involved in orchestrating Suharto's coup and in identifying those to be killed (Kim 2002 and many other sources). Sukarno, an immensely popular independence leader, remained nominal president until March 1967, when Suharto became acting president and established his "New Order" government.

Suharto ruled for thirty-one years and moved Indonesia firmly into the US and Western orbit. Economic conditions improved but Suharto was both deeply authoritarian and profoundly corrupt. He is believed to have stolen between $15 and $35 billion (Denny 2004). By the late 1990s, Indonesia was in a financial crisis, Suharto was aging, and the Cold War was over. A series of street demonstrations led to Suharto's resignation. Suharto's regime was authoritarian and corrupt, but stable. In the period that followed Suharto's rule, the era of Boellstorff's essay, stability was replaced by change.

Boellstorff ends this paragraph with the phrase "running amok." The idea of amok is important in the remainder of the essay. Running amok is a fairly common English phrase but has a particular meaning in the Indonesian context. Western scholars have frequently identified *amok* as a psychological syndrome specific to Indonesian and Malay contexts, and defined it as a period of "frenzied indiscriminate, homicidal aggression" (Spores 1988: 139). In one version this is explained by "an evil tiger spirit entering a person's body and compelling him or her to behave violently without conscious awareness" (Saint Martin 1999). However, the use of *amok* is also deeply bound up with the colonial administration of Indonesia and the medicalization of particular forms of behavior. Its meaning has changed depending on the context of its use (Imai et al. 2018; Hahn 1995; Kloos 2014).

to "localize" violence: "By this I mean exploring the full particularity of its multifarious occasions: how it is produced in certain circumstances; how it is deployed, represented, limited, imagined, ignored, or instigated; how it is identified, disciplined, interrogated, and, of course, punished" (Steedly 1999: 445–446). My only quibble with this alternative is that when violence is framed in terms of localization, a presumption that culture is local in the first instance grounds the analysis in the last instance—no matter how emphatically the constitutive role of the state, the legacy of the colonial encounter, or other translocal forces such as "world religions" enter the interpretive frame. In the cases at hand here, both the "deviant" masculinities and the cultural logics of the attackers drew their structuring assumptions from national and global discourses. Understanding these incidents can illuminate how the full particularity of violence's occasion can involve an imagined Indonesian community (Anderson 1983), rather than the ethnological categories (Javanese, Madurese, Buginese, etc.) that, however historicized and problematized, continue to dominate anthropological investigations of the archipelago (Boellstorff 2002). This article incorporates an attention to what was unique about these incidents (that they targeted non-normative men), with attention to national topographies of culture, towards the goal of investigating intersections of emotion and violence.[j, 5]

I wish to ask how emotion figures in violence understood as political. In the historical moment that I write emotion and political violence come together most starkly in the figure of the terrorist. The "terrorist" is the limit function of the emotion/violence nexus, and the terrorist's terror is by definition political, else the person is solely a mass murderer. Against claims that emotion is a precultural, even a cultural psychological response function, it is clear that the terror produced by political violence is a cultural phenomenon. This means its form is always historically and geographically specific. Political homophobia is the name I give to an emergent cultural logic linking emotion, sexuality, and political violence. It brings together the direct object of nonnormative Indonesian men with the indirect object of contemporary Indonesian public culture, making enraged violence against *gay* men intelligible and socially efficacious.[6]

---

5. Mary Steedly (1946–2018) was a Harvard anthropologist whose work focused on the Karo Batik region of Sumatra in Indonesia. While Steedly urges focus on the specific local context of violence, Boellstorff argues that although all violence is ultimately local, violence against non-normative men in Indonesia can only be understood in a national and international context.

The work of Benedict Anderson (1936–2015) is critical to Boellstorff. Anderson's work is discussed more extensively in note 3 of the Appadurai essay. Boellstorff's comment about "an imagined Indonesian community" refers to Anderson's concept of the imagined community described in his 1983 book of the same name. Anderson argued that printing in a common vernacular language is the basis for nationalism because it allows a large and diverse group of people (most of whom do not know each other) to imagine themselves to be united by a common language and shared ideas. In this context, Boellstorff argues that Indonesia is an imagined community. The more than 250 million Indonesians, living on more than 17,000 islands and speaking more than 300 languages imagine themselves to have a specific national identity and shared notions of masculinity. This idea is promoted by the government and elites through national education, media, and the use of the Bahasa Indonesian language (spoken as a first language by only 7 percent of the population) as the national tongue.

6. Boellstorff here mentions the historical moment in which he is writing and the anthropology of emotions. Both of these are important things to keep in mind.

This essay appeared in 2004, during a period that was both deeply troubled and somewhat optimistic. The 9/11 terror attacks and subsequent violence against Muslims in the United States were still fresh in people's minds. At the same time, the Cold War had ended relatively recently, and many rulers who had been critical figures in that conflict, including Suharto, were falling. For many throughout the world, this led to a sense of optimism. In this essay, Boellstorff takes great care to avoid anti-Muslim rhetoric and seems at least somewhat optimistic for the future of Indonesia. In a postscript written for the seventh edition of this text, Boellstorff discusses more recent events in Indonesia. Today, we live in far less optimistic times.

Through highlighting the role of national belonging in this violence, I suggest that norms for Indonesian national identity may be gaining a new masculinist cast. I also hope to foreclose reductive explanations in terms of Islam. While at present Islam may represent a necessary condition for these new forms of violence, it cannot explain their relationship to masculinity, emotion, and the public sphere. In reconfiguring official Islam's heterosexist rejection of male homosexuality and transgenderism into political homophobia, the perpetrators of this violence are not just expressing religious belief but reacting to a feeling of *malu*, a complex term that can be provisionally rendered as "shame." While informed by Islamic sexual norms, the context and timing of the Kaliurang and Solo incidents reveals a new problematic evoking these feelings. This is the sense that the potential for the nation to be represented by non-normative men challenges a nationalized masculinity, enabling what has long been understood to be a normative male response to malu—namely, the masculine and often collective enraged violence known in Indonesian as *amok*. By definition, amok is always a public act. The attackers in Kaliurang and Solo, who claimed to represent a post-Soeharto vision of the national, may have sought to shore up a perceived shameful threat to the nation through public violence directed at the events themselves. That it is these events which are considered shameful, and that violence is seen as their proper counter, indicates that these attackers' vision of the nation is normatively male. Emotion here can be used to divine politics.[k]

Political homophobia highlights how postcolonial heterosexuality is shaped by the state, but in ways specific to particular colonial legacies and national visions, and which therefore vary over time as well as space. A substantial literature now documents the massive effort undertaken by the Indonesian state to inculcate gendered ideologies of the ideal citizen, a national masculinity and femininity. Against the wide range of kinship forms found throughout the archipelago, the family principle (*azas kekeluargaan*), with its associated ideologies of "State Momism" (Suryakusuma 1996) and "State Fatherism," sets forth narrow visions of masculinity and femininity as the foundations of society.[l] Implicit is the heterosexist ideology linking these ideally gendered men and women into the citizen-family. As we see in nationalist literature going back to the 1920s, the idea of becoming a modern Indonesian is often framed in terms of a shift from arranged to "chosen" marriage (Alisjahbana 1966; Siegel 1997; Rodgers 1995). While there are still arranged marriages, and many that fall between arrangement and choice, the ideal of chosen marriage now dominates images of the proper Indonesian citizen. I have noted elsewhere (Boellstorff 2004a) that when marriage is arranged sexual orientation is secondary, but that when marriages are based on love and choice, sexuality becomes a new kind of problem. In contemporary Indonesia choice, to be national, must be heterosexual choice, and while both man and woman choose, the dominant ideology is that men pursue while the "choice" of the woman is secondarily that of refusal.[m] It is through heterosexuality that gendered self and nation articulate. In the new Indonesia, men who publicly appear to make improper choices threaten this gendered and sexualized logic of national belonging.[7]

The anthropology of emotions was becoming an important field of study in the late 1990s and early 2000s. Several major works appeared. These included major reviews and new essays by Catherine Lutz and Geoffrey White (1986), John Leavitt (1996), Lila Abu-Lughod and Catherine Lutz (1990), and Jeff Goodwin et al. (2001).

7. Boellstorff (and others) make an important assertion: the way that the state defines, and controls gender is one of the most fundamental patterning elements of social structure. This is close to a foundational statement for a gender-centered anthropological theory. Boellstorff asserts that heterosexual marriage choice and specific family gender roles are basic to the formation of the Indonesian state. Blackwood (2007) says: "Since the inception of Suharto's New Order in 1965, the Indonesian state has avidly pursued a policy of promoting nuclear families and motherhood. . . . During Suharto's rule (1966–1998), the state enshrined mother and wife as women's primary role and duty." Boellstorff's analysis owes much to Foucault's devel-

I come to the topic of political homophobia from a larger project in which I explore how Indonesians occupying *gay* and *lesbi* subject-positions are shaped by national discourse (Boellstorff 2003, 2005). It bears noting that so-called "traditional" homosexual or transgender roles, primarily limited to ritual and performance contexts, can still be found in many parts of Indonesia. *Gay* Indonesians occasionally draw upon these "traditional" sexualities to claim legitimacy (they are almost exclusively for men). In reality, however, few *gay* Indonesians identify with or even know of these "traditions": they see themselves as (to employ the Indonesian term), *modern*, part of a national community. These Indonesians are found across the archipelago, even in rural areas, and are more likely to be lower-class than members of the jet-setting elite that stands so frequently as trope of the "Third World" homosexual. It is in this sense, as persons whose sexualities are irreducible to locality or tradition, that *gay* Indonesians could be seen as a major, if unintended, success story of Soeharto's New Order—truly national subjectivities. *Gay* Indonesians are not marginal to the body politic, but a kind of distillation of national discourse. This is not an Indonesian version of "Queer Nation"; the impact of state ideology on *gay* Indonesians is not primarily at the level of politicization. Few *gay* Indonesians are involved in the kinds of political work exemplified by the failed Solo national meeting. For a dominant ideology to impact subjectivities, it is not necessary for that ideology to be loved or even clearly understood, as we see in Euro-American homosexualities, so shaped by sexological legacies of which many lesbian and *gay* Euro-Americans are unaware.[8]

HOMOPHOBIA AND HETEROSEXISM

Like much of Southeast Asia, Indonesia is often characterized as tolerant of homosexuality, bisexuality, and transgenderism. Like most myths this is a false belief that contains a grain of truth, and to identify this grain of truth I develop a distinction between "homophobia" and "heterosexism." Most behavioral sciences use "homophobia" as if it transparently reflects a set of real-world conditions. Psychological correlational studies employ measurements like the "Lesbian Internalized Homophobia Scale" that assume, for instance, that a lack of desire to affiliate with other lesbians and *gay* men, or a pleasure at being perceived by others as heterosexual, are a priori indicators of "internalized homophobia" (Szymanski et al. 2001: 34; see also Floyd 2000; Wright et al. 1999). In fact, the concept originated in the early 1970s. As Daniel Wickberg notes in his cultural history of the term, "unpacking the idea of homophobia reveals liberal norms and assumptions about personhood and social

---

opment of the ideas of biopower and control of sexuality in Western Europe. The government and elite institutions deploy education, media, language, and bureaucratization to create specific understandings of sexuality. This process is fundamental to a state's extension of power to create national citizens out of individuals with diverse and particularistic identities.

8. One important element that backgrounds this essay is that Indonesia is widely known for the diversity of its gender roles. For example, Boellstorff has just mentioned Bugunise ethnicity. Bugis society is well known for having five gender roles: Oroané, Makkunrai (cisgender men and women respectively), calalai and calabai (men who are female and women who are male respectively), and bissu (shamans who are androgynous) (Graham 2001 and many other sources). However, Boellstorff says few *gay* Indonesians have much understanding of this. Instead, their self-understanding derives from the way that the government has organized sexuality. By exerting its power to organize heterosexual households, the state has, as an unintended consequence, created new *gay* and *lesbi* identities as well. For Boellstorff, their existence is more of a testimony to the power of the state to control discourse than it is the survival of a far more variable sexuality.

Queer Nation is a LGBTQ political action organization founded in New York City in 1990. Boellstorff's point is that new *gay* and *lesbi* identities in Indonesia have not emerged as a reaction to oppression or as part of an attempt at political organization. Rather, they are a consequence of the state's exercise of biopower. In the last line, Boellstorff suggests that something similar happened in the West in the twentieth century.

order rather than just liberal attitudes toward homosexuality itself" (2000: 43). Homophobia links Western conceptions of shamed self and threatened society: later I discuss how malu and amok are linked in a similar fashion.[9]

The distinction between homophobia and heterosexism can provide a powerful conceptual rubric to address questions of violence—particularly if we employ the binarism not as a gloss on precultural reality but as embodying assumptions about politics and the self. If homophobia employs a Freudian problematic to locate antipathy in the individuated psyche, heterosexism employs a Gramscian problematic to locate antipathy in hegemony. Heterosexism refers to the belief that heterosexuality is the only natural or moral sexuality. It does not imply the gut level response that homophobia does; for instance, a bureaucratic structure may be heterosexist but it cannot be homophobic. It operates at the level of generalized belief and social sanction, rather than on an emotive plane. In the Euro-American context, this gives heterosexism a cultural currency that homophobia lacks. While few Euro-Americans would admit to being homophobic, many—for instance, much of the Religious Right in the United States—would openly affirm they are heterosexist, often through terms like pro-family. Homophobia and heterosexism form a binarism, building on distinctions between emotion/thought, personal/public, and ideational/material. While the binarism does not isomorphically diagnose a real-world division between two forms of oppression, it proves heuristically productive for understanding the imbrication of violence and emotion.[10]

In many cases homophobia and heterosexism feed off each other; heterosexism creates a climate where fear and hatred of non-normative sexualities and genders can take root, and homophobia creates a climate where heterosexuality is assumed to be superior. However, this is not necessarily the case in all times and places. De-linking homophobia and heterosexism gives us new perspectives on sexual inequality, not only in Indonesia but in other parts of Southeast Asia where there is a need for "a more refined model of cultural antipathy" towards homosexuality (Jackson 1999: 229). It is possible to have homophobia with little or no heterosexism—cases (like some Latin American contexts) where many forms of sexuality are recognized as natural, yet emotional violence against homosexual persons exists—and heterosexism with little or no homophobia, where heterosexuality is presumed superior to other sexualities, yet this does not lead to violence against homosexual persons.

This latter state of affairs has predominated in Indonesia until recently: heterosexism over homophobia. Since violence against *gay* men qua *gay* men is almost unknown in Indonesia, and since in addition the Indonesian Civil Code (based on the Dutch Civil Code, which is in turn based on the Napoleonic Code) has little to say about homosexuality and transgenderism[n] (and to my knowledge there have never

---

9. Thus, if terms like gay and lesbian are culturally dependent (in this essay *gay* versus gay) so too are terms like homophobia. They reference the particular conditions of Western society.

Boellstorff understands psychologists as assuming that homophobia is a natural aspect of sexuality. He, however, understands it as a consequence of specific Western understandings of shame and of the self.

10. Boellstorff argues that, in Western (and possibly other) understandings, homophobia is an emotional reaction originating in the individual human psyche. Heterosexism, however, is a hegemonic ideology promulgated by elites in order to exercise certain sorts of control and organization. For example, note the frequency of the word "family" in US conservative discourse. Prominent Christian conservative lobby groups include The American Family Association, the Faith and Family Alliance, the Family Research Council, and Focus on the Family. In these cases, it is a particular form of family that is being promoted. Boellstorff analytically separates heterosexist ideology from homophobia. However, harkening back to ideas from Durkheim and Lévi-Strauss, he identifies a binary structure through which heterosexism may implicate homophobia. Heterosexism as a public ideology expressed in material terms such as prohibiting gay marriage, and may connect to private, emotionally based ideas of homophobia. However, for Boellstorff this connection is contextual rather than inevitable. He says this binary is a useful tool to understand the overlap of violence and emotion.

been arrests for homosexuality in postcolonial Indonesia), Euro-American visitors often mis-recognize a "tolerant" culture. This is because for Euro-Americans the constant threat of violence is the disciplinary pedagogy margin-alizing non-normative sexualities and genders. (If in my home country of the United States I imagine walking down the street holding the hand of my male partner, what I fear is not that others will think me immoral, nor that they will enact laws against me, but that they will phys-ically assault me.) In the absence of homopho-bia, heterosexism is assumed to be absent as well. However, despite the fact that there is little homophobia in contemporary Indonesia, heterosexism is pervasive. The expectation that everyone will marry heterosexually is voiced in many belief systems across the archipelago, but gains added contemporary force from the state's portraying it as essential for becoming a modern citizen. The "tolerance" of homo-sexuality exists only because Indonesians keep these practices secret and do not publicly pro-claim homosexual identities.[11]

HOMOPHOBIA AS THUGGERY?

The potential sea-change in Indonesia is the masculinist drawing of a connection between homophobia and heterosexism, such that the former can stand as a condition of possibility for the latter—in a context where heterosexism has historically held a dominant cultural posi-tion without homophobia's aid. By exploring how changing masculine representations of the nation shape this shift from everyday hetero-sexism to political homophobia, I hope to avoid reducing political homophobia to either thug-gery or Islam. While we yet have no concrete data it is plausible that the attackers involved in the Kaliurang and Solo incidents were paid, as have been many of those involved in politi-cal violence in Indonesia since 1998. That per-sons were paid, however, does not mean that emotions were not involved (it appears that many men involved in the rape of ethnic Chi-nese women in Jakarta in 1998 were paid; yet their erections were no less real). I am partic-ularly keen to avoid treating Islam as source of political homophobia. The pivotal question of this article is not whether or not official Islam disapproves of homosexuality (as a heterosex-ist cosmology, it obviously does), but how and why Islamic (male) youth groups have at a cer-tain point in time and within the nation-state of Indonesia, transformed this heterosexism into homophobia. The homophobic reaction of these Islamic youth groups appears not as a spe-cifically religious response (those attacked were not in mosques or demanding religious recogni-tion) but as a reaction to feelings of *malu* asso-ciated with representations of the nation.[12]

---

11. Foucault (1979) wrote extensively on the role of discipline and the idea of the disciplinary society. Beginning with a reflection on Jeremy Bentham's idea of a panopticon (a prison in which all the actions of the prisoners are potentially viewable by an observer) Foucault argued that the prison, with its powers of obser-vation, judgment, and examination became the patterning element of society. This was particularly found in the "disciplinary pedagogy" of education. In a discussion of the organization of space, Foucault notes that the assignment of individual spaces in a classroom made "the education space function like a learning machine, but also as a machine for supervising, hierarchizing, rewarding" (1979: 147). In this passage, Boell-storff applies this idea broadly to society: the process of observation, judgment, and examination operates on the playground as well as in the classroom.

12. In May 1998, a series of riots broke out across Indonesia. The principal causes were economic, and their main result was Suharto's resignation. However, ethnic Chinese were particular targets for the rioters. Chinese people play a large role in the Indonesian economy and have often been targets of hostility and violence. In the 1998 attacks, more than 165 women, mostly ethnic Chinese, were raped in Jakarta and an additional 300 in other towns. However, as of 2018, not only have the perpetrators not been brought to justice, but, despite extensive documentation of the attacks, the government until recently has attempted to deny they took place (Wargadiredja 2017; Britton 2018). In early 2023, President Joko Widodo acknowledged that the 1998 riots and 11 other incidents involved a "gross violation of human rights" and expressed "regret." However, as of 2023,

It is true that in the Kaliurung and Solo incidents the perpetrators represented themselves as belonging to fundamentalist Muslim groups, and that Central Java is a hotbed of these groups. These groups have also attacked other social groups or places they associate with immorality, such as brothels and discos.° On one level, then, political homophobia is linked to a wider cultural dynamic where Islam represents an avenue for political struggle that includes conceptions of an Islamic polity (Hefner 2000). However, while to date Islam may be a necessary condition for political homophobia, it is not a sufficient condition and these incidents cannot be "read off" political Islam. Such an analysis could not explain why antipathy towards *gay* men should be expressed in an emotional and violent manner, rather than, say, the passing of an Islamic legal judgment (*fatwa*) or some form of non-violent social sanction. This linkage of Islam with violence is both an Orientalist stereotype (Lawrence 1998: 4) and a self-Orientalizing stereotype taken up by some "fundamentalist" Islamic groups: Muslim intellectuals in Indonesia have cautioned against taking this representation at face value (Wahid 1999). There are a wide range of Muslim groups and belief systems in contemporary Indonesia, many of which tolerate sexual and

gender minorities. Crucially, most *gay* Indonesians are themselves Muslim, and we lose sight of the rich cultural contexts in which they reconcile sexuality and faith if we treat Islam as direct source of political homophobia rather than a contributing (but not determining) factor. Indeed, it is unclear to what degree Islam is a confounding variable, since it is also the normative, majority religion (approximately ninety percent of Indonesians follow the Islamic faith; Indonesia is thus home to more Muslims than any other nation). In contexts where other religions dominate, it is typically the fundamentalist variants of that religion (Hinduism in India, Christianity in the United States) that have the cultural capital to employ violence, and in these cases it is also linked to masculinity (Hansen 1996).[13]

ENGENDERING VIOLENCE

In the rich body of anthropological work on emotion in Southeast Asia, a central conceptual category has been the Malay/Indonesian term *malu* (and its analogues; e.g., Javanese *isin*, Balinese *lek*, Bugis *sin*; Tagalog *hiya*). Malu typically appears in dictionaries translated as "shame" or "embarrassment," but the

---

no one has been brought to justice for their part in these attacks (Nugroho 2023, https://www.scmp .com/week-asia/people/article/3221871/indonesian-activist-lifts-lid-rape-chinese-women-may-1998-riots -it-was-new-low)

Note the care that Boellstorff takes to contextualize the violence and to avoid viewing it simply as a function of Islamic worldviews. Virtually all anthropologists would likely agree with Boellstorff. However, the opposing view: that Islamic ideology and practice are universally consistent and unalterably opposed to Western notions of individuality and liberty (and sexuality) has been a strong political force in the United States. It's probably best exemplified by Samuel Huntington's 1996 book *The Clash of Civilizations and the Remaking of the World Order*. In the wake of 9/11, many anthropologists thought that combating this view was extremely important (see for example Brown 2005; Hannerz 2015).

13. Boellstorff here uses both the idea of Orientalist stereotypes and self-orientalizing. Orientalist/Orientalism is a historic term that refers to Western artists and scholars who depict and study the Middle East. In 1978, Edward Said (1935–2003) a founder of postcolonial studies, published the pathbreaking work *Orientalism*. There, Said analyzed the ways Western depictions of Islam and the Middle East created a fantasy world of European imagination; a world that frequently reversed the mores and values of Europe. Orientalist work tended to view Middle Eastern societies as sensual, mystical, rigid, static, and, above all, other. Orientalist ideas fit well with works like Huntington's *Clash of Civilizations* (described above). Self-Orientalism reflects the fact that it is not only Westerners who are influenced by Orientalist depictions. Through colonialism, globalization, and media, people in the Middle East and Asia are exposed to and influenced by Orientalism as well (Ong 1999: 81). They may internalize and use these images both in self-understanding and in political action.

anthropological literature is unanimous in concluding this fails to represent the complexity of *malu* and its centrality to Southeast Asian conceptions of sociality. Long before Clifford Geertz construed Balinese polities as "theatre states" (Geertz 1980), he inaugurated the dramaturgical metaphor in an analysis of lek (the Balinese near-equivalent to malu). Phrasing lek as "stage fright," Geertz concluded that

> What is feared—mildly in most cases, intensely in a few—is that the public performance that is etiquette will be botched, that the social distance etiquette maintains will consequently collapse, and that the personality of the individual will break through to dissolve his standardized public identity. (Geertz 1973: 402)

It was from precisely this passage that Ward Keeler launched his critique of Geertz, based on his own study of isin (the Javanese near-equivalent to malu). For Keeler, the weakness of Geertz's metaphor was that it "implies a distance between actor and role, and so between self and social persona, which is misleading" (Keeler 1983: 161). In a manner foreshadowing Butler's performative theory of the constitution of the Euro-American gendered subject (Butler 1990), Keeler argued, in effect, that the actor comes into being as a social persona only when on stage. He concluded that isin is neither shame nor stage fright, but *an awareness of vulnerability in interaction* (p. 158). In my reading of the literature, and based upon my own ethnographic work, Keeler's analysis of Javanese isin is valid not only for Balinese lek but Indonesian malu and its other analogues. Indeed, there is general agreement that malu is nothing less than a key site at which Southeast Asians become social persons. In their review of the literature on malu, Collins and Behar conclude that it is "a highly productive concept that has effects in a wide array of personal and social realms," including the political domain (Collins & Behar 2000: 35). They also emphasize the linkages between malu and sexuality:

> As with the English concept of shame, malu is closely associated with sexuality. The Indo-

nesian word for genitals (*kemaluan*) echoes the English expression "private parts." Furthermore, sexually provocative behavior by self or others should elicit malu . . . Gender-inappropriate behavior causes both men and women to feel *malu*. A boy would feel malu if he behaved like a girl, for example by displaying tears in public. (p. 42)

But while sexuality can elicit malu in both men and women, "the most obvious gender difference in the construct of malu is in the appropriate response to being made malu. While women made malu are expected to become withdrawn or avoidant, crying out of the sight of others, men are expected to react aggressively" (p. 48). In the cases of political homophobia at issue here, we find not only a masculinist expression of malu, but a masculinist and politicized trigger of malu. While rarely openly discussed, many Indonesian men have had experiences of being seduced by other men—at religious boarding schools (*pesantren*), at a friend's home, in a park, or elsewhere. While men who think of themselves as *normal* rarely discuss such incidents, *gay* men have described them to me during fieldwork, as illustrated by the except below, from an informant recalling events near Kediri in East Java:

> Shall I tell the story? I used to live in the pesantren, from the last year of junior high school through until the end of high school. About four years it was at that time that I started to understand same-sex relations [*awali mengerti hubungan sejenis*] because I was seduced by my Koranic recitation teacher . . . I was 18 or 19 years old at the time and he was 25 years old. The first time we were together I didn't have any emotions [*belum rasa*] . . . When we were sleeping together he liked to hold me and he'd ejaculate . . . at the beginning I felt very uncomfortable [*risih*]. I didn't like feeling the sperm in his sarung . . . but he started asking me to hold his penis . . . eventually I started to like it . . . He had his own room, so we could do it easily. He was always very helpful to me in my studies; perhaps at the beginning he was

only sympathetic [*simpatik*] and eventually there arose desire [*timbul suka-suka*].

Here, my informant uses a language of emotion to describe a landscape of desire in which a *normal* man desires another man sexually. At the point when these sexual relations occurred, my informant did not yet think of himself as *gay*; it was one *normal* man seducing another. What is typical here is that the emotional response is of discomfort, not rage; when *gay* men talk about *normal* men who spurn their advances the reaction is described as one of refusal not violence. It appears that what is interpreted as "sexually provocative" or "gender-inappropriate" male behavior leads to violence when it involves staking a claim to civil society.[14]

That the sense of malu is masculinized can be seen not only in that the perpetrators were male, but that the response took the form of violent group attacks—of amok. This cultural logic that links malu to amok is of particular interest because if malu is a site of subject-formation, amok is typically understood to be its opposite: a gut reaction where the masculine self disappears into raw action (and often, into a crowd). The contrast is not interior versus exterior, since malu involves the public self, and amok is an intentional state, not just mindless physical action (it has been evoked, for instance, by resistance to colonialism). The distinction pivots not on interior versus exterior but self versus society. Amok is a gendered response to malu; it counters a sense of vulnerability in interaction with a sense of *invulnerability in action*. The question is: why, at this point in time, would acts by *gay* men to access civil society be perceived as initiating a chain of emotions beginning in malu and ending in amok? In these cases, the entry of male homosexuality into public discourse is framed as motivating a gut-level reaction of malu, as if one's own (male) social self is threatened. I am interested in this dynamic, in how political homophobia bridges malu and amok when a particular kind of nationalized masculinity is at stake. This may be because the nation is perceived to be in imminent danger of being represented by non-normative men.[15]

EMOTION AND MASCULINE SEXUALITY

While there is a male-specific typical reaction to malu, and while gender-inappropriate behavior can elicit malu, the range of acceptable masculinities has been quite wide in

---

14. Clifford Geertz, whose "Notes on a Balinese Cockfight" is included in this volume, wrote extensively on Indonesia. His work includes *Negara: The Theater State in Nineteenth Century Bali* (1980), *The Religion of Java* (1960), and many others. Geertz's analysis of Negara focuses on the idea that ritual and performance were central to (and virtually identical to) political power. If performance is identical to power, then failures of performance are to be greatly feared.

Philosopher and gender theorist Judith Butler (b. 1956) is known for her performative theory of gender. Butler argues that humans are always immediately social. Therefore, there is no biological sex that is not also gender. Gender is not something applied to biological sex. Sex/gender is not something one is or has, but rather something one does. Butler says: "Gender is the repeated stylization of the body, a set of repeated acts within a highly rigid regulatory frame that congeal over time to produce the appearance of substance, of a natural sort of being" (2014: 43–44).

Combining Butler and Geertz (along with Keeler's critique of Geertz) Boellstorff links performance, gender, and politics. This is modified in Boellstorff's description of a private homosexual encounter. In this case, the degree of malu felt by the narrator is not clear. However, since the encounter was private and since it had no known connection with the political realm, malu did not become amok.

15. This passage shows the significance of imagined community in Boellstorff's explanation of violence against gay men. While amok has often been described as an internal reaction to shame, or malu (a man is shamed, he broods over his shame and ultimately explodes in a murderous rage or amok), Boellstorff argues that in some manner, gay Indonesian men's quest for public recognition invokes a sense of malu in some heterosexual Muslim men, who perceive it as a threat to their national identity and respond with public violence that they define as amok. Boellstorff describes political homophobia as a "bridge between malu and amok.

many Indonesian contexts. For instance, in java, where the Kaliurang and Solo incidents occurred, "Pure" Javanese tradition does not condemn homosexuality and regards a very wide range of behavior, from he-man to rather (in [Euro-American] terms) "effeminate," as properly masculine' (Peacock 1968: 204). This has even included the political realm: the most notable recent example of this was the 1995 incident when Joop Ave, then Minister for Tourism, Post, and Communication under Soeharto, fled New Zealand after being accused of accosting a male staff member of the Carlton Hotel in Auckland. Despite widespread rumors that Ave was *gay*, he not only kept his post, but the mass media dismissed the "homo rumors" even while openly pondering why Ave had never married.P This was not simply due to journalistic fear of state reprisal; it reflected a general belief that so long as Ave did not publicly proclaim *gay* status, his possible sexual activities with men, while perhaps leading to gossip, did not threaten his public position.

Until recently the fact that men engage in public male-male sexuality (e.g., at a park, disco, or performance event) has not resulted in malu. For Indonesian men male-male sexuality has either been ignored, used contrastively to underscore one's own social propriety, been greeted with curiosity and even titillation, or been casually looked down upon. But it has not led to a personal feeling of malu that could justify violence. Historically, successful Indonesian masculinity has not hinged on a sole sexual attraction to women, so long as one eventually marries. Prior to marriage, same-sex encounters remain common (but almost never publicly acknowledged) in a wide range of contexts, from religious boarding schools to markets and shopping malls. Often these activities are construed not as "sex" but playing around (*main-main*), particularly if anal penetration does not take place. After marrying it is by no means unknown for men to continue to engage in homosex (or discover it for the first time); a lack of cultural salience for homosexuality and

gender segregation make it possible to hide such activities.

In this context where it is assumed all men will marry women, but also that they may have sex with other men and/or with warias, violence is almost never linked to homosexual erotics. Warias, while hardly celebrated, are an accepted part of the contemporary Indonesian social mosaic and can be found in a wide range of contexts, from salons to music videos (see Boellstorff 2004b). Acts of violence against *gay* men have been rare. When, for instance, an Indonesian man encounters another man expressing sexual interest in him—even in public—the man will typically either politely refuse or agree to the sexual encounter and keep quiet about it afterwards.[16]

I recall another incident from the Kediri region; I was in the company of a group of gay men from the area and two gay men from Surabaya. We were spending the evening in a part of the town plaza (*alun-alun*) where *gay* men meet for conversation and to find sexual partners. As often happens in such a place, other Indonesians could be found nearby—*normal* couples with children in strollers, groups of older men and women running late-night errands. Closest to us, however, were a group of young men sitting on a low wall under a tree. As we walked by, Amir—one of the *gay* men from Surabaya—struck up a conversation. The men were aged from 16 to 21 and had come to this part of the town square without realizing its significance. When they asked what we were doing in town, Amir explained that we had attended a meeting of the local *gay* group. In response to their blank stares, Amir calmly clarified what *gay* meant—and that he was *gay* himself and liked to have sex with men. The youths giggled but did not take offence; indeed, they remained all evening. One of them eventually pulled Amir aside to say that he was interested in having sex with men but did not want his friends to know about it. This story is not atypical: across Indonesia, street youths are a common feature of the public areas used by *gay* men, yet these youth

---

16. In Indonesia, violence against warias and gay people more broadly is growing. Today, people who are sexually nonconforming in Indonesia face increasing public hostility, violence, and legal persecution. There are raids on bars, spas, and homes. On December 6, 2022, the Indonesian parliament passed a law that effectively criminalized all same-sex relations, and attacked a wide range of civil rights.

typically do not accost them; they leave them alone, asking for cigarettes or pocket money at most, often having sexual relations with (or even becoming long-term partners of) *gay* men.

The pattern seems similar across the archipelago and across religious or local difference. On another occasion I was out on Saturday night with three *gay* men in the city of Singaraja in north Bali. We made our way to the park where *gay* men and warias often spend their evenings. I rode on the back of a motorcycle driven by one of the *gay* men; another motorcycle carried Made and Danny, two Balinese *gay* men very much in love. It was late but the park was still busy, with a mix of *gay* men, warias, and *normal* men, many sitting along the benches of a bus stop. I sat down on one bench with several warias and three *normal* men; at another bench two meters to my right, under a street-light, Made sat with his Danny in his lap, their caresses visible to all who drove or walked by.[17]

After a few moments one of the *normal* men, with long hair and a stocky, athletic body, sat down beside me and introduced himself as Gus. A few pleasantries passed our lips; then, silence. After a few moments Gus gestured towards a waria standing nearby and said "that one is pretty, like a normal woman" [*perempuan biasa*]. I asked "do you like to have sex with warias?" Gus replied "Yeah, sure, it's *normal*, because there is passion [*gairah*]." Then I pointed to Made, who was embracing Danny at the other bench, and asked "would you like a man like that, who isn't made up?" Gus shrugged and said "No, no thank you! I couldn't do that, because there is no passion to have sex with someone like that." Gus' reaction, like that of the youth in Kediri, was not homophobic. His desire for warias was not paired with an emotional repugnance towards *gay* men; he was not offended by Made and

Danny, and did not find my question insulting. Examples like these are infinitely more representative of contemporary Indonesian society than the Kaliurang incident: for an Indonesian man to attack another man because that other man expresses sexual interest in him, or because effeminate men appear in public, has been rare indeed.

The emergence of political homophobia indicates how the public presentation of male homosexuality and transgenderism can now occasion malu even if one does not participate oneself, because in the post-Soeharto era, masculinity is nationalized in a new way. With the nation under perceived threats of disintegration, attempts by non-normative men to access civil society can appear to threaten the nation itself While both *gay* homosexuality and waria transvestitism figure in this calculus, recall that waria are a publicly recognized social category. As Peter Jackson notes in the case of Thailand, under such a discursive regime male homosexuality can represent more of a danger than transgenderism, since it is more difficult to fit within a heterosexist logic where those who desire men must be effeminate (1999: 238). Male homosexuality is also more threatening than transvestitism due to the widespread Southeast Asian assumption that inner states should match exterior bodily presentations (Errington 1989: 76). Warias, who identify themselves as men with women's souls, properly display this inner mismatch in their cross-dressing. In contrast, gay men have a different kind of desire than normative men (they "desire the same"), but this inner deviation is not exteriorized; some are effeminate, but most are indistinguishable from *normal* men. The cultural expectation that exterior presentation should match inner state or belief has been politicized before; during the Soeharto years one of the most successful ways to create fear

---

17. These passages raise an important and thought-provoking question. Boellstorff's writing is interesting and rich. However, anthropology must consider the extent to which anecdotes are evidence, and this is not a simple question. Boellstorff's experience is that Indonesian men do not have strong emotional reactions to homosexual behavior, and he provides a series of stories and one or two quotes from interviews to support this contention. However, it is also true that in a 2020 survey, only 9 percent of Indonesians say that homosexuality should be accepted by society. This compares with 72 percent in the United States and 73 percent in the Philippines (Pew June 25, https://www.pewresearch.org/global/2020/06/25/global-divide-on-homosexuality-persists).

of a by-then nonexistent communist movement was to describe it as an "organization without shape" [*organisasi tanpa bentuk*]; that is, a collectivity whose exterior did not match its interior, just as it was supposed that individual communists were failing to exteriorize their political beliefs. With their difficult-to-read desires, *gay* men can be interpreted as a kind of masculinity *tanpa bentuk*—not when they make sexual propositions to other men in private, but when they appear to stake a public claim to civil society; that is, when they appear political. It may be for this reason that *gay* men have been the primary target of political homophobia, while warias and *lesbi* women have been attacked to date only by virtue of their association with *gay* men.[18]

CONCLUSION: THE EMERGENCE OF POLITICAL HOMOPHOBIA

It is in the Indonesian context, where heterosexism has predominated over homophobia, that the recent attacks gain such significance. For the Muslim youths involved in these attacks, the public presence of non-normative genders and sexualities became interpreted in phobic terms, as a psychic threat to proper masculinity. This made violence not only thinkable but sensible as an emotional "gut reaction" to what was now interpreted as an assault on the nation's manhood. We see a shift from an intellectual assumption, rarely voiced because taken for granted, that all Indonesians should marry heterosexually, to an emotional assumption, carried out with knives and clubs, that non-normative men threaten the nation's future. I term this a shift from everyday heterosexism to political homophobia, and the character of this emotional rage shows us that the nation envisioned by these attackers is normatively male. While all homophobia has political effects, the notion of "political homophobia" is useful for highlighting violence deployed as a means of controlling who can make claims to belonging. The violence of the Kaliurang and Solo incidents was directed at demands for inclusion in a new public sphere and not at the mundane romances and seductions of everyday life.[9, 19]

Alarmism is not the goal of this analysis, and I do not mean to suggest that political homophobia will become an everyday occurrence in Indonesia. There has been an increasing presence of *gay* men in Indonesian public culture, as illustrated by the 2004 hit movie *Arisan!*, which included a subplot concerning a *gay* man and featured two scenes of *gay* men kissing each other. However, the linkage between emotion and violence that these events have set in motion does not hinge on repetition. A single incident can have sustained emotional consequences for its intended indirect object; we see this in the World Trade Center attacks and the 1992 destruction of the Babri Mosque in India. Indeed, the Kaliurang and Solo incidents continue to affect gay Indonesians. We see this most clearly in Yogyakarta (near Kaliurang), an important center of *gay* community and publishing since the early 1980s; following

---

18. Here Boellstorff asserts that a critical source of political *malu* is a perception of the threat posed to the nation and that this threat is exacerbated by a deep Indonesian belief that people's outside states should reflect their internal realities. Thus, he argues that there should be less hostility to warias than to gay men.

It's worth stopping to wonder if there is a bit less to this than Boellstorff argues. From European antisemitism, the Red Scare accusations of Senator McCarthy in the 1950s, to the accusations of witchcraft that E. E. Evans-Pritchard documented among the Azande in the 1930s, the idea of a hidden enemy has often been a way to mobilize politics. People don't need profound beliefs about interior and exterior states to be moved to violence against those they perceive as different. It's also worth noting that there have been many attacks against warias in the past decade in Indonesia.

19. In the conclusion, Boellstorff returns us (indirectly) to the issues of hegemony and discourse. The issue, he argues, is not really who does what to whom in bed. Rather, it is the nature of Indonesian state ideology and what being properly Indonesian means. Because this is a public issue, the public claims of Indonesia's gay community are ultimately far more important than the physical actions and attractions of individual Indonesians.

the Kaliurang incident, *gay* organizations in that city ceased meeting and *gay* publications ceased production, beginning again only around mid-2003. A book launch held by Dédé Oetomo at a Muslim university in Yogyakarta in early November 2001 for a volume of his writings on homosexuality and Indonesian society took place without incident, but a second event to be held at a local bookstore was interrupted by the police, who prevented the event from taking place on the pretext that it would disturb public security.[r] More broadly, intermittent attacks on warias and gay men, including assaults on gay men in public places and incidents where waria are assaulted and their hair forcibly cut, have occurred in several parts of Indonesia, including Aceh, Bali and Java.[s] In 2004 a group of Muslim-identified youth arrived at the end of an event held near the city of Solo by the racy tabloid *X-Pos* to thank their *gay* readers; upon arriving they burned all the copies of the tabloid they could find, as the *gay* men present hid in their hotel rooms or fled the scene. Thus, while on the whole, there is little evidence that everyday homophobia is in on the rise, it remains an open question as to whether or not the increasing visibility of *gay* men will co-occur with greater violence (Oetomo 2001).[20]

Perhaps the most urgent question is how political homophobia will shape struggles over Indonesia's emerging post-Soeharto civil society. Historically *gay* men and warias have appeared only rarely in the political sphere either as topic of discussion or trope. When the latter has occurred, it has usually been to speak metaphorically of persons who change their opinions (like warias change their gender presentation). For instance, in a 1999 volume of essays concerned with demonstrating that Islam is incompatible with political violence (*kekerasan politik*), Abdurrahman Wahid—noted Muslim intellectual and recently President of Indonesia—spoke metaphorically of intellectuals changing their opinions as changing their sex, jokingly admonishing them not to become warias (Wahid 1999: 182).

Compare this with the situation two years later, when the populist and often anti-American newspaper *Rakyat Merdeka* (published from Jakarta) ran a front-page headline concerning U.S.-led attacks on the Taliban with the title *Amerika Bencong!*[t] (Bencong is a variant of banci (waria).) The headline was accompanied by a photograph of President George W. Bush doctored to include lipstick, earrings, and a leather jacket (Fig. 2). Here non-normative men stand not for shifting intellectual views but a compromised nation. The article claimed that the United States was a *béncong* because rather than challenging Osama bin Laden to a one-on-one duel, Bush had the audacity (*berani*) to invite its allies to attack Afghanistan *en masse* in search for him. In other words, the United States had no malu, no sense of vulnerability in interaction, and thus felt a rage—a sense of invulnerability in action—that compelled it to enroll others to join in amok violence. The United States is presented as operating under a nationalized intersection of manhood and emotion. It is the dynamic of the Kaliurang and Solo incidents, displaced into the figure of the non-normative male. Under a cultural logic of political homophobia, Bush-in-drag—representing a nation's failed masculinity—appears both violent and a proper target for violence. [Fig 2 (not included in this

---

20. Boellstorff here argues that a few highly repressive actions can have a profound effect. There are two points to be made here. First, this is the nature of hegemony. Analysts who focus on ideology note that, in any society, most people are obedient to the social order. A police state in which everyone is under surveillance and suffers immediate and direct consequences from violations of the norms of behavior, is unwieldy and expensive to operate (though China does seem to actually be trying). However, a hegemonic ideology and an occasional act of repression are almost as effective. Second, Boellstorff might well have been a bit more alarmist. Acts of direct repression against the LGBT community in Indonesia have steadily increased. This has included moves to ban depictions of LGBT people on TV and in other media. Indonesia's current president Joko Widodo (Jokowi) has been largely silent in the face of the increasing oppression of LGBT people and, in 2018 chose Ma'ruf Amin (b. 1943) a hard-line Islamic cleric as a running mate. In May 2019, Jokowi won a second term.

edition) has been described by Boellstorff in the paragraph above. Its caption reads: "From 'Rakyat Merdeka' newspaper, Oct. 7, 2001 issue. George W. Bush as emotional transvestite."] My hypothesis is that political homophobia may make this image intelligible to the Indonesian public regardless of religion. In place of national masculinity as benevolent and paternal (however violent in actual practice), we find it embattled, in danger of losing its very manhood. It is thus called upon to deflect this shame in a properly masculine manner, by violently striking down any representation of itself by homosexual, effeminate, or transvestite men. As Indonesia struggles through a period of tense uncertainty, anthropological attention to the public face of emotion and the heterosexist gendering of national belonging can contribute to a better understanding of how violence is not the "primordialist" suspicion of culture, but the working out of cultural logics of inequality and exclusion to their horrific but comprehensible conclusion.[21]

ACKNOWLEDGMENTS

Research was funded by the Social Science Research Council, the National Science Foundation, the Morrison Institute for Population Studies at Stanford University, and the Department of Cultural and Social Anthropology of Stanford University. This paper was largely written under the auspices of a Postdoctoral Fellowship in Southeast Asian Studies in the Department of Anthropology, Research School of Pacific and Asian Studies, at the Australian National University. I thank these institutions for their support. Helpful comments were provided by Edward Aspinall, Lena Avonius, John Ballard, Shelly Errington, Byron Good, Karl Heider, Andrew Kipnis, Johan Lindquist, Francesca Merlan, Bill Maurer, Dede Oetomo, Wilhelm Ostberg, Kathryn Robinson, Rupert Stasch, and the anonymous reviewers for Ethnos. A special thanks to Joshua Barker for his insightful commentary. All italicized terms are in Indonesian unless noted otherwise.

---

21. Boellstorff concludes that, since the fall of the Suharto regime in 1998, some young, heterosexist Muslim men perceive the public organization of people with non-normative gender expression as a threat to proper masculinity, and hence to the nation. They met this threat with political homophobia, and attacks on public events that support non-normative sexual and gender expression.

During the first and second decades of the twenty-first century, in the United States, there have been long-running political conflicts between supporters of gay rights and religious and cultural conservatives who argued that giving members of the LGBTQ community the same legal rights as heterosexuals endangered the nation. Although these debates encouraged conservative voters to go to the polls, and there have been many individual acts of violence against gay men and women, there have been no organized gangs of young conservative men attacking conferences of gay scholars or pride rallies as happened in Indonesia. However, some of the same tendencies that animated violence among Indonesian men were also visible among American conservatives. For example, during the lead-up to the 2007 elections, conservative commentators repeatedly charged that Obama was insufficiently masculine: Tucker Carlson 7/12/2007: "Well everyone knows that a book club is no place for a man. So why has Barak Obama suddenly turned into Oprah?" Joe Scarborough on Obama bowling 34/31/2008: "Oh, that's so dainty. Ugh." Don Imus 4/17/2008, comparing Obama to Hillary Clinton "And he's almost a bigger pussy than she is." Monica Crowley (*McLaughlin Group*) 5/17/2008: "He is way too much of a girly man to be president of the United States." Gender-based attacks on Obama have continued after his presidency. For example, a 2017 headline on the Neo-Nazi website Daily Stormer said: "Barak Obama is a Cocaine Sniffing Faggot" (Rogers [stormer author] 2017). According to David Frum, a former speech writer for George W. Bush, a large part of the audience for Fox News commentator Greg Gutfield (b. 1964) believes that "Obama *is* gay, that his marriage is a sham, and that Mrs. Obama leads a life of Marie Antoinette-like extravagance to compensate for her husband's neglect while he disports himself with his personal aides" (in Gabler 2012). Neil Gabler (2012) notes that gay-baiting has been a basic tactic of the Republican Party for generations. In the past few years, laws passed restricting LGBT+ medical treatment, school participation, bathroom use, speech, and books in states controlled by conservative legislatures have led to political refugees fleeing persecution in these states for other states (and in some cases, countries) that support their rights.

POSTSCRIPT, May 2019

[Because this essay deals so explicitly with current events and politics, and because there has been so much political change in Indonesia since its publication, we asked Professor Boellstorff to comment on events since the original publication of this essay]

In my view, to have one's work carried forth into new debates represents the greatest compliment that can be paid to a scholar. In that regard the inclusion of "The Emergence of Political Homophobia in Indonesia" in this volume on anthropological theory is an honor for which I am deeply thankful.

I am also of the view that scholarly work is situated in place and time; its value to future research is predicated, not stymied, by that contextual specificity. In that spirit "The Emergence of Political Homophobia in Indonesia" appears here in its original form. This postscript recounts the milieu in which the essay was written, and how it has linked up with further work, including work of my own. I also reflect on three ways in which this essay's argument might be useful in the 2020s and beyond.

I began work on what would become "The Emergence of Political Homophobia in Indonesia" in 2000, the year I received my PhD. Teaching in California and drafting early versions of *The Gay Archipelago* (Boellstorff 2005), I was in email contact with colleagues in Indonesia and was aware of unprecedented (at that point) attacks against *gay* men when holding quasi-public events. Parallel to working through my dissertation fieldwork materials, I started writing on the question of homophobia and violence. This led to conversations with a number of colleagues, including Johan Lindquist: our collaboration developed to the point that we coedited a special issue of the journal *Ethnos*, "Bodies of Emotion," in which this essay first appeared. In our introduction to that special issue, we emphasized:

The ultimate goal of this volume is to further develop analyses that treat emotion as cultural—and culturally specific—without ontologizing either the individual or social. It is to recognize that the dogged persistence of the individual/social binarism, despite longstanding and creative efforts to deconstruct it, is more than an intellectual fillip. It reveals deeply held assumptions (and not just Western ones) about the relationship between embodied versus transpersonal modes of being. (Boellstorff and Lindquist 2004: 438)

This core question of the individual/social binarism animates this essay's analytical distinction between heterosexism and homophobia.

It has been rewarding to see "The Emergence of Political Homophobia in Indonesia" brought into a number of debates and placed in conversation with new field sites (e.g., Currier 2010). There is value in analytical distinctions like that between heterosexism and homophobia. All languages need synonyms, but conceptual specificity can be crucial for theoretical work. My own conclusion while writing this essay was that conflating "homophobia" and "heterosexism" limits our ability to address key issues like selfhood, motivation, emotion, and collectivity as they impact society and politics.

For less happy reasons, this essay represents the first of a tetralogy of essays of my own (Boellstorff 2014, 2016, forthcoming). The acts of violence described in "The Emergence of Political Homophobia in Indonesia" were novel at the time—and that novelty must be emphasized, lest it be naturalized as having existed since time immemorial. But novelty has not resulted in cessation. Instead, these forms of violence have reappeared every few years since September 1999. In January 2016, they took on a horrific new form, truly unprecedented in that they have been sanctioned by the state and placed at the center of debates regarding Indonesia's national identity and societal future. The demonizing, scapegoating, and cruel rejection of what we can now term "LGBT Indonesians" has already resulted in massive oppression and discrimination. At the time I write this dynamic continues, as exemplified in the elevation of the virulently anti-LGBT Ma'ruf Amin to the Vice-Presidency in the 2019 election.

Sadly, then, one way in which this essay may be useful is in responding to an Indonesian context wherein LGBT citizens have become central to debates over national identity. A second resonance of this essay is with regard to questions of emotion and social action. Given the context of this collection, a third way to engage with this essay is with regard to anthropological theory generally. Despite some attempts to contain it within specific field sites, anthropological analysis can (and should) speak to wider debates. Overgeneralization and false comparison are to be avoided, but generalization and comparison done right extend ethnographic inquiry and place anthropological theory into interdisciplinary conversations and broader publics. I hope "The Emergence of Political Homophobia in Indonesia" will continue to participate in such debates, and contribute to the continuing relevance of anthropology to our shared human journey.

REFERENCES

Alisjahbana, Sutan Takdir. 1966. *Indonesia: Social and Cultural Revolution*. Kuala Lumpur: Oxford University Press.

Anderson, Benedict. 1983. *Imagined Communities: Reflections On the Origins and Spread of Nationalism*. London: Verso.

Anderson, Benedict R. O'G.(ed.). 2001. *Violence and the State in Suharto's Indonesia*. Ithaca: Southeast Asia Program Publications, Cornell University.

Aripurnami, Sita. 1996. "A Feminist Comment on the Sinetron Presentation of Indonesian Women." In *Fantasizing the Feminine in Indonesia*, ed. Laurie Sears. Durham: Duke University Press.

Barker, Joshua. 1998. "State of Fear: Controlling the Criminal Contagion in Suharto's New Order." *Indonesia* 66: 7–44.

Berman, Laine. 2000. "Surviving on the Streets of Java: Homeless Children's Narratives of Violence." *Discourse and Society* 11(2): 149–174.

Blackwood, Evelyn. 1995. "Senior Women, Model Mothers, and Dutiful Wives: Managing Gender Contradictions in a Minangkabau Village." In *Bewitching Women, Pious Men: Gender and Body Politics in Southeast Asia*, ed. Aihwa Ong & Michael G. Peletz. Berkeley: University of California Press.

Boellstorff, Tom. 2002. "Ethnolocality." *Asia Pacific Journal of Anthropology* 3(I): 24–48.

———. 2003. "Dubbing Culture: Indonesian Gay and Lesbi Subjectivities and Ethnography in an Already Globalized World." *American Ethnologist* 30(2): 225–242.

———. 2004a. "Zines and Zones of Desire: Mass Mediated Love, National Romance, and Sexual Citizenship in Gay Indonesia." *Journal of Asian Studies* 63(2): 367–402.

———. 2004b. "Playing Back the Nation: Waria, Indonesian Transvestites." *Cultural Anthropology* 19(2): 159–195.

———. 2005. *The Gay Archipelago: Sexuality and Nation in Indonesia*. Princeton: Princeton University Press.

———. 2014. "Lessons from the Notion of 'Moral Terrorism.'" In *Feelings at the Margins: Dealing with Violence, Stigma, and Isolation in Indonesia*, ed. Thomas Stodulka and Birgitt Röttger-Rössler, pp. 148–158. Frankfurt: Campus Verlag.

———. 2016. Against State Straightism: Five Principles for Including LGBT Indonesians. *E-International Relations*. https://www.e-ir.info/2016/03/21/against-state-straightism-five-principles-for-including-lgbt-indonesians.

———. Forthcoming. *Om Toleran Om*: Four Indonesian Reflections on Digital Heterosexism. *Media, Culture, and Society*.

Boellstorff, Tom, Johan Lindquist. 2004. "Bodies of Emotion: Rethinking Culture and Emotion through Southeast Asia." *Ethnos* 69(4): 437–444. https://doi.org/10.1080/0014184042000302290.

Brenner, Suzanne. 1998. *The Domestication of Desire: Women, Wealth, and Modernity in Java*. Princeton: Princeton University Press.

———. 1999. "On the Public Intimacy of the New Order: Images of Women in the Popular Indonesian Print Media." *Indonesia* 67: 13–37.

Butler, Judith. 1990. *Gender Trouble*. New York: Routledge.

Butt, L. 2001. "KB Kills: Political Violence, Birth Control, and the Baliem Valley Dani." *Asia Pacific Journal of Anthropology* 2(1): 63–86.

Collins, Elizabeth and Ernaldi Bahar. 2000. "To Know Shame: Malu and Its Uses in Malay Society." *Crossroads: An interdisciplinary Journal of Southeast Asian Studies*, 14(1): 35–69.

Currier, Ashley. 2010. "Political Homophobia in Postcolonial Namibia." *Gender and Society* 24(1): 110–129. doi:10.1177/0891243209354275.

Errington, Shelly. 1989. *Meaning and Power in a Southeast Asian Realm*. Princeton: Princeton University Press.

Floyd, Kory. 2000. "Affectionate Same-sex Touch: The Influence of Homophobia on Observers' Perceptions." *Journal of Social Psychology* 140(6): 774–788.

Geertz, Clifford. 1960. *The Religion of Java*. Glencoe, IL: Free Press.

———. 1973. "Person, Time and Conduct in Bali." *The Interpretation of Cultures*. New York: Basic Books.

———. 1980. *Negara: The Theatre State in Nineteenth-Century Bali*. Princeton: Princeton University Press.

George, Kenneth M. 1996. *Showing Signs if Violence: The Cultural Politics of a Twentieth-Century Headhunting Ritual*. Berkeley: University of California Press.

Hansen, Thomas B. 1996. "Recuperating Masculinity: Hindu Nationalism, Violence and the Exorcism of the Muslim 'Other.'" *Critique of Anthropology* 16(2): 137–172.

Hatley, Barbara. 1997. "Nation, 'Tradition,' and Constructions of the Feminine in Modern Indonesian Literature." In *Imagining Indonesia: Cultural Politics and Political Culture*, ed. Jim Schiller and Barbara Martin-Schiller. Athens: Ohio University Press.

Hefner, Robert W. 2000. *Civil Islam*. Princeton: Princeton University Press.

Idrus, Ilmi. 2001. "Marriage, Sex, and Violence." In *Love, Sex, and Power: Women in Southeast Asia*, ed. Susan Blackburn. Clayton, Australia: Monash Asia Institute.

Jackson, Peter A. 1999. "Tolerant but Unaccepting: The Myth of a Thai 'Gay Paradise.'" In *Genders and Sexualities in Modern Thailand*, ed. Peter A. Jackson & Nerida M. Cook. Chaing Mai: Silkworm Books.

Keeler, Ward. 1983. "Shame and Stage Fright in Java." *Ethos* 11(3): 152–165.

Lawrence, Bruce B. 1998. *Shattering the Myth: Islam Beyond Violence*. Princeton: Princeton University Press.

Nagengast, Carole. 1994. "Violence, Terror, and the Crisis of the State." *Annual Review of Anthropology* 23: 109–136.

Oetomo, Dede. 2001. "Gay Men in the Reformasi Era: Homophobic Violence Could be a By-product of the New Openness." *Inside Indonesia* 66 (https://www.insideindonesia.org, accessed May 17, 2004).

Peacock, James L. 1968. *Rites of Modernization: Symbolic and Soda! Aspects of Indonesian Proletarian Drama*. Chicago: University of Chicago Press.

Pemberton, John. 1994. *On the Subject of "Java."* Ithaca: Cornell University Press.

Rafael, Vicente L. (ed.) 1999. *Figures of Criminality in Indonesia, the Philippines, and Colonial Vietnam*. Ithaca: Cornell Southeast Asia Program.

Riches, David. 1986. The Phenomenon of Violence. In his edited *The Anthropology of Violence*. Oxford: Basil Blackwell.

Robinson, Geoffrey. 1995. *The Dark Side of Paradise: Political Violence in Bali*. Ithaca: Cornell University Press.

Robinson, Kathryn. 1989. "Choosing Contraception: Cultural Change and the Indonesian Family Planning Programme." In *Creating Indonesian Cultures*, ed. Paul Alexander. Sydney: Oceania Publications.

Rodgers, Susan (ed.). 1995. *Telling Lives, Telling History: Autobiography and Historical Imagination in Modem Indonesia*. Berkeley: University of California Press.

Sen, Krisna. 1998. "Indonesian Women at Work: Reframing the Subject." In *Gender and Power in Affluent Asia*, ed. Krishna Sen and Maila Stivens. London: Routledge.

Siegel, James. 1997, *Fetish, Recognition, Revolution*. Princeton: Princeton University Press.

———. 1998. *A New Criminal Type in Jakarta: Counter-Revolution Today*. Durham: Duke University Press.

Stasch, Rupert. 2001. "Giving Up Homicide: Korowai Experience of Witches and Police (West Papua)." *Oceania* 72: 33–52.

Steedly, Mary Margaret. 1999. "The State of Culture Theory in the Anthropology of Southeast Asia." *Annual Review of Anthropology* 28: 431–454.

Stoler, Ann Laura. 1995. *Race and the Education of Desire: Foucault's History of Sexuality and the Colonial Order of Things*. Durham: Duke University Press.

Suryakusuma, Julia I. 1996. "The State and Sexuality in New Order Indonesia." In *Fantasizing the Feminine in Indonesia*, ed. Laurie Sears. Durham: Duke University Press.

Szymanski, Dawn M., Barry Chung, and Kimberley F. Balsam. 2001. "Psychosocial Correlates of Internalized Homophobia in Lesbians." *Measurement and Evaluation in Counseling and Development* 34(1): 27–38.

Tiwon, Sylvia. 1996. "Models and Maniacs: Articulating the Female in Indonesia." In *Fantasizing the Feminine in Indonesia*, ed. Laurie Sears. Durham: Duke University Press.

Tsing, Anna Lowenhaupt. 1993. *In the Realm of the Diamond Queen: Marginality in an Out-of-the-way Place*. Princeton: Princeton University Press.

Wahid, Abdurrahman. 1999. *Tuhan Tidak Perlu Dibela* [God Does not Need to be Defended]. Yogyakarta: LKiS Yogyakarta.

Wessel, Ingrid and Georgia Wimhofer (eds.). 2001. *Violence in Indonesia*. Hamburg: Abera.

Wright, L., H. Adams, and J. Bernat. 1999. "Development and Validation of the Homophobia Scale." *Journal of Psychopathology and Behavioral Assessment* 21(4): 337–347.

Wickberg, Daniel. 2000. "Homophobia: On the Cultural History of an Idea." *Critical Inquiry* 27: 42–57.

AUTHOR'S NOTES

a. Of these terms, banci is the best known, but is somewhat derogatory; I use the preferred term waria (an amalgam of wanita ("woman") and pria ("man"). I italicize the term gay throughout to distinguish it from the English term "gay," to which gay is related but distinct. For consistency I italicize lesbi as well. Data on the Kaliurang incident is compiled from PlanetOut.com, 11/13/00 and 11/14/00, Detik.com 11/13/00, Kompas 11/12/00 and 11/14/00, GAYa Nusantara #77, Oetomo 2001, and direct testimony from witnesses.

b. According to witnesses, some of the motorcycles driven by the attackers also had stickers from the Muslim United Development Party or the Anti-Vice Movement (Gerakan Anti Maksiat or GAM) (Detik.com,

November 14, 2000). The Ka'bah is the holy shrine at the center of the Great Mosque of Mecca.

c. The statement was allegedly in Javanese (*lanang kok dandan wedok, banci metu*; in Indonesian this would be laki-laki kok dandan perempuan, banci keluar) (Dettik.com, November 14, 2000).

d. Detik.com, November 13, 2000.

e. GAYa Nusantara, 77: 16–17, 23.

f. While *lesbi* women groups and correspondents participate in this network, it is dominated by gay men.

g. Because of difficulties with attendance, this Congress was renamed a National Working Meeting (*Rapat Kerja Nasional*, shortened to *Rakernas*), and scheduled for September 10–11 so as to coincide with *September Cena* ("Joyous September") a large gay event held annually near the city of Solo (Central Java).

h. Two leaders of the groups, Hasan Mulachela and Boyamin, stated that "as citizens of Solo we cannot accept these practices a la Sodom and Gomorrah to take place in Solo. If the Lesbian and Gay National Meeting takes place in Solo that would publicize those practices" (*Kompas*, September 11, 1999). Mulachela also threatened to bring out "thousands of the Islamic community" to force the Congress to be cancelled (*Bernas*, September 11, 1999; Mulachela is also a member of the Pembaruan DPRD party fraction).

i. Many *gay* (also *lesbi* and *waria*) Indonesians who know of these two incidents see them as watershed moments when, for the first time, non-normative masculinity became the target of publicly articulated hatred and physical assault.

j. In a 1994 review article, Carol Nagengast noted that "[u]ntil relatively recently, few anthropologists examined violence and conflict between groups and the state and among groups within states" (Nagengast 1994: 110). Nagengast identified anthropology's focus on ostensibly self-contained communities at the expense of the nation as one reason for this lack of attention to violence outside domains of custom and tradition (112; see also Riches 1986). Also in 1994, John Pemberton presented anthropology with the image of Javanese peasants shoving each other aside over pieces of a cooked chicken in a *rebutan* or "struggle" (Pemberton 1994: 18, 213). By counterpoising this vignette to Geertz's use of the tranquil *selamatan* feast as master metaphor for Javanese culture (Geertz 1960),

Pemberton indexed the growing number of ethnographically-informed studies of violence in Indonesian societies (e.g., George 1996; Robinson 1995; Siegel 1998; Tsing 1993). More recently, scholars of Indonesia have responded to new and resurgent forms of violence following Soeharto's fall (e.g., Anderson 2001; Barker 1998; Rafael 1999; Stasch 2001; Wessel & Wimhofer 2001). Some of this scholarship provides insights on everyday violence, including domestic violence and its linkages to state violence (Berman 2000; Butt 2001; Idrus 2001). The primary emphasis, however, has been on `political violence.'

k. I am grateful to Joshua Barker for this turn of phrase, which originates in his insightful commentary on an earlier version of this paper, given at the 2001 meetings of the American Anthropological Association.

l. See, inter alia, Aripurnami 1996; Blackwood 1995; Brenner 1998, 1999; Hatley 1997; Robinson 1989; Sen 1998; Tiwon 1996.

m. It is therefore not surprising that *tomboi* call themselves *hunter* in some regions of Indonesia, particularly south Sulawesi. They use this term because they "hunt" feminine women as potential partners; they consider the act of initiating contact masculine.

n. Ann Stoler notes her own "long-term and failed efforts" to find any significant discussion of homosexuality in the colonial Dutch East Indies (Stoler 1995: 129).

o. See Oetomo 2001; "In Indonesia, Once Tolerant Islam Grows Rigid," New York Times, December 29, 2001.

p. See, for instance, the coverage of the incident in *Forum Keadilan* No. 3 (Year IV), May 25, 1995, pp. 12–20. Since most gay men marry women, Ave's bachelor status at 51 years of age was noteworthy.

q. This new political homophobia in Indonesia is thus quite different from (though not entirely unrelated to) the arrest and conviction in Malaysia of Anwar Ibrahim, former Deputy Prime Minister, on charges of sodomy and corruption.

r. Dédé Oetomo, personal communication.

s. For an example, see *Serambi Indonesia*, June 29, 1999. My thanks to Dédé Oetomo and Edward Aspinall for respectively bringing the Bali and Aceh incidents to my attention.

t. I thank Karl Heider for bringing this article to my attention.

Agency and Structure

Two extremely popular quotes are attributed to Margaret Mead: "Never doubt that a small group of thoughtful committed citizens can change the world. Indeed it is the only thing that ever has"; and "Always remember that you are absolutely unique. Just like everyone else." It saddens us to report that, although these lines are consistent with some of Mead's ideas, there are no specific sources for them or evidence that she ever actually said them. They appeared in print only after Mead's death. This is a good, if ironic, commentary on the position of anthropology with respect to the relationship of the individual to society.

In the late nineteenth and early twentieth centuries, European scholars such as Émile Durkheim specifically rejected the importance of the individual in social analysis. They preferred instead to focus on describing social roles and searching for social rules. For Durkheim, the study of the individual was the domain of psychology. Sociology (and anthropology) was to be concerned only with "social facts" and forces that cannot be reduced to individual actions or choices.

In the United States, perhaps because of broader social concerns, rejecting the role of the individual in culture was more problematic. Franz Boas argued that individuals could make a difference in society. Some of his students, such as Paul Radin (1883–1959), focused their studies on individuals (but took them to stand for their entire societies). Other Boas students, such as A. L. Kroeber, entirely dismissed the role of the individual. Leslie White argued that even the most famous people had no more influence than "a sack of sawdust" (1948: 113). These opposing viewpoints led to a contradiction at the core of much of American anthropology. On one hand, many anthropologists took bold political and social positions, usually opposing discrimination and violence. They clearly believed that their choices and actions mattered. On the other hand, ethnography and anthropological theory tended to minimize the role of the individual. For example, there is little scope for individual action in the neomaterialist or symbolic anthropological theories of the 1960s and 1970s.

However, beginning in the 1980s, anthropologists and sociologists began to reconsider the relationship of the individual and society. Just as an anthropology that ignored the individual had its origins in European work, so too did this reevaluation of an individual's importance. For the American anthropologists featured in this section, concern with the role of the individual in society has numerous critical sources. These include the Italian Marxist Antonio Gramsci (1891–1937), the French deconstructionist Jacques Derrida (1930–2004), and particularly the French and British sociologists Pierre Bourdieu (1930–2002) and Anthony Giddens (b. 1938). The work of many of these scholars has been described in detail elsewhere in this book. We refer you to those discussions for more information. Here we want to describe specifically how their work relates to the question of individual action versus social structure.

Gramsci argued that the focus of Marxist analysis (and political action) needed to move toward ideology. He examined the ways in which the ruling elites created the ways of thinking and acting he referred to as *hegemony*. However, Gramsci also proposed that there were counter-hegemonic forces in society. Individuals, in particular, "organic intellectuals," individuals arising within the working class, could be the vanguard of the revolution. Gramsci wrote that each person "contributes to sustain a conception of the world or to modify it, that is, to bring into being new modes of thought" (1989: 116). Gramsci had a profound influence on the work of the French Marxist Louis Althusser (1918–1990) (described in the introduction to "French Social Thought: Postmodernism and Practice"). Althusser proposed that there were numerous "ideological state apparatuses," such as schools, the media, trade unions, and churches. These promoted the hegemonic ideology of the elites but did not speak with a single voice. Rather, they promoted different versions of ideology, opening space for conflict among them and individual choice.

The work of Derrida and other proponents of literary deconstruction was also critical. They argued that meaning is constructed by insisting on the authority of certain interpretations and, at the same time, denying the validity of others. Deconstruction involved analyzing history and texts to expose the ways in which they were built and to recover the voices of those who had been silenced or whose history had been denied. One of the best-known examples of this work is James C. Scott's 1990 *Domination and the Arts of Resistance: Hidden Transcripts*. In this book, Scott explores the ways that oppressed peoples, such as slaves and prisoners, spoke their minds in the presence of oppressive power. Recognizing these forms of resistance is critical to ideas of individual agency, because if such subaltern people are simply filling social roles and obeying laws, their actions of resistance are rendered meaningless. Thus, a concern with individual actions dovetails nicely with the ideas of postmodern analysis that became popular in anthropology in the 1980s and 1990s.

Much writing on the relationship between agency and social structure is incorporated under the phrase *practice theory*. Perhaps the most direct source of work on practice theory is found in the writings of Bourdieu, Giddens, and Sherry Ortner (b. 1941), whose "Power and Projects: Reflections on Agency" is reprinted in essay 36 in this section. The main focus of practice theory is analyzing the relationship between structures of culture, such as class, family, and religion, and the way that people act within and upon those structures. A foundational assumption of practice theory is that there is a dynamic relationship between people and social structure.

Bourdieu was very influential in the development of practice theory. His two books *Outline of a Theory of Practice* (1977) and *The Logic of Practice* (1990) explained and elaborated on some of the fundamental concepts in practice theory. Bourdieu's ideas have been extensively described in essay 27. His focus on *habitus* combined a social-cultural framing for individual action with the acknowledgment that individual behavior is not simply the expression of their social group (class, ethnicity, and so on) but is also dependent on idiosyncratic individual life experience. Bourdieu recognized that individual lives are not reducible to their position in society and that the ways in which people experience their lives are critical to the reproduction of society.

British sociologist Anthony Giddens emphasized the interactive link between individual experience and social reproduction. Giddens has been extraordinarily prolific, writing on topics as diverse as postmodernity, globalization, and sexuality in modern societies. However, his theory of structuration is deeply concerned with the relationship of individual actions to the reproduction of social structures. Giddens argues that high-level macro structures of society cannot be understood without focusing on the micro-level actions of people's daily lives. He refers to these connections as "duality of structure" and notes that this relates to "the *fundamentally recursive character of social life, and expresses the mutual dependence of structure and agency*" (1979: 69, emphasis in the original). Social structure shapes individual action, but it can only be reproduced by the repetitive acts of living people. Thus, when people choose to ignore traditions or moral codes, or to change them, social structure changes (Gauntlett 2002: 102). This in turn further shapes individual actions.

The authors in this section provide different approaches to the problem of agency. Philippe Bourgois (b. 1956) received his PhD from Stanford University in 1980 and is currently a professor at the University of California, Los Angeles. Bourgois is well known for working in marginal communities in the United States. His early work analyzed labor and class relations in the banana industry on the border of Costa Rica and Panama. His second book, *In Search of Respect: Selling Crack in El Barrio*, was based on fieldwork among drug users in East Harlem in New York City. More recently, he has focused on homeless heroin addicts in San Francisco (*Righteous Dopefiend* [2009]) and police violence in Philadelphia (Karandinos et al. 2014). Bourgois has written extensively about subaltern populations and state violence.

In "From *Jíbaro* to Crack Dealer: Confronting the Restructuring of Capitalism in El Barrio" (essay 35), Bourgois draws on his fieldwork in East Harlem to explore the lives of second-generation Puerto Rican immigrants. In work strongly influenced by Gramsci and Althusser, Bourgois shows how the disappearance of working-class jobs in New York City has left these people with understandings and ideologies that are extremely ill adapted to jobs in the burgeoning service sector. In the 1970s, the British sociologist Paul Willis (b. 1945) showed how the culture of British education fitted working-class youths for factory jobs. Bourgois shows us one version of what might happen to those youths when their jobs disappear.

Ortner has been an important voice in anthropology since receiving her PhD from the University of Chicago in 1972. Her early work focused on symbolic anthropology and structuralism. Two of her essays from this era, "Is Female to Male as Nature Is to Culture?" (1972) and "On Key Symbols" (1973), are still widely read by graduate students in anthropology (the former is essay 21 in this book). In the 1980s, Ortner began to combine her interests in symbolic and interpretive anthropology with her reading of Bourdieu and Giddens. In "Anthropology since the 1960s," published in 1985, she surveyed developments in symbolic anthropology, cultural ecology, structuralism, and Marxist anthropology, concluding that the future direction of anthropology lay in studies that draw particularly from Marxist approaches but focus on issues of agency and structure.

Ortner has held academic positions at Sarah Lawrence College, the University of Michigan, and Columbia University. She is currently a professor of anthropology at the University of California, Los Angeles. Her fieldwork and research have focused on the Sherpas of Nepal (her books about them include *High Religion* [1989] and *Life and Death on Mt. Everest* [1999]), gender studies (*Sexual Meanings: The Cultural Construction of Gender and Sexuality* [1981] and *Making Gender: The Politics and Erotics of Culture* [1996]), her high school classmates (*New Jersey Dreaming: Capital, Culture, and the Class of '58* [2003]), and independent film directors and producers in New York and Los Angeles (*Not Hollywood: Independent Film at the Twilight of the American Dream* [2013]).

"Power and Projects: Reflections on Agency," featured here, is the final chapter of Ortner's 2006 book *Anthropology and Social Theory*. In this essay, she reflects on and analyzes the basic elements of practice theory. She particularly focuses on her own contributions to theory as well as those of Bourdieu, Giddens, and William H. Sewell Jr. (b. 1940). Ortner presents examples drawn from European fairy tales, Western evangelical missionaries and their Tswana converts in South Africa, and marriage choices among the Magar in Western Nepal to give readers an understanding of the meaning, scope, and limitations of ideas of agency and structure.

Our final selection (essay 37) is by Ruth Gomberg-Muñoz (b. 1975). Gomberg-Muñoz received her PhD from the University of Illinois, Chicago, where she worked with Alaka Wali, the founding director of the Center for Cultural Understanding and Change. She is currently assistant professor of anthropology at Loyola University, Chicago. In "Willing to Work: Agency and Vulnerability in an Undocumented Immigrant Network," Gomberg-Muñoz provides an extended ethnographic example of the meaning of agency and structure. She shows how structures like immigration policy, capitalist relations of production, and family dynamics are intertwined with the working styles and behavioral choices made by undocumented Mexican immigrant busboys working at Chicago-area restaurants. Gomberg-Muñoz's writing combines some of the traditional elements of anthropology, such as empathy for other people and a belief in the comprehensibility and dignity of those labeled as "other," with more recent concerns, such as ethnicity within the nation-state, class structure, gender, individual agency, and relations of power.

SUGGESTED READINGS

Bourdieu, Pierre. 1977. *Outline of a Theory of Practice*. Cambridge: Cambridge University Press.
  A difficult but rewarding discussion of Bourdieu's theory.
———. 1984. *Distinction: A Social Critique of the Judgement of Taste*. Cambridge, MA: Harvard University Press.
  Bourdieu's analysis of the way that taste and aesthetics are used and valued among members of the French bourgeoisie; an extended application of many of his ideas.

Bourgois, Philippe, and Jeffrey Schonberg. 2009. *Righteous Dopefiend*. Berkeley: University of California Press.
  Bourgois presents a moving and sympathetic portrait and analysis of homeless heroin addicts in San Francisco. The book is illustrated with powerful black-and-white images by photographer Schonberg.
Giddens, A. 1979. *Central Problems in Social Theory: Action, Structure and Contradiction in Social Analysis*. Berkeley: University of California Press.
  A collection of essays in which Giddens analyzes the roles of Marxist, interpretive, functionalist, and structuralist theories in sociology and presents his theory of structuration.
Ortner, Sherry. 1989. *High Religion: A Cultural and Political History of Sherpa Buddhism*. Princeton, NJ: Princeton University Press.
  Ortner provides an analysis of the history and practice of Buddhism among the Nepali Sherpas that is also an extended example of the use of practice theory in cultural analysis.
———. 2006. *Anthropology and Social Theory: Culture, Power, and the Acting Subject*. Durham, NC: Duke University Press.
  In this collection of essays, Ortner emphasizes agency and structure as she analyzes social class, race, and identity, as well as public culture and the media.
Willis, Paul. 1977. *Learning to Labor: How Working Class Kids Get Working Class Jobs*. New York: Columbia University Press.
  Willis's dark analysis of the British working class of the late 1960s and early 1970s focuses on the ways in which apparent rebellion leads to conformity.

35. From *Jíbaro* to Crack Dealer: Confronting the Restructuring of Capitalism in El Barrio

Philippe Bourgois (b. 1956)

FOLLOWING HIS YEAR and a half of field work in a rural coffee-growing country in the central highlands of Puerto Rico from 1948 through 1949, Eric R. Wolf warned that even the small farmers and coffee pickers in the most isolated and traditional rural barrio that he was studying "in the future will supply many hundreds of hands to the coast, to the towns, and to the United States" (Wolf 1956b, 231). Macroeconomic and political forces proved Wolf's warning to be an understatement. American industrial capital was provided with extraordinary incentives and local agricultural development in Puerto Rico atrophied at the same time that emigration to the factories of New York City was actively promoted. The ensuing exodus over the next three and a half decades of almost a third of Puerto Rico's total population resulted proportionally in one of the larger labor migrations in modern history.[1]

STRUCTURAL CONSTRAINTS OF THE NUYORICAN EXPERIENCE

The majority of the immigrants found employment in New York City's most vulnerable subsector of light manufacturing. They arrived precisely on the eve of the structural decimation of factory production in urban North America. Indeed, the post–World War II Puerto Rican experience provides almost a textbook illustration of what Wolf in his later work refers to as "the growth of ever more diverse proletarian diasporas" that "capitalist accumulation . . . continues to engender" as it spreads across the globe (1982a: 383). Perhaps most interesting and relevant for understanding Nuyorican ethnicity—that is, the experience of New York City-born and raised Puerto Ricans—are the contradictory ways that the "changing needs of capital . . . con-

---

From *Articulating Hidden Histories: Exploring the Influence of Eric R. Wolf* (1995)

1. This essay first appeared in *Articulating Hidden Histories* (Schneider and Rapp 1995), a collection of essays dedicated to exploring the legacy of Eric R. Wolf. Wolf is generally considered one of the most important Marxist-influenced anthropologists of the mid-twentieth century (see essay 31). He was particularly interested in the ways in which the expansion of capitalism has affected cultures throughout the world and explored this theme at length in his book *Europe and the People without History* (1982), a work widely considered a founding document of globalization theory. Globalization theory provides an intersection between capitalism, power, and meaning. Bourgois quotes freely from Wolf's work in the opening sections of this essay.

Here, Bourgois discusses how the economic opportunities for young working-class Puerto Rican men evaporated as the New York City economy changed in the 1980s. He shows how these young men attempt to negotiate their way through an unfamiliar cultural landscape in which they are ill-equipped to succeed. Bourgois's analysis illustrates the pressures and conflicts in an economic and social system subject to globalization. At the same time, he illustrates the ways in which people create and contest meaning.

tinuously produce and recreate symbolically marked 'cultural' distinctions" among "the new working classes" who have crisscrossed oceans and continents in their struggle for survival and dignity (Wolf 1982a: 379–380).[2]

Depending upon one's formal definition, over the past three or four generations, the Puerto Rican people—especially those living in New York—have passed through almost a half dozen distinct modes of production: (1) from small land-owning semi-subsistence peasantry or hacienda peons; (2) to export agricultural laborers on foreign-owned, capital-intensive plantations; (3) to factory workers in urban shantytowns; (4) to sweatshop workers in ghetto tenements; (5) to service sector employees in high-rise inner-city housing projects; (6) to underground economy entrepreneurs homeless on the street.[3]

This marathon sprint through economic history onto New York City's streets has been compounded ideologically by an overtly racist "cultural assault." Literally overnight the new immigrants—many of whom were enveloped in a *jíbaro* (hillbilly)-dominated culture emphasizing interpersonal webs of patriar-chal *respeto*—found themselves transformed into "racially" inferior cultural pariahs. Ever since their arrival they have been despised and humiliated with that virulence so characteristic of America's history of polarized race relations in the context of massive labor migrations. Even though the Puerto Rican experience is extreme, it is by no means unique. On the contrary, peoples all through the world and throughout history have been forced to traverse multiple modes of production and have suffered social dislocation.[4]

The historic structural transformations imposed upon the Puerto Rican *jíbaro* translate statistically into a tragic profile of unemployment, substance abuse, broken families, and devastated health in U.S. inner cities. No other ethnic group except perhaps Native Americans fares more poorly in the official statistics than do mainland U.S. Puerto Ricans. This is most pronounced for the majority cohort living in New York City where Puerto Ricans have the highest welfare dependency and poverty rates, the lowest labor force participation rates, and the fastest growing HIV infection rates of any group (Falcon 1992; Lambert 1990).

---

2. One of Wolf's key contentions is that the histories of oppressed peoples and minority groups are fundamental to understanding culture (Schneider and Rapp 1995: 7). Wolf sees such people as essential actors driving culture change—a theme he explores in *Peasant Wars of the Twentieth Century* (1969). Bourgois, by studying people from an impoverished neighborhood in New York City, is acting very much in the tradition of Wolf.

3. The *mode of production* is a fundamental Marxist concept. Briefly, a mode of production is a pattern that combines labor, the machines and raw materials that workers use, and the social and technical relations under which they use them (Suchting 1983: 76–77). Marx analyzed the history of Europe as a series of successive modes of production. His modes were Asiatic, ancient, feudal, and modern bourgeois (Lichtheim 1973: 151). In the first half of the twentieth century, Marxist scholars insisted that all societies could be characterized as belonging to one of these four modes. A critical innovation of the neo-Marxists scholars of the last third of the twentieth century was to expand the mode of production concept to include many societies that did not fit easily into Marx's original modes. This, however, tended to result in a great proliferation of new modes of production. Here Bourgois delineates a number of modes of production, none of which is found in the works of Marx, but each of which describes a pattern of labor, material, equipment, social, and technical relationships found in the modern world.

4. Note the polemical writing in this passage. Bourgois emphasizes the racist aspects of the immigrant experience, describing Puerto Rican immigrants as despised rather than welcomed. Bourgois believes that anthropologists have an obligation to analyze and publicize the violence and inequality underlying American society. In addition to working with crack dealers, Bourgois worked with homeless drug addicts in San Francisco (2009) and analyzed police violence in Philadelphia (2014).

Bourgois stresses that the Puerto Rican experience in New York City is not unique. The Boasian tradition in anthropology typically emphasized the unique characteristics of cultures. Marxists, on the other hand, tend to be more concerned with cultural similarities. Marxists claim that alienation and exploitation always lead to socio-political change.

THE ETHNOGRAPHIC SETTING

These contemporary expressions of historical dislocation formed the backdrop for my five years of participant-observation fieldwork on street culture in the "crack economy" during the late 1980s and early 1990s. For a total of approximately three and a half years I lived with my wife and young son in an irregularly heated, rat-filled tenement in East Harlem, better known locally as El Barrio or Spanish Harlem. This two-hundred-square-block neighborhood is visibly impoverished yet it is located in the heart of the richest city in the western hemisphere. Its vacant lots and crumbling abandoned tenements are literally a stone's throw from multimillion-dollar condominiums. Although one in three families survives on public assistance, the majority of El Barrio's 130,000 Puerto Rican and African American residents comprise the ranks of the "working poor." They eke out an uneasy subsistence in entry-level service and manufacturing jobs in a city with one of the highest costs of living in the world.[5]

In my ethnographic research, I explored the ideologies (i.e., the power-charged belief systems) that organize "common sense" on the street—what I call "street culture." Consequently, over the years, I interacted with and befriended the addicts, thieves, dealers, and con artists who comprise a minority proportion of El Barrio residents but who exercise hegemony over its public space. Specifically, I focused on a network of some twenty five street level crack dealers who operated on and around my block.

On the one hand, such an intensive examination of street participants risks exoticizing the neighborhood and may be interpreted as reinforcing violent stereotypes against Puerto Ricans. On the other hand, case studies of the "worthy poor" risk "normalizing" the experience of class and racial segregation and can mask the depths of human suffering that accompanies rapid economic restructuring. Furthermore, the legally employed majority of El Barrio residents has lost control of the streets and has retreated from daily life in the neighborhood. To understand the experience of living in the community, the ideologies of violence, opposition, and material pursuit which have established hegemony over street life— much to the dismay of most residents—have to be addressed systematically. Furthermore, on a subtle theoretical level, the "caricatural" responses to poverty and marginalization that the dealers and addicts represent provide privileged insight into processes that may be experienced in one form or another by major sectors of any vulnerable working-class population experiencing rapid structural change anywhere in the world and at any point in history. Once again, there is nothing structurally exceptional about the Puerto Rican experience except that the human costs involved are more clearly visible given the extent and rapidity with which Puerto Rican society has been absorbed by the United States and the particularly persistent virulence of American ideologies around "race" and culture.[6]

---

5. It is interesting to note that the economic changes that Bourgois discusses in this essay have accelerated over the past thirty years. Many of the neighborhoods Bourgois describes no longer exist. East Harlem is increasingly gentrified. In the first quarter of 2023, the median home price there was $780,000 (https://www.propertyshark.com/mason/market-trends/residential/nyc/manhattan/east-harlem). Many of its Puerto Rican and African American residents have been pushed out by rising rents and forced to relocate to other areas of New York City (see Padilla 2013).

6. This passage expresses several key concerns of current anthropology. The first is the notion of "exoticizing." To exoticize a group of people is to make them appear strange, and foreign, and, ultimately, to diminish their humanity. A group that is exotic doesn't have to be taken seriously. A second key concept is "privilege." A privileged insight is one that is to be taken more seriously because of the position of those who offer it. The word privilege used in this manner is often derogatory. For example, white males of European descent are held to have privileged positions. That is, for historical reasons, they are the ones whose voices and interpretations are granted the most credibility. Here, Bourgois speaks of the privileged voice of the crack dealers, an

My central concern is the relationship of the street dealers to the worlds of work—that is, the legal and illegal labor markets—that employ them and give meaning to their lives. The long-term structural transformation of New York from a manufacturing to a service economy is crucial to understanding this experience. Although economists, sociologists, and political scientists have argued extensively over the details of the statistics, most recognize that the dislocations caused by the erosion of the manufacturing sector are a driving force behind the economic polarization of urban America (Wilson 1987). They also specifically recognize that Puerto Ricans are the most vulnerable group in New York's structural adjustment because of their over-concentration in the least dynamic subsector within light manufacturing and because of their fragile incipient foot-hold in public sector and service employment (Rodriguez 1989).

Through my ethnographic data I hope to show the local-level implications of the global-level restructuring of capital and, in the process, give voice to some unrepentant victims. In a nutshell, I am arguing that the transformation from manufacturing to service employment—especially in the professional office work setting—is much more culturally disruptive than the already revealing statistics on reductions in income, employment, unionization, and worker's benefits would indicate. Low-level service sector employment engenders a humiliating ideological—or cultural—confrontation between a powerful corps of white office executives and their assistants versus a mass of poorly educated, alienated, "colored" workers.[7]

SHATTERED WORKING-CLASS DREAMS

All the crack dealers and addicts whom I have interviewed worked at one or more legal jobs in their early youth. In fact, most entered the labor market at a younger age than the typical American. Before they were twelve years old they were bagging groceries at the supermarket for tips, stocking beer off-the-books in local *bodegas,* or shining shoes. For example, Julio, the night manager at a video games arcade that sells five-dollar vials of crack on the block where I lived, pursued a traditional working-class dream in his early adolescence. With the support of his extended kin who were all immersed in a working-class "common sense," he dropped out of junior high school to work in a local garment factory[8]:

> I was like fourteen or fifteen playing hooky and pressing dresses and whatever they were

---

extremely unprivileged group of people. In this situation, they are to be taken seriously because their control of public spaces in the neighborhood and their position in society gives them special insight.

7. Notice two critical Marxist concerns in the previous two paragraphs. The first is the central importance of work. Marxists take production as the most basic patterning element of society. Marx wrote that "[people] begin to distinguish themselves from animals as soon as they begin to produce their means of subsistence" (these words appear in essay 4 in this volume). A Marxist analysis thus proceeds from labor to other aspects of life. For Bourgois, it is axiomatic that work is a critical source of meaning in people's lives. However, the fact that Marxist analysis starts with production does not necessarily mean that people inevitably experience their jobs as a source of meaning. For example, the working-class youth that the British social analyst Paul Willis (b. 1945) describes in *Learning to Labor* (1977), understand work as inherently meaningless and do not particularly care about the jobs they take: It's all just work. In that book, Willis shows how working-class understandings about labor and manhood, the schools, and governmental structures served to reproduce the working class of the 1970s. The rebellion of working-class youth, rather than threatening the economic system, supported it. Bourgois was strongly influenced by Willis and many points in this essay follow Willis's argument.

The second Marxist concern is the notion of conflict. For Marx, all societies (except the future communist utopia) are inherently riven by conflicts. History is the inexorable working out of these conflicts.

8. Note Bourgois's use of the phrase "common sense" in quotation marks (it has appeared twice so far and will appear another two times). The scare quotes emphasize that there is no universal common sense.

making on the steamer. They was cheap, cheap clothes.

My mother's sister was working there first and then her son, my cousin Hector—the one who's in jail now—was the one they hired first, because his mother agreed: "If you don't want to go to school, you gotta work."

So I started hanging out with him. I wasn't planning on working in the factory. I was supposed to be in school; but it just sort of happened.

Ironically, little Julio actually became the agent who physically moved the factory out of the inner city. In the process, he became merely one more of the 445,900 manufacturing workers in New York City to lose their jobs as factory employment dropped 50 percent from 1963 to 1983 (Romo and Schwartz 1993). Of course, instead of understanding himself as the victim of a structural transformation, Julio remembers with pleasure and even pride the extra income he earned for clearing the machines out of the factory space:

Them people had money, man. Because we helped them move out of the neighborhood. It took us two days—only me and my cousin, Hector. Wow! It was work. They gave us seventy bucks each.[9]

Almost all the crack dealers had similar tales of former factory jobs. For poor adolescents, the decision to drop out of school and become a marginal factory worker is attractive. It provides the employed youth with access to the childhood "necessities"—sneakers, basketballs, store-bought snacks—that sixteen-year-olds who stay in school cannot afford. In the descriptions of their first forays into legal factory-based employment, one hears clearly the extent to which they and their families subscribed to mainstream working-class ideologies about the dignity of engaging in "hard work" versus education.

Had these enterprising, early-adolescent workers from El Barrio not been confined to the weakest sector of manufacturing in a period of rapid job loss their teenage working-class dream might have stabilized. Instead, upon reaching their mid-twenties they discovered themselves to be unemployable high school dropouts. This painful realization of social marginalization expresses itself generationally as the working-class values of their families conflict violently with the reality of their hardcore lumpenization. They are constantly accused of slothfulness by their mothers and even by friends who have managed to maintain legal jobs. They do not have a regional perspective on the dearth of adequate entry-level jobs available to "functional illiterates" in New York City and they begin to suspect that they might indeed be "vago bons" (lazy bums) who do not *want* to work hard and help themselves. Confused, they take refuge in an alternate search for career, meaning, and ecstasy in substance abuse.[10]

Rather, what is "common sense" is dictated by economic structures and the mode of production. When these change, common sense changes as well.

9. In Marxist analysis, the structural factors that drive cultural change are often hidden from cultural participants. In this passage, we see Julio actively participating in the change that will lead to poverty for the people around him. Had Julio refused to take the job moving machinery he simply would have lost the income. Julio could not change the economic structures that led to the loss of manufacturing jobs.

10. The work of Antonio Gramsci (1891–1937) has influenced many modern Marxists, and the effect of Gramsci's ideas is found throughout this selection. Gramsci was a founder of the Italian Communist Party. Imprisoned from 1926 to 1934, he was released because of ill-health and died in 1937. Gramsci's key works are his prison notebooks, which, since they were written in part to avoid detection by prison censors, are extremely difficult to understand.

Gramsci's most important contribution to Marxism is the concept of *hegemony*, which he does not define with any precision. He most consistently uses hegemony to refer to a system of political and moral leadership in which the elite of a society use "intellectual devices to infuse its ideas of morality to gain the support of those who resist or may be neutral, to retain the support of those who consent to its rule" (Kurtz

Formerly, when most entry-level jobs were found in factories the contradiction between an oppositional street culture and traditional working-class, shop-floor culture was less pronounced—especially when the worksite was protected by a union. Factories are inevitably rife with confrontational hierarchies; nevertheless, on the shop floor, surrounded by older union workers, high school dropouts who are well versed in the latest and toughest street culture styles function effectively. In the factory, being tough and violently macho has high cultural value; a certain degree of opposition to the foreman and the "bossman" is expected and is considered appropriately masculine.

In contrast, this same oppositional street identity is nonfunctional in the service sector that has burgeoned in New York's finance driven economy because it does not allow for the humble, obedient, social interaction—often across gender lines—that professional office workers impose on their subordinates. A qualitative change characterizes the tenor of social interaction in office-based service sector employment. Workers in a mailroom or behind a photocopy machine cannot publicly maintain their cultural autonomy. Most concretely, they have no union; more subtly, there are few fellow workers surrounding them to insulate them and to provide them with a culturally based sense of class solidarity.[a] Instead they are besieged by supervisors and bosses from the alien, hostile, and obviously dominant culture. When these office managers are not intimidated by street culture, they ridicule it. Workers like Willie and Julio appear inarticulate to their professional supervisors when they try to imitate the language of power in the workplace and instead stumble pathetically over the enunciation of unfamiliar words. They cannot decipher the hastily scribbled instructions—rife with mysterious abbreviations—that are left for them by harried office managers. The "common sense" of white-collar work is foreign to them; they do not, for example, understand the logic for filing triplicate copies of memos or for postdating invoices. When they attempt to improvise or show initiative they fail miserably and instead appear inefficient—or even hostile—for failing to follow "clearly specified" instructions.[11]

Their "social skills" are even more inadequate than their limited professional capac-

1996: 106). In other words, hegemony is a system of ethical and political ideas propounded by a broad alliance of political and intellectual leaders and believed as "common sense" by the masses. The hegemony of a dominant class is created and reinforced in the institutions, social relations, and dominant ideas of a society (Sassoon 1991: 230).

In proposing a primary role for hegemony and intellectual leadership, Gramsci provided a counterbalance to the traditional Marxist emphasis on the fundamental importance of economic relations of production. The notion of hegemony has been attractive to Marxist anthropologists because it gives critical importance to the cultural realm. Gramsci's influence has been particularly felt in cultural studies and cultural production theory (see footnote 25).

The concept of hegemony plays a crucial role in this essay. Earlier, Bourgois spoke of the drug dealers' hegemony over street life in Spanish Harlem. In this passage, the working-class families of the crack dealers accept the far more powerful hegemonic ideology of America's elites: "common sense" about "hard work." The dealers themselves are at least partially accepting of these same ideologies and suspect that they are "vago bons."

In this passage Bourgois also discusses *lumpenization*. This comes from Marx's notion of the *lumpenproletariat*. Marx described the lumpenproletariat as comprising "ruined and adventurous off-shoots of the bourgeoisie, vagabonds, discharged soldiers, discharged jail-birds . . . pickpockets, brothel keepers, rag-pickers, beggars," etc. (Bottomore 1991: 327). Thus, the lumpenproletariat are the disinherited dregs of society. Their significance is twofold. First, since workers fear lumpenization, they will accept high levels of exploitation. Second, the lumpenproletariat is politically volatile. Since they are disaffected, they are easily drawn to political radicals and can be mobilized to challenge the power structure. Such challenges are as likely to come from the political right as the political left.

11. These passages reflect and update Willis's work in *Learning to Labor* (1977). Willis argued that the rebellion of working-class youth against their schools prepared them for the "tough and violently macho" life on the shop floor. However, Bourgois asks what happens when the shop floor disappears? The culture of rebellion that worked well for blue-collar laborers is completely inappropriate for service workers.

ities. They do not know how to look at their fellow co-service workers—let alone their supervisors—without intimidating them. They cannot walk down the hallway to the water fountain without unconsciously swaying their shoulders aggressively as if patrolling their home turf. Gender barriers are an even more culturally charged realm. They are repeatedly reprimanded for harassing female co-workers.[12]

The cultural clash between white "yuppie" power and inner-city "scrambling jive" in the service sector is much more than a difference of style. Service workers who are incapable of obeying the rules of interpersonal interaction dictated by professional office culture will never be upwardly mobile. In the high-rise office buildings of midtown Manhattan, newly employed inner-city high school dropouts suddenly realize that they look like idiotic buffoons to the men and women they work for. Once again, a gender dynamic exacerbates the confusion and sense of insult experienced by young, male inner-city employees because most supervisors in the lowest reaches of the service sector are women. Street culture does not allow males to be subordinate across gender lines.[13]

"GETTIN' DISSED"

On the street, the trauma of experiencing a threat to one's personal dignity has been frozen linguistically in the commonly used phrase "to diss" which is short for "to disrespect." Significantly, back in the coffee-hacienda highlands of Puerto Rico in 1949, Wolf had noted the importance of the traditional Puerto Rican concept of *respeto:* "The good owner 'respects' [*respeta*] the laborer." Wolf pointed specifically to the role "respect" plays in controlling labor power: "It is probably to the interest of the landowner to make concessions to his best workers, to deal with them on a respect basis, and to enmesh them in a network of mutual obligations" (Wolf 1956b: 235; see also Lauria 1964).[14]

Puerto Rican street dealers do not find "respect" in the entry-level service sector jobs that have increased twofold in New York's economy since the 1950s. On the contrary, they "get dissed" in their new jobs. Julio, for example, remembers the humiliation of his former work experiences as an "office boy," and he speaks of them in a race and gender-charged idiom:

I had a prejudiced boss. She was a fucking "ho'," Gloria. She was white. Her name was Christian. No, not Christian, Kirschman. I don't know if she was Jewish or not. When she was talking to people she would say, "He's illiterate."

So what I did one day was, I just looked up the word, "illiterate," in the dictionary and I saw that she's saying to her associates that I'm stupid or something!

Well, I am illiterate anyway.

---

12. Note that it is not only that workers like Willie and Julio do not know the language of the office, it is their habits of body as well. It is not only the way they talk, it is, literally, the way they walk. Pierre Bourdieu emphasized that *habitus* was not simply cultural information, it formed the body. Here, the walk of these workers provides an outstanding example.

13. This passage points up a crucial issue in Marxist analysis, and anthropology in general. The individuals in Bourgois's study seem to be in the iron grip of culture. Bourgois's subjects are frightening but somewhat attractive. This comes from the sense that they might be decent individuals trapped by forces beyond their control. In this paragraph, workers are "incapable" of obeying the rules of office culture and forbidden by Puerto Rican street culture from being subordinate to women. Does culture really compel us to this degree?

14. The theme of this section is the clash of cultures: the street culture of the crack dealers versus the office culture in which they seek employment. Notice that in the office setting, the critical dimension of the relationship of street culture to office culture is that the members of office-worker culture have power, and despite their desire for respect, crack dealers have none. Since the powerful do not need to understand the culture of those less powerful, office workers are not usually aware of their subordinates' desire for respect (and, if they were, would not know how to give it). This is exacerbated by the gender and race differences between the (mostly white female) office workers and the subjects (mostly brown or black male) of Bourgois's research.

The most profound dimension of Julio's humiliation was being obliged to look up in the dictionary the word used to insult him. In contrast, in the underground economy, he is sheltered from this kind of threat:

Big Pete [the crack house franchise owner], he would never disrespect me that way. He wouldn't tell me that because he's illiterate too. Plus I've got more education than him. I got a GED.

To succeed at Gloria Kirschman's magazine publishing company, Julio would have had to submit wholeheartedly to her professional cultural style but he was unwilling to compromise his street identity. He refused to accept her insults and he was unable to imitate her culture; hence, he was doomed to a marginal position behind a photocopy machine or at the mail meter. The job requirements in the service sector are largely cultural—that is, having a "good attitude"—therefore they conjugate powerfully with racism:

I wouldn't have mind that she said I was illiterate. What bothered me was that when she called on the telephone, she wouldn't want me to answer even if my supervisor who was the receptionist was not there. [Note how Julio is so low in the office hierarchy that his immediate supervisor is a receptionist.]

When she hears my voice it sounds like she's going to get a heart attack. She'd go, "Why are you answering the phones?"

That bitch just didn't like my Puerto Rican accent.

Julio's manner of resisting this insult to his cultural dignity exacerbated his marginal position in the labor hierarchy:

And then, when I did pick up the phone, I used to just sound *Porta'rrrican* on purpose.

In contrast to the old factory sweatshop positions, these just-above-minimum-wage office jobs require intense interpersonal contact with the middle and upper-middle classes. Proximal contact across class lines and the absence of a working-class autonomous space for eight hours a day in the office can be a claustrophobic experience for an otherwise ambitious, energetic, young inner-city worker.

Willie interpreted this requirement to obey white, middle-class norms as an affront to his dignity that specifically challenged his definition of masculinity:

I had a few jobs like that [referring to Julio's "telephone diss"] where you gotta take a lot of shit from bitches and be a wimp.

I didn't like it but I kept on working, because "Fuck it!" you don't want to fuck up the relationship. So you just be a punk [shrugging his shoulders dejectedly].

One alternative for surviving at a workplace that does not tolerate a street-based cultural identity is to become bicultural: to play politely by "the white woman's" rules downtown only to come home and revert to street culture within the safety of one's tenement or housing project at night. Tens of thousands of East Harlem residents manage this tightrope, but it often engenders accusations of betrayal and internalized racism on the part of neighbors and childhood friends who do not have—or do not want—these bicultural skills.

This is the case, for example, of Ray, a rival crack dealer whose black skin and tough street demeanor disqualify him from legal office work. He quit a "nickel-and-dime messenger job downtown" to sell crack full-time in his project stairway shortly after a white woman fled from him shrieking down the hallway of a high-rise office building. Ray and the terrified woman had ridden the elevator together and coincidentally Ray had stepped off on the same floor as her to make a delivery. Worse yet, Ray had been trying to act like a "debonair male" and suspected the contradiction between his inadequate appearance and his "chivalric" intentions was responsible for the woman's terror:

You know how you let a woman go off the elevator first? Well that's what I did to her but I may have looked a little shabby on the ends. Sometime my hair not combed. You know. So I could look a little sloppy to her maybe when I let her off first.

What Ray did not quite admit until I probed further is that he too had been intimidated by the lone white woman. He had been so disoriented by her tabooed, unsupervised proximity that he had forgotten to press the elevator button when he originally stepped on after her:

She went in the elevator first but then she just waits there to see what floor I press. She's playing like she don't know what floor she wants to go to because she wants to wait for me to press my floor. And I'm standing there and I forgot to press the button. I'm thinking about something else—I don't know what was the matter with me. And she's thinking like, "He's not pressing the button; I guess he's following me!"

As a crack dealer, Ray no longer has to confront this kind of confusing humiliation. Instead, he can righteously condemn his "successful" neighbors who work downtown for being ashamed of who they were born to be:

When you see someone go downtown and get a good job, if they be Puerto Rican, you see them fix up their hair and put some contact lens in their eyes. Then they fit in. And they do it! I seen it.

They turnovers. They people who want to be white. Man, if you call them in Spanish, it wind up a problem.

When they get nice jobs like that, all of a sudden, you know, they start talking proper.

SELF-DESTRUCTIVE RESISTANCE

Third and second-generation Spanish Harlem residents born into working-class families do not tolerate high levels of "exploitation." In the new jobs available to them, however, there are no class-based institutions to channel their resistance. They are caught in a technological time warp. They have developed contemporary mainstream American definitions of survival needs and emotional notions of job satisfaction. In short, they are "made in New York"; therefore, they are not "exploitable" or "degradable." Both their objective economic needs as well as their personal cultural dignities have to be satisfied by their jobs. They resist inadequate working conditions. Finally, they are acutely aware of their relative deprivation vis-à-vis the middle-level managers and wealthy executives whose intimate physical proximity they cannot escape at work.[15]

At the same time that young men like Julio, Willie, and Ray recognize how little power they have in the legal labor market, they do not accept their domination passively. They are resisting exploitation from positions of subordination. They are living the unequal power struggle that a growing body of anthropological and ethnographic literature is beginning to address (Bourgois in press; Foley 1990; Fordham 1988; Willis 1977; Wolf 1990b: 590).

Unfortunately, for people like Julio and Willie, the traditional modes of powerless resistance—foot dragging, disgruntlement, petty theft, and so forth—which might be appropriate in traditional peasant or even proletarian settings (see Scott 1985) contradict the fundamental "technological" requirement for enthusiastic "initiative" and "flexibility" that New York's finance-driven service sector demands. In manufacturing, resistance can be channeled through recognized institutions—unions—that often reinforce class consciousness. In fact, oppositionally defined cultural identities are so legitimate on the shop floor that they even serve to ritualize management/ worker confrontation.[16]

---

15. The implication, more important now than when Bourgois wrote this essay, is that immigrants, those not "made in New York" can be exploited in different, harsher ways. It is not only that their legal status may make them vulnerable. Their ideas about the meaning of work, proper working conditions, and acceptable treatment from employers have been formed under different social and economic systems. This too may make them more exploitable. Bourgois explores this later in the essay.

16. Here Bourgois focuses on class conflict, a fundamental theme in Marxist analysis. Whereas Émile Durkheim and the functionalist thinkers saw society as fundamentally cooperative, Marx saw it as characterized by conflict. This is illustrated in Bourgois's descriptions of factory workers.

In the service sector, however, there is no neutral way to express cultural nonconformity. Scowling on the way to brewing coffee for a supervisor results in an unsatisfactory end-of-year performance evaluation. Stealing on the job is just cause for instant job termination. Indeed, petty theft is the avenue for "powerless revenge" most favored by Willie and Julio. They both were skilled at manipulating the Pitney Bowes postage meter machines and at falsifying stationery inventory to skim "chump change."

More subtle, however, was the damage to Julio's work performance due to his constant concern lest Gloria Kirschman once again catch him off guard and "disrespect" him without his being immediately aware of the gravity of the insult. Consequently, when he was ordered to perform mysteriously specific tasks such as direct mailings of promotional materials that required particular combinations of folding, stuffing, or clipping, he activated his defense mechanisms. Julio had rarely received direct mail advertisements in his project apartment mailbox; consequently, the urgency and the precision with which his supervisor oversaw the logistics of these mailings appeared overbearingly oppressive and insulting. Gloria appeared almost superstitious in the rigor and anxiety with which she supervised each detail and Julio refused to accept the "flexibility" that these delicate mailings required—that is, late night binges of collating and re-collating to make bulk-rate postage deadlines coincide with the magazine's printing and sales deadlines. Furthermore, to Julio, it was offensive to have to bring over the assembled promotional packets to Gloria's home for a last-minute late-night inspection:

It would be late and I would be at the office to do these rush jobs: collate them, staple them, fold them in the correct way . . . whatever way she said. It was always different. And it had to be just the way she wanted it. I'd stuff them just the right way [making frantic shuffling motions with his hands] and then seal the shit.

I used to hate that. I would box it and take it to the 38th Street Post Office at 10:30 at night.

But then sometimes she would call me from home and I would have to bring papers up to her house on 79th Street and 3rd Avenue [Manhattan's silk stocking district] to double check.

And she would try to offer me something to eat and I would say, "No, thank you," because she would try to pay me with that shit. 'Cause she's a cheap bitch.

She'd say, "You want pizza, tea, or cookies?" She had those Pepperidge Farm cookies [wrinkling his face with disgust].

But I wouldn't accept anything from her.

I wasn't going to donate my time, man.

She thought I was illiterate. She thought I was stupid. Not me boy, charge *every penny*. From the moment I leave the office that's overtime all the way to her house. That's time and a half.

I used to exaggerate the hours. If I worked sixteen, I would put eighteen or twenty to see if I could get away with it. And I would

---

The sociologists Kingsley Davis (1908–1997) and Wilbert Moore (1914–1987) summarized the functionalist approach in "Some Principles of Stratification" (1944). In this work, they suggest that people work cooperatively at their level of competence and are rewarded appropriately for their efforts. The center of this model is consensus. We all work together, each doing his or her job, to produce a final product.

In Marxist analysis, on the other hand, factory production seems almost secondary to the struggle between workers and overseers on the factory floor. Workers are in conflict with managers and owners. Unable, in most circumstances, to openly rebel, they protest their condition through theft and small acts of sabotage. If these are not excessive, such acts are tolerated by owners as a cost of doing business. In fact, tolerating small amounts of theft is one way owners can keep wages low.

The critical issue for Bourgois's interlocutors is that in a factory, there is separation of the classes. Management and workers rarely meet face-to-face. Additionally, there are institutions such as unions that can channel worker hostility. This makes small acts of resistance possible. On the other hand, in an office, service workers are in constant contact with managers who demand that people form a "team" that expresses a "can-do" attitude. This means that they must suppress all insubordination or develop new and subtle ways of showing it.

get away with it. I'm not going to do that kind of shit for free.

And that bitch was crazy. She used to eat baby food. I know cause I saw her eating it with a spoon right out of the jar.

If Julio appeared to be a scowling, ungrateful, dishonest worker to Gloria, then Gloria herself looked almost perverted to Julio. What normal middle-aged woman would invite her twenty-year-old employee into her kitchen late at night and eat baby food in front of him?[17]

Julio's victories over his employer, Gloria, were **Pyrrhic**. In the cross-cultural confrontation taking place in the corridors of high-rise office buildings there is no ambiguity over who wields power. This unequal hierarchy is constantly reasserted through the mechanisms of cultural capital so foreign to participants in street culture. For example, when someone like Willie, Julio, or Ray is "terminated" for suspicion of theft, the personnel report registers an insulting notation: "lack of initiative," "inarticulate," or "no understanding of the purpose of the company." Julio correctly translates this information into street-English: "She's saying to her associates that I'm stupid!"[18]

Willie and Julio have no frame of reference to guide them through service employment because their social network only has experience with factory work. In their first factory jobs, both Willie and Julio were guided by older family members who were producing the very same products they were making. Still today, for example, Julio's mother is a sweatshop/homework seamstress and Willie's uncle is a factory foreman in the Midwestern town where his metal-chroming company relocated. In contrast, the only socialization available to Willie and Julio in the service sector comes from equally isolated and alienated fellow workers. Willie, for example, who has always been precocious in everything he has done in life—from dropping out of school, to engaging in street violence, to burglarizing, to selling drugs, to abusing women, to becoming a crack addict—immediately understood the impossibility of his supervisor's maintaining an objective quality control in the mailroom where he worked prior to being hired by Julio at the crack house:

I used to get there late, but the other workers wasn't never doing shit. They was *lazy* motherfuckers—even the supervisor.

---

17. Like the story above about Ray and the elevator, this story emphasizes the overlap between class and culture. In both stories, attempts to show respect or friendship are misinterpreted. In the first story, Ray's attempt to show respect to a woman on an elevator goes awry when she interprets his actions as those of an assailant. In this story, Gloria almost certainly understands herself as proffering a minimal degree of friendship. Julio interprets this as an insult.

It is interesting to note that Bourgois writes at a now-vanished moment in American history. In the late 1980s and early 1990s, computers, the internet, and automation had yet to be fully deployed in US industry. When this essay was written, a "mailroom" was a relatively large and important part of business in New York, and a direct mailing might still be handled by employees such as Gloria and Julio. Today, the vast majority of communication is electronic, and a direct mailing would almost certainly be handled by a different specialized firm.

Bourgois also wrote this essay during the American crack cocaine epidemic (roughly 1984–1993). During these years, the sale and use of crack cocaine as well as drug-related violence soared. New laws particularly the Anti-Drug Abuse Act of 1986 and the Violent Crime Control and Law Enforcement Act of 1994, led to harsh and automatic penalties for the possession and sale of marijuana and crack. This led to an enormous increase of inmates in the US prison system, particularly African Americans (Samaha 2014).

18. In this paragraph, Bourgois invokes Bourdieu's idea of cultural capital (see essay 27, note 9). Lamont and Lareau (1988: 155), interpreting Bourdieu, provide a useful definition of cultural capital: "institutionalized, i.e., widely shared, high-status cultural signals (attitudes, preferences, formal knowledge, behaviors, goods, and credentials) used for social and cultural exclusion."

"Pyrrhic victory": a victory at a cost so great it harms the victor, after King Pyruss of Epirus (318–272 BCE). King Pyruss was a strong opponent of Rome, and considered one of the great generals of his time. Even though victorious against Roman forces, several of these battles cost his army heavy casualties leading to the term.

They all be sitting, asking each other questions over the phone, and fooling with video games on the computer. And that's all you do at a place like that. My boss, Bill, be drinking on the sneak cue, and eating this bad-ass sausage.

Finally, the precarious tenure of entry-level jobs in the service sector was the immediate precipitating factor in Willie's and Julio's retreat from the legal labor market. When they were not fired for "bad attitude," they were laid off due to economic retrenchment. The companies employing them fluctuated with the unpredictable whims of rapidly changing "yuppie fashions." Julio, for example, lost two different positions in fragile companies that folded: (1) Gloria Kirschman's trendy magazine, and (2) a desktop-publishing house.

Surprisingly, in his accounts of being laid off Julio publicly admitted defeat and vulnerability. On repeated occasions I had seen Julio brave violence on the streets and in the crack house. I knew him capable of deliberate cruelty, such as refusing to pay for his fifteen-year-old girlfriend's abortion or of slowly breaking the wrist of an adolescent who had played a prank on him. Downtown, however, behind the computer terminal where he had held his last job "in printing," he had been crushed psychologically by the personnel officers who fired him. Ironically, I registered on my tape recorder his tale of frustration, humiliation, and self-blame for losing his last legal job as a printer only a week after recording with him a bravado-laced account of how he mugged a drunken Mexican immigrant in a nearby housing project:

I was with Rico and his girl, Daisy. We saw this Mexican . . . He was just probably drunk. I grabbed him by the back of the neck, and put my 007 [knife] in his back [making the motion of holding someone in a choke hold from behind]. Right here [pointing to his own lower back]. And I was jigging him *HARD* [grinning for emphasis at me and his girlfriend, who was listening, rapt with attention]!

I said: "*No te mueve cabron o te voy a picar como un pernil* [Don't move motherfucker or I'll stick you like a roast pork]." [More loud chuckles from Julio's girlfriend.] Yeah, yeah, like how you stab a pork shoulder when you want to put all the flavoring in the holes.

I wasn't playing, either, I was serious. I would have jigged him. And I'd regret it later, but I was looking at that gold ring he had. [Chuckle.]

The Mexican panicked. So I put him to the floor, poking him hard, and Rico's girl started searching him.

I said, "Yo, take that asshole's fucking ring too!"

After she took the ring we broke out. We sold the ring and then we cut-out on Daisy. We left her in the park, she didn't get even a cent. She helped for nothing. [More chuckling.][19]

As a knife-wielding mugger on the street, Julio could not contrast more dramatically with the panic-stricken employee begging for a second chance that legal employment had reduced him to:

I was more or less expecting it. But still, when I found out, I wanted to cry, man. My throat got dry, I was like . . . [waves his hands, and gasps as if struck by a panic attack].

They called me to the office, I was like, "Oh *shit!*"

I couldn't get through to them. I even told them, "I'll let you put me back to messenger; I will take less pay; just keep me employed. I need the money; I need to work. I got a family."

---

19. To his credit, Bourgois does not romanticize the central characters in this essay. They are capable of great cruelty and violence. However, in the logic of Marxist analysis, they are victims of economic and social forces beyond their control. More specifically, their surroundings have made them who they are. Thus, despite their actions, these young men are depicted in a sympathetic light. However, it is important to consider the issue of individual agency. Many thousands of people are subjected to the same conditions and virtually none of them sell drugs or break the wrists of children.

But they said, "Nope, nope, nope." I left. I just stood right outside the building; I was fucked, man. All choked up. *Me jodieron* [They jerked me].[20]

THE NEW IMMIGRANT ALTERNATIVE

The flooding of cocaine and then crack onto America's streets during the 1980s infused new energy into the underground economy, making drug dealing the most vibrant equal opportunity employer for Harlem youths. Normally, in order to fill jobs adequately in the expanding service sector, New York's legal economy should have to compete for the hearts and minds of the growing proportion of the inner city's "best and brightest" who are choosing to pursue more remunerative and culturally compatible careers in the underground economy. A wave of cheaper, more docile and disciplined new immigrant workers, however, is altering this labor power balance. These immigrants—largely undocumented—are key agents in New York's latest structural economic adjustment. Their presence allows low-wage employment to expand while social services retrench. This helps explain, for example, how the real value of the minimum wage could have declined by one-third in the 1980s while the federal government was able to decrease the proportion of its contribution to New York City's budget by over 50 percent (Berlin 1991: 10; Rosenbaum 1989: A1). The breakdown of the inner city's public sector is no longer an economic threat to the expansion of New York's economy because the labor force that these public subsidies maintain is increasingly irrelevant.[21]

Like the parents and grandparents of Julio and Willie, many of New York's newest immigrants are from remote rural communities or squalid shantytowns where meat is eaten only once a week, and where there is no running water or electricity. In downtown Manhattan many of these new immigrants are Chinese, but in East Harlem the vast majority are Mexicans from the rural states of Puebla and Guerrero. To them, New York's streets are still "paved in gold" if one works hard enough.

Half a century ago Julio's mother fled precisely the same living conditions these new immigrants are only just struggling to escape. Her reminiscences about childhood in her natal village reveal the trajectory of improved material conditions, cultural dislocation, and crushed working-class dreams that is propelling her second-generation son into a destructive street culture:

I loved that life in Puerto Rico, because it was a healthy, healthy, healthy life.

We always ate because my father always had work, and in those days the custom was to have a garden in your patio to grow food and everything that you ate.

We only ate meat on Sundays because everything was cultivated on the same little parcel of land. We didn't have a refrigerator, so we ate *bacalao* [salted codfish], which can stay outside, and a meat that they call old meat, *carne de vieja,* and sardines from a

---

20. These two stories are important because they demonstrate that, at some level, Julio understands the true nature of power. Julio is a violent and abusive individual capable of injuring another person without remorse. He is, however, easily defeated by people such as Gloria Kirschman, who would probably be terrified of him were they to meet on the streets of the barrio. The point is that ultimately power does not stem from the ability of individuals to threaten physical violence, but from the relations of production in which they are enmeshed. An office manager is able to demolish Julio because he realizes that, despite his bravado, they hold enormous power, and he holds almost none. For Marxists, although physical violence may be terrible, the worst sort of violence is structural—that is, the violence done to human beings that stems from exploitative and oppressive relationships built into a society's economy and class structure.

21. The process Bourgois describes in this paragraph is based on the idea that in a capitalist society, an individual's value is his or her contribution to capitalist production. Individuals who make no contribution have no value. Because they can be easily replaced by new immigrants, Julio and those like him have little economic value, and society need not care about them or expend much on their support.

can. But thanks to God, we never felt hunger. My mother made a lot of corn flour.

Some people have done better by coming here, but many people haven't. Even people from my barrio, who came trying to find a better life [*buen ambiente*] just found disaster. Married couples right from my neighborhood came only to have the husband run off with another woman.

In those days in Puerto Rico, when we were in poverty, life was better. Everyone will tell you life was healthier and you could trust people. Now you can't trust anybody.

What I like best was that we kept all our traditions . . . our feasts. In my village, everyone was either an Uncle or an Aunt. And when you walked by someone older, you had to ask for their blessing. It was respect. There was a lot of respect in those days. [Original in Spanish][22]

Ironically, at sixty, Julio's monolingual Spanish-speaking mother is the only one of her family who can still compete effectively with the new immigrants who are increasingly filling Manhattan's entry-level labor market. She ekes out a living on welfare in her high-rise housing project apartment by taking in sewing from undocumented garment industry subcontractors. Rather than bemoaning the structural adjustment which is destroying their capacity to survive on legal wages, street-bound Puerto Rican youths celebrate their "decision" to bank on the underground economy and to cultivate their street identities. Willie and Julio repeatedly assert their pride in their street careers. For example, one Saturday night after they finished their midnight shift at the crack house, I accompanied them on their way to purchase "El Sapo Verde" (The Green Toad), a twenty dollar bag of powder cocaine, sold by a reputable outfit three blocks away. While waiting for Julio and Willie to be "served" by the coke seller, I engaged three undocumented Mexican men drinking beer on a neighboring stoop in a conversation about finding work in New York. One of the new immigrants was already earning five hundred dollars a week fixing deep-fat-fry machines. He had a straightforward racist explanation for why Willie—who was standing next to me—was "unemployed":

OK, OK, I'll explain it to you in one word: Because the Puerto Ricans are brutes! [pointing at Willie] Brutes! Do you understand?

Puerto Ricans like to make easy money. They like to leech off the other people. But not us Mexicans! No way! We like to work for our money. We don't steal. We came here to work and that's all. [Original in Spanish]

Instead of physically assaulting the employed immigrant for insulting him, Willie turned the racist tirade into the basis for a new, generational-based "American-born," urban cultural pride. In fact, in his response, he ridiculed what he interpreted to be the hillbilly naiveté of the Mexicans who still believe in the "American Dream." He spoke slowly in street-English as if to mark sarcastically the contrast between his "savvy" Nuyorican identity versus the limited English proficiency of his detractor:

That's right, m'a man! We is real vermin lunatics that sell drugs. We don't want no part of society. "Fight the Power!"[b]

What do we wanna be working for? We rather live off the system. Gain weight, lay women.

When we was younger, we used to break our asses too. [Gesturing toward the Mexican men who were straining to understand his English] I had all kinds of stupid jobs too . . . advertising agencies . . . computers.

But not no more! Now we're in a rebellious stage. We rather evade taxes, make

---

22. Marxists hold that capitalism is a system of maximal exploitation because under capitalism, the individual is stripped of everything except his or her labor. This has sometimes led Marxists to romanticize non-capitalist systems of production. In this passage, Julio's mother reminisces about the beauty of life in Puerto Rico, forgetting for the moment that it was most likely the crushing poverty and misery of that life that caused her family to emigrate to New York City. Bourgois uses this rather long quote as a rhetorical device to emphasize the misery of relations of production in New York.

quick money and just survive. But we're not satisfied with that either. Ha![23]

CONCLUSION: ETHNOGRAPHY AND OPPRESSION

America was built on racial hierarchy and on blame-the-victim justifications for the existence of poverty and class distinctions. This makes it difficult to present ethnographic data from inner-city streets without falling prey to a "pornography of violence" or a racist voyeurism. The public "common sense" is not persuaded by a structural economic understanding of Willie's and Julio's "self-destruction." Even the victims themselves psychologize their unsatisfactory lives. Most concretely, political will and public policy ignore the fundamental structural economic facts of marginalization in America (see Romo and Schwartz 1993). Instead the first priority of federal and local social "welfare" agencies is to change the psychological—or at best the "cultural"—orientations of misguided individuals (Katz 1989).[24]

Unfortunately researchers in America have allowed the gap to grow between their hegemonically "liberal" intellectual community and an overwhelmingly conservative popular political culture. From the late 1970s through most of the 1980s, inner-city poverty was simply ignored by all but right-wing academics who filled a popular vacuum with scientifically flawed "best sellers" on the psychological and cultural causes of poverty in order to argue against the "poisonous" effect of public sector intervention (cf. Gilder 1982; Murray 1984). Their analyses coincide with the deep-seated individualistic, blame-the-victim values so cherished in American thought.

There is a theoretical and methodological basis for anthropology's reticence to confront devastating urban poverty in its front yard. Qualitative researchers prefer to avoid tackling taboo subjects such as personal violence, sexual abuse, addiction, alienation, self-destruction, and so forth, for fear of violating the tenets of cultural relativism and of contributing to popular racist stereotypes. Even the "new advocacy ethnography" which is confronting inner city social crises—homelessness, AIDS, teen pregnancy—in an engaged manner tends to present its "subjects" in an exclusively sympathetic framework (Dehavenon n.d.). The pragmatic realities of a new advocacy anthropology require published data to be politically crafted. A complex critical perspective therefore is often stifled by the necessity of contributing effectively and responsibly to a "policy debate." Defining policy as a political arena for engagement can demobilize both theory and practice.

Regardless of the political, scholarly, or personal motivations, anthropology's cautious and often self-censored approaches to social misery have obfuscated an ethnographic understanding of the multifaceted dynamics of the experience of oppression and ironically sometimes even have served to minimize the depths of human suffering involved. At the same time, there is a growing body of ethnographic literature at the intersection of educa-

---

23. Gramsci believed that subaltern populations, that is, those who are subordinate or held in positions of oppression and exploitation, produce "organic" intellectuals who develop counter-hegemonic ideas. In other words, the oppressed develop new notions of morality and leadership, as well as new alliances that redefine the cultural worlds in which they live. In Gramsci's thought, the organization of a counter-hegemony is critical to developing the revolutionary potential of the masses. In this passage, the recent Mexican immigrants echo the hegemonic ideas of bourgeois American society. Willie, in ridiculing these ideas and defying the "hard work makes success" logic of the Mexicans, offers a counter-hegemonic response.

24. In other words, social institutions serve to reinforce the hegemonic ideas of the power elites. The "cure" for Willie's radicalism, for instance, is to be found in social service organizations that will convince him of the virtues of "common sense" and "hard work." The phrase "pornography of violence" comes from the work of philosopher Abraham Kaplan (1918–1993). In his 1955 essay "Obscenity as an Esthetic Category," Kaplan wrote that "the pornography of violence is more widespread in our culture than all the other categories of obscenity put together" (1955: 557–558), a comment that now seems prescient.

tion and anthropology—sometimes referred to as cultural production theory—which provides insight into how contradictory and complicated forms of resistance often lead to personal self-destruction and community trauma (Foley 1990; Fordham 1988; MacLeod 1987; Willis 1977). Nevertheless, perhaps even these more self-consciously theoretical attempts to grapple with an unpleasant reality tend to glorify—or at least to overidentify with—the resistance theme in order to escape a "blame-the-victim" insinuation (see Bourgois 1989).

Much of the problem is rooted in the nature of the ethnographic endeavor itself. Engulfed in an overwhelming whirlpool of personal suffering it is often difficult for ethnographers to see the larger relationships structuring the jumble of human interaction around them. Structures of power and history cannot be touched or talked to. Empirically this makes it difficult to identify the urgent political economy relationships shaping everyday survival—whether they be public sector breakdown or economic restructuring. For my own part, in the heat of daily life on the street in El Barrio, I often experienced a confusing anger with the victims, the victimizers, and the wealthy industrialized society that generated such a record toll of unnecessary human suffering. For example, when confronted with a pregnant friend frantically smoking crack—and condemning her fetus to a postpartum life of shattered emotions and dulled brain cells—it was impossible for me to remember the history of her people's colonial terror and humiliation or to contextualize her position in New York's changing economy. Living the inferno of what America calls its "underclass," I—like my neighbors around me and like the pregnant crack addicts themselves—often blamed the victim. To overcome such a partial perspective when researching painful human contexts it is especially important to develop a sensitive political economy analysis that "articulates the hidden histories" of the peoples raking themselves over the coals of the latest forms of capitalism.[25]

REFERENCES

Berlin, Gordon. 1991. *The Poverty among Families: A Service Decategorization Response.* Photocopied report. New York: Manpower Demonstration Research Corporation.

Bourgois, Philippe. 1989. "Crack in Spanish Harlem: Culture and Economy in the Inner City." *Anthropology Today* 5: 6–11.

———. In press. *In Search of Respect: Selling Crack in Spanish Harlem.* New York: Cambridge University Press.

Dehavenon, Anna Lou, ed. n.d. *There Is No Place Like Home: The Anthropology of United States Homelessness and Housing.* Unpublished manuscript.

---

25. In this concluding paragraph, Bourgois struggles with the difficulties and realities of involved, urban anthropology. He is critical of both American society and of the failure of anthropologists to expose the underlying dynamics of oppression that perpetuate inequality. Throughout this essay, Bourgois has emphasized the social and economic forces that cause people to take actions that seem to perpetuate their oppression. Here, he strongly cautions anthropologists against blaming the victim and relates his own struggles when confronted by his pregnant friend smoking crack. However, while acknowledging the difficulties and harsh realities of this woman's life, can we accept that she bears no responsibility for her behavior?

The term "cultural production theory" is associated with the French Marxist Louis Althusser (1918–1990), Bourdieu, and Willis. Cultural production theory "seeks to explain how individual actions, carried out by the oppressed, and sometimes in direct response to an unjust system can actually benefit the maintenance of the system" (Howell 2013: 96). Willis's *Learning to Labor,* described in note 7, is one of the best-known examples of cultural production theory. The term *cultural production theory* has not proved popular. The theoretical position most frequently associated with Bourdieu is generally referred to as *practice theory.* A critical difference between cultural production theory and practice theory is that the latter gives far greater scope to individual agency.

Although Bourgois is critical of some aspects of politically engaged anthropology he has also written:

Writing against inequality is imperative. Denouncing injustice and oppression is not a naïve, old-fashioned anti-intellectual concern or a superannuated totalizing vision of Marxism. On the contrary, it is a vital historical task intellectually, because globalization has become synonymous with military intervention, market-driven poverty, and ecological destruction. It is impossible to understand what is going on anywhere without paying attention to the power dynamics that shape inequality everywhere. (Bourgois 2006: x–xi)

Falcon, Angelo. 1992. *Puerto Ricans and Other Latinos in New York City Today: A Statistical Profile*. New York: Pamphlet, Institute for Puerto Rican Policy.

Foley, Doug. 1990. *Learning Capitalist Culture: Deep in the Heart of Tejas*. Philadelphia: University of Pennsylvania.

Fordham, Signithia. 1988. "Racelessness as a Factor in Black Students' School Success: Pragmatic Strategy or Pyrrhic Victory?" *Harvard Educational Review* 53: 257–293.

Gilder, George. 1982. *Wealth and Poverty*. New York: Bantam.

Katz, Michael. 1989. *The Undeserving Poor: From the War on Poverty to the War on Welfare*. New York: Pantheon Press.

Lambert, Bruce. 1990. "AIDS Travels New York-Puerto Rico 'Air Bridge.'" *New York Times* (15 June): B1.

Lauria, Anthony, Jr. 1964. "'Respeto,' 'Relajo,' and Inter-Personal Relations in Puerto Rico." *Anthropological Quarterly* 37(2): 53–67.

Macleod, Jay. 1987. *Ain't No Makin' It: Leveled Aspirations in Low-Income Neighborhood*. Boulder, Colo.: Westview Press.

Murray, Charles. 1984. *Losing Ground: American Social Policy 1950–1980*. New York: Basic Books.

Rodriguez, Clara E. 1989. *Puerto Ricans: Born in the U.S.A.* Winchester, Mass: Unwin Hyman.

Romo, Frank, and Michael Schwartz. 1993. "The Coming of Post-Industrial Society Revisited: Manufacturing and the Prospects for a Service Based Economy." In *Explorations in Economic Sociology*. Richard Swedburg, ed., 335–373. New York: Russell Sage Foundation.

Rosenbaum, David E. 1989. "Bush and Congress Reach Accord Raising Minimum Wage to $4.25." *New York Times* (1 November): A1–A2.

Scott, James C. 1985. *Weapons of the Weak: Everyday Forms of Peasant Resistance*. New Haven: Yale University Press.

Willis, Paul. 1977. *Learning to Labor: How Working Class Kids Get Working Class Jobs*. New York: Columbia University Press.

Wilson, William Julius. 1987. *The Truly Disadvantaged: The Inner City, the Underclass, and Public Policy*. Chicago: University of Chicago Press.

Wolf, Eric R. 1956b. "San Jose: Subcultures of a Traditional Coffee Municipality." In *The People of Puerto Rico: A Study in Social Anthropology*, by Julian Steward et al., pt. 7, 171–264. Urbana: University of Illinois Press.

———. 1982a. *Europe and the People without History*. Berkeley, Los Angeles, London: University of California Press. (Translations: German, Italian, Spanish.)

———. 1990b. "Distinguished Lecture: Facing Power—Old Insights, New Questions." *American Anthropologist* 92:586–596.

AUTHOR'S NOTES

The author would like to thank the following institutions for their support: The Russel Sage Foundation, the Harry Frank Guggenheim Foundation, the Social Science Research Council, the National Institute on Drug Abuse, the Wenner-Gren Foundation for Anthropological Research, the United States Bureau of the Census, and San Francisco State University. Helpful critical comments by Jane Schneider and Rayna Rapp changed the shape of the article. Finally, none of this could have been written without Harold Otto's moral support and typing, as well as final work on the keyboard by Henry Ostendorf and Charles Pearson.

a. Significantly, there are subsectors of the service industry that are relatively unionized—such as hospital work and even custodial work—where there is a limited autonomous space for street culture and working-class resistance.

b. "Fight the Power" is a song composed by the rap group Public Enemy.

36. Power and Projects: Reflections on Agency[a]

Sherry Ortner (b. 1941)

THESE REFLECTIONS on "agency" are part of a larger project which centers on a concept I have called in other contexts "serious games" (Ortner 1996a, 1999a). The idea of serious games represented one attempt to build upon the important insights of "practice theory" but at the same time move beyond them. The fundamental assumption of practice theory is that culture (in a very broad sense) constructs people as particular kinds of social actors, but social actors, through their living, on-the-ground, variable practices, reproduce or transform—and usually some of each—the culture that made them. Reduced to bare bones like this, the idea sounds simple, but it is not. The theoretical elaboration and empirical application of the concepts of practice theory have both proven its power and shown its holes.[1]

Responding to this the idea of serious games was meant to move questions of practice theory in several new directions. As in practice theory social life in a serious games perspective is seen as something that is actively played, oriented toward culturally constituted goals and projects, and involving both routine practices and intentionalized action. But the serious games perspective, as I will elaborate in part in this chapter, allows us to bring into focus more complex forms of social relations—especially relations of power—and more complex dimensions of the subjectivity of social actors—especially for present purposes, those involving "intentionality" and "agency."[2]

From *Anthropology and Social Theory* (2006)

1. Ortner opens with a series of critical ideas that she will explore in this essay. *Agency* in the anthropological sense is the ability of individuals to act independently and make their own choices. No one has unlimited agency. Our choices are limited by our material and social worlds. If you are a white female in America, it is very difficult to choose to be an Asian male. If you are born into poverty, you cannot choose to grow up in the wealthy suburbs. Thus, agency always occurs within wider structures and social circumstances. The balance between agency and structure is a key area of study for Ortner and other practice theorists.

Practice theory is a broad term for theoretical positions founded in the works of Pierre Bourdieu, and the British sociologist Anthony Giddens (b. 1938). It also owes much to Michel Foucault, Louis Althusser (1918–1990), and other French Marxist and postmodern thinkers. Ortner is one of the foremost synthesizers of their work. Her seminal 1984 essay "Theory in Anthropology since the Sixties" is an early and important statement of practice theory in the United States. It critiqued the popular approaches of that era for their relative absence of focus on both social reproduction and individual choices.

Ortner introduces the idea of "serious games" in her 1996 book *Making Gender: The Politics and Erotics of Culture*. In this work she says that the idea of a game captures the fact that "life is culturally organized and constructed, in terms of defining categories of actors, rules and goals of the game" and that such games are serious because "power and inequality pervade the games of life in multiple ways" (1996: 12).

2. "Subjectivity" is a key concept in practice theory and in much of current anthropological discourse. The term is meant to capture both individual psychological processes and the social structures in which these occur. In her essay "Subjectivity and Cultural Critique" Ortner (2005: 31) defines subjectivity as "the ensemble of modes of perception, affect, thought, desire, fear, and so forth that animate acting subjects . . . as well [as] the cultural and social formations that shape, organize, and provoke these modes of affect, thought and so on."

A few notes before proceeding: First, I need to say immediately that serious games have nothing to do with formalistic game theory, popular in the harder social sciences.[b] Interpretations of social life by way of serious games involve neither game theory's formal modeling nor its assumption that a kind of universal rationality prevails in virtually all kinds of social behavior. On the contrary "serious games" are quite emphatically cultural formations rather than analysts' models. In addition, a serious games perspective assumes culturally variable (rather than universal) and subjectively complex (rather than predominantly rationalistic and self-interested) actors.

I also need to say that the idea of (serious) games is not in any way meant to be a substitute for a theory of large-scale social and cultural processes. Despite its appearance of concentrating on micro-politics, its ultimate purpose is always to understand the larger forces, formations, and transformations of social life. In the normal course of the kinds of social and cultural analyses in which I am interested, one actually works in the opposite direction, starting with those larger formations and then trying to work backwards toward their underlying serious games.

This chapter, however, is focused on one particular piece of the serious games idea, namely the question of actors' agency and intentionality noted earlier. Serious games always involve the play of actors seen as "agents." Yet there is something about the very word "agency" that calls to mind the autonomous, individualistic, Western actor. The very categories historically standing behind practice theory, the opposition between "structure" and "agency," seem to suggest a heroic individual—The Agent—up against a **Borg-like** entity called "Structure." But nothing could be further from the way I envisage social agents, which is that they are always involved in, and can never act outside of, the multiplicity of social relations in which they are enmeshed. Thus while all social actors are assumed to "have" agency, the idea of actors as always being engaged with others in the play of serious games is meant to make it virtually impossible to imagine that the agent is free, or is an unfettered individual.[3]

But the social embeddedness of agents, which is central to the idea of serious games, may take at least two forms. On the one hand the agent is always embedded in relations of (would-be) solidarity: family, friends, kin, spouses or partners, children, parents, teachers, allies, and so forth. It is important to note this point because some of the critics of the agency concept, those who see agency as a bourgeois and individualistic concept, focus largely on the ways in which the concept appears to slight the "good" embeddedness of agents, the contexts of solidarity that mitigate agency in its individualistic and selfish forms.

On the other hand, the agent is always enmeshed within relations of power, inequality, and competition. Without ignoring relationships of solidarity, the omnipresence of power and inequality in social life is central to the very definition of serious games. (While earlier versions of practice theory did not wholly ignore questions of power, it is safe to say that those questions were not at the core of the framework) This chapter focuses specifically on the relationship between agency and power.

Ortner mentions her "chapter" in many places in this essay. "Power and Projects: Reflections on Agency" is the final chapter of Ortner's 2006 book *Anthropology and Social Theory: Culture, Power, and the Acting Subject*.

3. Here Ortner confronts a problem with deep roots in anthropological theory and Western thinking: a tendency to dualism. Ortner wants to avoid the idea of binary opposition between agency and structure. Rather, she sees these as deeply enmeshed with each other. Giddens describes human social activities as "recursive." He writes: "They are not brought into being by social actors but continually recreated by them via the very means whereby they express themselves as actors" (1984: 2). [*The Constitution of Society: An Outline of the Theory of Structuration*.]

The **"Borg"** refers to a set of extraordinarily powerful, extremely hierarchical extra-terrestrial entities from the television series *Star Trek: The Next Generation* (1987–1994) as well as several movies. The Borg address other beings with variations on the ideas "resistance is futile" and "you will be assimilated."

THE AGENCY PROBLEM

The idea of "agency" is beset by many of the same problems as the idea of "the subject" (see Chapter 5, Ortner *Anthropology and Social Theory: Culture, Power, and the Acting Subject* (2006)). There is a certain kind of antihumanist thinker or writer who has a knee-jerk antipathy to any allusions to either of these suspect phenomena. But for a more nuanced representation of the kinds of intellectual anxieties that these categories provoke, I will turn to the excellent introduction to Ethnography and the Historical Imagination (hereafter EHI) by John and Jean Comaroff (1992). The Comaroffs are not what are conventionally called "antihumanists." They are not interested in banishing the social subject from their theoretical models, nor individuals from their ethnographic histories. They are not interested in arguing for structural or discursive causation as against the effects of the actions of theoretically defined subjects and historical actors. Nonetheless the Introduction to EHI can be characterized as a kind of extended worry over "the humanist turn" (36) and "our current conceptual obsession with agency" (37).[4]

In the introduction to EHI the Comaroffs are trying to develop a general theoretical framework for an anthropological history. They have two overarching concerns about an overemphasis on agency in anthropological and historical analysis. The first is that, unless very carefully handled, agency harks back to deep ethnocentrisms:

> Many anthropologists have been wary of ontologies that give precedence to individuals over contexts. For these rest on manifestly Western assumptions: among them, that human beings can triumph over their context through sheer force of will, [and] that economy, culture, and society are the aggregate product of individual action and intention. (10)

The second concern, and one that is in some ways more central to their project, is that too much focus on the agency of individuals and/or groups results in a gross oversimplification of the processes involved in history. This oversimplification itself takes at least two forms. The first is simply that the social and cultural forces in play in any historical engagement are infinitely more complex than what can be learned from looking at actors' intentions: "The 'motivation' of social practice . . . always exists at two distinct, if related, levels: first, the (culturally configured) needs and desires of human beings; and second, the pulse of collective forces that, empowered in complex ways, work through them" (36). It is the close examination and analysis of the "pulse of collective forces" that, in the Comaroffs' view, begin to

---

4. Jean Comaroff (b. 1946) and John Comaroff (b. 1945) are South African anthropologists who have been professors at the University of Chicago and Harvard. They are particularly known for their work on British colonialism and its aftermath among the Tswana people. The Comaroffs studied with Monica Wilson (1908–1982) and Isaac Schapera (1905–2003), who helped establish South African anthropology in the nineteen twenties and thirties. Wilson and Schapera were students of A. R. Radcliffe-Brown and Bronislaw Malinowski. The Comaroffs were opponents of apartheid and strongly influenced by Marxist thinking. In addition to postcolonialism, the Comaroffs' anthropology has been concerned with witchcraft, law, globalization, and hegemony.

John and Jean Comaroff are also the subjects of accusations and lawsuits concerning sexual harassment and abuse of power during their times at both University of Chicago and Harvard. As of summer 2023, Harvard is facing nine counts relating to sexual harassment and abuse of power by the Comaroffs and several other anthropology professors (Hamid and Schisgall 2023).

The "humanist turn" Ortner refers to here is a movement in the social sciences to "move beyond awareness of cultural differences and look for that which all human beings share" (Kozlarek 2011: 20, https://unesdoc.unesco.org/ark:/48223/pf0000213085_ara.locale=en). Proponents of the humanist turn argue that ideas about what it means to be human and what is dehumanizing are present in all cultures and that these can form the basis for political and social action. "Antihumanist," as it is used here, refers to theories that do not account for the individual subject such as those of Kroeber (essay 9), and Radcliffe-Brown (essay 15). However, this is an unusual use of the term. By conventional measure, all the authors represented in this volume are humanists. That is, they are all centered on understanding people without recourse to the divine or mystical.

get slighted when the weight of analytic effort gets shifted to "agency," and that results in a deeply inadequate account of what was actually going on.

[The problem] becomes particularly visible when we examine epochal movements like European colonialism, in which purposive, "heroic" action was a central motif, even a driving impulse. Yet, from our perspective, that impulse is not enough to account for the determination of the processes involved—or even to tell very much of the story. (36)

The second dimension of lost complexity is in some ways an extension of the first. If an analysis that is too focused on the intentionalities of actors loses sight of large-scale social and cultural forces in play, it also—the Comaroffs fear—loses sight of the complex, and highly unpredictable, relationship between intentions and outcomes. Specifically, they remind their readers of the importance, and prevalence, of unintended consequences in any historical process. Speaking of their *Of Revelation and Revolution* project (Jean and J. L. Comaroff 1991; J. L. and Jean Comaroff 1997) they emphasize the degree to which the processes of cultural transformation constantly worked in unanticipated ways: "The scattered signs retrieved in [the research] all pointed to wider social transformations borne *unwittingly* by the missionaries. In many respects these actually ran counter to their own desires and motives" (EHI, 36). The suggestion here is that "desires and motives" the stuff of intentionality and agency, are sometimes actually irrelevant to outcomes, but at the very least have a complicated and highly mediated relationship to outcomes. This complexity again, they fear, tends to get lost in the "obsession with agency."[5]

Speaking for myself, but also I think for many other theorists interested in questions of agency, I can only agree that these dangers are always potentially real. And there are no doubt certain kinds of work that fall into the various traps the Comaroffs describe. But an important body of theoretical work has been developed precisely to theorize the "desires and motives" and practices of real people in the social process (1) without "giving precedence to individuals over contexts"; (2) without importing Western assumptions such as the idea "that human beings can triumph over their context through sheer force of will, [or] that economy, culture, and society are the aggregate product of individual action and intention"; (3) without slighting "the pulse of collective forces"; and (4) always recognizing the ever-present likelihood of unintended consequences. The reader will recognize here the framework with which I began this essay (and this volume), the framework of practice theory within which neither "individuals" nor "social forces" have "precedence," but in which nonetheless there is a dynamic, powerful, and sometimes transformative relationship between the practices of real people and the structures of society, culture, and history.

Interestingly the idea of agency was not much developed in two of the three key texts of early practice theory: Pierre Bourdieu's *Outline of a Theory of Practice* (1977) and Marshall Sahlins's *Historical Metaphors and Mythical Realities* (1981). Although there are discussions in Bourdieu that see actors as exhibiting what we would think of as "agency," the term is not theorized in this or in his later elaboration of the theory (1990). This omission may be intentional, but speculations on this point (e.g., on a lingering antihumanism in Bourdieu's work) would carry us far beyond the

---

5. Much of twentieth-century anthropology was a reaction against the idea that individuals play a central role in culture and history. However, in popular culture, history has often been understood as the actions of great men and women. Anthropologists tended to argue against the importance of the individual. As we noted earlier in this book, Leslie White compared the Egyptian Pharaoh Ikhnaton to a sack of sawdust (essay 16, note 10).

The Comaroffs' *Of Revelation and Revolution* (1991, 1997) is a two-volume analysis of the history and current effects of the nineteenth and twentieth-century evangelization of the Southern Tswana people by British missionaries. The analysis focuses on the ways in which culture structures thought and the global context in which encounters between the Tswana and the evangelists occurred.

confines of this essay. It may also be relevant, however, that there is apparently no French term for what American and British social theorists mean by "agency," as I learned when I recently had a paper translated into French.[c] The term is also largely missing from Marshall Sahlins's book, in part I think because of the French influence on Sahlins's work, and in part because his interest in historical transformation led him to elaborate not on agents and agency, but on "events" and their dynamics.[6]

Agency was however important to the third of the founding texts, Anthony Giddens's *Central Problems in Social Theory* (1979). And it has been important to the work of the Americans who have continued to work on practice theory: William H. Sewell Jr. and myself.[d] The Anglo-American bias toward agency in the practice theory literature lends some credence to the idea that agency is a form of Western individualism. Yet I think it would be a grave mistake to dismiss agency as merely a piece of American ethno-psychology not transferable to other cultural contexts, or even to "humanity" in general. Let me probe more deeply into its theoretical and philosophical underpinnings.[7]

DEFINING AGENCY

The issues involved in defining agency are perhaps best approached by sorting out a series of components: (1) the question of whether or not agency inherently involves "intentions"; (2) the simultaneous universality and cultural constructedness of agency; and (3) the relationship between agency and "power." I will

say a few words about how each of these has been approached by others, and also indicate my own position on each.[e]

Before continuing let me reiterate that "agency" is never a thing in itself but is always part of a process of what Giddens calls structuration, the making and remaking of larger social and cultural formations. As I focus on defining agency in this section it may seem to be a kind of freestanding psychological object, but that (mis)impression will be corrected in the final section of the essay.

Intentionality

I begin with the question of intentionality because in some ways it gets to the heart of what agency means. "Intentionality" here is meant to include a wide range of states, both cognitive and emotional, and at various levels of consciousness, that are directed forward toward some end. Thus intentionality in agency might include highly conscious plots and plans and schemes; somewhat more nebulous aims, goals, and ideals; and finally desires, wants, and needs that may range from being deeply buried to quite consciously felt. In short intentionality as a concept is meant to include all the ways in which action is cognitively and emotionally pointed toward some purpose.

On this question theorists tend to fall out along a continuum. At one end are what I think of as "soft" definitions of agency, in which intention is not a central component. Examples include "A sense that the self is an authorized social being" (Ortner 1996a: 10); "the socio-culturally mediated capacity to act" (Ahearn

---

6. Marshall Sahlins (1930–2021) was a student of Leslie White and Morton Fried (1923–1986) who was deeply influenced by cultural ecology and the economics of Karl Polanyi (1886–1964). Like his mentors, Sahlins sees culture as a force that cannot be reduced to its constituent elements. However, he has also focused on culture as the result of history, environment, individual action, and chance. He distinguishes between "systemic agency," social structures that give some people power and deprive others of it, and "conjunctural agency," historic circumstances that coincidentally amplify the actions of individuals (Sahlins 2004). [*Apologies to Thucydides: Understanding History as Culture and Vice Versa.* Chicago: University of Chicago Press.]

7. Giddens calls his theoretical position *structuration*. Structuration examines the balance between agency and structure. Giddens argued that "structures as rules and resources are both the precondition and unintended outcome of people's agency" (Baert 1998: 104).

William H. Sewell Jr. (b. 1940) is a University of Chicago historian whose work has centered on France in the eighteenth and nineteenth centuries. Sewell argues for a history that is more informed by anthropological theory as well as an anthropology more attuned to historical detail. Sewell is strongly influenced by Bourdieu.

2001b: 112); "the property of those entities (i) that have some degree of control over their own behavior, (ii) whose actions in the world affect other entities' . . . and (iii) whose actions are the object of evaluation . . ." (Duranti 2004: 453); and "a stream of actual or contemplated causal interventions of corporeal beings in the ongoing process of events-in-the-world" (Giddens 1979: 55).[8]

In some cases people who provide such "soft" definitions do not address the question of intentionality at all. Giddens however does provide a discussion of the relationship between intentionality and agency. But it is in a sense a "soft" relationship. Giddens acknowledges "the intentional or purposive character of human behavior," but at the same time he emphasizes "'intentionality' as process. Such intentionality is a routine feature of human conduct, and does not imply that actors have definite goals consciously held in mind during the course of their activities" (1979: 56). In other words acknowledging intentionality as a general disposition of humans as agents is an acceptable position; seeing intentionality as "definite goals consciously held in the mind" is more problematic.[f] This is so for several reasons: First, because what are presented discursively by actors as intentions are often after-the-fact rationalizations (57); second, because—and here the problematic word is "conscious"—Giddens wants to leave space for the Freudian unconscious in a theory of action (58); and finally because—as the Comaroffs also argued—too much focus on explicit intentions obscures the fact that most social outcomes are in fact unintended consequences of action (59).

I do not disagree with these points. One has to be careful with intentionality for all the reasons Giddens (and the Comaroffs) noted. Yet if one is too soft on intentionality, one loses a distinction that I think needs to be maintained, between routine practices on the one hand, and "agency" seen precisely as more intentionalized action on the other.[9]

On the other end of the continuum are thinkers who make intention (in various senses) much more central to their concept of agency. For example, Charles Taylor, not in his paper on agency (1985a) but in "The Concept of a Person" (1985b: 99) says, "To say that things matter to agents is to say that we can attribute purposes, desires, aversions to them . . ." But the most developed presentation of this position is to be found in William H. Sewell Jr.'s by now classic paper, "A Theory of Structure: Duality, Agency, and Transformation" (1992). Sewell's definitions of agency are always full of intentions in the broadest sense, that is, always seem to be projected forward, if not toward "definite goals"; then at least in ways more actively motivated than is the case for routine practices. Thus he first defines agency as "the strivings and motivated transactions that constitute the experienced surface of social life" (2). He later defines "a capacity for agency" as a capacity "for desiring, for forming intentions, and for acting creatively" (20). Finally, in a discussion of the ways in which agency can be collective as well as individual, he says that "agency entails an ability to coordinate one's actions with others and against others, to form collective projects, to persuade, to coerce . . ." (21).[g, 10]

I share Sewell's "hard" conception of agency for the reason given above, namely,

---

8. Laura Ahearn (b. 1962) is linguistic and sociocultural anthropologist who has worked primarily in Nepal. She is particularly interested in issues of language, agency, and gender. Ahearn was a professor at Rutgers but now works for the consulting firm Social Impact.

9. For Ortner, the critical problem with the "soft" intentionality she has just discussed is that in these examples, human behavior seems to be simply a function of humans living in the world. A focus on soft intentionality leaves little room for the view that people actively pursue consciously chosen goals.

10. Charles Taylor (b. 1931) is a Canadian philosopher whose work opposes attempts to understand human society that are rooted in the natural sciences. Taylor also contests the idea, central to the work of Max Weber, that the world is becoming more rational and secular as well as less religious. Taylor argues that moral identity is fundamental to personal identity. Our moral identity, he argues, is defined by our fundamental evaluations

that it is the strong role of active (though not necessarily fully "conscious") intentionality in agency that, in my view, differentiates agency from routine practices. Of course there is not some hard and fast boundary between them; rather there is a kind of continuum between routine practices that proceed with little reflection and planning, and agentive acts that intervene in the world with something in mind (or in heart). But it seems worthwhile to try to maintain the distinction that defines the two ends of the spectrum.

The Cultural Construction of Agency

There is general agreement across all theorists that agency in some sense is universal, and is part of a fundamental humanness. William Sewell says explicitly that "a capacity for agency . . . is inherent in all humans" (1992: 20). Alessandro Duranti points out that "all languages have grammatical structures that seem designed to represent agency" (2004: 467). Charles Taylor simply uses "agent" interchangeably with person, self, and human being (1985a passim).[h, 11]

At the same time there is general agreement that agency is always culturally and historically constructed. Sewell uses the analogy of the capacity for language. Just as all humans have the capacity for language but must learn to speak a particular language, so all humans have a capacity for agency, but the specific forms it takes will vary in different times and places.

The authors vary in emphasizing different domains of social life as shapers of agency. Charles Taylor in a very general way, and Laura Ahearn and Alessandro Duranti in much more specific ways, focuses on the relationships between language and agency. For Giddens the most relevant level is that of social practices and interactions. Sewell importantly invokes "the schemas that are part of any cultural repertoire" that are both imposed and drawn upon in shaping forms of desire, courses of action, and so forth (1992: 8). The notion of cultural

schemas in this sense has been central to some of my own work as well, from my early discussion of "key scenarios" (Ortner 1973) to my work on (Sherpa) cultural schemas in *High Religion* (1989a). And finally, agency is differentially shaped, and also nourished or stunted, under different regimes of power, which brings us to the final dimension of defining agency.

The Relationship between Agency and Power

A number of theorists of agency do not spend much time on questions of power,[i] beyond a sort of general notion that agency is the capacity to affect things. In my own view, however, agency and social power in a relatively strong sense are very closely linked. Thus here I will quickly survey only those authors who give this question some systematic attention.

Laura Ahearn, first, opens her essay on "Language and Agency" (2001b) with the question, "why agency now?" and answers it in part by relating it to the emergence of social and political movements starting in the 1970s. This is to say that the emergence of a problematic of "agency" had its roots in questions of power from the outset.

Partly as a result of that history, "agency" came to be equated in many people's minds with the idea of "resistance." Ahearn rightly asserts, however, that "oppositional agency is only one of many forms of agency" (2001b: 115). Yet it is clear that questions of power more broadly conceived are central to Ahearn's thinking about agency. Her point is not that domination and resistance are irrelevant, but that that human emotions, and hence questions of agency, within relations of power and inequality are always complex and contradictory (2001b: 116; see also Chapter 1, this volume).

Where Ahearn addresses the complexity of motivations and intentionalities generated in relations of power, Giddens moves the discussion of agency and power back into his larger theory of structuration (1979). On the one

---

"intellectual and moral commitments that constitute us as knowers and judgers" (Calhoun 1998). Such evaluations "are at the core of our conception of what is a good, fulfilling life" (Maclure 2006).

11. Alessandro Duranti (b. 1950), a linguistic anthropologist (and former Dean of Social Sciences) at UCLA, works primarily in Samoa and has written extensively about agency and intentionality.

hand he argues that "the concept of action [a term he sometimes uses interchangeably with agency] is logically tied to that of power, where the latter notion is understood as transformative capacity" (88). On the other hand the transformative capacity of agents is only one dimension of how power operates in social systems. It also operates as what he distinguishes as "domination," that is, power as it is built into objectified structures like institutions and discourses. The two in turn are interconnected through his notion of the "duality of structure" (91–92), as mediated by "resources." But here the discussion gets rather murky.[12]

In his discussion of Giddens's notion of resources, Sewell assures us first that the confusion is not entirely in the mind of the reader: "I agree with Giddens that any notion of structure that ignores asymmetries of power is radically incomplete. But [using] an undertheorized notion of resources . . . succeeds merely in confusing things" (1992: 9). He then clarifies what is meant by resources, how these are implicated in power, and how all of this ties up with what we mean by agency:

However unequally resources may be distributed, some measure of both human and nonhuman resources are controlled by all members of society, no matter how destitute and oppressed. Indeed, part of what it means to conceive of human beings as agents is to conceive of them as empowered by access to resources of one kind or another. (1992: 9–10)

Sewell returns to issues of power in the article's section entitled "Agency." He argues (here in agreement with Giddens) that "agency is not opposed to, but . . . constituent of, structure" (1992: 20). It is here that he makes the point noted above about the universality of human agency. But he goes on to talk about power differentials and the ways in which they affect people's capacities for, and forms of, agency:

It is . . . important . . . to insist that the agency exercised by different persons is far from uniform, that agency differs enormously in both kind and extent. What kinds of desires people can have, what intentions they can form, and what sorts of creative transpositions they can carry out vary dramatically from one social world to another.
. . . Structures . . . empower agents differentially, which also implies that they embody the desires, intentions, and knowledge of agents differentially as well. Structures, and the human agencies they endow, are laden with differences power. (20–21)

Ahearn on the one hand and Giddens and Sewell on the other approach the nexus of agency and power quite differently. But my point is not so much to draw out the contrast (although that might be an interesting exercise), as simply to agree with all of them that a strong theory of agency (and more broadly a transformed theory of practice) must be closely linked with questions of power and inequality. The question for the rest of this chapter is the nature of that linkage.

Please note: Many of the major examples in the discussion that follows are drawn from the realm of gender. This was not entirely intentional; I did not initially set out to write an essay about agency as a gendered issue. There is no question, however, that in a great many cases the most vivid examples of the relationships between agency and power turn out to be found in the realm of gender relations. But of course questions of agency also go far beyond gender relations. Thus gender here stands not only for itself but for a range of other forms of power and inequality, as will become clear in the course of the discussion.[13]

12. Note here the similarity between Giddens and Foucault (see essay 28). Both discuss the relationship between power and discourse. Both Foucault and Giddens wrote in similar ways about the rise of the surveillance state and how prisons set the pattern for other kinds of discipline (see Giddens, *A Contemporary Critique of Historical Materialism*).

13. Part of Ortner's background is her work on gender and structuralism. One of her early works is the 1974 essay "Is Female to Male as Nature Is to Culture?" in which she presents a structural analysis of gender inequality (essay 21 in this volume). In the essay you are currently reading, Ortner uses examples from gen-

THREE MINI ESSAYS ON AGENCY AND POWER

Broadly speaking the notion of agency can be said to have two fields of meaning, both of which have been signaled in the preceding discussion. In one field of meaning "agency" is about intentionality and the pursuit of (culturally defined) projects.[j] In the other field of meaning agency is about power, about acting within relations of social inequality, asymmetry, and force. In fact "agency" is never merely one or the other. Its two "faces"—as (the pursuit of) "projects" or as (the exercise of or against) "power"—either blend or bleed into one another or else retain their distinctiveness but intertwine in a **Moebius**-type relationship. Moreover, power itself is double-edged, operating from above as domination and from below as resistance. The Moebius helix therefore becomes even more complex. All of this may seem rather dense; the examples to come are meant to play out what these points look like in practice.[14]

The Textual Construction of Agency

I begin with an interpretation of some Grimms' fairy tales.[k] I said above that, while in some sense agency is a capacity of all human beings, its form and, as it were, its distribution are always culturally constructed and maintained. Substantively, then, this exercise will allow us to see in some detail what might be called the politics of agency, the cultural work involved in constructing and distributing agency as part of the process of creating appropriately gendered,

and thus among other things differentially empowered, persons.[l]

The brothers Grimm reworked and wrote down the tales in a particular time and place— early-nineteenth-century Germany. One could certainly ask questions about the relationship between their acts of inscription and its historical context but that would be a very different exercise. One could also ask questions about the variable ways in which these tales were heard, interpreted, and used in ordinary social practice, but again that would be a very different exercise. Here I have a more modest purpose: I am simply interested in looking at what might be called the narrative politics involved in the construction of agency in a particular body of stories, something which, at least for me, virtually leaps out of the texts.[15]

As we shall see agency or its absence in the tales is expressed largely through an idiom of activity and passivity. Activity involves pursuing "projects"; passivity involves not simply refraining from pursuing projects, but refraining in a sense from even desiring to do so. I should note first that for the most part the only consistently active female characters in the tales are wicked—the wicked stepmothers and witches who have evil projects and seek by evil means to carry them out. I will return to them below. Here I want to focus on the heroines, the little girls and young princesses who are the protagonists of their stories.[m] Most of these heroines are in the mode of what the folklorist V. I. Propp (1968) calls "victim heroes": Although they are the protagonists the action of the story is moved along by virtue of bad things happening to them rather than by their initiating

---

der research. However, she attempts to transcend structural analysis. Rather than seeing structure and agency as a binary distinction that can be mediated by a third force, Ortner suggests that structure and agency are related aspects of a single process. Agency is, in some way, the acting out of structure, and structure is created by the ways in which it is acted out.

14. **"Moebius helix"** or Möbius strip: an object in three-dimensional space that appears to have two sides but in fact has only one. It is named for one of its discoverers, the German mathematician August Ferdinand Möbius (1790–1868). Here, Ortner uses it as an analogy to suggest that something that appears to have two aspects, in fact, has only one.

15. Ortner's first example is interesting: She analyzes a body of text rather than the actions of real people within a culture. There has been an accepted linkage between culture and text since Clifford Geertz's book *The Interpretation of Culture* (1973).

actions as in the case of the majority of male heroes. Thus passivity is to some extent built into most of these girls from the outset.

Yet a closer look at the tales shows that even many of these victim heroines take roles of active agency in the early parts of their stories. Though their initial misfortunes may have happened to them through outside agency, they sometimes seize the action and carry it along themselves, becoming—briefly—heroines in the active questing sense usually reserved for male heroes. But—and this is the crux of the (gendered) politics of agency—they are invariably punished for this. The action of the tales systematically, and often ruthlessly, forces them to renounce this active stance, forces them to renounce the possibility of formulating and enacting projects, even when those projects are altruistic.[16]

At the simplest level I take these stories to be tales of "passage," of moving from childhood to adulthood. For the boy heroes passage generally involves the successful enactment of agency—solving a problem, finding a lost object, slaying the dragon, rescuing the damsel in distress. For all of the female protagonists, however, passage almost exclusively involves the renunciation of agency. Agentic girls, girls who seize the action too much, are punished in one of two ways. The less common form of punishment, first, is the denial of passage to adulthood. Five of the tales have heroines who are fully active and fully successful in enacting their projects. In one version of "Little Red Riding Hood," for example, the girl and her grandmother get up on the roof and successfully kill the wolf and turn him into sausage. Or in "Hansel and Gretel" it is Gretel who kills the witch. In these and other cases of active and specifically successful heroism on the part of the heroine, the girl does not achieve what the vast majority of Grimms' heroines achieve—the mark of female adulthood, marriage.[n] Instead

she returns to her natal home at the end of the story, and does not achieve passage.

In the more common female tale the heroine gets married at the end. But if she has been at all active in the early part of the tale (and sometimes even if she has not), she must invariably pass through severe trials before being worthy of marrying the prince, or by implication, any man at all. These trials always involve symbols and practices of utter passivity and/or total inactivity, as well as practices of humility and subordination. In "Sweetheart Roland,"[o] she cleverly saves her skin at the beginning, and then saves both herself and her lover, but for her pains her lover betroths another woman. In response the heroine turns herself first into a stone (utterly inert), then into a flower (in which form she says she hopes to be stepped on and crushed), and finally cleans house for some time for a shepherd before marrying her sweetheart in the end. In "The Twelve Brothers" and "The Six Swans,"[p] the heroine actively sets out on a quest to rescue her brothers. Despite her good intentions, however, she causes her brothers damage as a result of her efforts to save them and goes through a seven year period of complete silence and solemnity (including in one case making shirts for her brothers and in the other case simply spinning for seven years) before getting married at the end.

If any sort of agency must be punished, even for "good" girls, the punishment is even worse for "bad" female characters, the witches and wicked stepmothers. These women are highly agentic: they have projects, plans, plots. Needless to say they all come to terrible ends. After trying and failing to kill Snow White, for example, the stepmother/witch is invited to the wedding of Snow White and the Prince, but once there she is forced to dance in red-hot slippers until she falls down dead. Since she and similar characters have done wicked things, their

---

16. Although the linkage between culture and text starts with interpretive anthropology, Ortner's essay is more a reflection of Althusser's ideas about social reproduction and her concept of key scenarios. In an important 1973 essay, "On Key Symbols," Ortner suggests that some symbols are key scenarios that formulate a "culture's basic means-ends relationships in actable forms" (1973: 1341). For example, if a text such as Grimms' fairy tales is a key scenario, then children will absorb culturally significant gender behaviors through reading or listening to the stories.

punishments seem justified on moral grounds, yet within the general pattern of punishing any sort of female agency, it seems fair to suggest that they are punished as much for their excessive agency as for its moral content.[17]

In sum we can see these tales as cultural formations that construct and distribute agency in particular ways, as part of the cultural politics of creating appropriately gendered persons in that particular time and place. From the actor's point of view, the "project" of the story is the project of growing up, of doing the appropriate things to become an adult man or woman. Within the cultural politics of gender difference and inequality that informs the tales, however, growing up means that both parties in this ultimately unequal relationship cannot "have" agency. This is couched in a language of (the complementary of) activity and passivity. The prince cannot be a hero if the princess can rescue herself.[q] Even worse the prince cannot be a hero if the princess can rescue him.[r]

But an examination of texts like the Grimms' fairy tales has narrowed our focus to the cultural construction of social subjects as agents (or not), that is, it has narrowed our focus to the culturally constituted psychology of players within serious games. For the rest of this chapter, however, I want to move to the broader level at which the relationship(s) between agency and power are organized into the serious games of culture and history in the first place.

Projects on the Edge of Power

I have long been interested in the question of how people sustain a culturally meaningful life in situations of large-scale domination by powerful others, including prominently slavery, colonialism, and racism. This was a central theme, for example, of *Life and Death on Mt. Everest* (Ortner 1999a), where I discussed the ways in which Sherpas, despite having been greatly affected by a century of intimate involvement in Himalayan mountaineering, nonetheless retain arenas of culturally

"authentic" life. By this I mean not that those arenas are untouched by the massive presence of mountaineering, but simply that they are shaped less by the mountaineering encounter and more by the Sherpas' own social and political relations, and by their own culturally constituted intentions, desires, and projects. We may shorthand this idea as cultural life "on the margins of power."

During this extended moment when the often linked histories of anthropology and colonialism are being worked out, and when the very practices of anthropology in light of those histories are being rethought, it seems important to pay attention to this question of cultural "authenticity" in the shadow of massive, and culturally (as well as physically) hostile, forms of power. One response by many anthropologists has been to emphasize the degree to which colonialism so formed and deformed the societies in question that what anthropologists have seen in later fieldwork has virtually no cultural authenticity at all, that it is largely a Western and/or colonial product. Clearly this position in its extreme form would tend to replicate at an intellectual level the sins of historical colonialism itself.[s] As against this position it seems important to seek different ways of thinking about these questions.[t]

The example of "power" for present purposes is colonialism in southern Africa, as discussed by Jean and John Comaroff in *Of Revelation and Revolution*, Volumes 1 and 2.[u] The Comaroffs brilliantly explore the "long conversation" between Methodist missionaries and Tswana subjects, and the ways in which over time Tswana consciousness has been transformed by the ideas and practices introduced by the missionaries.

Here however I wish to draw something different out of their material. In looking at their data I found it useful to distinguish broadly between two modalities of agency, as broached at the beginning of this section. In one modality agency is closely related to ideas of power, including both domination and resistance; in

---

17. Ortner discusses how agency is presented in these stories but not how these messages are received and acted on in real life. At the start of this section, Ortner discussed the two sides of agency: intentionality and power. The Grimms' fairy tales reflect the gendered power relationships of late eighteenth and early nineteenth century Europe but say nothing about intentionality—the use to which children then or today put those stories.

another it is closely related to ideas of intention, to people's (culturally constituted) projects in the world and their ability to engage and enact them. I must emphasize again that these are not two different "things," although I despair of a terminology that may seem to render them as such. At an epistemological level the contrast is between what I called earlier two fields of meaning. At the ethnographic level, however, what is at stake is a contrast between the workings of agency within massive power relations, like colonialism or racism, as opposed to the workings of agency in contexts in which such relations can be—however momentarily, however partially—held at bay. Here it is less a matter of things than a matter of contexts.

Let us return for a moment to the categories and say a bit more about agency as power. In probably the most common usage "agency" can be virtually synonymous with the forms of power people have at their disposal, their ability to act on their own behalf, influence other people and events, and maintain some kind of control in their own lives. Agency in this sense is relevant for both domination and resistance. People in positions of power "have"—legitimately or not—what might be thought of as "a lot of agency," but the dominated too always have certain capacities, and sometimes very significant capacities, to exercise some sort of influence over the ways in which events unfold. Resistance then is also a form of "power-agency," and by now we have a well-developed theoretical repertoire for examining it. It includes everything from outright rebellions at one end, to various forms of what James Scott (1985) so well called "foot dragging" in the middle, to—at the other end—a kind of complex and ambivalent acceptance of dominant categories and practices that are always

changed at the very moment they are adopted. Instances across the whole spectrum of "resistance" (although the Comaroffs eschew the term) can be found throughout the *Revelation and Revolution* opus, but it is the last type that is most central to it and most fully developed: ambivalent acceptance by many Tswana people of missionary categories and practices, together with a constant recasting and reframing of them in terms of their own ways of seeing and acting in the world.[18]

The agency of (unequal) power, of both domination and resistance, may be contrasted with the second major mode of agency noted earlier, that of intentions, purposes, and desires formulated in terms of culturally established "projects." This agency of projects is from certain points of view the most fundamental dimension of the idea of agency. It is this that is disrupted in and disallowed to subordinates, as in the example of what happens to active, intending girls in the Grimms' fairy tales. It is also this that flourishes as power for the powerful, whose domination of others is rarely an end in itself but is rather in the service of enacting their own projects. And finally it is this—an agency of projects—that the less powerful seek to nourish and protect by creating or protecting sites, literally or metaphorically, "on the margins of power."

What, then, would such cultural projects look like? Many are simple "goals" for individuals, as in the case of the fairy tale heroine who wishes to grow up, marry the prince, and live happily ever after. Here the notion of agency as individual "intention" and "desire" comes to the fore, although one must never lose sight of the fact that the goals are fully culturally constituted. But many projects are full-blown "serious games," involving the intense play of

---

18. James Scott (b. 1936) is the Sterling Professor of Political Science at Yale. In the 1980s, Scott was recognized for his studies of resistance to power by subordinate groups. Two of his best-known works are *Weapons of the Weak: Everyday Forms of Peasant Resistance* (1985) and *Domination and the Arts of Resistance: Hidden Transcripts* (1990). Scott argued that even in social situations such as slavery that seem to completely deny autonomy and power to people, resistance is never fully conquered. Scott searched for and celebrated such resistance. His ideas play a strong role in the similar insistence that, despite situations of inequality or oppression, all people still have some degree of agency. This argument carries over to his more recent work such as *Seeing Like a State* (2000) in which Scott analyzes the failure of state development plans. He argues that state plans to make people rational and governable fail because of the faulty assumptions such plans make about nature, science, power, and the agency of people within the state.

multiply positioned subjects pursuing cultural goals within a matrix of local inequalities and power differentials.

As an example of the latter let me turn to the extensive discussions of precolonial Tswana politics, kinship, and marriage (see especially J. L. Comaroff and Jean Comaroff 1981; J. L. Comaroff 1987 and Jean and J. L. Comaroff 1991: Chapter 4). Here we see the strong cultural value invested in male political careers, in which Tswana men seek to better their positions in relation to royal families, local rivals, and the like. We learn how these men seek to "eat" their rivals and to establish themselves as patrons with arrays of clients in their service. We see how kinship relations and marriage transactions are managed in relation to the furtherance of these careers.

This is an example first of all of agency primarily in the sense of the pursuit of (cultural) projects. It is not about heroic actors or unique individuals, nor is it about bourgeois strategizing; nor on the other hand is it entirely about routine everyday practices that proceed with little reflection. Rather it is about (relatively ordinary) life socially organized in terms of culturally constituted projects that infuse life with meaning and purpose. People seek to accomplish valued things within a framework of their own terms, their own categories of value.

But this is also not free agency. The political rivalries are themselves generated by various orders of social and political asymmetries and/or rivalries between chiefs and commoners, free men and serfs, fathers and sons, men and women, agnates and affines, and so on and so forth. The cultural desires or intentions, in other words, emerge from structurally defined differences of social categories and differentials of power. Thus as I stated above these cultural projects are themselves serious games, the social play of cultural goals organized in and around local relations of power. The point is thus not that the pursuit of cultural projects is something wholly innocent of power relations; quite the contrary, as we have just seen in the example of Tswana men's politics. But the point of making the distinction between agency-in-the-sense-of-power and an agency-in-the-sense-of-(the pursuit of)-proj-

ects is that the first is organized around the axis of domination and resistance, and thus defined to a great extent by the terms of the dominant party, while the second is defined by local logics of the good and the desirable and how to pursue them.

For a second, and slightly more complicated, example let us look at Tswana women. We learn from earlier Comaroff writings that women had some significant disadvantages within Tswana society. In the traditional division of labor women did all the agricultural work. The work was fairly laborious in itself, and its laboriousness was compounded by certain kinds of chiefly powers and chiefly demands in relation to agriculture. In addition women were culturally viewed and ritually remade as inferior and subordinate (Jean Comaroff 1985). It was a specific feature of the initiation rites that young girls were trained in "passive obedience" and "docile endurance" (Jean Comaroff 1985: n5, n6). The data here have very strong resonances with the European fairy tales discussed above. The Tswana rites constructed the girls precisely as subjects from whom any vestige of agency was ideally drained out.

Under these circumstances much of the "agency" of women that appears even in the earlier works is reactive to power, is an agency of "power-as-resistance." For example during the initiation rites, even as the women were constructed as docile bodies ready for sex, marriage, and hard agricultural labor, they expressed "resistance to established gender relations: provocative song and dance, intrusive noise and explicit accusation" (Jean Comaroff 1985: 117). And, although in the traditional context such gestures appear to have had relatively minor impact, Jean Comaroff suggests that they represented "a suppressed, but continuing undercurrent of female discontent in the precolonial system" that played a significant role in the "enthusiastic response of [Tswana] women to the Methodist mission" (1985: 118). Here, then, the agency of power-as-resistance moves toward the status of something more active, something resembling a "project." In embracing Methodism it would seem that many Tswana women began to embrace a vision of an alternative world that went beyond the reactive opposition to male and/or chiefly domination.[19]

In addition, however, we can perhaps tease out an agency of projects, a sense of women enacting their own (culturally constituted) intentions, even in the precolonial context. This is more difficult to see, in part because women were, as just noted, precisely not supposed to have agency in this sense. Yet there are hints in the texts that one could see women's relationship to their agricultural work, for example, in this light. Women not only did all the agricultural work, but they also "held fields in their own right as daughters or wives" (Jean Comaroff 1985: 64). They seem to have invested much pride and planning in their agricultural activities; occasionally they tried to evade or resist chiefly regulation of agricultural activities (J. L. Comaroff and Jean Comaroff 1997: 128); and finally, when the missionaries actively sought to make agriculture men's rather than women's work, the women strongly resisted this change (ibid.: 136–37). I call attention here less to the resistance itself, than to the likelihood that the resistance signaled an important arena of women's projects of pride and identity, with which the missionaries were interfering. Perhaps resistance is always of this nature: protecting projects, or indeed the right to have projects. I note again that the distinction between an agency of power and an agency of projects is largely heuristic. In practice they are often inseparable.

Both of these examples—of men's political practices and women's practices of fertility (there was a close cultural link between agricultural and physical fertility [Jean Comaroff 1985: 65])—are examples of what I am calling agency as (the pursuit of) projects. The agency of projects is not necessarily about domination and resistance, although there may be some of that going on. It is about people having desires that grow out of their own structures of life, including very centrally their own structures of inequality; it is in short about people playing, or trying to play, their own serious games even

as more powerful parties seek to devalue and even destroy them.

I said earlier that in some ways the notion of projects is perhaps the most fundamental dimension of the idea of agency. In the discussion of the Grimms' fairy tales "power" consisted of destroying the girls' agency precisely in the sense of their capacity to actively enact projects. In the present section I set the discussion at a different level, contrasting the forms of agency seen within the dialectics of domination and resistance, and the forms of agency seen when actors are engaged in cultural projects, serious games whose terms are not primarily set by the power dialectic. At issue once again is the importance of questioning the totalizing effect of formations like colonialism or racism, and of attempting to see the ways in which dominated actors retain "agency" in either mode—by resisting domination in a range of ways, but also by trying to sustain their own culturally constituted projects, to make or sustain a certain kind of cultural (or for that matter, personal) authenticity "on the margins of power."

The Elementary Structure of Agency

In the previous section I looked at agency-as-power and agency-as-projects almost as if they occupied two different spaces. This was an intentional move as I tried to think about the dynamics of local agency in the face of domination by outsiders and powerful others. Here however I wish to look at the organization of "projects" themselves and think about something that was hinted at in the case of Tswana men's politics: the ways in which the agency of projects, the agency involved in pursuing significant cultural ends, almost always, and almost necessarily, involves internal relationships of power. Marx saw the point quite clearly: very schematically, for capitalists to play the serious game of capitalism, to make a profit and defeat the competition, they had to subordinate and exploit workers. The agency of project intrinsically hinges on the agency of power.

---

19. The Comaroffs suggest that resistance expressed in song and dance underlie female discontent and a willingness to change or opt out of the culture by embracing the Methodist Church.

This little structure interrelating projects and power is extremely widespread. That is why I am calling it, with only slight tongue in cheek, "the elementary structure of agency." In this final section of the chapter I will begin by simply illustrating the way in which this structure plays out in a number of diverse ethnographic and historical cases. After presenting a few examples, however, I will complicate the picture by considering the instability of power relations, and thus the ways in which "resistance" lurks within this elementary structure, even if it is not always enacted.[20]

An example that is probably familiar to most anthropologists can be seen in the games of honor played between men in many cultures. The man's honor vis-a-vis his opponents' is enhanced or diminished depending on his ability to maintain his authority and control over "his" women and, to a lesser extent, "his" junior males. Success in the public arenas of honor depends on power in the private arenas of gender, family, and kinship.[v]

But not all cultural games are men's games (though, given a widespread masculinist bias cross-culturally, many are), and not all cultural games hinge on control of women (though, by the same reasoning, many do).[w] An example that hinges on a different power axis, and again one which could be drawn, with variations, from any number of cultures, would be the phenomenon of arranged marriage. The case I will use here is from Laura Ahearn's work (2001a) among some Magar people of Junigau village in Western Nepal.[x] Traditionally the people of the area in which Ahearn worked recognized three types of marriage: arranged marriage (the most prestigious); elopement (which entailed some loss of prestige for the family); and marriage-by-capture, a violent, barely legitimate affair held in very low esteem in which a man's kin group kidnapped the prospective "bride"

and brought her home for rape/consummation by the groom. A family gained prestige and respect in the community by arranging a good match for their child; this is "the (ideal) game." One could proceed to focus on the intricate politics of the negotiations *between* bride's and groom's kin, that is, on the game as it is played between the families. There is certainly a good deal of this, and it is indeed complex and delicate. But this focus diverts one's attention from the underlying power relations that make it possible: parents must have enough control and authority over their children to have them go along with the arrangements, and children have to be willing to accept the parents' choice of spouse.

It should be noted that the power differentials within what are supposed to be groups or social entities (here families) with shared goals are also the basis of the ultimate instability of all games. And it is here that we must introduce the third piece of the "elementary structure," the ever-present possibility of "resistance." The possibility of resistance is a more shadowy and of course not always realized part of the structure, but it is part of the structure nonetheless. This is true because subordinated actors are never wholly drained of agency except perhaps in fairy tales.

It is no doubt the case that playing the game tends to reproduce both the public structures of rules and assumptions, and the private subjectivity/consciousness/habitus of the players, and thus that playing the game—as Bourdieu unhappily and critically insists[y]—almost always results in social reproduction. Yet ultimately games do change, sometimes because of the entry of some externality that cannot be digested, but sometimes too because of the instability of the internal power relations on which successful play depends. Indeed, the externalities may prove indigestible precisely

---

20. Here Ortner proposes to look at agency-as-projects in relationship to power in society.

The title of this section is wordplay with two other famous works in anthropology: *The Elementary Forms of the Religious Life,* in French Les formes élémentaires de la vie religieuse (1912), by Émile Durkheim, and *Elementary Structures of Kinship,* in French, Les structures élémentaires de la parenté (1949), by Claude Lévi-Strauss. In these works, Durkheim and Lévi-Strauss searched for fundamental building blocks in the formation of religion and kinship respectively. Although Ortner is not pursuing the same goals as Durkheim or Lévi-Strauss, she believes some of the relationships of agency to power that she discusses "lurk" within every society.

because they empower some of the normally subordinated subjects, and open up the possibility of rebellions, great and small.

The Magar case nicely illustrates all this as well. The power and authority of parents over children is clearly unstable, since even within the traditional system young people could and did elope and foil their parents' plans, or a stubborn daughter could resist an arrangement and open herself up to capture. But Ahearn traces the injection into the system of a new technology, one that gave even more power to young people, and that further undermined the parents' abilities to control their children's marriages: writing. As younger Magar men and women became better educated, and gained control of the tool of literacy, the unprecedented social phenomenon of love letters burgeoned. Even though young men's and women's physical behavior was still closely monitored, letters could be exchanged, and young men and women were more and more able (and, in a sense, incited) to "arrange" their own marriages. Clearly the game was changing.[7, 21]

And one final example, in this case involving yet other power differentials: class and ethnicity. I draw the case from Nicole Constable's study of Filipina domestic workers in Hong Kong (1997). The dominant game here is the game of capitalist success, with ambitious young Hong Kong couples out in the workplace and in the market making money and seeking to establish very upscale lifestyles. This being the late modern, haute bourgeoisie, both husbands and wives have time-consuming careers, and their success depends on hired domestic labor for cleaning, entertaining, and most of all, child care. Enter the Filipina domestic workers, who of course have their own projects, pursuing the higher wages of Hong Kong to make better lives for their own families. The financial success of the power couple no doubt depends on their own hard work, social networking, and so forth. But it also depends, though much more invisibly, on their ability to control their domestic workers. In the Hong Kong case, as in many others, the power differential is exacerbated by the weak legal position of many of the workers, who either came in illegally, or overstayed their visa, or in some other way are vulnerable to the power of the state. At the same time the control of the workers by their bosses can be quite literal—Filipina maids are sometimes physically struck, sometimes locked in their rooms, or otherwise abused. The power of the employers seems virtually total.[22]

And yet, again, it is unstable, as all power relations ultimately are. While employers can be highly controlling, they also see themselves as enlightened modern subjects, and not as slave owners. Thus Filipina and other foreign domestic workers are given one day off a week, usually Sunday, and they have developed a practice of gathering in a particular square on Sundays. These gatherings have all the characteristics of Bakhtinian carnivals. Sociability is enjoyed, and cultural commonalities are celebrated. At the same time stories about the often unhappy working conditions are shared, mutual support is exchanged, and—most of all—information about "rights" and organizations that support them is made collectively available. Many of the women have become involved in organizations such as the Asian Domestic Workers Union or

---

21. Note that Ortner deals with ideas that are crucial to other theorists in this book. Compare Ortner's idea of "serious games" to Geertz's idea of "deep play" (essay 26). Like Geertz, Ortner is interested in the notion of a game. "Serious games" tell us about the distribution of power and the agency of actors in society. Ortner is also interested in the possibilities of change and conflict that result from new technologies. (We wonder how things have changed now that Magar men and women almost certainly have cell phones.) Compare this with White's ideas on the influence of technology (essay 16). Ortner is not a particular follower of either Geertz or White. However, comparing these different ideas can give you some perspective on how theorizing in anthropology has changed over the past century.

22. Nicole Constable (b. 1958) is a cultural anthropologist at the University of Pittsburgh. In addition to work on resistance and discipline among domestic workers, she has also written about email and internet marriages between women from Asia and US men (2003) and the lives of women migrant workers in Hong Kong (2014).

the United Filipinos in Hong Kong. Constable quotes various journalists complaining that the workers' power has grown too strong (1997: 164). While these views are greatly exaggerated, there is no doubt that many of the workers are no longer willing to tolerate bad treatment and have learned to stand up for their rights, individually and collectively. Once again, then, the game is changing.[23]

These examples are meant to make several points. The first, which I emphasized at the outset, concerns the ways in which games are not simply engagements between opposing families, groups, or classes, but are built upon power relations at a micro-level. These are often invisible in anthropologies that remain at the level of large-scale political formations—colonialism, the state, etc.—and do not as it were touch the ground. The second follows from the first: the internal power relations are so heavily policed precisely because they contain the potential to disrupt particular plays of the game in the case of individuals, and the very continuity of the game as a social and cultural formation over the long run. Yet finally we must come back to the distinction, yet also articulation, between an agency of projects and an agency of power. We have seen here how the exercise of power over subordinates is normally in the service of the pursuit of some project. Power is rarely an end in itself. But subordinates inevitably have projects of their own. These may be quite overt, as in the case of subordinated cultures under colonialism, or that of workers like the Filipina maids under global capitalism. Or they may be covert, as in the case of the "hidden transcripts" of slaves so well discussed by James Scott (1990), or in the more inchoate forms of dissatisfaction of women and wives often seen in apparently stable gender systems (see again Jean Comaroff 1985; Ahearn 2000; see also Ortner 2003, Chapter 11). Thus if power and the subordination of others is always in the service of some project, so too is resistance; the entire domination/resistance dialectic itself makes sense as the clash of people's projects, their culturally constituted intentions, desires, and goals.

BY WAY OF CONCLUSION

We have seen that at one level agency is a kind of property of social subjects. It is culturally shaped by way of the characteristics that are foregrounded as "agentic"—for example, activity versus passivity in the Grimms' fairy tales, or wild versus tame in American high school social classifications (Ortner 2003). And agency is almost always unequally distributed—some people get to "have" it and others not; some people get to have more and others less. In the first instance it thus appears largely as a quality invested in individuals.[aa, 24]

Yet individuals or persons or subjects are always embedded in webs of relations, whether of affection and solidarity, or of power and rivalry, or frequently of some mixture of the two. Whatever "agency" they seem to "have" as individuals is in reality something that is always in fact interactively negotiated. In this sense they are never free agents, not only in the sense that they do not have the freedom to formulate and realize their own goals in a social vacuum, but also in the sense that they do not have the ability to fully control those relations toward their own ends. As truly and inescapably social beings, they can only work within the many webs of relations that make up their social worlds.

---

23. "Bakhtinian carnivals" refers to the work of the Russian literary critic and philosopher Mikhail Bakhtin (1895–1975). Bakhtin viewed the pre-Lenten religious festivals of Carnival (in the US often called Mardi Gras) as action (or text) that subverts the dominant order through humor, sacrilege, and often eccentric behavior.

24. Ortner here refers to *New Jersey Dreaming: Capital, Culture, and the Class of '58* her 2003 analysis of her New Jersey high school class (Weequahic High School). In that work, she explores the effects of social class on people's lives. She shows that class members differentiated between "wild" and "tame" classmates. She says: "The wild/tame distinction can refer to the question of submissiveness or resistance to authority, which is its most explicit 'youth culture' reference. But it carries other references as well: dress and demeanor, active sexuality, and more" (2003: 96).

Further, while agency in the abstract sense appears as a property of (differentially empowered) subjects, it is best seen (again) less as a psychological property or capacity unto itself, and more as a disposition toward the enactment of "projects." From the point of view of the subject this disposition toward the enactment of projects appears as issuing from one's own desires: "I will . . ." But from the point of view of the cultural analyst it is the projects that define the desires in the first place. Thus the anthropology of "agency" is not only about how social subjects, as empowered or disempowered actors, play the games of their culture, but about laying bare what those cultural games are, about their ideological underpinnings, and about how the play of the game reproduces or transforms those underpinnings. Finally there is the question of the relationship between agency and power that has been the central theme of this chapter. At one level agency itself may be defined as a form of power; "agents" could easily be shorthanded simply as "empowered subjects." This point would work for the relatively simple Grimms' fairy-tale analysis where boys are constructed precisely as empowered subjects, "agents," while girls are systematically disempowered by having their agency deconstructed.[25]

But subsequent sections of this chapter revealed more complex relations between the two phenomena. In the section using the Comaroffs' material on Tswana men and women, I tried to make a distinction between Tswana agency as it plays out within the missionary-cum-colonial relationship, and agency as it plays out "on the margins" of that relationship. I called the first an "agency of power;" because it tends to be defined almost entirely by the domination-resistance dialectic, and thus almost entirely in the terms of the dominant party. I called the second an "agency of (cultural) projects." because I was calling attention to the ways in which Tswana men and women could or should be seen to be playing, or trying to play, their own serious games, defined more by their own values and ideals despite the colonial situation.

I find it useful to distinguish, and not just in situations of colonial domination, between agency as a form of power (including issues of the empowerment of the subject, the domination of others, the resistance to domination, and so forth) and agency as a form of intention and desire, as the pursuit of goals and the enactment of projects. I find it useful because, at the simplest level, they seem to me quite distinct usages of the term, distinct "fields of meaning." But I find it useful as well because, having pulled them apart, one can examine their articulations with one another. That is what I tried to show in the final section of this essay, in which I argued that, in the context of what I have been calling serious games, the pursuit of projects for some often entails, necessarily, the subordination of others. Yet those others, never fully drained of agency, have both powers and projects of their own, and resistance (from the most subtle to the most overt) is always a possibility. Both domination and resistance then are, it seems to me, always in the service of projects, of being allowed or empowered to pursue culturally meaningful goals and ends, whether for good or for ill.

REFERENCES

Ahearn, Laura. 2000. "Agency." *Journal of Linguistic Anthropology* 9(1–2): 12–15.
———. 2001a. *Invitations to love: Literacy, love letters, and social change in Nepal.* Ann Arbor: University of Michigan Press.
———. 2001b. "Language and agency." *Annual Review of Anthropology* 30: 109–137.
Bourdieu, Pierre. 1977. *Outline of a Theory of Practice.* Trans. R. Nice Stanford: Stanford University Press.
———. 1990. *The Logic of Practice.* Trans. R. Nice. Stanford: Stanford University Press.

---

25. The game is a powerful and somewhat deceptive metaphor for what Ortner has in mind. We think of people as active agents who play a game. However, the game defines the goals players strive for and structures the actions they are permitted or forbidden to take. Thus, in a real sense, the game creates its players: that is, their subjectivities are shaped by the game. Of course, you can choose whether you wish to play football or chess, but you cannot easily choose to not play the games of your culture such as being a citizen, a son or daughter, or finding a way to get some money.

Comaroff, Jean. 1985. *Body of Power, Spirit of Resistance: The Culture and History of a South African people*. Chicago: University of Chicago Press.

Comaroff, Jean, and John L. Comaroff. 1991. *Of Revelation and Revolution: Christianity, Colonialism, and Consciousness in South Africa*, Vol. 1. Chicago: University of Chicago Press.

Comaroff, John L. 1987. "Sui Genderis: Feminism, Kinship Theory, and Structural Domains." In *Gender and Kinship: Essays Toward a Unified Analysis*. J. F. Collier and S. J. Yanagisako eds., Pp. 53–85. Stanford: Stanford University Press.

Comaroff, John L., and Jean Comaroff. 1981. "The Management of Marriage in a Tswana Chiefdom." In *Essays on African Marriage in Southern Africa*. E. J. Krige and J. L. Comaroff, eds. Pp. 29–49. Capetown: Juta and Company.

———. 1992. *Ethnography and The Historical Imagination*. Boulder: Westview Press.

———. 1997. *Of Revelation and Revolution: The Dialectics of Modernity on a South African Frontier*, Vol. 2. Chicago: University of Chicago Press.

Constable, Nicole. 1997. *Maid to Order in Hong Kong: Stories of Filipina Workers*. Ithaca, NY: Cornell University Press.

Duranti, Alessandro. 2004. "Agency in language." In *A Companion to Linguistic Anthropology*. A. Duranti, ed. Pp. 451–473. Malden, Mass.: Blackwell.

Giddens, Anthony. 1979. *Central Problems in Social Theory: Action, Structure and Contradiction in Social Analysis*. Berkeley: University of California Press.

Ortner, Sherry B. 1973. "On Key Symbols." *American Anthropologist* 75: 1338–1346.

———. 1989a. *High Religion: A Cultural and Political History of Sherpa Buddhism*. Princeton: Princeton University Press.

———. 1996a. "Making Gender: Toward a Feminist, Minority, Postcolonial, Subaltern, etc., Theory of Practice." In *Making Gender: The Politics and Erotics of Culture*. S. B. Ortner, ed. Pp. 1–20. Boston: Beacon Press.

———. 1999a. *Life and Death on Mt. Everest: Sherpas and Himalayan Mountaineering*. Princeton: Princeton University Press.

———. 2003. *New Jersey Dreaming: Capital, Culture, and the Class of '58*. Durham, NC: Duke University Press.

Propp, V. I. 1968. *Morphology of the Folktale*. Trans. L. Scott. Austin: University of Texas Press.

Sahlins, Marshall. 1981. *Historical Metaphors and Mythical Realities: Structure in the Early History of the Sandwich Islands Kingdom*. Ann Arbor: University of Michigan Press.

Scott, James C. 1990. *Domination and the Arts of Resistance: Hidden Transcripts*. New Haven: Yale University Press.

Sewell, William H. 1992. "A Theory of Structure: Duality; Agency, and Transformation." *American Journal of Sociology* 98(1): 1–29.

Taylor, Charles. 1985a. "What is human agency?" In *Human Agency and Language: Philosophical Papers*, pp. 1: 1–44. Cambridge: Cambridge University Press.

———. 1985b. "The concept of a person." In *Human Agency and Language: Philosophical Papers*, pp. 1: 97–114. Cambridge: Cambridge University Press.

AUTHOR'S NOTES

a. I would like to thank Oscar Salemink and his colleagues and students at the Vrije Universiteit of Amsterdam for warm hospitality and helpful comments on an earlier draft of this paper. I would also like to thank Laura Ahearn, Andrew Apter, Alessandro Duranti, Antonius C. G. Robben, and Timothy Taylor for additional, extremely valuable and supportive, comments.

b. For a recent example within anthropology, however, see Acheson and Gardner 2004.

c. Given this, the occasional appearance of the term in English translations of Bourdieu's works may represent the translator's choice of terms. I believe the closest approximation in French for "agency" is "action;' which carries a somewhat different set of connotations. Bourdieu does however use the term "agent" interchangeably with actor; this does not seem to represent any significant theoretical point on his part.

d. There is also a growing body of work on agency in American archaeology, in which it has become something of a hot topic. See, e.g., Dobres and Robb (2000) and Dornan (2002).

e. I have not been able to cover all the thinkers who have tackled one or another aspect of the agency question. But I would mention in particular Keane (2003).

f. Duranti 2004 largely follows Giddens on this point. But in a forthcoming paper (2006) he moves toward the harder end of the spectrum.

g. Somewhere in between these softer and harder views of the role of intentionality in agency lies the question of improvisation, which has been a central category in practice theory from the beginning. In Bourdieu it represents the idea that the habitus, the internalized system of cultural dispositions toward action, is not a set of hard and fast rules, but rather a set of limits within which an actor can improvise. Yet improvisation itself has what can be thought of as a soft end and a hard end. At the soft end it is akin to improvisation in jazz—a kind of playing with the possibilities inherent in the musical form, for the sheer emotional and aesthetic pleasure of that play. But at the hard end it is closely tied to intentionality. The actor has some intention in mind; there is perhaps a standard cultural way of realizing that intention, but for some reason it is blocked; the actor thus improvises an alternative solution in order to realize that intention. Improvisation here is more like Lévi-Strauss's bricolage, the creative use of possibilities at hand to realize some goal or purpose. It is worth noting that most of Bourdieu's examples of improvisation are of this latter nature. See also the well-discussed story of the woman who climbed up a house in Holland et al. 1998.

h. See also Mohanty 1989.

i. I will not try to define power in any systematic way or this essay will be endless. My various uses of the term will be clear, I hope, from context.

j. I use "projects" in the Sartrean sense, especially as discussed in Search for a Method (Sartre 1968). This important book moves decisively away from Sartre's early emphasis on the freedom of the acting subject.

k. A condensed version of this discussion was published as a section of Ortner 1996a. The present, fuller, version of this discussion harks back to an unpublished working paper (Ortner 1991).

l. The tales have been interpreted many times over (see especially Bettelheim 1977); much of the more recent work has specifically focused on gender issues (e.g., Bottigheimer 1987; Barzelai 1990; Zipes 1993; Orenstein 2003).

m. Interestingly the tales divide almost evenly between those with male and those with female protagonists.

n. In "The Seven Ravens" the girl goes to seek her brothers, and finds and rescues them with great resourcefulness, virtually unassisted. In "The Robber Bridegroom" the girl is helped by an old woman, and between the two of them they bring about the execution of the robber and his band. And in "Fundevogel" the girl actively and resourcefully saves her brother from a wicked old woman.

o. A variant of "Fundevogel."

p. Variants of each other and of "The Seven Ravens."

q. See also my discussion of Shahbano in Chapter 1 of this volume.

r. It is worth reflecting for a moment on the different loci of power in the tales, and power's different relationships to "agency." Agency is directly equated with power in the case of the wicked stepmothers, but, in the case of the boys and girls, princes and princesses, the relationship between agency and power is more oblique and indirect. The "power" that endows boys with agency and drains it out of girls is not in the hands of any particular agent but is built into the larger cultural order as encoded, among other things, in the fairy tales. This provides a clear illustration of Giddens's distinction between power, which is interpersonal, and domination, which is structural. Obviously the two levels or modalities feed off one another—practices of power reproduce structural domination, while structural domination enables and, one might say, empowers, practices of power.

s. Said (1978) made the point that much of Western scholarship carries forward colonialist assumptions. Yet he probably did not envision the ironic situation that these kinds of colonialist assumptions are sometimes re-created by well-meaning scholars who are precisely trying to overcome them.

t. Probably the best body of work along alternative lines is Robin D. G. Kelley's work on African American popular, political, and musical culture (e.g., 1997).

u. This section is drawn from a paper called "Specifying Agency: The Comaroffs and their Critics." It was presented at the 1998 American Anthropological Association meetings on a panel devoted to Of Revelation and Revolution, Vol. 2. The Comaroffs wrote a response to all the papers, and the papers and the response were published as a special issue of interventions (2001). In the meetings version, and later the published version, of my paper, I formulated my comments as a critique of some of the discussions of the book. I do not wish to continue in that vein, in part because I am persuaded by some of the Comaroffs' defenses of their text in their rejoinder, and in part because, in the long run, I feel that we are on the same side of the intellectual and political issues in question, even if we approach them differently.

v. The classic references here are from the Mediterranean area as it was studied and interpreted in the sixties—see especially Peristiany 1966. I am aware of the critiques of the honor and shame literature, to the effect that honor and shame have been used to homogenize and stereotype an entire region (see especially Appadurai 1996). Nothing I say here is intended to stereotype the region, but only to illustrate through an ethnographically familiar pattern the ways in which one part of a cultural game—the competition between men—hinges on the subordination of others for its success.

w See Ortner 1981 for another example of the pattern, and also for an early attempt on my part to theorize the idea of an underlying "game." I am struck now by the coincidence of the date of that paper with the early practice theory literature.

x. Ahearn primarily examines the case in terms of issues of female agency; see also Kratz 2000. I am using Ahearn's material here to develop a slightly different point.

y. See, for example, the discussion of working class habitus in Distinction (1984).

z. Although from a historical or processual point of view one can say that "the game is changing," from an ethnographic point of view, at one point in time, it will appear as a conflict of cultural or historical games between parents and children (Ahearn, personal communication).

aa. Or groups. The question of group agency is less problematic than it appears. While groups do not have agency in the psychological sense (like individuals), groups surely have both "projects" and "power."

37. Willing to Work: Agency and Vulnerability in an Undocumented Immigrant Network

Ruth Gomberg-Muñoz (b. 1975)

THE BUSBOY SHOW

ON WEEKEND NIGHTS, when "Il Vino" (a large Chicago-area restaurant) is busy and the lounge is crowded with diners waiting for a table, five Mexican immigrant busboys get together to stock the bar.[a, b] I call this "the Busboy Show." First, the busboys load about 20 cases of beer and two bins of liquor onto a wheeled cart. Then they push this cart through the restaurant to the service station at the bar. Two or three of them will stay on the outside of the bar with the cart, and the other two or three will go behind the bar. The bartenders and servers get out of the way. Like a sped-up assembly line, one busboy will snatch a case of beer from the cart and throw it—literally, throw it into the air—to a second busboy standing closer to the bar. This busboy catches it easily and tosses it across the top of the bar, where a busboy standing behind the bar grabs it and throws it to a fourth busboy, who catches it and stacks it in front of the beer coolers. A final busboy will rip open the cases and stock beer in the coolers. They work lightning quick—it only takes them about one minute to empty the cart. Customers and restaurant employees gather around to watch, commenting on the busboys' strength and speed. The busboys enjoy the attention and ham it up for onlookers, prodding each other to go faster and faster. They also try to outdo one another by throwing the cases as high into the air as they can. Sometimes, when there's a new busboy, the other guys will throw him an empty case just to laugh as he juggles it in the air.

The Mexican busboys at Il Vino have a reputation as "the hardest workers that we have," in the words of their supervisors and coworkers alike. This association of Mexican immigrants with hard work is not unique to Il Vino.[c] In fact, the conception of Mexican immigrants as a laboring class has a long history in the United States, and for more than a century Mexican workers have often been considered a diligent, tractable segment of the U.S. work force (De Genova 2005; Gamio 1971; Gutierrez 1995; Heyman 2001). Ethnographic research shows that the perception of Mexican immigrants as hard workers continues to have popular currency (Coutin and Chock 1997; De Genova and Ramos Zayas 2003; Waldinger and Lichter 2003). In particular, many low-wage employers express their approval of Mexican immigrants' apparent willingness to do low-wage, low-status work (De Genova 2005; Neckerman and Kirschenman 1991; Waldinger and Lichter 2003). But where does this apparent willingness to work hard come from? And why would presumably permanent members of the low-wage labor force put so much effort into being hard workers?[1]

Recent ethnographic scholarship by Nicholas De Genova (2005), Christian Zlolniski (2006), and Josiah Heyman (2001) has considered how undocumented immigrants' labor practices are circumscribed by the state but negotiated and transformed through the activ-

From *American Anthropologist* (2010)

---

1. Gomberg-Muñoz draws readers in with an opening vignette, a technique that is similar to the opening employed by Clifford Geertz (essay 26) and Abu-Lughod (essay 33). Compare her analysis of Mexican migrants to the comparison drawn by Philippe Bourgois between first-generation Mexican immigrants and second-generation Puerto Rican immigrants (essay 35).

ities of workers, mangers, and state agents themselves (see also Brodkin 2007 and Smith-Nonini 2007). For example, De Genova's 2005 work explores the ways in which Mexican workers grapple with racialization, "illegalization," and labor subordination in a Chicago factory, while Zlolniski's 2006 ethnography examines labor flexibility and organized resistance efforts among immigrant janitors in California. Building on these studies, I consider in this article how a cohort of undocumented Mexican immigrants negotiates a social identity as hard, willing workers as they promote their labor and cultivate dignity and self-esteem.[2]

The purpose of this article is to provide an ethnographic description of workaday struggles that undocumented people wage to make their lives better—in light of serious constraint. I begin by briefly considering the interactions among culture, structure, and agency, in which undocumented immigrants respond to constraints by constructing certain norms and social identities, then I move on to ethnographic descriptions that show how and why a willingness to work hard is negotiated by undocumented workers on the restaurant floor. I particularly examine how workers establish norms of hard work discursively through teasing, peer pressure, and confrontation. Then I explore how behaviors that promote an ethic of hard work also give rise to contradictions among workers, as they struggle to reconcile their vulnerabilities with ideals of autonomy and bravery. Ultimately, I hope to show how categorical inequalities are simultaneously reproduced and resisted in the everyday activities of undocumented people, with both short-term and long-term implications.[3]

An attention to the workaday activities of undocumented immigrants complements existing literature on unauthorized labor migration that has tended to focus on macrolevel processes rather than microlevel lives (e.g., Heyman 1998; Kearney 2004; Massey et al. 1994; Massey et al. 2002; Ngai 2005; Portes and Walton 1981; Sassen 1988; but see Chavez 1992; Zlolniski 2006). By focusing on workers' agency, this research also advances scholarship that has criticized political-economic approaches to globalization and migration for being overly deterministic and "top down" (Basch et al. 1994; Fernandez-Kelly 1983; Mahler 1998). But an analysis of the interaction of agency and constraint avoids obscurantist treatments of local identity making that can mask implications of unequal power structures (see also Bourgois 2003; di Leonardo 1998; Durrenberger and Erem 2005). More broadly, as I examine how categorical inequalities are perpetuated and resisted in the everyday lives of marginalized workers, I hope to contribute, if only modestly, to anthropological theories of social reproduction and change. Finally, by focusing attention on the everyday lived realities of undocumented people, I seek to push past one-dimensional stereotypes of "illegal immigrants" as mere victims or criminal usurpers and emphasize their complex humanity.

"SOMETHING IS INSTILLED IN THEM FROM BIRTH, I THINK": ON CULTURE, STRUCTURE, AND WORKERS' AGENCY

The ethnographic focus of this article is a cohort of ten undocumented immigrant men: Alejandro, Alberto, Chuy, Lalo, Leonardo, Luis, Manuel, Omar, Rene, and Roberto.[d] All of these

---

2. Nicholas de Genova (b. 1968) is a geographer and anthropologist. He is Chair of the Department of Comparative Cultural Studies at the University of Houston. Much of his work is on Mexican immigrants in Chicago.

Christian Zlolniski (b. 1960) is an anthropologist at The University of Texas–Arlington who specializes in labor migration.

Josiah Heyman (b. 1958) is an anthropologist at the University of Texas–El Paso who works on border and immigration issues.

3. As with the other selections in this section of the book, Gomberg-Muñoz's work shows a strong influence from Pierre Bourdieu, Michel Foucault, and other scholars of history and practice. Gomberg-Muñoz positions her work as dealing with issues of structure and agency. *Structure* refers to the cultural and historical context in which individuals act and *agency* to their freedom of action within that structure.

men have worked as busboys in Chicago-area restaurants, and they all are members of the same transnational social network that moves between Chicago, Illinois, and Leon, Guanajuato, Mexico.[e] These workers differ meaningfully in their beliefs, experiences, and plans for the future, but they also have important things in common. They are friends, and in some cases brothers and cousins, who share the stigma of being "illegal aliens" and the dignity of being hard workers and family men. In this article, I examine how these workers use their agency to create a culture of hard work that is responsive to their particular structural vulnerabilities. But how to best conceptualize the everyday interactions of culture, structure, and agency remains an enduring anthropological problem.

In popular discourse, Mexican immigrants' work ethic is often attributed to their "culture" or "cultural background" (Gutierrez 1995; Moss and Tilly 2001; Waldinger and Lichter 2003). Not only coworkers and managers at restaurants like Il Vino but also my colleagues at the university have suggested that the busboys' work ethic "may be just cultural." This popular use of culture identifies work ethic as an essential, integral component of Mexican society, as this comment from Il Vino's manager shows: "They are just phenomenal workers. I don't know what it's like in Mexico, but something happens there. Something is instilled in them from birth I think" (conversation with author, March 11, 2008). But the idea that there is "just something" about Mexican culture that produces hard workers glosses over variation among Mexican workers, ignores the role of inequality in structuring labor conditions, and diminishes workers' agency on the job. Relatedly, this folk use of culture overlooks the historical subordination of Mexican workers in the United States that has given rise to an association between Mexican immigrant workers and a "willingness" to work hard. For example, Mexican workers in the United States are typically relegated not only to low-wage, low-status jobs but also frequently to piece-rate work, tem-porary contract labor, or nonunionized employment in which income and job security are directly tied to the degree of "hard work" that a worker puts forth (see Gamio 1971; Zlolniski 2006). In the end, the notion that a "Mexican work ethic" is an integral part of "Mexican culture" essentializes Mexican immigrant workers, naturalizing their historical subordination and reducing their work performances to a putative cultural inclination for socially degraded, back-breaking labor (for critiques of this use of culture, sec also di Leonardo 1998; Gershon and Taylor 2008).

While anthropological notions of "culture" usually avoid this kind of naturalization of inequality and difference, Arjun Appadurai (2004: 60) notes that in an anthropological sense culture has typically referred to "one or other kind of pastness"—beliefs and behaviors that are presumably traditional, slow to change, and permanently present in a local, bounded social group. This notion of "culture" has been criticized for assuming distinctions between groups of people—and homogeny within them—that are, at best, amorphous and fluid (Appadurai 1996, 2004; Douglas 2004; but see Rosenblatt 2004). Further, traditional anthropological conceptions of culture may diminish the role of Western domination and expansion in the creation, differentiation, and study of putatively bounded cultural groups (Gupta and Ferguson 1997). In response, anthropologists have increasingly turned their attention to the ways in which shared meanings and social identities are continuously created and recreated in everyday interactions (e.g., Gershon and Taylor 2008; Rao and Walton 2004; see also Willis 1977). A conception of culture as "those differences that either express, or set the groundwork for, the mobilization of group identities" (Appadurai 1996: 13) emphasizes the situational, dynamic construction of norms, boundaries, meanings, and group identities and the way that these take shape as part of broader economic and sociopolitical landscapes (Rao and Walton 2004; Sen 2004).[4]

---

4. The special province of anthropology is usually taken to be culture. However, cultural explanations have often posed a problem for anthropologists. In the popular imagination, and in much of the history of anthropology, culture refers to a body of knowledge and behavior that identifies a group of people. Although this idea still has some salience, anthropologists are increasingly troubled by the idea of culture as a single shared

Insofar as cultural differences are continuously created and interpreted by human actors, human agency produces culture (Ortner 2006; Rosenblatt 2004). Culture, agency, and structures of power are mutually influencing: agency produces culture as agency is shaped and constrained by cultural norms and boundaries; both culture and agency can affect structures of unequal power, as agency is differentially empowered or limited by structure in turn (Giddens 1993; Ortner 1997, 2006; Sewell 1992). When the concept of "agency" is applied to undocumented immigrants, who are highly circumscribed in their choices and activities, the question arises as to whether these workers are actually exercising their agency or are merely doing what they must to survive. This latter interpretation suggests that the highly controlled environment in which undocumented immigrants live and work largely deprives them of meaningful choice and agency.[f] But as Nandini Gunewardena and Ann Kingsolver (2007) note, while human agency represents power in a broad sense of capability for action, it is not reducible to empowerment. Rather, agency is the human capacity to exert some control over the conditions of one's existence; it is "the ability of people to affect their world" (Rosenblatt 2004: 461; see also Giddens 1993; Ortner 1997, 2006; Sewell 1992). Inequality differentially constrains the scope and effectiveness of agency (Ortner 2006; Sewell 1992), such that this small group of undocumented workers is unlikely to impact U.S. immigration policy or even change their subordinate status at the restaurant. Nevertheless, as I will show, they can and do effectively shape their work environment through their collective agency.[8, 5]

For example, when these workers throw cases of beer to each other (instead of simply and less spectacularly handing them off), they are achieving at least four interrelated effects. First, they are exerting control over how they are perceived by their white U.S. bosses, coworkers, and customers. This form of "impression management" (Goffman 1959) taps into U.S. folk culture notions of "Mexican work ethic," reinforcing an association of the Mexican staff with hard work and enhancing their job security at the restaurant. Second, they are cultivating norms of hard work amongst themselves, effectively creating a culture of work that shapes how each busboy approaches his work and perceives his labor. Third, they are responding to particular structural vulnerabilities—financial insecurity, racialization, and social stigmatization—and attempting to manage and reduce these vulnerabilities. Fourth, reproducing racialized stereotypes of "Mexican work ethic" can have the ultimate effect of reinforcing racial circumscription of the Mexican immigrant staff, an unintended but important outcome (see Tilly 1998 for a discussion of durable inequality).[6]

Denying workers agency risks reducing them to mere pawns and diminishing their capacity

---

body of knowledge and usually reject the notion that people behave as they do directly as a result of their culture. Here Gomberg-Muñoz is critical of the idea that "hard work" is simply part of Mexican culture. She argues that to believe so portrays "hard work" as a universal, intrinsic, and unchanging aspect of what it means to be Mexican (this is what Gomberg-Muñoz means by essentializing and naturalizing). She argues instead that the work ethic she documents is a product of the specific legal and economic position of illegal Mexican immigrants to the United States (as well as certain aspects of Mexican history and society). In other words, it is both the result of and contributes to the particular structures that organize the lives of her interlocutors, what Bourdieu referred to as "structured structures predisposed to function as structuring structures" (essay 27).

5. Note that Gomberg-Muñoz makes extensive use of the work of Sherry Ortner (see essay 36) as well as of two theorists also frequently referenced by Ortner: Anthony Giddens (b. 1938) and William Sewell (1909–2001). (For more information on these, see essay 36, note 7.)

6. The four points that Gomberg-Muñoz makes here present a good example of the interrelations of structure and agency, and in particular, of Giddens's theory of structuration. Structure places Mexican immigrants in a particular context. Within that context, these individuals may choose to make displays of hard work. These choices give them greater job security and forms part of their culture but also tends to reinforce the structures that place them in low-wage employment in the first place. Thus, the preconditions of their agency (their position

to affect social life. Conversely, emphasizing agency at the expense of structure can mask political and economic realities and obscure relations of domination and subordination. A conception of "agency" as effective, but not necessarily empowered, human action allows us to understand the meaningful activity of disempowered, marginalized, and subjugated people who act on their own behalf (see, e.g., Bourgois 2003; Willis 1977; Zlolniski 2003, 2006). This conception of agency also resembles Karl Marx's well-known observation that "men make their own history, but not of their own free will; not under circumstances they themselves have chosen" (1973: 146), which locates the prime mover of social reproduction and change in the activities of subordinated workers. The following sections explore in more detail how and why this group of undocumented workers exercises their collective agency to shape their relationships to work and society in the United States.[7]

"A LITTLE SOMETHING EXTRA": WILLINGNESS AS A SPECIAL FEATURE OF LABOR POWER

As early as 1907, Mexican workers began migrating to Chicago in large numbers to work in the city's burgeoning rail yards (De Genova 2005: 113). By the 1920s, Chicago had the largest population of Mexicans in the United States outside of the U.S. Southwest (Ready and Brown-Gort 2005), and Mexican workers constituted 43 percent of all railroad-track labor and 11 percent of employees in steel and meatpacking plants in the Chicago area (De Genova 2005: 114. The concentration of these industries on Chicago's South Side led to the settlement of major Mexican communities in South Side neighborhoods. While the meatpacking plants, steel mills, and rail yards that initially attracted Mexican workers to Chicago are now largely defunct, well-established transnational networks and an expanding service economy have meant a steady increase in the Mexican immigrant population of Chicago's city and suburbs over the past four decades (Ready and Brown-Gort 2005).

In postindustrial "global cities" like Chicago, highly educated and highly skilled workers have flourished economically, boosting demand for workers in low-end service industries like hospitality and maintenance (Calavita 1994; Gray 2004; Hondagneu-Sotelo 1994; Lamphere et al. 1994; Sassen 1988; Smith-Nonini 2007). Most service work cannot be exported, and service is one of the few industries that actually experiences growth in postindustrial regions. The service economy currently accounts for

---

within a particular context and structure) produce the unintended consequence of reinforcing the management's understanding of them as low-wage manual laborers.

McGee and Warms both held warehouse jobs as young men and we would like to add to Gomberg-Muñoz's four points: People also throw cases of merchandise because it's fun and helps pass the time.

7. Gomberg-Muñoz refers to one of the best-known quotes by Karl Marx. In *The Eighteenth Brumaire of Louis Bonaparte*, written in 1852, and analyzing the coup d'état staged by Charles Louis-Napoléon Bonaparte (1808–1873) in 1851. Marx (in a more poetic translation than Gomberg-Muñoz uses) says, "Men make their own history, but they do not make it as they please; they do not make it under self-selected circumstances, but under circumstances existing already, given and transmitted from the past. The tradition of all dead generations weighs like a nightmare on the brains of the living" (www.marxists.org). The 18 Brumaire, year 8, was the date on the French Revolutionary calendar on which Napoleon Bonaparte seized power from the French Revolutionary governing committee (the Directory). It corresponds to November 9, 1799. Charles Louis-Napoléon Bonaparte was a nephew of Napoleon Bonaparte (1769–1821). He was elected the first president of France in 1848, but not permitted by the Constitution to stand for a second term, he staged a self-coup, seizing power and proclaiming himself Emperor Napoleon III. In *The 18th Brumaire*, Marx explores the way that different factions within the French bourgeoisie gave up political liberty for increased access to wealth and power, as well as the acquiescence of the French peasantry to a government that did not represent their interests. Gomberg-Muñoz draws a parallel between Marx's understanding of the weakness of the peasantry and the actions of her interlocutors.

two-thirds of jobs in developed nations, and work in construction, maintenance, and hospitality is quickly overtaking manufacturing as the most important source of employment for low-skill workers in urban centers (Castells 2000; Massey et al. 1994; Smith-Nonini 2007: 199).

This has important implications for conditions of labor, as low-end service workers are often less constrained by mechanization and, largely lacking union protection, are highly vulnerable to repressive work conditions and low wages (Sassen-Koob 1981; Smith-Nonini 2007). The expansion of service economies also has important implications for the characteristics of workers themselves because the attractiveness of service labor power is often evaluated on subjective criteria such as work ethic and good attitude, behaviors that are in turn promoted by conditions of vulnerability and powerlessness (Moss and Tilly 2001; Sassen-Koob 1981; Waldinger and Lichter 2003; Zlolniski 2006). Being particularly powerless, undocumented immigrants make especially desirable service workers (Sassen-Koob 1981), and they comprise over 10 percent of the U.S. work force in low-end service industries such as construction labor (25 percent), grounds keeping and building maintenance (19 percent), and leisure and hospitality (17 percent), even though they account for only 5.4 percent of the total civilian labor force (Passel 2006; Passel and Cohn 2009).

Characteristics of the service economy and its work force are not givens but, rather, are continuously created through state activities and everyday interactions between workers and managers (Gray 2004; Zlolniski 2003; see Gibson-Graham 1996 for a critique of the "essentialization" of capitalism). As Mia Gray (2004) points out, there is nothing inherent to the service sector that renders some jobs high paying and others low paying. Rather, low wages in the service sector are the function of a confluence of factors, including the following: lack of unionization, social degradation of low-end service sector jobs, and policies that undermine organization efforts and differentiate sectors of the service labor force by race, gender, and immigration status (Fernandez-Kelly 1983; Fine 1996; Gray 2004; Heyman 2001; Kearney 2004; Stepick and Grenier 1994). Relatedly, as Zlolniski (2003, 2006) argues, the labor flexibility of immigrant workers is not an intrinsic characteristic but, rather, is continuously negotiated and challenged in interactions between managers and workers.

At restaurants like Il Vino, racialized immigration categories and work categories are mapped onto one another, and Mexican immigrants are segregated into the lowest-paid jobs: typically as busboys, line cooks, and dishwashers (see also Adler 2005; Fine 1996; Stepick and Grenier 1994). A willingness to be diligent and tractable is expected from the Mexican immigrant workers in these jobs; it is an essential feature of their labor. This comment from Julia, the general manager at Il Vino, represents management's perspective on the flexibility of the immigrant bus staff: "I think that we just look at them as busboys and they will do really whatever you ask them to do. From garbages to cleaning out toilets to—you know. So I think we're harder on them in that we take it for granted . . . and expect that they will do whatever we ask them to do" (conversation with author, March 11, 2008). This sentiment is echoed by other supervisors at restaurants in Chicago, who identify Mexican immigrants' willingness to do "whatever we ask" as an important component of their labor.

Extra work and flexible work have become part of the everyday routine for the Mexican immigrant busboys at Il Vino, resulting in an increased and diversified workload. On a regular work day, busboys serve water and bread, help servers carry food trays, put leftovers in carryout containers, clear tables of dirty dishes, and "turn over" tables when diners leave (removing dirty linens, dishes, and silverware and replacing them with clean ones). Each busboy is typically responsible for his own section. Sections can vary in size, but at Il Vino each busboy section is usually comprised of three smaller sections that each have one server and five four-person tables. In other words, on an average night, an Il Vino busboy is supporting three servers, fifteen tables, and sixty diners at once. When attending to their sections, busboys are expected to be quick, attentive, and helpful.

Nightly, in addition to busing tables, the busboys sweep and mop the restaurant; clean the bathrooms; empty the garbage cans; wipe down tables and chairs; set the tables; stock the server stations with water glasses, dishes, napkins, straws, and silverware; stock the front bar with beer, liquor, and glassware; and set up the banquet room for any parties the next day. Because it is nearly impossible to accomplish all of this while being attentive to their sections, the busboys often do not finish their work until two hours after Il Vino has closed for the evening. After busing, cleaning, and setting up, which are considered the busboys' regular duties, they are responsible for performing a myriad of other occasional tasks. Busboys unclog toilets, clean up martini-induced vomit, change customers' flat tires, trap mice, organize storage rooms, move furniture, paint, salt the parking lot when it snows, water the plants, and scrape gum from the bottom of tables. In a pinch, they can also be counted on to cook, bartend, and perform minor first aid.

The busboys at Il Vino have not always had such a heavy workload. Over the years, they have slowly assumed responsibility for more and more tasks by doing "extra" work, which can be initiated by management or by the workers themselves. Roberto explains, "If you're my boss and you tell me, 'You know what, cut the lawn, arrange the flowers, all that,' I'll do it for you. And I'll do a good job, and moreover I'll do a little extra so that, 'Wow!' You come back and, 'Oh, you surprised me!'" (conversation with author, June 17, 2008). While extra work is a source of complaint when the immigrant workers are talking among themselves, there is universal agreement that complaining to management should be avoided. In fact, workers often respond promptly and with energy, if not enthusiasm, when called on to do extra tasks. They demonstrate their "willingness to work" by performing extra work without complaint and with alacrity. The workers even have a name for this performance—*echándole ganas*— which literally means "putting desire in it" but can be roughly translated as "putting effort into it" or "putting your back into it." The workers at Il Vino are very conscious of the impression they make and explain that they have important incentives for *echándole ganas*.

Many workers, like Alejandro, Leonardo, and Omar, acknowledge and resent that their "willingness to work hard" is promoted by their undocumented status. Leonardo says, "When you come from Mexico and you don't have anything, all you have to offer is that you are a good worker and you want to better yourself" (conversation with author, March 4, 2008). Omar agrees and says that, for undocumented workers, being pliant can make the difference between keeping or losing a job: "They know we are illegal, so if I complain, what do you think they will say to me? 'There's the door if you don't like it'" (conversation with author, July 16, 2008). Yet these workers also believe that having a good work ethic can reduce or even overcome the vulnerability associated with being undocumented. Leonardo continues, "If you're a good worker, nothing, not even being illegal, will ever affect you" (conversation with author, March 4, 2008). Roberto adds that working hard enhances income and security: "Our job is as a busboy, right, but we also do construction, organizing, throwing stuff out, cleaning. . . . They save money because they don't have to pay people to do [extra tasks]. But the other side of it is that it benefits us too, you know? In money, in more hours. Those are benefits" (conversation with author, June 16, 2008). Performing a willingness to work hard promotes these workers' financial stability—a particularly important quality for undocumented people whose employment is frequently insecure and low paid.

Indeed, busboys receive both material and social inducements to work hard. The busboys earn tips from waiters and waitresses, who are more likely to tip generously when they are pleased with busboys' work performance, Tips are a significant component of the busboys' income: the busboys at Il Vino typically earn upward of one hundred dollars in tips alone on an average weekend night. This is a healthy supplement to their minimum-wage hourly pay. In addition to tips, the Mexican workers at Il Vino also receive considerable social esteem from their coworkers and managers, extending the benefits of working hard beyond economy and into the realm of autonomy and respect. For example, Rene observes that: "[The bosses] are always noticing who works and who doesn't work. And when you win them over, they don't watch you anymore, they give you—you win their respect" (conversation with author, July 13, 2008). As I explore in more depth later, gaining esteem for being a hard worker can enhance the dignity of undocumented immigrants who are highly stigmatized as "illegal aliens," while gaining autonomy and respect on the job may be particularly important for undocumented workers who are subject to constant and arbitrary supervision (see Romero 2002).[h]

Cultivating a reputation as hard workers has another important benefit: it can help undocumented workers carve out employment niches for themselves in the low-wage job market (see Tilly 1998 for a discussion of opportunity hoarding). When Alejandro arrived in the United States nearly 20 years ago, his father had promised to secure him a job in the restaurant where he worked as a cook. The "job" was washing dishes in the restaurant kitchen—for free. Alejandro explains that, "Just to get me a job [my dad] was like, 'Just try him out. If he works you can pay him, if not, then he'll learn.' They didn't pay me for the first month" (conversation with author, June 3, 2008). Twenty years later, Alejandro still works in restaurants. He has been a busboy, a busboy manager, and even a waiter during this time—and his calmness, seniority, and expertise have earned him the nickname "Buddha" among his friends. Alejandro has learned one thing well: he can capitalize on stereotypes about Mexican immigrants as hard workers to promote employment for himself and his friends. He describes one situation in particular, in which the popular pizza place where he worked had opened a second restaurant and hired a young, all-white bus staff:

> And [the managers] told me, "They cannot handle it, [and] there's twelve [of them]. I want you to go over there and teach them

how to work good." . . . I went down to the office and I said, "If you want to keep all these people working, you're going to need them. I can do, I'll bring five, six of my friends and we can do all this work. So you decide. You want to keep twelve people and not get the job done, or six guys and get the work done, and probably be cheaper for you." [The owner said,] "Done. Get them." [conversation with author, June 3, 2008]

Alejandro wielded stereotypes of Mexican immigrants as particularly hard workers to persuade his boss to hire his friends. Recruiting acquaintances for job openings is a common practice among immigrant workers, whose employers are largely content to let workers take charge of the hiring and training process (see Waldinger and Lichter 2003; Zlolniski 2006). For Alejandro and his co-immigrant friends, a "willingness to work hard" is a special feature of their labor power that they can strategically draw on to make their labor more attractive to employers.[8]

"MOVE IT! MOVE IT! PUT SOME EFFORT INTO IT!": NEGOTIATING NORMS OF HARD WORK ON THE JOB

Unlike the rest of the service staff, the busboys at Il Vino have no direct, formal manager. Instead, the most senior busboy is usually considered the de facto leader and is responsible for managing interactions between busboys and management staff. For the past ten years, Rene has been in this leadership position more often than anyone else. Rene is a quiet and good-humored man in his late twenties who is widely respected not only by the other busboys but also by the waitstaff, managers, and owners of Il Vino. Rene says that he does "not like to be the boss of anybody" (conversation with author, August 5, 2007) and prefers to lead by example; he can often be found in

---

8. These several paragraphs illustrate how the Mexican immigrants Gomberg-Muñoz interviews actively cultivate the stereotypes that help them find and keep jobs but also keep them in their positions as low-wage earners. At the same time, they secure and reinforce those positions, not only for themselves but for their children and friends, thus reproducing the conditions of labor across generations.

other busboys' sections, helping them serve water or clean tables. Rene is a highly motivated and efficient worker who often teases his coworkers over the walkie-talkie radios they carry. *"Córrele, córrele!"* or *"Échale ganas!"* he often tells them—[Move it, move it! Put some effort into it!].

The Mexican immigrant workers at Il Vino have several mechanisms through which they negotiate and enforce norms of hard work on the job, ranging from gentle teasing to outright confrontation. For these mechanisms to be effective, the workers must be committed to working as a team. The team-oriented organization of work for Il Vino busboys is encouraged by several factors, including the tendency of management to treat the workers as a homogeneous group, the system of tip distribution in which all busboys pool their tips and split them equally, and long-standing social ties among workers. Teamwork also has important benefits for workers: it is critical to getting their work done quickly and efficiently and diffuses stress by insulating individual group members and spreading responsibility and accountability throughout the group.

All of the immigrant busboys who work at Il Vino generally agree that having a team-oriented approach to work is the best quality that a busboy can have, while the worst busboys are those who act individualistically or who are bossy. As Roberto explains, even the so-called busboy leader is careful not to act bossy and to contribute his share to the workload; "Like for example if tomorrow is going to be really busy, 'Okay, you do this, you do this, I'll do this, you do this.' It's not just one person, no one person is going to come and say, 'Okay, I want—.' No. Everyone is equal, we discuss it, 'Yeah, okay, what do you think?' 'How about this?' Like that, 'Cool, let's get to work'" (conversation with author, July 17, 2007). But just working together is not enough; all busboys are expected to work at roughly the same level. Roberto explains: "When we work as a team, we all work together as though we were a motor and the cylinders are, 'toom, toom, toom.' But if just one is kind of fucked up, now you have to work more, and it's not fair that one guy is like that. And the complaints start,

'Hey man, what the fuck?'" (conversation with author, June 17, 2008). Slacking workers are not tolerated for long, and conformity to work norms is continually encouraged and enforced among the workers.

One of the primary mechanisms by which these workers encourage norms of hard work is the use of humor. New or slow workers are nicknamed "turtle" or "stupid" and teased about their poor work ethic. One worker known for moving a bit slower than the others was nicknamed "el Ferrari," and when the other guys wanted him to move faster, they would call over their walkie-talkie radios: "Hey Ferrari, vroom vroooo00m!" If a busboy's section appears dirty, or if a table needs water, another busboy might come to help him and say to the server, "Where's your busboy? You don't have a busboy tonight or what?" Teasing is particularly important for socializing new workers, who are often unaccustomed to such fast-paced work. Alejandro explains: "There was one guy, slow. Slow as a turtle . . . And we would joke around, like, 'Come on, move, Turtle.' Everybody calls him names. If they take it as a joke, they start to fit in, like, 'Oh my god, they call me a turtle, so I'm going to try to speed up a little more'" (conversation with author, June 3, 2008).

Goading each other into working harder is not always successful, and if one busboy consistently works more slowly than the rest, the other workers will adopt more serious measures to deal with the problem. When the restaurant is busy, the senior busboys will cover for the slow worker—this keeps management from noticing weakness in the work of the group. But when they are cleaning or setting up, the busboys may slow down their own work, or even stop working entirely, until the slow worker catches up. This puts serious pressure on the weak busboy. If the situation still does not improve, a sit-down discussion with the slacking worker may be in order. Luis explains that, "Look, there is a time and place to say something. Like when we stay and have a drink after work, we'll tell him, Listen, man, you suck, you sucked tonight. Try to do better." And among the Mexicans, we tell each other, right? . . . We trust each other to say, "Look, man, work harder, pick it up, okay?" (conversation with author, March 28, 2008).

In extreme cases, the busboys will stop covering for a slacking worker and allow his weakness to be exposed to management; this usually results in the weak busboy's dismissal. This is a last resort, however, and the workers prefer strategies that do not expose them to interference by management or risk the cohesion of their team.[9]

"WE WETBACKS ARE PEOPLE WHO LIKE TO WORK": CONSENT AND CONTRADICTION

I have so far described why and how undocumented Mexican restaurant workers perform social identities as hard workers on the job, but an important question remains: How do workers reconcile this identity with their broader values and beliefs? A comprehensive discussion of this question is outside the scope of this article (but see Gomberg-Muñoz in press), but in this final ethnographic section I examine how this cohort perceives itself in relation to wider narratives about immigration, work, and achievement in the United States. In particular, I explore how these workers reproduce and resist stereotypes about Mexican immigrants as they struggle to maximize their dignity and self esteem.[10]

Scholars of migration have considered the ways in which transmigration itself shapes the attainment of dignity and esteem. For example,

Jeffrey Cohen (2001) and Lynn Stephen (2007) have shown that transmigrant workers boost their social stature in communities of origin through remittances and participation in transnational projects (see also Smith 2006). One extension of this argument is that transmigrant workers decouple the performance of socially degraded work in the United States from their social identities, which are presumed to meaningfully reside in Mexico. Thus, Michael Piore has argued that:

> The temporary character of the migration flow appears to create a sharp distinction between work, on the one hand, and the social identity of the worker, on the other. The individual's social identity is located in the place of origin, the home community . . . From the perspective of the migrant, the work performed is essentially asocial: It is purely a means to an end. [1979: 54][11]

But my research indicates that undocumented workers do not leave their social identities at the border, even when they view their stay as temporary. Rather, work and social life in the United States are interactive spaces in which identities as men, friends, fathers, husbands, boyfriends, Mexicans, and workers are negotiated and transformed. Remittances and transnational projects are instrumental in helping workers attain financial security and respect in Mexico, but creating social identities on job sites in the United States is also

---

9. Gomberg-Muñoz shows that the workers actively take control away from the management, but they do so by policing their own behavior and that of new hires in ways that make them acceptable to the management. Thus, the workers exercise agency but do so within structures that maintain the fundamental inequality between the management and the workers. They exercise choice and a degree of power. This helps carve out space for them in the local economy but simultaneously reinforces their position of relative powerlessness.

10. Note the emphasis on behavior as performance in this passage. Olivier Klein, Russell Spears, and Stephen Reicher (2007) point out that social identity performances fill two functions: They strengthen individual and group identities, and they persuade their audiences to adopt specific behaviors. Both are evident in Gomberg-Muñoz's depiction of the busboys. The performances by the busboys create a particular identity for them as a group and the performances convince the managers of the value of hiring Mexican immigrants and allowing them to police themselves.

11. Jeffrey Cohen (b. 1961) is an anthropologist at Ohio State University who specializes in labor migration.
Lynn Stephen (b. 1956) is an anthropologist at the University of Oregon who works on the impact of globalization, migration, and nationalism. Michael Piore (b. 1940) is a professor of economics and political science at The Massachusetts Institute of Technology. He is a specialist in the study of labor markets.

important: it is a critical feature of workers' personhoods. But as they cultivate social identities, undocumented Mexican immigrants contend with pervasive stereotypes and profound stigmatization.

In recent years, highly publicized and polarizing debates about immigration have relegated perceptions of Mexican immigrants in the United States into two popular one-dimensional types.[i] The first stereotype can be identified as "Mexicans as illegal aliens." This conception of Mexican immigrants identifies them as iconic illegal aliens and stigmatizes them as lawless, unclean, and threatening interlopers who paradoxically steal jobs and leech public assistance (Coutin and Chock 1997; De Genova 2005; Massey et al. 2002; Suarez-Orozco and Suarez-Orozco 1995; Vila 2000). As the fodder of conservative cable-news shows, radio programs, and high-profile local political campaigns, this stereotype has wide popular currency (De Genova 2005; Golash-Boza 2009). As a result, Latin American immigrants in the United States have become especially vulnerable to social alienation, exploitation, harassment, and hate crimes (Pew Hispanic Center 2007; Suarez-Orozco and Suarez-Orozco 1995; Urbina 2009). According to federal crime statistics, hate crimes against Latinos in the United States surged 40 percent between 2003 and 2007—a period of heightened anti-immigrant sentiment (Urbina 2009).[12]

The second prevailing stereotype can be called "Mexicans as hard-working immigrants" (see also Heyman 2001). This conception of Mexican immigrants locates them in historical narratives of "America as a nation of immigrants" and "America as a land of opportunity." Mexican immigrants, even the undocumented, are portrayed as sympathetic figures who have earned a moral claim to U.S. citizenship by working hard to improve their lives just as generations before them have done (Coutin and Chock 1997). This stereotype emphasizes Mexican immigrants' religiosity, family orientation, and work ethic and is frequently promoted in immigrant rights discourses.[j] My research suggests that both of these stereotypes—"Mexicans as illegal aliens" and "Mexicans as hard-working immigrants"—continue to abound and are applied (sometimes simultaneously) to Mexican workers in restaurants like Il Vino.[13]

It is within this context that undocumented Mexican immigrants in the United States make sense of who they are and what they are doing. But as Heyman points out, "identifications are not the same as identities" (2001: 135), and workers develop complex and contradictory perceptions of themselves as they respond to external oppression, engage hegemonic narratives about immigration and "America," and construct social identities in the United States. It should not be surprising that undocumented workers take pains to distance themselves from notions that they are lawless, threatening, or unclean. In fact, workers have sophisticated responses to this stereotype, in which they

---

12. Inflammatory rhetoric aimed specifically at Mexican immigrants reached new extremes in the Republican presidential primary campaigns of 2015. For example, announcing his presidential bid on June 16, 2015, Donald Trump (b. 1946) said: "When Mexico sends its people, they're not sending their best. . . . They're sending people that have lots of problems and they're bringing those problems with [them]. They're bringing drugs. They're bringing crime. They're rapists" (Lee 2015). Similar claims continued through the Trump presidency and to the current day (Summer 2023). For example, on March 8, 2023, Trump falsely claimed that South American countries "are emptying out their prisons, insane asylums and mental institutions and sending their most heinous criminals to the United States" This claim has been fact checked by numerous agencies and found to be totally without evidence (for example https://www.factcheck.org/2023/03/factchecking-trumps -rally-fox-interview/).

13. As Gomberg-Muñoz might have predicted, Trump's claims (note 12) were met with both support by some and denunciation by others. Democratic candidate Hillary Clinton (b. 1947) responded that Republicans had "demonized hard-working immigrants" and tweeted "Hard-working, law-abiding immigrant families deserve a path to earned citizenship—not second class status" (@HillaryClinton, 9–16–2015). However, more than 8 years after the start of his first presidential campaign, and after tens of thousands of documented false or misleading claims, Trump continues to retain the devotion of a large percentage of the American public.

argue that they are victims, not perpetrators, of criminal behavior and that "dirty" labor requires bravery and stamina. In the following quote, Lalo expresses a widely held view that counters stereotypes of undocumented immigrants as criminal:

> Jumping the border, yes, it's a crime. But is it criminal? One thing is to kill, or steal something. Okay, I'm stealing something in the sense that I am on your land without permission, but I didn't come to kill, I didn't come to steal, I didn't come to hurt anyone. But they don't want to see it that way. So, yes, jumping the border, I know that I'm committing a crime, but it's not the same as if I work for you and you don't pay me. That is stealing. And we are human beings, and we should help each other, And you should pay me because I'm doing work for you. But you take advantage and don't pay me because I'm undocumented and I can't do anything about it. You just call immigration, or the police, and it's over. That's a robbery, any way you want to look at it. That's stealing, that's a crime. [conversation with author, August 1, 2007].

In this comment, Lalo not only reaffirms the image of the "hard-working Mexican" but also makes a moral argument against the abuse of undocumented labor. As the threat of immigration enforcement is ever present in the labor relations of undocumented workers, many workers like Lalo perceive such laws as tools in their exploitation (sec also Heyman 2001; Zlolniski 2003). In fact, these workers are angry at the way that undocumented status makes them vulnerable to exploitation, as this comment from Alejandro shows: "The bosses know you don't have papers, and they use [that knowledge]. That's why they pay you what they pay you, because you cannot ask for more money"

(conversation with author, June 3, 2008). In contrast to exploitative employers, undocumented workers emphasize that they have an ethical approach to getting ahead: good, old fashioned hard work.[14]

Undocumented workers valorize the integrity of hard work and draw strong boundaries against "suck-ups" (*barberos*) and U.S. workers, who they say will win the boss at any cost.[k] Rene explains, "I don't work hard to kiss ass. I don't want to be like, 'Look, boss, let me clean your shoes, let me do this,' you know? I just go to work, do my job, go home. American workers are like, 'How are you, boss? A chair, boss? A soda, boss?' . . . That's why I don't walk around kissing ass. I want respect at my job" (conversation with author, August 5, 2007).

These workers also associate dirty and difficult labor with bravery and self-worth. Luis says, "I think that an American is not worth as much as a Mexican, he doesn't work the same as a Mexican. It's like I told you, a Mexican takes risks and an American, if he sees that something is difficult or a job is dangerous, he won't do it . . . I think that's why the boss would rather hire illegals than Americans" (conversation with author, March 28, 2008). Emphasizing the idea that Mexican workers have an ethical approach to getting ahead renders hard work a moral activity that is worthy of dignity and respect. By equating willingness to work with integrity and bravery, workers convert socially degraded work into a source of self esteem.[15]

Undocumented Mexican workers have very high labor-force participation rates, and these workers attribute their employment opportunities to a combination of personal strengths and opportunity in the United States.[l] This comment from Leonardo shows how he situates "Mexican work ethic" in a narrative about opportunity in the United States: "We wetbacks are people who like to work and . . . to

---

14. In other words, workers develop counter-hegemonic narratives. The ideas of hegemony and counter-hegemony come from the work of Antonio Gramsci (1891–1937; see essay 35, note 10) but are common in work about agency.

15. Note that here Luis essentializes both Mexican and American workers. Thus, on the one hand, he justifies the dignity of doing hard labor but on the other, he perpetuates the image of the Mexican worker as fit primarily for such hard labor.

improve ourselves. . . . And when a Mexican comes here illegally and there are good opportunities, he will take advantage of them and improve himself" (conversation with author, March 4, 2008). Ironically, their very exclusion from the polity as undocumented immigrants supports a belief in "American" achievement ideology because the structural limitations these workers encounter are explained by their illegal status. For example, Lalo claims: "If I had papers, I would never be without work. But how many white guys do you see begging on the street corner who are strong, capable of working in a kitchen. . . . Why don't they work? They're lazy" (conversation with author, July 17, 2007). That is, to the extent that these workers experience exclusion from opportunities in the United States, they believe that they are excluded because they are not actually U.S. citizens. In spite of their resentment toward the ways in which undocumented status constrains their opportunities, these workers widely affirm a belief in "America as a land of opportunity."[16]

Cultivating a social identity as hard workers creates other contradictions for immigrant workers. For example, while they perform a willingness to work, they are reluctant to see themselves as deferential. In fact, they develop narratives that emphasize Mexican workers' physical bravery and resistance to abusive treatment. When these workers sit around together and have a beer, they relish telling "war stories" in which a Mexican worker heroically confronts an abusive boss. Like most war stories, these are probably exaggerated. Nevertheless, narratives about standing up to the boss, challenging him physically, and putting one's job at risk highlight workers' self-respect and reveal that their "willingness to work" has its limits.

These limits are particularly revealed when workers discuss their plans for the future: Alejandro, Rene, Chuy, Manuel, and Luis have all (unprompted) expressed a desire to get a union job. Tellingly, they state their goal as "getting a union job," as opposed to work as a union carpenter or brick-layer or electrician, indicating

that they are at least as concerned about being part of a union collective as they are about the work itself. For Rene, whose knowledge about union work is mostly derived from his electrician brother-in-law, the appeal of being in a union has as much to do with autonomy as job security. He explains that, "If I get a job with the union, then when somebody asks, 'Where do you work?' I can tell them, 'Oh, I'm Local 399,' instead of 'I work for this guy or that guy,' Then you don't belong to anybody, it's more of a professional job" (conversation with author, July 13, 2008). Workers' goals of unionization suggest that, under different circumstances, these "willing workers" might not be so different from more politicized immigrants described elsewhere (e.g., Brodkin 2007; Smith-Nonini 2007; Zlolniski 2003, 2006).

Cultivating a social identity as hard workers provides several short-term advantages for undocumented Mexican workers, including control over the composition and organization of their work group and a measure of financial stability and social esteem. Yet a reputation as hard workers also has long-term implications for undocumented Mexican workers. In the long run, reiterating racial stereotypes about Mexicans' putatively superior work ethic can reproduce their subordination, maintain categorical differentiation of the working class, and even set up the "hard workers" themselves for intensified exploitation (see also De Genova 2005; Tilly 1998; Willis 1977).

CONCLUSION: VULNERABILITY AND AGENCY

In the introduction to this article, I posed a question: Why would presumably permanent members of the low-wage labor force put so much effort into being hard workers? Part of the answer is related to political processes that create and maintain conditions of vulnerability vis-a-vis the capitalist state (De Genova 2005;

16. Gomberg-Muñoz makes a point with important political implications. She argues that immigrants perceive the United States as a land of limitless opportunity because they attribute their failures to their immigrant status rather than to structural factors that limit opportunities for all poor Americans and operate with particular force for racial and ethnic minorities.

Portes and Walton 1981; Sassen 1988). In the United States, a combination of border militarization and anti-immigrant policies has not reduced the flow of labor migration but, rather, has "illegalized" it, legitimizing exploitation of immigrant workers by making access to political, economic, and social resources a right of citizenship (De Genova 2005; Massey et al. 2002; Ngai 2005). National boundaries and immigration policies produce, reinforce, and reify the distinctions among "citizen," "legal immigrant," and "illegal alien" (Heyman 2001; Ngai 2005; Sassen 1988). Selective enforcement of the border and the globalization of all aspects of production except for labor renders persistent labor migration all but certain (Massey et al. 2002; Portes and Walton 1981). Thus, immigration policies do not stop labor migration; rather, they generate inequality among the labor force by assigning illegal status to a segment of the working class (Heyman 2001; Lipsitz 2005; Sassen-Koob 1981).

While the workers featured in this ethnography feel the impact of these policies acutely, they are not mere pawns of capitalist forces. Rather, they are workers who take an active role in cultivating well-being by negotiating norms of efficiency, self-motivation, and "willingness" at their U.S. jobsites. While this process has the benefit of making these workers more attractive to low-wage employers, it has the side effect of reproducing various exploitative aspects of their work, including intensification of their labor characterized by increasing workloads for the same pay.

Undocumented Mexican workers in the United States do not arrive freely able to position themselves as they choose in relation to U.S. social structure. Instead, they contend with powerful stereotypes and negotiate their identity and self-worth within these subjective constraints. While these workers are not immune either from the stigma of being "illegal aliens" or the stigma of doing "dirty work," they do not necessarily internalize these stigmatizations. In fact, they develop multiple and various strategies for protecting themselves psychologically and defending their dignity and self-esteem.

Undocumented workers are neither mere victims or criminals, nor inherently hard workers or liberated actors free from the constraints of nation-state boundaries or hegemonies. They are complicated people who actively and creatively engage in workaday struggles to make their lives better. As they contend with racial, legal, and class constraints, they cultivate financial and emotional well-being by developing social identities as hard workers who are worthy of dignity and respect. By establishing reputations as good workers, they maintain markets for their labor and sequester job opportunities for themselves and members of their social networks. Moreover, they cultivate an identity that is consistent with their values and resistant to the stigma associated with illegal immigration.[17]

REFERENCES CITED

Adler, Rachel. 2005. "Oye Compadre! The Chef Needs a Dishwasher: Yucatecan Men in the Dallas Restaurant Economy." *Urban Anthropology* 34(2,·3): 217–246.

Alvarez, Robert. 2005. *Mangos, Chiles, and Truckers: The Business of Transnationalism*. Minneapolis: University of Minnesota Press.

---

17. Gomberg-Muñoz's conclusion emphasizes points that she has made earlier in the essay. It also positions her writing within the grand tradition of American anthropology. Although Gomberg-Muñoz makes no specific call for political action here, it is hard to read her work without developing sympathy for the people she describes.

Since the days of Franz Boas and Bronislaw Malinowski, anthropology has frequently emphasized showing the rationality, dignity, and humanity of oppressed peoples and those labeled "primitive" or inferior by the dominant discourse in wealthy and powerful nations. A call to political action has always been implicit in this position. Since Boas's day, that call has been for equality and an end to what the anthropologist and ethicist Gerald Berreman (1930–2013) called "invidious distinctions imposed unalterably at birth upon whole categories of people to justify the unequal social distribution of power, livelihood, security, privilege, esteem, freedom—in short, life chances" (1972: 410).

Appadurai, Arjun. 1996. *Modernity at Large: Cultural Dimensions of Globalization*. Minneapolis: University of Minnesota Press.

———. 2004. "The Capacity to Aspire: Culture and the Terms of Recognition." In *Culture and Public Action*. Vijayendra Rao and Michael Walton, eds. Pp. 59–84. Delhi: Permanent Black.

Arias, Patricia. 2004. "Old Paradigms and New Scenarios in a Migratory Tradition: U.S. Migration from Guanajuato." In *Crossing the Border: Research from the Mexican Migration Project*. Jorge Durand and Douglas Massey, eds. Pp. 171–183. New York: Russell Sage Foundation.

Basch, Linda, Nina Glick Schiller, and Cristina Szanton Blanc. 1994. *Nations Unbound: Transnational Projects, Postcolonial Predicaments, and Deterritorialized Nation-States*. Amsterdam: Gordon and Breach Science Publishers.

Bourgois, Philippe. 2003[1996]. *In Search of Respect: Selling Crack in El Barrio*, 2nd edition. New York: Cambridge University Press.

Brodkin, Karen. 2007. *Making Democracy Matter: Identity and Activism in Los Angeles*. New Brunswick, NJ: Rutgers University Press.

Calavita, Kitty. 1994. "U.S. Immigration and Policy Responses: The Limits of Legislation." In *Controlling Immigration*. Wayne Cornelius, Philip Martin, and James Hollifield, eds. Pp. 55–82. Stanford: Stanford University Press.

Castells, Manuel. 2000[1996]. *The Rise of the Network Society*, 2nd edition. Malden, MA: Blackwell Publishing.

Chavez, Leo R. 1992. *Shadowed Lives: Undocumented Immigrants in American Society*. New York: Wadsworth.

Cohen, Jeffrey H. 2001. "Transnational Migration in Rural Oaxaca, Mexico: Dependency, Development, and the Household." *American Anthropologist* 103(4): 954–967.

Cordero-Guzman, Hector, Robert C. Smith, and Ramon Grosfoguel, eds.

———. 2001. *Migration, Transnationalization, and Race in a Changing New York*. Philadelphia, PA: Temple University Press.

Cornelius, Wayne. 1989. "Impacts of the 1986 U.S. Immigration Law on Emigration from Rural Mexican Sending Communities." *Population and Development Review* 15: 689–705.

Coutin, Susan Bibler, and Phyllis Pease Chock. 1997. "Your Friend, the Illegal." Definition and Paradox in Newspaper Accounts of U.S. Immigration Reform. *Identities* 2(1–2): 123–148.

De Genova, Nicholas. 2005. *Working the Boundaries: Race, Space, and "Illegality" in Mexican Chicago*. Durham, NC: Duke University Press.

De Genova, Nicholas, and Ana Y. Ramos-Zayas. 2003. *Latino Crossings: Mexicans, Puerto Ricans, and the Politics of Race and Citizenship*. New York: Routledge.

di Leonardo, Micaela. 1998. *Exotics at Home: Anthropologies, Others, and American Modernity*. Chicago: University of Chicago Press.

Douglas, Mary. 2004. "Traditional Culture—Let's Hear No More about It." In *Culture and Public Action*. Vijayendra Rao and Michael Walton, eds. Pp. 85–109. Delhi: Permanent Black.

Durrenberger, E. Paul, and Suzan Erem. 2005. *Class Acts: An Anthropology of Service Workers and Their Union*. Boulder: Paradigm Press.

Fernandez-Kelly, Maria Patricia. 1983. *For We Are Sold, I and My People: Women and Industry in Mexico's Frontier*. Albany: University of New York Press.

Fine, Gary Alan. 1996. *Kitchens: The Culture of Restaurant Work*. Berkeley: University of California Press.

Gamio, Manuel. 1971[1930]. *Mexican Immigration to the United States: A Study of Human Migration and Adjustment*. New York: Dover.

Gershon, Ilana, and Janelle S. Taylor. 2008. Introduction to "In Focus: Culture in the Spaces of No Culture." *American Anthropologist* 110 (4): 417–421.

Gibson-Graham, J. K. 1996. *The End of Capitalism (As We Knew It): A Feminist Critique of Political Economy*. Minneapolis: University of Minnesota Press.

Giddens, Anthony. 1993. "Problems of Action and Structure." In *The Giddens Reader*. Philip Cassell, ed. Pp. 88–175. Stanford: Stanford University Press.

Goffman, Erving. 1959. *The Presentation of Self in Everyday Life*. New York: Anchor.

Golash-Boza, Tanya. 2009. "A Confluence of Interests in Immigration Enforcement: How Politicians, the Media, and Corporations Profit from Immigration Policies Destined to Fail." *Sociology Compass* 3: 293–294.

Gomberg-Munoz, Ruth. In press. *Labor and Legality: Life in a Mexican Immigrant Network*. New York: Oxford University Press.

Gray, Mia. 2004. "The Social Construction of the Service Sector: Institutional Structures and Labour Market Outcomes." *Geoforum* 35: 23–34.

Guarnizo, Luis Eduardo, and Michael Peter Smith. 1998. "The Locations of Transnationalism." In *Transnationalism from Below*. Michael Peter Smith and Luis Eduardo Guarnizo, eds. Pp. 3–34. New Brunswick, NJ: Transaction.

Gunewardena, Nandini, and Ann Kingsolver. 2007. "Introduction." In *The Gender of Globalization: Women Navigating Cultural and Economic Marginalization*. Nandini Gunewardena and Ann Kingsolver, eds. Pp. 3–21. Santa Fe, NM: School for Advanced Research Press.

Gupta, Akhil, and James Ferguson. 1997. "Discipline and Practice: 'The Field' as Site, Method, and Location in Anthropology." In *Anthropological Locations: Boundaries and Grounds of a Field Science*. Akhil

Gupta and James Ferguson, eds. Pp. 1–46. Berkeley: University of California Press.

Gutierrez, David G. 1995. *Walls and Mirrors: Mexican Americans, Mexican Immigrants, and the Politics of Ethnicity.* Berkeley: University of California Press.

Heyman, Josiah McC. 1998. "State Effects on Labor Exploitation: The INS and Undocumented Immigrants at the Mexico United States Border." *Critique of Anthropology* 18(2): 157–180.

———. 2001. "Class and Classification at the U.S.–Mexico Border." *Human Organization* 60(2): 128–140. Hondagneu-Sotelo, Pierrette.

———. 1994. *Gendered Transitions: Mexican Experiences of Immigration.* Berkeley: University of California Press.

———. 2001. *Domestica: Immigrant Workers Cleaning and Caring in the Shadows of Affluence.* Berkeley: University of California Press.

Kearney, Michael. 2004. "The Classifying and Value-Filtering Missions of Borders." *Anthropological Theory* 4(2): 131–156.

Lamphere, Louise, Alex Stepick, and Guillermo Grenier. 1994. "Introduction." In *Newcomers in the Workplace: Immigrants and the Restructuring of the U.S. Economy.* Louise Lamphere, Alex Stepick, and Guillermo Grenier, eds. Pp. 1–21. Philadelphia, PA: Temple University Press.

Lipsitz, George. 2005. "Foreword." In *Mangos, Chiles and Truckers: The Business of Transnationalism.* Minneapolis: University of Minnesota Press.

Mahler, Sarah J. 1998. "Theoretical and Empirical Contributions toward a Research Agenda for Transnationalism." In *Transnationalism from Below.* Michael Peter Smith and Luis Eduardo Guarnizo, eds. Pp. 64–102. New Brunswick, NJ: Transaction Publishers.

Marx, Karl. 1973[1852]. "The Eighteenth Brumaire of Louis Bonaparte." In *Political Writings,* vol. 2: Surveys from Exile. David Fembach, ed. Pp. 143–249. New York: Penguin Books.

Massey, Douglas, Joaquin Arango, Graeme Hugo, Ali Kouaouchi, Adela Pellegrino, and J. Edward Taylor. 1994. "An Evaluation of International Migration Theory: The North American Case." *Population and Development Review* 20: 699–751.

Massey, Douglas, Jorge Durand, and Nolan J. Malone. 2002. *Beyond Smoke and Mirrors: Mexican Immigration in an Era of Economic Integration.* New York: Russell Sage Foundation.

Mehta, Chirag, Nik Theodore, Iliana Mora, and Jennifer Wade. 2002. *Chicago's Undocumented Immigrants: An Analysis of Wages, Working Conditions, and Economic Contributions.* Chicago: UIC Center for Urban Economic Development.

Moss, Philip, and Chris Tilly. 2001. *Stories Employers Tell: Race, Skill, and Hiring in America.* New York: Russell Sage Foundation.

Neckerman, Kathryn, and Joleen Kirschenman. 1991. "Hiring Strategies, Racial Bias, and Inner City Workers." *Social Problems* 38(4): 433–447.

Ngai, Mac. 2005. *Impossible Subjects: Illegal Aliens and the Making of Modern America.* Princeton: Princeton University Press.

Omi, Michael, and Howard Winant. 1994. *Racial Formation in the United States from the 1960s to the 1990s.* New York: Routledge.

Ortner, Sherry. 1997. "Thick Resistance: Death and the Cultural Construction of Agency in Himalayan Mountaineering. Special issue, "The Fate of 'Culture': Geertz and Beyond," *Representations* 59: 135–162.

———. 2006. *Anthropology and Social Theory: Culture, Power, and the Acting Subject.* Durham, NC: Duke University Press.

Passel, Jeffrey. 2006. Size and Characteristics of the Unauthorized Migrant Population in the U.S. Estimates Based on the March 2005 *Current Population Survey.* Washington, DC: Pew Hispanic Center. https://pewhispanic.org/reports/report.php?ReportID=61, accessed November 1, 2009.

Passel, Jeffrey, and D'Vera Cohn. 2009. *A Portrait of Unauthorized Immigration in the United States.* Washington, DC: Pew Hispanic Center. https://pewhispanic.org/files/reports/107.pdf, accessed August 13, 2009.

Pedraza, Silvia, and Ruben G. Rumbaut. 1996. *Origins and Destinies: Immigration, Race, and Ethnicity in America.* New York: Wadsworth.

Pew Hispanic Center. 2007. National Survey of Latinos: As Illegal Immigration Issue Heats Up, Hispanics Feel a Chill. https://pewhispanic.org/reports/report.php?ReportID=84, accessed December 12, 2008.

Piore, Michael. 1979. *Birds of Passage: Migrant Labor and Industrial Societies.* New York: Cambridge University Press.

Portes, Alejandro, and Ruben Rumbaut. 1996. *Immigrant America: A Portrait.* Berkeley: University of California Press.

Portes, Alejandro, and John Walton. 1981. *Labor, Class, and the International System.* New York: Academic Press.

Rao, Vijayendra, and Michael Walton. 2004. "Culture and Public Action: Relationality, Equality of Agency, and Development." In *Culture and Public Action.* Vijayendra Rao and Michael Walton, eds. Pp. 336. Delhi: Permanent Black.

Ready, Timothy, and Allert Brown-Gort. 2005. *The State of Latino Chicago: This Is Home Now.* South Bend: Institute for Latino Studies, University of Notre Dame. https://latinostudies.nd.edu/pubs/pubs/StateofLatino-final.pdf, accessed July 10, 2007.

Romero, Mary. 2002. *Maid in the U.S.A.* New York: Routledge.

Rosenblatt, Daniel. 2004. "An Anthropology Made Safe for Culture: Patterns of Practice and the Politics of Difference in Ruth Benedict." *American Anthropologist* 106(3): 459–472.

Sassen, Saskia. 1988. *The Mobility of Labor and Capital: A Study in International Investment and Labor Flow.* Cambridge: Cambridge University Press.

Sassen-Koob, Saskia. 1981. "Towards a Conceptualization of Immigrant Labor." *Social Problems* 29(1): 65–85.

Sen, Amartya. 2004. "How Does Culture Matter?." In *Culture and Public Action.* Vijayendra Rao and Michael Walton, eds. Pp. 37–58. Delhi: Permanent Black.

Sewell, William H. 1992. "A Theory of Structure: Duality, Agency, and Transformation." *The American Journal of Sociology* 98(1): 1–29.

Smith, Robert C. 2006. *Mexican New York: Transnational Lives of New Immigrants.* Berkeley: University of California Press.

Smith-Nonini, Sandy. 2007. "Sticking to the Union: Anthropologists and 'Union Maids' in San Francisco." In *The Gender of Globalization: Women Navigating Cultural and Economic Marginalization.* Nandini Gunewardena and Ann Kingsolver, eds. Pp. 197–214. Santa Fe, NM: School for Advanced Research Press.

Steinberg, Stephen. 2005. "Immigration, African Americans, and Race Discourse." *New Politics* 10(3). https://www.wpunj.edu/newpol/issue39/Steinberg39.htm, accessed August 13, 2009.

Stephen, Lynn. 2007. *Transborder Lives: Indigenous Oaxacans in Mexico, California, and Oregon.* Durham, NC: Duke University Press.

Stepick, Alex, and Guillermo Grenier, with Hafidh A. Hafidh, Sue Chaffee, and Debbie Draznin. 1994. "The View from the Back of the House: Restaurants and Hotels in Miami." In *Newcomers in the Workplace: Immigrants and the Restructuring of the U.S. Economy.* Louise Lamphere, Alex Stepick, and Guillermo Grenier, eds. Pp. 181–198. Philadelphia, PA: Temple University Press.

Suarez-Orozco, Carola, and Marcelo Suarez-Orozco. 1995. *Transformations: Immigration, Family Life, and Achievement Motivation among Latino Adolescents.* Stanford: University of Stanford Press.

Tilly, Charles. 1998. *Durable Inequality.* Berkeley: University of California Press.

Urbina, Ian. 2009. After Pennsylvania Trial, Tensions Simmer over Race. *New York Times,* May 16: A18.

Vila, Pablo. 2000. *Crossing Borders, Reinforcing Borders: Social Categories, Metaphors, and Narrative Identities on the U.S–Mexico Frontier.* Austin: University of Texas Press.

Waldinger, Roger, and Michael Lichter. 2003. *How the Other Half Works: Immigration and the Social Organization of Labor.* Berkeley: University of California Press.

Willis, Paul. 1977. *Learning to Labor: How Working Class Kids Get Working-Class Jobs.* New York: Columbia University Press.

Zlolniski, Christian. 2003. "Labor Control and Resistance of Mexican Immigrant Janitors in Silicon Valley." *Human Organization* 62(1): 39–49.

———. 2006. *Janitors, Street Vendors, and Activists: The Lives of Mexican Immigrants in Silicon Valley.* Berkeley: University of California Press.

AUTHOR'S NOTES

a. Acknowledgements. I am very grateful to all of the ethnographic participants who contributed to this research. I am also indebted to Molly Doane, Josiah Heyman, Tom Boellstorff, and the anonymous AA reviewers, all of whom read this manuscript and offered valuable insights and suggestions. This material is based on work supported by the National Science Foundation under Grant No. 0718696.

b. These workers are real people—not composites—and I have changed all names, nicknames, and identifying details of people and places to protect their anonymity. While there are many large-scale restaurants in the Chicago area that could easily fit Il Vino's description, the establishment that I describe here is a fictitious composite of several different restaurants. I have tried to capture the scale, pace, economy, and culture of the real-life restaurant where most of these men work or have worked, but the details have all been changed. Most ethnographic data collection took place between August of 2007 and January of 2009. Interviews with immigrant workers were conducted in Spanish except for those with Alejandro, who prefers English. Interviews with immigrants' coworkers and managers were all conducted in English.

c. Scholars can choose from several different words to describe foreign-born workers in the United States, including *immigrant, migrant, transmigrant, and transborder* (see De Genova 2005 and Stephen 2007). Each term addresses a particular nuance in the relationship of mobile workers to the nation-state, and each has its own merits and drawbacks. I use the term immigrant when I describe my ethnographic participants for two related reasons. First, many of them are long-term, if not permanent, settlers in the United States, and migrant and transmigrant suggest an element of mobility or impermanence that does not accurately reflect their situations. Second, my research focuses on workers' daily activities in Chicago and less on their transnational and migration experiences per se. I use transmigrant when referring to transnationalist scholarship or transnational workers generally.

d. As is typical in high-end restaurants, the bus staff at Il Vino is all male. Mexican immigrant women have lower labor-force participation rates than their male counterparts and, when employed, tend to be concentrated in the lowest-paying jobs and in private households (Hondagneu-Sotelo 1994, 2001; Mehta et al. 2002).

e. The state of Guanajuato is part of a region known as the Bajio, an area of Mexico that has the distinction of being populous and well-integrated in national and international markets. Migration of Bajio workers to the United States is more than a century old; it began in earnest during the early 20th century, accelerated in midcentury, and continues today. There are long-standing webs of transnational networks between the Bajio region of Mexico and the United States; many of the workers featured here are second and even third-generation transmigrants. For more on the Bajio as a "sending" region, see Arias 2004; Cornelius 1989; Massey et al. 2002. For more on transnational social networks, see Alvarez 2005; Basch et al. 1994; Guarnizo and Smith 1999 Cordero-Guzman et al. 2001; Smith 2006.

f. I am indebted to anonymous reviewer #4 for proposing this objection.

g. This is a simple conception of structure, culture, and agency that will undoubtedly fail to satisfy some scholars who are concerned with more nuanced considerations of each term. For more developed theoretical discussions of the interaction of structure, culture, and agency, see Giddens 1993; Ortner 2006 and Sewell 1992.

h. Of course, being esteemed for being a hard worker and being stigmatized are not contradictory. Gutierrez (1995) points out that the fodder of negative stereotypes about Mexicans—docility, tractability, uncleanliness came to be seen as great virtues of a low wage labor force in the United States. During U.S. immigration hearings of the early 20th century, Mex-

icans were repeatedly identified as a labor force whose racial characteristics made them ideally suited for arduous and low-paying work (Gutierrez 1995; Pedraza and Rumbaut 1996).

i. It is important to note that these stereotypes—and, in Chicago, the term Mexican as well—not only apply to workers from Mexico but also to immigrants from Latin America generally. When Latin American immigrants come to the United States, they are ascribed into the racial category of "Latino" or "Hispanic" that subsumes actual regional, class, ethnic, and national differences (Omi and Winant 1994; Portes and Rumbaut 1996). Because of the large Mexican population in Chicago, Latin American workers are often referred to as "Mexican," regardless of their actual national origin.

j. The "work ethic" of Latin American immigrants is often invoked to contrast them with African American workers, reinforcing racist stereotypes and economic marginalization of both groups but to the particular detriment of the latter (see Steinberg 2005; Waldinger and Lichter 2003).

k. These workers frequently conflate "American" with "white." Because of intense racial segregation of African Americans in the Chicago area, these workers have very little contact with African Americans and do not tend to see them as competitors in the labor market.

l. The labor-force participation rate of undocumented Latino immigrants in the Chicago area is estimated to be 90 percent, compared to 69 percent for the total metro-area population (Mehta et al. 2002). Nationally, the labor-force participation rate for undocumented immigrant men is estimated to be 94 percent, compared with 83 percent for U.S.-born men (Passel and Cohn 2009).

Phenomenological Anthropology and the Anthropology of the Good

The engagement of anthropology with philosophy has been both long and deep. Greg Urban (2013: 592) notes that Boas developed American anthropology partially in response to Immanuel Kant's (1724–1804) *Critique of Pure Reason*. Ruth Benedict's ideas about the Apollonian and Dionysian owe a deep debt to Fredrick Nietzsche's (1844–1900) *The Birth of Tragedy*, and Pierre Bourdieu, who referred to social science in general and anthropology in particular as "fieldwork in philosophy," was a student of the Marxist philosopher Louis Althusser (1918–1990) and was even more deeply influenced by the phenomenologist and existentialist Maurice Merleau-Ponty (1980–1961). In this section, we explore two current trends in philosophical anthropology, phenomenological anthropology, and its related field, the anthropology of the good.

The philosophical schools of phenomenology and existentialism have their roots in the work of Edmund Husserl (1859–1938) and his mentor Franz Brentano (1838–1917). Many of the most widely recognized philosophers of the twentieth century either were students of Husserl or were profoundly influenced by his work. Martin Heidegger, Emmanuel Levinas (1906–1995), and Edith Stein (1891–1942, also known as Teresia Benedicta a Cruce, the patron saint of Europe), were among his students. Those who studied with these students or considered Husserl's insights to have an impact on their philosophy included Max Scheler, Hannah Arendt, Jean-Paul Sartre, Simone de Beauvoir, Maurice Merleau-Ponty, Herbert Marcuse, Kurt Godel, Jacques Derrida, and a great many others.

In general, phenomenologists focus on the study of human consciousness and understand our experience of the world as arising from that consciousness. We cannot understand the physical world as existing separately from our consciousness of it (that's not to say that it doesn't have such an existence, but only that we cannot understand it; we have no point to view it from). Thus phenomenology occupies a midground between objectivity and subjectivity. Phenomenologists therefore focus on the ways people experience and interact with their social worlds. The key phenomenological technique that Husserl proposed for achieving this focus was what he called the *epoché*, a term he borrowed from the ancient Greek skeptical philosophers. *Epoché* is a sort of bracketing in which the philosopher attempts to suspend judgment about objects, relationships, people, and events in an attempt to examine phenomena as they appear in our immediate, prereflective experience.

The phenomenological emphasis on experience leads to a concern with embodiment. Our bodies and our physical brains are always implicated in our experience and our understandings. Whereas René Descartes famously said, "I think therefore I am," thus separating the mind from the body and prioritizing the mind as where the humanness of humanity lies, phenomenologists and existentialists reverse this formulation: I am, therefore I think, or, in Jean-Paul Sartre's famous formulation, existence precedes essence. In saying this, they reject mind-body dualism, focusing instead on the interconnectedness and inseparability of thinking and being. This rejection of dualities and focus on the ambiguous ways in which categories such as subject and object, interiority and exteriority, or emic and etic blend and merge is typical of phenomenological approaches.

Desjarlais and Throop (2011) identify three threads within phenomenological anthropology, the hermeneutic, the critical, and the existential. The first of these is focused on the ways in which people make meaning and how they interpret and engage with issues such as selfhood, agency, pain, and morality. Anthropologists working in this vein often explore both the meaning-making of the people they work with and their own relationship to them. While hermeneutic phenomenology is focused on questions of interpretation, critical phenomenology examines the way people experience their lives in the context of the cultural, political, and discursive contexts in which their lives and experiences are set. It explores the ways that the structure of power informs individual and cultural experience. Existential phenomenology, the third strain, focuses on the "existential demands, constraints, dilemmas, potentialities, uncertainties, and the 'struggle for being' that figure into what it means to be human" (Desjarlais and Throop 2011: 93). It focuses on the choices people make, the implications of these choices, and their understanding of freedom and constraint. In this context, Sarah Bakewell's (2016: 33–34) attempt to summarize what existentialists do may be useful:

> —Existentialists concern themselves with *individual concrete human existence.*
> —They consider human existence different from the kind of being other things have. Other entities are what they are but as a human I am whatever I choose to make of myself at every moment. I am *free*—
> —And therefore, I am *responsible* for everything I do; a dizzying fact which causes
> —an *anxiety* inseparable from human existence itself.
> —On the other hand, I am only free within *situations* which can include factors in my own biology and psychology, as well as physical, historical, and social variables of the world into which I have been thrown.
> —Despite the limitations, I always want more. I am passionately involved in personal *projects* of all kinds.
> —Human existence is thus *ambiguous*; at once boxed in by borders and yet transcendent and exhilarating.
> —An existentialist who is also *phenomenological* provides no easy rules for dealing with this condition but instead concentrates on *describing* lived experience as it presents itself.
> —By describing experience well, he or she hopes to understand this existence and awaken us to ways of living more *authentic* lives.

Desjarlais and Throop also offer several critiques of phenomenology and phenomenological anthropology. They note that first of all, phenomenology is so broad and open to interpretation that there tends to be as many different forms of phenomenology as there are phenomenologists. Beyond this they find that critiques fault phenomenology for epistemological problems and for lack of sufficient attention to the political and socioeconomic forces that condition life. However, phenomenologists never claim to be able to think like a native. Instead, they rely on people's detailed accounts of their experiences and understandings, and they pay close attention to their own positioning. It is true that phenomenologists focus on experience rather than deep structures of inequality and oppression. However, understanding experience can in itself be highly political, and many phenomenologists and existentialists of the twentieth century were deeply engaged in politics.

Our example of phenomenology, "Ambivalent Happiness and Virtuous Suffering" by Jason Throop, fits somewhere between the hermeneutic and existentialist schools of phenomenology. It examines and reflects on understandings of happiness on Yap, a Pacific island in the Federated States of Micronesia (and one well known in anthropology). Current-day Americans and many others tend to have an almost wholly positive view of happiness. We tend to consider it a critical goal of life and tell our children things like, "We don't care what you do; we just want you to be happy." Yapese have a much more complex relationship with happiness. As they reflect on their own experiences of happiness and those of their community members, they critique the connection between happiness and selfishness. For them, happiness conflicts with community solidarity. This solidarity is built through what Throop terms *virtuous suffering*. Yet, perhaps ironically, such virtuous suffering leads, if not exactly to happiness, perhaps to contentment.

C. Jason Throop was born in Halifax, Nova Scotia, and raised in Ottawa, Ontario. He is in currently professor and chair of the Department of Anthropology at the University of California,

Los Angeles, where he also received his doctorate in 2005. His dissertation committee members included Alessandro Duranti and Cheryl Mattingly.

ANTHROPOLOGY OF THE GOOD

Tolstoy begins *Anna Karenina*, "Happy families are all alike; every unhappy family is unhappy in its own way." The anthropology of the good, in some sense, reverses Tolstoy's dictum. The anthropology of the good is not about happiness exactly. But it is about the things, ideas, and actions that make a good life and, critically, about the struggle of individuals to achieve, to whatever extent they can, that good life.

The anthropology of the good was both identified and promoted in two widely read essays; the first, by Joel Robbins, appeared in 2013, and the second, by Sherry Ortner, in 2016. Both essays argue that a key concern of anthropologists since the late 1980s has been the nature and lives of people suffering under regimes of oppression. Robbins refers to this as "the suffering subject" and Ortner as "dark anthropology." This sort of anthropology has focused on economic forces, particularly neoliberalism and globalization, and on the ways that these have negatively impacted the communities that many anthropologists study. Robbins identifies the focus of anthropology as "the subject living in pain, in poverty, or under conditions of violence or oppression" (2013: 448).

Robbins goes on to note that one effect of anthropology's focus on suffering was to subtly shift anthropological attention from analytic distance and critical comparison to "empathic connection and moral witnessing based on human unity" (2013: 453). Such moral witnessing is based on deeply held and universalistic convictions of what should happen. Most Western intellectuals hold that human beings have inherent rights to be free of trauma and suffering. We tend to define progress as that which moves us in the direction of these freedoms. Robbins, of course, is not trying to argue against freedom or in favor of suffering. However, if every analysis is focused around suffering and oppression, locates these primarily in colonialism and the neoliberal order, and emphasizes empathy with the oppressed and the search for social justice, the result is a flattening of anthropological discourse. Pace Tolstoy, all unhappy societies are alike (or, at least, are analyzed by anthropologists as being alike), and the search for happiness, or at least a good life, becomes problematic.

Robbins points out that the focus on suffering also draws us away from anthropology's historical goal: the understanding of ways of living that are truly different. He writes:

> At its best, anthropology . . . [before the 1980s based] itself on the promise that the discovery of other ways of living might teach us the limits of our own, and might lead us to a vision of a world that was better than ours in ways we could not on our own imagine. As David Schneider once put it, "one of the fundamental fantasies of anthropology is that somewhere there must be a life really worth living" (1967: viii). (2013: 456)

Both Robbins and Ortner see one of the current trends in anthropology as a movement precisely back in this direction. They see this expressed in new work that focuses on issues such as "value, morality, imagination, well-being, empathy, care, the gift, hope, time and change" (Robbins 2013: 457).

Thus, in some senses, the anthropology of the good returns us to the critical historical concern of anthropologists: How do people in different societies live? In particular, it focuses on what living a decent life means in different places and at different times. However, the anthropology of the good is also informed by a wealth of theoretical perspectives that were relatively rare in earlier anthropology. The first of these concerns is issues of power, structure, and agency. These are described in some detail in the introduction to the last section of this book. However, it is good to keep Marx's famous dictum in mind (and in doing so, we follow both Leacock and Gomberg-

Muñoz in this book). In the opening of *The Eighteenth Brumaire of Louis Bonaparte* (1852), Marx writes: "Men make their own history, but they do not make it as they please; they do not make it under self-selected circumstances but under circumstances existing already, given and transmitted from the past." Marx is saying that we are not completely free to choose the life we live. We must make our choices within the context in which we find ourselves. Thus, although everyone, even the slave or the prisoner, has some ability to choose the life they will live, our choices are made within a nexus of power and structure that gives much greater freedom and ability to some than to others. Or, as Marx continues: "The tradition of all dead generations weighs like a nightmare on the brains of the living."

The second perspective is that to study the good, or morality, or value, or the other elements that Robbins identifies, anthropologists need to consider what these things are and, perhaps even more importantly, how we (and how the people who are the subjects of this sort of anthropology) know what they are. But this is no simple matter. Questions such as "What is the nature of good?" or "How do we know if an action is moral?" have been central concerns of philosophy since before the time of Socrates. Thus, when anthropologists engage with people's attempt to live good lives in whatever conditions they find themselves, they are necessarily engaging with philosophy as well. The anthropology of the good rapidly merges into philosophical anthropology. Or, as anthropologist Susan Mazur-Stommen put it on a Quora forum, "one way to think of anthropology is as applied philosophy."

Anthropologists of the good draw from an extremely wide variety of philosophical traditions, from the classical Greeks to the work of analytic philosophers like Ludwig Wittgenstein (1889–1951), postanalytic philosophers such as Stanley Cavell (1926–2018), and political philosophers like Hannah Arendt (1906–1975). Despite this diversity, it may prove useful to have a broad framework for the philosophy of morality, ethics, and virtue. Historically, there are three general positions in these fields: the consequentialist, the deontological, and the Aristotelian.

Consequentialism is the idea that acts can be judged as moral or immoral depending on their outcome. Probably the best-known form of consequentialism is utilitarianism. Utilitarians argue that decision-making should be rational and consistent and that it should be based on achieving the greatest good for the greatest number. In other words, the outcome of a decision is the most important factor in judging its value or morality. Of course, this doesn't tell us what good actually is, only that we should strive to maximize it. Perhaps the best-known current-day utilitarian is Princeton University professor of bioethics Peter Singer (b. 1972).

A second approach to morality is called deontology. The word comes from the Greek for "duty" (*deon*), and deontology's fundamental premise is that morality and ethics should be duty or rule based. Thus, actions are good or bad to the degree that they correspond to rules and obligations, irrespective of their consequences. Immanuel Kant (1724–1804) is among the most widely known deontological philosophers. He argued that it was the motives of a person carrying out an action rather than the consequences of the deed that made an action right or wrong. However, Kant also couched this in terms of a categorical imperative. Kant explained the meaning of the categorical imperative in several ways, but two of the best known are "act only in accordance with that maxim through which you can at the same time will that it become a universal law" (G 4:421) and "never act in such a way that we treat humanity, whether in ourselves or others, as a means only but always as an end in itself" (Johnson and Cureton 2019). The political philosopher John Rawls (1921–2002) was (primarily) a contemporary deontological thinker.

The third ethical framework is referred to as Aristotelian or virtue ethics. As the name implies, much of virtue ethics goes back to the work of Aristotle. For Aristotle, neither consequences nor rules nor morality as an abstract concept mattered much. Instead, cultivating ethics and living a good life were about the possession of the right character traits. J. N. Hooker (1996: 10–11) writes that Aristotle had no notion of moral obligation but rather saw people as good or bad in the same way a tool was good or bad: a good life was one that performed its function well. But what is life's function? For Aristotle, it was to apprehend and manifest qualities like beauty, trust, loyalty, and courage. Although many critical thinkers in philosophy in the past century have been staunch critics of virtue ethics, it has undergone a revival in recent decades, and it seems in some ways very well suited to anthropology. For many, a key difficulty in virtue ethics is the fact that different societies have different ideas of virtue. But it's that same characteristic that makes it so appealing to anthropologists. Because different societies have different ideas of virtue, virtue ethics operates well in a context of cultural relativism. Current-day philosophers concerned with virtue ethics include Christine Swanton (b. 1947) and Julia Annas (b. 1946). However, for the anthropologists whose work we present in this section, Stanley Cavell's thinking is critical. Cavell's ideas are described in essay 38 by Veena Das and in our notes to that essay.

Veena Das (b. 1945) was trained at the University of Delhi in India and taught there for more than thirty years. She has been the Krieger-Eisenhower Professor of Anthropology at Johns Hopkins University since 2000. Das has been critically interested in Indian ethnography, particularly as it relates to health and disease and to violence. However, she has also been strongly drawn to both Indian and Western philosophy and has brought these into her work in profound ways. She writes that she is

> driven by the task to understand the everyday as a site on which we see the closeness of both the ordinary and its violation. My ethnographic task has been to track the traces of each in the other. My work owes everything to the inspiration I get from the great philosopher Stanley Cavell and his mode of reading the texts of Ludwig Wittgenstein. A claim I make is that the moral task of securing the everyday is what connects my interlocutors in the field with the task of leading words home that I take to be the essence of Cavell and Wittgenstein's philosophy. (2009)

"Leading words home" refers to Wittgenstein's remark, "What we do is to bring words back from their metaphysical to their everyday use." Referring to this, Cavell says that it's "as if our words are away, not at home, and it takes the best efforts of philosophy to recognize when and where our words have strayed into metaphysics" (in Parini 1985: 117). These ideas provided Das with her focus on thinking about the concrete human experiences of hope, striving, desire, and becoming, in a context grounded in history and in the everyday as well as in the human need to ask questions that cannot be easily or definitively answered.

Our selection from Das, "Engaging the Life of the Other: Love and Everyday Life," comes from Michael Lambek's 2010 edited volume *Ordinary Ethics: Anthropology, Language, and Action*. It explores how Kuldip and Saba, a Hindu boy and a Muslim girl, fall in love and attempt to make a space for their marriage and their lives together in a community in India in which Hindus and Muslims are members of mutually suspicious subcommunities and where the political context encourages antagonism between Hindu and Muslim. This essay forms part of Das's larger project of understanding the meanings of religious violence in India.

In some ways, the work of anthropologists such as Throop and Das returns anthropology to the foundation built by Boas and Malinowski. Both try to seek out and accurately document lives and cultures that are different from their own as objectively as they can. But they do so in ways that are deeply empathic and allow us to grasp the meanings, the rationalities, and the structures that both constrain the lives of those they study and offer new possibilities. Their work allows us to join the people they write about, if only for a moment, in the process of becoming. They allow us to rediscover yet again what Franz Boas observed in 1883: that the value of a person lies in *herzensbildung*, that is, in the cultivation, education, and nobleness of the heart.

SUGGESTED READINGS

Fischer, Edward F. 2014. *The Good Life: Aspiration, Dignity, and the Anthropology of Wellbeing*. Stanford, CA: Stanford University Press.
    Fischer compares ideas of the good life in Germany and Guatemala. He finds commonalities in needs for aspiration, opportunity, dignity, and purpose.
Jackson, Michael. 2013. *The Wherewithal of Life: Ethics, Migration, and the Question of Well-Being*. Berkeley: University of California Press.
    A phenomenological account of three migrant men in three countries: a Ugandan in Copenhagen, a Mexican in Boston, and a man from Burkina Faso in Amsterdam. Jackson explores the balance between the moral claims of family and kin and the promises of personal fulfillment.
Heintz, Monica. 2009. *The Anthropology of Moralities*. New York: Berghahn.
    A collection of ten essays from key authors examining morality in diverse places including Russia, Uzbekistan, Vietnam, and Ireland.
Kleinman, Arthur. 2011. *What Really Matters: Living a Moral Life amidst Uncertainty and Danger*. Oxford: Oxford University Press.
    Medical anthropologist Arthur Kleinman tells how six people he had known (and a seventh, the early-twentieth-century psychologist and anthropologist W. H. R. Rivers) faced war, illness, and injury, circumstances in which they were forced to consider what really matters.
Lambek, Michael, ed. 2010. *Ordinary Ethics: Anthropology, Language, and Action*. New York: Fordham University Press.
    A collection of twenty essays from key current authors. Topics include ethics of speaking, responsibility and agency, and punishment and personal dignity.
Lambek, Michael, Veena Das, Didier Fassin, and Webb Keane. 2015. *Four Lectures on Ethics: Anthropological Perspectives*. Chicago: HAU Books.
    An important work on anthropological understandings of morality and ordinary ethics from four of the key thinkers in this field.
Mahmood, Saba. 2011. *Politics of Piety: The Islamic Revival and the Feminist Subject*. Princeton, NJ: Princeton University Press.
    Mahmood explores grassroots pietist movements in Cairo, Egypt. She shows the linkages between the ethical and political and considers the ways in which such movements challenge anthropologists to rethink assumptions about liberal politics, patriarchy, and freedom.
Ortner, Sherry B. 2016. "Dark Anthropology and Its Others." *HAU: Journal of Ethnographic Theory* 6(1): 47–73.
    A critical article in which Ortner traces the development of the anthropology of suffering, its connections with economics and governmentality, and the increasing importance of anthropologies of the good.
Ram, Kalpana, and Christopher Houston. 2015. *Phenomenology in Anthropology: A Sense of Perspective*. Bloomington: Indiana University Press.
    A series of essays by well-known phenomenological anthropologists covering a wide range of topics.
Robbins, Joel. 2004. *Becoming Sinners: Christianity and Moral Torment in a Papua New Guinea Society*. Berkeley: University of California Press.
    Robbins's research on the Urapmin of New Guinea shows how conversion to Christianity affected culture and connected with preexisting cultural themes.
Yoshimi, Jeff, Philip Walsh, and Patrick Londen. 2023. *Horizons of Phenomenology: Essays on the State of the Field and Its Applications*. Chaim: Springer.
    A collection of essays providing a series of perspectives on phenomenology. Includes a section on anthropology and archaeology.

38. Engaging the Life of the Other: Love and Everyday Life

Veena Das (b. 1945)

I BEGIN THIS ESSAY with the simple proposition that everyday life is the site in which the life of the other is engaged. I try to work out the implications of such a proposition for the moral striving I observe in low-income neighborhoods in Delhi, where, in collaboration with a group of researchers, I have been engaged in understanding urban transformations for the last ten years. What is at stake for me here is both the idea of the everyday and our picture of what is constitutive of moral striving. Due to the breadth of its semantic meanings, everyday life can be understood in many ways. Everyday life might, for instance, be thought of as the site of routine and habit, within which strategic contests for culturally approved goods such as honor or prestige take place. For others, everyday life provides the site through which the projects of state power or given scripts of normativity can be resisted (see Gardiner 2000 for a succinct discussion of these issues). I have argued in recent years that our attachment to routines and habit is inflected by another affect—that of the experience of the everyday as also the site of trance, illusion, and danger (Das 2007). The mutual shadowing of the ordinary and skepticism in my view defines the character of the everyday, so that to secure the everyday, far from being something we might take for granted, might be thought of as an achievement.[1]

My view of moral life is deeply influenced by a notion of the everyday in which how I respond to the claims of the other, as well as how I allow myself to be claimed by the other, defines the work of self-formation. In the philosophical writings of Stanley Cavell, the realization of these moral ideas, or what he calls the picture of Emersonian perfectionism, is not premised on a pregiven, objectively agreed-upon idea of the common good or on virtues that have a vocabulary of their own but rather envisions a moral striving that in its uncertainty and its attention to the concrete specificity of the other is simply a dimension of everyday life (Cavell 1990). In this picture of spiritual becoming, what one seeks is not to ascend to some higher ideal but to give birth to what sometimes Cavell is moved to call an adjacent self—a striving in which the eventual everyday emerges in a relation of next-ness to the actual everyday (Critchley 2005). Against the dominant understanding of morality as the capacity to form moral judgments in which the crucial requirement is that we should be able to take an abstract, non-subjective vantage position from which we can orient ourselves to the world, I argue that recourse to such an ideal position often results in evading the imperative to be attentive to the suffering of the other. I am arguing not that there is no room for moral judgments in our lives or that people do not

From *Ordinary Ethics: Anthropology, Language, and Action* (2010)

1. In her 2007 book, *Life and Words: Violence and the Descent into the Ordinary*, Das examines the violence that followed the partition of India and Pakistan in 1947 and the violence the followed the assassination of Indira Gandhi in 1984. She explores how the survivors of violence integrate this "poisonous knowledge" into their everyday lives. She emphasizes the agency involved both in silence and in speech. Das further explores how the founding violence of Indian partition is repeatedly expressed in the role of violence in maintaining the state. Thus, her concern is how people create their lives with the knowledge of and against an ongoing history of violence.

apply abstract standards derived from, say, a rule of conduct found in what they consider to be authoritative traditions but rather that whole areas of moral life remain obscure if our picture of morality remains tied to some version of following rules.[2]

In order to give conceptual and empirical depth to the notion of next-ness or an adjacent self as the aim of moral striving, I wish to develop what used to be called an extended case study of the marriage of a Hindu man and a Muslim woman in one of the low-income neighborhoods in Delhi. I offer this case study not as an example of larger social processes of, say, social change or social conflict but rather as a mode of engaging a singularity through which I can show how a range of complex forces brought into being by the simple fact of a boy and girl having fallen in love fold

themselves into intimate relations and come to define what Henrietta Moore calls "intimate aspirations" (personal correspondence). In the later Wittgenstein we have a stringent critique of the notion that the correct projection of a concept is already laid before us—thus, he says, when we assume that we know what following a rule means, we have a picture of a rigid line or grid on which our actions will move. Yet this picture produces only the buried mythology of our language (Wittgenstein 1953).[a, 3]

What would be the opposite of this notion of "projection" along the imagery of an ideally rigid rail line? We could draw upon Foucault's notion of eventalization, which he argues is a way of lightening the weight of causal thinking in our intellectual projects, of interrupting given constants and instead thinking of gestures, acts, and discourses through which the

---

2. Stanley Cavell (1926–1981) was a Harvard-based philosopher who focused on "ordinary language philosophy." He argued that philosophers should focus on the things that ordinary human beings cannot help thinking about. Cavell wondered, for example, if "others really know the nature of one's own experience, or whether good and bad are relative. . . . [These and other questions are examples of] . . . human willingness to allow questions for itself which it cannot answer with satisfaction" (Cavell 1984: 9). Cavell often wrote about Hollywood films and other works of fiction.

The American transcendentalist Ralph Waldo Emerson (1803–1882) proposed that the goal of life was the achievement of higher forms. For Cavell, this meant a striving for an "attainable but unattained" self; a self that is always "on the way" (Goodman 2018). This is similar to what Das, in this essay, calls the "adjacent self."

3. Ludwig Wittgenstein (1889–1951), often considered one of the twentieth century's most influential philosophers, is particularly important to Das. Wittgenstein is perhaps best known for his contributions to the philosophy of language and his work on private language and rule following. He argues that philosophical problems often have their root in misunderstandings of the logic of language.

Alterman (2003: 327) describes what he calls Wittgenstein's "community view" of rule-following: "an individual applies rules in a finite number of instances, but an infinite number of rules may be compatible with any such finite set of applications. The conclusion is that there is no fact of the matter as to which rule someone is following." In other words, on the one hand, people live in a world bounded by rules (like don't marry a Muslim) but on the other, rules are, by their nature, multiple and overlapping. In their daily lives, people must find ways to act in accordance with the rules (and justify their actions to their community members) but at the same time find ways to interpret the rules that allow them agency to pursue projects that might, in some interpretations, violate the rules.

Henrietta Moore (DBE, FBA FAcSS) (b. 1957) is a British social anthropologist at University College, London. Moore has studied global economic development and is the Director of the Institute for Global Prosperity. She promotes the role of diversity and environment in the generation of wealth. Moore is also (increasingly) a public intellectual, speaking on topics including Brexit and the provision of a universal living wage. Moore, incidentally, has also edited a collection of essays in anthropological theory (2006), centering on epistemology. In an essay on books, Moore has written: "The question of whether you can ever escape your family, your culture, your gender runs like a golden thread through all of my writing on feminism and anthropology, as it does indeed through the writing and scholarship of all feminists. It is our true inheritance" (2012).

Das has written extensive footnotes for this essay. They often include definitions of terms that might be unfamiliar to the reader. We have lettered the footnotes and placed them at the end of the essay. We urge readers to look at them.

imagery of the rigid line on which action will unfold can be made to stop (Foucault 1996).[b] One ethnographic mode of writing that we could draw from Wittgenstein is to think of the scenic as capturing a particular way in which a mode of conversation or a course of action is dramatized so that various voices (that of the child, of the skeptic, of common sense, or the philosopher) are allowed expression (Wittgenstein 1953). Using the idea of a scene, I hope to show how something as simple as a Hindu boy having fallen in love with a Muslim girl becomes a seed scattered in the soil of the everyday. It carries within it the potential to unleash great violence—but also an opportunity for intimate aspirations to be realized by all who have to re-create their relations around the couple. While I will try to frame this kind of nascent happening with an account of political affects to show how such an act can morph into Hindu-Muslim violence, how it can become the subject of police investigations, court cases, and parliamentary inquiries, I will also carry it into the life of this couple, whom I call Kuldip and Saba and their relationships. My descriptions of the mode of engaging this event in the everyday will, however, take the form of scenic descriptions that evoke Wittgenstein's scenes of instruction (as in a child learning to read) or dramatizations of skeptical doubt (as in the parable of the boiling pot). I hope that, by presenting the singularity of this case in this mode, I will be able to show how the notion of next-ness or the adjacent self allows for some calming of the turbulent potential of this event. It is a picture of moral perfectionism as a striving—the play of uncertainty, doubt, and the deepening of intimate relations within a whole weave of life.[4]

THE EXPLOSIVE POTENTIAL OF HINDU-MUSLIM MARRIAGES

The potential for violence in Hindu-Muslim relations involving the sexuality of women is a long-standing theme of political rhetoric in India and has been addressed in administrative and judicial practices through the concern for "public order." Deepak Mehta (2009) has analyzed how exchanges of insults between Hindus and Muslims in the public sphere were articulated around the themes of the sexualized body of the Prophet, the emasculation of the men of the other group, and slights concerning the sexuality and purity of women. He analyzes the genres of insult and shows how they were written not so much to evade the British censor as to be recognized in the eyes of the colonial state as literatures of insult. However, heaping insults and humiliation on the other is only part of the story—the other part is the theme of desire that crosses the normative boundaries of religion, which has fascinated poets, writers, and film-makers. Within this field of desire, fraught with the possibilities of tremendous violence, how are loving couples enabled to negotiate the treacherous waters of Hindu-Muslim sensibilities, the difficult realm of law, and the dense kinship universe of each person?

In her recent work on love marriages in Delhi, Perveez Mody (2008) offers the notion of

---

4. Sanna Tirkkonen (2015: 16) writes that *eventalization* is a strategy by which "[w]e can show that an issue or practice we are dealing with and wish to call into question stands on an unstable foundation. By doing so we can point out that it is merely an event whose disappearance is just as possible as its existence." Foucault himself put it less formally. He said that eventalization was a strategy to show that things "weren't as necessary as all that" (Foucault 1991: 76).

Das's introduction has been couched in dense philosophical language but harkens back to critical themes in anthropology that return to Boasian ideas and articulate with structure and agency frameworks. Culture is a historical process that is continually created through the actions of individual men and women. It is a framework, but a broad, shifting, and unstable one. Norms and values exist but are multiple and contradictory. Consequently, individuals make choices looking to create themselves within their understandings of possible futures. In this way society is reproduced. But this reproduction is tenuous, and the possibilities of individual and collective disaster are often very real.

"not-community" to depict the complex inter-action between law, publicity, and intimacy. She argues that ideas of liberal citizenship are both enabled and punctured by new forms of intimacy, as demonstrated in the legal trajectories through which such issues are addressed in India. In a fascinating account of how the law negotiates the sensitivities around Hindu-Muslim relations, Mody's work brings out the contradictions embodied in legislative acts, such as the Special Marriage Act of 1872 in the colonial period, that, on the one hand, provided legal protection for individuals who chose to marry without parental consent and yet, on the other, constrained these choices by various other qualifications—specifically, by restricting the law's application to those who explicitly renounced membership in any religious community. Not only at the legislative level but also at the level of police procedure, adjudication, and public-interest litigation, the ambivalence regarding Hindu-Muslim marriages often bursts into publicity of one sort or another, as is evident both in the literature of the nineteenth century and in the newspaper and other reportage in our own times.[c] For such couples, negotiating the terrain of parental consent, community approval, or even a complete break with previous kinship relations might bring into play a whole range of affects that are the stuff of cinema and literature. Most anthropologists have been reluctant to explore the profound implications of such a situation. Even Mody, because she was constrained to follow cases

that had already burst into national publicity, is not able to show us how questions of ethics, morality, and intimate aspirations are negotiated outside the realm of publicity, though she does show that, when couples are successful in getting parental consent, they are careful to maintain a fiction of "arranged marriage."

Jonathan Parry (2001) writes of the ubiquity of marriages and liaisons that cut across caste and community among the Satnamis of Chattisgarh, but he points out that these cases pertain to secondary marriages.[d] As far as primary marriages are concerned, the norms of caste endogamy are maintained. Parry seems to suggest that, within these parameters, the contrast between normative marriages and non-normative ones was not so stark in that region until the Bhilai Steel Plant (BSP), a Public Sector Undertaking, took it upon itself to intervene to ensure the stability of marriages. Parry's descriptions of such marriages leave one with the impression that there is not much affective stake in marriage until one realizes that the basis of his conclusion is "public talk" and gossip among men, which might leave little room for expressions of emotions of intimacy. It seems safe to say that one gets little help from the anthropological literature on how marriages outside the norms of caste and community create new forms of subjectivation at the level of the local. What kinds of shifts in subjectivity can one detect as marriages across caste and community become a matter that lies between kinship and politics?[5]

---

5. A detailed description of the social order of India is beyond the scope of this work. However, it is useful for readers to have a basic outline of some of the critical divisions in Indian society. Two of these are the religious differentiation between Hindus and Muslims and the divisions among Hindus that are often referred to as "caste." Both Hindu and Muslim communities have very long histories in India. In the colonial era (1858–1947), Britain controlled the modern nations of Pakistan, India, and Bangladesh. At the time of independence in 1947, in a political move that remains highly controversial, Britain divided its possessions into a majority Hindu India and a majority Muslim Pakistan. The act of division led to communal violence that displaced well over ten million people and may have led to the deaths of two million. In 1971, in another violent conflagration, Bangladesh won its independence from Pakistan. Today, Hindus in Pakistan constitute only a small percentage of the population, but some two hundred million Muslims live in India and constitute about 14 percent of its population.

Hindu India is divided by caste (readers should be aware that both the terms "Hindu" and "caste" are controversial). Castes are religiously justified, hierarchically ranked groups. They are ideally endogamous (members may only marry members of their own caste) and contact with lower ranked castes is understood as polluting to members of higher-ranked castes (see Mary Douglas, essay 24, for more information about caste). The Satnamis of Chattisgarh are a caste and religious group from the Center East of India. This group was founded by a member of the Chamar (leatherworking) caste and is accorded extremely low status by most Hindus.

In order to demonstrate that Hindu-Muslim marriages continue to carry a potential for violence, I will give a recent example from a political pamphlet distributed by Akhil Bharati Vidyarthi Parishad (ABVP), the student wing of the Bharatiya Janata Party (BJP), known for its militant defense of a Hindu nationalism that has consistently put into question Muslim belonging to the nation.[e] The pamphlet shows how the anxieties around terrorism and Islamic *jihad* that have gained fresh ground due to both global and national discourses on terrorism and security are folded into the older rhetoric of the Muslim tendency to "seduce" young and gullible Hindu girls.[6]

The pamphlet, written in English, which was distributed to students at the prestigious Jawaharlal Nehru University in 2009, following much publicity in the print and electronic media, carried the following warning:

Few days back a Malayalam Daily; Kerala Kaumudi exposed shocking revelations about a jihadi organization named "Love Jihad" which has been conveniently ignored by rest of the media. The allegation that Muslim men entice Hindu and Christian women into marriage for reasons other than love, as part of an Islamist conspiracy, has recently been investigated by Kerala Police and has brought out some ugly details. The August 31 issue of Kerala's foremost newspaper, Malayalam Manorama, carried an extensive report on how a Pakistan-based terrorist organization is planning, abetting and financing the enticement of college students from different communities in the State to become cannon fodder for its

jihad in India. The report terms such young women as "Love Bombs."

The exposé continues:

Trapping naive Hindu girls in the web of love in order to convert to Islam is the modus operandi of the said organization. Already more than 4000 girls have been converted to Islam by these Jihadi Romeos. Special branch of Police started investigation when marriages of such large scales were reported within last 6 months. As per the instructions of this organization, the recruits need to trap a Hindu girl each within the time frame of 2 weeks and brainwash her to get converted and then get married with her within 6 months. Special instructions to breed at least 4 kids have also been issued. If the target doesn't get trapped within first 2 weeks, they are instructed to leave her and move on to another girl. College students and working girls should be the prime target. Having completed their mission the organization will give 1 lakh Rupees and Financial help for the youth to start a business. Free mobile phone, bikes and fashionable dresses are offered to them as tools for the mission. Money for this "Love Jihad" comes from the Middle East. Each district has its own zonal chairman to oversee the mission. Prior to College admission they make a list of Hindu girls with their details, and target those who they feel are vulnerable and easy to be brainwashed.[7]

This pamphlet was based upon newspaper reports in both regional and national dailies.

---

6. The Bharatiya Janata Party (BJP) is a populist Hindu Nationalist political party. Founded in 1980 it was the successor to several other Hindu Nationalist political parties. The BJP is one of the most powerful political organizations in India. Atal Bihari Vajpayee (1924–2018), Indian Prime Minister from 1998 to 2004, and Narendra Modi (b. 1950), Prime Minister from 2014 both are members of the BJP. The BJP promotes the idea of Hindutva or Hindu-ness. Hindutva is the notion that India is defined by a common Hindu way of life and style of thinking. They contrast this with Muslim ways of thinking. Rana Ayyub (2018), writes that Narendra Modi's government "routinely disseminates fake news, targeting and demonizing Indian Muslims." In May 2019, Modi was reelected Prime Minister and the BJP captured 56 percent of the Indian Parliament winning 303 parliamentary seats. However, in the 2024 election, the BJP party won only 240 seats, dealing a blow to Modi's political power.

7. A *lakh* rupees is 100,000 rupees. A lakh is a common unit for counting money in India.

The issue came up when the Kerala High Court was hearing the anticipatory bail petitions of two young Muslim men, Sirajjudin and Shahan Sha, on the charges that they had abducted two girls from a local college and had forcibly converted them to Islam. The parents of the girls had brought a habeas corpus petition before the court. In the course of hearing the anticipatory bail petition, the court had observed that every citizen is entitled to "freedom of conscience and the right to freely profess and propagate religion as enshrined in Article 25 of the Constitution." "This right," the court further observed, "did not extend to the right to compel people professing a religion to convert to another religion." As this event unfolded, it spread to a hearing in the Karnataka High Court and a police inquiry into the activities of the alleged Love Jihad organization, as well as the People's Front of India, a Muslim group alleged to be involved in funding these activities. The police did not find any organization by the name of Love Jihad—nevertheless, the Deputy General of Police (DGP) reported in court that a spurt in conversions of Hindu and Christian girls was suspected and would be investigated in greater detail. A militant Hindu Rights Group, Sri Ram Sene, announced that it would send 150 party activists to keep an eye on suspicious activities of couples and immediately stop any "love jihad" activity they might identify. Members of Catholic organizations in Kerala also took notice of these events. K. S. Samson, the head of the Kochi based organization Christian Association of Social Action, announced that it would cooperate with the Vishwa Hindu Parishad (a right-wing Hindu group) to identify girls who were being forcibly converted from Hinduism and would expect reciprocal co-op-

eration for saving Christian girls. An unnamed police officer is reported to have stated that certain fundamentalist groups that have been carrying out vigilante attacks against couples who marry outside their respective communities have now started using the label "love jihad" to justify their attacks.[f, 8]

I point to such pamphlets and forms of publicity to indicate that an aura of suspicion surrounds marriages that cut across communities, especially the Hindu-Muslim divide. While there might be intensification of rumors and a heightened sense of danger at some moments and at others the intensity might wane, people in the neighborhoods in Delhi and other places are very aware of the potential for violence that such marriages might unleash. In two of the neighborhoods in Delhi in which I conducted fieldwork, local peace committees, composed of Hindus, Muslims, and Sikhs, have been created at the initiative of the local police, in association with the neighborhood branch of the Congress Party; they work to track down rumors and to mobilize support to defuse any violence that might escalate in response to local or even national events. I don't want to suggest that members of the police force always play a peace-maintaining role or that some political parties are more tolerant or, as the local parlance would have it, "secular" in accepting such marriages than others, but there are interesting local histories that account for different sensibilities even at the level of the neighborhood.[8] In the context of tracking some of the publicity materials that these committees have generated, I learned about nine cases of Hindu-Muslim marriage, as well as other intercaste marriages that created considerable tension in the two neighborhoods in the last eight years. In addition, there are elopements

---

8. The claim that there was a "Love Jihad" aimed at Hindu women was baseless, but common, with court cases and accusations appearing in several Indian states in the late 2000s and early 2010s. Charu Gupta (2009) notes that the pattern of accusations is similar to one that happened in the 1920s. However, the context here is important. In 2008, there were twelve coordinated Islamic terror attacks in India. The attacks were spread across four days, from November 26 to November 29, killing 179 (including 9 attackers) and wounding 300. Saying "26/11" in India has some of the same resonance that speaking of 9/11 does in the United States (and has been the subject of movies and television). Thus, at the time when these accusations were made, it was easy to incite anti-Muslim sentiments. In 2020, several Indian states passed statutes aimed at outlawing Love Jihad (with very little evidence of its actual existence). https://blogs.loc.gov/law/2021/03/falqs-the-controversy-over-marriage-and-anti-conversion-laws-in-india.

or rumors of affairs across caste boundaries or even within the same community. For the purposes of this essay, however, I shall look only at the cases of Hindu-Muslim marriage. As I describe the manner in which social relations were continuously reconfigured in this one case, I make only occasional reference to the other cases. However, my discussion is informed by the wider field of forces that operate in them all. My technique of description is to place myself within an imminent and emerging story, depicting scenes of conversation, evasion, fear, and elation, rather than taking a transcendental view from a distance after the story has already acquired clarity. I was sometimes accompanied by my research assistant and colleague, Purshottam, who has been collecting statistical data on a panel of households in the area for the Institute for Socio-economic Research on Development and Democracy (ISERDD), a research organization dedicated to longtime research and advocacy on behalf of the poor, of which I am a founding member. Purshottam and I often visited Bhagwanpur Kheda, a low-income neighborhood in East Delhi, together, and sometimes we would end up talking to Kuldip's family together. I also stopped often to have tea with women who were sitting in the street, making small objects for sale, chatting, or simply "taking in the sun" in the winter months. Since 2000 I have visited these neighborhoods at least twice a year, but the story is drawn from 1998 to 2000, when I conducted intensive fieldwork in this area. I use the ethnographic present when I am able to draw directly from my field notes.[9]

A STRANGER IN MY HOUSE

Purshottam and I were walking down the street when Leela Devi's sister-in-law, Savita, happened to open the door of their house. She insisted that we come in to have a cup of tea. Leela Devi is not home today—normally, being the eldest women in the house, she is the one to greet us and give us news of what has been happening. It is clear that Savita is bursting to tell us something. (This and other conversations all took place in Hindi and have been translated by me.)

SAVITA. Did you know that Kuldip [Leela Devi's eldest son] has gotten married?

VEENA. No, when did that happen? Congratulations. Where are the sweets?

SAVITA. What congratulations? He has brought a Muslim girl into the house [lit., has made a Muslim girl sit in the house]. No one in the neighborhood knows. They are both constantly running here and there [*idhar udhar bhag rahen hain*], hiding from her parents, who are threatening to kill Kuldip and they [the parents of the girl] have also lodged a police case of abduction. Didn't sister [Leela] tell you?

Over the next few days, we visit Leela Devi several times, because she seems anxious to talk and keeps calling both of us to come and visit her—yet when we meet, she can only skirt around the issue. Thus what we can gather are broken fragments.

It is afternoon, and Leela Devi, Purshottam, and I are sitting in the open courtyard while she washes some clothes. Suddenly there is a flurry of movement, as sounds of loud knocking erupt. Before we can react, Leela Devi has gotten up, wiped her hands, rushed us into a little adjoining room, where old TVs and a broken sofa are piled up, and locked the door from outside. I can hear some kind of contentious conversation taking place. Leela Devi sounds placatory, saying he is not here—he was ill—that is why he has not returned your money, but he will. Finally the men leave, but their threats hang in the air. It turns out that these were two tough men sent by some people from whom Kuldip has taken credit. When Leela

9. The Congress Party: The Indian National Congress, a political party founded in 1885 as a Nationalist, Independence movement. In the 1920s, it was led by Mahatma Mohandas Gandhi (1869–1948). Since the country's independence in 1949, nine of India's fourteen prime ministers since independence have come from the Congress Party.

Devi finally comes to open the door of our room, I can see that she is trembling.[10]

She tells us the following story:

You know how good Kuldip was in his studies. He got a scholarship to ITT. [The Indian Institute of Technology is an elite engineering school. As it happens, Kuldip's scholarship was not to ITT but to ITI, one of several Indian Technical Institutes set up by the government as vocational training centers. These are highly valued by families in lower-income neighborhoods, but they train students to be technicians, not engineers. This pattern of slight deception about his accomplishments was typical of Kuldip's stories about himself.] But he did not complete that degree, because he set up a tutorial college in partnership with a friend. He said, "I can make much more money setting up a college on my own." But his partner deceived him. He ran away with the money they made jointly. See how brilliant he is; his photograph is in the papers. [She shows me an advertisement in a two-sheet tabloid called Careers Today that has Kuldip's photograph.] Now the moneylenders are after him. What between these moneylenders and the RSS guys,[h] we are afraid to leave the house.

I mutter something about how sorry I am and say that if they need any help they should tell me. But she continues to talk, almost to herself:

For the last two years, things have just not worked out. Earlier my husband got so many TVs and cassette players to repair. [A room had been built as an extension of the house and as a storefront for the repair shop.] But now he does not get much business. For the last two years there has been this *chakkar* between my son and Saba. We did not know, but his grandfather knew. And in truth he encouraged Kuldip.

It is hard to translate the term *chakkar*, but its meaning in this context might best be conveyed as a tangled web. What did the encouragement of the grandfather mean? I had learned earlier that the grandfather, who was a retired employee of the postal department, was considered relatively well off by local standards because he had both a regular pension and other sources of income. One of these was from a local shrine in small urban settlement (*kasba*), where the ancestral home was located. It seems that, after the Partition of India, many Muslims from this town either migrated to Pakistan voluntarily or were forced to leave because of the communal violence. One such family was the shrine keeper of a local *pir* (saintly master), about whom not much was known. The shrine remained abandoned for awhile, but someone used to go and light a *diya* (earthen lamp) every evening on it. One day a visitor, who did not know that the overgrown, abandoned site was a shrine, had gone to relieve himself there at night, but the *diya* chased him away. The very same night, Kuldip's grandfather dreamed that the spirit of the Pir, named Bhooray Khan, had come into him, and he took upon himself the task of becoming the manager of the shrine. He cleaned up the place and slowly, through the medium of dreams, he began to construct the history of the local Pir. He has since filled in details, making his own biography of the Pir, on the model of the usual *urs*[i] stories of a Muslim saint who is handsome and pious. He is on way to his betrothed's house when some village women plead with him to rescue their cattle from a group of raiding bandits. The handsome young man agrees to do so but dies in the ensuing fight with the bandits, though he is able to restore their cattle to the women and is consequently consecrated as a Pir. According to the grandfather, he also received the boon of being able to cure various ailments. Although he has never studied Arabic, he can dream of Qur'anic *ayats* (verses); he then recites them over a glass of water or another material

---

10. As Das's essay develops, consider how she describes Kuldip. What kind of a person is he? How does Das present him? Is he a sympathetic character?

object, with which he can cure ailments. It is not clear from his description whether he sees the verses or hears them, but in any case he says he gets knowledge—sometimes he calls this knowledge *gyan* and sometimes *ilm*. Both terms can have generic and specific meanings in the context of healing cults but are differently anchored to Hindu and Islamic ideas of knowledge, respectively. His son, Kuldip's father, has also inherited this ability to dream cures. The family, however, considers itself to be firmly Hindu. Kuldip's mother and father are devout worshippers of the mother goddess, Vaishno-Devi, who demands vegetarianism of them. The grandfather and the children are exempt from these requirements placed by the mother goddess. The grandchildren, Kuldip and his siblings, have not inherited this ability to dream. The grandfather believes that each grandchild will show his disposition and that nothing can be imposed by way of an impersonal religious belief.[11]

Therefore, I suspect, when Kuldip fell in love with Saba he confided in his grandfather, relating the difficulties they were facing and the fact that they were both hesitant whether they would be able to withstand the pressures that are built into a marriage outside one's community, especially a Hindu-Muslim marriage. I will let Kuldip speak about this. The occasion was a poignant one, since, after hiding from Saba's relatives and running all over north India from one sympathetic relative to another, sometimes Kuldip's, sometimes Saba's, and living in various cheap hotels, they had run out of money. Saba was pregnant and soon to give birth. Meanwhile, negotiations between various relatives had been continuing, so that Saba felt reassured that her parents or brother would not risk a communal confrontation by killing Kuldip or her, as they had earlier threatened to do. Kuldip's mother invited them to come back. This was now more than a year after they had first eloped.

KULDIP. When I first saw her, I did not even notice her very much. Actually, one of my friends was going out with a girl. He used to ask me to come with him, and his girl friend brought Saba along so that they would not be conspicuous—a girl and a boy alone attract the attention of all kinds of bad people. I do not know how it happened, but then I knew that she was the only one in the world for me. But I did not know if she would be able to stand the rigors of a true love [*saccha pyar*].

SABA. First I was offended, but then his sincerity won me over. Still, it was difficult, because everyone in my family knows how I have immersed myself in the verses of the Qur'an. I was the first girl in my family to have learned how to read the whole Qur'an. I know only enough Arabic to recognize the verses and to recite them, but I am not like others, who learn just a few verses. So I knew how hurt and upset my father and brother would be. But once I acknowledged to myself that I loved him, I thought that this is what I must do—this is what I have to do [*yeh to karna bi karna hai*].[j]

The story that followed is similar to other stories of strategies followed by couples to combine the resources of helpful kin and friends and to somehow get the protection of the law to evade the feared violence that such a marriage can generate (Mody 2008). Thus, for instance, before Kuldip and Saba eloped they took care to leave a written statement with the local police station through a lawyer, with copies in the hands of some friends, to the effect that Saba was voluntarily leaving with Kuldip in order to get married. Saba feared that her father might lodge a complaint of abduction against Kuldip (which he did), and she was advised that such a letter would come in handy against police harassment or criminal charges,

---

11. To summarize, Kuldip, his parents, and his paternal grandparents all understand themselves as Hindu. However, Kuldip's grandfather cares for the shrine associated with a Sufi Islamic saint. Kuldip's father and grandfather claim mystical powers to cure illness for both Hindus and Muslims based on their connection with the Muslim saint.

were they to be levied against Kuldip. Like many other eloping couples, they had first gone to the Tis Hazari Court in Old Delhi in order to get married under the Special Marriage Act of 1954, but, as Mody has described in her book, it is not a straightforward matter for an eloping couple to get married in the court. The banns of the intention to marry have to be publicly posted for thirty days in advance, in addition to the requirement of several official forms of certification, including one from the local police station testifying to residence of the couple in a neighborhood in Delhi.[k, 12]

Many young men of the RSS or other Hindu fronts monitor these banns in order to prevent such marriages. Recall that the Sri Ram Sene said that they would send 150 activists to stop "love jihad" marriages and the comment of the anonymous policeman I cited earlier that this threat should be seen as a continuation of the usual strategies of threatening and intimidating couples from different religions who wish to marry. However, Mody also points out that there are various kinds of services offered in the courts that are not part of the formal legal system but have nevertheless become a part of the everyday life of the court. One of these services is that of the Arya Samaj, a Hindu reform organization that has historically combined a progressive agenda of Hindu reform with a strong anti-Muslim stance and a program for reconverting Muslims to their "original" Hindu state. Even E. J. Brill's *First Encyclopedia of Islam, 1913–1936*, in its chapter on India, mentions that the Arya Samaj had been active in the work of reconversion and that the Rajput Shuddhi Society (Rajput Purification Society), which was affiliated with it, had brought 1,052 Rajput Muslims into the Hindu fold between 1907 and 1910 (Houtsma et al. 1993).

In any case, with the help of some friends, Kuldip and Saba were able to contact a local Arya Samaj priest, who offered to convert Saba to Hinduism and to perform an Arya Samaj wedding for them, which would be recognized by the court. Thus they could simply register their marriage rather than have to wait for the court procedures. Both Kuldip and Saba pointed out to me that this was not the only option they tried.[13]

SABA. I really had no objection to being converted—I thought if one of us has to do it, why not me? They gave me a different name—Seema—not too different from my own name, so that I would not become disoriented. The priest actually told me that it is customary for all Hindu girls to get a new name on marriage. There was not much ritual or anything—just *yag* [in Sanskrit, *yajna*, fire sacrifice]—and circumambulation round the fire and putting vermilion in the parting of my hair. Kuldip said to me, "Don't take anything to heart—this is just for legal purposes. No one is going to stop you from reading the Qur'an or saying your *namaz*."[l] But still it was interesting [using the English word] that no temple would agree to marry us—only the Arya Samaj agreed.[14]

KULDIP. Actually we also tried the mosque. I wanted to become a Muslim, but there they insisted that we must bring an affidavit

---

12. Tis Hazari is a neighborhood in Delhi. It has long been the site of courts with jurisdiction over Central and West Delhi. The focus here is on how Kuldip and Saba attempt to negotiate a way forward in their life together using the resources at hand. These include the municipal authorities, communal organizations, and sympathetic relatives.

13. Note that Kuldip and Saba are using Arya Samaj to subvert the organization's intentions. The organization understands Indian Muslims (and Christians) as Hindus who have been converted. It wishes to reconvert them to Hinduism. Kuldip and Saba are not truly interested in returning Saba to Hindu practice. They are simply looking for a safe way to get married.

14. While Das has told us that she is using pseudonyms, the change of first name is significant. In India, the first name "Saba" immediately identifies its holder as Muslim.

signed in a court that I was willing to be converted out of my own free will. The **mufti** of Fatehpur Sikri told me that I would have to study the Qur'an for at least three months before I could know that I wanted to accept Islam and before they could assure themselves that it was a genuine case of wanting to convert and not simply a ruse for getting married. Actually, all these are excuses—these days no one wants to take a risk [using the word *risk* in English].[15]

SABA. All these are just excuses for doing nothing—to cover up the fact that they don't want the hassle. They think the RSS guys will come and take *panga* [a colloquial expression meaning to pick a fight]. And then they don't want to deal with irate parents. The fact is that my parents are very conscious of their high caste status—we are Rajputs, and Kuldip comes from a lower caste.

KULDIP. Oh yes, this is a *kaum* [community] that should welcome those like me who genuinely want to accept Islam, because this community grew by conversions. Only later did they come to realize that someone like me who has received the light of Islam is like a gift from above [*uppar wale ki den*]—like a precious newborn—to be received on one's eyelashes [an expression denoting extreme delicacy]. But they were bothered about caste and parents and RSS.[16]

I wanted to talk more, but there were always interruptions. I give some further texture to Kuldip's intriguing references to his attraction to Islam, as well as its relation to the manner in which his father's and grandfather's unstable relations to Islam played in the life of the household, by stitching together several short conversations from different times after Kuldip

and Saba had moved back into Kuldip's parents' house and after the birth of a son to Saba.

LEELA DEVI. I do not know when our days will turn. I pray day and night to Mata Rani [the mother goddess], saying, "Don't turn your face away from us." Earlier my husband used to have visions of her, and she used to guide him—do this; do that. But now there is no business—everyone gets new TVs and no one seems in need of repair.[17]

VEENA. Is she angry because something wrong has been done?

LEELA DEVI. Who is to say? It is the mother's wish. I keep trying to divine what is the matter. Is it because Saba might have become a Hindu? But who can take away the *samskara* she has? [*Samskara* refers to the impressions formed on one's being from the intimate environment in which one grows up—the term also refers in more specific way to rites of passage.] So I thought maybe when she is lighting the evening lamp [at the domestic altar]—or maybe she does something not quite right in the puja [ritual worship]—so I tactfully stopped her from doing that. Maybe He [her husband—a common way of referring to one's husband, since it is taboo for a woman to pronounce her husband's name] has started drinking. He might even be eating meat. He is inclined that way, though the goddess has imposed very strict dietary restrictions on him. People criticize me for bringing Kuldip and Saba home—the RSS boys are after us. I told one of them, "You can get many people to defend your Hindu *dharma*. But as for me, I am a mother. Where will I get my son again if I lose him?" I say, "Mata Rani, forgive me—don't punish me for loving my son."

---

15. A **Mufti** is an Islamic legal expert.

16. Here, Das (using quotes from her interlocutors) points to the overlap of Hindu and Muslim beliefs in people's actual lives. Caste is an aspect of Hindu social organization. As Muslims, Saba's parents, in theory, should have no interest in Kuldip's caste background. However, Saba cites this as a key reason her parents do not want her to marry Kuldip.

17. Earlier, Das has told us that Leela Devi is a devotee of Vaishno Devi. Mata Rani is an alternate name for the same goddess.

Here, with a different inflection, Saba:

> Though I told you that, when they did all that *shuddhi* [purification] and conversion, both Kuldip and I knew that this was just for the marriage, it did have some influence on me. I began seriously to learn how to do puja. It moved me to think that this is what Kuldip grew up watching and doing—and then I thought that, so long as I do not perform sajda [the Islamic term for prostration]^m before another god, I do not offend against Allah's glory. I would fold my hands and bow my head in respect, but I would not touch my head to the altar. That is why I thought I have not rejected Islam. Allah too knows and blesses lovers. [*Aashikon par to Allah bhi fida hai*-lit., even Allah is enchanted by lovers.]

On yet another occasion, sitting in the barsati (a room on the side of the open terrace) that had been now assigned to Kuldip and Saba as a "Muslim" or "Islamic" space (since the family did not make the subtle distinctions that scholars make between the two) and having tea:

> SABA. But then Mummy Ji [referring to Kuldip's mother] began to be somehow uneasy with my performing puja and all. She said, "You have learned to read the Qur'an and to say the *namaz* since you were such a little girl—how can we take away from you all your *samskara*? Maybe the goddess herself does not want us to take you away from what is dear to your heart and from your Allah."

> KULDIP. Here in the *barsati* we keep the Qur'an and everyone supports Saba—they know she has to perform the rite at the right time. Anyway, women are not allowed to go to the mosque, so all that has to be done at home.

> VEENA. And you, how do you relate to all this?

> KULDIP. Well, I have also started reading the *namaz*.

> SABA (*interrupting*). Actually, that was really quite amazing. Papa Ji [Kuldip's father] says

he can dream the right *ayat* to be read when he makes a cure. But he is under some kind of order from Mata Rani not to say Bismillah. I have watched him perform all this, and I cannot understand how Allah *mian* does his work.^n But He [referring to Kuldip] is like he's intoxicated with this [*is cheez ka nasha chad gaya hai*]. The other night he woke me up at three in the morning and said, "Teach me how to read the *namaz*." I said, "Now?" And he said, "Yes." I can tell you I know how long it takes even for a person born a Muslim to learn the proper way of reading the *namaz*—but he seems to pick up so fast. It is hard to know what Allah wants.

> VEENA (*to Kuldip*). So do you think of yourself as Muslim now or as Hindu? Or does it not matter?

> KULDIP. I am a Muslim now. Of course, I stand with my mother when she performs *arti* [waving of lamps and chanting] in the evening before the image of the goddess. I too used to be a complete devotee of the goddess. And of course I will take part in the annual *shraddha* rituals to honor the ancestors. But sitting in temples or making offerings—all that is over. Now I think that something compels me to learn more about Islam. I go and hang about in the mosque. I have talked to the elders there, and they now see that the light of Islam has come into me. They now agree that a great mistake was made in not admitting me earlier—but now I have recited the *kalma* [profession of faith].

Saba corrects him to say *kalima*, and he recites for me *La Illaha Illallah Muhammadur Rasullullah*, "There is no God but God, and Mohammad is his Prophet." Then he says shyly that Arabic does not yet sit on his tongue properly.

It turned out that each person in the family was trying to make slow shifts in his or her orientation to the divine, to prayer, and to ritual performances, as well as adjustments in the question of to which community he or she belonged. Kuldip's mother became closer to the goddess as she tried to see that anything that angered the goddess in relation to the presence of a Muslim girl in the home was somehow neutralized. Her husband, who had earlier been able to dream both in an Islamic and in a Hindu idiom, felt the weight of betrayal toward the goddess. But he was losing his ability to cure, so he shifted his allegiance to a local Sufi *baba* (an honorific for a holy or wise older man) known as *khichdi baba*. Khichdi is a popular dish of rice and lentils, but in popular parlance it also refers to an unruly mix.[o] Once when I was talking to Kuldip's grandfather, he said that, since Allah had given them small bounties such as the blessing of the *pir*, he was now demanding what was due to him (*apna hisab le rahen hain*). Kuldip took on the Islamic name Mohammad as a sign of his commitment to Islam but limited its use to the mosque or among Saba's relatives. His grandfather had a dream in which a new *basti* (settlement) was being formed, in which he saw a mosque and, like a watermark on a sheet of paper, a temple behind it.[p] Consulting a book on how to interpret dreams from an Islamic perspective, he informed me that the dream was a good omen, since if you see a new *basti* with a mosque and a market it means Allah has blessed a new endeavor—as for the temple, he could not say. Dreams, he tells me, are the last bit of prophecy Allah has bestowed on humans, provided you know how to interpret them, for Iblis (Satan) also uses dreams to delude men.[18]

As I indicated earlier, Kuldip had something of a trickster quality, as in being able to make ITI appear as IIT or in managing his debts with the dexterity of a gambler—taking loans from one type of person (a relative) and to pay off another (a moneylender). Perhaps this is why the grandfather was relieved to have a good dream. However, Kuldip's luck did not hold for long—there was added pressure from his uncle and aunt, who shared the house with his parents, because his unsettled debts were creating a scandal in the neighborhood. Kuldip had gone a long way toward "becoming Muslim" but had neither been circumcised nor partaken of beef—the two ultimate tests in local understanding that conversion is complete. After one particularly ugly event, in which one of his creditors threatened to have him beaten up, he left with Saba and their son for Aligarh, where some of her relatives stay in a Muslim neighborhood and where he was able take on a Muslim identity (name, beard, and regular prayers in the mosque, while still avoiding beef and deferring circumcision). Although I could not meet Saba and him after they left, they maintained regular contact with the family, and his mother told me that the creditors had forcibly placed a family on the top floor, who paid regular rent to the creditors and were expected to stay until the debt was paid off. Kuldip's four younger brothers became the major conduits for contact between the parents and his family. In addition, tentative gift exchanges between the affines were established by each side, sending appropriate gifts of sweets from the market for *diwali* and *id ul-nabi*, the two major festivals of Hindus and Muslims. Kuldip's younger brother laughingly told me that Kuldip was trying to put Saba in purdah, to observe the veil, and that Saba was vigorously resisting on the grounds that even her orthodox father had failed to do that. After a year had passed, I heard rumors that Kuldip had failed to establish himself economically, that a tutorial college he had set up with borrowed money in Aligarh had failed, and that he might be returning to his parents' house. The first indication of this was that he had sent his son to spend the summer in Delhi.[q, 19]

---

18. In these passages, Das shows that even in this community, divided into two contentious factions with a long history of disputes and even given the intense political hostility to marriages that cross ethnic and religious lines; people are far more than automatons sitting at structural points in their societies. Instead, they interpret, reinterpret, and engage in acts of creativity to fashion a path that allows them to reconcile opposites and create a good, morally decent life (in their own understandings of the terms) based in the realities of the people who make up their families.

19. We love Das's description of Kuldip as "something of a trickster." However, there are two things to be said: first, Kuldip's life is representative of that of many poor people; he gets by in various ways, sometimes through the use of deception. Second, the very things that Das praises implicitly, the flexibility and porous

Not all such marriages across religion or caste seem to show the same complexity. While marriages across communities are by no means rare, the reactions range from quiet acceptance to violent fights. Thus, for instance, Namita, a girl from the **baniya** caste fell in love with a Muslim boy from the same neighborhood, eloped with him, and converted to Islam. Her parents would have nothing to do with her and had cut all connections, but she was hopeful that over time they would forgive her. By contrast, when a Hindu girl, Sonia, ran away with a hawker, a Hindu from a similar lower-caste background, it was not caste or religion that was the issue but the sheer fact of her running away and the question of family honor. Her mother and uncle (her father had abandoned her mother) lodged a case of abduction with the police on the grounds that she was a minor. The couple was produced in court, where Sonia alleged that her mother was trying to engage her in prostitution and that was why she was opposing their marriage. Her mother was reduced to silence and amazement that such coarse language could (as she said) "come out of her daughter's mouth." The court ordered Sonia to be placed in Nari Niketan (a government-run custodial home for girls and women who might have been raped, who have been rescued from brothels, or who are otherwise in danger of being sexually or physically violated) until she attained legal majority. The family then relented and withdrew the case, which legally then ended in a "compromise."[r, 20]

I do not wish to go into the full geography of these cases here, although an understanding of the changing forms of intimacy in urban India would require us to do that. Instead, my aim is to reflect more deeply on the case of Kuldip and Saba to ask what moral projects might be embedded in everyday life in the context of the agonistic belonging of Hindus and Muslims as neighbors in the same local worlds (see Singh 2009)—local worlds that are, however, inflected with national and even transnational imaginaries that shape Hindu and Muslim identities. What idea of everyday life might we propose here? And how might our understanding of the moral depart from the idea of morality as the capacity to make abstract moral judgments or to deploy a vocabulary that marks off the domain of the moral from everyday life?

EVERYDAY LIFE AS AN ACHIEVEMENT

The term everyday covers a wide range of meanings: it tends to perform different kinds of functions in the oeuvre of different writers. Rather than attempt to give an account of these different theoretical positions, here I will show how two specific intuitions about the everyday become important sites for understanding the sense of the moral as the generation of an adjacent self, as we have seen in the case of Kuldip and Saba. In his magisterial work on the everyday, Fernand Braudel (1979) speaks of the coordination of the durability of the long term with the minute fluctuations of low-level occurrences. Behind the visible institutions of state and market, Braudel was interested in the "basic activity which went on everywhere," the volume of which he called "fantastic." What Braudel tries to do for material life, covering the rich zone that he calls "infra-economics," one could do for the moral life. The big events that become visible because of their capacity to break into the public realm have both an antecedent life and an afterlife. These eventologies of the ordinary in the light of what comes after, as Shane Vogel (2009) elegantly puts it, require one to wait patiently to track how something new might be born. In the case of Kuldip and Saba, we see that there isn't one single conversion as a turning away from a previous mode of life but rather a slow flowering of the discovery of how Saba might become the daughter by marriage of a home in which the identities Hindu and Muslim are in an unstable relation to one another. Moreover, we see that Islam holds an attrac-

---

nature of the community are the factors that allow Kuldip to do this.

20. **"Baniya caste"**: a merchant/moneylender group. Baniya are Vaishya. Thus, they are members of one of the higher "twice born" castes.

tion for Kuldip, though the specific dimensions of Islam with which he finds affinity will come only later. Each member of the family is given an opportunity to learn how to inhabit this newness, and I have tried to track closely and respectfully, to the extent that they would allow me, the ordinary moments interwoven with extraordinary events, such as Kuldip's desire in the middle of the night to learn how to say the *namaz*, or Kuldip's grandfather's dream that a new *basti* was being formed and his vision of a mosque and an old ruined temple that is never completely erased, a scene that he could interpret as a harbinger of good things to come.[21]

There is another vision of the everyday in both Freud and Austin, which Cavell describes as "not being awake." In his words, "each harbors, within sensibilities apparently otherwise so opposite, a sense of human beings in their everyday existence as not alive to themselves, or not awake to their lives" (Cavell 2005c: 214). What it is to become awake to one's life might be thought of by analogy with Cavell's

reading of Thoreau and his pond—of Thoreau taking the time to relate a hundred details, such as the transformation of water into ice or the significance to be found in bubbles within the ice. This attentiveness to minute shifts in actions and dispositions is one way in which to inhabit the everyday: one sees something like it in the changes Kuldip's mother notices through the mediation of her mother goddess or in what Saba tries to bring about in herself so that she can connect to Kuldip's childhood. There are, of course, pressures from the lack of money, and one could hardly hold Kuldip up as some kind of moral exemplar. But, beyond his attempts to elude his debtors and perhaps a bit of cheating here and a bit of misrepresentation there, his love for Saba brings a possibility for newness into being. This is the possibility that, even when the national rhetoric is vitiated by a vision of a strong Hindu state in which the presence of Muslims is barely tolerated, a small community of love can come about and, at least in some lives, break the solidity of oppositional identities.[22]

---

21. Fernand Braudel (1902–1985) was a French historian and a key influence on many anthropologists, including Das. Braudel was a critical figure in the *Annales* school of French history, so called because it is associated with the journal *Annales d'histoire économique et sociale,* founded in 1929. Rather than focusing on specific individuals or political decisions, *Annales* historians emphasized social and cultural history. He focused on capturing the realities of the lives of average people in Europe from the fifteenth through eighteenth centuries. In his 1950 address to the College de France, Braudel said: "Everything must be recaptured and relocated in the general framework of history . . . so that we may respect the unity of history which is also the unity of life (Braudel 1980: 16). He pursued this goal in works such as *The Structures of Everyday Life: The Limits of the Possible* (1981).

Profound time depth played an important role in Braudel's work. In addition to focusing on short-term and medium-term processes, Braudel argued that there were extremely long historical patterns, what he called the *"longue durée,"* which were critical to understanding people's lives. He wrote: "Cycles, intercycles, structural crises may mask the regularities and continuities of systems (some would call them cultures)—that is, of old habits of thought and action, of frameworks that strenuously resist dying, however illogical (Braudel and Wallerstein 2009: 180).

Shane Vogel (b. 1975) is a professor of English and Cultural Studies at Indiana University. He has written analyses of the work of Das and the anthropologist Kathleen Stewart (b. 1951). Vogel writes that we should not consider everyday life as the ordinary punctuated by unusual interruptions, but instead consider how "the event is woven into the everyday, tentacle-like as Das puts it, shaping ordinary scenes and practices" (Vogel 2009: 252).

22. Henry David Thoreau (1817–1862) was an American transcendentalist philosopher and essayist. In July 1845 Thoreau moved into a cabin he had built by himself on Walden Pond in Eastern Massachusetts (on land owned by Emerson, see note 2). Thoreau spent the next 26 months at the pond, observing nature and contemplating the relationship among people, nature, and society. His book about the experience, *Walden* published in 1854, is a classic of American literature.

In 1972, in *The Senses of Walden,* Cavell contemplates Thoreau's project. Cavell connects the acquisition of knowledge with the loss of identity and selfhood. He sees Thoreau as resisting this trend by minute attention

In a provocative essay on evil and love, Leo Bersani (2008) asks whether love can overcome evil. He invites us to think of a different way to conceptualize love, and indeed relatedness. Developing Freud's great insight that, in love, to find an object is always to refind it, Bersani argues that love is inseparable from memory. Thus the loved object is already a bearer of other memories (of the mother, of an infantile idealized self)—it cannot, despite claims to the contrary, provide an openness to the other. Bersani makes the extraordinary claim that the "beloved becomes the lover as a result of being loved" and thus defines the task of love as embracing the reality of the other as one's own. In other words, what one has to overcome in love is, first, the inability to love oneself and hence the inability to love the other. Without going into the full development of his argument, what I take from Bersani's remarkable essay is the idea that love provides us with the opportunity to realize our "virtual being," which is not the idealized infantile self but rather, in my vocabulary, an adjacent self that is allowed to come into being. That course entails losses that we might even mourn—the most important loss being the security of anchorage in a solid, given identity. I find it salutary to understand that, in this urban environment, in this household struggling with everyday wants and needs, this labor of opening oneself to a different vision of what it might be to receive the other should be performed. Even before the marriage, there were indications in this household that Hindus and Muslims are not completely locked inside their identities; that perhaps constitutes the condition of possibility for such love to be born and to find a home. It is a picture of the moral in which we might lose the profundity of moral statements through which much of philosophy, theology, and religion (including that of the religious experts in these very neighborhoods) stages the moral. What we gain is the simple capacity to inhabit the everyday and to perform the labor of discovering what it is to engage the life of the other.[23]

What, then, of the scholarship on Hindu-Muslim relations that has long argued that there is a profound history of hostility between Hindus and Muslims, within which the only hope for peace lies in settling for relationships in the "marketplace"? In Louis Dumont's famous formulation:

> we are faced with a reunion of men divided into two groups who devalorize each other's values and who are nevertheless associated. The association, quite inadequately studied, has had a profound effect on Hindu society and has created Muslim society of quite a special type, a hybrid type which we are scarcely in a position to characterize, except by saying that, lying beneath the ultimate or Islamic values are other values presupposed by actual behaviour . . . [there is a] permanence of psychological dispositions to the extent that each Muslim, Christian, or Lingayat has something of the Hindu in him. (1980: 211)

It is interesting that Dumont does not ask himself whether there might be a "Muslim," for

---

to nature and himself. Gerald Burns (2013), commenting on *The Senses of Walden* notes that "Cavell stops short of calling Thoreau's life in the woods a project of self-formation, but that is what it comes down to."

23. Leo Bersani (1931–2022) was a literary theorist and professor of French at the University of California, Berkeley. The quote from Bersani occurs in his discussion of Socrates idea of Platonic love. Here is the longer quote from Bersani's book *Intimacies* (2008). "The beloved becomes the lover as a result of being loved. How? Just as lovers are, according to Socrates 'startled' when they see an image of what they had glimpsed in heaven, so the boy begins by being 'amazed at the exceptional friendship the lover offers him.' The boy's beauty makes desire flow so abundantly in the lover that 'it overflows and runs away outside him.' 'Think,' Socrates explains, 'how a breeze or an echo bounces back from a smooth solid object to its source; that is how the stream of beauty goes back to the beautiful boy and sets him aflutter.'" (page 85). Continuing: "The lover's desire is not that which he fails to recognize as his; rather, it is the reality of the other that he remembers and embraces as his own." Das proposes that in falling in love, the Hindu Kuldip and Muslim Saba rise above their previous identities and begin to develop new possibilities that transcend the Hindu-Muslim division.

instance, within the "Hindu." Nor does he imagine that a traffic in categories might be normal in the social life of nations and persons.[24]

The thesis of "devalorization" has a strong hold on many scholars. Thus, though many scholars have provided evidence of so-called "syncretic" practices in folk religion, Peter van der Veer (1994) has cautioned against reading a history of harmony or mutual respect into these practices. Instead, he argues that Hindus seek out Muslim shrines not as an expression of devotion but because they assume that, like untouchables, Muslim healers are able to master the spirit world and to expel malign spirits. He then goes on to conclude that the Muslim practice of saint worship is thus incorporated into impure practices typical of lower castes in a Hindu worldview. A major problem with his analysis is that it slips too easily between the figure of the *pir* and the figure of the *amil*, or healer who uses the occult. Others have shown that relations between Hindu devotees and Muslim *pirs* are much more nuanced (Saheb 1998; Werbner and Basu 1998). Another problem, from the perspective of this essay, is that terms such as "the Hindu worldview" are so totalizing that they leave little room for an exploration of the moral projects people might pursue because they assume that all the steps are already taken or that following rules is like following a pregiven grid.[25]

To pay attention to the possibilities for both hurt and care within the contentious memories Hindus and Muslims have of each other, possibilities that increase or decrease in intensity along with the larger political projects within which their identities are implicated, is to assume neither that we can find solace in such binary oppositions as faith and ideology (Nandy 1990) nor that all relationships across the Hindu-Muslim divide are doomed to failure from the start. Instead, we might pay attention to the manner in which moral striving shows up in everyday labors of caring for the other, even in contexts where a mutual antagonism defines the relation—or, as Bhrigupati Singh (2009) formulates the issue, where the relation between neighbors might be defined as one of "agonistic belonging," in which one locked in conflict with another at one level might find that there are other thresholds of life in which one becomes, despite all expectations, attracted to that other.

ACKNOWLEDGMENTS

I am very grateful to my colleagues at ISERDD and especially to Purshottam for their help and cooperation. I thank Webb Keane and Michael Lambek for comments and discussions on the broader questions of ethics. My ongoing con-

---

24. Louis Dumont (1911–1988) was a French anthropologist. His most famous work is *Homo Hierarchicus* (1974, French orig. 1966) in which he explores Indian caste as a totalizing ideological system based on the relative, non-competitive ranking of homogeneously conceived mutually exclusive, and mutually interdependent social groupings. Dumont argues that this is a fundamentally different way of understanding society than the individualism and the notions of human equality that are present in the West, which he terms "Homo aequalis." Dumont argues that economy and politics are secondary to ideological considerations of purity and impurity in Indian thinking.

25. In her conclusion, Das contrasts the concept of "devalorization" with her own work. Although caste hierarchy and the contentious relations between Muslims and Hindus are part of the structure of Indian society, individuals navigate the fields of emotion, economics, the desire for prestige or simple survival within this matrix in ways that cross structural lines. It may be true, for example, that Hindu Indians sometimes see worship at Muslim shrines as similar to lower-caste practices. However, that is not inevitable. In making their lives, the families of Kuldip and Saba have had to modify the ways in which they understand each other and the world. They have been able to do this at least partly because there were connections between the Muslim and Hindu communities that they could draw on. These included both family ties (such as the fact that Kuldip's grandfather had a specific relationship with a Muslim shrine) and associational links (such as the Arya Samaj . . . an organization that, is, in theory, anti-Muslim). They have had to re-create themselves in ways that value the relationship between Kuldip and Saba. This is a form of moral striving in the creation of everyday life. However, this is not only different from the formal moral codes of their society, it defies them.

versations with friends in Baltimore and Delhi, especially Bhrigupati Singh, Sylvain Perdigon, Sidharthan Maunaguru, Naveeda Khan, Deborah Poole, Michael Moon, Aaron Goodfellow, Deepak Mehta, Rita Brara, Pratiksha Baxi, and Roma Chatterji, have helped shape my thinking on issues relating to kinship, sexuality, and sovereignty. The persons I name as Kuldip and Saba and their respective families were excellent teachers on matters of religion and love, for which I am grateful for more than can be said here. My thanks to Helen Tartar for her amazing editorial eye.

REFERENCES

Basu, K. K. 1949. "Hindu-Muslim Marriages." *Indian Law Review*: 24–36.

Baxi, Pratiksha. 2008. *The Hostile Witness and Public Secrecy in Rape Trials in India*. Paper presented at the panel "Interrogating the Governance of Intimate Violence: Social Movements, State Presences, Legal Process." Law and Social Sciences Research Network (LASSNET) Conference, Delhi, January 10.

Bersani, Leo. 2008. "The Power of Evil and the Power of Love." In *Intimacies*, eds. Leo Bersani and Adam Philips, pp. 57–89. Chicago: University of Chicago Press.

Braudel, Fernand. 1979. *Civilization and Capitalism, 15th to 18th Century: The Structures of Everyday Life*. Trans. Sien Reynolds. Rev. ed. Berkeley: University of California Press.

Cavell, Stanley. 1990. *Conditions Handsome and Unhandsome: The Constitution of Emersonian Perfectionism*. Chicago: University of Chicago Press.

———. 2005c. "Thoreau Thinks of Ponds, Heidegger of Rivers." In *Philosophy the Day after Tomorrow*, ed. Cavell, pp. 213–236. Cambridge: Harvard University Press.

Chowdhry, Prem. 1997. "Enforcing Cultural Codes: Gender and Violence in Northern India." *Economic and Political Weekly*, May 10: 1019–1028.

Critchley, Simon. 2005. "Cavell's 'Romanticism' and Cavell's Romanticism." In *Contending with Stanley Cavell*, ed. Russell B. Goodman, pp. 37–55. New York: Oxford University Press.

Das, Veena. 2007. *Life and Words: Violence and the Descent into the Ordinary*. Berkeley: University of California Press.

Dumont, Louis. 1980 [1969]. *Homo Hieararchicus: The Caste System and Its Implications*. Chicago: University of Chicago Press.

Foucault, Michel. 1996. *Foucault Live: Interviews, 1966–84*, ed. Sylvère Lotringer. Cambridge: MIT Press.

Gardiner, Michael E. 2000. *Critiques of Everyday Life*. New York: Routledge.

Houtsma, Martijn, Thomas A. J. Wesnick, E. Lévi Provencal, H. A. R. Gibb, and W. Heffening, eds. 1993. *E. J. Brill's First Encyclopedia of Islam, 1913–1936*. Leiden: Brill.

Kaur, Ravinder. 2004. "Across Region Marriages: Poverty, Female Migration and the Sex Ratio." *Economic and Political Weekly* 39(25): 2595–2603.

Mehta, Deepak. 1996. "Circumcision, Body and Community." *Contributions to Indian Sociology*, n.s. 30(2): 215–243.

———. 2000. "Circumcision, Body, Masculinity: The Ritual Wound and Collective Violence." In *Violence and Subjectivity*, ed. Veena Das, Arthur Kleinman, Mamphela Ramphele, and Pamela Reynolds, pp. 79–102. Berkeley: University of California Press.

Mody, Perveez. 2008. *The Intimate State: Love Marriages and the Law in Delhi*. New Delhi: Routledge.

Nandy, Ashis. 1990. "The Politics of Secularism and the Recovery of Religious Tolerance." In *Mirrors of Violence: Communities, Riots and Survivors*, ed. Veena Das, pp. 69–93. New Delhi: Oxford University Press.

Parry, Jonathan. 2001. "Ankalui's Errant Wife: Sex, Marriage and Industry in Contemporary Chhattisgarh." *Modern Asian Studies Review* 35(4): 783–820, 1986.

Saheb, S. A. A. 1998. "A Festival of Flags: Hindu Muslim Devotion and Sacralising of Localism at the Shrine of Nagar-e-sharif in Tamilnadu." In *Embodying Charisma: Modernity, Locality and Performing of Emotion in Sufi Shrines*, ed. Pnina Weber and Helene Basu, pp. 51–62. London: Routledge.

Singh, Bhrigupati. 2009. "Gods and Grains: Lives of Desire in Rural Central India." PhD dissertation. Department of Anthropology. Johns Hopkins University.

Veer, Peter van der. 1994. *Religious Nationalism: Hindus and Muslims in India*. Berkeley: University of California Press.

Vogel, Shane. 2009. "By the Light of What Comes After: Eventologies of the Ordinary." *Women and Performance: A Journal of Feminist Theory* 19(2): 247–263.

Werbner, Pnina, and Helene Basu. 1998. *Embodying Charisma: Modernity, Locality and Performing of Emotion in Sufi Shrines*. London: Routledge.

Wittgenstein, Ludwig. 1953. *Philosophical Investigations*. trans. G. E. M. Anscombe. New York: Macmillan.

AUTHOR'S NOTES

a. Para. 219 of *Philosophical Investigations* states: "'All the steps are already taken' means: I no longer have any choice. . . . But if something of this sort really were the case, how would it help? No; my description only made sense if it was understood symbolically. I should have said: This is how it strikes me."

b. Foucault is worth citing in some detail here. He says that eventalization "means making visible a *singularity* at places where there is a temptation to evoke a historical constant, an immediate anthropological trait or an obviousness that imposes itself uniformly on all . . . as a way of lightening the weight of causality, 'eventalization' thus works by constructing around a singular event analyzed as process a 'polygon' or rather a 'polyhedron' of intelligibility, the number of whose faces is not given in advance and can never properly be taken as finite" (Foucault 1996: 277).

c The question of dissolving a marriage in which one spouse has converted to Islam has received considerable attention in law, though at the level of adjudication rather than legislation. Thus, for instance, Basu (1949) discusses the landmark cases from the 1920s on this issue. The legislative acts formulated to address the question of forcible abduction of women during the Partition brought a whole range of anxieties, fears, and fantasies into being around the issue of Hindu-Muslim marriages in the public domain (Das 2007).

d. The work of the historian Prem Chowdhry establishes that the tolerance for intercommunity marriages has declined in modernity, at least in north India, though reliance on cases that come up in caste *panchayatsi*, or courts, predisposes one to ignore those who continue to live in the recesses of everyday life. See Chowdhry (1997). In fact, Ravinder Kaur has argued that there are long-established traditions in certain parts of Haryana in which wives were brought from regions as far away as Bengal and Assam, though the pressure of a declining sex ratio has increased the demand for wives from outside in Punjab and Haryana (Kaur 2004).

e. I am grateful to Pratiksha Baxi for sending me material pertaining to this controversy.

f. Details of the various episodes, including the court hearings, can be found in *Indian Muslim*, October 27, 2009. Downloaded from https://twocircles.net hoo9 Oct 27.

g. It is common in north India for English-speaking persons to speak of someone as "communal" or "secular," or even to insert these English words within Hindi sentences, as in "Voh admi bahut secular hai" ("that man is very secular"). I am afraid that my own writing might have imbibed these modes of speaking, and I thank Michael Lambek for gently pointing out those errors.

h. RSS refers to the Rashtriya Swayamsevak Sangh, a Hindu nationalist organization affiliated with the BJP and generally hostile to the rights granted to Muslims in the Indian polity. On the local level, branches of the RSS are often involved in preventing cross-religious marriages by intimidation.

i. Urs (lit. "nuptial ceremony") refers to the celebration of the death anniversaries of various pirs, celebrated at the site of their tombs. The saints, far from dying, are believed to reach the zenith of their spiritual life on this occasion. The biography of the pir is recited or sung on this and other occasions. It has a standard plot structure, which involves a journey on the occasion of the pir's marriage that is interrupted to offer help to an oppressed figure and in the course of which the pir meets a heroic death.

j. I note a further thought here, though I cannot develop it fully for lack of space. The expression Saba used has some resonance with the upper-caste Hindu notion, popularized by popular Hindi cinema and television serials, that a chaste woman falls in love only once and that true love is to be found only once in a lifetime.

k. Many Internet sites where couples can discuss their problems and seek advice have grown up in recent years. See https://sukhdukh.com, for instance. [editors' note: this website not in existence as of May 2019]

l. *Namaz* (in Urdu) refers to the five prayers offered by Muslims to Allah by reading prescribed sections from the Qur'an and is considered to be one of the five pillars of Islam.

m. The rules for prostration and correct forms of worship are laid out in the 3md sura of the Qur'an, entitled As-Sajda. They are also the subject of many fatawas issued by the Dar-ul-uloom and by local muftis.

n. The honorific *mian* is often added to *Allah* among South Asian Muslims. The term *Bismillah* is an abbreviation of the longer phrase *b-ismillahi r-raqmi-ini r-rahim*. "In the name of God, most gracious, most merciful." It is recited before every *sura* of the Qur'an except the ninth *sura*, which includes the famous sword verse, according to which Muslims are exhorted to kill any pagan they encounter—though it must be remembered that the command was given in the context of the battle of Tabuk, as my Muslim friends in this neighborhood never tire of reminding me. The fact that Kuldip's grandfather could dream of the *ayats* of the Qur'an but could not say *Bismillah* because of the command of the goddess could mean several things. It could mean that, though he recites the verses, he does not do so with full allegiance to Islam. It could have the darker meaning that the verses he recites are the verses, or are seen as similar to the verses, in the ninth *sura*, in which God's anger against pagans is most evident, and that he uses these verses by trapping the anger that lies in the words to overcome the disease or perhaps to perform harmful magic. This point was somewhat dangerous to pursue, hence Saba takes leave of the interpretation by referring to the mysterious ways of Allah.

o. In addition to well-known regional shrines of *pirs*, numerous shrines are not known outside the small *kasbas*, or urban neighborhoods. Sometimes the *pir* is known both by a Hindu name and by a Muslim name and may have functionaries from both communities. At other times, as in this case, either a Muslim family or a Hindu one might officiate as the main ritual functionary at the shrine. See Saheb (1998).

p. The analogy of the watermark is mine. He used the term *mandir ka saaya jaisa*, "as if there were the shadow of a temple" his gesture of moving his hands in slow motion from one side to another as he talked of this scene reminded me of a watermark.

q. Their son had not yet been circumcised. However, among many Indian Muslim communities, the ritual of circumcision is customarily performed when the child is a bit older. Mehta (2000) has described how the ritual of circumcision called *Musahamami* ("making a Muslim") among the Ansaris includes a verbal statement addressed to the child to the effect that until that day he was a Hindu and now he is going to become a Muslim. The fascinating account shows how the social memory of conversion might thus be encoded in ritual language.

r. Although compromise is not legal in the case of rape, and thus court records do not ever state that a compromise was reached, Baxi (2008), in her remarkable work on the adjudication of rape in the district courts in Gujarat, notes that the courts regularly arrived at this solution, partly in recognition of the fact that parents will sometimes register criminal charges of abduction and rape against a man, even if their daughter has left voluntarily with him, in order to "punish" the girl and her lover. In such cases, courts are aware that the courtroom is being used to avenge the honor of the family rather than to seek justice. Alternatively, the courts recognize that parents might have already "recovered" the girl, who, due to the long time it takes for a case to be adjudicated in court, might now be married to someone else and settled in her conjugal home. This is not to deny that a settlement might be the result of pressure put on the courts by men in power, especially if the girl comes from a lower-status family that does not have the means to make court appearances over such a long period of time.

39. Ambivalent Happiness and Virtuous Suffering

C. Jason Throop

> One of the fundamental fantasies of anthropology is that somewhere there must be a life really worth living.
>
> —DAVID SCHNEIDER, 1967

THIS SARDONIC REFLECTION on one of the core fantasies motivating anthropological fieldwork is found in a brief two-page foreword that David Schneider penned to introduce Roy Wagner's book *The Curse of the Souw* (1967).[a] The statement, classically Schneiderian in terms of its deeply ironic tone and scope, could very well have served as a preface to Schneider's own ethnographic research on Yap, however. As a member of the Harvard Yap Expedition—one of twenty-one "expeditions" launched as part of the Coordinated Investigation of Micronesian Anthropology (CIMA)—Schneider was required to contribute ethnographic data that would help to better understand, and ideally "solve," the problem of "rapid depopulation" on the island. During the period of Japanese colonial rule, depopulation had accelerated to such an extent that in 1924 "the Japanese delegation to the League of Nations Permanent Mandates Commission was criticized regarding the 'alarming' danger of 'extinction' of the Yapese native population" (Bashkow 1991: 195).[b] As Ira Bashkow notes, at this time perhaps the

most famous anthropological statement on de-population in indigenous communities was that of W. H. R. Rivers, who had argued that "underlying" the "more obvious causes" of depopulation, such as "the new diseases and poisons," was a "psychological factor": the "loss of interest in life" caused by colonial disruptions in the religious and economic institutions that had previously motivated vigorous native pursuits. (Bashkow 1991: 187)

A strikingly similar perspective was voiced, Bashkow observes, by Japanese colonial administrators, who, in responding to the League of Nations commission, had "apparently convinced themselves that 'psychologically, the natives were absolutely indifferent to their extinction'" (ibid.: 195). That the Yapese themselves may have no longer been able to hold on to the belief that their own lives were "really worth living," and that there could be significant psychological "factors" at the root of such a radical form of world-collapse, established the backdrop against which Schneider's fieldwork on the island was cast.[1]

From *HAU: Journal of Ethnographic Theory* (2015)

1. Throop opens with references to David Schneider (1918–1995), a founder of symbolic anthropology. Schneider was a recognized authority on Yap. However, Schneider is remembered today for his contributions to symbolic anthropology, especially his work on kinship as a symbolic rather than a biological system. References to Schneider's work appear many times in this book. You can find out more information about him

While Schneider's research eventually led him to the conclusion that "the population had begun a 'slow but steady' increase" and that "the Yapese suffered no Riversian 'loss of the will to live'" (ibid.: 227), as his fieldnotes attest, he was deeply unsettled by his inability to attune to the affective expectations and responses of his Yapese "informants" as he tried to establish "rapport" with them. In contrast to the tonality of many of his own idealized romantic and humanistic impulses prior to entering the field, Schneider discovered quite quickly that the Yapese "were not blissfully sexual, nor loyally communal, nor politically easygoing, and not by a long stretch were they egalitarian" (ibid.: 226). Nor were they, in any straightforward sense of the term at least, "happy."

A Life Really Worth Living

What makes a life "really worth living," and what, if anything, does "happiness" have to do with it? As detailed in Walker and Kavedžija's introduction to this collection, the relationship between understandings of happiness as *eudaimonia* (a form of human flourishing) or *hedonia* (a specifiable emotional feeling) has structured many debates about happiness in contemporary social scientific and philosophical accounts. From a phenomenological perspective, however, "happiness" is taken to be an intermediary phenomenon (Throop 2009a; cf. Jackson 1998) that manifests neither strictly in terms of a generalized capacity for flourishing nor as an interiorized state. It is considered instead a modality of being, a felicitous form of attunement, attachment, and attention, which orients persons to themselves, others, events, situations, and the world in particular sorts of ways. To put it differently, happiness in such a view is understood as an existential orientation to self, other, and world, rather than as a particular mode of living well or feeling good.[2]

As Michael Jackson (2011) argues when speaking of the related concept of "well-being," however, such felicitous attunements are never settled states of existence (see also Jackson 2013; cf. Corsín Jiménez 2008; Mathews and Izquierdo 2009; Thin 2012). They arise and dissipate, flow and ebb, constrict and expand in ways that are never simply coterminous with, nor necessarily predictable from, the dictates of culturally constituted expectations and desires that inform putatively shared understandings of what constitutes the parameters of a good life or the discernible qualities of hedonic feelings. Rather, such positive attunements are always haunted by "insufficiency and loss," as well as by a basic "condition of existential dissatisfaction" that marks the ever-present discontinuities "between who we are and what we might become" (Jackson 2011: ix).[3]

---

in note 19 in essay 15 by Radcliffe-Brown. Yap had a long history of colonization that included the Portuguese, Spanish, Germans, and Japanese. The Japanese colonial era began in 1922 and ended in 1945.

2. This essay first appeared in a special issue of the journal *HAU: The Journal of Ethnographic Theory* called "Happiness: Horizons of Purpose," edited by Iza Kavedžija and Harry Walker. In their introduction, they comment that "in the ancient world, happiness was understood with reference to a . . . [broad] conception of human flourishing or *eudaimonia* implying a relatively objective evaluation of a whole life, with particular reference to the practice of virtue: a happy life, simply put, was a life of virtue" (2015: 8). Throop will mention other essays in this special issue numerous times in this essay. When he does, we will provide the essay titles in notes.

Throop moves the discussion from the dichotomy between happiness as an idealized lifestyle or happiness as a specific sensation of joy to what he calls an intermediary phenomenon. In a 2009 essay, Throop, discussing the psychologist and philosopher William James (1842–1910), identifies intermediary experience as "the barely graspable and yet still palpable transitive parts of the stream of consciousness that serve as the connective tissue between more clearly defined thoughts, ideas, images, feelings, and sensation" (2009: 536). Thinking about the characteristics of this "connective tissue" provides a pathway into states of consciousness that push people to perceive and experience the world in certain ways.

3. Michael Jackson (b. 1940) is a New Zealand–born poet, novelist, and anthropologist who has been a critical thinker in existential and phenomenological anthropology. Writing with Albert Piette (b. 1960), a French existentialist and phenomenological anthropologist, Jackson says, "We live not in stable states, with

That we could be happier, that things that should make us happy sometimes do not, that we are not happy in the right way, measure, or degree, that some forms of happiness may be incommensurate with other forms of joy we may yet equally desire, that our happiness is not shared by others, that our own happiness may actually diminish possibilities for happiness in others, or, even worse, that it may only be possible by means of others' unhappiness and suffering—all of these are existential possibilities that not only inhabit the background of any foregrounded experience of happiness (see also Vigh 2015), they also at times break through to unsettle and transform it. Happiness in the context of those concrete specificities of situated encounters in which singular and complex beings engage with one another and their surrounding world is thus seldom experienced without some degree of ambivalence, ambiguity, and instability.[4]

The Spirit of Happiness

Having witnessed the effects of cultural dissolution at the hands of four differing colonial administrations (Spanish, German, Japanese, and American), Schneider's adopted Yapese "father" embodied in a particularly striking way the tonality of despairing "unhappiness" that seemed to permeate everyday life in the wake

of the US Navy's "liberation" of the island. As Bashkow describes it,

> Annually performing ceremonies that no one else remembered, Tannengin regarded the forgetting of customs as an actual threat to Yapese survival, because words to be spoken to the spirits were "lost and cannot be recovered." Lamenting depopulation—the people had died around him—he wondered if the spirits of fertility had not already "all gone away from Yap." (1991: 211)

And indeed, as Schneider's "father" well knew, the "words to be spoken to the spirits" were of paramount concern given that they not only facilitated communication with them but also helped to ensure their "happiness." As Schneider later famously observed, when confronted with a significant problem, the "head of the lineage" must **divine** "to locate a happy ancestral spirit, and on finding one, . . . [beseech] that ancestral spirit to intercede on behalf of its living lineage with the generalized spirit who can effect the cure for the illness, improve the fishing, make the woman pregnant, and so on" (1984: 15–16). Such efforts to discern and maintain the relative "happiness" of spirits, Schneider argued, were considered crucial to ensuring the wellbeing of individuals, families, and communities alike.[5]

---

fixed identities, but experimentally—*en passage* between different narratives and worldviews, as well as different modes of being—participants and observers, in relation to others and yet alone, physically grounded yet lost in thought, filled with life yet bound to die, looking back and looking forward. . . . What characterizes the existentialist-phenomenological perspective is not only a refusal to reduce human experience to a priori categories such as the social, the cultural, the biological, or the historical, but a determination to open our minds to domains of experience that fall outside of or defy the rubrics with which intellectuals typically seek to contain or cover what William James called 'the undifferentiated plenum' of lived experience or what Virginia Wolf spoke of as 'moments of being'" (2015: 9, 11). Elsewhere, Jackson writes, "Existential anthropology assigns to our capacity to act responsively to the world and to project ourselves onto it the same determinative power that orthodox social science assigns to culture, class, gender and history. . . . Before any coherent account is rendered, any meaning proposed, any explanation offered, or belief embraced, there exists an ontologically 'primitive' imperative to act in some way or other in response to the actions of others or the world at large—to be a who rather than merely a what" (2015: 174).

4. The essay by Heinrik Vigh to which Throop refers appeared in the same edited volume as this essay. It discusses the visions of happiness of young militiamen who had fought in the 1988–1989 civil war in Guinea Bissau in West Africa.

5. **"Divine"**: in this context means to use a magical or spiritual technique to discover something.

Concern for the "happiness" of spirits was also echoed in the reflections of Liffer, one of two women on the island who was known to still be able to communicate with spirits at the time at which I conducted the bulk of my fieldwork in the early to mid-2000s. In her late eighties, thin with short well-cropped hair, sharp features, and penetrating dark eyes, Liffer spoke quietly, but with a confidence that reflected the fact that people had approached her cautiously for many years, with respect, knowing that she had the ability to communicate with spirits (*ngathaliy*). When recounting her life story to me, Liffer recalled that the spirits (*thagiith*) first came to her when she left her natal village to move in with her husband and her husband's family. Her own family had not blessed the marriage and had cut off all ties with her in the wake of her decision to marry a man they did not first approve of. Liffer was only nineteen when all of this happened (about a decade prior to Schneider's arrival on the island). Not long after her family abandoned her, Liffer became terribly sick and remained incapacitated for the better part of three months.[6]

As her illness showed little sign of abating, her mother-in-law, who had kept a close eye on her throughout her affliction, decided that her sickness was a symptom of *ngathaliy*. Since her mother-in-law had some previous experience calling the spirits, she offered to help. Frightened but unsure what else to do (or in fact if she had any choice in the matter), Liffer accepted the offer. Sitting down facing her directly, her mother-in-law looked deep into her eyes and instructed her not to resist, before beginning to utter in a repetitive and rhythmic fashion the phrase *moey moey* ("come, come"). As the spirit entered her body, Liffer recalled yawning and feeling a cold sensation running down the length of her spine, and then apparently nothing more until the spirit left her.

When she regained consciousness, her mother-in-law explained that the spirit who possessed her was her deceased father, who said that he had come on account of the sickness from which his *kanaawoq* ("host"; literally "path") was suffering. The spirit then explained that the way to cure her sickness was for Liffer to return to her natal estate and to have her family make sweet-scented flower necklaces, as well as gather food and other valuables that could be then used to propitiate him. When her natal family eventually complied with the spirit's request, her father's spirit was *falfalaen'* ("happy"), she reported, because there were now "good feelings in the estate" (*feal' ea laen ii yaen' ko tabinaew*). Her father's spirit had been acting out of "compassion" (*runguy*) for her, she explained, and was not "angry" (*puwaen'*) at the other members of her family who had abandoned her. Other spirits may and do act quite differently, however. The happiness of spirits is, it seems, a precarious achievement.[7]

Precarious Happiness

As Sara Ahmed (2010) points out in her excellent book on the topic, the instability and contingency of the English term "happiness" is captured in its etymological roots. The lexeme is derived from the Middle English word "hap," a term that refers to chance. In its earliest derivations, the word "happy" originally referred to "having good 'hap' or fortune,'" to be lucky or fortunate" (ibid.: 22). According to Ahmed, the term "happy" was first used to refer to chance and contingency, to the fact that something beyond our control has happened to us—in this particular case, something good. Ahmed suggests, however, that the inherent contingency once tied to the meaning of the term "happiness"—its precariousness—has been slowly lost over time. No longer thought

---

6. The use of native terms throughout this essay is typical of phenomenological writing. It harkens back to the Sapir-Whorfian idea that experience and language are closely linked. An anthropologist who wants to get close to the experience of others must therefore be highly aware of local languages and the ambiguities of translation.

7. Liffer's story is typical of the initiation tales of healers presented in ethnographies of many different cultures: a person becomes a spiritual healer after being cured of a spirit-caused disease. The critical element here is the way the story focuses on whether or not the spirit is happy.

to be exclusively connected to unpredictability and chance, happiness has become deemed an internalized condition or state of being that can be cultivated or produced through our actions, choices, efforts, and work. As such, happiness is now deemed a state of the self that is produced through the self's efforts. A failure in happiness can thus quite easily be read back as a failure of the self.[c, 8]

A primary goal of Ahmed's theoretical interventions into contemporary understandings and uses of happiness is to reclaim the contingency entailed in its original formulations. In so doing, she hopes to expand its range of possibility. She also aims to show how "unhappiness" can significantly unsettle and reveal aspects of our taken-for-granted assumptions about the world that may in fact limit the range of possibilities for happiness in the context of our own and others' lives. In this respect, she argues, "we need to think about unhappiness as more than a feeling that needs to be overcome" (ibid.: 217). It is only when this happens, she suggests, that we can, "witness happiness as a possibility that acquires significance by being a possibility alongside others . . . [and accordingly] can value happiness for its precariousness, as something that comes and goes, as life does" (ibid.: 219). In Ahmed's estimation, such a view of happiness is only rendered properly visible, however, when the variable "'worldly' question of happenings" that define the limits, contingencies, and possibilities of happiness is given careful consideration.[9]

Worldly Happenings

Paer was a large woman with pure white hair in her late sixties living in a **midcaste** village on the east coast of Yap. Married three times, with four children, and recently widowed, she walked with a visible limp that required her to use a cane to get around. On this particular day, Paer sat on the veranda of her house, avoiding my gaze, looking out over her garden. She had planted this garden close to the house, she explained, to reduce the distance she had to walk to get food when her grandson was visiting. Her leg was hurting a lot these days and it was just not possible for her to get to her favorite taro patches and gardens without some help.[10]

Her present pain seemed to be evocative of the traces of past suffering, however; at that moment our conversation shifted rather abruptly, I thought, to her memories of gardening for the Japanese soldiers during the war. "During that war, there was great suffering, that was put upon us," she exclaimed.

Very great suffering that the Japanese gave to us. We all stayed and we all worked. And there was work and that is how it went. We went to work and we all, we all cooked for

---

8. Sara Ahmed (b. 1969) is a well-known feminist and queer theorist. Her partner is the anthropologist Sarah Franklin (b. 1960), also well known as a gender theorist. Abu-Lughod references Franklin, and we discuss her in our note 8 in essay 33.

9. Consider the ways that Throop's and Ahmed's ideas of happiness challenge basic assumptions of much of American popular thought. We tend to think of happiness as an internal state possible under virtually any circumstances. Think of Bobby McFerrin singing "Don't Worry Be Happy" (though the song is not without ambiguity). The American orator, sometimes dubbed "The Great Agnostic," Robert G. Ingersoll (1833–1899) wrote: "Happiness is the only good. The time to be happy is now. The place to be happy is here. The way to be happy is to make others so." Ingersol proposed this as the creed of a secular religion. Most Americans remain more religious than Ingersoll, but his creed might well be the majority opinion in the United States.

10. Note Throop's distinctive style, which reflects his phenomenological approach: he describes the physical location of this encounter, places himself in it, and tells us some things about Paer—she has pain and avoids meeting his eyes. We've seen ethnographers place themselves within their texts numerous times in this book (Geertz, Rosaldo, Abu Lughod) but never with this degree of detail.

"Midcaste": According to Schneider, Yap society is hierarchical and divided into seven castes. These are further divided into three endogamous upper castes and four endogamous lower castes, with lower caste villages paying tribute to villages of higher rank.

them . . . , so in the morning we ate [whatever we could] and then off to work . . . in the gardens [to get] food for the Japanese.

After a long pause, my field assistant Manna interjected, "Very hard work was put in." "Very hard," Paer continued.

Those Japanese I tell you, very hard work there. You could not because . . . you were working it didn't matter . . . you see, you would work and [even if] there is pain in your back and you cannot stand up, you are told to return to work because they are watching . . . and they will beat you.

While the suffering associated with Japanese forced labor camps was brutal, the end of the war did not, however, mark the end of Paer's pain. "Myself, my life, there has been very intense suffering in my life, from long ago [before the war] to present." Not only did she lose her first husband in a car accident, but her efforts to pursue renewed possibilities for living were shattered yet again when her second husband beat her so badly that she had to end the marriage and return to her parents' village. While unwilling to say much about those years, she explained that through it all she somehow managed to find the wherewithal to keep going for the sake of her children. After a few years of struggling to make do in her parents' village, she eventually met the man who would become her third husband. While they, too, often struggled, argued, and fought, his final succumbing to cancer was perhaps the most devastating experience of her life.[11]

While Paer believed that she had done the best she could have given the circumstances that were thrown her way, she had reached the limit of what she could bear. As she confided,

I got married and I became pregnant, myself and my children, we lived together, . . . [and] I helped my [family's] and my children's life

[as best I could]. But [then] there was my [last] husband who died so right now there is nothing that I can do, I stay and I wait for the time that I will [die].

Reflecting upon her situation in the wake of her third husband's passing, she characterized herself as having lost the ability to "hope." "I usually try a bit you know," she explained,

[but] now I have no more responsibilities [my husband is dead and my children have grown] . . . if there is something [to do], I make every effort to do it . . . [if] there is something [to do] I try my best to garden . . . [for instance] if there is someone [visiting] who is hungry I don't like that they will [go] hungry, but, at present I am [mostly] living idly, perhaps I have lost hope, or I don't know what.

The fact that she had worked, endured, and persevered in the face of suffering was for Paer, as it was for many of the people I spoke to in the context of my research, something of significant moral worth (see Throop 2010a). Regardless of its perceived moral value, however, such experiences did not in the end bring her "happiness." They only resulted in her experiencing on a daily basis, now that she was close to the end of her life, a painful loss of hope.

Attunement, Attachment, and Attention

Key to phenomenological approaches to lived experience is the idea, first articulated by Edmund Husserl ([1913] 1962), that individuals are continually shifting between differing "attitudes"—or what Clifford Geertz (1973) termed "perspectives"—in the context of their engagements with their social and physical worlds. It is by means of what Husserl termed "acts of phenomenological modification" that individuals come to transform their orientations to experience: from despairing to hopeful

---

11. Note the way that Throop keeps the reader present in the ethnographic scene. He tells us how he is thinking in the moment (he thinks that Paer shifts the scene abruptly), he reports a long pause, and he brings his previously unmentioned field assistant into the conversation. He provides long quotes from Paer. This gives the writing an immediacy that is different from most other essays in this book. Throughout the rest of the essay, Throop alternates ethnographic sections and sections focusing on theory and analysis.

perspectives on a given situation, for example (see Throop 2003, 2010a, 2010b, 2015; Duranti 2009a, 2009b, 2010).[12]

Differing phenomenological modifications can, however, have greater or lesser transformational effects on the experience of particular objects, acts, events, and persons. Some modifications are radical enough to transform an experience of an object to such an extent that it is no longer experienced as the "same" object at all—shifting between the incommensurable images of the Rubin Face/Vase Illusion being one good example. Other modifications may be quite subtle, however. Such attenuated shifts in perspective include everyday and ongoing fluctuations in attention by means of which different properties of an object come into focus: noticing the smooth surface of an actual vase after appreciating its amber coloring, for instance. Subtler modifications are also entailed in those moments where an object is experienced as the "same" object existing under

different conditions through time—such as when it becomes apparent that the same vase placed in different lighting is actually a hue of brownish-red (see Throop 2015).

Whether radical or subtle, such shifts in orientation to objects of experience necessarily involve what are often unnoticed alterations in forms of understanding, feeling, emotion, and mood that color the experience of a given object, action, event, situation, or person moment by moment. Such everyday acts of modification Husserl termed "intentional modifications" (see Husserl [1913] 1962; Duranti 2009a, 2009b). In Husserlian terms, "intentional modifications" refers to the ways in which consciousness is directed toward given objects of experience (e.g., intentionality).[d] "Intentional modifications" implies, in short, that consciousness constitutes objects of experience by means of particular, and shifting, acts of judgment, feeling, sensing, imagining, remembering, anticipating, or perceiving.[13]

---

12. Edmund Husserl (1859–1938) was a founder of phenomenology and one of the most important philosophers of the twentieth century. Husserl focused on understanding consciousness. He noted that "consciousness is always consciousness of something"; that is, consciousness can never be separated from intentionality or from the world of experience. Husserl begins with the idea of a "natural attitude," the seemingly commonsense assumption that the world is something that exists separate from one's self and that one's consciousness is located in this world. Husserl proposes adopting a phenomenological attitude characterized by bracketing that he calls *epoché*. In bracketing, all judgment and certainty are withheld, and we attempt to grasp the material world and what happens in it with as little preconception as possible. For Husserl, this practice allows us to move closer to understanding our lived experience. Presenting this lived experience is one of Throop's goals in this essay.

In *The Interpretation of Cultures*, Geertz writes, "A perspective is a mode of seeing in that extended sense of 'see' in which it means 'discern,' 'apprehend,' 'understand,' or 'grasp.' It is a particular way of looking at life, a particular manner of construing the world" (1973: 110).

13. Throop cites Duranti several times in this essay. Alessandro Duranti (b. 1950) is a linguist and Distinguished Research Professor of Anthropology at UCLA. Duranti (2009: 208) presents an example of intentional modification similar to Throop's using a book: "At one moment, while we are typing or reading in our study, we might be barely aware of the books that are on our desk even though they are in front of us and within our peripheral vision. But as we decide that we need to consult one of the books, we start to relate to them in a different way. As we glance at the books we match each one against the memory that we have of the book that we are trying to find. We find ourselves quickly examining each book in terms of the color of its cover or in terms of its thickness. . . . We might stop and think about the fact that one of those books is the one that is overdue at a university library and that another one is the book that someone gave us for our birthday and we haven't read yet. . . . Throughout these moments, as our gaze moves from one book to the next . . . it is not just our attention that is continuously shifting. The way we are disposed toward what we see or touch also shifts. At any given moment, each of those books is the same object that was in front of us a few seconds earlier; in other words, that is, our perception of it as a physical object has not changed (e.g., its color, weight, or smell has not changed in any perceivable way), but our consideration of the way we direct our attention to it has changed. These shifts in our ways of thinking of, feeling about, or coming in contact with the same object is what Husserl called 'intentional modifications' (Husserl 1931, 1989)." Duranti adds: "The concept

The surrounding world is never a neutral canvas upon which subjects freely paint their experiences, however. The world itself also draws us in, has a hold on us, and pulls our attention toward it. Attention, as Husserl argued, is "pulled" or "affected" by worldly happenings, events, situations, and relations (Husserl [1918–26] 2001; see Throop and Duranti 2014). Accordingly, depending on the context, at any given moment, we may be drawn to notice or engage with certain aspects of a given situation and not others. We are thus, as Jarrett Zigon argues, attuned to the "diverse and particular relationships that make possible the vast diversity of ways of living we find in the social world" (2014: 22).[e, 14]

Happiness, as a form of attunement and intentional modification that transforms perspectives on the world, thus organizes attention in particular sorts of ways. Happiness brings attention to certain aspects of the world that would not otherwise be noticed in other emotional or mood-inflected orientations. It also covers over aspects of the world that would be disclosed in other, non-happy modes of being. As such, happiness significantly shapes the contours of the world, as well as those possibilities for action, attachment, attention, and attunement that are encountered within it. According to Ahmed (2010), who also productively draws from Husserl in her approach to happiness, such modes of "affective interest" shape the horizons of an individual's embodied experience, cares, and concerns, and the range of practical actions enfolded within them.

To say that happiness is a form of attunement that organizes attention, redefining what is salient and desirable, in the process reconfiguring the experience of particular situations, interactions, persons, or objects, is another way of saying that happiness establishes horizons. The phenomenological notion of horizon highlights the existential fact that humans are necessarily embodied, finite, and positioned beings who are never able to exhaust their experience of the world in which they are emplaced, "as there is always something more yet to come, a side yet to see, an aspect, quality, action, or interaction yet to experience" (Desjarlais and Throop 2011: 90). Happiness, its pursuit or realization, thus significantly organizes what it is that individuals attend to, how they attend to it, as well as what they ignore. It is, of course, necessary in this regard to recall that particular horizons are defined for us, as much as by us, and that social, cultural, political, economic, and historical processes are always significantly at work in partially shaping the sedimented, habituated parameters of particular lifeworlds. This includes affectively configured horizons as well.[15]

Horizons of Happiness

Over the course of my fieldwork, Tamag, a short and athletic man in his late fifties, had become a close friend whom I often visited whenever I had the chance to make the thirty- to forty-minute drive up to the northern municipality of Maap. Known for his good-natured affa-

---

of intentional modification is important because it makes evident the role that human subjects play in meaning-making through intentionality."

14. Jarrett Zigon is the Linda Porterfield Chair in Bioethics and Professor of Anthropology at the University of Virginia. His work focuses on ethics.

15. Tadashi Ogawa and Bret Davis (2000: 147) provide a useful description of Husserl's ideas of inner and outer horizon: "The inner horizon means the opening-up of a thing's inner individual phenomena and the relations between these phenomena. For example, a house cannot simply appear all at once in a single instant. A house can appear only through the moments in which the parts of the house appear, namely, the door, windows, roof, walls, and so forth. . . . Thus the thing 'house' appears together with the manifestation of its internal referential relations. The same could be said about the outer horizon of the appearance of the house. A house appears with the earth on which it is built, the yard and garden of the house. . . . The house refers by transcending itself into the wider space of the world."

Be sure to read Throop's endnote v on attunements. It is critical to understanding the next section of the essay.

bility, Tamag was a thoughtful, socially astute observer, with much to say about the contemporary challenges Yapese communities are facing. During one such visit, sitting together in the comfortable shade of his newly built rest house (*koeyeeng*) overlooking the ocean, I listened intently as Tamag reflected on the difficulty he and others were having motivating the village youth to participate in community work projects, such as their village's current effort to replace the roof on the village men's house (*faeluw*). The problem, Tamag suggested, was one of *falfalaen'* ("happiness"). Rather confused by the statement, I asked him to elaborate. Whereas community work had traditionally been a non-negotiable obligation that took priority over all other considerations, he explained, for the younger generations it seemed that the self-sacrifice implicated in such community-mandated forms of service was increasingly at odds with the youth's growing desire to feel only "happiness" (*falfalaen'*) in their lives. While it was certainly enjoyable to feel "happy" (*falfalaen'*), a major problem with aspiring to be happy at all times, Tamag lamented, was that individuals who are always happy will never directly embody suffering (*gaafgow u fithik ea dooway*). Without directly experiencing suffering, he reasoned, an individual will never be able to effectively cultivate feelings of *runguy* ("compassion") for others who may yet still be suffering.

All of this was not to say, Tamag reassured me, that there were not times in his own life when he felt *falfalaen'* or desired to be "happy." In fact, he fondly remembered moments of playing with friends and cousins during his childhood as times when he felt some of his greatest contentment. The fact remained, however, that such experiences of "happiness" were fleeting and contingent affairs that arose in the wake of an absence of responsibility to and for others. Experiences of *falfalaen'* did not, therefore, in his estimation, significantly impact his attachments and obligations to friends, family, and community. Such moral bonds were

instead defined, he believed, by his experiences of *suffering-for* others in the context of effortful work in the village and for his family (see the discussion of axes of "virtue" in relation to happiness in Walker and Kavedžija 2015).[16]

Even though still at times sought after and valued modes of being, "contentment" and "happiness" (*falfalaen'*) were in Tamag's case modes of attunement that limit horizons of compassionate responsivity to others in the community who may be suffering (*gaafgow*). One of the key logical assumptions undergirding his reflections was that if an individual is *falfalaen'* ("happy"), he or she is not focused on the wellbeing of others. The attention of such "happy" individuals will not be drawn, as Ahmed might say, to others' "unhappiness." Individuals who are *falfalaen'* are instead characterized as focusing their attention solely upon their own success, wellbeing, and comfort. Social attachments are thus neglected in the wake of happiness's horizon. In short, a key moral question arising in the face of such forms of self-focused happiness is: If others are still suffering, how can you claim to be happy?[f]

The Unhappiness of Happiness

According to Ahmed, conventionalized forms of happiness that give shape to particular "horizons of experience" are affective forms of orientation that often result from an unquestioned inheritance. The normative standards, values, and assumptions embedded in such affective orientations narrow the horizon of what counts as happiness for any given individual or group (cf. Laidlaw 2008). Conventional forms of happiness recurrently focus our attention to particular objects, actions, and situations and not others, in the process bringing definition and prominence to particular possibilities and relations and not others. If particular horizons of experience are defined by such an affective narrowing of attention, then, Ahmed asks, "what kind of world takes shape when happiness provides the horizon?" (2010:14). And perhaps

---

16. In their introduction to the volume of essays in which this essay appears, Walker and Kavedžija propose three axes for apprehending and interrogating happiness in any society—scope: who can hope to be happy and why, virtue: what is the relationship between happiness and virtue, and responsibility: who is responsible for whose happiness. Throop will explore each of these.

more pointedly, whose happiness counts in the shaping of such a horizon?

"The promise of happiness is what makes certain objects proximate, affecting how the world gathers around us," Ahmed suggests (ibid.). And yet, on the flip side, happiness also causes objects and others to recede from our view. Most significantly, this includes those objects, others, and situations that threaten to diminish our happiness. As Ahmed explains,

> Happiness might play a crucial role in shaping our near sphere, the world that takes shape around us, as a world of familiar things. Objects that give us pleasure take up residence within our bodily horizon. To have "our likes" means certain things are gathered around us . . . [conversely] awayness might help establish the edges of our horizon; in rejecting the proximity of certain objects, we define the places that we know we do not wish to go, the things we do not wish to have, touch, taste, hear, feel, see, those things we do not want to keep within reach. (2010: 24)

Happiness augments attachments to felicitous objects as much as it diminishes attachments to infelicitous ones.

Facing toward some horizons and away from others, happiness is a form of attunement, attachment, and attention that foregrounds some events, relations, and objects, while necessarily backgrounding others. Walking quickly past a homeless man on the street while averting our eyes, turning the channel on the TV so as not to hear about the latest onslaught of tragic news, avoiding "touchy subjects" in conversations with family and friends, dwelling in the happiness of places or times now long past or in the future possibility of a happiness yet to come—all are routine ways that happiness is guarded and guards, thus limiting and defining our proximity to the suffering of others or to those unhappy situations or relations that

might threaten happiness (even if such happiness is only ever an anticipated goal). Happiness may mask the roots of suffering as well. As Ahmed argues, "Happiness can work to cover over unhappiness, in part by covering over its causes, such that to refuse to take cover can allow unhappiness to emerge" (ibid.: 87).[17]

Happiness can define and narrow worldly horizons, thus excluding others, objects, events, and acts from a person's purview. It can also cover over or mask unhappiness and its roots. As Lauren Berlant (2011) claims, the very pursuit of happiness as a means of attaining "the good life" may also be implicated in forms of "cruel optimism," wherein objects of desire become themselves the primary obstacles to present and future flourishing. Happiness is, however, only one of many possible experiences of "affect" that may be attached to the "structure of relationality" characterizing Berlant's view of optimism. As she explains,

> Whatever the experience of optimism is in particular, then, the affective structure of an optimistic attachment involves a sustaining inclination to return to the scene of fantasy that enables you to expect that this time, nearness to this thing will help you or a world to become different in just the right way. But again, optimism is cruel when the object/scene that ignites a sense of possibility actually makes it impossible to attain the expansive transformation for which a person or a people risks striving. (2011: 2)

Even though Berlant explicitly distances herself from Ahmed, whom she sees as dealing primarily with emotion and not "affect," that is, with "the feeling of optimism itself" rather than the diffuse and uneven atmospherics implicated in the "optimism of attachment" (ibid.: 12), she certainly seems to share her suspicion that happiness may be implicated in binding people to particular "modes of life that threaten their well-being" (ibid.: 16). Her anal-

---

17. Ahmed writes this line in the context of an argument for a "feminist consciousness." She says that "[the] process of consciousness raising involves not simply becoming conscious of unhappiness but also achieving (with others) better ways of understanding unhappiness." (Ahmed 2010: 97). For both Throop and Ahmed, the frame or horizon of happiness affects how we are in the world and our actions in a recursive, self-reinforcing cycle.

ysis of the global obesity epidemic as a form of "slow death" is one powerful example.[18]

A Slow Death

> This disease is terrible . . . it is just a terrible disease . . . it doesn't . . . the one thing I don't like about it is that it doesn't just kill you right there. It slowly, you know, . . . kills you little by little. One body part goes, then this, this, this, this . . . same . . . same . . . and that is worse . . . that is the pain . . . the painful part of it.

The once assertive, self-assured, and at times intimidating young man whom I often saw stumbling around town in a half-drunken stupor, always sporting his ubiquitous sunglasses and baseball cap, had been reduced at the time that he uttered these words to a skinny, glassy-eyed, feeble man now facing the very real possibility of his own death. As he spoke these words to me, lying there on his hospital bed the day before he was to leave for Guam for treatment for his failing kidneys (Yap State Memorial Hospital has no dialysis machines), all of Chep's previous bravado and intensity seemed to have been drained from his being. As he explained to me, his diabetes had progressed to the point where his right leg had been amputated above the knee, his eyesight was steadily deteriorating, and his kidneys were failing. He also had a "bad heart" and there were problems with his "veins," which were not, as he put it, "letting enough blood through." As a result, he was suffering from shortness of breath. He could barely sit up in bed without feeling dizzy and faint. Standing up was simply out of the question.

As we spoke together in the poorly lit space of his hospital room, Chep knew that he did not have long to live, and, tragically, he was right; he died a few months later in a much better lit hospital room in Guam. Largely immobile, weak, at times disoriented, in constant pain, and unsure of his future, Chep spent much of his last days contemplating the events and circumstances that led up to the onset of his illness. As he recalled,

> My diabetes I think it is definitely the . . . the lifestyle the way I used to have to uh . . . do things . . . I think . . . ah alcohol is the one thing that is not good for that . . . and I had so much alcohol when I was growing up . . . and . . . like twenty years or the last twenty years when I started drinking before I stopped . . . it didn't bother me at the time. I didn't even feel anything. And I kept on doing it and people kept telling me, "Hey, you have to slow down, you're sick . . . " "Who said?" . . . um . . . I really, I really, I really don't know when . . . until I knew that I could not do it . . . I was so sick, I couldn't do it . . . so [it is only then that] I stopped.

The simple truth was that Chep enjoyed drinking. It did not matter to him if the doctor told him to stop because he was sick or if he happened to hurt or disappoint his family when he was drunk. (He would often abandon his wife and children, disappearing for days when off on a bender.) The bottom line was that drinking made him "happy." It made him feel like his life was really worth living. When he was drunk, he asserted, he was *falfalaen'*—all of his worries, anxieties, and concerns faded away. That is, until his diabetes progressed to the point where he was far too sick to even consider taking another sip. By that point, however, his possibility for second chances had run out.

The tragic results of Chep's abiding in the "happiness" that he experienced while drinking resonated with what many voiced to be the narrowly present-focused temporal horizon that experiences of *falfalaen'* are prone to engender. Indeed, when people spoke to me about "happiness," their own and others', they often characterized it as a fleeting state of being in which one is no longer adequately oriented to either past or future concerns. To be *falfalaen'* in this moment is thus to forget the suffering of the past, not only one's own suffering but also the

---

18. Lauren Berlant (1957–2021) was a philosopher and literary critic. *Cruel Optimism* (2011) is one of her most important books. There she examines how cultural goals, in particular, the American ideal of the good life, encourage people to act against their own best interests.

suffering of others, one's family, one's community, and one's ancestors. It is to forget Schneider's "father's" concern for the happiness of spirits. The restricted temporal reach of experiences of *falfalaen'* also obscures its precariousness in the face of an always-unpredictable future. It thus also covers over the contingency of happiness, as Ahmed would put it.[8]

In contrast to the narrow temporal horizons that *falfalaen'* putatively foregrounds, experiences of suffering (*gaafgow*) are understood to offer an extended existential vista onto both past situations and future happenings. Suffering, its avoidance, and "suffering-for" the benefit of others were in fact explicitly held to give rise to possibilities for appropriately planning and thinking through what can be done in the present in the service of bettering one's family's and community's position in future generations. Suffering was also a way to tangibly connect one's present suffering with the suffering of others who have also worked to better those material and social conditions that define an individual's, family's, or community's contemporary existence. This includes the day-to-day efforts of those who suffer alongside each other in the present, as much as it does those whose past suffering has paved the way for current possibilities for prosperity and wellbeing. Indeed, each "estate" or *tabinaew* within a given village in Yap, along with all the various house foundations, taro patches, and gardens associated with it, was traditionally understood to be invested with particularized histories and ranks that reflect the labor of differing successive clans upon the land (see Labby 1976; Schneider 1984; Throop 2010a). "The place established by estate ancestors within this order," Jim Egan observes, was directly "bound to the land upon which they lived, imbuing its soil with essences that were passed on to the very taro grown within it" (1998: 45).

Suffering was thus generally deemed virtuous by local standards to the extent that it helped to orient individuals, families, and communities to future horizons of possibility and past legacies of effortful sacrifice. In so doing, suffering defines extended horizons of experience, and accordingly gives rise to possibilities for "hope" (*athapaag*). This is not the hope that suffering will be transformed without remainder into future happiness. It is instead more akin to the hope that Jackson (2011) sees as rooted in an existential dissatisfaction that traverses the expanse of who we are, who we have been, and who we might yet still become.[19]

Recognizing past suffering, acknowledging the ongoing suffering of others, as well as being attuned to the ever-present possibility of an arrival of unwanted future suffering, are each aspects of the moral worth of *gaafgow* ("suffering") that actively bring into relief the precariousness of "happiness," as well as its limited intersubjective and temporal scope. "Happiness" (*falfalaen'*), while still at times valued, falls short in its capacity to organize horizons of experience that enable those forms of belonging, caring, and striving that best define moral modes of being in Yapese communities. It is important to note here, however, that the sense of precariousness articulated in such ambivalent moral framings of *falfalaen'*, especially when understood against the background of virtuous suffering, is rather differently pitched than Ahmed's call to value the "hap" of happiness—that is, its fragility and instability. For Ahmed it is precisely the "hap" of happiness that illuminates its value in disclosing possibilities. From a Yapese perspective, such precariousness is instead understood to be a temporal attribute of happiness that problematically narrows possibilities for social connection, responsibility, and care—possibilities that extend well beyond the contingencies of present relations and situations to those of previous and forthcoming generations.[20]

---

19. Jackson explores existential dissatisfaction in *Life within Limits* (2011), a book about people in Sierra Leone, the site of Jackson's initial fieldwork. He defines existential dissatisfaction as "the quest for the unknown something or someone without which one's life feels incomplete" (2011: 169).

20. Earlier, Throop, following Ahmed, focused on the "hap" of happiness, the idea that the root of the word happiness originally referred to chance or luck. In phenomenological terms, a critical reader might

The Being of Happiness

The precariousness of happiness, whether it is considered a desired or problematic aspect of its phenomenological manifestation, evokes again questions about the relation between feeling and being happy. If feeling happiness can lead us astray, is it possible to live a good life without happiness? Are living a good life and living a happy life commensurable as modes of being? As Ahmed points out, for Aristotle, who took happiness to be an ultimate good or virtue, happiness cannot be "reduced to good feeling" (2010: 36). Rather, "happiness or *eudaimonia* refers to 'the good life' or the virtuous life, which is a life-long project" (ibid.). To say that happiness is not reducible to a specifiable good feeling in Aristotle's view is not to say, however, that happiness does not involve feelings (see also Lambek 2015). "The virtuous agent will not only feel pleasure and pain where appropriate, in relation to the right objects, but will also experience the right amount of such feeling, where the right amount is the 'mean', which means not too much or too little" (Ahmed 2010: 36). The relationship between feeling and being happy, that is, between hedonic and *eudaimonic* perspectives on happiness, is one that pivots not only on the relative degree to which happiness can be understood to saturate a given moment of existence, but also on the temporal expanse of happiness itself (what Walker and Kaveždija 2015 term the "scope" of happiness). If the good life is a "life-long project" and happy feelings are precarious and fleeting, then clearly, while the experience of happiness may be considered by some to be a necessary condition of living well, it can never in itself be a sufficient one. In short, there must be more to life than happiness if life is to be lived "well." And yet, is it really accurate to say that the experience of happiness is always temporally and situationally bound to such an extent that it cannot be anything otherwise than fleeting and ephemeral? What of happiness that extends within, between, and beyond generations? What of the happiness of spirits?[21]

If happiness is a felicitous modality of being, a form of attunement, attachment, and attention that orients us to others, events, situations, and the world in particular sorts of ways, how might the horizons of "happiness" variously expand or contract? In terms of its positively inflected affective tonalities, happiness as a hedonic experience certainly ranges in duration, focus, and intensity as it manifests in particularized emotional experiences and more diffuse moods. When it is experienced as an emotion, happiness is a narrowly temporally bounded and positively valenced embodied feeling that is registered at an intensity that is strong enough to both catch and direct our attention to specific and specifiable contexts, situations, occurrences, objects, actions, and people. As an emotion, happiness is often, though not always, also reflexively available to us. We not only feel happy; we may recognize that we are happy. We may also recognize what or who is causing us to feel that way.[22]

Happiness is not always so clearly rendered nor closely tethered to the immediate contexts in which we find ourselves enmeshed, however. It may in fact be distinctly decoupled from them. We may find ourselves feeling happy for no good reason or encounter others who seem happy despite the horrible circumstances they are in. We may also remain only vaguely aware of our happily mooded state as we move through obstacles and challenges with an ease that is not normally possible for us. In these

---

consider whether suffering also has a chance or luck aspect. Is happiness truly more fragile, more unstable than suffering?

21. The Michael Lambek (b. 1940) essay *Le bonheur suisse, again* (2015) that Throop refers to uses the life history of a single Swiss farmer to consider issues of individual and collective happiness as well as the relationship of happiness to virtue.

22. Note the phenomenological emphasis in this paragraph. Throop creates an *epoché* around happiness and tries to think about what happiness is from context or object.

contexts, happiness arises in situations that should evoke unhappiness or perhaps other more neutral or negative feelings. This form of happiness, as Ahmed terms it, is "unattributed happiness" (2010: 25). In my terminology, this would be an instance of happiness expressing itself as a mood (Throop 2014).[23]

Seldom the endpoint of our reflection, moods are instead the existential medium through which our reflections take shape (Throop 2012, 2014). As E. Valentine Daniel suggests, moods connote "a state of feeling—usually vague, diffuse, and enduring, a disposition toward the world at any particular time yet with a timeless quality to it" (2000: 333). As a vague, yet enduring, "disposition toward the world," a mood provides the existential expanse within which reflection is deployed. To be in a mood is thus to inhabit a vague and diffuse orientation toward the world that suffuses our every perception, action, and reaction to it. In short, mood is our being, being affected and attuned (see Throop 2009a, 2009b, 2012, 2014).

Accordingly, when we are "in" a mood, let's say a "happy mood," the line between our subjective experience and the intersubjective world that surrounds us is often significantly blurred. As Geertz famously observed,

> Moods vary only in intensity: they go nowhere. They spring from certain circumstances but they are responsive to no ends. Like fogs, they just settle and lift; like scents, suffuse and evaporate. When present moods are totalistic: if one is sad everything and everybody seems dreary; if one is gay everything and everybody seems splendid. (1973: 97)

In this sense, happy moods are atmospheric. According to Ahmed, an atmosphere is "a feeling of what is around, which might be affective in its murkiness or fuzziness, as

a surrounding influence which does not quite generate its own form" (2010: 40). And yet, the atmospheric quality of a happy mood is only ever made tangible from a particular point of view. As Ahmed argues, "If we are always in some way or another moody, then what we will receive as an impression will depend on our affective situation" (ibid.). In this capacity, we can understand a happy mood to be a dispersive and ongoing mode of attuning our attention to salient aspects of our own and others' ways of being, as well as to the situations within which we find ourselves emplaced. This is true, however, as much for happy moods as it is for unhappy ones.

Atmospheric Ambivalence

Even despite the moral problematization of the horizons of *falfalaen'* in Yapese communities, individuals' everyday dealings often disclosed what seemed to me to be traces of tangible moods of happiness that were legible in stories, jokes, and exchanges between family and friends. Simple forms of copresence also often bore the glimmers of subtler forms of happy attunement. Moments of sitting quietly together on the veranda with a family member, attending a celebration, barbecue, or traditional dance, or even enjoying the taste of a good betel nut with a friend were all situations that seemed to be palpably imbued with an atmospheric mood of happiness. The presence of infants and toddlers also seemed to soften and yet enliven the mood of those caring for them, again bringing into being possibilities for experiences that might fall into the range of the felicitous. Moments of satisfaction arising in wake of having participated in a particularly successful fishing trip or when having completing a given work project were also often intersubjectively discernible, even if subtly so. For the most part, however, such moods were sel-

---

23. Throop provides an extensive discussion of moods in a 2014 essay, "Moral Moods." There he links his ideas of mood and of "intermediary experience." He quotes Husserl's most famous (and also infamous, for his support of the Nazis and later unwillingness to repudiate them) student, Martin Heidegger (1889–1976): "A mood assails us. It comes neither from the 'outside' nor the 'inside,' but arises out of being-in-the-world, as a way of such being" (2014: 69). In his earlier essay on intermediary states, he also turns to Heidegger and his concept of being-in-the-world, what he calls *Dasein*. "The idea is . . . that the foundation of our existence is one that lies in-between, in an intermediate zone of experience that is not yet solely subjective or objective" (537).

dom if ever explicitly remarked upon. Nor were they brought up as examples of *falfalaen'* ("happiness"). When people did explicitly comment upon such moods, they almost always did so indirectly through deploying an idiomatic metaphorical allusion to fair meteorological conditions: for example, *Ke manigiil yifung ea doba* ("There is excellent weather today").[24]

While talk of experiences of suffering came with relative ease for the majority of people I knew, most individuals had difficulty talking openly about their experiences of *falfalaen'*. In fact, even when I asked people directly about it, by far the most typical response was for individuals to simply deny that they had experienced much, if any, "happiness" in their lives. In the words of Tina, a hardworking woman in her early sixties who was suffering with chronic pain in her back, hands, and knees,,[*sic*] "I don't think there is anything in my life that brought me much happiness. . . . There is a lot of sadness in my life, lots of sadness and suffering, perhaps I have forgotten about the happiness since there was so little of it."

Of those few individuals who did have something specific to say about happiness, many spoke of experiences they had during their childhood. Being carefree and unencumbered by the responsibilities, duties, and expectations of adulthood stood out for them as a time in their lives when they were *falfalaen'*. Having limited social obligations, having fun, and playing were often foregrounded as being key to their experience of "happiness" at that particular time in their lives. As Buulyal, a single woman in her late thirties, phrased it,

In my life, the only time I remember feeling *falfalaen'* was when I was a child, six or seven years old. At that time I had yet to go to elementary school and I was sent to stay with my grandparents. My parents and siblings were not there. But I was happy. At that time I was enrolled in the Head Start Program for preschoolers. Everyday I would wash and eat by myself before heading up the hill to school. At school I learnt songs and stories,

I got to draw with crayons, and play. I was really happy with what I was doing.

Other individuals located experiences of "happiness" in those spaces and places where they were able to find some solitude. This often arose in the context of what seemed to me to be rather depersonalized accounts of individuals' experiences walking along village paths, spending time in gardens, or out at sea alone. For many who spoke of *falfalaen'* in such terms, the emphasis was most often placed on how such spaces provided them with a chance to get away from others, to reflect, be peaceful and calm. For instance, Dammal, a low-caste woman in her early fifties, responded as follows when asked when she was most happy,

Just sitting somewhere. When I was little I liked going out to sea. I wanted to sit and look around and listen to the waves. I went with my uncle once, that was happiness. People might call other things happiness, like hanging around with a lot of people. Yes, there is happiness in it, but it doesn't last. It will be for only a short while before it is over. But that . . . if I listen to the singing of the birds while gardening or walking through the forest and when I come back home I can still hear the sound that lingers in my mind. . . . Happiness in my life are the moments I am alone listening to everything around me. If there's nothing to do, I can just sit. I will not get bored. I do like being around people and talking to them, but it is when there's no one around that I'm happy.

Still others voiced experiencing happiness in the context of their work. As Gonop, a village chief in his early sixties, explained to me,

My work, I really enjoy it and I would say that the happiest I have been in my life has been while I was working. That is the thing that brings me the most happiness. It is true that there is a lot of suffering associated with work but my mind does not dwell on it. I try

---

24. Are the moods that Throop discusses here best thought of as happiness or as contentment? Can we distinguish between the two phenomenologically? Consider this question as you read the quotes from Throop's Yapese interlocutors below.

not to think about suffering, the pain, or the things that hurt. It doesn't matter what you do, there is suffering in work, but I think there is also some happiness.

Statements concerning an overall lack of "happiness" in one's life, narratives that restrict "happiness" to the context of experiences that were had in childhood, or claims that "happiness" arises in situations where one is able to find isolated reflective solitude all resonate with the view that *falfalaen'* is a mode of worldly attunement in which moral responsibilities, long-term projects, past debts, and current social obligations are avoided, backgrounded, or ignored (cf. again Walker and Kavedžija's (2015) discussion of the axes of "responsibility" and "virtue"). Gonop's characterization brings to light, however, a more complicated articulation in which suffering, pain, hardship, effortful striving, and work are interlaced with experiences of "happiness." In this view, "happiness" is not realized in a pure state. Its horizons are not uniform. *Falfalaen'* does not only exist, in other words, in suffering's absence. It is instead intermixed with other embodied modes of being, most pointedly those associated with work. In this respect, *falfalaen'* was deemed as at times potentially blended with experiences of *magaer*, a local term that designates the effort, fatigue, or feelings of physical exertion that arise from hard work or service (see Throop 2010a: 61–67).

When speaking of work and the effortful suffering associated with it, many individuals explained to me that such forms of work-induced suffering, particularly in the case of collective work projects, played a significant role in fostering strong bonds of attachment in the family, the village, and the broader community. The phrase used to describe such forms of attachment when speaking at the level of the village was *amiithuun ea binaw*, literally, "pain of the village" or "the village's pain" (Throop 2008, 2010a). Having participated in my share of village work projects over the years, I understood quite well the bodily aches, soreness, and pains associated with the demands of physical labor associated with them. That mutual suffering that arose from

working together could foster shared horizons of purpose, attachment, accomplishment, and social belonging seemed rather reasonable to me in light of such experiences. The way that "happiness" could arise within such efforts took a bit longer to sink in.

As far as my own embodied understanding of possibilities of a "happiness" born of, and interlaced with, collective work was concerned, it was not until the summer of 2005, when I spent the better part of my visit helping the men in my village reconstruct a community meeting house (*p'eebaay*), that I came to understand the possibility of happiness arising in the midst of backbreaking labor. Particularly salient to me at the time was the fact that the activity of working itself seemed to play a role in mollifying building tensions in the village. These had arisen in the wake of a heated meeting that had occurred a few days prior wherein the chiefs had vocally chastised some villagers for failing to show up regularly to help out with village work. This concern was voiced, as Tamag's had been, in the register of a selfish striving for "happiness" on the part of those who had been absent. I reflected on the experience in my fieldnotes in the following terms,

> As far as I could tell, there was no discernible tension and the work continued with the same vigor as it had the previous days. In fact, I would say that this was the first time that I really understood from a first-hand perspective how the power of collective work, effort, and exertion could foster a sense of connectedness within the community. At the time this insight occurred to me, we were all working to pull the large carved mahogany trunks that are to be the main weight-bearing posts for the *p'eebaay*—posts that will hopefully last for the next thirty to forty years and that will have been put in place through the collective effort of all of the men of the village. As we pulled on ropes affixed to the end of the logs, we chanted in a call and response fashion, first *Iy gamow!* ["We together"], then *Ke bowchuw!*, ["A little more"]. Straining with all of our collective power, we managed to slowly move the logs, a few feet at a time, into position.

Amidst grunts and groans were laughter and smiles. The feeling of sore, tightening, tiring, and later aching muscles was intermixed with feelings of happiness, amusement, and belonging. (August 11, 2005)

Again the specific goal was not to experience *falfalaen'* through work. Nor was "happiness" understood to be that which sediments social belonging in such contexts. Collective suffering and pain were instead thought to be at the root of such forms of social intimacy. While not deemed to be a specific goal or outcome of collective effortful work, "happiness" remained, however, a possibility as an aspect, layering, or lamination of it. In this way, *falfalaen'* is part of a more complex attunement that also includes horizons established in and through *suffering-for* and—*with* others.[25]

CONCLUSION

In this article, I have tried to make the case that "happiness" should not be understood strictly as either a generalized capacity for flourishing or as an interiorized state. It is instead a form of intermediary experience: an existential orientation that brings into being certain possibilities for articulating relations between self, other, and world. If we are to think of happiness as a felicitous mode of attunement, attachment, and attention that configures the contours of the horizons of our experience, then it might well be true that there are aspects of happiness that mark it as an existential possibility of our shared human condition. As such, happiness, like hope or empathy, might evidence an existential structure that is somehow traceable across individuals, contexts, historical time periods, and cultures. That happiness may manifest in the intensity and contextual speci-

ficity of an emotion or may diffusely permeate one's perspective on the world in the form of an intermediary experience like a mood seems to suggest, however, that whatever its existential structure might entail, happiness is not, and can never be, a singular or static phenomenon. Furthermore, the complexity of happiness may be amplified by its combinatorial laminations with other affective and embodied forms. Even in its "purer" realizations, however, happiness is always a dynamic affective formation that shifts, intensifies, diminishes, and transmutes through time. While it seems clear that the contents or objects made relevant by happiness may also vary from one individual to the next and one community or historical period to another, the experiential horizons defined by happiness may further differ, and be differently valued, in significant ways (see Walker and Kavedžija (2015)). For instance, while the precariousness of happiness might in one context give rise to a generative opening up of possibilities, in yet another it may be deemed to foreclose them.

In the case of Yapese communities, orientations to "happiness" are ambivalent. In the lives of the people I got to know best, it was certainly true that subtle, often unmarked and unremarkable, felicitous moods arose in the context of everyday moments of being together, talking, or eating with family and friends. It was also true that experiences that might be recognized as "happiness" further arose, in somewhat more complex ways, in the context of effortful striving to collectively endure the pain and suffering associated with community work obligations. And yet, in the Yapese context, "happiness" is still largely understood to be an experience that narrowly focuses attention to the self's cares and concerns, in the process making less prominent the struggles and suffering of others.

---

25. Note Throop's move into a description of his experiences in Yap at this point in the essay. This dovetails nicely with his existential and phenomenological perspective. We can compare Throop's personal narrative with those of Geertz and Rosaldo earlier in the book. Geertz uses his narrative in "The Raid" to situate himself as a credible expert. Rosaldo argues that it is only because of his experiences that he could understand Ilongot headhunting. Throop does neither of these. Neither does he claim that his experiences allow him to see like a native. Instead, he presents his experiences as a moment of empathy that allows him a personal glimpse of the relationship between moments of happiness, suffering and pain, and the Yapese vision of what a good life might be.

The experience of *suffering-for* others, in contrast, is taken to define a rather different horizon of experience in which there is a distinct foregrounding of attunements to past suffering, compassion for present suffering, and effortful work to better one's family's and one's community's wellbeing in the future. As such, we can understand "happiness" in the context of this particular configuration to be a mode of attunement, attachment, and attention that narrowly defines horizons, in the process excluding others, objects, events, and acts from the self's purview. The trouble with "happiness," in this account, is that it takes our attention away from the unhappiness of others (including spirits), the unhappiness of previous generations, and the precariousness of our own happiness, which is in the end always fleeting and fragile.

As is evident in the case of Ahmed's and Berlant's writings, local framings are not the only accounts that trouble the horizons established by happiness. For Ahmed, happiness is characterized as entailing normative assumptions and values that take our attention away from the unhappiness of others. For Berlant, happiness is an affective modulation of optimistic attachment that may in fact be considered cruel to the extent that its very pursuit directly limits possibilities for its actual attainment. Even the most expansive forms of happiness may have thus a constrictive, and perhaps cruel, side.

To conclude, I think it is worth reflecting briefly again on one of the more compelling arguments made by Ahmed in her efforts to return to the original meaning of happiness, a meaning that foregrounds the "hap" or happenstance of happiness. This is a meaning that arguably shifts us away from the narrow horizons that conventionalized forms of happiness define. When the contingency and precariousness of happiness are foregrounded, Ahmed argues, we open a place for possibility, singularity, and difference to arise in the ways that happiness is articulated for ourselves and for those others who may or may not share our particular horizons of experience. While contingent, such forms of happiness may thus be more expansive than those realized within the parameters of normative visions of the good life. Such an orientation to the "hap" of happiness arguably opens a space to come into contact with ways of being that are not simply replications of our own normative understandings of what happiness entails. It is also an orientation to happiness that does not occlude the realities and possibilities of unhappiness. And yet, while a contingent understanding of happiness resonates well with Yapese framings, the putative virtues of the horizons provided by it do not.

Happiness is not alone in evoking such possibilities, however. As Emmanuel Levinas (1998) argues, suffering may also open and not foreclose our own possibilities for being, being with others, and being morally attuned. According to Levinas, in the presence of another's suffering, suffering that is not and can never be my own, there is a recurrent refusal of my attempts to domesticate another's pain to the self-sameness of my being. The suffering in the other, and the suffering that arises in me as the suffering of compassion for the other's suffering, are foundationally incommensurate experiences that are yet articulated through the call to responsibility that they each evoke.[26]

---

26. Emmanuel Levinas (1906–1995) was a Lithuanian-born French existentialist. Levinas studied with Husserl in Germany and knew and admired Heidegger (before the latter became a Nazi). He was among the first to introduce Husserl and Heidegger to the non–German-speaking world, translating one of Husserl's works into French. For Levinas, the face-to-face encounter with the Other forms the basis of ethics. And ethics forms the basis for philosophy. Lisbeth Lipari writes: "Levinas theorizes that the ethical relation originates in the asymmetrical subordination of self to other, wherein the priority of the other always comes first. . . . Ethics, according to Levinas, begins with the renunciation of the self's right to be in favor, always of the other. The self is called to responsibility for the other before it is free, and the face is the manifestation of the ethical exigency that is woven into the very structure of human being" (2012: 229). Levinas anchors ethics and philosophy ultimately in the epiphany of the face-to-face encounter with the Other. This leads him to say that philosophy must ultimately be rooted in the "wisdom of love" not the "love of wisdom," which he understands as "responsibility to and for the other" (Burggraeve 2002: 83). Following Levinas, the idea of the other and thoughtful consideration of the other and otherness needs to be foregrounded in anthropology in particular and life in general.

Meaningful *suffering-for* another in the form of compassion results from our experiencing the asymmetry evidenced so forcefully, so palpably, in the face of the other's pain. In confronting the stark impenetrability of pain, the integrity of another being is revealed against the intimate backdrop of our own self-experience. It is in this primordial orientation "for-the-other" as suffering other and not as an object or thing—that is, as a living being and not a thing to be used—that there exists an ethical obligation, Levinas argues, "prior to the statements of propositions, communicative information and narrative" (ibid.: 166). Such an understanding of the moral worth of suffering resonates with a number of Yapese sensibilities and assumptions.

Some forms of suffering, like some forms of happiness, it seems, hold existential possibilities for opening up orientations to alternate ways of being. The problem remaining to be understood, however, is whether or not the possibilities for being revealed within the horizons of the "hap" of happiness and the unassumability of suffering disclose commensurate excesses and singularities, or if instead, as I suspect, each in its own way defines a distinctive horizon of experience that opens upon a unique region of being.[27]

ACKNOWLEDGMENTS

I would like to thank Iza Kavedžija, Harry Walker, and the rest of the participants at the original London School of Economics and Political Science workshop on "Happiness" for their substantial comments and critiques. Thanks are also due to five anonymous reviewers and to my student Christopher Stephan for providing significant suggestions on how to improve the piece.

REFERENCES

Ahmed, Sara. 2010. *The Promise of Happiness*. Durham, NC: Duke University Press.

Bashkow, Ira. 1991. "The Dynamics of Rapport in a Colonial Situation: David Schneider's Fieldwork on the Islands of Yap." In *Colonial Situations: Essays on the Contextualization of Ethnographic Knowledge*, edited by George W. Stocking Jr., 170–242. Madison: University of Wisconsin Press.

Berlant, Lauren. 2011. *Cruel Optimism*. Durham, NC: Duke University Press.

Daniel, E. Valentine. 2000. "Mood, Moment, and Mind." In *Violence and Subjectivity*, edited by Veena Das, Arthur Kleinman, Mamphela Ramphele, and Pamela Reynolds, 333–66. Berkeley: University of California Press.

Corsín Jiménez, Alberto. 2008. *Culture and Well-Being: Anthropological Approaches to Freedom and Political Ethics*. London: Pluto.

Desjarlais, Robert, and Jason Throop. 2011. "Phenomenological Approaches in Anthropology." *Annual Review of Anthropology* 40: 87–102.

Duranti, Alessandro. 2009a. "The Relevance of Husserl's Theory to Language Socialization." *Journal of Linguistic Anthropology* 19(2): 205–26.

———. 2009b. "The Force of Language and Its Temporal Unfolding." In *Language in Life and a Life in Language: Jacob Mey—a Festschrift*, edited by Kenneth Turner and Bruce Fraser, 63–71. Bingley, UK: Emerald Group Publishers.

———. 2010. "Husserl, Intersubjectivity and Anthropology." *Anthropological Theory* 10(1): 1–20.

Egan, Jim. 1998. "Taro, Fish, and Funerals: Transformations in the Yapese Cultural Topography of Wealth." PhD thesis, University of California, Irvine.

Geertz, Clifford. 1973. *The Interpretation of Cultures*. New York: Basic Books.

Heidegger, Martin. 1995 [1929/1930]. *The Fundamental Concepts of Metaphysics: World, Finitude, Solitude*. Translated by William McNeill and Nicholas Walker. Bloomington: Indiana University Press.

Hunt, Edward E., Jr., Nathaniel R. Kidder, and David M. Schneider. 1954. "The depopulation of Yap." *Human Biology* 26: 21–51.

Husserl, Edmund. 1962 [1913]. *Ideas: General Introduction to a Pure Phenomenology*. Translated by W. R. Boyce Gibson. New York: Collier Books.

---

27. In these last paragraphs, Throop makes a strong existential turn. He ends with the idea of a "unique region of being." This likely refers to Heidegger's later work in which he discusses human consciousness as a clearing in the midst of all things of the universe through which the world mystically understands itself. Being, or *Dasein*, flows through this clearing but is an abstract force that can have infinite manifestations. Heidegger (1977, orig. 1954) uses these ideas to think about technology. Throop uses them to think anthropologically about cultural similarities and differences in the experience of happiness and suffering.

———. 2001 [1918–1926]. *Analyses Concerning Passive and Active Synthesis: Lectures on Transcendental Logic*. Translated by Anthony J. Steinbock. Dordrecht: Kluwer Academic Press.

Jackson, Michael. 1998. *Minima Ethnographica: Intersubjectivity and the Anthropological Project*. Chicago: University of Chicago Press.

———. 2011. *Life within Limits: Well-Being in a World of Want*. Durham, NC: Duke University Press.

———. 2013. *The Wherewithal of Life: Ethics, Migration, and the Question of Well-Being*. Berkeley: University of California Press.

Labby, David. 1976. *The Demystification of Yap: Dialectics of Culture on a Micronesian Island*. Chicago: University of Chicago Press.

Laidlaw, J. 2008. "The Intension and Extension of Well-Being: Transformation in Diaspora Jain Understandings of Non-violence." In *Culture and Well-Being: Anthropological Approaches to Freedom and Political Ethics*, edited by Alberto Corsín Jiménez, 156–79. London: Pluto.

Levinas, Emmanuel. 1998. *Entre Nous: On Thinking-of-the-Other*. Translated by Michael B. Mith and Barbara Harshav. New York: Columbia University Press.

Lutz, Catherine. 1988. *Unnatural Emotions: Everyday Sentiment on a Micronesian Atoll and Their Challenge to Western Theory*. Chicago: University of Chicago Press.

Mathews, Gordon, and Carolina Izquierdo, eds. 2009. *Pursuits of Happiness: Well-Being in Anthropological Perspective*. New York: Berghahn.

Robbins, Joel. 2013. "Beyond the Suffering Subject: Toward an Anthropology of the Good." *Journal of the Royal Anthropological Institute*, n.s., 19(3): 447–62.

Rose, Nikolas. 2006. *The Politics of Life Itself*. Princeton, NJ: Princeton University Press.

Schneider, David M. 1955. "Abortion and Depopulation on a Pacific Island." In *Health, Culture, and Community*, edited by Benjamin D. Paul, 211–35. New York: Russell Sage Foundation.

———. 1967. "Foreword." In *The Curse of the Souw*, Roy Wagner, vii–viii. Chicago: University of Chicago Press.

———. 1984. *A Critique of the Study of Kinship*. Ann Arbor: University of Michigan Press.

Thin, Neil. 2012. *Social Happiness: Theory into Policy and Practice*. Bristol: Policy Press.

Throop, C. Jason. 2003. "Articulating Experience." *Anthropological Theory* 3(2): 219–41.

———. 2008. "From Pain to Virtue: Dysphoric Sensations and Moral Sensibilities in Yap (Waqab), Federated States of Micronesia." *Journal of Transcultural Psychiatry* 45(2): 253–86.

———. 2009a. "Intermediary Varieties of Experience." *Ethnos* 74(4): 535–58.

———. 2009b. "Interpretation and the Limits of Interpretability: On Rethinking Clifford Geertz's Semiotics of Religious Experience." *Journal of North African Studies* 14(3/4): 369–84.

———. 2010a. *Suffering and Sentiment: Exploring the Vicissitudes of Empathy and Pain in Yap*. Berkeley: University of California Press.

———. 2010b. "Latitudes of Loss: On the Vicissitudes of Empathy." *American Ethnologist* 37(4): 771–82.

———. 2012. "On Inaccessibility and Vulnerability: Some Horizons of Compatibility between Phenomenology and Psychoanalysis." *Ethos* 40(1): 75–96.

———. 2014. "Moral Moods." *Ethos* 42(1): 65–83.

———. 2015. "Sacred Suffering: A Phenomenological Anthropological Perspective." In *Phenomenology in Anthropology: A Sense of Perspective*, edited by Kalpana Ram and Christopher Houston, 68–89. Bloomington: Indiana University Press.

Throop, C. Jason, and Alessandro Duranti. 2014. "Attention, Ritual Glitches, and Attentional Pull: The President and the Queen." *Phenomenology and Cognitive Sciences*. Online First.

Zigon, Jarrett. 2014. "Attunement and Fidelity: Two Ontological Conditions for Morally Being-in-the-World." *Ethos* 42(1): 16–30.

AUTHOR'S NOTES

a. Joel Robbins (2013) references this same quote as a means to illuminate critical differences between so-called "savage slot" and "suffering slot" ethnography.

b. Estimates of precolonial population on the island range anywhere from 28,000 to 50,000 inhabitants (Hunt, Kidder, and Schneider 1954; Schneider 1955; Labby 1976). By the time of the first census conducted by the Catholic mission in 1899, however, the population had shrunk to just under 8000. Yap's population reached an all-time low during the American Navy's first census in the wake of the Japanese occupation in 1946, with merely 2478 inhabitants (Hunt, Kidder, and Schneider 1954; Egan 1998).

c. With the global circulation of psychiatric mood disorders, and the psychopharmaceutical management and "enhancement" of moods to fit within a range of the "happy," an ongoing diagnostic accounting of such failures of the self (which we should also note all too easily takes attention away from other political, social, and economic failures) is quite arguably one of the defining marks of our contemporary situation. To preserve the integrity of the self's wellbeing, the locus of failure is increasingly construed as one of neurobiological deficiency or malfunction (see Rose 2006).

d. The term "intentional" is used here in reference to the phenomenological concept of intentionality, which refers to the "aboutness" of consciousness as directed toward particular objects of experience.

e. My use of "attunement" throughout this article resonates strongly with Zigon's articulation of the concept, which builds directly upon Heidegger's original formulation (ibid.). As Heidegger explains, "Attunements are the fundamental ways in which we find ourselves disposed in such and such a way. Attunements are the 'how' [*Wie*] according to which one is in such and such a way. Certainly we often take this 'one is in such and such a way'. . . as something indifferent, in contrast to what we intend to do, what we are occupied with, or what will happen to us. And yet this 'one is in such and such a way' is not—is never—simply a consequence or side-effect of our thinking, doing, and acting And precisely those attunements to which we pay no heed at all, the attunements we least observe, those attunements which attune us in such a way that we feel as though there is no attunement there at all, as though we were not attuned in any way at all—these attunements are the most powerful" ([1929/30] 1995: 67–68).

f. It is interesting to note in this regard that the Yapese term that can be most easily glossed as "selfishness" (fal'ngaak) can be literally translated as "his or her goodness-wellbeing." Why would goodness or wellbeing be directly associated with self-centeredness? There are a number of cognate Yapese morphemes that carry the connotation of "good" or "well" (fal, feal', faal, and fael') that are also used to designate morally problematic states of being. These include fal'ngaak ("selfish"), fal'fal'l'ugun ("liar, falsehood"), and fael' ("to fool someone"). On the positive end of the spectrum are the terms faalngin ("propitious act, abstention, or sacrifice"), fal'eag ("to create, build, or repair"), fal'egin ("to fix or mend"), falaaqaab ("fortunate, lucky"), and falfalaen' ("happiness, contentment"). Even in the

case of these more positively valenced terms, however, there are notable connotations of lack, contingency, imperfection, and sacrifice implicated in them. Bridging between these polarities is the term falaay, which may refer to either "beneficial medicine" or "harmful magic" depending on the context. That the same morphemic root is used to designate terms for happiness, good fortune, beneficial medicine, harmful magic, falsehood, and selfishness is quite striking and not, I think, arbitrary.

g. A similar such ambivalent characterization of the narrow temporal horizons of happiness is also detailed in Catherine Lutz's classic ethnographic work on emotions on the nearby Micronesian atoll of Ifaluk. As Lutz observes, in Ifaluk, "happiness/excitement" is often seen to be a "dangerous, socially disruptive" emotion (1988: 145). "In this regard, the concept of *ker* (happiness/excitement) plays what is, from an American perspective, a paradoxical role. Happiness/excitement is an emotion people see as pleasant but amoral. It is often, in fact, immoral because someone who is happy/excited is more likely to be unafraid of other people. While this lack of fear may lead them to laugh and talk with people, it may also make them misbehave or walk around showing off or 'acting like a big shot' (*gabos fetal*)" (ibid.: 167). Accordingly, whereas "American approaches to child rearing and emotion elevate happiness to an important position, setting it out as an absolute necessity for the good or health child (and adult), the Ifaluk view happiness/excitement as something that must be carefully monitored and sometimes halted in children" (ibid.).

Decolonization and Whiteness

The vast majority of anthropologists in the late nineteenth and the first half of the twentieth centuries were among the most liberal thinkers of their era. In particular, the followers of Boas tended to believe in the value and rationality of all cultures and the biological and psychological equality of all people. Even before Boas, men like Louis Henry Morgan and E. B. Tylor, though undoubtedly racist by current standards, were far less racist than most of their white American and European peers. However, like all of us today, they were men and women of their era, and like all of us today, they could not fully escape the understandings, prejudices, and blind spots of their time. They tended, especially Boas and his students, to be progressives in the late-nineteenth- and early-twentieth-century meaning of the term. They held that social reform, science, technology, and economic development would lead to a better, fairer, more just world. And they thought that this was true across all cultures. On December 23, 1883, on Baffin Island, Boas wrote:

> The fear of traditions and old customs is deeply implanted in mankind, and in the same way as it regulates life here, it halts all progress for us. I believe it is a difficult struggle for every individual and every people to give up traditions and follow the path to truth. The Eskimo are sitting around me, their mouths filled with raw seal liver (the spot of blood on the back of the paper shows you how I joined in). (Cole 1983: 33)

Note Boas's progressivism. To create a better world, ultimately "every people" should "give up tradition." A few days later on January 22, 1884, he wrote:

> I do *not* want a German professorship. . . . I should much prefer to live in America in order to be able to further those ideas for which I live. . . . What I want to live and die for, is equal rights for all, equal possibilities to learn and work for poor and rich alike! (Cole 1983: 37)

Equal rights and possibilities for all were heroic, universalist ideas, and Boas and many twentieth-century anthropologists of all backgrounds did their best to live them. However, doing so implied assimilationism. Boas, speaking of immigrants to the United States, wrote that "assimilation is thus as inevitable as it is desirable; it is impossible for immigrants we receive to remain permanently in separate groups" (Boas 1921: 3). Boas recognized that racism would make assimilation much more difficult for black Americans and Native Americans. For the former, he believed that ultimately intermarriage would be the best way around intractable racism. For the latter, he strongly supported cultural preservation as a form of protection against the violence of white settlers and the government.

The late-nineteenth-century Western notion of progress and the belief in the value of assimilation had interesting implications for the relationship between anthropology and colonialism. On the one hand, many anthropologists were deeply critical of colonial practices. In most cases, they stood for the worth, dignity, rationality, and value of indigenous peoples and cultures at a time when these were dismissed and disregarded. They were frequently loathed and sometimes banned by colonial administrators. They often saw colonialism and imperialism as a naked grab for money and power. Boas, for example, challenged Americans to imagine what their reaction would be if China had colonized New England using the same justifications that the British had used:

I think this problem will become clear if we imagine the Chinese coming here and finding square miles of land in northern New York and New England lying waste, owned but not used. Would they not be entitled, on the same grounds on which we base our colonial claims, to say that they have no land at home and that for the sake of the welfare of humanity they will till the soil that we do not know how to utilize? (quoted in Liss 2015 Franz Boas Papers)

However, at the same time, Boas's position on imperialism was murky (Liss 2015). He and other anthropologists developed projects in American colonial possessions. Though they often recognized it as brutally exploitative, anthropologists tended not to challenge colonialism directly. Not that it would have mattered. It pays to remember that from the late nineteenth to mid-twentieth century, there were never more than a few hundred professional anthropologists in the world. One anthropologist in the 1930s noted that he became an anthropologist partly because there were only fifty in the United States, while colonialism was a world-historical force involving hundreds of millions of people.

After World War II, anthropology, like so much else, began to change rapidly. The relationship between anthropologists, those they studied, and anthropological understandings of their own governments, imperialism, colonialism, and race began to shift dramatically. This was the result of the convergence of several different factors. In no particular order, they included wars of national liberation and the end of direct colonialism in many places in Africa and South Asia, the emergence of groups of younger anthropologists trained after World War II and more heavily influenced by Marx, the Vietnam War and US involvement in other conflicts throughout the globe, the civil rights movement in the United States, and the women's liberation movement in the United States and Europe.

By the early 1960s, anthropologists were becoming increasingly politically engaged, almost always promoting the interests of indigenous people or campaigning for left-leaning causes. Sol Tax (1907–1995) and Marshall Sahlins (1930–1921) were examples of politically engaged anthropologists of this era. Among many other things (including founding the journal *Current Anthropology*), Tax was one of the main organizers of the 1961 American Indian Chicago Conference that brought over four hundred Native Americans from ninety different communities together and resulted in the drafting of a Declaration of Indian Purpose, later presented to President Kennedy (Hauptman and Campesi 1988). Tax and his students developed what they called "action anthropology." Tax said that action anthropology had two goals, first, to "help a group of people solve a problem," and second, for the anthropologist to "learn something in the process." He noted that the action anthropologist "refuses to ever think or to say that the people involved are for him a means of advancing his knowledge; and he refuses to think or say that he is simply applying science to the solution of those people's problems" (1975: 515).

Sahlins developed and practiced the idea of the "teach-in," a type of protest against the war in Vietnam based on the sit-ins used in the civil rights movement. Sahlins's idea was that rather than striking to protest the war or demonstrating, faculty would hold sessions that included lectures, films, and music aimed at understanding the Vietnam War's colonial context and protesting it. The first teach-in was held at the University of Michigan in March 1965. By the end of that year, teach-ins had been held at more than 120 colleges and universities. A national teach-in held in Washington, DC, reached an audience of over one hundred thousand (DeBennedetti 1990: 108, 115).

As some anthropologists became increasingly politicized, they began to examine the relationship between anthropology and colonialism and to question anthropology's colonial entanglements (Thomas 1991). By the late 1960s and early 1970s, this led to a series of publications examining the role that anthropology had played in the colonial endeavor. Among the first of these was by Kathleen Gough (1925–1990). Gough was trained in the British structuralist tradition but was very heavily influenced by Marxism. In her 1968 essay "Anthropology and Imperialism," she wrote:

Anthropology is a child of Western imperialism. It has its roots in the humanist visions of the Enlightenment, but as a university discipline and a modern science it came into its own in the last decades of the nineteenth century. This was a period in which the Western nations were making their final push to bring practically the whole pre-industrial non-Western world under their political and economic control. (1956: 12–13)

Gough noted that anthropologists generally accepted the colonialist/imperialist framework in which they were implicated. "Anthropologists were of higher social status than their informants; they were usually of the dominant race, and they were protected by imperial law; yet, living closely with native peoples, they tended to take their part and to try to protect them against the worst forms of imperialist exploitation" (1968: 13).

Gough issued a call for anthropologists to consider the ways their discipline interacted with colonialism and the effects on both anthropology and anthropology's subjects. In the next few years, numerous works considered these relationships. These included the German-Mexican anthropologist Rudolfo Stavenhagen's (1932–2016) call to decolonize the social sciences in general and anthropology in particular (1971; perhaps the first use of the word *decolonize* as a critique of social science), Saudi Arabian–born anthropologist Talal Asad's (b. 1932) 1973 edited volume *Anthropology and the Colonial Encounter* analyzing the relationship between anthropology and British colonialism, and Diane Lewis's (1931–2015) analysis of anthropology and colonialism (1973). Lewis, a pioneering black anthropologist, concluded that colonialism, which she linked directly with white supremacy, "structured the relationship between anthropologists and non-Western peoples" and that anthropologists pursued their work "in the interests of the colonizers" and "in terms of the concepts and theories they developed" (1973: 590).

On the one hand, as the many replies to Lewis's 1973 article published alongside it show, the exact nature of the relationship between anthropology and colonialism was, and remains, controversial. On the other hand, these and other essays brought the issue to the table, where it has remained, with greater or lesser intensity, ever since. However, in the half century since Stavenhagen's, Lewis's, and Asad's work appeared, several converging trends have led to increasing focus on colonialism and white supremacy. One of these was the rise of a neoliberal economic global order in the 1980s.

In the 1980s, several works influenced by world systems theory had a strong impact on people with an interest in colonialism and white supremacy, in particular, Eric Wolf's *Europe and the People without History* and Sidney Mintz's *Sweetness and Power*. One of the leading scholars representing this trend was Michel-Rolph Trouillot, who was both a student of Mintz and an important voice in the movement to study white supremacy and anthropology's role within it (see essay 30). By the end of the twentieth century, political, economic, and technological changes were releasing the forces of global capitalism on the world, often with devastating effects on the communities anthropologists studied, and increasingly on countries where a newer generation of anthropologists originated.

A second trend in anthropology is demographic change. In the fifty years between 1970 and 2020, the demographics of the United States and other wealthy nations changed dramatically. In 1990, for example, 76 percent of the population of the US identified as white. In the 2020 census, that had dropped to just over 64 percent (Jones et al. 2021). Similarly, while the majority of American anthropologists are still white, those numbers are also changing. In 1995, 75 percent of new anthropology doctorates went to whites but only 63.6 percent in 2007 (https://decasia.org/academic_culture/2009/11/race-and-white-dominance-in-american-anthropology/index.html).

Just as anthropology is slowly becoming more ethnically diverse, so too male dominance in the field has been changing over the past fifty years. The number of women earning doctorates in anthropology started to grow in the 1970s and passed the number of men earning degrees in 2007, when women earned 55–60 percent of the new doctoral degrees in anthropology (https://decasia.org/academic_cul ture/2009/09/gender-imbalance-in-anthropology/index.html). During this same period, anthropologists born in countries outside of the US and Western Europe have become more common. It is not surprising that these new generations of anthropologists should turn a critical eye on both the engagement of anthropology with colonialism and whiteness as an anthropological category.

The idea that anthropology itself needed to be decolonized dates back to the early 1970s but was given new impetus in the early 1990s with the publication of *Decolonizing Anthropology: Moving Further toward an Anthropology of Liberation* in 1991 (issued in a second and third edition in 1999 and 2010). The book was a collection of essays by influential anthropologists of the era including its editor Faye V. Harrison, Michael L. Blakey, Deborah D'Amico-Samuels, and Edmond Gordon, among others. Harrison was president of the Association of Black Anthropologists at the time the book was published. Many of the other contributors to the volume were also black anthropologists.

The movement to decolonize anthropology turned many of the discipline's analytic tools on anthropology itself. It asked important questions about the relationship between anthropologists and the communities they worked in and about whose voices were heard and whose were suppressed. It strove to reformulate anthropology as a discipline of liberation. According to A. Lynn Bolles, Professor of Women's Studies at the University of Maryland, decolonization means

> taking seriously the critiques and theories of anthropology's peripheral allies such as feminist activists and policy makers. It also incorporates the idea that global racial apartheid is the foundation of social, economic, and gender inequalities. . . . [It] entails looking beyond the colonizers' perspectives and using the frames of reference of those being studied. . . . To decolonize anthropology means to recognize and confront the discipline's colonial legacies, which have led to the marginalization and exploitation of indigenous people and their knowledge. (2023: 519)

Other influential works in the decolonization movement include Maori anthropologist Linda Tuhiwai Smith's 1999 *Decolonizing Methodologies* in which she proposes the implementation of research methodologies based on Maori understandings of the world and *Decolonizing the University* (2018), edited by Gurminder Bhambra, Dalia Gebrial, and Kerem Nişancioğlu, an edited volume of essays that examines the university as part of colonial empires and settler colonialism. The authors call for a reorganization of the university that crosses boundaries between disciplines, between universities and communities, and between nations.

By the early 2020s, decolonization had become a central concern of many anthropologists. This is perhaps best shown by Akhil Gupta's (b. 1959) 2021 presidential address, delivered at the annual meeting of the American Anthropological Association in Baltimore and later published as "Decolonizing US Anthropology" (2022), coauthored with Jessie Stoolman. In the address, Gupta wonders, "How would US anthropology have been different had the founding generations conceptualized the discipline as a decolonizing project?" (2022: 778). After a deeply critical analysis of the history of American anthropology, Gupta proposes that current-day anthropologists interrogate colonial legacies and structures by asking a series of questions. These include, What should we study "in order to become an antiracist and anticolonial discipline?" What methods are needed to make anthropology a decolonizing science? What practices should departments use to decolonize the discipline? "How would decolonizing practices shape the interactions between anthropological researchers and their subjects?" How should decolonization affect how authorship of anthropological work is assigned? And how do we decolonize pedagogy and the canon? (2022: 786). Gupta coupled his call to decolonize with a written apology to indigenous communities. Gupta appeared with Lee Baker (b. 1966), Shannon Speed (b. 1964), and other discussants who also gave provocative presentations.

Gupta's address was well received by many anthropologists but also raised more controversy than presidential addresses usually do (see, for example, the five essays in the commentary section of *American Anthropologist*, March 2023 edition). Many objected to Gupta's characterizations of earlier generations of anthropologists. For example, Herbert Lewis (b. 1934), an emeritus professor at the University of Wisconsin, wrote a critical letter that was cosigned by seventy anthropologists. Lewis wrote,

Current critics ignore, or possibly are ignorant of, the work of thousands of anthropologists over the better part of a century. They are censuring the intellectual record of attempts at understanding human life and invaluable records of human thought, creativity, activity, and struggle. They tend to do this without actually reading the works. (2022)

Another critic accused Gupta and his discussants of assuming that "anthropologists can be reduced to their racial identity" and pointed out that "one advantage of couching your argument in terms of anti-racism is the implication that people who disagree with you are, consciously or unconsciously, apologists for racism" (Stoll 2023).

We will make one comment concerning Gupta and Stoolman's question about what would have happened if the founders of anthropology had thought of it as a decolonizing project. To us, the answer seems obvious: anthropology would not exist today as an academic discipline. All of us are people of our eras, no more or less than Boas and Mead one hundred years ago. Most anthropologists of a century ago were probably about as radical as they could be and still survive in universities. In 1919, Boas was censured by the American Anthropological Association for saying that anthropologists should not spy for the government. In 1968, Kathleen Gough was an activist against the Vietnam War and published her essay calling anthropology the child of colonialism. In 1970, she was fired by Simon Fraser University. Her dismissal was certainly related to her publications and political activities (Jorgensen 1993). Even today, as state governments ban ethnicity as a factor in college admissions, shut down diversity and inclusion offices on state university campuses, and ban high school AP courses in African American history, it is not clear that anthropology conceived of as an anticolonial, antiracist, decolonizing project can have a robust future outside of elite private institutions.

Our selection on decolonizing anthropology is by Audra Simpson (b. 1969), professor of anthropology at Columbia University. Simpson is a citizen of the Kahnawa:ke Mohawk Nation, located on the south shore of the St. Lawrence River only a few miles from Montreal. In her award-winning book *Mohawk Interruptus: Political Life across the Borders of Settler States* (2014) and elsewhere, Simpson develops the notion of refusal as an act of political defiance. In that book, she writes,

> I am interested in . . . ways in which Kahnawa'kehró:non [the people of Kanhnawa:ke] had *refused* the authority of the state at almost every turn and in doing so reinstantiated a different political authority . . . how refusal worked in everyday encounters to enunciate repeatedly to themselves and to outsiders: "This is who we are; this is who you are; These are my rights." (2014: 106)

Simpson differentiates refusal from resistance. For her, resistance is a weapon of the weak that reinscribes inequality. Refusal, on the other hand, "interrupts the smooth operation of power, denying resumed authority and remaking historical narratives (Ferguson 2015). Simpson applies the idea of refusal to her own work as well. She tells us only certain things about the Kahnawa'kehró:non, declining to give us a window into many of the internal debates and operations of the nation and drawing strict lines between what she is willing to say in print and what she is not.

The study of whiteness and white privilege is a second trend that grew increasingly important in the late 1980s and early 1990s. For many social scientists in the late nineteenth and the twentieth centuries, whiteness was invisible. The vast majority of them were white, and they understood their experience as white people to be normal and mainstream. They viewed racial minorities and ethnic groups as contrasted with this baseline of white normality. There were some notable exceptions to this, particularly the work of W. E. B. Du Bois, Frantz Fanon, and other black scholars. For example, in a poetic and penetrating 1910 essay, republished in 1920, "The Souls of White Folk" (a riff on the title of his 1903 book *The Souls of Black Folk*), Du Bois identifies whiteness as a distinctive ethnic identity as having been discovered in the nineteenth and twentieth centuries. He continues:

> This assumption that of all the hues of God, whiteness alone is inherently and obviously better than brownness or tan leads to curious acts; even the sweeter souls of the dominant world as they discourse with me on weather, weal, and woe are continually playing above their actual words an obligato of tune and tone, saying:
>
> "My poor, un-white thing! Weep not nor rage. I know, too well, that the curse of God lies heavy on you. Why? That is not for me to say, but be brave! Do your work in your lowly sphere, praying the good Lord that into heaven above, where all is love, you may, one day, be born-white!"

Du Bois's work, and that of other black authors, was marginalized and often ignored outside of the African diaspora (in Du Bois's case, this marginalization was further augmented by his openly Marxist politics and support of Stalinist Russia; see, for example, his description of Stalin as a "great man"; Du Bois 1953). However, in the late 1980s and the 1990s, the same forces that had led to the emergence of the decolonization movement also spawned a renewed examination of whiteness. This occurred not only in anthropology but also in other social science fields such as sociology and history. Some of the influential works of this era include bell hooks's (1952–2021) *Black Looks: Race and Representation* (1992), which examines whiteness from a black perspective; Peggy McIntosh's (b. 1934) "White Privilege: Unpacking the Invisible Knapsack" (1989), in which McIntosh, a white academic, describes how she came to understand the advantages given to her by whiteness; and Charles W. Mills's (1951–2021) *The Racial Contract* (1997), which argues that racism is a fundamental feature of Western political systems.

Whiteness studies tend to focus on several critical areas. Colorblindness studies focus on the "invisibility of whiteness to those who possess it" (McDermott and Ferguson 2022). Such studies explore the ways that such invisibility is connected to the denial of both current and historical white privilege, as well as white resistance, in the name of equality, to any attempts to redress the historical effect of racist policies. A related field of research concerns both the way that white people feel about their identity and the intersections between white identity, gender, social class, and religious identity.

Another key field within whiteness studies explores the ways that white supremacy is encoded and reproduced in societies. Research in this area focuses on how the assumptions of whiteness and white cultural norms are basic constructs behind political, economic, and social institutions. Examples of work in this area include studies of how government policies reinforce racial divisions and inequality and the ways that "white norming," the generally unconscious implementation of cultural expectations and organizational policies, systematically benefit white people (Chandler and Wiborg 2022).

A third field considers the history of whiteness, particularly the way European immigrants who were frequently not considered to be white by the white Anglo-Saxon Protestants who controlled the reins of wealth and power in the United States became white. Two popular works in this genre are Michael Ignatiev's 1995 *How the Irish Became White* and Karen Brodkin's *How Jews Became White Folks and What That Says about Race in America* (1998). This literature is somewhat problematic since Irish and Jewish people could usually become white in ways that are typically denied to others who are not phenotypically white. Ashley "Woody" Doane (2008: 88) notes that "what is less contentious is that European immigrants learned what it *meant* to be white in the United States, especially with respect to establishing themselves in contrast to African Americans."

The second essay in this section, "To Protect and Serve Whiteness" by Orisanmi Burton, is from the whiteness studies perspective. It examines how white supremacy and the threat of violence are present in policing, even when police behave in thoroughly competent and professional ways. Burton is a professor at American University. His broader work examines state repression and grassroots resistance. He focuses on "prisons as sites of low-intensity counterinsurgency warfare, waged by and through the state in order to reproduce racial and gender hierarchies, manage political dissent, and facilitate the accumulation of capital in times of crisis" (Besteman et al. 2018). He has recently published a book on prisons and policing, focusing on black radicalism and the series of rebellions that shook New York prisons in the 1970s.

We believe that decolonialization and whiteness are important perspectives and provide new insights into current-day society, world history, and the discipline of anthropology. We fully support research and writing in these areas. Further, we have always wanted to see anthropology as a discipline in which scholars of all backgrounds feel welcome and appreciated. We are aware that has not always been the case.

The decolonization and whiteness theoretical perspectives are among the most openly political theoretical positions in anthropology today. Anthropologists *should* take moral positions, and as we have seen throughout this volume, they have a long history of political involvement. This, we think, is proper. But anthropology is greater than politics and the concerns of the moment. The six groups of questions that Gupta raised in his 2021 presidential address are important and worthy of study. We hope that many anthropologists heed his call to think deeply and creatively about them. However, an anthropology focused primarily on these would be limiting and ineffective.

Anthropology must continue to be what it has been since at least the days of Boas, a discipline that asks big questions and a form of fieldwork in philosophy. *Other* has become a sort of bad word in some corners of anthropology and academia. But anthropology must reclaim the idea of the other. Because ultimately, no matter who you are, where you're from, or any attribute you have, you live in a world of others. The human experience is an experience of other people and other cultures. As Clifford Geertz, quoting a Javanese proverb (and speaking of Javanese understandings) said, it's a world of other fields and other grasshoppers (1973: 53). The job of anthropology, in its many forms, guises, perspectives, theories, and paradigms, is to explore, hopefully with humility and respect, what it means to be human. That means thinking about who we are as individuals and as members of society and who others are, as individuals and members of society. It means working to understand other perspectives on meaning and other ways of seeing the world. It means thinking about similarity and about difference.

Like virtually everyone else of their era, McGee and Warms, as graduate students in the 1980s, could not have imagined the world of today. In 1985, a supercomputer weighed 5,500 pounds. Today, a smartphone weighs about six ounces and is more than one hundred times more powerful (Steele 2022). In 1982, there were 450 million phones in the world, and a three-minute discount-rate call from New York to Japan cost $4.43 ($14.42 in late 2023 dollars). Today there are more than fifteen billion phones in the world, almost two for every human being. Even in very poor nations, many people are likely to have smartphones. And the price of a three-minute call to anywhere using a service such as WhatsApp is, for all practical purposes, too small to calculate. In 1985, China's total economy was about one-fourteenth the size of the United States' total economy. Today it is the world's second largest and about 70 percent the size of the United States' total economy. At the same time, globalized products and chains are now found the world over. You can order Pizza Hut at more than one thousand shops in China and many, many more in about one hundred additional countries, including Nepal, Kazakhstan, Sri Lanka, and Mauritius. It's easy to get Thai food in Zurich or Geneva, and there are numerous places to eat fondue in Bangkok. Hollywood products are designed with the Chinese audience in mind, and American kids grow up devoted to *Dragon Ball Z* and *One Piece*. The world has become interconnected and culture homogenized in ways that people in the 1980s could not have imagined. At the same time, these technologies and the cultural knowledge they enable have not led to greater understanding. In many ways, it seems like people's conceptions of meaning and reality are as far or further apart now than they were forty years ago. The need for us to think about ourselves and others, to think about culture, to try to understand what it is, how it works, and how it is experienced has only become more valuable.

No one can know what life will be like in the last third of the twenty-first century, which is about as far from us now as the 1980s are behind us. We cannot know the technologies, triumphs, disasters, acts of violence, and acts of reconciliation that will shape the lives of people born in the 2050s and 2060s. We can't know their ideas about race, or colonialism, or anything else. But it would be very surprising if the core job of anthropology, to think about ourselves and others, to strive to understand culture and how we, whoever we are, and people different from ourselves see the world, was not still a critical task facing humanity.

SUGGESTED READINGS

Argyrou, Vassos. 2002. *Anthropology and the Will to Meaning: A Postcolonial Critique.* Sterling, VA: Pluto Press.
   In a densely argued critique, Argyrou proposes that in searching for comprehension of other cultures, anthropologists are driven by an idea of "sameness" that inadvertently both denies and reproduces racism.
Asad, Talal. 1973. *Anthropology and the Colonial Encounter.* New York: Humanities Press.
   Early collection of essays charting the relationship between anthropology and colonialism.
Frankenberg, Ruth. 1993. *White Women, Race Matters: The Social Construction of Whiteness.* Hoboken, NJ: Routledge.
   Foundational document in studies of whiteness. Frankenberg focuses on the experiences of white women in the United States and how they are structured by unspoken barely recognized racism.
Harrison, Faye V. 1997. *Decolonizing Anthropology: Moving Further toward an Anthropology of Liberation.* 2nd ed. Arlington, VA: American Anthropological Association.
   Landmark collection of essays on the relationship of anthropology and colonialism.
McIntosh, Peggy. 1989. "White Privilege: Unpacking the Invisible Knapsack." *Peace and Freedom Magazine*, July/August. https://nationalseedproject.org/key-seed-texts/white-privilege-unpacking-the-invisible-knapsack.
   A famous early statement about the existence and nature of white privilege.
Simpson, Audra. 2014. *Mohawk Interruptus: Political Life across the Borders of Settler States.* Durham, NC: Duke University Press.
   Simpson's book-length exploration of refusal as a response to settler colonialism.
Tuhiwai, Linda. *Decolonizing Methodologies: Research and Indigenous Peoples.* New York: Zed Books, 1999.
   Exploration of anthropological methodology from an indigenous perspective.
Wolf, Patrick. 2006. "Settler Colonialism and the Elimination of the Native." *Journal of Genocide Research* 8(4): 387–409.
   Foundational statement about the enduring nature of settler colonialism and the inevitability of oppression associated with it.

40. The Ruse of Consent and the Anatomy of "Refusal": Cases from Indigenous North America and Australia

Audra Simpson (b. 1969)

ONE MIGHT TRY TO resist writing an article on ethnographies of the political with direct recourse to the political present. Doing so might risk elevating elements of the moment and then sacrificing the theory-building project with a dizzying and contaminating arbitrariness of the present—a present whose significance is yet to be determined. Furthermore, an analysis that starts with things formally political, and in this, specifically electoral, and presidential in the U.S. might make these risks of contamination especially acute. "Are things really as they seem?" "Is this in fact, a fact, and one that will endure?" Yet, how to make sense of the very un-statesman-like behaviour of a President who bragged of sexual assault, mocked a physically disabled journalist, campaigned on a "nativist" platform that called out the foreign, qualified them as "bad people" (re: Muslims, Mexican and presumably criminal border crossers) and did so with jeering support? How to make sense of the significance of this discursive and now legal practice of xenophobia, with no reflection on how such claims to argument are also claims to place and claims out of history? How could he—a person descended from immigrants, settlers of a second and third order—make determinations on the content of other peoples' character and right of passage to this place? How can anyone really make these determinations, save for actual Indigenous people? One would have to imagine that there are no Indigenous political orders in place to make such loud, public statements or that Indigenous peoples simply do not matter if settlers are in their place.[1]

Here, I am being deliberately provocative in order to press upon the claim of formal politics in contemporary settler colonial societies and territories, which accrue and implement their power through thin, triumphalist and erroneous claims to place and to history. In doing so, they make natives out of immigrants and ghosts, "descendants" out of "spurious" claimants, criminals out of natives. Yet, it may be at this moment where electoralism lays bare the faulty premise of settler colonial states and the very architecture of history, politics and sentiment that allow for easy, reductionist answers to profound problems of justice, of what may be irreconcilable issues. This is the spurious claim of a colonial past, that stays in the past, of a populace that consents via an electoral system to be governed, and the speculative "truthiness" of these claims to territory itself. The half-truths, the non-truths have piled up

---

From *Postcolonial Studies* (2017)

1. This essay was written in the first year of the Trump presidency (2017), and Simpson is reacting with outrage to that political moment. As we have noted (Gomberg-Muñoz, essay 37, note 12), from the earliest days of his presidential campaign, Donald Trump (b. 1946) made false and derogatory claims about immigrants. As of 2024, he continues to make such claims, as do many other Republican officials. From Simpson's position as an Indigenous person, Trump, as well as most people living in North America, are immigrants. If anyone would have the right to comment on new immigrants, it is Indigenous people, not the descendants of immigrants, all of whom Simpson refers to as "settlers." Simpson notes that Trump would have to believe that Indigenous Americans do not matter at all to speak as he has. Compared to the number of times he has spoken about immigrants, Trump has had relatively little to say about Native Americans; however, much of what he has said and done, Native people have interpreted as derogatory and opposed to Native interests (see, for example, Smith 2020; CBS 2017).

and are pointing fingers at everyone as if to say "check this," verify that, and this industry of fact checking around the claims of the new Republican regime arc back to the original false claims of the settler: a right to territory and a right to govern. So, it is perhaps then a most appropriate time to reflect upon the present and ask about the imagination of the political under conditions of falsehood.[2]

In this article, I consider what I frame as a "not easy answer" to the problem of political will and politics in settler colonial societies. These are societies defined by the coloniality of their past and their presents, and thus are societies beset by ongoing inequalities and structural violence that demand justice. Yet, the problem of justice imagines "recognition"

to be the philosophical and institutional remedy to matters of "historical injustice"—to matters of dispossession, violence, and as the Introduction to this set of articles indicates, matters of inequality and thus of power. In this piece, I offer a deepening of earlier arguments I have made about recognition, about its presumed infallibility and centrality to matters of justice. "Refusal" rather than recognition is an option for producing and maintaining alternative structures of thought, politics and traditions away from and in critical relationship to states. In this piece, I use ethnographic examples to deepen this earlier argument about the generative alternative that refusal may play not only as a political practice but also as a mode of analysis.[3]

---

2. Settler colonialism is one of Simpson's key analytical tools. Lorenzo Veracini (2013) explored the history of the idea of settler colonialism. He notes that up until the 1960s, historians tended to view settlement and colonialism as entirely different categories. This involved viewing places where Europeans (and others) colonized and settled as unoccupied or unutilized land, in effect completely ignoring Indigenous presence. Ideas began to shift in the 1960s, particularly under the influence of the French-Algerian War of 1954–1962, which resulted in almost a million Europeans who had settled in colonial Algeria in the nineteenth century fleeing the country.

McKay et al. (2020), building on work by the Australian anthropologist Patrick Wolfe (1949–2016), provide a useful definition of settler colonialism: "Settler colonialism describe[s] the logic and operation of power when colonizers arrive and settle on lands already inhabited by members of another group. Importantly, settler colonialism operates through a logic of elimination, seeking to eradicate the original inhabitants through violence and other genocidal acts and to replace the existing spiritual, epistemological, political, social, and ecological systems with those of settler society. . . . Thus, settler colonialism functions as a structure of society rather than a past event." According to Wolfe (2006), settler colonialism is not universally genocidal but always necessitates a logic of elimination. These definitions explain what Simpson is saying. The United States and Canada, and really all countries in the Americas and many others besides, position colonialism and settlement as something that happened in the past. Whatever injustices were committed in that era have little to do with present-day life. Theorists of settler colonialism insist that settler colonialism is a basic patterning structure always active in every society that has Indigenous minorities. As such, it determines relationships of inequality broadly rather than only with Indigenous people.

Simpson uses the word *truthiness*, which in its modern connotation means something that has the emotional quality of feeling true, regardless of its facticity. The word was coined with this meaning in 2005 by comedian and television personality Stephen Colbert (b. 1964).

3. Simpson's essay comes from an issue of the journal *Postcolonial Studies* that focuses on recognition, power, and coloniality. It includes an introduction written by Samantha Balaton-Chrimes, a Senior Lecturer in International Studies at Deakin University, Melbourne Australia, and Victoria Stead, a Senior Research Fellow at Deakin University. Recognition has long been a key concept in political theory in general and multiculturalism in particular. In a foundational essay, the Canadian philosopher Charles Taylor (b. 1931) argues for a close linkage between recognition and both individual and group identity. He writes, "The need . . . for *recognition* . . . is one of the driving forces behind nationalist movements in politics."

Taylor saw recognition as a key prerequisite for true multiculturalism and misrecognition as a form of oppression. He wrote, "Misrecognition shows not just a lack of due respect. It can inflict a grievous wound, saddling its victims with a crippling self-hatred. Due recognition is not just a courtesy we owe people. It is a vital human need" (1992: 25–26). Balaton-Chrimes and Stead, as well as Simpson, take issue with Taylor's emphasis on recognition. They argue that in settler-colonial contexts, "recognition functions, not as a

The implicit backdrop for this argument is the aforementioned political present, and the particularity of electoralism in settler states. Electoralism, predicated on the notion of political will communicated through a vote, seems upended in this moment. "We did not vote for him" some would say, in a popular sense. My focus, however, is not on the failures of an electoral college system or perhaps errors in polling methodology, but the deeper issue that is obfuscated by the apparent agreed-upon nature of voting-as-consent or as expression of political will. If indigeneity is taken to be a social and political fact, all other arguments based on right to land are rendered spurious. This process of making land one's own, against Indigenous political orders—what Manu Vimalassery has recently called "the counter-sovereignty" of settler projects, which orient against Indigenous sovereignty—animates this argument as well.[a] Energised by this approach to the legal history of United States settler laws of dispossession, however, I argue above all against the practice of reduction, both in our analysis and in our political imaginations, to "recognition." "Recognition" is seen as the *sine qua non* if not the end point, the orgasm of justice today.[b] This overstatement of its possibility is in part because complex politics have been rendered in reduced forms that imagine "flat (dehistoricized) pluralism."[c]

By "recognition," I mean the political practice, rooted in philosophical formula of seeing, unencumbered, what and who is before you— seeing as one ought to be seen, in a way that is consistent with one's sense of self and property. What this translates into in legal contexts, for questions of justice, is the affirmation of one's (inherent) rights by the state. But these are states, in colonial contexts, that were born only through the devices of lethal force and dispossession and, in the case of the United States, economic and political enslavement of particular populations.[d] These broad but particular and differently experienced racial histories bear upon the present in significant ways. In this piece, I focus on the particular way in which law in colonial contexts enforced Indigenous dispossession and then, granted freedom through the legal tricks of consent and citizenship. For Native people, this ruse of consent marks the inherent impossibility of that freedom after dispossession, a freedom I argue is actually theft.[e] This because of the trickery of "consent" in colonial contexts, which papers over the very conditions of force and violence that beget "consent." Treaty-making is one such case that I will discuss. The long view of history, that in settler colonial contexts is actually always short, invokes a fundamental hegemony of interpretation such as viewing the "signing" of agreements as full and robust consent, and consent as justice. In such political configurations, there are no further matters to be discussed. Time starts anew; the matter is done. We know with the analytic of settler colonialism that matters are not done, that oppressive structures survive agreements. Yet, in spite of the problematic historical, philosophical and legal basis of settler societies, "recognition" appears to be the only political game in town, and with that comes the presumed unassailability of electoral politics as a device for not only representation, no matter how mediated and concessionary it may be, but also the recognition of rights and the exercising of rights.

Rather than recognition and its ruse of consent, I have proposed elsewhere a political alternative of refusal.[f] This article moves with recourse to ethnographic and legal cases to a deeper exposition of that alternative, one that also articulates to the present. In order to get at the architecture of this argument, I will consider the way in which I came to the concept of refusal in order to work through both the material of "the field," and the field of analytic possibilities that availed themselves to the study as I started to write it up.[4]

---

mechanism for the amelioration of colonialism's effects but *as a means through which those effects are reproduced*" (Balaton-Chrimes and Stead 2017: 2). Simpson argues here that refusal constitutes an alternative pathway both for justice and maintaining alternative politics and structures of thought. For Simpson's comments on Taylor's ideas, see Simpson (2014: 20).

4. To recap, Simpson has argued that questions of legitimacy and justice in the United States and Canada, both of which she identifies as settler-colonial societies, have been analyzed using the concept of recognition of different ethnic and racial groups and of people as individual citizens who have certain rights. She

REFUSAL: A BRIEF RETROSPECTIVE

When I first conceived of the project that would become my book *Mohawk Interruptus: Political Life Across the Borders of Settler States*, my plan was a study of nationhood and citizenship among an Indigenous people in North America who are resolutely committed to jurisdiction over territories of various forms.[8] Their own object was and is territory in a material sense. This encompassed their "land," but also a territory of ideas, of the past, present and future, and, most vigorously, their membership within the polity itself. All of this effort is made as they travel across various borders and boundaries upon their territories.[5]

Kahnawa'kehró:non[h] assert their histories in the face of bordered contestation of those claims by liberal, democratic and *still settling* states. Because these are my own people, I had a very strong a priori "ethnographic sense" of what was going on; I was *paying attention* for years before my formal fieldwork began. Our band council (tribal council) was evicting non-native people from the community in order to enforce a 50% blood quantum requirement for membership that was vigorously debated, contested, embraced and defended. These processes were symptoms of something more than

an episodic bout of intolerance or failure of liberal subjectivity and I wanted to know "why?" But more than asking, "why are these more than perceived failures of liberal, settler normativity?"—which seemed obvious enough—I asked, "why is this happening now?" and "where is it coming from?" I looked for linkages between land, law and governance within and beyond the reserve. The project turned into something else when I encountered the archive and did interviews—when "observations" and the materials from the community took form in dense, identifiable lines of argument, stances and theories themselves. Suddenly, I had something else, a colonial history of what had seemed so very "eventful" and episodic, but was in fact processual and structural, and which presented no containable, predictable and diagnostic "easy answer." These processes defied reduction and ethnographic containment—this was not a matter of "flat pluralism" or "factionalised, tribal politics." In fact, what was before me was a study in difficulty, a study of constraint and of contradictions. There was no way to describe or theorise what was crucial, which was the very deliberate actions that people were making in the face of the expectation that they consent to their own elimination, to having their land taken, their lives controlled and their stories told for them.[i, 6]

---

then argues that the nation and the social order are legitimized through elections and electoral politics because the ability to vote is held to guarantee that the state has the consent of those it governs. However, at least as it pertains to Indigenous people, Simpson refers to this consent as a ruse and a trick because it ignores the history of subjugation and eliminationist policies to which Indigenous people have been subject. Simpson argues, "For Native people, this ruse of consent marks the inherent impossibility of that freedom after dispossession, a freedom I argue is actually theft." Rather than participating in this settler-colonizer system, Simpson proposes a policy of refusal, which she details in the next section.

5. *Mohawk Interruptus: Political Life across the Borders of Settler States*, published in 2014, is Simpson's book-length treatment of some of the issues she discusses in this essay. Simpson's book was very well received, winning several awards, including the Native American and Indigenous Studies Association Best First Book Award and the Laura Romero First Book Prize from the American Studies Association. Her work has had a strong influence on other scholars (Murarka 2021).

6. Simpson begins her discussion with observations of her own people, the Kahnawa'kehró:non. Kahnawà:ke refers to the Mohawk Kahnawà:ke First Nations Reserve, located on the south bank of the St. Lawrence Seaway, about a twenty-minute drive from downtown Montreal. The Kahnawà:ke reserve is an area of about 18.5 square miles and has a population of roughly eight thousand. It is one of several Mohawk territories in Canada and the United States. Kahnawà:ke has a long history of territory loss and encroachment by non-Natives. A relatively recent and traumatic example of this was the loss of about 10 percent of Kahnawà:ke territory during the building of the St. Lawrence Seaway in the late 1950s. This was not only a territorial loss

"Refusal" was a stance but also a theory of the political that was being pronounced over and over again.[j] It emerged in my own writing and through observation of Kahnawà:ke action but also through the words of people. I would hear, "enough is enough," "it's not us it's them," and—in a commentary on the international border—"the white man put that there, not us." The people of Kahnawà:ke used every opportunity to remind each other, and especially non-native people, that this is our land, that there are other political orders and possibilities, and that a heightened sensitivity to matters of love and jurisdiction within the polity was also linked to longer waits at borders, awkward (to say the least) interactions with cashiers upon taking our Indian status cards for tax exemption,[k] and deeply difficult personal decisions. I also saw that these discourses and actions, and these matters of moral and political habit, were articulated quite perfectly to larger actions by the Iroquois Confederacy (Haudenosaunee) through time. As such, there was an historical and contemporary push for broader efforts to demand recognition of existing agreements as well as simultaneous refusals to play various games of the state (voting, paying taxes at times and serving in the military).[l, 7]

Thus, if there was a "structure" of settler colonialism that was discernible through time, there was also a structure of refusal. These refusals were symptomatic of that structure and manifested in the games of settler colonial governance, and in particular, the play that would signal consent. Paramount among these refusals is citizenship itself, the aforementioned actions that would signal consent and belonging within a settler political system and would move Mohawks out of their own sovereignty into an ambit of "consent" and with that, settler citizenship and the promise of whiteness. All of this pointed analytically to the deeply unequal scene of articulation that people were thrown into and were remaking through the quotidian and the grand.[8]

This deeply unequal scene of articulation that I am describing may be understood as the "settler colonial present," a present that purported newness, that owned time and was punctured repeatedly by Mohawk sensibilities, practices and by their continued life itself.[m] Thus, the demand of Indigenous life upon this

---

but altered their relationship with the St. Lawrence River, which was critical to their cultural identity.

The idea (or accusation) of "flat pluralism" is a critique of recognition theory. In the introduction to these essays, Balaton-Chrimes and Stead argue that *"flat* pluralism" (emphasis in the original) ignores the violent nature of conflict between Indigenous people and colonizers, and the struggles of the former for recognition, as well as ignoring the possibility that some cultural differences are so large that they are seen and understood only with great difficulty, if at all.

Simpson's path of discovery begins when she starts to examine why the band council began to enforce a 50 percent blood requirement for tribal membership and the factors that triggered this event. She discovers that this is part of an ongoing colonial history that has no easy answer and claims that what people are doing cannot be described let alone theorized. This is somewhat similar to but further reaching than Rosaldo's claim about Ilongot headhunting (essay 29). Can anthropologists accept that there are things that cannot be described or theorized?

7. Simpson provides two footnotes here about the broader history of the idea of refusal. In note j, she mentions Herman Melville's (1819–1891) 1853 short story "Bartleby, the Scrivener." Melville writes about an office employee who, though at first diligent, begins responding to every request with "I would prefer not to." Since his request is phrased so modestly, his workmates and supervisors acquiesce. When his boss leaves, Bartleby refuses to move and is arrested. Ultimately, Bartleby, refusing to eat, starves to death in jail.

8. Simpson refers to the actions of colonial settlers as "games." She'll use the term another four times in the essay and once in an endnote. Her usage carries a little of Sherry Ortner's idea of serious games (essay 36). Simpson's use of the word is aimed at the actions of settler-colonialist individuals and governments. To not play the game is to refuse to accept the legitimacy of the state. However, since ultimately the state holds a monopoly of power, opting out is often impossible. For example, you must obey the laws promulgated by the government or face the consequences of not doing so whether you vote or not.

"settler present" was temporal, those that were supposedly sequestered in the past were pushing upon the present and this push upon the temporal was and is political. How could the claims that the state was making upon history, upon law, upon governance work factually, if not ethically, if Mohawks were demanding that treaties[n] be upheld and Indigenous passports be honoured, if they expected that controversial internal decisions to exclude be respected? Their demands are tied to refusals to disappear or acquiesce to state legitimacy and power. They push up against the desire of the liberal state to consider its governance just. By this, I mean a state whose existence is borne of cruel and dispossessive time, yet still seems to own time, and thus is able to posture as a liberal state, "we are not discriminatory (anymore), so neither shall you discriminate."[9]

What such requirements involve is a forgetting that the state's very being creates the problems that that [*sic*] Indian reserves must manage, and yet, states act as though this is not a matter at all—even though this vexed, very important non-mythical origin story of fundamental dispossession is everywhere and nowhere. So, the implicit demand to forget, through the operation of "consent" and "citizenship," is challenged by the counter that Indigenous people represent simply by (a) living and (b) knowing this. In living and knowing themselves as such, they pose a demand upon the newness of the present, as well as a knotty reminder of something else. That "something else" is the ongoing work of dispossession, and its handmaiden of failed assimilation. Indigenous peoples are reminders, sometimes indecipherable announcements of other orders, other authorities, and an earlier time that has not fully passed. "Settler time" is revealed as the fiction of the presumed neutrality of time itself, demonstrating the dominance of the present by some over others, and the unequal power to define what matters, who matters, what pasts are alive and when they die.

How then are those who are targeted for elimination to articulate their politics within the exigencies of settler time and settler governance? How are they to demonstrate the vitality of their historical consciousness of this as something that is not natural or neutral? How to articulate political projects of pre-existing political traditions if one has been offered a half-life of civilisation in exchange for land? To do these things, they refuse to consent to the apparatus of the state. And in time with that, I refused then, and still do now, to tell the internal story of their struggle. But I consent to telling the story of their constraint.

That became the point to needle through, and then stitch with. The context of the broader argument I was making about the interruptive capacity of Indigenous political life was historical as much as it was contemporary and anticipatory. After reviewing the Mohawk and settler history that framed the debates and contestations that prompted the study, there came a deep pragmatism—the realisation that this would never be read fairly. The mess of internal struggle over issues structured fundamentally by dispossession is our business. And yet, I wanted to talk about our business just enough so that it could be understood that this is a difficult situation. Bringing in blood quantum is a difficult situation, dealing with gendered and raced discrimination was at times excruciating and painful, with older, legal and Victorian sensibilities of exclusion internalised and naturalised by some and contested vigorously by others. As such, I spent as much time outlining the territorial and political context to the moment of exclusion that prompted the research: why a 50% blood quantum requirement? Why the eviction of non-Indians? Why

---

9. Simpson, in endnote n discusses the treaties she refers to in this passage, in particular, the "'Two-Row' wampum treaty." Some additional information about this treaty will help your reading. The Two Row Wampum Treaty was an agreement made in 1613 between the Dutch government and the Haudenosaunee (Iroquois). It was one of the earliest treaties made between Europeans and native North Americans. The Haudenosaunee understand it as the basis for all later treaties with the French, British, US, and Canadian governments. The treaty requires that the Haudenosaunee be treated as equal partners with Europeans and that they be permitted to pursue their own forms of culture, government, and society on their own lands without outside interference.

a **"Moratorium on Mixed Marriages"**? These are excisions on agreed-upon standards of contemporary liberal freedom—the freedom to be who you want to be, marry who you want, do what you want, unencumbered. What is the context for this? My attention to the contextual webbing was rendered here in vernacular terms: "let's not pretend." Let us not pretend that there is an even playing field for interpretation. Let us not pretend that "the Iroquois" are not already pre-figured, that their actions are going to be interpreted fairly or that we do not push on all of these processes, fully. So I refused to pretend that potential readers, many of whom are in my field and subfield, would give it a fair read, would get it, were I to lay it bare. Furthermore, I was not talking about kinship charts, ceremony, ritual cycles or Mohawk verb structure. And do not get me wrong, I do not cite these classic interests of the subfield of "Iroquois Studies" because

these interests are not important or do not bear on interests to community itself, but because I was interested in what was not of interest to anthropology or political science and theory—the mess of what people were talking about, struggling with, trying to think through and beyond. There was no place in the existing literature for this material. So, I refused to be that thick description prose-master—the one that would reveal in florid detail the ways in which these things were being sorted out, the internal mechanisms of deliberation and discord. As such, my ethnographic "refusal" operated at the level of the text: deliberate, willful, and, like the people I was working with and the process I was documenting, very aware of its context of articulation. That settler context includes a deep suspicion of Indigenous peoples, and at times, as we saw during the so-called Oka Crisis of 1990, a deep hatred for the Haudenosaunee.[o, 10]

---

10. **"Moratorium on mixed marriages"**: Starting in 1981, the Mohawk Council of Kahnawà:ke announced a "moratorium on mixed marriages." The tribal government declared that such marriages would not be recognized on Kahnawà:ke land and people involved in them would not have residency rights. The ban was not enforced until the 2010s when the council began to take active steps to evict people with less than 50 percent blood quantum. This resulted in lawsuits in which those being evicted sued to prevent their removal. In 2018, the Quebec Superior Court struck down provisions of Kahnawà:ke law that required residents to move and suspended other membership rights. The council determined not to appeal the ruling. Note that this neatly illustrates the point made in our note 8. You may refuse to vote or participate in government, but you must still obey the laws and judgments of the government or face often harsh consequences.

The Oka Crisis, or the Mohawk Resistance at Kanesatake, was a seventy-eight-day standoff (11 July–26 September 1990) between Mohawk protesters, Quebec police, and the Canadian Army. It took place near the town of Oka, about forty miles from downtown Montreal. The conflict was sparked by the proposed expansion of a golf course and the development of townhomes on disputed land that included a Kanyen'kehà:ka burial ground. After Corporal Marcel Lemay, a Quebec provincial police officer, was killed in gunfire as the police attacked protesters who had closed a bridge, tensions increased as thousands joined the protest. The army was called in, and the protest ended. The golf course expansion was canceled, and the land was purchased by the Canadian government. However, there has since been legal transfer of the land to the Mohawks of Kanesatake. During and before the crisis, Canadian politicians and media personalities made profoundly racist comments including suggesting murdering the protesters. The radio host Simon Bédard said: "You go in there with the army, and you clean it all up. Fifty deaths, 100 deaths, 125 deaths, it's done. We can put that behind us and go on." The statement returned to haunt him in 2008 when he was forced to resign as a political candidate after these comments were aired (CBC 2008). Note that this was years before Simpson wrote this essay and indicates that by 2008 it had become much less acceptable to say such things. But, of course, that doesn't mean that people didn't think them.

Simpson writes that she won't be taken seriously because she was not discussing "kinship charts, ceremony, ritual cycles or Mohawk verb structure." However, Simpson's topic in this essay is within the mainstream of Native American and Indigenous studies. She rightly points out that topics like kinship charts were areas of concern in classic ethnography. But they haven't been much written about in the last fifty years. *American Indian Quarterly* is a core journal in Native American studies. In 2017, the year Simpson's article appeared, they published almost no essays on any of the classic topics Simpson mentions. Instead, they published essays on tribal sovereignty (Precht 2017), racism and aboriginal protest in Canada (Rutherford 2017),

How then to describe or theorise that which is cognisant of its own space of articulation? How to write about matters when one is deeply aware of the history that governs apprehension? This was the rub and the challenge and this was also a way of listening and anticipating that opened up a theoretical possibility for imagining and writing the political ethnographically. But also, differently.[p] Here was a writing strategy and an analytic that stood outside of the repetitive stance of "resistance" that, again and again, over-inscribed the state with its power to determine what mattered,[q] for thinking beyond what counted through the channel of "recognition,"[r] and moved away from while pointing to the over-determined effective capacity of the state. This was the "hard no"—the refusal that operated ethnographically in time with those whose lives and actions determined the argument.[11]

The people I worked with and belong to know all of this. The condition of Indigeneity globally is, partially, to know this, because to be Indigenous is to be structured into this position of scarcity, of defence of your attachment to land and country and water, as well as the politics and so-called metaphysics—the liveliness of those places—to live the understanding of that loss or defence against further loss. So, in fact, more than the cost of a fair ethnographic and interpretive reading is at risk. Indigenous peoples are grappling with the fiction of justice and its comingling with recognition while pushing for justice and its comingling with the failures of recognition, so I also could not let the work that I did harm us. I had to think very longitudinally about this. Struggles by and for land, for rights, for gender justice are central in Indigenous North America. And with that comes the promise of reparative or transitional justice through the impossible but therapeutic fallacy of "reconciliation," as a key mode of recognition politics. This is the political language game and largely state-driven performance art that attempts to move elements of history forward in order to "move on" from the past, to transition out of one period of history into another, better one. This dramaturgical solution appears as macro (and philosophical) antidote to the so-called problems of the past—"historical injustice," the error of bad moral judgement and action, before. And yet, of course, these grounded issues of land loss and legal exclusions fan out to and from the global. This is not particular to Kahnawà:ke, to Haudenosaunee peoples, and can be found in Indigenous ethnography and cultural criticism elsewhere.[s, 12]

BEEN CAUGHT STEALING[t]

Let us now talk about the "elsewhere." In her book, *The White Possessive*, Aileen Moreton-Robinson revisits the famous, interpretive debate between anthropologists Gananath Obeyesekere (1992) and Marshall Sahlins (1995).[u] Here, the concern was the right way to think about the death of Captain Cook in 1779 in Kealakekua Bay in Hawai'i, and specifically

the experience of Native American elected officials (Schroedel and Aslanian 2017), Indigenous collectives (Warrior 2017), and other similar topics.

11. Simpson here makes a critical differentiation between resistance and refusal. She argues that the idea of resistance gives too much power to the hegemony of the state. Refusal proposes independence from state action and the pursuit of a separate course, regardless of the state. Refusal might also suggest an all-or-none stance concerning relations with the state. Resistance might be more a question of degree. We should note that refusal, and sometimes even resistance, is only possible to the degree that the state, which controls overwhelming wealth and power, permits it. Refusal or resistance in the face of absolutist state power tends to lead to death or imprisonment. Both liberal and autocratic states use these tools, but liberal states are far more likely to allow a greater range of refusal or resistance than autocratic ones. For example, the price of resistance or refusal in fascist or Stalinist states was usually imprisonment and death.

12. Dramaturgy is the study of the composition and presentation of drama for the theater. Simpson is saying that settler culture offers a performance of recognition and reconciliation as a solution to the political and social issues of Indigenous peoples. She says that her subjects reject this performance.

the eighteenth-century interpretation of his death by the Indigenous people of that place, the Kanaka Maoli: was he a god, was he an invader? Was he sacrificed, was he murdered? How did "the natives think" about him?[v]

This was a tired exchange that met in questions of structure, not historical harm or justice. "How the anthropologists think" was more an exercise in choosing the "right way" or the correct way to think about order and interpretation. The Geonpul cultural critic and theorist Moreton-Robinson revisits this question of interpretation with recourse to those that saw Cook and their stories of his arrival on another Indigenous coast and in another land. Her presentation and analysis of the narratives offer a gorgeous triangulation between accounts and a variance in interpretation. She centres the Bubu Gujin elder Hobbles Danaiyairi's version of Cook (as told to Deborah Bird Rose) within structure, but the structure of theft and all that it entailed: violence, killing (what Danaiyairi called "cleaning the country") and erecting "buildings."[w] Here, he stated:

I know you been stealing country belong to mefellow. Australia. What we call Australia, that's for Aboriginal people. But him been take it away. You been take the land, you been take the mineral, take the gold, everything. Take it up this Big England.[x]

Suddenly, "how Natives think" is not a presumptive claim of interpretive ownership; it is a statement of theft, in raw form.[13]

"You been take the land, you been take the mineral, take the gold, everything." What does one do with this sort of knowledge? Here, I am not even interested in the motivations of the perpetrators, who work for and are of "Big England," nor the anthropological exchange itself, but with the suppositional exercise in the ways in which that statement of fact must have moved though Bubu Gujin' consciousness and informed action. Let us think about that. Bird Rose calls the stories of Cook a "saga" that explained and sorted the past and also accounted crucially for (settler) law, for its contingency, its randomness and its cruelty.[y] Hobbles Danairayi argues:

We the one boss for the land. Because I know. You been coverem up me gotem big swag [concealing the people and the truth]. Government been coverem up me. Coverm over. That's why he been pinch it away, that land. Because we know you mob now . . . You'll have to agree with us, agree with the people, people on the land. You gonna agree because Aboriginal owning.[z]

Everything is achieved in this statement: an Indigenous indictment of theft, a command for justice, an invocation of the facticity and un-deniability of it all. He claims ownership of territory, he marks theft, he points to takeover of that territory and twins it with the durability of white sociality. The ascent of the settler state is marked ("we know you mob now"), as if to say, "we know you are a thing now." These are the facts, these our undeniable facts, let them stand next to the mytho-production of a settler state—"we know" you are for Big England.[aa] Hobbles Danaiyari knows that these people were and still are descended from foreigners. This is settler time now, they own time, they determine official history. And yet, there is still a "we" from the land that was taken, wrongfully, that can know of these machinations. There is no disappearance there; in fact, there is a con-

---

13. We have mentioned the 1990s debate between Gananath Obeyesekere (b. 1930) and Marshal Sahlins (1930–2021) in Wolf, essay 31, note 26. It was an important moment in the anthropology of the 1990s. Aileen Moreton-Robinson (b. 1956) is a Australian sociologist and a member of the Goenpul people, an Australian Indigenous group whose historical lands were near Brisbane. Deborah Bird-Rose (1946–2018) was an ethnographer who worked with Australian Aboriginal people and was particularly interested in history and colonialism. Hobbles Danaiyairi (1925–1988) was a community leader, lawman, and political activist of the Mudburra people, Aboriginal Australians of the Northern Territory. Bird-Rose considered Danaiyairi a mentor. The quote here comes from a 1982 interview with him.

As Simpson notes below, Danaiyairi, in conversations with Bird Rose, does not talk about the historic Captain Cook but rather uses Cook to represent a "range of Europeans" and the laws and policies they have made.

versation among them about this new mob. As if to cut through any sense of either indigenous disappearance or consent to this all, he ends with the staggering empirical demand: "You gonna agree because Aboriginal owning."[14]

This is as if to say here: "only an unreasonable, possibly not smart person could deny this common-sense facticity." And yet . . . here we are again. This is what he is left with, as there is a need to tell this story of Cook, as well as the ambushes, the violence, the other stories of his territory. There is the temporality of disavowal, where he has to explain these matters, probably over and over again. This is no way a reflection on Bird Rose, or to assign her a space of ignorance; clearly, she was ahead of many curves and thankfully so. We are better for her fantastic archive of conversations with him on the landscape and history of his place. But one must ask following this brief discussion of his narrative, what does it then make for? What kind of activity or posture towards the state? Bird Rose's piece presented Danairayi's statement and analysis of the theft of land as an ongoing basis of Australian statehood. She assigns the person of Captain Cook, in Danairayi's analysis, to a space of consolidation, representing a "range of Europeans" who are represented in his person as well as their law. This is a law and a person that are revealed to be "greedy, violent, and unprincipled."[bb, 15]

I dwell here in Danaiyairi's history of Cook for all that it tells us and also for what it may do. Bird Rose states that the stories consolidate what Danaiyairi knows of white people, of invasion, of settlement (or in fact form his knowledge of places and events), but I am interested in them because they make a strong statement against disappearance or consent. In longer form, they archive the violence and theft of various kinds that mark the emergence of a new, relentless "mob" (settlers), including indigenous "responses" that may get glossed as "agency" but are deep instantiations of life in the face of death.[cc] Bird Rose organises these stories as evidence of two legal and moral orders (Indigenous and Settler) as well as accounts of various kinds of the past. Their commitment again to the refusal to die, to lose the truth and to roll over bears upon the larger argument here because it is this historical consciousness that animates the various armed resistances (lasting until the 1920s) that we hear about in those territories as well.[16]

Similarly, with Haudenosaunee people, the treaties as well as moments when land was lost or almost reclaimed are held on to, pointed to, acted upon, and the loss remembered, retold and reminded to form political consciousness and structure posture and action.[dd] A recent example of this from this [*sic*] would be the Haudenosaunee chief Deskaheh's attempt to

---

14. Danaiyairi's position was complex. In other places, he argued for a future based on social equality between Aboriginal people and other Australians. He said: "We're not trying to push you back to London and big England, but what's your feeling? You the one been making lot of mistake, but we can be join in, white, and black, and yellow. This a big country, and we been mix em up [people]. We're on this land now. We can be friendly, join in, be friends, mates, together" (Bird Rose 2007).

15. The idea that settlers were greedy, violent, and unprincipled is foundational to most recent academic history and anthropology. However, popular culture is another matter. As debates over education in the early 2020s have shown, a heroic and purely positive accounting of history has the support of many in the United States, and some state governments have attempted to enforce it in K–12 education. For example, in 2023, Florida public schools were instructed to teach students that some black people benefited from slavery because it taught them useful skills. Attacks on course content at universities have been less specific but, also in Florida, a 2023 law bans public universities in that state from offering general education core classes that "distort significant events," teach "identity politics," or "are based on theories that systemic racism, sexism, oppression, and privilege are inherent in the institutions of the United States and were created to maintain social, political, and economic inequities" (Planas 2023; Florida State Senate 2023).

16. Questions of agency and life in the face of death often go hand in hand. See, for example, Primo Levi (1919–1987), Viktor Frankl (1905–1997) in particular, and Holocaust literature in general.

gain recognition of the Six Nations Confederacy within the League of Nations in the 1920s. [ee] Here, his valiant, four-year effort on behalf of Haudenosaunee in Europe was based upon our sovereignty and obligations the Crown owed us as treaty signatories. Canada's aggressive assimilation policy pushed him and Haudenosaunee people to this point of refusal, but a refusal that carried with it a demand for recognition. This was a refusal of Canada within our governmental affairs, of their theft of our wampum belts and their invasion of Six Nations, [ff] of the right of Chiefs and Clan mothers to govern at Six Nations. This refusal of settler invasion and governance led us to seek international recognition as a sovereign nation-state for Haudenosaunee people. [gg] The bid for recognition as a nation-state did not succeed, and the sad and bitter death the **condoled chief**, Deskaheh (Levi General) suffered upon his return to North America, on the American side of the border, is attributed in our communities to the border itself. His wife could not cross the border from Canada to the United States to get him his (Indian) medicine where he lay dying in the home of the Tuscarora Chief Clinton Rickard because of state regulations that rendered her, a person of the Six Nations, an alien who could not enter the U.S. [17]

This fairly recent story, steeped in facticity for us, a story of refusal and recognition and of terrific political effort, demonstrates the possibility of history and of so-called failure as incitements to not only mobilise, but also maintain structures away from domination. We tried, maybe it did not work, the end was not the one we wanted, but it was an [sic] incredibly hard fought and, we know, right. "We know you are wrong, you are not honoring agreements, we refuse to play this game anymore." We refused to take more abuse and disrespect from Canada—they had dismantled the traditional government at Six Nations reserve and seized the wampum belts that encode our governance system—so we went International. What then does one do? If one knows law has been contravened (yours or theirs) and you know you stand outside of law but law tries to capture you through citizenship. Do you then consent to notions of "just law," of "just governance"? Is this possible in an ongoing context of theft's disavowal not to mention its ongoing life? While there is the lawful theft of your governance system, your land to ponder, to live through? Recall the last words I quoted from Danaiyairi: "You gonna agree because Aboriginal owning." It is just this sort of deep cognisance of differing social and historical facts that make for the posture of refusal. "Refusal" holds on to a truth, structures this truth as stance, and as the revenge of consent.

When I deploy the term "revenge" I am hailing an act of historical consciousness, of asserting this against the grain and thus, avenging the prior of wrongdoing. "Revenge" does not mean individuated harm inflicted on a perpetrator in a transaction that renders "justice." In my usage here, I mean avenging

17. Levi General (1873–1925) was a Haudenosaunee chief who was given the title Deskaheh. He was one of the most important Haudenosaunee political leaders of his era. Among other things, he traveled to London in 1921 and to Geneva in 1923 to campaign for recognition of the Haudenosaunee as an independent nation. He was a popular speaker in Europe, Canada, and the United States and a powerful spokesperson against assimilation. Though he did gain some support in his quest for Haudenosaunee recognition, particularly from delegates from Ireland, Persia, Panama, and Estonia (Catapano 2007: 228), his quest was chimerical. The league was dominated by Britain and France, and they would not permit the sort of challenge Deskaheh represented. He was never able to address the League of Nations. Deskaheh traveled with George P. Decker (1861–1935), an attorney who had a long-standing interest in Native land claims and frequently defended Indigenous clients. Decker's interest in Indigenous people in general and the Haudenosaunee in particular was inspired by his teenage reading of Lewis Henry Morgan's *The League of the Iroquois* (Koch 1992). After the failure of Deskaheh's campaign for recognition, the Canadian government, likely in reprisal for his agitation, replaced the Haudenosaunee government. Clinton Rickard (1882–1971) was a Tuscaroran chief and the founder of the Indian Defense League, which has been particularly concerned with the rights of Indigenous people to cross borders.

A **condoled chief** is one who sits on the Grand Council of the Haudenosaunee Confederacy. They are "condoled" because they are appointed at a condolence ceremony after the death of a previous chief.

a prior of injustice and pointing to its life in the present.[hh] This is the act itself of knowingly refusing the inequity of interpretive possibility, pointing to its presumptive falsity of recognition via contractual thinking. This is to revenge the wrongdoing of history and interpretation ethnographically and analytically.[18]

Here, I want to introduce the conceit of contractual thinking and practice. In making a "contract," two parties knowingly abstract themselves out of their own context to enter into an agreement.[ii] A paradigmatic example of this are "treaties." In North America, they serve as the model of the social and political contract in the "new world" and are in many cases, the foundational document of colonial recognition, the mechanism by which Indigenous peoplehood and political order as "nationhood" are first recognised and affirmed. Kevin Bruyneel has argued that treaties were so important to a kind of power-sharing that their cessation in 1871 marks "post-colonial time."[jj] Here, we should add that the temporality of "post-colonial," although used in his work in a more Fanonian sense, eludes the North American and other settler colonial cases: "they" never left, the native never disappeared,[kk] even if this is an aspiration of the "post" colonial. But nonetheless, treaties are central to contractual thinking in Native history and politics,

regardless of the fact that there was profound difference of interpretation of these treaties by Indigenous peoples and settler governments; most treaties were for land cessions, and many were signed under duress. These conditions were sometimes so forceful that had they been conditions of equal standing they probably would not have been signed in the first place, yet they represent legal forms of incontrovertible rights to land, to resources and to jurisdiction.[ll] Regardless of intent, regardless of interpretation, they represent agreement and recognition; they are forms of covenant-making that bind. And that is where consent is bound with recognition, and refusal both symptomatic of interpretive truth itself and a mechanism for other possibilities.[19]

REFUSING AN EASY ANSWER

I want to now turn briefly to another possibility, and do so with an anthropological case in order to round out these modes of refusing that I am sorting through and analysing. I will return to treaties again, further into this piece. But before I do, I want to discuss *Barrio Libre: Criminalizing States and Delinquent Refusals of the New Frontier*, by Gilberto Rosas. In this work, Rosas

---

18. "'Contractual thinking' is defined as an intersubjective understanding between the government and citizens that there exists an interdependent reciprocal relationship in which the vital interest of each side is considered ultimately inseparable from its responsibility to the other" (Pan 2008: 52).

19. The term *Fanonian* refers to the thinking of Frantz Fanon (1925–1961), a psychiatrist and political philosopher. Fanon was born on the Caribbean Island of Martinique but left when he was eighteen. He fought with the Free French in World War II and returned to France for his medical training. Fanon was a key theorist of anticolonialism. He understood colonization not only as economic exploitation but also in terms of the psychological damage it caused. In *Black Skin, White Masks* (1952), he explored the double consciousness and psychological subordination of colonized people. He wrote with deep insight about the ways the colonized internalize the understandings of the colonizers and the self-loathing that can result. *The Wretched of the Earth* (1961) became a key text of revolutionary movements. It examined and supported the role of violence in fighting colonialism and freeing colonized people from both physical and psychological oppression. Fanon wrote that violence unites the colonized and "at the individual level . . . is a cleansing force. It rids the colonized people of their inferiority complex, of their passive and despairing attitude. In emboldens them, and restores confidence" (2004: 148, Richard Philcox translation). Fanon was known for his role in the Algerian War of Independence from France (1954–1962). He led a French psychiatric hospital in Algeria starting in 1953 but soon decided he could not support the French government, even in that capacity. He joined the FLN (National Liberation Front), the organization fighting against France. He was soon expelled from Algeria but continued to represent the FLN until shortly before his death.

takes on the structuring role of neoliberalism and capitalism in the production of criminals.ᵐᵐ This is a deep ethnography of crossing the border from what is now Mexico into the United States. His interlocutors are youth who are pushed and moved through borders not of their making by forces of capital but also of their own will. They move through sewers, through filth, in passages that are dangerous and decrepit and hold nothing but uncertainty on the other side. Yet, in spite of this uncertainty and discomfort, they move, and their posture while doing so is one of non-consent as well of at times, flagrant and ostentatious cruelty in passage.ⁿⁿ They call themselves "Barrio Libre," denizens of the free neighbourhood. This is a space without constraint under conditions of "neoliberal sovereignty-making," a sovereignty-making that is incomplete, that in its commitment to free trade (and not people) can cook people in the desert.ᵒᵒ This militarisation and violent precarity of life's passage (and possible death, horrible death, body slicing death through or beyond the border) is what Rosas names neoliberal sovereignty's incomplete, but "violent affirmation."ᵖᵖ In spite of the precarity of life through the border, the youth that Rosa worked with feel freedom: deeply, linguistically and behaviourally. Their own force upon others is a manifestation of this unvanquished and internal script of refusal. Here, Rosas describes their geopolitics, their mapping and their stance:

> Barrio Libre was more than a free-floating geography, superimposed over a dominant one . . . to belong to it was an expansive, furious refusal of normativity, an enraged subversion of the respective sovereignties of the U.S. and Mexico that seeped from under the new frontier.�q�q

What of these politics? Is this an agreed-upon "resistance?" Is this "resilience," with lives and bodies contorting to withstand and accommodate the pain and structures of injustice?ʳʳ They inflict pain. They walk through shit to get to where they are going. They get arrested. They get deported. They run and climb and get killed, fleeing from officers. Their refusal to see this condition as anything other than a state of freedom is a refusal for us, as well, of the easy answer. There is nothing "easy" in the stories that Rosas tells, or in the analysis that he performs in his book, and this reflects the context and scene of the youths' articulation. They are walking through indeterminacy, through pain, refusing to die or to let go of a sense of themselves as a collective that does this sort of thing. In doing so, they inhabit a posture of profound self-determination even in conditions of danger and precarity, where a state perceives them to be criminal in their very act of movement.[20]

In the previous section, I used an example of history to think through law as it makes theft legal in another colonial context. This is the magic of settler time, and the arbitrary power of settler law, and of course law itself. But first, there are temporal and geographic differences that need to be accounted for when thinking across eighteenth-century Australia (retold in the twentieth) and twenty-first-century Mexico (as told and seen in the twenty-first). Not only are individual interlocutors and characters and knowledge systems different but the scenes of these studies are different. The matrix of two colonial projects also requires accounting—"Mexico" as an artefact of Spanish Empire and now articulated within global capital and U.S. neoliberalism, "Australia" as an independent child of British Empire, articulating as well through global, neoliberal imper-

---

20. Gilberto Rosas (b. 1968) is an anthropologist currently at the University of Illinois, Urbana-Champaign. *Barrio Libre* (2012) is an ethnographic account of the US-Mexican border at Nogales, Arizona, and Sonora. The youth Rosas describes have lives of extraordinary danger and violence. Simpson's endnote refers to a passage in which a member of the group is cut in half in a train accident. However, they are also gang members. They make money by robbing or demanding payments from undocumented immigrants trying to cross the border, or by ferrying drugs (for example, Rosas 2012: 63). Rosas says they use theft, violence, and bribery to survive. Thus, they derive their livelihoods by exploiting the border, preying on people less powerful than themselves. Although they refuse Mexican and US authority, their actions support these authorities by making the border more difficult to cross.

atives. Those are glosses on tremendously nuanced macro histories. When we scale down to the stories and lives that are told to us by Bird Rose's interlocutor Hobbles Danaiyairi and Rosas's youth, there is a ready reading for refusal of various sorts. Some of the ethnographic matter is similar in will and intent. I now turn to "law" in order to round out these cases but also to further think through the specificity of consent in settler governance and its structuring relationship to refusal.

THE RUSE OF CONSENT

Would you consent to have your land taken? Are the treaties I described earlier a model for thinking through just relations on stolen land? The trick of law in settler spaces is to pretend that this in fact was not a theft that all parties consented to this fully and that appropriation of land was in fact just. And thus, matters are settled. Recent work by Heidi Stark unmasks the conceit of this as fact with recourse to events in what is now American and Indigenous history.[ss] Stark's thesis is the following: the nascent U.S. and Canada constructed Indigenous people (mostly men) as criminal in order to mask their own criminality. They did so by actually converting treaties from Indigenous understandings of forms of relationship (often called "renewal") to contracts and land cessions. By interpreting these agreements as contracts, they set up conditions for outright war through the sanctioning of constant incursions upon Indigenous land. These incursions "rendered unlawful the moment they violated the treaties that authorized their presence across Indigenous lands."[tt] She then offers in painstaking detail accounts of the hangings and the incarcerations of predominantly indigenous men as they resisted these wrongful interpretations of treaty: everywhere from Modoc country, to Tsilhqot'in in what is now British Columbia, to Dakota territory in what is now Minnesota. Native male bodies were hanged, were shot, were incarcerated for the purposes of a land grab, but this land grab was also achieved in part by the interpretive move by the state: the move from the model of relationship to contract, with the subsequent move to inevitable contravention and the production of criminality. Stark then argues, this was the making and the masking of a "criminal empire."[uu] This "criminal empire" was driven by a desire for land and resources, achieved through the force of violence and executed and sealed through contractual thinking and law—a law that masked settler state criminality while producing Indians as criminals.[21]

I articulate Stark's account and analysis to Rosas's ethnography and also to Danaiyairi's interviews because they all point to the press of states and law as they do their work of "governing" and fail, at points, to achieve "perfect settler sovereignty," "neoliberal sovereignty" or what some might perceive as simply "governance." The practices and techniques of institutional "recognition," of bringing peoples [sic] presumed alterity into the ambit of the state through the devices of treaty, of contract, later of citizenship itself, the mechanisms of rights appear to offer fairness, protection a form of justice. All of these techniques also require concession to the authority of foreign and dispossessing political will but also serve to diminish the authority and sovereignty (even when recognised, ever so slightly), of robust Indigenous political orders. These varying accounts have demonstrated state's effort to enclose life for land and sometimes their failure at this, but

---

21. It is a well-documented fact that the United States and Canada have violated treaties made with Indigenous people. However, part of what is at stake in Simpson's description is the understanding of the word *treaty*. Stark sees treaties as descriptions of ongoing relationships rather than contractual obligations. She charges that Europeans portrayed them to Indians as ongoing relationships but then treated the treaties as contractual obligations, thus criminalizing Indian actions. But is this an accurate understanding of either European or Native actions? Some treaties are agreements made between parties that consider themselves equal actors. The Two Row Wampum Treaty of 1613 mentioned earlier might be something close to this. Others are documents in which the winners of military actions dictate terms to the vanquished (like the Treaty of Versailles imposed on Germany after World War I). Consent and negotiation are part of the first kind of treaty, but not in any meaningful sense of the second.

also in broad strokes, a kind of cunning practice of recognition and governance.[vv] In this, I mean a calculating effort to (in Lisa Ford's terms) perform territorial rationality, jurisdiction and governance by any legal and discursive means necessary,[ww] but also to (in my terms) steal while making those who you steal from, the criminal. This is the ruse of consent, they did not consent to this fully, they know this, it is the liberal move again and again to pretend as if this ruse of consent signals freedom and the free will to consent to this. It is a ruse laid bare in these electoral moments in the U.S.A, when people are starting to point to where they think "the facts" lie—where the origin stories are, and what the sturdiness of those stories is—all motivated by the specious grasp on both ethics and truth-telling by the current regime. These double moves are the conditions as well, for and of refusal.[22]

The ethnographic and historical cases here point to the multiple ways in which contractual thinking and dispossession have produced historical consciousness in indigenous people that pushes against the contained, diagnostic language of politics (or perhaps political science itself) and rendered refusal an expression of this consciousness. Refusal is a symptom, a practice, a possibility for doing things differently, for thinking beyond the recognition paradigm that is the agreed-upon "antidote" for rendering justice in deeply unequal scenes of articulation. A master and a slave are unequal. One owns the other. Seeking oneself in the gaze of another can be a fallacy of endless suffering if not in and of itself an impossibility. Will they see me as I ought to be seen? Turning away, as Coulthard has argued, and as I have argued

and demonstrated in *Mohawk Interruptus*, is a technique, is a possibility.[xx] Every possibility is not in the gaze or the minds of the master, nor is the hope of mutuality (underwritten by a hope for sincerity) something that all seek. History is also littered with those painful, disappointing, mobilising stories of so many failed attempts at justice, and also at times, refusal. Why keep trying? One might wonder. This practice of refusal, one of various sorts, revenges the conceit of easy politics, of the very notion that Indigenous peoples had all things been equal would have consented to have things taken, things stolen from them. I have charted this out in this brief thesis on refusal. Rosas' interlocutors smash these categorical imperatives, what I call the "easy answers." The people I work with refuse the eliminatory efforts of the state. They operate as nationals in a scene of wardship and dispossession. They are different from Rosas' interlocutors, but they operate from a similar and flagrantly self-assured position, utterly escaping the answer that is easy to record or to analyse. My ethnographic and analytical prerogative is to make the practice of ethnography itself a refusal in time with theirs.

ACKNOWLEDGMENTS

I am eternally grateful to Sam Balaton-Chrimes and Victoria Stead for inviting me to write this work for the Against Recognition workshop at Deakin University in 2016. It benefitted greatly from the discussion of a lively and exacting interdisciplinary group of theorists and social scientists. I am grateful as well to Carole McGranahan, Robert Nichols, Elisa

---

22. Lisa Ford is a Australian legal historian whose work focuses on "jurisdictional politics in the United States and the British empire to 1850."

When Simpson talks about refusal, the USA, and electoral politics in this paragraph, she almost certainly has in mind the notion that the "people who are starting to point to the sturdiness of stories" are liberals attacking the lies and immorality of the Trump administration. They felt unrepresented by the results of the 2016 presidential election and as a result had begun to see the 2016 election as a ruse. However, readers might consider whether claims that electoral politics are a sort of ruse to which they don't consent better characterize the current political right. They might recall Trump's October 20, 2016, preelection statement that he would not accept the election results if he lost. He argued that any outcome other than a win would indicate that the election was fraudulent. As of 2024, he continues to claim that the 2020 election was a ruse. In general, the declaration that electoral politics and the rights of citizenship are ruses designed to camouflage domination has not historically been a prelude to freedom. It's been a call to autocracy and fascism.

Lobo and Erica Weiss for reading and commenting upon an abbreviated version of this article that was published as Audra Simpson, "Consent's Revenge," *Cultural Anthropology* 31(3), 2016, pp 326–333. Audiences and seminarists at Stony Brook University, New School for Social Research, York University, New York University, University of Illinois-Chicago, Stanford University, University of Victoria and Trent University helped my thinking along, as did the really engaged conference goers at the "Crossroads in Cultural Studies" conference in 2016 in Sydney, Australia, where a version of this piece served as Keynote. The engaged and gently directive comments of one external reviewer strengthened the claims and the arc of the piece as well. Any mistakes are my own.

AUTHOR'S NOTES

a. Manu Vimalassery, "Counter Sovereignty," *J19* 2(1), 2014, pp 142–148.

b. Audra Simpson, "Whither Settler Colonialism?," *Settler Colonial Studies* 6(4), 2016, pp 438–445.

c. See Introduction (this volume) Balaton-Chrimes and Stead, p XX (12 my copy).

d. The logic of racial enslavement does extend to Indigenous peoples as well, and the same may be argued for what is now Australia with regard to "station" labour provided by Aboriginal peoples. Tim Rowse, *White Power, White Flour: From Rations to Citizenship in Central Australia*, Cambridge: Cambridge University Press, 2002.

e. For a nuanced account of the history of dispossession and dispossessive thought (as "recursive practice") in political theory, please see Robert Nichols, "Theft Is Property! The Recursive Logic of Dispossession," *Political Theory*, 2017, pp 1–26.

f. Audra Simpson, *Mohawk Interruptus: Political Life Across the Borders of Settler States*, Durham, NC: Duke University Press, 2014; Simpson, "Whither Settler Colonialism?"

g. Simpson, *Mohawk Interruptus*.

h. "People of Kahnawà:ke."

i. For exposition on this key definitional point on settler colonialism (contra other colonialisms), namely the need for the elimination of Indigenous people in order to secure their land, see Patrick Wolfe, "Settler Colonialism and the Elimination of the Native," *Journal of Genocide Research* 8(4), 2006, pp 387–409.

j. There is a related literature in political theory that pronounces and theorises this position; see Andrew Lamas, Todd Wilson and Peter N Funke (eds), *The Great Refusal: Herbert Marcuse and Contempo-rary Social Movements*, Philadelphia: Temple University Press, 2016. Also relevant is a Western anarchist tradition of negative solidarities of refusal. See, for example, this summary and analysis from Julius Gavroche in the online anarchist blog "Autonomies" vis-à-vis the "occupy movement," https://autonomies.org/pt/2015/07/the-refusal-of-sovereignty-an-anarchist-reading-of-occupy-movements. An older, American iteration of "refusal" is articulated in Herman Melville, "Bartleby, the Scrivener. A Story of Wall street," *Putnam's Monthly* II(XI), 1853, pp 546–557; Concluded II(XII), pp 609–615. My thanks to Joshua Moses for bringing the Bartelby piece to my attention and Banu Bargu for pressing me on anarchist traditions of theorising a cognate form of opposition to force.

k. For a specific account of this issue from Kahnawa'kehró:non, see "Mohawks are Getting Tired of Explaining to Cashiers Why they Don't pay the QST" [Quebec Sales Tax Exemption]. https://montrealga zette.com/news/mohawks-are-getting-tired-of-explain ing-to-cashiers-why-they-dont-have-to-pay-qst.

l. See the legal case of Warren Green's opposition to conscription in the Second World War discussed in Paul C Rosier, *Serving their Country: American Indian Politics and Patriotism in the 20th Century*, Cambridge: Harvard University Press, 2009, p 95. Green did not on principle object to military service; he objected in principle to Haudenosaunee people being treated as American citizens rather than "imperium imperio" a nation within a nation. He agreed to act as a test case for the Haudenosaunee and lost the case. The ruling came down in November 1941.

m. Kevin Bruyneel, *The Third Space of Sovereignty: The Postcolonial Politics of U.S.-Indigenous Relations*, Minneapolis: University of Minnesota Press, 2007. See also Lorenzo Veracini, *The Settler Colonial Present*, Houndmills: Palgrave Macmillan, 2015.

n. As a member nation in the (six-nation) Iroquois Confederacy, Mohawks have entered into treaties with other first nations, with the Dutch, the British and the French. Among the most popular and referenced is the Kahswentha or "Two-Row" wampum treaty with the Dutch. This treaty images non-invasive but coexisting political orders that share space. Imaged as two discrete vessels sailing along side of each other on a shared sea of purple wampum, the "Two Row" is on a belt woven from wampum. Wampum are quahog shells rendered into beads that were woven into a narrative and were used to render these belts as either "mnemonic devices" or texts for knowledge retention and reminder in communities or [sic?] treaties and agreements. The "Two Row" wampum treaty is one of the earliest that Haudenosaunee have entered in with settlers and one of the most violated. It is still held up as a model of just relations, however, between native and non-native people for its acknowledgement of shared territory and commitment to stay on separate courses in shared territory.

o. "Haudenosaunee" is "people of the Longhouse" (people who build a house, Mohawk). This was heard and translated into French and popularised through time as "Iroquois." Haudenosaunee or Iroquois refers to the confederation of six nations (Tuscarora, Seneca, Cayuga, Onondaga, Oneida, Mohawk). Kahnawà:ke Mohawks are of the easternmost nation, whose role was and is imagined as "Keepers of the Eastern Door" of the metaphoric and geographical Longhouse that extended across what is now the Northeastern United States

p. Audra Simpson, "On Ethnographic Refusal: Indigeneity, 'Voice' and Colonial Citizenship," *Junctures: The Journal for Thematic Dialogue* 9, 2007, pp 67–80. The article was heavily revised and is currently the fourth chapter of Simpson, *Mohawk Interruptus.*

q. Lila Abu-Lughod, "The Romance of Resistance: Tracing Transformations of Power Through Bedouin Women," *American Ethnologist* 17(1), 1990, pp 41–55.

r. Glen Coulthard, *Red Skin, White Masks: Rejecting the Colonial Politics of Recognition*, Minneapolis: University of Minnesota Press, 2014; Elizabeth A Povinelli, *The Cunning of Recognition: Indigenous Alterities and Australian Multiculturalism*, Durham, NC: Duke University Press, 2002; Simpson, Mohawk Interruptus.

s. For an ethnographic account and analysis of Six Nations' 2007 reclamation of land titled to them, and taken from them, after the American Revolution in what is now Ontario, Canada, see Theresa McCarthy, *In Divided Unity: Haudenosaunee Reclamation at Grand River*, Albuquerque: University of Arizona Press, 2016.

t. This is a nod to the Jane's Addiction song written by Perry Farrell and Eric Avery by the same name (1990). It first appeared on their album *Ritual de lo Habitual* (Warner Brothers).

u. Aileen Moreton-Robinson, *The White Possessive: Property, Power and Indigenous Sovereignty*, Minneapolis: University of Minnesota Press, 2014; Gananath Obeyesekere, *The Apotheosis of Captain Cook: European Mythmaking in the Pacific*, Princeton, NJ: Princeton University Press, 1992; Marshall Sahlins, *How "Natives" Think: About Captain Cook, For Example*, Chicago, IL: University of Chicago Press. 1995.

v. Sahlins, *How "Natives" Think.*

w. The context of the sentences in which "buildings" occurs suggests these mean sturdy dwellings or perhaps settlements, for example: "[Cook] . . . he's got a big building now up in Darwin, up in Katherine. He starting building up now. And my people here, they don't got a building. 'Nother people and 'nother people still wondering about for land." Quoted in Deborah Bird Rose, "The Saga of Captain Cook: Morality in Aboriginal and European Law," *Australian Aboriginal Studies* 2, 1984, p 34.

x. Moreton-Robinson, *The White Possessive*, p 117. See Bird Rose, "The Saga of Capitan Cook" for the longer account from which Moreton-Robinson quotes.

y. Rose, "The Saga of Captain Cook."

z. In Rose, "The Saga of Captain Cook," p 34 (emphasis mine).

aa. See also Lisa Ford, *Settler Sovereignty: Jurisdiction and Indigenous People in America and Australia 1786–1836*, Cambridge: Harvard University Press, 2010. Ford's comparative history of the legal production of this mytho-discursive form of "perfect settler sovereignty" in Georgia and New South Wales in the late eighteenth and early nineteenth century reads well alongside Vimalassery, "Counter-Sovereignty."

bb. Rose, "The Saga of Captain Cook," p 34.

cc. The violence or possibility and record of death is not one-sided. For an account of the centrality of violence in what is now the American southwest for multiple First Nations, Spanish and Anglo settlers in the eighteenth and nineteenth century, see Ned Blackhawk, *Violence Over the Land: Indians and Empires in the Early American West*, Cambridge: Harvard University Press, 2006.

dd. Carole McGranahan, "Refusal and the Gift of Citizenship," *Cultural Anthropology* 31(3), 2006, pp 334–341; Elisa J Sobo, "Theorizing (Vaccine) Refusal: Through the Looking Glass," *Cultural Anthropology* 31(3), 2016, pp 351–358.

ee. "Deskaheh" is his title. His name was Levi General.

ff. See note xxii for exposition of "wampum" and "wampum belts."

gg. Rick Monture, *We Share Our Matters: Two Centuries of Writing and Resistance at Six Nations of the Grand River*, Winnipeg: University of Manitoba Press, 2014, pp 107–140; Simpson, *Mohawk Interruptus*, pp 135–137.

hh. Thanks to Elisa Sobo for pushing me on this.

ii. I am deeply indebted to both Robert Nichols and Sherene Razack for their thinking on the coloniality of the contract. I am taking it in a different direction here, but their work has led me to this point. See Robert Nichols, "Indigeneity and the Social Contract Today," *Philosophy & Social Criticism* 39(2), 2013, pp 165–186; Robert Nichols, "Contract and Usurpation," in Audra Simpson and Andrea Smith (eds), *Theorizing Native Studies*, Durham, NC: Duke University Press, 2014, pp 99–121; Sherene Razack, "The Murder of Pamela George," in Sherene Razack (ed.), *Race, Space and the Law: Unmapping a White Settler Society*, Toronto: Between the Lines Press, 2002, pp 121–147.

jj. Bruyneel, *The Third Space of Sovereignty.*

kk. My disagreement with this temporalisation is indebted to Wolfe "Settler Colonialism and the Elimination of the Native," and more fully explicated in regard to Canadian settler colonialism in Simpson, *Mohawk Interruptus.*

ll. James Daschuk, *Clearing the Plains: Disease, Politics of Starvation and the Loss of Aboriginal Life*, Regina: University of Regina Press, 2013; Robert Innes, *Elder Brother and the Law of the People: Contemporary Kinship and Cowessess First Nation*, Winnipeg: University of Manitoba Press, 2013; Scott Lyons, *X Marks: Native Signatures of Assent*, Minneapolis: University of Minnesota Press, 2010.

mm. Gilberto Rosas, *Barrio Libre: Criminalizing States and Delinquent Refusals of the New Frontier*, Durham, NC: Duke University Press, 2012.

nn. Rosas, *Barrio Libre*, p 99.

oo. Rosas, *Barrio Libre*, p 100.

pp. Rosas, *Barrio Libre*, p 105.

qq. Rosas, *Barrio Libre*, p 109.

rr. For an important analysis of the production of affects of pleasurable vulnerability and "resilience" (as curatorial end-game) in discussions over a Chicago housing project museum, see Catherine Fennell, "The Museum of Resilience: Raising a Sympathetic Public in Post-Welfare Chicago," *Cultural Anthropology* 27(4), 2012, pp 641–666.

ss. Heidi Kiiwetinepinesiik Stark, "Criminal Empire: the Making of the Savage in a Lawless Land," *Theory & Event* 19(4), 2016. https://muse.jhu.edu/article/633282.

tt. Stark, "Criminal Empire," p 2.

uu. Stark, "Criminal Empire," p 2.

vv. I am hailing Elizabeth Povinelli's rendering of the term in the context of multicultural Australia, in The Cunning of Recognition, an ethnographic account of the machinations of governance where "historical wrongdoing" is the matter repair, yet because of the operations of capital, cannot be too deep. So, the logic of recognition operates in very quiet, calculating ways to make it impossible to repair too much (i.e. return land).

ww. Ford, *Settler Sovereignty*.

xx. Coulthard, *Red Skins, White Masks*; Simpson, *Mohawk Interruptus*.

41. To Protect and Serve Whiteness

Orisanmi Burton (b. 1981)

INTRODUCTION

CRITICS OF POLICING often utter the phrase, "To Protect and Serve," in order to point out the gap between discourses of ethical policing and practices of punitive policing in black communities. This refrain, deployed at some moments with irony and at others with supplication, reveals a widespread comprehension that black communities are not the subjects of police protection, but the objects of police coercion and that individuals belonging to the category of black—whether by virtue of phenotype, family history, economic status, or geographic location—are not citizens for whom the public good is extended.[a] As the title of this article makes clear, I suggest this tagline is woefully incomplete and that a more appropriate representation of the policing function is "To Protect and Serve whiteness."[1]

The present moment has presented an opening for appraisals and critiques of policing and its relationship to race. During the summer of 2014, police killings of Eric Garner and Michael Brown—both unarmed black men—stimulated widespread protests and political organization. These mobilizations were informed and inflected by the long durée of resistance against antiblack police violence (Williams 2015). Since the 1990s, the application of "order–maintenance," a pervasive policing philosophy that prioritizes low-level "quality of life" violations over violent crimes has been subjected to sustained criticism for the harm it has inflicted on black communities (Giroux 2003; Harcourt 2001; Herbert 2001; Howell 2009; Wacquant 2009b).[b] Touted by law enforcement enthusiasts as a proven method for enhancing public safety (Bratton and Knobler 2009), critics argue that order–maintenance functions as a "social cleansing strategy" for eliminating undesirable populations (Smith 2001).[2]

From *North American Dialogue* (2015)

1. The "Protect and Serve" slogan was first used by the Los Angeles Police Department in the 1950s. It was the winning entry of a contest to choose a slogan for the department. It has since been adopted by police departments across the country and it is a popular description of what the police are supposed to do. However, it is also deceptive. The courts have repeatedly found that police departments have no legal obligation to protect citizens (Cyrus 2022; Ragland 2021).

2. 2014 was an important moment in the history of race in the United States, particularly as it pertained to policing black communities. It was a time of relative peace and prosperity. The Great Recession of 2008 had ended, and most American troops had been withdrawn from Iraq and Afghanistan. However, smartphones and social media had begun to change cultures worldwide. In the United States, Apple introduced the iPhone in 2007. By 2014, 53 percent of the US population owned smartphones (Statistica 2018), and this meant that well over 150 million Americans had the ability to capture live video almost instantly. At the same time, a network of social media websites had also grown. Facebook, YouTube, and Instagram had all been founded within the past decade and by 2014 reached most American families. Police brutality against black communities was nothing new, but now it could be witnessed almost in real time. The deaths of Eric Garner (1970–2014) and Michael Brown (1996–2014) were key examples of this. Burton provides some details of these deaths later in the essay, but it will be useful to have a basic idea now.

This analysis shifts the locus of critique away from the problems of "racially discriminatory" policing practices and "excessive" police force. Although it is critically important for scholars and activists to uncover, critique, and interrupt these forms of structural and direct state violence, the conceptual differentiation between mundane and excessive acts of police abuse betrays a general incapacity to think about extrajudicial antiblack violence as imbricated in policing itself. As Martinot and Sexton (2003:172) argue, policing is a "regime of violence that operates in two registers, terror and the seduction into the fraudulent ethics of social order; a double economy of terror, structured by a ritual of incessant performance." A black person is killed by a police officer, security guard, or vigilante every 28 h (MXGM 2013), while past and present order–maintenance regimes inflict an incalculable number of non-lethal,

civil, and human rights abuses against black people every day (CCR 2012). Thus on the one hand, extrajudicial violence occurs so often that it has become a banal fact of American life. While on the other hand, the aggregate effect of order–maintenance policing is nothing short of extraordinary. The problematization of "police brutality" tacitly naturalizes the forms of psychic violence, dehumanization, and dispossession inflicted in routine and professional encounters between police and black people.[3]

This article opens with an account of a mundane instance of racialized police violence; an encounter I observed in which the officers involved performed their duties with the utmost professionalism, yet still enacted antiblack violence. Next I assert that policing in the United States is always already racialized policing. It is an enterprise centrally concerned with the protection of whiteness and the regulation of

---

On July 17, 2024, New York City police officers tried to arrest Garner, age forty-three, on suspicion of illegally selling single cigarettes. Officer Daniel Pantaleo (b. ca. 1985) placed his arm around Garner's neck and wrestled him to the ground where he was pinned by multiple officers. Garner repeatedly told officers he could not breathe before losing consciousness. Officers left Garner on the sidewalk for seven minutes waiting for an ambulance to arrive. He was pronounced dead an hour later. Pantaleo was brought before a grand jury, which refused to indict him. Garner's family sued New York City for wrongful death, eventually settling for $5.9 million (Costello 2018; Mazza 2018; Goodman 2015). A 2019 disciplinary hearing for Pantaleo led to his dismissal from the NYPD.

Michael Brown, an eighteen-year-old black teen, and his friend Dorian Johnson were walking in the middle of Canfield Drive, a two-lane street in Ferguson, Missouri, a suburb of St. Louis. They were stopped by Ferguson police officer Darren Wilson, who was driving his department-issued Chevy Tahoe SUV, and ordered them to move off the street. Exactly what happened is controversial. The basic facts are that Wilson got out of his vehicle, and he and Brown struggled. Brown ran at least 180 feet from Wilson's car but then turned and came back toward Wilson. Wilson fired a total of twelve shots, at least six of which hit Brown, who was unarmed. Brown was killed by a shot to the top of his head. The entire incident took place in under two minutes, but Brown's body lay in the street for four hours before it was removed (USDOJ 2015). A grand jury declined to indict Wilson. Brown's family sued the city for wrongful death, eventually receiving a settlement of about $1.5 million (Salter 2017; Goldgeier 2017).

Both Garner and Brown's deaths became catalysts for enduring protest movements. Through the fall of 2014, there were repeated protests in Ferguson. These were supported by numerous demonstrations and protests around the country. The Black Lives Matter movement had started earlier but galvanized around the Garner and Brown killings. Despite extraordinarily detailed investigations, the details of the Brown case remain controversial. However, ultimately exactly what happened to Brown may not have mattered much. The protests that followed his death were driven by frustrations over decades of predatory policing in Ferguson and other places.

For "long durée," which Burton uses twice in this essay, see essay 38, Das, note 21.

---

3. Naturalization of psychic violence: Naturalization is a key concept. Daniel Chandler and Rod Munday (2020) provide a useful definition. Naturalization is "the process by which culturally specific worldviews which are constructed socio-historically come to be phenomenally experienced by those within a culture as natural, normal, self-evident common sense, and are thus taken for granted as universal."

Steve Martinot (b. 1939) is a philosopher who has written extensively about race and white supremacy.

black life. I then present a genealogy of the order–maintenance approach, and of policing more broadly, through an examination of slave patrols in the US south. I argue that not only is policing an instrument of law enforcement, but that it also shapes and maintains racial meanings. I close by demonstrating that the extra-judicial killings of Eric Garner and Michael Brown, which sparked widespread unrest, occurred within a milieu of pervasive structural violence and that the intensification of political mobilization around policing, although sparked by direct acts of police violence, are in fact a generalized rejection of policing itself.[4]

A MUNDANE ACCOUNT OF RACIALIZED POLICE VIOLENCE

On a Thursday afternoon in April of 2015, my wife J and I took our 3-year-old son to play in Community Center Park, an idyllic outdoor space in Chapel Hill, North Carolina. The park features a vast expanse of open space, play equipment for children, a rose garden, a jogging path, basketball courts, a stream, hiking trails, and picnic tables situated beneath oak trees. The community center stands adjacent to

the parking lot and features public restrooms, indoor basketball courts, and a swimming pool.

On this particular day, the park was not heavily attended. I saw a man sipping from a Starbucks cup as he tracked his child on the jungle gym; a woman thumbing away on her phone while playing catch with three children; but I soon became transfixed with a teenager who was playing outside by himself. I watched as this black boy, about 16 years of age, repeatedly ran and then tumbled into summersaults. He leapt to his feet, thrusting his hands into the air. He climbed and then jumped off boulders. With each jump he executed an air kick or air punch. Upon landing these moves he confidently proclaimed, "I am the greatest," or "I'm the best in the world." I noticed that others were also looking at the boy. Their faces revealed a range of expressions—from amused to annoyed, yet the boy was undaunted. I smiled to myself, thinking about how nice it would feel to be so uninhibited. I looked down to find that my son was also staring at the boy, but on his face was a look of awe. He was clearly impressed by the boy's athleticism.

My family began to leave about 30 min later, but before heading to our car we walked over to meet the boy. He greeted us politely, introducing himself as TK. Now that we were close,

---

4. The term *structural violence* was first used by Johan Galtung (1930–2024), a Norwegian sociologist, in a 1969 essay, "Violence, Peace, and Peace Research." Galtung argued that the term *structural violence* described situations in which social structures disadvantage groups of people. Galtung wrote,

> When one husband beats his wife there is a clear case of personal violence but when one million husbands keep one million wives in ignorance there is structural violence. Correspondingly, in a society where life expectancy is twice as high in the upper class as in the lower class, violence is exercised even if there are no concrete actors one can point to directly attacking others, as when one person kills another. (1969: 171)

Scholars have studied how social structures such as sexism, racism, and homophobia have systemically disadvantaged groups of people. Structural violence also highlights the historical roots of inequality. For instance, to understand inequality in the United States, one must also consider the country's history of slavery and discrimination against immigrants. Paul Farmer (1959–2022) was an anthropologist and medical doctor who worked primarily in Haiti. Farmer and others founded Partners in Health, an international nonprofit organization that builds hospitals and promotes grassroots health care. Farmer, a MacArthur grant winner, was the author of numerous books for popular audiences that helped make *structural violence* a common term in social science and popular discourse. Farmer wrote,

> Structural violence is violence exerted systematically—that is, indirectly—by everyone who belongs to a certain social order. . . . In short, the concept of structural violence is intended to inform the study of the social machinery of oppression. Oppression is a result of many conditions, not the least of which reside in consciousness. We will therefore need to examine . . . the roles played by the erasure of historical memory . . . as enabling the conditions of structures that are both "sinful" and ostensibly "nobody's fault." (2004: 307)

I saw that TK was wearing a World Wrestling Federation belt, the kind with a giant golden crest in the center. Suddenly, his behavior made sense. TK was an aspiring wrestler who was using the park to practice his form and showmanship. He bent over and gently shook my son's little hand. Smiling, TK took off his wrestling belt and let my son hold it. Before we left, he told us that he would be the best wrestler in the world one day.

Moments later, as we made our way to the parking lot, a man emerged from the community center, dashing toward us. "I'm sorry to bother you," he said, "but did that man threaten you?"

"What?" I blurted, startled and confused by the question.

"Did he threaten you?" the man asked again. "We received a complaint that he is threatening people."

"No," J said. "We were just talking to him. He is very sweet. He is having fun and pretending to be a wrestler. Our son wanted to meet him so we brought him over to talk."

"Oh, well we had several complaints," the man said. "But sorry to bother you," he added, walking away.

J and I looked at each other and shook our heads, wordlessly acknowledging the racial subtext to this exchange. I was about to get in the car, but she thought to go back to TK in order to contact a guardian. After about 5 min of waiting by the car with our son I spotted a police car pulling into the parking lot. Knowing, without having to be told, that they had arrived for TK, I picked up my son and walked over to where he and J were standing. She was leaving a voicemail for someone. I told TK that the police were coming to talk to him and asked if it was okay if we could stand next to him. He nodded silently. Moments later, two uniformed officers crossed the parking lot, walking directly to TK. When they asked his name, TK with his head slightly bowed, responded with his full first and last name. This simple gesture of disclosing his given name as opposed to his nickname spoke volumes. It signaled that TK knew the drill so to speak. He knew the proper way to engage with state authority. Perhaps he had been coached, as I once was. The officers also appraised us, but before they could ask we told them we were his friends. Satisfied, they turned back to TK, verbally assuring him that he was not in trouble. They asked him where he lived. TK told them his street address, which was just minutes from the park.

"Is your mother at home?" an officer asked. J again interjected, telling the two officers that she left a voicemail on his mother's phone.

"Do you come out here a lot?" the officer asked TK. "Yes sir," TK said.

The officers then asked permission to walk him home. He verbally agreed. And so TK left the park, escorted by two officers, one at each side. I did not follow them. Instead, I watched as they walked away. I felt a profound mixture of anger and sadness, unable to wrap my mind around how it was possible that I could feel compelled to introduce my son to this young man, to shake his hand and speak to him, while someone else could interpret him as a threat. Once TK was beyond my view, I saw that the other park guests had been watching us. One of them, a white man, was sitting on a picnic table, smoking a cigarette, an unambiguous violation of both park rules and a city ordinance.[5]

PROTECTING WHITENESS/ POLICING BLACKNESS

The police did not threaten, or brutalize, or kill TK. But what he experienced was racialized police violence. His play was perceived as

---

5. TK's story is powerful because, in addition to being well told, it's so very mundane. Almost anyone reading this essay who has taken children to play in a public park can imagine exactly what Bunton is describing. The killing of Tamir Rice (2002–2014) was a tragic example of a similar event On November 22, 2014, Rice, a twelve-year-old black boy, was killed in Cleveland, Ohio, by Timothy Loehmann, a white police officer. Officers Loehmann and Frank Garmback were responding to a police dispatch call regarding a black male with a gun. Rice was playing with a toy gun outside a public recreation center. Loehmann shot him almost immediately upon arriving on the scene. Rice died the following day. Several months after the incident a grand jury declined to indict Loehmann, but in 2017 Loehmann was fired by the Cleveland Police Department for not revealing reports from a job with a previous police department who deemed him emotionally unstable and unfit for duty.

a threat, and for that he was questioned and expelled from a public space by state agents authorized to use lethal force. The insistent question of whether or not the officers involved acted out of conscious or unconscious anti-black bias is irrelevant because in their role as police officers they are structurally placed in opposition to blackness.

In using the terms "blackness" and "whiteness" I am not attempting to reify historically contingent categories of human difference. Nor am I seeking to reduce the actual range of racial and ethnic identities, identifications and experiences into an uncomplicated binary. Rather, I seek to enunciate two of the paradigmatic locations on the socio-historical hierarchy that structure the modern world (Fanon 1967; Reyes 2009; Smith 2012; Wilderson III 2010).[c] Drawing on scholarship in Critical Whiteness Studies (Frankenberg 1997; Harris 1993; Lipsitz 2006; Roediger 1994), I conceptualize whiteness as a structural position atop the racial order and blackness as that which must always be policed. Whiteness extols capital accumulation over all other objectives and it afflicts its proprietors with a twin condition of blindness and aphasia, inhibiting their capacity to recognize the discriminatory public policies, or name the forms of genocidal violence that make whiteness possible. And because it requires public recognition and acceptance of its norms and values, whiteness places a premium on social homogenization. Whiteness is simultaneously produced by and productive of the hegemonic structure of white supremacy—a racially ordered regime of dominance.[6]

As a mode of social life, whiteness is not exclusively tied to white bodies. To the contrary, whiteness is all-too-often desired, pursued, and even inhabited (albeit tenuously) by phenotypically non-white people. In other words, white supremacy is a multicultural project (Rodríguez 2011; Smith 2012). But whiteness always stands on tenuous ground. It requires constant maintenance amidst the unbroken tradition of black resistance and recursive political–economic crises. These disruptions produce moments like the current one, moments in which whiteness threatens to become visible as a problem.

Blackness too is constituted by particular affective, ethical and political ways of inhabiting the world (Lipsitz 2011; Vargas 2006; Vargas 2010). However, the present analysis is specifically concerned with the ways in people who inhabit black bodies become floating signifiers for threat that require policing. Judith Butler, responding to an earlier moment in which policing came under scrutiny, draws upon Fanon (1967) to theorize the fear induced by the gendered black body:

> The black body is circumscribed as dangerous, prior to any gesture, any raising of the hand, and the infantilized white reader is positioned in the scene as one who is helpless in relation to that black body, as one definitely in need of protection by his/her mother or, perhaps, the police. The fear is that some physical distance will be crossed, and the virgin sanctity of whiteness will be endangered by that proximity. The police are thus structurally placed to protect whiteness against violence, where violence is the imminent action of that black male body. (Butler 1993:18)

Thinking through TK's encounter using Butler's conceptualization, we see that TK did not need to intentionally threaten anyone. His very being was a threat. His black body became a "phobogenic object" (Fanon 1967:151) that disrupted white public space.[7]

---

6. Aphasia: the inability to understand speech. Burton is saying that the structural position of whiteness makes it impossible for people to either see the discrimination that is plainly in front of them or understand what is said to them about it. Note the subtlety of Burton's argument. He does not say all white people see the world this way. He says it is a characteristic of the structural position of whiteness, which may characterize individuals, white or not, to a greater or lesser extent.

7. Judith Butler (b. 1956) is an eminent theorist of gender. She is discussed in our introduction to "Gender" and in essay 34 by Boellstorff, note 14. Butler makes these comments in a brief essay on another incident of police violence, the Rodney King beating. Rodney King (1965–2012) was brutally beaten by Los Angeles police officers on March 3, 1991. The incident was caught on videotape by a local resident. The next year, the acquit-

Although Butler provides us with an indispensible conceptualization of the black male body as immanently threatening, black women and gender non-conforming people are also interpellated as objects of policing. Under New York's Stop and Frisk program, black women and black men are stopped by police at comparable rates (Crenshaw et al. 2015). Not only are black women routinely subjected to physical brutality and killed during police encounters, they also experience forms of physiological and psychological punishment that are distinct from those typically enacted against black men. These forms of patriarchal police violence include sexual threats and intimidation, groping and/or bodily penetration under the guise of "performing a thorough search," rapes and sexual assaults, failure to protect black women who are being assaulted, failure to attend to injuries or illnesses leading to further injury or death, and arresting or otherwise punishing black women who seek the protection of the police from an abusive intimate partner (Crenshaw et al. 2015; Law 2014; Richie 2012).

Research into the brain's limbic system has yielded a preponderance of empirical evidence showing that black bodies are seen to represent physical danger and are thus experienced as threats (Chekroud et al. 2014; Phelps et al. 2000). Additionally, the legal archive provides extensive testimonial material to this effect. Take, for example, the Grand Jury testimony of Darren Wilson, the officer with the Ferguson Police Department (FPD) who shot unarmed black teenager, Michael Brown, to death, sparking an initial wave of unrest that suddenly rendered the violence of policing and the problem of whiteness visible. Wilson's justification for killing Brown evinces what Waytz et al. (2014) call "superhumanization bias"—the attribution of supernatural, extrasensory, and/or magical capacities to phenotypically black people. Wilson narrated his fear for his life in language that imbued Brown with the capacity to expand his body mass and run through bullets:

> I shoot another round of shots. . . . At this point it looked like he was almost bulking up to run through the shots, like it was making him mad that I'm shooting at him. And the face that he had was looking [*sic*] straight through me, like I wasn't even there, I wasn't even anything in his way. (N.A. 2014:228)

Furthermore, Wilson's discursive juxtaposition of Brown's inviolable black body with his

---

tal of the officers involved sparked days of protest and rioting in Los Angeles. As in Ferguson, the disturbances were more about decades of unfair policing than the specifics of the Rodney King incident.

A "phobogenic object" is one that inspires fear simply by existing. Butler's comments refer to a famous passage in *Black Skin, White Masks*, Frantz Fanon's examination of the psychology of race. In chapter 5, Fanon explores the othering and opposition experienced by blacks in white-dominated society from an existential perspective. Fanon's entry point is comments he hears children make about him: "Look, a Negro! . . . Mama, see the Negro! I'm frightened" (1986: 112, orig. 1952). Fanon determines to laugh at this but finds himself unable. He writes,

> I could no longer laugh because I already knew that there were legends, stories, history, and above all *historicity*. . . . I was responsible at the same time for my body, for my race, for my ancestors. I subjected myself to an objective examination, I discovered my blackness, my ethnic characteristics; and I was battered down by tom-toms, cannibalism, intellectual deficiency, fetichism, racial defects, slave-ships, and above all else, above all: "Sho' good eatin'."

In other words, Fanon understands himself as colonized, as defined by the prejudice and ignorance of unavoidable white others even though he also experiences himself as a sophisticated, highly educated professional who not only fought for France's survival during World War II but has dedicated his life to helping others. Fanon's experiences, refined by his reading of Jean-Paul Sartre's *Anti-Semite and Jew* (1946), lead him to existential reflections on the nature of blackness.

By the way, in the original French, the phrase that Charles Markman, Fanon's translator, renders as "Sho' good eatin'" is "Y' a bon banania." It refers to a print advertisement for a popular French breakfast drink that featured a black French soldier speaking in a cliché accent. Advertisements featuring "Y'a bon" ran from the early twentieth century through the 1960s.

For more on Fanon, see Simpson, essay 40, note 22.

own defenseless, almost phantasmal whiteness typifies the dialectics of the racial myth: white virtue requires black threat. As Fine and Ruglis (2009:21) note, "the strategic production of whiteness as security, innocence, and merit teeters dangerously and precariously upon the exclusion and containment of black and Brown bodies." In Wilson's account, Brown was not unarmed. His body was a lethal object. It was driving the action, shaping the terms of the encounter, and compelling the inevitability of its own annihilation. Wilson was merely reacting to the situation:

> He had started to lean forward . . . like he was going to just tackle me, just go right through me . . . I saw the last [bullet] go into him. And then when it went into him, the demeanor on his face went blank, the aggression was gone, it was gone, I mean, I knew he stopped, the threat was stopped." (N.A. 2014:229)

A GENEALOGY OF "ORDER-MAINTENANCE" POLICING IN NORTH AMERICA

During the past 30 years, "order–maintenance policing," alternatively known as "broken windows policing," has imparted the veneer of scientific legitimacy to the antiblack policing function by couching the social liquidation of undesirable populations in the vernacular of public safety. First conceptualized in 1982 by conservative intellectuals James Q. Wilson and George L. Kelling, the order–maintenance approach asserts that public disorder and violent crime are "inextricably linked, in a kind of developmental sequence" (Wilson and Kelling 1982:3). Wilson and Kelling argue that policing undesirable acts such as public urination, public drunkenness, and vagrancy, as well as the undesirable people who perpetrate these acts, will deter "serious crime."[d] Although both

of these foundational premises have been thoroughly disputed (Harcourt 2001; Rosenfeld 2002; Taylor 2001), order–maintenance policing has ascended to the level of law enforcement common sense (Wacquant 2009a).[8]

Order–maintenance policing is nothing new. Indeed in their elaboration of the concept, Wilson and Kelling pine for a return to the style of policing prevalent "during the earliest days of the nation" in which night watchmen "[maintained] order against the chief threats to order—fire, wild animals, and disreputable behavior" (Wilson and Kelling 1982:2). But here the duo neglects to unambiguously reference another chief threat to order: the nation's enslaved black population. Following Bass (2001), Hadden (2001), Reichel (1988), and Williams (2007), I argue that in order to understand policing and the order–maintenance imperative as foundationally antiblack we must account for the evolution of modern policing through southern slave patrols. As we will see, policing and the order–maintenance imperative developed in the slave holding states out of the need to curtail black mobility, punish minor affronts to white supremacy, and guard against the ever-present threat of black insurrection.

In the early 1700s, planters in South Carolina found themselves outnumbered by a ballooning slave population and vulnerable to organized slave revolt. Inspired by the Barbados Slave Act of 1661, which established the legal basis for classifying slaves as chattel property, Carolina planters passed a 1704 law creating the first slave patrol (Hadden 2001). These patrols were organized groups of armed white men who roamed the territory, policing and surveilling the black population—enslaved and free alike. According to the law, patrolling was intended "to prevent such insurrections and mischief as from the great number of slaves we have reason to suspect may happen when the greater part of the inhabitants are drawn together" (Henry

---

8. James Q. Wilson (1931–2012) was a leading political scientist, presidential advisor during the Reagan administration, and textbook coauthor. He was an advocate for the "war on drugs." George L. Kelling (1935–2019) was a criminologist at Rutgers and Harvard. Wilson and Kelling's "broken windows theory" was particularly influential in New York City in the 1990s where it was adopted by Police Commissioner William Bratton (b. 1947) and then Mayor Rudy Giuliani (b. 1944).

1914:31). As they searched homes, checked "papers," dispersed gatherings, apprehended fugitives, and meted out corporal punishment for non-compliance, patrollers sought to occlude the possibility of black private space and black resistance. Black spaces and black bodies were to remain visible, yet isolated and exploitable by a white policing public:

> The duties of this patrol were to visit each plantation in its beat at least once per month, chastising any slave found absenting himself from home without a pass, administering twenty lashes as a maximum; to search the negro dwellings, confiscating any firearms that might be in the home or any goods that they might have good reason to believe have been stolen; to enter any tippling house or any other house whatever, where any one of them might have seen a slave enter. Any fowls or provisions found in the hands of any negro who is away from home without a ticket might be appropriated to the patrolman's own use. (Henry 1914:33)

The policing powers of slave patrols developed gradually, through an accretion of laws that responded to shifting social, political and economic conditions and an unbroken tradition of black resistance (Genovese 1992). Following the lead of South Carolina, patrols formed in North Carolina, Georgia, Virginia, and throughout the southern colonies. A law passed in Virginia in 1705 granted citizens of the commonwealth the right to "kill or destroy" runaway slaves without fear of legal reprisal (Reichel 1988:57). The Fugitive Slave Law of 1793 empowered slave owners to "seize and arrest" fugitive slaves from across states lines, expanding the geography of policing powers in North America.

Initially, free white men, mostly of meager social standing, were conscripted from militias and legally compelled to participate in the patrol system, but by 1734 slave patrols were populated by a broad range of southern white society. They also began receiving remuneration for patrolling, an important step in the long durée of police professionalization (Hadden 2001). The policing of slaves was a powerful symbolic force in the constitution of racial meanings. It signaled to whites that, whether or not they profited directly from slavery, the defense of white supremacy and the regulation of black mobility was their civic obligation. Whiteness, and white masculinity in particular, became tied to the capacity to control and enact violence upon black bodies. The Fugitive Slave Act of 1850 helped to formalize this relation by penalizing whites that failed to capture and return escaped slaves.[9]

Following the conclusion of the Civil War, the passage of the 13th amendment abolished de jure chattel slavery but legally *preserved* the master/slave relationship under a new logic of racial criminalization (James 2005). But even partial abolition, along with the passage of the 14th amendment, placed the "intelligibility and collectivity of whiteness" in crisis (Omi and Winant 2014:76). The beleaguered structure of white supremacy required new forms of antiblack violence in order to sustain itself. As Hadden (2001) notes, the duty of meting out this violence shifted from slave patrollers to Klansmen and policemen.

With the passage of the Black Codes during the post-reconstruction period, "crime" became a cipher for blackness. In what was perhaps a precursor to modern order–maintenance policing, officers were tasked with enforcing newly emerging laws against mundane acts of vagrancy, unemployment, loitering, and public

---

9. The fugitive slave laws and acts of 1793 and 1850 made it legal for owners and their agents to pursue slaves who escaped to free states. There were critical differences between the 1793 law and the 1850 act. The 1793 law made the kidnapping and return of escaped slaves legal. However, the 1850 law, engineered by US senators Daniel Webster (1782–1852) of Massachusetts and Henry Clay (1777–1852) of Kentucky as part of a compromise that brought California into the Union, committed the federal government to an active role in supporting the kidnapping and return of escaped slaves and enacted heavy penalties for anyone who interfered with the process. The 1850 law sowed deep hardship and fear not only among escaped slaves but also among free blacks who were also exposed to kidnapping and sale into slavery. Outrages committed in enforcing the act also helped galvanize northern opposition to slavery.

drunkenness. These laws were enforced almost exclusively against blacks (Davis 1998). Once ensnared in the criminal justice system, black prison–slaves were leased to individuals and corporations. They were also exploited directly by state governments and once again forced to labor on plantations, in mines, and on chain gangs (Blackmon 2009). As Du Bois (1999:698) notes, "in no part of the modern world has there been so open and conscious a traffic in crime for deliberate social degradation and private profit as in the South since slavery." This legally codified system of racial criminalization, which ensnared roughly 800,000 black men and women between 1865 and 1942 (Blackmon 2009), could not have functioned without hypervigilant, antiblack policing.[10]

Antiblack policing was not solely a southern phenomenon. In the US north during the 19th century, bars and clubs that were reputed to encourage race mixture became frequent sites of white riots and mass (black) arrests (Roediger 1991:103). During the opening decades of the 20th century, police violence often took the form of selective enforcement. Communities of European immigrants, many of questionable whiteness, enacted organized violence against black migrants seeking to settle in northern urban centers. Riots, bombings, murders, and

intimidation were pervasive, in part because in many cases, the police openly supported these acts and neglected to arrest the assailants (Massey 1993; Sugrue 2014).[11]

In his book *The Condemnation of Blackness*, Khalil Gibran Muhammad (2010:227) argues that early 20th century "vice districts"—spaces where drugs, alcohol, and prostitution were permitted—formed in northern black ghettos with the "active support of politicians and police officers." Selective police enforcement helped to forge the enduring link between spaces of criminality and immorality and black spaces. Muhammad also demonstrates that in the 1930s, the emergence of crime statistics and the FBI's Uniform Crime Reports lent scientific credence to the already pervasive notion that blacks were an innately criminal population. The circulation of this narrative as science was enabled by crime "experts," who presented this overrepresentation of blacks in the crime reporting tables as empirical evidence of disproportionate criminality, foreclosing the possibility that the figures reflected racially discriminatory policing.[12]

As Dylan Rodríguez (2012:105) notes, "the diverse and complex practices of police violence are not only inseparable from the institutional evolution of policing in the last half century,

---

10. Convict leasing began in the Southern states before the Civil War and continued in various forms until it was abolished by the federal government in 1941. In convict leasing, mostly black men, arrested for mostly trivial offenses, worked under brutal conditions for plantation and factory owners. The wages they earned went almost entirely to the states that imprisoned them. Men caught in this system suffered physical tortures and depredations and lived under conditions that were often as harsh or harsher than those of slavery, though prison sentences did end and bondage was not hereditary (Smith 2021).

11. In the first decades of the twentieth century, white mobs repeatedly rioted against black people and property, killing hundreds. The best known of these riots was the destruction of "Black Wall Street" in Tulsa, Oklahoma, in 1921, but it was far from the only example. Others that happened between 1917 and 1927 include East St. Louis, Illinois; Chester, Pennsylvania; Lexington, Kentucky; Ocoee, Florida; Little Rock, Arkansas; and Poughkeepsie, New York. In all these cases, police provided little protection to black people or property and in some cases sided openly with the white rioters (Hochschild 2022).

12. Khalil Gibran Muhammad (b. 1972) is the Ford Foundation Professor of History, Race, and Public Policy at Harvard's Kennedy School of Public Policy and Government. The book Burton references here won the American Studies Association award for most outstanding book in 2011. Muhammad's work explores the complex relationship between perceptions of blackness and criminality, particularly in Philadelphia in the early twentieth century. He argues that progressive reformers rejected the social Darwinist idea that black people were biologically predisposed to criminality, instead showing that crime had social and economic sources. However, this shift from the biological to cultural resulted not only in affirming the link between criminality and blackness but giving it the force of social science, leading to aggressive and often violent policing.

they are essential to the very institutional integrity and identity of the U.S. police regime writ large."[e] History shows us that policing in North America is always already racialized policing. Its historical development has been inflected by white supremacy, here conceptualized not as a discreet historical moment, but as an ongoing regime that requires constant reformulation and maintenance. Policing performs this maintenance by monitoring and shoring up the fault lines between the deserving, innocent and presumed white "us" and the ungovernable, guilty and irredeemably black "them." In the following section, I assert that contemporary policing continues to serve this function through both "excessive" acts of violence and banal forms of daily regulation.

LINKING THE EXCESSIVE TO THE MUNDANE IN ORDER-MAINTENANCE REGIMES

Beginning in 2014, widespread political unrest emerged around the issue of antiblack police violence in the United States. These mobilizations—protests, riots, teach-ins, walk-outs, civil disobedience, writing, art, and the formation of new organizations—were most immediately sparked by two widely publicized killings of unarmed black men by police. On July 17, 2014, Eric Garner, a 43-year-old, unarmed black man was choked to death by the New York Police Department (NYPD) officer Daniel Pantaleo. A bystander-recorded video of the homicide was uploaded to YouTube, showing four NYPD officers pinning the non-resistant Garner to the ground as Pantaleo held him in a chokehold for 15 s. Before his death, Garner yells, "I can't breathe" 11 times. Less than 1 month later, on August 9, 2014, in Ferguson, Missouri, Michael Brown, an unarmed black teenager, was shot at least six times by Officer Darren Wilson. Then, in a cruel act of public

punishment, the FPD allowed Brown's lifeless body to lay in the street for 4.5 h, while residents of Ferguson watched in horror. Two separate Grand Juries would later rule that neither killing warranted criminal charges.

These two acts of policing, although brutal, were tragically mundane. In his article "Why We Won't Wait," historian Robin Kelley memorializes eight of the black women, men, and children who were killed by police "while we waited" for the Grand Jury's decision in the Wilson case. He articulates the inevitability of antiblack police killings by describing the deceased as "just a stack of dead bodies that rises every time we blink" (Kelley 2014:1). Striking a similar chord, Poet Claudia Rankine (2015) argues that the flow of daily life in America is modulated by the recurrent production of black death:

> We live in a country where Americans assimilate corpses in their daily comings and goings. Dead blacks are a part of normal life here. Dying in ship hulls, tossed into the Atlantic, hanging from trees, beaten, shot in churches, gunned down by the police or warehoused in prisons: Historically, there is no quotidian without the enslaved, chained or dead black body to gaze upon or to hear about or to position a self against.

The ritual of state-sanctioned antiblack violence remains largely unnamed by the general public. The unbroken tradition of black resistance against the violence of policing has thus far proven unable to remedy the problem of whiteness and the twin afflictions of blindness and aphasia it induces. It is instructive that in this age of "big data," in which virtually all facets of social life are collected, measured, and traded as currency, the number of killings by police is not even an official category of knowledge.[f] I ask, what could be more mundane than that for which we cannot name?[13]

What did generate widespread public indignation was the disproportionate response to the

---

13. The *Washington Post* began tracking killings by police in 2015. As of June 21, 2024, the paper had tracked 9,767 such killings. Their analysis shows that although about half of all those killed by police were white, black people were killed at more than twice the rate of whites. Police kill 2.4 white people per million of the white population per year but 6.1 per million of the black population per year. You can see the *Washington Post* database at https://www.washingtonpost.com/graphics/investigations/police-shootings-database.

protesters and rioters by law enforcement. On August 16, 2014, Missouri Governor Jay Nixon declared a State of Emergency in Ferguson. That night the FPD and the National Guard patrolled the streets of Ferguson with an array of armored vehicles and military arsenals. This indignation, rendered legible through hours of media debate, orbited around the notion of police excess. Police had "too many weapons," they were using "too much force," and it was costing taxpayers "too much money." But this critique of excessive police force naturalizes the antiblack policing function and obfuscates the ways in which the violence of policing is enacted as standard operating procedure, even when a given encounter does not immediately produce a brutalized or lifeless black body.

The killings of both Eric Garner and Michael Brown stemmed from order–maintenance approaches. Garner lived and died in Tompkinsville, a working class neighborhood inhabited primarily by people of color and recent immigrants. He was allegedly selling unlicensed cigarettes, a misdemeanor offense under New York State Law. Under the logic of order–maintenance, Garner's activity on that block was an invitation for violent crime and thus his removal from the landscape was imperative. Ironically, the police were the ones who brought violence to the situation, a predictable effect of the order–maintenance approach (Herbert 2001; Howell 2009; Parenti 1999; Smith 2001). Before Pantaleo choked him to death, the camera phone video captures Garner saying, "every time you see me, you're harassing me."[g, h] Garner was accustomed to being policed, as are millions of black, Latino, and South Asian people in New York City.

In 2011, under the order–maintenance regime of former New York City Mayor Michael Bloomberg and Police Chief Raymond Kelley, 685,724 people were stopped, questioned, and frisked by the NYPD. Eighty-four percent of them were black and Latino and 90 percent of them were totally innocent (CCR 2012). The experience of being targeted by police, often more than once, has profound psychological effects. In his Op-Ed for the *New York Times*, Nicholas Peart, a Harlem resident who is young, black, and male describes what it's like to live under an order–maintenance regime. After being stopped, frisked, and threatened three times between 2006 and 2010, Peart writes:

> After the third incident I worried when police cars drove by; I was afraid I would be stopped and searched or that something worse would happen. I dress better if I go downtown. I don't hang out with friends outside my neighbor-hood in Harlem as much as I used to. Essentially, I incorporated into my daily life the sense that I might find myself up against a wall or on the ground with an officer's gun at my head.[i]

During one encounter with the NYPD, Peart was accosted while leaving his apartment building. Officers confiscated his keys, wallet, and cellphone. They then used his key and attempted to enter his apartment, an (illegal) act that "terrified" his 18-year-old sister, who was in the apartment at the time. The way in which Peart narrates his lack of autonomy over his body and domicile, his fear of being "out of place," and his acute awareness of his own vulnerability to premature death conveys the extent to which order–maintenance policing reenacts the practices and imperatives of slave patrolling. Although couched in colorblind language, order–maintenance criminalizes black association, occludes black private space, and confines black bodies within a milieu of pervasive state violence. "For a black man in his 20s like me," Peart continues, "it's just a fact of life in New York."[14]

---

14. 2011 was the peak year for New York's Stop and Frisk program. In 2008, the Center for Constitutional Rights (CCR) filed a class-action lawsuit against the City of New York arguing that stop and frisk policies constituted unconstitutional racial profiling. On August 12, 2013, a federal judge found in favor of the CCR, determining that New York's program was unconstitutional. Stop and Frisk actions had begun to decline before the judgment but fell dramatically afterward. By 2014, they had dropped to 45,728. The decline continued, reaching a low of 8,947 in 2021 but rising to 15,102 in 2022. In 2011, fewer than 12 percent of stops resulted in arrests or summons. In 2022, this had risen to 35 percent. However, the racial composition of those stopped

Although Michael Brown's killing was the spark that incited the first wave of political unrest in Ferguson, Missouri, the US Department of Justice "Investigation of the Ferguson Police Department"[j] found that residents of that city have been living under a racially exploitative policing regime for years. In 2013, Ferguson's municipal court issued over 9000 arrest warrants stemming from cases involving minor infractions such as parking, traffic, and housing code violations (USDOJ 2015:3). These violations were not equally distributed throughout Ferguson's population. The city is 67 percent black, yet black people account for 90 percent of citations, 85 percent of vehicle stops and 93 percent of arrests (USDOJ 2015:62). The prosaic transgression that inaugurated Brown's deadly encounter with Darren Wilson was a "Manner of Walking in Roadway" violation, an act for which 95 percent citations are issued to black people (USDOJ 2015:4).

Although FDP records do not explicitly identify race as a pretext for code enforcement, the system's race–neutral façade is undermined by the explicitly antiblack emails that circulated among FDP commanders and municipal court staff between 2008 and 2011 (USDOJ 2015). As the Ferguson Report notes, the FPD sees its black residents "less as constituents to be protected than as potential offenders and sources of revenue" (USDOJ 2015:2).[k] Thus, Ferguson's order–maintenance regime finds its prototype in the Black Codes, with the notable exception that direct wealth extraction has supplanted labor exploitation as the dominant mode of statecraft.[15]

We have seen that the cognitive and conceptual divide between police violence and the normal functioning of policing is unworkable in relation to blackness. The rolling procession of black people killed by observable acts of police aggression unfolds in concert with a repertoire of seductive antiblack policing policies, strategies, and tactics. Although couched in color-blind language, order–maintenance policing has imparted renewed legitimacy to the well-worn imperatives that animated 18th and 19th century slave patrols: the incapacitation of blackness, the fragmentation of black association, and the criminalization of black life.

CONCLUSION

After TK's expulsion from the park, I walked back across the parking lot and entered the Community Center. There, I found the staff member who initially approached us about TK. He was standing near the entrance, gazing out of the window.

"Did you call the police on that kid?" I asked.

"Yes," he replied after hesitating a few moments. "We received a complaint." I could tell that the directness of my question startled him and in that moment I became acutely aware of my own blackness, the fact that I was about 12 inches taller than this white man, and of the very real possibility that I might become the next threat that required policing. Almost out of habit, I made a conscious effort to prevent my voice and my body language from communicating the extent of the anger I felt in my gut.

"Did you even bother to talk to him first?" I continued, in a measured tone. "You ran into the parking lot to speak to my wife and I but you never even spoke to TK. You never even asked him what he was doing. Why is that?"

There was a brief pause and I could tell he was considering something carefully. In that moment, I found myself wondering whether

---

remains unchanged. In 2011, 51 percent of those stopped were black, and in 2023, 59 percent were black (NYCLU 2023). An analysis by the Brennan Center for justice showed that there was no relationship between the crime rate in New York City and Stop and Frisk policies. Crime did not rise as the number of people stopped drastically declined (Cullen and Grawert 2016).

15. The emails that Burton refers to are available from NPR and are truly vile. Two examples are a June 2011 email about a man who wanted to get "welfare" for his dogs because they are "mixed in color, unemployed, lazy, can't speak English and have no frigging clue who their Daddies are" and a November 2008 email predicting that Barack Obama would not be president very long because "what black man holds a steady job for four years" (Hernandez 2015).

or not he knew about Freddie Gray, the young man who, days earlier, had died in police custody after "making suspicious eye-contact," then running from police.[16]

"Yes, I see your point," he said finally. "But it was out of my hands, it's our policy to . . . "

"But this is a *Community Center*," I interrupted, losing my cool. "There was no reason to get the police involved!" I wanted to explain so much to him: like how often black people, and black youth in particular, are treated as threats; and about that time, when I was TK's age, that me and a friend were arrested by a mounted police for "sitting-while-black"; and about how minor police encounters routinely escalate to brutal or deadly police encounters when they involve black people. But I was resentful for needing to explain these things and I could feel my anger getting the best of me. I simply turned and walked back to the car where my family was waiting.

As the three of us drove home I thought about the anger that was still with me. I was angry with the would-be victim that was threatened by TK, but who didn't even bother to stick around and explain him or herself. I was angry at community center policy for resorting to policing as the default way to manage patron discomfort, thereby abnegating any meaningful notion of "community." I was angry for my son, because in a few years, when he ceases to be seen as innocent, he will need to become hyperaware of how others perceive him. But most of all, I was angry with myself. I should have followed TK and the officers all the way home so as to ensure that he was treated as a dignified human being and not an object. In that moment, I should have acted as if his well-being was solely my responsibility, because it was.

Following that day, my son and I frequented Community Center Park in the hopes of spotting TK. I wanted to make sure he was okay. Finally, about 2 weeks later, I saw him in roughly the same spot as when I first laid eyes on him. This time he was not jumping, or yelling, or performing air kicks, or proclaiming himself the greatest in the world, he was just sitting quietly by himself watching other kids play.[17]

ACKNOWLEDGMENTS

I am thankful to Professor Charles Price for his constant support and guidance. I am also indebted to Professor Alvaro Reyes, whose course "Racialization in the U.S. City" was a major inspiration for this work. I would also like to thank Vincent Joos, Ben Rubin, Willie J. Wright, and Nikhil Umesh for commenting on earlier drafts of this work. Finally, I would like to thank Professor Patricia J. Williams, Professor Ann Stoler, and all of the participants in the "Racial Formations and Justice" Seminar at the 2015 Institute for Critical Social Inquiry. Those lectures, conversations, and debates helped shape my thinking and approach.

REFERENCES

Bass, Sandra. 2001. "Policing Space, Policing Race: Social Control Imperatives And Police Discretionary Decisions." *Social Justice* 28(1) 156–176.

Blackmon, Douglas A. 2009. *Slavery By Another Name: The Re-Enslavement Of Black Americans From The Civil War To World War II.* New York: Anchor.

Bratton, William, and Peter Knobler. 2009. *The Turnaround: How America's Top Cop Reversed the Crime Epidemic.* New York: Random House.

---

16. Freddie Gray (1989–2015) fled from police in Baltimore. Officers pursued and arrested him. He was found to be carrying a spring-assisted knife, which the arresting officer incorrectly claimed was illegal. Gray was transported in a police van to Baltimore's Western District Station and was unconscious on arrival. Gray died of his injuries a week later. Gray's hands and legs were bound during his transport, but he was not secured in the vehicle. Experts believe that his fatal injuries resulted from his head forcefully hitting the hard interior surfaces of the transport vehicle. The officers involved faced a variety of charges related to the case. Three of the six went to trial and were acquitted. Charges were dropped against the others (USDOJ 2017).

17. At the conclusion of this essay, Burton describes how TK has modified his public behavior to bring it in line with white expectations for black behavior in the park. The dictates of white supremacy have molded his body and shaped his behavior.

Butler, Judith. 1993. Endangered/Endangering: Schematic Racism And White Paranoia. *Reading Rodney King/Reading Urban Uprising*:15–22.

CCR. 2012. *Stop and Frisk: The Human Impact.* Center for Constitutional Rights.

CCRB (New York City Civilian Complaint Review Board). 2014. *A Mutated Rule: Lack of Enforcement In the Face of Persistent Chokehold Complaints in New York City.*

Chekroud, Adam Mourad, Jim A. C. Everett, Holly Bridge, and Miles Hewstone. 2014. A Review Of Neuroimaging Studies Of Race-Related Prejudice: Does Amygdala Response Reflect Threat? *Frontiers in Human Neuroscience* 8.

Christie, Nils. 2004. *A Suitable Amount of Crime.* New York: Psychology Press.

Crenshaw, Kimberle Williams, Andrea J. Ritchie, Rachel Anspach, and Rachel Gilmer. 2015. *SAYHERNAME: Resisting Police Violence Against Black Women.* African American Policy Forum.

Davis, Angela Y. 1998. "From The Prison Of Slavery To The Slavery Of Prison: Frederick Douglass And The Convict Lease System." In *The Angela Y. Davis Reader,* ed. Joy James, 74–95. Malden, MA: Blackwell.

Davis, Mike. 2006. *City of Quartz: Excavating the Future in Los Angeles.* New ed. London; New York: Verso.

Du Bois, W. E. B. 1999. *Black Reconstruction in America, 1860–1880.* Simon & Schuster.

Fanon, Frantz. 1967. *Black Skin, White Masks.* Berkeley: Grove Press.

Fine, Michelle, and Jessica Ruglis. 2009. "Circuits And Consequences Of Dispossession: The Racialized Realignment Of The Public Sphere For Us Youth." *Transforming Anthropology,* 17(1):20–33.

Frankenberg, Ruth. 1997. *Displacing Whiteness: Essays In Social And Cultural Criticism.* Durham, NC: Duke University Press.

Genovese, Eugene D. 1992. *From Rebellion To Revolution: Afro-American Slave Revolts In The Making Of The Modern World.* Baton Rouge: LSU Press.

Giroux, Henry A. 2003. "Zero Tolerance, Domestic Militarization, And The War Against Youth." *Social Justice,* 30(2):59–65.

Hadden, Sally E. 2001. *Slave Patrols: Law And Violence In Virginia And The Carolinas.* Vol. 138. Cambridge: Harvard University Press.

Harcourt, Bernard E. 2001. *Illusion of Order: The False Promise of Broken Windows Policing.* Cambridge: Harvard University Press.

Harris, Cheryl I. 1993. "Whiteness As Property." *Harvard Law Review,* 106(8):1707–1791.

Harvey, Thomas, John McAnnar, Michael-John Voss, Megan Conn, Sean Janda, and Sophia Keskey. 2014. *ArchCity Defenders: Municipal Courts White Paper.* St. Louis, MO: ArchCity Defenders.

Henry, Howell Meadoes. 1914. *The Police Control Of The Slave In South Carolina.* Nashville: Vanderbilt University.

Herbert, Steve. 2001. "Policing the Contemporary City: Fixing Broken Windows Or Shoring Up Neo-Liberalism?" *Theoretical Criminology,* 5(4):445–466.

Howell, K. Babe. 2009. "Broken Lives from Broken Windows: The Hidden Costs of Aggressive Order-Maintenance Policing." *New York University Review of Law & Social Change,* 33:271.

James, Joy. 2005. *The New Abolitionists: (Neo) Slave Narratives And Contemporary Prison Writings.* Albany: SUNY Press.

Kelley, Robin D.G. 2014. "Why We Won't Wait: Resisting the War Against the Black and Brown Underclass." *Counterpunch.* Vol. 2015. Petrolla: Counterpunch. https://www.counterpunch.org/2014/11/25/why-we-wont-wait.

Law, Victoria. 2014. "Against Carceral Feminism." *Jacobin.* https://www.jacobinmag.com/2014/10/against-carceral-feminism.

Lipsitz, George. 2006. *The Possessive Investment In Whiteness: How White People Profit From Identity Politics.* Philadelphia: Temple University Press.

Lipsitz, George. 2011. *How Racism Takes Place.* Philadelphia: Temple University Press.

Martinot, Steve, and Jared Sexton. 2003. "The Avant-Garde of White Supremacy." *Social Identities,* 9(2):169–181.

Massey, Douglas S. 1993. *American Apartheid: Segregation And The Making Of The Underclass.* Cambridge: Harvard University Press.

Muhammad, Khalil Gibran. 2010. *The Condemnation Of Blackness: Race, Crime, And The Making Of Modern Urban America.* Cambridge: Harvard University Press.

MXGM. 2013. *Operation Ghetto Storm: 2012 Annual Report on the Extrajudicial Killing of Black People.* Malcolm X Grassroots Movement.

N.A. 2014. Case: State of Missouri v. Darren Wilson transcript of: Grand Jury. St. Louis: Gore Perry. Omi, Michael, and Howard Winant. 2014. Racial Formation in the United States. New York: Routledge.

Parenti, Christian. 1999. *Lockdown America: Police And Prisons In The Age Of Crisis.* London; New York: Verso Books.

Phelps, Elizabeth A., Kevin J. O'Connor, William A. Cunningham, E. Sumie Funayama, J. Christopher Gatenby, John C. Gore, and Mahzarin R. Banaji. 2000. "Performance On Indirect Measures Of Race Evaluation Predicts Amygdala Activation." *Journal of Cognitive Neuroscience,* 12(5):729–738.

Rankine, Claudia. 2015. "The Condition of Black Life Is One of Mourning." *New York Times Magazine.* New York: The New York Times Company. https://www.nytimes.com/2015/06/22/magazine/the-condition-of-black-life-is-one-of-mourning.html?_r=0.

Reichel, Philip L. 1988. "Southern Slave Patrols As A Transitional Police Type." *American Journal of Police*, 7:51.

Reyes, Alvaro. 2009. "Can't Go Home Again: Sovereign Entanglements and the Black Radical Tradition in the 20th Century." Durham: Duke University.

Richie, Beth E. 2012. *Arrested Justice: Black Women, Violence, and America's Prison Nation*. New York: NYU Press.

Rodríguez, Dylan. 2011. "The Black Presidential Non-Slave: Genocide and the Present Tense of Racial Slavery." *Political Power and Social Theory*, 22:17–50.

Rodríguez, Dylan. 2012. "De-Provincialising Police Violence: On The Recent Events At UC Davis." *Race & Class*, 54(1):99–109.

Roediger, David. 1991. *The Wages of Whiteness*. Vol. 133: New York: Verso.

Roediger, David R. 1994. *Towards the Abolition of Whiteness: Essays on Race, Politics, and Working Class History*. New York: Verso.

Rosenfeld, Richard. 2002. "Crime Decline in Context." In *Contexts* 1(25): 25–34.

Smith, Andrea. 2012. "Indigeneity, Settler Colonialism, White Supremacy." In *Racial Formation in the Twenty-First Century*, ed. Daniel Martinez HoSang, Oneka LaBennett, and Laura Pulido, 66–90. Berkeley: University of California Press.

Smith, Neil. 2001. "Global Social Cleansing: Postliberal Revanchism And The Export Of Zero Tolerance." *Social Justice*, 28(3):68–74.

Sugrue, Thomas J. 2014. *The Origins Of The Urban Crisis: Race And Inequality In Postwar Detroit*. Princeton, NJ: Princeton University Press.

Taylor, Ralph B. 2001. *Breaking Away From Broken Windows: Baltimore Neighborhoods And The Nationwide Fight Against Crime, Grime, Fear, And Decline*. Boulder, CO: Westview Press.

USDOJ. 2015. *Investigation of the Ferguson Police Department*. Washington, DC: United States Department of Justice Civil Rights Division.

Vargas, João H. Costa. 2006. *Catching Hell In The City Of Angels: Life And Meanings Of Blackness In South Central Los Angeles*. Minneapolis: University of Minnesota Press.

Vargas, João H. Costa. 2010. *Never Meant to Survive: Genocide and Utopias in Black Diaspora Communities*. Lanham: Rowman & Littlefield.

Wacquant, Loïc. 2009a. *Prisons Of Poverty*. Minneapolis: University of Minnesota Press.

Wacquant, Loïc. 2009b. *Punishing The Poor: The Neoliberal Government Of Social Insecurity*. Durham: Duke University Press.

Waytz, Adam, Kelly Marie Hoffman, and Sophie Trawalter. 2014. "A Superhumanization Bias in Whites' Perceptions of Blacks." *Social Psychological and Personality Science* 6(3).

Wilderson, III, Frank B. 2010. *Red, White & Black: Cinema And The Structure Of Us Antagonisms*. Durham, NC: Duke University Press.

Williams, Bianca C. 2015. "#BlackLivesMatter: Anti-Black Racism, Police Violence, and Resistance. Fieldsights." Society for Cultural Anthropology, June 19.

Williams, Kristian. 2007. *Our Enemies In Blue: Police And Power In America*. Cambridge: South End Press.

Wilson, James Q., and George L. Kelling. 1982. "Broken Windows." *Atlantic Monthly*, 249(3):29–38.

AUTHOR'S NOTES

a. It is instructive that in 1950s, when the Los Angeles Police Department (LAPD) adopted this phrase as its official motto, LAPD Police Chief William Parker at the same time wielded the organization as a weapon in his racial crusade against "interracial vice," public housing, and a drug epidemic that was conveniently localized in black South Central and Latino East Los Angeles (Davis 2006).

b. Order–maintenance has also had devastating impacts on LGBTQ people, homeless people, youth, non-citizens, Muslim communities, and South Asian communities.

c. This article is concerned with how policing shapes relations between whiteness and blackness, but as Smith (2012), Wilderson (2010), and many others have argued, the category of native also constitutes a paradigmatic racial category.

d. I have placed this term in scare quotes because normative criminological discourse employs a very narrow state-sanctioned definition of what constitutes a crime. For a thorough critique see Christie (2004).

e. Rodriguez also suggests that a robust genealogy of racialized policing in North America should account for colonial military outfits, Texas Rangers, and white citizens militias, which targeted colonial subjects and native populations as objects of control. I would also add that in addition to slave patrolling, the institution of policing was formalized through the regulation European immigrants, particularly the Irish, in the urban US north. However, as these groups were gradually incorporated into whiteness their oppressive relationship to policing changed.

f. The US Department of Justice does not keep complete records of officer-involved shootings.

g. New York Daily News. 2015. "Original Eric Garner Fatal Arrest Video." YouTube.com.

h. Although the NYPD Patrol Guide has prohibited chokeholds since 1994, they too are routine. A 2014 report revealed that 1128 chokehold complaints have been reported since 2009 (CCRB 2014).

i. Peart, Nicholas K. 2011. "Why Is the N.Y.P.D. After Me?" The New York Times, 12/17/2011.

j. Hereafter cited as the Ferguson Report.

k. ArchCity Defender, a St. Louis-based non-profit organization, found that municipal fines and court fees were the second largest source of revenue for the City of Ferguson. See: Harvey et al. (2014).

References

Abbott, Dorothy. 1991. "Recovering Zora Neale Hurston's Work." *Frontiers: A Journal of Women's Studies* 12(1): 174–181.

Abraham, Gary A. 1992. *Max Weber and the Jewish Question*. Urbana: University of Illinois Press.

Abrahams, Roger D. 1974. "Black Talking on the Streets." In *Explorations in the Ethnography of Speaking*, edited by Richard Bauman and Joel Sherzer, 240–262. Cambridge: Cambridge University Press.

Abu-Lughod, Lila. 1991. "Writing against Culture." In *Recapturing Anthropology: Working in the Present*, edited by Richard G. Fox, 137–162. Santa Fe, NM: SAR Press.

———. 1995. "A Tale of Two Pregnancies." In *Women Writing Culture*, edited by Ruth Behar and Deborah A. Gordon, 339–349. Berkeley: University of California Press.

Adams, R. M. 1966. *The Evolution of Urban Society*. Chicago: Aldine.

Adams, Richard N. 1975. *Energy and Structure: A Theory of Social Power*. Austin: University of Texas Press.

Agamben, Giorgio. 1993. *Infancy and History: The Destruction of Experience*. London: Verso.

Agar, Michael H. 1980. *The Professional Stranger: An Informal Introduction to Ethnography*. New York: Academic Press.

Ahmed, Sarah. 2010. *The Promise of Happiness*. Durham, NC: Duke University Press.

Allen, Joe. 2020. "The Return of the 'Hamburgs'? White Vigilantes, the Chicago Police, and Anti-Fascism in Chicago." *Counterpunch*, June 14. https://www.counterpunch.org/2020/06/16/the-return-of-the-hamburgs-white-vigilantes-the-chicago-police-and-anti-fascism-in-chicago.

Allen, N. J. 2013. "Mauss, Marcel." In *Theory in Social and Cultural Anthropology: An Encyclopedia*, edited by R. Jon McGee and Richard L. Warms, 533–537. Thousand Oaks, CA: Sage.

Alterman, Anton. 2003. Review of *Wittgenstein, Rules and Institutions*, by David Bloor. *Jerusalem Philosophical Quarterly* 52 (July): 327–332.

Anderson, Carol. 2017. *White Rage: The Unspoken Truth of Our Racial Divide*. New York: Bloomsbury.

Anderson, Mark. 2014. "Ruth Benedict, Boasian Anthropology, and the Problem of the Color Line." *History and Anthropology* 25(3): 395–414.

Anonymous. 1850. *Every-day Wonder; or Facts in Physiology Which All Should Know*. London: John van Vorst.

Antonio, Robert J., and Alessandro Bonanno. 2000. "A New Global Capitalism? From 'Americanism and Fordism' to 'Americanization-Globalization.'" *American Studies* 41(2/3): 33–77.

Applebaum, Herbert, ed. 1987. *Perspectives in Cultural Anthropology*. Albany: State University of New York Press.

Ardrey, Robert. 1961. *African Genesis*. New York: Atheneum.

Arendt, Hannah. 1958. *The Human Condition*. Chicago: University of Chicago Press.

Asad, Talal. 1973. *Anthropology and the Colonial Encounter*. London: Ithaca Press.

Atkinson, J. J. 1903. *Primal Law*. London: Longmans, Green.

Axelrod, Robert. 1984. *The Evolution of Cooperation*. New York: Basic Books.

Babb, Florence. 2013. "Feminist Anthropology." In *Theory in Social and Cultural Anthropology: An Encyclopedia*, edited by R. Jon McGee and Richard L. Warms, 258–261. Thousand Oaks, CA: Sage.

Bachofen, Johann Jakob. 1992 [1861]. "Das Mutterrecht." Translated by Ralph Manheim. In *Myth, Religion and Mother Right: Selected Writings of J. J. Bachofen*. Princeton, NJ: Princeton University Press.

Baert, Patrick. 1998. *Social Theory in the Twentieth Century*. Cambridge: Polity Press.

Bakewell, Sarah. 2016. *At The Existentialist Café: Freedom, Being, and Apricot Cocktails*. New York: Other Press.

Baktin, Mickhail M. 1984. *Rabalais and His World*. Bloomington: Indiana University Press.

Balaton-Chrimes, Samantha, and Victoria Stead. 2017. "Recognition, Power and Coloniality." *Postcolonial Studies* 20(1): 1–17.

Barash, D. 1979. *The Whisperings Within*. New York: Harper & Row.

Barnes, Harry E. 1960. Foreword to *Essays in the Science of Culture in Honor of Leslie A. White*, edited by Gertrude E. Dole and Robert L. Carneiro, xi–xvi. New York: Crowell.

Barnouw, Victor. 1957. "The Amiable Side of 'Patterns of Culture.'" *American Anthropologist* 59(3): 532–536.

Barrett, Richard A. 1989. "The Paradoxical Anthropology of Leslie White." *American Anthropologist* 91(4): 986–999.

Barrett, Timothy. 2018. "Bourdieu, Hysteresis, and Shame: Spinal Cord Injury and the Gendered Habitus." *Men and Masculinities* 21(1): 35–55.

Barton, Ruth. 1998. "'Husley, Lubbock, and Half a Dozen Others': Professionals and Gentlemen in the Formation of the X Club 1851–1864." *History of Science Society* 89(3): 410–440.

Bataille, Georges. 1988–1991. *The Accursed Share: An Essay on General Economy*. New York: Zone Books.

Bateson, Gregory. 1958 [1936]. *Naven*. Palo Alto, CA: Stanford University Press.

Bateson, Gregory, and Margaret Mead. 1942. *Balinese Character: A Photographic Analysis*. New York: New York Academy of Sciences.

Bateson, M. C. 1984. *With a Daughter's Eye: A Memoir of Margaret Mead and Gregory Bateson*. New York: William Morrow.

Baudrillard, Jean. 1994. *Simulacra and Simulation*. Ann Arbor: University of Michigan Press.

Bauer, Bruno. 1974 [1841–1842]. *Kritik der Evangelischen Geschichte der Synoptiken*. New York: Hildesheim.

Beardsley, Richard K. 1976. "An Appraisal of Leslie A. White's Scholarly Influence." *American Anthropologist* 78(3): 617–620.

Beatty, Aidan. 2021. "The Two Irish Wives of Friedrich Engels." *Socialist History* 2021(60): 5–22.

Behar, Ruth. 1995. "Introduction: Out of Exile." In *Women Writing Culture*, edited by Ruth Behar and Deborah A. Gordon, 1–29. Berkeley: University of California Press.

Behar, Ruth, and Deborah A. Gordon, eds. 1995. *Women Writing Culture*. Berkeley: University of California Press.

Belk, Russell W. 1975. "Variables and Consumer Behavior." *Journal of Consumer Research* 2(3): 157–164.

Bell, V. 1993. *Interrogating Incest: Feminism, Foucault, and the Law*. London: Routledge.

Benedict, Ruth Fulton. 1930. "Psychological Types in the Cultures of the Southwest." In *Proceedings of the Twenty-Third International Congress of Americanists* [held at New York, September 17–22, 1928], 572–581. Lancaster, PA: Science Press Printing.

———. 1934a. "Anthropology and the Abnormal." *Journal of General Psychology* 10(2): 59–82.

———. 1934b. *Patterns of Culture*. Boston and New York: Houghton Mifflin.

———. 1940. *Race: Science and Politics*. New York: Modern Age Books.

———. 1946. *The Chrysanthemum and the Sword: Patterns of Japanese Culture*. Boston: Houghton Mifflin.

———. 1948. "Anthropology and the Humanities." *American Anthropologist* 50(4): 585–593.

Benedict, Ruth Fulton, and Gene Weltfish. 1943. *The Races of Mankind*. New York: Public Affairs Committee.

Benjamin, Walter. 1969 [1936]. "The Work of Art in the Age of Mechanical Reproduction." In *Illuminations*, edited by H. Arendt, 217–252. New York: Schocken.

Bennett, W. J., and M. Nagai. 1953. "The Japanese Critique of the Methodology of Benedict's Chrysanthemum and the Sword." *American Antiquity* 9:208–219.

Bentham, Jeremy. 1789. *An Introduction to the Principles of Morals and Legislation*. London: T. Payne.

Ben-Zvi, Yael. 2007. "Where Did Red Go? Lewis Henry Morgan's Evolutionary Inheritance and the US Racial Imagination." *New Centennial Review* 7(2): 201–229.

Berlin, Brent. 1973. "Folk Systematics in Relation to Biological Classification and Nomenclature." *Annual Review of Ecology and Systematics* 4:259–271.

Berlin, Brent O., Dennis Breedlove, and Peter Raven. 1973. "General Principles of Classification and Nomenclature in Folk Biology." *American Anthropologist* 75:214–242.

———. 1974. *Principles of Tzeltal Plant Classification*. New York: Academic Press.

Berlin, Brent, and Paul Kay. 1969. *Basic Color Terms: Their Universality and Evolution*. Berkeley: University of California Press.

Bermeo, Sarah, David Leblang, and Gabriela N. Alverio. 2022. "Rural Poverty, Climate Change, and Family Migration from Guatemala." Brookings Institution, April 4. https://www.brookings.edu/arti cles/rural-poverty-climate-change-and-family-migration-from-guatemala.

Bernstein, Jay H. 2002. "First Recipients of Anthropological Doctorates in the United States, 1891– 1930." *American Anthropologist* 104(2): 551–564.

Berreman, Gerald. 1972. "Race, Caste, and Other Invidious Distinctions in Social Stratification." *Race and Class* 13(4): 385–414.

Bersani, Leo, and Adam Phillips. 2008. *Intimacies*. Chicago: University of Chicago Press.

Besteman, Catherine, Karina Biondi, and Orisanmi Burton. 2018. "Authority, Confinement, Solidarity, and Dissent." PoLAR Online. https://polarjournal.org/2018/10/18/authority-confinement-solidarity -and-dissent-2.

Bertalanffy. Ludwig von. 1968. *General Systems Theory*. New York: George Braziller.

Bettelheim, Bruno. 1955. *Symbolic Wounds: Puberty Rites and the Envious Male*. London: Thames & Hudson.

Bharati, Agehananda. 1970. "The Hindu Renaissance and Its Apologetic Patterns." *Journal of Asian Studies* 29(2): 267–287.

Biletzki, Anat, and Anat Matar. 2018. "Ludwig Wittgenstein." In *Stanford Encyclopedia of Philosophy*. https://plato.stanford.edu/archives/sum2018/entries/wittgenstein.

Bird Rose, Deborah. 2007. "Hobbles Danayarri (1925–1988)." In *Australian Dictionary of Biography*, vol. 17. https://adb.anu.edu.au/biography/danayarri-hobbles-12397/text22285.

Blackburn, J. 1994. *Daisy Bates in the Desert: A Woman's Life among the Aborigines*. London: Secker and Warburg.

Blackhawk, Ned. 2008. *Violence over the Land: Indians and Empires in the Early American West*. Cambridge, MA: Harvard University Press.

Blackwood, Evelyn. 2007. "Regulation of Sexuality in Indonesian Discourse: Normative Gender, Criminal Law, and Shifting Strategies of Control." *Culture, Health & Sexuality* 9(3): 293–307.

Blaze, Alex. 2008. "I Heard That Barack Obama Fellow Is Something of a . . . Faggot." Bilerico Project. https://bilerico.lgbtqnation.com/2008/06/i_heard_that_barack_obama_fellow_is_some.php. Retrieved May 30, 2019.

Boas, Franz. 1896. "The Limitations of the Comparative Method in Anthropology." *Science*, n.s., 4:901–908.

———. 1901. "The Mind of Primitive Man." *Journal of American Folklore* 14(52): 1–11.

———. 1906. "Some Philological Aspects of Anthropological Research." *Science* 25:921–933.

———. 1911. *Handbook of American Indian Languages*. Part 1. Bureau of American Ethnology, Bulletin 40. Washington, DC: Smithsonian Institution.

———. 1912. "Changes in the Bodily Form of Descendants of Immigrants." *American Anthropologist* 14(3): 530–562.

———. 1919. "Scientists as Spies." *The Nation* 109:797.

———. 1921. "The Great Melting Pot and Its Problem," *New York Times Book Review and Magazine*, February 6: 3.

———. 1938. "An Anthropologist's Credo." *The Nation* 147(9): 201–204.

———. 1974a [1938]. "The Background of My Early Thinking." In *A Franz Boas Reader: The Shaping of American Anthropology, 1883–1911*, edited by George W. Stocking, 41–42. Chicago: University of Chicago Press.

———. 1974b. "The Principles of Ethnological Classification." In *A Franz Boas Reader: The Shaping of American Anthropology, 1883–1911*, edited by George W. Stocking, 61–67. Chicago: University of Chicago Press.

Boas, Franz, and C. Kamba Simango. 1922. "Tales and Proverbs of the Vandau of Portuguese South Africa." *Journal of American Folklore* 35(136): 151–204.

Boellstorff, Tom. 2007. *A Coincidence of Desires: Anthropology, Queer Studies, Indonesia*. Durham, NC: Duke University Press.

Bolles, A. Lynn. 1994. Review of *Decolonizing Anthropology: Moving Further toward an Anthropology for Liberation*, by Faye V. Harrison. *American Ethnologist* 21(4): 900–901.

———. 2023. "Decolonizing Anthropology." *American Ethnologist* 50(3): 519–522.

Boorstin, Daniel J. 1983. *The Discoverers*. New York: Random House.

Booth, Melinda. 2006. "Charlotte Osgood Mason: Politics of Misrepresentation." *Oakland University Journal* 10:49–66.

Bordelon, Pam. 1997. "New Tracks on Dust Tracks: Toward a Reassessment of the Life of Zora Neale Hurston." *African American Review* 31(1): 5–21.

Borghol, Nada, Matthew Suderman, Wendy McArdle, Ariane Racine, Michael Hallett, Marcus Pembrey, Clyde Hertzman, Chris Power, and Moshe Szyf. 2012. "Associations with Early-Life Socio-Economic Position in Adult DNA Methylation." *International Journal of Epidemiology* 41(1): 62–74.

Borrello, Mark. 2008. *Dogma, Heresy, and Conversion: Vero Copner Wynne-Edward's Crusade and the Levels of Selection Debate.* New Haven, CT: Yale University Press.

Bottomore, T. 1991. "Lumpenproletariat." In *A Dictionary of Marxist Thought,* edited by T. Bottomore, 327. Oxford: Basil Blackwell.

Bourdieu, Pierre. 1977. *Outline of a Theory of Practice.* Translated by Richard Nice. Cambridge: Cambridge University Press.

Bourdieu, Pierre, and Jean-Claude Passeron. 1990 [1970]. *Reproduction in Education, Society, and Culture.* 2nd ed. London: Sage.

Bourgois, Philippe. 1995. "From Jíbaro to Crack Dealer: Confronting the Restructuring of Capitalism in El Barrio." In *Articulating Hidden Histories: Exploring the Influence of Eric R. Wolf,* edited by Jane Schneider and Rayna Rapp, 125–141. Berkeley: University of California Press.

———. 2006. Foreword to *Engaged Observer: Anthropology, Advocacy, and Activism,* edited by Victoria Stanford and Asale Angel-Ajani, ix–xii. New Brunswick, NJ: Rutgers University Press.

Bourgois, Philippe, and Jeff Schonberg. 2009. *Righteous Dopefiend.* Berkeley: University of California Press.

Boyd, Valarie. 2003. *Wrapped in Rainbows: The Life of Zora Neale Hurston.* New York: Scribner.

Boyne, Roy. 1966. "Structuralism." In *The Blackwell Companion to Social Theory,* edited by Bryan S. Turner, 194–220. Oxford: Blackwell.

Braudel, Fernand. 1980. *On History.* Chicago: University of Chicago.

———. 1992. *The Structures of Everyday Life: The Limits of the Possible.* New York: Harper & Row.

———. 2009. "History and the Social Sciences: The Longue Durée." Translated by Immanuel Wallerstein. *Review (Fernand Braudel Center),* 32(2): 171–203.

Breslin, Meg McSherry. 1998. "Valerio Valeri, 53, U. of C. Professor." *Chicago Tribune,* May 5.

Briggs, Jean L. 1970. *Never in Anger: Portrait of an Eskimo Family.* Cambridge, MA: Harvard University Press.

Brillouin, Leon. 1956. *Science and Information Theory.* New York: Academic Press.

Britton, Jack. 2018. "20 Years Later, Victims of Indonesia's May 1998 Riots Are Still Waiting for Justice." *The Diplomat,* May 18. https://thediplomat.com/2018/05/20-years-later-victims-of-indonesias-may-1998-riots-are-still-waiting-for-justice. Retrieved May 30, 2019.

Brodkin, Karen. 1998. *How Jews Became White Folks and What That Says about Race in America.* New Brunswick, NJ: Rutgers University Press.

Brown, Dee. 1971. *Bury My Heart at Wounded Knee.* New York: Holt, Rinehart and Winston.

Brown, Jerram L. 1983. "Cooperation—A Biologist's Dilemma." *Advances in the Study of Behavior* 13:1–37.

Brown, Keith. 2005. "Samuel Huntington, Meet the Nuer: Kinship, Local Knowledge and the Clash of Civilizations." In *Why America's Top Pundits Are Wrong: Anthropologists Talk Back,* edited by Catherine Besteman and Hugh Gusterson, 43–59. Berkeley: University of California.

Brown, Norman O. 1959. *Life against Death: The Psychoanalytical Meaning of History.* Middletown, CT: Wesleyan University Press.

Bucher, Bernadette, and Claude Lévi-Strauss. 1985. "An Interview with Claude Lévi-Strauss 30 June 1982." *American Ethnologist* 12(2): 360–368.

Bücher, Karl. 1968 [1901]. *Industrial Evolution.* New York: Augustus M. Kelley.

Buffon, Georges Louis Leclerc. 1752–1799. *Histoire naturelle, générale et particulier.* Paris: L'Imprimerie Royale.

Bulmer, Ralph. 1967. "Why Is the Cassowary Not a Bird? A Problem of Zoological Taxonomy among the Karam of the New Guinea Highlands." *Man* 2(1): 5–25.

Burggraeve, Roger. 2002. *The Wisdom of Love in the Service of Love: Emmanuel Levinas on Justice, Peace, and Human Rights.* Milwaukee, WI: Marquette University Press.

Burke, Kenneth. 1989. *On Symbols and Society.* Chicago: University of Chicago Press.

Burkholder, Zoe. 2006. "Franz Boas and Anti-Racist Education." *Anthropology News,* October, 24–25.

Burns, Gerald. 2013. Review of *Thoreau's Importance for Philosophy,* edited by Rick Anthony Furtak, Jonathan Ellsworth, James D. Reid. *Notre Dame Philosophical Reviews,* February 11.

Butler, Judith. 1990. *Gender Trouble: Feminism and the Subversion of Identity*. New York: Routledge.

———. 2004. *Undoing Gender*. New York: Routledge.

Byrne, Patrick H. 1997. *Analysis and Science in Aristotle*. Albany: State University of New York Press.

Caffrey, Margaret, and Patricia Francis. 2006. *To Cherish the Life of the World: The Selected Letters of Margaret Mead*. New York: Basic Books.

Cairnes, J. E. 1875. "Mr Spencer on Social Evolution." *Fortnightly Review* 17:63–82.

Calhoun, Craig. 1998. "Strong Evaluation and the Self. Taylor, Charles (b. 1931)." In *Routledge Encyclopedia of Philosophy*. Taylor and Francis. https://www.rep.routledge.com/articles/biographical/taylor-charles-1931/v-1/sections/strong-evaluation-and-the-self.

"Campaign Finance Key Players: The Riady Family." 1998. *Washington Post*, March 4. https://www.washingtonpost.com/wp-srv/politics/special/campfin/players/riady.htm.

Cancian, Frank. 1965. *Economics and Prestige in a Maya Community: The Religious Cargo System in Zinacantan*. Stanford, CA: Stanford University Press.

Carneiro, Robert L., ed. 1967. *The Evolution of Society: Selections from Herbert Spencer's Principles of Sociology*. Chicago: University of Chicago Press.

———. 1970. "A Theory of the Origin of the State." *Science* 169:733–738.

———. 2004. "Leslie White." In *Totems and Teachers: Key Figures in the History of Anthropology*, edited by Sydel Silverman, 151–176. Lanham, MD: AltaMira Press.

Carstairs, George M. 1956. "Hinjra and Jiryan: Two Derivatives of Hindu Attitudes to Sexuality." *British Journal of Medical Psychology* 29:128–138.

———. 1957. *The Twice Born: A Study of a Community of High-Caste Hindus*. London: Hogarth Press.

Caspari, Rachel. 2003. "From Types to Populations: A Century of Race, Physical Anthropology, and the American Anthropological Association." *American Anthropologist* 105(1): 65–76.

Casson, Ronald W. 1983. "Schemata in Cognitive Anthropology." *Annual Reviews of Anthropology* 12:429–462.

Castells, Manuel. 2010. *The Rise of the Network Society*. Malden, MA: Wiley-Blackwell.

Catapano, Andrea L. 2007. "The Rising of the Ongwehònwe: Sovereignty, Identity, and Representation on the Six Nations Reserve." *Dissertation in History*, Stony Brook University.

Cavell, Stanley. 1988. *Themes Out of School: Effects and Causes*. Chicago: University of Chicago.

———. 1985. "A Capra Moment." *Humanities* 6(4): 3–7.

———. 1972. *The Senses of Walden*. New York: Viking.

———. 2004. *Cities of Words: Pedagogical Letters on a Register of the Moral Life*. Cambridge, MA: Harvard University Press.

CBC. 2008. "Quebec Liberal Candidate Resigns over Mohawk Comments." September 11. https://www.cbc.ca/news/canada/montreal/quebec-liberal-candidate-resigns-over-mohawk-comments-1.737631.

CBS. 2017. "Native Americans Respond to Trump's Pocahontas Comment." November 27. https://www.cbsnews.com/news/native-americans-respond-to-trumps-pocahontas-comment.

Chagnon, Napoleon. 1968. *The Fierce People*. New York: Holt, Rinehart and Winston.

Chagnon, Napoleon, and William Irons. 1979. *Evolutionary Biology and Human Social Behavior: An Anthropological Perspective*. North Scituate, MA: Duxbury Press.

Chambers, E. 1977. Review of *Energy and Structure: A Theory of Social*, by Power Richard Newbold Adams. *American Anthropologist* 79:451–452.

Chandler, Jennifer, and Erica Wilborg. 2021. "Whiteness Norms." In *Encyclopedia of Critical Whiteness Studies in Education*, edited by Zacchary A. Casey, 714–782. Brill.

Childe, V. Gordon. 1942. *What Happened in History*. Baltimore, MD: Penguin.

Chodorow, Nancy. 1974. "Family Structure and Feminine Personality." In *Woman, Culture, and Society*, edited by Michelle Rosaldo and Louise Lamphere, 43–66. Palo Alto, CA: Stanford University Press.

Chomsky, Noam. 1995. "Language and Nature." *Mind* 104(413): 1–61.

Clark, Peter. 2013. "Ian Cunnison Obituary." *The Guardian*, August 27. https://www.theguardian.com/science/2013/aug/27/ian-cunnison.

Clayton, Blake C. 2015. *Market Madness: A Century of Oil Panics, Crises, and Crashes*. Oxford: Oxford University Press.

Clifford, James, and George E. Marcus, eds. 1986. *Writing Culture: The Poetics and Politics of Ethnography*. Berkeley: University of California Press.

Coghlan, Andy. 2010. "Genes Marked by Stress Make Grandchildren Mentally Ill." *New Scientist*, no. 2785 (November 6).

Cole, Douglas. 1983. "'The Value of a Person Lies in His Herzensbildung,' Franz Boas' Baffin Island Letter-Diary, 1883–1884." In *Observers Observed: Essays on Ethnographic Fieldwork*, edited by George Stocking, 13–52. Madison: University of Wisconsin.

Collier, Jane F. 1974. "Women in Politics." In *Woman, Culture, and Society*, edited by Michelle Rosaldo and Louise Lamphere, 89–96. Palo Alto, CA: Stanford University Press.

Collier, Jane F., and Sylvia Yanagisako, eds. 1987. *Gender and Kinship*. Palo Alto, CA: Stanford University Press.

Comisión para Esclarecimiento Histórico (Guatamala). 1998. *Guatemala, Memory of Silence; Report of the Commission for Historical Clarification, Conclusions and Recommendations*. Guatemala, Guatemala CEH.

Comptroller General of the United States. 1976. Letter to Senator Charles H. Percy. https://www.gao.gov/assets/ggd-75–94.pdf.

Comte, August. 1975 [1922]. "Plan of the Scientific Operations Necessary for Reorganizing Society." In *Auguste Comte and Positivism: The Essential Writings*, edited by Gertrud Lenzer, 9–69. New York: Harper Torchbooks.

Condorcet, Jean-Antoine-Nicolas de Caritat, Marquis de. 1902 [1794]. *Esquisse d'un tableau historique des progre`s de l'esprit humain*. Paris: Bibliotheque Nationale.

Conkey, Margaret, and Janet Spector. 1984. "Archaeology and the Study of Gender." *Advances in Archaeological Method and Theory* 7:1–38.

Conklin, Harold C. 1954. "The Relation of Hanunóo Culture to the Plant World." PhD diss., Yale University.

Copeland, Lennie. 1985. *Going International: How to Make Friends and Deal Effectively in the Global Marketplace*. New York: Random House.

Coquery-Vidrovitch, Catherine. 1978. "Researches on an African Mode of Production." In *Relations of Production: Marxist Approaches to Economic Anthropology*, edited by David Sedden, 261–288. London: Frank Cass.

Corbett, Michael, Julia Corbett-Hemeyer, and J. Matthew Wilson. 2014. *Politics and Religion in the United States*. 2nd ed. New York: Routledge.

Corning, Peter A. 1982. "Durkheim and Spencer." *British Journal of Sociology* 33(3): 359–382.

Cosmides, Leda, and John T. Tooby. 1997. "Evolutionary Psychology: A Primer." Center for Evolutionary Psychology, University of California, Santa Barbara. https://www.cep.ucsb.edu/primer.html.

Costello, Andrew. 2018. "A Closer Look at the Eric Garner Incident: The New York Police Department Should Review Its Policy Instead of Trying Its Police Officer." *Journal of Criminal Justice and Law* 2(2). https://doi.org/10.21428/b6e95092.b9012c5f.

Cotera, María Eugenia. 2008. "'Lyin' up a Nation': Zora Neale Hurston and the Literary Uses of the Folk." In *Native Speakers*, edited by María Eugenia Cotera, 71–102. Austin: University of Texas.

Cottell, Fran, and Marianne Mueller. 2020. "From Pain to Pleasure: Panopticon Dreams and Pentagon Petal." In *Bentham and the Arts*, edited by Anthony Julius, Malcolm Quinn, and Philip Schofield, 244–269. London: UCL Press.

Cotterrell, Roger. 1999. *Emile Durkheim: Law in a Moral Domain*. Stanford, CA: Stanford University Press.

Crick, Jen, Malini Suchak, Timothy M. Eppley, Matthew W. Campbell, and Frans B. M. de Waal. 2013. "The Roles of Food Quality and Sex in Chimpanzee Sharing Behavior (Pan Troglodytes)." *Behaviour* 150(11): 1–22.

Crosby, Alfred W. 1989. *America's Forgotten Pandemic: The Influenza of 1918*. Cambridge: Cambridge University Press.

Csordas, Thomas J. 1994. *The Sacred Self: A Cultural Phenomenology of Charismatic Healing*. Berkeley: University of California Press.

Cullen, James, and Ames Grawert. 2016. "Fact Sheet: Stop and Frisk's Effect on Crime in New York City." Brennan Center for Justice. https://www.brennancenter.org/our-work/research-reports/fact-sheet-stop-and-frisks-effect-crime-new-york-city.

Cyrus, Ramenda. 2022. "Police Have No Duty to Protect the Public." *American Prospect*, April 18. https://prospect.org/justice/police-have-no-duty-to-protect-the-public.

D'Andrade, Roy. 1995. *The Development of Cognitive Anthropology*. Cambridge: Cambridge University Press.

Darnell, Regna. 2001. *Invisible Genealogies: A History of Americanist Anthropology*. Lincoln: University of Nebraska Press.

———. 2015. *The Franz Boas Papers*. Vol. 1, *Franz Boas as Public Intellectual—Theory, Ethnography, Activism*. Lincoln: University of Nebraska Press.

Darnell, Regna, Joshua Smith, Michelle Hamilton, and Robert L. A. Hancock. 2015. *Franz Boas on War and Empire: The Making of a Public Intellectual*. Lincoln: University of Nebraska Press.

Darwin, Charles. 1842. *The Structure and Distribution of Coral Reefs*. London: Smith, Elder.

———. 1858. "On the Tendency of Species to Form Varieties; and on the Perpetuation of Varieties and Species by Natural Means of Selection." *Journal of the Linnean Society* 3:45–62.

———. 1871. *The Descent of Man and Selection in Relation to Sex*. London: John Murray.

———. 1883 [1868]. *The Variation of Animals and Plants under Domestication*. 2nd ed. New York: D. Appleton.

———. 1952 [1839]. *Journal of Researches*. Reprint; New York: Hafner.

———. 1988 [1859]. *On the Origin of Species*. New York: New York University Press.

Das, Veena. 2009. "Veena Das." John Simon Guggenheim Memorial Foundation. https://www.gf.org /fellows/all-fellows/veena-das. Retrieved May, 30 2019.

Dasent, G. W. 1903. *Popular Tales from the Norse*. Edinburgh: David Douglas.

Davidson, Arnold I. 2005. "Ethics as Ascetics: Foucault, the History of Ethics, and Ancient Thought." In *The Cambridge Companion to Foucault*, edited by Gary Gutting, 123–149. Cambridge: Cambridge University Press.

Davis, Kingsley, and Wilbert E. Moore. 1944. "Some Principles of Statification." *American Sociological Review* 10(2): 242–249.

———. 1953. "Replies to Tumin." *American Sociological Review* 18:394–396.

Dawkins, Richard. 1976. *The Selfish Gene*. New York: Oxford University Press.

Deacon, Desley. 1999. *Elsie Clews Parsons: Inventing Modern Life*. Chicago: University of Chicago Press.

De Beauvoir, Simone. 1952. *The Second Sex*. Edited and Translated by H. M. Parshley. New York: Knopf.

DeBenedetti, Charles. 1990. *An American Ordeal: The Antiwar Movement of the Vietnam Era*. Syracuse, NY: Syracuse University Press.

Deflem, Mathieu. 1991. "Ritual, Anti-Structure, and Religion: A Discussion of Victor Turner's Processual Symbolic Analysis." *Journal for the Scientific Study of Religion* 30(1): 1–25.

Delegorgue, Adulphe. 1847 [1990]. *Travels in Southern Africa*. Durbin: Killie Campbell Africana Library; Pietermaritzburg: University of Natal Press.

Deleuze, Gilles, and Félix Gauttari. 1987. *A Thousand Plateaus: Capitalism and Schizophrenia*. Minneapolis: University of Minnesota Press.

Deloria, Vine, Jr. 1969. *Custer Died for Your Sins: An Indian Manifesto*. New York: Macmillan.

Denny, Charlotte. 2004. "Suharto, Marcos and Mobuto Head Corruption Table with $50bn Scams." *The Guardian*, March 26.

Dentan, Robert Knox. 1968. *The Semai: A Nonviolent People of Malaya*. New York: Holt, Rinehart and Winston.

Derrida, Jacques. 1992. *Given Time: 1. Counterfeit Money*. Chicago: University of Chicago Press.

Derry, George H. 1902. "The Personal Side of Herbert Spencer." *Sewanee Review* 10(1): 1–11.

Desjarlis, Robert, and C. Jason Throop. 2011. "Phenomenological Approaches in Anthropology." *Annual Review of Anthropology* 40:87–102.

Desmond, Adrian. 2001. "Redefining the X Axis: 'Professionals,' 'Amateurs' and the Making of Mid-Victorian Biology: A Progress Report." *Journal of the History of Biology* 34(1): 3–50.

Devereux, G. 1961. "Shamans as Neurotics." *American Anthropologist* 63:1088–1090.

Devons, Ely, and Max Gluckman. 1964. "Conclusion: Modes and Consequences of Limiting a Field of Study." In *Closed Systems and Open Minds*, edited by Max Gluckman, 254–259. Chicago: Aldine.

Dewalt, Billie R. 1975. "Changes in the Cargo Systems of MesoAmerica." *Anthropological Quarterly* 48(2): 87–105.

Dewey, John. 1922. *Human Nature and Conduct: An Introduction to Social Psychology*. New York: Holt.

Diamond, Jared M. 1987. "The Worst Mistake in the History of the Human Race." *Discover* 8:64–66.

Diamond, Stanley, ed. 1960. *Culture in History: Essays in Honor of Paul Radin*. New York: Columbia University Press.

Di Giovine, Michael A. 2009. *The Heritage-Scape: UNESCO, World Heritage, and Tourism*. Lanham, MD: Lexington.

Digrius, D. M. 2016. Review of *The Franz Boas Papers: V.1: Franz Boas as Public Intellectual—Theory, Ethnography, Activism*, edited by Regna Darnell, Michelle Hamilton, Robert L. A. Hancock, and Joshua Smith. *Choice: Current Reviews for Academic Libraries* 53(6): 908.

Di Leonardo, Micaela. 1991. "Introduction to Gender, Culture, and Political Economy: Feminist Anthropology in Historical Perspective." In *Gender at the Crossroads of Knowledge*, edited by Micaela di Leonardo, 1–48. Berkeley: University of California Press.

Dillon, Wilton S. 1980. "Margaret Mead and Government." *American Anthropologist* 82(2): 319–339.

Doane, Ashley. 2008. "Whiteness." In *International Encyclopedia of the Social Sciences*, 2nd ed., edited by William A. Darity Jr., 87–89. Detroit: Macmillan Reference.

Dolgin, Janet L., David S. Kemnitzer, and David M. Schneider. 1977. *Symbolic Anthropology*. New York: Columbia University Press.

Dollard, John. 1939. "The Dozens: Dialect of Insult." *American Imago* 1(1): 3–25.

Douglas, Mary. 1966. *Purity and Danger: An Analysis of the Concepts of Pollution and Taboo*. London: Routledge and Kegan Paul.

———. 1970. *Natural Symbols: Explorations in Cosmology*. New York: Pantheon.

———. 1992. *Risk and Blame: Essays in Cultural Theory*. London: Routledge.

Drake, St. Clair. 1980. "Anthropology and the Black Experience." *Black Scholar* 11(7): 2–31.

Du Bois, W. E. B. 1920. *Darkwater: Voices from within the Veil*. New York: Harcourt, Brace and Howe.

———. 1953. "On Stalin." National Guardian. https://www.marxists.org/reference/archive/stalin/biographies/1953/03/16.htm.

Duménil, Gérard, and Dominique Lévy. 2011. *The Crisis of Neoliberalism*. Cambridge, MA: Harvard University Press.

Dumont, Louis. 1974. *Homo Hierarchius: The Caste System and Its Implication*. Chicago: University of Chicago Press.

Dupré, Wilhelm. 1969. "Paul Joachim Shebesta (1887–1967)." *History of Religions* 8(3): 260–266.

Duranti, Alessandro. 2009. "The Relevance of Husserl's Theory to Language Socialization." *Journal of Linguistic Anthropology* 19(2): 205–226.

Durkheim, Émile. 1928. *Le socialisme: Sa définition, ses débuts, la doctrine saint-simonienne*. Paris: F. Alcan.

———. 1933 [1893]. *The Division of Labor in Society*. Translated by George Simpson. New York: Macmillan.

———. 1951 [1897]. *Suicide: A Study in Sociology*. Translated by Jon A. Spaulding and George Simpson. New York: Free Press.

———. 1965 [1912]. *The Elementary Forms of the Religious Life*. Translated by Joseph Swain. New York: Free Press.

Durkheim, Émile, and Marcel Mauss. 1963 [1903]. *Primitive Classification*. Translated by Rodney Needham. Chicago: University of Chicago Press.

Dworkin, Andrea. 1987. *Intercourse*. New York: Free Press.

Early, Timothy K. 1987. "Chiefdoms in Archaeological and Ethnohistorical Perspective." *Annual Review of Anthropology* 16:279–308.

Easton, David. 1953. *The Political System: An Inquiry into the State of Political Science*. New York: Knopf.

Eco, Umberto. 1997. "Murder in Chicago." *New York Review of Books*, April 10.

Egan, Timothy. 2023. *A Fever in the Heartland: The Ku Klux Klan's Plot to Take over America, and the Woman Who Stopped Them*. New York: Viking.

Elkin, A. P. 1941. "Native Languages and the Field Worker in Australia." *American Anthropologist* 43(1): 89–94.

———. 1956. "A. R. Radcliffe-Brown." *Oceania* 26(4): 239–251.

Elliott, Paul. 2012. "Felix Gauttari's Desiring Machine." *The I. B. Tauris Blog*. https://theibtaurisblog.com/2012/09/17/felix-guattari-and-the-desiring-machine. Retrieved May 30, 2019.

Engels, Friedrich. 1949 [1888]. *Ludwig Feuerbach and the End of Classical German Philosophy*. Moscow: Foreign Languages Publishing House.

———. 1972 [1884]. *The Origin of the Family, Private Property, and the State*. New York: Pathfinder Press.

Equal Justice Initiative. 2015. *Lynching in America: Confronting the Legacy of Racial Terror Supplement: Lynchings by County*. Montgomery, AL: Equal Justice Initiative.

———. 2019. "Remembering Black Veterans Targeted for Racial Terror Lynchings." November 11. https://eji.org/news/remembering-black-veterans-and-racial-terror-lynchings.

Erickson, Paul A., and Liam D. Murphy. 1998. *A History of Anthropological Theory*. Peterborough, ON: Broadview Press.

Evans-Pritchard, E. E. 1940. *The Nuer: A Description of the Modes of Livelihood and Political Institutions of a Nilotic People*. Oxford: Oxford University Press.

————. 1951a. *Kinship and Marriage among the Nuer*. Oxford: Clarendon Press.

————. 1951b. *Social Anthropology*. New York: Free Press.

————. 1956. *Nuer Religion*. Oxford: Clarendon Press.

Fanon, Frantz. 1986. *Black Skin, White Masks*. London: Pluto.

Fardon, Richard. 2007. "Dame Mary Douglas." *The Guardian*, May 18. https://www.theguardian.com/news/2007/may/18/guardianobituaries.obituaries.

Ferguson, Kennan. 2015. "Refusing Settler Colonialism: Simpson's Mohawk Interruptus." *Theory & Event* 18(4).

Fernandez, Manny, and Christine Hauser. 2015. "Texas Mother Teaches Textbook Company a Lesson on Accuracy." *New York Times*, October 6, A10.

Fessler, Daniel. 1995. "A Small Field with a Lot of Hornets: An Exploration of Shame, Motivation, and Social Control." PhD diss., University of California, San Diego.

Firth, Raymond. 1925. "Economic Psychology of the Maori." *Journal of the Royal Anthropological Institute* 55 (July–December): 340–362.

————. 1964. "The Place of Malinowski in the History of Economic Anthropology." In *Man and Culture: An Evaluation of the Work of Bronislaw Malinowski*, edited by Raymond Firth, 209–227. New York: Harper & Row.

————. 1973. *Symbols, Public and Private*. Ithaca, NY: Cornell University Press.

Fitzpatrick, Vincent. 1989. *H. L. Mencken*. New York: Continuum.

Flannery, Kent V. 1972. "The Cultural Evolution of Civilizations." *Annual Review of Ecological Systems* 3:399–426.

Florida State Senate. 2023. An Act Relating to Higher Education. https://www.flsenate.gov/Session/Bill/2023/266/BillText/er/HTML.

Food and Agriculture Organization of the United Nations, Statistics Division. N.d. FAOSTAT. https://faostat3.-fao.org/download/FB/FBS/E.

Fortes, Meyer, and E. E. Evans-Pritchard. 1967 [1940]. *African Political Systems*. London: Oxford University Press.

Foster, George. 1967. *Tzintzuntzan: Mexican Peasants in a Changing World*. Boston: Little, Brown.

Foucault, Michel. 1965 [1961]. *Madness and Civilization*. New York: Pantheon.

————. 1972. *The Archaeology of Knowledge*. Translated by A. M. Sheridan Smith. New York: Harper Colophon.

————. 1978. *The History of Sexuality*. Vol. 1, *An Introduction*. New York: Pantheon.

————. 1979. *Discipline and Punish: The Birth of the Prison*. New York: Vintage.

————. 1980. "Truth and Power." In *Power/Knowledge: Selected Interviews and Other Writings, 1972–1977*, by Michel Foucault, edited by Colin Gordon, 109–133. New York: Pantheon.

————. 1991. *The Foucault Effect: Studies in Governmentality: With Two Lectures by and an Interview with Michel Foucault*. Edited by Graham Burchell, Colin Gordon, and Peter Miller. Chicago: University of Chicago Press.

Fournier, Marcel. 2006. *Marcel Mauss: A Biography*. Princeton, NJ: Princeton University Press.

Fox, Richard G. 1991. *Recapturing Anthropology: Working in the Present*. Santa Fe: School of American Research Press.

Fox, Robin. 1972. "In the Beginning: Aspects of Hominid Behavioral Evolution." In *Perspectives on Human Evolution*, edited by Sherwood L. Washburn and Phyllis Dolhinow, 358–381. New York: Holt, Rinehart and Winston.

Frake, Charles O. 1961. "The Diagnosis of Disease among the Subanun of Mindanao." *American Anthropologist* 63:113–132.

————. 1962. "The Ethnographic Study of Cognitive Systems." In *Anthropology and Human Behavior*, edited by Thomas Gladwin and William D. Sturtevant, 72–85. Washington, DC: Anthropological Society of Washington.

Frank, G. 1997. "Jews, Multiculturalism, and Boasian Anthropology." *American Anthropologist* 99(4): 731–745.

Frazer, James George. 1911–1915 [1890]. *The Golden Bough: A Study in Magic and Religion*. 3rd ed. London: Macmillan.

Freeman, Derek. 1983. *Margaret Mead and Samoa: The Making and Unmaking of an Anthropological Myth*. Cambridge, MA: Harvard University Press.

Frère, Bruno. 2004. "Genetic Structuralism, Psychological Sociology and Pragmatic Social Actor Theory, Proposals for a Convergence of French Sociologies." *Theory, Culture, Society* 21(3): 85–99.

Freud, Sigmund. 1939. *Moses and Monotheism*. Translated by Katherine Jones. London: Hogarth Press.

————. 1950 [1913]. *Totem and Taboo: Some Points of Agreement between the Mental Lives of Savages and Neurotics*. Translated by James Strachey. New York: Norton.

————. 1960 [1905]. *Jokes and Their Relation to the Unconscious*. Translated by James Strachey. New York: Norton.

————. 1961 [1930]. *Civilization and Its Discontents*. Translated by James Strachey. New York: Norton.

————. 1961 [1928]. *The Future of an Illusion*. Translated by James Strachey. New York: Norton.

————. 1963 [1900]. *On Dreams*. Translated by James Strachey. New York: Norton.

Fried, Morton. 1967. *The Evolution of Political Society*. New York: Random House.

Friedl, Ernestine. 1975. *Women and Men: An Anthropologist's View*. New York: Holt, Rinehart and Winston.

Friedman, Jonathan. 1974. "Marxism, Structuralism, and Vulgar Materialism." *Man* 9(3): 444–469.

————. 1987. "An Interview with Eric Wolf." *Current Anthropology* 28(1): 107–118.

Frye, Northrop. 1964. *The Educated Imagination*. Bloomington: Indiana University Press.

Fukui, Nanako. 1999. "Background Research for The Chrysanthemum and the Sword." *Dialectical Anthropology* 24(2): 173–180.

Fukuyama, Francis. 1989. "The End of History?" *National Interest* 16 (Summer): 3–18.

Funnell, Warwick. 2001. "Distortions of History, Accounting and the Paradox of Werner Sombart." *Abacus* 37(1): 55–78.

Furnivall, John Sydenham. 1947. *Colonial Policy and Practice: A Comparative Study of Burma and Netherlands India*. Cambridge: Cambridge University Press.

Gabbatiss, Josh. 2017. "Is Violence Embedded in Our DNA?" *Sapiens*, July 12.

Gabler, Neal. 2012. "What's Behind the Right's 'Obama Is Gay' Conspiracy?" *The Nation*, October 23.

Gadamer, Hans-Georg. 1975. *Truth and Method*. Translated by Garren Burden and John Cumming. New York: Seabury Press.

Galton, Francis. 1869. *Hereditary Genius: An Inquiry into Its Laws and Consequences*. London: Macmillan.

————. 1883. *Inquiries into Human Faculty and Its Development*. New York: Macmillan.

Gardner, Helen, and Robin J. Wilson. 1993. "Thomas Archer Hirst—Mathematician Xtravagant V. London in the 1860s." *American Mathematical Monthly* 100(9): 827–834.

Gardner, Robert. 1965. *Dead Birds* (motion picture). United States: Film Study Center.

Gauntlett, David. 2002. *Media, Gender and Identity: An Introduction*. London: Routledge.

Geertz, Clifford. 1960. *The Religion of Java*. Glencoe, IL: Free Press.

————. 1963a. *Agricultural Involution: The Processes of Ecological Change in Indonesia*. Berkeley: University of California Press.

————. 1963b. *Peddlers and Princes: Social Development and Economic Change in Two Indonesian Towns*. Chicago: University of Chicago Press.

————. 1973. *The Interpretation of Cultures*. New York: Basic Books.

————. 1974. "From the Native's Point of View: On the Nature of Anthropological Understanding." *Bulletin of the American Academy of Arts and Sciences* 28(1): 26–45.

————. 1975. "On the Nature of Anthropological Understanding." *American Scientist* 63(1): 47–53.

————. 1980. *Negara: The Theatre State in Nineteenth-Century Bali*. Princeton, NJ: Princeton University Press.

————. 1984. "Distinguished Lecture: Anti Anti-Relativism." *American Anthropologist* 86(2): 273–278.

————. 1986. "Making Experience Authoring Selves." In *The Anthropology of Experience*, edited by Victor W. Turner and Edward M. Bruner, 373–380. Urbana: University of Illinois Press.

Geoghegan, William H. 1976. "Polytypy in Folk Biological Taxonomies." *American Ethnologist* 3(3): 469–480.

German, Mike. 2020. "The FBI Warned for Years That Police Are Cozy with the Far Right. Is No One Listening?" *The Guardian*, August 28.

Gerth, H. H., and C. Wright Mills. 1946. "Introduction: The Man and His Work." In *From Max Weber: Essays in Sociology*, edited by H. H. Gerth and C. Wright Mills, 1–74. New York: Oxford University Press.

Geschiere, Peter. 2011. "Autochthony, Citizenship, and Exclusion—Paradoxes in the Politics of Belonging in Africa and Europe." *Indiana Journal of Global Legal Studies* 18(1): 321–339.

Gibbon, Edward. 1942 [1776–1788]. *The Decline and Fall of the Roman Empire*. New York: E. P. Dutton.

Giddens, Anthony. 1979. *Central Problems in Social Theory: Action, Structure and Contradiction in Social Analysis*. Berkeley: University of California Press.

————. 1985. *A Contemporary Critique of Historical Materialism.* Berkeley: University of California Press.

Gillis, John R. 2000. "Our Virtual Families: Toward a Cultural Understanding of Modern Family Life." Working Paper No. 2. Emory Center for Myth and Ritual in American Life, Department of History, Rutgers University.

Gleick, James. 1987. *Chaos: Making a New Science.* New York: Viking.

Gluckman, Max. 1940. "Analysis of a Social Situation in Modern Zululand." *Bantu Studies* 14(1): 1–30.

————. 1947. "Malinowski's Contribution to Social Anthropology." *African Studies* 6:57–76.

————. 1949. "Malinowski's Sociological Theories." Rhodes-Livingstone Paper 16. Rhodes-Livingstone Institute, Livingstone, Northern Rhodesia.

————. 1954. *Rituals of Rebellion in South-East Africa.* The Frazer Lecture 1952. Manchester: Manchester University Press.

————. 1956. *Custom and Conflict in Africa.* Glencoe, IL: Free Press.

————. 1967 [1956]. "The Peace in the Feud." In *Custom and Conflict in Africa*, 2–26. New York: Barnes & Noble.

Gluckman, Max, and I. Schapera. 1960. "Dr. Winifred Hoernlé: An Appreciation." *Africa* 30(3): 262–263.

Gmelch, George. 1971. "Baseball Magic." *Trans-action* 8(8): 39–41.

Goldenweiser, Alexander. 1910. "Totemism: An Analytical Study." *Journal of American Folklore* 23:179.

————. 1913. "The Principle of Limited Possibilities in the Development of Culture." *Journal of American Folklore* 26(101): 259–290.

————. 1917. "The Autonomy of the Social." *American Anthropologist* 19(3): 447–449.

Goldgeier, Kathy. 2017. "Michael Brown's Parents Settle Wrongful Death Lawsuit with Ferguson, Mo." NPR, June 20. https://www.npr.org/sections/thetwo-way/2017/06/20/533738274/michael-browns-parents-settle-wrongful-death-lawsuit-with-ferguson-mo.

Goodenough, Ward. 1956. "Componential Analysis and the Study of Meaning." *Language* 32:195–216.

————. 1995. *The Expansive Moment: Anthropology in Britain and Africa, 1918–1970.* Cambridge: Cambridge University Press.

Goodison, Sean E. 2022. *Local Police Departments Personnel, 2020.* NCJ 305187. https://bjs.ojp.gov/sites/g/files/xyckuh236/files/media/document/lpdp20.pdf.

Goodman, J. David. 2015. "Eric Garner Case Is Settled by New York City for $5.9 Million." *New York Times.* https://www.nytimes.com/2015/07/14/nyregion/eric-garner-case-is-settled-by-new-york-city-for-5-9-million.html.

Goodman, Russell. 2018. "Ralph Waldo Emerson." In *Stanford Encyclopedia of Philosophy.* https://plato.stanford.edu/entries/emerson/ https://plato.stanford.edu/entries/emerson. Retrieved May 30, 2019.

Goodwin, Jeff, James M. Jasper, and Francesca Polletta, eds. 2001. *Passionate Politics: Emotions and Social Movements.* Chicago: University of Chicago Press.

Goodwin, Marjorie. 1990. *He-Said-She-Said: Talk as Social Organization among Black Children.* Bloomington: Indiana University Press.

Goody, Jack. 1995. *The Expansive Moment: Anthropology in Britain and Africa, 1918–1970.* Cambridge: Cambridge University Press.

Gopal, Sena Desai. 2015. "Selling the Sacred Cow: India's Contentious Beef Industry." *The Atlantic*, February 12.

Gordon, Robert, and Cameron Wesson. 2013. "Max Gluckman." In *Theory in Social and Cultural Anthropology: An Encyclopedia*, edited by R. Jon McGee and Richard L. Warms, 336–340. Thousand Oaks, CA: Sage.

Gorer, Geoffrey, and John Rickman. 1962 [1949]. *The People of Great Russia: A Psychological Study.* New York: Norton.

Gough, Kathleen. 1956. "Brahmin Kinship in a Tamil Village." *American Anthropologist* 58(8): 826–853.

————. 1968. "Anthropology and Imperialism." *Monthly Review.* 19(11): 12–27.

Gould, Stephen Jay. 1981. *The Mismeasure of Man.* New York: Norton.

————. 1989. *Wonderful Life: The Burgess Shale and the Nature of History.* New York: Norton.

————. 1994. "Cabinet Museums Revisited." *Natural History* 103(1): 12–20.

Graebner, F. 1911. *Die Methode der Ethnologie.* Heidelberg: C. Winter.

Graham, Ruth. 2024. "Southern Baptists Vote to Oppose Use of IVF." *New York Times*, June 12.

Graham, Sharyn. 2001. "Negotiating Gender: Calalai' in Bugis Society." *Intersections: Gender, History and Culture in the Asian Context*, no. 6.

Gramsci, Antonio. 1989. "Prison Notebooks." In *An Anthology of Western Marxism*, edited by Roger Gottlieb, 112–119. New York: Oxford.

———. 1992 [1930–1932]. *Prison Notebooks*. Vol. 2. New York: Columbia University Press.

———. 1994. *Letters from Prison*. Edited by Frank Rosengarten. Translated by Raymond Rosenthal. New York: Columbia University Press.

Grant, Madison. 1916. *The Passing of the Great Race; or, the Racial Basis of European History*. New York: Scribner.

Graves, Robert. 1948. *The White Goddess*. New York: Vintage.

Greenblatt, Stephen. 2011. *The Swerve: How the World Became Modern*. W. W. Norton.

Gross, Feliks. 1986. "Young Malinowski and His Later Years." *American Ethnologist* 13(3): 556–570.

Guatemala Human Rights Commission. N.d. "History of Guatemala." https://www.ghrc-usa.org /resources/fast-facts. Retrieved May 30, 2019.

Gunder-Frank, A. 1966. "The Development of Underdevelopment." *Monthly Review* 18(4): 17–31.

Gupta, Akhil, and Jessie Stoolman. 2022. "Decolonizing US Anthropology." *American Anthropologist*, 124(4): 778–799.

Gupta, Charu. 2009. "Hindu Women, Muslim Men: Love Jihad and Conversions." *Economic and Political Weekly* 44(51): 13–15.

Gutting, Gary. 2005. *Foucault: A Very Short Introduction*. Second edition. Oxford: Oxford University Press.

Hager, Lori D. 1997. "Sex and Gender in Paleoanthropology." In *Women in Human Evolution*, edited by Lori Hager, 1–28. New York: Routledge.

Hahn, Robert A. 1995. *Sickness and Healing: An Anthropological Perspective*. New Haven, CT: Yale University Press.

Hall, Calvin S., and Gardner Lindzey. 1978. *Theories of Personality*. 3rd ed. New York: Wiley.

Halstead, Fred. 1969. "A Further Alarm Signal from Chicago: An Open Letter from Fred Halstead." https://www.marxists.org/history/etol/document/swp-us/idb/swp-pc-min/1969-Sep%20 1970-Jun/62-Further-alarm-signal-from-Chicago-dec-15–1969.pdf.

Hamid, Rahem D., and Elias J. Schisgall. 2023. "Judge Allows Most Counts in Comaroff Harassment Lawsuit against Harvard to Proceed." *Harvard Crimson*, April 4. https://www.thecrimson.com/arti cle/2023/4/4/comaroff-lawsuit-proceeds.

Handler, Richard. 1991. "An Interview with Clifford Geertz." *Current Anthropology* 32(5): 603–613.

Hannerz, Ulf. 2015. "Writing Futures: An Anthropologist's View of Global Scenarios." *Current Anthropology* 56(6): 797–818.

Hansen, Karen Tranberg. 2015. "Urban Research in a Hostile Setting: Godfrey Wilson in Broken Hill, Northern Rhodesia 1938–1940" *Kronos* 41(November): 193–214.

Hardin, Garrett. 1968. "The Tragedy of the Commons." *Science* 162(December 13): 1243–1248.

Hardy, Barbara. 2006. "Writing a Critic's Biography." *George Eliot-George Henry Lewes Studies*, nos. 50/51: 110–124.

Harries, Patrick. 1981. "The Anthropologist as Historian and Liberal: H. A. Junod and the Thonga." *Journal of South African Studies* 8(1): 37–50.

Harris, Marvin. 1964. *The Nature of Cultural Things*. New York: Random House.

———. 1968. *The Rise of Anthropological Theory*. New York: Thomas Y. Crowell.

———. 1974. *Cows, Pigs, Wars, and Witches: The Riddles of Culture*. New York: Random House.

———. 1977. *Cannibals and Kings: The Origins of Culture*. New York: Random House.

———. 1978. "India's Sacred Cow." *Human Nature* 1(2): 28–36.

———. 1979. *Cultural Materialism: The Struggle for a Science of Culture*. New York: Random House.

———. 1981. *America Now: The Anthropology of a Changing Culture*. New York: Simon & Schuster.

———. 1985. *Good to Eat: Riddles of Food and Culture*. New York: Simon & Schuster.

———. 1994. "Cultural Materialism Is Alive and Well and Won't Go Away Until Something Better Comes Along." In *Assessing Cultural Anthropology*, edited by R. Borofsky, 62–76. New York: McGraw-Hill.

Harrison, Faye V., ed. 1991. *Decolonizing Anthropology: Moving Further toward an Anthropology for Liberation*. Washington, DC: American Anthropological Association, Association of Black Anthropologists.

Harrison, Lawrence E. 1992. *Who Prospers? How Cultural Values Shape Economic and Political Success*. New York: Basic Books.

Harrison, Lawrence E., and Samuel Huntington, eds. 2001. *Culture Matters: How Values Shape Human Progress*. New York: Basic.

Harte, Julia, and Alexandra Ulmer. 2022. "U.S. Police Trainers with Far-Right Ties Are Teaching Hundreds of Cops." Reuters, May 6. https://www.reuters.com/investigates/special-report/usa-police-extremism.

Harvey, David. 2010. *The Enigma of Capital: And the Crisis of Capitalism*. Oxford: Oxford University Press.

Hauptman, Laurence M., and Jack Campisi. 1988. "The Voice of Eastern Indians: The American Indian Chicago Conference of 1961 and the Movement for Federal Recognition." *Proceedings of the American Philosophical Society* 132(4): 316–329.

Heidegger, Martin. 1977. *The Question concerning Technology, and Other Essays*. New York: Harper & Row.

Hemenway, Robert. 1980. *Zora Neale Hurston: A Literary Biography*. Urbana: University of Illinois Press.

Henry, Granville C. 1993. *Forms of Concrescence: Alfred North Whitehead's Philosophy and Computer Programming Structures*. Cranbury, NJ: Associated University Presses.

Henry, Meghan, et al. 2018. *The 2018 Annual Homeless Assessment Report (AHAR) to Congress*. Washington, DC: US Department of Housing and Urban Development.

Herdt, Gilbert. 1984. *Ritualized Homosexuality in Melanesia*. Berkeley: University of California Press.

Hernandez, Rigoberto. 2015. "Here Are the Racist Emails Ferguson Officials Passed Around." NPR *Codeswitch*. https://www.npr.org/sections/codeswitch/2015/03/04/390725377/here-are-the-racist-emails-ferguson-officials-passed-around.

Herskovits, Melville. 1957. "Some Further Notes on Franz Boas' Arctic Expedition." *American Anthropologist* 59:112–116.

Hertz, Robert. 1973 [1909]. "The Pre-eminence of the Right Hand: A Study in Religious Polarity." In *Right and Left: Essays on Dual Symbolic Classification*, edited by Rodney Needham, 3–31. Chicago: University of Chicago Press.

Hewitt, Nancy A., ed. 2010. *No Permanent Waves: Recasting Histories of U.S. Feminism*. New Brunswick, NJ: Rutgers University Press.

Hill, K. 1988. "Macronutrient Modifications of Optimal Foraging Theory: An Approach Using Indifference Curves Applied to Some Modern Foragers." *Human Ecology* 16:157–197.

Hill, Kim, Hillard Kaplan, Kristen Hawkes, and A. Magdalena Hurtado. 1987. "Foraging Decisions among Aché Hunter-Gatherers: New Data and Implications for Optimal Foraging Models." *Ethnology and Sociobiology* 8:1–36.

Hirschman, Charles, Samuel Preston, and Vu Mahn Loi. 1995. "Vietnamese Casualties during the American War: A New Estimate." *Population and Development Review* 21(4): 783–812.

Hobbes, Thomas. 1983 [1651]. *Leviathan*. London: Dent.

Hochschild, Adam. 2022. *American Midnight: The Great War, a Violent Peace, and Democracy's Forgotten Crisis*. New York: Mariner Books.

Hockett, Charles F. 1973. *Man's Place in Nature*. New York: McGraw-Hill.

Hodgson, Geoffrey. 2004. "Veblen and Darwinism." *International Review of Sociology* 14(3): 343–361.

Hoebel, E. Adamson. 1949. *Man in the Primitive World: An Introduction to Anthropology*. New York: McGraw-Hill.

Hoernle, Agnes Winnifred. 1925. "The Social Organization of the Nama Hottentots of Southwest Africa." *American Anthropologist* 27(1): 1–24.

Hoey, Brian. 2013. "Roy Rappaport." In *Theory in Social and Cultural Anthropology*, edited by R. Jon McGee and Richard L. Warms, 2:685–688. Los Angeles, CA: Sage Reference.

Hofstede, Geert. 1991. *Cultures and Organizations: Software of the Mind*. New York: McGraw-Hill.

Hoijer, Harry. 1954. *Language in Culture*. Chicago: University of Chicago Press.

Holborow, Marnie. 2007. "Language, Ideology and Neoliberalism." *Language and Politics* 6(1): 51–73.

Holles, Everett R. 1975. "A.C.L.U Says F.B.I. Funded 'Army' to Terrorize Young War Dissidents." *New York Times*, June 27.

Holmes, Evelyn. 2022. "Chicago Police Department Swears in 80 New Officers, Reflecting Diversity Efforts." ABC 7 Eyewitness News, March 29. https://abc7chicago.com/chicago-police-department-cpd-recruiting-diversity/11690613.

Holmes, G. 1914. "Areas of American Culture Characterization Tentatively Outlined as an Aid in the Study of Antiquities." *American Anthropologist* 16:413–416.

Hooker, J. N. 1996. *Three Kinds of Ethics*. Pittsburgh, PA: Carnegie Mellon University Press.

hooks, bell. 1981. *Ain't I a Woman: Black Women and Feminism*. Boston: South End Press.

Horton, Scott. 2011. "In Defense of Flogging: Six Questions for Peter Moskos." *Harper's*, July 21. https://harpers.org/2011/07/in-defense-of-flogging-six-questions-for-peter-moskos.

"House Votes to Repeal and Eventually Replace Obamacare." 2015. Reuters, February 3. https://www.reuters.com/article/us-usa-congress-obamacare-idINKBN0L72JS20150204.

Howell, Angela McMillan. 2013. *Raised Up Down Yonder: Growing Up Black in Rural Alabama*. Jackson: University of Mississippi Press.

Howells, Robin. 2017. "J'aime a voir l'univers people: Re-enchanting the World in Bernardin de Saint-Pierre." *Modern Language Review* 112(2): 341–361.

Hoxie, Frederick E. 1995. *Parading through History: The Making of the Crow Nation in America, 1805–1935*. Cambridge: Cambridge University Press.

Hsu, Francis L. K. 1980. "Margaret Mead and Psychological Anthropology." *American Anthropologist* 82(2): 349–353.

Huang, Kathy. 2016. "Tales of the Waria: Inside Indonesia's Third-Gender Community." HuffPost, February 2. https://www.huffpost.com/entry/tales-of-the-waria-indonesia_b_1546629. Retrieved May 30, 2019.

Huizinga, Johan. 1949. *Homo Ludens*. New York: Routledge.

Human Rights Watch. 2019. "India: Vigilante 'Cow Protection' Groups Attack Minorities." https://www.hrw.org/news/2019/02/19/india-vigilante-cow-protection-groups-attack-minorities.

———. 2023. "Guatemala, Events of 2022." https://www.hrw.org/world-report/2023/country-chapters/guatemala.

Humboldt, Alexander von. 1874 [1845–1862]. *Kosmos*. Stuttgart: J. G. Cotta.

Humboldt, Wilhelm von. 1963. *Humanist without a Portfolio: An Anthology of the Writings of Wilhelm von Humboldt*. Translated by Marianne Cowen. Detroit: Wayne State University Press.

Hume, Brad D. 2008. "Quantifying Characters: Polygenist Anthropologists and the Hardening of Heredity." *Journal of the History of Biology* 41:119–158.

Hunt, Tristam. 2009. *Marx's General: The Revolutionary Life of Friedrich Engels*. Metropolitan Books.

Huntington, Samuel P. 1996. *Clash of Civilizations and the Remaking of the World Order*. New York: Simon & Schuster.

Hurston, Zora Neale. 1928. "How It Feels to Be Colored Me." *World Tomorrow* 11 (May): 215–216.

———. 1934. "Characteristics of Negro Expression." In *Negro: An Anthology*, edited by Nancy Cunard, 39–46.

———. 1935. *Mules and Men*. Philadelphia: J. B. Lippincott.

———. 1943. "High John De Conquer." *American Mercury* 57:450–458.

Hurston, Zora Neale, and Robert Hemenway. 1984. *Dust Tracks on a Road: An Autobiography*. Urbana: University of Illinois Press.

Hurston, Zora Neale, and Carla Kaplan. 2002. *Zora Neale Hurston: A Life in Letters*. New York: Doubleday.

Hurteau, Pierre. 1993. "Catholic Moral Discourses on Male Sodomy and Masturbation in the Seventeenth and Eighteenth Centuries." *Journal of the History of Sexuality* 4(1): 1–26.

Hutchins, Edwin. 1994. *Cognition in the Wild*. Cambridge, MA: MIT Press.

Hyatt, Marshall. 1990. *Franz Boas, Social Activist: The Dynamics of Ethnicity*. New York: Greenwood Press.

Hymes, Dell. 1972. *Reinventing Anthropology*. New York: Pantheon.

Ibn Khaldun. 1989. *Muqaddimah, or Introduction to History*. Translated by Franz Rosenthal. Princeton, NJ: Princeton University Press.

Ignatiev, Noel. 1995. *How the Irish Became White*. New York: Routledge.

Imai, Hissei, Yusuke Ogawa, Kiyohito Okumiya, and Kozo Matsubayashi. 2018. "Amok: A Mirror of Time and People. A Historical Review of the Literature." *History of Psychiatry* 30(1): 38–57.

Ingold, Tim. 1986. *Evolution and Social Life*. Cambridge: Cambridge University Press.

Isaac, G. L. 1978. "The Food Sharing Behavior of Protohuman Hominids." *Scientific American* 238:90–108.

Iyengar, Rishi. 2015. "India Stays World's Top Beef Exporter Despite New Bans on Slaughtering Cows." *Time*, April 23.

Jacknis, Ira. 2002. "The First Boasian: Alfred Kroeber and Franz Boas, 1896–1905." *American Anthropologist* 104(2): 520–529.

Jackson, Michael D. 2010. "'Doing Justice to Life': A Conversation with Social Anthropologist Michael D. Jackson." Harvard Divinity School, March 17. https://hds.harvard.edu/news/2010/03/17 /doing-justice-to-life-a-conversation-with-social-anthropologist-mich#. Retrieved May 30, 2019.

Jameson, Fredric. 1991. *Postmodernism; or, The Cultural Logic of Late Capitalism*. Durham, NC: Duke University Press.

Jenkins, Sally. 2012. "Why Are Jim Thorpe's Olympic Records Still Not Recognized?" *Smithsonian*, July. https://www.smithsonianmag.com/history/why-are-jim-thorpes-olympic-records-still-not-rec ognized-130986336.

Jha, Stefania Ruzsits. 1995. "Michael Polanyi's Integrative Philosophy." PhD diss., Harvard University.

———. 1996. "Michael Polanyi's Integrative Philosophy." *Polanyiana* 5(2): 36–65.

Jirousek, Lori. "'That Commonality of Feeling': Hurston, Hybridity, and Ethnography." *African American Review* 38(3): 417–427.

Johns, Timothy. 1999. "The Chemical Ecology of Human Ingestive Behaviors." *Annual Review of Anthropology* 28:27–50.

Johnson, Robert, and Adam Cureton. 2019. "Kant's Moral Philosophy." In *Stanford Encyclopedia of Philosophy*. https://plato.stanford.edu/entries/kant-moral. Retrieved May 30, 2019.

Jonassen, Frederick B. 1990. "Lucian's 'Saturnalia,' the Land of Cockaigne, and the Mummers' Plays." *Folklore* 101(1): 58–68.

Jones, Nicholas, Rachel Marks, Roberto Ramirez, and Merarys Rio-Vargas. 2021. "2020 Census Illuminates Racial and Ethnic Composition of the Country." https://www.census.gov/library/sto ries/2021/08/improved-race-ethnicity-measures-reveal-united-states-population-much-more-multi racial.html.

Jorgensen, Joseph G. 1993. "Kathleen Gough's Fight against the Consequences of Class and Imperialism on Campus." *Anthropologica* 35(2): 227–234.

Jouvenel, Bertrand de. 1949. *On Power: Its Nature and the History of Its Growth*. New York: Viking.

Jung, Carl Gustave. 1971 [1923]. *Psychological Types*. Princeton, NJ: Princeton University Press.

Kan, Sergei. 1986. "The 19th Century Tlingit Potlatch: A New Perspective." *American Ethnologist* 13(2): 191–212.

Kanno-Youngs, Zolan, and Caitlin Dickerson. 2019. "Asylum Seekers Face New Restraints under Latest Trump Orders." *New York Times*, April 29.

Kapferer, Bruce. 2006. "Situations, Crisis, and the Anthropology of the Concrete: The Contribution of Max Gluckman." In *The Manchester School: Practiced and Ethnographic Praxis in Anthropology*, edited by T. M. S. Evens and Don Handleman, 118–158. New York: Berghahn.

Kaplan, Abraham. 1955. "Obscenity as an Esthetic Category." *Law and Contemporary Problems* 20:544–559.

Kaplan, David, and Robert A. Manners. 1972. *Cultural Theory*. Englewood Cliffs, NJ: Prentice Hall.

Kaplan, Robert. 1994. "The Coming Anarchy." *Atlantic Monthly* 273(2): 44–76.

Karandinos, George, Laurie Hart, Fernando Castrillo, and Philippe Bourgois. 2014. "The Moral Economy of Violence in the US Inner City." *Current Anthropology* 55(1): 1–22.

Karp, Ivan, and Kent Maynard. 1983. "Reading the Nuer." *Current Anthropology* 24(4): 481–503.

Kenyatta, Jomo. 1979 [1938]. *Facing Mount Kenya: The Traditional Life of the Gikuyu*. London: Heinemann.

Keys, Ancel. 1943. "Physical Performance in Relation to Diet." *Federation Proceedings* 2:164–187.

———. 1946. "Nutrition and Capacity for Work." *Occupational Medicine* 2:536–545.

Kim, Jaechun. 2002. "U.S. Covert Action in Indonesia in the 1960s: Assessing the Motives and Consequences." *Journal of International and Area Studies* 9(2): 63–85.

King, Lily. 2014. *Euphoria: A Novel*. New York: Atlantic Monthly Press.

Kirchhoff, Paul. 1935 [1955]. "Principles of Clanship in Human Society." *Davidson Journal of Anthropology* 1:1–10.

Klein, Olivier, Russell Spears, and Stephen Reicher. 2007. "Social Identity Performance: Extending the Strategic Side of SIDE." *Personality and Social Psychology Review* 11(1): 1–18.

Klingmann, Anna. 2007. *Brandscapes: Architecture in the Experience Economy*. Cambridge, MA: MIT Press.

Kloos, David. 2014. "A Crazy State: Violence, Psychiatry, and Colonialism in Aceh, Indonesia, ca. 1910–1942." *Bijdrangen tot de Taal-, Lande-en Volkenkunde* 170(1): 25–65.

Koch, Robert G. 1992. "George P. Decker and Chief Deskaheh." *The Crooked Lake Review* 54. https://www.crookedlakereview.com/articles/34_66/54sept1992/54koch.html.

Komenda, Ed. 2018. "Orville Brettman Tied to Right-Wing Extremist Group That Bombed Elgin Church: Grand Jury Testimony." *Northwest Herald*, March 10. https://www.shawlocal.com/2018/03/07/orville-brettman-tied-to-right-wing-extremist-group-that-bombed-elgin-church-grand-jury-testimony/aqw4f33.

Kondo, Dorinne K. 1990. *Crafting Selves: Power, Gender, and Discourses of Identity in a Japanese Workplace*. Chicago: University of Chicago.

Kormondy, E. J., and D. E. Brown. 1998. *Fundamentals of Human Ecology*. Upper Saddle River, NJ: Prentice Hall.

Kozlarek, Oliver. 2011. "The Humanist Turn in the Social and Cultural Sciences and the Commitment to Criticism." *Taiwan Journal of East Asian Studies* 8(2): 17–36.

Kraut, Richard. 2018. "Aristotle's Ethics." In *Stanford Encyclopedia of Philosophy*. https://plato.stanford.edu/entries/aristotle-ethics. Retrieved, May 31, 2019.

Kroeber, A. L. 1901. "Decorative Symbolism of the Arapaho." *American Anthropologist* 3:308–336.

———. 1917. "The Superorganic." *American Anthropologist* 19:163–213.

———. 1925. *Handbook of the Indians of California*. Bulletin 78. Washington, DC: Smithsonian Institution, Bureau of American Ethnology.

———. 1939. *Cultural and Natural Areas of Native North America*. Berkeley: University of California Press.

———. 1940. "Psychotic Factors in Shamanism." *Character and Personality* 8:204–215.

———. 1948. *Anthropology: Race Language, Culture, Psychology, Prehistory*. New York: Harcourt, Brace and World.

———. 1957. *Style and Civilizations*. Berkeley: University of California Press.

———. 1959. "The History of Personality in Anthropology." *American Anthropologist* 61(3): 398–404.

Kroeber, Alfred Louis, and Clyde Kluckhohn. 1950. "Culture: A Critical Review of Concepts and Definitions." *Papers of the Peabody Museum of American Archaeology and Ethnology* 47(1), Harvard University.

Kuhn, Thomas S. 1962. *The Structure of Scientific Revolutions*. Chicago: University of Chicago Press.

Kuklick, H. 1991. *The Savage Within: The Social History of British Anthropology, 1885–1945*. Cambridge: Cambridge University Press.

Kuper, Adam. 1982. "Lineage Theory: A Critical Retrospect." *Annual Review of Anthropology* 11:71–95.

Kurtz, Donald V. 1996. "Hegemony and Anthropology: Gramsci, Exegesis, Reinterpretations." *Critique of Anthropology* 16(2): 103–135.

Kvale, Steiner, ed. 1992. *Psychology and Postmodernism*. Newbury Park, CA: Sage.

Labov, William. 1972. *Language in the Inner City: Studies in the Black English Vernacular*. Philadelphia: University of Pennsylvania Press.

LaCapra, Dominick. 1972. *Emile Durkheim: Sociologist and Philosopher*. Ithaca, NY: Cornell University Press.

Lacoste, Yves. 1984. *Ibn Khaldoun: The Birth of History and the Past of the Third World*. London: Verso.

Laertius, Diogenes. 1925. *Lives of Eminent Philosophers*. Loeb Classical Library 184. Cambridge, MA: Harvard University Press.

Lafitau, Joseph-François. 1724. *Mœurs des Sauvages Ameriquains*. Paris: Saugrain.

Laland, Kevin, John Odling-Smee, and Sean Myles. 2010. "How Culture Shaped the Human Genome: Bringing Genetics and the Human Sciences Together." *Nature Reviews Genetics* 11(2): 137–148.

Lamont, Michelle, and Annette Lareau. 1988. "Cultural Capital: Allusions, Gaps and Glissandos in Recent Theoretical Developments." *Sociological Theory* 6(2): 153–168.

Lamphere, Louise. 1987. "The Struggle to Reshape Our Thinking about Gender." In *The Impact of Feminist Research in the Academy*, edited by Christie Farnham, 11–33. Bloomington: Indiana University Press.

———. 1989. "Feminist Anthropology: The Legacy of Elsie Clews Parsons." *American Ethnologist* 16(3): 518–533.

———. 1992. "Gladys Reichard among the Navajo." *Frontiers: A Journal of Women Studies* 12(3): 78–115.

———. 2004. "Unofficial Histories: A Vision of Anthropology from the Margins." *American Anthropologist* 106(1): 126–139.

Latour, Bruno. 2002. "Gabriel Tarde and the End of the Social." In *The Social in Question: New Bearings in History and the Social Sciences*, edited by P. Joyce, 117–132. New York: Routledge, 2002.

———. 2005. *Reassembling the Social: An Introduction to Actor-Network-Theory*. Oxford: Oxford University Press.

Lavery, David. 2001. "The Imagination of Insurance: Wallace Stevens and Benjamin Lee Whorf at The Hartford." *Legal Studies Forum* 24(3–4): 481–492.

Leach, Edmund R. 1954. *Political Systems of Highland Burma: A Study of Kachin Social Structure.* London: London School of Economics and Political Science.

———. 1976. *Claude Lévi-Strauss.* New York: Penguin.

———. 1984. "Glimpses of the Unmentionable in the History of British Social Anthropology." In *Annual Review of Anthropology*, edited by Bernard Siegel, Alan Beals, and Stephen Tyler, 13:1–23. Palo Alto, CA: Annual Reviews.

Leacock, Eleanor. 1983. "Interpreting the Origins of Gender Inequality: Conceptual and Historical Problems." *Dialectical Anthropology* 7(4): 263–284.

Leaf, Murray J. 1979. *Man, Mind, and Science: A History of Anthropology.* New York: Columbia University Press.

Le Bon, Gustave. 1977 [1895]. *The Crowd: A Study of the Popular Mind.* New York: Penguin.

Lee, Michelle Ye Hee. 2015. "Donald Trump's False Comments connecting Mexican Immigrants and Crime." *Washington Post*, July 8. https://www.washingtonpost.com/news/fact-checker/wp/2015/07/08/donald-trumps-false-comments-connecting-mexican-immigrants-and-crime.

Lehman, David. 1992. "Paul de Man: The Plot Thickens." *New York Times*, May 24.

Lesser, Alexander. 1981. "Franz Boas." In *Totems and Teachers: Perspectives on the History of Anthropology*, edited by Sydel Silverman, 1–31. New York: Columbia University Press.

Lett, James. 1987. *The Human Enterprise: A Critical Introduction to Anthropological Theory.* Boulder, CO: Westview Press.

———. 1997. *Science, Reason and Anthropology: The Principles of Rational Inquiry.* Lanham, MD: Rowman & Littlefield.

Levine, Norman. 1987. "The German Historical School of Law and the Origins of Historical Materialism." *Journal of the History of Ideas* 48(3): 431–451.

LeVine, Robert A. 2007. "Ethnographic Studies of Childhood: A Historical Overview." *American Anthropologist* 109(2): 247–260.

Lévi-Strauss, Claude. 1951. "Language and the Analysis of Social Laws." *American Anthropologist* 53(2): 155–163.

———. 1963a. "The Effectiveness of Symbols." In *Structural Anthropology*, 186–205. New York: Basic Books.

———. 1963b. "Structural Analysis in Linguistics and in Anthropology." In *Structural Anthropology*, 31–54. New York: Basic Books.

———. 1967. *Les structures élémentaires de la parenté.* 2nd ed. Paris and The Hague: Mouton.

———. 1969 [1949]. *The Elementary Structures of Kinship.* Rev. ed. Boston: Beacon Press.

———. 1969. *The Raw and the Cooked.* New York: Harper & Row.

———. 1973. *From Honey to Ashes.* Chicago: University of Chicago Press.

———. 1987. *Introduction to the Works of Marcel Mauss.* Translated by Felicity Baker. London: Routledge and Kegan Paul.

Lévy-Bruhl, Lucien. 1966 [1910]. *How Natives Think.* Translated by Lillian A. Clare. New York: Washington Square Press.

Lewis, Diane. 1973. "Anthropology and Colonialism." *Current Anthropology.* 15(5): 581–602.

Lewis, Herbert S. 1998. "The Misrepresentation of Anthropology and Its Consequences." *American Anthropologist* 100(3): 716–731.

———. 2001. "The Passion of Franz Boas." *American Anthropologist* 103(2): 447–467.

———. 2022. "Open Letter, on the Counterfactual History of Anthropology." *HOAN* 21 (March). https://easaonline.org/downloads/networks/hoan/HOAN_Newsletter_21j-202112_Lewis_Open_Letter_AAA.pdf.

Lichtheim, G. 1973. "Marx and the Asiatic Mode of Production." In *Karl Marx*, edited by Tom Bottomore, 151–171. Englewood Cliffs, NJ: Prentice Hall.

Lilla, Mark. 1998. "The Politics of Jacques Derrida." *New York Review of Books* 45(11): 36–41.

Lipari, Lisbeth. 2012. "Rhetoric's Other: Levinas, Listening, and the Ethical Response." *Philosophy & Rhetoric* 45(3): 227–245. https://doi.org/10.5325/philrhet.45.3.0227.

Litonjua, M. D. 2001. "The State in Development Theory: The Philippines under Marcos." *Philippine Studies* 49(3): 368–398.

Lobel, Diana. 2011. *The Quest for God and the Good: World Philosophy as Living Experience.* New York: Columbia University Press.

Locke, John. 1824 [1690]. *An Essay Concerning Human Understanding*. London: Rivington. https://oll .libertyfund.org/titles/761. Retrieved April 10, 2016.

Lomawaima, K. Tsianina. 1994. *They Called It Prairie Light: The Story of Chilocco Indian School*. Lincoln: University of Nebraska Press.

Lorenz, Konrad. 1952. *King Solomon's Ring: New Light on Animal Ways*. Translated by Marjorie Kerr Wilson. New York: Crowell.

———. 1966. *On Aggression*. New York: Harcourt, Brace and World.

Lorenzini, Daniele. 2015. "What Is a 'Regime of Truth'?" *Le foucaldien*. 1/1. DOI: 10.16995/lefou.2.

Lounsbury, Floyd. 1956. "A Semantic Analysis of the Pawnee Kinship Usage." *Language* 32:158–194.

Lovejoy, C. Owen. 1981. "The Origin of Man." *Science* 211:341–350.

Lowe, Donald. 1995. *The Body in Late-Capitalist USA*. Durham, NC: Duke University Press.

Lowie, Robert H. 1913. "Military Societies of the Crow Indians." *Anthropological Papers of the American Museum of Natural History* 11:145–217.

———. 1920. *Primitive Society*. New York: Liveright.

———. 1928. "A Note on Relationship Terminologies." *American Anthropologist* 30(2): 263–267.

———. 1937. *The History of Ethnological Theory*. New York: Holt, Rinehart and Winston.

———. 1946a. Review of *A Scientific Theory of Culture and Other Essays*, by Bronislaw Malinowski. *American Anthropologist* 48(1): 118–119.

———. 1946b. "Evolution in Cultural Anthropology: A Reply to Leslie White." *American Anthropologist* 48(2): 223–233.

———. 1947. *Primitive Society*. New York: Liveright.

Lubbock, Sir John. 1865. *Prehistoric Times: As Illustrated by Ancient Remains and the Manners and Customs of Modern Savages*. London: Williams and Norgate.

———. 1870. *Origin of Civilization and the Primitive Condition of Man: Mental and Social Condition of Savages*. London: Longmans, Green.

Lucretius. 1916. *De Rerum Natura*. Translated by William Ellery Leonard. New York: E. P. Dutton.

Lucy, John. 1993. *Reflexive Language: Reported Speech and Metapragmatics*. Cambridge: Cambridge University Press.

———. 1997. "Linguistic Relativity." *Annual Reviews of Anthropology* 26:291–312.

———. 2004. "Language, Culture, and Mind in Comparative Perspective." In *Language, Culture, and Mind*, edited by Michel Achard and Suzanne Kemmer, 1–22. Stanford, CA: CSLI Publications.

Lummis, C. Douglas. 1982. *A New Look at "The Chrysanthemum and the Sword."* Tokyo: Shohakusha.

Lutkehaus, N. C. 1995. "Margaret Mead and the 'Rustling-of-the-Wind-in-the-Palm-Trees-School' of Ethnographic Writing." In *Women Writing Culture*, edited by R. Behar and D. A. Gordon, 186–201. Berkeley: University of California Press.

Lutz, Catherine A., and Lila Abu-Lughod, eds. 1990. *Language and the Politics of Emotion*. New York: Cambridge University Press.

Lutz, Catherine, and Geoffrey M. White. 1986. "The Anthropology of Emotions." *Annual Review of Anthropology* 15:405–436.

Lyell, Sir Charles. 1834. *Principles of Geology*. London: J. Murray.

———. 1863. *The Geological Evidences of the Antiquity of Man*. Philadelphia: G. W. Childs.

Lyotard, Jean-François. 1984. *The Postmodern Condition: A Report on Knowledge*. Minneapolis: University of Minnesota Press.

MacCormack, Carol P. 1980. "Nature, Culture, and Gender: A Critique." In *Nature, Culture, and Gender*, edited by Carol P. MacCormack and Marilyn Strathern, 1–24. Cambridge: Cambridge University Press.

Macintosh, Sir James. 1828 [1799]. *A Discourse on the Study of the Law of Nature and Nations*. London: H. Goode.

Maclure, Jocelyn. 2016. "Charles Taylor: A Strong Evaluator." In *Due Course*. https://induecourse.ca /charles-taylor-a-strong-evaluator. Retrieved May 31, 2019.

Maillet, Benoit de. 1748. *Telliamed, ou, Entretiens d'un philosophe indien avec un missionaire franc¸ ois sur le diminution de la mer, la formation de la terre, l'origine de l'homme, etc*. Amsterdam: L'Honore.

Maine, H. S. 1963. *Ancient Law: Its Connection with the Early History of Society and Its Relation to Modern Ideas*. Boston: Beacon Press.

Malcolm, Janet. 2007. *Two Lives: Gertrude and Alice*. New Haven, CT: Yale University Press.

Malefijt, Annemarie de Waal. 1974. *Images of Man: A History of Anthropological Thought*. New York: Knopf.

————. 1989. *Religion and Culture: An Introduction to Anthropology of Religion*. Prospect Heights, IL: Waveland Press.

Malikail, J. S. 1981. "A Philosophy of Mind Adequate for Discourse on Morality: Iris Murdoch's Critique." *Journal of Educational Thought* 15(1): 61–72.

Malinowski, Bronislaw. 1922. *Argonauts of the Western Pacific*. New York: E. P. Dutton.

————. 1929a. "Practical Anthropology." *Africa* 2:22–38.

————. 1929b. *The Sexual Life of Savages in Northwestern Melanesia*. London: Routledge.

————. 1935. *Coral Gardens and Their Magic*. New York: American Book Company.

————. 1939. "The Group and the Individual in Functional Analysis." *American Journal of Sociology* 44:938–964.

————. 1954 [1925]. *Magic, Science and Religion, and Other Essays*. New York: Doubleday.

————. 1955 [1927]. *Sex and Repression in Savage Society*. New York: Meridian.

————. 1967. *A Diary in the Strict Sense of the Term*. New York: Harcourt, Brace and World.

Malotki, Ekkehart. 1983. *Hopi Time: A Linguistic Analysis of the Temporal Concepts in the Hopi Language*. Trends in Linguistics, Studies and Monographs 20. Berlin: Mouton.

Malthus, Thomas Robert. 1926 [1798]. *An Essay on the Principles of Population as It Affects the Future Improvement of Society with Remarks on the Speculations of Mr. Godwin, M. Condorcet, and Other Writers*. London: Macmillan.

Mandel, Ernest. 1990. "Karl Marx." In *Marxian Economics*, edited by John Eatwell, Murray Milgate, and Peter Newman, 1–38. London: Palgrave.

Manganaro, Marc, ed. 1990. *Modernist Anthropology: From Fieldwork to Text*. Princeton, NJ: Princeton University Press.

Manners, David. 1973. "Obituary of Julian Steward." *American Ethnologist* 75:886–903.

Marcus, George. 1992. "Cultural Anthropology at Rice since the 1980s." Provost lecture, February 17, 1992. https://www.ruf.rice.edu/-anth/research/marcus-provost-lecture.htm.

Marcus, George E., and Dick Cushman. 1982. "Ethnographies as Texts." *Annual Reviews of Anthropology* 11:25–69.

Marsland, Rebecca. 2013. "Pondo Pins and Nyakyusa Hammers: Monica and Godfrey in Bunyakyusa." In *Inside African Anthropology: Monica Wilson and Her Interpreters*, edited by Andrew Bank and Leslie J. Bank, 129–161. Cambridge: Cambridge University Press.

Marx, Karl. 1930 [1867]. *Capital: A Critique of Political Economy*. 4th ed. Translated by Paul Eden and Paul Ceder. New York: E. P. Dutton.

Marx, Karl. 1952. "The Eighteenth Brumaire of Louis Bonaparte." Marxists.org. https://www.marxists.org/archive/marx/works/1852/18th-brumaire. Retrieved August 20, 2019.

————. 1963 [1844]. "On the Jewish Question." In *Karl Marx: Early Writings*, edited by T. B. Bottomore, 3–40. New York: McGraw-Hill.

————. 1993 [1858]. *Grundrisse: Foundations of the Critique of Political Economy (Rough Draft)*. New York: Penguin Classics.

Marx, Karl, and Friedrich Engels. 1970 [1846]. *The German Ideology: Part One with Selections from Parts Two and Three, Together with Marx's Introduction to A Critique of Political Economy*. Edited by C. J. Arthur. New York: International Publishing.

————. 1972 [1848]. "The Communist Manifesto." In *Karl Marx: Essential Writings*, edited by Fredrick L. Bender, 240–263. New York: Harper & Row.

————. 1975 [1845]. *The Holy Family: Or, Critique of Critical Criticism: Against Bruno Bauer and Company*. Moscow: Progress Publishers.

Maskara, Shreya. 2021. "Cow Protection Legislation and Vigilante Violence in India." ACLED, May 3. https://acleddata.com/2021/05/03/cow-protection-legislation-and-vigilante-violence-in-india.

Mason, Otis. 1895. "Similarities in Culture." *American Anthropologist* 8:101–117.

Mattingly, Cheryl. 2010. *The Paradox of Hope: Journeys through a Clinical Borderland*. Berkeley: University of California.

————. 2014. *Moral Laboratories: Family Peril and the Struggle for a Good Life*. Oakland: University of California.

————. 2017. "Cheryl Mattingly." John Simon Guggenheim Memorial Foundation. https://www.gf.org/fellows/all-fellows/cheryl-mattingly. Retrieved May 31, 2019.

Mauss, Marcel. 1925. "In Memoriam. L'oeuvre inedited de Durkheim et de ses collaborateurs." *L'Année sociologique*, n.s., 1:8–29.

————. 1935. "Les techniques du corps" [The techniques of the Body]. *Journal de psychologie normal et pathologique* 32:271–293.

———. 1947. *Manuel d'ethnographie*. Paris: Payot.

———. 2000 [1925]. *The Gift: Forms and Functions of Exchange in Archaic Societies*. Translated by W. D. Halls. New York: Norton.

———. 2009. *Techniques, Technology and Civilisation*. New York: Durkheim Press/Berghahn Books.

Mazur-Stommen, Susan. 2018. Comments to "What is the relationship between philosophy and cultural anthropology? How are they similar/different." Quora. https://www.quora.com/What-is-the-relationship-between-philosophy-and-cultural-anthropology-How-are-they-similar-different. Retrieved June 4, 2019.

Mazza, Joe. 2018. "The Eric Garner Incident: Sentinel Calls for Greater Scholarly Support in Policymaking." *Journal of Criminal Justice and Law* 2(2). https://doi.org/10.21428/b6e95092.b820d350.

McDermott, Monica, and Annie Ferguson. 2022. "Sociology of Whiteness." *Annual Review of Sociology* 48(1): 257–276.

McDowell, Nancy. 1980. "The Oceanic Ethnography of Margaret Mead." *American Anthropologist* 82(2): 278–303.

McGee, R. Jon. 2002. *Watching Lacandon Maya Lives*. Boston: Allyn & Bacon.

McGuire, Joseph D. 1900. "In Memoriam: Frank Hamilton Cushing." *American Anthropologist* 2(2): 354–380.

McKay, Dwanna L., Kirsten Vinyeta, and Kari Marie Norgaard. 2020. "Theorizing Race and Settler Colonialism within U.S. Sociology." *Sociology Compass* 14(9).

McLaren, Angus. 1974. "Some Secular Attitudes toward Sexual Behavior in France: 1760–1860." *French Historical Studies* 8(4): 604–625.

McLennan, John Ferguson. 1865. *Primitive Marriage: An Inquiry into the Origin of the Form of Capture in Marriage Ceremonies*. Edinburgh: A. and C. Black.

McWhorter, John. 2011. "The Root: Zora Neale Hurston Was a Conservative." NPR, January 5. https://www.npr.org/2011/01/05/132674087/the-root-zora-neale-hurston-was-a-conservative. Retrieved May 31, 2019.

———. 2014. *The Language Hoax: Why the World Looks the Same in Any Language*. New York: Oxford Press.

Mead, Margaret. 1928. *Coming of Age in Samoa: A Psychological Study of Primitive Youth for Western Civilization*. New York: William Morrow.

———. 1930. *Growing Up in New Guinea: A Comparative Study of Primitive Education*. New York: William Morrow.

———. 1935. *Sex and Temperament in Three Primitive Societies*. New York: William Morrow.

———. 1939. "Native Languages as Field-Work Tools." *American Anthropologist* 41(2): 189–205.

———. 1949. *Male and Female: A Study of the Sexes in a Changing World*. New York: William Morrow.

———. 1956. *New Lives for Old; Cultural Transformation—Manus, 1928–1953*. New York: Morrow.

———. 1959. *An Anthropologist at Work*. New York: Avon.

Melina, Remy. 2011. "Why Do Dogs Walk in Circles before Lying Down?" Live Science, March 28. https://www.livescience.com/33160-why-do-dogs-walk-in-circles-before-lying-down.html. Retrieved May 31, 2019.

Mercier, Charles. 1883. "Mr. H. Spencer's Classification of Cognitions." *Mind* 8(30): 260–267.

Merry, Sally E. 2006. *Human Rights and Gender Violence: Translating International Law into Local Justice*. Chicago: University of Chicago.

Métraux, Rhoda B., and Margaret Mead. 1955. *Themes in French Culture: A Preface to a Study of French Community*. Stanford, CA: Stanford University Press.

Metzger, D. 1965. Review of *The Nature of Cultural Things*, by Marvin Harris. *American Anthropologist* 67(5): 1293–1296.

Miller, Jacques-Alain, and Richard Miller. 1987. "Jeremy Bentham's Panoptic Device." *October* 41 (Summer): 3–29.

Miller, James, and Jim Miller. 2000. *The Passion of Michel Foucault*. Cambridge, MA: Harvard University Press.

Modell, Judith Schachter. 1983. *Ruth Benedict: Patterns of a Life*. Philadelphia: University of Pennsylvania Press.

Montagu, Ashley. 1980. *Sociobiology Examined*. Oxford: Oxford University Press.

Moore, Henrietta L. 1994. *A Passion for Difference: Essays in Anthropology and Gender*. Bloomington: Indiana University Press.

————. 2012. "The Books that Inspired Henrietta Moore." *LSE Review of Books*, June 24. https://blogs. lse.ac.uk/lsereviewofbooks/2012/06/24/the-books-that-inspired-henrietta-moore. Retrieved May 31, 2019.

Moore, Henrietta, and Todd Sanders. 2006. *Anthropology in Theory: Issues in Epistemology*. Malden, MA: Blackwell.

Moore, Kimberley C. 2018. "Lynchings, Klan Activity Part of Polk's History." *The Ledger*, May 7. https://www.theledger.com/news/20180505/lynchings-klan-activity-part-of-polks-history. Retrieved May 31, 2019.

Morgan, Elaine. 1972. *The Descent of Woman*. New York: Stein and Day.

————. 1982. *The Aquatic Ape*. New York: Stein and Day.

Morgan, Lewis Henry. 1871. *Systems of Consanguinity and Affinity of the Human Family*. Smithsonian Contributions to Knowledge 17. Washington, DC: Smithsonian Institution.

————. 1910 [1877]. *Ancient Society or Researches in the Line of Human Progress from Savagery to Barbarism to Civilization*. Chicago: Charles H. Kerr.

————. 1966 [1851]. *League of the Ho-dé-no-sau-nee or Iroquois*. New York: B. Franklin.

Morgen, Sandra. 1989. "Gender and Anthropology: Introductory Essay." In *Gender and Anthropology: Critical Reviews for Research and Teaching*, edited by Sandra Morgen, 1–20. Washington, DC: American Anthropological Association.

Morrison, Toni. 1987. *Beloved*. New York: Knopf.

Morton, Samuel G. 1839. *Crania Americana*. Philadelphia: J. Dobson.

————. 1844. *Crania Aegyptica*. Philadelphia: J. Penington.

Müller, F. Max. 1977 [1856]. *Comparative Mythology*. New York: Arno Press.

Murarka, Shubhra. 2021. Review of *Mohawk Interruptus: Political Life across the Border of Settler States*, by Audra Simpson. *JASO: Online Journal of the Anthropological Society of Oxford* 13(2): 195–200.

Murdoch, Iris. 1970. *The Sovereignty of Good*. New York: Ark Paperbacks.

Murdock, George Peter. 1947. "Bifurcate Merging, A Test of Five Theories." *American Anthropologist* 49(1): 56–68.

————. 1951. "British Social Anthropology." *American Anthropologist* 53:465–473.

————. 1959. "Evolution in Social Organization." In *Evolution and Anthropology*, edited by B. Meggers, 126–145. Washington, DC: Anthropological Society of Washington.

————. 1960 [1949]. *Social Structure*. New York: Macmillan.

Murphy, Robert F. 1994. "The Dialectics of Deeds and Words." In *Assessing Cultural Anthropology*, edited by R. Borofsky, 55–61. New York: McGraw-Hill.

————. 2004. "Julian H. Steward." In *Totems and Teachers: Key Figures in the History of Anthropology*, edited by Sydel Silverman, 125–149. New York: AltaMira Press.

Nadel, S. F. 1954. *Nupe Religion*. London: Routledge and Kegan Paul.

Nanda, Serena. 1990. *Neither Man nor Woman: The Hijras of India*. Belmont, CA: Wadsworth.

Naroll, Raoul. 1961. Review of *Evolution and Culture*, by Marshall D. Sahlins and Elman R. Service. *American Anthropologist* 63(2): 389–392.

Newman, Fred, and Lois Holzman. 1993. *Lev Vygotsky: Revolutionary Scientist*. New York: Routledge.

New York Society for Ethical Culture (NYSFEC). N.d. "What Is Ethical Culture?" https://www.nysec. org/whatis. Retrieved April 15, 2016.

Nichols, Roger L. 1996. Review of *Parading through History: The Making of the Crow Nation in America, 1805–1935*, by Frederick E. Hoxie. *Reviews in American History* 24(3): 407–411.

Nietzsche, Friedrich. 1954 [1883–1885]. *Thus Spake Zarathustra*. New York: Modern Library.

————. 1956 [1871/1887]. *The Birth of Tragedy and On the Genealogy of Morals*. Garden City, NY: Doubleday.

————. 1967 [1901]. *The Will to Power*. New York: Vintage.

————. 1968 [1895]. "The Antichrist." In *The Portable Nietzsche*, edited by Walter Kaufman, 565–656. New York: Penguin.

————. 1974 [1882]. *The Gay Science*. New York: Vintage.

Northrup, F. S. C. 1947. *The Logic of the Sciences and the Humanities*. New York: Macmillan.

NYCLU (ACLU of New York). 2023. "Stop and Frisk Data." NYCLU. https://www.nyclu.org/en/stop -and-frisk-data, https://www.nyclu.org/en/closer-look-stop-and-frisk-nyc.

NYPD (New York Police Department). 2012. "Police Officer Frequently Asked Questions." https:// www.nyc.gov/site/nypd/careers/police-officers/faqs-hiring-pos.page.

Obeyesekere, Gananath. 1981. *Medusa's Hair: An Essay on Personal Symbols and Religious Experience*. Chicago: University of Chicago Press.

————. 1992. *The Apotheosis of Captain Cook: European Mythmaking in the Pacific*. Princeton, NJ: Princeton University Press.

O'Brien, Jean M. 2010. *Firsting and Lasting: Writing Indians out of Existence in New England*. University of Minnesota Press.

O'Dell, Tom, and Peter Billings. 2005. *Experiencescapes: Tourism, Culture and Economy*. Copenhagen: Copenhagen Business School Press.

Ogawa, Tadashi, and Bret Davis. 2000. "The Horizonal Character of Phenomena and the Shining-Forth of Things." *Research in Phenomenology* 30:146–157.

O'Laughlin, Bridget. 1975. "Marxist Approaches in Anthropology." In *Annual Review of Anthropology*, edited by Bernard Siegel, Alan Beals, and Stephen Tyler, 4:341–370. Palo Alto, CA: Annual Reviews.

Ollion, Etienne. 2012. "Pierre Bourdieu." Oxford Bibliographies. https://www.oxfordbibliographies.com/view/document/obo-978019 9756384/obo-9780199756384–0083.xml.

O'Meara, J. Tim. 1989. "Anthropology as Empirical Science." *American Anthropologist* 91:354–369.

Ong, Aihwa. 1999. *Flexible Citizenship: The Logic of Transnationality*. Durham, NC: Duke University Press.

Opler, Morris E. 1967. "Franz Boas: Religion and Theory." *American Anthropologist* 69(6): 741–745.

Oppenheimer, Franz. 1914. *The State: Its History and Development Viewed Sociologically*. Translated by John M. Gitterman. Indianapolis: Bobbs-Merrill.

Orlove, Benjamin S. 1980. "Ecological Anthropology." In *Annual Review of Anthropology*, edited by Bernard Siegel, Alan Beals, and Stephen Tyler, 9:235–273. Palo Alto, CA: Annual Reviews.

Ortner, Sherry B. 1972. "Is Female to Male as Nature Is to Nurture?." In *Women, Culture, and Society*, edited by Michelle Rosaldo and Louise Lamphere, 67–80. Palo Alto, CA: Stanford University Press.

————. 1973. "On Key Symbols." *American Anthropologist* 75:1338–1346.

————. 1975. "Gods' Bodies, Gods' Food: A Symbolic Analysis of Sherpa Ritual." In *The Interpretation of Symbolism*, edited by Ray Willis, 133–167. New York: Wiley.

————. 1984. "Theory in Anthropology since the Sixties." *Comparative Studies in Society and History* 26(1): 126–166.

————. 1989. "Gender Hegemonies." *Cultural Critique*, 14: 35–80. https://doi.org/10.2307/1354292.

————. 1996. "So, Is Female to Male as Nature Is to Culture?" In *Making Gender: The Politics and Erotics of Culture*. Boston: Beacon Press, 173–180.

————. 2003. *New Jersey Dreaming: Capital, Culture, and the Class of '58*. Durham, NC: Duke University Press.

————. 2005. "Subjectivity and Cultural Critique." *Anthropological Theory* 5(1): 31–52.

————. 2006. *Anthropology and Social Theory: Culture, Power, and the Acting Subject*. Durham, NC: Duke University Press.

Ortner, Sherry B., and Harriet Whitehead. 1981a. "Introduction: Accounting for Sexual Meanings." In *Sexual Meanings: The Cultural Construction of Gender and Sexuality*, 1–27. Cambridge: Cambridge University Press.

————. 1981b. *Sexual Meanings: The Cultural Construction of Gender and Sexuality*. Cambridge: Cambridge University Press.

Ospovat, Dov. 1976. "The Influence of Karl Ernst von Baer's Embryology, 1828–1859: A Reappraisal in Light of Richard Owen's and William B. Carpenter's 'Palaeontological Application of Von Baer's Law.'" *Journal of the History of Biology* 9(1): 1–28.

Owen, David. 1994. *Maturity and Modernity: Nietzsche, Weber, Foucault and the Ambivalence of Reason*. New York: Routledge.

Padilla, Andrew. 2013. El Barrio Tours (film with independent distribution).

Pan, Chengxin. 2008. "Contractual Thinking and Responsible Government in China: A Constructivist Framework for Analysis." *China Review* 8(2): 49–75.

Parezo, Nancy J. 2007. "Reassessing Anthropology's Maverick: The Archaeological Fieldwork of Frank Hamilton Cushing." *American Ethnologist* 34(3): 575–580.

Parini, Jay. 1985. "The Importance of Stanley Cavell." *Hudson Review* 38(1): 115–119.

Parsons, Elsie C. 1936. "The House Clan Complex of the Pueblos." In *Essays in Anthropology: Presented to A. L. Kroeber in Celebration of His Sixtieth Birthday, June 11, 1936*, edited by Robert H. Lowie, 229–231. Berkeley: University of California Press.

Pathe, R. A. 1988. "Gene Weltfish." In *Women Anthropologists: A Biographical Dictionary*, edited by Ute Gacs, Aisha Khan, Jerrie McIntyre, and Ruth Weinberg, 372–381. New York: Greenwood Press.

Paulme, Denise. 1960. *Femmes d'Afrique Noire*. Paris: Mouton.

Peace, William J. 1993. "Leslie White and Evolutionary Theory." *Dialectical Anthropology* 18(2): 123–151.

———. 1998. "Bernhard Stern, Leslie A. White, and an Anthropological Appraisal of the Russian Revolution." *American Anthropologist* 100(1): 84–93.

———. 2004. *Leslie A. White: Evolution and Revolution in Anthropology*. Omaha: University of Nebraska Press.

———. 2007. "Leslie A. White and the Socio-Politics of War." *Histories of Anthropology Annual* 3:1–21.

Peace, William, and David H. Price. 2001. "The Cold War Context of the FBI's Investigation of Leslie A. White." *American Anthropologist* 103(1): 164–167.

Pew Research Center. 2013. "The Global Divide on Homosexuality." June 4. https://www.pewresearch .org/global/2013/06/04/the-global-divide-on-homosexuality. Retrieved May 31, 2019.

———. 2015. "Cell Phones in Africa: Communication Lifeline." April 15. https://www.pewresearch .org/global/2015/04/15/cell-phones-in-africa-communication-lifeline.

Pike, Kenneth. 1954. *Language in Relation to a Unified Theory of the Structure of Human Behavior*. Vol. 1. Glendale, CA: Summer Institute of Linguistics.

Pinker, Steven. 1994. *The Language Instinct: How the Mind Creates Language*. New York: HarperCollins.

Planas, Antonio. 2023. "New Florida Standards Teach Students That Some Black People Benefited from Slavery Because It Taught Useful Skills." NBC News, July 20. https://www.nbcnews.com /news/us-news/new-florida-standards-teach-black-people-benefited-slavery-taught-usef-rcna95418.

Plato. 1993. *Republic*. Translated by Robin Waterfield. Oxford: Oxford University Press.

Polanyi, Karl. 1944. *The Great Transformation*. Boston: Beacon.

Polanyi, Karl, Conrad M. Arensberg, and Harry W. Pearson. 1957. *Trade and Market in the Early Empires: Economies in History and Theory*. Glencoe, IL: Free Press.

Pollak, Richard. 1997. *The Creation of Dr. B: A Biography of Bruno Bettelheim*. New York: Simon & Schuster.

Pollis, Carol A. 1987. "The Apparatus of Sexuality: Reflections on Foucault's Contributions to the Study of Sex in History." *Journal of Sex Research* 23(3): 401–408.

Precht, J. 2017. "Asserting Tribal Sovereignty through Compact Negotiations: A Case Study of the Coushatta Tribe of Louisiana." *American Indian Quarterly* 41(1): 67–92.

Preece, Harold. 1936. "The Negro Folk Cult." *The Crisis* 43(12): 364–365.

Price, David. 2000. "Anthropologists as Spies." *The Nation* 271(16): 24–27.

———. 2004. *Threatening Anthropology: McCarthyism and the FBI's Harassment of Activist Anthropologists*. Durham, NC: Duke University Press.

———. 2011. "How the CIA and Pentagon Harnessed Anthropological Research during the Second World War and Cold War with Little Critical Notice." *Journal of Anthropological Research* 67(3): 333–356.

Pritchett, Anthony. 2007. *Friends for Life, Friends for Death: Cohorts and Consciousness among the Lunda-Ndembu*. Charlottesville: University of Virginia Press.

Pruetz, J. D., and P. Bertolani. 2007. "Savanna Chimpanzees, *Pan troglodytes verus*, Hunt with Tools." *Current Biology* 17:412–417.

Putnam, Robert D. 2000. *Bowling Alone: The Collapse and Revival of American Community*. New York: Simon & Schuster.

Pyyhtinen, Olli. 2014. *The Gift and Its Paradoxes: Beyond Mauss*. Surrey, UK: Ashgate.

Quetelet, Adolphe. 1848. *Du système sociale et des lois qui le régissent*. Paris: Guillaumin.

———. 1968 [1835]. *A Treatise on Man and the Development of His Faculties*. New York: B. Franklin.

Quinn, Naomi. 2006. "The Self." *Anthropological Theory* 6(3): 362–384.

Rabinow, Paul. 1977. *Reflections on Fieldwork in Morocco*. Berkeley: University of California Press.

———. 1986. "Representations Are Social Facts: Modernity and Postmodernity in Anthropology." In *Writing Culture: The Poetics and Politics of Ethnography*, edited by James Clifford and George Marcus, 234–261. Berkeley: University of California Press.

"Race in Malaysia: Failing to Spread the Wealth." 2005. *The Economist*, April 25. https://www.econo mist.com/node/4323219.

Radcliffe-Brown, A. R. 1924. "The Mother's Brother in South Africa." *South African Journal of Science* 21:542–555.

———. 1964 [1922]. *The Andaman Islanders*. New York: Free Press.

———. 1965a [1940]. "On Joking Relationships." *In Structure and Function in Primitive Society*, 90–104. New York: Free Press.

———. 1965b [1935]. "On the Concept of Function in Social Science." *In Structure and Function in Primitive Society*, 178–187. New York: Free Press.

Radin, Paul. 1911. "Description of a Winnebago Funeral." *American Anthropologist* 13(3): 437–444.

———. 1924. "Ojibwa Ethnological Chit Chat." *American Anthropologist* 26(4): 491–530.

———, ed. 1926. *Crashing Thunder: The Autobiography of an American Indian*. New York: Appleton.

———. 1957 [1927]. *Primitive Man as Philosopher*. 2nd ed. New York: Dover Publications.

Ragland, Alex. 2021. "A Review of 'to Protect and Serve.'" *Georgetown University Undergraduate Law Review*, May 10. https://guulr.com/2021/05/10/a-review-of-to-protect-and-serve.

Rappaport, Roy A. 1967. *Pigs for the Ancestors*. New Haven, CT: Yale University Press.

———. 1971. "Ritual, Sanctity, and Cybernetics." *American Anthropologist* 73(1): 59–76.

———. 1984. *Pigs for the Ancestors*. 2nd ed. New Haven, CT: Yale University Press.

———. 1994. "Humanity's Evolution and Anthropology's Future." In *Assessing Cultural Anthropology*, edited by R. Borofsky, 153–167. New York: McGraw-Hill.

"Rates on Overseas Phone Calls Decline." 1982. *New York Times*, May 19, 14.

Rawson, Claude. 1994. "The Masks of M. Foucault." *Sewanee Review* 102(3): 471–476.

Reiter, Rayna, ed. 1975. *Toward an Anthropology of Women*. New York: Monthly Review Press.

Resek, Carl. 1960. *Lewis Henry Morgan: American Scholar*. Chicago: University of Chicago Press.

Ricardo, David. 1817. *On the Principles of Political Economy and Taxation*. London: John Murray.

Ringel, Gail. 1979. "The Kawkiutl Potlatch: History, Economics, and Symbols." *Ethnohistory* 26(4): 347–362.

Ritzer, George. 1992. *Sociological Theory*. 3rd ed. New York: McGraw-Hill.

Rivers, W. H. R. 1900. "A Genealogical Method of Collecting Social and Vital Statistics." *Journal of the Anthropological Institute*, n.s., 3:74–82.

———. 1910. "The Genealogical Method of Anthropological Inquiry." *Sociological Review* 3:1–12.

Robbins, Joel. 2013. "Beyond the Suffering Subject: Toward an Anthropology of the Good." *Journal of the Royal Anthropological Institute* 19(3): 447–462.

"Robert Kuok [#114, The World's Richest People]." 2006. The World's Billionaires.

Rogers, Lee. 2017. "Barack Obama Is a Cocaine Sniffing Faggot Says New Biography." *Daily Stormer*, May 4.

Roheim, Geza. 1971 [1925]. *Australian Totemism: A Psychoanalytic Study in Anthropology*. New York: Humanities Press.

Romanucci-Ross, Lola. 2001. "Celebrants and the Celebrity: Biography as Trope." *American Anthropologist* 103(4): 1174–1178.

Rorty, Richard, ed. 1967. *The Linguistic Turn: Essays in Philosophical Method*. Chicago: University of Chicago.

———. 1979. *Philosophy and the Mirror of Knowledge*. Princeton, NJ: Princeton University Press.

Rosaldo, Michelle. 1974. "Women, Culture, and Society: A Theoretical Overview." In *Women, Culture, and Society*, edited by Michelle Rosaldo and Louise Lamphere, 14–42. Palo Alto, CA: Stanford University Press.

Rosaldo, Michelle, and Louise Lamphere, eds. 1974. *Women, Culture, and Society*. Palo Alto, CA: Stanford University Press.

———. 1980. *Knowledge and Passion: Ilongot Notions of Self and Social Life*. Cambridge: Cambridge University Press.

Rosas, Gilberto. 2012. *Barrio Libre: Criminalizing States and Delinquent Refusals of the New Frontier*. Durham: Duke University Press.

Roscoe, Paul. 2014. "The End of War in Papua New Guinea: 'Crime' and 'Tribal Warfare' in Post-Colonial States." *Anthropologica* 56(2): 327–339.

Rose, David G. 2018. "How Islamists Stigmatise Indonesia's Transgender Waria." *South China Morning Post*, September 16.

Rosenberg, Daniel. 2017. "Taming the Minotaur: Bertrand de Jouvenel on Liberty and Authority." *Perspectives on Political Science* 46(2): 118–126.

Rosenberg, Rosalind. 2004. *Changing the Subject: How the Women of Columbia Shaped the Way We Think about Sex and Politics*. New York: Columbia University Press.

Roughley, A. R. 2003. "Textual Surveillance: The Double Eyes (and I's) of George Bataille's Story of the Eye." *Rhizomes: Cultural Studies in Emerging Knowledge* 6.

Rousseau, Jean-Jacques. 1974 [1762]. *Émile*. Translated by Barbara Foxley. New York: E. P. Dutton.

Rowe, Dorothy. 2005. "Money, Modernity, and Melancholia in the Writings of Georg Simmel." *Critical Studies* 25:27–38.

Rubin, Gayle S. 1984. "Thinking Sex: Notes for a Radical Theory of the Politics of Sexuality." In *Pleasure and Danger: Exploring Female Sexuality*, edited by Carole S. Vance, 3–44. New York: Routledge.

Ruddick, Nicholas. 2007. "Courtship with a Club: Wife-Capture in Prehistoric Fiction, 1865–1914." *Yearbook of English Studies*: 37(2): 45–63.

Rutherford, Scott. 2017. "'We Have Bigotry All Right-but No Alabamas': Racism and Aboriginal Protest in Canada during the 1960s." *American Indian Quarterly* 41(2): 158–179.

Ryang, Sonia. 2004. "Chrysanthemum's Strange Life: Ruth Benedict in Postwar Japan." Occasional Paper 32. Japan Policy Research Institute. https://www.jpri.org/publications/occasionalpapers/op32.html.

Rylko-Bauer, Barbara, Merrill Singer, and John van Willigen. 2006. "Reclaiming Applied Anthropology: Its Past, Present, and Future." *American Anthropologist* 108(1): 178–190.

Sacks, K. 1979. *Sisters and Wives: The Past and Future of Sexual Equality*. Westport, CT: Greenwood Press.

Safianow, Allen. 1988. "'Konklave in Kokomo' Revisited." *The Historian* 50(3): 329–347.

Sahlins, Marshall D. 1964. "Culture and Environment: The Study of Cultural Ecology." In *Horizons of Anthropology*, edited by Sol Tax, 132–147. Chicago: Aldine.

———. 1968. *Tribesmen*. Englewood Cliffs, NJ: Prentice Hall.

———. 1972. *Stone Age Economics*. Chicago: Aldine.

———. 1976. *The Use and Abuse of Biology: An Anthropological Critique of Sociobiology*. Ann Arbor: University of Michigan Press.

Sahlins, Marshall D., and Elman R. Service. 1960. *Evolution and Culture*. Ann Arbor: University of Michigan Press.

Said, Edward. 1978. *Orientalism*. New York: Pantheon.

Saint Martin, Manuel L. 1999. "Running Amok: A Modern Perspective on a Culture-Bound Syndrome." Primary Care Companion, *Journal of Clinical Psychiatry* 1(3): 66–70.

Salamone, Frank. 2014. "His Eyes Were Watching Her: Papa Franz Boas, Zora Neale Hurston, and Anthropology." *Anthropos* 109:217–224.

Salazar-Lopez, Leila. 2011. "A Call to Protest the Belo Monte Dam, June 19th and 20th." Amazon Watch, June 15. https://amazonwatch.org/news/2011/0615-protest-the-belo-monte-dam. Retrieved November 16, 2015.

Saletin, William. 2021. "Americans Don't Want to Defund the Police. Here's What They Do Want." *Slate*, October 17. https://slate.com/news-and-politics/2021/10/police-reform-polls-white-black-crime.html.

Salter, Jim. 2017. "Ferguson Attorney: Brown Family Settlement $1.5 Million." *AP*. June 23. https://apnews.com/general-news-24f52e10c5db47fbbee037df230d8819.

Samaha, Albert. 2014. "Cheaper, More Addictive, and Highly Profitable: How Crack Took Over NYC in the '80s." *Village Voice*, August 12. https://www.villagevoice.com/news/cheaper-more-addictive-and-highly-profitable-how-crack-took-over-nyc-in-the-80s-6664480.

Sanday, Peggy Reeves. 1980. "Margaret Mead's View of Sex Roles in Her Own and Other Societies." *American Anthropologist* 82(2): 340–348.

———. 1981. *Female Power and Male Dominance: On the Origins of Sexual Inequality*. New York: Cambridge University Press.

Sanday, Peggy Reeves, and Ruth Gallagher Goodenough, eds. 1990. *Beyond the Second Sex: New Directions in the Anthropology of Gender*. Philadelphia: University of Pennsylvania Press.

Sangren, Steven P. 1988. "Rhetoric and the Authority of Ethnography." *Current Anthropology* 29(3): 405–435.

Sapir, Edward. 1924. "Culture, Genuine and Spurious." *American Journal of Sociology* 29:401–429.

———. 1934. "Symbolism." In *Encyclopedia of the Social Sciences* 14:492–495. New York: Macmillan.

Sartre, Jean-Paul. 1946. *Réflexions Sur La Question Juive [Anti-Semite and Jew]*. Paris: Gallinard.

———. 1956. *Being and Nothingness: An Essay on Phenomenological Ontology*. New York: Philosophical Library.

———. 1989 [1946]. "Existentialism Is a Humanism." In *Existentialism from Dostoevsky to Sartre*, edited by Walter Kaufman. New York: Meridian.

Sassoon, A. S. 1991. "Hegemony." In *A Dictionary of Marxist Thought*, edited by T. Bottomore, 229–231. Oxford: Basil Blackwell.

Sauer, Carl Ortwin. 1968. *Northern Mists*. Berkeley: University of California Press.

Sawicki, J. 1991. *Disciplining Foucault: Feminism, Power, and the Body*. New York: Routledge.

Scheper-Hughes, Nancy. 1979. *Saints, Scholars, and Schizophrenics: Mental Illness in Rural Ireland.* Berkeley: University of California Press.

———. 1989. "Death without Weeping." *Natural History* 98:8–16.

———. 1992. *Death without Weeping: The Violence of Everyday Life in Brazil.* Berkeley: University of California Press.

———. 1995. "The Primacy of the Ethical: Propositions for a Militant Anthropology." *Current Anthropology* 36(3): 409–420.

Scheutz, Jenny. 2020. "Rethinking Homeownership Incentives to Improve Household Financial Security and Shrink the Racial Wealth Gap." Brookings Institution, December 9. https://www .brookings.edu/articles/rethinking-homeownership-incentives-to-improve-household-financial-se curity-and-shrink-the-racial-wealth-gap.

Schneider, David M. 1968. *American Kinship: A Cultural Account.* Englewood Cliffs, NJ: Prentice Hall.

Schneider, Jane, and Rayna Rapp, eds. 1995. *Articulating Hidden Histories: Exploring the Influence of Eric R. Wolf.* Berkeley: University of California Press.

Schott, Rudiger. 1976. "More on Marx and Morgan." *Current Anthropology* 17(4): 731–734.

Schroedel, Jean R., and Aslanian Artour. 2017. "A Case Study of Descriptive Representation: The Experience of Native American Elected Officials in South Dakota." *American Indian Quarterly* 41(3): 250–286.

Schumpeter, Joseph A. 1942. *Capitalism, Socialism, and Democracy.* New York: Harper and Brothers.

Scott, David. 1997. "Leibniz and the Two Clocks." *Journal of the History of Ideas* 58(3): 445–463.

Scott, James. 1985. *Weapons of the Weak: Everyday Forms of Peasant Resistance.* New Haven, CT: Yale University Press.

———. 1990. *Domination and the Arts of Resistance: Hidden Transcripts.* New Haven, CT: Yale University Press.

———. 2000. *Seeing Like a State.* New Haven, CT: Yale University Press.

Seligman, Charles G. 1910. *The Melanesians of British New Guinea.* Cambridge: Cambridge University Press.

Selsam, Howard, and Harry Martel. 1963. *Reader in Marxist Philosophy.* New York: International Publishers.

Service, Elman R. 1962. *Primitive Social Organization: An Evolutionary Perspective.* New York: Random House.

———. 1963. *Profiles in Ethnology.* New York: Harper & Row.

———. 1976. "Leslie Alvin White, 1900–1975." *American Anthropologist* 78(3): 612–617.

———. 1981. "The Mind of Lewis H. Morgan." *Current Anthropology* 22:25–31.

———. 1988. "Morton Herbert Fried (1923–1986)." *American Anthropologist* 90(1): 148–152.

Shankman, Paul. 2009. *The Trashing of Margaret Mead: Anatomy of an Anthropological Controversy.* Madison: University of Wisconsin Press.

Shankman, Paul, and Angela Thieman Dino. 2001. "The FBI File of Leslie A. White." *American Anthropologist* 103(1): 161–164.

Shannon, Claude. 1948. "A Mathematical Theory of Communication." *Bell System Technical Journal* 27:379–423.

Shipp, E. R. 1980. "Prof. Gene Weltfish Dead at 78; Was a Target of Anti-Red Drives." *New York Times,* August 5, B101.

Shokeid, Moshe. 2004. "Max Gluckman and the Making of Israeli Anthropology." *Ethnos* 69(3): 387–410.

Silk, Joan B., Sarah F. Brosnan, Joseph Henrich, Susan P. Lambeth, and Steven Shapiro. 2013. "Chimpanzees Share Food for Many Reasons: The Role of Kinship, Reciprocity, Social Bonds and Harassment on Food Transfers." *Animal Behavior* 85(5): 941–947.

Silverman, J. 1967. "Shamanism and Acute Schizophrenia." *American Anthropologist* 69:21–31.

Silverstein, Michael. 1993. "Metapragmatic Discourse and Metapragmatic Function." In *Reflexive Language: Reported Speech and Metapragmatics,* edited by John A. Lucy, 33–58. Cambridge: Cambridge University Press.

Simmel, Georg. 1971. *On Individuality and Social Forms: Selected Writings.* Chicago: University of Chicago.

Simoons, Frederick J. 1979. "Questions in the Sacred-Cow Controversy [and comments and reply]." *Current Anthropology* 20(3): 467–493.

———. 1981. *Eat Not This Flesh: Food Avoidances in the Old World.* Westport, CT: Greenwood Press.

Simpson, Audra. 2014. *Mohawk Interruptus: Political Life across the Borders of Settler States.* Durham, NC: Duke University Press.

Slater, Robert B. 1998–1999. "The First Black Faculty Members at the Nation's Highest-Ranked Universities." *Journal of Blacks in Higher Education* 22 (Winter): 97–106.

Sloan, Richard P. 2006. "Trivializing the Transcendent: What Can Science Really Tell Us about Faith?" *Christianity Today*, August 1.

Smith, Adam. 1976 [1776]. *An Inquiry into the Nature and Causes of the Wealth of Nations.* Oxford: Clarendon Press.

Smith, Anna V. 2020. "Trump's Impact on Indian Country over Four Years." *High Country News*, December 16. https://www.hcn.org/articles/indigenous-affairs-trumps-impact-on-indian-country-over-four-years.

Smith, Clint. 2021. *How the Word Is Passed: A Reckoning with the History of Slavery across America.* New York: Little, Brown.

Smith, Daniel, and John Protevi. 2018. "Gilles Deleuze." In *Stanford Encyclopedia of Philosophy.* https://plato.stanford.edu/entries/deleuze. Retrieved May 31, 2019.

Smith, Grafton Elliot. 1928. *In the Beginning: The Origin of Civilization.* New York: Morrow.

Smith, Watson, and John M. Roberts. 1954. "Zuni Law, a Field of Values." *Papers of the Peabody Museum* 3(1). Cambridge, MA: Harvard University Press.

Sokefeld, Martin. 1999. "Debating Self, Identity, and Culture in Anthropology." *Current Anthropology* 40(4): 417–448.

Solecki, R., and C. Wagley. 1963. "William Duncan Strong (1899–1962)." *American Anthropologist* 65(5): 1102–1111.

Spencer, Herbert. 1851. *Social Statics: Or, the Conditions Essential to Human Happiness Specified, and the First of Them Developed.* London: John Chapman.

———. 1859. "What Knowledge Is of Most Worth?" *Westminster Review* 72:1–41.

———. 1860. "The Social Organism." *Westminster Review*, n.s., 17:51–68.

———. 1873–1934. *Descriptive Sociology.* 13 vols. New York: Appleton-Century-Crofts.

———. 1884. *Man versus the State.* London: Williams and Norgate. https://www.econlib.org/library/LFBooks/Spencer/spnMvS0.html. Accessed April 9, 2016.

———. 1898 [1864]. *Principles of Biology.* New York: D. Appleton.

———. 1898 [1874]. *The Principles of Sociology.* Vol. 1. New York: D. Appleton.

———. 1902. *Facts and Comments.* New York: D. Appleton.

———. 1904. *An Autobiography: Herbert Spencer.* New York: D. Appleton.

———. 1961 [1873]. *The Study of Sociology.* Ann Arbor: University of Michigan Press.

———. 1969 [1851]. *Social Statics: The Conditions Essential to Human Happiness Specified, and the First of Them Developed.* New York: A. M. Kelley.

———. 1975 [1885]. *The Principles of Sociology.* Westport, CT: Greenwood Press.

Spencer, Leon P. 2013. *Toward an African Church in Mozambique: Kamba Simango and the Protestant Community in Manica and Sofala, 1892–1945.* Luwinga Mzuzu, Malawi: Mzuni Press.

Spier, Leslie, A. Irving Hallowell, and Stanley S. Newman, eds. 1941. *Language, Culture, and Personality: Essays in Memory of Edward Sapir.* Menasha, WI: Sapir Memorial Publication Fund.

Spinoza, Baruch. 1930 [1677]. *Ethics.* London: Oxford University Press.

Spores, John C. 1988. *Running Amok: An Historical Inquiry.* Athens: Ohio University Center for International Studies.

Spradley, James P. 1979. *The Ethnographic Interview.* New York: Holt, Rinehart and Winston.

———. 1980. *Participant Observation.* New York: Holt, Rinehart and Winston.

———, ed. 1987. *Culture and Cognition.* New York: Waveland Press.

Srinivas, M. N. 1952. *Religion and Society among the Coorgs of South India.* Oxford: Oxford University Press.

Statistica. 2018. "Smartphone Penetration Rate as Share of the Population in the United States from 2010 to 2021." https://www.statista.com/statistics/201183/forecast-of-smartphone-penetration-in-the-us.

Stavenhagen, Rodolfo. 1971. "Decolonializing Applied Social Sciences." *Human Organization* 30(4): 333–344.

Steele, Chandra. 2022. "Space Wars: 80s CRAY-2 Supercomputer vs. Modern-Day iPhone." *Wired*, November 23. https://www.pcmag.com/news/space-wars-the-cray-2-supercomputer-vs-the-iphone-12.

Steffen, L. H. 1989. *The Sovereignty of the Good.* Masterplots II: Nonfiction Series, 1–5.

Steward, Julian. 1939. "Changes in Shoshonean Indian Culture." *Scientific Monthly* 49(6): 524–537.

———. 1955. *Theory of Culture Change: The Methodology of Multilinear Evolution*. Urbana: University of Illinois Press.

Stirner, Max. 1918 [1844]. *The Ego and Its Own*. Translated by Steven T. Byington. New York: Boni and Liveright.

St. John, Graham. 2008. "Victor Turner and Contemporary Cultural Performance: An Introduction." In *Victor Turner and Contemporary Cultural Performance*, edited by Graham St. John, 1–37. New York: Berghahn.

Stocking, G. 1968. "The Scientific Reaction against Cultural Anthropology, 1917–1920." In *Race, Culture, and Evolution: Essays in the History of Anthropology*, 270–307. New York: Free Press.

———. 1974. *The Shaping of American Anthropology, 1883–1911*. New York: Basic Books.

———. 1983. *Observers Observed*. Madison: University of Wisconsin Press.

———. 1984. *Functionalism Historicized: Essays on British Social Anthropology*. Madison: University of Wisconsin Press.

———. 1987. *Victorian Anthropology*. New York: Free Press.

———. 1992. "Ideas and Institutions in American Anthropology: Thoughts toward a History of the Interwar Years." In *The Ethnographer's Magic and Other Essays in the History of Anthropology*, 114–177. Madison: University of Wisconsin Press.

———. 1995. *After Tylor: British Social Anthropology, 1888–1951*. Madison: University of Wisconsin Press.

Stoler, Ann Laura. 1989. "Making Empire Respectable: The Politics of Race and Sexual Morality in 20th-Century Colonial Cultures." *American Ethnologist* 16(4): 634–660.

———. 1995. *Race and the Education of Desire: Foucault's History of Sexuality and the Colonial Order of Things*. Durham, NC: Duke University Press.

———. 2002. *Carnal Knowledge and Imperial Power: Race and the Intimate in Colonial Rule*. Berkeley: University of California Press.

Stoll, David. 2023. "Decolonizing Anthropology—or Racializing It?" *Chronicle of Higher Education*, November 7. https://www.chronicle.com/article/decolonizing-anthropology-or-racializing-it.

Stoller, Paul. 1989. *The Taste of Ethnographic Things: The Senses in Anthropology*. Philadelphia: University of Pennsylvania Press.

Stopp, M., and G. Mitchell. 2010. "'Our Amazing Visitors': Catherine Cartwright's Account of Labrador Inuit in England." *Arctic* 63(4): 399–413.

Strauss, Claudia, and Naomi Quinn. 1994. "A Cognitive/Cultural Anthropology." In *Assessing Cultural Anthropology*, edited by Robert Borofsky, 284–300. New York: McGraw-Hill.

Strauss, David Friedrich. 1892. *The Life of Jesus*. 2nd ed. Translated by George Eliot. London: Swan and Sonnenschein.

Strawson, Galen. 2004. "Against Narrativity." *Ratio* 17(4): 428–452.

Strong, W. D. 1994. *Labrador Winter: The Ethnographic Journals of William Duncan Strong, 1927–1928*. Edited by Eleanor Leacock. Washington, DC: Smithsonian Institution Press.

Sturtevant, William C. 1964. "Studies in Ethnoscience." *American Anthropologist* 66:99–131.

Suchting, W. A. 1983. *Marx: An Introduction*. New York: New York University Press.

Sumner, William Graham. 1963a [1914]. *The Challenge of Facts and Other Essays*. Edited by Albert G. Keller. New Haven, CT: Yale University Press.

———. 1963b [1914]. "The Concentration of Wealth: Its Economic Justification." In *The Challenge of Facts and Other Essays*, edited by Albert G. Keller, 79–90. New Haven, CT: Yale University Press.

"Sumner, William Graham." 1967. *National Cyclopedia of American Biography* 25:8–9. Clifton, NJ: J. T. White.

Sumner, William Graham, and Albert G. Keller. 1927. *The Science of Society*. New Haven, CT: Yale University Press.

Sumser, Robert. 1992. "'Erziehung.' The Family and the Regulation of Sexuality in the Late German Enlightenment." *German Studies Review* 15(3): 455–474.

Tanner, Nancy, and Adrienne Zihlman. 1976. "Women in Evolution, Part I: Innovation and Selection in Human Origins." *Signs* 2(3).

Tax, Sol. 1958. "The Fox Project." *Human Organization* 17:17–19.

———. 1960. "Action Anthropology." In *Documentary History of the Fox Project, 1948–1959*, edited by Fred Gearing, Robert McC. Netting, and Lisa R. Peattie, 167–171. Chicago: University of Chicago Press.

———. 1975. "Action Anthropology." *Current Anthropology* 16(4): 514–517.

Taylor, Charles. 1979. "Interpretation and the Sciences of Man." In *Interpretive Social Science: A Reader*, edited by Paul Rabinow and W. M. Sullivan, 25–71. Berkeley: University of California Press.

———. 1992. "The Politics of Recognition." In *Multiculturalism: Examining the Politics of Recognition*, edited by A. Gutmann, 25–73. Princeton: Princeton University Press.

Taylor, Michael W. 2007. *The Philosophy of Herbert Spencer*. New York: Continuum.

Taylor, William Cooke. 1840. *The Natural History of Society in the Barbarous and Civilized State*. New York: Appleton.

Thapan, Meenakshi. 2002. "Pierre Bourdieu (1930–2002): A Personal Tribute." *Economic and Political Weekly* 37(9): 826–828.

Thomas, Elizabeth Marshall. 1959. *The Harmless People*. New York: Knopf.

Thomas, Nicholas. 1991. *Entangled Objects: Exchange, Material Culture, and Colonialism in the Pacific*. Cambridge, MA: Harvard University Press.

Thompson, John B. 1984. *Critical Hermeneutics: A Study in the Thought of Paul Ricoeur and Jurgen Habermas*. Cambridge: Cambridge University Press.

Thoreau, Henry David. 1854. *Walden or Life in the Woods*. Boston: Ticknor and Fields.

Throop, C. Jason. 2014. "Moral Moods." *Ethos* 42(1): 65–83.

Thrush, Coll. 2014. "The Iceberg and the Cathedral: Encounter, Entanglement, and Isuma in Inuit London." *Journal of British Studies* 53(1): 59–79.

Tirkkonen, Sanna. 2015. "Foucault's Understanding of Critique and Modernity." In *Engaging Foucault*, edited by Adriana Zaharijevic, Igor Cvejic, and Mark Losoncz, 1:12–23. Belgrade (Serbia): Institute for Philosophy and Social Theory.

Todorov, Tzvetzn. 1987. *Literature and Its Theorists: A Personal View of Twentieth-Century Criticism*. Translated by Catherine Porter. Ithaca, NY: Cornell University Press.

Tönnies, Ferdinand Julius. 1957 [1887]. *Gemeinschaft und Gesellschaft, Community and Society*. East Lansing: Michigan State University Press.

Tooker, Elizabeth. 1992. "Lewis H. Morgan and His Contemporaries." *American Anthropologist* 94(2): 357–375.

Toro, Juan Ruiz. N.d. "Puerto Rico's Operation Bootstrap." Modern Latin America. https://library.brown.edu/create/modernlatinamerica/chapters/chapter-12-strategies-for-economic-developmen/puerto-ricos-operation-bootstrap. Retrieved May 31, 2019.

Torres Colón, Gabriel Alejandro, and Charles A. Hobbs. 2015. "The Intertwining of Culture and Nature: Franz Boas, John Dewey, and Deweyan Strands of American Anthropology." *Journal of the History of Ideas* 76(1): 139–163.

Tozzer, Alfred M. 1909. "The Putnam Anniversary." *American Anthropologist* 11(2): 285–288.

Trautmann, Thomas, and Karl Sanford Kabelac. 1994. "The Library of Lewis Henry Morgan and Mary Elizabeth Morgan." *Transactions of the American Philosophical Society* 84(6/7): i–336.

Turgot, Anne-Robert-Jacques. 1973 [1750]. *Turgot on Progress, Sociology and Economics: A Philosophical Review of the Successive Advances of the Human Mind, On Universal History [and] Reflections on the Formation and the Distribution of Wealth*. Translated by Roland L. Meek. Cambridge: Cambridge University Press.

Turnbull, C. 1961. *The Forest People*. New York: Simon & Schuster.

———. 1972. *The Mountain People*. New York: Simon & Schuster.

Turner, Edith. 1987. *The Spirit and the Drum: A Memoir of Africa*. Tucson: University of Arizona Press.

———. 1992. *Experiencing Ritual: A New Interpretation of African Healing*. Philadelphia: University of Pennsylvania Press.

———. 2006. *Heart of Lightness: The Life Story of an Anthropologist*. New York: Berghahn.

———. 2012. *Communitas: The Anthropology of Collective Joy*. New York: Palgrave Macmillan.

Turner, Jonathan H., Leonard Beeghley, and Charles H. Powers. 1989. *The Emergence of Sociological Theory*. Belmont, CA: Wadsworth.

Turner, Victor. 1967a. "Betwixt and Between: The Liminal Period in Rites of Passage." In *The Forest of Symbols: Aspects of Ndembu Ritual*, 93–111. Ithaca, NY: Cornell University Press.

———. 1967b. *The Forest of Symbols: Aspects of Ndembu Ritual*. Ithaca, NY: Cornell University Press.

———. 1967c. "Ritual Symbolism, Morality, and Social Structure among the Ndembu." In *African Systems of Thought*, edited by M. Fortes and G. Dieterlen, 48–58. London: Oxford University Press.

———. 1969. *The Ritual Process: Structure and Antistructure*. Chicago: Aldine.

Tyler, Stephen. 1969. *Cognitive Anthropology*. New York: Holt, Rinehart and Winston.

———. 1978. *The Said and the Unsaid: Mind, Meaning, and Culture*. New York: Academic Press.

Tylor, Sir Edward Burnett. 1861. *Anahuac: Or Mexico and the Mexicans, Ancient and Modern*. London: Longman, Green, Longman, & Roberts.

———. 1871. *Primitive Culture*. London: John Murray.

———. 1876. "Oaths and Ordeals." *Popular Science Monthly* 9 (July).

———. 1889. "On a Method of Investigating the Development of Institutions; Applied to Laws of Marriage and Descent." *Journal of the Royal Anthropological Institute* 18:245–269.

———. 1920. *Primitive Culture*. 2nd ed. London: John Murray.

"Union Wages in 1928." 1928. *Monthly Labor Review*. 27(5): 10–18.

United Nations. 1993. Declaration on the Elimination of Violence Against Women. United Nations A/RES/48/104.

United Nations High Commission for Refugees (UNHCR). 2019. "Figures at a Glance." https://www.unhcr.org/en-us/figures-at-a-glance.html. Retrieved September 16, 2019.

Urban, Greg. 2013. "Neo-Kantianism." In *Theory in Social and Cultural Anthropology: An Encyclopedia*, edited by R. Jon McGee and Richard L. Warms, 590–593. Thousand Oaks, CA: Sage.

USDC (United States Department of Commerce, Bureau of the Census). 1972. *Supplementary Report: Race of the Population of the United States, by States: 1970*. https://www2.census.gov/library/publications/decennial/1970/pc-s1-supplementary-reports/pc-s1-11.pdf.

USDOJ (United States Department of Justice). 2015. *Department of Justice Report Regarding the Criminal Investigation into the Shooting Death of Michael Brown by Ferguson, Missouri Police Officer Darren Wilson*. https://www.justice.gov/sites/default/files/opa/press-releases/attachments/2015/03/04/doj_report_on_shooting_of_michael_brown_1.pdf.

USDOJ (United States Department of Justice). 2017. *Federal Official Decline Prosecution in the Death of Freddie Gray*. https://www.justice.gov/opa/pr/federal-officials-decline-prosecution-death-freddie-gray.

United States Department of Labor Statistics. 1929. *Wages and Hours of Labor in the Lumber Industry in the United States: 1928*. Washington, DC: Government Printing Office.

United States Department of State. N.d. *Bureau of International Narcotics and Law Enforcement Affairs: Guatemala Summary*. https://www.state.gov/bureau-of-international-narcotics-and-law-enforcement-affairs-work-by-country/guatemala-summary.

Vaid, Urvashi. 1993. "Speech at the March on Washington." Gifts of Speech. https://gos.sbc.edu/w/vaid.html. Retrieved September 27, 2010.

Van Dyke, Virginia. 2009. "The Khalistan Movement in Punjab, India and the Post-Military Era: Structural Change and New Political Compulsions." *Asian Survey* 49(6): 975–997.

Van Gennep, Arnold. 1960 [1909]. *The Rites of Passage*. Translated by Monica Vizedom and Gabrielle L. Caffee. Chicago: University of Chicago Press.

Van Ginkel, R. 1992. "Typically Dutch . . . Ruth Benedict on the 'National Character' of the Netherlanders." *Netherlands' Journal of Social Sciences* 28(1): 50–71.

Veblen, Thorstein. 1912 [1899]. *The Theory of the Leisure Class: An Economic Study of Institutions*. New York: Viking.

Veracini, Lorenzo. 2013. "'Settler Colonialism': Career of a Concept." *Journal of Imperial and Commonwealth History* 41(2): 313–333.

Vico, Giambattista. 1984 [1774]. *The New Science of Giambattista Vico*. Translated by Thomas Goddard Bergin and Max Harold Fisch. Ithaca, NY: Cornell University Press.

Vogel, Shane. 2010. "By the Light of What Comes After: Eventologies of the Ordinary." *Women and Performance: A Journal of Feminist Theory* 19(2): 247–260.

Wacquant, Loïc. 2004. "Pointers on Pierre Bourdieu and Democratic Politics." *Constellations* 11(1): 3–15.

———. 2008. "Pierre Bourdieu." In *Key Sociological Thinkers*, edited by Rob Stones, 2nd ed., 261–277. London: Palgrave Macmillan.

Walker, J. C. 1986. "Romanticizing Resistance, Romanticizing Culture: Problems in Willis's Theory of Cultural Production." *British Journal of Sociology of Education* 7(1): 59–80.

Wallace, Anthony F. C. 1956a. "Mazeway Resynthesis: A Biocultural Theory of Religious Inspiration." *Transactions of the New York Academy of Science* 13:626–636.

———. 1956b. "Revitalization Movements: Some Theoretical Considerations for Their Comparative Study." *American Anthropologist* 58(2): 264–281.

Wallenchinsky, David, and Irving Wallace, eds. 1975. *The People's Almanac*. Garden City, NY: Doubleday.

Wallerstein, I. 1974. *The Modern World-System: Capitalist Agriculture and the Origins of the European World-Economy in the Sixteenth Century*. New York: Academic Press.

Ward, Nicole, and Jeanne Batalova. 2023. "Refugees and Asylees in the United States." Migration Policy Institute, June 15. https://www.migrationpolicy.org/article/refugees-and-asylees-united-states.

Wargadiredja, Arzia T. 2017. "Indonesia's Mass Rape Victims Are Waiting for Justice That May Never Come." Vice, May 21. https://www.vice.com/en_us/article/qvdk3q/indonesias-mass-rape-victims-are-waiting-for-justice-that-may-never-come. Retrieved May 31, 2019.

Warrior, Carol Edelman. 2017. "Indigenous Collectives: A Meditation on Fixity and Flexibility." *American Indian Quarterly* 41(4): 368–392.

Washburn, Sherwood, and C. Lancaster. 1968. "The Evolution of Hunting." In *Man the Hunter*, edited by R. B. Lee and Irven DeVore, 293–303. Chicago: Aldine.

Weber, Max. 1949. *The Methodology of the Social Sciences*. Glencoe, IL: Free Press.

———. 1958 [1930]. *The Protestant Ethic and the Spirit of Capitalism*. Translated by Talcott Parsons. New York: Scribner.

———. 1978. *Economy and Society: An Outline of Interpretive Sociology*. Edited by Guenther Roth and Claus Wittich. Translated by Ephraim Fischoff. Berkeley: University of California Press.

———. 1993 [1920]. *The Sociology of Religion*. Boston: Beacon Press.

White, Edmund. 2014. *Inside a Pearl: My Years in Paris*. London: Bloomsbury.

White, Leslie A. 1930. "An Anthropological Appraisal of the Russian Revolution." *New Masses*: 14–16.

———. 1943. "Energy and the Evolution of Culture." *American Anthropologist* 43:335–356.

———. 1945a. "'Diffusion vs. Evolution': An Anti-Evolutionist Fallacy." *American Anthropologist* 47(1): 339–356.

———. 1945b. "History, Evolutionism, and Functionalism: Three Types of Interpretation of Culture." *Southwestern Journal of Anthropology* 1(2): 221–248.

———. 1948. "Ikhnaton: The Great Man vs. the Culture Process." *Journal of the American Oriental Society* 68(2): 91–114.

———. 1957. Review of *Theory of Culture Change*, by Julian Haynes Steward. *American Anthropologist* 59(3): 540–542.

———. 1959a. "The Concept of Culture." *American Anthropologist* 61(2): 227–251.

———. 1959b. *The Evolution of Culture*. New York: McGraw-Hill.

———. 1975. *The Concept of Cultural Systems: A Key to Understanding Tribes and Nations*. New York: Columbia University Press.

Whorf, Benjamin Lee. 1956. *Language, Thought and Reality*. Cambridge, MA: MIT Press.

Wierzbicka, Anna. 2005. "Empirical Universals of Language as a Basis for the Study of Other Human Universals and as a Tool for Exploring Cross-Cultural Differences." *Ethos* 33(2): 256–291.

Wiessner, Polly, and Nitze Pupu. 2012. "Toward Peace: Foreign Arms and Indigenous Institutions in a Papua New Guinea Society." *Science* 337(6102): 1651–1654.

Willis, P. 1983. "Cultural Production and Theories of Reproduction." In *Race, Class and Education*, edited by L. Barton and S. Walker, 107–138. London: Croom Helm.

Wilson, Monica. 1950. "Nyakyusa Kinship." In *African Systems of Kinship and Marriage*, edited by A. R. Radcliffe Brown, 111–139. London: Oxford University Press.

Wissler, Clark. 1917. *The American Indian: An Introduction to the Anthropology of the New World*. New York: D. C. McMurtrie.

———. 1926. *The Relation of Nature to Man in Aboriginal America*. New York: Oxford University Press.

Wittgenstein, Ludwig. 2001. *Philosophical Investigations*. 3rd ed. Oxford: Blackwell.

Wolf, Eric R. 1959. *Sons of the Shaking Earth*. Chicago: University of Chicago Press.

———. 1966. *Peasants*. Englewood Cliffs, NJ: Prentice Hall.

———. 1969. *Peasant Wars of the Twentieth Century*. New York: Harper & Row.

———. 1982. *Europe and the People without History*. Berkeley: University of California Press.

———. 1999. *Envisioning Power: Ideologies of Dominance and Crisis*. Berkeley: University of California.

———. 2004. "Alfred L. Kroeber." In *Totems and Teachers: Perspectives on the History of Anthropology*, 2nd ed., edited by Sydel Silverman, 27–49. New York: AltiMira.

Wolf, Eric R., and Joseph G. Jorgensen. 1970. "Anthropology on the Warpath in Thailand." *New York Review of Books*, November 19, 26–35.

Wolfe, Patrick. 2006. "Settler Colonialism and the Elimination of the Native." *Journal of Genocide Research* 8(4): 387–409.

Wrangham, Richard. 2009. *Catching Fire: How Cooking Made Us Human*. New York: Basic Books.

Wright, Johnson Kent. 2006. Review of *Iselin contra Rousseau: Sociable Patriotism and the History of Mankind*, by Béla Kapossy. *Journal of Modern History* 80(3): 620–621.

Wright, Richard. 1937. Review of *Their Eyes Were Watching God*, by Zora Neale Hurston. *New Masses*, October 5, 22–23.

Wundt, Wilhelm Max. 1904 [1874]. *Principles of Physiological Psychology*. Translated by Edward Bradford Titchener. New York: Macmillan.

———. 1916 [1912]. *Elements of Folk Psychology: Outlines of a Psychological History of the Development of Mankind*. New York: Macmillan.

Yanagisako, Sylvia, and Jane Collier. 1987. "Toward a Unified Analysis of Gender and Kinship." In *Gender and Kinship: Essays toward a Unified Analysis*, ed. Sylvia Yanagisako and Jane Collier, 14–50. Palo Alto, CA: Stanford University Press.

Young, Michael W. 2004. *Malinowski: Odyssey of an Anthropologist, 1884–1920*. New Haven, CT: Yale University Press.

Zuberi, Tukufu, and Eduardo Bonilla-Silva. 2008. *White Logic, White Methods: Racism and Methodology*. Lanham, MD: Rowman & Littlefield.

Zumwalt, Rosemary L. 2013. "The Shaping of Intellectual Identity and Discipline through Charismatic Leaders: Franz Boas and Alan Dundes." *Western Folklore* 72(2): 131–179.

Credits

Lila Abu-Lughod, "A Tale of Two Pregnancies," in *Women Writing Culture*, ed. Ruth Behar and Deborah A. Gordon (Berkeley: University of California Press, 1995): 339–349.

Arjun Appadurai, "Disjuncture and Difference in the Global Cultural Economy," *Public Culture* 2, no. 2 (1990): 1–24. Copyright © 1990 by Arjun Appadurai. All rights reserved. Republished by permission of the copyright holder and the publisher, Duke University Press. www.dukeupress.edu.

Ruth Fulton Benedict, "The Science of Custom," *The Century Magazine* 117, no. 6 (1929): 641–649.

Franz Boas, "The Methods of Ethnology," *American Anthropologist* 22, no. 4 (October–December 1920): 311–321.

Tom Boellstorff, "2004 The Emergence of Political Homophobia in Indonesia: Masculinity and National Belonging." *Ethnos* 69(4): 465–486. Copyright © 2004.

Pierre Bourdieu, "Structures, *Habitus*, Practices," in *The Logic of Practice*, trans. Richard Nice (Stanford, CA: Stanford University Press, 1990 [1980]): 52–65. Copyright © 1989 by Polity Press. All rights reserved. Used with permission of Stanford University Press, www.sup.org.

Philippe Bourgois, "From Jíbaro to Crack Dealer: Confronting the Restructuring of Capitalism in El Barrio," in *Articulating Hidden Histories: Exploring the Influence of Eric R. Wolf*, ed. Jane Schneider and Rayna Rapp (Berkeley: University of California Press, 1995): 125–141.

Orasanmi Burton, "To Protect and Serve Whiteness," *North American Dialogue* 18(2): 38–50, ISSN 1556-4819. © 2015 by the American Anthropological Association. All rights reserved.

Veena Das, "Engaging in the Life of the Other: Love and Everyday Life," in *Ordinary Ethics: Anthropology, Language and Action*, ed. Michael Lambek, 376–399 (New York: Fordham University Press, 2010). Copyright © 2010. Reproduced with the permission of Fordham University Press.

Mary Douglas, "External Boundaries," in *Purity and Danger: An Analysis of the Concepts of Pollution and Taboo* (London: Routledge & Kegan Paul, 1966): 114–128. Copyright © 1966 by Mary Douglas. Reproduced by permission of Taylor & Francis Books UK.

Émile Durkheim, "What Is a Social Fact?," in *The Rules of the Sociological Method*, ed. George E. G. Catlin, trans. Sarah A. Solovay and John H. Mueller. First copyrighted in 1938 by University of Chicago; copyright reassigned to George E. G. Catlin. Copyright 1938 by George E. G. Catlin; renewed 1966 by Sarah A. Solovay, John H. Mueller, and George E. G. Catlin. Reprinted with the permission of The Free Press, a Division of Simon & Schuster, Inc. All rights reserved.

Michel Foucault, "The Incitement to Discourse," from *The History of Sexuality*, Vol. 1, *An Introduction*, by Michel Foucault, trans. Robert Hurley, translation copyright

Clifford Geertz, "Deep Play: Notes on the Balinese Cockfight," *Daedalus* 134, no. 4 (2005): 56–86. Originally published in 1972. Reprinted by permission of MIT Press Journals.

Ruth Gomberg-Muñoz, "Willing to Work: Agency and Vulnerability in an Undocumented Immigrant Network," *American Anthropologist* volume 112, issue 2 (2010): 295–307. Reproduced by permission of the American Anthropological Association from *American Anthropologist*. Not for sale or further reproduction.

Marvin Harris, Nirmal K. Bose, Morton Klass, Joan P. Mencher, Kalervo Oberg, Marvin K. Opler, Wayne Suttles, and Andrew P. Vayda, "The Cultural Ecology of India's Sacred Cattle [and Comments and Replies]," *Current Anthropology* 7, no. 1 (1966): 51–66. Published by the University of Chicago Press on behalf of Wenner-Gren Foundation for Anthropological Research, http://www .jstor.org/stable/2740230.

Zora Neale Hurston, Chapter 4 [pp. 59–75] from *Mules and Men* by Zora Neale Hurston. Copyright 1935 by Zora Neale Hurston; renewed © 1963 by John C. Hurston and Joel Hurston. Reprinted by permission of HarperCollins Publishers.

Alfred L. Kroeber, "On the Principle of Order in Civilization as Exemplified by Changes of Fashion," *American Anthropologist*, n.s., 21, no. 3 (1919): 235–263.

Eleanor Leacock, "Interpreting the Origins of Gender Inequality: Conceptual and Historical Problems," *Dialectical Anthropology* 7, no. 4 (February 1983): 263–284. With kind permission from Springer Science+Business Media.

Claude Lévi-Strauss, "Four Winnebago Myths: A Structural Sketch," in *Culture in History: Essays in Honor of Paul Radin*, ed. Stanley Diamond (New York: Columbia University, 1960). Copyright © Columbia University Press. Reprinted with permission of the publisher.

Bronislaw Malinowski, "The Essentials of the Kula," in *Argonauts of the Western Pacific* (New York: E. P. Dutton, 1922): 81–104.

Karl Marx and Friedrich Engels, "Feuerbach: Opposition of the Materialist and Idealist Outlook" [1846], in *The German Ideology: Part I, with Selections from Parts II and III, Together with Marx's "Introduction to a Critique of Political Economy,"* ed. C. J. Arthur. Translation of Part I, copyright © by International Publishers Co., Inc., 1947; revised translation of Part I © by Lawrence & Wishart, 1970. Reprinted by permission of International Publishers, New York.

Marcel Mauss, excerpts from *The Gift: Forms and Functions of Exchange in Archaic Societies*, trans. Ian Cunnison (New York: W. W. Norton, 1967): 31–45, 76–81. Originally published in 1925, copyright © by Routledge & Kegan Paul, 1954. Reproduced by permission of Taylor & Francis Books UK.

Margaret Mead, "Introduction," in *Coming of Age in Samoa* (New York: HarperCollins, 2011): 3–11. Copyright © 1928, 1949, 1955, 1961, 1973 by Margaret Mead. Reprinted by permission of HarperCollins Publishers.

Lewis Henry Morgan, "Ethnical Periods," in *Ancient Society* (New York: Henry Holt and Company, 1877).

Sherry Ortner, "Is Female to Male as Nature Is to Culture?" was originally published in *Feminist Studies*, 1972, Volume 1, No. 2, pp. 5–31, by permission of the publisher, Feminist Studies, Inc.

Sherry Ortner, "Power and Projects: Reflections on Agency," in *Anthropology and Social Theory: Culture, Power, and the Acting Subject*, pp. 130–153. Copyright ©

A. R. Radcliffe-Brown, "On Joking Relationships," *Africa: Journal of the International African Institute* 13, no. 3 (1940): 195–210. Copyright © 1940 International Africa Institute. Reproduced with permission of Cambridge University Press.

Roy Rappaport, "Ritual Regulation of Environmental Relations among a New Guinea People," *Ethnology* 6, no. 1 (1967): 17–30. Copyright © 1967. Reprinted with permission.

Renato Rosaldo, *Culture and Truth.* Copyright © 1989, 1993 by Renato Rosaldo. Reprinted by permission of Beacon Press, Boston.

Audra Simpson, "The Ruse of Consent and the Anatomy of Refusal: Cases from Indigenous North America and Australia," *Postcolonial Studies* 20, no. 1 (2017): 18–33.

Sally Slocum, "Woman the Gatherer: Male Bias in Anthropology," in *Toward an Anthropology of Women*, ed. Rayna R. Reiter (New York and London: Monthly Review Press, 1975). Copyright © 1975 by Rayna R. Reiter. Republished with permission of Monthly Review Press.

Herbert Spencer, "The Social Organism," *The Westminster Review* (January 1860); reprinted in Herbert Spencer, *Essays: Scientific, Political, and Speculative*, 3 vols. (London and New York, 1892).

Julian Steward, "The Patrilineal Band," in *Theory of Culture Change: The Methodology of Multilinear Evolution*. Copyright © 1955 by the Board of Trustees of the University of Illinois. Renewed 1983 by Jane C. Steward. Used with permission of the University of Illinois Press.

C. Jason Throop, "Ambivalent Happiness and Virtuous Suffering," *HAU Journal of Ethnographic Theory* 5, no. 3 (2015): 45–68.

Michel-Rolph Trouillot, "Anthropology and the Savage Slot: The Poetics and Politics of Otherness" in *Recapturing Anthropology: Working in the Present*, ed. Richard G. Fox (Santa Fe: School of American Research Press, 1991): 17–44.

Victor Turner, "Symbols in Ndembu Ritual," in *The Forest of Symbols* (1967). Copyright 1967 by Cornell University. Used by permission of the publisher, Cornell University Press.

Sir Edward Burnett Tylor, "The Science of Culture," in *Primitive Culture: Researches into the Development of Mythology, Philosophy, Religion, Art, and Custom*, vol. 1. (London: John Murray, 1871).

Max Weber, "Class, Status, Party," trans. H. H. Gerth and C. Wright Mills, *Politics* 1, no. 9 (1944): 271–278. Originally published in *Economy and Society*, 1922. Copyright © October 1944, by Politics Publishing Co.

Leslie White, "Energy and the Evolution of Culture," *American Anthropologist* 45, no. 3 (July– September 1943): 335–356.

Benjamin L. Whorf, "The Relation of Habitual Thought and Behavior to Language," in *Language, Culture, and Personality: Essays in Memory of Edward Sapir*, ed. Leslie Spier, A. Irving Hallowell, Stanley S. Newman (Menasha, WI: Sapir Memorial Publication Fund, 1941): 134–59. Originally published in *American Anthropologist* 21, no. 3 (1919): 235–63.

Eric Wolf, "Distinguished Lecture: Facing Power, Old Insights, New Questions." Reproduced by permission of the American Anthropological Association from *American Anthropologist* volume 92, issue 3 (1990): 586–596.

Index

Burns, Lizzy, 70n13
Burns, Mary, 70n13
Burton, Orisanmi, "To Protect and Serve Whiteness," 722–23, 743–57
Bush, George W., 602–3, 603n
Butler, Judith, 597, 598n14, 747–48, 747n7; *Gender Trouble*, 575

Calderón de la Barca, Pedro, 123, 123n23
Cambridge University, 213, 215
Campanella, Tommaso, 511, 511n13
capital, Bourdieu's concept of, 458n9, 623n18
capitalism: and immigration, 613; origins of, 119n18; Protestantism and, 86–87, 119n18, 290n25, 470n4, 492n8; and sexuality, 469n2; and the simulacrum, 565, 565n30; Spencer's naturalization of, 29n; White on, 269n; Wolf on, 533, 536, 547, 613–14, 613n; women's status under, 384–86, 385n18, 385n19
Carlson, Tucker, 603n
Carlyle, Thomas, 19n
Carneiro, Robert, 275n40
Carstairs, George Morris, 402, 402n16
Cartier, Jacques, 511, 511n13
Cartwright, George, 512, 513n17, 522n35
Castañeda, Carlos, 510, 510n
caste, 119–21, 119n17, 121n21, 400–403, 400n14, 401n, 678n, 691n24, 699n10
Castro Faria, Luiz de, 329
Catholic Church, 20n, 142n, 171n20, 205n19, 393, 470, 470n4, 471n, 472n, 509n11, 680
Catilina, Lucius Sergius, 116, 116n12
Cato Institute, 24n7

cattle, prohibition on killing, 295, 297–311
Cavell, Stanley, 2, 672, 673, 675, 676n2, 689, 690n22
Cervantes, Miguel de, 464n22
Chagnon, Napoleon, 275n40, 388, 531
Chaillie, R., 86
Chandler, Daniel, 744n3
chaos theory, 569, 569n
charisma, 87, 112n4, 310
Charles I, King, 20n
Charles II, King, 20n
Charles V, Emperor (Charles I of Spain), 520
Chicago World's Fair (1893). *See* World's Columbian Exposition
Childe, V. Gordon, 16, 261n13, 262n14, 262n15, 264n17
children: in American culture, 173–75, 173n, 175n5, 180n14; enculturation of, 91, 91n6, 135–37, 149n18, 150n19, 167, 173–80, 355; Lacanian psychology of, 554n9; nature associated with, 353; neo-Freudian psychology of, 173n; "primitive" peoples likened to, 28n, 135, 149n18, 396n4, 397–98; sexuality of, 475–77, 477n13
China Beach (television show), 516, 517n23
The China Syndrome (film), 566n31
Chodorow, Nancy, 355, 361
Chomsky, Noam, 211n
Christianity: critiques of, 51n17, 65n, 67n4, 74n24, 120n20; and heterosexism, 594n10; Ilongot headhunters and, 490–91; the West identified with, 518–19, 519n29; and white supremacy, 190n. *See also* Catholic Church; Protestantism
class: English Civil War and, 20n; *habitus* and,

460–62, 461n15, 462n16; individuals in relation to, 70n14; lumpenproletariat, 563, 564n27, 618n10; Marxist theory of, 116n11; Marx's theory of, 16, 67n4, 70n14, 78, 79n32, 112n4, 114n8, 114n9; and sexuality, 469n2; social and political struggles associated with, 78–79, 79n32, 115–17, 116n12, 117n13, 267n27; Spencer on, 20, 23, 23n7, 27, 30; Weber's theory of, 86, 112–17, 112n4, 114n8, 114n9, 116n11; White and, 267–68, 267n27; working/laboring, 611, 616n7, 618n11; in the workplace, 622n, 623n17
classical civilizations. *See* Greece and Rome
Clay, Henry, 750n
Cleargreen, 510n
Clews, Henry, 148n13
Clifford, James, *Writing Culture*, 504n4, 516n23, 524n, 527n, 533, 537n6
Clinton, Hillary, 603n, 660n13
Cobb, William Montague, 138
cockfights, 392, 426–46
cognitive anthropology, 85, 151n20, 314n3, 332–33, 391, 545n19, 546n20. *See also* thought/mind
Cohen, Jeffrey, 659, 659n11
Colbert, Stephen, 726n2
Cold War, 112n3, 590n, 591n6
Cole, Fay-Cooper, 256n
collective conscience, 20n, 23n6, 83–85, 92n8, 94n10, 133, 229n18, 245n21, 259n10, 330, 453n3, 467n, 555
Collins, Elizabeth, 597
colonialism: anthropology's role in, 216, 238n7, 325n28, 402n16, 640, 717–20; avoidance of the issue of, 302n7; Boas's